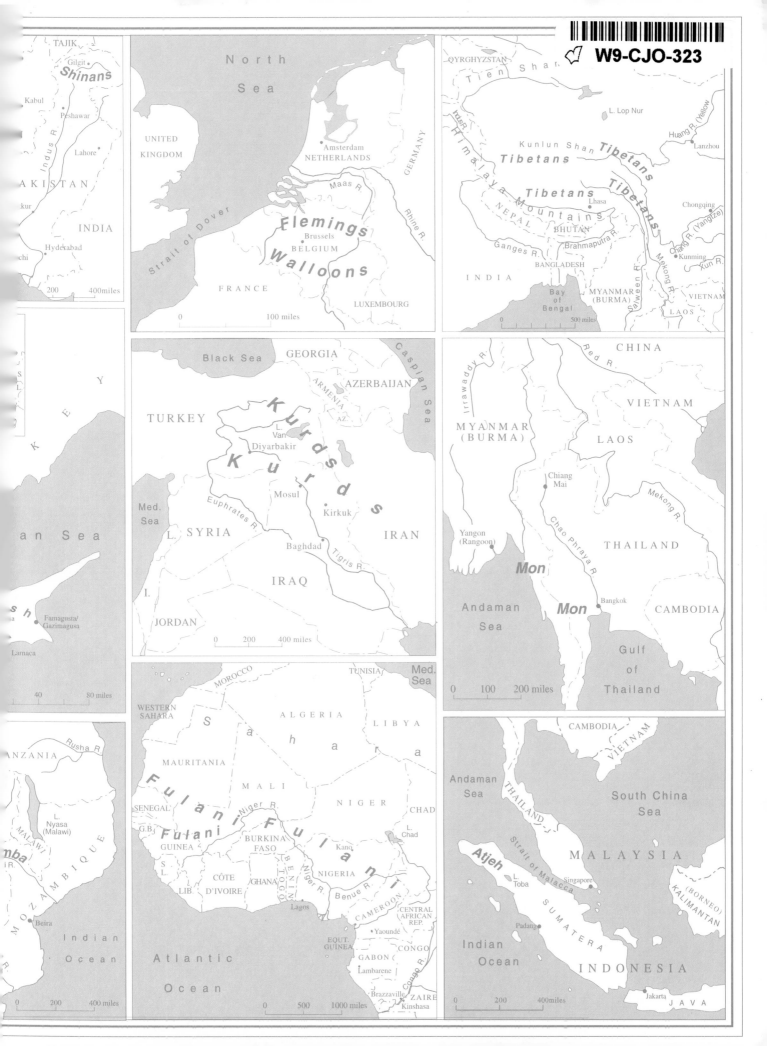

Map 1 — Pakistan/India (upper left)

TAJIK
Shinans
Kabul
Peshawar
Gilgit
Lahore
Indus R.
PAKISTAN
INDIA
Hyderabad
kur
chi

200   400 miles

Map 2 — Netherlands/Belgium

North Sea
UNITED KINGDOM
Amsterdam
NETHERLANDS
GERMANY
Maas R.
Rhine R.
Strait of Dover
Flemings
Brussels
BELGIUM
Walloons
FRANCE
LUXEMBOURG

0   100 miles

Map 3 — Central Asia/Tibet

QYRGHYZSTAN
Tien Shan
L. Lop Nur
Huang R. (Yellow)
IndsR
Himalaya Mountains
Kunlun Shan
Tibetans
Tibetans
Tibetans
Tibetans
Lanzhou
Lhasa
Chongqing
NEPAL
BHUTAN
Chang R. (Yangtze)
Ganges R.
Brahmaputra R.
Kunming
Xun R.
INDIA
BANGLADESH
Bay of Bengal
MYANMAR (BURMA)
VIETNAM
LAOS

0   500 miles

Map 4 — Kurds / Middle East

Black Sea
GEORGIA
Caspian Sea
ARMENIA
AZERBAIJAN
AZ.
TURKEY
Kurds
Kurds
L. Van
Diyarbakir
Med. Sea
Euphrates R.
Mosul
Kirkuk
SYRIA
I.
Baghdad
Tigris R.
IRAN
IRAQ
JORDAN

0   200   400 miles

Map 5 — Myanmar/Thailand (Mon)

CHINA
Irrawaddy R.
Red R.
VIETNAM
MYANMAR (BURMA)
LAOS
Chiang Mai
Mekong R.
Yangon (Rangoon)
Chao Phraya R.
THAILAND
Mon
Bangkok
Mon
Andaman Sea
CAMBODIA
Gulf of Thailand

0   100   200 miles

Map 6 — Cyprus (left)

K E Y
an Sea
sh
Famagusta/ Gazimagusa
sa
Larnaca

40   80 miles

Map 7 — Africa (Fulani / Sahara)

MOROCCO
TUNISIA
Med. Sea
WESTERN SAHARA
ALGERIA
LIBYA
Sahara
MAURITANIA
MALI
NIGER
CHAD
Fulani
SENEGAL
Niger R.
G.B.
Fulani
Fulani
BURKINA FASO
Kano
L. Chad
GUINEA
BENIN
S.L.
NIGERIA
LIB.
CÔTE D'IVOIRE
GHANA
TOGO
Niger R.
Benue R.
CAMEROON
Lagos
CENTRAL AFRICAN REP.
EQUT. GUINEA
Yaoundé
GABON
CONGO
Lambarene
Congo R.
ZAIRE
Brazzaville
Kinshasa
Atlantic Ocean

0   500   1000 miles

Map 8 — Mozambique/Malawi (lower left)

TANZANIA
Rusha R.
MALAWI
Nyasa (Malawi)
nba
iR
MOZAMBIQUE
mba
Beira
Indian Ocean

0   200   400 miles

Map 9 — Indonesia/Malaysia (Atjeh)

CAMBODIA
VIETNAM
Andaman Sea
THAILAND
South China Sea
Strait of Malacca
Atjeh
MALAYSIA
L. Toba
Singapore
(BORNEO) KALIMANTAN
SUMATERA
Padang
Indian Ocean
INDONESIA
JAVA
Jakarta

0   200   400 miles

THE ENCYCLOPEDIA OF THE
PEOPLES OF THE WORLD

THE ENCYCLOPEDIA OF THE
PEOPLES OF THE WORLD

EDITED BY
AMIRAM GONEN

A Henry Holt Reference Book

HENRY HOLT AND COMPANY

NEW YORK

A Henry Holt Reference Book
Henry Holt and Company, Inc.
Publishers since 1866
115 West 18th Street
New York, New York 10011

First published in the United States in 1993 by
Henry Holt and Company, Inc.
Published in Canada by Fitzhenry & Whiteside Ltd.,
91 Granton Drive, Richmond Hill, Ontario L4B 2N5.

Library of Congress Cataloging-in-Publication Data

The Encyclopedia of the peoples of the world / edited by Amiram
        Gonen. — 1st American ed.
          p.   cm.   —   (A Henry Holt reference book)
        1. Ethnic Groups — Encyclopedias. 2. Indigenous peoples —
        Encyclopedias.   I. Gonen, Amiram.   II.   Series.
        GN495 . 4 . E53   1993   93–22942
        305.8'003—dc20   CIP
ISBN 0–8050–2256–2

First American Edition — 1993

Printed in Germany
All first editions are printed on acid-free paper. ∞

10   9   8   7   6   5   4   3   2   1

EDITORS AND CONTRIBUTORS

MICHEL ABITBUL, Ph.D.   *North Africa*

Professor of African Studies,
The Hebrew University of Jerusalem.

VIVIENNE BURSTEIN-SHEER, Ph.D.   *South Africa*

Lecturer in African Studies,
The Hebrew University of Jerusalem.

PETER DEMANT, Ph.D.   *The Middle East and Western Europe*

Research Associate,
The Harry S. Truman Research Institute,
The Hebrew University of Jerusalem.

SILVIA ELGUEA, M.A.   *Mexico, Central and South America*

Lecturer, Ramapo College of New Jersey, and
Associate Professor, Metropolitan Autonomous University, Mexico.

NAMDI ELLEH, M.Arch.   *Central America*

Researcher, University of Wisconsin, Milwaukee.

EDOUARD A. ELOI, JR., M.S.   *South America*

Academic Coordinator, International Training Center,
Ramapo College of New Jersey.

NIZA FABRE, Ph.D.   *South America*

Assistant Professor of American Studies,
Ramapo College of New Jersey.

BERNARDO GANDULLA, Ph.D.   *South America*

Professor of History,
The University of Buenos Aires.

MOSHE GEMER, Ph.D.   *Eastern Europe, Northern and Central Asia*
Lecturer in Middle Eastern History,
Tel Aviv University and The Open University.

RUTH GINEO, M.A.
Researcher in African Studies,
The Harry S. Truman Research Institute,
The Hebrew University of Jerusalem.

West Africa

AMIRAM GONEN, Ph.D.
Associate Professor of Geography,
The Hebrew University of Jerusalem.

North America and Western Europe

ARI GORLIN, B.A.
Researcher, Jerusalem.

Papua New Guinea

BARBARA GREEN, M.A.
Reseacher in African Studies,
The Hebrew University of Jerusalem.

Southern and Central Africa

HADASSA GROSSMAN, Ph.D.
Lecturer in History, Tel Aviv University, and
Fellow at The Harry S. Truman Research Institute,
The Hebrew University of Jerusalem.

Brazil

ADRIANA GUEVARA DE VAN OUDENALLEN, D.D.S.
Researcher, University of Wisconsin, Milwaukee.

South America

DAVID HAMBURGER, B.A.
Researcher in History, Jerusalem.

Southeast Asia

NAOMI HAZAN, Ph.D.
Associate Professor of African Studies,
The Hebrew University of Jerusalem.

Africa

HOWARD HOROWITZ, Ph.D.
Associate Professor of Geography,
Ramapo College of New Jersey.

The Caribbean, Central and South America

JEFFREY KALMAN, B.A   *Central America*
Researcher, Ramapo College of New Jersey.

STEVEN KAPLAN, Ph.D.   *East Africa*
Associate Professor, Chairman of the African Studies Dept.,
The Hebrew University of Jerusalem.

DAVID KENNEDY, B.A.   *Nepal*
Researcher in Anthropology, Montreal.

VLADIMIR EMMANUILOVICH KHANIN, Ph.D.   *East Africa*
Senior Lecturer in Political Science,
Zaporozhye Branch, St. Petersburg Institute of Politics.

KONSTANTIN LERNER, Ph.D.   *Central Asia*
Researcher in Asian and African Studies,
The Hebrew University of Jerusalem.

MOSHE MAOZ, Ph.D.   *Middle East*
Professor of Middle Eastern Studies,
The Hebrew University of Jerusalem.

CHRISTOPH MARX, Ph.D.   *East Africa*
Lecturer in African History,
Tel Aviv University.

YOLANDA PRIETO, Ph.D.   *Cuba*
Associate Professor of Sociology,
Ramapo College of New Jersey.

GALIA SABAR-FRIEDMAN, Ph.D.   *East Africa*
Lecturer in African Studies,
The Hebrew University of Jerusalem.

MARWYN SAMUELS, Ph.D.   *East and South Asia*
Professor of Geography,
Syracuse University.

ROHAN SAXENA, M.A.   *India*
Researcher, Jerusalem.

AVRAHAM SHAFIR, B.A.   *Eastern Europe*
Researcher in Slavic Studies, Jerusalem.

LEONARDO SINKMAN, Ph.D.   *Argentina and Uruguay*
Fellow Researcher. The Harry S. Truman Institute,
The Hebrew University of Jerusalem.

ANNA MARIA FUND PATRONDE SMITH, Ph.D.   *South America*
Professor of History,
University of Buenos Aires.

MICHAEL SOFER, Ph.D.   *Oceania*
Lecturer in Geography,
Tel Aviv University.

TAMAR SOFFER, B.A.   *Maps*
Cartographer, The Hebrew University of Jerusalem.

DAVID STEA, Ph.D.   *Mexico, Central and South America,*
Professor, U.S. International University and
University of the Americas, Mexico;
Director, International Center for Culture and Environment, Mexico;
Visiting Professor, Ramapo College of New Jersey.

MARIO SZNAJDER, Ph.D.   *Chile, Bolivia, and Peru*
Lecturer in Political Science,
The Hebrew University of Jerusalem.

CAROLINE HAIYAN TONG, M.A.   *China*
Researcher in Political Science, Syracuse University.

BOAZ TSAIRI, M.A.   *Native Peoples of North America*
Regional Development and Economic Consultant
to the Gitksan Wet'suwet'en Nations, British Columbia, Canada,
and The Hebrew University of Jerusalem.

HARRY VAN OUDENALLEN, M.Arch.   *Central and South America*
Professor of Architecture,
University of Wisconsin, Milwaukee.

MICHAEL VOLODARSKY, Ph.D.   *The Caucasus, and Iran*
Lecturer, Tel Aviv University.

GEOFFREY WIGODER, Ph.D.   *Jews*
Former Director of the Oral History Department,
Institute of Contemporary Jewry,
The Hebrew University of Jerusalem.

BORIS DOV YAROSHEVSKI, Ph.D.   *Russia*
Lecturer, The Center of East European and Soviet Studies,
Tel Aviv University.

MICHAEL ZAND, Ph.D.   *Central Asia*
Professor, Institute of Asian and African Studies,
The Hebrew University of Jerusalem.

AYALA ZINGER, M.A.   *East Africa*
Researcher in African Studies,
The Harry S. Truman Research Institute,
The Hebrew University of Jerusalem.

THOMAS ZITELMANN, Ph.D.   *East Africa*
Visiting Research Fellow, The Institute of German History, Tel Aviv University.

FOREWORD

A world that is far more complex and fluid has emerged in the past half century. The worldwide cultural landscape has been transformed by the revival of ethnic nationalism, with many peoples claiming and fighting for political freedom and territorial integrity on the basis of ethnic identity and solidarity. Not a day passes without ethnicity and multiculturalism rising to the forefront of the news. It is an underlying cause of political change and social and economic development. Peoples who have been buried for years under the cover of large empires, or who have been living under the umbrella of nation-states dominated by others have emerged as viable national entities.

The general reader of current world affairs is puzzled — who are these people? Where do they live? What is their culture? What religion do they practice? What is their history? What is their role as a minority or majority? What political or economic status are they striving for? The purpose of this encyclopedia is to provide concise answers to such questions. In most entries the reader can find the various names of a people or an ethnic group, population figures, location, language, religion, main economic occupations, and some history, where ethnic circumstances are relevant.

WHO IS INCLUDED?

This encyclopedia includes only contemporary peoples and ethnic groups; it does not include those peoples who have existed in antiquity and recent history or who have assimilated into other cultures. Nevertheless, peoples currently in the process of assimilating are included.

Who is included and why? No attempt has been made to develop and use a single definition of what constitutes a people or an ethnic group. In general, however, some criteria have been used, either alone or in combination: common history; distinct language; shared traditions, religion, or folklore; common identity maintained in the face of strong pressures to assimilate; self-designation; and territorial concentration.

In recent decades many new nation-states have been formed as a result of decolonization. Colonialism carved Africa into political territories and ethnic divisions are now being superceded by allegiance to new national identities. Though Kenya is comprised of many ethnically defined peoples, a common Kenyan identity has recently emerged.

Therefore, in this Encyclopedia separate nation-states have their own entries as well as does each of the ethnic groups they comprise. In such entries the reader is provided an opportunity to confront the ethnic fabric underlying the economic, social, and political structure of such multi-ethnic nation-states.

Size of population is not a criterion for inclusion into the Encyclopedia. Some entries deal with small ethnic groups who, though seemingly insignificant in number, are a distinct cultural entity or had significant impact in the past and therefore merit inclusion. Conversely, some subdivisions of peoples in the form of tribes, clans, or religious communities were not included as entries despite their size, because they do not constitute a distinct ethnic entity. Thus, the Christian Copts in Egypt, though of a sizable number, are included in the entry on Egyptians. Religion often is compounded with ethnicity. Some religious communities, such as the Parsis in Bombay, India, have developed a cultural identity and unity and are thus treated as an ethnic group; others are merely a religious denomination within an ethnically homogeneous people.

NAMES

Names of entries are generally assigned based on common usage. Indigenous names are used when appropriate. Self-designated names, when known, can be found in parentheses next to the common name. Should a reader wish to search for a people or an ethnic group by a self designation (denoted by s.d.) or alternative spelling, the index is an invaluable resource, as it is both rich and extensive. In areas such as Southeast Asia, where each ethnic group has been named differently by local rulers, neighbors, and Europeans, in addition to their self-designation, the easiest way to locate the group in the Encyclopedia would be through the index.

When spelling place names, common usage is generally adhered to. However, in some recently independent countries, where there has been a trend to reform the spelling of the place names, some entries echo these changes. The people we know as Kazakhs now prefer that their name be written Qazaq, a form that more accurately reflects the pronunciation of the name.

POPULATION FIGURES

Though every attempt has been made to provide accurate population figures, many countries have not had an updated ethnically-based census taken since the 1960s. Some figures are, therefore, inexact. Ethnic groups in many countries have never had a census taken and the population figures are estimates, based on a rough projection of prior data.

MAPS

There are about 250 maps throughout the Encyclopedia showing the location of selected peoples and ethnic groups. The maps are simple, self-evident, and clear. Some of the peoples selected to be depicted on maps are little known or cut across state boundaries. When an ethnic group is concentrated in a small area, its location is denoted by an asterix. The maps provide the reader with an invaluable tool for understanding the geographical context of peoples and ethnic groups, including those that have been made famous by the evening news.

SELECT BIBLIOGRAPHY

A select bibliography is found at the end of this Encyclopedia. It includes mostly books covering several peoples of a region or of a cultural category. A few of the books deal with one people, such as the Kurds, when there is special interest in them in current affairs.

The bibliography is organized by continents and, where appropriate, by regions within the continents.

The bibliography only includes books in English.

VARIOUS SIGNS HAVE BEEN USED IN THE ENCYCLOPEDIA:

SMALL CAPS: *A cross reference to an entry in the Encyclopedia.*

s.d.: *Self-designation, the name used by the people themselves.*

( ): *Alternative names and self-designation other than the one used in the entry.*

A

ABADJA   A subgroup of the IBO.

ABADZEKH   A subgroup of the ADYGHEANS. (see also CHERKESS)

ABAKAN TATARS   see KHAKASS.

ABAM   A subgroup of the IBO.

ABAT-KIZHI   see SHORS.

ABAZIANS   (Circassians, s.d. Abaza) An ethnic group living in the northern Caucasus, in the upper basin of the Kuban and Zelenchuk Rivers. In 1989 they numbered about 34,000: some 24,000 in the Qarachai-Circassian Autonomous *Oblast* and some 10,000 in Turkey and other former regions of the Ottoman empire where, together with other north Caucasian ethnic groups, they were resettled between 1859 and 1864 and are known as Circassians (see CHERKESS).

They are closely related to the ABKHAZIANS and their language belongs to the Abkhazo-Adyghean branch of the Ibero-Caucasian family. The Abazians adopted Sunni Islam of the Hanafi school in the fifteenth century.

The Abazians are divided into two subgroups: TAPANTA (i.e., valley folk) and ASHKHAZWA (i.e., mountain dwellers), each with its own dialect. The Tapanta dialect adopted a Roman alphabet in 1932; since 1939 it has employed a Cyrillic script.

Until the fifteenth century the Abazians, who lived on the Black Sea coast between the Bzyb River and the site of the modern town of Tuapse (between the UBYKHS and the ABKHAZIANS) were largely assimilated by Abkhazian tribes. In the fifteenth and sixteenth centuries they settled in the northern Caucasus, where they are under the cultural influence of their Adyghean neighbors. Ethnographically, they are now almost indistinguishable from the KABARDIANS. Their traditional economy is based on agriculture and stock-raising.

ABDALI   (Durrani) A subgroup of the PASHTUN.

ABE   (Abbe, Abbey) A people living in the area surrounding the town of Agboville in the Côte d'Ivoire. Their language is related to those spoken in the lagoon area, and they share many social structures with the AKAN.

Having resisted early colonization attempts by the FRENCH at the end of the nineteenth century, the Abe were only subdued after a failed uprising in 1910.

ABELAM   An ethnic group of around 50,000 living in the Sepik River region of northern Papua New Guinea. Their language is part of the Sepik region group. The Abelam religion centers upon the life-cycle, with the initiation of boys standing out as an important event. Their economy is based mainly upon the growing of vegetables such as yams and sweet potatoes, and cash crops such as coffee and cocoa. They practice slash and burn cultivation.

Abelam

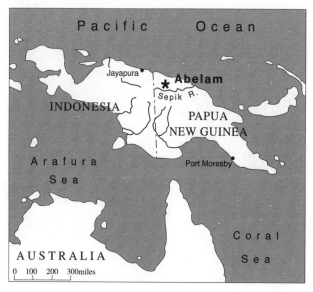

ABENAKI   see ABNAKI.

ABIDJI   An ethnic group living in the lagoon area of the Côte d'Ivoire.

ABIHKI   see CREEK.

ABIPON   A subgroup of the GUAYCURU living in Argentina.

ABISSA   A subgroup of the MABA.

ABITIBI   (Abitibiwinni) A Native North American people of about 700, found mostly in two small bands in Ontario and Quebec, Canada. They speak an Algonkian dialect.

ABKHAZIANS   (s.d. Apswa) A people located on the Black Sea coast south of the main Caucasian chain between the Psou and Inguzi Rivers. According to the 1989 Soviet census they number over 100,000 in the former Soviet Union, of whom some 90,000 live in the Abkhazian Autonomous Republic (capital, Sukhumi) of Georgia, and some 3,000 in Achara, near Batumi, Georgia; 30,000 can also be found in Turkey and former territories of the Ottoman Empire, where they were resettled in the 1860s and 1870s together with other northern Caucasian peoples and are known as Circassians (see CHERKESS).

The Abkhazian language belongs to the Abkhazo-Adyghean branch of the Ibero-Caucasian family. For centuries the Georgian literary language was used both officially and by the church. An Abkhazian alphabet, based on the Cyrillic alphabet, was created in 1862. It

Abkhazians

was replaced by the Roman alphabet in 1926, the Georgian alphabet in 1938, and again by the Cyrillic alphabet in 1954. During the twentieth century, a literary language and written literature, whose main founder was Dimitry Gulia, emerged alongside the Abkhazians' rich and ancient folklore. Abkhazians are divided into two main subgroups, BZYBIAN (Gudantian) and ABZHUI, each with its own dialect. The Abkhazian literary language is based on the ABZHUI dialect.

The Eastern Orthodox rite, common among the Abkhazians, was adopted in 523 C.E. During the fifteenth and sixteenth centuries, many adopted Sunni Islam of the Hanafi school. The traditional economy is based on agriculture, cattle breeding (goat breeding in the mountains), bee-keeping, and hunting; in recent times tea, tobacco, and citrus cultivation have been added. The Abkhazian Autonomous Republic also boasts of various industries and a large resort area along the Black Sea coast.

In the middle of the first millennium B.C.E., Abkhazian tribes constituted part of the ancient Kolkhidian kingdom; they formed a part of the west Georgian state of Lazika from the fourth to sixth centuries C.E. An Akhazian kingdom, comprised of both Abkhazians and the inhabitants of western Georgia, lasted from the eighth to the tenth centuries, when it was absorbed by the united Georgian kingdom. Ottoman hegemony over the region was achieved over the next three hundred years. In 1810 the region came under Russian rule, but was only annexed formally to the Russian Empire in 1867. In 1922, in the aftermath of the Russian Revolution, an Abkhazian republic was created. This was reconstituted as the Abkhazian Autonomous Republic, an administrative part of the Georgian Republic, in 1931. With the collapse of the Soviet Union a movement advocating Abkhazian secession from Georgia emerged. Only 20 percent of Abkhazia's population is Abkhazian, the remainder defining themselves mainly as GEORGIANS. (see also ABAZIANS, TURKS)

ABNAKI   (Abenaki) A small Native North American band of about 200, many of whom reside in Quebec, Canada, centered on the Abnakis de Wolinak Reserve. In culture and language they are related to the PENOBOSCOT and PASSAMAQUODDY.

ABOR   see ADI.

ABOURE   (Abure) An ethnic group living in the lagoon area in the southeastern region of the Côte d'Ivoire.

ABRON see BRONG.

ABSAROKA see CROW.

ABUJHMARIA (Hill Maria) An ethnic group living in Abujhmar, in the Bastar district of Madhya Pradesh, India. They number some 11,000 (the 1981 census counted them with the GOND, to whom they are related). Their language is similar to Gond, a member of the Dravidian family of languages.

Abujhmaria houses are constructed of timber and bamboo and have thatched roofs; villages are situated on hill slopes or in valleys near a freshwater source. Sites are occupied for two to three years and the surrounding land cultivated, using the slash and burn method. When the land is no longer arable, the villagers relocate their village to a new site. The Abujhmaria also practice hunting, fishing, and animal husbandry (pigs, poultry), and collect forest produce, mainly for their own consumption. Most Abujhmaria villages are uniclan.

ABUNG (Lampong) A generic term for a group of peoples numbering about 500,000 and including MARINGGAI, PAMINGGIR, and PUBIAN (Pabean), living along the coast of south-central Sumatra, Indonesia. Since the area they inhabit is called Lampung, they are sometimes referred to as Lampong. They speak either Malay or a Malay dialect but their traditional script has fallen into disuse. They still preserve their traditional religion although certain elements, such as head-hunting and human sacrifice, have been replaced by ritual dances and buffalo sacrifices respectively at the instigation of the colonial government of the DUTCH. Another once important aspect of their religious rituals was the construction of towering megaliths as ritual centers. While these are no longer erected, their presence indicates early Abung settlement in the area. Whereas the DUTCH were not entirely successful in their bid to rid the Abung of various practices, they now appear to be succumbing to the influence of contemporary Indonesian society.

The Abung peoples originated in the Sumatra highlands but were forced to the coast by growing opposition to their head-hunting raids. They now engage in slash and burn cultivation of rice, although the best fields are reserved for pepper. Only pepper and certain products gathered in the jungle are used in trade. Social stratification is of primary importance but, through performing certain rituals, upward mobility is allowed and even encouraged.

ABUSEMEN An ethnic group living in Chad. They are related to the KOUKA, MIDOGO, and BULALA.

ABZHUI A subgroup of the ABKHAZIANS.

ACADIANS, ACADIENS see CANADIANS, QUEBECOIS.

ACHAGUA A South American Indian people living in the Caqueta region of southeastern Colombia. They subsist primarily from agriculture, their staple crop being bitter manioc. Villagers usually live in a single large communal house. (see also VENEZUELANS, COLOMBIANS)

ACHANG (Maingtha, Monghsa, s.d. Ngachang) A Tibeto-Burman group numbering c.20,000 who inhabit the Chinese-Burman border area. With the influx of ethnic CHINESE into their territory and the ensuing loss of agricultural land, the Achang increasingly find employment as skilled laborers among the SHAN, with whom they share many cultural components. (see also KACHIN)

ACHAR see AJAR.

ACHHICK (Hill Garo) A subgroup of the GARO.

ACHIM see AKIM.

ACHINESE see ATJEHNESE.

ACHIOLARE A Luo-speaking group living in Sudan.

ACHOLI A people living in the north of Uganda, on the high plain of Acholi, east of the Nile River. A small part of their territory extends into the Sudan. They speak a Western Nilotic language which carries traces of Eastern Nilotic and Central Sudanese influence.

They have a mixed economy of agriculture (millet, sesame, sweet potatoes, ground nuts, cassava, and beans), and livestock-breeding. Before the arrival of the Europeans, they were expert iron-workers.

The Acholi have a patrilinear clan-structure and live in polgynous households, with a bilateral family-structure. Their society is stratified, being subdivided into commoners and aristocracy. The Acholi were divided into several independent groups, which never established political unity. A chiefdom usually consisted of one, sometimes several villages, most of which were large, mainly for reasons of defense. In the course of the twentieth century this settlement pattern became obsolete when the Ugandan state suppressed raiding, thereby eliminating the reason for fortified settlements. The settlement pattern now is much more dispersed.

Like most Nilotic-speakers, the Acholi worship a remote creator god (*juok*), Lubango , custodian of the social order. Other spirits, the *jok*, intervene in everyday life and are usually connected with specific places, where shrines are erected for them. Of great importance is the ancestor cult. Rituals performed at ancestral shrines are aimed at influencing the ancestor spirits to bring wealth and rich harvests. The *rwot*, or supreme chief, was usually also the rainmaker. His authority sprang largely from this ceremonial and religious function, and he seems to have had mostly ritual rather than administrative functions. The office was hereditary. There are also professional healers (*ajwaka*) among the Acholi. (see also LANGO, UGANDANS)

ACHUARA   A subgroup of the JIVARO.

ACHUMAWI   A small Native North American people, many of whom live in northeast California, U.S.A., on the Likely Federal Reservation and on the Lookout Rancheria, both in Modoc County. They form part of the PIT RIVER TRIBE.

ACWABO   see CHAUBO.

ADA   A subgroup of the ADANGBE.

ADAL   see AFAR.

ADAMPA   see ADANGBE.

ADANGBE   (Adampa, Adangme, or Dangme) A people numbering around 510,000, living along the coast and in the Accra plain of southeast Ghana. They are associated with the GA and are closely related to the EWE. The SHAI, found primarily in the Accra District or the eastern region between Accra and the Volta region, the KROBO (Klo), who live along the right bank of the Volta River, and the ADA, KPONG, NINGO, OSUDOKUA, and PRAMPRAM, are all identified as Adangbe.

ADARE   see HARAGE. (see also ETHIOPIANS, SOMALIS)

ADELE   An ethnic group living in central Togo. (see also TOGOLESE)

A'DHAM   A subgroup of the RHADE

ADI   (Abor) An ethnic group numbering about 35,000 living in Arunachal Pradesh, India. They speak Abor, a member of the Tibeto-Burman family of languages. The most prominent subgroups of the Adi are the BORI, BOMO-JANBO, MIMAT, AIENG, PASSI, MINYONG, PADAM, MILANG, PANGGEE, and SIMONG.

The ASSAMESE in the plains of the Brahmaputra valley gave the name "Abor" to a tribe of independent hillmen (today known as the Adi) who lived on the southern slopes of the Himalayan range between the rivers Dihing and Subansiri in the Siang District of Arunachal Pradesh. The Adi claimed supremacy over all the mountain ranges between Assam and Tibet, and levied contributions from their lowland, less martial, neighbors. During the period of rule by the BRITISH, the British government sent many punitive expedition to subdue these powerful tribes of the Northeastern Frontier.

The Adi practice slash and burn agriculture to raise rice, cotton, tobacco, maize, ginger, red pepper, edible roots, pumpkins, sugarcane, and opium.

ADIJA   see BUBI.

ADIOUKRU, ADJUKRU   see ADYUKRU.

ADIYAN   An ethnic group numbering 10,000 (1981) living in the states of Kerala, Karnataka, and Tamil Nadu, India. They speak dialects of the Kannada and Malayalam languages of the Dravidian family. The name "Adiyan" may have been derived from the Sanskrit "Adi," meaning "original" or "aboriginal."

Adangbe

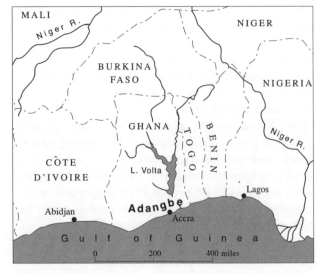

Previously regarded as untouchables, the Adiyan were formerly agricultural serfs and are today low-paid agricultural laborers.

The Adiyan celebrate Hindu festivals, but have no separate temples of their own.

ADJA An ethnic group living in southern Benin and in the Aneho and Atakpame areas of Togo. Their language is Adja.

They believe that they are a branch of the YORUBA that migrated from Oyo in present day Nigeria in the thirteenth century and settled in Tado and later in Notse, in present day Togo. One branch of Adja that migrated southward in the eighteenth century became the EWE people, while another group founded the Allada kingdom in present day Benin. (see also EWE)

ADOUMA An ethnic group living in Gabon, along the left bank of the upper Ogooue River in the area of Latoursville.

ADOYMARA A subgroup of the AFAR.

AD SAWRA A subgroup of the TIGRE.

AD SHEIKH A subgroup of the TIGRE.

ADYGHE see ADYGHEANS, BALKAR, CHERKESS, KABARDIANS.

ADYGHEANS (s.d. Adyghe) In its widest sense, "Adyghean" is used to designate three north-Caucasian peoples, the Adygheans, KABARDINIANS, and Circassians (see CHERKESS), who all call their language Adygheabze. The language of the Adygheans proper is termed "Lower Adyghe" (the Adyghe themselves also call it Kakh); it belongs to the Abkhazo-Adyghean branch of the Ibero-Caucasian family. The literary language is based on the Temizgoi dialect; in 1918 it adopted the Arabic alphabet, in 1927 it was changed to the Roman, and in 1938, to the Russian (Cyrillic) alphabet.

The Adygheans live in the Adyghean Autonomous *Oblast*, or region (established in 1922, administrative center Maikop) in the western part of North Caucasus; in the Karachai-Circassian Autonomous *Oblast*; and along the Black Sea coast. Between 1859 and 1864 a considerable number of Adygheans were resettled in Turkey and in other Near and Middle East states of the Ottoman empire, where they are known as Circassians (see CHERKESS). According to the Soviet census of 1989 they numbered almost 125,000, about 95,000 of whom live in the Adyghean *Oblast*.

During the sixth and seventh centuries Eastern Orthodox Christianity from the Byzantine and Georgia began to spread among the Adygheans. Since the fifteenth century, they have been Sunni Muslims of the Hanafi stream.

The main subgroups are ABADZEKH, BESLENEY, BJE-DUKH, EGER-UTAKAI, KHATU-KAI, MACHOSHEI, NATUKHAI, SHAPSUG, TEMIRGOI; the Adygheans in the Adyghean *Oblast* are mostly descendants of the BJEDUKH and TEMIRGOI. They have a rich folklore with a written literature that emerged in the 1930s.

The population is mainly rural and its traditional economy is based on agriculture, cattle-raising, and horticulture.

ADYUKRU (Adjukru, Adioukru) An ethnic group living in the Côte d'Ivoire in the coastal region along the western part of the Ebrie lagoon, near the town of Dabou. In 1970 they numbered about 30,000. Although they are of KRU origin, their social structure and culture have been influenced by their lagoon neighbors. Their main occupation is palm oil production.

ADYUMBA An ethnic group living in Gabon on the banks of Nazereth Bay near the mouth of the Ogooue River. They were originally a MPONGWE clan.

AETA A southern subgroup of the NEGRITOS of the Philippines.

AFAR (Danakil, Adal) A people numbering about 2 million living in southern Eritrea, eastern Ethiopia, and in Djibouti, in the lowland deserts west of the Red Sea. They speak an eastern Cushitic language and are Sunni Muslims. The non-urban Afar are mostly nomadic pastoralists. They herd camels, cattle, goats, and sheep, usually in the vicinity of their encampments, located near sources of water. In addition to the pastoral economy, they were involved in mining the salt in the subsea level saline lakes of the Danakil depression in the East African Rift Valley. They were also involved in the slave trade practiced by ARABS in this part of Africa, and were famous as a warlike people.

The Afar were divided into four states or sultanates, each further divided into chiefdoms which are divided among smaller kinship or territorial groups. Distinction is made between two ancestor-related groups, the ASAYMARA ("red") and the ADOYMARA ("white"). The former is considered of higher status and lived mainly

An Afar woman herding cattle in Ethiopia

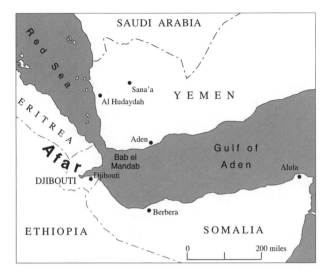

Afar

in the interior. Currently both groups are dispersed over Afar territory and the status distinction is less marked.

There was longstanding hostility between the Muslim Afar of the lowland desert and the Christian AMHARA of the inland mountains of Ethiopia. When the Amhara empire expanded eastward into the lowlands, efforts were made to integrate the Afar into the Ethiopian state. Both sedenterization of the Afar and turning them from pastoralists into agriculturalists were tried, but often in vain. Hostility prevailed, and was rekindled when the Muslim peoples in Eritrea rebelled against Ethiopian rule.

Numbering about 200,000, the Afar of Djibouti are the second largest people in that country after the ISSA. Most live in the north. Traditionally, most of the economic power in Djibouti, as well as political dominance, was in the hands of the ISSA. The FRENCH attempted to alter this power structure, and from the early 1960s the Afar were permitted to control the country's government under the leadership of Ali Aref Bourhan. Djibouti, as the last European possession in Africa, received its independence from France in 1979. Since independence, Afar ethnic rivalry with the dominant ISSA is the main economic and political feature of the country, and the main concern of the Afar.

In Ethiopia, although the Afar are a comparatively small population, they are of central importance. In current political jargon they are known as the "strategical nomads." They played a central role in the expansion and recession of the late medieval Islamic states between the Christian empire and the Red Sea, and up to the nineteenth century they controlled the trading

routes between the empire, the Red Sea, and the Somali coast (Zeyla). There are also Afar living around the Eritrean port of Assab, nowadays central for Ethiopian access to the sea, and subject to special agreements between Ethiopia and Eritrea.

The segmentary social structure found an outlet among present political affiliations. Afar opposition to the Mengistu government centered around the Afar Liberation Front (AFL) of Ali Mirrah, the former sultan of Aussa, while his internal opponents, founding the Afar National Liberation Movement (ANLM), successfully negotiated self-adminstration with the former government. A recent offspring of the ANLM is the Afar Revolutionary Democratic Movement (ARDU). A movement named Ugogomo/Revolution cooperated with the old regime. In 1991 the ruling EPRDF/TPLF founded the Afar Democratic Union (ADU). (see also DJIBOUTIANS, ERITREANS, ETHIOPIANS, ISSA, SOMALI)

AFATIME   see AVATIME.

AFGHANS   1. Appellation of the PASHTUN used by most of their neighbors and, mainly through the mediation of Persian, in European non-scholarly terminology. 2. Unifying appellation applied within Afghanistan to members of all ethnic groups inhabiting the country (AIMAQ, AIMAQ-I DIGAR, BALUCHIS, FARSIVAN, GAVARI, KUTANANS, GHORBATIS, GUJAR, HAZARA, ISHKASHIMI, JALALI, MONGOLS, MUNJANI, NURESTANIS, ORMURI, PARACHI, PASHAI, PASHTUN, PIKRAJE, QAZAQ, QIZILBASH, QYRGHYZ, RUSHANI, SHADIBAZ, SANGLICHI, SHEIKHMOHAMMEDIS, SHUGHNI, TAJIK, TATARS, TIRAHI, TURKMEN, UZBEKS, VAKHI, VANGVALAN, ZEBAKI). This usage is intended to define the country's ethnic groups as forming the nation of Afghanistan, the "Land of the Afghans," and is presently in use almost exclusively among the educated strata of the urban population.

The population of Afghanistan is estimated at around 13 million, but an accurate national census has been extremely difficult to obtain. This is mainly due to the ongoing civil wars and the mass emigrations that have escalated since the beginning of the 1980s. It is estimated that one-sixth of the population fled to Pakistan after the Soviets entered Afghanistan in 1979. Nearly 20 percent of the population live in urban areas and the majority of this number live in the capital, Kabul. Roughly 50 percent of the population consists of the PASHTUN; the TAJIKS make up about 30 percent, and the UZBEKS account for between 5 and 10 percent.

The official languages of Afghanistan are Dari and Pashto, and although the latter is used for literary purposes, Dari is most commonly used in everyday life. Most Afghan are Sunni Muslims, with about 10 percent adhering to Shi'ite Islam. From roughly the third century B.C.E., Buddhism was the dominant religion in the area until the seventh-century influx of Islam from western Asia, and the latter has remained the dominant religion ever since.

Afghans have traditionally subsisted on crops such as wheat, rice, potatoes, and corn, as well as local fruit and nut production. The main cash crops consist of dried fruit and nuts. The ravages of war have increasingly damaged both agriculture and trade.

Afghanistan first found unity as a nation under the rule of Ahmad Shah Abdal in 1747. The area was eventually colonized by the BRITISH after the First Afghan War (1838-1842). Throughout this period, the RUSSIANS were also trying to gain control and in 1907 an Anglo-Russian agreement was signed which gave Afghans their own government (still influenced by the BRITISH). There was much turmoil throughout the twentieth century, resulting in many turnovers of power. The constitutional monarchy established in 1964 was ended by a coup in 1973. By 1978 the USSR was backing the People's Democratic Party of Afghanistan, who were in power. Beginning in the 1980s, a widespread rebellion against the Soviet-backed government grew into a civil war and by the end of the decade an estimated 1 million Afghans had been killed. The Soviet-backed regime was ousted, but there is still much turmoil between the different factions over the balance of power. (see also PASHTUN)

AFLENDA   A subgroup of the TIGRE.

AFRAN QALLUU   (Oborra, Ala, Nole, Jarso) A division of the eastern OROMO.

AFRIDI   A subgroup of the PASHTUN.

AFRIKANERS   The Afrikaner population of South Africa originated in an amalgam of DUTCH, GERMANS, BELGIANS, and FRENCH (Huguenots), who came as settlers from the seventeenth century. They number around 3 million and constitute about 65 percent of the white and 10 percent of the total population of South Africa. The Afrikaans language derives from Dutch and is distinctly Dutch-flavored (particularly in its noun forms), although it has simplified the Dutch grammar and has incorporated many loan-words both from English and from local African languages.

Prior to the twentieth century, the Afrikaners were a rural people, accounting for the fact that the terms "Afrikaners" and "Boers" (lit. farmers) have historically been synonymous appellations. Today under 8 percent of Afrikaners are involved in agricultural occupations; around 20 percent are manual and blue-collar workers; and around 70 percent are involved in white-collar occupations. Afrikaners are scattered throughout South Africa, with the largest concentrations in the urban areas in the Transvaal, in the Orange Free States, and in the northern Cape. The province of Natal probably has the smallest concentration of Afrikaner settlement.

The Afrikaners are Christians, the majority of whom are members of one of the three Dutch Reformed Churches in South Africa; the Nederduitse Gereformeerde Kerk (c.70 percent of Afrikaners); the Nederduitsch Hervormde Kerk (c.13 percent); and the Gereformeerde Kerk (c.6 percent). The last is the most conservative of the three, and is also called the Dopper Church in analogy with the inverted cup (*dopper*) used to extinguish candles. Gereformeerde Kerk members call themselves Doppers since they aim at "extinguishing the light" (or "the fire") "of the French Revolution."

Afrikaner history in South Africa began in 1652 with the establishment of a refreshment station at the Cape by the Dutch East India Company. Since barter with the local inhabitants (primarily KHOIKHOI) failed to ensure adequate supplies to meet growing Company demands, immigration from Europe was encouraged. DUTCH, GERMANS, and FRENCH Huguenots took advantage of the free passage offered and became the first *freeburgers* in South Africa (and the forefathers of modern-day Afrikaners). From an early date, extensive agriculture became the norm. From here on, the settlers' chronic hunger for land and labor dominated their relations with local peoples. A series of wars, first against the KHOIKHOI and then against the XHOSA, accompanied the expansion of the eastern frontier. Political hegemony over the Cape colony passed to the BRITISH in 1795, the DUTCH in 1803, and back to the BRITISH in 1806.

Opposing BRITISH rule, especially the establishment of circuit courts in which (white) masters could be sued by their (black) servants, and the emancipation of slaves (which, according to their Manifesto, was "contrary to the laws of God and nature"), sections of the Afrikaner population trekked east and north, out of the jurisdiction of the Cape Colony. This Great Trek, which began in 1835, was in four main streams of

"Voortrekkers." The last was led by Piet Retief, author of the Voortrekkers' Manifesto. He and a number of his followers were slaughtered while negotiating for land with the ZULU under Dingaan. Andries Pretorius's retaliatory campaign and the overwhelming defeat of the ZULU in the Battle of Blood River in 1837 later became a focal point of twentieth-century Afrikaner nationalist ideology. Following a further series of military campaigns against the more recalcitrant local peoples (the Boers sometimes being supported by black allies like the ROLONG and GRIQUA), the Voortrekkers established the Boer republics of Natalia (in present-day Natal), the Orange Free State and the mineral-rich South African Republic (present-day Transvaal). Natalia's independence was extremely shortlived, while the latter two republics were incorporated into the Union of South Africa in 1910, following their defeat in the Anglo-Boer War of 1899–1902. Prompted primarily by British designs on the mineral wealth of the republics, the war was hard and bitter. While British troops vastly outnumbered the Boers, the latter's strategy of guerrilla warfare postponed their defeat for three years. During the course of the war the BRITISH interned thousands of Boer women and children in concentration camps: 26,000 perished there, primarily as a result of epidemic diseases.

Prior to the Boer War, the Afrikaner population was primarily rural. In the Boer republics families were isolated in vast farms and the accepted social pattern was one in which "each man fled the tyranny of his neighbor's smoke." The main social units were the family, the church, and the commando (a semi-formal citizen's army unit mobilized in times of need and disbanded thereafter). Boer society was patriarchal and egalitarian. There were no intraracial class distinctions, and social status was primarily determined by learning. Education was "Bible education," taught mainly at home by parents and private religious tutors or in the few state schools. Within this system, church ministers held the highest social status, and moral, social and political standards and norms were largely determined by the Dutch Reformed Church.

In the aftermath of the Boer War, Afrikaners streamed to the cities in consequence of the BRITISH military strategy of farm burning and land devastation during the war, and an agricultural crisis at the turn of the century stemming from the cyclical recurrence of drought and Rinderpest disease. In 1904 for example, only 6 percent of Afrikaners were urbanized; by 1946, 44 percent of Afrikaners lived in the cities; and by 1960, 76 percent of the Afrikaner population were per-

manent urban dwellers. This steady stream of unskilled Afrikaners into the urban areas brought them into direct social contact (and economic competition) with the equally rapidly urbanizing unskilled African population; and this within the English-dominated economic system. By 1930, more than one-sixth of the white population were defined as being "very poor," the vast majority of these "poor whites" being Afrikaners. It was in a two-flanked offensive against both inter-racial class allegiances for the Afrikaner proletariat and anglicization by the more economically successful Afrikaners that the Afrikaner nationalist movement arose in the 1930s. The nationalist offensive was both material and ideological, including active trade union involvement and the support of Afrikaner businesses, together with the promotion of the exclusivist nationalist ideology of Christian-Nationalism. The Dutch Reformed Church as well as a slew of newly-formed political, economic, and cultural organizations, orchestrated the nationalist endeavor.

The ideology of Christian-Nationalism was a blend of seventeenth-century Dutch Calvinism and ethnic nationalism according to which the Afrikaners are a Chosen People, elected by God to fulfill a specific calling in South Africa, one which focuses on the reconstitution of pre-ordained organic nations from the present undifferentiated masses (specifically analoguous with the chaos of the time of the Tower of Babel). Afrikaner history is thus sacred history. The Great Trek was a second Exodus while the Battle of Blood River was promoted as a clear confirmation of election and calling, still commemorated as the Day of the Covenant (in reference to Pretorius's oath to hold the day forever holy should the Voortrekkers defeat the ZULU). And within the framework of this ideology, redemption was finally achieved by the election of the Christian-Nationalist *Nasionale* Party to office in 1948.

The Afrikaners have ruled South Africa since that date, imposing a Christian-Nationalist superstructure in the form of apartheid on all of the population. In the late 1980s, in response to the search for a new dispensation under prime ministers Botha and De Klerk, a large number of Afrikaner organizations have emerged, striving for the creation of a whites-only Afrikaner *Volksstad* or *Boerestaat* in part of South Africa; a white homeland in which the Afrikaner faithful may live. (see also SOUTH AFRICANS)

AFSHAR An ethnic group living in southern Iran in the Kerman province and in the southern Zagros area between Shiraz and Hamadan. Small groups of Afshar are also to be found in Turkey and in Afghanistan (near Kabul). A rough estimate puts them at numbering about 500,000. The Afshar language belongs to the southwestern (Oghuz) group of the Turkic family of languages. Similar to Azerbaijani, it is unwritten, Persian being used as the literary language. The Afshar are Shi'ite Muslims.

The Afshar are semi-nomads, engaged in long distance cattle- and sheep-breeding and agriculture. The appellation Afshar (in the form of Awshar) was first mentioned in the late eleventh century. They played an important role in the military and administrative history of Iran. The most prominent political figure of Afshar origin was the celebrated eighteenth-century warrior, later shah of Iran, Nadir.

Afshar

AFU   An ethnic group living in Nigeria.

AFUNU   A subgroup of the TIV. (see also CHOKOSSI)

AGAIDUKA   see SHOSHONE.

AGARIA   A people numbering almost 70,000 (1981) living in the Maikal range in the Mandla, Raipur, and Bilaspur districts of Madhya Pradesh, India. They speak Mundari and Kherwari, dialects belonging to the Austro-Asiatic family of languages.

The name Agaria is closely connected with the Hindi and Sanskrit for "fire" ("Ag" and "Agni"). The Agaria, traditionally iron-smelters, claim that their first ancestor made the first plowshare. They worship Lohasur, the iron demon they believe dwells in smelting kilns.

They live dispersed over the countryside, with their small smithies widely distributed. They have various customs and traditions, including family names, in common with the GOND. (see also PANIKA)

AGAW   (Agow, Agew) A people numbering 500,000 (1980s), living in the southern Gojjam and part of the Gondar regions of Ethiopia. They speak Khamir (Khamtanga), a central Cushitic language, but are linguistically and culturally also strongly amharized. They are Ethiopian Orthodox Christians. The Agaw are plow-using agriculturalists.

The present Agaw are related to an historically once much more important population who became largely amharized over the centuries. From 1137 to 1270 a Christian Agaw-based line of emperors, the Zagwe dynasty, ruled the Ethiopian Empire. Particularly noted was the emperor Lalibela, during whose reign the famous rock-hewn churches were built. (see also ETHIOPIANS, QEMANT)

AGNAGAN   An ethnic group of about 4,000 people, living along the border valleys of Western Togo. They have retained their traditional religious beliefs. (see also TOGOLESE)

AGNI   (Anyi) A people of the AKAN grouping numbering approximately 584,000 and living in the Côte d'Ivoire east of the Comoe River, along the border with Ghana. They speak the Twi language and are mostly Christians. Their family structure is based on matrilineal descent.

The Agni were among the first peoples in the Côte d'Ivoire to come into contact with Europeans and to adopt Western cultural forms.

Although they attempted to resist colonial rule by the FRENCH in the late nineteenth century, the FRENCH encouraged them in their conflict with the BAULE people in an attempt to weaken the latter's political power. A conflict with the economically successful EHOTILE in the 1950s climaxed in a failed Agni attempt at secession prior to independence. (see also IVOIREANS)

AGOLINU   A subgroup of the FON.

AGTA   see NEGRITOS.

AGUA CAHUILLA   see CAHUILLA.

AGUARUNA   A subgroup of the JIVARO.

AGUATEC   A subgroup of the MAYA.

AGUL   An ethnic group of the central mountain part of southeast Daghestan. According to the 1989 Soviet census they numbered 20,000. They became Sunni Muslims of the Shafi'i stream not earlier than the sixteenth century, after the Arab conquest of the Caucasus. The Agul language belongs to the Lezgian group of the Daghestan branch of the Ibero-Caucassian family; it is unwritten and Lezgian is used as the literary language.

The Agul inhabit four isolated canyons connected by narrow paths. The first road to their region was built in 1936. Today the main Agul connections are with the LEZGIN.

Agul villages are located on slopes and consist of three or four blocks; two- to three-storey stone houses standing side by side; the village usually contains a fortress.

The national dress is of the common Daghestani type (men wear a Circassian coat, felt cloak, and sheep skin coat; women, a long dress, wide trousers, and a head scarf).

The traditional economy is based on sheep-breeding, agriculture, carpet-making, and smithery.

AGUSAN MANOBO   An ethnic group living along the Agusan River on the northeast side of Mindanao, an island in the Philippines. No updated official data are available, but a gradual decline in numbers has been noted and it can be assumed that modernizing tendencies have taken their toll on the Manobo way of life.

The Manobo language is a member of the Malayo-Polynesian family. They practice a traditional native religion, and have been strongly influenced by Christian missionaries. The name "Manobo" means both "hillmen" and "unbaptized." They subsist from slash and burn agriculture, cultivating tubers, rice, and maize. Their diet is supplemented by wild pig, python, birds, and fish.

The Agusan Manobo share many characteristics with surrounding ethnic groups, notably the BAGOBO and MANDAYA.

AHAM   A subgroup of the IBO.

AHLON BASSILA   An ethnic group living in central Togo. (see also TOGOLESE)

AHMADIS   see PAKISTANIS.

AHORI   A subgroup of the YORUBA living in Nigeria.

AHOULAN   A group of Ewe-speakers living around the Togolese capital of Lome and along that country's border with Ghana. Their main occupation is fishing.

AHT   see NOOTKA.

AIANLU   A subgroup of the KHAMSE.

AIENG   A subgroup of the ADI.

AIMAQ   ("tribe/clan" in Mongol and eastern Turkish; also referred to as Chahar ["four" in Persian] Aimaq) Collective name for four clans of Afghanistan inhabiting the western part of the central massif (the Ghur) of Afghanistan and in eastern Iran (where they are known as BARBARI). Groups included under this listing are the FIRUZKUHI, residing north of the Hari Rud river; the TAIMANI, south of it; the JAMSHIDI, in Kusht; and the HAZARA DEH-I ZAINAT (not to be confused with the HAZARA) in Qal'a-i Naw. The total number of Aimaq is estimated as between 500,000 and 830,000. The usual form of self-designation is by name of clan and not by the collective name of [Chahar] Aimaq.

The Aimaq speak several dialects of Dari (the official name of Persian in Afghanistan) with a heavy admixture of Turkic and partly Mongol. They are Sunni Muslims of the Hanafi religious school.

The TAIMURI, who live separated from the Aimaq astride the Afghano-Iranian border, are included by some scholars within this grouping.

The Aimaq are most probably descendants of Turco-Mongol tribes who settled in the area following the Mongol conquest and mixed with the local Iranian population. Their economy is based on agriculture and cattle-breeding. During the winter they live in permanent villages but move annually to summer camps with their flocks of sheep and goats. Most of them use as their summer shelter the Central Asian *yurt* (tent) rather than the black tents used by other nomadic groups in Afghanistan.

AIMAQ-I DIGAR   (lit. "another Aimaq") Common appellation for five loosely connected ethnic groups of northern and northeastern Afghanistan, named so in their aggregate to be distinguished from the AIMAQ ethnic groups. The Aimaq-i Digar consist of:

TIMURI (Taimuri): estimated number 33,000 (all figures here date from the 1970s);

TAHIRI: estimated number 17,000;

ZURI: estimated number 15,000;

MALIKI: estimated number 12,000;

MISHMAST: estimated number 5,000.

All Aimaq-i Digar ethnic groups speak varying dialects of Dari (the Persian spoken in Afghanistan). They are Sunni Muslims of the Hanafi religious stream. They are semi-nomads; some subgroups have become sedentarized or tend to sedenterization.

The TAHIRI tends also to dispersion, being scattered from the main habitat of all the Aimaq-i Digar up to the central southeastern area of Farah. (see also AFGHANS)

AIMELLE A subgroup of the GURAGE.

AINU The approximately 17,000–24,000 Ainu are the remnants of an indigenous people of Japan, living mainly in Japan's northernmost island of Hokkaido and in the southern part of the Russian island of Sakhalin. Little is known of their origins, but it is generally surmised that they are descended from a proto-Caucasoid group who possessed a Neolithic culture and migrated to Japan in prehistoric times. They once

Ainu

occupied all of Japan, but were pushed northward over the centuries by Japanese expansion.

Unlike other East Asian peoples, the Ainu have wavy brown hair and light skins. Because of their abundant body hair, they are referred to as "the hairy ones."

Their spoken language, consisting of several dialects, is unrelated to any known linguistic family. There is no written language, but songs and stories are transmitted orally from generation to generation.

The Ainu practice a traditional religion, worshiping many gods of the mountains, land, sky, and sea. One distinctive feature of the Ainu religion is the bear cult.

Early Ainu life was based on a hunting-gathering economy. Since 1868, there has been a steady process of assimilation into the larger JAPANESE community, and they have increasingly adopted Japanese housing, clothing, food, and other aspects of life and economy. Ainu customs survive only in certain villages, and traditional dress and religious objects are used only on ceremonial occasions.

The Ainu population is dwindling rapidly due to intermarriage and assimilation. Only a small percentage is of unmixed blood. They are economically among the poorest groups in Japan, and unemployment remains high.

AIRUM A nomadic subgroup of the AZERBAIJANI.

AISSORES see ASSYRIANS.

AIT ATTA A confederation of peoples, most of whom are of Berber origin, with some berberized ARABS and blacks, who live in the south-central Atlas mountains of Morocco. Their region is situated between the Dra River in the west, the Dades, Todra, and Reris Rivers in the north, and the Ziz River in the east. The geographic center of the Ait Atta region is located near the Sarho massif, their place of origin, and the oasis of Tazzarine.

In 1960 they numbered approximately 150,000. They speak the Berber language and are Muslims. Their kinship system is based on the principle of common descent from a single sixteenth-century ancestor. The Ait Atta are nomadic pastoralists, dispersed over a large territory, and retain many of their traditions.

In the early nineteenth century the Ait Atta expanded from the Darho towards the Dra oasis. Some clans, especially the AIT KABBAS, resisted colonization by the FRENCH in the late nineteenth and early twentieth centuries. They lost their independence only in 1933.

After Morocco became independent from FRENCH rule in 1956, most of the Ait Atta supported the Berber-based political party. Among Ait Atta clans are groups known as HARATIN, dark-skinned people who suffered from Perber racism. Following Moroccan independence the HARATIN migrated in large numbers to cities such as Marrakesh and Casablanca, and as a result became wealthier, while the Ait Atta remained in rural areas.

AIT KABBAS   A clan of the AIT ATTA.

AIZO   An ethnic group scattered in small villages around the town of Ouida in Benin. They number around 10,000 and are largely assimilated into the larger FON and ADJA populations.

AJAR   (s.d. Achar) A Georgian ethnic group living on the northeast coast of the Black Sea (southwest Georgia). They speak Gurian, a dialect of Georgian with many lexical borrowings from Turkish and, through Turkish, from Persian and Arabic. They gradually converted from East Orthodox Christianity to Islam mainly during the seventeenth and eighteenth centuries, their territory being part of the Ottoman empire until 1878 when it was ceded to Russia.

Between 1918 and 1921 the territory of the Ajar (Achara, Ajaristan), changed hands, first to the BRITISH and next to the then-independent Georgian republic. In 1921 the Ajarian Soviet Autonomous Republic was proclaimed within the framework of the Georgian Soviet Socialist Republic.

The Soviet census of 1926 listed the Ajar, then numbering over 70,000, as a separate ethnic group. However, from 1930 they were officially regarded as GEORGIANS.

The Ajar are settled in two natural climatic areas: on the coast and littoral terraces, with a developed subtropical agriculture and vast health resorts (lower Achara); and in the mountainous zone (mountain Achara), with a stock-raising economy. Achara's administrative, industrial, and cultural center is the port city of Batumi. (see also GEORGIANS)

AJAVA   see YAO.

AKA   (s.d. Hrusso) A group numbering 12,500 (1981), living at an altitude of 3,000 to 6,000 feet in the sub-Himalayan region of Arunachal Pradesh, India. Their language belongs to the Tibeto-Burman family.

The Aka are of Mongoloid stock. Aka men tie their hair in the middle of the head in a knot, while the women wear it at the back. They practice the shifting cultivation mode of agriculture; their staple foods are maize and millet.

AKA-BALE   An ethnic group living in the Andaman Islands in the Indian Ocean. They subsist on fishing, gathering, and small-scale cultivation.

AKA-BEA   An ethnic group living in the Andaman Islands in the Indian Ocean. They subsist on fishing, gathering, and small-scale cultivation.

AKA-BO   An ethnic group living in the Andaman Islands in the Indian Ocean. They subsist on fishing, gathering, and small-scale cultivation.

AKA-JERU   An ethnic group living in the Andaman Islands in the Indian Ocean. They subsist on fishing, gathering, and small-scale cultivation.

AKA-KEDE   An ethnic group living in the Andaman Islands in the Indian Ocean. They subsist on fishing, gathering, and small-scale cultivation.

AKA-KOL   An ethnic group living in the Andaman Islands in the Indian Ocean. They subsist on fishing, gathering, and small-scale cultivation.

AKA-KORA   An ethnic group living in the Andaman Islands in the Indian Ocean. They subsist on fishing, gathering, and small-scale cultivation.

AKAN   A major group of peoples of West Africa. Most Akan live in Ghana. According to their tradition, they originated in the Adanse region around Lake Bosumtwi in Ghana. They speak Akan and are divided into numerous and distinct subgroups including the AKIM, AKUAPEM, AKYEM, KWAHU, ASHANTI, BRONG, DENKYIRA, ASSIN, NZEMA, and FANTE. (see also AGNI, IVOIREANS, GHANAIANS)

AKEBOU   An ethnic group numbering around 17,000 living in the Plateaux Region in Togo. They are not affiliated to any larger ethnic group and have intermingled with the AKPOSSO. (see also TOGOLESE)

AKHA   (Kaw, Kha Ko) An ethnic group numbering over 100,000 located primarily in the Yunnan Province of China. Akha communities also exist in the mountainous border regions of Burma, Thailand, and Laos. Ethnographers report either seven or nine sub-

An Akha woman in northern Thailand

groups of Akha, including the PULI, TYITSO, AKHO, NU-QUAY, JEN G'WE, and HTEU LA, but all groups speak dialects of a common Tibeto-Burman language and share the belief that they are descended from seven brothers who once lived in south Yunnan. The Akha language has no native script, but missionaries in Burma have devised several scripts for the various dialects.

Despite slight regional differences, the Akha have a strong sense of identity and their villages, which they

Akha

frequently relocate, are connected by a series of paths. Slash and burn agricultural techniques are used to raise food crops and tobacco. They also gather local roots and insects to supplement their diet. In recent years, many Akha villages have begun raising opium which they trade to local Chinese merchants for food and tools.

The Akha practice ancestor worship and animal sacrifice. A corpse may be kept in the home prior to internment for as long as two months, during which magical rites and sacrifices are performed.

AKHO a subgroup of the AKHA.

AKH-U see LATI.

AKHVAKH (s.d. Ashwad) An ethnic group numbering some 4,000, living in the mountains of north-west Daghestan. They have been Sunni Muslims of the Shafi'i stream since the sixteenth century. The Akhvakh language belongs to the Andi subgroup of the Avar-Andi-Dido group of the Daghestan branch of the Ibero-Caucasian family. It is unwritten, Avarian being used as the literary language.

The Akhvakh are undergoing an intensive process of integration within the AVAR. One vivid manifestation of their ethno-cultural consolidation is the use of the term "AVAR" by the Akhvakh as another self-designation. They do not appear in Soviet/Russian official ethnographic nomenclature as an ethnic group in their own right, but are regarded as a subgroup of the AVAR. Accordingly, they are listed as AVAR on their identity cards.

Until recent times, Akhvakh women were known by the water pitchers which they made with beeswax. The traditional economy includes agriculture and cattle-breeding. National dress is of the common Daghestani type (see AGUL).

AKIKUYU see KIKUYU.

AKIM (Akyem, Achim) A major Akan-speaking group living in the Atewa hills and along the Birin River between the towns of Kibi and Oda, Ghana. They believe that they originated in the modern Adansi area from which they migrated eastward under pressure from the DENKYIRA in the seventeenth century. During the eighteenth and nineteenth centuries they paid tribute to the ASHANTI. The Akim are divided into three major divisions: AKYEM ABUAKWA, the largest; AKYEM KOTOKU; and the southernmost and smallest division, the AKYEM BOSUME. (see also AKAN)

AKIT A subgroup of the KUBU.

AKLIL A subgroup of the GURAGE.

AKNADA see TINDIANS.

AKOKO A subgroup of the YORUBA living in Nigeria.

AKPOSSO An ethnic group living in the mountainous area of the Plateaux Region in Togo and across the border in Ghana. In 1983 they numbered around 52,000. They have no centralized political framework.

The Akposso were pushed into their current area in the nineteenth century by the ASHANTI and EWE. Later in that century they were involved in a series of wars with the ASHANTI, in which they were defeated. The arrival of the BRITISH in the area and their victory over the ASHANTI enabled the Akposso to descend from the mountains and to reoccupy their foothill villages.

Today the Akposso cultivate cocoa and coffee. (see also AKEBOU, TOGOLESE)

AKUAPEM (Akuapim) An AKAN people living in the eastern Region of Ghana, northeast of the capital, Accra. In the eighteenth and nineteenth centuries they were dominated by the ASHANTI and paid tribute to their kingdom. (see also AKAN)

AKUNAKUNA A subgroup of the IBIBIO.

AKUWEYA-YACHI An ethnic group living in Nigeria.

AKWE A Native South American group living in Brazil.

AKYEM A subgroup of the AKAN, living in Ghana.

AKYEM ABUAKWA, AKYEM BOSUME, AKYEM KOTOKUSEE Subgroups of the AKIM.

ALABA A people numbering 100,000 (1980s) who live along the eastern bank of the Bilate River in the southern Shoa Province of Ethiopia. Their language belongs to the eastern Cushitic group, and they are Sunni Muslims, culturally and linguistically related to the HADIYA. The Alaba are agriculturalists and cattle-raisers. (see also ETHIOPIANS)

ALABAMA An Algonkian-speaking Native North American group whose approximately eighty-eight members are scattered today across Louisiana and Oklahoma, and in Texas, where they are found on the Alabama-Coushatta State Reservation in Polk County. They joined with the CREEK and other Indian tribes in the Creek Wars against the United States. The tribe was forced to move to the Indian Territory (Oklahoma) in 1836.

ALACALUF A nomadic Native American people living along the coast and offshore islands of Chile and Tierra del Fuego. They subsist by collecting mussels and shellfish, fishing, and hunting seals and porpoises.

ALACHUA see SEMINOLE.

ALAK A Mon-Khmer group numbering about 2,000 living in southern Laos. They worship spirits.

The Alak engage primarily in slash and burn cultivation of rice, but areca trees, betel nuts, and tobacco are also grown.

ALANGAN An ethnic group numbering several thousand who live in the mountainous northern interior of the island of Mindoro in the Philippines. They speak Mangyan, a Malayo-Polynesian language. They are the least-modernized group on Mindoro, retaining traditional forms of dress (bark cloth); some still lead a seminomadic existence as hunters and food-gatherers.

ALAWITES see LEBANESE, SYRIANS.

ALBANIANS (s.d. Shqiptiar) There are over 5 million Albanians, of whom 2.9 million live in Albania (where they constitute 90 percent of the population), and some 1.7 million in former Yugoslavia, mainly in the adjacent province of Kosovo (1.3 million), where they constitute 80 percent of the population. Sizable communities are also found in northwest Greece, Italy, Turkey, and the U.S.A.

The Albanians are believed to be descendants of the aboriginal inhabitants of the western Balkan peninsula, who were compressed into their present-day mountain homeland by the Slavs. Albanian is an Indo-European language, and is the only living representative of its group. It is believed to be descended from ancient Illyrian. Its main dialects are Gheg, spoken in Tirana, the capital, and in the north, and Tosk, spoken in the south. The dialects differ slightly in vocabulary and pronunciation.

This linguistic division corresponds to anthropological differences. The GHEGS and the TOSKS differ markedly in outlook and social behaviour, the GHEGS having better preserved national characteristics.

Like other mountain dwellers, the Albanians, especially the GHEGS, were fiercely independent and resisted any external authority. Tribal loyalties and structure persisted until World War II at least, at which time the overwhelming majority of Albanians were Sunni Muslims, according to Italian statistics. A Greek Orthodox minority, concentrated in the north and south, was the second largest community (c.15 percent), but Albanians in Greece and Italy belong predominantly to this denomination. A Roman Catholic community (c.8 percent) was concentrated around Scutari.

The Albanians never formed a state of their own until the twentieth century. During their long history, they were either under the rule of other powers — Byzantines, SERBS, BULGARIANS, BOSNIANS, Normans, Venetians, and Ottomans — each of which promoted its own religion, or lived in their inaccessible mountains as independent tribes who shifted alliances among themselves and with the neighboring states whom they often supplied with mercenaries. Charles of Anjou was the first, and, until the twentieth century, the only monarch, to adopt the title "King of Albania," after he conquered the Albanian coast in 1272.

The Ottoman conquest of Albania, begun in 1385, was completed only in 1571. Apart from the country's rugged terrain and the resistance of Venice, they were thwarted by a series of local revolts. The most famous of these, between 1443 and 1470, was led by Skanderbeg, who was proclaimed a hero by the Albanian national movement in the nineteenth century.

Although they established their "*pax turcica*," the Ottomans never succeeded in extending their direct rule beyond the coastal plain and the lowlands. The mountain tribes, especially in the north, were left to their own devices as long as they kept the peace and supplied irregulars (one man per household) to the Ottoman army. Landlords in the lowlands, on the other hand, were fully absorbed into the Ottoman military administrative structure (the *timar*). Conversion to Islam was never a condition of this absorption and the

Albanians

islamization of the Albanians did not gain momentum until the eighteenth century.

Muslim Albanians were, and considered themselves, a part of the *stadtsvolk* of the Ottoman Empire, and as such contributed far beyond their share in the population to its expansion, maintenance, and survival. An Albanian nationalism was first formulated in 1878, with the establishment of the "Albanian League for the Defense of the Rights of the Albanian People," which was actually instigated by the Ottoman authorities to influence the decisions of the Congress of Berlin. Yet, until the creation of an independent Albania in 1913, Albanian nationalism remained in an embryonic stage, striving for autonomy within the Ottoman Empire rather than for an independent state. The creation of Albania in 1913 was more the result of Italian and Austro-Hungarian efforts (both resisted any significant strengthening of Serbia and Greece) than of local nationalist activity.

After World War I, Albania's independence was recognized, but the first years of the new state were marked by internal struggles. In 1924 Ahmed Zog seized power with Yugoslav help, proclaimed Albania a republic and declared himself president. In 1928 he proclaimed Albania a monarchy with himself as king. In the 1920s and 1930s, a series of treaties with Italy placed Albania under Italian protection in all but name. Still, in 1939 Mussolini conquered the country.

Following World War II a Communist regime, headed by Enver Hoxha, was established in Albania. A staunch Stalinist, Hoxha broke with the Soviet Union in 1959 and with the People's Republic of China in 1975 for their "revisionism." Albania was declared, "the world's first atheist state," and was closed to the outside world, thus making it the poorest and most underdeveloped country in Europe. Following his death in 1985, his heirs, headed by Ramiz Alia, cautiously attempted to open the country to the world and started a slow process of liberalization, but the collapse of the Communist regimes in Eastern Europe soon brought down that of Albania as well.

In Yugoslavia, Tito recognized Kosovo's Albanian majority by declaring the region an Autonomous Province within Serbia. Following his death, however, and with the general rise of nationalism in Yugoslavia, tension and ethnic conflict developed in Kosovo. In 1989 Serbia dissolved the Autonomous Province of Kosovo and placed the territory under martial law. (see also CAUCASIANS, UDI)

ALENSAW   A subgroup of the IBO.

ALEUT A Native North American group which, along with Indians and INUIT, comprises the original inhabitants of pre-contact North America. There are about ten thousand Aleut today scattered among thirteen islands of the Aleut chain. Their first major contact with a non-native group was with the RUSSIANS, who took into slavery or killed many of them.

Today they form part of the Alaskan Native community and live mainly from fishing. The different Aleut villages are bound together in the Aleut Corporation centered in Anchorage, U.S.A. (see also GREENLANDERS)

ALFUR The collective name for the indigenous inhabitants of the large but sparsely populated island of Halmahera (also Djailolo) in northeastern Indonesia. The entire population of the island, estimated at about 150,000, is divided into some thirty tribes of different racial, cultural, and linguistic stock.

Historically, the inhabitants were generally dominated by the Muslim sultans of the small outlying islands of Ternate and Tidore who played a prominent role in the spice trade. Only recently, however, has the population begun to adopt Christianity and Islam, and indigenous beliefs in spirits remain strong. The southern groups on Halmahera speak Malayo-Polynesian languages, while the northern groups (and the TERNATANS and TIDORESE) speak languages unlike other Indonesian languages. They are generally classified as a separate North Halmaheran language family although possible ties have been surmised with the languages of New Guinea and the AUSTRALIAN ABORIGINES. Racially, the former group possesses Mongoloid features; the latter group is similar to the Melanesians.

Hunting, fishing, and gathering are important to both groups, but the coastal peoples have also adopted slash and burn cultivation of rice to supplement their diet.

ALGERIANS (s.d. Jaziriyyun) An Arab people numbering 26 million inhabiting Algeria, a country in North Africa. They are mostly Arabic-speakers (Algerian dialect); there is an important minority of BERBERS. French remains an important second language in spite of attempts at Arabization. Since the departure of one million French colonists, the population consists nearly exclusively of Muslims (Sunni Malikites except for Ibadites in the Mzab).

Until the TURKS established suzerainty over the whole territory in the sixteenth century, Algerians did not form a unified nation: east Algeria (the Constantinois) shared a common history with Tunisia, while the west shared much of its history with Morocco. The Algerians are very unevenly distributed between: a relatively densely settled Mediterranean margin (in particular the central and oriental Tell) where the surplus population of overpopulated Berber mountain villages flowed over into the plains; and the nearly empty desert, where nomads who constitute 2.5 percent of the country's population are spread over 90 percent of the area. In spite of the fact that petroleum and natural gas, Algeria's major export earners, are found mostly in the south, the Sahara population shows a migratory deficit towards the cities. Urbanization has now risen to 40 percent or more.

Algerians form a very young population struggling to build a viable society in the face of inclement natural circumstances (aridity, deforestation, and erosion) and severe social and ethnic problems. Meager economic opportunities have driven more than one million Algerians abroad to France.

The Algerians may descend from a mixture of indigenous BERBERS and colonizing Phoenicians and Carthaginians. Later they were partially subdued and colonized by Rome. Irrigation and slave labor turned North Africa into the Western Empire's richest agricultural province, which was lost in the turmoil of tribal revolts and Vandal invasions of the fourth-fifth centuries. Algerians received their strongest imprint in the seventh century from the conquering ARABS, who defeated the indigenous BERBERS and brought complete islamization and incomplete arabization. ARABS became the ruling elite, but Islam remained a minority religion until the eleventh century, when competition between Sunni and Shi'ite dynasties in North Africa led the Egyptian-based Fatimids to send destructive Bani Hilal nomad-settlers westward: they devastated the Maghreb, and are blamed for a fateful decline in agricultural and city life, and growth of pastoralism. After having lived under Saharan Berber kingdoms of the Almoravids and Almohads, Algerians were, from the thirteenth to the sixteenth centuries, partitioned between Moroccan and Tunisian dynasties. The "Barbary coast" was next contested between the SPANIARDS and TURKS, and won by the latter: Algeria became an Ottoman province and a corsairs' den whose lords grew rich from ransoming Christian prisoners. After 1671 Algiers was a quasi-independent backwater.

In 1830 military intervention by the FRENCH led to the conquest of Algiers, provoking the fall of Ottoman overlordship throughout the whole of Algeria. But it took France time to decide what to do with its colony. A revolt in the Oran region where the Marabou serif

Abd el-Kader created a strictly Islamic state and initiated a holy war, ended in capitulation, and lasting French occupation. Sporadic tribal or Islamic revolts in the later nineteenth century were powerless to prevent the massive colonization by which France consolidated its hold. Colonial policy toward Muslims wavered between a tendency towards assimilation, sedentarization, and modernization on the one hand, and open subordination on the other. France systematically discriminated in favor of its *colons*, who transformed the Algerian countryside. By the 1930s they formed 2 percent of the rural population but owned one-quarter of all cultivated lands. However, most Europeans were city-dwellers: FRENCH, other Europeans (ITALIANS, SPANIARDS, MALTESE), and naturalized JEWS ultimately totaled nearly one million.

Meanwhile the Muslim Algerians developed a national consciousness of their own, but the *colons* blocked even the slightest emancipation. After World War II, a restricted Muslim elite obtained a partial franchise, and complete equalization was broached for all. Hopes for peaceful improvement of the Muslims' position and the closure of social-economic gap were gone. Decades of French rule had created an underdeveloped Algerian society. After a series of more limited (and cruelly suppressed) regional revolts, in 1954 the FLN (National Liberation Front) launched a full-scale war of independence. The armed insurrection was harshly repressed, but meanwhile the FLN gained wide international recognition.

Without hope of a military victory, the FLN combined international action with terrorism and strengthened its institutions. Meanwhile the European settlers rejected any compromise, armed themselves, and contemplated secession. After a particularly violent war (which may have cost up to one million civilian lives), Algerians obtained full independence in 1962. As French *colons* departed, their estates became the booty for a new Arab bourgeoisie. The new rulers installed an authoritarian, one-party, socialized state, mixed from the onset with a dose of Islamic symbolism. Yet for all its proclaimed hegemony, the FLN failed to reform itself into a mass vanguard party. Houari Boumediene's rule (1965–1978) symbolized the concentration of power in the sovereign state, which from the late 1970s found it increasingly hard to fulfill the people's economic aspirations, or to lay a firm basis for a collective Algerian identity. The ideological vacuum has been filled by an increasingly vocal Islamic fundamentalist movement: the religious majority of the Algerians has never been secularized. Under Chadli Ben-

jedid's leadership (1978–1992), the FLN has attempted to prop up the economy and repossess Islamic elements from fundamentalists.

The expansion of education and industrialization (paid for by natural gas revenues) has not succeeded in keeping pace with the Algerians' high rate of population growth and rapid urbanization. By the mid-1980s economic development remained unspectacular and the party's image became tarnished. The absence of legal ways to express the growing discontent with the functioning of state and profiteering by new classes gave rise to social unrest. In 1988 massive riots, initiated by youth movements, forced the regime to permit political pluralism. This raised hopes for a democratic opening profiting three major tendencies: the intellectuals' and women's movements demanding secularization and modernization, BERBERS demanding ethnic-linguistic pluralism, and anti-Western fundamentalists seeking a conservative religious-political program. Of these three, the fundamentalists are by far the strongest. In 1990 the Islamic Front won the municipal elections, defeating the FLN for the first time. In an atmosphere of religious intolerance and growing destabilization, the Islamic Front seemed on the verge of taking over the Algerian state. In 1991, after violent demonstrations, the army proclaimed a state of emergency, cracked down on the fundamentalist leadership, and delayed legislative elections. However, in Algeria's first-ever free elections the Islamic Front won by an overwhelming margin. Soon afterward, in 1992, the army took over, disbanded the Islamic Front, and began to persecute the fundamentalists.

ALGONKIANS (Algonquin) A Native North American people living in the Province of Quebec, Canada. Although the Algonkian language is one of the most widely spoken in North America, the Algonkian nation is relatively small, comprising today only about 4,000 members. They engage in hunting, fishing, and forestry.

ALIFURU   SEE AMBONESE.

ALIKOZAI   A subgroup of the PASHTUN.

ALIZAI   A subgroup of the PASHTUN.

ALKALI LAKE   SEE SHUSWAP.

ALLAN   SEE BALKAR, OSSET, QARACHAI.

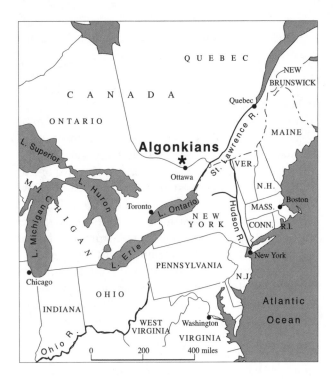

Algonkians

ALLAR A group numbering 350 living in Pal-ghat, Kerala State, India. They are nomadic food-gatherers, and worship trees, plants, rocks, and streams.

ALMO A subgroup of the MARAKWET.

ALORESE Inhabitants of the Indonesian island of Alor, with a population of about 150,000. They speak a variety of languages and dialects divided into seven linguistic groups, Abui, Adang, Kamang, Kawel, Kelong, Kolana, and Kui-Kramang, all belonging to the Austronesian family of languages. Most Alorese have converted to Christianity although there are some Muslim communities along the coast and significant inland communities retaining traditional beliefs.

They are primarily agriculturalists who cultivate corn and raise small livestock such as pigs, goats, and chickens. Wealth is sometimes measured by the number of Javanese drums possessed.

Whereas coastal Alorese have a lengthy history of contact with JAVANESE traders and DUTCH and POR-TUGUESE from the colonial authorities, those residing in the remote interior of the island are often still isolated from the outside world except for sporadic visits by Christian missionaries.

ALSATIANS (s.d. Alsaciens, Elsaesser) The 1.5 million Alsatians and 2.3 million Lorraines constitute a regional-cultural subdivision of the contemporary FRENCH people, living in southeast France, in the Alsace-Lorraine region. They are predominantly Catholic. While French is spoken in Lorraine and in the larger Alsatian towns, German dialects and culture connect the Alsatians to GERMANS beyond the Rhine no less than to France.

Alsace-Lorraine (Elsasz-Lothringen) was acquired by France in the seventeenth century, and then formed part of Germany from the Franco-Prussian war of 1871 until the end of World War I. For France the loss created a permanent focus of irridentism, while Germany followed a policy of forced assimilation, prohibiting both the use of French and the existence of regional (often Catholic) Alsatian associations which strove for a degree of local self-government. France recaptured the province in 1918, but autonomist tendencies remained strong; yet Alsatian identification with the FRENCH progressed apace.

The Alsatians were annexed under occupation by the Germans during World War II, but were reattached to France after liberation. Although this was welcomed by the population, French attempts to impose lay schools and the French language spurred an autonomist movement. A slower pace of acculturation has since been adopted.

ALTAI (s.d. Altay-Kizhi) The name used by Soviet Russian authorities to describe a group of Turkic tribes living in the Kuznetskii and Ala Tau Mountains on the southeast border of the Russian Federation. In 1989 there were 72,000 Altai in the Soviet Union, 85 percent of whom constitute about 30 percent of the population of the Gorno-Altai Autonomous Province. After three failed attempts to provide their language with an alphabet, a Cyrillic one was finally adopted.

The Altai were originally nomadic tribes of the Siberian steppes who submitted to and formed part of the different regional empires. As a result of colonization by the RUSSIANS they were pushed out of their ancestral pastures and hunting grounds into the mountains where, unable to pursue their traditional livelihood, many became bonded agricultural laborers. They are still engaged primarily in agriculture.

In 1922 the Soviet authorities formed the Altai-Oirot Autonomous Province, which in 1948 was renamed Gorno-Altai and the people named Altai. The present Altai include the CHELKAN, KUMANDIN, and TUBA.

Altai

At the time of the Russian conquest, the Altai practiced Mahayana Buddhism. During Russian rule, some converted to Russian Orthodoxy, but many returned to Lamaism in the twentieth century as an expression of anti-Russian sentiment, while some Altai, particularly the TELEUT group, converted to Islam.

ALTAY-KIZHI   see ALTAI.

ALUR   A people living in the forested savanna of northwest Uganda and in a remote part of northeast Zaire, northwest of Lake Mobutu. They speak a Western Nilotic language.

The Alur own large herds of cattle, but they are also agriculturalists who practice shifting cultivation, producing sorghum, maize, eleusine, sesame, bananas, beans, and tobacco. Those Alur who live on the shores of Lake Albert are also occupied in fishing.

Their society is subdivided into groups and subgroups, and there are two kinds of clans, aristocrats and commoners. The exogamous clans also constitute geographical units and are the basis of the social and political organization. The basic social unit is the village, which consists of a circle of 10-15 huts and is usually situated on a hill. Only the villages of the chiefs are fortified. The office of chief is both hereditary and the highest political position, and his prominence is indicated by certain privileges and by the size of his house and herds. The chief fills the offices of judge and rainmaker. Prominent persons have more than one wife.

Their religion is very similar to that of the ACHOLI. Several spirits (*jol*) are localized in rocks and rivers or embodied in snakes. Ancestor shrines are built in the shape of a miniature hut and situated inside the village. The Alur also have a rainmaker, who is usually the chief, and healers.

The Alur have partially assimilated enclaves of the OKEBO and LENDU, originally Sudanese-speaking people, mainly living in Zaire. They gained influence in the region because of their ability to mediate in ethnic conflicts. (see also UGANDANS, ZAIREANS)

AMAR   see HAMMAR.

AMARAR   A Bedawiye-speaking subgroup of the BEJA.

AMARROO   (Badittu, Koyra) An ethnic group of 70,000 (1980s) living to the east of Lake Chamo in eastern Gemu Gofa province, Ethiopia. Their language, sometimes called Koyra, is related to Kachami and belongs to the Omotic language cluster. The Amarroo adhere to traditional beliefs.

The mountainous kingdom of Amarroo was integrated into the Ethiopian empire at the end of the nineteenth century. The Amarroo practice terrace agriculture (barley, cabbage, pulses).

AMBAMBA   see OBAMBA.

AMBAQUISTAS   A subgroup of the KIMBUNDU.

AMBE   An ethnic group living in northeastern Zaire.

AMBO I   An ethnic group living in southeast Zambia and along both sides of the border between Angola and Namibia. They are Oshidonga-speakers and both Christians and adherents of traditional religions. In Angola they comprise 3 percent of the population; in Zambia, 1 percent. Most Ambo are nomadic cattle-raisers. In Angola they were the main suppliers of beef for the central highlands.

Ambo society was divided into communities consisting of one to three hundred families organized in a clan system and ruled by a king (the last king was defeated by the PORTUGUESE in 1915).

AMBO II (Bwamba) A people living in southwest Uganda, in the forest area. They speak Bulibuli and Bwezi, two languages belonging to two linguistic groups within the Western Lacustrine Bantu languages. The Ambo proper speak Bulibuli (or Amba). The Bwezi vernacular is related to the Toro language.

The Ambo used to be hunters but have changed to agriculture, today also in a commercialized form, growing cash crops such as coffee. For their subsistence they produce plantains, cassava, and sweet potatoes.

The basic social unit is the village, which is grouped around one kinship unit and may contain between 50 and 500 persons. The kinship structure is a patrilineal, exogamous lineage system. One segment consists of people having between four and seven ancestor generations in common (maximal lineage). No clan contains both Bulibuli and Bwezi lineages, but there are bilateral connections between Bwezi and Bulibuli lineages in the way of quasi-kinship relations. Clans have no continuous area of settlement and the maximal lineage is the largest localized segment of a clan. Minorities, like the Vonoma and Mvuba-language groups, are socially integrated and culturally assimilated. A small minority of PYGMIES have been integrated, but they are still hunters.

The Ambo have no central political authority, and constitute a segmentary society without chiefs. There is no institution for enforcement of decisions, which are carried out through the bonds of solidarity and loyalty. Elders exercise no influence, but theirs is a rudimentary, although unstable, clientele-system.

The NYORO and TORO both laid claim to overlordship of the Ambo but could never put it into practice. During the colonial era the Ambo were considered part of the TORO for administrative purposes.

The Christianization of the Ambo took longer than that of other groups. They never had a uniform pantheon of gods, leaving much space for local variants.

AMBONESE (Alifuru, South Moluccans; s.d. Orang Ambon, Orang Maluka Selatan) Inhabitants of the Central (not South) Moluccan Archipelago in Indonesia. They number about 750,000, with sizable communities in Jakarta and in the Netherlands. Most speak a Malay dialect although a native Ambonese collection of dialects is still used in the interior of the islands of Ceram and Buru. They are primarily Christians and Muslims who have incorporated traditional ancestor worship into their beliefs. Most Ambonese now believe that while God is responsible for the universe, it is the spirits of departed ancestors who intervene in

daily life. A third religion, Agama Nunusaku, is also prevalent; it incorporates Christian, Muslim, and traditional beliefs. Common to adherents of all faiths, however, is the sense of ethnic exclusivity. Only Ambonese may participate in local services; non-natives are forbidden entrance to local churches and mosques.

Wild sago is an important economic staple, but yams, cassava, and taro are also cultivated in garden plots. Historically, the islands are famous for their spices, including cloves and nutmeg, and these are still cultivated as cash crops. There is some fishing too.

The islands were known to Europe as early as Roman times for their spices (the term Spice Islands was often used to describe them). For over two millennia traders came to the islands, influencing the local culture and introducing Christianity and Islam. The Ambonese were the mainstay of the colonial army and administration of the DUTCH; years of contact with the outside world made them the most educated of Indonesia's ethnic groups. They later rejected independence in 1950 and attempted to declare their own Republic of the South Moluccas, but this was overrun by Indonesia and many inhabitants fled to the Netherlands as refugees.

In the Netherlands, the Ambonese declined to integrate into the predominant culture, and blamed the Dutch government for the collapse of the South Moluccan Republic. Tensions peaked in the mid-1970s when various separatist groups committed a series of startling terrorist attacks in the Netherlands to force the government to pressure Indonesia to grant the South Moluccas independence.

AMERICANS The people of the United States of America, constituting a heterogenous population of almost 250 million, living in a federation of fifty states extending from the Atlantic to the Pacific Oceans (and including the states of Alaska and Hawaii). Alongside the small indigenous population of Native Americans, many ethnic, linguistic, and religious groups are represented, while several uniquely American cultural groups have also emerged.

The non-native population of the United States can be classed into several categories. The majority is of European descent. Some are descended from early settlers of North America who arrived prior to independence in 1776 or in the early years of statehood. They are mainly BRITISH, DUTCH, and FRENCH. SPANIARDS, many of whom intermingled with the indigenous population, constitute a distinct category. Other categories are the descendants of immigrants who flocked to the country at the turn of the century, seeking economic, social, political, and religious refuge. These include IRISH, ITALIANS, JEWS, SLAVS, GERMANS, and others, who retain a sense of community within the larger American people.

Some 40 million African-Americans have made a significant contribution to the development of an American culture: in addition, their struggle for liberty and equality has helped shape American social, economic, and political history. They are descendants of slaves brought from Africa to the United States to work the great plantations of the South. Recently they have been joined by new immigrants from Africa and the Caribbean. Hispanics, or Latino-Americans, numbering over 20 million, are the fastest growing category among the Americans. These recent waves of immigrants coming mainly to the southwest seek economic opportunities and political asylum.

Asian Americans, mainly CHINESE and JAPANESE in origin, first arrived in the West Coast in the mid-nineteenth century where they found work as menial laborers. Despite attempts to exclude them from participation in American life (the CHINESE were barred from immigrating between 1882 and 1943) and to ban the movement of some, like the JAPANESE, in wartime, their numbers have grown and they have been joined by an influx of refugees from Southeast Asia since the mid-1970s. There are also sizeable groups of South Asians (mainly INDIANS and PAKISTANIS), and Pacific Islanders.

Some uniquely American groups have emerged from the waves of immigrant communities. Important among these are the Creoles of the southeastern coast, the Sea Islanders of the eastern seaboard, and the Amish of Pennsylvania. The five million Mormons of Utah and the Rocky Mountain states, although not an ethnic group, are another example of a distinctive American-based culture that has emerged.

English, the official language of the United States, is spoken by the overwhelming majority of the population, but in many of the numerous immigrant communities it is studied as a second language. Spanish is also an important language and is co-official with English in the state of New Mexico. In addition, most European and many Asian and African languages are spoken. Although the number of speakers of Native American languages has been in a marked decline, many are still spoken regionally, with some, like Navajo, having as many as 200,000 speakers.

Although American and British English are mutually intelligible, they differ in both pronunciation and spelling, the American variant having been subject to a somewhat simplified orthography and the influence of immigrants' pronunciation patterns. Even within the United States there are regional differences of pronunciation, making it possible to pinpoint a speaker's place of origin with some degree of proximity.

The religious beliefs of Americans are equally diverse. Most follow some form of Christianity: there are almost 90 million Protestants and 60 million Roman Catholics, as well as adherents of the Eastern Orthodox rite. The Jewish community of the United States is the largest in the world and there are significant and growing Muslim, Hindu, Buddhist, and Sikh communities. Many members of the African-American community have retained or reverted to traditional beliefs such as Santeria, and the Native American peoples have, to some degree, retained their traditional beliefs. Officially, America adheres strictly to the separation of church and state, and the society is predominantly secular. At the same time religious symbols abound in the daily life of Americans, albeit in a secular form; Christmas is universally accepted as a holiday, and there are also some American holidays of both religious and national nature.

Since the turn of the century, this once predominantly agricultural society has been transformed into an industrial, technological, and mercantile society which, coupled with abundant natural resources, has made Americans one of the wealthiest national groups in the world. While most Americans are employed in industry and trade, the service sector is also of particular importance.

American food, clothing, and arts can be experienced around the world and have come to represent "Western Culture." American fashions such as jeans are, in many developing countries, regarded as a status symbol. American fastfood chains and beverages can be found advertised in many a language and alphabet around the world. New York is one of the world's great cultural capitals, with every art form represented. While California is the center of the entertainment industry worldwide, the jazz traditions of African-Americans of the southeast have set a trend in contemporary music.

The first Americans are believed to have settled in the present United States some 30,000 years ago. They fanned out across the diverse geographical regions, creating tribal societies and nations. The arrival of the first Europeans to the United States has also been the subject of some speculation although the first of the modern settlements were established only after Christopher Columbus's voyages to the western hemisphere in 1492. Four nations, Britain, France, Spain, and the Netherlands, vied for control of the region, Britain becoming the dominant power on the eastern seaboard. Many of the first settlers, such as the Pilgrims of Plymouth Rock, were refugees fleeing religious persecution; others were traders and merchants who recognized the vast wealth of this unexploited region. With the influx of European settlers, particularly in New England and Virginia, came a certain degree of self-rule. What were initially peaceful relations with the indigenous peoples occasionally became hostile as the burgeoning immigrant population made encroachments on their land and livelihood.

In the South, large plantations were established based on the exploitation of imported African slave laborers. While the first settlers were ENGLISH, SCOTTISH, and IRISH, there was also an influx of FRENCH, GERMANS, and other Europeans. In the southwest, then under Spanish control, settlers intermingled with slave laborers and the native population, forming the core of the current Hispanic component of Americans.

With increased prosperity came a sense of distinction from Europe. Despite local political autonomy, the colonists considered themselves exploited by Britain, and sought to administer the colonies themselves. As tensions increased, so did the call for independence by thinkers such as Thomas Paine, Benjamin Franklin, and Thomas Jefferson, who sought to create a federal republic out of the colonies. Gathered together in the Continental Congress (1775–1776), they resolved that "These colonies are, and of right ought to be, free and independent states." Two days later, on 4 July, 1776, they issued the Declaration of Independence, sparking the Revolutionary War which led to the formation of the United States of America.

The following years saw the split of American opinion among Liberals, Radicals, and Conservatives, each with its own vision of the type of government to be adopted by the infant state. A compromise was reached in the Constitution of 1788 which still remains the basis of American political life. Written to "form a more perfect union, establish justice, ensure domestic tranquility, provide for the common defense, promote the general welfare, and to secure the blessings of liberty to ourselves and our posterity," it failed to liberate the millions of enslaved African-Americans. In 1791 ten amendments were made ensuring such liberties as freedom of religion, speech, the press, and the right to trial by jury. Known as the Bill of Rights, they were later echoed in the liberal constitutions of other countries but were not always put into practice in the United

States. Expansion into lands inhabited by Native American peoples continued and the African-American population remained largely enslaved. Another question debated was regionalism and the rights of states against the federal government, matters which eventually erupted in the Civil War of 1861–1865.

Nonetheless, Americans prospered and expanded to the west. New immigrants poured in from Europe as more territories were annexed, including the Louisiana Purchase, Texas, and California. As new territories were opened to settlement, the indigenous inhabitants were largely ignored and their rights violated. Waving the banner of "Manifest Destiny," and with a pioneering frontier spirit, Americans spread from the Atlantic to the Pacific Ocean.

One of the most pressing problems facing Americans in the nineteenth century was the slavery question. It had long been abolished in the north but was vital to the Southern economy. The debate over this and the degree to which states were to control internal affairs led to the secession of the South and the establishment of the slave-holding Confederate States of America in 1861. The objective of a united American nation was finally achieved with the surrender of the Southern states in 1865, and the government began a policy of reconstruction to reintegrate the South.

The years following the Civil War saw the arrival of millions of immigrants from Europe and Asia. European immigrants came through the northeastern states, particularly the port of entry at Ellis Island, New York, where IRISH fleeing famine, ITALIANS fleeing poverty and JEWS fleeing pogroms came in their millions at the turn of the century. On the West Coast, Asian immigrants found employment, settling in San Francisco and Los Angeles. Filipinos, having served in the American Navy since 1901, settled in cities with naval traditions. These new immigrants were gradually absorbed into the new American society. At the same time, they contributed much to the evolving American culture and were vital to the emergence of the contemporary industrial and commercial economy.

America emerged from its relative isolation into a world power during the two World Wars. Prosperity saw the emergence of a new middle class culture, where suburbia and the automobile have become important elements. The 1960s witnessed a transformation in American social and political life, when the popular struggle for civil rights of African-Americans became widespread, embracing also the struggle for the rights of women, children, homosexuals, the disabled, and Native Americans.

Still, contemporary America is a land of ethnic contrasts, a composite of many parts. Each group has made its contribution to the culture of the country and become a part of the emerging American supra-ethnicity. Once deemed a melting pot, America can best be described today as a cultural mosaic.

AMERICO-LIBERIANS (Settlers, Afro-Americans) The name given to around 15,000 black individuals who were settled in Liberia at the beginning of the nineteenth century by the American Colonization Society. The Americo-Liberians number about 450,000, including a large number of local ethnic groups with whom they intermarried over the years. Some originated in Barbados. Nearly half were slaves who were freed by their masters on condition that they emigrated.

In Liberia they formed communities along the Saint Paul River, from Robertsport in the northwest to Harper in the southeast. Although some intermarried with local Africans, most tended to attach themselves, often as farm laborers, to American settlements. The language of the Americo-Liberians is English and they are mostly Methodist Christians.

The Americo-Liberians formed the ruling elite in Liberia for about 150 years. The local ethnic groups were usually hostile towards their new rulers, who competed with them in trade. In 1915 the KRU people revolted against them but were defeated with American assistance.

In 1980 their hegemony was abolished in a coup led by Samuel Doe, a member of the KRAHN people. (see also BASSA, LIBERIANS, VAI)

AMHARA A people numbering 12 million (1984) living in the central Ethiopian highlands of Gondar, Gojjam, western Wollo, and northern Shoa, and also found in other areas, both rural and urban, of Ethiopia. The figure includes linguistically amharized population groups (most notably OROMO).

The Amharic language (also Amharinya) belongs to the southern Semitic (Ethio-Semitic) group, combining a southern Semitic vocabulary with a Cushitic syntax. The Amhara are mainly Ethiopian Orthodox Christians, but there is also a Muslim Amharic-speaking population, the JABARTI. The Amhara are mainly highland agriculturalists who produce grains and use the plow. Although farming can be considered their traditional occupation, their dominant political position has always been linked to military and administrative exploits and careers. Considered the core population of Ethiopia, the Amhara people's culture has largely de-

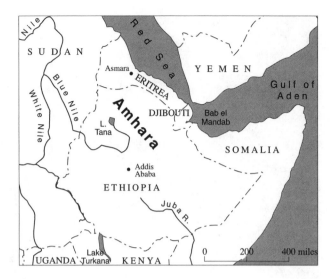

Amhara

termined the image of the "ETHIOPIANS." The formation of the Amhara was closely connected with the development and expansion of the Ethiopian empire from the second half of the thirteenth century and the spread of vernacular Amharic as the royal language (together with the written Ge'ez of the church). The use of Amharic paralleled the military and political expansion of the imperial state. A probable factor in its diffusion was the intermarriage of military settlers with local women.

The geographic spread of the Amhara language and culture came to a halt during the sixteenth century, when the OROMO occupied the southern parts of the central Ethiopian highlands. The isolated Amharic principality of Shoa, at the southern fringe of the empire, became in the second half of the nineteenth century a starting point for a new expansion toward the south. Since the shaping of modern Ethiopia in its current borders by Menelik II, the social institutions of the Amhara, their culture, and their language spread over the newly acquired territory. They were dominant as military and administrators living in newly established garrison towns, armed settlers who subdued dependent populations, and within the Ethiopian Orthodox Church. Since 1955 Amharic has had the status of an official language. The spread of modern education, including the literacy campaigns under the regime of Mengistu Haile Mariam, have contributed to recent processes of amharization.

Communal and village life among the Amhara is strongly influenced by the Ethiopian Orthodox Church, with the parish as the principal communal unit. Voluntary and self-help associations, which char-

An Amhara priest with the Holy Scriptures, written in Ge'ez

above: Traditional Anadarko teepees
below: Andalusian women in southern Spain

acterized the organization of a parish, also spread in urban contexts. In the rural communities, land was held in unalienable collective ownership of the extended peasant families, and heritage in landrights followed an ambilateral pattern. Rights in tribute and surplus labor were temporally distributed inside the hierarchical power structures which linked the territory, the people, and the nobility with the empire's overall structures.

The social and political institutions of the Amhara had a crucial influence on the development of institutions which linked the south of Ethiopia with the political centre in Addis Ababa. The tribal and clan structures, and the way in which leadership was temporarily elected among some southern peoples, were alien to the Amhara. They installed dominant landholders and established the hereditary office of local chief to represent the administration among his kin and people. Concerning the definitions of rights to land, the legal system of the Amhara became a strong incentive for the spread of the Amharic language. (see also AFAR, ETHIOPIANS)

AMI   An ethnic group of approximately 150,000 living in eastern Taiwan. They are one of the few indigenous peoples in Taiwan to retain their own language. The Ami are fishermen and hunters, but also cultivate rice. Recently private land ownership has replaced co-operative ownership. Religious practices include the ritual slaughter of pigs and chickens.

ANADARKO   A small Native North American group residing today in Oklahoma in the Caddo Federal Trust Area. Together with the CADDO they number about 1,400 persons.

ANANG   A subgroup of the IBIBIO.

ANASAZI   SEE PUEBLO INDIANS.

ANDALUSIANS   (the name may stem from the Vandals) Seven million Andalusians inhabit Spain's southern region, situated between the Sierra Morena and the Sierra Nevada. This area remained longest in Muslim hands and still evinces Moorish influences, including the architecture of Córdoba, Seville, and Granada, which during the Middle Ages were major Muslim cities. Folklore, in particular flamenco dances, songs, and religious processions, still survives.

Demographically, the Andalusian population remained overwhelmingly Spanish, with relatively small

Andalusians

minorities of ARABS, BERBERS, and JEWS. Most of Andalusia was reconquered for Christendom in the twelfth century. Granada, the last Muslim stronghold, fell in 1492. The Andalusians are the poorest of the SPANIARDS. Underindustrialized, they suffer one of Europe's top unemployment rates. A quarter of the population is still engaged in agriculture, often as part-time laborers. Creating equal employment is the foremost aim of an Andalusian autonomist movement, the Partido Andalucista, which also strives (within the framework of the Spanish state) to obtain recognition of the Andalusians' specific culture and of their links with North Africa. Distinctly Andalusian communities still live in Morocco, descendants of Morisco refugees forced to leave Spain in the fifteenth and sixteenth centuries. (see also SPANIARDS)

ANDAMANESE   A ethnic group living in the Andaman Islands, India. Once the majority of the population in that chain, their numbers are now very low. Until recently, they were a typical semi-nomadic hunting and food-gathering tribe, traditionally also fishermen. They are now settled in Strait Island.

ANDH   An ethnic group numbering 239,000 (1981), living in the states of Andhra Pradesh, Madhya Pradesh, and Maharashtra, India. They speak Marathi, a language of the Indo-Aryan family. They are divided into two subgroups, the Andh proper and the SHADU ANDH, who do not intermarry.

Most of the Andh are engaged in agriculture; some also as laborers.

ANDI (s.d. Qwannaw) An ethnic group in northwest Daghestan numbering an estimated 8,000. They are Sunni Muslims of the Shafii religious stream, who converted to Islam between the thirteenth and fifteenth centuries. Their language belongs to the Avar-Andi-Dido group of the Ibero-Caucasian linguistic family. Andi is unwritten, and Avarian is used as a literary language. In the twentieth century, after highways were built in the mountains, the process of assimilation of the Andi into the AVAR began. The Andi have been regarded by Soviet ethnographers as an Avarian group which preserves its own language and some ethnographic peculiarities as, for example, the traditional two-storey stone house with its stone-fenced yard. The Andi were known in the Caucasus as makers of black felt cloaks. Other traditional occupations are cattle- and sheep-breeding, horticulture, and handicrafts.

ANDORRANS The 55,000 inhabitants of the small principality of Andorra, situated in the Pyrenees between France and Spain. They are Roman Catholics and speak Catalan, Spanish, and French. Since 1278, Andorra has been ruled by the FRENCH (represented by the president of France) and the SPANIARDS (represented by the bishopric of Urgel). Some 20 percent of the workforce is engaged in agriculture but tourism is also an important industry because of the country's status as a tax-free haven.

In recent years, there has been an increase in Andorran wishes to assert greater independence.

ANE see MINA.

ANFILLO see MAO.

ANGAMI (s.d. Tengima) One of the largest ethnic groups of NAGA, numbering 63,000 (1981), living in the Manipur and Nagaland states of India. Their language belongs to the Tibeto-Burman family.

Economically, the Angami are the most prosperous tribe in Nagaland, and land in their area is owned both privately and collectively. Their villages are situated mostly on hilltops, and they are excellent terrace cultivators. (see also CHAKHESANG, NAGA)

ANGAS A subgroup of the TIV.

ANGHIDY see TINDIANS.

ANGKOLA A subgroup of the BATAK living in the interior highlands of the Indonesian island of Sumatra.

ANGOLANS The 10 million inhabitants of Angola are primarily a rural people; only 25 percent of Angolans live in urban areas. They are divided into eight distinct ethno-linguistic groups: the OVIMBUNDU of the central highlands; the MBUNDU of the districts of Luanda, Malange, and Kwnaza in the northeast; the KONGO of Cabinda and Uige provinces of northern Angola; the LUNDA-CHOKWE of eastern Angola; the NYANYEKE-HUMBE of the Huile and Cuene provinces; the OVAMBO of the extreme south; the GANGUELA of eastern Angola near the Zambezi and Langwebulu rivers; and the HERERO of the extreme southeast near the border with Namibia. In addition to Portuguese, various African languages are spoken such as Kikongo, Umbundu, Kimbundu, Lunda-Louvale, and the languages of the pastoral HERERO and the AMBO.

Angola has one of the richest mineral reserves in southern Africa. Petroleum and diamonds constitute the backbone of its economy and it is the second largest exporter of hydrocarbons in Africa. Industrial activity is centered on producing equipment for the petroleum industry, but also includes food processing, textiles, steel, and electrical equipment. Agricultural production has been seriously disrupted by the constant state of war and the nationalization of the European plantations. The main cash crop is coffee but sisal, cotton, palm oil, and sugar are also grown and exported.

The Angolans achieved independence from Portugal after a long and violent civil war which began in 1961 and was led by the National Front for the Liberation of Angola (FNLA) whose supporters were of the KONGO group; the Popular Movement for the Liberation of Angola (MPLA), supported by the MBUNDU people; and the National Union for the Total Independence of Angola (UNITA), dominated by the OVIMBUNDU. A characteristic of these organizations was their external basis of support. The MPLA was supported by the Soviet Union, UNITA received aid from China and South Africa, and the FNLA was backed by western and prowestern governments. Although all three groups were fighting a common adversary, they were never able to unite and, even after independence was achieved following the coup in Portugal in 1974, the conflict between the three movements continued.

The tensions between the movements exploded into a civil war, each side still receiving considerable aid from foreign governments.

The MPLA, led by Agostinho Neto, took over the government in 1976. Following the Marxist-Leninist model, it immediately sought to concentrate power in its own hands in the form of a one-party state and therefore did not allow any form of opposition to operate. As a result the other movements resorted to force. As the FNLA had been seriously weakened because of its defeat during the civil war, UNITA became the main source of opposition.

Supported by South Africa, the United States, and other conservative African and Middle Eastern governments, UNITA launched attacks on a variety of targets. South Africa's 1984 proposal to withdraw troops from Angola precipitated a series of peace talks which lasted throughout the decade. In spite of a peace agreement between UNITA and the government, signed in March 1991, sustained peace has not been achieved.

ANGOLARES   see SAO TOME AND PRINCIPE.

ANIA   A division of the eastern OROMO.

AN'KALYN   A subgroup of the CHUKCHI.

ANKWAI   A subgroup of the TIV.

ANNAMESE   see VIETNAMESE.

ANTANDROY   A tribal division of the MALAGASY.

ANTANKARANA   A tribal division of the MALAGASY.

ANTANOSY   A tribal division of the MALAGASY.

ANTEIFASY   A tribal division of the MALAGASY.

ANTEIMORO   A tribal division of the MALAGASY.

ANTIGUANS AND BARBUDANS   The people of Antigua and Barbuda, an independent island state in the eastern Caribbean Sea. They number about 65,000. First colonized by the BRITISH in 1632, the islands achieved independence in 1981. Most of the inhabitants are descendants of black Africans brought as slaves to work the extensive sugar and cotton plantations. They speak an English patois and are predominantly Anglicans. There is a small oil refinery on the island but tourism is the most important factor of the local economy.

ANTILLEANS   see SAINT VINCENT AND THE GRENADINES, THE PEOPLE OF.

ANTIPA   A subgroup of the JIVARO.

ANU   see LUTZU.

ANUAK   (Yambo) An ethnic group, numbering several tens of thousands, who live on the banks of the Sobat River and its tributaries in the Gambela region of western Ethiopia. Their language belongs to the Nilotic group and they practice traditional beliefs and Christianity (various missionary denominations).

The Anuak are settled agriculturalists, fishermen, and occasional hunters. Their social structure linked noble clans, which provided the village headmen, with commoners. They were one of the first Nilotic groups to obtain guns, in the late nineteenth century. Since the 1980s the Anuak have been affected by resettlement schemes for the AMHARA and TIGRAY peoples in Ethiopia. (see also ETHIOPIANS)

ANU CHU   see MONTAGNARDS. (see also JARAI)

ANUTA ISLANDERS   A Polynesian-speaking people inhabiting the small island of Anuta, one of the easternmost of the Solomon Islands. They are thought to have originated from Tonga and Wallis Island.

ANZANG   see RENGMA.

AO   (Aurh; s.d. Ni-so-meh, Sa-mai-na) An ethnic group numbering 105,000 (1981), living in the Mokokchung district of Nagaland, India. They are divided into three linguistic subgroups: Chonglee, Chungke, and Mong-sen.

Ao houses are constructed along the mountain ridges on platforms above the ground and arranged in regular streets. Each village contributes two or three members to a council of elders. They are an endogamous people, although intermarriage is becoming more widespread.

The Ao practice slash and burn cultivation. (see also LOTHA, NAGA)

APACHE   A collectivity of Native North American groups speaking Athapaskan, which includes the ARAVAIPA, CHIRICAHUA, CIBECUE, JICARILLA, KIOWA, LIPAN, and MESCALERO. There are approximately 10,000 Apache. They were originally scattered across the southwest United States including the West Texas plain.

The Apache culture was originally based on hunting and gathering but after contact with the SPANIARDS they became traders as well. For almost sixty years the Apache fought a war with the United States Army. The last Apache group, which surrendered to the U.S. army in 1886, was led by Geronimo, who spent the rest of his life in exile in Florida.

Apache

Today the Apache are found in Oklahoma, New Mexico, and Arizona. The so-called White Mountain Apache in Arizona own and operate a ski resort which gives them a higher standard of living than other Apache tribes. The Apache Reservation is now partly flooded by the Coolidge Dam. (see also ATHAPASKAN)

APACHICILA   see SEMINOLE.

APALACHEE   see SEMINOLE.

APALAI   (Aparai) A South American Indian group numbering a few hundreds, living in the north of the State of Pará, in Brazil. Some have never been seen by outsiders. Their language belongs to the Carib family.

APARAI   see APALAI.

APA TANI   An ethnic group numbering 17,000 (1981), they live in seven villages along the banks of the Kali River in the Subansiri District, Arunachal Pradesh, India. Their language belongs to the Tibeto-Burman family.

Of Paleo-Mongoloid stock, the Apa Tani are a settled group, practicing the most modern method of terraced paddy cultivation (animal traction was unknown to them until 1945). Their houses, clustered together in well laid-out streets, are built from the region's abundant bamboo and pinewood. Paddy-straw is used to thatch the roofs. Before 1947 the concept of money was unknown to them; Apa Tani wealth is measured in terms of oxen.

APAYAO   (s.d. Isneg) An ethnic group numbering about 15,000, who live along the Apayao and Matalag Rivers in Apayao Subprovince in northern Luzon, an island in the Philippines. Their language belongs to the Iloko-Cagayan branch of Northern Philippine languages.

Formerly headhunters, the Apayao subsist on slash and burn cultivation, rice being the staple crop, followed by tubers and sugarcane. Permanent settlements consist of small hamlets. Leadership among the Apayao is based upon personal achievements and is not inherited.

The Apayao traditional religion centers around a large pantheon of spirits. (see also MANDAYA)

APINAYE   A South American Indian group living in the Goiás region of Brazil. They speak a Ge language. They subsist primarily from agriculture, supplemented by hunting, gathering, and fishing.

APINDJI   An ethnic group living on the east side of the middle N'Gounie River, Gabon. Their native religious cult was adopted by the FANG in the twentieth century, but some Apindji have converted to Catholicism as a result of extensive missionary activity. Many Apindji migrated to other regions of the country during the colonial period.

APSWA   see ABKHAZIANS.

AQA-JARI   see KUHGILU.

AQSULUQ   A subgroup of the UIGHUR.

ARAB AL-ASWAD   see JABELAWI.

ARABS   (s.d. al-Arab) The approximately 175 million Arabs form a diverse group of predominantly Muslim peoples living in countries where Arabic is the official and written language, and where one of the many Arabic dialects is spoken. The language is a

South Semitic tongue related to modern Amharic, Hebrew, and Aramaic. The oldest surviving inscription in Arabic dates from the fourth century C.E. Arabic is written from right to left in a cursive script that lends itself to many ornamental uses. It is the world's sixth largest mother-tongue and the language of religion for another 750 million Muslims.

Arab minorities live in Israel (750,000); Ceuta and Melilla (10,000); southeast Turkey (550,000); southwest Iran (750,000); East Africa (Ethiopia, Djibouti, and Somalia: 90,000); West Africa (Senegal, Mali, and Niger: 200,000); central Africa (Chad and Nigeria: 500,000; Uganda, Kenya, Tanzania: 70,000); Madagascar (20,000); Afghanistan (25,000); and Indonesia (90,000).

More recent migration has brought many Arabs to Europe, with 1.5 million (including BERBERS) in France alone; and to the United States (450,000), Argentine (60,000), Brazil (50,000), Chile (50,000), and Canada (90,000). The continuity of the Arab world is interrupted by the presence in its midst of a mosaic of non-Arab minorities: ASSYRIANS, KURDS, CHERKESS, ARMENIANS, BERBERS, JEWS, GYPSIES. Some of these are partially arabized.

In ancient times Arabic-speakers were confined to the Arab peninsula between the Red Sea and the Persian Gulf, although nomads from the Arabian desert occasionally sedentarized and mixed with Aramaic-speaking populations in Syria-Palestine and Mesopotamia. Pre-islamic Arabs lived pastoral lives based on camel-herding and caravan trade. Then, as mostly now, they were organized in patriarchal clans and tribes. Early Arab history can be seen as a drawn-out process of sedentarization of nomads. Their pivotal trading position helped some pre-islamic Arab tribal kingdoms to power.

Muhammad, the founder of Islam, established a theocratic statelet in the town of Medina in the Hijaz province in 622, then went on to conquer and convert the whole Arab peninsula. His successors clashed with the Byzantine and Sassanid (Persian) empires. Within one century, by persuasion and coercion, Arabs next spread the message of Islam westward to North Africa and into Spain, eastward to Persia, Afghanistan, the Indus Valley, and Central Asia, and later south along the East African coast. The Arab world is thus divided into two broad regions, the Maghrib ("west") west of the Nile and the Mashriq ("east") to the east. They brought their language with them and created permanent settlements. The first Arab cities, Kufa, Basra, Fustat (Old Cairo), and Qayrawan (Kairouan), were originally camping sites of Arab armies which in time became foci of arabization.

Nomad Arab culture mixed with existent sedentary cultures. Of particular importance was the literary and artistic influence of Persian culture. The ruling Muslim Arabs initially constituted a minority but over the centuries, became the large majority, Christian Arabs re-

Arabs

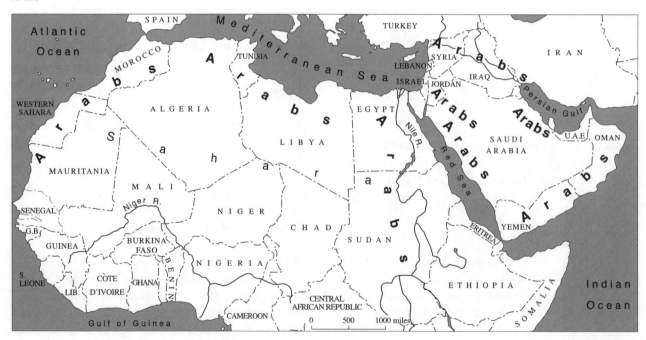

above left: A Moroccan Arab
above right: An Egyptian Arab
bottom: Beduin Arabs in the Sinai

taining regionally contiguous blocks in Lebanon, Egypt, Palestine, Syria, and Iraq.

Today some 90 percent of Arabs are Muslim. Islam is a strictly monotheistic religion; its five "pillars" are the confession of the believer's submission to Allah (God), daily prayer, charity, fasting in the month of Ramadan, and pilgrimage to Mecca. Not only a religious doctrine, Islam is also a system of rules and attitudes permeating the whole of life. It places emphasis on the creation of a righteous community of believers. Muhammad is considered the last in a line of prophets that includes biblical figures. His successors (*caliphs*) were at once spiritual arbiters and emperors. The succession of the fourth *caliph* was the cause of an enduring schism in Islam: Muhammad's son-in-law Ali was denied the caliphate and was killed with his sons. Mu'awiyya, the victor, founded the first dynasty, the Damascus-based Ummayads (661–750), who ruled a still purely Arab-dominated empire, with privileges for ethnic Arabs.

The majority of the Muslim community who accepted the principle of community-endorsed succession, and went along with Mu'awiyya's title to the caliphate, are known as Sunnis. The faction of 'Ali seceded from the main branch of Islam and formed the Shi'ites who claim that succession must run in Muhammad's lineage. In time they developed a more emotional, eschatological, and messianic Islam, and became a revolutionary catalyst in the Muslim world. Shi'ite sects are nowadays mainly found in Lebanon, Syria, and Iraq. The Abbasids who superseded the Umayyads (750–1258) created a more universalist Muslim commonwealth; converts were fictitiously attached to Arab tribes and thus had equal rights. This was the Golden Age to which Arabs nostalgically look back. Baghdad became the capital of a common Arab-Persian-Hellenistic-based civilization, which assimilated Greek philosophy and science, employed JEWS, Christians, PERSIANS, and INDIANS, and developed medicine, mathematics, historiography, poetry, architecture, and much else.

The classical Arab period came to an end in 1258 when Baghdad was destroyed by MONGOLS. The later Middle Ages saw the incursions of Turkic and Mongol invaders from Central Asia who destroyed cities and irreparably damaged delicate irrigation networks in the Arab East. Outlying provinces seceded; Sicily, Malta, and Spain were lost to Western Christendom. After 1500 new sea routes diverted Western trade from the Arab transit zone, turning the Middle East into a backwater and precipitating economic ruin. The Arab world entered a long period of decline under Ottoman Turkish rule.

However, the change of master had little ethnic or linguistic effect, although Arabic became differentiated into a number of dialects. While in the east Persians rejected arabization, Arab influence continued to spread throughout Africa. By 1050 tribal invasions of the Bani Hilal from Arabia wrought widespread destruction in the Maghrib. South Morocco and Mauritania were conquered, arabized, and islamicized in the fourteenth and fifteenth centuries. Arabs took over Nubia in the fifteenth century, and from Sudan infiltrated West Africa where Arab populations mingled with local blacks.

In the nineteenth century, European colonization of the largely Ottoman-dominated Arab world began. The opening of the Suez Canal in 1869 made the Arab world the strategic axis linking Europe to the East. While the Ottoman Empire formally retained its independence, Arab territories in North Africa fell under European administration. In Algeria and Libya this was accompanied by a process of substantial European population settlement; important commercial communities also settled in Egypt.

In 1916 the Arabs in the Hijaz broke into open revolt against Turkish rule. However, despite promises by the BRITISH to support an independent Arab kingdom, France and Britain after World War I carved the Ottoman empire into mandates. The action of the imperial powers inflamed anti-Western feeling in the region, but only after World War II did most Arab countries gain independence. By then, however, the borders drawn by the colonial powers had engendered separate Arab sub-nations. State-bound bureaucracies and nascent local power elites have since tended to keep the Arab world divided in multiple states. Besides the pan-Arab longing for a common political framework, marked national patriotisms are now in evidence. Concrete attempts at creating a unitary Arab state have repeatedly been frustrated. The Arab League, created in 1945 at British instigation, has little practical significance.

Since the beginning of the twentieth century, the dominant economic factor has been the exploration, extraction, and sale of oil in specific parts of the Arab region, which contains two-thirds of proven world reserves. However, the tribute the world pays Arab owners for tapping their fossil energy does not automatically create generalized prosperity: only a small portion is productively invested in the Arab states. While wealth has generated Arab influence on world politics and economy, it has also deepened social gaps between the haves and have-nots in Arab society and destabilized inter-Arab relations.

Arab societies are still predominantly traditional. They are marked by severe differences in gender roles and the subservience of women to men. Family life tends to be patriarchal and authoritarian, and the mores of keeping women secluded at home and away from public life (e.g., by the veil), although decreasing, are still strong. (see also AFAR, AIT ATTA, ALGERIANS, BAHRAINIS, BEJA, DJOHEINA, EGYPTIANS, HASSAUNA, IRAQIS, ISRAELIS, JORDANIANS, KURDS, KUWAITIS, LEBANESE, LIBYANS, MALTESE, MOROCCANS, MZABITES, OMANIS, PALESTINIANS, QATARIS, SAUDI ARABS, SUDANESE, SYRIANS, TANZANIANS, TUNISIANS, UNITED ARAB EMIRATES ARABS)

ARABS OF CENTRAL ASIA   see ARABS.

ARAGO   An ethnic group living in Nigeria.

ARAKANESE   see MAGH, TIPRA.

ARANDA   Groups of Aranda-speaking AUSTRALIAN ABORIGINES living in the central Northern Territory. Originally nomadic hunters, they are now becoming increasingly settled.

A-RAP   A subgroup of the JARAI.

ARAPAHO   A Native North American ethnic group residing today in three states: Montana, Oklahoma, and Wyoming, U.S.A.

Originating in the upper Mississippi Plain, they moved south with their allies, the CHEYENNE, during the sixteenth and seventeenth centuries. In 1867 they moved to the Oklahoma Territory and in 1890 sold their reservation to the United States government.

Today the Arapaho number about 5,000 persons, many of whom live on the Federal Northern Cheyenne Reservation in Montana, the Federal Wind River Reservation in Wyoming, and the Cheyenne and Arapaho Tribes Federal Trust Area in Oklahoma. The Montana Reservation houses the Wind River outdoor activity center for North American Indian Heritage, which has been run by the Arapaho for several years.

ARAPICO   A subgroup of the JIVARO.

ARARA   A South American Indian group numbering a few hundreds, living in the territory of Rondônia,

north Brazil. Their mortality rate has increased upon contact with outsiders.

ARAUCANIANS   A South American Indian people living mainly in the center and south of Chile, between the Choapa river and the Reloncavi Gulf. They constitute around 2 percent of the population of modern Chile (some 250,000). Some Araucanian groups settled in the Northern Patagonic lands in Argentina after crossing the Andes as a result of long wars in Chile.

They are divided into three main groups: the PICUNCHE, originally living north of the Itata River; the main group, the MAPUCHE, between the Itata and Tolten Rivers; and the HUILICHE, between the Tolten River and the Reloncavi Gulf. The Araucanian language is part of the Andean Equatorian language grouping.

The Araucanians subsisted on agriculture, growing vegetables, collecting fruits, fishing, hunting, and tending and pasturing the chillihueque (a llama-related camelid). Originally they were loosely organized in tribes (*levo*) and families were polygamic.

The confrontation with the SPANIARDS brought about the closing of ranks and the establishment of politico-

Araucanians

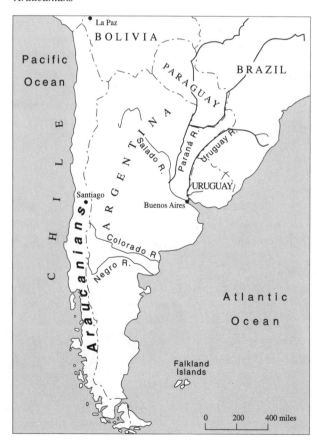

above: Mapuche Araucanians with a cattle cart in central Chile
below: An Araucanian cattle market in central Chile

military organizations by the different Araucanian tribes, strengthening the *cacique* (chieftain) position. It was the epic poem, *La Araucana* (1569, 1588, and 1589), by a Spanish soldier, Alonso de Ercilla y Zuñiga, about the conquest of Chile and the war against the Araucanians, that brought the name and the fame of Araucanian warriors to Spain and Europe at the end of the sixteenth century.

The protacted war became a main factor in the shaping of the CHILEANS as a people and a nationality. The SPANIARDS succeeded in overcoming the PICUNCHE during the sixteenth and seventeenth centuries. The HUILICHE later assimilated with settlers and immigrants, but the MAPUCHE offered long term resistance. The prolonged conflict contributed to the isolation of Chile, absorbed much of the resources of the land, and made it less attractive for settling than other parts of Spanish America. On the other hand, it provided Spanish-Chilean society with a cohesive factor that precluded civil wars and strife of the kind that took place in Peru.

Arauco resistance continued after Chile achieved independence (1818) and only during the Pacific war with Peru and Bolivia were troops sent (1880–1882) into Araucania to subdue the last strongholds.

After their military defeat, thousands of Araucanian families were granted land for cultivation by the government. The Chilean settling of Araucania led to the modernization of the MAPUCHE and their migration to the larger cities of the country.

The problem of the Mapuche lands has not yet been satisfactorily settled and periodically groups of Araucanians protest and organize politically for the return of land they consider their own. During the leftwing popular unity government of Salvador Allende (1970–1973), an agrarian reform was implemented in Mapuche lands too, which was discontinued after General Pinochet's military coup. With redemocratization in Chile (1990) further land claims have been raised by Mapuche leaders. (see also CHILEANS, TEHUELCHE)

ARAVAIPA   A subgroup of the APACHE.

ARAWAK   (Locono) A Native South American group living on the Caribbean coast of easternmost Venezuela. They are agriculturalists and some keep slaves. They speak the Arawak language, which they share with other native groups in the region.

The Arawak were the indigenous inhabitants of many of the Antillean islands, the Bahamas, and

Trinidad, but they were driven away by the CARIB. Soon after the Spanish conquest, they were practically extinct. (see also BAHAMIANS, BARBADIANS, CAMPA, COLOMBIANS, DOMINICANS, GOAJIRA, JAMAICANS, MANAO, NETHERLANDS ANTILLEANS, PUERTO RICANS, TRINIDADIANS AND TOBAGOANS, VENEZUELANS)

ARAWE   see SENGSENG.

ARBORE   An ethnic group numbering about 10,000, who live on the northwest banks of Lake Stephanie in western Sidamo Province, Ethiopia. Their language belongs to the eastern Cushitic group, and they adhere to traditional beliefs.

The Arbore are pastoral cattle-raisers: they were formerly engaged in the ivory trade. Their social structure is marked by age- and generation-grading. (see also ETHIOPIANS, OROMO)

ARCHI   (s.d. Arshishtib, Arshashdul) An ethnic group numbering about 1,000, dwelling between the AVAR and the LEZGI in Daghestan, in the eastern Caucasus mountains. They have been Sunni Muslims of the Shafi'i stream since the sixteenth century.

The Archi language is regarded as a member of the Lezgian group of the Ibero-Caucasian family. It is unwritten, and Avarian is used as the literary language. The Archi also speak Lak.

Ethnographically, the Archi are similar to the AVAR. They do not appear in the Soviet/Russian official ethnographic nomenclature as a separate ethnic group, but are regarded as part of the greater AVAR people. Accordingly, they are listed as AVAR on their identity cards.

The Archi live in traditional two- or three-storey stone houses of the same structure as in the whole Avarian ethnic territory (on the basin of the Sulak River and its four tributaries). Archi women wear the *chukhta*, a special headdress decorated with silver coins. Their traditional economy includes sheep-breeding and agriculture.

ARGENTINES   (s.d. Argentinos) About two-thirds of the 33 million Argentines reside in the humid pampa plains which comprises about 22 percent of the national territory, where Argentina's productive capacity is concentrated.

The distribution of population is highly uneven, over one-third living within the metropolitan area of Buenos Aires. The other clusters of population in Argentina are the oasis settlements of the Andean Piedmont.

It was the activity of the conquering SPANIARDS and of the later *criollo* (their Argentine-born descendants) which contributed to the present situation of low density population, and generated three varieties of response among the indigenous inhabitants. The nomadic people, less developed and structurally weaker, tended to abandon the conquered regions in an attempt to defend their ever-shrinking hunting and gathering territories. This process of retreat resulted in interminable quarrels among themselves for domination of the remaining land. Other groups chose to actively resist, a decision which deeply altered their cultural bases. The third variant in this pattern of response was at first incorporation, or coerced integration, into the colonial system, and later colonization of the indigenous peoples during the period following independence. The communities subjugated in this way were precisely those of the northeast who were most developed within Argentine territory. They were exploited as workers in the *ecomiendas* (estates), drastically reducing their numbers and leading to cultural extinction. Loss of ethnic identity was also produced by ethnic mixing, prevailing up to the present day in marginal zones along the Bolivian and Chilean borders, resulting in hybrid and highly acculturated, non-indigenous populations.

Many indigenous groups were victims of massacres at the hands of the Spanish conquerors. Others died in battle against Spanish domination, in what became known as the Great Uprising, during the seventeenth century.

Today the majority of Argentines are of unmixed European descent. In the humid pampa the population is exclusively European, mostly descendants of families who arrived in Argentina after 1850. Under 3 percent of the population is pure Indian, and the proportion of blacks is negligible. The Argentine territory was originally settled from Peru, Paraguay, or Chile. Asuncion was the primary settlement center from which the SPANIARDS spread over much of the surrounding territory, especially along the Paraguay-Paraná-Plata River system. Northwest Argentina was occupied by people who came from Lima. The main route of settlement followed the old Inca road to Tucumán. A strong flow of immigrants from Chile in more recent times has supplemented the population of the oases from Mendoza to Neuquen, and people of Chilean origin are the principal settlers of the eastern Andean border in southern Patagonia.

South American Indian groups exist in Argentina, although their number is much reduced. The GUARANI,
CHANA, KAINGANG, and CHARRUA groups inhabited the shores of the Paraná and Uruguay Rivers. Available information about these groups is largely historical, since most of those living in these areas were conquered by the Europeans and other Indian groups that had adopted the horse. In the pampa, Patagonia, and Tierra del Fuego, indigenous groups included the TEHUELCHE and ONA.

The indigenous people of the Cuyo Region (Mendoza, San Juan, and San Luis) are known only through Spanish chronicles of the colonial era, when a policy of conquest resulted in their mass transfer to the *encomiendas*. North of San Juan lived the Huarpe Allenticac, in Mendoza, the Huarpe Millcayac, and in San Luis, the Huarpe Puntanos. All manifested powerful Inca influence; they were sedentary, lived in stone houses, and practiced agriculture and gathering (carob trees).

During the Spanish colonial period, the economy of the eastern Piedmont settlements was linked to the highlands and the west coast. The Argentine plains produced just one item of importance to the highland centers: the mule, an animal that made possible the transportation of goods over rugged mountain trails at high altitudes. In this region there were seminomadic herders of cattle and mules who established no permanent settlements. These were the *gauchos*, who also played an important role in developing the humid pampa where pastoral settlement was concentrated. When wheat farming was introduced near the end of the eighteenth century, it was scorned by the vast majority of settlers and left for tenant-farmers. Wheat was raised near the Paraná and Plata Rivers, and on the pampa within a twenty five-mile radius of Buenos Aires. With the mass European immigration that started in the 1880s, the grasslands of Argentina, with their modern agriculture for export, entered a period of spectacular development and the country was integrated into the world economy as purveyor of foodstuffs.

Immigration to the pampa began in earnest in the 1840s when GERMANS arrived as immigrants. A population of roughly 500,000 in 1810 grew to 1.8 million as the first census was concluded in 1869. Between 1857 and 1900 some 2 million immigrants arrived in Buenos Aires and 800,000 departed, a net increase of 1.2 million. From the 1870s a handful of European colonists became pioneers in growing wheat and speedily progressed from cultivation for the local market to massive export. It was only then, toward the end of the 1880s, that the Argentine ranching oligarchy began to favor mass immigration, which had hardly been necessary for a less labor-intensive pastoral economy. At first, settlement projects were undertaken by private foreign companies with governmental assistance. In this way the initiatives of leaders of migrant groups resulted in the establishment of lasting links at the local level between Argentina and Europe. In the case of the French colony of Pingue, in the southern pampas of Argentina, the early colonists recruited only immigrants from Averyon, their native province. The Welsh colony of Chubut in Patagonia supplied successive waves of migration that were usually recruited from the same districts in Wales from which the first settlers originated.

The great intercontinental migration to Latin America between 1854 and 1924 brought 11 million people, over half of whom settled in Argentina. The majority of the immigrants were ITALIANS, followed numerically by SPANIARDS, POLES, RUSSIANS, FRENCH, and GERMANS. Up to 1890 Argentina attracted more ITALIANS than either the United States or Brazil. Between 1900 and 1905 Argentina experienced another increase in Italian immigration, which maintained predominance throughout almost the entire period of mass immigration, and attracted a higher percentage of southern than of northern ITALIANS. Deficiencies in official statistics notwithstanding, it is generally accepted that during the period 1888–1914 over 2.5 million people settled in Argentina. A little over 4 percent of these came from the Middle East and North Africa (some 104,000). In the decade following World War I, there was a large Polish immigration, which represented the largest national group up to 1940. Russian immigration was high between the end of the nineteenth century and the beginning of the twentieth, and again in the decade following World War I. They continued to be the most rural foreign ethnic group in Argentina in 1914. The majority of Russian immigrants were German-speakers from the Volga, while others were JEWS. In this same period there were major immigrations from Germany and East European countries, including a large proportion of JEWS.

Argentina gained independence in 1816 but civil unrest marked the years 1829–1862. A liberal oligarchical regime succeeded in developing the economy, and soon the country was known as one of the most modernized nations in Latin America. By 1930 it led the continent in gross national product per capita, foreign trade, literacy, urbanization, area of farmland per person, and claimed the smallest proportion of the labor force employed in agriculture. The rapid economic growth prior to 1930 was aided by both the agro-export oriented economy and the political stability of almost seventy years of uninterrupted constitutional government.

However, since 1930 Argentina's economic growth has been sporadic and military intervention and dictatorship have been frequent. Peronist populism marked a new political and social era, characterized by a strong nationalist movement of workers and popular mass mobilization disputing the traditional oligarchical rule. After the fall of the first two Peronist governments, lack of political legitimacy and the consolidation of factional business and trades-union elites enabled authoritarian restorations that weakened the party representative system. With no legitimate source of authority, dictatorships took power in the 1960s and 1970s, the last of which, a regime based on military terror against civilian sectors, ruled from 1976 to 1983. The restoration of democracy in 1983 has paved the way for changes in civilian political organizations that may hold out prospects for political stability.

ARGOBA   An ethnic group numbering 50,000 (1984) who live in eastern Ethiopia, north of the town of Ankober and east of the town of Harar. Their language belongs to the southern Semitic (Ethio-Semitic) group; they are Sunni Muslims.

Sedentary peasants, the Argoba descend from the population of the medieval Islamic state of Ifat (Awfat), an area now mainly inhabited by Oromo-speakers. Islamization of the Argoba began during the ninth century. (see also ETHIOPIANS)

ARI   A people numbering 110,000 (1980s), divided into ten groups, who live east of the Mago River in central Gemu Gofa province, Ethiopia. Their language belongs to the Omotic group. They adhere to traditional beliefs.

The Ari are ensete-farmers, using the hoe and the digging-stick.

ARIAAL   A subgroup of the RENDILLE.

ARIBI   An ethnic group living in Mauritania.

ARIKARA   (Ricara, Ree) A small Native North American group living today on the Fort Berthold Federal Reservation in North Dakota, numbering 2,000 persons. They were not a nomadic people, but lived along the Missouri River in fixed village settlements of earth lodges rather than teepees, growing corn and squash and hunting buffalo seasonally. Culturally they were related to the MANDAN and HIDATSA. In the 1830s a smallpox epidemic devastated their population. A few years later they were moved by the United States army to their present location. (see also HIDATSA)

ARLENG see MIKIR.

ARMENIANS (s.d. Hay) A people living mainly in Armenia, in the southern part of the Transcaucasus, as well as in nearly 100 countries, mainly the Middle East, North and South America, and West Europe (mostly in France). The estimated total number of Armenians is about 6 million, of whom, according to the 1989 Soviet census, 4.6 million live within the former USSR.

The Armenian language forms an independent group of the Indo-European family and consists of three strata: the classical literary language, Grabar, dating from the fifth century; Middle Armenian (used mainly in the kingdom of Cilicia in the northeast Mediterranean); and New Armenian (Ashkharabar), which has existed since the nineteenth century and is represented by two variants of the literary language, East (former USSR and also Iran) and West (the remaining diaspora), based on two different dialect groups. The Armenian alphabet was invented by Saint Mesrop Mashtots at the beginning of the fifth century.

Armenia was the first country in the world to proclaim Christianity its state religion (297–301). Today most Armenians belong to the Armenian Apostolic church with its center in Echmiadzin (near Yerevan). There are also groups of Catholic and Protestant Armenians, as well as Armenian-speaking Muslims in northeast Turkey (in the region of Hemshin).

The Armenian people came into being at the beginning of the first millennium B.C.E. at the junction of the Upper Euphrates and Aratsani Rivers. Their ancestors peopled Hittite and Hurrite states and later the state of Urartu. In the seventh century B.C.E. the first Armenian dynasty, the Yervanids, appeared. They were conquered by Media, Achaemenid Iran, and the Seleucids. In 189 B.C.E. two independent Armenian states were proclaimed; in the first century B.C.E., under Tigran II, the country became an empire extending from the Caucasus mountains to the Middle East, but lost its annexed territory at the end of that century during a war between Rome and Parthia. In 397 the Armenian kingdom was divided between Iran and Rome. From 438 to 481, the Armenians waged a religious war against the Sassanid states which tried to convert them by force to Zoroastrianism. Over the following centuries Armenia was invaded by ARABS, Seljuk TURKS, MONGOLS, Ottoman TURKS, and others, with brief periods of independence, including the twelfth- to fourteenth-century kingdom of Cilicia.

Russia annexed a part of Persian Armenia in 1828–1829. Turkish Armenia became an arena of massacres; between 1894 and 1896, 500,000 Armenians were killed. During World War I there were 1.5 million Armenian victims. Hundreds of thousands fled the country and swelled the Armenian diaspora, which had existed since the Middle Ages. In 1918 an independent republic was proclaimed in former Russian Armenia, but was abolished by the Communists, who established in its place the Armenian Soviet Socialist Republic (1920). After World War II about 200,000 Armenians from the diaspora settled in Armenia. The flow became much slower after 1949, and from the late 1960s it was reversed, many Armenians migrating to North America.

With the eclipse of the USSR tension erupted between Azerbaijan and Armenia over the Nagorno Qarabakh Autonomous *Oblast* (region) of Azerbaijan, inhabited predominantly by Armenians. The tension developed into a continuing military conflict. As a result, virtually all Armenians who lived in Azerbaijan (with the exception of those in Nagorno Qarabakh) left, mostly for Armenia, but also for Russia and other neighboring non-Muslim countries.

The Armenians possess a rich and original culture, with developed branches of historiography, religious and secular poetry, music, and architecture. Their traditional economy was based on viticulture, horticulture, and cattle-breeding. Stone-cutting, carpet-weaving, and jewelry are among the most ancient handicrafts. (see also MESKH, SYRIANS, TURKS)

ARO A subgroup of the IBO.

ARSHASHDUL see ARCHI.

ARSHISHTIB see ARCHI.

ARSI A division of the OROMO living in the Arussi, Bale, and northern Sidamo provinces of Ethiopia.

ARU (Aru Islanders) Inhabitants of the Aru Islands in the Banda Sea, eastern Indonesia. They number about 20,000 and are apparently of Papuan extraction. Because of the importance of the islands to the spice trade since the fifteenth century, there has been a considerable influx of external ethnic elements, most notably MALAYS. There are slightly more Muslims than Christians among the Aru Islanders.

For the most part, the economy consists of sago gathering and subsistence agriculture, with occasional hunting to supplement the diet. They also export pearls and feathers from the abundant birds of paradise found on their island, but trade is generally monopolized by larger neighboring groups, particularly the BUGINESE and MACASSARESE.

ARUA A South American Indian group numbering a few hundred, living in the territory of Rondônia, north Brazil, close to the border with Bolivia.

ARUBANS The inhabitants of the Caribbean island of Aruba, located just north of the Venezuelan coast, which seceded from the Netherlands Antilles in 1986. While still under a governor appointed by the DUTCH, they are scheduled for complete independence in 1996. The island has 63,000 inhabitants, predominantly Roman Catholics, most concentrated in and around the capital, Oranjestad. Their official language is Dutch, but Papiamento, a mixture of Spanish, Portuguese, and Dutch, is most frequently spoken. Oil refining, the economic base of Aruba until its refinery closed in 1985, has been supplanted by tourism as the major income source for inhabitants of this semi-arid island.

ARUSHA A people living in northern Tanzania to the west of Mount Mery. They are estimated to number over 150,000. Originally and linguistically part of the MASAAI people, they belong to the Nilotic branch of the Nile-Saharian language family. Unlike the MASAAI, however, who are shepherds, the Arusha's main occupation is intensive agriculture, making them economically and culturally more similar to their Bantu neighbors.

ASAMAT An ethnic group of about 40,000 living in southwestern Irian Jaya, the Indonesian part of the island of New Guinea. They speak an indigenous language of their own. They are hunters, gatherers, and fishermen, and they are ardent believers in spirits.

ASAYMARA A subgroup of the AFAR.

ASERAWANUA A subgroup of the LAKI.

ASHANTI (Asante) An Akan-speaking people living in central Ghana. Their main city is Kumasi. Some are Christians, while others retain their traditional religious beliefs.

Although their origins are obscure they seem to have migrated from the south in the seventeenth century in small kin-groupings and to have settled on a junction of two northern trade routes, where they formed the Ashanti state. Their new location gave them the opportunity to become involved in trade and accumulate wealth. Gold became extremely important both economically and politically. The Golden Stool of the Asantehene, the Ashanti king, became the symbol of Ashanti power and unity.

During the eighteenth century the Ashanti empire expanded and neighboring groups were conquered. In the nineteenth century the Ashanti began to open trade routes to the coast and came into conflict with the Europeans and their African allies on the coast.

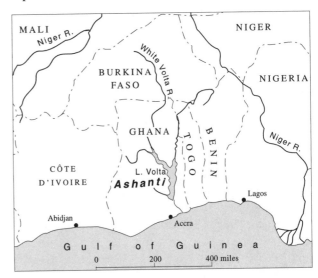

Ashanti

Towards the end of the nineteenth century the BRITISH conquered and razed Kumasi. Later, they exiled the Asantehene and officially became their rulers. In 1901 the Ashanti region was made part of the British colony of the Gold Coast.

Although the BRITISH ruled most of the Gold Coast indirectly, through local chiefs, they governed the region of the abolished Ashanti state directly. In 1919 they allowed the Ashanti king to return and the Ashanti Union was recreated. However, it was never again a sovereign power. With the return of the king the BRITISH shifted to indirect rule through the local authority. This new situation created confusion among the Ashanti, who were not sure to whom their loyalty should be given.

The Ashanti kept their national pride throughout the colonial period and in 1954, three years before the Gold Coast gained its independence, they formed a national liberation movement which opposed a unitary independent state and asserted the Ashanti right to self-determination. Some Ashanti leaders demanded complete secession; others wanted autonomy in a federal framework.

These demands soon led to violence in the major cites. The Ashanti movement posed a serious obstacle to the leading party of the Gold Coast, the Convention People's Party (CPP), headed by Kwame Nkrumah. However, the CPP managed to exploit sub-regional rivalries and divisions within the ranks of the chiefs and thus to install its own political machine in the Ashanti region.

In 1957 the Gold Coast became independent and its name was changed to Ghana. The CPP won the elections and Kwame Nkrumah became Ghana's first president.

After independence the Ashanti joined other opposition groups and often opposed the different regimes. However they acted in cooperation with other ethnic groups and the demand for autonomy or secession grew weaker. In the years 1969–1978 Ghana's leaders were Ashanti. (see also AKAN, FANTE)

ASHKENAZIM   see ISRAELIS, JEWS.

ASHKHAZWA   A subgroup of the ABAZIANS.

ASHKUN   One of several tribes grouped together as NURESTANIS.

ASHWAD   see AKHVAKH.

AS MU'ALLIM   A subgroup of the TIGRE.

ASSALE   A subgroup of the HASSAUNA.

ASSAMESE   A people numbering 15 million, constituting the dominant ethnic group of the Indian state of Assam. They can also be found in surrounding states of northeast India. Although the Assamese are a Mongoloid people, closely related to the SHAN of Burma, their language belongs to the Indo-European family and is similar to Bengali. In the past 600 years, a rich Assamese literature has evolved independent of any of the surrounding cultural traditions. The study of this literature, particularly the works of Sankar Dal, its foremost poet, is considered an essential part of an Assamese classical education.

Some two-thirds of the Assamese are Hindus. The rest are mainly Muslims and are known as GARIA.

About 90 percent of the Assamese engage in agriculture. Rice is the most common crop, but local tea, which accounts for over half India's total production, is by the far the most profitable. Three distinctive Assamese festivals all share agricultural roots. Assamese women are also known as talented weavers, and a woman's status is often measured by her adeptness at this craft.

ASSIN   (Asen) An Akan-speaking group living in the central region of Ghana. (see also AKAN)

ASSINIBOIN   (Rocky Mountain Sioux) A Native North American people numbering 6,000 equally divided between Alberta, Canada on the Stoney (Wesley and Chiniquay) Reserves, and Montana, U.S.A., where many live on the Fort Belknap and Fort Peck Federal Reservations. Originally they were nomadic buffalo hunters living in teepees. Like other plains groups, they suffered from the smallpox epidemic of 1835–1836.

ASSYRIANS   The Assyrians are a people of Semitic origin, one of the Middle East's many religious minorities which have developed a quasi-ethnic identity. They are Nestorians, members of the "Ancient Church of the East" who form the eastern part of the Church of Antioch, which originated from a schism about the nature of Jesus at the Third Ecumenical Council in Ephesus in 431. Nestorius, the Syrian-born patriarch of Constantinople, taught that Jesus had two distinct natures. The official Byzantine church rejected this doctrine; but Nestorianism came to dominate churches to the east of the Byzantine Empire, in modern Iraq and Iran. Nestorians (also called Aissores) kept to their East Syriac (neo-Aramaic) language and to this day continue to use a distinct dialect and script.

By the late eighteenth century, most Mosul-plain Nestorians had converted to Catholicism (the uniate Chaldean Church), leaving a diminished Nestorian community in Kurdistan between Lakes Van (in modern Turkey) and Urmia (in modern Iran). From 1830 to 1933, the Nestorians suffered a string of tragedies. Missionary efforts by the Church of England initiated a long-lasting Nestorian bond with the BRITISH, but as a result of this association, they developed a national identity, asserting that "Assyria" (Northern Iraq) was their ancestral home, and clamoring for independence. This in turn provoked Ottoman and Kurdish attacks.

In 1915–1917, Russian advances into Ottoman territory emboldened the Assyrians to rebel against the TURKS. When the RUSSIANS retreated, the Assyrians found themselves in danger. Of the 100,000 who attempted to flee to the British-occupied Kermanshah-Qazvin region in 1918, only half survived. They were resettled by the BRITISH in northern Iraq. Plans failed for an independent Assyrian state. The British mandate in Iraq employed Assyrians, who had a martial reputation, in their armed levies, using them for suppressing Kurdish revolts.

This "collaboration" jeopardized their position once more when Iraq became independent. With the advent of national rule in Iraq, Assyrian leaders insisted on the creation of an autonomous national home for the Assyrians in Iraq. But in 1933, Iraqi troops and Kurdish, Yazidi, and Arab groups destroyed sixty of their villages, killing thousands. Assyrians who tried to flee to Syria were massacred at the Euphrates crossing. Most Assyrians then left Iraq for the U.S.A.

As few as 30,000 Assyrians still live in Iraq. Most moved to Baghdad with the onset of the Kurdish rebellion in the 1950s. Another 20,000 live in the extreme northwest of Iran, west of Lake Urmia, although most have migrated to Tehran. Their largest concentration is in Chicago, U.S.A.

After World War I many Nestorian Assyrians in Iraq and Iran converted to the Chaldean church. Chaldeans, speaking Arabic but retaining Syriac liturgy, form the largest Christian group in Iraq, living in the northeast (Zakhu and Dohuk) and in Baghdad. Today there are around 500,000 Assyrians worldwide.

ASUR   An ethnic group numbering 12,000 (1981), living in Bihar and West Bengal, India. They speak Mundari, a dialect belonging to the Austro-Asiatic family of languages. The Asur are related to the MUNDA, AGARIA GOND, and KHARIA. They adhere to their traditional religion.

The Asur's pre-Aryan origins are reflected in the linguistic term *a-sur*, an opposite of the Sanskrit *sur*, meaning "valorous." Some scholars regard them as related to the Mohanjodaro civilization dating back to 3,500 B.C.E.

Their prime occupation was at one time iron-smelting, but with the coming of steel mills, they have become agriculturalists, raising potatoes and grains by a method of shifting cultivation. They also work as laborers.

The Asur social system is based on tracing lineage back to a common ancestor. (see also HO)

ASURINI   A South American Indian group numbering a few hundred, living in the state of Pará, north Brazil. Their language belongs to the Tupi family. They have no fixed settlements.

ATA I   A subgroup of the TURKMEN.

ATA II   (Dugbatang) An ethnic group living in northwestern Davao Province of Mindanao, an island of the Philippines. Their language belongs to the local Manobo grouping of Malayo-Polynesian languages.

The Ata are slash and burn agriculturalists who grow rice, tubers, and corn.

ATACAMA   (Atacameño) A South American Indian people living in the Atacama Desert in northern Chile.

Atacama

They subsist primarily from agriculture, with maize as the staple crop. They raise dogs, guinea pigs, and llamas, and hunt.

Their native language has been lost due to a high degree of assimilation into the dominant Spanish culture.

ATA ENDE   see ENDE.

ATAHORI ROTE   see ROTINESE.

ATA KIWAN   see SOLORESE.

ATAOUAT   A small Mon-Khmer group in southern Laos who employ slash and burn methods to cultivate rice.

ATASI   see CREEK.

ATA SIKKA   see SIKKA.

ATA TANA 'AI   A subgroup of the SIKKA.

ATAYAL   An ethnic group living in north-central Taiwan. No statistical data is available regarding the current population. They speak two distinct languages, Atayal and Sedeq. One of the most feared warrior tribes in the area, they live in subterranean housing and are primarily an agricultural people, although they also hunt and fish. A bridal dowry is paid in pigs, embroidered clothing, and in conches, which serve as a currency.

ATEN   An ethnic group living in Nigeria.

ATHABASKAN   see ATHAPASKAN.

ATHAPASKAN   (Athabaskan) An Athapaskan-speaking Native North American group living in the sub-arctic forest in British Columbia, the Yukon, western Northwest Territories, and northern Alberta, Canada. This grouping includes the DENE, BEAVER, SLAVE, and WET'SUWET'EN ethnic groups.

Other Native North American peoples speaking dialects of Athapaskan, the NAVAJO and APACHE, live in the southwest United States. However, some Athapaskan-speaking peoples are no longer part of the Athapaskan cultural grouping. The only original plains Indians who speak an Athapaskan dialect are members of the SARCEE of Alberta, Canada. (see also DENE)

ATI   A northern subgroup of the NEGRITOS of the Philippines.

ATJEHNESE   (Achinese) A people numbering some 2 million occupying the Atjeh province in the northern part of the Indonesian island of Sumatera (Sumatra). Primarily a coastal people, they have made settlement incursions inland, mainly along the banks of rivers, and are sometimes classified as two distinct groups, the UREUENG BAROLI (lowland people) and the UREUENG TUNONG (hill people). Their language is part of the Malayan subfamily of Austronesian languages, closely-related to Cham of mainland Southeast Asia. The Atjehnese are Muslims. Vestiges of pre-Islamic religious beliefs have survived only in a diluted form.

The Atjehnese are essentially agriculturalists, with rice being the staple crop. Other important crops include corn and sugarcane. while coffee, rubber, and pepper are cultivated primarily for their trading value. Some cattle are also raised, while fishing provides an important supplement to the diet. At the same time, industry and trade are of disproportional importance to the local economy, and crafts such as metallurgy, pottery-making, boat-building, and weaving are particularly important.

Atjehnese

An Atjehnese sultanate apparently originated from the coastal Buddhist kingdom of Poli, of which mention is made as early as 500 C.E. Political power gradually moved to the banks of the Atjeh River, where it was firmly established by the early sixteenth century and which, at some points, dominated most of Sumatera. Fiercely independent, the Atjehnese were only subdued by the colonial administration of the DUTCH in 1903, and then only ruled by a military administration for fifteen years. Atjeh was never reoccupied following the recovery of Indonesia from the JAPANESE after World War II; until the independence of Indonesia it was ruled by the Islamic modernist movement. Rebellion against the centralized Indonesian government broke out in 1953, and Atjeh was only incorporated into Indonesia as a province in 1961.

ATNA An Athapaskan-speaking Native North American group numbering a few hundred persons, many of whom live in two villages, Copper Center and Gulkana, in the Copper River Basin, southern Alaska, U.S.A. Unlike many such groups, they can still rely on their traditional food sources of moose, caribou, and salmon.

ATONI (Timorese; s.d. Atoin Pah Meto) A people estimated as numbering under a million, living on the Indonesian island of Timor. The INDONESIANS refer to them as Orang Timor Asli (native Timorese) to distinguish them from other inhabitants of the island who are mostly recent immigrants. They speak an Austronesian language. A Dutch-devised script is in limited use, primarily by missionaries. Traditional beliefs have been recently supplanted by Christianity: Protestantism in the former Dutch-ruled areas and Catholicism in the former Portuguese-ruled areas. Native religious elements are still strong, however, and have been integrated into the Christian belief system.

Once primarily slash and burn cultivators of rice and corn, the Atoni have devastated much of what was once arable land and are becoming increasingly dependent on raising livestock and gathering forest products. They are also famous for their fine woven cloth. Economic instability on the island, however, and the ongoing civil war led by Catholic EAST TIMORESE insurgents (many of whom are Atoni), have caused considerable emigration to neighboring islands.

The Atoni are culturally and linguistically distinct from their neighbors and in the past were often the victims of slaving raids. Small sultanates were established in the sixteenth century, some of which managed to oppose colonial rule until the early twentieth century. Colonialism by both the DUTCH and the PORTUGUESE was a divisive factor among them, and its repercussions are still felt in the civil war on the island.

ATSI A subgroup of the KACHIN.

ATSINA see GROS VENTRE.

ATSUGEWI A Native North American group numbering a few hundred, many of whom live in northeast California, U.S.A., on the Likely Federal Reservation and on the Lookout Rancheria, both in Modoc County. They form part of the PIT RIVER people.

ATTIE (Akie) A people living in the Côte d'Ivoire, north of the capital, Abidjan, and west of the Comoe River. Their language is related to the languages spoken in the lagoon area but they are socially similar to the AGNI and BAULE. Most of the Attie are Christians; they are active in coffee and cocoa cultivation. They never had centralized states; their political unit is the village. Age groups are important in their social structure.

ATTINGOLA A subgroup of the GORONTALO.

AUCA A small South American Indian group found in the West Amazonian region of Ecuador, where the foothills of the Andean mountains flatten into tropical forest. Their name is derived from a derogatory Quechuan term meaning "wild." There are about 1,000 Auca, mostly living on reservations, where they have been christianized. A group of about 100 Auca still rejects acculturation.

The Auca language is unwritten and tribal history is handed down orally. Their main weapon is the spear.

AUK see TLINGIT.

AUKH see CHECHEN.

AUP An ethnic group living on the Indonesian island of Kalimantan (Borneo). (see also DAYAK)

AURH see AO.

AUSHI see USHI.

AUSTRALIAN ABORIGINES A term currently used to denote the Australoid race which inhabited Australia, including Tasmania, at the time of its discovery by Europeans. Present archeological evidence establishes that this race arrived in Australia at least 40,000 years ago. The present definition of an Aboriginal is "a person of Aboriginal descent who identifies as an Aboriginal and is accepted as such by the community in which he lives." The 1986 Australian national

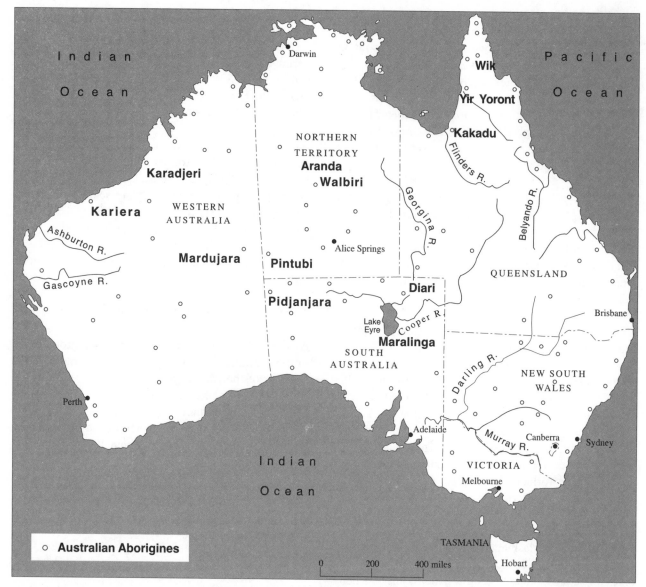

Australian Aborigines

census counted 228,000 Australian Aborigines, or 1.5 percent of the population, with fewer than 25 percent living in cities of more than 100,000 people, and one-third living in rural areas (over twice the rural concentration of the total population). They are dispersed all over Australia with the highest concentration in Queensland, and the highest share of the population in the Northern Territory.

The key unit of social and economic organization among the Aborigines is the "band" (or horde), which may consist of up to fifty people. "Tribe" is used to denote a society of bands with a language or dialect in common, and which has some responsibility for social rites. The population size of such tribal units among the Australian Aborigines varies from a few hundred to about 2,000. Some of the better known tribal societies are the ARANDA, GIDJINGALI, WALBIRI, and DALABON in the Northern Territory, the KARADJERI in Western Australia, the KAKADU in Queensland, and the PIDJANJARA and MARALINGA in South Australia. With the coming of the Europeans, many Aboriginal societies were liquidated and their members dispersed or killed. Contact between the two groups was uneven, coming much later to some areas of the continent than to others, and thus some Aboriginal societies have remained traditionally oriented up to the present day. Some have combined Christianity with Aboriginal traditional beliefs and practices.

above: Australian Aborigine children in a modern setting
below: Australian Aborigines performing a traditional dance

All present-day Australian Aboriginal languages are believed to be descended from a single proto-Australian language. In pre-European times the Aborigines spoke more than 200 distinct languages with numerous dialects. The vast majority of the Australian Aboriginal languages are close to extinction. Many are already extinct in areas of dense European settlement. Most of the languages still in full daily use in Aboriginal communities have only a few hundred speakers each.

The traditional hunting economy remains viable in some areas where hunting techniques and the social organization of subsistence production have remained largely unaltered. However, in many other areas European technology has been adopted and adapted to Aboriginal needs (guns are used for hunting, boats for fishing, and motor vehicles for transportation), resulting in raised efficiency of the traditional economic system. Increasing numbers of Aborigines are moving into towns in search of paid employment. This shift has not necessarily improved their economic conditions, and high levels of unemployment and poverty are common among urban Aboriginal communities. In rural areas they are usually employed on cattle ranches.

At the time of contact the Aboriginal population was estimated to range from 300,000 to 700,000. The impact of BRITISH who came as settlers from the end of the eighteenth century was disastrous for traditional Aboriginal society. Although the official policy of the first settlers was to establish peaceful relationships with the Aboriginal inhabitants of the colony, the latter gradually fell victim to violent confrontations with the settlers. Sheep and cattle supplanted the game animals on which the Aborigines depended for their food supply. They lost control over the land due to the spread of European settlement. Many Aboriginal groups were unable to continue their traditional hunting and gathering life, which resulted in malnutrition and starvation. In many cases Aboriginals were simply removed from their land. Moreover, diseases brought by the Europeans, previously unknown among Aborigines, also took their toll. By the end of the nineteenth century, special reserves of unwanted land were established in an attempt to protect the Aborigines, but the Aboriginal population continued to decline throughout the early decades of the twentieth century.

In 1977 the Aboriginal Land Rights (Northern Territory) Act came into operation. It granted recognition to Aboriginal land right claims in the Northern Territory and made provision for traditional Aboriginal owners to exercise substantial control over activities on their land, including mineral exploration and mining. This allows them to benefit economically from the use of the land. Other significant areas of land have been transferred to Aboriginal ownership. In South Australia, too, land rights have been granted to the Australian Aboriginals. (see also AUSTRALIANS)

AUSTRALIANS The 17 million inhabitants of the Australian continent and the island of Tasmania. They speak English and the majority are Christians. Of the total population, 85 percent is urban, about 60 percent of whom reside in the five major urban centers, Sydney, Melbourne, Brisbane, Perth, and Adelaide.

The earliest inhabitants of Australia migrated from the Asian mainland along the Indonesian archipelago. Their descendants were known as AUSTRALIAN ABORIGINES. The second wave of settlers were Europeans, at first mostly convicts sent from Britain in the last quarter of the eighteenth century. Contact between the estimated 300,000 Aborigines and the European settlers led, through epidemics and persecution, to a rapid decline in the numbers of Aborigines, and it is only recently that this has risen to more than 200,000.

It was not until the 1850s gold rushes that Australia's population grew substantially. In that decade more than 500,000 people arrived. Immigrants came mainly from Britain, the colonial power ruling Australia, and from other European countries, mostly Central Europe and Scandinavia. After World War II, immigration restrictions on non-Europeans were gradually relaxed and the resulting large-scale immigration produced a dramatic change in Australian society, as a result of the arrival of 3 million settlers from more than sixty nations. At the end of the 1970s the immigration policy had become more restrictive. Together with a reduction in total numbers since the early 1980s, there has also been a considerable change in the origin of the settlers. In the early 1970s Europeans constituted about 70 percent of the total immigration, while by the late 1980s they represented less than one-third of annual arrivals. Asian immigration has become dominant, about one-half of the total, mostly from Vietnam, the Philippines, and Malaysia. In the 1970s India, Lebanon, and Turkey were dominant among the countries of origin of Asian settlers.

The most noticeable feature of the Australian population distribution is the concentration of people in the east, southeast, and southwest of the continent. The densely populated areas, mainly the southeast coastal lowlands which were historically most attractive to European settlers, constitute only

17 percent of Australia's land area but contain 87 percent of the population. The major urban concentrations and the main manufacturing activities are located in these areas, which are also characterized by intensive agricultural production and some mining. The remaining areas, in the north, central-east, and west, contain all arid and semi-arid lands and are characterized by very sparse settlement, including several huge uninhabited areas known as the "outback."

In 1901 the former British colonies of New South Wales, Victoria, Queensland, South Australia, Western Australia, and Tasmania were federated under the name of the Commonwealth of Australia. The designation "colonies" was at the same time changed to "states," except for the Northern Territory, which was transferred from South Australia to the Commonwealth as a "territory" in 1911. In the same year the Commonwealth acquired from the state of New South Wales the Canberra site for the Australian capital.

Traditionally Australian wealth was derived from agricultural production, especially pastoral development but also wheat. Pastoral industries, producing meat and wool, still play a major role in the Australian economy, although mining has developed substantially, particularly since the 1950s. Gold-mining encouraged a number of waves of immigration especially in the 1850s and between 1890 and 1910. However, iron ore, copper, lead, zinc, and a wide range of other minerals are produced in large quantities in different locations around the continent. In the cities industrial production is prominent.

AUSTRIANS (s.d. Oesterreicher) A people of German language and civilization, numbering 7.5 million, most of them Catholic Christians. Austria's position astride the Danube valley made it the natural crossroads of central Europe. This explains historically strong foreign influences, more marked in densely populated Lower Austria than in the isolated alpine Higher Austria, where a landlocked mountainous geography stimulated marked regional cultural particularisms. The Tyroleans are considered most authentic, and regard themselves as a seperate group; SOUTH TYROLEANS live as a minority in northern Italy. In the regions of Carinthia and Styria a number of Slovenian villages exist, while Burgenland includes Hungarian and Croatian minorities.

For a long time Austria did not signify a people as much as a geographical entity. The Romans organized this region, the basis of prehistoric Celtic civilization,

as a fortified frontier against Germanic invasion, but to no avail. In the eighth century, Charlemagne instructed the BAVARIANS to conquer the Alps, which resulted in the region's linguistic and cultural (though not physical) germanification. Austria was reorganized as *Ostmark* (eastern frontier) of the Germanic empire against the HUNGARIANS (and later the TURKS). From the thirteenth century Austria developed territorially from an ill-defined collection of original Habsburg regions; yet no Austrian nation as such existed before the twentieth century. The Austrian empire proper came into its own after the splitting of the Habsburg family estate among the Spanish and German branches in 1555. By the nineteenth century Austria had grown into the center of a sprawling multinational empire, eight times the size of its current territory, and ruling over CZECHS, SLOVAKS, HUNGARIANS, CROATS, SERBS, SLOVENES, POLES, Ruthenians, JEWS, BOSNIANS, ROMANIANS, and many others. But "Austrians" as such did not yet exist.

Culturally, the Austrian (after 1866, Austro-Hungarian) Empire contributed to baroque art and classical music. In the nineteenth century, Vienna was the capital of central European civilization. However, the Austrians were ruling an empire which was an unintegrated collection of tongues, religions, and ethnicities, kept together by monarchy and bureaucracy.

The empire's dismemberment in 1919 left modern Austria a more homogeneous germanic and Catholic state. Consequently, Austrians gravitated towards Germany, and in the 1930s developed first a fascist-type dictatorship and then a strong Nazi movement of their own. The 1938 *Anschluss* led to denial of any Austrian particularism: paradoxically this stimulated a specifically Austrian nationalism. After 1945 the Austrians built their own neutral, democratic parliamentarian and mixed-economy welfare state, with marked trade union and church influences.

AVAGANA A subgroup of the PASHTUN.

AVAR (s.d. Magharulae: "mountaineers") One of the peoples of Daghestan. According to the 1989 Soviet census they numbered 604,000. However, official Soviet/Russian demographic statistics include in this number thirteen small, closely-related Avar-Andi-Dido groups in the northwest part of the mountain region of Daghestan, in the Sulak River basin and its four tributaries, the Avatian, Andian, Kazikumukhian, and Kara Koisu Rivers. The Avar ethnographic territory divides Daghestan into two parts. Some Avar live in northern Azerbaijan where, until the nineteenth century, they

Austrians

formed "free communities," maintaining contact with the Avar Khanate in Daghestan. They are Sunni Muslims of the Shafi'i school; their islamization apparently began in the tenth and eleventh centuries, but was completed only in the sixteenth century.

The Avar language belongs to the Avar-Andi-Dido subgroup of the Ibero-Caucasian language family. Since the late Middle Ages the Avar-Andi-Dido ethnic association had common military forces using Bolmats ("military language"), a specific language based on the Khunzakh dialect of Avar. Later it became the base for a literary language and a lingua franca for the whole group of closely-related peoples. Already in the fifteenth century (or according to some sources, the seventeenth), an attempt was made to compile an Avar script based on the Arabic one. In 1920 a simplified script, also Arabic-based, was introduced, and was replaced in 1928 by a Roman-based and in 1938 by a Cyrillic-based script. The first attempts at literary creation in Avar had begun as early as the late eighteenth-early nineteenth centuries. There is now a well-developed literature in this language.

Traditional Avar villages are located on steep slopes; stone houses consist of two to three storeys and fortress-like towers. Cattle are kept on the ground floor; the roof of one house serves as the courtyard for another, upper, house.

Traditional dress includes the felt cloak and quilted coat. Women wear the *chikhta*, a special headdress. The Avar economy includes cattle-breeding, horticulture; leather goods, wooden objects, and metal work. (see also ANDI, AKHVAKH, ARCHI, BAGULAL, BEZHTIN, BOTLIKH, CHAMALAL, DIDO, GINUKHAN, KARATI, KHVARASH, TINDIANS)

AVATIME (Afatime) An ethnic group originating in central Togo, who now form an enclave in EWE territory in the Volta Region of Ghana.

AVIKAM An ethnic group living in the westernmost part of the lagoon area of the Côte d'Ivoire.

AWATIXA see GROS VENTRE.

AWEMBA, AYEMBA see BEMBA.

AWHAFIA A subgroup of the IBO.

AWHAWZARA A subgroup of the IBO.

AWOIN An ethnic group living in the Western Region of Ghana along the Côte d'Ivoire border. They belong to the AGNI-BAULE subgroup of the AKAN grouping.

AWSHAR see AFSHAR.

AWTANZO A subgroup of the IBO.

AWUNA (Anlo) A subgroup of the EWE.

AYDA see OYDA.

AYMARA A South American Indian people of about 1.5. million living mainly in Bolivia and Peru on the high Andean plateau around Lake Titicaca. Several subgroups of South American Indians make up the Aymara people, and these can be found in Bolivia, northern Chile, and Peru. Speaking the Aymara language and located in the central Andes mountains, these include the CANCHI, CARANGA, CHARCA, COLLAGUA, LUPACA, OMASUYO, PACSA, QUILLACA, and UBINE groups. The COLLAHUAYA speak both Aymara and Quechua as well as Machchajjayai. The primary occupation of the Aymara people is agriculture, severely limited by the harsh soil and climatic conditions of the Andes. Herds of llama and alpaca are kept by some farmers. They also engage in fishing using huge rafts made of reeds.

The Aymara created the Tiwanaku empire, the first in the Andean area, which expanded as far as the central and southern coasts of Peru and northern Chile. The Aymara kingdoms dominated the central highlands from the end of the twelfth century until the arrival of the SPANISH in the sixteenth century. There were seven such kingdoms with their colonies in different ecological zones covering a territory from just south of Cuzco into the northern highlands of present-day Bolivia. The Aymara were very wealthy and dominated the altiplano region around the southern end of Lake Titicaca.

The Quechuan-speaking Inca struggled to conquer the Aymara, finally annexing them to the empire by allowing them a degree of independence which they eventually lost. The Inca emperor Viracocha invaded the Aymara territory in 1430 and incorporated it into his empire. The two largest Aymara states, Colla and Lupaca, were consequently destabilized.

Sixteenth century Spanish *conquistadores* and gold-seekers opened the door to Catholic indoctrination of the Aymara but the effort did not completely erase indigenous religions: thus, there are still people who practice earlier forms of religion in different parts of

An Aymara basket merchant

the Andes. The fundamental social unit in Aymara society is the extended family, members of which live together in a kinship commune presided over by a chief (usually the eldest male extended family member) as leader of the family.

While Spanish is now the official language of the Andean countries, Aymara continues to be the dominant language in parts of La Paz and Oruro provinces of Bolivia, yet linguistic boundaries with the Quechua language are blurred. Aymara is also spoken in Peru and northern Chile, Quechua being the major language of most of the remainder of the Andean highlands. African slaves in the Yungas area were Aymara-speakers and their descendants, who represent a very small black presence in Bolivia, continue to speak Aymara and maintain a black-Aymara subculture.

During the colonial period, attempts, only partially successful, to create uniform policies for the Andean region included the imposition of Quechua as the only indigenous language permitted to be spoken. Thus, while some areas managed to retain their Aymara language, others had to change to Quechua. In consequence, who spoke what language, and its relation to their original ethnic affiliation, was relatively accidental. Cultural differentiation was therefore blurred, differences between ethnic groups having less to do with language and ethnicity than with geographical location. (see also BOLIVIANS, COLOMBIANS)

AYOKAWA   A subgroup of the HAUSA.

AYOU   An ethnic group living on the Indonesian island of Kalimantan (Borneo). (see also DAYAK)

AYS   see SEMINOLE.

AZANDE   (sing. Zande) A people numbering 360,000 who live in the Sudan and in the Republic of Zaire. They speak Zande, which belongs to the Adamawa branch of the Niger-Congo family of languages. Today most Azande are involved in agriculture as well as cattle-herding. Most of the Azande people follow local African religions, and a small number profess Christianity.

The Azande conquered and absorbed many ethnic groups of the Congo River basin in the eighteenth and nineteenth centuries with their military prowess and sophisticated political organization. At the end of the nineteenth century they advanced into southwestern Sudan, absorbing the BONGO, MORU, and

NDOGO as well as other small groups, but their main home is still Zaire. In the 1920s the British colonial administration resettled most of the Azande along roads in an effort to combat diseases that were killing off Azande cattle. In the 1940s a new scheme was developed to resettle most of the Azande people and to improve their agricultural methods. (see also CENTRAL AFRICAN REPUBLIC, PEOPLE OF THE, SUDANESE, ZAIREANS)

AZARZIR   A subgroup of the MAURE.

AZERBAIJANI   A Turkic people living in Azerbaijan and northwest Iran (Iranian Azerbaijan). Besides Iranian Azerbaijan, a considerable number also live in the cities of Tehran and Qum, and in the Khoraban province. The estimated number of Azerbaijani in Iran is about 15 million; the number in the former USSR according to the Soviet 1989 census was 6.8 million concentrated mainly in Azerbaijan. A considerable number also live in Daghestan and Georgia. The division of the Azerbaijani-inhabited area into two political parts became an accomplished fact in 1828 following a series of wars between Iran and the Russian Empire.

Azerbaijani

The Azerbaijani language belongs to the Oghuz group of Turkic languages. In Iran it uses the Arabic script with a few additions; this script was also used in the USSR until 1929, when it was shifted to the Roman and in 1939 to the Cyrillic script. Nowadays there is a trend to return to the Roman-based alphabet. They are predominantly Shi'ite Muslims, with a few enclaves of Sunnis of the Shafi'i school in the northern part of Azerbaijan. The latter are culturally assimilated breakoffs of various Daghestani ethnic groups. Like other Turkic peoples, the Azerbaijani hold oral epics and poetry in high regard, and the art of the *ashug* (reciters) is highly praised. They are also proud of their written literature, particularly poetry of the Middle Ages.

The origins of the Azerbaijani have been traced to the fusion of indigenous Iranian populations with Turkic Oghuz nomads who arrived in Azerbaijan mainly in the eleventh century.

For centuries Azerbaijan was ruled by the ARABS and the MONGOLS. In 1918 Russian Azerbaijan was proclaimed an independent republic. However, in 1920 it was conquered by Soviet troops and became the Azerbaijan Soviet Socialist Republic. During World War II Iranian Azerbaijan was occupied by Soviet troops, who encouraged an autonomist movement there, and by the end of 1945 the Soviet-backed autonomy of Azerbaijan within the framework of Iran was proclaimed, which survived only for about a year.

For centuries the majority of Azerbaijani were occupied in agriculture and cattle-breeding, crafts and trading. Many areas of Azerbaijan are arid semi-deserts and plains. Agriculture and especially the growing of cotton were based on irrigation and animal husbandry on seasonal migrations from the plains to mountain pasturelands. The nomads among the Azerbaijani (including ethnic groups of AIRUM, PADAR, SHAHSEVEN),

settled on the land in the first quarter of the twentieth century.

In the second half of the nineteenth century there emerged an intelligentsia which acquired a European (i.e., Russian) education and advocated a Muslim nationalist reform. The development of an oil industry, particularly the Baku oil fields, created national classes of bourgeoisie and workers. Under the impact of the Russian, Persian, and Turkish revolutions of 1905–1907 Azerbaijani nationalists developed political ideas, which for the first time focused on their own political-cultural identity.

During the seven decades of Soviet rule in Azerbaijan a tremendous social change produced new industries, towns, a reconstituted way of life, and new institutions. However, Azerbaijani grievances against this imposed modernization gradually grew and became the basis for a mass public protest movement in the 1980s.

Since 1988 an armed Armenian-Azerbaijani conflict had been waged for Nagorno Qarabakh, an autonomous *Oblast* (region) within the framework of Azerbaijan, inhabited mainly by ARMENIANS, in which hundreds of people from both sides were killed. Since then about 200,000 Azerbaijani previously living in Armenia have left for Azerbaijan. At the end of 1992 Azerbaijan announced its decision to withdraw from the Commonwealth of Independent States. (see also PADAR)

AZERI   see AZERBAIJANI.

AZJAR   A subgroup of the KEL AHAGGAR. (see also TUAREG)

B

BABALIA   An Arabic-speaking subgroup of the BU-LALA.

BABILLE   An Oromo-speaking ethnic group living in Ethiopia.

BABINE   A Native North American group of WET'SUWET'EN splinter bands, numbering about 2,000 persons, many of whom live in four villages along the shore of Babine Lake in the north-central part of British Columbia, Canada. They maintain to this day a clan form of social organization which they share with the WET'SUWET'EN, from whom they separated at the beginning of this century. (see also CARRIER)

BABUISSI   see BUISSI.

BACAIRI   A South American Indian people living in the Xingu region of Brazil. They subsist primarily from agriculture and fishing, although hunting and gathering are also important. They are noted for transplanting and irrigating wild fruit trees. Guest houses in each village facilitate intertribal trade.

BADA   An ethnic group living in the mountainous central region of the Indonesian island of Sulawesi (Celebes). (see also TORADJA)

BADAGA   A Dravidian people numbering about 146,000 living in the Nilgiri hills north of Madras in the Indian state of Tamil Nadu. In their own language, Badaga, their name means "northerners"; they are thought to have migrated to their present home between the twelfth and sixteenth centuries.

The Badaga are traditionally divided into six distinct castes ranging from priests to servants. Their economy is based on agriculture (the two highest castes are vegetarian), with rice the predominant crop. Other grains, vegetables, and potatoes are also grown. They fre-quently barter their agricultural produce with neighboring peoples who in return herd their buffalo.

BADAWACCO   A subgroup of the HADIYA.

BADE   A subgroup of the FULANI.

BADI   see NAT.

BADITTU   see AMARROO.

BADOUMA   An ethnic group living in Gabon.

BADU   An Akan-speaking group living in Ghana.

BADUI   (s.d. Urang Kanekes, Urang Rawajan, Urang Parahiang) An ethnic group of fewer than 2,000 living in thirty-five villages along the northern slopes of the Kendeng Mountains in western Java (Djawa), an island of Indonesia. They speak an archaic form of Sundanese but have no script, the art of writing being proscribed by their religion. An indigenous writing system does exist, but its use is limited to the priesthood at religious ceremonies. Their religion consists of an intricate mythology accompanied by countless taboos. Three villages are entirely forbidden to outsiders (Badui Dalam) and the inhabitants are forbidden to cultivate cash crops, eat four-legged animals, domesticate any animals but chickens, use fertilizer, use any but traditional herbal medicines, etc. These three villages are surrounded by the other thirty-two villages (Badui Luar) which also possess a rigid series of prohibitions regarding the use of food, color, etc. There are apparently strict sexual restrictions as well; the average Badui family has only 1.5 children. Other INDONESIANS hold the Badui, particularly the Badui Dalam, in high regard, and politicians frequently consult with them on issues of national importance.

BAFIA   An ethnic group living in the central-eastern region of Cameroon. They engage primarily in farming and fishing.

BAFOUR   An ethnic group living in Mauritania.

BAGA   An ethnic group living in lower Guinea. In recent decades they have been largely assimilated into the dominant SUSU population.

BAGAFORE   An ethnic group living in Guinea.

BAGAJE   A subgroup of the FULANI.

BAGAM   An ethnic group living in Cameroon.

BAGANDA   see GANDA.

BAGATA   An ethnic group numbering 91,000 (1981) living in Andhra Pradesh and Orissa, India. They speak Oriya, a language belonging to the Indo-Aryan family.

Originally soldiers by profession, today the Bagata are agriculturists. They subsist on the collection and sale of minor forest produce.

BAGGARA   An Arab people estimated at numbering c.600,000, living in northern Sudan. They are Muslims claiming descent from a southern Arabian people. Principal subgroups of the Baggara include the RIZAY-GAT and the TAAISHA in Darfur Province and the HOMR, HAWAZMA, MESSIRIYYAH and SELIMA in southern Kordofan Province. The HAWAZMA and SELIMA are mainly sedentary, differing in various ways from the nomadic cattle-raising Baggara. The HOMR and RIZAYGAT move southward during the dry season to territories controlled by the DINKA, NUER, and SHILLUK.

The Baggara were active slave traders until the beginning of the twentieth century, since when some have been occupied in cattle-raiding. They are regarded as a buffer group between the northeast and southwest parts of Sudan, and have a history of tense relations with both sides.

BAGIELLE   see BAYELE.

BAGOBO   An ethnic group numbering about 50,000, living in an area between the upper Palangi and Davao Rivers on the island of Mindanao in the Philippines. They speak Obo, a member of the local Manobo family of languages.

The Bagobo are predominantly an agricultural society, using the slash and burn method and frequently changing the sites of their fields. The advent of commercial logging has caused considerabe damage to their hunting grounds.

They adhere to a traditional religion, worshiping a supreme god known as Manama.

BAGULAL   (s.d. depending on *auls*, or villages). An ethnic group of northwest Daghestan, estimated as numbering 4,500. Their language belongs to the Daghestani branch of the Ibero-Caucasian family. It is unwritten, and Avarian is used as a literary language.

The Bagulal have been Sunni Muslims of the Shafi'i stream since the sixteenth century. They were not recognized in Soviet/Russian official ethnography as an ethnic group in their own right, but were regarded as a subgroup of the AVAR. Accordingly, their identity cards list them as AVAR. Intensive ethnic integration of all Avarian subgroups in the twentieth century has resulted in the Bagulal themselves using the term "AVAR" as a self-designation (together with more specific self-designations in territorial terms).

The Bagulal live in distinctive one-storey houses with courtyards which comprise auxiliary buildings. In ancient *auls* special strongholds were built side by side with the traditional Daghestani stone towers. Their economy is based on agriculture, horticulture, and cattle-raising.

BAHAMIANS   The inhabitants of the Commonwealth of the Bahamas, a large island group located off southeast Florida, northeast of Cuba. Thirty of their 700 islands and cays are inhabited. Most of the population is concentrated on the islands of Great Abaco, Grand Bahama, and especially New Providence, where the capital, Nassau, is located.

The 1990 population, estimated at just over 250,000, is predominantly black or a European-African mixture, of whom about one-third are Baptists, one-quarter Anglicans, and one-quarter Roman Catholics. Bahamian culture is characterized by exuberant celebrations: the best known is the "Junkanoo" parade that takes place on New Year and Boxing Days, when local people march and dance to rhythms of African origin, against a musical background of cow bells and drums.

The Bahamas, site of the first landing of Columbus, were originally inhabited by native ARAWAK. The first British settlements were established in the 1600s. During the American Revolution, loyalists fled there together with their slaves, establishing both the basis for what is now a substantial part of the Bahamian population and a plantation economy later ended by British abolition of slavery in 1834. Since independence, Bahamians have been ruled by a white minority; opposition of the black majority to this system, however, is increasing.

Tourism, which occupies two-thirds of the work force, and financial services currently contribute to a rapidly expanding Bahamian economy. Less important contributors to the economy include agriculture, including bananas, citrus fruit, and vegetables, and oil.

BAHARLU   A subgroup of the KHAMSE.

BAHNAR   The largest and most wide-spread Mon-Khmer group of the central highlands in Vietnam, numbering about 120,000. The Bahnar language was supplied with a romanized script by French missionaries in 1935.

The Bahnar are primarily slash and burn cultivators of rice who also raise fruit and vegetables and hunt. Certain Bahnar specialize in various trades and act as merchants, lawyers and medical professionals.

The Bahnar prospered during the French colonial period and are currently one of the most acculturated Montagnard ethnic groups. They served in the French military and civil administration and were the foremost advocates of Montagnard ethnonationalism during the colonial and later the South Vietnamese periods.

Their religion places importance on ghosts and spirits and a second language of obscure origins is sometimes used in certain religious rituals.

The RENGAO, numbering 6,000, are generally considered a mixed Sedang-Bahnar subgroup. Other Bahnar subgroups include the JOLONG, KONKO, KREM, ROH and TOLO. (see also HROY)

BAHR   see PEAR.

BAHRAINIS   An Arab people consisting of about two-thirds of the total population (500,000) of the state of Bahrain, situated in the Persian Gulf. For Gulf principalities, where the 1970s oil boom led to a demand for labor, this percentage is high; the reason is that, possessing smaller oil reserves than its neighbors, Bahrain has remained a minor producer with less need to import guest workers. IRANIANS, INDIANS, PAKISTANIS, other ARABS, and Europeans make up the rest of the population.

Bahrain is noteworthy for its Shi'ite majority of nearly 60 percent, many of them of Iranian descent. Most others are Sunnis.

Bahrain has functioned as an island station since Sumerian times. The region was islamicized in the eighth century; maritime trade in the Gulf was disrupted in 1514 by the arrival of the PORTUGUESE. Bahrain was ruled by Iran from 1602 until 1783, when the presently ruling (Sunni) al-Khalifah family took control. Iranian influence still accounts for the tiny archipelago's preponderant Shi'ism.

In 1861 Bahrain became a British protectorate, and after Britain's retreat from Aden, its main pillar in the region. However, its small but well educated (and militant) labor class also made it harder to control. The ruling al-Khalifas suppressed attempts at installing a parliament. Upon reaching independence in 1971, Bahrain chose to remain outside the United Arab Emirates. Iran lays claim to Bahrain, and in 1978 Khomeini's Iran called on Bahraini Shi'ites to destabilize Bahrain's absolute monarchy.

From 1934 oil has been Bahrain's main export. The traditional pearl industry has nearly disappeared. By 1980 Bahrain had taken over ownership of the Bahrain Petroleum Company and now features one of the Middle East's largest refineries. Bahrain is developing into a service center for Gulf trade and shipping, as well as the main banking center of the Gulf. It has, however, suffered from the 1991 Gulf War, which caused not only pollution but also a massive draining of foreign capital.

BAI   (Pai, Po, LaBhu, Minchia; s.d. Ber Deser, Shua Bern Ni) Numbering an estimated 1.1 million, the Bai constitute the largest concentrated minority group in the Yunnan Province of southwest China, in the Dali Autonomous District.

Their ancestors, believed to have been the original settlers of the area, founded their own state of Dali (Tali) in 937 C.E., but it was destroyed by the Mongols in the thirteenth century.

The Bai language, a member of the Tibeto-Burmese language group, has borrowed extensively from Han Chinese. Many Bai speak and write Chinese since, until recently, they had no written language of their own.

Buddhism is the predominant religion, although local deities, ancestral spirits, and Taoist gods are also worshipped.

For centuries, the Bai have lived peacefully with their neighbors, the Han CHINESE; similar lifestyles have enabled close contact and even intermarriage between the groups. At the same time, the Bai have retained distinctive cultural characteristics, most noticeably in their language, religious beliefs, marriage customs, and dress. Unique social and kinship organizations are based on the village and extended family.

About 90 percent of the Bai engage in agriculture, growing rice, sugarcane, vegetables, and fruit. Many are also skilled craftsmen.

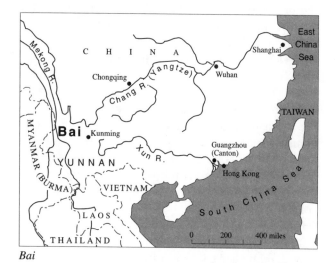

Bai

BAIGA   A people numbering 255,000 (1981) living in the Eastern Satpura hills in the Mandla, Balaghat, and Bilaspur districts of Madhya Pradesh, Bihar, Maharashtra, Orissa, and West Bengal, India. They speak Hindi and Chhatisgarhi, languages belonging to the Indo-Aryan family of languages, and are related to the BINJHWAR and BHAINA.

The Baiga are Hindus, and worship a number of gods. Their villages are located upon hilltops and amid thick jungles. They are expert hunters and basket-makers. (see also BHUIYA, BINJHWAR, PANIKA)

BAINOUK   A subgroup of the DIOLA.

BAISO   An ethnic group living in Ethiopia. They speak an Eastern Cushitic language.

BAJANS   see BARBADIANS.

BAJAU LAUT   (Sama, Palaqua) An ethnic group totaling c.50,000, one-third of whom live in the Sulu Archipelago of the Philippines, while the others are dispersed throughout eastern Indonesia and Borneo.

They speak a Samal dialect, which can be understood by most Samal speakers, and call themselves Sama Laut or Sama Mandelaut (Sea Samal). The most seafaring of the Samal-speaking peoples, they live among other coastal peoples, usually in villages built on piles over the sea or in communities of houseboats

tied to one another. They fish in large groups, using their catches both for self-subsistence and for trading purposes.

The Bajau Laut have a history of being exploited by other groups, and neighboring groups refer to them by derogatory terms. Once known as a society of boat people who were always on the move, they have in recent years begun to live in more permanent coastal villages. They are a very unorthodox Muslim group who observe the Islamic calender but do not center themselves around a mosque and are considered pagan by others. They have many ceremonies to evoke spirits (some of which are evil spirits called *saitan*).

BAJUN   A clan of the SOMALI.

BAJUWI   (Bajui; s.d. Bajuwej) An ethnic group of SHUGHNI inhabiting the valley of the Bajuw River in the Mountain Badakhshan Autonomous *Oblast* (Region) of Tajikistan. No statistical data are available, but a rough estimate would put them at several hundred. They speak a dialect of Shughni sometimes regarded as a language of its own, and belong to the Isma'ili sect of Islam. They are mountain agriculturalists. (see also SHUGHNI)

BAKA   A nomadic subgroup of the BEJA.

BAKANIQUI   An ethnic group living in Gabon.

BAKARWAL   A Muslim group living in Kashmir, India. Ethnically and linguistically akin to the PATHAN, the Bakarwal, whose name means "goat-rearers," are pastoralists. They migrate every year with their flocks to the cool high ranges of Kashmir and return to the warm plains of Jammu as October approaches, to avoid the cold weather.

The Bakarwal, together with the GUJAR, are represented in the Jammu and Kashmir parliament. They were the first to resist the 1947 and 1965–1966 invasions of the Pakistani army.

BAKEDI   see TESO.

BAKELE   see KELE.

BAKHSAN   A subgroup of the BALKAR.

BAKHTIARI   A people inhabiting the Bakhtiari mountains west of Esfahan and the foothills of the eastern Khuzistan Valley in Iran. Their number is estimated as over 600,000, subdivided into two groups of clans, the HAFT LANG and the CHAHAR (CHAR) LANG. The people as a whole is headed by *ilkhani*, assisted by an *ilbeq*. Clan heads are known as *kalantars*.

The Bakhtiari language belongs to the West Iranian subgroup of the Iranian language family and combines several non-written dialects.

Bakhtiari are Shi'ite Muslims. Most lead a nomadic life. Pastures and livestock are almost the only source of livelihood. According to season, the Bakhtiari either roam seeking pastures in the plains, or escape from the summer heat to high mountain pastures in the north. Bakhtiari women enjoy complete equality of rights within the family.

Until the 1920s the *ilkhani* possessed administrative power. From the 1930s his influence diminished due to steps taken by the government of Iran aimed at weakening the traditional structure of ethnic groups inhabiting Iran, for the sake of centralization. Following World War II, however, the role of the *kalantars* became more prominent.

Bakhtiari

The Bakhtiari played an essential part in the political life of Iran during the Iranian revolution of 1905–1911, when they helped the Constitutionalists in Tehran to dethrone Muhammad Ali (1907–1909). Later, the Bakhtiari initiated the establishment of the federation of southern peoples (1921–1924), but were defeated and forced to submit to the central government. During recent decades their influence in Iran has been relatively insignificant. They did not take an active part in the Islamic revolution of 1979. However, the revolution brought about a drastic destabilization of the traditional ethnic structure and a rapid decrease of the role of the clan heads caused by the introduction of strict Islamic revolutionary cadres on every tribal level and the establishment of cooperatives.

The Bakhtiari possess a rich narrative poetic and musical folklore. Their carpets are highly valued.

BAKONGO   see KONGO.

BAKOS   see BAYELE.

BAKOSSI   see KOSSI.

BAKOTA   see KOTA.

BAKOUKOUYA   A subgroup of the TEKE.

BAKU   An ethnic group living in the mountainous central region of the Indonesian island of Sulawesi (Celebes). (see also TORADJA)

BAKWERI   see KWERI.

BALAESAN   An ethnic group living on the Indonesian island of Kalimantan (Borneo). (see also DAYAK)

BALANGINGI   An ethnic group numbering an estimated 15,000 living in the Sulu-Sanghe area from Mindanao to Borneo and Sulawesi (Celebes) in the Philippine Islands and Indonesia. They are believed to be one of the strongest groups of this region, with their own history dating back to the early nineteenth century. Originally slavers and pirates, they were weakened by Spanish colonialization and eventually forced into a more submissive marine-based life with the invasion of the United States.

They are Muslims, who believe that the spirits of the dead remain on earth, and speak an eastern Samal dialect. Their name derives from their island of origin.

Balangingi villages are frequently located near coral reefs and mangrove swampland, housing between 100 to 600 people and centered around the local mosque.

Theirs is a marine-based economy, and houses are usually built on stilts on sites where high tides will cover the ground beneath. Agriculture is another source of subsistence (corn, cassava, rice, bananas, and the production of copra, or dried coconut kernels).

above: A market in Den Pasar, Bali, Indonesia
below: Balinese men watching a cock-fight in a temple in Bali

BALANTA, BALANTE   see LANTA.

BALANTAK   (Kosian, Mian Balantak) An ethnic group numbering about 30,000 living along the tip of the eastern peninsula of the Indonesian island of Sulawesi (Celebes). They speak an Austronesian language. Both Christianity and Islam began to win adherents among them in the early twentieth century. They cultivate rice, yams, taro, corn, and millet.

BALENGE   see LENGI.

BALEYA   see LEYA.

BALI   A subgroup of the TIKAR.

BALINESE   Predominant population of the large Indonesian island of Bali. They number over two million. The Balinese language is a Malayo-Polynesian language distinct from Javanese, whose script it utilizes. Contemporary Balinese publications also make use of the Roman alphabet. The island of Bali never underwent a process of islamization, and the traditional religion, sometimes known as *agama tirta* (the religion of water) is particularly strong. It is of Indian origin although native elements are present. There are numerous deities, some nameless, who are worshipped with elaborate rituals including prayers, music and dance, trances, and token offerings of food and flowers. Today, tourists flock to Bali to witness these ceremonies, which make use of richly embellished costumes and elaborate dance sequences.

Balinese agriculture consists primarily of rice, corn, and cassava. There are also some tobacco plantations introduced by CHINESE who came as traders in the nineteenth century. The Balinese have attained a high level of craftsmanship in gold and silver work, woodcarving, painting, and the manufacture of ritual objects such as musical instruments and masks. These have gained renown worldwide.

The cultural history of the Balinese can generally be traced to both indigenous and Indian roots. Brahman groups arrived directly from India between the eighth and eleventh centuries and JAVANESE who were Hindus in the succeeding 400 years. With the collapse of the Javanese Madjipahat empire in the late 1400s, Javanese aristocrats and religious leaders fled to Bali as refugees, enhancing the local culture with Hindu elements. No less important to the preservation of a unique Balinese society were the liberal policies of the colonial administration of the DUTCH in the nineteenth

century. They discouraged missionary activity and commercial exploitation, hoping to preserve a rich and varied heritage. Only upon the independence of Indonesia in 1950 have the Balinese benefited from some degree of modernization and mass education.

BALKAR   (s.d. Tanlu: "mountaineers") An ethnic group inhabiting the northern slopes of the Central Caucasian Ridge, in the ravines of the Baksan, Cheghem, and Cherek Rivers in the south (mountainous) and southwest of the Kabardino-Balkar Republic of Russia. In 1989 they numbered 89,000, 70,000 of whom lived in the Kabardino-Balkar Republic. They have been Sunni Muslims of the Hanafi religious school since the late eighteenth century, with remnants of traditional religion and some elements of Christian beliefs, the latter due to a certain spread of Christianity among them before their islamization.

The Balkar language belongs to the Turkic family of languages and is closely connected to the Qarachaian language. The joint literary language for these two ethnic groups was finally shaped in the 1960s after about forty years of struggle between unifying and separating tendencies. From 1925 to 1938 the Roman alphabet was used, but since 1938, the Cyrillic.

The ethnogenesis of the Balkar is uncertain. The prevailing opinion is that they resulted from the merging of the Turkish OYPCHAQ with the aboriginal ADGYHEANS and ALLAN.

The Balkar are divided into subregional groups: the BAKHSAN (whose dialect became the main base for the literary language), the CHEGMLY, and the MALKARLY. The name of this latter group was used as a general name for the ethnic group as a whole. In 1921 the Balkar, together with the KABARDINIANS, were given the administrative status of an autonomous *oblast* (region), which was transformed in 1936 into the Kabardino-Balkar Autonomous Socialist Republic. In 1943 the Balkar were deported by the Soviet authorities to Central Asia. Accordingly, the Kabardino-Balkar Republic was reduced to the Kabardin Republic. The Balkar were returned by a 1957 decree of the Supreme Soviet of the USSR, by which the Kabardino-Balkar Autonomous Republic was re-established, It was renamed the Kabardino-Balkar Republic with the eclipse of the USSR. At the end of December 1991, the Balkar voted by referendum to proclaim a separate Balkar Republic, but officially the previous administration is still in force.

Ethnographically the Balkar are similar to the neighboring KABARDINIANS. Their dwellings and stone towers are preserved in their mountain villages. The traditional economy centers around sheep-, cattle-, and horse-breeding, and home handicrafts. (see also QARACHAI)

BALKHIQI   see GYPSIES.

BALOCH   see BALUCH.

BALONG   An ethnic group living in Cameroon.

BALOUMBOU   An ethnic group living in Gabon.

BALUBA   see LUBA.

BALUCH   (s.d. Baloch) A people inhabiting the southeast Iranian provinces of Baluchistan and Sistan, the Pakistani province of Baluchistan, and southwest Afghanistan. Dispersed groups of Baluch live in the adjacent regions of the above countries, and also in India, Turkmenistan, the Persian Gulf emirates, and as far as Kenya and the Zanzibar region of Tanzania. Overall estimates of the number of Baluch vary from 3 to 5 million.

The overwhelming majority of Baluch are Sunni Muslims of the Hanafi school. Some few in the northwest of Iranian Baluchistan are Shi'ites (since the sixteenth century) and a group in Pakistani Baluchistan have from the early seventeenth century formed a Muslim sect known as Zikri.

The Baluchi language belongs to the northwest group of Iranian languages and uses the Arabic script. The system of writing and literary language are still in the process of development, but their folklore, both poetic and prose, is rich. Written literature dates back to the 1870s. The main rostra for literary production are

either monolingual Baluchi periodicals or, in Pakistan, bilingual Baluchi-Urdu publications.

Most are nomads, raising mainly sheep, goats, and camels, and cultivating small plots of land for fruit, vegetables, grain, and fodder. They live in encampments of tents made of black goat-hair and mats woven of dried leaves. The sedentary Baluch engage in agriculture, growing mainly grain, dates, beans, and also vegetables and fruits. They live predominantly in mud-brick houses. Men's wear consists of wide baggy trousers, long shirts, and turbans; women wear wide one-piece embroidered frocks with center-pockets.

There are many Baluch tribes, numbering from a few hundred to tens of thousands of families: some are of non-Baluch origin and became Baluch relatively recently. A specific case are the Brahni-Baluch equibilinguals who may at times identify themselves as Baluch and at times as Brahni.

The earliest mention of the Baluch, dating from the eighth to tenth centuries, places them in areas mainly to the north or northeast of their present habitat. Evidently, the Baluch came to their present day territory in several waves of migration in the eleventh to fourteenth centuries.

The famous Baluchi carpets are woven mainly by Baluch groups residing in Sistan and Khorasan. (see also AFGHANS, JATS II, PAKISTANIS)

BALUD   see BILAAN.

BAMA   see BURMANS.

BAMANA   see BAMBARA.

BAMBANA   An ethnic group living in Gabon.

BAMBARA   (Bamana) A people living mainly in Mali, where they number around 2.5 million people or 31 percent of the population. They occupy the central part of Mali from Nara and Nioro in the north to the Côte d'Ivoire border in the south. They also live in Senegal, the Côte d'Ivoire and Guinea, where they constitute only a small percentage of the population.

Many Bambara have converted to Islam although in some areas they cling to their traditional culture and religion. Their language, Bamana-ka, is the lingua franca in a large part of Mali.

According to their tradition the Bambara originated in the region of Toron, near the sources of the Milo and Baoule Rivers. In fact, the migration northward

Baluch

from this region was made by a Bambara family (the Coulibaly) whose ancestors founded two Bambara kingdoms in the seventeenth century in the regions of Segou and Kaarta.

In the middle of the nineteenth century the two kingdoms were conquered by El Hadj Omar, the Muslim leader of a *jihad* (Muslim holy war) movement, who belonged to the TUKULOR and lived in the region of Futa Toro (modern northern Senegal and southern Mauritania).

At the end of the nineteenth century the FRENCH conquered the two kingdoms. During the French colonial period and after the independence of Mali the Bambara became dominant in the administrative and political systems.

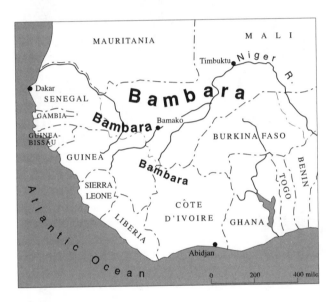

Bambara

The extended family is the basic social unit of the Bambara. It includes all male members, their wives and their children. A chief controls the extended family, which is divided into nuclear families. All family members worship the same ancestor and all legal matters are resolved inside the family unit. Agriculture is the main Bambara occupation and is considered to be the most highly valued work. (see also IVOIREANS, MALIANS)

BAMILEKE   A people living in the west province of Cameroon. They number about 3.1 million or 27 percent of the country's population. They are divided into several subgroups, each of which is controlled by a powerful chief.

The original Bamileke region was colonized first by the GERMANS and after World War I by the BRITISH. During this period, demographic pressure caused many

Bamileke to migrate to the urban centers of the country where they became a significant factor in the national economy. The Bamileke joined and overwhelmingly supported the Union des Populations Camerounaises (UPC), a political party in the French part of Cameroon that was the first to demand independence in French West Africa.

Because of their success in and dominance of the business sector, the Bamileke were often subject to hostility and jealousy from other native ethnic groups in the regions to which they migrated. This envy has continued in the post-independence era and culminated in the Tombel massacre of 1967 in which over 230 Bamileke were killed by KOSSI. (see also CAMEROONIANS, KOSSI)

BAMITABA   An ethnic group living in Cameroon.

BANABANS   A Micronesian-speaking ethnic group numbering about 3,500, originally natives of Ocean (Banaba) Island situated just south of the equator in the west Pacific Ocean. Today most Banabans live on Rambi Island in the northeast part of the Fiji group.

Ocean Island is a phosphate island, part of the former colony of Gilbert and Ellice Islands, most of whose population was deported to the Carolines, Nauru, and Gilbert Islands during occupation by the JAPANESE in World War II. After the war the British Phosphate Company managed to prevent the Banabans from being repatriated and to have them all transported to Rambi Island. There they are paid some form of royalty for phosphate production, but they consider themselves exiled and are anxious to return. The phosphates on Ocean Island have been almost completely mined; the soil has been contaminated and it is of little use for agriculture.

BANASU   An ethnic group living in the mountainous central region of the Indonesian island of Sulawesi (Celebes). (see also TORADJA)

BANAUE   A subgroup of the IFUGAO.

BANAWA   An ethnic group living in the mountainous central region of the Indonesian island of Sulawesi (Celebes). (see also TORADJA)

BANDA   The largest ethnic group of the Central African Republic, where they number approximately 800,000, or 30 percent of the population. They are found in the center and east of the country with smaller numbers also found in Zaire and Cameroon. The

above: Banabans on Rambi Island, Fiji
below: Bontok farmers in their terraced fields, Luzon, the Philippines

Banda arrived at their present location from the Sudan in the nineteenth century. As a result of slave raids from the north and east they split into numerous subgroups which dispersed over a wide area.

Although during the FRENCH colonial period the Banda were not politically active, they suffered repression following independence as the historical enemies of dictator Jean-Bedel Bokassa's ethnic group, the MBAKA. Following anti-Bokassa demonstrations in 1979, the army entered Banda neighborhoods in the capital and killed as many as 200 people.

Subgroups include the DAKPA, LANGBA, LINDA, N'GAO, NDRE, TOGBO, and YAKPA in the Central African Republic and the NGBAKA, who live along the Ubangi River in the northeastern corner of Zaire. (see also CENTRAL AFRICAN REPUBLIC, PEOPLE OF THE)

BANDI   see GHANDI.

BANDJABI   (Nzabi) An ethnic group living in southeastern Gabon between the Louesse and Nyanga Rivers and in the area between the Upper Ogooue and the Upper N'Gounie. Some Bandjabi are Christians and some practice traditional religions. Not much is known about them prior to the nineteenth century. In the late nineteenth century they were engaged in commerce. In the early twentieth century the Bandjabi unsuccessfully resisted colonization by the FRENCH.

BANE   An ethnic group living in Cameroon.

BANERO   An ethnic group numbering a few thousand, living in the Sepik River basin in northern Papua New Guinea. They speak an indigenous Papuan language. They live on tropical fruits, vegetables, and fishing: pig-raising is also quite common. They believe in spirits and practice magic in religious rituals.

BANGASH   A subgroup of the PASHTUN.

BANGGAI   (Aki) An ethnic group numbering over 100,000 living in the Banggai Archipelago off the Indonesian island of Sulawesi (Celebes). They are divided into two subgroups, the MIAN SEA-SEA and the MIAN BANGGAI, each speaking a dialect of Aki, an Austronesian language.

Both Christianity and Islam began to win adherents among them in the early twentieth century. They cultivate yams, taro, corn, sago, bananas, and vegetables.

BANGI   An ethnic group related to the MBOCHI, living in Congo.

BANGLADESHIS   A term referring to all the peoples who live in Bangladesh. Nearly all the population are BENGALIS, with about 2 percent consisting of Muslim BIHARA, Burman "hill people," and a variety of foreign settlers. Nearly 90 percent of the population are Sunni Muslims, while the rest are mainly Hindus and a small number are Buddhists or Christians. With a population of 120 million and an estimated annual population growth of 2.5 percent, Bangladesh is one of the world's most densely populated countries.

The national language is Bengali, an Indo-Aryan language belonging to the Indo-European family. It is spoken by nearly all Bangladeshis, while Urdu, an Indian language, is spoken in the cities where there is a large number of Indian migrant workers. About 10 percent of the population live in cities; the rest live in rural communities in which agriculture is the dominant occupation. Rice, along with a variety of fruits and vegetables, is the main subsistence crop, while jute is grown as a cash crop, sold raw or made into a variety of products. Nearly 70 percent of all Bangladeshi export revenues come from the sale of jute and jute products, making the industry very important to the increasingly unstable economy.

The area now known as Bangladesh was once the eastern part of Bang, where the Hindus flourished for nearly 700 years, beginning in the fourth century C.E. The Muslims took control of the area in the thirteenth century and held it for 500 years, withstanding attacks by Turkic peoples and AFGHANS. In the early part of the eighteenth century, the BRITISH gained control of the area. Tension was created between the Muslims, who did not accept British rule, and the Hindus, who did. In 1905, the BRITISH sectioned off the area now known as Bangladesh as a Muslim state, a decision they later rescinded as a result of a mainly Hindu public outcry.

Muslims became increasingly adamant about securing a separate state, and this led to the partition of British India into Pakistan and India at the time of independence in 1947. Pakistan was divided into two parts that were separated by India; West Pakistan, the dominant half, and East Pakistan, which is the area now known as Bangladesh. After thirty years of West Pakistani control, Bangladesh (with Indian Army help) won independence from West Pakistan in 1971. (see also BENGALIS)

BANGWAKETSE   see NGWAKETSE.

BANHUN   see BANYUN.

BANIAN   A clan of the SOMALI.

BANIARA   A mostly Muslim ethnic group living in Kashmir, India; a small number are Hindus. Not an agricultural group, the Baniara make bronze and brass utensils (a typical Hindu occupation in that area) and are also money-lenders.

BANIWA   (Baniua) A South American Indian group living near the the Icana River, in the State of Amazon, north Brazil, on both sides of the border with Venezuela.

   Their language belongs to the Arawak family. Together with the TUKANA they form the most important group of the area, and both have dominated and enslaved the MAKU group, who were the original inhabitants of the area.

BANJARA   An ethnic group numbering 11,000 (1981), living in Bihar and Orissa, in India. They speak Rajasthani, a dialect belonging to the Indo-Aryan family of languages.

BANJOGI   see PANKHO.

BANKWAL   A subgroup of the TIV.

BANNA   An ethnic group closely related to the HAMMAR.

Bannock

BANNOCK   A small Native North American group of hunter-gatherers in the Great Basin, United States, numbering about 2,000 persons. Today many live on the Fort Hall Federal Reservation in Idaho, U.S.A. They are related to the SHOSHONE.

BANOUM   An ethnic group living around the town of Foumban in the West Province, Cameroon. They are primarily Muslim. They had a kingdom of their own in the precolonial era, and its architecture is today an important tourist attraction in Cameroon.

BANTJEA see TORADJA.

BANTU   see EMBU, GWERE, HAYA, KENYANS, MANYEMA, MBERE, MERU, NGUNI, PADHOLA, SAMIA, SOMALI, SOTHO, SOUTH AFRICANS, TANZANIANS, THARAKA, TSQNGA, UGANDANS.

BANU MGUILD   A Berber group living in the center of Morocco in the upper ridges of the Middle Atlas mountains. They are Muslims and speak a Berber language.

   They rebelled against the FRENCH together with other Berber peoples of the Middle Atlas in 1913. Later, they were permitted to keep their own judicial system.

BANYORO see NYORO.

BANYULI see NYULI.

BANYUN   (Banhun) An ethnic group living in the southern Casamance area of Guinea-Bissau. They practice their traditional religion and their main occupation is agriculture.

BAOULE, BAWLE   see BAULE.

BAPEDI   see PEDI.

BAPOUNOU   see POUNOU.

BAQISH   One of four tribes comprising the MAMASAN.

BARA   A tribal division of the MALAGASY.

BARABAIG   An ethnic group of Nilotes, numbering 36,000, living in the Rift Valley and the adjacent highlands of Tanzania. They are the largest of several ethnic groups, some of whom call themselves Tatog (Datog). Their language belongs to the Afro-Asiatic family.

Above from left to right: a Crow Indian, (Montana U.S.A.); a Kayapo Indian (Brazil); a Sioux Indian (Pine Ridge Reservation). Center from left to right: a Maya Indian (Chiapas, Mexico); an Assiniboin chief (the Rocky Mountains); a Yanomami child (Brazil). Below from left to right: a Navajo Indian (Arizona, U.S.A.); a Quechua Indian (the Andean highlands); A Kamayura Indian (Brazil).

The Golden Stool of the Ashanti

The *Sika Dwa Kofi* ("stool born on Friday"), the famous "Golden Stool" of the ashanti of Ghana, Togo, and the Côte d'Ivoire, is not actually a functional stool; rather, it is a gilded footstool on which various ornaments and trophies are mounted. Traditionally, not even the Ashanti king (known as the *Asantehene*) was permitted to sit on the stool, which represented the welfare and continuity of the entire nation. The Golden Stool was not simply a cult object; it was also the most important symbol of the sovereignty of the *Asantehene*.

Popular tradition proposes that a priest received the Golden Stool from the heavens; he then placed it on the knees of Osei Tutu, the founder of the Ashanti state. Since that time, it has been the source of legitimacy and authority for all Ashanti sovereigns, and its conferral on the new ruler is the final affirmation of the transfer of wealth and power from the previous *Asantehene* to his successor.

The ASHANTI handle the Golden Stool with the greatest respect. During public events, it is carried by attendants, who grasp the bronze and gold bells dangling from its sides. It is richly adorned with gilded ribbons and plaster masks of famous kings and generals vanquished and beheaded by the ASHANTI. As the symbol of the unity of all ASHANTI, it represents the object in which the *Sunsum*, the soul of the nation, resides.

One can only speculate about the Golden Stool's age. As early as 1817 a British traveler described a royal stool covered entirely with gold and exhibited under a magnificent canopy. During the late nineteenth century the Golden Stool was the focus of many dramatic events. The BRITISH exiled the *Asantehene* in 1896; they then seized the Golden Stool and hid it. Several years later the new British governor of the Gold Coast Colony (now Ghana) demanded that the stool be given to him as his throne: a symbolic gesture that was intended to provide him with a tangible sign of his authority over the ASHANTI. This act of sacrilege only roused their indignation and spurred a last, desperate revolt against their colonial masters. While the BRITISH suppressed the revolt (and officially proclaimed the Ashanti's territory a Crown Colony) in

Ashanti dignitaries assembled on the occasion of the death-day of the Okyehne (King) of Kibi. They are carrying ornate gilded scepters.

1901, the Golden Stool was never delivered to the governor. Instead, it was slowly forgotten, until it was discovered accidentally by workmen. They dismantled the golden cover and removed the golden bells to melt them down and sell them.

When word of this reached the ASHANTI, they were infuriated. Although the culprits were arrested and severely punished, the damage to the Golden Stool was irreparable. It was decided, instead, to construct a new Golden Stool, incorporating surviving elements of the old one.

Since then, the new stool has been venerated much like its predecessor. To this day it is displayed on festive occasions, such as the yearly Odwira ceremony, held for the "purification of the nation" and in

The Okyehne with grass in his mouth, symbolizing the prohibition against eating or talking during ceremonies.

mourners' procession accompanies the Okyehne of Kibi. After the death of an Ashanti king various memorial rites are held, which ay last up to seven days.

he Golden Stool of the Ashanti, placed sideways on a chair. The golden ornaments epresent the defeated enemies of the Ashanti.

honor of the deceased Ashanti kings. The Golden Stool is now transported by the king's three most senior stoolbearers. These men occupy a special position in the community and are not subject to jurisdiction. Any attack upon them is punishable by death.

Stools play an important role in the ceremonial life of the ASHANTI. A stool is carved to mark a dignitary's accession to high office and is then used by the official thereafter. An official of outstanding merit, who passes away during his term of office, is bathed and seated on the stool prior to his funeral. The stool is then painted black (using a paste including soot, blood, animal fat, and egg yolk) in the presence of the Golden Stool and brought into the "House of the Throne Stool," where it is kept together with the stools of other deceased dignitaries. The black stools are believed to house the souls of ancestors. Regular sacrifices to them are said to curry the favor of the deceased: on important occasions special propitiation ceremonies are held before the stools to invoke the intervention of ancestors for the benefit of the community. In this way, the stools serve as a reminder to the living of the deeds of revered ancestors.

The Cross of Agadez

No collector of traditional Islamic ornaments remains unmoved at the mention of the many ornate amulets made in the Sahara Desert, particularly the Cross of Agadez, the noted Berber ornament. Both its outline and the cross imposed upon it have led to (often farfetched) speculations about the survival of some form of Christianity in the Sahara and the spread of early Christianity among the region's nomadic peoples.

While Christianity was certainly a decisive cultural influence in the Sahara region until the Arab conquest in the late seventh century, one imaginative interpretation of the Cross of Agadez proposes that at least some of the Sahara's nomads are decended from Christian Crusaders, who retained only their most important religious symbol, the cross, while abandoning all other signs of their European origins. Theories such as this do not, however, withstand critical investigation.

The geometrical motifs of the Saharan peoples' ornaments are strikingly different from other Arabic-Islamic styles typically found in North Africa. Among nomadic peoples the cross recurs frequently, most notably on the large ornamental plates, originating in the Egyptian oasis of Siwa, and worn only by girls in preparation for marriage. The cross motif is also evident on rings and other ornaments made in Siwa.

Many other traditional Berber motifs seem to have evolved from the cross, including the rhombus, the swastika, the eight-pointed star, and the diagonal and double cross. In fact, the cross itself merely a variant of other traditional geometric Berber motifs found on ornamen in Siwa and other Berber regions and not a Christian symbol. Similar motifs ca be found in the prehistoric rock drawing of the area.

Among the ornamental forms commonly found among the TUAREG are the so called *tcherot* amulets made of sheet silver. These serve both as ornaments and protection against evil spirits. The characteristic amulet-container is a small rectangular box flattened at the edges: its outline corresponds to that of a complete goat skin. Tuareg smiths, who created leathe as well as metal ornaments, were said to have had intimate knowledge of the nature of demons and their effect on the working of the world. Among their clients they had the reputation of possessing especially potent means of protecting against evil spirits. Many believed, therefore, that

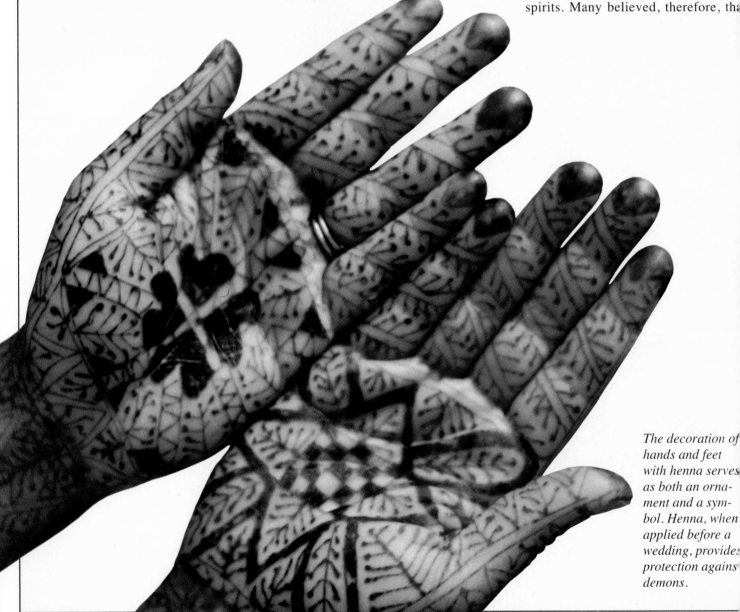

The decoration of hands and feet with henna serves as both an ornament and a symbol. Henna, when applied before a wedding, provides protection against demons.

amulets made by them guaranteed optimal protection to their wearers.

The names given by the artisans to their ornaments attest to the close relationship between the nomads of the Sahara and nature. Besides the sun, moon, and stars, representations of certain desert animals and even their tracks occupy an important place within the decorative motifs of these nomads. For those unfamiliar with the flora and fauna of the Sahara, however, it is often difficult to recognize in the ornamental and arabesque designs a "gazelle," a "scorpion," or even "camel urine."

Another common motif, particularly on the *tcherot* amulets is the "sandal of the prophet," clearly an Islamic symbol in light of its reference to Muhammad, the founder of Islam. This particular motif is found throughout North Africa, and recent research has shown that the "sandal of the prophet" motif bears similarities to all other foot- or shoe-shaped amulets found throughout the Islamic world.

Indeed, the motif of footprints of heroes, holy persons, demons, and gods is prevalent worldwide. The human foot, together with its protective footwear, was always considered a protection against evil. The "sandal of the prophet" motif thus reveals itself as the Islamic version of ancient designs belonging to the early history of mankind.

The hamsa (hand amulet), originating in the pre-Islamic era, represents the five fundaments of Islam: creed, prayer, the giving of alms, fasting, and the haj (pilgrimage to Mecca).

A Haratin Berber in festive attire, including fine garments and numerous silver amulets. Representations of hands, feet, footwear (in particular the "sandal of the prophet"), plants, animals, and even coins, protect against demons and the "evil eye."

Several Cuna women sit together working on their famous mola blouses.

Molakana: The Magnificent Handicrafts of Panama

The CUNA, who live on the Atlantic coast of Panama, wear strikingly colorful garments. Most notable is *mola* (plural: *molakana*), a woman's blouse with front and back decorated in vibrant colors and abstract geometric designs of figurative meaning. Designs are created by sewing different pieces of material on top of each other. Each Cuna woman posesses about five *molakana*. Until the 1970s only used *molakana* were sold to tourists or salesmen, but today they are coveted by tourists and collectors alike and are sold to art galleries, boutiques, and department stores in America, Europe, and Japan.

The *mola* is the only part of their tradi-tional women's costumes now produced by the CUNA themselves: the skirt, head-cover, and rich ornaments that complete the outfit are bought ready-made from foreign salesmen in Panama or Colombia. While contemporary Cuna costumes are fashioned according to European styles, we know from travelers' reports, dating from the seventeenth century, that Cuna men usually went naked except for a penis-sheath, and the women wore only a cotton skirt. Only on festive occasions would men wear a cotton garment. In those days, the CUNA lived in the interior of Panama and in northwestern Colombia, where excessive clothing would have hin-dered them in the hot and humid climate.

During the nineteenth century, Cuna culture changed profoundly. Their area of settlement spread toward the Atlantic Ocean and the numerous coral islands dotting the coast. There they attained a modest affluence by producing coconuts for market and were able to buy goods, such as iron utensils and gold ornaments, from European settlers across the narrow isthmus, on the Pacific coast. As a resu of these contacts with the outside worl Cuna costumes developed alon European lines. The men adopted shirt trousers, and hats (supplemented on fe tive occasions with ties and jackets); th women wore skirts, blouses, and hea coverings. While the wearing of golde nose-rings fell into disuse among th men, the women retained and eve embellished their rich gold and pearl jev elry.

The *mola* first appeared at the end the nineteenth century. Meaning "mater al" or "dress," it is a short- sleeved ga ment with two quadratic areas in front ar back. Young girls are instructed by the mothers in the art of sewing designs the *mola* and the completion of one's fir *mola* is an occasion for great prid Sometimes the seamstress invents h own patterns; at other times she choos one from journals. The design is the drawn with chalk on a piece of materi before it is cut and sewn.

A beginner usually starts with small

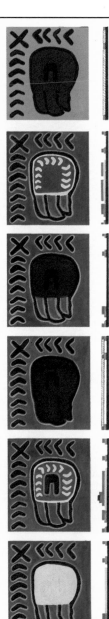

The stages in the processing of a mola. The mola is made of several continuous layers of material sewn one above the other. From these layers, the main design is cut and sewn. The detailed ornamentation is executed by putting on layers of brightly colored material, which are gradually cut out and sewn in. An experienced artist cuts and sews several layers of material simultaneously.

Traditional motifs are often found in combination with contemporary technological phenomena. The subject matter extends from local animals to U.S. Navy helicopters.

pieces of material, on which cut figures of animals or similar items are sewn; a master craftswomen is able to work on several pieces simultaneously. Older *molakana* designs tend to appear abstract and geometrical, but for the CUNA they represent tangible objects such as trees, animals, or arrowheads.

In earlier times, representations of wrapping-paper and merchandise designs were popular. These were faithfully copied together with the European script on them. In addition, there are designs invented by the maker; these represent a wide variety of subjects, including animals, plants, festive scenes, and mythological figures. At the same time, any design is acceptable as long as it is beautiful and festive. Today it is not uncommon to find modern appliances, automobiles, and even helicopters. Newer *molakana* are generally reserved for use at ceremonies and festivals.

Among the CUNA, women are strictly controlled and idleness is discouraged. Women are expected to use any free time left over from duties in the home or the fields in producing *molakana*. Even during official public occasions, such as ceremonial gatherings of the entire population, which may last many hours, Cuna women are busy embroidering the festive *molokana* for which they have become world-renowned.

An Evenki tent. Like other Siberian peoples, the Evenki are pastoral nomads, who wander with their herds of reindeer.

Shamanism: Ecstasy and the Healing of Illnesses

Shamanism is a phenomenon that has shaped the religious life of almost all Eurasian and Central Asian people, regardless of their specific creed or beliefs. It propounds the existence of numerous spirits and recognizes a human aptitude to communicate with them. Despite its being displaced by mainstream religions (for example, by Christianity among the LAPPS and several Siberian peoples, by Islam among the TURKS, and by Buddhism among the MONGOLS), shamanism has been preserved by the peoples of northern and eastern Siberia and of northeastern China, in particular among the EVENKI.

An old Evenki woman bakes unleavened bread in the traditional manner; the Evenki learnt this art from the Qazaqs.

Several male and female shamans remain active among them.

The shaman is a mediator between the community and the spirit world. While in a trance he or she makes contact, often with the help of an animal "familiar," with helpful spirits. The shaman's role includes: invoking spirits, who communicate through the shaman as a medium; the assuaging or expelling of hostile spirits; conducting the souls of the deceased to their destined place in the other world; and returning the souls of the ill from the other world.

The shaman is a much sought-after healer. The shaman's vocation is often revealed during a severe illness. The healing process will only commence once the candidate has consented to accept the new role of shaman. Often the initiation process includes abduction by spirits or a dismembering and resurrection of the shaman's body. Through this experience initiates are familiarized with their spirit protectors. The shaman's skills are frequently inherited; the initiate befriends

e protector spirits of ancestors (usually
e grandfather or grandmother from the
ther's side).

The most conspicuous accoutrements of
ae shamans are their costumes and
rums, often produced collectively by the
ommunity. The costume is generally
ecorated with cosmological drawings,
irrors, metal pieces, and other items
esigned to drive away evil spirits or
tract helpful ones. The community is
so represented in the costume.

Despite their special position as religious
unctionaries, shamans pursue a similar
festyle to other members of their commu-
ity, and are often found as hunters, fisher-
en, herdsmen, and cultivators. Although
eir protection of the community is indis-
ensible, they gain, at best, a very modest
come for these services.

The EVENKI of Inner Mongolia are
mong the those people who have best
etained elements of shamanism. The fol-
owing eyewitness account expresses the
ower of their shamans:

A famous shaman attracted the envy of
is colleagues after healing a dying man.
When his colleagues attempted to kill
im, the shaman called on his protective
pirits to help divert their attacks. As a
esult of the diversion, a horse and cow
ere killed instantly. The shaman then
voked the powers of his protective spirit
slay the leader of his adversaries. The
dversary, realizing death was imminent,
ansformed himself into a ghost and
ppeared before his own grandfather,
om whom he had inherited his powers.
longside his grandfather was the spirit
f a young woman who had died in
ildbirth. At once, the shaman real-
ed what he had done to merit
eath. At his own initiation rite,
is elderly teacher failed to
all upon the spirit of this
oman. Only now was she
king revenge. By perform-
g the necessary acts of con-
ition to the spirit of the
oung woman, the dying
haman was revived.

The conflicting relationship
etween shaman and spirit
uides is so fragile that careless
onduct or improper use of ritu-
ls by the shaman may render the
pirits dangerous. Therefore, most
hamans consider their office an
ndesirable and tedious burden. Much as
ey are praised for their successes, they

A depiction of spirits encountering shamans (from a Chinese drawing).

are often criticized and even punished for
their failures.

Evenki stories of the great deeds of past
shamans, mostly women, abound. In the
past the power and influence of shamans
were much greater, and the risks they
took upon failure were far more severe.
One legend, with many versions, tells of
the shaman woman Nishan originally
from the banks of the Nisgai River.
Having resurrected a young man killed in
an accident, news of her powers spread
throughout China. Eager to verify the stories about the woman, a Chinese emperor
of the Manchurian Qing dynasty summoned her to heal one of his ailing relatives. Yet, despite all her attempts, the
woman failed and her patient died. The
infuriated emperor denounced the woman
as a charlatan and had her cast to her
death down a deep well. According to the
legend, her guiding spirits were transferred to the powerful Evenki shamans,
where they still reside today.

An Evenki woman wearing a traditional cap and holding a drum. The shaman's drum helps produce the trance.

The Voodoo Possession Cult of the Ewe

The phenomenon of possession, often inaccurately defined as a "trance" or "ecstasy," is known worldwide. Most societies believe in the existence of ghosts, who may possess individuals. The posessed then become vehicles for the possessing entities.

Possession is sometimes considered an illness from which the affected person may be cured through the ritual of exorcism. At other times it is seen as an indication that the ghosts have chosen the affected person as a servant, dancer, or priest. Through "initiation," a ritual induction, the possessed person becomes a member of the cultic congregation and enters into an enduring relationship with the spirits. This latter belief is exemplified among the cults of the Zar in the Sudan, the Pepo on the coast of East Africa, the Bori and Holey of the HAUSA and SONGHAI, and the Voodoo cult of the EWE in Togo and Ghana.

In addition to the highest god, Mawu, who secluded himself from human affairs soon after the creation, the EWE also worship ancestors and ghosts. Ancestors function as moral models and guard the villages from which they themselves once departed as "good deceased." Ghosts, on the other hand, are considered immoral and unpredictable. They are associated with the environment (forests, deserts, savannahs, and rivers) and represent animals, foreign nations, illnesses, and natural phenomena such as thunderstorms or rainbows.

The EWE believe in a predestined association between each individual and certain ghosts. Some people are spared a dramatic encounter with their ghosts, whereas others are subjected to attacks by the ghosts and recover their health only when initiated into a cult in the ghost's honour. During initiation, the individual learns to turn "troublesome ghosts" into "helpful ghosts." Novices are taught the characteristics and preferences of the ghost, and a symbiotic relationship is developed whereby the initiated person adapts (usually through dance) to the ghost (embodiment) and erects a sanctuary, where the ghost can find repose during the periods

The possession ritual of the Ewe usually starts in the afternoon and finishes late at night. The public sits at the edge of the dancing area.

A dancer is seized by a slave-ghost of the savannah. Her costume, steps, and gestures, resemble those of the peoples of the north.

The priest, Ino Sotodji, and his Mami Wata altar. The items heaped here are not for regular use: rather, they create the ambience through which the ghost of the White Woman may be captured.

when it is not embodied in its human associate.

Under the leadership of experienced priests, the cult enacts its possession rituals. First, the dancers allow themselves to succumb to fear, lust, and other powerful emotions. Then, just before the actual seizure takes place, a brief state of calm and relaxation is experienced by many of the dancers, described by some as if they have suddenly "become empty." It is only now that the first possession symptoms appear. At first, only the participant's hands and feet begin to tremble. Soon, however, the whole body enters a state of hyper-mobility. The possessed dancer succumbs to trembling and cramps, and unknowingly begins to shout, sing, and cry. Eventually the dancers lose consciousness. Helpers ensure that they cause themselves and others no bodily harm.

After embodiment by the ghosts, the possessed persons enter the sanctuaries, considered to be the "homes" of the ghosts. There they change their clothes. Some put on the costumes of other tribes while others dress up in shirts, skirts, wigs, or hats. Still others carry items representative of the ghosts by which they have been possessed: brooms (ghosts of the household), wooden guns (ghosts of the hunt), teapots (ghosts of slaves), or combs and mirrors (the ghost of the White Woman).

In subsequent dances, gestures, steps, language, and costumes merge into a complex artistic performance, indicative of the ghosts' preferences and characteristics. This usually lasts several hours; the drums are then silenced and the atmosphere becomes festive. At the end of the dance the possessed almost always fall to the ground unconcious and their "emptied" bodies are carried to a remote resting place. When they recover, they do not remember having been possessed.

The possession ritual can be interpreted as a discovery of the world of the unknown, with the possessed serving as mediators between this, the known world and the unknown. The menace of the unknown is ritualized and tamed, and thereby incorporated into the individual and public realm. Furthermore, by adopting the role of mediators between the two worlds, individuals can ritually distinguish themselves from the rest of society.

The Ginseng Seekers of the Changpai Mountains

Genuine ginseng, the *Panax Ginseng C.A. Mayer*, grows in the Changpai Mountains of Manchuria, in eastern Russia, and in vast areas of Korea. It is a rather inconspicuous, sensitive, bright-green plant, with five finger-shaped feathered leaves and small whitish-yellow blossoms. It is famous for its large, bittersweet root, which supposedly has remarkable healing powers. The root is perennial and can attain a considerable age.

Many popular legends have been woven around the ginseng root in the course of centuries of ginseng-seeking. When seekers find a root of which the inner part is decayed, they believe that the soul of the plant has escaped. Roots of an advanced age are supposed to be able to transform themselves into human beings, animals, or inanimate objects with the power to help or punish their possessor. These, and similar, ideas can be traced to the biological peculiarities of the plant; others are connected with traditional Chinese beliefs.

Ginseng's medicinal properties made it economically significant. Centuries ago, peasants in the impoverished areas of Central Asia roamed the Changpai Mountains, earning a living searching for ginseng. Wild ginseng was almost extinct by the middle of the nineteenth century, so the importance of cultivating ginseng increased. To this day, however, HAN CHINESE peasants in northeastern China continue to search for ginseng during the autumn months, when the plant bears red seeds and and is easily detected in the dense forest undergrowth.

In former times the ginseng search was a dangerous undertaking, reserved only for men. In the thick mountain forests, they were under constant threat from wild animals and bandits. Ginseng seekers adhered to strict rules, and during the search they were forbidden to shout, used a secret vocabulary, and bestowed special honors upon protective spirits. This demonstrates the typical Chinese connection between trade and local religious beliefs. These ideas and rites linked the men among the

A ginseng root is wrapped with moss, soil, and bark and tied up.

ginseng-seekers' guilds that served to protect their interests. Today such guilds no longer exist, but the traditional search is still practiced. Since only a handful of experienced seekers go out on their own, searches usually take place in groups structured hierarchically.

Mystical visions during the ginseng search play an important role. In their dreams the seekers are shown places where they might find ginseng roots. Before one is allowed to dig out a root it must have a

red ribbon bound around it. The ginseng is then wrapped with the bark of a tree and carried away. Signs left on trees provide information to any subsequent seekers about the character of the find and the number of participants. Positive and negative injunctions regulate conduct in case of an unsuccessful search.

Before, during, and after the search the ginseng seekers offer sacrifices in honor of the mountain spirits and their protecting patron, Lao Batou. According to legend

A Han woman from Kumming.

Representation of a ginseng spirit on a wrapper produced by the cigarette firm "Shennue."

An old ginseng seeker meets a ginseng spirit (a drawing by Hui Juan).

his legendary ginseng seeker died of unger in the deep mountain forests. hortly before his death he left a message nat informed his successors of his destiny. hey buried his corpse and since then have vorshiped him. Thus, he became the pro- ecting spirit of the ginseng seekers, and ales and songs of his heroic deeds still cir- ulate.

While the beliefs of the ginseng seekers ave not been sufficiently researched, hinese folklorists have been studying them for some thirty years. Some tell of the experiences of ginseng seekers in the mountains, of helpful or vengeful spirits, and of sepisodes in the search for ginseng. According to one such tale, during the period of the Qing Dynasty of China, northeastern Manchuria was temporarily closed to the HAN and illegal ginseng seek- ers were exposed to the danger of being detected and punished. Other tales resem- ble the records of the visions that play such an important role in the search. The world of the ginseng spirits in these tales is paral- lel to the imagined human world beyond, and many ginseng spirits are believed to be the souls of deceased ginseng seekers. In all tales, many early beliefs about ginseng have been perserved. Although contempo- rary ginseng seekers are not always aware of these beliefs, ginseng tales, alongside the representation of ginseng in popular art, transmit the wisdom of the ginseng seekers and continue to shape the folklore of the Changpai Mountains.

A historical photograph of a Shinto priest wearing a traditional ceremonial costume.

Path of the Gods: Shinto Mythology

Elements of Shinto mythology still affect the everyday life of the JAPANESE. It almost seems as if "the path of the gods" has experienced a renaissance since the defeat of State Shintoism in 1945. Shinto myths were first recorded in the eighth century C.E., most notably in the *Kojiki* (Chronicle of Old Happenings, 712 C.E.) and in the *Nihongi* (Japanese Annals, 720 c.e.). These myths served to legitimize the Japanese state's ruling Tenno Dynasty. In these myths scholars of the imperial court documented the royal family's claim to have inherited their right to rule from time immemorial. However, with the collapse of the imperial prerogative during the Japanese Middle Ages, the ancient annals, and with them the myths, lapsed into obscurity.

Modern Japan, confronted with internal political problems and growing external threats since the eighteenth century, returned to ancient traditions, hoping to revive Japanese political and cultural mores. In 1868, during the Meiji Restoration, it seemed that this aim had been achieved. Once again the old myths provided legitimacy to the Emperor's rule. The end of the nineteenth century witnessed the promotion of State Shintoism, a religious philosophy promulgating imperial authority. The concept

A torii, or gateway, on an island near Hiroshima. Through it leads the path to the shrine of Itsukushima.

survived until 1945, when the JAPANESE surrendered to the Allied forces at the end of World War II.

Even in modern Japan, however, the Shinto concept of the world, developed in antiquity, has not been forgotten. Shinto mythology was, from its beginning, politically motivated but source documents also indicate that the single continuous myth that was created was culled from various traditional sources.

Japanese mythology contains no storie about the creation of the human race. It account of the creation of the world i also rather sparse. Only with the firs divine couple, Izanagi (the first god) an Izanami (his sister, the first goddess) does the mythological narrative reall gain substance.

Izanagi and Izanami created the firs

Japanese pilgrims visiting a Shinto temple.

Priests play music at the Aoi Matsuri cel-ebration, celebrating the divine descent of the emperor.

An ancient Shinto shrine in the modern city of Tokyo.

nd and then erected a heavenly pillar as symbol of the world's center. Thereafter, ey united as a couple in a complex wed-ng-rite. During the birth of their child, e fire god, Izanami burned herself and ed. Upon following his beloved wife to the terrible kingdom of death, Yomi Kuni, Izanagi is horrified to discover at her corpse has already decomposed. the remains crouch terrible demons

and only with considerable effort does Izanagi succeed in saving himself from these monsters. With an immense boulder, he then blocked the entrance to the cave leading to the kingdom of death and recit-ed the divorce formula.

Izanami became the goddess of death; with her, death came to this world. So as to cleanse himself from the impurity of death — the fear of impurity is a cornerstone of

the Shinto religion — Izanagi washed him-self in a river. From the union of Izanagi and the River several prominent Shinto deities emerged, among them the all-important trinity: the storm god, Susanoo; the moon god, Tsukiyomi; and the sun goddess, Amaterasu. The last was to become the ancestor-goddess of the Japanese imperial dynasty. Because of his impetuous behavior, Susanoo was ban-ished to the underworld by Izanagi.

Fearing her brother's wrath, Amaterasu, the sun goddess hid in a cave and the world became dark. Although she is even-tually lured back to her rightful place by the other gods and the light is restored, Susanoo's taunts earn him further banish-ment to the underworld (to be distin-guished from the kingdom of the dead presided over by Izanami). Susanoo's descendant, Okuninushi, "the Great Sovereign" ruled the heavens until an assembly of the gods induced him to abdi-cate. He then retired to his palace, later the great shrine of Izunu which, after the Ise shrine dedicated to Amaterasu, is con-sidered the most important Shinto sanctu-ary in Japan.

From this point, Shinto mythology is essential in legitimizing the imperial sys-tem. Amaterasu authorizes her grandson, Ningi No Mikoto, to descend from heaven and govern the earth, a role assigned to his descendants for all times. A descendant of Ningi eventually founded the Japanese Empire, concluding the era of the gods and inaugurating the human era.

Peoples of India

The Barabaig constitute a cattle-herding society. Their domesticated animals include a strain of zebu as well as sheep, cows, goats, and donkeys. Cow's milk, prepared in different ways, is their traditional staple diet. They also cultivate the land (maize in particular), hunt, and gather wild foodstuffs (mainly honey) to supplement their diet.

The social structure of the Barabaig is based on patrilineal clans and families which are often polygamous. This structure has affected the type of traditional Barabaig settlement, causing it to be made up of individual homesteads usually built far apart.

The traditional clothing of women is a leather cape and skirt (*bangwende*); men used to wear a red ocher-dyed toga, the wearing of which was officially banned in 1968. They profess traditional African religions.

BARAKI   see ORMURI.

BARAKZAI   A subgroup of the PASHTUN.

BARBADIANS   (s.d. Bajans) The inhabitants of Barbados, a Caribbean island located north of Venezuela and an independent member of the British Commonwealth. They number more than 250,000, making Barbados one of the most densely populated countries in the world. Although nearly all are English-speaking Christians (40 percent Anglicans), marriage is exceptional, with some 70 percent of births out of wedlock. More than one-quarter of the population is under 15. Ninety percent of the population is black, the remainder consisting of whites, mulattos, and a substantial East Indian minority. Half the island's income is generated by tourism, with sugar and rum also produced.

Evidence indicates that the SPANIARDS landed on this island in 1518, and had exterminated the peaceful Arawak population by 1536. With the British takeover and the establishment of plantations, slaves were introduced in the early 1600s, and continued to produce substantial income for their British masters until 1838, four years after slavery was abolished. Barbados joined the West Indies Federation in 1958 and achieved independence in 1966.

BARBARI   (Berberi) A group related to the HAZARA of Afghanistan but living in Iran, in the Torbat-e Jam district of the province of Khorasan. No population data are available, but a rough estimation puts them at several thousand. They are thought to have migrated to their present habitation from Afghanistan in the nineteenth century. In the 1920s a small group of Barbaris also lived in Turkmenistan. Nothing is known of their presence there after that period. (see also AIMAQ, HAZARA)

BARBUDANS   see ANTIGUANS AND BARBUDANS.

BARETUMA   A subgroup of the OROMO.

BARGISTA   see ORMURI.

BARIA   (Nara) An ethnic group numbering 50,000 (1980s), who live north of the Gash River in southwest Eritrea. They speak Nara, a Nilotic language. The Baria are Sunni Muslims. They are sedentary agriculturalists. The academic ethnic label "Baria" (Bareya) has in Amharic the literal meaning of "slave," denoting the status of the Baria (and the adjacent KUNAMA) in the eyes of their dominant neighbors. (see also ETHIOPIANS, ERITREANS)

BARIBA   (s.d. Batomba) A people living in northern Benin. They number about 400,000, 8.5 percent of the country's population. They practice traditional religions but have been gradually converting to Islam.

In the late eighteenth century they achieved autonomy from the YORUBA of Oyo and formed a number of kingdoms in the Borgou region. The colonization of Benin, then Dahomey, by the FRENCH in the late nineteenth century and the imposition of an artificial Anglo-French border brought an end to Bariba trade in the region and destroyed their economic power. During the colonial period the Bariba territory was neglected by the FRENCH and lagged behind the rest of the country in economic and political development. The reforms that followed the end of World War II allowed the formation of political parties and the Bariba and other northern groups soon organized themselves as a northern-interests party, turning the political scene into an ethnic battle ground. The south-north cleavage continues to manifest itself in independent Benin's politics. (see also BENINIANS)

BARKA   A small ethnic group living in western Burkina Faso. (see also BURKINABES)

BARLAS   see UZBEKS.

BARMA   An ethnic group living in Chad around the town of Massenga along the Chari River and in the region of the capital, Ndjamena. In 1964 they numbered

35,000. The Barma are mostly Muslims, though they retain pre-Islamic customs and rites. Their main occupation is agriculture.

The Barma established the Baguirmi kingdom in the sixteenth century around the town of Massenga which served as its capital. The kingdom was under constant pressure and had to pay tribute to the neighboring kingdoms of Bornu to the west and Ouadai to the east. In the late nineteenth century the kingdom was destroyed by Rabah, a Sudanese slave raider who built an empire in Central Africa.

BARMAN   see BORO-KACHARI.

BAROTSE, BAROZI BAROZWI   see RUZWI.

BARTANGI   An ethnic group inhabiting a small area along the Bartang river in the Mountain Badakhshani region of Tajikistan. Their estimated number (in the early 1970s) was 5,000.

The Bartangi language belongs to the Pamiri division of Iranian languages. It has two main dialects, Basidi (with a Bardari subdialect) and Raumedi-Sipanji. Bartangi is unwritten, with Tajik used as the literary language. Although recognized as a specific ethnic group, the Bartangi have been regarded officially since the 1930s as part of a broader Tajik people. They are followers of the Isma'ili sect of Islam, with a small fraction of Sunni Muslims of the Hanafi school. The date of their islamization is unknown, but cannot be earlier than the eleventh century.

The Bartangi live in small villages of between ten and fifty extended families, built mainly in the valley or on the slopes at the feet of mountains. Their dress is now semi-European but retains traditional elements. Their diet is predominantly vegetarian, with meat reserved for festive occasions. Their traditional occupation is grain and legume farming on small terraced plots, with some sheep-, goat-, and cattle-breeding.

BARTHAPLAYA   see NYINBA.

BARUE   see BARWE.

BARWE   (Barue) An ethnic group belonging to the SHONA grouping of peoples. They live south of the Zambezi River in Mozambique.

After breaking away from the Mwene Mutapa empire in the sixteenth century, they gained control of the interior trade routes of southern Africa. This led to a complex relationship with the PORTUGUESE, traders and colonialists in the region. While they sometimes allied themselves with the PORTUGUESE to obtain guns and subdue their mutual enemies, increased contacts caused Barwe culture to languish, and they conducted several anti-Portuguese rebellions to assert their independence. The fiercest of these occurred in 1917, when the Barwe organized a coalition of neighboring groups against their Portuguese overlords.

BASA   A subgroup of the TIV.

BASEDA   An ethnic group living in Benin.

BASERI   A subgroup of the KHAMSE.

BASHIRI   A subgroup of the KHAMSE.

BASHKIRS   (s.d. Bashqort) A Turkic people, concentrated mainly in the Bashqortstan Republic of Russia between the middle Volga River and the Ural mountains, as well as in some localities in the eastern regions of Russia. In 1989 they numbered 1.5 million. They are Sunni Muslims of the Hanafi school who converted to Islam before the thirteenth century. The Bashkir language belongs to one of the Qypchaq-Bulgar groups of Turkic languages. As a literary language Bashkir emerged only in the twentieth century. Until 1928 it used the Arabic alphabet, from 1928 to 1939 the Roman, and since 1939 the Cyrillic alphabets.

The Bashkirs emerged from the amalgamation of various ethnic groups, mostly of Turkic origin. Bashkirs were under the rule of the Golden Horde, then of the Kazan, Siberian, and Noghai khanates. At the beginning of the seventeenth century, RUSSIANS penetrated into Bashkir lands and gradually subdued the people over the following 200 years. After the 1917 Bolshevik Revolution the Bashkirs established their own government, but in 1920 the Soviet authorities succeeded in dominating them and in 1922 the Bashkir Autonomous Soviet Republic was created.

At the beginning of the twentieth century traditional lifestyles and occupations were still widespread among the Bashkirs. Those in the eastern plain areas of Bashqortstan were semi-nomadic shepherds, living in wooden dwellings and migrating in summer to grazing lands, where they lived in tents. Those of the central mountain zone spent winter in wooden dwellings but moved in summer to temporary wooden shelters. They were hunters, wood cutters, and beekeepers. Bashkirs of the northern areas, farmers and beekeepers, did not migrate in summer to temporary quarters.

In Soviet times a large number of industrial plants were built in Bashqortstan, accompanied by a massive influx of immigrants, particularly RUSSIANS and TATARS; many Bashkirs who remained in the rural areas saw themselves at a disadvantage vis-a-vis this urban population. In 1990, 25 percent of the population of Ufa, the capital, was Tatar, 58 percent Russian, 8 percent other minorities, and only 9 percent Bashkir.

The Bashkirs sustain an ambiguous relationship with the neighboring TATARS. This latent conflict has continued for many years, reflecting the complex mutual dependency of the two peoples. By the end of the 1980s there were 1.2 million TATARS in Bashqortstan, i.e., 34 percent of the total population. Some Tatar public figures emphasize that TATARS were instrumental in extending the revolution to Bashqortstan at the beginning of the twentieth century, and in creating arts and culture there. Moreover, they claim that the population of the western Bashkir areas, Bashkir-Tatar bilinguals, are not Bashkir. The Bashkirs deny these claims, countering that the backwardness of eastern Bashqortstan, where the population speaks only Bashkir, is to be ascribed to Tatar economic, political, and linguistic hegemony. They also cite Tatar assimilation of Bashkirs.

The Tatar-Bashkir relationship was aggravated with the proclamation of the Republic of Bashqortstan in the summer of 1990, when Bashkir and Russian were declared the official languages of the republic. Tatar demands to elevate the Tatar language to the same level in Bashqortstan have so far been denied.

A specific subgroup of the Bashkirs is the NAGAIBAK (s.d. Noghaibak), Bashkirs professing Eastern Orthodox Christianity.

BASHQORT   see BASHKIR.

BASKETO   An ethnic group numbering 50,000 (1980s), who live in dense population clusters on both sides of the upper stream of the Mago River in central Gemu Gofa Province, Ethiopia. Their language belongs to the Omotic group. They adhere to traditional beliefs and their main occupation is the intensified cultivation of grain and ensete.

BASOTHO   see SOTHO, SOUTHERN SOTHO.

BASQUES   (s.d. Euskaldun) A people numbering 2.5 million, who live on both the French (200,000) and the Spanish (2.3 million) side of the West Pyrenees, in a country of 21,000 sq.km they call Euskadi: the Labourd (Lapurdi), Bas-Navarrais (Baxe Nabarra), and

Soule (Ziberoa) departements in France, and the Spanish provinces of Vizcaya (Bizkaia), Guipozcoa (Gupuzkoa), Navarre (Naparra), and Alava (Araba). Of unknown origin, they may be the remnant of a prehistoric population which occupied a larger area of Aragon and Old Castile, and with whom they show some physical continuity.

Their unique pre-Indo European language, Euskara, possibly related to either the Caucasian or the Berber languages, is still spoken by 680,000 Basques. Basque literature can be traced back over the past 500 years.

The Basques have an extended family structure, and are known for their archaic social traditions, magical ceremonies and dances, and rich oral folklore. The Roman conquest influenced their vocabulary. The disappearance of paganism is variously dated to either the tenth or the seventeenth century. In the later Middle Ages, the Basque counties fell under Castilian suzerainty, enjoying an autonomous judical system. The overpopulation of their constricted territory always stimulated emigration, in particular to the Americas.

During the sixteenth to the eighteenth centuries the Basques actively participated in Spain's colonization of Latin America.

In the nineteenth century heavy industrialization attracted non-Basque (Spanish) labor, which threatened Basque culture and caused the rise of Basque nationalism in industrial areas, leading in the 1880s to a revival of the

Basques

written language and its literature. However, Basque as a spoken language was in retreat until the 1960s.

Both France and Spain have attempted forcible assimilation of the Basques, but only in Spain has the Basque question deteriorated into a major national conflict. After being defeated by the Nationalists in the 1936–1939 Civil War, the Basques lost the last vestiges of their autonomy. The Franco regime followed a policy of acculturation, proscribed the Basque language and folklore, and repressed the Basque church. The Catholic church laid the basis for a Basque movement; Catholic schools in outlying rural areas started to teach Basque.

In 1954 the independence movement ETA (Euskadi Ta Askatasuna, "Basque Homeland and Freedom") was established. Its violent tactics in the late Franco era provoked heavy-handed police repression, which in turn increased popular goodwill for the guerrillas. The Basque cause was espoused by the clergy, illegal trade unions, and parties, as well as by professionals and intellectuals. Show-trials underlined the Basque sense of alienation from the Spanish state. Economic recession has further nourished their sense of grievance.

Post-Franco Spain of the 1980s has legalized the Basque language and attempted decentralization. Today a regional Basque government is autonomous in educational and cultural matters, although the predominantly Basque northern Navarre is excluded from this arrangement. The extreme left-nationalist wing of the Basque movement (Herri Batasuna) is the only party insisting upon complete secession. It garners about one-sixth of the Basque vote. However, after a moderate majority of Basques had accepted regional autonomy in a referendum, many former ETA militants joined legal parties, and the violent ETA-military wing has found itself relatively isolated. Spain's central government has lately been successful in stamping out terrorism, in cooperation with France, whose own Basque population has also radicalized under ETA influence. In contrast to Spanish Basques, the Basques of France have never been granted any autonomy. (see also SPANIARDS)

BASSA A Kru-speaking people living mainly in Grand Bassa County, Liberia, and in small numbers in the Marshall and River Cess Territories. They number about 400,000, or 16 percent of the population. Most maintained their traditional religion even after the arrival of the AMERICO-LIBERIANS in the nineteenth century. Despite their location, few Bassa were assimi-lated into the coastal culture dominated by the AMERICO-LIBERIANS, and as late as 1952 most were administered only indirectly. Only a handful participate in the country's administration or commerce and the majority are still employed in agriculture. The Bassa were not directly involved in the 1980 coup by the KRAHN nor in the ongoing civil war. (see also LIBERIANS)

BASSA-BAKOKO A people living in Cameroon. For centuries they inhabited the coastal areas before being pushed inland by the DUALA. Some are Christians and some practice traditional religions.

During the period of colonization they fought against the GERMANS who were trying to penetrate into the hinterland. When the GERMANS finally managed to control the area, the Bassa-Bakoko were used as forced labor on the Duala-Yaounde railway. After World War I Cameroon's territory was divided between the FRENCH and the BRITISH, with the Bassa-Bakoko region going to France. During the colonial period many Bassa-Bakoko turned to the local Protestant mission to receive a European oriented education.

In the decolonization era most of the Bassa-Bakoko supported the Union des Populations Camerounaises (UPC), the political party which called for the end of French rule. During the late 1950s and early 1960s the Bassa-Bakoko participated in a rebellion against the FRENCH that continued after independence in 1960 in opposition to the Cameroon government. The rebellion was finally crushed with the help of French soldiers in the mid-1960s. (see also CAMEROONIANS)

BASSA-KOMO A subgroup of the TIV.

BASSARI An ethnic group living in central Togo, northwest of the town of Sokode, where they number around 33,000, and in small numbers in neighboring Ghana. They live together with the MOSSI and GURMA groups who assimilated into the dominant Bassari culture.

The Bassari never had a centralized state and lived in isolated villages. Once blacksmiths, they were forced into agriculture by the German colonial administration prior to World War I. (see also TENDA)

BASSILA An ethnic group living in central Togo.

BATA An ethnic group living in Nigeria.

BATAK I (Batta) A proto-Malayan people numbering c.4 million inhabiting the interior highlands of north-central Sumatera (Sumatra), an island in Indonesia, particularly in the area surrounding Lake Toba. They are divided into several groups including the ANGKOLA, KARO, MANDAILING, PAKPAK (Dairi), SIMALUNGUN (Timur), and TOBA, but all share language, traditions, and a belief in descent from a common ancestor. Differences between the subgroups have recently been aggravated by widespread conversions to both Christianity and Islam, artificial political divisions of territory, and urbanization. The most westernized and urbanized of these groups is the TOBA; Protestantism has made its greatest inroads among them and they are currently most involved of all Batak groups in the administration of the republic of Indonesia. The KARO have best retained their traditional mode of life.

Of the 4 million speakers of Batak, the Karo dialect with its c.1 million speakers is often classified as a distinct language. Even among the TOBA who have since emigrated from the Batak lands, links with ancestral villages remain strong.

Traditional Batak employment centers mainly on agriculture with rice being the staple crop. Herding is also important although the consumption of meat is generally reserved for feasts. They are also skilled metalworkers and carvers working a variety of materials including wood, bone, bark, and shells, and competent weavers who employ tie-dye techniques to give brilliant colors to their fabrics. The term "batik" used to describe a dyeing method in which fabric is covered by wax, is derived from Batak. Rich ornamentation is integral to Batak culture although certain practices such as teeth filing and tattooing have fallen into disuse.

The Batak lived in relative seclusion until recently, due in part to their reputation as brutal warriors and cannibals.

There has, in the past, been significant contact with Hindu groups which influenced their indigenous religious beliefs and led to the creation of a local script, based on (but noticeably different from) the Devangari script. They also had a complex legal system presided over by a council of village elders; those found guilty of severe crimes such as incest were punished by being eaten by the villagers. Traditional religious beliefs still persist, largely because of the group's seclusion, although the influence of the Hindu cosmology is evident. Ceremonies include sacrifices, made from a ritual breed of horses, to appease ancestors and deceased notables. The Batak have only a nebulous conception of an afterlife, but ceremonies connected with death and burial are of pri-

Batak I and Batak II

mary importance. Expensive rites involving bones and skulls are generally reserved for the wealthy and influential.

BATAK II   (Tinitianese) An ethnic group numbering a few thousand, living in northeastern Palawan, an island in the Western Philippines. They speak a Malayo-Polynesian language with close ties to the Central Bisayan group of Philippine languages, especially Tagbanuwa and Palawano.

The Batak are hunters and gatherers, who practice limited dry rice slash and burn agriculture. They are semi-nomads (believed by some to be related to the NEGRITOS) who live in barrios along the coast. They have good relations with the neighboring Christians, with whom they work on coconut plantations.

BATAMMARIBE   An ethnic group related to the SOMBA living in Benin.

BATANGAN   An ethnic group numbering several thousand who live in the rugged central uplands of the island of Mindoro, in the Philippines. They speak Mangyan, a language which belongs to the Malayo-Polynesian family.

They still wear bark cloth and in some places lead a semi-nomadic existence relying primarily on hunting and gathering for subsistence.

BATEK, BATEK DE, BATEK NONG, BATEK TE
Subgroups of the SEMANG.

BATEKE   see TEKE.

BATHONGA   see TONGA, NGUNI.

BATHUDI   An ethnic group numbering 150,000 (1981) living in Bihar (where they are a minor tribe) and Orissa, India. They are related to the Bauris, Bagodis, and Bhoois.

The Bathudi are Hindus. Brahman priests officiate at their ceremonies. They dwell in hilly, wooded areas, and are traditionally fishermen.

BATIN   An ethnic group numbering about 100,000 living along the Tembesi River in western Sumatera (Sumatra), Indonesia. They are Malay-speaking Muslims who cultivate rice and recently rubber. Although they are sometimes thought to be MALAYS with strong cultural influences from the MINANGKABAU, a distinctive Batin identity has recently begun to emerge and the term Djambi Malay is sometimes used as a national self-designation.

BATJANESE   Indigenous inhabitants of the Batjan Archipelago off the coast of Halmahera, an island in northeastern Indonesia. They represent 15 percent of the archipelago's total population of about 150,000. They are divided between Christians and Muslims.

BATOKA   see TONGA, NGUNI.

BATOMBA   see BARIBA.

BATSANGUI   see TSANGUI.

BATSBA NAKH   see BATSBI.

BATSBI   (s.d. Batsba Nakh, "Batsbi people") An ethnic group estimated as numbering 3,000 living in eastern Georgia, in the village of Zemo (Upper) Alvani. Some Batsbi families live also in Telavi and Tbilisi, Georgia. The Batsbi language belongs to the Veinakhian branch of the Ibero-Caucasian family. It is unwritten, and Georgian is used as the literary language.

Until the nineteenth century the Batsbi lived in the mountainous territory of the Georgian province of Mta-Tusheti (Mountain Tusheti), hence Tsova-Tushi, another, incorrect, name for the people. Later they resettled in the above-mentioned village.

The Batsbi are Eastern Orthodox Christians. Their traditional economy is based on cattle-breeding: in winter and spring in the Alazani River valley, and in summer on the mountain meadows of the upper course of the Kakhetian and Tush Alazani Rivers.

BATSWANA   see TSWANA.

BATTA   see BATAK.

BAU   An ethnic group living in the mountainous central region of the Indonesian island of Sulawesi (Celebes). (see also TORADJA)

BAULE   (Baoulé or Bawlé) An AKAN group living in the center of the Côte d'Ivoire between the Comoe and Bandama Rivers. They number about 1.9 million people, 19 percent of the total population. Their language is Twi.

In the nineteenth century the Baule were middlemen in the trade between the savanna and the coast. They had no centralized political framework but unsuccessfully resisted French colonization of their region in the late nineteenth and early twentieth centuries.

After World War II, when the FRENCH allowed party politics in their colonies, the first party of the Côte d'Ivoire, the Parti Democratique de la Côte d'Ivoire (PDCI), was established by a wealthy Baule farmer, Félix Houphouet Boigny, who was to become the Côte d'Ivoire's first president. The PDCI gained considerable support from the Baule people and led the country to independence in 1960. Although the PDCI is still the country's only party, Houphouet Boigny has tried to benefit all ethnic groups. Nonetheless, the Baule political and economic role in the Côte d'Ivoire is out of proportion to their number. (see also IVOIREANS)

BAVARIANS   (s.d. Bayern) A distinctive historical and cultural group, numbering 11 million, within the German people, inhabiting southern Germany. Their collective identity goes back to the twelfth-century beginnings of the Wittelsbach dynasty, which remained in power until the post-World War I revolution. They are predominantly Catholic, with a Protestant minority. In the nineteenth century, the Bavarians lost their independence and were annexed to the new Germany, but they have remained its most particularistic element. They still manifest a certain degree of regional patriotism.

Popular culture survives in Oberbayern costumes, beer and music *Feste*, and in religious folklore such as the Oberammergau passion play. (see also AUSTRIANS, GERMANS)

BAVARMA   see VARMA.

BAVI   A subgroup of the KUHGILU.

BAVOUNGOU   see VOUNOU.

BAWEAN ISLANDERS   (s.d. Orang Babian) Inhabitants of the Bawean islands off the coast of the island of Madura, Indonesia. They number about 20,000 and are primarily MADURESE, although they have mixed with other Indonesian ethnic groups such as the MACASSARESE and BUGINESE.

The Baweans consider themselves a distinct people. They are Muslims who engage in agriculture and fishing. Singapore boasts a sizable community of Bawean Islanders.

BAYA   (Gbaya, Gbeya) The second largest ethnic group in the Central African Republic, numbering around 800,000 and constituting about 30 percent of the population. The Baya inhabit most of the western part of the country and some also live in Cameroon. They speak a language called Baya; some are Christians while others practice traditional religions. They migrated to their present location at the beginning of the nineteenth century from Cameroon and Nigeria under FULANI military pressure.

At the end of the nineteenth century the FRENCH enforced a head tax on the region and sent the Baya to forced labor. During World War I the Baya were under German rule but since this was only nominal, it was a period of relief for the Baya. After the war the Baya territory came under French colonial rule. The Baya, who had a tradition of armed resistance and who had been at war with the FULANI for most of the second part of the nineteenth century, did not accept French rule quietly.

In 1928 they formed the Kongo Wara movement whose purpose was to resist labor recruitment and taxation. The movement included almost all the Baya and until 1931 there were severe outbreaks of violence in Baya's rural area which required considerable armed force to suppress.

After independence the Baya were not dominant in politics. The despotic ruler of the independent Central African Republic, Jean-Bedel Bokassa, gained their support by appointing a Baya as his military chief, but this support was only temporary since the appointed

Baya was later executed after being accused of planning a coup.

The MANDJIA who live on the Ubanguian Plateau are a subgroup of the Baya. (see also CENTRAL AFRICAN REPUBLIC, PEOPLE OF THE)

BAYEKE   see YEKE.

BAYELE   (Yele, Bagielli; s.d. Bakos) A group of PYGMIES living in Equatorial Guinea along the banks of Rio Campo and in the northwest and northeast of Rio Muni. They also live in Cameroon, where they are called Bagielli. They speak a Bujeba dialect. (see also EQUATORIAL GUINEANS)

BAYERN   see BAVARIANS.

BAYSO   (Gidicho) An ethnic group for whom no statistical data are available, living on the island of Gidicho in Lake Abaya in the northern Sidamo Province, Ethiopia. They are close neighbors of the Omotic-speaking GATAMI, although they themselves speak an eastern Cushitic language related to southern Somali dialects. The Bayso are agriculturalists.

BAZANTCHE   An ethnic group living in Benin.

BEAFADA   see BIAFADA.

BEAVER   A small Native North American Athapaskan-speaking group located in the northwestern part of British Columbia, Canada. At present, as in the past, they support themselves by means of hunting and gathering food. Many also work in the forest industry. (see also ATHAPASKAN, CARRIER)

BEDE   A subgroup of the KANURI.

BEDIA   An ethnic group numbering 90,000 (1981), who live in Hazaribagh, Ranchi, and Singhbhum in the states of Bihar and West Bengal, India. Dwelling in upland regions, they depend on dry cultivation.

BEDUANA   A subgroup of the JAKUN.

BEDUIN   see ARABS, IRAQIS, JORDANIANS, MOROCCANS, QATARIS, SAUDI ARABS, SYRIANS, UNITED ARAB EMIRATES, YEMENITES.

BEIR   A small ethnic group of the southern SUDANESE people. Their language is one of the Sudanic languages of the Nilotic group (Beir branch). The Beir live southwest of the ANUAK people on the Pibor River. Most are nomads professing traditional African religions.

BEJA A people numbering an estimated 1.2 million, living in northeast Sudan, where they represent 6 percent of the total population. The majority of the Beja belong to one of three Bedawiye-speaking groups: the BISHARIN, AMARAR, and HADENDOWA. The latter are the largest and most powerful, and are influential in the flourising agricultural development of the Tawkar delta, along the Red Sea coast. The BISHARIN cover the largest territory and are situated on the Atbarah River in the south, with small nomadic groups in the bleak northern ranges of the Red Sea Hills. The AMARAR live between the BISHARIN and the HADENDOWA. Some Beja are still nomads, keeping sheep, goats, camels, and cattle. Another Beja subgroup is the BAKA, most of whom are nomads professing Islam.

The ancestors of the Beja, a Cushitic group of herdsmen, arrived in the eastern Sudan between 4000 to 2500 B.C.E. Today, having undergone a long and intensive process of arabization, they have mixed with other Arab groups and adhere to Islam. (see also BENI AMER, EGYPTIANS, ETHIOPIANS, ERITREANS)

BELANDA A subgroup of the JAKUN.

BELANG A subgroup of the MINAHASAN.

BELAUAN see PALAU ISLANDERS.

BELGEN, BELGES, see BELGIANS.

BELGIANS (s.d. Belgen, Belges) The population of Belgium, numbering 11 million, divided between two distinct ethno-linguistical communities, the Germanic FLEMINGS and the Romanic WALLOONS. Most Belgians are Catholic.

The Flemish-Walloon divide goes back to Roman times. After a period of romanization in Gaul, Frankish invasions in the fifth century advanced to a line from Maastricht to Dunkirk. By the year 1000, this boundary had frozen into a permanent language frontier. In the fourteenth century, the Burgundian dukes coalesced the Seventeen Provinces into the Low Countries (or "nether lands"), a rich and highly urbanized region with a mixed Dutch-French population.

In the sixteenth century, after the Burgundian Circle passed into Habsburg possession and hence into Spanish hands, Spanish efforts to suppress Protestantism

Belgians

led to revolt and independence of the northern part of the Netherlands. Spain reimposed Catholicism in its southern zone, and the cultural elite moved north. The French Revolution brought judical and administrative modernization and stimulated industry, but also cemented French as the elite language. In 1830 an anti-Dutch revolt led by a coalition of conservative Flemish clergy and liberal Walloon bourgeoisie brought about the united Belgian kingdom, bilingual in theory but French-dominated in fact.

From the beginning the Belgians were beset by chronic ethnic disunity. Unilinguism was adopted in administration, education, etc., according to the dominant language in each region. However, only in the 1930s were the two languages treated equally. A completely Flemish-educated elite came of age after World War II. The language struggle exacerbated in the 1960s: it has led to Belgium's progressive federalization, with cultural-educational autonomy and separate institutions for both communities and a special status for Brussels. Recently, each linguistic community has established its own legislature and executive, independent from the national center. Although community problems remain unresolved, no party is demanding the breakup of Belgium, and regionalist parties declined in the 1980s. In 1993 Belgium became a federal state, composed of Flanders, Wallonia, and Brussels. (see also FLEMINGS, WALLOONS)

BELISI A subgroup of the NGUNI.

BELIZEANS The inhabitants of Belize, formerly British Honduras, located on the coast of the Caribbean Sea south of Mexico and east of Guatemala. About 50 percent of the approximately 230,000 Belizeans are of African descent. *Mestizos* (people of mixed races) and INDIANS make up the next largest groups, with East Indians and Europeans rounding out the population.

Largely rural peasants in the recent past, the Belizeans have become increasingly urbanized: almost half live in Belize City, and a smaller number in Belmopan, the new capital. The official language is English, but both Spanish and Mayan are spoken by some peoples; major religions are Roman Catholicism and Protestanatism.

In 1862, the colony of British Honduras came into existence. Its status was disputed between Britain and Spain until the mid-nineteenth century. British Honduras experienced brief prosperity before World War I, but remained undeveloped. Mexico eventually recognized British dominion over the small territory, but Guatemala continued to claim British Honduras: until independence, Guatamalan maps labeled Belize "territory illegally held by Great Britain." British Hondurans (as they were then called) drafted their first constitution in 1964, but did not achieve full independence until 1981, when a second constitution was ratified. Today, although actual confrontations are rare, the old territorial dispute with Guatemala continues.

Agriculture is the most important sector of the Belizean economy, producing sugar, fruit, rice, and tobacco. Belizeans also manufacture clothing, beverages, and construction materials. Their limited international trade is principally with the United States, Great Britain, and Canada.

BELLA BELLA see HAISLA.

BELLA COOLA (Tallion) A West Coast Native North American group of about 1,100 persons, many of whom live in a small fishing village halfway between Prince Rupert and Vancouver, British Columbia, Canada. They lived in cedar plank houses, and were well known in the past as skilled carvers of totem poles. Today many members of the group still earn their livelihood from ocean-fishing of salmon.

BEMBA (Awemba, Ayemba, Wemba, Muemba) An ethnic group living in northeastern Zambia. Numbering nearly 8 million, they constitute 15 percent of that country's population, although one-third of all ZAM-BIANS speak their language, Chibemba. Missions associated with the Catholic church and various Protestant millennarian movements have had considerable success among the Bemba although their traditional religion, which worships a supreme deity, a hunting god, and ancestral spirits (particularly important are the spirits of past chiefs), is also widespread.

Traditionally, the Bemba followed a system of matrilineal descent. Their chiefdoms, although autonomous, owed allegiance to one ruler, the Chitumukulu. Similarly, there was a hierarchy of clans, the highest being the crocodile clan, which were divided into houses and paired, each partner helping the other in performing rituals and in everyday life; marriage between paired clans was encouraged.

The early Bemba were renown as hunters and warriors. They often raided their neighbours and absorbed them to expand their realm. This resulted in Bemba involvement in the ivory, copper and slave trade in East Africa and along the Indian Ocean. With the development of copper mines in Zambia during the British colonial period, Bemba flocked to the mines and soon constituted the majority of the workforce.

The Bemba participated in the establishment of the Zambian African National Congress (ZANC) and the breakaway United National Independence Party (UNIP) concentrated in Bemba territory in the copper mining region, and sometimes regarded as a Bemba party. Zambia's first president, Kenneth Kaunda, was a Bemba. (see also MUKULU, UNGA, ZAMBIANS, ZAIREANS)

BEMBE A people living in Congo. They are related to the KONGO and speak their language.

BENA A Bantu-speaking ethnic group living in Tanzania.

BENA MAIA see BENA MAIN.

BENA MAIN (Bena Maia) An ethnic group living in Angola.

BENA MUKULU see MUKULU.

BENCHO An ethnic group numbering 130,000 (1980s), who live east of the Gurafarda River in western Kefa Province, Ethiopia. They adhere to traditional beliefs. Together with the SHE and the MERE, the Bencho once formed a polity under a *beneshtato* (king of the Bencho), and many Bencho also lived among the SHEKO.

BENDE   A subgroup of the NYAMWEZI.

BENGALIS   The term refers to speakers of Bengali, an Indo-Aryan language believed to be descended from ancient Sanskrit, which belongs to the Indo-European family. Numbering an estimated 175 million, they mainly inhabit the state of West Bengal, a federal state within India; Bangladesh; and other surrounding areas. Ninety-eight percent of the population of Bangladesh are Bengali-speakers; nearly 85 percent of Bengalis live in rural villages, or *mauzas*, established by the BRITISH for bureaucratic reasons during colonial times. Houses are usually made of mud from local rivers and are slightly elevated to avoid floods during seasonal monsoons.

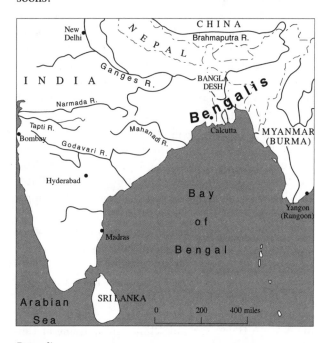

Bengalis

The two major religions of the Bengalis are Hinduism and Islam. The separation between West Bengal and Bangladesh is evident in the composition of these two religions. Hinduism is the dominant religion in West Bengal, practiced by 80 percent of the population; the remaining 20 percent are Muslims, while in Bangladesh Islam is practiced by 90 percent of the population. Bengali Hindus practice a modern strain of Vedantic Hinduism. The Hindu clergy comes from the highest Brahman castes. They believe in reincarnation and in cremation as the means by which the soul is released from the body. Bengali Muslims belong to the Sunni sect and follow the Hanafi school. Members of the Muslim clergy are volunteers who undergo rigorous

training. The Muslims bury their dead in the belief that the deceased is merely in a transitional state until the Day of Judgment. Hindu society is divided into a caste system in which the dominant caste usually controls the governing body. Among both Hindus and Muslims, elders are still respected as community leaders and decision makers. Both religions have had considerable influence on the arts and music among all Bengalis.

About 70 percent of the Bengalis work in agriculture, with wet-rice and jute as the main crops. Their traditional weaving industries once thrived, but were eventually ruined by industrialization, introduced by the BRITISH in India. (see also also BANGLADESHIS)

BENGUENTANOS, BENGUET IGOROTS   see IBALOI.

BENI AMER   (Beja) An ethnic group numbering 125,000 (1989) living in the lowland border areas of northern Eritrea and the eastern Sudan. They speak Bedawiye and Arabic and are Sunni Muslims. The Beni Amer are nomadic pastoralists (camels, cattle) clustering around a federation of tribes belonging to the BEJA, the largest non-Arabic ethnic group inhabiting the deserts between the Nile River and the Red Sea. Their islamization began during the ninth century.

The Beni Amer cluster is today a stronghold of the islamic (*Sufi*) Khatmiyya brotherhood. The ruling Beni Amer and their vassals once formed a patron-client relationship.

BENI HASSAN   see SANHADJA.

BENINIANS   (Beninois) The people of Benin, independent since August 1960, number c.5 million, of whom about 60 percent are rural. They consist of a number of ethnic groups, including the FON and the YORUBA of the southern and central regions, the BARIBA and the SOMBA of the north, the GUN, who are related to the FON, and the KILINGA, who are related to the BARIBA.

The official language of Benin is French, but Fon is the most widely-spoken. Sixty-five percent of the Beninians practice traditional religions, 15 percent are Christians, and 13 percent are Muslims.

Benin's economy is divided into the formal sector covering government, relatively modern industry, and agriculture, and an informal sector consisting of basic food production and cross-border trade with Nigeria, on which Benin is highly dependent. Agriculture accounts for over two-fifths of Benin's GDP and occupies more than two-thirds of the working population.

The Beninians were ruled by the FRENCH from the beginning of the twentieth century, at which time the country was called Dahomey after the great kingdom that controlled the area in precolonial times. During the colonial period Dahomey was largely neglected by the FRENCH. However, it served as a source of African administrators for large parts of French-ruled West Africa and a relatively large number of Beninians studied abroad.

The FON and YORUBA of the south enjoyed educational advantages while the northern peoples such as the BARIBA and the SOMBA were less westernized. After independence, the existence of a large educated elite in a country with a slow and underdeveloped economy caused great instability in Benin's political life, which was dominated by a continuing struggle between regional elites. Three main forces in the country have been struggling for power since the colonial period: the southern peoples who formed their own party after World War II, led by Migan Apithy; the northern peoples, led by Robert Maga; and the peoples living in the central region around the city of Abomey.

Until 1972 there was a series of military coups followed by a long period of Mathiew Kerekou's military rule. In 1989, following severe popular unrest, Kerekou reluctantly agreed to begin a process of democratization. In 1991 the first multiparty elections since independence took place, and Nicepore Soglo was elected president.

BENISHANGUL   A term describing 8,000 (1980s) Nilotic Berta-speakers living in the northern highlands (Belashangul) of Ethiopia's Western Wallage Province, bordering on Sudan. Since the 1980s, the ethnic composition of the area has been affected by resettlement programs for members of the TIGRAY and AMHARA of Ethiopia.

BENI WAIL   A subgroup of the HASSAUNA.

BENTENAN   A subgroup of the MINAHASAN.

BERBA   An ethnic group related to the SOMBA living in Benin.

BERBERS   (s.d. Tamazight) A people descended from the pre-Arab inhabitants of the Maghreb; their name derives from the Roman term for barbarians, "Barbara" (Barbary) being used for the North African coast. Berbers speak widely divergent and mutually unintelligible languages belonging to the Hamitic group. A majority of those who at one time spoke Berber have adopted Arabic as their language and assimilated into the Arab majority. Berbers are Muslims, but retain a specific cult of saints and their tombs, where prayer is considered to have healing effects. They also have distinct customary law, weaving styles, and agricultural techniques. Most are monogamous. As many as 11 million may be living in North Africa, the Sahara, and the West African Sahel. Berbers have conserved their distinctiveness best in inaccessible mountain areas — such as the Aures, Greater Kabylia, Rif, and the High Atlas — and deserts (Mzab, Hoggar).

In antiquity Berber Numidian kingdoms allied with the Carthaginians, from whom the Berbers adopted agricultural and metallurgic technology, and accepted Semitic deities. In the seventh century, Berber tribes put up vigorous resistance against the ARABS before being won over to Islam. Eventually they were instrumental in the Muslim conquest of Spain in the eighth century. However, discrimination by the dominant ARABS stimulated heresies among the Berbers: thus the Kharijites chased the ARABS from the central Maghreb and in the eighth and ninth centuries founded the Ibadi kingdom of Tahert. Shi'ism was popular among the SANHADJA and Qutama of Lesser Kabylia. In the eleventh and twelfth century, Berbers founded the puritanical

Berbers

above left: Berber women in Morocco
above right: A Berber street scene
bottom: Berbers visting a sacred tomb

Islamic dynasties of the Almoravids and the Almohads, whose realm stretched from Central Spain to sub-Sahara Africa.

Berbers are organized in tribes, generally united in confederations which were more often than not beyond the reach of the central government's tax-enforcing authority; such tribes used to engage in internecine warfare until the FRENCH pacified them in the 1880s.

Today Morocco houses the largest concentration of Berbers, some 6.5 million. The principal tribes are the RIF in the north, the BERRABER (Imazighen) in the center, and the SHLEUH in the south. The Rif in particular has remained a neglected and only superficially controlled region. Berber tribes played a prominent role in the 1920–1926 revolt of Abdelkrim against the FRENCH.

Although Moroccan Berbers are mostly rural, Marrakesh is a Berber city which until the 1950s lived under Glaoui Berber rule. While RIF Berbers are agriculturalists, the BERRABER practice transhumance. Protected granaries in their permanent villages have a characteristic pattern. SHLEUH engage in terrace cultivation and husbandry. On the borderland of the Moroccan steppe and the Sahara live the HARRATIN, who cultivate oases and are looked down upon by other Berbers. They are often active in low-status professions such as tanning, and are ascribed magical powers.

Four million Berbers live in Algeria. The FRENCH attempted to stimulate Arab-Berber tensions; the latter are today struggling for cultural self-determination. Important groups are the KABYLES in the Jurjura, the MZAB, and the TUAREG. Smaller Berber group live in Tunisia and in Libya, where Berber life is localized in small oases and villages.

The scarcity of resources has forced many Berbers to leave their villages for the city; many have crossed to Europe, where they form a significant migrant worker community. (see also AIT ATTA, ALGERIANS, ARABS, BANU MGUILD, CANARY ISLANDERS, EGYPTIANS, KABYLE, KEL AHAGGAR, MALIANS, MALTESE, MASMUDA, MAURITANIANS, MZABITES, NIGERIENS, OULED DELIM, SANHADJA, TUNISIANS, TUAREG, ZAYYAN, ZEMMOUR)

BER DESER   see BAI.

BEREMBUN   A subgroup of the JAKUN.

BERI   see BIDEYAT.

BERMUDANS   Over 60 percent of the 60,000 inhabitants of Bermuda, a British colony of islands in the western Atlantic Ocean, are of black African origin, the remainder being of European (mainly BRITISH or PORTUGUESE) descent; religious affiliation is to a variety of Christian denominations. English is universally spoken. Tourism and an offshore financial sector stimulated by the absence of income and corporate taxes are the major foreign income earners.

BERN NI   see BAI.

BERRABER   A subgroup of the BERBERS.

BERTA   An ethnic group numbering 5,000 (1982), who live south of the Blue Nile River, in the border areas of the Blue Nile Province of Sudan and Western Wallagga Province of Ethiopia. Their language, Berta, belongs to the Nilotic group, and they also speak Arabic. They are Sunni Muslims.

The Berta are sedentary agriculturalists. Until the first part of the nineteenth century, they were part of the population of the eastern Sudanese empire of Funj. (see also ETHIOPIANS)

BERTI   An ethnic group related to the ZAGHAWA.

BESERMEN   see UDMURT.

BESHADA   An ethnic group closely related to the HAMMAR.

BESLENEY   A subgroup of the ADYGHEANS.

BESOA   An ethnic group living in the mountainous central region of the Indonesian island of Sulawesi (Celebes). (see also TORADJA).

BESOM   An ethnic group related to the SANGA living in Congo.

BESOURBA   An ethnic group related to the SOMBA living in Benin.

BET ASGEDE   A subgroup of the TIGRE.

BETANIMENA   A tribal division of the MALAGASY.

BETE   (Magwe) A Kru-speaking people living in some 800 villages in the Côte d'Ivoire, around the towns of Daloa, Soubre, and Gagnoa. They number about 200,000. Their society is patrilineal and patrilocal.

They probably migrated to their current location from the west in the seventeenth century and drove away the GAGU, DIDA, and GURO who inhabited the area. In the late nineteenth century they tried to resist French colonization but were finally suppressed in 1906. During the colonial period they began to cultivate coffee and cocoa and many migrated to the capital, Abidjan.

BETI-PAHOUIN   see FANG.

BET JUK   A subgroup of the TIGRE.

BETSILEO   A tribal division of the MALAGASY.

BETSIMISARAKA   A tribal division of the MALAGASY.

BEZANOZANO   (Tankay) A tribal division of the MALAGASY.

BEZHTIN   (s.d. Kapucha, Bezhita) An ethnic group inhabiting three *auls* (villages) in northwest Daghestan. Their total number is estimated at 2,500.

The Bezhtin language belongs to the Daghestani branch of the Ibero-Caucasian family. It is unwritten, and Avarian is used as the literary language. They have been Sunni Muslims of the Shafi'i stream since no earlier than the sixteenth century.

Since the 1930s the Bezhtin have been officially regarded as a subgroup of the AVAR people. They are undergoing an intensive process of consolidation within the AVAR.

The traditional Bezhtin three- or four-storey stone houses often share a common roof, a feature probably influenced by their southern neighbors, the GEORGIANS. Bezhtin women wear a special headscarf and shawl. The traditional economy is based on sheep-herding and market-gardening, especially of potatoes.

BHACA   see NGUNI.

BHAINA   A group numbering 40,000 (1981), found in the Bilaspur district of Madhya Pradesh and in Maharashtra, India. The Bhaina are Hindus. Said to be adept sorcerers, some are magicians and village priests while others engage in agriculture.

BHARIA   A people numbering 197,000 (1981), who live in the Chhindwara, Jawalpur, and Bilaspur districts of Madhya Pradesh and Maharashtra, India. Having lived side-by-side for generations with the more influential and prosperous GOND, the Bharia have much in common with this group.

The Bharia are Hindu, but worship the snake and tiger in addition to the Hindu pantheon. Their principal deity is named Bhimsen.

Simple agriculturists, they collect minor forest produce. Their social organization is based on democratic principles, and the verdict of the village council is accepted as the final word in disputes. The Bharia bury as well as cremate their dead and observe a ten-day period of mourning.

BHATTRA   A ethnic group of 117,000 (1981), living in Bastar and south of Raipur in Madhya Pradesh and Maharashtra, India. They speak Oriya, a member of the Indo-Aryan family of languages.

The Bhattra worship a god of hunting and hold an annual ceremony on the fifteenth day of the month of Asarh (June) to propitiate the spirits of their ancestors. They live in exogamic totemic clans, and are cultivators, farm laborers, and village watchmen.

BHIL   A people numbering over 7 million (1981), dwelling in the states of Andhra Pradesh, Gujarat (where they are the largest ethnic group), Madhya Pradesh, Rajasthan, Maharashtra, Tripura, and Karnataka, India.

They speak a number of languages belonging to the Indo-Aryan family, such as Rajasthani, Gujarati, Khandeshi, and Marathi, but the general character of the dialect remains Gujarati.

Bhil

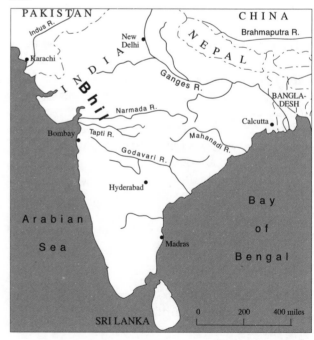

The Bhil were originally a tribe of food-gatherers and slash and burn cultivators and, until 1947, a ruling ethnic group. Bhil rajas permitted Konkni immigrants from the plains to settle in their hill domains, allowing them to follow the prosperous occupation of agriculture and exacting various forced levies, while they themselves continued to pursue forest-based occupations. However, the Bhil today are predominantly farmers. They are also expert in wielding the bow and arrow and the sword.

The Bhil have played a valorous part in Indian history. To safeguard their freedom, they fought the Moguls, the Maratha, and the British. Adjustment to the various regional cultural patterns may have lost them their common cultural heritage, but they have not lost the consciousness of a common origin and a basic unity.

Clan exogamy is strictly observed, but they may not marry outside their own group. (see also BHILALA)

BHILALA   A people numbering 85,000 (1981) living in the Dhar, Jhabua, and West Nimar districts of Madhya Pradesh, India. They are considered a mixed caste originating from alliances between immigrant Rajput and BHIL of the Madhya Bharat region. A Hindu group, they worship the common Hindu deities but each family has its own guardian deity to whom special reverence is paid.

The Bhilala are known for beautifully embroidered garments of different colors. Tattooing is common among them. They always carry bows and arrows. Their primary occupation is land cultivation, and some Bhilala are substantial farmers; but a large number are employed as farm and forest laborers. Some have even taken government jobs.

BHOTIA   see BHUTANESE, SIKKIMESE.

BHUINA   see BHUIYA.

BHUIYA   (Bhuinhar, Bhumia) A people numbering 208,000 (1981) found in the Surguja and Raigarh districts of Madhya Pradesh and in Bihar, Bengal, and Orissa, India. They speak Oriya and local Hindi dialects belonging to the Indo-Aryan family of languages. They are a Hindu group related to the BAIGA. The Bhuiya venerate the sun, and nearly all worship the cobra.

Previously practicing shifting cultivation, the Bhuiya are now used to settled cultivation. They are also occupied in agricultural and forest labor, and as priests for other groups.

BHUMIA   see BHUIYA.

BHUMIJ   A people numbering 528,000 (1981) found in Singhbhum, Hazaribagh, Ranchi, and Dhanbad in the states of Bihar, Orissa, and West Bengal, India. They speak Mundari with local variations and also a polyglot of Oriya, Bengali, and a variation of Hindi. They are related to the MUNDA.

The Bhumij are a Hindu group, worshipping in Shiva temples and offering sacrifices to village deities. They also worship their ancestors.

A proto-Australoid group, they live by agriculture, fishing, hunting, and gathering forest produce. Their houses are spacious with two to five rooms, but have no windows as protection against the cold.

BHUSKA   A small ethnic group located in the northern Indian state of Uttar Pradesh. Chiefly engaged in fishing, hunting, and farming, they are known for their traditional witchcraft.

BHUTANESE   (Bhotia) The dominant people of the small kingdom of Bhutan wedged between India and China. The Bhutanese are also found along the Indian borders with Tibet and Nepal. Their total population is about 900,000. The term "Bhot" means Tibet and it is thought that this people originated in that country, as evidenced by the Tibeto-Burman dialect they speak. In contemporary India, however, other non-Tibetans occupying the same region are also referred to as Bhotia.

Most Bhutanese are Tibetan Buddhists although Bon, a shamanist religion predating Buddhism, is also common, particularly in the remote regions of the Himalayas.

The Bhutanese are semi-nomadic and live in small, remote villages often separated by rugged mountain terrain which makes communications virtually impossible. There they engage in terrace agriculture, growing rice and other grains and herding yak. Traditionally they traded their produce in Tibet for salt, wool, and livestock but this has become increasingly difficult since the Chinese occupation of that country.

Modernization has brought about other changes in the established Bhutanese lifestyle. Until the early 1960s they lived in a feudal society governed by a hereditary aristocracy and the enslavement of other peoples taken in battle was common. In 1960 the government of Bhutan abolished slavery and emancipated women, steps that were immediately adopted in the Bhutanese-settled regions of India as well.

BHUTIA   see LEPCHA, SIKKIMESE.

BIADJU   An ethnic group living on the Indonesian island of Kalimantan (Borneo). (see also DAYAK)

BIAFADA   (Beafada) An ethnic group living in Guinea-Bissau, north of Bambadinca. In the nineteenth century they resisted FULANI penetrations from the Futa-Jallon region. They also tried to resist colonization but their territory was conquered by the PORTUGUESE in the early twentieth century. (see also GUINEA-BISSAU, THE PEOPLE OF)

BIAR   An ethnic group of approximately 8,000 located in the Indian states of Madhya Pradesh and Uttar Pradesh. They engage mostly in construction.

BIBRI   A Central American Indian group inhabiting the southern Caribbean region of Costa Rica, in the Talamanca Valley and the nearby area of Cocles. Some Bibri live in Salitre and Cabgra.

BIDAYUH   An ethnic group living on the Indonesian island of Kalimantan (Borneo). (see also DAYAK)

BIDEYAT   (s.d. Beri) An ethnic group numbering about 15,000 living in Chad, in the Fada region in Ennedi. Their language is Baele and they are subdivided into a number of clans.

BIDIDI   A subgroup of the TSWANA.

BIDYOGO   An ethnic group living in Guinea-Bissau.

BIET   A subgroup of the MNONG.

BIG BEAR BAND   see CREE.

BIH   (Pih) A Malayo-Polynesian group numbering about 8,000 living in the hilly region of southern Vietnam. They engage in paddy cultivation of rice and in the manufacture of pottery.

BIHARA   An ethnic group living in Bangladesh, where they constitute two percent of the population. Descended from Burmese hill tribes, they have adopted Islam.

BILAAN   (Balud, Takogan, Tumanao) An ethnic group numbering c.50,000, inhabiting the coastal area of the Davao Gulf of Mindanao, an island in the Philippines. Previously, they lived in the mountains but were forced to migrate by the AMERICANS.

The Bilaan speak a Southern Philippine language similar Tagabili and Tiruray. They practice slash and burn agriculture growing rice, millet, and maize; the latter is quickly becoming the staple crop. They adhere to their traditional religion, which has parallels with that of the BAGOBO.

BILALA   see BULALA.

BILIN   (Bogos) An ethnic group numbering 100,000 (1980s), who live in the Hamasien area of central Eritrea. They speak Bilin and Tigre, members of the central Cushitic language group. Until the second half of the nineteenth century, they were Ethiopian Orthodox Christians, but since then have shifted to Sunni Islam with a smaller number becoming Roman Catholics. The Bilin are sedentary agriculturalists who use the plow. (see also ERITREANS)

BILLAVA   see HALE PAIKA.

BIMANESE   (s.d. Dou Bima) Predominant ethnic group of the eastern half of the island of Sumbawa, Indonesia. They number about 200,000 and are virtually all Muslims. Rice cultivation is the primary economic activity. They speak a Malayo-Polynesian language related to the language of the SAVUNESE, the inhabitants of the Savu islands.

BINJHIA   An ethnic group numbering 18,000 (1981) living in Bihar, Uttar Pradesh, Madhya Pradesh, and Orissa, India. They speak Mundari, a dialect belonging to the Austroasiatic family of languages.

An endogamous group, they are settled wet and upland cultivators. They do not yoke cows, but use cow and buffalo milk.

The construction of the Rourkela steel plant in Bihar has brought some prosperity to the group, and the opening of a railway line connecting the centers of Ranchi and Rourkela has further improved their material condition by providing steady work and contract labor.

BINJHWAR   A people of 98,000 (1981) living in the Raipur and Bilaspur districts of Madhya Pradesh and Maharashtra, India. They speak Chhattisgarhi, a member of the Indo-Aryan family of languages.

A Bideyat woman living along the coast of Lake Chad, Niger

The Binjhwar are a Dravidian group, considered an offshoot of the BAIGA of the Mandla and Balaghat districts. They are, in fact, the landowners of the BAIGA.

BIRHOR A people inhabiting the Chota Nagpur plateau along the border of the states of Bihar and Madyha Pradesh in northern India. The Birhor language is a member of the Munda family of languages. They possess a theocratic political structure with clans governed by a priest. They believe that illnesses are caused by hostile spirits, and the clan leader is sometimes called to placate these spirits with elaborate rituals.

The Birhor were originally nomadic hunters and gathers (possibly cannibals as well) and some still maintain this lifestyle. Due to the extensive deforestation of their traditional home, a large number have abandoned their former occupations in favor of sedentary slash and burn agriculture.

BIRIFOR An ethnic group living in Burkina Faso near Diebougou and the Black Volta River along that country's border with Ghana. They speak Mole.

BIROM A subgroup of the TIV.

BIRWA A subgroup of the SOTHO.

BISA A Chibemba-speaking group numbering about 125,000 living in the central part of eastern Zambia. Some are Christians while others still practice their traditional religion. The Bisa are organized matrilineary.

In the nineteenth century, the Bisa were particularly involved in the trade of ivory, copper, slaves, and homespun cloth; agriculture, including cotton cultivation, was another important occupation.

Because of the disunity of the various Bisa chiefdoms, they were overrun by the BEMBA in the ninteenth century; their culture, religion, and social organization still preserve a marked Bemba influence. Other groups who took advantage of Bisa disunity to attack their territory were the NGONI and LUNDA. (see also BUSANI, TAMBO)

BISANO see BUSANI.

BISAYA An ethnic group numbering about 50,000, living in northern Borneo (Kalimantan), in the Malaysian province of Sabah, where they are primarily Muslim, and in Sarawak where they are either Christians or adhere to their traditional religion. They cultivate rice and engage in hunting and gathering.

BISHARIN A Bedawiye-speaking subgroup of the BEJA.

BIWATI see MUNDUGMOR.

BIYOBE A subgroup of the SOMBA.

BJEDUKH A subgroup of the ADYGHEANS. (see also CHERKESS)

BLACKFOOT (Blackfeet) A Native American group composed of three tribes of plains Indians: the BLOOD, the PAGAN, and the Blackfoot. The latter currently refer to themselves as SIKSIKA. Originally distributed over the great plains east of the Rocky Mountains on both sides of the U.S.-Canada border, they now live on reservations in Alberta and Montana.

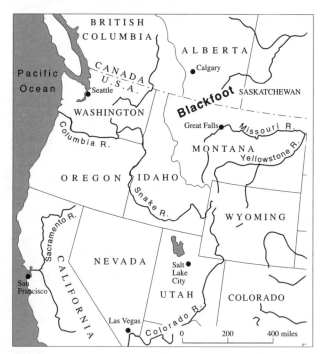

Blackfoot

BLGARI see BULGARIANS.

BLO A subgroup of the RHADE.

BLOOD One of three Native American tribes which compose the BLACKFOOT nation.

BOA An ethnic group living in the Haut-Zaire region of Zaire.

BOALEMO A subgroup of the GORONTALO.

BOANO   An ethnic group living on the Indonesian island of Kalimantan (Borneo). (see also DAYAK)

BOAZI   An ethnic group numbering a few thousand, living in the Fly River basin in southwestern Papua New Guinea. They speak Boazi, an indigenous regional language. They subsist on fishing and hunting. Their traditional religion is mixed with Christian influences.

BOBO   (s.d. Bwaba) An ethnic group living in the Dedougou and Bobo Dioulasso regions of western Burkina Faso and along the Burkina Faso-Mali border. They speak Bwamu.

BODHA   A small ethnic group living on the Indonesian island of Lombok, immediately east of Java. Although they are the indigenous inhabitants of the island, they are rapidly becoming extinct due to assimilation and acculturation. They speak a Sasak dialect and are Muslims, with vestiges of ancestor worship persisting in certain isolated locales.

BOERS   see AFRIKANERS.

BOFI   An ethnic group living in the Boda area of the Central African Republic.

BOGOMILS   see BULGARIANS.

BOGOS   see BILIN.

BOHANE   A subgroup of the CHARRUA.

BOIR-AHMADI   A subgroup of the KUHGILU.

BOKI   A subgroup of the IBIBIO.

BOKOKO   A subgroup of the TIV.

BOLAANG MONGONDOW   A people numbering under 2 million inhabiting the northern peninsula of the Indonesian island of Sulawesi (Celebes). They speak an Austronesian language and are predominantly Muslims. About 10 percent of the population are Protestants. They grow rice, sago, yams, and cassava, and raise small livestock.

BOLEWA   A subgroup of the KANURI.

BOLIVIANS   Numbering nearly 7.5 million, the inhabitants of Bolivia speak three main languages: Spanish, Aymara, and Quechua. During Spanish colonial times and part of the post-independence period, the Indians were denied the right to speak Spanish. The result is that as late as 1950 only a third of the population spoke Spanish fluently while 64 percent spoke an Indian language or dialect.

Traditionally Bolivians were classified in their national census according to racial types: Indian, *cholo* (mixed Indian and white), and white. In this classification whites were those of European extraction and constituted the Bolivian upper classes. *Cholos* include Indian-white mixed persons and Indians who speak fluent Spanish, have abandoned the Indian way of dressing, live in cities, and have acquired a certain degree of professional skill. The Indian classification includes the largely unskilled, black population that speaks an Indian language and constitutes the majority of Bolivians. This stratification was created by the Spanish invasion and colonization, the white conquerors and their descendants becoming the upper, and the *cholos* the intermediate, social strata.

Bolivian Indians are divided into three main groups: Andean (the majority), living in the highlands and valleys; Pampeano, living in the northern and central-western lowlands; and Guaranico, living in the southwestern lowlands. The Andean Indians speak two main languages which define them as members of the two large groups, AYMARA and QUECHUA. Aymara-speaking Indians are the original inhabitants of the Titicaca (north) plateau between the Andes (west) and the Cordillera Real (east) and Lake Poopo and the Uyuni salt marshes (south). The founders of the Tiahuanaco civilization on the shore of Lake Titicaca (probably in the second half of the first millennium C.E.) were Aymara-speaking Indians. The QUECHUA are the descendants of the Inca conquerors (second half of the fifteenth century) and the local population who adopted the language of the empire. Both groups are subdivided into numerous local-geographical groups possessing different styles of dress.

The AYMARA and QUECHUA population of Bolivia still regards itself as the true heirs of the Inca empire and the whites as usurpers. There is much diffidence and lack of will to communicate and provide information on the Indian side, beyond the language problem, probably as a result of the bitter historical experience of conquest and dominance by the SPANIARDS and later by the Bolivian upper classes.

Bolivians are predominantly Roman Catholics. Protestantism is present within the white population.

above: At the witch market, La Paz, Bolivia
below: Bolivians in the cloth market, La Paz, Bolivia

Indian Catholicism is frequently found mixed with pre-Columbian pagan rites and festivals.

Most Bolivians (60 percent) inhabit the *altiplano* (highlands of Western Bolivia) at heights of around 12,000 feet above sea level. The climatic conditions are harsh but the area is rich in minerals and the Indians had established a developed agriculture-based society in pre-Columbian times. Around 25 percent of the Bolivians inhabit the *yungas* or mountain valleys in the eastern slopes of the Cordillera Real at a height of 6,000 feet. This is an intensive agricultural area where most of Bolivian coca is produced. Since coca leaves are traditionally used by the Indian and *cholo* altiplano population to overcome fatigue, cold, hunger, and perhaps provide a certain feeling of wellbeing, the cultivation and trade of coca, with other crops, has provided an incentive for population spread into the *yungas*. Lately, international narcotraffic has found in Bolivia one of the main sources of supply of coca leaves. The Oriente (east) lowlands of Bolivia are sparsely populated, although they cover most of the country.

The Bolivian white population is predominantly urban, while most of the Indians are part of the rural and mining sectors. Bolivia's troubled political history did not provide much ground for social, economic, and national integration between the population groups until the 1950s. The revolution of April 1952 brought the Movement of National Revolution (MNR) and Victor Paz Estenssoro to power. As president, he nationalized the tin mines, reduced the army in favor of the popular militia, proclaimed universal suffrage, and, in the wake of land claims by the Indians, launched an agrarian reform.

The MNR governments lasted, through reelection, from 1952 to 1964 and its policies modernized and integrated Bolivian society. In 1964 a military coup took over and military governments were in power in Bolivia until 1982. Since then the redemocratization process is being built on the basis of strong neo-liberal economic stabilization policies.

BOLON   An ethnic group living in the Orodara region, southwest of Bobo Dioulasso, in Burkina Faso.

BOMA   An ethnic group living in the Mai-Ndombe area of Zaire, along the Zaire River, north of the Kasai River.

BOMBO   An ethnic group related to the SANGA living in Congo.

BOMO-JANBO   A subgroup of the ADI.

BOMVANA   A subgroup of the NGUNI.

BOMVU   A subgroup of the NGUNI.

BONDO   A MUNDA group numbering 5,000 and related to the GADABA living in the southern part of the Indian state of Orissa. They engage in slash and burn agriculture and terrace cultivation of rice. They also raise cattle, pigs, and chickens to supplement their diet, and fish the stagnant waters of the rice paddies. (see also KONYAK)

BONE   A subgroup of the GORONTALO.

BONGO   see AZANDE.

BONGOM   see KELE.

BONI   An ethnic group numbering c.3,000 living in the forest hinterland between the port of Lamu and the Somali border, in eastern Kenya. The Boni are hunter-gatherers (in the vicinity of waterholes). Their language belongs to the Sam group of languages. Boni attempts to cultivate land have been few and unsuccessful.

BONO   see BRONG.

BONOM   see MONOM.

BONTOK   (Igorot, Guianes) An ethnic group numbering c.150,000, living in the deep canyon country along the Upper Chico River in northern Luzon, an island in the Philippines.

The Bontok language belongs to a subgroup of the northern Luzon group of Philippine languages. There is marked cultural diversity among speakers of Bontok, although they share a common history and rituals.

The Bontok practice wet-rice terracing along with the slash and burn cultivation of sweet potatoes, maize, millet, and beans. Headhunting used to be the means of obtaining power, but since it is no longer practiced, power is held by the wealthiest members of any given village.

The Bontok believe that ancestral spirits live in the mountains surrounding their villages. The afterlife is similar to life on earth and the calls of certain birds are the voices of these spirits. They believe in a supreme being who is referred to as "Lumawig."

BORANA   A southern division of the OROMO living in southern Sidamo, Ethiopia, and in northern Kenya.

· *A Bororo (Cattle Fulani) woman in Niger*

Bontok

BORI   A subgroup of the ADI.

BORINQUENOS   see PUERTO RICANS.

BORO   see BORO-KACHARI, DIMASA-KACHARI.

BORODA   A subgroup of the GAMO.

BORO-KACHARI   A people numbering 610,000 (1971), found in Assam, India. Their language is Assamese-Burmese, of the Tibeto-Chinese family.

The Boro-Kachari, characteristically Mongoloid in appearance, are a branch of the Great Bodo group of the Indo-Mongoloid family and constitute 45.4 percent of Assam's population. They are not a homogeneous ethnic group, and are known by different names in different parts of Assam: MECH, Sonowal, Thengal Kachari, Boro, Dimasa, and Barman. It is considered likely that they brought the art of rearing silkworms to India.

A Hindu group, they have two main deities, Bathou (analogous to Shiva of the Hindu trinity) and Mainao (also called Buli Buri; the goddess of wealth). They also worship many other deities.

The Boro-Kachari live in compact villages of reed, jungle grass, and split bamboo dwellings surrounded by barriers. They are predominantly agriculturalists, cultivating paddy, and are especially skilful in constructing irrigation canals and earthwork embankments for diverting water from river beds into their ricefields. (see also DIMASA-KACHARI)

BORON   see BRONG.

BORORO I   A South American Indian group living in the State of Mato Grosso, central-west Brazil. Formerly a numerically important group occupying a wide area of savanna, they have been reduced to several hundreds as a result of the aggressive advance of modern developers into their lands. Their language does not fit into any of the larger families, but their culture ties them to the Ge group.

BORORO II   An ethnic group of the Cattle Fulani living in Nigeria where they number about 1.6 million, or 1.5 percent of Nigeria's population. (see also FULANI)

BOROT   A subgroup of the MARAKWET.

BORUCA   (Brunka) A Central American Indian group living in the southern Pacific region of Costa Rica. Their main clusters of settlement are in Boruca, Curre, and Maiz.

BOSHA   (Busa, Garo) An ethnic group numbering 10,000 (1980s) who live in northwest Kefa Province, Ethiopia. They are Sunni Muslims. The Bosha formed a small polity south of Janjero. During the first part of the nineteenth century, Bosha was included in the OROMO kingdom of Jimma.

BOSNIAN MUSLIMS   (s.d. Bosnaki) Of the 2.15 million Bosnian Muslims, 2 million represent 47 percent of the population of the former Yugoslav republic of Bosnia-Herzegovina. The rest of the population (totaling some 4.4 million) is divided among approximately 34 percent Greek Orthodox SERBS, and 18 percent Roman Catholic CROATS. The three groups, who are anthropologically, ethnically, and linguistically identical, share common customs (with the exception of those based on religion) as well as social structures and values. During the second half of the twentieth century, growing assimilation (including intermarriage) was the norm. Yet in the civil war of 1992 the religious divide proved to be the strongest factor, and served as the only basis for nationalism.

Bosnia-Herzegovina, like its neighbors, Serbia and Croatia, was settled by Slavic tribes during the sixth and seventh centuries. However, the Slavs of Bosnia-Herzegovina were late in consolidating a unified political and cultural entity because they were subject to political and religio-cultural pressures from the two neighboring kingdoms. Only in the thirteenth century was a strong state created in Bosnia-Herzegovina, which reached its zenith during the rule of Tvrtko I (1353–1391), who assumed the title of king.

To withstand these pressures from east and west and to emphasize their independence, the Bosnian rulers adopted the Bogomil church (which originated in Bulgaria) and encouraged its spread. Yet the growing Ottoman threat made them turn for help to the west and yield to the pope's demands to suppress the "heresy." This in turn facilitated the final Ottoman conquest of the country (1461–1483) and its incorporation into the empire. It is believed that following the Ottoman conquest the bulk of the Bogomil following, as well as most of the nobility, converted to Islam, thus creating a massive Muslim population in Bosnia-Herzegovina.

During the Ottoman period the Bosnian Muslims were members of the *stadtsvolk* and as such contributed their share to the empire's administration and military.

Bosnian Muslims

In Bosnia-Herzegovina itself they formed the majority in the cities, and former *bojars* (nobles) continued to rule the country as Ottoman officials, and since the seventeenth century as almost completely autonomous rulers. In the nineteenth century these Muslim *beks* and *agas* led a series of revolts against the attempts at modernization and centralization of the central authorities. The last of these revolts sparked off the great Balkan crisis of 1875–1878, following which Bosnia-Herzegovina was put under Austro-Hungarian administration.

During the period of Austro-Hungarian rule (1878–1918) and that of the new kingdom of Yugoslavia (1918–1941), the Muslims lost first their political and then — due to agrarian reforms promulgated by Yugoslavia — their economic superiority and tended to abstain from the new national politics. Under Austro-Hungarian encouragement they developed their own communal institutions, which were kept apart from those of the rest of the Muslims in Yugoslavia, during the monarchy. The strong efforts by both SERBS and CROATS to woo the Muslims to their fold failed, as was clearly demonstrated in the 1953 census when only 3.9 percent of the Muslims declared themselves SERBS and less than 1.7 percent CROATS. The fact that almost 94.5 percent of the Muslims did not declare their nationality served as a justification for Tito to establish a separate People's Republic of Bosnia and Herzegovina.

Paradoxically, the Communist regime in Yugoslavia seems to have promulgated a modern national identity and nationalism among the Bosnian Muslims. Until World War II the Muslims were the most conservative and least modernized community. The reforms promulgated by Tito, the forced opening-up of the community to outside contact, the rapid development of education, and the secularization process, taught Bosnian Muslims to express their identity in secular, nationalist terms, and showed them that only they were really interested in a separate Bosnian entity. The disintegration of Yugoslavia and the civil war in 1992 seem to have brought this process to its fruition. (see also BULGARIANS, SERBS)

BOTLIKH (s.d. Buykhatly, genitive of Buykhe, the name of a village) An ethnic group estimated at between 2,000 and 3,000 living in northwest Daghestan. Their language belongs to the Daghestan branch of the Ibero-Caucasian family and has recently been regarded by some scholars as a dialect of Andi. It is unwritten, and Avarian is used as the literary language. They have been Sunni Muslims since the sixteenth century.

The Botlikh are officially regarded as a subgroup of the greater AVAR people. Today they too call themselves AVAR and are undergoing an intensive process of consolidation with this group.

The Botlikh are known as makers of large ceramic pitchers for wine; the headdress traditional for women in all ethnic groups of the Sulak basin is distinguished among the Botlikh by its specific "horned" style. Their traditional economy is based upon: sheep-breeding; horticulture and market-gardening; and handicrafts.

BOTOCUDO A South American Indian group living in the State of Minas Gerais, near the State of Espírito Santo, southeast Brazil. They are marked by lip and ear disks, and they have resisted incursions for 300 years. They are skilled game-hunters. Some scholars classify them with the KAINGANG and XOKLENG groups. It is believed that the several thousand Indians of the GEUREN group are descendants of the Botocudo.

BOUA An ethnic group living in Chad around their traditional capital, the town of Kobrol, along the Chari River.

BOUT A Mon-Khmer group living in Vietnam at the junction of the Lao and Cambodian borders. Only one source notes the existence of the Bout as a distinct ethnic group.

BOUZON An ethnic group living in Niger.

BOWLI An ethnic group living in Ghana, in the Volta Region, east of Lake Volta. Their language is Bowiri.

BOZHI LUDI see CANADIANS.

BOZO An ethnic group living in Mali, along the Middle Niger River. Their main occupation is fishing.

BRAHMAN A large ethnic group living in Nepal. They are not regarded as aborigines of Nepal, but as migrants from India. Their language is Nepali.

The Brahman are considered to be of Aryan stock. The upper stratum consists of Parbatiya Upadhyaya and Kumai Brahman. Jaishi are regarded as lower Brahman. Except for the Jaishi, most Brahman act as priests, and are supposed to be familiar with the scriptures and with Sanskrit. However, they are at liberty to choose another occupation. Their staple food varies from rice to wheat and maize, depending upon the agricultural products of the place where they live.

Some Brahman are vegetarian. They are high-caste Hindus by birth, and all their social customs are guided by the Hindu scriptures.

BRAHUI A people living in Pakistan and also in Afghanistan and Iran with estimated populations of 1.5 million, 200,000, and 10,000 respectively. In Pakistan they live mainly in the Sind and Baluchistan provinces, with Kalat in Baluchistan as their central city. They are bilingual, speaking the Baluchi language as well as their native Dravidian tongue, and the majority are Sunni Muslims.

The Brahui are bound together by their blood lineage, and although they have in the past separated themselves from the surrounding cultures, they are more frequently found joining into the national community. British colonial rule diminished the power of the *sadars* (hereditary village chiefs), subsequently creating a dependency of the Brahui on the national government. Once known as nomadic shepherds, they are now mainly occupied in sedentary agriculture.

BRAME An ethnic group living in Guinea-Bissau between Canchungo and Bula on the right bank of the Mansoa River. They are related to the PAPEL and MANJACO peoples. Most Brame practice traditional religions. (see also GUINEA-BISSAU, THE PEOPLE OF)

BRANG An ethnic group living on the Indonesian island of Kalimantan (Borneo). (see also DAYAK)

BRAO (Love) A Mon-Khmer group numbering 40,000 living in a sweep of territory encompassing northern Cambodia, southern Laos, and eastern Thai-

Brahui

land. They practice slash and burn agriculture and produce pottery.

BRAZILIANS (Brasileiros) The 153 million inhabitants of Brazil are an ethnically mixed people, due to the interbreeding of indigenous and immigrant peoples.

The Brazilians speak Portuguese, although in Brazil it has developed into a version quite different from the original language. Many factors have contributed to this change: the local dialects of Indian tribes, the African languages spoken by blacks, the contribution of European and Asian immigrants, and the ever-present influence of the United States.

The three major racial groups are: indigenous Indians who lived in the forests prior to the country's discovery by the Europeans; white Europeans, first the PORTUGUESE, then other European immigrants; black Africans brought over as slaves. All possible mixtures exist today in Brazil as a result of this situation throughout the past four centuries. Their offspring are called *mestizo* (white and Indian), *mulatto* (white and black), *mameluco* (PORTUGUESE and Indian), *cafuso* (Indian and black). To these were added other peoples who came to Brazil at different periods.

Originally the Indians were dispersed throughout the country, but as the PORTUGUESE began to take possession of the land, they were pushed further and further into the inland jungle. Thus the coastline was mainly populated by whites, and the interior contained Indian villages. The conquest of the Indians inland by the white *bandeirantes* (those who carried the flag, or *bandeira* in Portuguese) can be seen as either a heroic battle against nature, vegetation, animals, and the hostile Indians, or as the cruel and systematic extermination of Indian lives, villages, and traditions.

Today the Indians, who form approximately 1–2 percent of the population, are concentrated in settlements sponsored by the government and mostly run by missions, or live in their villages, mainly in the north and northeast; very few still inhabit the jungle, and some of these have never been seen by the white man. The best-known Indian groups are the GUARANI, TUPI, CARIB, AKWE, KAYAPO, and GE. The Indian groups are classified according to their language family, although some groups use an unclassified language. Their numbers vary from several thousands to a few dozen.

European settlement in Brazil dates back to the sixteenth century with the Portuguese conquest. However, the main influx of immigrants took place at the end of the nineteenth and the beginning of the twentieth centuries. ITALIANS, PORTUGUESE, SPANIARDS, GERMANS, JAPANESE, POLES, and others came during that period: their number is estimated at more than 4.5 million. They settled mostly along the coastline, in Rio de Janeiro, São Paulo, and in the southern Brazilian states. Most of the first factories built from 1890 were manned by immigrants. The textile industry and the coffee plants owe their existence and their prosperity to immigrants. They and their descendants had a strong influence on the formation of present-day Brazilians at all levels: cuisine, music, and arts are all witness to the rich contribution made by immigrants to Brazil. Today the descendants of GERMANS, ITALIANS, and JAPANESE are well represented in the Brazilian elite.

Descended from slaves brought from Africa, Brazil's black population played an important role in Brazilian life at many levels even before their emancipation in 1889. The influence of their traditions is strongly felt in the country's spicy cuisine, in its internationally popular music, in rites which originate in their religion, and in the *capoeira*, a mixture of ritual dance, fencing, and martial art. They are mostly concentrated in the Brazilian state of Bahia ("the Rome of the Negroes"). Many successful Brazilians prominent today in the country's political and cultural life have ancestors who came to Brazil as slaves. Bahia is also the cradle of Afro-Bahian religious rituals and ceremonies: the *candomble*, *macumba,* and *nago* traditions. For example, the Festival of Iemanjá (the Queen of the Seas) has become an important date and a popular celebration in Salvador, Bahia's capital.

The population distribution in such a large country varies according to region: the north and northeast are less densely populated than the southeast or the south, where the coastline offered a natural attraction to people landing in Brazil. Very roughly, it can be said that the whites predominate in the southern states, due to the large number of European immigrants who settled there, mainly during the nineteenth century. The Indians and their descendants live mostly in the Amazon basin, although they are also scattered throughout the country. Blacks live mainly in the northeastern and central areas of Brazil, which boasted a prominent slave population up to their official emancipation.

The history of Brazil has had a direct impact on the development of the country's social and cultural patterns. After having been a Portuguese colony for nearly 300 years, Brazilians saw the arrival of Portugal's king João VI in 1807, when he fled the imminent invasion of his country by enemy forces. He brought with him some of the aristocratic customs of the royal

above left: A woman in Bahia, Brazil
above right: The Carnival
below: A market in Manaus, Brazil

court. Thirteen years later he was called back to Lisbon, and left the crown in his son's hands. In 1822 Pedro I declared Brazil a sovereign empire, cutting it loose from the mother-country without bloodshed. He and his son Pedro II ruled the empire until 1889, when the country was proclaimed a federated republic.

The northern region of Brazil consists of the states of Rondonia, Acre, Amazonas, Roraima, Pará, Amapá, and Tocantins, with a population of approximately 10 million inhabitants. The northeast includes the states of Maranhao, Piaui, Ceará, Rio Grande do Norte, Paraíba, Pernambuco, Alagoas, Sergipe, and Bahia, with 44 million people. The southeast with its four states, Minas Gerais, Espírito Santo, Rio de Janeiro, and São Paulo, is the economic core of Brazil, with a population of 67 million. The south comprises the states of Paraná, Santa Catarina, and Rio Grande do Sul, with a population of 23 million. Finally, the central west area with the states of Mato Grosso, Goias, and Brasília, the country's capital, has 10 million inhabitants.

BREIZ   see BRETONS.

BRETONS   (s.d. Breiz) Of the 3 million Bretons, who form a distinct component of the FRENCH, c.600,000 continue to speak their old Gaelic language which is related to Gaelic Irish, Welsh, and Highland Scottish. In their rough and isolated land on the Atlantic coast, fishing and agriculture continue to dominate daily life. Industrialization never succeeded here, hence Brittany's chronic economic crisis. The survival of many traditions and customs (bards remembering old songs, musical instruments, costumes, Celtic mythology, and pre-Christian elements in the veneration of saints) may be related to Brittany's economic backwardness.

In the first century B.C.E., Roman conquest opened the area, then known as Armorica, to broad romanization. In the fifth and sixth centuries, the area was invaded by Celts fleeing the Germanic tribes' invasion of England. The Breton language achieved its maximal extension in the tenth century, but has dwindled since then. Brittany's Celtic heritage has maintained itself most strongly along its southern coast, where the language remains alive.

Brittany declined in the nineteenth century; poverty sent many Bretons into emigration. It is now an old-fashioned rural province. (see also WELSH)

BRITISH   The British are the inhabitants of the United Kingdom of Great Britain (England, Wales, and Scotland) and Northern Ireland. The islands are densely populated, with a total of 57 million inhabitants. The British are divided into a number of peoples: ENGLISH, SCOTS, WELSH, and NORTHERN IRISH, culturally different but allied by politics and history.

Until 900 years ago, the British Isles were periodically invaded from the European continent. The first to come, in prehistoric times, were the Celts, who were pushed farther inland by later arrivals. Today they preponderate only in Wales and the Scottish Highlands, but many cultural relics testify to their former preeminence. The same holds true for the Romans, whose range of influence subsequently determined the area inhabited by the ENGLISH. The next wave consisted of Germanic colonists: Angles, Saxons, and Jutes constitute the single most important substratum of the modern British. The last invasion was that of the Normans in 1066.

The ENGLISH soon became predominant among the British. They subjugated the WELSH and after a long process finally absorbed Wales in the sixteenth century. In 1707 the ENGLISH united with the SCOTS to form Great Britain. Ireland, however, was treated as a colony, until fully integrated by 1801. A long struggle for independence resulted in 1920 in the partition of Ireland, with the NORTHERN IRISH remaining attached to Great Britain.

In the course of time, an overall British identity has developed. However, since 1700 many British people have emigrated. Most have gone to the United States, smaller contingents to what were to become the "white dominions": Canada, Australia, New Zealand, South Africa. The British empire laid the basis for a prodigious expansion of English as the world's foremost lingua franca. (see also ENGLISH, SCOTS, WELSH)

BRONG   (Abron, Boron or Bono) An Akan-speaking people living mainly in the Brong-Ahafo region of Ghana, between the Côte d'Ivoire border and the Volta River. They have a matrilineal society but never had a centralized political structure. (see also AKAN)

BRU   (Leu) A Mon-Khmer group numbering about 1,000, living in central Vietnam.

BRUNEIANS   Inhabitants of the small sultanate of Brunei (Negara Brunei Darussalam), numbering fewer than 300,000. They are divided among two enclaves along the northern coast of the island of Borneo. Two-thirds of the population are MALAYS, one-fifth is CHINESE, and the remainder consists of a variety of indigenous peoples. The MALAYS are Muslims, and there are sizable Buddhist, Christian, and traditional religious communities. Islam is the official state religion, and Islamic law dominates the political and social life of the country.

The Bruneian economy is based on oil, but agriculture also plays a part, with the chief crops being rice, bananas, and cassava. Because of the immense oil revenues, the Sultan of Brunei is the world's wealthiest person. He has done much to improve local conditions, and the standard of living in Brunei is among the highest in the world. There has, however, been some opposition to his policies favoring Muslims and ethnic MALAYS over other ethnic groups.

Despite its small size, Brunei once dominated the entire island of Borneo (Kalimantan) and neighboring islands, including parts of the Philippines. In 1888, a treaty was signed making Brunei a protectorate of Great Britain. Independence was granted in 1984. Britain still has considerable control over the local economy and foreign affairs as does the Dutch-owned Shell oil company, which has developed the extensive Seria field since 1929. In recent years, Japan's Mitsubishi corporation has begun developing natural gas resources.

BUBI (Adija, Ediye) An ethnic group numbering about 15,000, living in the Fernando Po Region of Equatorial Guinea. They speak a Bantu language which has developed four distinct dialects. Their society is matrilineal and is divided according to the social function of the individual.

Spanish attempts to colonize the region in the late nineteenth century encountered Bubi resistance. The Bubi became politically active in the 1960s and created the "Union Bubi" to separate their region from that of the Rio Muni and escape FANG domination. Although they had Spanish support against the FANG, they were not successful, and Equatorial Guinea became a single, independent state in 1968. (see also EQUATORIAL GUINEANS)

BUDDU An ethnic group living in Uganda, on the western shore of Lake Victoria.

BUDGA see BUDJA.

BUDJA (Budya, Budga) An ethnic group living in the Mutoko area of northwestern Zimbabwe. They are a subgroup of the KOREKORE, itself a member of the SHONA family of peoples.

In the 1880s, the Budja defended themselves against PORTUGUESE colonialists. Budja chief Mutoka signed a concession with the British South African Company in 1890, but his refusal to pay taxes led to a British invasion of his territory in 1895.

BUDUKH An ethnic group estimated as numbering 2,000, living in the Shakdag mountain region of northern Azerbaijan. The Bukukh language belongs to the Daghestan branch of the Ibero-Caucasian family. It is unwritten, and Azerbaijan is used as the literary language. They are Sunni Muslims of the Shafi'i stream, apparently since the sixteenth century.

The Budukh are under the cultural and ethnographic influence of the AZERBAIJANI. Their ancient villages are located on steep slopes and consist of several blocks inhabited by family-related groups. The stone houses have two storeys in the front and one in the rear. Dwelling rooms are on the second storey. Their traditional economy includes distant sheep-breeding and terrace agriculture.

BUDUMA A subgroup of the YEDINA.

BUDYA see BUDJA.

BUEM An ethnic group living in the Volta Region, Ghana. (see also TOGOLESE)

BUGABO One of the eight "early states" of the HAYA.

BUGI see BUGINESE.

BUGINESE (Bugi) An ethnic group living in the southern peninsula of the island of Sulawesi (Celebes), Indonesia. Numbering about 3 million, they are closely related to the MACASSARESE, and share with them most cultural components. The Buginese language has long had a native script, apparently adopted from Malay. They have been Muslims since the seventeenth century.

Fertile land, seamanship, and a reputation as competent warriors enabled the establishment of a powerful Buginese kingdom in the precolonial period. Despite their decline since the arrival of the DUTCH in the fifteenth century, the Buginese remained an influential group in their region, and their cultural influence is felt on many of the smaller, neighboring peoples. (see also also MACASSARESE, MORI)

Buginese

BUHID A Malayo-Polynesian ethnic group numbering about 10,000 living in the southern mountainous interior of the island of Mindoro in the Philippines. They are one group of speakers of the Mangyan language.

BUISSI (Babuissi) An ethnic group living in the upper Nyanga River basin of Gabon, and in smaller numbers in the Congo.

BUJEBA (Mabea) An ethnic group living in Equatorial Guinea. (see also EQUATORIAL GUINEANS)

BUKAR An ethnic group living on the Indonesian island of Kalimantan (Borneo). (see also DAYAK)

BUKHARA'I see GYPSIES.

BUKHARANS OF SIBERIA see TATARS.

BUKIDNON (s.d. Higaonan: "mountain dwellers") An ethnic group numbering c.100,000 native to the great plains of the Bukidnon Plateau of northern Mindanao, an island in the Philippines. Their language is a member of the Manobo family of languages.

Before the advent of Christian missionaries, Bukidnon villages were ruled over by *datus* (sultans), who usually had many wives, were relatively wealthy, and served to judge disputes; *datus* have now lost much of their power. Previously a war-like people, with warriors dressed in elaborate embroidered costumes, the Bukidnon retain their pantheon of nature spirits.

BUKIT An ethnic group living on the Indonesian island of Kalimantan (Borneo). (see also DAYAK)

BUKITAN see PUNAM.

BUKSA An ethnic group of 32,000 (1981) living in Uttar Pradesh, India. They are Hindus, and are regarded as a cognate (most probably an earlier offshoot) of the THARU. The Buksa claim to be the main inhabitants of the Tarai and Bhabar areas of Uttar Pradesh, which they say they settled about 1,000 years ago. Many of their legends trace their descent from Rajputs.

Earlier, the Buksa led a transmigrant life dependent upon shifting cultivation, but now have taken to settled community life.

BUKUSU A subgroup of the LUHYA, numbering some 25,000, living in western Kenya. Unlike other LUHYA groups, they are pastoralists as well as agriculturalists.

BULALA (Bilala) An ethnic group of Arabic origin living in the Lake Firti region of Chad. They number over 200,000, some of whom live as nomads among the DAZA. The Bulala speak a Kouka dialect. They are

Bukidnon

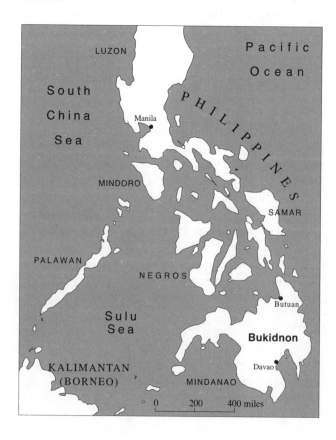

mostly Muslim but have retained a variety of pre-Islamic rites. Their main occupation is agriculture.

The Arabic-speaking BABALIA living north of Chad's capital of Ndjamena are a subgroup of the Bulala.

BULALAKAO   see HANUNOO.

BULGARIANS   (Bolgarians; s.d. Blgari) The 9 million Bulgarians live mainly in Bulgaria, where they form over 87 percent of the population, with small groups living in neighbouring Romania, Moldova and the Ukraine. Emigrant communities can be found in Russia, the United States, and other countries. The 1.8 million Macedonians of former Yugoslavia, living mainly in Macedonia, where they form about 70 percent of the population, are considered by the Bulgarians as part of the Bulgarian people.

Bulgarian belongs to the southern branch of the Slavic languages and is divided into several dialects. It is the oldest Slavic literary language and one of its old dialects formed the basis for Church Slavonic, the liturgical language in which Slavic Orthodox services are still held. Modern literary Bulgarian was formed in the nineteenth century and is based on the dialect of Sofia.

The Bulgarian Church, to which most Bulgarians adhere, is an independent branch of the Orthodox Church. The Pomaks (s.d. Pamatsi) are Bulgarian-speaking Muslims, who live mainly in the central and western Rhodope mountains. They are believed to be descendants of the Bogomils, who adopted Islam in the sixteenth and seventeenth centuries. The Bogomils were a Christian sect which originated in Bulgaria and were persecuted by both the Orthodox and the Catholic churches as heretics. BOSNIAN MUSLIMS are also mainly descendants of Bosnian Bogomils. The number of the Pomaks is estimated at 300,000, although from 1878 they have never appeared separately in Bulgarian statistics. In the mid-nineteenth century, however, they were estimated to number between 400,000 and 500,000, i.e., about a quarter of the population.

Slavic tribes settled the area between the Danube River and the Adriatic Sea in the sixth and seventh centuries C.E. They seem to have forced out or annihilated many of the original Thraco-Illyrian, Latin, and Greek inhabitants of the area and assimilated the rest. In 679 the Bulgars conquered present-day northeast Bulgaria and founded their state. The Bulgars (or Bulghars) were originally Turkic nomads who roamed the steppes north of the Black and Caspian Seas and were gradually assimilated by the more numerous Slavs. They killed the Byzantine emperor and even besieged Constantinople. Their king Boris I (852–889) was baptized in 856, and in 870 converted his people to Orthodox Christianity, taking the title of czar. Under Simon (893–927) the first Bulgarian state reached its zenith, ruling over the areas between the Danube and the Adriatic and Aegean Seas. After Simon's death, however, his state declined rapidly and returned to Byzantine rule.

The second Bulgarian state was established in 1185, following a successful general revolt by the Bulgars and the VLACHS. Under Ivan Assen II (1318–1341) it reached its zenith but soon declined again. In 1330 the SERBS conquered Macedonia. In 1340 the Ottomans began their campaign against Bulgaria and by 1396 all Bulgaria and Macedonia was under their direct rule. It remained so for 482 years.

Under Ottoman rule the Bulgarians were part of the "Greek Orthodox nation" (*Rum milleti*), which was under the authority of the (Greek) Patriarchate of Constantinople. This gave rise to a slow hellenization of the Bulgarians, especially of the educated social strata. Thus, when Bulgarian nationalism made its appearance, it was directed against the Greek influence more than against the TURKS. With Russian encouragement, Bulgarian nationalists revived the literary language and the Cyrillic alphabet (for a while Bulgarian was written in Greek letters) and established schools in which it was the language of instruction. A forty-year struggle ended in 1870, when the sultan re-established the autonomy of the Bulgarian Church from Constantinople. From here to demands of political independence the distance was short.

In 1876 a rising was cruelly crushed by the Ottomans, which led to RUSSIAN military intervention. The treaty of San Stepano which concluded the Russo-Ottoman War of 1877 provided for the establishment of an independent Bulgaria in its widest borders, including eastern Thrace and Macedonia. The Congress of Berlin, however, introduced cardinal changes. A principality of Bulgaria under Ottoman suzerainty was established north of the Balkan mountains and an autonomous province of Rumelia to their south, within the Ottoman empire. Thrace and Macedonia remained under direct Ottoman rule. In 1885, however, the province of Rumelia was de facto united with Bulgaria. In 1908, following the Young Turk revolution, Ferdinand, the prince of Bulgaria, proclaimed the country's independence and took the title of czar.

In 1912 the Bulgarians, in coalition with the SERBS and the GREEKS, attacked the Ottomans and conquered

Thrace and Macedonia. However, as the three could not agree on the division of the spoils, the Bulgarians attacked their former allies in 1913, and Romania then attacked Bulgaria. Defeated, Bulgaria had to give up most of Macedonia to Serbia. In World War I Bulgaria fought on the side of the Central powers against Serbia, and lost some of its territory. It fought on the Axis side in World War II, and Germany fulfilled all its territorial demands, although Bulgaria never declared war on the Soviet Union, due to the overwhelming pro-Russian sentiments in the country.

In 1944 Soviet forces invaded Bulgaria, and by 1947 a communist regime was in power in Sofia. Since then, until its collapse in 1990, Bulgaria's communist regime was one of the strictest and most loyal to Moscow in Eastern Europe.

BULGARIAN TATARS   see CRIMEAN TATARS.

BULGEDA   A subgroup of the TOUBOU.

BULI   A subgroup of the SAWAI.

BULIP   see STIENG.

BULOM   (Sherbro) An ethnic group living in Sierra Leone. In the late sixteenth century their territory was cut in two by the TEMNE who were pushing toward the coast.

The northern branch of the Bulom today occupies parts of the Kambia and Port Loko Districts and has been assimilated by the TEMNE and SUSU. The southern and larger branch, known as SHERBRO, occupies most of the coastal area of Sierra Leone. This branch has been largely absorbed by the MENDE. Some Bulom are Christians, while others practice traditional religions.

BULU   An ethnic group related to the FANG, living in southern Cameroon. Their main occupation is agriculture. In the precolonial era they served as middlemen in the European slave trade. They unsuccessfully resisted colonization by the GERMANS in the late nineteenth century. Following World War I, the Bulu territory fell to the FRENCH.

In the 1950s the Bulu manifested hostility towards the successful BAMILEKE who migrated to the south. The Bulu have been well represented in the political administration of Cameroon since 1982 in spite of their small number, through President Paul Biya, himself a Bulu.

BUME   see NYANGATOM.

BUNE   A subgroup of the YORUBA living in Nigeria.

BUNGAN-BULIT   An ethnic group living on the Indonesian island of Kalimantan (Borneo). (see also DAYAK)

BUNGKU   An ethnic group living on the Indonesian island of Sulawesi (Celebes) and the outlying island of Wowoni. They speak a Filipino-related language and are Muslims with vestiges of some traditional beliefs. They have migrated to the coast from their original mountain homeland.

BUNGOMEK   (Bonam) A subgroup of the SABAOT.

BUNHRAN   A subgroup of the IFUGAO.

BUNUR   A subgroup of the MNONG.

BUOL   A subgroup of the GORONTALO.

BURA   A subgroup of the TIV.

BURGHER   Name given to the 50,000 descendants of the original DUTCH colonial settlers of Sri Lanka (Ceylon) who have since mingled with later settlers from England and other countries. The Burghers constitute an upper middle class in Sri Lanka, employed in government and commerce. (see also SRI LANKANS)

BURJI   An ethnic group numbering 50,000 (1980s) who live south of the Amarroo hills in northwest Sidamo Province, Ethiopia. Their language belongs to the eastern Cushitic group, and they adhere to traditional beliefs and to Sunni Islam. The Burji are sedentary agriculturalists. After their inclusion into the Ethiopian empire (1900), some Burji settled in northern Kenya (Mount Marsabit). (see also ETHIOPIANS)

BURKINABES   The name for the 9 million inhabitants of the former Upper Volta, now Burkina Faso, independent since 1960. About half the population belongs to the MOSSI ethnic group, living in the northeast and central parts of the country. They are divided into four subgroups after the four pre-colonial Mossi kingdoms. While some Mossi chiefs have converted to Islam, most practice traditional religions. Other groups include the BOBO, BARKA, DYULA, and SAMO in western Burkina Faso, SENUFO and LOBI in the southwest, GRUSI and related groups in the south, FULANI in the north, GURMA in the east, and BUSANI in the southeast. More than 50 percent of the Burkinabes practice traditional religions, around 30 percent are Muslims, and only 1 percent are Christians. The official language is French, but Mossi and Dyula are most widely-spoken. Only 10 percent of the population live in urban centers, and over 85 percent are engaged in agriculture.

The relatively high population density combined with poor soil and the Côte d'Ivoire's demand for labor has resulted in substantial migration. Every year around 450,000 Burkinabes leave the county to work in the Côte d'Ivoire and Ghana; from 50,000 to 100,000 do not return.

The FRENCH occupied the territory of present day Burkina Faso, then called Upper Volta, in the late nineteenth century. Until 1947 it was ruled together with the Côte d'Ivoire as a single territory, but with the post-war establishment of African political parties, MOSSI chiefs demanded the separation of Upper Volta from the Côte d'Ivoire to increase their political power. In this way the Mossi party gained considerable political power and dominated all political institutions created by the colonial administration. During the 1950s a group of young MOSSI, resentful of the chiefs' power, created their own party.

The main division in Upper Volta was between the east and the west, but within each region there was a further division between traditionalists and their opponents. Around the capital of Ouagadougou in the east lived about 2 million MOSSI, largely adherents of traditional religions and mostly obedient to their chiefs. In the west there was a similar number of BOBO and other peoples: Muslims around the town of Bobo-Dioulasso and adherents of traditional religions in the rural areas. Cultural, geographic, and economic ties between the peoples of the two regions were weak.

At independence the strongest party was the Union Democratique Voltaique led by Maurice Yameogo, himself a MOSSI, who attempted to curb ethnic and regional separatism by forbidding all ethnic associations. After independence Yameogo banned all opposition parties and Burkina Faso became a one-party state. Although in the thirty years since independence Burkina Faso has been politically unstable, with power moving from civilian to military hands, the ethnic factor played only a minor role in the country. In 1991 a process of democratization began with the emergence of new political groups.

BURMANS (Burmese, Myanmarese; s.d. Bama) The 43 million inhabitants of Burma, renamed Myanmar in 1990, include several peoples. The Burmans mostly inhabit the central plain of Myanmar, formed by the Irrawaddy and Salween Rivers. Other smaller peoples, including the KAREN, KACHIN, CHIN, and SHAN, live in the hills and mountains surrounding the great central plain.

Burmese, which is spoken by over two-thirds of the population, is a part of the Tibeto-Burmese language grouping, a subgroup of the Sino-Tibetan family of languages. Some of the languages spoken in the mountains, such as Kachin and Chin, do not belong to the Sino-Tibetan family.

Myanmar is primarily a rural country where settlement is in villages with little or no infrastructure. In the central plain, wet-rice cultivation is the dominant means of subsistence and is entirely for domestic consumption. In the hills and mountains, slash and burn agriculture produces dry rice, cotton, maize, and peanuts. Fishing and lumber are two important commercial activities, while industry is almost nonexistent.

The overwhelming majority of Burmans (approximately 94 percent) are Theravada Buddhists. There are also some Christians, primarily among the KAREN, KACHIN, and CHIN. Muslims and Hindus are a very small minority.

The Burmans migrated south from Yunnan approximately 3,000 years ago. The first monarch, Kin Anawratha, set up a Burman kingdom in the eleventh century C.E. and made Theravada Buddhism the official religion of his kingdom. Two centuries later Kublai Khan's rule in the north shifted Burmese rule to its present location.

After three Anglo-Burman wars, Burma became a province of India under the BRITISH. During World War II, the JAPANESE conquered the country; in 1948 Burma became an independent state. The Union of Burma, now known as Myanmar, has been divided by ethnic strife and political unrest since gaining independence. Currently, a military government maintains strict control over the country's fifteen states and provinces despite elections, which gave a majority of votes to the opposition.

BURMAWA A subgroup of the TIV.

BURMESE see BURMANS.

BURUM see PURUM.

BURUNDIANS The population of Burundi in East Africa, numbering 5.5 million, is divided mainly between the HUTU (85 percent), TUTSI (14 percent), and TWA (1 percent) peoples. The HUTU and the TWA inhabited the region long before the TUTSI arrived in the fourteenth century from the area of the OROMO people in Ethiopia. The TUTSI became the ruling elite over the HUTU majority.

More than 60 percent of the Burundians are Christians, mainly Roman Catholics, less than 40 percent adhere to traditional beliefs, and about 1 percent are Muslims. More than 90 percent of the working population is engaged in agriculture.

In the late nineteenth century the GERMANS occupied Burundi. After World War I the BELGIANS received the colony as a League of Nations mandated territory including neighboring Rwanda. Like the GERMANS before them, the BELGIANS ruled the Burundians indirectly through an intermediate princely class of the TUTSI. Before independence in 1962 the BELGIANS held elections in Burundi. The head of the winning party was murdered immediately after the elections and his party proved unable to contain the ethnic tensions. The monarchy emerged as the only source of legitimacy of both the TUTSI and the HUTU.

In 1965 tensions reached a climax as a result of a coup attempt made by the HUTU-dominated gendarmerie and the ensuing massacre of the HUTU political elite and thousands of their rural supporters. These events ended any significant political participation of the HUTU for many years. A year later the monarchy was abolished in a coup carried out by the TUTSI, who became increasingly dominant in the government.

In 1972, after an attempted Hutu rebellion in which a few thousand TUTSI were killed, the government responded with a large-scale massacre of HUTU, especially the educated class. Estimates of the number of dead vary from 80,000 to 250,000. About 200,000 HUTU fled the country and all HUTU were eliminated from the armed forces.

Ethnic tensions continued to exist after 1972 and in 1988 erupted again in the north of the country when groups of HUTU, claiming TUTSI provocation, slaughtered hundreds of TUTSI. The TUTSI-dominated army was sent to restore order and in the following days more large-scale massacres took place.

The political situation remained tense until in mid-1989 the president, a member of the TUTSI, announced plans to combat all forms of discrimination against the HUTU. A commission for national unity was established and as a result twelve of the twenty-three portofolios in the government were given to HUTU ministers. However, the army was still reluctant to allow HUTU to enter its ranks.

BURUSHASKI, BURUSHO see HUNZUKUT.

BURYAT-MONGOLS see BURYATS.

BURYATS (Buryat-Mongols) A Mongol people numbering 422,000 (1981) whose state, the Buryat Autonomous Republic, part of Russia, borders on both Mongolia and the Yakut Autonomous Republic.

The Buryat language belongs to the North Mongolian family of languages. In the eighteenth century it was written in both the Mongolian and the Cyrillic alphabets, but in 1938 the Soviet authorities instituted sole use of the latter.

The two Buryat tribes, Saradol and Salair-Ozon, arrived in the area at the beginning of the thirteenth century under the command of Genghis Khan and his brother Ozon. They absorbed some of the neighboring nomad Mongol and Turkic tribes in the vicinity.

Buryats

Traditionally shamanists, many Buryats were converted to Buddhism and, since the Russian occupation in the beginning of the seventeenth century, to Russian Orthodox Christianity. Originally horse-breeding nomads, the Buryats subsist nowadays mainly on forestry and wood-related industries, as well as cattle-, sheep- and horse-raising, fur-trapping, and coal-mining.

BUSA   An ethnic group living in Nigeria. (see also BOSHA)

BUSANGA   see BUSANI.

BUSANI   (Bisa, Bisano, Busanga) An ethnic group living in Burkina Faso, along the White Volta River below Tenkodogo and in small numbers across the border in Ghana and Togo. They speak a Mande language. (see also BURKINABES)

BUSAWA   A subgroup of the FULANI.

BUSHMEN   see SAN, SOUTH AFRICANS.

BUSH NEGROES   see FRENCH GUIANESE, SURINAMESE.

BUTONESE   Inhabitants of the island of Butung off the coast of southern Sulawesi (Celebes), an island of Indonesia. They number almost half a million, including the many Butonese who have migrated to the farflung islands of Indonesia. They are entirely Muslim and speak an Austronesian language related to some languages of the Philippines. Wolio, the dialect used by the aristocracy, is considered the official language and has a script.

Today, the Butonese are primarily agriculturalists who cultivate corn and limited amounts of rice and yams. They are also competent sailors who have traded throughout the Indonesian archipelago. This, coupled with piracy, enabled them to establish the powerful sultanate of Butung, which controlled the neighboring islands and extensive parts of southern Sulawesi. Conquest by the DUTCH in the early twentieth century led to the introduction of cotton as a cash crop.

BUYI   (Bouyi, Puyi, Chung-chia). The approximately 2.1 million Buyi live almost exclusively in the Guizhou Province of southwest China. Their language, similar to Dai, had no written form until the Chinese government provided one based on the Latin alphabet. Many Buyi are sinicized and have adopted the Chinese language.

One of the several theories accounting for their origins holds that they descend from Han CHINESE banished to Guizhou in early times; another theory claims

that they are descended from DAI forced by Han CHINESE expansion to abandon rich agricultural lands for the poorer valleys of Guizhou.

Their culture and religion are similar to that of the local CHINESE. Some are polytheists; others are Buddhist or Christian.

Most Buyi are peasants, cultivating rice, wheat, corn, and some cash crops. They preserve their traditional dress and are famous for their skill in wax-printing.

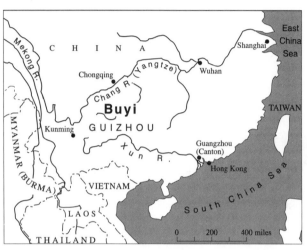

Buyi

BUYKHATLY   see BOTLIKH.

BUYU   An ethnic group living in the mountainous central region of the Indonesian island of Sulawesi (Celebes). (see also TORADJA).

BWABA   see BOBO.

BWAMBA   see AMBO.

BWILE   A Chibemba-speaking group living along the eastern shore of Lake Mweru on the northern border of Zambia. Some practice traditional religions while others are Christians. Their primary occupation is fishing.

The Bwile were conquered by the LUNDA in the eighteenth century.

BYELORUSSIANS   (s.d. Belarussi) Of the approximately 10.1 million Byelorussians, more than four-fifths live in Belarus. The remainder live mainly in neighboring Russia, the Ukraine, Lithuania, and Poland. There are sizable communities of Byelorussian migrants in Britain, Canada, and the U.S.A. as well.

The Byelorussian language is an East Slavic tongue closely related to Ukrainian and Russian. It possesses three dialects: southwestern, northwestern, and central. The latter was used to create the literary language, which is written in the Cyrillic alphabet.

There is a marked difference between the eastern Byelorussians, who have been influenced mainly by the RUSSIANS and belong to the Russian Orthodox Church, and the west Byelorussians, who have been influenced by the POLES and belong mainly to the United Lutheran Church. A separate group are the Poleshchuk, who live in the Pripet marshes and are a transitional group between the Byelorussians and the UKRAINIANS.

The Byelorussians are descendents of Slavic tribes, who settled between the second and the fifth centuries on the western shores of the Dvina, the Upper Dnieper, the Neman, and the Pripet Rivers and assimilated the Baltic tribes who had inhabited the area from at least Iron Age times. Three large tribal groups subsequently developed: the Dregovichi, the Radimichi, and the Krivichi. In the ninth century these were incorporated into the ancient Russian state of Kiev, from which emerged the three East Slavic nations of RUSSIANS, UKRAINIANS, and Byelorussians.

In the second half of the thirteenth century the area was conquered by the MONGOLS and attacked by the Teutonic Order. It was subsequently under foreign rule for several centuries, first by LITHUANIANS and then by POLES. As a result, the ancestors of the Byelorussians were separated from those of the other East Slavic peoples, and began to develop distinctive customs, culture, and language.

The Catholic Lithuanian-Polish rulers tried to enforce papal authority on their Eastern Orthodox, East Slavic subjects. The majority of landowners converted to the Catholic faith, and were subsequently polonized. The majority of the peasantry, however, retained their Eastern Orthodox identity.

In the wars that swept the region in the seventeenth century, the area suffered devastation, famine, and epidemics, which caused the population to decrease by almost half. The Northern War of 1700–1721 caused a further decline in population.

The partition of Poland brought all Byelorussians under Russian rule after 1772. In their centralizing efforts the Russian authorities attempted to assimilate the Byelorussians as they had assimilated the UKRAINIANS. In 1840 it was even forbidden to use the term "Byelorussian."

Industrialization and urbanization in the nineteenth century created the socio-economic base for national revival, which began, as in many other countries, with the creation of literature in the Byelorussian language; the publication of Viccenti Rovinski's novel *Anaide* is considered to mark this point. By the time of the 1917 revolution, however, the Byelorussian national movement was still in an embryonic stage, and the creation of the Soviet Socialist Republic of Byelorussia was carried out by the Bolshevik government in Moscow. This republic included the eastern parts of Byelorussia. The western parts were annexed from Poland in 1939, following the Molotov-Ribbentrop agreement.

Although Byelorussian self-identity was reinforced during the Soviet period, no separatist nationalist movement such as that of the Ukraine developed in Byelorussia. Its independence following the disintegration of the USSR in 1991 was, therefore, as the creation of the republic had been, an external act rather than a response to internal demands and developments. (see also RUSSIANS, UKRAINIANS)

BZYBIANS   (Gudantians) A subgroup of the ABKHAZIANS.

C

CABECARE A Central American Indian group inhabiting the southern Caribbean region of Costa Rica, in the areas of Moravia de Chirripo, Estrella, San Jose de Cabecar, Telire, and Pacuare. A cluster of Cabecare live in Ujarraz.

CABERRE A Native South American group living in Venezuela.

CABRAIS see KABRE.

CADDO A Native North American nation numbering some 1,500. Originally buffalo hunters and cultivators of maize from the Texas Plain, they moved to the Indian Territory of Oklahoma in 1872. Today they share the Caddo Tribe Federal Trust Area with the ANADARKO.

CAETE One of the TUPINAMBA groups of southeastern Brazil.

CAFAYATE A chiefdom of the DIAGUITA.

CAFUSO A Native South American group living in Brazil.

CAGABA A South American Indian people living along the Caribbean coast of Venezuela. They subsist primarily from agriculture, using irrigation to grow bitter manioc and fruit trees. They also work and trade in gold and copper. They are governed by powerful chiefs or kings.

CAHUILLA (Agua Cahuilla) A Native North American group numbering a few hundred whose native tongue is Uto-Aztecan. Originally small-game hunters and cultivators of maize from southern California, many live today on the Cahuilla Federal Reservation in Riverside County, California, U.S.A.

CAJUNS see AMERICANS, QUEBECOIS.

CALEDONIANS see SCOTS.

CALO see KALO.

CALPANQUI An OTAVALO group.

CAMACAN A South American Indian people living in the highlands parallel to the Atlantic coast of Brazil. They cultivate maize, sweet potatoes, and manioc. Hunting and fishing are also important activities.

CAMBODIANS see KHMER.

CAMEROONIANS The people of Cameroon, in central West Africa, estimated to number about 11.5 million. They are divided into several ethnic groups, including BAMILEKE in the west, FANG and the BASSA-BAKOKO in the center and south, FULANI and several related groups called KIRDI in the north, MBUM and BAYA in the center and east, and DUALA along the coast. All these ethnic groups are further subdivided into smaller subgroups who are culturally and linguistically related.

Cameroon's population is unevenly distributed with concentrations in the west and south-central region and in the Sudanese savanna of the north. The peoples of the west and south have been influenced by Christianity and Western education and culture; northerners are either Muslims or adherents of local religions who have largely retained their traditional way of life. The western and southern regions are also more urbanized and industrialized while the north has remained economically undeveloped. Another major contrast is between anglophone north-west Cameroon, ruled by the BRITISH in the colonial period, and the much larger, more populous francophone area of former French Cameroon. The impact of rule by the BRITISH and

FRENCH is still evident in education, commerce, law, etc.

While Cameroon's official languages are French and English, the languages most spoken are Beti-Pahouin and Bamileke. Forty percent of the population are Christians, 39 percent follow traditional religions, while 2 percent are Muslims.

Cameroon was a German colony until World War I. Following Germany's defeat it was divided as a mandate between France and Britain. After World War II, the FRENCH allowed party politics to develop. The first political party to emerge in French Cameroon was the UPC, which demanded independence and supported unification with British Cameroon. It was supported mainly by the BAMILEKE and DUALA, who were related to ethnic groups in the British part of Cameroon. Violent incidents in the 1950s led the FRENCH to ban the UPC, but the movement simply went underground to continue the struggle for independence. At independence the strongest, and later sole party, was the Union Camerounais of Ahmadou Ahidjo, a Muslim from the north who became the country's first president in 1960. Meanwhile violence broke out again, mainly in the Bamileke areas, over the dissatisfaction of urban BAMILEKE at unemployment and overcrowded living conditions. Later known as the Bamileke revolt, it was joined by the BASSA-BAKOKO, and only suppressed in the mid-1960s with the help of French troops. Ethnic incidents involving the BAMILEKE continued to occur sporadically, culminating in the Tombel Massacre of 1967 in which 230 BAMILEKE were killed.

The two parts of Cameroon became federated in 1961 and were unified in 1972. Ahidjo handed over his responsibilities to Paul Biya in 1982. Since 1991 there has been violent civil unrest and demand for political reform and democratization.

CAMPA   A South American Indian group living in the mountains of Peru. They speak an Arawak dialect and cultivate maize, sweet manioc, beans, peanuts, potatoes, and peppers. They hunt, gather, and engage extensively in trade.

CAMROUNAIS   see CAMEROONIANS.

CANADIANS   There are nearly 27 million Canadians, of whom about one quarter are of BRITISH descent and one quarter of FRENCH descent. The remainder are primarily of mixed European descent (ITALIANS, GREEKS, PORTUGUESE, UKRANIANS), and there are also sizable Asian (particularly on the West Coast) and African communities. About 5 percent of Canadians are either Native Americans, INUIT, or METIS, a group of mixed Indian and French descent. The majority of Canadians speak English. Most French Canadians have preserved their own French language and culture and are predominantly Roman Catholic; English Canadians generally adhere to Protestant denominations, one of the most important being the United Church of Canada.

About three-quarters of all Canadians are urban-dwellers, but agriculture, forestry, and fishing are of importance, particularly in the central prairie provinces and along the Atlantic seaboard.

The question of what constitutes a distinctly Canadian identity is one that has troubled Canadians in this century. French Canadians link their heritage to that of seventeenth-century French colonists. English Canadians, however, are wedged between two dominant yet closely related cultures, that of Britain, the former colonial power, and that of the United States, their influential neighbor to the south. Canada is a constitutional monarchy, with the British sovereign serving as titular head of state. Until the 1980s its constitution could be amended only by an act of British Parliament. At the same time, American business and culture dominate contemporary Canada: almost 70 percent of all Canadians live within 100 miles of the American border and 90 percent within 200 miles. There has, however, been an attempt to forge a uniquely Canadian culture based on cultural activity and sport. A specifically Canadian literary genre has flourished and a uniquely Canadian painting style is exemplified by the work of several artists known as the Group of Seven, active in the 1920s and 1930s; hockey is universally recognized as the national pastime.

Because of enormous waves of immigrants in recent years, Canada has adopted a policy of multiculturalism, by which each ethnic community is encouraged to preserve its heritage as part of a larger Canadian mosaic. Among these communities are the Acadians, descendants of the original French settlers who first arrived in Canada in 1604; they today number close to 250,000. They are found mostly in the northern half of the Canadian province of New Brunswick (sometimes known as Acadia). Smaller communities exist in Nova Scotia and Prince Edward Island. They are devout Catholics, and generally speak an archaic variant of French at home. In certain areas of New Brunswick with a mixed French- and English-speaking population, a hybrid dialect known as Chiac has emerged.

The FRENCH established permanent settlements between 1632 and 1634. Over the next century, the territory repeatedly changed hands between Britain and France. Ultimate British control, achieved in 1755, resulted in the mass deportation of the local population to French colonies in Louisiana and the West Indies. Fewer than 3,000 Acadians remained in Canada, either as refugees in neighboring Quebec or in British prison camps. They were eventually released, and it is their descendants who constitute today's Acadians.

The Doukhobors, a group of ethnic UKRAINIANS numbering about 25,000, live primarily in western Canada. Smaller communities are dispersed throughout North America; one such subgroup, the Molokans, are found primarily in California, where they number 20,000 and are rapidly integrating into the surrounding society. Although the Doukhobors are primarily a religious group, they have maintained a distinctive society in Canada and have preserved the Ukrainian language, their unique religious beliefs, dietary customs, and a strong sense of community. They believe that God is present in each individual and that established church ritual is unnecessary to attain redemption. They practice vegetarianism, eschew tobacco and alcohol, and live according to the motto "Toil and Peaceful Life." They are avowed pacifists and favor a communal society.

Most Doukhobors emigrated to Canada in 1899. In recent years they have begun a slow process of assimilation into the wider society. Crafts include Slavic embroidery, wood carving, and a rich traditional of choral music.

In the mid-1800s, Canada was granted internal self-rule. Independence was achieved through a lengthy process in 1867. A century later, in the 1970s, Quebecois secessionist sentiment sparked a series of violent acts aimed at furthering the cause of independence. Since that time, tensions between the English and French communities have smoldered under the surface, sometimes threatening to erupt. Notable threats to the unity of the country occurred during both world wars (the FRENCH opposed conscription) and from the late 1960s to the present when a separatist party became an important factor in the provincial politics of French-dominated Quebec. Recently, regionalism and even separatism have been felt in other parts of the country as well, sparked both by the sudden upturn in the local economy (as in western Canada since the discovery of oil) and a reluctance to allow concessions to Quebec in order to preserve the country. At the same time, indigenous groups have demanded that their rights be recog-

nized and that they be granted autonomy. Until now, attempts to rewrite the constitution to the satisfaction of all Canadians have ended in failure.

CANARY ISLANDERS   The 1.6 million inhabitants of the Canary Islands, which are located in the Atlantic Ocean off the northwest African coast, consist primarily of the descendants of indigenous inhabitants (BERBERS from northwest Africa) and Spanish settlers. The Canary Islands have, since 1982, been an autonomous community in the Spanish state, by which they were conquered in the fifteenth century. The people speak Spanish, although their pronunciation is significantly different from mainland Spanish. They refer to mainland SPANIARDS as *peninsulares* or *godos*. The islanders are overwhelmingly Roman Catholic in religious affiliation. Tourism and construction have replaced farming as the most important economic activities.

CANCHI   A subgroup of the AYMARA.

CAO   A Mon-Khmer group living along the upper basin of the Song Boung River on the Vietnamese-Laos border. They engage in slash and burn cultivation of rice.

CAPAHA   see QUAPAW.

CAPE VERDEANS   The people of the islands of Cape Verde, estimated as numbering some 1 million. Only 347,000 actually live in Cape Verde; the rest have emigrated, mainly to the United States, the Netherlands, Italy, and Portugal. The nine inhabited islands of Cape Verde are located in the Atlantic Ocean near the western coast of Africa.

Ethnically, the Cape Verdeans are descendants of intermarriage between African slaves and European, mainly PORTUGUESE, settlers. About 97 percent are Roman Catholics and 1 percent Protestants. They speak a Portuguese Creole (Crioulo) which is archaic in form and influenced by African vocabulary, syntax, and pronunciation.

The PORTUGUESE arrived in the uninhabited archipelago in the fifteenth century and the islands later became a station in the Atlantic slave-trade. During the twentieth century many Cape Verdeans were still used as laborers by the PORTUGUESE under slavelike conditions. Some were sent to another Portuguese colony, Guinea-Bissau, and became a leading force in its decolonization struggle. Following independence in

1975, the PAICV (Partido Africano da Independencia de Cabo Verde), the party that emerged from the Cape Verde liberation movement, dominated the country and converted it into a single-party state. Negotiations were begun with Guinea-Bissau, dominated after independence by Cape-Verdeans, over unification of the two countries, but a 1980 coup in Guinea-Bissau put an end to Cape Verdean domination and unification plans were halted.

In 1990 Cape Verde became a multi-party state. Elections held in 1991 brought a new president to office. (see also LANTA, GUINEA-BISSAU, THE PEOPLE OF)

CAPRIVIAN   An ethnic group, numbering about 47,000 and largely agricultural, living in the extreme northeast of Namibia. (see also NAMBIANS)

CARA   A Native South American group living in Ecuador.

CARABUELO   An OTAVALO people.

CARACAS   A Native South American group living in Venezuela.

CARELIANS   see FINNS.

CARIB   A Central American Indian group, from whom the name "Caribbean Sea" is taken. They lived in the Antilles and along parts of the South American coast prior to the Spanish conquest. The Carib, who engaged in extensive warfare, were expanding their territories from the mainland to the Antilles when the SPANIARDS arrived. Most pure-blooded Carib perished from exotic diseases or overwork, or were exterminated during the conquest. As is the case with other groups in this area, the remaining Carib, many of whom intermarried with other ethnic groups, are scattered over a number of South American countries, including Brazil, Colombia, Guyana, and the Lesser Antilles. No estimates of their population are available. (see also BRAZILIANS, COLOMBIANS, DOMINICANS, NETHERLANDS CASTILIANS, SPANIARDS)

CARIJONA   A South American Indian people living in the Caqueta region of southeastern Colombia. They subsist from agriculture, a task generally reserved for women. Crops include bitter and sweet manioc, maize, sweet potatoes, beans, and peppers. They also engage in hunting, fishing, and gathering. They live in large communal houses.

CARIRI   (Kiriri) A South American Indian group numbering around 1,000, living in the State of Bahia, northeastern Brazil. They are supported by government aid. Having lost most of their own culture, they are well integrated into the local area.

CARNAGA   A subgroup of the AYMARA.

CARRIER   A Native North American group numbering about 9,000 persons whose name was given to them by the FRENCH in the early eighteenth century. The name relates to the fact that widows in this group carried the bones of their husbands on their backs for a year. Many Carrier bands have rejected the name, preferring instead to identify with their traditional tribal designations.

In the 1960s several villages of Carrier north of Prince George, British Columbia, were relocated when their lands were flooded to provide hydro-electric power.

CASTILIANS   (s.d. Castilianos) One of the major components of the Spanish people, inhabiting Castile, the central part of Spain. In the Middle Ages, their kings were among the instigators of the crusade against Muslim Spain (the *reconquista*) which became the central organizing principle of Spanish society. With the conquest of most of southern Spain, the Castilians formed the largest nation on the Iberian peninsula. With the unification of Castile and Aragon

Castilians and Catalans

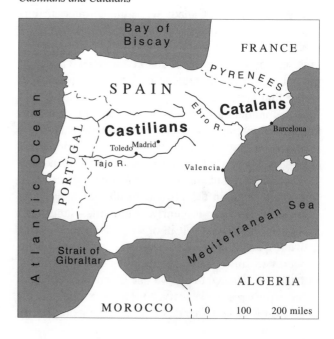

in the late fifteenth century, Castilians became politically and culturally Spain's most prominent population group and their further development was entwined with that of Spain as a whole. Castilian has become the modern Spanish language. (see also SPANIARDS)

CATALANS   The 7.2 million Catalans live in Catalonia, a province of northeast Spain located in the triangle between the Pyrenees, the Ebro River and the Mediterranean Sea, as well as in the Balearic Islands, Andorra, and southeast France. Their language is related to Spanish (Castilian) and to South French tongues. Catalan areas are among Spain's most advanced, and contain some of its most important tourist centers.

Catalan particularism has deep historical roots, and is epitomized by the perpetual competition of Catalan Barcelona with Castilian Madrid. Romanized since the second century B.C.E., the Catalans became under Charlemagne a Christian bulwark against the Moors. Economically flourishing from the tenth century, they began to develop a separate language and culture. Their hour of glory was connected foremost with the expansion of the prosperous and independent merchant republic of Barcelona in the western Mediterranean, dominating the Balearics, Sicily, Sardinia and Corsica in the fourteenth century.

Later, Catalans fell under the dominion of the demographically and economically stronger CASTILIANS. They were spared the general Spanish decline from the late seventeenth and eighteenth centuries. A literary revival among middle class intellectuals fueled a strong Catalan nationalist movement. Catalan political parties played a major role in Spain's Second Republic (1932–1936), and were largely allied with the Republican (anti-Franco) side in the 1936–1939 Civil War. Defeat ushered in a long period of oppression. The Franco dictatorship (1939–1975) banned even the private use of the Catalan language as a danger to "national consciousness," and drove Catalan press and political parties underground. The Catalans were discriminated against economically and underrepresented in the bureaucracy and army. Although the cultural policy was cautiously liberalized in the 1950s, instruction in Catalan remained prohibited, and actual use of Catalan showed signs of decline. In the 1960s progressive Catholic church circles, too, began to support Catalan regionalist demands; the Montserrat cloister became a Catalan national symbol.

The struggle of the Catalans for autonomy has been waged in the main by non-violent means. After Franco's death, the use of the Catalan language was legalized. Like the BASQUES, GALICIANS, and ANDALUSIANS, the Catalans obtained a large measure of regional autonomy in the 1970s. (see also SPANIARDS)

CATAWBA   A Native North American nation numbering a few hundred persons. They were traditionally cultivators of maize. In the 1860s some moved to Oklahoma, while the rest stayed in South Carolina, where they continue to enjoy their traditional rights.

CAYAPAS   (Kayapas, s.d. Chachi: "strong and valiant men") A small Indian group residing in the riparian forests of Esmeraldas Province, near the northwest coast of Ecuador; alongside the Cayapas River, its tributaries and adjacent streams; populations of Cayapas today can be found alongside the Onzole, the Estero de Camarones, the Zapallo Grande, the San Miguel, and the Santiago Rivers. They originally lived in the Andean region of what is now Ecuador. When the SPANIARDS arrived in the early 1500s, the Cayapas escaped to the northern coastal plain and foothills. They speak a language called Cha'palaachi.

The Cayapas founded towns, such as Punta de Venado on the Cayapas River, but they visit these towns only for weddings and burials. They spend most of their time in the forests.

In early colonial times, the SPANIARDS began to impose Christianity upon the Cayapas, but met strong resistance. However, disease and the encroachment of

Cayapas

other peoples gradually weakened the Cayapas, and eventually they were converted to Christianity, although their culture retains distinctive traces of their former beliefs.

The number of Cayapas Indians has continued to decline in recent years. In 1984, they numbered between 7,000 and 8,000; in the early 1990s, the population had fallen to about 3,000. They have suffered from a lack of civil rights and of protection from their non-Indian neighbors, and their territory has been encroached upon by lumber companies that have cut down, and built roads through, much of their forest. They have recently formed a confederation of communities to deal with the increasing contact with modern society that has disrupted their traditional culture.

CAYAPO   see KAYAPO.

CAYUGA   A Native North American people living in New York and Oklahoma and forming part of the IROQUOIS CONFEDERACY.

CELE   A subgroup of the NGUNI.

CENTRAL AFRICAN REPUBLIC, THE PEOPLE OF THE   Inhabitants of the Central African Republic (CAR), which gained independence in 1960. The estimated population is 2.8 million, concentrated mainly in the western half of the country; large areas of the east are virtually uninhabited. The population consists of about eighty ethnic groups, most of whom arrived in several waves of migration during the eighteenth and nineteenth centuries. The largest ethnic group is the BANDA, located in the center and east; the BAYA inhabit the north and west; AZANDE, the southeast; SARA, the dominant ethnic group in Chad, the north; MANDJIA, the center; MBUM, the northwest, MBAKA, the southwest; riverine groups (YAKOMBA, SANGO, and GBANZIRI), along the Ubangi River; and PYGMIES, the extreme southwest. About 60 percent of the population adhere to traditional religions, 35 percent are Christians, and 5 percent are Muslims. The official languages are French and Sango, a lingua franca during the colonial period and adopted as a national language.

Of the country's ethnic groups, the riverine groups have played and still play a dominant social, economic, and political role. Although they constitute only about 5 percent of the total population, during the French colonial period they held more than 60 percent of the administrative and civil positions in the colony and they continued to dominate the country after independence.

Upon independence, a Baya-dominated political party took control and banned all opposition parties. In 1965, a MBAKA, Jean-Bedel Bokassa, took power in a military coup. Initial Baya support, received for appointing a BAYA as his head of the army, was lost following the appointee's execution. Bokassa's despotic rule was ended by a bloodless coup in 1979 and the first president regained power. Although the Central African Republic is still a one-party state, there has been popular pressure for political reform.

CEWA   see CHEWA.

CHABA   A subgroup of the EGBA.

CHACHI   see CAYAPAS.

CHADIANS   The people of Chad, numbering 5.5 million, mostly live in the southern half of the country. Around 50 percent are Muslims, 7 percent are Christians, and the rest adhere to traditional religions. The official language of Chad is French and the most widely spoken languages are Arabic and Sara.

Chad is one of the poorest and least developed countries in Africa. Its history since independence from the FRENCH in 1960 has been dominated by a lack of common interests and understanding between the peoples of the south and those of the north. The north is predominantly Islamic and the peoples living there are mainly nomadic or semi-momadic pastoralists of Arab origin; Arabic is the language of trade and is superimposed on local languages. There are two main ethnic groups divided into numerous clans — the HASSAUNA of the northwest and the DJOHEINA of the northeast — and ethnic rivalries in the north are strong.

The south of Chad is a smaller, better watered, and more heavily populated area. Most of its inhabitants belong to the SARA people, a population of sedentary cultivators. The SARA are subdivided into several linguistically and culturally related groups. The other inhabitants of the south belong to numerous fragmented ethnic groups, the main ones of which are the MOUNDANG, TOUBOURI, MASA, MUSGUM, MASALIT, and the MABA and the LISI, both of which are also each subdivided into several subgroups.

Since the end of World War II, the people of the south have became modernized and westernized. Literacy advanced rapidly and Christianity attracted many adherents. By contrast, the northern peoples had shown reluctance toward modern education and clung to Islam. As a result, after independence most of the administrators and civil servants came from the south. The northern people, who were willing to accept French colonial rule, were not ready to be dominated by the southerners. This conflict between north and south made Chadian politics extremely unstable. Since independence there have been three civil wars in Chad which resulted in French intervention.

CHAGA (Chagga) A people of southeastern Tanzania; numbering close to 800,000, they are the third largest ethnic group in Tanzania. The Chaga language belongs to the Highland Cluster of the Bantu group of the Niger-Kordofan family of languages. The core of Chagaland (Uchaga) is situated on the southern slope of the Mount Kilimanjaro.

A good climate, well watered soil, and favorable ecological conditions made it possible for the Chaga to practice intensive irrigated agriculture with the use of natural fertilizers. The Chaga grow bananas, as well as some cash crops (mainly coffee).

Chaga families are patrilineal and very often polygamous. Their traditional society is egalitarian, based on age groups, and eschews slavery. During the precolonial period the Chaga were divided into about thirty independent chiefdoms, some of which competed for control over the caravan trade with the coast. The Chaga are among the most modernized ethnic groups of Tanzania, and are actively involved in the coffee trade, wage labour, and modern education, as well as in local and national politics. The spiritual life of the Chaga center on Roman Catholicism as well as on Lutheran Protestantism.

CHAHA A subgroup of the GURAGE.

CHAHAR AIMAQ see AIMAQ.

CHAHAR (CHAR) LANG A clan of the BAKHTIARI.

CHAKHESANG An ethnic group living in the Phek district of Nagaland, India. They speak Angami and Sema.

The Chakhesang are an Indo-Mongoloid people formerly designated Eastern ANGAMI by the BRITISH since they follow most Angami customs and intermarry with them. The name is a combination of the prefixes of the subtribes CHAKHUMA, KHEZAMA (these two are Southern ANGAMI), and SANGTAM, selected in 1948 when they merged.

They practice terrace wet cultivation and double cropping.

CHAKHUMA A subgroup of the CHAKHESANG.

CHAKMA A group numbering 75,000 (1981) living in northeast hill tracts of the Chittagong in Assam, Meghalaya, Mizoram, Tripura, and West Bengal, India. They speak Bengali, a language of the Indo-Aryan family.

They are Buddhist and also observe many of their indigenous rites, especially during birth, marriage, and cremation. They have their own script and religious literature called the *Taras*.

The Chakma and other hill peoples in this region are ethnically different from the settled populations. A Mongoloid people, they are culturally similar to the hill people of the area extending from Tibet to Thailand.

Chakma houses are built entirely of bamboo on a high bamboo platform raised about twelve feet from the ground. Their main occupation and source of livelihood is agriculture, and they practice a unique form of hillside cultivation, raising paddy, melon, cucumber, chili, eggplant, maize, sesame, and cotton seeds, all mixed together. Each crop comes out in its own season and is harvested without further sowings. The plow was introduced by the riverside Chakma in the nineteenth century, but in the interior slash and burn cultivation continues as the only practical method of agriculture. The Chakma are also good weavers.

CHAM An ethnic group numbering about 125,000 living in southern Vietnam and Cambodia. Their language, Cham, is a member of the Malayo-Polynesian family of languages. Despite their relatively small numbers today, the Cham state of Champa in southern Vietnam, which flourished until the fifteenth century had a remarkable impact on the surrounding peoples who later adopted many of its cultural innovations. The Cham were among the first regional peoples to devise their own alphabet based on an Indian script. It is still in use today although the French colonial authorities introduced a romanized script which is rapidly gaining popularity.

At the heyday of the Champa empire, two cultural influences predominated, the Hindu culture of India, and Islam. Today, Vietnamese Cham practice somewhat distorted versions of both Hinduism and Islam, each religion influencing the rites and dogmas of the

A Chamula woman in Chiapas, Mexico

Cham

other. The Cham of Cambodia adhere to a more orthodox version of Islam.

The separation of the Cham across the international border dates from the invasion by the VIETNAMESE of Champa in 1471. Most freemen and aristocrats fled to Cambodia while the poorer peasantry remained in Vietnam. There they continue to engage in market agriculture, although difficult terrain and weather conditions hinder the cultivation of rice. Over the centuries both Vietnamese and Cambodian Cham have assimilated into the surrounding cultures and their language has generally been abandoned except in remote communities. Only recently has there been a revival of Cham ethnic pride, spurred on by governmental promises of ethnic autonomy. In the early 1960s a shadowy Front for the Liberation of Champa was established. (see also HROY)

CHAMALAL   An ethnic group, estimated as numbering 5,000, living in northwest Daghestan, in the basin of the Andian Koisu tributary of the Sulak River. Their language belongs to the Avar-Andi-Dido group of the Ibero-Caucasian family. It is unwritten, and Avarian is used as the literary language. The Chamalal have been Sunni Muslims of the Shafi'i school since the sixteenth century.

Since the 1930s, the Chamalal have been regarded as a subgroup of the greater AVAR people. They are currently involved in the process of intensive integration of all related groups living on Avarian ethnic territory. Today, in addition to "Chamalal" they call themselves "AVAR."

Their traditional economy includes agriculture, horticulture, cattle-breeding, and home-based industry.

CHAMARRO   see MARIANA ISLANDERS.

CHAMBA   A subgroup of the TIV.

CHAMBRI   An ethnic group numbering a few thousand, living on an island mountain in the Sepik River basin area of northern Papua New Guinea. They speak an indigenous local language. They subsist from fish, which they catch off their island. While most are Catholics, they still believe that all power stems from the spirits of the dead.

CHAMORROS   An indigenous ethnic group numbering 100,000, living in Guam (80,000) and in the nearby Mariana Islands (20,000) in the Pacific Ocean. They speak Chamorro (an Austronesian language mixed with Spanish, Tagalog [Filipino], and English) among themselves, and English in their contacts with outsiders. They are predominantly Roman Catholic.

CHAMULA   The Chamula are an indigenous Tzotzil-speaking people of highland Chiapas, Mexico. Approximately 40,000 in number, they are centered in the village of San Juan Chamula, northwest of the town of San Cristobal de las Casas. Nominally Roman Catholic, their religious practices include pre-contact elements: they believe, for example, that Christ rose from the cross to become the sun; their pre-Lenten carnival marks not just the Christian event, but the five "lost days" of the ancient Mayan "long count" calendar, as well.

In spite of fierce resistant to invading SPANIARDS in 1524, the Chamula were subdued by 1528, after which they were forced to work for Spanish landholders. Disappointed by the results of the war of independence, still economically oppressed, and unable to identify with the new Mexico, the Chamula engaged in rebellion in 1869. Throughout the twentieth century, until quite recently, town-dwelling Chamula were treated as racial and cultural inferiors by the *mestizo* population. Recent reports indicate that the atmosphere is changing toward greater social acceptance of Indians, but increasing poverty among these highland agrarian people now forces men to leave their homeland in search of work. (See also MAYA)

CHAN (s.d. Lazi) An ethnic group settled mainly in Turkey in seven villages between the basin of the Chozokh River and the Black Sea coast, and partly in the Ajarian region of Georgia. The Chan were Eastern Orthodox Christians from the sixth until the sixteenth century, when they became Sunni Muslims of the Hanafi school. Their number can be roughly estimated as several thousand.

The languages of the Chan and the MEGREL are now regarded as two dialects of Megrel-Chan (otherwise Zan, after the ancient name used by both groups), which belongs to the Kartvelian branch of the Ibero-Caucasian family. The Chan in Georgia use Georgian as their literary language, and those in Turkey use Turkish. Their main occupations are agriculture, fishing, and trade.

In scholarly literature, the term Laz is sometimes used as a synonym for the name Chan, and the term Zan is used as a unifying designation for both the Chan and the MEGREL.

CHANA A Native South American group living in Argentina.

CHANG A NAGA group living in the hills of Nagaland on the border between eastern India and northwestern Myanmar (Burma).

CHAOBON (s.d. Niakuoll) A Mon-Khmer ethnic group numbering about 3,000, living in central Thailand. They are considered to have arrived in the area prior to the DAI, but have since adopted Buddhism and agricultural methods from the DAI. A few remote communities still practice slash and burn cultivation.

CHARA An ethnic group numbering 15,000 who live between the Dintsha and Omo Rivers in eastern Kefar Province, Ethiopia. Their language belongs to the Omotic group, and they adhere to traditional beliefs. The Chara are grain- and ensete-farmers.

CHARCA A subgroup of the AYMARA.

CHARRUA An almost extinct South American Indian group of Uruguay. The name "Charrua" is generic and includes the GENOA, YARO, BOHANE, and MIHUENE. The MIHUENE lived in the Argentinian province of Entre Rios. They were hunters and gatherers, and therefore nomadic, practicing very primitive ceramic arts. The Charrua culture has been almost entirely absorbed; vir-tually all now known about them comes from colonial chronicles and archeology. (see also ARGENTINES)

CHAUBO (Acwabo) An ethnic group living in Mozambique, in the lower Zambezi River basin, on the left bank of the river. They speak a Lomwe dialect. The Chaubo were originally part of the Maravi Empire.

CHAUDHRI An ethnic group numbering approximately 250,000 inhabiting the state of Gujarat in western India. They are predominantly agriculturalists.

CHAVANTE see XAVANTE.

CHAVCHU A subgroup of the CHUKCHI.

CHAVCHYVAV A subgroup of the KORYAK. They were traditionally fishermen.

CHAZICHE A subgroup of the TEHUELCHE.

CHECHEN (s.d. Nokhchiy) A people living in the central Caucasus, mostly between the middle course of the Terek River and the main Caucasian Ridge, in west Daghestan. In 1989 their total number was 960,000, of whom 734,000 lived in the Chechen-Ingush Autonomous Republic.

During the seventh and eighth centuries the Chechen accepted Eastern Orthodox Christianity under the influence of Georgia, but since the sixteenth and seventeenth centuries they have been Sunni Muslims of the Hanafi school.

The Chechen language belongs to the Vakh (or Veinakh) branch of the Ibero-Caucasian family. Their script was first based on the Roman alphabet (1925), but since 1938 the Cyrillic alphabet has been used.

Historically, the Chechen were divided into regional tribal communities (MICHIK, QACHALYQ, AUKH, ICHKERI, etc.) living in the mountains, in two-storey stone houses with cattle housed on the ground floor; in some *auls* (villages), medieval stone towers of three to five storeys for both fighting and dwelling have been preserved.

In the sixteenth and seventeenth centuries Chechen began to settle on the plains in the basin of the Terek, Sungha, and Argun Rivers.

One of the tribal communities, the QARBULAQ, numbering about 40,000, migrated to the Ottoman empire and is now dispersed in the various Middle East states which came into existence with the collapse of the empire. Together with other representatives of North Caucasian ethnic groups, they are known in those areas as Circassians (see CHERKESS).

Chechen under the leadership of Shamil resisted Russian expansion but in 1859 were included in the Russian empire; in 1936 the Chechen-Ingush Autonomous Republic was established.

In 1944 it was abolished and the people deported to Qazaqstan and Siberia; in 1957 the Chechen were returned to their ethnic territory. With the disbandment of the USSR, the Chechen proclaimed their independence, which has remained to a great extent only formal.

Chechen

Their traditional economy centers around cattle-breeding and agriculture; recently, oil-extracting and a refining industry have been added.

CHECHI   see CZECHS.

CHEGMLY   A subgroup of the BALKAR.

CHEHALI   A Native North American ethnic group numbering about 1,000 persons, many of whom live in Washington State on the Chehali Federal Indian Reservation. They are part of the Northwest Coast Indian culture, residing in plank houses, raising totem poles, and living traditionally by fishing (salmon and sea mammals).

Today they operate a successful salmon hatchery and many of their members work in the forest industry. Following the smallpox epidemic that assailed the CHI-

NOOK people in the early nineteenth century, its many survivors joined the Chehali.

CHELKAN   A group living in the Kuznetskii and Ala Tau Mountains on the southeast border of the Russian Federation. They are classified as ALTAI.

CHEMWAL   A subgroup of the NANDI.

CHENCHU   An ethnic group numbering 29,000 (1981), found in Andhra Pradesh, Karnataka, and Orissa, India. They speak Telugu, a dialect of the Dravidian family of languages.

The Chenchu are food-gatherers and hunters, expert honey-collectors, and bamboo cutters. They inhabit the denser forest regions of the above-mentioned states, living in hive-shaped huts with wattle walls.

CHENG   A Mon-Khmer group, closely related to the OY, living in southern Laos. They cultivate rice both in paddies and by slash and burn methods.

CHEPANG   An ethnic group living in the Lothar Khola region and valleys of Male Khola in the Mahabharat range in Nepal. They speak a Tibeto-Burman language.

The Chepang are a Hindu group of Mongolian stock. They have no subcastes. Their primary occupation is the cultivation of maize and millet, and their homes are fashioned of tree-branches. They trap birds and collect forest produce such as nettles. Some also fish and practice animal husbandry. The barter system is still extant among the Chepang.

CHERANGANY   A subgroup of the MARAKWET.

CHERKESS   1. In traditional Muslim geographic and historiographic literature (in Turkish *Cherkas*, in Persian *Charkas*, in Arabic collectively *Sharkasi*), and since the thirteenth century also as a general designation of the Adyghean ethnic groups, the contemporary ADYGHEANS, KABARDINIANS, and Cherkess. The name of one of the ancient Adyghean tribes, the Kerkete, is evidently reflected in this term.

2. The collective name for the members of the north Caucasian ethnic groups who emigrated in 1859–1864 to the Ottoman Empire and now dwell in Turkey and other Middle East states, where they are known as Circassians. They include the greater part of the historically western Cherkess tribes (ABADZEKH, BJEDUKH,

NATUKHAI, SHAPSUG, etc.) and also parts of the ABAZIANS, CHECHEN, and INGUSH.

3. An ethnic group (s.d. Adyghe) living in the basin of the Greater and Small Zelenchuk Rivers in the Karachai-Cherkess Autonomous Region of Russia (established in 1922, administrative center Cerkessk). In 1989 they numbered 52,000.

The contemporary Cherkess are descendants of the KABARDIANS who resettled in the first half of the nineteenth century in the upper basin of the Kuban river. They speak Kabardian (or Kabardino-Cherkess; in scholarly terminology also High Adyghe; see also KABARDIANS).

The Cherkess have been Sunni Muslims of the Hanafi school since the sixteenth century and are a mostly rural group.

CHERO

(Cheru, Cherwa, Barahazar) An ethnic group numbering 54,000 (1981), living in the Palamau, Shahabad, Champaran, Monghyr, Ranchi, Santal Parganas, and Gaya districts of Bihar and West Bengal, India. They speak Bihari, a dialect belonging to the Indo-Aryan family of languages.

The Chero are a Hindu group, with Brahman priests officiating at their weddings. They live in mud houses, with part of the dwelling used as a barn for cattle and another part used to store farm tools and grain.

CHEROKEE

A large Native North American group numbering about 50,000, living in Oklahoma and North Carolina. They quickly adopted many features of European-American culture, as evidenced in their developing their own alphabet and cultivating large farms which, before the civil war in the United States, utilized black slaves.

In 1838–1839 the Cherokee, with the exception of one band, were removed to the Indian Territory of Oklahoma, 1,200 miles west of their ancient home. This forced march, which claimed 4,000 victims, is referred to by the Cherokee as the Trail of Tears.

Some Cherokee sold their land in Oklahoma at the beginning of this century. Today they live in the Cherokee Federal Reservation in North Carolina and on the Cherokee Federal Trust Area in Oklahoma. They run a heritage centre which includes a museum and a representation of a traditional village. Many Cherokee served in the U.S. armed forces during World War II.

CHEWA

(Cewa) A Nyanja-speaking group living in eastern Zambia, the Tete district of Mozambique,

Cherokee and Cheyenne

and southern Malawi. The total Chewa population for these three countries is about 300,000, divided between Christians, Muslims, and ancestor-worshipers. The Chewa follow a system of matrilineal descent and inheritance with the chief as ultimate owner of all village land. He would distribute the land to his headmen who would, in turn, divide it among the villagers. Villagers could sell their produce but not their land, and paid tribute to the headman. Domestic slavery was also part of Chewa social and economic life. In addition to agriculture, they were involved in trade.

The Chewa descend from Maravi who emigrated from the Congo Basin before the sixteenth century to Lake Malawi and then to the Zambezi River. In the eighteenth century they seceded from the Maravi and moved to the Blantyre and Ncheu Districts in Mozambique. Some remained there while other groups moved farther west. Many members of one such group, under Mwase of Kasungu, converted to Islam. Another group, led by Mkanda, went north and settled on both sides of the Zambian border. The colonial government failed to unite the Chewa under Mkanda.

The Chewa in Mozambique came from Katanga in the late fifteenth century. They played an important role in the Tete district during Mozambique's struggle for independence.

The ZIMBA are a Chewa subgroup. (see also MALAWIANS, MOZAMBICANS, NGONI, NSENGA, ZAMBIANS)

CHE WONG   A subgroup of the SENOI.

CHEYENNE   A Native North American nation numbering today under 10,000. They originally lived in Minnesota, but were forced to move to the Black Hills of South Dakota. The Cheyenne consist of two major bands, the Northern and the Southern. The latter were closely associated with the ARAPAHO, today sharing the same reservation in Oklahoma. The Northern Cheyenne were associated with the SIOUX Indians of the Northern Plains and were their allies at the battle of the Little Big Horn where the forces of General George A. Custer were wiped out.

Subsequently the Northern Cheyenne were forced to move to Oklahoma but under the leadership of Chiefs Little Wolf and Dull Knife they managed to escape to Montana, where they live today on the Northern Cheyenne Federal Indian Reservation.

CHHAZANG   A Buddhist group inhabiting the Himachal Pradesh state of northern India. Their culture has been heavily influenced by that of Tibet.

CHIAPAS   A Native American people living in southern Mexico. (see also MEXICANS)

CHIBCHA   A South American Indian group concentrated primarily in Colombia, in the region of present day Bogotá and Tunja. They manifested one of the most sophisticated forms of government and leadership prior to the Spanish conquests. The destruction of their political structure by the SPANIARDS in the sixteenth century led to a gradual decline in the use of the Chibcha languages.

Chibcha social structure is fundamentally matrilineal and succession to chieftancy is based on this system, while land is inherited patrilineally. Traditional religion was strong, and numerous shrines were built in honor of the gods. The economy was based on agriculture, crafts, and weaving; products of these activities were exchanged with neighboring states for gold, which was used in temple decoration and hoarded by the chiefs in the form of lavish jewelry as symbols of status. (see also COLOMBIANS, GUAYMI)

CHICKAHOMINY   A small Native North American group, one of the constituent members of the Powhatan Confederacy, living in King William County, Virginia, on the Mattapowni State Reservation.

CHICKASAW   A Native North American group originally from lower Mississippi, numbering today about 10,000. Traditionally they lived in thatched dwellings. After signing a treaty with the United States in 1837 they moved to the Indian Territory of Oklahoma. Many live today in the Chickasaw Tribe Federal Trust Area near Ardmore, Oklahoma.

CHIK BARAIK   An ethnic group of Bihar numbering 53,000 (1981), living in Ranchi, Bihar, and in West Bengal, India.

The economy of the Chik Baraik is forest-based. Their traditional occupation is weaving, and they also hunt and forage. They usually have scattered houses with two or three families living in each.

CHIKUNDA   An ethnic group living in eastern Zambia (where they number 9,000), northern Zimbabwe, and along the lower Zambezi River in Mozambique. Their language, Nyungwe, is a combination of Shona and Nyanja. Although lacking a common ethnic heritage, they united into a cohesive group with its own customs and traditions. The Chikunda mounted slaving raids against their neighbors and served in the Portuguese army.

CHIL   see KIL.

CHILAPA   A subgroup of the JIVARO.

CHILCOTIN   (Tsilkotin) A Native North American group living in south-central British Columbia, Canada, numbering today about 1,700 persons. Many members work away from the reserve but they supplement their income by traditional hunting and fishing.

CHILEANS   The people of Chile, estimated at more than 13 million (1992), are predominantly white, although, since the sixteenth-century conquest of the country by Spain, they have assimilated by intermarriage with ARAUCANIANS and other local Indian populations. The Chileans are Spanish-speaking, although some immigrant communities tend to preserve their original languages.

Isolation and distance contributed to the development of a particular Chilean identity in South America during the period of Spanish colonization (sixteenth to nineteenth centuries). The war of independence

A Chilean woman in Temuco, Chile

(1810–1818), the establishment of an autocratic republic (1833), and the wars against the Peruvian-Bolivian confederation (1836–1839) and the Pacific War between Bolivia, Chile, and Peru (1879–1883), as a result of which Chile conquered the nitrate-rich areas of Atacama and Tarapaca, strengthened Chilean nationalism. Until the mid-nineteenth century immigration to Chile was mainly Spanish (BASQUES, CASTILIANS, and ANDALUSIANS) but since 1848 German immigration was officially encouraged and large groups of settlers arrived in the Valdivia and Llanquihue regions in the south. During the nineteenth and the beginning of the twentieth centuries European immigration increased; groups of ITALIANS, FRENCH, BRITISH, SWISS, AUSTRIANS, CROATIANS, JEWS, and ARABS settled in the country. Since immigration was controlled, the incoming groups integrated easily and were seldom perceived as a menace to the Chilean nation. Cultural pluralism, the liberal and associative nature of Chilean nationalism, a relatively strong democratic tradition, and the presence of a clear socio-economic cleavage precluded the appearance of ethnic strife in Chile.

The Indian population (estimated at 2 percent of the population) is mostly Araucanian, speaks Mapuche, its own language, and Spanish, and lives in central south Chile between the Biobio and the Tolten Rivers. The largest Chilean community outside Chile is found in Argentina where the main group of workers in Patagonia was Chilean until many of them were expelled in the 1970s as a result of growing tension between the countries that almost led to war in 1978. Other large groups of Chileans live in the poorer suburbs of Buenos Aires. Ninety percent of the population live in the central valley, a fertile strip of land between the Andean mountains and the coastal range.

Most Chileans are Roman Catholics. Tolerance and the separation of church and state (1925) have allowed for religious pluralism and many Chileans are adopting different forms of Protestantism. There is a small Jewish community (c.10,000), and a number of Muslims have recently built a mosque in Santiago.

Since colonial times Chileans have been divided into upper and lower classes. The Chilean man of the people is the *roto* ("broken one"), characterized popularly as poor, hardworking, with a good sense of humour and a fondness for wine. More than 83 percent of the Chileans are part of the urban sector, with the remainder still part of the rural sector. *Huasos*, or Chilean cowboys, are famous for their horsemanship, proudly demonstrated in Chilean rodeos, but traditional ways of life are fast giving way to modernity. The middle class developed rapidly after the 1930s and took an active part in the country's socio-economic and political life. The predominance of the socio-economic cleavage — reflected in the political crisis of the 1970s during which the Chileans polarized in terms of Left and Right, destroying the economy and democracy — brought about military dictatorship and economic stabilization policies that affected the middle and lower classes. Redemocratization in the 1990s is being carried out on the basis of national reconciliation and social development. (see also ARAUCANIANS)

CHIMBA   A subgroup of the HERERO.

CHIMBU   An ethnic group of more than 60,000 living in the mountains of central Papua New Guinea. They speak an indigenous regional language. While they have no formally organized priesthood or worship, their ceremonies center on appealing to ancestral spirits. Their economy is based upon the cultivation of various fruits and vegetables, among which the sweet potato is most prominent, and upon the production of coffee.

CHIN   see BURMANS.

CHINESE   China's fifty-six identifiable ethnic groups inhabit the most populous country on earth, containing over 1,000 million people. By far the largest ethnic group is the Han, who are often simply (if somewhat inaccurately) refered to as "the Chinese." Numbering 937 million (1982), they make up 93 percent of the population and are the dominant culture. They inhabit all provinces, municipalities, and autonomous regions within China, and sizeable Han communities can also be found in Thailand, Malaysia, Indonesia, Singapore and Hong Kong (in both of which they constitute a majority), Vietnam, Burma, the Philippines, and Cambodia, as well as in countries outside Asia.

Most of these expatriate communities are descended from farmers and fishermen of the coastal provinces of southeast China, whose migration to the other countries of Southeast Asia reached its peak during the 1920s.

The Han Chinese language belongs to the Sino-Tibetan language family. Its ideographic script derives from second millennium B.C.E. pictographs, although the oldest written records (inscriptions on bronze, stone, bone, and tortoise shells) date back at least 3,500 to 4,000 years. There is no doubt that this non-

above: Working in the ricefields near Guilin, China
below: Practicing Tai Chi in the morning, Dali, China

phonetic script contributed greatly to the continuity and unification of Chinese culture. Despite significant changes over the centuries, its use as a literary language continues today.

Sharp regional and cultural differences, including major variations in spoken Chinese, are often as great as among many European nationalities. Numerous different dialects, many unintelligible to the others, can be classified into seven principal groups: Mandarin (the largest, spoken by some 70 percent), Wu (spoken in Shanghai and the surrounding environs), Gan (Kan); Xiang (Hsiang); Yue (Cantonese); Kejia (Hakka); and Min. The official spoken language of China, Putonghua (meaning "common language," or "standard Chinese"), is derived from northern Mandarin, particularly the Beijing dialect. Most Han speak and understand it, as do many minority nationalities.

A combination of various beliefs and religions is characteristic of the Han. Taoism and Confucianism, both of Chinese origin, and Buddhism are the most common, but ancestor worship is also of particular importance.

Although the Han form a great homogeneous group sharing the same culture, traditions, and written language, they are dispersed over such a large and diverse country that it is impossible to expect them to share a uniform lifestyle. They often characterize themselves by their native regions: northerners are usually tall and well-built; southerners are generally small, wiry, and soft-spoken.

Northern Mandarins are often described as proud, honest, and straightforward; people in the northwest are traditionally characterized as simple, conservative, and thrifty. Southerners, especially people from Shanghai and neighboring regions, are considered pragmatic, crafty, and smart, while the Cantonese are often referred to as clannish, diligent, unyielding, and eager to embrace new ideas. Just as dialects are indicative of distinct geographic regions, so music, art, and cuisine also vary from place to place. There are also obvious differences in economic development, educational and living standards, and various other aspects among the Han of different regions. Coastal areas are generally more developed and industrialized than the interior; people in the south are generally more prosperous and educated than those of the northwest.

Some 80 percent of the Han still engage in agriculture, although an increasing number have found work in industry, trade, and other economic sectors. Various crafts are also highly developed.

The complex ethnic history of the Han, spanning many centuries, is generally traced as beginning with the farming tribes of the Yellow and Yangtze River basins who created a neolithic culture in the second and third millennia B.C.E.

China was first unified under the Qin dynasty (221–207 B.C.E.), while the formative years of the Han nationality were during the Han dynasty (206 B.C.E.–220 C.E.), which provided the group's self-designation. Early settlement in the Yellow and Wei Rivers regions, often known as "the cradle of Chinese civilization," soon expanded eastward, and then to the south and southwest. Such expansion was generally accompanied by the forced assimilation of other ethnic groups. It was under the Tang dynasty (618–907) that China became the cultural and economic center of Asia, with commerce and trade flourishing and a series of successful wars in Central Asia and Korea.

Although the Han have dominated China during most of the country's history, two foreign dynasties, the Mongolian Yuan (1271–1368) and the Manchurian Qing (1644–1911), also ruled. The MANCHU in particular adopted Chinese culture, laws, and bureacratic procedures.

The Communists — who came to power under the leadership of Mao Zhedong in 1949, after nearly four turbulent decades of internecine conflict in China subsequent to the overthrow of the Manchus — launched a program of rapid industrialization and socialization until the economic crisis of the early 1960s forced a period of retrenchment and recovery lasting until 1965. In that year Mao launched the Cultural Revolution, a movement that oversaw attacks on bureaucrats, intellectuals, scientists, and individuals or groups with any foreign connections, and also encompassed a massive rustication movement whereby some 60 million people (mostly aged between sixteen and thirty) were moved from existing population centers in an effort to relocate industries, provide human resources for agriculture, reclaim land in remote areas, settle borderlands, promote sinicization (the settlement of Han Chinese in ethnic minority areas where they do not traditionally constitute a majority of the population), and relieve urban food and housing shortages. Despite the Communists' sinicization policy, the Han remain a minority in the relatively sparsely-populated north and west of the country.

China'a fifty-five ethnic minorities had a total population of 66.5 million in 1982, the single largest minority group being the ZHUANG (a Buddhist people related to the DAI and concentrated in Guangxi, Yunnan, and

Guangdong), who number over 13 million (1984). Other minority groups with more than 5 million members are: the HUI, Chinese-speaking Muslims numbering some 7.2 million and found mainly in Ningxia, Gansu, Henan, and Hebe; the UIGUR, 6 million Turkic Muslims found in Xinjiang; the YI, a 5.5 million-strong Buddhist people related to the TIBETANS, who inhabit Yunnan, Sichuan, and Guizhou; and the 5 million MIAO of Guizhou, Hunan, Yunnan, and Guangxi. China's 3.8 million TIBETANS are concentrated in Tibet (invaded and occupied by China in 1950), Qinghai, and Sichuan.

Several other ethnic minorities had populations estimated to be more than 1 million in 1984: these include the MONGOLIANS, with a population of 3.4 million; the MANCHU, 2.8 million; the BUYI, 2.1 million; the KOREANS, 1.8 million; the DONG, 1.4 million; the YAO, 1.4 million; and the Bai, 1.1 million. China's population of QAZAQS was estimated at 908,000 in 1984. In addition, China contains minority communities of DAUR, LAHU, LI, LISU, NAXI, SALAR, SHE, SHUI, SIBO, DAI, TU, and WA.

Ethnic minorities enjoyed exemption from nationally imposed birth limits until 1982, whereafter the renewed drive to limit births included them but allowed them as many as four children per couple in comparison to the one-child norm expected of the Han.

Having made significant steps towards normalizing relations with the capitalist West (a process fueled by the parties' mutual distrust of Soviet intentions) during the 1970s, China has expanded its attempts to modernize its industry, agriculture, national defense, and science and technology.

However, liberalization has remained strictly confined to the economic sphere; China remains a gerentocratic Communist dictatorship, as evidenced by the violent suppression by the military of peaceful pro-democracy student demonstrators in Tianenman Square in Beijing, the Chinese capital, in 1989. This action was condemned by China's Western trading partners and many countries imposed sanctions on Chinese trade as a result, but the perceived economic benefits of access to the huge Chinese market led to almost all sanctions being rescinded. (see also THAI)

CHINGATHAN   A small ethnic group found in the northern region of the state of Kerala in southern India. They engage mostly in the gathering of wild honey.

CHING-PO   see SINGHPO.

CHINOOK   A small Native North American group which was originally one of the largest of the Pacific northwest. Most of the tribe was wiped out in a smallpox epidemic in the 1830s. The survivors joined the CHEHALI, who now live on the Federal Indian Reservation in Washington State.

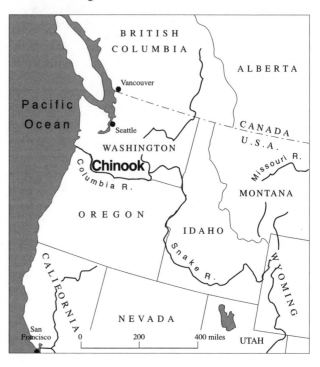

Chinook

CHIPEWYAN   A Native North American group living in the Mackenzie River Delta, Northwest Territories and in northern Alberta, Canada. They number about 1,700 persons. On account of their location they are the intermediaries between the INUIT to the north and the Woodland CREE to the south. The unemployment rate in their communities is one of the highest in Canada. Many attempt to follow their traditional practices of hunting and trapping.

CHIPPEWA   (Ojibway) One of the largest Native North American peoples, numbering more than 100,000 in Canada and 70,000 in the United States. They are concentrated in dozens of communities across Quebec, Ontario, Manitoba, and Saskatchewan in Canada and in Minnesota, Wisconsin, and North Dakota in the United States.

Traditionally they were hunters and gatherers but some of their bands also cultivated maize and wild rice. Their traditional dwellings were wigwams (tents covered by birch bark). They were also known for their birch bark canoes.

A warrior people, the Chippewa were allies of the British in their wars against the United States. In 1812 the Chippewa succeeded in destroying the city of Detroit. At present the Chippewa are embroiled in land claims and fishing-rights disputes with the federal and state governments in Wisconsin. Violence erupted over these issues in 1989 and 1990.

CHIQUITO   A South American Indian people living in the lowlands of Bolivia. Agriculture is their mainstay, their main crops being sweet manioc, maize, pineapples, sweet potatoes, beans, cotton, and peppers. They supplement their diet with hunting, fishing, and gathering.

Originally part of the GUARANI people of Paraguay, they migrated to their present home at the time of the Portuguese conquest of Brazil.

CHIRICAHUA   A subgroup of the APACHE.

CHIRIGUANOS   An ethnic group of South American Indians living in the Chiquisaca and Tarija regions of Bolivia. During the colonial period they numbered 200,000, but by the beginning of the twentieth century this number had been reduced to 25,000 and has since dropped to several thousands. The reduction in numbers was caused by the aggressive, often violent, intrusion of cattle-farming into their maize-farming areas. Two such encounters, in 1875 and 1892, led to an expulsion of the Chiriguanos to Argentina, to work in cattle ranches there. Some took refuge in missions.

Another contributing factor to massive migration of Chiriguanos from their area of origin was the Chaco War of 1932–1935 between Bolivia and Paraguay. Caught in the crossfire, many Chiriguanos fled to Argentina or Paraguay.

CHIRIMA   An ethnic group living in Mozambique.

CHIRUMBA   A subgroup of the SHONA.

CHISHINGA   A Chibemba-speaking group numbering about 85,000, living in the region north of Lake Bangweulu in Zambia. During the nineteenth century they produced iron. Some profess Christianity, while others adhere to traditional religions. They follow a matrilineal descent system. Their origins can be traced to the LUBA empire of southeast Zaire. They were conquered by the BEMBA in the early 1890s.

CHITIMACHA   A Native North American group numbering several hundred, originally resident in Mississippi but living today on the Chitimacha Federal Indian Reservation in Louisiana, United States.

CHITRALI   A small Muslim group found in the mountainous region of northern Tajikistan and in Pakistan.

CHIZEZURU   see ZEZURU.

CHOCTAW   A large Native North American group originally living in the southeast Mississippi Valley. Today there are about 30,000 Choctaw, 6,000 still living on their original territory on the Choctaw Federal Indian Reservation in Neshoba County, in Mississippi, and most of the rest in the Choctaw Federal Trust Area in Pushmataha and Latimer Counties in Oklahoma.

Traditionally, they depended for their livelihood on fishing and the cultivation of maize. They were among the first Native American groups to move to Oklahoma, which in their language (Algonkian) means "Red Men."

Language retention amongst the Choctaw has been and continues to be greater than among most other Native American groups. On the reservation in Mississippi more than 1,000 members are employed in the car assembly plant which is Choctaw-owned and operated.

CHODHARA   A people numbering between 15,000 and 20,000 found in the state of Gujarat in western India. They are primarily agriculturalists.

CHOISEUL ISLANDERS   An ethnic group of approximately 10,000 living in the Solomon Islands, in the southwest Pacific Ocean. Their main area is Choiseul Island. They speak four indigenous regional languages. Their subsistence is based on slash and burn cultivation, with the main crop being taro. Their traditional religious beliefs have been replaced by Christianity.

CHOKOSSI   (s.d. Afunu) An ethnic group living in the Sansanne-Mango and Dpaong areas of Togo, where they number around 26,000, and in small numbers in Ghana. Their language, Afunu, is a Baule dialect. They mostly practice their traditional religion, but there is a significant Muslim minority. Their social organization is highly stratified.

In the precolonial era, a Chokossi kingdom with its capital in Sansanne-Mango dominated the neighboring MOBA, GURMA, and GUANG. After initial resistance to the GERMANS in Togo, they eventually assisted them in the conquest of the remainder of the country.

Despite their relatively small numbers, the Chokossi are well-represented in Togo's administration and politics.

CHOKWE (Tshokwe) An ethnic group living in eastern Angola, where they number around 500,000; in northwest Zambia, where they number around 27,000, and in the southern part of the Shaba (Katanga) Region, Zaire. They were originally a seminomadic matrilineal society that was ruled by the LUNDA for centuries. They rebelled in the nineteenth century and had a decade of independence from 1885 to 1895.

During Zaire's post-independence "Katanga crisis," the Chokwe, together with the LUBA, organized the Balubakat party to oppose Katanga's secession. They later came to resent the central government for exploiting Katanga's natural wealth without re-investing in the region. (see also ZAIREANS)

CHONG A Mon-Khmer group numbering about 5,000, mostly inhabiting the region along the southern border of Cambodia and Thailand. The Chong are believed to have once occupied a much larger territory but have since assimilated into the dominant KHMER society. The SAOCH are considered descendants of the Chong who have resisted assimilation.

CHONO A nomadic South American Indian people living along the coast and offshore islands of Chile and Tierra del Fuego. They subsist by collecting mussels and shellfish, fishing, and hunting seals and porpoises.

CHONTAL A small Mayan group inhabiting parts of the state of Oaxaca in Mexico. Their pre-Columbian ancestors were less culturally advanced and much less powerful than the neighboring ZAPOTEC.

The Chontal are divided into Highland and Lowland subgroups. The language of the more isolated Highland Chontal manifests some resemblance to Aztec tongues, but in the absence of written records it is not known whether the Chontal were conquered, or simply influenced linguistically, by the Aztec. As is the case with many other indigenous groups in southern Mexico, they remain largely outside mainstream Mexican society. Although some have been taught to read and

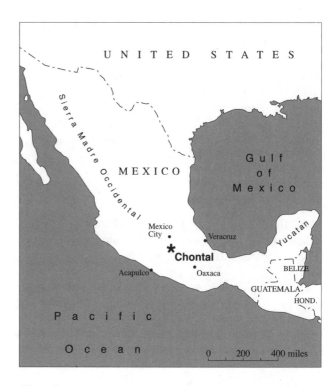

Chontal

write Spanish by governmental rural educators, they generally speak Chontal in their homes.

In spite of their traditional orientation, the Chontal have incorporated many Mexican cultural elements and aspects of the Spanish language itself into everyday life: their language is now so mixed in practice that it is hard to say what is Spanish and what is Chontal. While older folk usually speak pure Chontal, some younger adults find themselves, with prolonged mixing of languages, fluent in neither.

The Chontal have two forms of religious observance: public and private. The public is the Roman Catholic ritual; the private, the religion inherited from their remote ancestors. Catholic observance is, as with many other Mexican Indians, strongly influenced by the indigenous religion. As the sun was the most important of their original deities, it is in their view analogous to Christ, as is the moon to the Virgin Mary. This is in part their interpretation of Catholic ritual which, as it was once celebrated in Latin and now in Spanish, is poorly understood. They practice their indigenous rituals at home or in woodland caves: they believe that they are thus placating the devil. (see also MAYA, MEXICANS)

CHONYI A subgroup of the MIJIKENDA.

CHOPI A Lomwe-speaking group living along the Inhambane and Gaza coasts in Mozambique. Although some practice traditional religions, many have attended Methodist and Catholic schools and are Christians.

When the PORTUGUESE entered Inhambabe in 1870, the Chopi looked to them for support against the SHANGAAN. Yet despite initial friendly relations, the Chopi later became involved in non-violent protests against Portuguese rule. Famed for their unique musical instruments, they wrote many songs ridiculing the colonial PORTUGUESE. (see also MOZAMBICANS)

CHOROTE A tribe of the MATACO-MATAGUAYO.

CHOROTEGA A Native American group living in Costa Rica.

CHORTI A subgroup of the MAYA.

CHRAU A Mon-Khmer group numbering about 15,000, living in southern Vietnam, in the region surrounding Ho Chi Minh City (Saigon).

CHRU see CHURU.

CHUCHUGASTA A chiefdom of the DIAGUITA.

CHUKA A subgroup of the MERU.

CHUKCHANSI A small Native North American group living today in Table Mountain, California.

CHUKCHI An ethnic group living in the Chukchi Peninsula in northeastern Siberia, situated at the northeastern extremity of Asia. They number about 16,000 and form only 15 percent of the population of the Chukchi Autonomous *Okrug* (District) of Russia. In 1926, 70 percent of the Chukchi were nomads, but today most are settled, although some remain semi-nomadic.

The Chukchi language is closely related to and mutually intelligible with the Koryak and Helmen languages. Since 1931 it has utilized the Cyrillic alphabet.

The Chukchi are divided into the CHAVCHU, nomadic and semi-nomadic reindeer-herders, and the AN'KALYN, settled coastal fishers and fur-trappers. Today they are also employed in local mining. Despite pressure from the RUSSIANS, they have preserved their traditional rituals.

CHULIKATTA see MISHMI.

CHULUPI A tribe of the MATACO-MATAGUAYO.

CHUMASH A Native North American group numbering about 300. At the time of contact with the SPANISH in the eighteenth century, they numbered more than 20,000 and quickly adopted Spanish farming customs. Today the remaining members of the group live on the Santa Ynez Federal Reservation in Santa Barbara County, California.

CHURAHI A Hindu people living in the Chamba District of the northern Indian state of Himachal Pradesh.

CHURU (Chru) A Malayo-Polynesian group numbering about 10,000 living in the mountains of southern Vietnam. The Churu were the only Hill (Montagnard) people to have developed their own script, based on an Indian script, prior to the colonial period.

CHUTIA (Dibongiya) A people inhabiting the western part of the Indian state of Assam. They speak a

Chukchi

Sino-Tibetan language. Once the dominant ethnic group of the region, their status has decreased in recent years.

CHUTIYA An ethnic group living in Arunachal Pradesh and Assam in eastern India.

CHU TY A subgroup of the JARAI.

CHUUK ISLANDERS (Chuukese) A Micronesian-speaking people of about 52,000 who inhabit the Chuuk (formely Truk) island group, fourteen main volcanic islands scattered within a forty mile-wide lagoon located at the center of the Caroline island chain. Early in the twentieth century they were administered by Germany, from 1920 by the JAPANESE, and from 1945 by the United States. At present the island group is a member state of the Federated States of Micronesia, associated with the United States. Their society is based on a number of matrilineal clans which regulate marriage. They are mainly Roman Catholics. They conduct a basic subsistence cultivation in which breadfruit is the main crop, supplemented by fishing.

CHUVASH About half the approximately 1.8 million Chuvash live in the Chuvash Autonomous Republic, which is part of Russia. Large numbers of Chuvash reside in the neighboring Tatar and Bashkir Autonomous Republics as well as in the environs of Ulianovsk, Kuibyshev (now Samara), and Saratov. Other Chuvash emigrated to Siberia during the nineteenth and twentieth centuries.

The Chuvash language belongs to the Turkic family, but as the only representative of a separate branch of that linguistic group, it is not understood by speakers of the other Turkic languages. Anthropologically the Chuvash combine European and Mongolian elements. They are divided into Viryal (Upper) and Anatri (Lower) Chuvash, corresponding to the dialect division. The Anatri dialect was used in the 1870s to establish the literary language, which uses the Cyrillic alphabet. They claim and are believed by some researchers to be the descendants of the Volga-Bulgars, a claim also made by the TATARS and disputed by other scholars. The Chuvash as such figure in historical sources from the fifteenth century, when they were under Tatar domination.

In 1551 the Chuvash lands were annexed by the RUSSIANS. In the first half of the eighteenth century the Chuvash were forced to abandon their own religious practices in favor of Russian Orthodox Christianity.

The traditional occupations of the Chuvash were farming and cattle raising. Until the 1917 Revolution

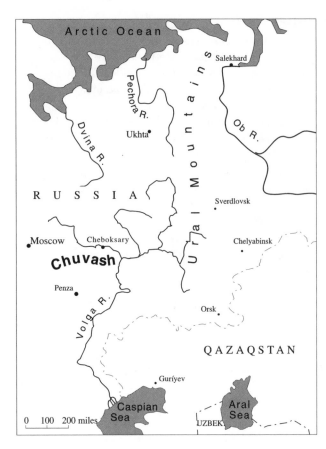

Chuvash

they were dispersed in rural communities and led a traditional way of life. During the Soviet period, and especially since World War II, a growing number of Chuvash have found industrial work in the cities. Some still engage in their traditional folk arts: choral singing, embroidery, artistic weaving, and wood carving.

CHYSH-KIZHI see SHORS.

CIBECUE A subgroup of the APACHE.

CIL A subgroup of the MNONG.

CINTA LARGA A South American Indian group living in the State of Mato Grosso, central-west Brazil. The several dozen individuals have very few outside contacts.

CIRCASSIANS see CHERKESS.

COCAMA A Tupi-speaking South American Indian group living in the upper Amazon region in Brazil. They are on the verge of extinction.

COCHINESE   see VIETNAMESE.

COCOPAH   A small Native North American nation, many of whom live in the Cocopah Federal Indian Reservation in Yuma County, southeastern California.

COFAN   A South American Indian group of about 500, living in several villages along the headwaters of the Aguarico and San Miguel Rivers in eastern Ecuador, on the border with Colombia. They speak their own language. Although they have to some extent become acculturated, they continue to depend upon shamanism to resolve conflicts and cure illness.

COLLAGUA   A subgroup of the AYMARA.

COLLAHUAYA   A subgroup of the AYMARA.

COLOMBIANS   The 27 million inhabitants of Colombia, a country in northwest South America, between the Caribbean Sea and the Pacific Ocean. Prior to the Spanish conquest in 1512, the CHIBCHA Indians, concentrated in the western mountain regions, were the dominant ethnic group of the area. Today's population is derived from intermarriages of Indians with SPANIARDS and African immigrants. It is estimated that almost one-half of the population is composed of combined European and Amerindian origins, while about one-fifth are of mixed European and African ancestry. Colombians are predominantly Spanish-speaking. There are also several indigenous languages, whose speakers include such major ethnic groups as the AYMARA, ARAWAK, CHIBCHA, CARIB, QUECHUA, TUPI-GUARANI, and YURUMANGUI. The vast majority of Colombians are Roman Catholic.

As inhabitants of the only country in Latin America with both Caribbean and Pacific coastlines, Colombians enjoy one of the world's most varied ecologies, ranging from the high Andes to Amazonia, with an acompanying enormous variety of plant and animal life. Mineral resources, whose exploitation is government-controlled, are abundant, and fossil fuel reserves, if not plentiful, are present in at least some quantity. However, only 5 percent of the land, predominantly located in highland valleys, is arable, and 30 percent is permanent pasture. Colombia's lack of suitable agricultural land, combined with one of the highest birth and population growth rates in Latin America, has led to substantial rural-to-urban migration: as a result, a country two-thirds rural in the late 1950s was almost two-thirds urban just thirty years later. Many migrants to urban areas live in irregular settlements called *barrios populares*.

Colombians grow such staple food crops as beans, bananas, cassava, corn, potatoes, and rice; tobacco is also produced for domestic consumption. While the best-known and principal legal export cash crop is coffee, coca, as refined cocaine, produces twice the export income. Coca, used to make a stimulating tea by Indians in Andean Highlands, is processed into cocaine for export by other people in other areas. Forestry and manufacturing, the latter diversified and 75 percent hydroelectric-powered, are significant. While they also manufacture transport equipment, Colombians suffer from inadequate transportation infrastructure, especially in rural areas: less than a third of the road network is paved. While literacy is relatively high, Colombians also suffer a shortage of trained professionals, especially in medicine: a variety of contagious and non contagious diseases, therefore, remain a problem.

Over 200 years after the Spanish conquest in 1525, the *audiencia* of Santa Fe de Bogotá, incorporated into the viceroyalty of Peru in 1559, was transferred to the viceroyalty of New Granada (1740), which was created by combining the land areas now comprising Colombia, Ecuador, and Venezuela. South-American-born creoles, feeling their prosperity threatened by continued subjugation to Spain, fomented early resistance to Spanish rule in the form of the Comunero Revolt of 1781. After independence was achieved in 1821, New Granada became the Republic of Gran Colombia, which lasted until 1830.

Continuing conflict between the Liberal and Conservative parties, which began in the latter half of the nineteenth century and continued into the mid-twentieth, had earlier resulted in an "alternating governments" agreement, restored in 1958. Colombian life, however, has been plagued by recent and continuing violence, in part political and in part related to international traffic in narcotics centered in the city of Medellín.

COLVILLE   A small Native North American group of the Salishan-speaking group living today in Ferry and Okanogan Counties in Washington State. They are related to the LILLOOET and the COMOX in British Columbia, Canada.

COMANCHE   A Native North American group originally living in the northern plain of Texas. Historically the Comanche were known as the best horsemen and cavalry among the Plains Indians. In the eighteenth and nineteenth centuries they were one of the largest and strongest tribes of the southern Plains Indians. For two centuries they prevented the northward expansion of the SPANIARDS and the MEXICANS.

In 1874 the Comanche were removed to the Oklahoma Territory. Over the course of the nineteenth century their numbers declined dramatically. Today there are about 4,000 Comanche, many of whom live on the Comanche Tribe's Federal Trust Area in Oklahoma.

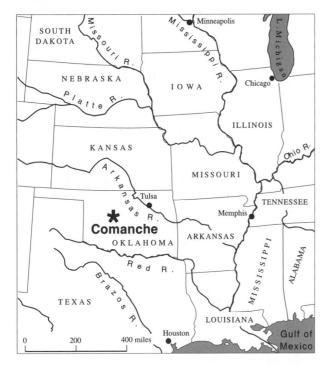

Comanche

COMECHINGON AND SANAVIRON   A remnant of an indigenous group who inhabited what is now the province of Cordoba, in Argentina.

COMORIANS   The 475,000 Comorians inhabit the Federal Islamic Republic of the Comoros, situated in the Mozambique Channel between Madagascar and the African mainland. They are of mixed African, Arab, and Malagasy descent. Their language, Shaafi Islam (Comorian), is a variant of Swahili, heavily influenced by Arabic; it is written in Arabic characters. The population is predominantly Muslim and there is a small Christian community, generally the remnant of the once-extensive French colonial presence. Some 80 percent of the population engages in agriculture.

The Comorians voted for independence from France in a referendum conducted in 1974. Only the people of

the southernmost island of Mayotte voted to remain part of France. Independence was declared unilaterally in 1975 for all the islands. Mayotte, however, is still governed by France, causing some tensions between the two countries.

COMOX   A Native North American group numbering about 1,000, many of whom live in the southwestern part of British Columbia, Canada. Traditionally they were dependent upon salmon fishing for their livelihood, and many still retain their fishing sites. (see also COLVILLE)

CONGOLESE   The people of Congo are estimated to number nearly 2.1 million. The main ethnic groups are the VILI on the coast, the KONGO, centered in the capital, Brazzaville, and the TEKE, MBOCHI, and SANGA of the plateaux of the center and north of the country. Each of these ethnic groups is subdivided into several linguistically and culturally related groups. About 50 percent of the Congolese practice traditional religions and the rest are mainly Christians. The official language of Congo is French while the most widely spoken languages are Kikongo (the language of the KONGO people) and Teke.

The Congolese gained their independence from the FRENCH in 1960. Since then the politics of the country have been characterized by ethnic divisions, mainly between the northern and southern peoples but also among the peoples of the north themselves. The first two presidents of Congo came from the south but after 1968 there were three northern presidents who gave priority to the development of the northern areas. Some of the northern peoples also felt that they had been neglected by the government. In 1990 popular resentment of the government and the severe economic crisis forced the president to agree to a democratization process. A national conference was formed and became a sovereign body.

COOK ISLANDERS   Polynesian-speaking MAORIS, numbering about 40,000, 19,000 of whom inhabit fifteen small islands in the southern Pacific Ocean. The Cook Islands form a self-governing state in association with New Zealand. The remainder (21,000) of the Cook Islanders live in New Zealand. They are Christians of different denominations. Over 90 percent of the Cook Islands' population are engaged in farming (coconuts, bananas, and citrus) and fishing. In recent years tourism has become the most important source of national income.

COPATAZA   A subgroup of the JIVARO.

COPTS   see EGYPTIANS.

COR I   A subgroup of the JARAI. (see also SEDANG)

COR II   A subgroup of the SEMANG.

CORNISH   (s.d. Kernow) Many of the inhabitants of the county of Cornwall in southwest England have evolved linguistic and cultural traditions distinct from those of the ENGLISH mainstream. There has been a recent revival of the Cornish language, which became extinct in the mid-eighteenth century, and many locals now speak this as well as English. Their Wesleyan Methodism is leavened with folklore and customs which refer back to pre-Christian beliefs. The local economy is founded on farming, tin and copper mining, fishing, and tourism.

CORSICANS   With 250,000 inhabitants, Corsica has always been a poor island, traditionally divided between inland sedentary villages and transient pastoralists. Poverty has driven most Corsicans to emigrate to France and Italy.

The Corsicans are predominantly Catholic. After a long history of domination by the Genoese, the Corsicans have been ruled by France since 1768. French became the official language, though Corsicans have continued to speak an Italian dialect, and retain more Italian cultural traits.

They are still characterized by extended families, clientelism, and vendettas. France pacified endemic pirates, but only the Revolution brought full integration into the French nation, stimulated by the successes of the island's most famous son, Napoleon Bonaparte. Throughout the nineteenth century, Corsicans sought social advance in army service or emigration: many participated in France's colonial expansion. One hundred thousand settled in Algeria; their repatriation in the 1960s became a factor in Corsica's economic modernization.

Nowadays, the economic crisis mostly affects the rural interior; tourism brings in income, but also provokes criticism of "internal colonialism." Nationalist agitation has expressed itself in terrorism. In the 1980s, the FRENCH declared an amnesty, and started a devolution of powers to regional organizations. Corsican autonomy was widened in 1991.

COSSACKS   (Zaporozhtsy)   see UKRAINIANS.

COSSACKS   see QAZAQ.

COSTA RICANS   (s.d. Ticois) The estimated 3 million inhabitants of Costa Rica, a Latin American state. About 95 percent inherit varying mixtures of the *mestizo* blend of Spanish conquerors and colonists with Indians, including some African roots.

People of many other nationalities and cultures have immigrated to Costa Rica: between 1870 and 1920, 20–25 percent of population growth could be attributed to immigration. Since 1920 its effect has been minor.

The official religion is Roman Catholicism, practiced by 90 percent of the population. Although its base has been seriously undermined in the last twenty years by the evangelical movement, the Catholic church is still the most powerful institution after the government. It played a central role in shaping the country's social-democratic fabric and has also been instrumental in legitimizing the social-welfare state. The degree to which the public sector has assumed responsibility for social welfare (education, health, social assistance) compares with that of many European states. The Costa Rican government is also economically active, having extended public-sector control to such areas as banking, petroleum refining, and utilities.

Despite the wholesale decimation of indigenous populations during the early colonial period, Costa Rica still has a dozen ethnic groups, plus two ethnic-descendant groups. Only six native languages have survived the last 500 years of colonization. Current estimates of the Indian population range from 11,000 to 19,000. Most of the official Indian Reserves are in the Cordillera de Talamanca, near the Panamanian border, although other reserves are found further north along the Pacific coast.

Not only are these Costa Rican natives isolated from the dominant society: they are isolated from each other, both by geographical seclusion and by cultural differences. These Indians practice traditional shifting cultivation, an ecologically sound use of forest resources when the population density is low. The most serious environmental problems are the loss of their reserve land and exploitation of natural resources within their reserves. Existing legislation protecting Indian cultures and their natural resources has been weakly and inconsistently applied. Mining laws and exploration for petroleum directly affect Indian reserves. State involvement in mining could easily circumvent the legislative intent to protect Indian lands and people. The Talamanca Indian groups negotiated an agreement with the government to permit petroleum exploration and exploitation on Indian reserves; however, it is uncertain that the agreement will effectively protect Indian culture and land.

The Indian population represents under 1 percent of Costa Ricans. In the southern Caribbean region there are two main Indian groups: the CABECARE inhabit the regions of Moravia de Chirripo, Estrella, San Jose de Cabecar, Telire, and Pacuare, while the BIBRI live in the Talamanca valley and the nearby area of Cocles. The GUATUSO and MALEKU are found in the northern Caribbean region in the population centers of El Sol, Tonjibe, and Margarita on the Guatuso plains. The MISKITO (Sambos Mosquitos) occasionally visit the Guatuso region during migratory phases. The BORUCA (Brunka) live in the southern Pacific region, principally in Boruca, Curre, and Maiz. Also in the region are the TERRABA (Terbi) in the Terraba area. A group of CABECARE live in Ujarraz, while some BIBRI live in Salitre and Cabagra. The GUAYMI have population centers in Guaymi de Coto Brus, Abrojos-Montezuma, and Conte Burica along the Panamanian border.

Ethnic groups considered as descendants of native Indian populations include the CHOROTEGA populations in Matumbu, Matambuguito, Guatil, Santa Barbara, Hondores in Guanacaste province; and a small group of HUETARES-PACACUAS in Quitirrise de Mora and Zapaton de Puriscal of the central region.

COTABATO MANOBO (Dulangon, Tudag) An ethnic group located in the southwestern highlands of Cotabato, mainly in the Kulaman Plateau, on the Philippine island of Mindanao. Their language belongs to the Manobo family. They are agriculturalists and also utilize wood from nearby forests to produce goods for sale. Their scattered settlements, consist of small thatched houses on piles, with up to twenty houses in a group.

The Cotabato Manobo hold a belief in a supreme being named Namola for whom the soul strives after death. To ease this process, the dead are buried half-covered by earth; their houses are burned. In 1971 world attention was drawn to the existence of a tiny (numbering c.70) group named the Tasaday, distantly related to the Cotabato Manobo, and said to be the remnants of a Stone Age people. This conclusion has now been dismissed, although it is apparent that they are relatively less developed than other peoples on Mindanao. Anthropological facts about the Tasaday remain to be studied before they can be classified among the peoples of the Philippines.

COTE D'IVOIRE, THE PEOPLE OF THE   see IVOIREANS.

COURONIANS   see LATVIANS.

COWICHAN   A relatively large Native North American group scattered along the coast of British Columbia and on Vancouver Island.

Traditionally they have lived as fishers and by hunting sea mammals. Today many of them work in the forest industry and on commercial fishing boats.

CREE   A large Native North American group numbering more than 100,000, making it the largest such group in Canada. They live in Quebec, Ontario, Manitoba, Saskatchewan, and Alberta. Most of the Cree were Woodland Indians, while those living in Saskatchewan and southern Alberta were Plains Indians.

The Big Bear Band in Saskatchewan was the last band of Plains Indians to enter a reserve and the only group to enter into a violent conflict with the Canadian authorities. Many of the current Canadian Native leaders, such as Ovide Mercredi, Chief of the Assembly of First Nations in Canada, are Cree.

In Quebec, after a long struggle with both provincial and federal governments, the Cree living in the James Bay Area accepted financial compensation for the con-

Cree

fiscation of that part of their land which was flooded by the large hydro-electric project in northern Quebec. They used part of the funds to purchase an airline and run it under the name of Air Creebec, making the Cree the only Native American people to own and run its own airline. In 1980 they successfully opposed the construction of Phase II of the James Bay Hydro-Electric Project.

Due to the large number of Cree speakers, the language is in wide use today. Newspapers, books, and journals are published in Cree and it is even used in computer programs. (see also LUBICON)

CREEK   (Abihki, Atasi) A large Native North American tribe originally living in Georgia and Alabama. They are also known as the Creek Nation or Confederacy. They were removed to Oklahoma in the 1830s and until 1906 they had their own Creek Nation government. Due to their large numbers and strong cultural commitment they managed to preserve their language and traditions. Today there are about 45,000, mostly living in the Creek Tribe Federal Trust Area in Hughes and Tulsa Counties, Oklahoma, U.S.A.

CRIMEAN TATARS   (s.d. Qyrym Tatarlyi or Qyrymly Tatar) An ethnic group numbering approximately 350,000 now living partly on the Crimean peninsula (administratively the Crimean *Oblast* of Ukraine) and partly dispersed in other areas of the CIS, mainly in Uzbekistan. Their language belongs to the Qypchaq group of Turkic languages and consists of three dialects: the southern (coastal), central, and northern (or steppe). The southern differs considerably from the others, and bears a resemblance to Turkish. Classical literary Crimean Tatar is very close to classical Osmanli Turkish. Reformed and simplified by Isma'il Gasprinsky (Gaspraly), the language became, under the name Turki, the model for the Turkic modernist press in the Russian Empire (late nineteenth-early twentieth centuries). In the 1920s to 1930s, Soviet literary Crimean Tatar was reshaped around the central dialect. The Arabic script was used until 1929, when it was replaced by a Roman one, which in 1938 was replaced by Cyrillic.

The Crimean Tatars are Sunni Muslims of the Hanafi school. Their origins can be traced back to the thirteenth century, with the arrival of the Golden Horde TATARS to the inner steppes of the Crimean peninsula. The apparently relatively tiny indigenous population, the Qypchaq, whose presence in the area has been recorded since the eleventh century, were soon ab-

sorbed by the new arrivals. Non-Turkic people, such as GREEKS and Goths, were also slowly assimilated, as well as many Slavs brought to Crimea as captives during the endless wars of the Crimean Tatar *khans* with their neighbors. With the annexation of Crimea by the RUSSIANS in 1772–1783, the Christian population of the area was moved from the peninsula to areas which the government wished to develop. This led to the conversion to Islam and subsequent tatarization of many Crimean Christians, mostly GREEKS of the coastal region.

The massive Slav immigration at the beginning of the nineteenth century caused Russian-encouraged Crimean Tatar migration to the Ottoman empire, which was accelerated by the Crimean War (1853–1856) in which the Ottoman empire joined with Britain, France, and Sardinia against Russia. As a result, after a century of Russian rule, the Crimean Tatar population had fallen from about 500,000 to 200,000. Most of those who went to Turkish regions of the Ottoman empire were assimilated into the Turkish population. However, of the descendants of those who migrated to non-Turkish parts of the Ottoman empire, 25,000 still identify themselves as Tatars in modern Romania (the Dobrudjan Tatars) and 10,000 in Bulgaria. The 34,000 who identified themselves as Tatars in Turkey in the 1980s may be descendants of Crimean Tatars or of Tatars who settled as individuals inspired by pan-Turkist ideology at the beginning of the twentieth century and in small groups after the 1917 Revolution in Russia. When the Soviets established the Crimean Autonomous Republic in 1921, only about 25 percent of its population were Tatars: the others were predominantly RUSSIANS and UKRAINIANS.

In May 1944 the Crimean Tatars remaining in Crimea were deported for alleged mass collaboration with the Nazis during the German occupation of Crimea (1941–1944). They were resettled in Central Asia, mainly in Uzbekistan, as farmers. Half perished en route to exile. From the end of the 1950s they were allowed by the Soviet authorities to publish their own newspaper and books in Tashkent and Uzbekistan. By a 1967 Soviet decree they were collectively rehabilitated, i.e., cleared of the accusation of collaboration. However, they were not allowed to return to the Crimea, the administration of which had been transferred in 1954 from Russia to the Ukraine as an *oblast* (district), and where massive settling of Slavs in many of the previous areas of Crimean Tatar habitation had already begun in 1944. The struggle of Crimean Tatars for return to the Crimea, backed by the dissident

above: A Croat celebration in Dubrovnik, Croatia
below: Croats in Dubrovnik, Croatia

movement of Russian intellectuals, has been one of the most dramatic phenomena of national movements in the USSR from the late 1960s through the 1980s. Many Crimean Tatars were imprisoned. Even when the decision was taken in November 1990 to permit the return of Crimea to the Tatars, its implementation was postponed by the authorities until 1991–1996. However, they began to resettle in Crimea of their own accord; they were met with hostility on the part of the Slav population.

As a result of the massive 1944 deportation, Crimean Tatars have lost much of their traditional life-style (except for their cuisine). They have undergone an intense process of assimilation into Russian culture. Virtually all speak both Russian and Crimean Tatar, and for many of the younger generation the former is their first language.

CRNO GORTSI   see MONTENEGRINS.

CROATS   (s.d. Hrvati) Most of the approximately 6 million Croats live in Croatia, on the Adriatic coast in the northwestern part of former Yugoslavia. About 800,000 lived in neighboring Bosnia-Herzegovina where they formed about a fifth of the population before the civil war that began in 1991. About 300,000 lived in Serbia. The war has caused extensive upheaval and population movements. About 200,000 Croats live overseas, mainly in North America and Australia, to which they immigrated after World War II.

Croatian is a Slavic language belonging to the Indo-European family. It is very close to Serbian and in fact forms with it a single language called Serbo-Croat. However, the Croats, due to their Roman Catholic heritage, use the Roman alphabet, while their neighbors and rivals, the SERBS, use the Cyrillic.

Until the end of the nineteenth century the Croats preserved the framework of the *zadruga* (extended family), three or four generations living in one household, with the father or grandfather as its head (*domachin*). Production and consumption were shared by all members of the *zadruga*. Subsequent socio-economic developments of this and the last century have caused the disintegration of the *zadruga*, particularly in towns.

Slavic tribes migrated to the Panonian plains in south central Europe in the early first millennium C.E. After crossing the Carpathian Mountains, the ancestors of the Croats settled mainly in the plains of the Drava and Sava Rivers as well as in the Dalmatian uplands, near the Adriatic Sea. In the ninth century they were converted to Christianity by Roman Catholic missionaries, unlike the neighboring SERBS, who converted to Greek Orthodox Christianity.

In 880 Branislav became the first independent duke of Croatia. Kresimir II, surnamed The Great (1000–1035), conquered a large part of Dalmatia, including some Italian ports on the Adriatic coast. By then the Croats had built a strong fleet, which they used first for piracy and later for trade, thus coming into conflict with Venice, the emerging maritime power on the Adriatic Sea. By the end of the eleventh century, under King Zvonimir, Croatia was one of the strongest powers in the Balkans.

In 1102 Croatia became part of the kingdom of Hungary by a personal union, but retained its autonomy under its own *Ban* (ruler). In the sixteenth century Croatia, as part of Hungary (both threatened by the Ottomans), became a Habsburg possession. By the early seventeenth century, the major part of Croatia was under Ottoman rule. Only a narrow strip in western Croatia remained under Austrian and Hungarian rule. However, the peace treaty of Carlowitz (1699) gave all of Croatia to the Habsburgs. Here, the Croats preserved until 1840 a measure of internal autonomy and used the Croatian language for official purposes, until an attempt to introduce Hungarian as the official language sparked off a revival of Croatian national aspirations followed by the emergence of a movement calling for the union of all southern Slavs. These were the aims of the 1848 rebellion, which was suppressed quickly. The late nineteenth century saw the steady growth of the movement striving for autonomy and for a southern Slav political entity.

In 1917 a Croatian Committee in Exile in London signed the Corfu Declaration with representatives of the Serbian government, which provided for the unification of the southern Slavs of Austria-Hungary with the independent states of Serbia and Montenegro. This led to the establishment in 1918 of the kingdom of Yugoslavia; however, the Croats were soon disappointed by their inferior role in the new kingdom. Croatian nationalism, led by Stjepan Radic and his Croatian Peasant Party, came out against Serbian ascendancy in the kingdom. Radic's assassination in 1928 deepened Croat antagonism to the SERBS.

In World War II the *Ustase*, a Croat fascist movement led by Ante Pavelic, utilized the German occupation of Yugoslavia in April 1941 to proclaim an independent Croatian state within the broadest possible borders. This state pursued a policy of expulsion and extermination of ethnic minorities, mainly SERBS, JEWS, and GYPSIES. The *Ustase* were allied with the GERMANS and fought against both Yugoslav resistance movements: that led by the monarchist government–in–exile in London and the communist one led by Tito (himself a Croat).

In 1946 the People's Republic of Croatia was established as one of Yugoslavia's six federated republics. Under Tito all nationalist movements were suppressed. Following his death in 1980, however, the long rivalry between the SERBS and Croats erupted once again. In the summer of 1991 Croatia proclaimed its complete independence and seceded from Yugoslavia. The SERBS reacted by force, starting a war which led the major powers to recognize independent Croatia. Later, in 1992, the Croats of Bosnia-Herzegovina became involved in a civil war between Croats, SERBS, and BOSNIAN MUSLIMS. (see also SERBS, SLOVENES)

CROW (Absaroka) A Native North American group numbering about 6,500, many of whom live in the state of Montana. They originally inhabited the Yellowstone area and parts of the Dakotas. Throughout the nineteenth century they suffered heavy losses at the hands of the SIOUX.

The Crow were one of the original Native North American groups practicing the Sun Dance religion, and it is still part of their religious belief system. In August they host an annual powwow, or meeting, which is the largest such gathering of Plains Indians of the U.S.A. and Canada today. The Crow Reservation is now partly flooded by the Yellowtail Dam.

CUA (Khua) A Mon-Khmer group living in the hilly area of central Vietnam.

CUBANS The 11 million inhabitants of Cuba, the largest of the Caribbean islands, located at the nexus of the three sea lanes of the Atlantic Ocean, the Gulf of Mexico, and the Caribbean Sea. Another 1.5 million Cubans live outside the country, mainly in the United States. They descend from the merging of various groups since the time of colonization: Ciboneyes and Taino Indians inhabiting the island at the time of discovery; SPANIARDS, the colonizers; black slaves from Africa; and, to some extent, CHINESE immigrants who arrived in the middle of the 1800s.

After several decades of colonization, most of the Indian population had disappeared, due to epidemics, genocide, and forced labor. Those who survived generally adopted Spanish culture after attaining freedom. Indian women often intermarried due to the shortage of women among the Spanish settlers.

The white population consisted initially of the Spanish *conquistadores*, and the traffic of Spanish migrants to and from Cuba was constant ever since the conquest. These SPANIARDS were mainly from Andalusia, the Canary Islands, and Asturia.

The first black slaves from Africa came to Cuba in the early sixteenth century. Havana became an important slave market and by the mid-1800s blacks outnumbered whites. Black slaves came from West Africa, mainly from Senegal and also the Congo, but the largest and most influential African group in Cuba were the YORUBA, originally from southwestern Nigeria. The presence of the YORUBA in Cuban culture is still felt today through food, music, and other national expressions.

Faced with a growing black population, the SPANIARDS tried to promote white immigration to the island, with little success. Advisors to the Crown then recommended the importation of Chinese workers, having heard that the CHINESE were strong and would be good substitutes for black slaves. The CHINESE came to Cuba as indentured servants to work in the sugar cane fields. This labor trade was organized similarly to the slave trade that preceded it, with companies specifically devoted to exploit the new lucrative business. The CHINESE were indeed enterprising, and later many climbed the commercial ladders. Most Chinese immigrants were male, and they widely practiced intermarriage, mainly to white *criollo* women (i.e., of Spanish ancestry born in the New World).

Ethnic and racial issues had been largely obscured by political divisions between *criollos* and SPANIARDS or other foreigners during colonial and republican times. However, racism was present in Cuban society. Before 1959, blacks were excluded from most of the better beaches, hotels, and places of entertainment patronized by AMERICANS or upper class Cubans. Race was related to social class. The upper and middle classes of republican times were mostly white. Similarly, blacks and mulattoes predominated in the poorest sectors of society. Among non-whites, possession of "white features" was a major predicator of social class mobility. There was a sizable number of mulatto Cubans, mainly in the professions, who were part of the middle or upper middle classes in Cuba.

The national language of the Cuban people is Spanish. The idiomatic expressions and the distinctive accent are, some say, reminiscent of Andalusia. There is also a great deal of African influence in Cuban Spanish, and some Taino words have survived. Due to the proximity and the influence of the United States, many English words have been introduced into the language.

In the 1950s about 85 percent of the population claimed Catholicism as their religion. Nominally, this was probably correct; however, the Catholic clergy estimated that only 10 percent were practicing Catholics. The Catholic church in Cuba never had the following it enjoyed in other Latin American countries. The practice of Catholicism was mainly an urban and upper and middle class phenomenon. However, most Cuban cultural attitudes and values are clearly based on Catholicism. Among the poorer classes, Catholicism was mixed with Afro-Cuban religions: Santeria includes a number of cults related to its participants' ethnic background and some forms have incorporated elements of Catholic ritual, with Catholic saints having been given African names.

The Protestant presence in Cuba goes back to the late 1800s and was clearly influenced by contact with the United States. The number of Protestants in Cuba grew after the U.S. occupation in 1898–1902. By the 1950s the Southern Baptist, Methodist, Presbyterian, and Episcopalian denominations were well established in Cuba. Protestantism appealed to lower and lower-middle income groups, and, despite American influence, the Protestant clergy were more sympathetic to the aims of the Socialist Revolution than were Catholics.

The Revolution of 1959, led by Fidel Castro, introduced revolutionary changes; after about a year, the principal aim of the government to reduce social and economic inequalities was welcomed by the poor and working class majority but rejected by most upper and middle class people. As a result of this national conflict and the strong U.S. sanctions against Cuba (including a long-lasting economic blockade), a massive exodus of primarily white upper and middle class Cubans started in the 1960s. These migrants were accepted as political refugees by the United States. More recent migrants from Cuba are representative of the island's population composition.

An important characteristic of the Cuban people is their strong sense of nationalism, the roots of which go back to *criollo* struggles to distinguish themselves from the SPANIARDS at all levels, including artistic expression, scientific pursuits, and politics. The attempts to forge *Cubania* (i.e. "Cuban-ness") continued for a long time, as Cuba was the last of the Spanish territories in the Americas to obtain its freedom. After independence from Spain in 1898, and free from a brief North American intervention that lasted until 1902, Cubans continued to express their nationalism during republican times by denouncing U.S. economic and political penetration in Cuba.

In Miami, which has the largest concentration of Cubans outside of Cuba, radical nationalism is also the political ideology that has informed the activities of anti-Castro, anti-Communist groups. However, more and more moderate voices on both sides of the strait of Florida aspire to use nationalism as a vehicle to promote a constructive dialogue geared towards solving Cuba's many pressing problems.

CUMANANGOTO A Native South American group living in Venezuela.

CUNA A South American Indian people living in Panama. Once possessing a complex religious and caste system, they now subsist as village agriculturalists. They raise pigs and chickens for trade. Due to acculturation, Western dress has all but replaced native clothing. Their religion exhibits traditional and shamanist tendencies.

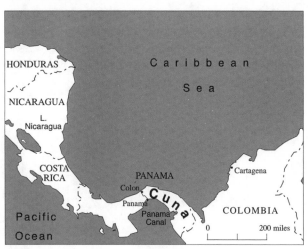

Cuna

CURAÇAO, THE PEOPLE OF The island of Curaçao, part of the Netherlands Antilles, is a Dutch dependency in the Caribbean Sea, off the north coast of Venezuela. The population of some 150,000 is primarily of black African origin (Curaçao was the center of the Caribbean slave trade during the colonial period), although over forty other nationalities are represented. Although the official language is Dutch, Papiamento, a lingua franca evolved from Dutch and English with the addition of French, Spanish, Portuguese, Arawak, and African words, is also spoken, as is English.

The economy is founded on the island's oil refineries, which serve to stimulate other economic activities such as shipbuilding, air traffic, and commerce.

above: A Turkish Cypriot potter
below: A Greek Cypriot farmer

CUSULIMA   A subgroup of the JIVARO.

CUYO   A Native South American group living in Argentina.

CYMRU   see WELSH.

CYPRIOTS   The inhabitants of the island of Cyprus in the eastern Mediterranean are divided along ethnic lines between Greek and Turkish Cypriots. Each group feels part of its respective nation and celebrates the national and religious holidays associated with its "motherland." Of the some 700,000 Cypriots, 80 percent are Greek Orthodox GREEKS and 18 percent Sunni Muslim TURKS. There are a few thousand ARMENIANS and Maronites. TURKS and GREEKS lived dispersed over all the island and one-sixth of the villages were mixed until 1974, when Cyprus was effectively partitioned by a Turkish invasion.

Cyprus was colonized by GREEKS by 1000 B.C.E. or earlier. Other conquerors followed: Phoenicians, the Ptolemies, and Romans. Christianized in the first century, Cyprus had its own independent patriarchate within the Byzantine empire. Cyprus came under Latin rule, first French, then Venetian, from the twelfth century to 1571, when the TURKS took over. Muslims settled in lieu of the Westerners, in particular in the northeast corner, but were much more tolerant toward their Orthodox Greek subjects than their predecessors had been. In the eighteenth century, the Orthodox *ethnarch* became responsible for taxation of the GREEKS, thus starting the political and economic preponderance of the church which continues until today. As Greek nationalism awakened and inflamed Greek Cypriots as well, church leaders led the struggle for *enosis*, or unification with Greece; yet throughout most of the Ottoman period, peaceful coexistence between the communities was the rule, although social contact between Greek and Turkish Cypriots was limited. In 1878 Cyprus came under British administration (under continued Ottoman suzerainty) as a naval base against Russia. Turkey relinquished its claim to Cyprus in 1923.

After Turkish independence, thousands of Turkish Cypriots left for Turkey, changing Cyprus's demographic balance to its current ratio. Greek Cypriots welcomed the BRITISH in the hope that the latter would enable *enosis*; TURKS in the hope they would prevent it, since *enosis* would transform the TURKS into a vulnerable minority. However, from the 1930s, Britain faced an anti-colonial struggle in Cyprus. Greek anti-fascist

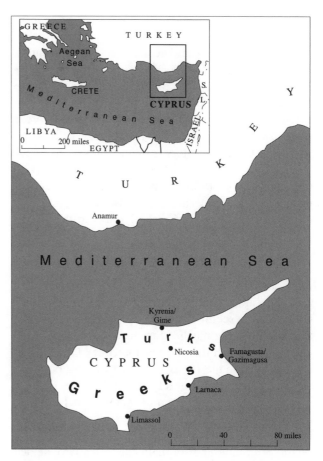

Cypriots

resistance in World War II inspired new *enosis* hopes. For Greek Cypriots, Crete served as an example of a Greek island that had obtained *enosis* after a century of revolts. For Turkish Cypriots, however, Crete exemplified the prospect of forced expulsion of Muslims. While GREEKS advocated freedom of movement and settlement throughout the island, the TURKS feared that such an arrangement would perpetuate their minority status; they therefore advocated ethnic segregation, and eventually *taksim* (partition). Radicalization of the Greek Right reached new levels in the 1950s with the election of the fiercely pro-*enosis* Michael Mouskos as Archbishop Makarios III, vying in pro-Hellenism with Giorgios Grivas's underground militant organization EOKA. Their intransigence made any constitutional compromise short of *enosis* unattainable. In 1960, the BRITISH decided to grant Cyprus limited independence; by then, however, too much blood had been spilt for either community to desire continued cohabitation with the other. A consociational constitution was adopted, but no Cypriot security force could be established. Community clashes broke out in 1963. The

TURKS, victims of violent Greek attacks, moved to fortified villages. Their enclaves were blockaded by the GREEKS, and they became economically dependent on mainland Turkey. Thus de facto partition started.

In 1974, a coup against Makarios encouraged by the Greek colonels, who aimed at annexing Cyprus, triggered a Turkish invasion. Mutual massacres and forced population removals ensued in factual partition: 62 percent of Cypriot territory is in the hands of the Greek Cypriots, 38 percent under the control of the Turkish Cypriots who in 1983 unilaterally declared independence. Tens of thousands of Turkish Cypriots fled to North Cyprus; 200,000 Greek Cypriots to the Greek-held South. This development has transferred the problem from one of powersharing to the question of how to build federal links between two territorially separated ethnic communities. United Nations peace-keeping forces along a buffer zone monitor the split island.

The Greek sector is relatively prosperous, with a standard of living much higher than mainland Greece. Having integrated its refugees, the Greek Cypriot sector recovered in the 1980s, with a new tourist boom on which its economy largely depends. The Turkish Cypriot sector suffers from an international boycott, declining tourism, and a stagnant economy; incomes here are four times lower than in the Greek Cypriot sector. Still, thousands of mainland TURKS have settled in formerly Greek homes, raising the Turkish Cypriot population to 153,000.

From 1976 the UN has sponsored peace talks. The Greeks Cypriots demanded a strong bi-communal federation. The Turkish Cypriots seemed in no hurry. Negotiations continued throughout the 1980s, but were mostly deadlocked, and as time passes, partition is becoming entrenched.

CZECHS (s.d. Cehi) The 11.3 million Czechs live mainly in Czechoslovakia and in adjacent areas in neighbouring Poland, Slovakia, and Austria. Expatriate communities are to be found in North America and Eastern and Western Europe.

The Czech language belongs to the Western group of the Slavic languages. It is closely related to, and mutually intelligible with, Slovak. It has been a literary language since the fifteenth century and uses the Roman alphabet. Until the nineteenth century Czech was also the literary language of the SLOVAKS.

Closely related to the SLOVAKS in origin, language, and religion (both peoples are Catholic), the Czechs differ from them culturally. Their predominant cultural influence for centuries was German, while that of the Slovaks was Hungarian. The Czechs are among the most westernized Slavic peoples (rivaled only by the SLOVENES), as well as the most advanced educationally, culturally, and economically, with widespread industrialization.

The Czechs are descendants of Slavic tribes that settled Bohemia and Moravia in the fifth and sixth centuries C.E. Their name has been adopted from an eponymous tribe which inhabited central Bohemia. By the ninth century, tribal states emerged, of which the strongest, Great Moravia, was formed in the basin of the Morava River, through which runs a central trade route from the Baltic to the Adriatic Sea. It expanded all over Bohemia and Moravia, part of Slovakia, the southern part of today's Poland, and the western part of Hungary. At that time the country was christianized, and after a long period of vacillation between Rome and Constantinople, it accepted Catholicism, first with a Slavonic and later with the Latin rite.

At the beginning of the tenth century, Great Moravia collapsed under the attacks of the HUNGARIANS. It was the turn of the Pvemysl dynasty, who ruled the Czechs from their castle in Praha (Prague), to unite Bohemia and later Moravia as well under their rule. The Pvemysl rulers (895–1306) tied Bohemia to the Holy Roman Empire, within which they received the title "King of Bohemia." They invited a large number of German settlers and made Prague into one of the greatest centers of culture and learning of that period.

With the extinction of the native dynasty, the kingdom of Bohemia was ruled by the House of Luxembourg (1310–1437). Karl, King of Bohemia, was from 1355 also Karl (Charles) IV, emperor of the Holy Roman Empire. He made Prague his capital, embellishing it and founded its university. After his death, however, the country became embroiled in the Reformation struggles. The execution in 1405 of Jan Hus, who had called for church reforms, split the country between Catholics and Hussites.

The election of Ferdinand I of Habsburg in the sixteenth century began almost 400 years of Habsburg rule (until 1918). During the Thirty Years' War the Habsburgs and Catholicism became entrenched in Bohemia and Moravia, followed by germanization of the country's cultural life.

Czech nationalism began to develop in the early 1800s, at first in cooperation with German nationalism, but during the revolutions of 1848 their ways parted, when the German constituent assembly in Frankfurt declared Bohemia and Moravia part of the German fatherland. During the nineteenth century Czech nation-

above: Czech men in Prague
below: Czech women in Prague

alists shifted their stress from autonomy within the Habsburg empire to independence from it. They also forged ties with the other Slavs of the empire, and especially with the SLOVAKS, which resulted in the creation of Czechoslovakia in 1918.

In this new state the Czechs, numbering twice as many as the SLOVAKS and more advanced socio-economically, became the dominant element. This created strong resentment among the SLOVAKS. The presence of many GERMANS (some 2.5 million) and HUNGARIANS under the democratic regime of Czechoslovakia (which granted free political expression to the diverse national elements) was used as an excuse by the Nazis for the dismemberment of Czechoslovakia following the Munich accord of 1938.

After World War II Czechoslovakia was reconstituted and the GERMANS were expelled. A communist regime was installed in Prague in 1948 and the country became part of the Soviet bloc. In 1968 the short-lived "Prague Spring" (an attempt to reform the communist regime along more liberal lines) was crushed by Soviet troops. Since then, until the regime's collapse in 1990, Czechoslovakia was one of the most rigidly Communist countries in Eastern Europe. In 1969 it was transformed from a unitary state into a federation of two republics. Following the end of communism and the rise of Slovak (and to some extent Czech) nationalism, the two component republics of Czechoslovakia decided to sever their federal links and became separate independent states in January 1993. (see also SLOVAKS)

D

DABA An ethnic group classed among the KIRDI groups, living in Chad.

DAFI A small ethnic group living in Burkina Faso.

DAFLA (s.d. Nishang, Nisi) An ethnic group of 22,500 (1981) living in the Subansiri region of Arunachal Pradesh, India. Their language belongs to the Tibeto-Burman family.

The Dafla are a martial people who practice polygamy. Their houses are long, sometimes 2,000 feet in length. The walls are made of twilled mat and the floor of flattened bamboo. More than ten families sometimes occupy a house, with each wife having her own separate establishment.

Shifting cultivation is the only method practiced, the principal crops being paddy and millet. Their staple is rice, supplemented by fish, the meat of various animals, edible tubers, and leafy vegetables.

DAGABA (Dagari, Dagati) An ethnic group of the MOLE-DAGBANI, living mainly in the Upper Region-West of Ghana. Some also live in the Côte d'Ivoire and Burkina Faso. (see also MOLE-DAGBANI)

DAGANA A subgroup of the HASSAUNA.

DAGARI, DAGATI see DAGABA.

DAGBAMBA, DAGBON see DAGOMBA.

DAGOMBA (Dagbon, s.d. Dagbamba) An ethnic group living in northern Ghana and in Togo. They speak the Dagbane language and their society is patrilineal.

In precolonial times, they inhabited the kingdom of the MOLE-DAGBANI, which was conquered by the GERMANS in the late nineteeth century and divided between German Togoland and the British Gold Coast, now Ghana. With the defeat of Germany in World War I all Dagomba territory came under the rule of the BRITISH. (see also MOLE-DAGBANI)

DAHAYAT A people numbering about 450,000, found mainly in the Indian state of Madhya Pradesh. They are closely related to the KOL and are Hindus. During the period of India's princely states they played an important role in civil administration and in court-related ritual.

DAI The approximately 840,000 Dai are concentrated primarily in the Yunnan Province of southwest China. They can also be found as TAI in Thailand, Burma, Laos, and Vietnam.

The Dai culture originated south of the Yangtze River in present-day south-central China some 3,000 years ago. They were forced south by Han Chinese expansionism. The Dai are closely related to the THAIS; their language is one of the Tai languages with a written form based on the ancient Indian script.

Buddhism is the predominant religion, and most young men spend some time as monks. In many villages, Buddhist temples or monasteries serve as social and religious centers. Traditional religious beliefs are also common.

The Dai live in wooden houses built on stilts. They engage mainly in plow-farming. Historical documents dating from the ninth century record the use of elephants and cattle in agriculture. The introduction of irrigation systems enabled extensive cultivation of rice.

In most respects, the Dai have maintained their distinctive ethnic characteristics, including dress, religion, and language. (see also HANI, SHAN)

DAJU A people living in Sudan, numbering an estimated 20,000. They live in the southwestern Darfur Province in the western Nuba Mountains of Kordofan Province and in isolated areas on the border with

Chad. The Daju speak an Eastern Sudanic language, which belongs to the Nilo-Saharan language family. Some speak Arabic.

The Daju are farmers and cattle-raisers. Most are Muslims, although they retain a high percentage of pre-Islamic religious beliefs and rites.

DAKARKARI A subgroup of the FULANI.

DAKOTA see SIOUX.

DAKPA A subgroup of the BANDA.

DALABON An Australian Aboriginal group living in the Northern Territory of Australia. (see also AUSTRALIAN ABORIGINES)

DAMARA A Nama-speaking group numbering 100,000, living in western Namibia. Their main occupation is agriculture. (see also NAMIBIANS)

DAMBONO An ethnic group related to the KOTA living in Gabon.

DAMELI An ethnic group living in the Chitral region of North Pakistan. No population data are available, but a rough estimation puts them at several hundred.

Their language is regarded as linking the Nurestani languages to the central subgroup of the Dardic group of Indo-Iranian languages of the Indo-European family. It is unwritten, and Urdu is used as the official language of writing and education. The Dameli belong to the Isma'ili sect of Islam and are sedentary agriculturalists.

DAMI see DIME.

DAMPELASA An ethnic group living on the Indonesian island of Kalimantan (Borneo). (see also DAYAK)

DAN (Gio) An ethnic group living in Nimba County, Liberia, where they number about 200,000, and in the extreme west of the Côte d'Ivoire, around the towns of Man and Dabane, where they number around 150,000. They mostly practice traditional religions and have resisted Islamic influence. In the Côte d'Ivoire the Dan unsuccessfully resisted French colonization in the early twentieth century. The YACOUBA are a subgroup of the Dan.

In Liberia, the Dan, known as Gio, have sided with the MANO and the KISSI against the KRAHN in that country's ongoing civil war. Many have fled to the Côte d'Ivoire and Guinea as a result of the fighting. (see also IVOIREANS)

DANAKIL see AFAR.

DANES The 5 million inhabitants of Denmark, predominantly Lutheran Protestants. Their language belongs to the Scandinavian branch of the Germanic languages. One quarter of all Danes live in Copenhagen. Modern Danes are said to descend from the tribe of Danes who, in the sixth century, arrived from Sweden and merged with the indigenous Jutes and FRISIANS. All Danish-speaking groups were unified in Denmark in the ninth century. Originally southern Sweden was part of this realm, which joined in expeditions of the Vikings who plundered the French and Spanish coasts and conquered Normandy and part of England. Danish seamen wreaked havoc on the Carolingian empire, and destroyed Celtic kingdoms in the British Isles (Danish was spoken in parts of England until the twelfth century). The pagan Germanic religion long subsisted among Danes. By the tenth and eleventh centuries, however, they finally gave in to Christianity.

In the late Middle Ages Danish power extended over Norway and Sweden as well as over Pomerania, Courland, and Estland on the Baltic coast. Later, the ethnically half German Schleswig-Holstein duchies were united under the Danish crown. The loss of Sweden in 1523 started three centuries of Danish-Swedish enmity. The adoption of Lutheranism entrenched permanent German cultural hegemony. In the mid-seventeenth century, however, disastrous wars against Sweden destroyed Danish supremacy in the Baltic for good. Danes ceased being a great power, a decline not made good even by the Danish-Norwegian union in 1720.

The Danes lost Norway to Sweden in 1815. In the nineteenth century the southern duchies of Schleswig-Holstein became bound up with the GERMANS' nationalistic aspirations. While North Schleswig had remained Danish, Holstein was becoming predominantly German. Overall, the German element was growing at the expense of the Danish. The duchies' substantial and influential German minority sought autonomy from Denmark, while the Schleswig Danes wished to thwart the germanization process. In 1864 Denmark lost the whole of Schleswig-Holstein (representing 40 percent of its territory) to Prussia. The late nineteenth century was a period of deprivation for the Danes now included in Germany, which followed a policy of germanification. Tens of thousands migrated to Denmark or overseas.

After World War I, only the Danish-populated zones of northern Schleswig reverted to Denmark after a referendum; Southern Schleswig joined Germany. Today the 50,000–60,000 (8–10 percent) Danish-identified citizens in South Schleswig are well integrated.

DANGME   see ADANGBE.

DANI   An ethnic group of some 110,000 living in the mountainous area around the Balim River in eastern Irian Jaya, the Indonesian part of the island of New Guinea. They speak various related indigenous languages. Their subsistence is largely based upon the growing of sweet potatoes and the raising of pigs. While today many Dani are practicing Christians, their traditional religious beliefs centered around the spirits of their dead. The majority of their rituals are war-related.

DANJO   A subgroup of the SEMANG.

DANOA   (Haddad) An ethnic group of forty clans totaling c.100,000, scattered throughout northern Chad. Thirty percent live in Kanem region. The Danoa have no native language and adopt the language current in the areas they inhabit. They rarely intermarry with other ethnic groups.

DANWAR   A ethnic group living in Inner Terai (Sindhuli), Terai (Sirah), and eastern hilly regions of Nepal. They are Hindus, and also worship other gods. Intercaste marriage is forbidden.

The Danwar subsist on farming, fishing, cattle breeding, and selling goats and buffalo. They are almost all illiterate.

DARASA   (Gedicho) A people numbering 500,000, who live to the east of Lake Abaya in northern Sidamo Province, Ethiopia. Their language belongs to the éastern Cushitic group and they are Sunni Muslims, with some being Ethiopian Orthodox Christians and others adherents to traditional beliefs. The Darasa are agriculturalists (grain, ensete) who also plant coffee as a cash crop. Their social and political structure was formerly characterized by clans, councils of elders, and age- and generation-grading similar to the system of the OROMO. (see also ETHIOPIANS, OROMO)

DARD   see KOHISTANI.

DARGIN   (Darghin; s.d. Dargwa) An ethnic group living in the mountains of central Daghestan, between the Caspian Sea coast and the Qaziqumukh Koisu River basin. The total number of those defined by official Soviet/Russian ethnography as Dargin is 30,000. Together with the QUBACHI and QAITAGH groups, most Dargin are Sunni Muslims of the Shafi'i school, with the exception of two *auls* (villages) which are Shi'ite. Their islamization began in the eleventh century and was completed no earlier than the sixteenth.

The Dargin language belongs to the central group of the Daghestani branch of the Ibero-Caucasian family. It has been a literary language since at least the nineteenth century. Until 1928 its alphabet was based on the Arabic script; in 1928 a new alphabet was created on the Roman base; this was changed in 1938 to the Cyrillic script.

A feudal state existed in the non-mountainous region of the Dargin ethnic territory, the Qaitagh Umitsiate (principality), which was included in the Russian empire in 1820; in the mountains there were independent clans, numbering at first four and later, by the beginning of the nineteenth century, ten. The Dargin were finally subjugated by Russia in 1844.

Dargin stone houses in the mountain regions are of the Daghestani type and possess two and more storeys; those in the lower regions have one or more storeys. The style of dress for men resembles that of other Daghestani groups (Circassian coat, felt cloak); women wear long dresses, wide trousers, and the *chikrit* headdress characteristic of mountainous Daghestan. The traditional economy is based on agriculture, horticulture, semi-nomadic sheep-breeding, cattle-breeding, and cottage industries.

DARGWA   see DARGIN, QUBACHI.

DARIBI   An ethnic group of approximately 5,000 living in the volcanic plateaus of the Purari River region of south-central Papua New Guinea. They speak an indigenous regional language. Although not affiliated with any religious belief, they fear ghosts. Their main crop is the sweet potato and they practice slash and burn cultivation.

DAROOD   A clan of the SOMALI.

DASHAN   see KACHIN.

DASSA   A subgroup of the YORUBA living in Benin.

DASSANETCH   (Geleba, Merille, Reshevat) An ethnic group numbering 35,000 (1980s), who live north of Lake Turkana in the southern Gemu Gofa Province, on the Ethiopian-Kenyan border. Their language belongs to the eastern Cushitic group and they adhere to traditional beliefs. The Dassanetch are agriculturalists (sorghum) and cattle-raisers. Their social structure is marked by age- and generation-grading.

DAUR   (Dayur) An ethnic group, estimated as numbering 100,000, inhabiting the Heilongjiang Province, Inner Mongolia, and the Xinjiang Autonomous Region in northern China.

Their Mongolian dialect preserves elements found in thirteenth-century Mongolian documents. Since the Daur live in three distinct areas, three dialects have emerged, although grammar and vocabulary have remained essentially the same. During the Qing dynasty (1644–1911) the Daur used the Manchurian script; since the 1910s they have adopted Chinese.

Prior to the seventeenth century, the Daur lived in the valleys of the Amur River. They were later resettled by the Chinese government in the Nonni River region in the south, where the majority of Daur now live.

Most Daur adhere to shamanist beliefs although some are also Tibetan Buddhists. Once nomadic woodland hunters and herdsmen, they are generally engaged now in agriculture, logging, hunting, stock-raising, and horse-breeding. Most Daur villages are populated by inter-related families, but there is a taboo on marriage between people bearing the same surname.

DAURAWA   A subgroup of the HAUSA.

DA VACH   see HRE.

DAYAK   Generic term for a wide range of ethnic groups living on the island of Borneo (Kalimantan), which is divided between Indonesia and Malaysia, who have preserved traditional religious beliefs. They are thought to number 2 million. Most engage in slash and burn cultivation of rice, fishing, hunting, and gathering.

The IBAN (Sea Dayak) are among the best known of Dayak groups. They are not in fact a coastal people but inhabit the hills adjoining the coastal region: the name Sea Dayak was given to them by the DUTCH and refers to their reputation, dating from the mid-nineteenth century, as cruel pirates. They number close to 250,000.

Dayak

The IBAN speak a Malay dialect and practice a religion based on the ritual cultivation of rice. The supreme deity, Sengalang Burong, is represented in the form of a local hawk and is associated with headhunting. As in most traditional Indonesian religions, the cult of the dead is of particular significance.

Whereas rubber is rapidly becoming an important cash crop, slash and burn cultivation of hill rice remains of unequaled importance to the social and economic as well as religious life of the IBAN. Young men also migrate to other islands in search of wealth, but they maintain strong ties with their villages and generally return.

Headhunting only stopped among the IBAN in the years following World War II. Nonetheless, warfare against neighboring peoples is still common, as is the capture and enslavement of neighboring women and children. Recent attempts by both the Indonesian government as well as Christian missionary groups have had some success in stemming these practices.

"Land Dayak" (Bidayuh) is a generic term for many small non-Muslim and non-Christian groups inhabiting the inland regions of the Malaysian province of Sarawak and the Indonesian province of West Kalimantan, located in the western half of Borneo. There are approximately 250,000 Land Dayak, divided into numerous tribes, among them the AUP, AYOU, BRANG, BUKAR, DESA, ENGKROH, ENGRAT (Mingrat), GROGO, JAGOI, KADUP, KUAP, LARA, LUNDU, MANYUKEI, MUALANG, SAMARAHAN, SARAMBAU, SAU, SEDUMAK, SELAKAN, SENNAH, SENTAH, SIBUNGO, SIDIN, SIGU, SIMPOKE, SINGGIE, and TAUP.

Each tribe has its own indigenous culture although all share common elements, including cultural influence by foreign populations such as the MALAYS, JAVANESE, and CHINESE. For many years they had been exploited by these groups, and the Land Dayak reportedly suffer from a sense of inferiority instilled in them during years of abuse. Unlike the closely related IBAN, the Land Dyak are relatively peaceful, although ritual headhunting was once common among some groups. Today they engage primarily in subsistence agriculture and in the cultivation of rubber and coffee. Iron-working is also an important occupation, as is trading for salt with the coastal peoples.

The MAANYAN DAYAK are a group living along the Patai River and its tributaries. They number about 35,000, divided into four subgroups sharing a common language and religious beliefs (Kaharingan) centering on the spirits of the dead and of nature. They engage primarily in the slash and burn cultivation of rice and fruit and in fishing. Rubber and lumber are important cash crops. Over 75 percent practice Kaharingan, and about 20 percent are Christians. There is also a small Muslim community.

"NGADJU" (Biadju, Oloh Kahayan) is used as a generic term for a group of Dayak peoples living along the rivers of southern Borneo. Groups include the BI-ADJU, BUKIT, DUSUN, KAHAYAN, KATINGAN, KOTAWARINGAN, LAWANGAN, MAANYAN, MURUNG, PATAI, SARUYAN, SIANG, SIONG, TABUYAN, TAMAN, and TAMOAN. These people are slash and burn cultivators of rice, who also engage in fishing and some hunting. They make baskets and pottery, weave, and work iron. Among the crafts engaged in are tattooing and wood carving. The NGADJU speak numerous languages and dialects and have various religious beliefs. Most groups adhere to a dualistic godhead, consisting of a male god of the heavens and a female god of the underworld.

"OT DANUM DAYAK" is used as a general designation for approximately 30,000 inhabitants of central Borneo. They are divided into several tribes, including the DOHOI, PANANJOI, and TABAHOI, but are closely related culturally. They speak mutually intelligible dialects of the same language, and share common religious beliefs, including a myth of divine origin explaining their division into different tribes. They engage in slash and burn cultivation of rice and are renowned for their rattan craftwork. Once warlike, a ceremonial peace concluded among all local Dayak groups in the 1890s is of considerable importance today for religious reasons. Some OT DANUM DAYAKS have converted to Christianity.

Due to coastal Malay influence, many Dayak have converted to Islam in recent years. Although they generally retain their traditional languages for some generations, they often call themselves "Orang Melayu" to differentiate themselves from pagan Dayak groups.

Although the Dayak are generally sedentary, there are several nomadic groups whose names are sometimes prefixed with Ot. These include, in addition to the OT DANUM DAYAK, the OT BALUI, OT MARUWEI, OT SIAU, and OT USU. Other nomadic groups include the BUNGAN-BULIT, MELATUNG, PANJAWANG, PUNAN, and PUNAN KARAHL.

DAY-KUNDI   A subgroup of the HAZARA.

DAZA   (Dazagada) A clan of the TOUBOU.

DEBBA   A subgroup of the MABA.

DEI   A Kru-speaking group living in Bomi County, Liberia. The Dei were the first people to come into contact with the AMERICO-LIBERIANS. (see also LIBERIANS)

DEKKER   A subgroup of the MABA.

DELAWARE   A Native North American group originating on the east coast of the United States, numbering today about 3,000. They now live mostly in Oklahoma, with 1,000 in Ontario, Canada.

The history of the Delaware is typical of that of North America's aboriginal peoples. After a series of violent conflicts with the BRITISH and the AMERICANS, they were forced to move to Ohio. After the War of 1812 war they were removed to the Indian Territory of Oklahoma, where they now live on the Federal Trust Area of the Delaware Indian Tribes of Western Oklahoma.

DEMONARA   A subgroup of the SOLORESE.

DENE   (Athapaskan) The Dene, numbering approximately 80,000, are one of the largest groups of Native peoples in North America. They occupy most of the Yukon Territory, central Alaska, and the western part of the Northwest Territories in Canada.

In contrast with many other Indian groups, the Dene nation has maintained its traditional way of life. Athapaskan, the Dene language, is in wide use today even among the younger generation. The Dene have been very successful in pressing their land claims against the Canadian government. The first Native member of

Parliament was a Dene woman from the Yukon Territory. (see also ATHAPASKAN)

DENKYIRA   An AKAN group living in the Western Region of Ghana. In precolonial times they had the most powerful state in the region until it was conquered by the ASHANTI in 1701.

DEORI   An ethnic group numbering 37,000 (1987), living in Arunachal Pradesh and Assam, India. They speak Tibetan, a member of the Tibeto-Burman family of languages.

The Deori are one of the four divisions of the CHUTIA, who established independent principalities in the upper regions of the Brahmaputra. They are Hindus and also worship household deities. Clan exogamy is strictly followed.

Of Mongol stock, the Deori are a riverine group. Their houses are constructed facing the river. They are pile dwellers, and a typical Deori house can accommodate more than forty persons. They are agriculturalists, and rice is their staple food.

DESA   An ethnic group living on the Indonesian island of Kalimantan (Borneo). (see also DAYAK)

DEUTSCHE   see GERMANS.

DHANGAR   An ethnic group living in Jhapa, Biratnagar, Saptari, Mahottari, and Sarlahi, in Nepal. They use the Devanagari script.

Their main occupation is agriculture but they also rear cattle and fowl. They are skilled in making cane and bamboo household utensils.

DHANKA   (Tadvi Bhil) An ethnic group numbering 255,000 (1981), living in Panch Mahals, Broach, Baroda, and West Khandesh in the states of Gujarat, Maharashtra, and Rajasthan, in India. They speak Bhili, a dialect belonging to the Indo-Aryan family of languages.

The Dhanka worship a supreme god, although they also respect local gods.

Agriculture and forest labor are the main occupations of Dhanka living in the plains. They collect forest produce such as gum, honey, and leaves of trees for making country cigars, and also collect timber from the jungle for export. Their staple food is rice and millet.

DHANWAR   (Dhanuhar) An ethnic group numbering 104,000 (1981), living in the hill country of Bilaspur in Madhya Pradesh and Maharashtra, India. They speak Kurukh, belonging to the Dravidian family of languages, and Chhattisgarhi, one of the Indo-Aryan languages.

The Dhanwar are Hindus. Their principal deities are Thakur Deo, the god of agriculture, and Dulha Deo, the god of the family and the hearth.

DHIMAL   (Maulik) A people found in northern India and in eastern Nepal. Their language belongs to the Tibeto-Burman family of languages. Mostly farmers and herders, some find employment in the tea plantations of Darjeeling.

DHUNDIA   A people numbering about 500,000, living in the state of Gujarat in western India. They engage primarily in agriculture.

DHURIA   A subgroup of the NAGESIA.

DHURWA   (s.d. Parja) An ethnic group numbering 22,000 (1961), living in the Bastar district of Madhya Pradesh, India.

The Dhurwa practice shifting cultivation and supplement their income by selling forest produce and by working as day-laborers for the local public works department. They observe no dietary restrictions beyond avoiding beef and totemic animals or plants.

Dhurwa villages in the interior are uniclan; they are isolated and have little contact with other groups. The Dhurwa do not interdine or intermarry with other tribes.

DIAGUITA   A South American Indian group who inhabited the Calchaqui Valley in Salta, the Tucumáni region of the Calchaqui and Santa Maria Valleys, and almost all of the provinces of Catamarca, La Rioja, and North San Juan in Argentine.

They appear to have been organized into chiefdoms centering on eight to ten townships. One such chiefdom, the YOCAVIL, occupying part of Santa Maria, had some ten towns on the Aconquija slopes. The PULARE inhabited the northern Calchaqui Valley (the towns of Chicoana and Atapsi, and the Lucaracatao ravine). Other ethnic subgroups such as the PACCIOCA, CHUCHUGASTA, and CAFAYATE lived between the Yocavil and the territories of the PULARE.

DIAN   An ethnic group related to the LOBI living in Burkina Faso.

DIARI An Australian Aboriginal group found in northeastern South Australia in the vicinity of Lake Eyre. They are hunters and gatherers. (See also AUSTRALIAN ABORIGINES)

DIAWONDO A small ethnic group living in Mali.

DIBONGIYA see CHUTIA.

DIDA A Kru-speaking ethnic group living in the south central Côte d'Ivoire. Many support the early twentieth-century movement of William Wade Harris, an African Christian prophet.

The traditional Dida political organization was always decentralized. They resisted colonization by the FRENCH until the end of World War I. After World War II they began cultivating cash crops such as coffee and cocoa. In the late 1950s there were ethnic tensions in this region between the Dida and DYULA and BAULE immigrants.

DIDAYI A small group of Munda-speaking farmers, numbering about 3,000, living in the Indian state of Orissa.

DIDINGA A group living in southwestern Sudan, south of the Toposa area, forming the slopes of the hills named after them. They are estimated at about 20,000 and speak a Sudanic language of the Nilotic group (Beir branch). The Didinga both herd cattle and cultivate land. Most adhere to local African beliefs.

DIDO (s.d. Tsez) An ethnic group inhabiting the mountains of northwest Daghestan, estimated as numbering 7,000. They are Sunni Muslims of the Shafi'i school, evidently since no earlier than the sixteenth century. Their language belongs to the Avar-Andi-Dido group of the Ibero-Caucasian family. It is unwritten, and Avarian is used as the literary language.

The Dido are presently undergoing a process of intensive ethnic consolidation into the AVAR grouping. Today the ethnic term "AVAR" is used by the Dido side by side with the term "Tsez" as their self-designation.

The traditional Dido tall stone house, with its two-pitch roof, shows the Georgian cultural influence. Large earrings reaching the shoulders are a specific part of Dido women's attire. The traditional economy is based on sheep-herding.

DIGARU see MISHMI.

DIGIL A clan of the SOMALI.

DIGO A subgroup of the MIJIKENDA.

DIGOR see OSSET.

DIHÁRIA (Kisan Korwa) A subgroup of the KORWA.

DIJIOKO A subgroup of the SARA.

DIMASA see BORO-KACHARI.

DIMASA-KACHARI An ethnic group numbering 40,000 (1971), found in North Kachar Hill District in Assam, India. Their language belongs to the Tibeto-Burman family of languages.

The Dimasa-Kachari belong to the Boro grouping of people which includes the BORO-KACHARI, MECH, RABHA, LALUNG, and KOCH of Assam. Their original home is believed to have been western China near the headwaters of the Yangtze and Hwang Rivers. They are Hindus.

Their main occupation is agriculture and they practice slash and burn cultivation. Plains Dimasa practice wet-land cultivation.

DIME (Dami) A small ethnic group numbering a few thousand who live to the west of the Mago River in central Gemu Gofa Province, Ethiopia. Their language is a member of the Omotic group and they adhere to traditional beliefs.

The Dime are sedentary agriculturalists (planting teff on the highlands) and cattle-raisers (in the lowlands), living in stone houses and terracing their fields. Epidemics and emigration have both taken their toll of the Dime population.

DINDE A subgroup of the SARA.

DINKA A people living in southern Sudan, estimated at about 3 million (some one-eighth of the total population of Sudan). They are considered the single largest ethnic group in the south of the country (40 percent of the population). Some Dinka live in Ethiopia and Kenya. They speak a Nilotic language, and the majority follow the traditional Dinka religion, while others have converted to Christianity.

Cattle are the basic economic unit and also enter widely into Dinka religious beliefs and customs. The importance of the Dinka in Sudan's modern history is mainly due to John Garang, a Dinka who has led the southern peoples of Sudan in a long and bloody

Dinka

war against the Sudanese government. (see also SU-DANESE)

DIOLA   (Jola) An ethnic group living around the mouth of the Casamance River in Senegal, where they number 620,000, or 9 percent of the population, and in the Fomi areas south of Bitang Bolon in the Gambia, where they number 49,000, or 7 percent of the popula-

Diola

tion. Their language, Diola, is one of six official languages in Senegal. They are mainly Christians with only a handful of Muslims dispersed among the total population.

The Diola had no centralized political framework. During the colonial period (the FRENCH occupied Senegal: the BRITISH, the Gambia) many young Diola migrated to urban centers and their traditional culture was deeply influenced by Western education, Christianity, and Islam.

Since Senegal's independence, the Diola have been prominent in a regionalist movement of peoples living in Casamance, protesting the central government's neglect of their region due to its relative seclusion (it is separated from the rest of the country by the state of the Gambia). Violent incidents have occurred sporadically since the early 1980s.

The BAINOUK and BALANTE are subgroups of the Diola. (see also GAMBIANS, SENEGALESE)

DIONKOR   (Diongor) A Nilotic-speaking ethnic group in central Chad closely related to the HADJERAY.

DIR   A clan of the SOMALI.

DIRI   An ethnic group living in the principality of Dir, in North Pakistan. No population data are available, but a rough estimation puts them at several thousand. Their language consists of several cognate dialects, one of which, Bashkarik, is used by linguists as the appelation of this language in general. It belongs to the Dardic group of Indo-Iranian languages. It is unwritten, and Urdu is used as the official language of writing and education, with Pashto used for oral communication with non-Diri.

The Diri are Sunni Muslims of the Hanafi school and are sedentary agriculturalists. Since the seventeenth century they have been under the two-level hereditary rule of a family of the Akhund-Khel Pashtun clan. The lower level consists of *khans* who belong to the ruling family, each of whom possesses his own fief and all of whom regard themselves as vassals of the head of the ruling family.

DIVARA   SEE HALE PAIKA.

DIVEHI   SEE MALDIVIANS.

DIZI   (Dizu) An ethnic group numbering 25,000 who live in the Maji mountains in southern Kefa Province, Ethiopia. They adhere to traditional beliefs. After its inclusion into the Ethiopian empire in 1898, the Dizi territory became a frontier area for dealings in ivory, slaves, and arms.

DJALLONKE see YALUNKA.

DJAMBI MALAY see BATIN.

DJANE A clan of the DJOHEINA.

DJEM A subgroup of the MABA.

DJERMA (Dyerma, Zerma, Zarma) A subgroup of the SONGHAI living along the Niger River valley from Djenne in Mali to Gaya in Niger. There are also some Djerma in the Nikki-Kandi area of Benin. They speak Djerma and are mostly Muslims.

Their common identity was strengthened by their war with the FULANI, who conquered a large part of their lands in the nineteenth century. By the end of that century, however, they had regained their territory.

In precolonial times Djerma society was composed of semi-autonomous village-states. The Djerma did not resist French colonization at the end of the nineteenth century. During the colonial period and after independence the Djerma migrated in large numbers to Ghana and the Côte d'Ivoire to seek work. (see also NIGERIENS)

DJIBOUTIANS Inhabitants of Djibouti, the former French territory of the AFAR and ISSA in East Africa, numbering approximately 450,000. The official languages of the country are Arabic and French and the population is predominantly Muslim.

The Djiboutians are composed of four main groups: AFAR, ISSA, ARABS (mostly YEMENIS), and Europeans. Most of the population is concentrated in the vicinity of the capital, Djibouti. Although some still maintain their traditional occupations, primarily cattle-herding and agriculture, the overwhelming majority are currently employed by the government or foreign companies.

Djibouti's history is one of internecine squabbles. The ISSA, constituting almost 50 percent of the population, are closely related to the SOMALI, while the AFAR, with almost 40 percent of the population, are part of a larger group of AFAR found in neighboring Ethiopia. Both countries have made territorial claims on Djibouti (since renounced). Other elements which further exacerbate the situation are the harsh climatic

conditions in this small country: 90 percent of the land is uninhabitable desert and less than 10 percent is suitable for grazing cattle; its strategic location in the Horn of Africa and its invaluable port at the entrance to the Red Sea; and French colonial policy, which favored the AFAR.

Colonization efforts by the FRENCH only began in 1862, continuing until 1900. Because of its strategic value Djibouti was long a major outpost of the French Foreign Legion, and in 1977 it became the last country in continental Africa to achieve independence. French and other European interests are still strong and almost 70 percent of the workforce is employed in providing services to FRENCH and other European nationals stationed in the country. Although the population has enjoyed a minor economic boom with the reopening of the Suez Canal in 1975, the territory shows little opportunity for serious economic development. Ethnic stability is maintained by a constitutional provision whereby the president must be an ISSA and the prime minister an AFAR, but drought, lack of development, and conflict throughout the Horn of Africa threaten this country's stability and independence.

DJIMINI An ethnic group living in the Côte d'Ivoire between the Comoe and Nzi Rivers on the southern fringe of Senufo territory. Their language is closely related to that of the SENUFO.

DJOHEINA A group of seminomadic Arab clans, numbering around 350,000, which moved to Chad from the Nile Valley in Sudan in waves of migration between the fourteenth and nineteenth centuries. The Djoheina are divided into several clans, among the most important of whom are the MISIRIE ("Egyptians") who live in the Ouadai region.

Until recently, the MISIRIE fought against neighboring groups, and many joined the guerrilla bands that operated against Chad's first president, Ngarta Tombalaye.

Other groups include: the SALAMAT ARABS living between the Chari River and Ouadai; the RIGEZAT, who extend from the the Oudai region to Sudan's Darfur region; the OULED RACHID living throughout the Batha Valley and in the southern Baguirmi region; the OULED HEMAT, found throughout the eastern part of the country; the DJANE; and the KHOZZAM. (see also CHADIANS)

DLAMINI A SWAZI clan.

A Djerma potter in Niger

DOBRUJAN TATAR   see CRIMEAN TATARS.

DOBU ISLANDERS   An ethnic group numbering a few thousand living on Dobu Island, part of an archipelago just off the southeastern coast of Papua New Guinea. Their language, which is spoken on the island as well as off by a few more thousand, is an indigenous local language.

The Dobu area is now intensely christianized and village churches are an integral part of community life. They believe in a rich mythology made up of many legends containing magical spells. Their main crop is yams and they practice slash and burn cultivation.

DODOTH   A people inhabiting the northeast region of Uganda. Their language is close to that of the KARAMOJONG and the TESO peoples and belongs to the Eastern Nilotic subgroup of the Nilo-Saharan language family.

The Dodoth are cattle-herders. Cattle are the focal point of their cultural and social life and the measurement of wealth. Political alliances and marriages are sealed with cattle. Agriculture is of secondary importance.

The kinship structure is one of patrilineal clans, which were originally exogamous. The Dodoth live in scattered settlements but not in villages. They have a broad age-set system, consisting of men, sometimes of different ages, who are initiated together. The oldest age-set is that of "elders," those who were the most influential. During the colonial era chiefs were introduced by the British.

The Dodoth were orginally part of the KARAMOJONG, whom they regard as close kin. They recognise only one remote god, Akuj, who does not intervene in everyday life. Today they are largely Christians, with a minority belonging to the Muslim faith. (see also KARAMOJONG)

DOGHOSIE   An ethnic group living in Burkina Faso.

DOGON   An ethnic group living on the Bandiagra plateau east of Mopti, in Mali. They number about 240,000, some 3 percent of that country's population. They speak a distinct language called Dogon. They mostly practice traditional religions but are slowly converting to Islam.

At the beginning of the fourteenth century the Dogon escaped the pressure of Muslim groups by build-

ing their villages on the Bandiagara cliffs between Bandiagara and Douentza.

There they developed a unique and productive system to overcome the agricultural difficulties of the region. The Dogon are also famous for their artistic abilities and their art is considered to be among the best in West Africa.

During the period of decolonization they formed their own political party but were not dominant in politics, either during decolonization or after Mali's independence. (see also MALIANS)

DOG RIB   A Native North American group numbering today about 2,500, many of whom live in an isolated community on the Mackenzie River Delta, Northwest Territories, Canada.

Many still hunt and trap, their traditional means of earning a livelihood.

DOHOI   An ethnic group living on the Indonesian island of Kalimantan (Borneo). (see also DAYAK)

DOLAGO   An ethnic group living in the mountainous central region of the Indonesian island of Sulawesi (Celebes). (see also TORADJA)

DOLGAN   (s.d. Tya-Kikhi, Sakha) The 5,500 Dolgan are the descendants of several EVENKI (Tungus) clans who adopted a dialect of the Turkic-speaking

Dolgan

YAKUT. They form the basic population of the Taymyr Autonomous *Okrug* (Province) of the Russian Federation, north of the Arctic Circle.

The Dolgan migrated from the southwest to their present area of residence in the eighteenth century. Before the 1917 Revolution they were nomadic reindeer-herders and hunters. Under the Soviet regime they were made to abandon nomadism and nowadays subsist on agriculture and dairy-farming. (see also NGANASAN, YAKUT)

DOMETE   see OMETO.

DOMINICA ISLANDERS   The people of the Commonwealth of Dominica, an independent state of the Windward Islands located in the Caribbean Sea. They number some 86,000. The island was first colonized by the FRENCH in 1727, who ceded it to the BRITISH in 1763. The majority of Dominica Islanders are descendants of African slaves brought to the island to work on the extensive coffee and sugar plantations established during French colonization. However, there also exists a significant community descended from the indigenous CARIB Indian population, who have been able to preserve their identity through the establishment of a reserve where they are able to practice their traditional lifestyle. English is the main language, with a French patois also commonly spoken. About 90 percent of the population is Roman Catholic. Agriculture and tourism constitute the island's economic mainstays.

DOMINICANS   The people of the Dominican Republic, numbering over 7 million, occupy the eastern two-thirds of the island of Hispaniola; the western third of the island is inhabited by HAITIANS. Another million Dominicans have emigrated, especially to the United States and Venezuela. In the U.S. they have formed distinct neighborhood communities in urban areas such as New York City. They speak Spanish.

Most Dominicans are Roman Catholics, but evangelical Protestants are increasing in number, especially along the eastern Samana Peninsula. Many rural Dominicans are not frequent churchgoers; compared to other Latin American nations, there are relatively few churches in rural areas.

When Columbus founded his first settlements in the "New World" on this island, he encountered large numbers of Tainos, part of the Arawak societies that also inhabited neighboring islands in the Greater Antilles. These people were reduced to virtual extinction in less than half a century as victims of introduced diseases, slaughter, hunger, harsh labor, and suicide. As the Tainos died off, the island was occupied by colonists from Spain and by slaves from Africa; the intermixing of these groups over the course of five centuries has produced the Dominican people, a Spanish-speaking mixed-race culture, which has assimilated diverse groups of immigrants from other Spanish colonies, such as the Canary Islands.

The history of the Dominicans has been marked by many periods of colonization and war. Columbus moved the administrative center of Hispaniola to Santo Domingo on the south coast in 1496. For one generation, Hispaniola was the focal point of the emerging Spanish empire in the New World, but the streambank gold deposits were depleted by the mid-1500s. For several hundred years, population was small and economic development was negligible. When the Dominican Republic gained its independence from Spain in 1821, it was occupied by Haiti almost immediately (1822–1844). Spain annexed the island again in 1861, and a second War of the Restoration was fought to regain independence in 1865. As a politically weak country, the Dominican Republic sought assistance from the United States, and even requested annexation to the United States in 1870. In fact, the United States did assume control of the the Dominican Republic on several occasions over the last century; from 1916 to 1924 U.S. troops governed the island, and as recently as 1965 U.S. Marines intervened to install a friendly government.

Between 1930 and 1961 the Dominican Republic was ruled by the military dictator, General Rafael Trujillo; he encouraged a rapid build-up of the capital city Santo Domingo (temporarily renamed Ciudad Trujillo) and also shifted populations into designated rural areas and toward the Haitian border, where tension culminated in a massacre of over 10,000 Haitian squatters in 1937. Since Trujillo's assassination, Dominican politics have been dominated primarily by long-time President Juan Balaguer, who has held the office for most of the last three decades.

The Dominican population has grown rapidly in the twentieth century (at an annual rate of between 2 and 3 percent), and has shifted dramatically towards Santo Domingo. Until the 1930s the largest percentage of the population was in the central valley region, and Santiago was the largest city; today greater Santo Domingo has over 3 million people, nearly half of the nation's total, and is five times large than greater Santiago.

In rural areas most people live in simple houses alongside unpaved roads; most frequently, rural homes are built of timber from the native "royal palm" tree, with thatched roofing also made from palm. Small garden plots are typically found alongside each rural home, providing a reliable food supply throughout the year. Few rural homes have running water; a common roadside sight is a boy fetching water with the help of a donkey. In urban areas, houses are more likely to be built of cement block walls with corrugated metal roofing. Santo Domingo, in particular, is a city of stark contrasts, with luxurious, middle-class neighborhoods, and dense squatter settlements.

DOMPU (s.d. Dou Dompu) The predominant ethnic group of the central isthmus of the island of Sumbawa, Indonesia. They number about 25,000 and are virtually all Muslims. Rice cultivation is their primary economic activity. They speak Biman.

DON COSSACKS see UKRAINIANS.

DONDO I An ethnic group living in Zimbabwe.

DONDO II An ethnic group related to the KONGO living in Congo.

DONG (also Tong, Tung, Tong-chia) The estimated 1.4 million Dong live mainly in the Guizhou, Hunan, and Guanxi Provinces of southwest China. They first appeared in China during the Sung dynasty (960–1127) and soon moved south, possibly as a result of Mongol incursions.

Dong

Their language is a member of the Zhuang-Dong group of the Sino-Tibetan family. The influence of the Han CHINESE can be seen in their extensive borrowing from Chinese and the use, until recently, of the Chinese ideographic script. In 1958, the Chinese government provided them with their own writing system based on the Roman alphabet.

The Dong economy is largely dependent on agriculture and forestry. Their major crops include rice, wheat, corn, tobacco, and cotton. The influence of other local ethnic groups such as the YAO, MIAO, and others, can be seen in their architecture. They live at intermediate elevation in houses built on pilings. Pagoda-like drum towers are usually the center of village social life and celebrations. Little is known about Dong religious beliefs.

DONGGALA An ethnic group living in the mountainous central region of the Indonesian island of Sulawesi (Celebes). (see also TORADJA)

DONGGO (s.d. Dou Donggo) An ethnic group numbering about 15,000, living in six mountain villages in the eastern part of the island of Sumbawa, Indonesia. They speak a Biman dialect and have preserved their traditional religion based on ancestor worship. Rituals center around sacred stones where the gods are believed to meet for intercourse.

Slash and burn cultivation of rice is their primary economic occupation, but wild boar and birds are also hunted. The DUTCH introduced coffee as a cash crop.

DONGOLAWI see JABELAWI.

DONGOLAWIN, DANGLA A subgroup of the NUBIANS.

DONGXIANG (Tonghsiang) The approximately 280,000 Dongxiang are concentrated primarily in the Gansu province of northwest China. While there is no adequate historical documentation to account for their origins, it is generally believed that they are descended from MONGOLIANS who converted to Islam under the influence of neighboring Muslims. Since the Buddhist majority of MONGOLIANS regarded them as religious traitors, they were forced to migrate to their present home. Historically, they were also called "Mongolian Hui Hui" (i.e., Mongolian Muslims).

Their language, a member of the Mongolian family, has borrowed extensively from Chinese. Many

Dongxiang speak Chinese, and it is commonly used in writing.

Most Dongxiang are Muslims, and that religion exercises great influence on their daily life. They engage mainly in agriculture, growing potatoes, wheat, and barley. Their lifestyle and culture have much in common with the neighboring HUI.

DORLA An ethnic group that numbered nearly 15,000 in the 1941 census, found in various locations in Madhya Pradesh, India. They are related to the KOYA of Andhra Pradesh.

The name "Dorla" is regarded as a corrupt form of the word *doralu*, a plural of *dora*, meaning a chieftain or a prominent individual. They are expert bowmen, and their main occupation is agriculture and food-gathering.

DORLA SATAM   see KOYA.

DOROSIE   (Dorobe) see LOBI.

DORZE An ethnic group numbering 45,000 (1980s) who live to the west of Lake Abaya in the eastern Gemu Gofa Province, Ethiopia. Their language belongs to the Omotic group, and they adhere to traditional beliefs. The Dorze used to be farmers (extensive terrace agriculture), merchants, and mercenaries, hiring themselves out to neighboring Ometo states.

Their social and political structure was based on clans, individual (male) competition for ranks, and elected leadership. After inclusion into the Ethiopian empire, they became urbanized, and today more than half are town-dwellers.

DOU BIMA   see BIMANESE.

DOU DOMPU   see DOMPU.

DOU DONGGO   see DONGGO.

DOU HAWU   see SAYUNESE.

DOUKHOBORS   see CANADIANS.

DREGOVICHI   see BYELORUSSIANS.

DRUZE (Arabic: Duruz; s.d. Muwahhidun, Unitarists) An ethnic-religious group living dispersed in communities in Lebanon, Syria, and Israel. Smaller groups live in Jordan, West Africa, the United States, Canada, and Latin America.

The Druze are adherents of an esoteric religion which originated during the eleventh century as a splinter from the Shi'ite Isma'ili sect. The sect was introduced by the missionary ad-Darazi who proclaimed that the ruling Fatimid sultan al-Hakim was an incarnation of God. The Druze religion contains Gnostic and other pre-Islamic influences, including a belief in the transmigration of souls.

The imposition of al-Hakim's cult failed in Egypt; the Druze were persecuted and fled to Syria, where they survived in isolated mountain enclaves near Mount Hermon and in particular Mount Lebanon, the Matn, and Shouf, regions which were also Maronite-populated. Persecuted by Muslims and Maronites, over the centuries the Druze developed a distinct cultural identity, marked by strong bonds of solidarity and a military orientation. Longstanding isolation coupled with a unique culture turned this religious group into an Arabic-speaking ethnic group. In the seventeenth century many Druze migrated to Galilee and Mount Carmel in Palestine. Their major shrines are Hasbaya in Lebanon and the grave of their prophet Shueib (Jethro) in Galilee.

Baba al-din al-Muqtana gave the Druze religion its orthodox form and created its canon of inspired letters. Soon the Druze became a closed community keeping its doctrines secret. Its deeper tenets are only known to a hierarchy of initiates, the *uqqal*, who are distinguished from the masses, the *juhhal*. Druze ethics emphasize mutual help and truthfulness vis-a-vis other Druze; Druze women enjoy greater freedom than Muslim women.

Druze history has been one not only of retrenchment and periodic self-assertion against outsiders, but also of internal violence. In the sixteenth century, the Druze supported the Ottoman conquest and were rewarded with semi-autonomous status under the Druze Ma'anid dynasty (1517–1697). From time to time Druze emirs made bids at de facto independence; subsequent Druze history is one of intermittent anti-Turkish revolts, such as under Fakr ad-Din II. From the late seventeenth until the early nineteenth century the Shihabi dynasty was predominant. In this period, the Maronites developed a feudal structure, partly under Druze overlordship. This sowed the seeds of future rivalry. Bashir II (1788–1840) temporarily succeeded in making himself independent from the Ottoman Empire, but interfactional warring weakened the Druze, while Ma-

above: Druze villagers in the Golan
below: Druze elders in Lebanon

ronites grew in numbers and strength, and gained many converts. In 1841 civil war broke out between the two groups. In 1860 a new Christian revolt for land reform in the mixed Christian-Druze Shouf region was cruelly suppressed, and 10,000 were massacred in communal violence. France sent an expeditionary force to protect the Christians and enforced a special semi-autonomous status for Christian Mount Lebanon within the Ottoman Empire. Severly repressed, the Druze had their hegemony broken, and half of them left for the Hawran in southern Syria, where they drove out the original population and continued to enjoy a measure of autonomy.

The dismemberment of the Ottoman Empire after World War I dispersed the Druze over three countries. However, in spite of their self-definition, the Druze have not sought statehood. Today as many as 200,000 Druze live in Lebanon, where, allied with the PALESTINIANS in the 1975 civil war, they were beaten by Syrian intervention. Israeli withdrawal from the Shouf region in 1983 led to Druze/Maronite massacres.

The largest Druze concentration dwells in Syria (300,000, or 3.5 percent of the country's population). In 1920 Jabal al-Duruz (the Druze Mountain) was organized by France as a separate state led by the al-Atrash family. An anti-French revolt mixing Druze particularism with pan-Arabism was suppressed in 1925–1927. In the 1930s the Druze territory was finally integrated in Syria, but the region remained neglected. However, Druze youth succeeded in advancing through the army hierarchy.

Israel's 70,000 Druze live mainly in the Galilee and on Mount Carmel. They serve in the Israeli army and police, and by throwing in their lot with the JEWS have won better treatment than Muslim or Christian ARABS. Alienation is nevertheless noticeable in the younger generation, some of whom see themselves as ARABS of the Druze religion. (see also ISRAELIS, LEBANESE, PALESTINIANS, SYRIANS)

DUAISH   A subgroup of the MAURE.

DUALA   An ethnic group living in the coastal area of Cameroon. They are mostly Christians, and their language, Duala, was used by missionaries in the area as the lingua franca for the coastal peoples of Cameroon. In the precolonial period the Duala were middlemen in the slave trade with the Europeans.

In the late nineteenth century the Duala king, as the representative of all the peoples in the region, signed a treaty allowing Germany to annex all of Cameroon. After World War I the Duala territory came under French rule. During the colonial period the Duala sold some of their lands to BAMILEKE and to Europeans and, since independence, they have gradually lost economic and political power in their region.

DUANE   A Mon-Khmer group living in Vietnam and Laos. They are often identified with the JEH, MENAM, NOAR, and SAYAN.

DUBLA   An ethnic group numbering 500,000 (1981), found in the states of Gujarat, Goa, Karnataka, Maharashtra, and the union territory of Daman and Diu, in India. They speak Bhili and Tibetan, languages belonging to the Indo-Aryan and the Tibeto-Burman groupings respectively. Most are Hindus.

A long period of oppression by Rajput and other outlaws, as well as high taxes, brought the Dubla to such a state of indebtedness that they could be sold by one landowner to another. Their plight attracted Mahatma Gandhi's attention and led to the de jure abolition of agricultural serfdom in 1923. Most Dubla now live by agricultural labor.

DUFF ISLANDERS   A Polynesian-speaking ethnic group numbering several hundred, who inhabit a chain of small volcanic islands which form part of the Solomon Islands. The principal island is Taumako.

DUGBATANG   see ATA.

DUKKAWA   A subgroup of the FULANI.

DULANGON   see COTABATO MANOBO.

DUMA   A subgroup of the KARANGA.

DUMBUSEYA   A Shona-speaking group of unknown origins living in the Zwishaware region of Zimbabwe. They descend from refugee SHONA who fled the NGUNI in the 1830s.

DUNGAN   see HUI.

DUONG   A subgroup of the SEMANG.

DURRANI   A subgroup of the PASHTUN.

DURUMA   A subgroup of the MIJIKENDA.

DURU-VERRE   An ethnic group living in Cameroon.

DUSHMAN-ZIARI   One of four tribes comprising the MAMASAN.

DUSUN   (s.d. Tuhun Ngaavi, Kadazan) A people numbering around 400,000 living in the Malaysian province of Sabah on the island of Kalimantan (Borneo), where they constitute the largest single ethnic group. They continue to practice their traditional religion, although contact with the federal Malaysian government has brought them increasingly closer to Islam. They engage primarily in the cultivation of rice, although techniques differ according to geographical conditions. They also raise water buffalo, pigs, chickens, and ducks.

The Dusun have had considerable contact with CHINESE, INDIANS, and MALAYS, who have come as traders to the island for over 2,000 years. Rule by the Buddhist state of Srivijaya, the Hindu state of Majapahit, Catholic Portugal, and Protestant Britain have all affected the established cultural norms. Today, Malaysia is the dominant cultural influence, and Malay norms are being imposed on the Dusun. (see also DAYAK)

DUTCH   (s.d. Nederlanders) The 15 million Dutch live in the Netherlands, one of the world's most densely populated countries. Standard Dutch is a West Germanic language derived from the dialect of Holland, with strong Flemish and Brabantine influences. Counting the FLEMINGS of Belgium, Dutch is spoken by over 20 million people. The FRISIANS of the northern Netherlands speak a separate language. The Dutch used to be rather homogeneous ethnically, but fragmented religiously. The Protestants (themselves divided over a large number of churches and sects), who now represent some 31 percent of the population, have traditionally been dominant, but are now outnumbered by Catholics (38 percent); the remaining third of the population is distributed among a wide variety of denominations.

The "Old" minorities, Huguenots and JEWS (most of the latter perished in World War II), were those who had fled to the Netherlands to escape religious persecution. In recent decades, SPANIARDS, PORTUGUESE, TURKS, INDONESIANS MOROCCANS, SURINAMESE, and West Indians have constituted new minorities:

these already account for 6.5 percent of the population of the Netherlands.

There are marked regional differences among the Dutch, with Holland proper dominating economically and culturally. Cosmopolitan Amsterdam contrasts with conservative Zealand and Overijssel.

The Dutch descend from three West Germanic populations, FRISIANS, Franks, and Saxons, who in the eighth century adopted Christianity. The Dutch remained an undefined collection of fiefs of the Holy Roman Empire until attached, in the fifteenth century, to the Burgundians' burgeoning territories. Under the Habsburgs, absolutism, religious persecution of Protestants, and economic exploitation triggered a successful anti-Spanish revolt which gave rise to the United Provinces, the Dutch political entity, in 1579.

The Dutch built their prosperity on mercantile shipping in Scandinavia and profited from the shift of trade routes from the Mediterranean to the Atlantic to create a network of colonies in the East and West Indies. The influx of a Flemish cultural elite helped make the seventeenth century Holland's Golden Age, when art, science, and tolerant humanistic thought flourished despite Calvinist intolerance.

Spain succeeded in restoring Catholicism to the southern Dutch provinces, which became part of the Netherlands in 1648. The Rhine-Meuse delta has since remained a major divide between the Catholic south and the Protestant north.

By the end of the seventeenth century the Dutch had lost their great power status. Economic revival later in the nineteenth century precipitated internal social tensions. Together with the emancipation of the Catholics, these developments gave birth to a unique arrangement of four "pillars": Protestant, Catholic, liberal, and socialist, which were in fact complex, closed subcultures, each with its separate parties, schools, trade unions, media, etc. Cross-contact was minimal, and allocations were decided by negotiations and compromises between each pillar's elites. This power-sharing system survived until the 1960s.

The 1970s saw the influx of 500,000 foreign workers, who created a conglomerate of minorities. Although racist antiforeigner movements such as those manifested in neighboring countries have hardly taken root among the indigenous Dutch, integration cannot be said to have been very successful to date.

DUWABLAS   A subgroup of the KUBU.

DUWAMISH   A small Native North American Salishan-speaking group, living today in northwest Washington, U.S.A. Many members earn their living in the forest industry, supplemented by fishing in the summer months.

DYAWARA   An ethnic group living in Mali.

DYE   A subgroup of the SOMBA.

DYERMA   see DJERMA.

DYULA   The designation of a group of MANDINKA spread over a large part of the West African savanna, whose occupation is trade. Their language, Dyula, is the common trade language in most of West Africa, and the word itself means "itinerant trader" in that language. The Dyula are Muslims. The term "Dyula" is often used to describe all Muslim traders of whatever ethnic or cultural background.

In pre-colonial times their commercial networks stretched from Senegal to Nigeria and from Timbuktu in Mali to the northern Côte d'Ivoire. When European powers began to colonize West Africa, the Dyula expanded into the new towns that were built in the coastal area.

E

EAST TIMORESE   The inhabitants of the former Portuguese colony of East Timor and the enclave of Oe-cussi surrounding the capital, Dili, which was annexed by Indonesia in 1975. They are primarily Roman Catholics, and religion has played an important role in the emergence of a national identity distinguishing them from other ethnic groups (and sometimes members of the same ethnic group) living in the western half of the island.

The TETUM and ATONI are the predominant ethnic groups in East Timor. Unlike the peoples of neighboring islands, they are of Austronesian descent and speak Austronesian languages. They also differ from other neighboring groups in that they are overwhelmingly Catholic, the result of over 350 years of Portuguese colonization. During the period of decolonization, the East Timorese fiercely opposed Indonesian annexation of their territory, preferring to establish an independent state there. The population, once estimated at about 1 million, has been radically reduced as a result of an ongoing civil war between militant secessionists and Indonesian government forces.

EBRIE   An ethnic group living along the Ebrie Lagoon near Abidjan, the capital of the Côte d'Ivoire. They are mostly Christians.

The Ebrie were forced to the coastal area by the AGNI in the mid-eighteenth century. Although they never had a centralized political framework, their inclusive political unit being the village, they are now well integrated into the Côte d'Ivoire's modern economy and society. (see also IVOIREANS)

ECUADORIANS   The people of Ecuador, the fourth smallest country in South America, numbering more than 11 million. Nearly 80 percent of the population are Indians or *mestizo* (mixed Indian and European — mainly SPANIARDS). About one tenth of the population is of African origin, brought as slaves to work on tropical plantations in the coastal region. Only 10 to 15 percent of Ecuadorians are of European, mainly Spanish, origin, since Ecuador never attracted significant European immigration. There is a certain percentage of mulattoes (mixed African and European) and a larger percentage of *montuvios* (mixed Indian and African) along the coast. The division between white, *mestizo,* and Indian is drawn according to linguistic, socio-economic, and cultural criteria. The Spanish-speaking upper and middle class, the western-oriented part of the population, regardless of ethnic origin, is considered white. *Mestizos* are bilingual (mainly Spanish and Quechua), middle or lower middle class, and bi-cultural. The Indian part of the population speaks mainly Quechua (the language of the Inca empire that conquered the area in the second half of the fifteenth century) and Amazonian Indian languages.

More than half the population resides in the Sierra (Andean highlands between the Cordillera Occidental and the Cordillera Oriental) at altitudes of up to 9,000 ft., while the second largest group (around 46 percent) lives in the coastal plain. The rest, almost all Indians, lives in the Oriente region — the Andean eastern slopes and the Amazon basin. In this area the major groups are the AUSHURI and the JIVARO, the latter famous for using blowpipes with poisoned darts and for their custom of shrinking the heads of enemies killed in war. A tiny minority of Ecuadorians (0.5 percentage) lives in the Galápagos Islands, known locally as the Archipiélago de Colón.

Ecuadorian coastal Indian tribes such as the PUNA, ESMERALDA, and HUANCAVILCA and their mountain counterparts, the CARA, QUITU, and PURUHA, preserved a certain measure of cultural identity within the Inca empire. In 1525 the Inca emperor Huayna Capac divided his realm between his two sons, Huascar, who received the south (the territories of modern Peru and Bolivia), and Atahualpa, who received the northern kingdom of Quito. Although Atahualpa won the ensuing civil war,

above: An Ecuadorian mother and child
below: A market in Quito, Ecuador

he was captured and put to death by his allies, Spanish *conquistadores* under Francisco Pizarro, after having converted to Catholicism (1533). Atahualpa's death enabled the Spanish to assume control over the country and to establish themselves as the ruling classes. The city of San Francisco de Quito was founded in 1534 over Indian ruins; Guayaquil was founded in 1535. The *audiencia* of Quito became part of the viceroyalty of Peru but in the eighteenth century its administration was transferred to the viceroyalty of Nueva Granada, centered in Bogotá.

Ecuadorian demands for independence were first heard in Quito in 1809. In the ensuing struggle against Spain the territory of Quito's *audiencia* was finally liberated by Bolívar's army in the Battle of Pichincha (1822) and incorporated as the southern department of the republic of Gran Colombia. In 1830 it seceded and became the republic of Ecuador.

Since then the Ecuadorians have suffered from a series of dictatorships, military interventions, political turmoil and limited democracy during most of the past century. Despite the separation of church and state, attained by the liberals at the beginning of this century, and a certain degree of modernization, socio-economic cleavages still divide Ecuadorians. The Indians masses remain particularly indigent with many working small plots of land on large *haciendas* (farms), where they are paid very little. Even those who own some land in the Andes Mountains only subsist with difficulty. Free agricultural communities founded in colonial times own the least fertile lands, which have since become exhausted. Whereas some Indians migrate to the cities to improve their lot, they generally converge on the poorest urban sectors, furthering social and cultural problems. Modernization, agricultural exports (fruit, cocoa, and coffee), mineral exploitation, and petroleum have brought some prosperity to the country, but social pressures have produced populist politics and conservative and military reactions.

In 1979 Ecuador adopted a democratic constitution: elections have been held regularly since then. However, as in other Andean countries, the onerous combination of historic, ethnic, and socio-economic divisions have encumbered the emergence of a strong national identity.

EDANADAN CHETTI   A small ethnic group found in the southern Indian state of Kerala. They are primarily agriculturalists.

EDDA   A subgroup of the IBO.

EDIYE   see BUBI.

EDO   An ethnic group living in the Bendel State, Nigeria. (see also NIGERIANS)

EESTLASED   see ESTONIANS.

EFIK   A subgroup of the IBIBIO.

EGBA   A YORUBA subgroup living around the Nigerian capital, Lagos. Mostly Christians, they were the first YORUBA people to have contacts with European missionaries.

Following a civil war among the YORUBA in the early nineteeth century, the Egba migrated from the city of Ibadan and formed a kingdom in their present homeland. Their loss of independence to the BRITISH in 1914 was followed by a disastrous failed revolt in 1918.

Because of their proximity to Lagos, many Egba have become successful businessmen.

The CHABA, ITSHA, KETU, MANAGO, and MANIGRI of Benin are subgroups of the Egba. (see also YORUBA)

EGEDE   An ethnic group living in Nigeria.

EGER-UTAKAI   A subgroup of the ADYGHEANS.

EGGAN   A subgroup of the TIV.

EGYPTIANS   (s.d. Misriyyun) Densely concentrated in the Nile Valley and Delta of North Africa, the 55 million Egyptians constitute the largest Arab nation. They speak a particular Arabic dialect and are predominantly Sunni Muslims (90 percent). The remainder are adherents of the Coptic Church, a Christian denomination described as monophysite, i.e., attributing a single nature to Jesus and emphasising his divinity.

Copts live in Upper Egypt, Asyut, and Luxor, and in Cairo and Alexandria. As an endogamous group, the Copts have best preserved the Hamitic strain of the ancient Egyptians, and bear a close physical resemblance to them. Since the eighteenth century a handful of Copts accepted Catholic dogma, organizing themselves in a uniate church. Although many Copts were traditionally financial inspectors in the civil service, managers of tax farms, and bankers, most have remained poor, and there have been complaints of discrimination at the hands of the Muslim majority.

Roughly 200,000 NUBIANS lived between Aswan in southern Egypt and the Dongola region in Sudan be-

above: An Egyptian operating a traditional water pump near the Nile river
below: Egyptians on a traditional boat (falucca) on the Nile River

fore being resettled near Kom Ombo when Lake Nasser was flooded. They converted to Christianity in the sixth century, then to Islam in the fourteenth century. Smaller ethnic groups include the non-Arab nomadic BEJA along the Sudanese border and BERBERS in the Siwa oasis in the Western Desert.

Despite a remarkably high birthrate — Egypt's population grows by one million every nine months — population control campaigns have little effect. Forty-three percent of the population is still rural, and villagers moving to the city often retain their rural-type networks. Thus Cairo, with 10 million inhabitants, is the very prototype of the overcrowded Third World megalopolis. Housing shortages have forced one million inhabitants to seek shelter in Cairo's cemeteries, aptly called the "City of the Dead." The capital links the two inhabitable parts of the country, the Delta and the Nile Valley (the remaining 97 percent of Egypt is desert). The Aswan Dam, completed in 1971, has created a water reserve which precludes future droughts, permits perennial irrigation, and has enabled a 30–40 percent increase in cultivation. Cotton remains a major export.

Despite strenuous efforts to increase productivity and income, Egypt's burgeoning population has to make do with ever less. The economy is reliant on the Suez Canal and the remittances of two million citizens working abroad; Egypt has long become an importer rather than an exporter of food and is reliant on foreign wheat.

Since the unification of Upper and Lower Egypt (c.3100 B.C.E.) the country was ruled by a succession of thirty dynasties. These pre-Arab Pharaonic Egyptians spoke a Hamitic African language with strong Semitic influences. Their hieroglyphic script already appeared with the first dynasty.

After a long, rather self-contained history, Egypt finally succumbed to more powerful neighbors, in the last millennium B.C.E. Assyrians, PERSIANS, GREEKS, and Romans each contributed to the current heterogeneity of the population as they conquered and settled the prosperous Nile region. Some communities were assimilated into the local culture; others, notably GREEKS and JEWS, formed important diaspora communities in Alexandria and other cities.

The final decline of ancient Egypt's rich culture came with the advent of Christianity in the fourth century. Temples were closed, hieroglyphic texts were abandoned, and Greek became the official and administrative language. Still, the language of ancient Egypt has been preserved until today in Coptic, used mainly as a liturgical language but still spoken in some remote villages in Upper Egypt and written in a variant Greek script.

With the division of the Roman Empire into Eastern and Western realms, Egypt found itself under the rule of the Byzantines. However, corruption, steep exactions of tax farmers from the peasantry, and persecution of monophysites, all nourished resentment against Constantinople. Most of Egypt's Christians therefore welcomed the Arab conquest of the country in 641 as a means of liberating themselves from an oppressive regime.

The subsequent process of islamization constituted the biggest rupture and cultural discontinuity in Egyptian history. The Mediterranean economic circuit was interrupted and Egyptian history became intertwined with that of the Muslim world. Large-scale immigration of the invaders stimulated steady arabization: Arabic became the official language in the eighth century; Coptic went out of daily use by c.1000.

Despite expectations to the contrary, taxation continued to be heavy during the Umayyad and Abbasid caliphates. But several Coptic revolts were harshly suppressed and Islam had established itself as the dominant religion by the eighth century, promoted, to some degree, by partial tax exemptions for Muslims. Under the Tulunid dynasty (868–905) Egypt enjoyed a brief spell of independence, but Egypt's heyday came under the Shi'ite Fatimid dynasty (969–1171), which founded Cairo as their administrative capital. Salah ad-Din (Saladin; 1137–1193), a Kurd who defeated Crusader kingdoms in Syria and Palestine, established the succeeding Ayyubid dynasty and restored Sunni orthodoxy. In 1250 Mamelukes (Turkish slave-praetorian soldiers) took power. Transit trade between Mediterranean Europe and the Red Sea was stimulated by the crusades, but suddenly ruined by the discovery in 1498 of the Cape of Good Hope route. In 1516, the Ottomans conquered Egypt, beginning three centuries of neglect during which the irrigation canals from the Nile fell into disrepair and the country was reduced to poverty.

Soon after Napoleon Bonaparte's invasion of Egypt in 1798, Muhammad Ali (1769–1849), a Macedonian general of Albanian descent seized power and seceded, for all practical purposes, from the Ottoman Empire. He undertook an ambitious program of modernizing the administration, army, educational system, and economy. Egypt's traditional agriculture, based on the inundation of fields with Nile waters, was progressively brought under control by a system of canals, permitting the introduction of cotton production and industries. He also laid the groundwork for the digging of the Suez Canal, but when it was opened in 1869 the project's exorbitant cost had ruined Egypt's finances and brought the country under British influence. Nationalist anti-British incidents promoted by the military and intellectuals only served to entrench British hegemony; Britain occupied Egypt in 1882 to protect the flow of cheap Egyptian cotton to British textile factories.

Nonetheless, popular discontent continued to be expressed in the demands of the nationalist opposition for the departure of the British troops, the installation of a parliament, and independence. Although Britain officially suspended its protectorate after World War I, in effect it retained control, provoking further pan-Arab and Egyptian nationalism in the 1930s.

The defeat of the Egyptian army by Israel in 1948 undermined the prestige of the monarchy. In 1952 a group of Free Officers seized power, deposed the king, and declared a republic. Under Gamal Abdel Nasser, Egypt acquired the trappings of a one-party system, but the nationalization of industries and businesses led to the emigration of large and economically important minority communities of GREEKS and JEWS. Having obtained the departure of British troops, in 1956 Nasser nationalized the Suez Canal, provoking a three-pronged attack by France, Britain, and Israel. In the June 1967 war Egypt lost the Sinai peninsula to Israel; the ensuing war of attrition along the Suez Canal led to the wholesale depopulation of canal cities.

Nasser's successor, the pragmatic and pro-Western Anwar as-Sadat, opened war on Israel in October 1973; but later became the first Arab head of state to conclude a peace treaty with Israel as well. The Suez Canal, closed since 1967, was reopened in 1975, promising a brighter economic future for Egypt, but Sadat's peace accord with Israel earned him the enmity of other Arab states. He was assassinated in 1981 by Muslim fundamentalists opposed to peace with Israel. By the late 1980s, under Hosni Mubarak, ties with other Arab states were restored and the 1990–1991 Persian Gulf crisis enabled Egypt to regain its leading role in the Arab world.

Egyptians have a well-established intellectual reputation and provide the Arab world with religious and secular publications, novels, movies, and radio broadcasts. The growth of Islamic and Coptic militancy, however, has increased domestic tensions and threatens continued peaceful communal coexistence. Currently, radical fundamentalist groups are threatening Egypt's social fabric. (see also ARABS)

EHOTILE   An Akan-speaking group living in the Côte d'Ivoire.

EHOUE   An ethnic group numbering about 33,000 living in the Mono Region of Togo.

EINALLU   (Inanlu) A subgroup of the KHAMSE.

EIPO   An ethnic group numbering a few thousand living in central Irian Jaya, the Indonesian part of the island of New Guinea. Their indigenous language consists of three dialects. They are fervent believers in the presence of mythical, often monstrous, figures. Their subsistence is based upon the cultivation of various fruits and vegetables.

EJAGHAM   A subgroup of the IBIBIO.

EKITI   A subgroup of the YORUBA living in Nigeria.

EKKPAHIA   A subgroup of the IBO.

EKO   A subgroup of the YORUBA living in Nigeria.

EKOT   An ethnic group living in Cameroon.

EKURI   A subgroup of the IBIBIO.

ELEKE BEYE   see NEGIDAL.

ELGEYO   (Keyo) A Kalenjin-speaking group occupying a narrow strip of land on the western bank of the Kerio River in Kenya. Numbering over 245,000, they constitute about 1 percent of that country's population. Most of them live in the Elgeyo-Marakwet District, an area ranging in altitude from 3,500 to 8,500 feet and surrounded by a forest belt.

The Elgeyo practice mixed farming, growing maize, groundnuts, coffee, wheat, pawpaws, and bananas, and keep cattle, goats, and sheep. Cattle are particularly valued in their culture, although their land was never suitable for herding. Their methods of cattle husbandry are similar to those of the NANDI.

Due to the lack of traditional employment opportunities during their warrior years, a large percentage of young Elgeyo men joined the colonial police and army. (see also KALENJIN)

EL'KAN BEYENIN see NEGIDAL.

ELLENOI see GREEKS.

ELSAESSER see ALSATIANS.

EMBU A people living in the Embu province of Kenya, on the south eastern slopes of Mount Kenya. Their language, Embu, links them with other Central Bantu-speaking peoples of East Africa.

They are estimated to number about 350,000. Most Embu are Christians, belonging to either European denominations or African Independent Churches.

Embu

Oral tradition is a very developed and important part of Embu culture. According to legend, they are descendants of a brother and sister who committed incest and were expelled from their home. They founded a new home and their children became the "children of Embu."

Their main economic pursuit is agriculture. Good agricultural land ranges in altitude between 4,000 and 7,000 feet and consists of volcanic soils. Coffee, tea, and pyrethrum are the main cash crops grown, while maize, beans, cabbage, and other vegetables are cultivated as food crops.

ENCASSAR see SAHWI.

ENDE (s.d. Ata Ende) An ethnic group numbering about 50,000, living in the central region of the Indonesian island of Flores. They speak a Western Austronesian language related to the Bima language.

Two culturally distinct groups of Ende can be discerned: coastal and mountain Endenese. The former, numbering about 25,000, were influenced by the Islamic JAVANESE who arrived on their island in the sixteenth and seventeenth centuries. They are virtually all Muslims, and both Javanese and Portuguese elements are noticeable in their culture. Mountain Ende, due to their remote habitat, have preserved their traditional religion and culture.

The Ende engage primarily in slash and burn cultivation of rice and corn. Coconuts are raised as a cash crop and there are some domestic animals.

A short-lived Ende sultanate was established by the DUTCH toward the end of the eighteenth century to protect their interests on Flores from the PORTUGUESE.

ENDO A subgroup of the MARAKWET.

ENENGA An Omyene-speaking group living in the area around Lake Zile, Gabon. They are divided among Christians and adherents of traditional religions.

ENGGANESE (s.d. Etaka) The indigenous inhabitants of the island of Enggano in Indonesia. Diseases introduced by European traders resulted in a sharp decline in the island's native population in the mid-nineteenth century. Whereas in the 1860s they numbered about 6,500, today there are only a few hundred. Currently other groups dominate the island, which has since been declared a rehabilitation center for juveniles from other parts of Indonesia. The decimation of the Engganese is reflected in loss of their traditional religion and Islam. Christianity, introduced in 1902, is now the predominant religion. Similarly, agriculture was all but abandoned, with woodwork and trade being contemporary economic staples.

ENGKROH An ethnic group living on the Indonesian island of Kalimantan (Borneo). (see also DAYAK)

ENGLISH A people of 44 million living in England in the British Isles. Descendants of the English can also be found in former territories and dependencies of the British Empire around the globe. In England, the population is very urbanized and density is high. Major centers include London and other big cities in the plains and the mining and industrial regions of Lancashire and Yorkshire. The majority of English adhere to the Anglican Church. They speak English, a language belonging to the West Germanic group of Indo-European languages, but heavily influenced by the languages of the various peoples who conquered and settled in England in the past.

The English population is descended from a fusion of the original Celtic population with a succession of invaders throughout the first millennium C.E. Roman colonization brought Christianity in its wake. In the fifth and sixth centuries Germanic invasions from Denmark led to the settlement of Jutes and Angles in Kent and in East Anglia-Northumbria-Mercia, and of Saxons in Sussex and Essex (and thence to Middlesex and Wessex). The settlers brought their language with them; old English derived directly from Saxon. The Celts found refuge in Wales (where Gaelic has maintained itself) and Cornwall (where it died out two hundred years ago). In 1066 a Norman invasion under William the Conqueror (c.1028–1087) imposed feudalism and opened the country to French cultural influence, including on the English language.

The Plantagenet kings (1154–1399) developed a centralized monarchy, but were forced to share sovereignty with their subjects as represented by Parliament. In 1215 John Lackland (1167–1216) signed the Magna Carta, which laid the ground for a tradition of respect for civil liberties and equality before the law. Parliament had power to impeach the highest-placed, and on occasion even deposed the king. In time the House of Commons (representing the gentry and urban interests, and responsible for taxation) became more powerful than the semi-independent magnates and bishops in the House of Lords.

In the Middle Ages, the basis was laid for future English prosperity: serfdom was abolished, the expansion of sheep-breeding boosted the manufacture and trading of fabrics, and trade passed from foreigners (JEWS, GERMANS, and ITALIANS) into English hands. In 1534, after Henry VIII failed to obtain papal approval of his divorce, the Tudor monarchy broke with Rome and imposed a national English religion, Anglicanism, a unique amalgam of Protestant theology and Catholic liturgy. The Glorious Revolution of 1688 eliminated the possibility of a Catholic succession to the throne and created a constitutional monarchy. Parliament had become the real master of politics.

The English became the world's leading merchants, expanding colonial possessions, penetrating Spanish America, and gaining a monopoly on the lucrative slave traffic. England became the cradle of industrial capitalism and the center of the world's largest colonial empire. From 1750 the industrial revolution led to a rapid increase in both population and urbanization so that England was the world's most industrialized nation throughout most of the nineteenth century. At the same time, however, the unfettered expansion of crude capitalism resulted in substandard living conditions for the working classes. This gave rise to trade unions and labor movements, which became one of the driving forces of political reform. The parliamentary franchise was broadened to first the middle classes, and subsequently the working classes.

In the late nineteenth century English industrial productivity trailed behind the AMERICANS, GERMANS, and JAPANESE. Colonial disengagement, particularly after World War II, gradually reduced England to medium power status. In the 1950s and 1960s, successive Labor governments created a "capitalist welfare state," paid for by nationalizations and high taxes.

Since the late 1970s the consensus was broken by a rightist backlash against permissiveness, unemployment, trade unions, and immigration. The emancipation of the colonies resulted in an influx of more than one million IRISH, INDIANS, PAKISTANIS, Caribbean islanders, Africans, etc. Concentrated in the poorest quarters of the largest cities, their presence often provoked ethnic riots — in particular where ethnic tension mixed with social unrest. (see also BRITISH, SCOTS, WELSH)

ENGRAT (Mingrat) An ethnic group living on the Indonesian island of Kalimantan (Borneo). (see also DAYAK)

ENNAKOR A subgroup of the GURAGE.

ENNEMOR A subgroup of the GURAGE.

ENT (s.d. Enete) Numbering about 100, the Ent are the remainder of a larger population in north and central Siberia in the Russian Federation which has been assimilated by the NENETS, SELKUP, DOLGANS, and RUSSIANS. The Ent language belongs to the Samoyedic group of the Uralic family of languages and is closely related to Nenets and Nganasan. It has no alphabet and Russian is used as the literary language.

EPAN A subgroup of the RHADÉ.

EQUATORIAL GUINEANS A people living in the island of Bioko and in Rio Muni on the central African mainland. Although they are estimated to number only about 350,000, the ethnic composition is unusually complex. In Rio Muni the predominant group is the FANG, while in Bioko, the BUBI are the original inhabitants. Other smaller ethnic groups in Equatorial Guinea include the BAYELE, the LENGI, and the BUJEBA, and there is a small population of PYGMIES in northern Rio Muni. In recent years, continental Rio Munians, mainly FANG, flocked to Bioko where they now dominate the civil and military services. Whereas the official language of Equatorial Guinea is Spanish, in Rio Muni the lingua franca is Fang while in Bioko it is Bubi. Around 94 percent of the Equatorial Guineans are Catholic. They became independent from Spain in 1968.

The political life of Equatorial Guinea has been characterized since the colonial period by sharp ethnic cleavages and regional conflicts mainly between the FANG of Rio Muni and the BUBI of Bioko. The BUBI, who are less numerous, underwent a process of westernization and modernization during the colonial period as a result of considerable investments by the SPANIARDS in the development of their region. As independence neared, the pro-Spanish BUBI came to fear domination from the more politically active but underdeveloped FANG and formed a separatist movement. Their efforts to establish a separate state failed however, and in 1968 a leader of the FANG, Francisco Macias Nguema, became Equatorial Guinea's first president. During his brutal dictatorship, which lasted until 1979, about one-third of the population fled the country. Although the BUBI saw his rule as a FANG takeover, his persecutions were not aimed only at the BUBI, and many members of his own ethnic group suffered during his rule. Even after Nguema was deposed in a military coup, the FANG continued to dominate political life in the country. The regime, while somewhat more moderate, continued to be dictatorial.

ERAVALLAN (Villu Vedan) An ethnic group numbering about 1,000 living in the southern Indian states of Kerala and Tamil Nadu. They speak a Dravidian dialect and have preserved their traditional religion. They subsist on hunting and, increasingly, farming.

ERIE A Native North American group numbering no more than a few hundred, living in Oklahoma. At the time of contact the Erie were a large group dwelling around southwest Lake Erie, but they were almost entirely exterminated by warriors of the IRO-QUOIS CONFEDERACY. The few survivors were taken in by the CONESTOGA and the SENECA.

ERITREANS The 2.6 million inhabitants (1984) of Eritrea which became independent from Ethiopia in 1993. The Eritreans consist of nine ethno-linguistic groups: RASHA'IDA, BARIA, KUNAMA, BEJA, TIGRE, TIGRAY, BILIN, SAHO, and AFAR. Two of these groups (TIGRAY, AFAR) can also be found in Ethiopia.

The Eritrean People's Liberation Front (EPLF) fought a thirty-year war for independence from Ethiopia, claiming a long legacy of self-government. This was true, to some degree, for the small population of the harbor city of Massawa, which since the late sixteenth century was loosely attached to the Ottoman empire. However, a distinct Eritrean entity only emerged during the period of Italian colonization (1885–1942). Eritrea only became an Ethopian province in 1962, however, the Muslim and Tigrinya-speaking majorities did not acquiesce to the politics of Amhara cultural and political dominance, a factor which contributed considerably to Eritrean nationalism. Massive Ethiopian military offensives against Eritrean guerrillas between the years 1977 and 1978 caused more than 500,000 Eritreans to flee the region, mainly to the Sudan, and unwittingly popularized the national cause. In 1991 the EPLF, the EPRDF (Ethiopian People's Revolutionary Democratic Front) and the TPLF (Tigray People's Liberation Front) agreed on Eritrea's de facto independence, which was recognized by the Ethiopian government after a referendum in 1993. (see also ETHIOPIANS)

ERSARY A subgroup of the TURKMEN.

ERZYA The eastern subgroup of the MORDVIN.

ESA An ethnic group related to the EDO living in Nigeria.

ESHIRA (Echira, Shira) A Bantu people living along the Atlantic coast of southwest Gabon. They number about 250,000 and constitute about one fifth of Gabon's total population. They speak Eshira.

ESKIMO see INUIT, GREENLANDERS.

ESMERALDA A Native South American group living in Ecuador.

ESPAGNOLES see SPANIARDS.

ESTONIANS (s.d. Eestlased) There are about 1.5 million Estonians, the overwhelming majority of whom live in Estonia and adjacent areas in Latvia and Russia. Sizable communities in western Europe and North America date back to the two world wars and their aftermath.

The Estonian language belongs to the Finnic branch of the Uralian languages and is mutually intelligible with Finnish. It has three distinct dialects: the northern, which is the most widely spoken, the southern, and the northeastern, which is closest to Finnish. Both northern and southern dialects of Estonian have been written (in the Roman alphabet) since the thirteenth century, however, the current literary language, which emerged in the nineteenth century, is based solely on the northern dialect.

Although closely related ethnically and linguistically to the FINNS, different historical experiences have made the Estonians a culturally distinct people. Whereas the FINNS were heavily influenced by the SWEDES and are, as a result, culturally similar to the peoples of other Scandinavian nations, the GERMANS were the predominant cultural influence on the Estonians. Remnants of the Finnish roots of Estonian culture can, however, still be found in local folklore; the Estonian national epic, the *Kalevipseg*, is highly reminiscent of the Finnish *Kalevala*.

Although most Estonians belong to the Lutheran Church, a small minority, known as Setu, follow the Russian Orthodox rite. Concentrated around Lake Peipus, Estonia's eastern border with Russia, the Setu form a distinct cultural group with a separate self-identity and dialect.

An ancient people, the Estonians are first mentioned by Tacitus. In the ninth century C.E. Vikings raided Estonia on their way to Russia. Sweden, Denmark, and Russia later tried to conquer and convert the Estonians in the eleventh and twelfth centuries, but only in the first half of the thirteenth century did the Estonians adopt Christianity. At that time southern Estonia and northern Latvia (then known as Livonia), were overrun by the Order of the Knights of the Sword (later part of the Teutonic Order); the Danish king conquered northern Estonia.

In 1346 the king of Denmark sold his part of Estonia to the Teutonic Order. Upon the Order's dissolution in 1561, Poland and Sweden vied for control of the Baltic countries, with the latter emerging victorious in 1629. By then, the three centuries of German rule had made a marked impact on the country. Bishoprics, estates, and later cities were established, creating a German nobil-ity and a predominantly German class of burghers. Native Estonian peasants were pressed into serfdom.

In the Northern War of 1701–1721 the SWEDES lost the Baltic provinces to Russia. Czar Alexander I (reigned 1801–1825) officially liberated the Estonian peasantry from serfdom, but only under Alexander II (reigned 1855–1881) were they granted rights such as freedom of movement and released from the jurisdiction of landowners and from compulsory unpaid labor. Industrialization and urbanization generated enormous socio-economic changes in the Estonian population which, with the spread of education and the revival of Estonian literature, created the infrastructure for Estonian nationalism.

This nationalism, however, only fully matured in response to efforts at russification during the reigns of Alexander III (1881–1894) and Nicholas II (1894–1917). At first Estonians were delighted that this russification had enfeebled German culture and influence, but they soon became increasingly alienated from Russia as well. In the wake of the 1917 revolution, Estonia declared itself independent and enlisted foreign aid in resisting attempts at annexation by the Soviet regime. Following the Ribbentrop-Molotov agreement of 1939, Estonia, like the other Baltic states, was forced to accept Soviet bases on its territory, the first in a rapid series of stages that led to its annexation by the Soviet Union, where it was given the status of a union republic.

During the Soviet period, rapid industrialization of the northern part of the country was followed by urbanization and internal migration from the agricultural south. As a result, the overwhelming majority of Estonians now live in the north. Industrialization and efforts by the Soviet authorities also caused an influx of RUSSIANS into Estonia — ethnic RUSSIANS now constitute c.20 percent of the population.

In the liberal atmosphere of Mikhail Gorbachev's policies of *perestroika* and *glasnost*, Estonian nationalists struggled for secession from the Soviet Union and complete independence. Independence was achieved in 1991, upon the dissolution of the USSR.

ETAKA see ENGGANESE.

ETCHE A subgroup of the IBO.

ETHIOPIANS In the political sense, the Ethiopians are the inhabitants of the state of Ethiopia as shaped during the reign of Emperor Menelik II (1889–1913). Its boundaries excluded the territory of the former Italian colony of Eritrea, which in 1952 formed a federation with Ethiopia; it was annexed as a province in 1962. In 1991, after thirty years of guerrilla and civil war, a new Ethiopian government acquiesced to Eritrean independence. However, in a cultural sense, many ERITREANS share characteristics and historical legacies with the peoples of northern Ethiopia.

The 50 million Ethiopians belong to many ethnic groups. The two major peoples of the north, the AMHARA and the TIGRAY, are linked to the legacy of the Ethiopian empire and the Ethiopian Orthodox Church, whereas the peoples of southern Ethiopia only joined the modern Ethiopian nation-state at the turn of the twentieth century. For a long time the AMHARA dominated Ethiopia's political history; however, after fifteen years of civil war against the central government under Mengistu Haile Mariam (1974–1991), the Ethiopian People's Revolutionary Democratic Front (EPRDF) and its parent organization, the Tigray People's Liberation Front (TPLF), assumed power in Ethiopia's capital, Addis Ababa. As a result, the country is now undergoing a difficult process of renegotiating relations between the central state and its ethnic groups. Sixty-five ethno-linguistic groups have been formally recognized as nationalities, with self-administration on the level of district proposed for forty-seven nationalities. While together with other ethnic groups the TPLF opposed the traditional Amhara domination of the state, they still favor the continuity of Ethiopia as a unified state.

Although Ethiopia is often identified with Christianity, at present the largest religious group is Sunni Muslim (45 percent). Amharic-speaking Muslims are sometimes called *Jabarti,* while among the OROMO, Muslims were sometimes called *Nagade* (trader, stranger). About 40 percent of the population belong to the Ethiopian Orthodox (Tehawido) Church. There are also significant Protestant (Mekane Yesus Church) and Roman Catholic minorities. Between 5 and 15 percent of the population adhere to traditional beliefs. Until recently, there was a sizeable Jewish minority of c.50,000 called Falashas (strangers; s.d. Beta Israel). Probably descended from judaized AGAW tribes, by 1991 most had emigrated to Israel. A separate community, the Falashmura, comprises Falashas who adopted Christianity in the recent past. Many are now trying to return to Judaism and migrate to Israel.

Ethno-linguistic groups among Ethiopians belong to two language families, the Afro-Asiatic and the Nilo-Saharan. In addition, small numbers of non-Africans (YEMENIS, INDIANS, ITALIANS, GREEKS, ARMENIANS) have settled in Ethiopia. The Afro-Asiatic family consists of some few speakers of Arabic dialects (Rasha'ida, Jebelawin), in the region bordering northern Sudan and speakers of the Southern Semitic (Ethio-Semitic; Tigre, Tigray, Amhara, Gurage, Adare, Argoba, Gafat) and Cushitic (Hamito-Semitic) languages (Northern Cushitic: Beja; Central Cushitic: Agaw; Eastern Cushitic: Saho, Afar, Somali, Baiso, Oromo, Konso, Gidole, Arbore, Waraza, Tsama, Sidamo, Alaba, Darasa, Hadya, Kambata, Burji, Geleba). There are also speakers of Omotic (Western Cushitic) languages (major language clusters: Kefa-Janjero, Gimira-Maji, Omato, Ari-Banna). The latter includes more than sixty distinct ethnic groups and thirty groups of unidentified status. The Nilo-Saharan family contains speakers of Nilotic languages (Baria, Kunama, Berta, Gumuz, Koma, Nuer, Anuak, Majangir, Maban, Mekan, Suri, Surma, Nyanyatom). In some literature peoples belonging to Omotic and Nilotic language groups are sometimes pejoratively termed Shankalla (Shangalla).

Among northern Ethiopians the continuity of a state polity, Axum (today on Eritrean territory), can be traced from the first century C.E. The Axum empire was converted to monophysite (Ethiopian Orthodox) Christianity during the fourth century. The legacy of the state and church and its literature (written in the Ge'ez language and in Ethiopian script) is particularly linked related to the history of the TIGRAY and AMHARA. Many myths regarding the early Ethiopian state reach back "thousands of years," and are linked to the initiation process into the church. They include the story of a romantic encounter between King Solomon and the Queen of Sheba (believed to be in Ethiopia). Their son, Menelik I, became ruler over the country. The Christian AMHARA and TIGRAY came to believe in their special role as the legitimate holders of political power in a holy empire with indefinite borders. The myth of the Solomonic dynasty was reassumed by several recent Ethiopian emperors, among them Menelik II and Haile Selassie.

Over the centuries, the seat of political power shifted southward, and other ethnically and religiously heterogeneous populations were absorbed into the empire. From the fourteenth century Ethiopia gradually integrated the Jewish principalities in Semien and Dambea; by the turn of the sixteenth century several Muslim principalities in the south (Awfat, Dawaro, Arababni, Hadya, Sharha, Bali, Dara) were included in the empire after a fierce power struggle between the Christian empire and the Mus-

above left: An Ethiopian woman carrying a jug
above right: An Ethiopian woman with her camel
below: The market and gallows in Bati, Ethiopia

lim lowland state of Adal and its allies (SOMALI, AFAR, OROMO).

The term *Itiopia* has been in use since at least the fifteenth century to describe the scope of the empire and to distinguish its population from its neighbors. In medieval European texts "Ethiopian" came to denote all people with a dark skin. Deriving from the Greek *aitiopos* ("burned faces"), it was used in translations of the Bible as an equivalent for the Hebrew *Kush*. Until the nineteenth century, *Itiopia,* was used synonymously with the Arabic *Habash* (Abyssinia, Abyssinians).

From the later half of the nineteenth century, as a byproduct of imperial expansion, political centralization, and the confrontation with European colonialism, attempts were made to popularize the idea of being "Ethiopian" and to develop a sense of patriotism and national identity distinguished from regional and ethnic loyalties. This idea of Ethiopian nationalism was bolstered among intellectuals and other politically minded people by Menelik II's victory over the ITALIANS at Adawa (1896), and by resistance against Italian efforts at colonization (1935–1941). It was hindered, however, by the injustices linked with imperial expansion and the obvious dominance of the AMHARA. During the reign of Emperor Lij Yasu (1913–1916) an unsuccessful attempt was made to reconstruct relations between the competing ethnic groups and to incorporate the Muslim peoples of the south (AFAR, SOMALI, OROMO). The ITALIANS were later able to exploit this situation during their short colonial interlude.

During Haile Selassie's rule (1916–1974), attempts at "amharization," particularly among the emerging middle class, were used to forge a core population identifying solely with Ethiopia. While amharization became an integral part of the politics of modernization, it also elicited antagonism among non-Amhara peoples and encouraged them to assert their own identities. During the 1960s, self-help organizations encouraged road-construction, literacy campaigns, education, etc. among the TIGRAY, OROMO, GURAGE, KAMBATA, and HADIYA. These networks of organized ethnicity would often provide the basis for "national movements," which began emerging in the 1970s.

The monarchy of Haile Selassie was overthrown in 1974 and a military government under Mengistu Haile Mariam assumed power. Under Mengistu, Ethiopia formally adopted Marxism-Leninism, animating earlier discussions of the "nationality question." Practical politics, however, favored further centralization and cultural amharization in the name of Ethiopian unity, and

fueled simmering ethnic conflicts. In a short time, the government found itself in conflict with national liberation movements fighting for increased government participation and even independence for ERITREANS, TIGRAY, AFARS, OROMO, SIDAMO, and SOMALI.

A coalition of many of these groups ousted Mariam in June 1991. The new Ethiopian government, led by the EPRDF/TPLF is currently claiming to favor decentralization and has encouraged the formation of ethnic organizations. At the same time, such organizations are sanctioned only insofar as they are linked to the umbrella organization of the EPRDF. (see also AMHARA, ERITREANS, OROMO, SOMALI)

ETON An ethnic group living in Cameroon. They are related to the FANG.

EUSKALDUN SEE BASQUES.

EVALVUE An Akan-speaking group living in southwestern Ghana.

EVEN (Lamut) The 13,000 Even live in several north Siberian areas of the Magadan and Kamchatka Provinces and the Yakut Republic of the Russian Federation. They are closely related to the EVENKI in origin, language, and culture, and were considered to be part of them. Originally shamanist, they formally converted to Russian Orthodox Christianity in the nineteenth century but retained their shamanist rituals.

Previously engaged in reindeer-herding, hunting, and fishing, under the Soviet regime many Even turned to farming and husbandry. A Cyrillic alphabet was created for them in 1930. (see also YAKUT)

EVENKI (Tungus) Most of the 30,000 Evenki live in the north of central Siberia in the Evenki Autonomous District of Russia's Krasnoyarsk Province; 13,000 can also be found in northwest China. Their language belongs to the Tungus group of the Manchu-Tungus linguistic family and is divided into three dialects: northern, southern, and eastern. In 1931 they adopted the Roman alphabet; this was replaced in 1937 by the Cyrillic alphabet. Few publications, however, have appeared in the Evenki language, and Russian is used as the literary language.

The Evenki migrated from the Baikal area to their present location in the eleventh century; in the seventeenth century they were annexed to the Russian Empire. Although they adhere to the Russian Orthodox

Evenki

rite, they have retained various shamanist elements in their religious practices and beliefs.

The Evenki were originally divided into northern and southern groups. The former were hunters and reindeer-herders, the latter horse- and cattle-breeders. Under the Soviet regime the nomadic Evenki were forced to adopt a sedentary way of life, and are now engaged also in agriculture, livestock-raising, and fur-farming. (see also NGANASAN)

EWAB ISLANDERS   see KEI.

EWE   A people forming a branch of the ADJA peoples. The historic homeland of the Ewe lies between the Volta River in Ghana and the Mono River in Togo; in southeastern Ghana they number around 1.7 million people or 13 percent of the population; in southern Togo they number around 1.5 million or 44 percent of the population. A smaller number of Ewe live in southwest Benin. Although the Ewe adhere to traditional African religions, Christianity was introduced in colonial times and has become increasingly popular in recent years. Only a few are Muslims.

The Ewe separated from the ADJA in the early seventeenth century, when they began migrating southward. As a segmentary society, they never developed a centralized state structure. They were conquered between 1885 and 1914 by the BRITISH in the Gold Coast (present-day Ghana) and the GERMANS in Togo. After World War I, German-controlled eastern Eweland became part of French Togo; the remainder was given to the BRITISH either as a mandate or as part of the Gold Coast colony.

Several pan-Ewe movements in the Gold Coast and French Togo were formed to protest the partition of the Ewe territory among the colonial powers. They demanded to be united under a single colonial administration to serve as forerunner of an independent Ewe state. Despite efforts by the Trusteeship Council of the United Nations in the 1940s and 1950s to resolve the Ewe problem, both Ghana and Togo gained independence while the Ewe remained separated by an international border. The Togo Ewe, having taken advantage of Western education during the colonial period, dominated that country's civil service both under the German and French administration and after independence. The Ghanaian Ewe, however, opposed the centralized colonial and independent governments on ethnic grounds and have preserved the pan-Ewe notion.

Two subgroups of the Ewe are the AWUNA (Anlo), numbering about 5,000 who live along the coast between the Volta River and the Togolese-Ghana border, and the OUTACHI who live in the Ansho and Tabligbo regions of Togo. (see also ADJA, GHANAIANS, TOGOLESE)

EWONDO   A subgroup of the FANG.

EZHA   A subgroup of the GURAGE.

EZIAMA   A subgroup of the IBO.

EZZA   A subgroup of the IBO.

F

FALASHA see ETHIOPIANS.

FALASHMURA see ETHIOPIANS.

FALI An ethnic group classed among the KIRDI groups, living in Chad.

FALKLAND ISLANDERS The 2,000 inhabitants of the Falkland Islands, an archipelago in the South Atlantic Ocean off the coast of Argentina, are primarily BRITISH. Most engage in sheep-rearing, although there are indications that there are large oil and gas deposits in the region; these may alter the islands' traditional economy. Argentina, which calls the islands the Malvinas and claims them as its own, attempted to assert sovereignty by invading the islands in 1982. Britain recaptured the islands soon after, and there are currently over 4,000 British troops still stationed there.

FANG (Pahouin, Beti-Pahouin, Pangwe, Pamue) A people living mainly in northern Gabon in the Woleu Ntem region where they number around 330,000, some 30 percent of the country's population. They are also found in the East, Center, and South provinces of Cameroon, and in eastern Equatorial Guinea. They speak the Fang language. Most Fang converted to Catholic and Protestant Christianity after World War I as a result of extensive missionary activity in their religion. Only a small minority still adhere to traditional religions.

During the eighteenth century the Fang lived in the grassy plateaux of the Sanag and Lom Rivers in Cameroon. According to their tradition, they were forced by invaders to move southward and westward to the forest regions. There they became elephant hunters and began to trade ivory with the coastal area. They also cultivated forest crops such as bananas and oil palms. Because of the exhaustion of elephant herds and arable soil, however, they did not stay long in one

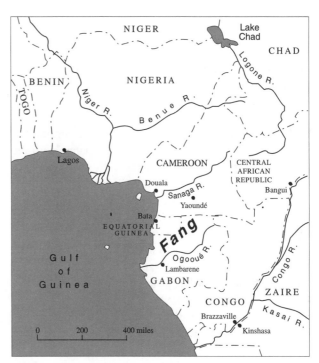

Fang

location. Every fifteen years they relocated to new villages, driving out or absorbing the original inhabitants in the process.

During the nineteenth century the Fang found it more profitable to sell their ivory directly to European traders on the coast rather than employing the services of other groups such as the KELE, SEKE, and MPONGWE as middlemen. Some Fang migrated to the coastal region, but they often came into violent conflict with European traders, local peoples, and the new French administration which had been established on the Gabonese coast at the time.

In the early twentieth century the FRENCH began to penetrate the hinterland and arrived in Fang territory, where they quickly suppressed Fang resistance. French colonial rule was established in the area on the eve of

World War I, while the Fang in present-day Equatorial Guinea were governed by the SPANIARDS. Under both colonial powers the Fang suffered greatly from forced labor, famine, and diseases. Their customary means of sustenance were largely abandoned in favor of the cultivation of cocoa and coffee as cash crops.

In the 1940s, the *Alar Ayong* movement was formed to unite the Fang into a single nation. Although it failed to establish a Fang nation-state, it did succeed in restoring Fang self-esteem. During decolonization and independence, the Fang were politically active in both Gabon and Equatorial Guinea and managed to dominate the latter despite Spanish support for BUBI nationalism.

The EWONDO of Cameroon are the largest subgroup of the Fang and speak their own, eponymous language. Another Fang subgroup is the NTUM. (see also EQUATORIAL GUINEANS, GABONESE)

FANTE (Fanti, Fantyn) An Akan-speaking coastal group living in the Central Region of Ghana. With the arrival of missionaries in their region in the nineteenth century many adopted Protestant Christianity .

By the early nineteenth century the Fante dominated the Ghanaian coast from Winneba to the Pra River. Although they were never united as one polity, they often cooperated in time of danger and their region was the only coastal area not dominated by the ASHANTI state. Despite a period of rapprochement between the ASHANTI and the Fante, however, the two groups began competing over control of the coastal-inland trade. Tensions increased when the Fante began providing refuge to Ashanti rebels. The ASHANTI responded by declaring war against the Fante. After ten years of fighting the Ashanti victory was complete. Soon after, the BRITISH arrived in the region and found the Fante natural allies against the ASHANTI. Fante leaders signed a treaty with Britain by which their region became a British protectorate. Only towards the end of the nineteenth century did they realize that they had relinquished their independence and vainly tried to oust the BRITISH. The Fante Confederacy Movement, established in 1871, sought to unite all the coastal peoples of the Gold Coast to defend them from other ethnic groups.

By the turn of the century the BRITISH had established the colony of the Gold Coast (now Ghana) and implemented indirect rule over the Fante. Intervention in internal Fante affairs was limited until the 1930s, and Fante chiefs maintained considerable autonomy. British intervention expanded, however, after the 1930s, providing momentum for local demands for independence. In 1957 the Gold Coast colony became the independent state of Ghana. The Fante had played a prominent role in the independence movement but, unlike the ASHANTI, did not demand autonomy in the new state. Since independence, they have played only a minor role in Ghanaian politics. (see also AKAN, GHANAIANS)

FANYANI An ethnic group related to the KOTOKO living in Chad.

FARARI see GYPSIES.

FARONESE (s.d. Foroyskt) The 30,000 inhabitants of the Faroe (Far Oer) archipelago are citizens of the Kingdom of Denmark. Their language is closley related to Icelandic. They engage in fishing, agriculture, sheep-herding, and down-collecting.

FARSIVAN (Parsivan, Parsiban; contraction of Farsizaban: "Persian-speaking") An ethnic group living in the western part of Afghanistan. They can also be found in the areas of Ghazni and Qandahur and in various towns in southern Afghanistan. They are estimated as numbering about 600,000 and are Shi'ite Muslims. They speak several western dialects and subdialects of Dari (the Persian spoken in Afghanistan), and use its literary form in writing.

Predominantly peasants, the Farsivan engage in agriculture; town-dwellers are craftsmen and traders. In Western scholarly literature they are sometimes erroneously confused with TAJIKS. (see also AFGHANS)

FEREIDAN A subgroup of the GEORGIANS descended from east GEORGIANS (Kakh) who were forcibly resettled by Shah Abbas I the Safavid (1581–1628) in the inner regions of Iran and converted from Christianity to Shi'ite Islam. There are several thousand Fereidan living mainly in villages near Esfahan.

At home they still preserve the Georgian language in a specific Fereidan dialect, one of the few (together with Ingiloi and Imerkhevian) Georgian dialects used only outside Georgia. (see also GEORGIANS)

FIJI ISLANDERS The c.750,000 inhabitants of the Fiji Islands, a chain of some one hundred islands located in the southwest Pacific Ocean, northeast of Australia. The Fiji group comprises four main islands: Viti Levu (where 70 percent of the population live), Vanua Levu, Tavaeuni, and Kandavu. First settled approximately 3,500 years ago, the islands came to serve as a launching ground for exploration and settlement in the Pacific Ocean, toward the islands now known as Polynesia.

Native Fijians make up only 48 percent of the archipelago's total population. INDIANS, descended from immigrants brought by the British colonial government to work in the sugarcane plantations, form another 46 percent. Native Fijians speak a Melanesian language with several regional dialects, of which Bau is considered the official. The majority are Christians, with Wesleyan Methodism being the leading denomination.

The traditional Fijian economy is agricultural and village-based, with taro, yams, cassava, and sweet potatoes as staples. Copra is a major cash crop, especially on the smaller islands, and fishing is increasingly important.

The clan (*mataquil*) is the social division which formed the major landholding entity on the cession of the Fiji Islands to Britain. In recent years there has been migration from villages, especially in the periphery, towards urban centers and an increasing tendency to leave the communal village framework to work the land as independent farmers. Within villages commercial production is on the increase and a considerable number of the independent farmers cultivate sugar, the dominant cash crop in Fiji, which has been traditionally grown by Indo-Fijians.

The traditional institution of the Great Council of Chiefs is still influential in the political arena and even day-to-day life. At the same time, racial diversity, compounded by former British colonial policies, have left Fiji a legacy of ethnic unrest. Native Fijians own over 80 percent of the land, while over 90 percent of the sugar cultivation, Fiji's largest export, is produced by INDIANS, most often on land leased from Native Fijians. This ethnic division has taken political shape since independence. The government is dominated by Fijians and run by some of the highest ranking native chiefs; the opposition is dominated by Indo-Fijians. Tensions climaxed after the 1987 general election when the ruling government was defeated by an Indian-dominated coalition. A military coup ousted the coalition government and a new interim government was promptly formed. Under the new administration Fiji declared itself a republic and withdrew from the British Commonwealth. The influence of the army has decreased since 1991.

FILASTINIYYUN   see PALESTINIANS.

FILIPINOS see PHILIPPINES, THE PEOPLE OF THE.

FINNS   (s.d. Suomalaiset; the term "Finns" derives from ancient sources describing LAPPS as Fenni or Phinoi) Of the 5 million citizens of Finland, 4.5 million are ethnic FINNS speaking Suomi (Finnish), a language belonging to the Finno-Ugric group; 9 percent are ethnically SWEDES. Ninety-five percent of the population is Lutheran Christian. Finland is a sparsely populated country of lakes and forests (the largest population concentrations are found in the south) and many Finns live in isolated settlements. Only 40 percent are urbanized: most Finns engage in agriculture and the timber industry.

The common ancestors of the Volga-Kama-Ural Finno-Ugric peoples reached the Baltic coast before the first century C.E. Between then and the eighth century, Finnish tribes of hunters and fishers migrated into present-day Finland. Here they separated into four tribes: the Kainulaiset (Kvanes), who settled east of the Gulf of Bothnia, the Hamalaiset (Tavastes), who chose the lake district, the Varsinais (Suomalaiset), who originally settled in southwest Finland, and the Karjalaiset (Carelians), living around Lakes Ladoga and Onega. In the process, the Finns forced the indigenous LAPPS northward.

Finnish raids against the SWEDES in the twelfth century, provoked the SWEDES to call a "crusade" against the shamanist Finns. Upon conquering the country the SWEDES introduced Catholicism and, from the thirteenth to eighteenth centuries, sent colonists to Finland. Swedish culture had a significant impact on the Finns but did not prevent the emergence of a rich local culture exemplified by the epic national poem, the *Kalevala*.

The expansion of Finnish areas of settlement northward in the fifteenth and sixteenth centuries drove the LAPPS even further from their original territory. This colonization of the north (a process which continues today) led to the introduction of feudalism. Around 1600 a peasant revolt, the "War of the Cudgels," was suppressed by the SWEDES, who used the occasion to impose a new Lutheran ruling stratum. By the eighteenth century, however, Swedish influence weakened. The Finnish language, virtually abandoned by the ruling classes, once again became accepted.

During the Napoleonic wars, Sweden's role was supplanted by Russia, which invaded Finland and annexed it in 1809. Reconstituted as a Grand Duchy, the Russian administration was at first mindful of preserving Swedish-Finnish institutions and privileges. However, the emergence of Finnish nationalism in the nineteenth century prompted attempts at forcible russification.

above left: Finns in a coffee shop
above right: A Finnish vegetable vendor
below: Finnish women in the vegetable market

This only augmented Finnish enmity toward Russia: the Russian Revolution of 1917 provided the occasion to declare Finland an independent republic.

In the post-World War I reshuffling of borders, Finland lost part of Carelia to the Soviet Union. After the secret Soviet-German pact of 1939, the Soviets forced the Finns to cede another piece of Carelia, causing them to seek the military backing of Nazi Germany. In punishment for siding with Germany, the Finns were forced to cede even more territory to the Soviet Union after World War II. Since 1917, they have lost 10 percent of their original territory, suffered massive destruction and loss of life, and were forced to absorb 500,000 Carelian refugees. Only absolute neutrality during the Cold War saved them from further Soviet encroachments.

Initially undertaken to pay off war debts to the Soviet Union, land reform and industrialization have allowed Finland to develop into a social-democratic capitalist society with a high standard of living.

FIOME (Gorowa) A people numbering about 35,000, living in the wet highlands in central Tanzania. The Fiome language belongs to the Cushitic group of the Nilo-Saharan family. The Fiome, are closely related to the IRAQW people in origin, language, and culture.

FIPA A people inhabiting the border regions of Tanzania and nothern Zambia, between Lakes Tanganyika and Rukwa. They acquired their present name from the Fipa Plateau, which is the heart of their ethnic territory. They number between 250,000 and 300,000. The Fipa language belongs to the Southern Highland Bantu group of the Niger-Kordofan family.

The traditional agriculture of the Fipa is based on the system of land-clearing for temporary cultivation. The common crop is millet, which requires cooperative labour for its production. The Fipa are also believed to have brought smelting and iron forging to the region.

FIRUZKUHI A subgroup of the AIMAQ.

FLATHEAD A Native North American nation numbering about 4,000, many of whom live on the Federal Indian Reservation in Montana, United States. They comprise the most easterly part of the SALISHAN group. The Flathead Reservation is now partly flooded by the Kerr Dam.

FLEMINGS (s.d. Vlamingen) Strictly speaking, "Flemings" refers to the inhabitants of Flanders (in the Middle Ages, a French county). By extension, the term is used for all speakers of Dutch dialects in northern Belgium. They number 5.6 million and form 57 percent of the BELGIANS. Although they share the same origin as the DUTCH, pre-Germanic Celtic relics are stronger in Flanders than in Holland. As a result of traditions of communal autonomy and centuries of isolation, regional contrasts are striking. Spanish influences are strongest in Antwerp, while the Kemps have remained a conservative, poor, and isolated region with traditionally powerful abbeys.

The various distinct Flemish dialects have, in recent years, been supplanted by standard Dutch. French, too, has made major inroads on dialect use, particularly in southern Flanders, incorporated by France in the seventeenth century, with a population of 90,000 thoroughly gallicized Flemings. Similarly, Brussels, originally a Flemish city, is now largely French-speaking.

Flanders prospered during the Middle Ages. Towns such as Bruges, Ghent, and Ypres became important economic centers because of their well-developed linen industry and trade. Independent from France since the fourteenth century, Flanders became the prize acquisition of the Burgundian dukes, who united the Netherlands. During the Reformation, Flanders was ruled by the Habsburgs in Madrid, who ensured the survival of Catholicism during the Protestant Reformation.

Flathead

In 1830 the Flemings joined the French-speaking WALLOONS to form Belgium. Although most BELGIANS spoke Flemish and the constitution guaranteed the choice of language, French came to dominate the bureaucracy, courts, and education and made encroachments on Flemish language and culture. Most government officials were French-speaking; their inabilty to make themselves understood in Flemish led them to neglect the Flemish regions in favor of Wallonia. By the mid-nineteenth century Flanders, never having developed industry, was an impoverished region. Many well-to-do Flemings came to adopt French, intensifying the ethnic struggle and giving it the added dimension of a class struggle.

Although the Flemish national movement is as old as Belgium itself, its objectives, including the adoption of Standard Dutch as spoken in Netherlands as the official language, were only formulated in 1900. During World War I nationalists promoted "activism" — the collaboration of Flemings with the GERMANS in occupied Belgium — provoking an anti-Flemish backlash after 1918. The introduction of democracy, however, also promoted the growth of nationalism between the world wars. The Flemish language, until then largely confined to the lower classes (it was also used privately among middle class familes) was finally recognized as the official language of Flanders and a Flemish University was legalized.

Meanwhile, the Brussels problem was festering: massive French immigration to the city turned it into a French-speaking island in Flemish territory. The Vlaamsch Nationaal Verbond and other extreme rightwing groups flirted with fascism and collaborated with the Nazis during World War II. In the postwar years Flemish grievances focused on French economic dominance and the growing use of French in Brussels.

In the 1960s the Flemings surpassed the WALLOONS economically and Antwerp supplanted Wallonia as Belgium's main industrial zone. The upsurge of the moderately right wing federalist Volksunie (People's Union) dates from this period. Under Flemish pressure, the language frontier was formalized and French advances in the Brussels region were frozen. These new arrangements left a significant French-speaking community under Flemish administrations; by distributing official functions to speakers of both languages only, it seemed that the Flemings were now receiving prefered treatment, kindling Walloon and Brussels countermovements.

A far-reaching constitution, adopted in 1970, instituted cultural autonomy for both communities. The movement to federalize Belgium has led to the establishment of a separate Flemish parliament with authority increasingly superseding that of Brussels. Flemish grievances have thus largely been met, and the Flemings are becoming the dominant constituent in Belgium. Yet in recent years the moderate nationalists have come under fire from the more extremist Vlaams Blok, which had some electoral success in 1991. Xenophobic themes in the Flemish movement are expressed in racist agitation against foreign (mainly Mediterranean) workers. (see also BELGIANS, DUTCH, WALLOONS)

FOI An ethnic group of about 5,000 living in the mountainous area of central Papua New Guinea. They speak an indigenous regional language. They are fishermen and hunters as well as cultivators of various garden crops. The Foi are famous for their highly developed artform of ceremonial song and poetry.

FOKENG (Bafokeng) A subgroup of the SOTHO.

FON The major people in Benin, numbering c.1.8 million, about 40 percent of Benin's population. They are found throughout central and southern Benin and in Togo along the southern border area. They speak Fon and practice traditional religions. The Fon are culturally related to the ADJA. They are famous for their art, particularly sculpture.

In the pre-colonial period the Fon were the foremost ethnic group of one of West Africa's most powerful and well organized states, the kingdom of Dahomey. Established in the seventeenth century, Dahomey expanded to the coast in the eighteenth century, gaining access to European trade, especially the slave trade. By the end of the nineteenth century Dahomey was conquered by the FRENCH.

During the colonial period the FRENCH favored the Fon region and they enjoyed many educational privileges. They played an important role in the French colonial administration and were later prominent in independent Benin's civil service. Many Fon emigrated to other parts of French Africa or France.

The MAHI, a Fon subgroup living in Benin north of Abomey between the Oueme River and the Dassa hills, established their own kingdom in the seventeenth century. Over the following 200 years, before French colonization, they were the prime target for Dahomey slave raids. Other Fon subgroups are the AGOLINU and the GUN, which has its own subgroups, the GUEMENU and TOFINU. (see also BENINIANS)

FONDI An ethnic group related to the FANG living in Cameroon.

FONGWE A subgroup of the TUMBUKA.

FORE An ethnic group numbering some 25,000 living in the mountainous area of eastern Papua New Guinea. They speak an indigenous language composed of three principal dialects. Although they have no official religion, they are known to believe in a world of spirits. Their economy is based upon slash and burn horticulture, pig-raising, and hunting.

FOROYSKT see FARONESE.

FORROS see SAO TOME AND PRINCIPE, THE PEOPLE OF.

FOX A Native North American group numbering about 1,500, many of whom live in Kansas, Iowa, and Oklahoma, in the United States. They originally inhabited Illinois but were driven out by the FRENCH and later the AMERICANS to Oklahoma where most of them live today.

FRAFRA An ethnic group living in the Upper Region-East of Ghana near the Burkina Faso border. (see also MOLE-DAGBANI)

FRENCH (s.d. Français) Most of the 56 million citizens of France are French. Their language, French, is a Romance language derived from vulgar Latin dialects as spoken in northern Gaul (*langue d'oil*), in particular in the Ile de France region around Paris. During the Renaissance, French was imposed as the official language; it has since become a prestigious element of French collective identity. In the Middle Ages and again throughout the eighteenth and nineteenth centuries it functioned as the international language of culture and diplomacy. Although French has long been standardized, there are still many regional dialects.

There are also a number of ethnically non-French bilingual groups living in the periphery of France. In the Middle Ages, the dialects of southern Gaul (*langue d'oc*) gave rise to a separate culture; surviving occitan dialects (Provençal) can still be heard in the Provence, Languedoc, Gascony, and elsewhere. Along the Atlantic coast their are communities of BRETONS and BASQUES, each struggling to preserve their own languages and cultures, while on the Mediterranean island of Corsica, calls for independence have been raised on the basis of ethno-linguistic and cultural claims.

From the seventeenth century, the French created one of the world's largest colonial empires; French settlers and cultural missions spread French language and culture around the world. As a result, c.90 million people are French-speakers today. Besides being an official language in Belgium, Switzerland, and Canada, French is widely spoken in the Val d'Aosta (Italy), in North Africa (the Maghreb), West Africa, Madagascar, the Caribbean, French Guiana, New Caledonia, and the Pacific islands. Most French are Catholic.

Modern French descend from a mixture of populations, the oldest stratum being prehistoric Celts. In the second and first century B.C.E., the Romans conquered Gaul and exerted a culturally formative, although demographically negligible, influence. Germanic invaders (West Goths, Burgundians, Longobards, Alemans, and Franks) were more numerous, but they too were absorbed into the Gallo-Roman culture. Infiltrating from the northeast and adopting Christianity in the sixth century, Franks became the dominant ethnic group and gave the French their name. However, a specific French consciousness did not appear until the twelfth century, when northern France was unified by a succession of kings who established their power over outlying provinces. Efforts to expel the ENGLISH from western France during the Hundred Years' War did much to institute a collective French identity.

France went on to forge a centralized new entity, incorporating Normandy and eventually other provinces such as the Provence and Brittany. From the seventeenth century, French kings attempted to assimilate the periphery by imposing linguistic and religious uniformity, becoming, in the process, Europe's foremost power.

During the eighteenth century the social and intellectual influence of the bourgeoisie advanced; intellectuals criticized France's increasingly obsolescent *ancien régime*, which perpetuated the power of the aristocracy. The French Revolution (1789) abolished feudal particularism, achieved a high degree of unity, created a radically democratic regime, and empowered the bourgeoisie. The empire of Napoleon Bonaparte (1804–1815) revolutionized the whole of Europe.

Throughout the nineteenth century, the French continued to experiment with a variety of political arrangements. This was also an era of extraordinary cultural creativity. But while Paris remained the cultural capital of Europe, the French were demographically and economically overtaken by the more industrialized GERMANS. The catastrophic Franco-Prussian War (1870) ushered in the democratic Third Republic, but

French people

the loss of Alsace-Lorraine also fired French irredentism.

Although France emerged victorious from World War I, the disastrous consequences of the war fostered a defeatist attitude among many French; during World War II some collaborated with the Nazi occupation forces. At the same time, many French sought to restore their independence and integrity and formed several underground movements such as the *Maquis*, whose exploits against the GERMANS are now legendary.

Political instability and divisive colonial wars abroad marked the postwar era. It took the leadership of outstanding statesmen such as President Charles de Gaulle (1890–1970) to take drastic measures, such as ending French rule in Algeria, to provide a modicum of stability. Nonetheless, both the right and the left were dissatisfied with the turn of affairs in France — the May revolt in Paris (the "metaphysical revolution") of 1968 signaled the profound disillusionment of the young with the French government.

Past decades have witnessed the modernization of French economic and social life. Today France is quite industrialized, but most French remain small-town dwellers, with a strong rural element, making them one of Western Europe's most agrarian nations. After a long period of stagnation, the population is growing again, but France is still much less densely populated than most of its neighbors.

In recent years France has experienced the mass influx of immigrants from North Africa (1.5 million), as well as PORTUGUESE, SPANIARDS (600,000), and ITALIANS (600,000), and Africans. The demographic weight (3 percent) and conspicuous presence of non-European Muslims on France's social map have nourished xenophobic nationalist movements.

French culture has become synonymous with a high quality of life. This achievement, however, has had its price with the "high" culture of court and capital affecting provincial and popular cultures. Whereas historically the center tried to gallicize peripheral regions such as French Flanders, Normandy, Provence, and Alsace-Lorraine, such centralization has provoked regionalist reactions against Paris. Burgundy has retained an individuality reflecting its Middle Kingdom past and Swiss influence remains perceptible in the Franche Comte and the Jura; the proximity of Italy can be felt in Savoy and the Dauphine. Complete assimilation has clearly failed among the BRETONS, BASQUES, and CORSICANS.

FRENCH CANADIANS   see CANADIANS, QUEBECOIS.

FRENCH GUIANESE   The inhabitants of French Guiana (Guyane Française), along with those of Guyana and Suriname, have neither Spanish nor Portuguese roots: rather, the first European settlers were FRENCH, ENGLISH, and DUTCH. The population of French Guiana, an area one-sixth that of France, numbers 100,000. The largest group is the mixed-race creoles, who account for 72 percent of the population: the remainder are Bush Negroes, descendants of escaped African slaves (6.4 percent), Amerindians (4.2 percent), Asians, Europeans, and other minorities (including BRAZILIANS), totalling just over 17 percent. French is the official language, spoken by nearly all the population except the Amerindians.

The interior of the country is sparsely populated: there are areas of Amerindian settlement in the Haut-Maroni and Haut-Oyapoc. Half the population lives in Cayenne, the capital and chief port.

French Guiana has become infamous in popular lore as a French prison colony, especially because of the description of, Devil's Island, in active use from 1859 through 1945, in Henri Charriere's novel *Papillon*. A less well-known, but more positive aspect of French Guianese history, was the pioneering clerical community at Mana, active from 1827 through 1846, which inaugurated formal education for freed black slaves and women.

Possession of French Guiana, sighted by Christopher Columbus in 1498, was disputed by the FRENCH, DUTCH and BRITISH in the seventeenth century. French Guiana was the name applied to the territory awarded to France by the Peace of Breda (1667). Disputes resumed in 1809 with Brazilian and British claims, but the territory remained FRENCH. With the discovery of gold in 1853, frontier disputes started anew with Brazil and Suriname (the latter still claims an area in southwest French Guiana, west of the Maroni River). In 1946 the colony became an overseas department of France. Political movements have arisen among the French Guianese for greater autonomy.

FRENCH POLYNESIANS   A Polynesian people representing about 83 percent of the total population (1990: 199,000) of French Polynesia, in the southeast Pacific Ocean. They inhabit thirty-five volcanic islands and 183 atolls in five archipelagos: Society, Austral (Tubuai), Tuamotu, Gambier, and Marquesas. The capital, Papeete, located on the main island of Tahiti in the Society group, is inhabited by some 86 percent of the total population. The population of French Polynesia includes minorities of FRENCH, other Europeans, and

CHINESE. The language is Tahitian and Christianity is the principal religion, with the Protestant Evangelical church as the largest denomination.

French Polynesia has been an Overseas Territory of France since 1957; it gained increased local autonomy in 1977. Although French law governs land tenure, in practice the old Polynesian system of joint land ownership still largely prevails today. Over 85 percent of the land is in Polynesian hands, a large amount of which is leased to the Chinese minority. The French government is responsible for conducting the external affairs of the territory, although by a constitutional settlement of 1990, the territorial government was enabled to enter into treaties with other Pacific states.

The economy of the islands is dominated by income from France. Agriculture and fishing provide most of French Polynesian exports. Coconuts and vanilla are the principal cash crops. Tourism is a main foreign exchange earner but it is currently affected by adverse environmental consequences from nuclear testing — underground nuclear tests have taken place on the island of Moruroa for more than twenty years. (See also TAHITIANS)

FRISIANS Between 300,000 and 400,000 inhabitants of Frisia, a northeastern province of the Netherlands with a total population of some 600,000, are Frisians; another 300,000 Frisian-speakers may dwell outside Frisia. Their language, spoken only in Frisia proper, on a few Danish islands, and in a few places in North Germany, is distinct from Dutch and considered closer to English. Education in Frisian is currently ac-

Frisians

cepted in the Netherlands. The Frisian economy is still largely rural: their pedigree cattle are world famous.

The Frisians stem from the Germanic Inguaeons, a Baltic tribe. In Roman times Frisians lived around the Dutch Shallows (Wadden) Sea, and expanded southward into West Flanders. In the eighth century they lost their independence, and adopted Christianity. After the Viking conquests, two Frisian realms emerged, one in Kennemerland (soon absorbed by Holland), the other extending from Frisia proper into Overijssel, Groningen, and Northern Germany. In the fifteenth century all of Frisia was absorbed by Holland. Since that time, areas in which Frisian is spoken have diminished with the loss of both West Frisia in Holland and East Frisia in Germany. The early twentieth century witnessed a certain revival of Frisian culture. Currently cultural autonomy is the aim of the nationalist party which garners c.6 percent of the vote. (see also DANES, DUTCH)

FRIULANS A subgroup of the ITALIANS, more than one million Friulans inhabit a predominantly agrarian and densely populated region in northeast Italy which until 1919 formed part of the Austrian Empire (Trieste). A Rhato-Latin dialect is spoken here, descending from Cisalpine Gallo-Roman. Their region constitutes an autonomous area within Italy. A minority SLOVENES live in the eastern part of the Friulan region.

FULANI (Fula, Peul, Fulbe) A people of unknown origins living in West Africa. Most live in northern Nigeria where, together with the HAUSA, they number 30.5 million. They are also found in Mali (1.6 million), Guinea (1.4 million), Cameroon (1.1 million), Senegal (1 million), Niger (950,000), Burkina Faso (550,000), Guinea-Bissau (210,000), and in smaller numbers in Ghana, Mauritania, Sierra Leone, Togo, and Chad. There are two types of Fulani: nomadic Cattle Fulani, and Town Fulani, who are traders. They speak Fulfulde and were among the first African groups to embrace Islam.

The Fulani have lighter skins than neighboring tribes, and their origins have therefore been the source of much speculation, none of it conclusive. In the early eighteenth century, they migrated to Futa-Jallon in northern Guinea, fought their neighbors, and established emirates. This was known as their first *jihad* (Islamic holy war) movement.

During the sixteenth century the Fulani settled in the states occupied by the HAUSA, where they served as religious counsellors. Since HAUSA kings were only nominally Muslim and the Fulani were orthodox, toward the end of the eighteenth century the latter demanded an Islamic reform. When the HAUSA did not oblige, the Fulani, led by Uthman dan Fodio, declared a *jihad* and rebelled against them. The revolt was joined by other subjects of the HAUSA who hated the despotic kings, and by non-Muslim nomadic Fulani. By 1810, the Fulani dominated the HAUSA and the *jihad* movement spread eastward to northern Cameroon and southward to the Yoruba states. The *jihad* resulted in a heightened Islamic awareness in northern Nigeria and served as a unifying factor for the HAUSA and the Fulani. In the modern history of Nigeria they are referred to as one people.

The Fulani of Mali live mainly in the great inland delta of the Niger River, in the Mopti region. In Guinea they live mainly in the Futa-Djallon region where they created a centralized state in the eighteenth century and maintained a dominant position throughout most of the colonial period. During decolonization the Fulani formed their own political party but with the rise of Ahmed Sekou Touré's Parti Democratique de Guinée it lost much of its power. Sekou Touré, who became Guinea's first president after independence in 1958, tried to combat tribalism and accused the Fulani of keeping up ethnic conflicts. His hostility toward the Fulani continued after independence and culminated in the execution of 500 Fulani in 1976 for allegedly participating in a conspiracy against him.

The Fulani of Cameroon live in the northern part of the country which they conquered during the nineteenth-century *jihad*. They were influential during the colonial period and rallied behind Cameroon's President Ahmadou Ahidjo after independence in 1960. With Ahidjo's resignation in 1982 the Fulani's social, economic, and political influence declined.

Most Fulani living in Niger migrated to that country from Nigeria during the colonial period. They live mainly along the Niger River. In Burkina Faso they are concentrated in the north and east and in Guinea-Bissau they live in a wide area between the towns of Gabu and Bafata.

The Fulani are subdivided into smaller groups: BADE, BAGAJE, BUSAWA, DAKARKARI, DUKKAWA, FAKKAWA, GUNGAWA, JABA, JANJI, KAGOMA, KAGORO, KAMBARI, KUDAWA, KUTURMI, KWATAWA, LOPAWA, SHANGAWA, WAJA, and ZABARMA. Another large subgroup of the Fulani, the BORORO, numbering around 1.5 million, lives mainly in Niger and Chad but are also found in Nigeria and Cameroon. Unlike other Fulani groups, the BORORO refused to accept Islam in the early nineteenth century. (see also GAMBIANS, GUINEA-BISSAU, THE PEOPLE OF,

Fulani

GUINEANS, HAUSA, HAUSA-FULANI, MALIANS, MAURITANIANS, NIGERIANS, NIGERIENS, SENEGALESE, SIERRA LEONEANS, TUKULOR)

FULERU An ethnic group living in the eastern highlands of Zaire. Before Belgian colonization they were organized in a single state.

FULNIO A South American Indian group living in the State of Pernambuco, northeast Brazil. They number a few thousand and, like the MASHACALI but unlike most other groups, have maintained their own culture, language, and religion. Most live in government-sponsored shelters, except for several hundred Indians who live dispersed throughout the area.

FUNG An ethnic group of northern Sudan who inhabit the land on either side of the Blue Nile River, upstream of Sannar. The Fung language belongs to the Northern Nilotic family. They are Muslims and engage both in agriculture and in cattle-herding.

FUR An ethnic group numbering an estimated 55,000, found mainly in the central Darfur Province in the northern part of Sudan. Their language belongs to the Nilo-Saharan family. Linguistically as well as culturally the Fur are considered to be indigenous to the mountain range of Jabal Marrah. They are Muslims and engage in cattle-herding and agriculture.

Compared with other Sudanese women, Fur women have a high degree of economic independence, as demonstrated by their right to own land and cattle and to sell or give away their possessions.

The history of the Fur people is one of power. A ruling dynasty of partly Arab origin arose during the seventeenth century and established a Fur sultanate that lasted until 1916.

FURILOCHE   A subgroup of the TEHUELCHE.

FURU   An ethnic group related to the MBOCHI living in Congo.

FWE   An ethnic group related to the TONGA living in Zambia.

G

GA An ethnic group closely related to the ADANGBE, numbering around 510,000, and living in Ghana, mostly in the capital, Accra, and the towns of Labadi, Nungua, Teshi, and Tema. According to Ga tradition, they migrated to their present region from Nigeria in the sixteenth century. In the precolonial era, they had thriving trade with the Europeans, but their patrilineal society never had a centralized political framework.

In Ghanaian politics, the Ga were particularly supportive of the United National Convention whose leader organized the coup against Ghana's first president Kwame Nkrumah, in 1966. From then until 1969 a member of the Ga ruled Ghana. (see also MINA)

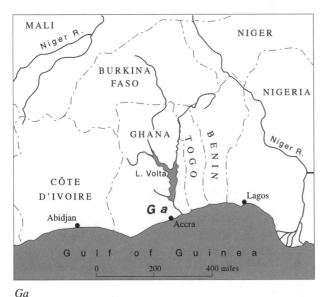

Ga

GABERI An ethnic group related to the KOTOKO living in Chad.

GABONESE The people of Gabon on the west coast of Africa number an estimated 1.2 million. They have the highest level of income per head in sub-Saharan Africa. Much of the rural population is concentrated in the Woleu N'Tem region, where coffee and cocoa are the main cash crops. The main ethnic groups which constitute the Gabonese people are the FANG (30 percent), ESHIRA (20 percent), the M'Bete-speaking peoples (15 percent), the KOTA (13 percent), and the Omyene-speaking peoples (5 percent). Each of these groups is further subdivided. More than 50 percent of the Gabonese live in urban areas; about 60 percent of the Gabonese are Christians, mostly Catholic, about 40 percent adhere to traditional religions, and fewer than 1 percent are Muslims.

The Gabonese became independent from colonial rule by the FRENCH in August 1960. During the following years, political life was unstable. Since 1968, however, the country was ruled by a stable one-party regime headed by Omar Bongo until, in 1990, popular unrest resulted in a democratization process and the creation of opposition parties. In general, Gabon has avoided ethnic conflict, even during its unstable years.

GABRA A southern division of the OROMO, living east of Lake Turkana in northern Kenya. They are camel-herders.

GADABA An ethnic group numbering 60,000 (1981), living in Andhra Pradesh, Madhya Pradesh, and Orissa, India. Their language, Gadaba, belongs to the Mundari group of the Austro-Asiatic and Dravidian language families.

The Gadaba live in compact, settled villages. Traditionally, they are plow cultivators in the plains and practice slash and burn cultivation in the hilly tracts. They collect firewood from the forests for sale. Hunting, food-gathering, and fishing also supplement their economy. They are now engaged in stone-cutting and earthwork, and also serve as agricultural laborers and farm servants. (see also PORJA)

GADABURSI A clan of the SOMALI.

GADALA   A subgroup of the SANHADJA.

GADAN   see GADDANG.

GADDANES   see GADDANG.

GADDANG   (Gadan, Gaddanes, Iraya, Yrraya) A group of non-Christian Gaddang who live in scattered settlements in and around the middle Cagayan Valley of Luzon, an island in the Philippines. They number a few thousand. The Gaddang believe that they descend from a common ancestor named Pangafu. They are slash and burn agriculturalists, cultivating dry rice, legumes, tubers, garlic, and tobacco. They live in autonomous settlements ruled by influential headhunter-warriors.

GADDI   A tribe numbering 77,000 (1981), found in Himachal Pradesh and Punjab, India. Their dialect of Western Pahari belongs to the Indo-Aryan family of languages. They are Hindu.

The Gaddi dwell in the mountains during the summer and migrate to the plains in the winter, a pattern common to pastoral tribes with flocks of sheep and goats in other parts of India. The Gaddi of Chamba Valley, Himachal Pradesh, follow their hereditary occupation of milk-vending.

GADE   A subgroup of the TIV.

GADULIYA LOHAR   A nomadic group of Rajasthani-speaking Hindus found in the Indian state of Rajasthan. Most are employed as laborers, particularly in specialized fields such as metalwork.

GAFAT   (Gobat) An ethnic group numbering several thousand who live east of Lake Tana in Gondar Province, Ethiopia. They are speakers of Amharic and are Ethiopian Christians. "Gafat" is a regional caste-name for smiths and potters among the AMHARA of Ibnat.

The Gafat are the remnant of a population linked to the medieval kingdom of Damot (south of the Blue Nile River). Fleeing from the OROMO, the Gafat founded the kingdom of Bizamo (north of the Blue Nile) during the sixteenth century. In the 1940s the Gafat language was thought to be nearly extinct. (see also ETHIOPIANS)

GAGAUZ   A Turkic people living mainly in Moldova (200,000), as well as in the Ukraine, Bulgaria (10,000), and Romania (5,000). Although their origins are obscure, their name and the similarities between their language and Anatolian Turkish has led scholars to hold that the Gagauz are descended from Oguz tribes who migrated to the steppes north of the Black Sea. In recorded history, however, they are only mentioned as Orthodox Christian peasants. In the nineteenth century, many migrated from the Ottoman province of Dobrudja, south of the lower Danube River, northward to Bessarabia.

Under Soviet rule, the Gagauz were denied their own autonomous region and schooling in their language. With the disintegration of the USSR, the Gagauz proclaimed the district of Moldava, in which they constituted a majority, to be autonomous.

GAGON   An ethnic group living in the Côte d'Ivoire. They are related to the DAN. (see also IVOIRE-ANS)

GAGU   (Gban) An ethnic group numbering around 20,000 living in south-central Côte d'Ivoire. They are in the process of assimilating into the culture of the GURO.

GAHUKU-GAMA   An ethnic group numbering around 15,000 living in the mountainous area of eastern Papua New Guinea. They speak an indigenous language; many are multi-lingual. While they are hunters and gatherers, they also produce garden crops. Their religious affinity is minimal, although Lutheran missionaries have been attempting to convert them to Christianity since the 1930s.

GAINJ   An ethnic group of a few thousand living in the mountainous area of central Papua New Guinea. They speak an indigenous local language and practice slash and burn cultivation. They believe that evil spirits inhabit the skies above them.

GALALARESE   An ethnic group closely related to the TOBELORESE, living on the Indonesian island of Halmahera.

GALICIANS   (s.d. Gallegos) The language and culture of the 2.5 million Galicians, who live in an isolated region of northwest Spain, are related to those of the PORTUGUESE. In the Middle Ages, the town Santiago de Compostela, which houses the presumed remains of Saint James, was a major European pilgrimage center. Galicia has remained a poor and backward region subsisting on fishing and agriculture. More than 1.5 million Galicians emigrated to the Americas, Europe, and to richer regions in Spain.

Galician culture has enjoyed a revival in the twentieth century and there is a growing nationalist movement with aspirations to greater autonomy. Within a framework of nationwide decentralization in Spain, Galicians have recently attained regional self-government. (see also SPANIARDS)

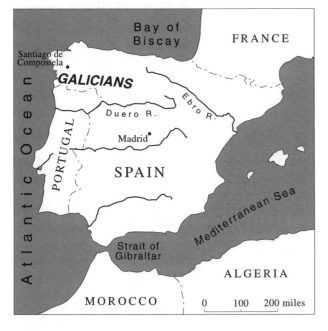

Galicians

GALLA   see OROMO.

GALLEGO   see GALICIANS.

GALOA   (Galwa) An ethnic group living on Lambarene Island and along the Ogooue River, Gabon. They speak Myene and are mostly Christians, but some adhere to traditional religions.

The Galoa were organized in a kingdom prior to colonization by the FRENCH. In the nineteenth century their king allowed FRENCH, BRITISH, and GERMANS to trade in his territories in order to eliminate middlemen from the NKOMI and ORUNGU on the coast. When his successor tried, however, to resist colonization, he was deported to Dakar (Senegal).

The Galoa joined the American and European missions, acquiring skills which enabled them to serve as agents of European firms and in the French colonial administration.

GALONG   A small ethnic group of paleo-Mongoloid stock, numbering 9,000 (1981), who inhabit the fertile, flatter land in the lower Siyom, Sipu, and Simen valleys of the Siang District, Arunachal Pradesh, India. The largest Galong village is Kombong, with a population of more than 1,000. Their dialect is closely related to the Adi language.

Shifting cultivation is practiced extensively. Rice, the staple food, is supplemented by millet and maize.

GAMBIANS   The people of the Gambia in West Africa are divided among a number of ethnic groups, the principal of which are the MALINKE, FULANI, WOLOF, DIOLA, and SONINKE. Each has its own language, but the country's official language is English. About 85 percent are Muslims, the rest are mainly Christians, with a small number who adhere to traditional religions.

The Gambia is one of Africa's smallest states. It is a semi-enclave in Senegal, but Gambian history and colonial experience differ from those of the SENEGALESE. The Gambians became independent from colonial rule by the BRITISH in February 1965. The People's Progressive Party (PPP), the dominant party since independence, has tried to integrate all ethnic groups despite its initial identification with the MALINKE. The Gambia's democratic and peaceful political life was interupted in 1981 by an attempted coup against the president, Dawda Jawara, which was averted with the intervention of the Senegalese army. As a result, the Senegambian confederation was established. It was dissolved in 1990, mainly because of Gambian fear of domination by the more numerous SENEGALESE.

GAMBIRI   (Tregami) One of several tribes grouped together as NURESTANIS.

GAMIT   A people numbering 362,000 (1981), living in the Surat district in Gujarat, Karnataka, and Maharashtra, India. Their dialect, Bhili, belongs to the Indo-Aryan family of languages.

GAMO   (Gamu) A people numbering 470,000 (1980s) who live in the highlands west of Lake Abaya in eastern Gemu Gofa province, Ethiopia. They speak Welamo and adhere to traditional beliefs. "Gamo" is also a generalized (pejorative) term given by the AMHARA to peoples living in the highlands west of Lake Abaya.

GAN   An ethnic group related to the LOBI living in Burkina Faso along the Bougouriba River, between Bobo Dioulasso and Gaoua.

GANDA (Baganda) A people living in Uganda, in the area northwest of Lake Victoria, between the Nile and Katonga Rivers. Numbering 2.2 million (1967), they are the largest single ethnic group in Uganda, comprising more than 15 percent of the population. Their language, Luganda, belongs to the Eastern Lacustrine Bantu languages. It was the earliest such language to be standardized and is the most widely used of all indigenous Ugandan languages: 39 percent of UGANDANS can speak this tongue.

Ganda

The Ganda are agriculturalists, growing plantains (their main food) vegetables, sugar-cane, coffee, and bananas. The latter crop allowed the Ganda to live a sedentary life, which in turn enabled a high population density. Livestock-herding is of minor importance and does not have the same position in their culture as it does among the northern cattle-herding Nilotic-speakers. The Ganda build and use boats in the areas bordering the lakes, especially on the Sese Islands, where fishing and inland trading are a main economic activity. They once had large fleets of war canoes.

The Ganda lived in villages centered around the chief's residence. With the growing importance of state officials and the declining influence of the chiefs, the settlement pattern became more dispersed. Villages are located on hills and consist of thirty to eighty homesteads. The Ganda have a clan-structure, with about thirty different clans. Originally they constituted a stratified society of peasants and pastoralists, but these dividing lines have become blurred.

The Ganda were politically organized within the kingdom of Buganda, from which modern Uganda derived its name. Their king (*kabaka*) had unlimited powers and governors ruled the various regions in his name. His court was administered by a hierachically-structured and specialized group of royal officials, making Buganda the most sophisticated centralized political organization in the area. The *kabaka*'s person was surrounded by elaborate rituals. During the colonial era a chiefs' council (*lukiko*) was instituted to check his power.

Early in the sixteenth century the HIMA, cattle-herders from the north, invaded the area and imposed their rule on the agricultural Ganda. The two groups soon merged into one people. Their kingdom, Buganda, expanded from a core area on the shores of Lake Victoria and incorporated areas which belonged to other Hima-ruled kingdoms. In the eighteenth century Buganda became the strongest power in the region, expanding at the expense of the declining Bunyoro kingdom. Nevertheless, Buganda did not cover all the areas where Luganda is spoken, Busoga and Kisiba remaining formally independent. The kings of Buganda retained some kind of rule over adjacent countries, which were subject to frequent raids and wars, stabilizing the king's rule in his own country and enhancing his prestige. Some neighboring regions were absorbed into the Buganda kingdom and their population assimilated, as happened with the SESE, inhabitants of the Sese Islands in Lake Victoria. In 1966 the king, Mutesa II, was expelled and one year later Buganda was abolished as a kingdom.

The Buganda kingdom was the core area of what later became the British Protectorate of Uganda, and the Ganda were the earliest and most intensively exposed to European influences. Their literacy rate is the highest in the country and they were therefore overrepresented in the administration during the time of the Protectorate. They rapidly switched to cash crop production, mostly coffee and cotton, supported by a new system of freehold land tenure introduced by the BRITISH.

During the last quarter of the nineteenth century, a new generation of chiefs emerged, largely Christianized and open to new incentives. This enhanced the Ganda's preparedness to adopt to new economic and administrative methods. They became the main African agents for spreading British colonial rule. One of the most notable military achievements was the conquest of the land of the TESO by the Ganda army leader, Kakungulu, in 1897, with the tacit support of the BRITISH, who took over the area in 1907.

The greater part of the population is Christian, but there is a small Muslim minority. Their indigenous religion was similar to that of their neighbors, consisting mainly of ancestor-worship and the belief in a a remote supreme being, as well as spirits and gods, whose worship was conducted by religious specialists. (see also SOGA, TESO, UGANDANS, YUMA)

GANDULE A Native South American group living in Venezuela.

GANE A subgroup of the SAWAI.

GANGILA see GANJULE.

GANGUELA A people numbering about 330,000 living near the Zambezi and Lungwebulu Rivers of eastern Angola. They are divided among Christians and adherents of traditional religions. Although the Ganguela engaged in agriculture and hunting, they were especially well known as capable fishermen. Their economic, social, and religious structures and rituals revolve around fishing, with certain rituals performed to appease the fisherman's guardian spirit.

The Ganguela were organized into some twenty small, decentralized subgroups such as the LOVALE, LUENA, and LUCHAZI, and were overrun by their more powerful neighbors, the LUNDA-CHOKWE and OVIMBUNDU. (see also ANGOLANS)

GANJULE (Gangila) An ethnic group numbering 3,000 (1980s) who live on three islands (Dana, Dano, and Ganjule) of Lake Chamo on the border between the Gemu Gofa and Sidamo Provinces in Ethiopia. They speak Kachami, a language of the Omotic grouping, and adhere to traditional beliefs. The Ganjule are fishermen, with fields on the mainland.

GANTI An ethnic group living in the mountainous central region of the Indonesian island of Sulawesi (Celebes). (see also TORADJA)

GANZA, GUNZA see KOMA.

GAOSHAN (Kaoshan) The collective name of a group of indigenous peoples, numbering a few thousand, living on the island of Taiwan, off the southeast coast of China. Several theories account for the origins of the Gaoshan, who are considered to be the descendants of the most ancient inhabitants of Taiwan: the Yue tribes of ancient China who migrated to Taiwan and were later joined by other peoples from the Ryukyu Islands, Indonesia, and the Philippines.

The distinctive dialects composing the Gaoshan language are related to Indonesian. They have no writing system of their own.

Most Gaoshan believe in ghosts and spirits; ancestor worship is also widespread. Their main occupation, the cultivation of rice, millet, taro, and sweet potatoes, is complemented by hunting and fishing.

The Gaoshan put up heroic resistance to the Japanese occupation of Taiwan between the years 1895 and 1945.

GAR A subgroup of the MNONG.

GARDULLA see GIDOLE.

GARIA I A group of ASSAMESE who adopted Islam in the seventeenth century. They number about five million, and are found mainly in the eastern Indian state of Assam.

GARIA II (s.d. Sumau) An ethnic group of a few thousand living on the northern coast of Papua New Guinea. They speak an indigenous regional language. They are gardeners whose chief crops are yams and bananas.

GARO I see BOSHA.

GARO II (Mandai) An ethnic group living in Bangladesh. They are divided among two main groupings, the ACHHICK, or Hill Garo, who dwell in heavily-forested regions, and the LAMDANI, or Plains Garo, who live at the foot of the Garo Hills in the district of Mymensing.

The Garo adhere to their traditional religion; their society is matriarchal. Their economy is based on agriculture.

GARRI A subgroup of the OROMO.

GARUDI see NAT.

GARWE An ethnic group living in Zimbabwe.

GARWI An ethnic group living in the mountains of the Swat region of northern Pakistan. No population data are available, but a rough estimate puts them at several thousand. Their language belongs to the Dardic group of Indo-Iranian languages. Garwi and Bashkarik (see DIRI), are usually regarded as two dialects of one language. Garwi is unwritten, and Urdu is used as the official language of writing and education, with Pashto used for oral communication with non-Garwi.

The Garwi are Sunni Muslims of the Hanafi school and are sedentary agriculturists.

GATAMI (Kachem) An ethnic group numbering 6,000 (1980s), who live on a southern island of Lake Abaya on the border between the Gemu Gofa and Sidamo Provinces, Ethiopia. Their language, sometimes called Kachama, belongs to the Omotic grouping and they adhere to traditional beliefs. The Gatami are weavers, fishermen, and hippopotamus hunters; they also have fields on the mainland.

GAUWADA An ethnic group numbering 35,000 (1980s), who live east of the Woito River in southeast Gemu Gofa Province, Ethiopia. They are speakers of an eastern Cushitic language and adhere to traditional beliefs. The Gauwada are agriculturalists (grains, ensete) and cattle-raisers.

GAVARI A subgroup of the AFGHANS.

GAVIAO A South American Indian group living in the State of Mato Grosso, central-west Brazil. Together with the SURUI they amount to a few hundred individuals. Both groups speak the same language.

GAWAR An ethnic group inhabiting a few villages in the Kunar valley in Afghanistan and Pakistan. No population data are available, although rough estimates of their number vary between several hundred and 3,000. Their language, Gawarbati, belongs to the central subgroup of Dardic languages of the Indo-Iranian group of the Indo-European family of languages. It is unwritten, Pashto (and in Pakistan also Urdu) being used as the literary language.

The Gawar are sedentary agriculturalists. Some have settled in the Bajaur area. A process of steady assimilation into the PASHTUN has been noted.

GAYO An ethnic group occupying the Gayo highlands in the Atjeh province of the Indonesian island of Sumatera (Sumatra). Although little research has yet been conducted about the Gayo (their remote territory has precluded contact until this century), they appar-

ently represent a proto-Malayasian strata of the island's population and have close linguistic and cultural ties with the BATAK. They have been Muslims since the seventeenth century as a result of contact and subjugation by the ATJEHNESE, but pre-Islamic beliefs are also important. The Gayo engage primarily in rice cultivation and herding.

GBANDE see GHANDI.

GBANZIRI An ethnic group living in the Central African Republic. (see also CENTRAL AFRICAN REPUBLIC, THE PEOPLES OF THE)

GBAYA, GBEYA see BAYA.

GEBE A subgroup of the SAWAI.

GEBUSI An ethnic group of approximately 500 living in the Strickland River region in central Papua New Guinea. They speak an indigenous regional language. They are producers of sago and bananas, and are hunters and fishermen. Their cosmos is occupied by many different spirits, prominent among which are the true spirits who answer many of nature's menacing questions.

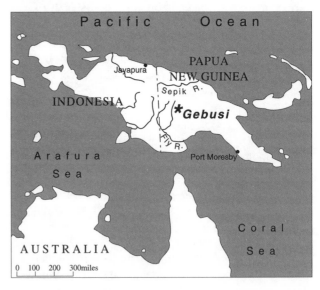

Gebusi

GEDICHO see DARASA.

GELEBA see DASSANETCH, ETHIOPIANS.

GENOA A subgroup of the CHARRUA.

GEORGIANS (s.d. Kartveli) A people living in the Republic of Georgia, in the central part of the Transcaucasus, until 1991 one of the union republics of the USSR. According to the Soviet 1989 census, there were 4 million Georgians, but this number included the AJAR as a subgroup of the Georgians, while the MEGREL and SVAN were also considered as parts of the broader Georgian nation.

The overwhelming majority of Georgians are Eastern Orthodox Christians (since the fourth century). A smaller number profess Catholicism; three Georgian ethnic subgroups, the AJAR, INGILOI, and FEREIDAN, are Muslims.

The Georgian language, Kartuli, belongs to the Kartvelian branch of the Ibero-Caucasian family of languages.

Within the boundaries of Georgia there are fifteen Georgian ethnolinguistic regions, divided between west and east and mountain and valley. Each area takes its name from the name of the main Georgian tribe settled in the region and its dialect. Although residual, tribal differences still exist.

The main lowland areas in eastern Georgia are Kartli, located in the basin of the Kura river, with Tbilisi the capital city as its main center, and Kakheti, located in the basin of the Alazani and Iori Rivers, with the city of Telavi as main center. The main mountain areas are Tusheti and Khevsureti. The west Georgia areas are Imereti (center), Kutaisi, the second largest city of Georgia, Racha, Guria, in the basin of the Vioni River (ancient Fasis), and Achara, on the Black Sea shore, in the area of the port of Batumi.

Georgian is the single ancient written language of the Ibero-Caucasian family. It is also the literary language for MEGREL and SVAN. The Georgian alphabet has been used since the fifth century; its origin has been traced back to the Greek and Aramaic alphabets, which were used in the first to the third centuries in Georgia. The earliest-known examples of Georgian literature date back to the late fifth and mid-sixth centuries.

During the tenth to twelfth centuries Georgia reached the highest level of its political and cultural development. *The Man in the Panther's Skin*, a poem by Shota Rustaveli, was written toward the end of the twelfth century.

In the fifteenth century the Georgian kingdom was divided into several political units. In 1801 the east-Georgian kingdom was abolished and Georgia was included in the Russian empire. Other parts of Georgia came under Russian rule between 1803 and 1878. Georgia's independence was restored in the period

1917–1921, in the aftermath of the Russian revolution; in 1922 it became part of the Transcaucasian Socialist Federative Soviet Republic, and from 1936 it was a Soviet Socialist Republic. In 1991 Georgia declared its independence.

The capital of Georgia from the third to the beginning of the sixth century was Armazg-Mzcheta; since then it has been Tbilisi. (see also MESKH)

GERA A subgroup of the OROMO.

GERE An ethnic group living in the Côte d'Ivoire.

GERKID A subgroup of the NUBIANS.

GERMANS (s.d. Deutsche) The 78 million Germans live in recently unified Germany: 49 percent are Protestant and 44 percent Catholic. They speak German, a West Germanic language also spoken in a variety of dialects in neighboring countries by AUSTRIANS, SWISS, French ALSATIANS, as well as by 15,000–20,000 Germans in the Danish province of North Schleswig. German-speakers are also found in Eastern Europe, the U.S.A., Brazil, and Argentina. Due to the fact that between 1700 and 1933 some 7 million Germans migrated to other countries, German-speakers may total 100 million worldwide.

The Germans descend from Indo-European peoples such as Franks, Saxons, and BAVARIANS who, in the first centuries B.C.E., expanded along the North and Baltic Seas. Confrontation with the Romans was the first formative influence: Rhineland's ancient urban culture is a Roman contribution. Germany came into being in the ninth century in the eastern area of Charlemagne's partitioned empire, which eventually evolved into the Holy Roman Empire. However, German emperors failed to establish strong authority and their realm was fragmented into several power-bases. In the Middle Ages Hanseatic towns dominated northern Europe economically. From the thirteenth century population and economic growth led to commercial expansion into and colonization of Poland, Bohemia, and Hungary. As Germans extended their hold over the eastern frontier, they germanized and christianized the local population. Of great importance was the colonization of the Baltic regions of Prussia under the Order of the Teutonic Knights.

In the sixteenth century Martin Luther and other Germans were among the vanguard of the Reformation, a formative moment of Germany's national consciousness. However, the Counter-Reformation succeeded in reclaiming southern Germany for Catholicism. Wars of religion, in particular the Thirty Years' War (1618–1648), left the country fragmented in hundreds of disconnected and weak principalities for centuries. The Napoleonic invasions destroyed feudalism and serfdom but simultaneously catalyzed a nationalist reaction led by Prussia, the dominant political and military power of northern Germany.

Mid-nineteenth century attempts to unify Germans by means of a liberal revolution fell through. It took another generation before Prussian chancellor Otto von Bismarck succeeded, around 1870, in imposing unity and welding together the different German regions (except for the Habsburg-dominated Austrian territories) into one empire. Rapidly industrializing and with a growing population, it became at once Europe's foremost political, economic, and military power. German culture dominated European philosophy, social and natural sciences, and technology. Latecomers in the imperial race for colonies, they directed their energies toward Central Europe. World War I resulted in defeat, territorial losses, and revolution. The 1920s' Weimar Republic lacked domestic legitimacy. In the early 1930s, the National Socialists came to power on a program of hyper-nationalism, and established a dictatorial regime led by Adolf Hitler. A combination of terror by state, party, and security organs, and a corporate economy efficiently crushed all opposition. The Nazis launched Germany on a course of militarization and unlimited expansion.

After World War II Germany was laid waste and occupied by the Allied powers. They divided it into Western and Eastern zones, which soon matured into the Federal Republic of Germany (FRG) and German Democratic Republic (GDR), respectively.

After the war, 10 million ethnic Germans — often centuries-old communities — were expelled from Central and Eastern Europe, throwing back the ethnic border between the Germans and the Slavs to the Oder-Neise line: 7 million from Posen, Silesia, Pomerania, and East Prussia (now part of Poland), and another 350,000 from Poland in its prewar borders, 2 million Sudeten Germans from Czechoskovakia, 200,000 from Hungary, 140,000 from Yugoslavia, 123,000 from Romanian Transylvania, 400,000 from the Soviet Union, in particular the Baltic republics. In addition, four million GDR citizens fled west before the erection of the Berlin Wall in 1961. In the 1980s hundreds of thousands more Germans entered Germany from the GDR and Eastern Europe. Two million Volga Germans in Russia remain in a category of their own. Deported en masse as collaborators in 1941–1942 to Qazaqstan and Saratov, they have been rehabilitated but not allowed to return to their former territory; 150,000 have migrated to Germany while the remainder have assimilated into their Russian-speaking surroundings.

The huge refugee population has been rather smoothly integrated. Germans rebuilt their society in two new countries. But while the Communist GDR never succeeded in fostering sufficient loyalty among its subjects, the capitalist FRG evolved into a viable polity, undergoing rapid economic growth in the 1950s and 1960s and creating once again one of the world's richest and most developed societies. In recent years the end of the Cold War, the fall of the Berlin wall, and the reabsorption of the impoverished former GDR compel Germans to concentrate their energies nearer at home. Meanwhile, a very liberal immigration policy has turned Germany into Europe's country with the most foreigners. Already hosting 6 million TURKS, KURDS, ITALIANS, GREEKS, South Slavs, GYPSIES, etc., some Germans felt threatened by the looming arrival of East Europeans. Economic difficulties, compounded by the hardships incurred by the integration of their East German compatriots, have stimulated violent neo-Nazi antiforeigner outbursts.

GERRI, GERRI-MERO　Subgroups of the OROMO.

GEUREN　A South American Indian people numbering several thousand, living in Brazil. They are believed to be descended from the BOTOCUDO.

GHANAIANS　The people of Ghana, West Africa, estimated as numbering over 15 million. About one-third live in urban areas, but most of the population is concentrated in the southern part of the country. The Ghanaian people consists of over seventy-five ethnic groups, each of which speaks a different dialect. The main ethnic groups are the AKAN (44 percent), including several subgroups, of which the largest is the ASHANTI around the city of Kumasi; the MOLE-DAGBANI ethnic groups (16 percent) in the north; the EWE (13 percent) in the east; the GA and ADANGBE (8 percent) in the south; the GUAN (7 percent) in the northeast; the GURMA (3.5 percent) in the east; and the GRUSI groups (3.5 percent).

About 43 percent of Ghanaians are Christians, 38 percent adhere to traditional religions, and the rest are Muslims. The official language of Ghana is English, while the most widely spoken languages are Akan and Mole-Dagbani.

The Ghanaians were the first people in sub-Saharan Africa to become independent from colonial rule when they gained independence from the BRITISH in 1957. The main opposition to Kwame Nkrumah's party, the Convention People's Party (CPP), came from the ASHANTI, who demanded autonomy and even secession. Nkrumah succeeded in creating a Ghanaian identity and in minimizing ethnic conflicts. After his fall in a military coup in 1966, although Ghana's politics became very unstable and military coups followed periods of civilian rule, serious ethnic conflicts have been avoided. The ASHANTI continued in opposition to most of Ghana's governments, but they acted in cooperation with other ethnic groups, and the demand for autonomy or secession grew weaker.

In the early 1990s demands for political reforms and democratization were raised by large segments of the Ghanaian people.

GHANDI (Bandi or Gbande) A Mande-speaking group numbering around 75,000, living in Lofa County, Liberia. (see also LIBERIANS)

GHASI An ethnic group related to the ORAON and MUNDA, living in the Chhotanagpur region, Bihar, India.

Experts at manufacturing drums and lacquer bangles, the Ghasi are also fishermen. They are very poor and largely illiterate.

GHEGS A subgroup of the ALBANIANS.

GHILZAI A subgroup of the PASHTUN.

GHORBATI (Ghorbat) An ethnic group living dispersed in Afghanistan. Their estimated number in the early 1980s was about 600 families, i.e., about 3,000. Most speak a language named Ghorbati or Qazulagi, which belongs to the Iranian group of the Indo-European family of languages. Some speak an unspecified language named Magadi. Practically all adult Ghorbati are equibilinguals or equitrilinguals, using Pashto and/or Dari (the Persian spoken in Afghanistan) as well as their own language.

The Ghorbati are Shi'ite Muslims; according to some sources, some of them are Sunnis of the Hanafi school. They are peripatetics, i.e., non-pastoral nomads. The main male occupations are shop-keeping, making sieves and drums, and shoe-repairing; main female occupations are peddling and folk healing. (see also AFGHAN, JATS II)

GHURVAT see GYPSIES.

GIAI see NHANG.

GIBANA A subgroup of the MIJIKENDA.

GIDICHO see BAYSO.

GIDJINGALI An Australian Aboriginal group living in the Northern Territory, Australia. (see also AUSTRALIAN ABORIGINES)

GIDOLE (Gardulla) An ethnic group, numbering 35,000 (1980s), who live south of Lake Chamo, in the southeast Gemu Gofa Province, Ethiopia. They are speakers of an eastern Cushitic language and are Sunni Muslims, with some following Ethiopian Christianity or traditional beliefs. The Gidole are agriculturalists (grains, ensete). (see also ETHIOPIANS)

GIKUYU see KIKUYU.

GILAK A people living in the Gilan province of Iran on the southwest shore of the Caspian Sea. Their estimated number (mid-1970s) was 1.9 million. Their language belongs to the northwestern subgroup of the Iranian group of the Indo-European family of languages. It is practically unwritten; some very small-scale attempts at using it as a written language were

Gilak

undertaken in the 1940s but soon abandoned. Persian is used as the language of writing and education. The main occupations of the Gilak are rice-, tea-, and tobacco-growing, silkworm cultivation, and fishing.

The Gilak were ruled by local dynasties until the shah of Iran, Abbas I the Safavid (1587–1629) incorporated them in 1592 into his empire.

GILBERT ISLANDERS (Gilbertese) A Micronesian-speaking people numbering about 70,000, who inhabit the sixteen Gilbert Islands, located just south of the equator in the west-central Pacific Ocean. They make up the majority of the population of the State of Kiribati, whose total population is 75,000. The Gilbertese, 30,000 of whom inhabit the island of Tarawa, are mostly Christians. They are not uniform in their social organization. The northern Gilbert Islanders have a traditional Polynesian social stratification while the southerners lack it. Their main economic resource until the end of the 1970s was valuable deposits of phosphate on Ocean Island. Now their economy relies on copra production and foreign aid, with the government as the main employer.

GIMPU An ethnic group living in the mountainous central region of the Indonesian island of Sulawesi (Celebes). (see also TORADJA)

GINUKH An ethnic group living in one *aul* (village) in the mountains of West Daghestan, numbering about 200. They are Sunni Muslims of the Shafi'i school (since no earlier than the sixteenth to seventeenth centuries). Their language belongs to the Daghestani branch of the Ibero-Caucasian family. In recent decades it has been regarded by some scholars as a dialect of the Dido language. It is unwritten, and Avarian is used as the literary language.

The Ginukh are undergoing an intensive process of ethnic consolidation into the AVAR and today the ethnic term "AVAR" is used by them as a self-designation as well as the term "Ginukh." Their traditional economy is based on sheep-breeding.

GIO see DAN.

GIRAVARU A subgroup of the MALDIVIANS, descended from the first wave of TAMIL who settled the islands.

GIRIAMA A subgroup of the MIJIKENDA.

GISU A people living in Uganda, in the area southeast of Mount Elgon, a fertile region with very high rainfall which sustains a dense settlement pattern, the highest in Uganda. They were driven into the mountains from their original home in the plains by the MASAAI and NANDI. Their language belongs to the Eastern Lacustrine group of Bantu languages.

The Gisu are sedentary agriculturalists growing plantains, millet, and sweet potatoes, as well as maize, coffee, and cotton as cash crops. Cattle-breeding is of minor importance. Because of the high population density and the immense pressure on the land, many Gisu left their original country and moved to the cities or to plantations where they make a living as wage laborers.

The Gisu live in polgynous households. Their kinship structure is that of exogamous patrilineal clans, which are not united under any political authority. The clan-elders constitute the highest authority. The Gisu practice initiation with circumcision for both sexes.

The ancestor cult is of great importance in their religious beliefs; the Gisu also worship spirits, said to dwell in rocks, waterfalls, and snakes.

GITKSAN A Native North American group numbering about 5,000, living in six villages along the Skeena River in north-central British Columbia, Canada.

Their dialect is of the Tsimshian group, closely related to that of the NISHGA and coastal TSIMSHIAN. They were converted to Catholicism only in 1890. In the last decade they have succeeded in gaining significant rights to their ancient territory of about 20,000 km².

They still maintain a well-functioning clan system. Many of them own their own salmon fishing boats and also work in the forest industry. Approximately half the Gitksan live off the Reserve. (see also TSIMSHIAN)

GIZIGA A subgroup of the KIRDI.

GLANGALI (Granggali) An ethnic group living in one village named Glangal (Granggal) in the Pech Valley of Afghanistan. No exact data on their number are available, although a rough estimate puts them at about 1,000.

The Glangali language belongs to the Dardic group of Indo-Iranian languages. It is unwritten, Pashto being used as the written language. Speakers of the Ningalami dialect, once spoken in the village of Ningalam, not far from Glangal, have apparently completely switched over to Pashto. The Glangali are

above: A traditionally-decorated Gitksan school, British Columbia, Canada
below: Gitksan chiefs, British Columbia, Canada

Sunni Muslims of the Hanafi school. They are sedentary agriculturalists.

GLAVUDA   A subgroup of the TIV.

GLIDYI   An ethnic group related to the EWE living in southern Togo.

GNAU An ethnic group of approximately 1,000 living in northern Papua New Guinea. They speak an indigenous local language. Their economy is based upon hunting, gathering, and the cultivation of crops such as sago. Although they practice no formal religion, they do believe in a wide range of spirits and myths. Among their important rituals are the initiation ceremonies of boys and girls.

GOAJIRA   An Arawak-speaking South American Indian people occupying the Goajira Peninsula in Colombia. They have adopted the breeding of European livestock while still maintaining an aboriginal culture. Status is now measured in cattle-wealth. Shamanism and traditional mythologies have survived.

GOBAT   see GAFAT.

GOBIR   A subgroup of the HAUSA.

GODIE   An ethnic group living in southwest Côte d'Ivoire, around the town of Lakota. They belong to the KRU ethnic grouping and are closely related to the DIDA.

GODOBERI   (s.d. Ghibdiri Adomi: "people of the village Ghidu") A people numbering 2,000 inhabiting the mountains of northwest Daghestan. They have been Sunni Muslims since the ARABS conquered the Caucasus in the seventh and eighth centuries. The Godoberi language belongs to the Daghestani branch of the Ibero-Caucasian family. It is unwritten and Andi is used as the literary language. The Godoberi are a subgroup of the AVAR.
   Their traditional economy is based on sheep- and cattle-breeding and horticulture.

GOFA   A people numbering 160,000 (1980s) who live in the western highlands of the Gemu Gofa Province, Ethiopia. They are speakers of Welamo and adhere to traditional beliefs. "Gofa" is a generalized term which includes the former polities of the Sala (Zala) and Uba. The Gofa plant cereals on terraced fields, and near their homesteads they cultivate ensete, cabbage, tobacco, millet, and maize.

GOGO   (Ugogo) A people inhabiting the thorn-scrub plain of central Tanzania. According to the 1967 census, they numbered 360,000. The Gogo are considered to be quite recent occupants of the region called Wagogo. The Gogo language belongs to the Central Tanzanian sub-group of the Bantu Niger-Kodofan family of languages.
   The Gogo are cultivators as well as shepherds. Their herds of cattle dominate the social and economic life of the community. Cultivation is based on the system of shifting agriculture. Millet is cultivated on the larger plots, cleared from scrub; for maize, tobacco, and groundnuts smaller plots are tilled. Their fields are usually close to their dwellings. The Gogo have no distinct villages. Their houses are spread thinly over a wide area. (see also TANZANIANS)

GOGODALA   An ethnic group of approximately 5,000 living in the Fly River basin in southern Papua New Guinea. They speak an indigenous regional language. In a process that began in the 1930s, nearly all of their traditional beliefs as well as their religious ceremonies have been replaced by Christian beliefs and rituals.

GOGOT   A subgroup of the GURAGE.

GOKLEN   A subgroup of the TURKMEN.

GOLA   An ethnic group living in Lofa, Grand Cape Mount, Bomi, and Montserando Counties, Liberia. Gola are also found in Sierra Leone.
   The Gola resisted attempts by AMERICO-LIBERIANS to colonize their region in the late nineteenth century. Only in 1905, after twenty-five years of fighting, did they sign a treaty with the Liberian goverment. (see also LIBERIANS)

GOMA   A subgroup of the OROMO.

GOND   A people numbering 7.5 million (1981), living in the states of Madhya Pradesh, Andhra Pradesh, Bihar, Orissa, Gujarat, Karnataka, West Bengal, and Maharashtra, India. Their language, Gondwani, belongs to the Dravidian family.
   The Gond are regarded as a primarily Dravidian people who crossed into their present abode from the

Gond

south through Bastar and Chanda. The area prospered under Gond rulers, who encouraged irrigation and agriculture, until Maratha armies conquered Gondwana, as the country was known, and plundered it.

A Hindu people, the Gond worship other family and village gods. Their society can be divided into three classes: the aristocracy, or Raj Gond; tenants, known as Dust Gond; and laborers, called Kamias. These are further divided into clans, each with its own totem. Joint families, known as *Bhaiband*, manage day-to-day affairs and hold the agricultural land in common ownership.

Slash and burn is the usual method of cultivation; crops raised include maize, millet, black-gram, paddy, oil seeds, wheat, chickpeas, and flax. Irrigation is almost unknown, and drinking water is fetched from running streams. Cows are held in religious regard and hence are not yoked to the plow.

Tribal conventions prohibit the sale of property, even though the government does not forbid it. The concept of holding landed property in common and the denial of an individual's right to sell the land in his possession are both ancient tribal laws which cannot be rescinded by legislature. (see also KAMAR, MAJHWAR, MURIA, PANIKA, PARDHAN)

GONGA (Shinasha) An ethnic group numbering 25,000 (1980s) who live in southern Gojjam Province, Ethiopia. The Gonga are the northernmost

speakers of an Omotic language. They adhere to traditional beliefs and Ethiopian Orthodox Christianity. Until the late nineteenth century, they formed a small kingdom.

GOODENOUGH ISLANDERS An ethnic group of approximately 15,000 living on an island off the northeastern tip of Papua New Guinea. The four languages which they speak are all indigenous local languages. They are gardeners, their principal crop being yams. Although the target of diligent missionary work for over 100 years, the Islanders still possess many of their magic-related traditional religious beliefs.

GORAIT An ethnic group numbering 7,500 (1981), living in Bihar and West Bengal, India. Their dialect is similar to Mundari.

The Gorait are occupied primarily in agriculture; a secondary occupation is foraging. On festive occasions they are hired to play drums. They worship a number of gods.

GORALE SEE POLES.

GORONTALO (Holontalo) An ethnic group numbering slightly under half a million, living in the northern peninsula of the Indonesian island of Sulawesi (Celebes). They speak several dialects, all related to languages of the Philippines. Their traditional religion has been supplanted by Islam. Economic activity centers around slash and burn cultivation of rice, corn, and

Gorontalo

sago, fishing, and collecting rattan. Some Gorontalo groups are well-known for their adeptness in the manufacture of colorful cloth and silk clothing.

In the past a Gorontalo kingdom was dominated by the TERNATANS. From the late seventeenth century until the Dutch occupation in the late nineteenth century, the Gorontalo formed a federation called the Lima Pahala (League of Five Brothers) with neighboring peoples.

Gorontalo subgroups include the ATTINGOLA, BOALEMO, BONE, BUOL, KWANDANG, LIMBOTO, and SOEWAWA.

GOUIN An ethnic group related to the SENUFO living in the Bañfuro area of Burkina Faso.

GOULAYE A subgroup of the SARA.

GOVE A generic term for several unrelated Shona-speaking groups living in Zimbabwe. Gove groups living along the Zambezi Valley are related to the KOREKORE; those living north of Harare are a branch of the ZEZURU; Gove in the Shurugwi district are a subgroup of the KARANGA.

GOVERA A subgroup of the KARANGA.

GOWA An ethnic group related to the TONGA living in Zambia.

GRANGGALO see GLANGALI.

GREBO An ethnic group numbering about 200,000, living in Grand Gedeh, Maryland, and Sinoe Counties, Liberia. They speak the Kru language. (see also LIBERIANS)

GREEK CYPRIOTS see CYPRIOTS.

GREEKS (s.d. Ellenoi) The overwhelming majority of Greeks live in Greece (10.2 million, or 96 percent of the population), in Cyprus (567,000, or 80 percent), in southern Albania (about 250,000), and in European Turkey, mainly Istanbul. Sizeable Greek communities are to be found in Western Europe, the Commonwealth of Independent States (about 360,000), North and South America, and Australia. The large Greek diaspora in the Middle East has mainly repatriated to Greece or emigrated to other destinations since the 1950s.

The Greek language forms a branch of its own within the Indo-European linguistic family. It is divided into many dialects, those of Crete and Cyprus being the most remote from the standard literary form. Greek is the oldest written language in Europe, written in its own alphabet, which was derived from Hebrew and later formed the basis for both the Roman and Cyrillic alphabets in which all European languages are written. With such a long history, Greek gave rise to several literary forms. Modern literary Greek tries to combine different elements of these forms while not moving too far from the colloquial dialects, mainly of Athens.

Greek tribes arrived in present-day Greece during the second half of the second millennium B.C.E. in several waves. From there they spread across the Aegean islands to the western rim of Anatolia. These areas, together with Crete and Cyprus, formed the classical Greek world, which developed a civilization that became the basis for the modern Western one. In later centuries the Greeks colonized parts of the Mediterranean, mainly southern Italy and eastern Sicily, and the Black Sea shores.

The conquests of Alexander the Great at once widened the horizons of the Greek world and laid foundations for the fusion of civilizations into what became known as Hellenistic civilization, but at the same time pushed Greece itself to the margins of the new Hellenistic world. The marginalization of Greece was completed under the Roman empire. With the partition of the Roman empire, the eastern half gradually moved away from Latin to Greek, under the Byzantine Empire.

Greek was the first language into which the Bible was translated, and it was the main language of the early Christian church long before Latin. The Byzantine Empire developed a civilization of its own, one of the most illustrious in history, which was absorbed by many of the neighboring Slavic peoples (including the RUSSIANS). The end of the Byzantine empire came with the fall of Constantinople to the Ottomans in 1453. However, within the Greek world under the Ottoman empire the center remained in Constantinople/Istanbul. The Ottomans placed all Eastern Orthodox Christians under the authority of the Patriarch of Constantinople. Greece continued to be marginal as before.

However, it was in Greece that in 1770 Russian-instigated uprisings against the Ottomans occurred. This had little to do with demands for independence, or with nationalism. By the 1820s, the situation had changed. The influence of nationalist slogans, the French Revolution, and the admiration for ancient Greece by European, and later Greek, Romanticists all created a national consciousness which, fed by the weakness of the Ottoman Empire, produced the revolt

above: A Greek dancing troupe
below: A Greek farmer

of 1821 and led to the War of Independence of 1821–1829, in which interventions by Britain, France, and Russia created an independent little Greece on a small part of the territory inhabited by Greeks.

For the first time since the late fourth century B.C.E., mainland Greece, or more precisely Athens, became a center of the Greek world, although it remained for decades secondary to Constantinople. Greeks from outside Greece refused to come and serve the new kingdom. Many Greek diplomats and adminstrators continued to be in the service of the Ottoman Sultan. For most Greeks "inside," Constantinople remained the acknowledged center and its liberation their greatest aspiration.

Their hope (the *magali*, or "great idea") was to re-unite all the territories regarded as the Greek homeland, forming classical (ancient) Greece as well as the Byzantine heartland. Many hoped for the reconquest of Constantinople, and the transfer of the capital to it from Athens: others hoped to re-establish the Byzantine empire.

The leaders and rulers of the new Greek state did their best to expand its borders. In 1864 Britain transferred the Ionian islands to Greece. In 1881, Greece received Thessaly, to the north. Following the Balkan wars Greece annexed Crete, almost all the Aegean islands (except the Dodecanese islands, annexed by Italy in 1912 and ceded to Greece in 1948), Epirus, and part of Macedonia, including Thessaloniki. Greece joined the Entente Powers in World War I in 1917, and gained Western Thrace as well as part of the Aegean coast of Anatolia, including the city of Smyrna.

In 1921 Greece, pushed by Britain, launched an offensive against the Turkish nationalists led by Mustafa Kemal Ataturk, but were defeated and thrown out of Anatolia, which became Turkish Izmir. Following this disaster the monarchy was overthrown and a republic proclaimed. The monarchy was reinstated only in 1936. Following the Greco-Turkish War a general exchange of population was carried out, in which over a million Greek Orthodox inhabitants of Turkey, many of whom did not speak Greek at all, were transferred to Greece, while a similar number of Muslim inhabitants of Greece were transferred to Turkey.

Following World War II, in which Greece was occupied by the Axis powers, British troops landed in Athens and restored the royal government. Simultaneously the Communists established their own regime in Thessaloniki. The civil war that followed ended only in 1949 and left deep wounds in the social and political fabric. The Left remained compromised for more than

a generation, and once it started to gain in strength again, a military junta carried out a coup in April 1967. When the king opposed them, they sent him into exile and abolished the monarchy in 1973. In 1974 the junta lost control and democracy was restored to Greece.

The Greeks of Cyprus (then about 79 percent of the population), who had been passive through Ottoman and British rule (since 1878) started after World War II to demand British withdrawal and union (*enosis*) with Greece. From the mid-1950s this was backed by the armed activity of an underground led by a general from Greece. The Turkish minority objected to union with Greece, and in 1960 Cyprus was given independence as a binational republic, under guarantees from Britain, Greece, and Turkey. However, as the Greeks did not give up their wish for *enosis* and the Turkish resolve to block it remained as strong as before, several crises, accompanied by rounds of clashes, occurred in the 1960s. In 1974 Greek extremists carried out a coup, backed, if not masterminded, by the junta in Greece, to unite with Greece. In response Turkey intervened militarily, forcefully divided the island, and established a Turkish Republic of Northern Cyprus. (see also CYPRIOTS, TURKS)

GREENLANDERS The 57,000 inhabitants of Greenland, a Danish dependency located between the North Atlantic and the Polar Sea on the world's largest island. They are predominantly INUIT (Eskimos). Fishing, hunting, and mining are the main occupations, with the small European population concentrated in administration and skilled services.

This former colony became self-governing after a referendum favoring home rule in 1979. With self-government came increased official usage of the Greenlandic language, an Eskimo-Aleut dialect. The territory is now called Kalaallit Nunaat and the capital is called Nuuk.

GRENADIANS The 84,000 inhabitants of Grenada, the smallest independent nation in the western hemisphere, comprising three islands north of Trinidad in the Caribbean Sea. They are predominantly descendants of black African slaves, who worked the islands' extensive sugar and spice plantations under British colonial rule. English is the official language and Roman Catholicism is the religion of 60 percent of the islanders; the rest are Protestants. Exports of agricultural products are the main source of foreign exchange. Grenada became independent in 1974. American military intervention following an internal military coup in 1983 led to the restoration of democratic government in late 1984.

GROGO   An ethnic group living on the Indonesian island of Kalimantan (Borneo). (see also DAYAK)

GROS VENTRE   (Atsina, Awatixa) A Native North American group who originally inhabited the plains of Montana, U.S.A., and southern Saskatchewan, Canada.

Today they share the Fort Belknap Federal Reservation with the ASSINIBOIN.

GRUSI   (Grunshi) A generic term for several small ethnic subgroups: the KASENA, MO, NUNUMA, SISALA, TAMPOLENSE, and VAGALA, living in the Northern and Upper Regions of Ghana and in Burkina Faso. (see also BURKINABES, GHANAIANS, MOLE-DAGBANI)

GUADELOUPEANS   Inhabitants of a French Overseas Department located among the Lesser Antilles in the Caribbean Sea. Guadeloupe has a population of some 400,000, mainly descendants of black African slaves who worked on the island's sugar and banana plantations. The people are mostly Roman Catholic and a Creole dialect is widely spoken, although French is the official language. Sugar and bananas are the mainstays of the local economy, which is heavily dependent on trade with the FRENCH. There is increasing agitation for greater autonomy from France.

GUAHIBLO   A Native South American group living in Venezuela.

GUAITACA   A nomadic South American Indian people living in the savanna of southeastern Colombia, southern Venezuela, and Brazil. They are hunters and gatherers and speak an unclassified language. Agriculture is completely unknown to them.

GUAJAJARA   A South American Indian group living in the area of the Pindare and Grajau Rivers, in the State of Maranhao, northeast Brazil. They number a few thousand and speak a language of the Tupi language family.

The Guajajara live dispersed in tens of villages. Many developers have been attracted to their region due to its vegetation, with the consequent peril to Indian possessions and lives.

GUAJIRO   A Native South American group living in Venezuela.

GUALAQUIZZA   A subgroup of the JIVARO.

GUAMONTEY   A nomadic South American Indian people living in the lower reaches of the Orinoco River. They are almost entirely dependent on the river for their subsistence, fishing and hunting river animals from their dugout canoes. They also gather eggs, roots, and seeds.

GUAN   (Guang, Gwan) An ethnic group living in Ghana in a curve extending from Gonja in the Northern Region to Krakye and Larteh in the Eastern Region and to Senya Bereku in the Central Region. The Guan language is related to that of the AKAN. Some Guan are also found in Togo.

The KRANCHI, who live on the peninsula between the main Volta River and the Oti arm of Lake Volta, are a Guan subgroup. (see also GHANAIANS)

GUARANI   Speakers of a South American Indian language scattered in the States of Paraná, Santa Catarina, and Rio Grande do Sul, close to Brazil's border with Argentina and Paraguay. One group is the TUPI-GUARANI, who inhabit Argentina, Bolivia, Brazil, Colombia, Paraguay, and Peru, and speak a language divided into fifty or sixty dialects. Other important groups are the KAIWA, MBUA, and NANDEVA.

The Guarani are mostly farmers, fishermen, and coastal sailors; their society is based on strong extended families. The search for gold brought the

Guajajara

SPANIARDS into contact with the Guarani and, as was the case with most South American aboriginal communities, this contact had an unfavorable impact on them, devastating their population and weakening their traditional way of life. (see also ARGENTINES, BRAZILIANS, CHIQUITO, PARAGUAYANS)

GUATEMALANS The 7.7. million inhabitants of Guatemala, about 55 percent of whom are indigenous Central American MAYA, with 42 percent, termed "Ladino," primarily European and Indian *mestizos*. People of mixed white and black ancestry form the small remaining percentage. While many of the Indians speak a Mayan dialect, most are bilingual, and the official language is Spanish. The population is predominantly Roman Catholic, with many indigenous peoples practicing their own versions of Christianity; there are small groups of Protestants and JEWS.

While about two-thirds of the population is rural, the highest population density is in Guatemala City, its surroundings, the highland plateau, and the south coast. Agriculture, the basic market activity of Guatemalans, propelled strong economic growth in the 1970s. Agriculture employs one-fourth of the total work force and generates more than three-fifths of all exports, including coffee, sugar, cotton, and fresh meat. Guatemalans also raise cattle, pigs, and sheep, yet production of basic grains such as corn is not sufficient for the population.

Two-fifths of the country's area is covered with forests, from which Guatemalans obtain lumber and chicle (for chewing gum). Fishing provides little for export, and mining is underdeveloped, as is industry, giving employment to only one-seventh of the population. Construction activity increased after the 1976 earthquake, but later declined once again.

Politically, the recent history of the Guatemalans has been characterized by violence, which has damaged the country economically through reductions in tourism and international investments. Their culture is mixed, belonging to both the Hispanic-American and ancient indigenous worlds, as described by Nobel prizewinner Miguel Angel Astiurias. Traditional dances, music, religious rites, and games survive in Indian regions. The modern sector, however, does less well: despite free compulsory primary education, many children do not go to school, resulting in 50 percent illiteracy in the cities and 70 percent in rural areas. More than one-quarter of the population has no access to medical care.

For two millennia after the indigenous Guatemalans began to adopt sedentary agriculture, beginning about 2500 B.C.E., villages grew in size and sophistication. Guatemala and neighboring areas of Yucatan and Chiapas in contemporary Mexico were the cradles of the impressive Mayan civilization that lasted until the tenth century C.E. Half a millennium after urban Mayan civilization began its decline, the descendants of the early MAYA were conquered by the SPANIARDS, beginning in 1523. During the colonial period, Guatemala's economy was reduced to agriculture, producing cocoa and indigo for export with the labor of Indians and blacks.

After Central American independence from Spain was declared in 1821, Guatemalans briefly became part of the short-lived Mexican Empire. Since the collapse of the empire in 1823 Guatemalans have lived through a succession of authoritarian regimes, revolutions, and coups. The 1970s witnessed an escalation of political violence, coupled with the effects of a 1974 volcanic eruption and a 1976 earthquake. Rightwing terrorism decimated the rural MAYA population, an act which led to global condemnation of Guatemala for human rights violations during the late 1970s and 1980s. Although the re-establishmeant of civilian government in 1986 was accompanied by the incorporation of human rights guarantees into the constitution, violence, at a lesser level, has continued.

GUATO A nomadic South American Indian people living along the upper Paraguay River. They traditionally harvested wild rice and occasionally grew maize and manioc along the river banks. They are on the verge of extinction.

GUATUSO A Central American Indian group living in the northern Caribbean region of Costa Rica. This small group is found on the Guatuso plains, near the towns of El Sol, Tonjibe, and Margurita.

GUAYAKI A Tupi-speaking South American Indian people living in the forests of eastern Paraguay. They subsist from hunting, fishing, and the gathering of pindo palm products. They practice neither agriculture nor the building of permanent settlements.

GUAYCURU The indigenous inhabitants of Argentina, who live in the Chaco area and part of the northern areas of Santiago del Estero and Santa Fe. The group consists of the TOBA, MOCOVI, ABIPON, and PILAGA subgroups. The pure Guaycuru were rapidly exterminated after the Spanish conquest; the warrior

Guayaki

ABIPON were largely exterminated during the eighteenth and nineteenth centuries.

GUAYMI   A Chibcha-speaking South American Indian people of the Caribbean lowlands of western Panama and Costa Rica. They are now almost completely extinct. (see also COSTA RICANS)

GUAYUPE   A Native South American group living in Venezuela.

GUDE   A subgroup of the TIV.

GUEMBE   (Valley Tonga, We) A Tonga-speaking ethnic group living in the Guembe Valley, Zambia. Because most of their region is infested with tsetse flies, they did not keep cattle but were agriculturalists.

In 1908 the Guembe resisted the British South Africa Company's imposition of taxes. They protested again in the 1950s, this time against a dam built on Lake Kariba which flooded their lands. As a result, 29,000 people were resettled, 6,000 as far as 100 miles away. The government has since aided the Guembe to develop a fishing industry near Lake Kariba. (see also TONGA)

GUEMENU   A subgroup of the GUN. (see also FON)

GUERE   An ethnic group living in west-central Côte d'Ivoire. They belong to the KRU ethnic grouping and are closely related to the WOBE.

The Guere never had a centralized political organization. Until recently most were subsistence farmers but there has been a recent move to cash crops. They have also begun migrating to other regions of the Côte d'Ivoire.

GUEREN   A South American Indian group living in the State of Bahía, northeast Brazil. Completely assimilated, the several thousand Gueren are believed to descend from BOTOCUDO Indians of the area.

GUERZE   see KPELLE.

GUHANA   An Arab group living in northern Sudan. (see also SUDANESE)

GUIANES   see BONTOK.

GUINEA-BISSAU, THE PEOPLE OF   The inhabitants of this West African state number an estimated 1 million and consist of several ethnic groups. The largest of these is the LANTA, who constitute 32 percent of the population. They live north and south of the Geba River and most adhere to traditional religions. The FULANI live in the center of the country, the MANJACO in the area south of the Cacheu River and north of the Mansoa River, and the MALINKE live in the north. Other smaller ethnic groups are the PAPEL, BANYUM, BIAFADA, BIDYOGO, and BRAME. The official language of Guinea-Bissau is Portuguese. The most widely-spoken languages are Creole, Balanta, and Fulani. About 54 percent of the population adhere to traditional religions, 38 percent are Muslims, and 8 percent are Christians, mainly Catholics.

Guinea-Bissau gained its independence from the PORTUGUESE in 1974. During the colonial period the PORTUGUESE brought to Guinea-Bissau a large number of CAPE VERDEANS to serve as work inspectors for local groups, mainly the LANTA. After independence these CAPE VERDEANS, who had educational advantages over the locals, dominated Guinea-Bissau's politics. This situation continued until 1980, when a Papel military coup supported by the LANTA, put an end to Cape-Verdean domination. Since then a large number of LANTA, PAPEL, and MANJACO have been appointed to high positions in the government and administration.

In 1991, following popular unrest, the regime declared a democratization process to be launched during 1993.

GUINEANS   The people of Guinea, West Africa, number under 6 million. Most are concentrated in the plateau area of central Guinea; 75 percent live in rural areas. Almost half the Guineans belong to the MANDE ethnic groups, of which the most important is the MALINKE. The SUSU, who belong to the MANDE, are subdivided into a number of groups and live along the coast. Another major ethnic group is the FULANI, who constitute 28 percent of the population. Both the MANDE and the FULANI live in the north and center of the country. The FULANI are concentrated mainly in the Futa Djallon region.

The remainder of the Guineans belong to about fifteen smaller ethnic groups. Ninety-five percent are Muslims. The official language of the country is French while the most widely spoken languages are Malinke and Fulani.

The Guineans gained their independence from the FRENCH in 1958. During decolonization the FULANI formed their own party. With the rise of the Parti Democratique de Guinée led by a MALINKE, Ahmed Sekou Touré, the Fulani party lost most of its power. Sekou Touré led his country to independence. He tried to fight tribalism and accused the FULANI of keeping up ethnic conflicts. After independence his hostility toward the FULANI continued and in 1976 he arrested and executed over 500 FULANI in response to an alleged conspiracy against him.

The army has been in power since 1984, following Sekou Touré's death.

GUISNAY   A subgroup of the MATACO-MATAGUAYO.

GUJAR   (Gujjar, Gurjar, Gujur) A people living in northwest India, north Pakistan, and north and northeast Afghanistan. No statistical data are available; rough estimates of their number vary between several tens of thousands to a few hundred thousand. It is known, however, that the bulk of the Gujar live in India and Pakistan, with about 10,000 in Afghanistan. The Gujari language belongs to the Indian group of the Indo-Iranian family of languages. Some scholars regard it as a dialect of Rajasthani. While some writings in Gujari exist, using the Urdu adaptation of the Arabic alphabet, it is predominantly an unwritten language. In Pakistan Urdu is used as the literary language, in India, Hindi, and in Afghanistan, Dari, the local version of Persian.

The Gujar of Pakistan and Afghanistan are Sunni Muslims of the Hanafi school, while in India most are Hindu, with some adhering to Sunni Islam. The date of their conversion to Islam is uncertain; the process seems to have lasted from the eleventh to the seventeenth centuries. The Muslim Gujar observe many Hindu practices.

Both Muslim and Hindu Gujar are divided into many clans. The Hindu Gujar are sedentary agriculturalists, while the Muslim Gujar of India and Pakistan are seasonal nomads: during their sedentary season they live in windowless one-room houses. Afghanistani Gujar are mainly pastoral nomads with flocks of goats. (see also AFGHANS, GYPSIES)

GUJARATI   The inhabitants of the Indian state of Gujarat. The term can also refer to people originating from that state who speak the Gujarati language but live elsewhere. According to the 1981 census the population of Gujarat was 34 million, of whom 91 percent were Gujarati-speakers. Hindus constitute 89.5 percent of the population, Muslims, 9.5 percent, and Jains, 1 percent.

Although the Gujarati language belongs to the Indo-Aryan family, it is also partly Prakrit and partly Sanskrit in origin.

Gujarat has experienced rapid industrialization, but agriculture still forms the backbone of its economy. It has also become prominent in dairy products. Historically, Gujaratis have been excellent entrepreneurs and have traded with many foreign countries.

GUJI   see GYPSIES.

GUJJI   A southern division of the OROMO living in northern Sidamo, Ethiopia.

GULGULIA   A small nomadic group found in the state of Bihar in eastern India. They live from hunting, begging, and part-time agricultural work. They also gather herbs from which they concoct traditional medicines.

GUMIS   see GUMUZ.

GUMMO   A subgroup of the OROMO.

GUMUZ   (Gumis) An ethnic group numbering 35,000 (1980s), who live in the lowlands of the northwestern Ethiopian border with the Sudan. They speak a Nilotic language, and are divided between Sunni Muslims, Ethiopian Orthodox Christians, and adherents to traditional beliefs.

The Gumuz are sedentary agriculturalists, practicing shifting cultivation, with sorghum as their staple. Until the first half of the twentieth century, they were forced to defend themselves against slavers. (see also ETHIOPIANS, SHANKILA)

GUN   A subgroup of the FON. (see also BENINIANS)

GUNGAWA   A subgroup of the FULANI.

GURAGE   A people numbering 1.5 million (1985) who live in the southwestern part of the Shoa Region in central Ethiopia. They speak a southern Semitic (Ethio-Semitic) language and adhere to Christianity (Ethiopian Orthodox, with a Roman Catholic minority), Sunni Islam, and traditional beliefs.

The Gurage are traditionally sedentary agriculturalists whose staple crop is the "false banana" (ensete edule).

The historical ethnic formation of the Gurage is linked to several waves of migration of speakers of southern Semitic languages, including the late medieval establishment of military colonies of the empire of the ETHIOPIANS. The "seven houses" of the western Gurage (CHAHA, ENNEMOR, EZHA, GYETO, MUHER, AKLIL, WALANI-WORIRO) formed a federation before becoming again part of the Ethiopian empire (1889). Northern Gurage include the AIMELLEL, SODDO, and GOGOT; eastern Gurage subgroups include the SILTI, URIRO, ULBARAG, ENNAKOR, and WALANE.

Country-town migration is high among the Gurage. They are firmly established in urban settings. Among the rural Gurage traditional forms of cooperative labor have become successfully integrated into efforts at modernization. (see also ETHIOPIANS)

GURENSE   see NANKASI.

GURGURA   A subgroup of the OROMO.

GURIA   A subgroup of the YEDINA.

GURKHA   (Gurkhali) Not strictly an ethnic group, the Gurkha are NEPALESE (mostly GURUNG, but also MAGAR, TAMANG, SUNWAR, LIMBU, and RAI) who enlisted in the British colonial army in the mid-nineteenth century.

They believe that they are descended from the warlike Rajputs of Chittaur in Rajasthan. The Gurkha kingdom was first conquered by the Shah Thakuri dynasty in the sixteenth century. In the eighteenth century the kingdom spread into what is now Nepal, reaching as far as China and Tibet.

The Gurkha played a considerable role in most conflicts involving the BRITISH, beginning with the Indian Mutiny of 1857–1858 and culminating in World War II, when there were almost 250,000 Gurkha troops fighting on the side of the Allies. With the postwar decline of the British Empire, the number of Gurkha troops has declined considerably; today, most are stationed in Hong Kong, scheduled to be returned to China by 1999.

Most Gurkha returned to Nepal, where they had difficulties reintegrating into the local culture because of their years of exposure to the outside world. In the 1980s there was some agitation by the repatriates for a measure of autonomy in Nepal so that their more modern, pro-Western, and martial culture could be allowed to continue to develop in a specific cultural framework.

GURMA   An ethnic group living in Ghana, near the Togo border, where they number about 500,000, in Burkina Faso, between the Mossi areas and the Niger River, where they number about 450,000, and in Togo, in the Sahsanne-Mango and Dapaong regions, where they number about 170,000. They mostly adhere to traditional beliefs. (see also BURKINABES, GHANAIANS, TOGOLESE)

GURO   (s.d. Kweni) A Mande-speaking group living in the west-central area of the Côte d'Ivoire. In 1968 they numbered about 110,000.

Patrilineal Guro had no centralized political organization. Their common identity began to develop only during French colonization in the late nineteenth century. Despite their resistance, they were finally subdued in the early twentieth century. (see also IVOIREANS)

GURRA   A subgroup of the OROMO.

GURUNG   An ethnic group of Nepal, who speak a language belonging to the Tibetan family. They are Buddhists of Mongol stock. The main occupation of the Gurung in the Lamjung district is agriculture. However, since this is a difficult enterprise at high altitudes, their economic condition is poor, despite their hard work. (see also GURKHA)

GURURUMBA   An ethnic group of a few thousand, living in the Asaro River valley in central Papua New Guinea. They speak an indigenous local language. They are hunters, gatherers, and slash and burn cultivators. They believe that bodily fluids and spiritual entities control the workings of the world. Their most celebrated ceremony is the pig festival, which is attended by thousands of people.

GUYANESE   The approximately 800,000 inhabitants of Guyana (formerly British Guiana), located along the northern Atlantic coast of South America,

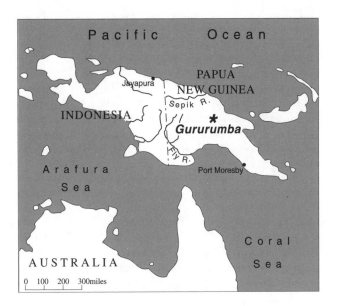

Gururumba

east of Venezuela. Guyana, whose official name is the Cooperative Republic of Guyana, is partly below sea level, protected from Atlantic flooding by a sea wall. Fifty percent of the population is composed of descendants of INDIANS and Southeast Asian laborers brought to the country in the mid-1800s to work on the sugar plantations. Of the other half of the population, just over 30 percent are directly descended from black slaves, while the remainder is composed of racially mixed people and smaller minorities of CHINESE, BRITISH, PORTUGUESE, and other Europeans. The capital, Georgetown, has a population of 72,000.

The official language is English, but racial variation is reflected in cultural, religious, and linguistic diversity. About half the people are Hindus or Muslims, one-third are Protestants, and one-sixth are Roman Catholic.

Most of the population is rural, with one-third of the people engaged in agriculture, and another third in mining. Major crops include rice, coffee, and citrus fruits. While the most important mineral product is bauxite, manganese and small quantities of gold and diamonds are also extracted.

What eventually became British Guiana, and later Guyana, was first explored by Sir Walter Raleigh in 1595 and 1617. During the 1600s, Guyanese territory was a subject of dispute among the DUTCH, FRENCH, and BRITISH, but following the Congress of Vienna (1814–1815), the land was divided into three colonies: a British, a French, and a Dutch one. Plantation sugar, produced by black slaves, formed the economic base

of Guyana well into the 1800s. After the abolition of slavery in the 1830s, the British began to import East Indians, at very low wages, to maintain plantation crop production. Discontent with British domination began about 1900, but did not reach serious proportions until the conclusion of World War II.

In 1953, in response to the Indian-led People's Progressive Party (PPP), Britain granted limited self-government; after the PPP's election victory, Britain suspended the constitution, accusing the PPP of communist leanings. The PPP, which split along ethnic lines in 1955, managed in 1964 to return briefly to power under a new constitution, but was defeated by the largely black People's National Congress (PNC) in 1964. Following independence in 1966, the Guyanese established South America's first Marxist state, nationalizing much of commerce and industry.

GWAGU   see KWEGU.

GWAMBA   see TSONGA.

GWAN   see GUAN.

GWANDARA   A subgroup of the TIV.

GWARI   A subgroup of the TIV.

GWE   A people living in southeast Uganda, in an area which is inhabited by other small groups such as the SAMIA, TESO, and PADHOLA. Their language belongs to the Eastern Lacustrine Bantu group. The Gwe are, like the SAMIA, culturally related to the LUHYA peoples of Kenya.

GWERE   An ethnic group living in the southeast of Uganda, south of the TESO. They are one of the smaller Bantu ethnic groups in Uganda. Their language, Lugweri, belongs to the group of Eastern Lacustrine Bantu languages, and is increasingly being replaced by Luganda, the language of the GANDA.

Some Gwere have assimilated into the PADHOLA and have been incorporated into their lineage system. Nevertheless, the Gwere are culturally related to the SOGA. (see also PADHOLA)

GYETO   A subgroup of the GURAGE.

GYPSIES   (in Europe s.d. Roma) An internationally dispersed, partially nomadic, minority population originating in India. Worldwide they number 8–10 million, 6–7 million of whom live scattered throughout Europe. Population data are approximations: authorities tend to play down real numbers, and many Gypsies either register under other nationalities or not at all. Other groups live in the United States, India, Pakistan, and elsewhere. Their language, Romani, is divided into many mutually unintelligible dialects. Today many no longer speak it. In general, Gypsies have converted to the religion of their surroundings. Gypsy social organization is based on extended families. They belong to a large number of tribes differentiated according to occupation.

Gypsies used to be characterized by their unconventional lifestyle; today only one-tenth continue to lead a semi-nomadic existence. Most Gypsies are extremely poor, with high illiteracy and death rates. As their traditional itinerant trades (horse trading, tinkering, smithing, music) become less in demand, many have resorted to begging and crime. Measures taken against Gypsies have included compulsory settlement, forced adoption, forcible referral of children to institutions, and forced sterilization.

Little is known about Gypsy history. Leaving North India (now Pakistan) for unknown reasons in the tenth century or earlier, and migrating through Persia and the Arab and Byzantine empires, they reached Eastern Europe between the thirteenth and fifteenth centuries and Western Europe a century later. In the Ottoman Balkan, Gypsies were exploited as slaves (half a million were still living as serfs in Romania in the nineteenth century). The church was often hostile because it associated them with magical practices such as palmistry. In the early modern period attempts were made to "discipline" them. England, France, and Spain all tried banishment or deported Gypsies to colonies overseas. In the early 1940s, the Nazis exterminated 400,000–500,000 Gypsies as undesirable aliens, a genocide unrecognized and unrecompensated in most instances. Since the 1970s Gypsies have become more assertive and have begun to organize in the International Romani Union, as well as in various civil rights and socio-cultural groupings. They are rediscovering their identity everywhere and undergoing a national revival, as apparent in publications, music, theater, and a greater willingness to register as Gypsies. European authorities have moved to stop discrimination against Gypsies in education, employment, and social security.

Four million Roma live in the Balkans and Eastern Europe. In Bulgaria, Hungary, the Czech Republic, Slovakia, and Romania, they represent about 5 percent of the population. Post–World War II Communist regimes have either ignored their Gypsy minorities or treated them without much sensitivity. Nomadic groups were forced to assimilate and settle, although Gypsy sedentarization most often failed. Gypsy cultural associations were prohibited. After the popular anti-Communist revolts of 1989, the situation has deteriorated: victims of popular prejudice, sometimes lacking rights, Gypsies have become the scapegoat of emerging nationalisms, facing violence as well as veiled threats of expulsions. Yet Eastern Europe has become the focus of the Roma movement: Gypsy organizations are mushrooming everywhere.

In Hungary there are 560,000 Gypsies. In the Nograd region, they constitute 12 percent of the population. Hungary has abandoned its enforced assimilation policy.

In Romania, the 760,000 Gypsies form one of the largest and most deprived national minorities. Some still travel with their wagons and horses; they are much harassed. Their yearly pilgrimage festival at the Bistritza monastery has become a focal point of ethnic expression, since Gypsy associations are prohibited. Hundreds of thousands fled to Germany, but many were sent back.

In Bulgaria (475,000 Gypsies), successive regimes have combined social-economic amelioration with cultural oppression, in particular of the Muslim Roma, who were coerced into assimilation.

Treatment of the 410,000 Gypsies in former Czechoslovakia was very bad. Authorities fought high Gypsy birthrates with compulsory sterilization. In Slovakia, where most Gypsies live, they have been subject to forcible dispersion; conditions are hardly better for the 150,000 in the Czech Republic.

The 850,000 Gypsies in former Yugoslavia are Europe's largest Gypsy community. In 1981 they were granted official equal nationality status. With broadcasts, publications, and cultural clubs, they were politically and culturally advanced. In the largely Albanian-inahabited Kosovo region of Serbia, where Gypsies are Muslims, some schools teach Romani, but many Gypsies migrated to the well-to-do north, where as servants, casual laborers, and second-hand clothing traders, they continued to suffer social discrimination. Recent explosions of ethnic hatred also affect Gypsies.

Smaller Gypsy groups live in Albania (62,000) and Poland (70,000), where the public attitude remains negative.

Half the 530,000 Gypsies of the Commonwealth of Independent States live in Russia, where nomadism is outlawed. They work as seasonal laborers and street traders. In Asia, the related Luli have long been recognized as a national minority of Indian origin. Substantial minorities dwell in the Ukraine and Moldova. Together with the Jugi, they have been estimated as numbering 20,000, of whom six-sevenths are Jugi.

New waves of migration to Western Europe, in particular to Germany, have brought in 500,000 Gypsies, whose small communities often lack the means for caravan sites. The largest group is France's 260,000, particularly numerous in the Midi region; 100,000 are wandering Gypsies (Manush) who traditionally lived from door-to-door sales until these were outlawed in 1972, leading to increased Gypsy involvement in crime.

Germany's 85,000 Gypsies (Sinti) attained some political leverage in the 1980s, when the Federal Republic of Germany officially recognized the Nazi genocide against them. Claims cases for war crimes reparations have been underway ever since. However, the arrival of refugees from Romania has exacerbated ethnic tensions and fuelled racist attacks.

Britain's 90,000 Gypsies are subject to continuous evictions. The 18,000 "Travellers" in Ireland, who move in little caravans of tinsmiths and horsetraders, are not ethnic Gypsies and may be descendants of the impoverished aristocracy (or, conversely, of the poorest classes).

The 40,000 Gypsies indigenous to the Netherlands are relatively well off, profiting from special caravan sites. Smaller groups eke out a living in Belgium (20,000), Scandinavia (33,000), and Switzerland (35,000).

More than 1 million Gypsies live in Southern Europe, where the largest group are Spain's 850,000 Gypsies, mostly unregistered, illiterate, unemployed slum-dwellers. Another 100,000 live in Portugal. Most of Italy's 120,000 Gypsies live in central Italy, the target of public hostility. Greece hosts 140,000 Roma. The situation is particularly acute for 45,000 Muslim Gypsies not eligible for citizenship, and enticed to convert to the Greek Orthodox Church, which functions as an entrance ticket to Greek society.

Turkey's 545,000 Gypsies are forced into a scavenging existence, although some work in industry or as shoeshines, street-sweepers, porters, or singers and dancers. Many travel between Greece and Turkey. Submitting to superficial assimilation, they continue to speak Romani among themselves.

JAT (also Guji and Gujar) is the general term in Afghanistan for several gypsy-like groups of tinkers, musicians, tradesmen, and fortune-tellers. Their number is estimated as a few thousand; they speak several Indo-Aryan languages, and also Pashto and/or Dari

(the Persian spoken in Afghanistan). The Jat are, at least outwardly, Sunni Muslims of the Hanafi school.

Another group represented both in Central Asia (Uzbekistan and Tajikistan) and in the north of Afghanistan is that designated by host populations as Jugi or Jogi (Central Asian and Afghanistani pronunciations respectively). A group of Jugi is also registered in the Astarabad and Mazandaran regions of Iran. No population data are available for the three groupings, but they are few in number. In Central Asia they call themselves "Mugat" or, in their secret argot, "Ghurvat." The latter term can also be used as an umbrella name for all peripatetic groups of Central Asia, including the Luli, Mazang, and Qavol. It is not known whether these self-designations have been retained by the Jugi of Afghanistan and Iran.

At least outwardly, the Gypsies of Central Asia and Afghanistan are Sunni Muslims of the Hanafi school and the Jugi of Iran are Shi'ite Muslims. The Luli and Jugi of Central Asia deny having any other language save Uzbek and Tajik respectively, but the Jogi of Afghanistan, who are fluent in both these languages, possess a language of their own known as Magatibai. No details are available which could aid in its classification. The Central Asian Jugi also use an argot named Zaboni Mugati or Jugigi. Grammatically Tajik, lexically non-Tajik and non-Uzbek, it is used as a secret form of communication.

The Jugi began to settle in quarters of their own, known as *jugikhona* (the house of Jugi) on the outskirts of Bukhara and Samarkand apparently no earlier than the early nineteenth century. Many sedentary Jugi turned to making wooden kitchen utensils and cheap jewelry while continuing traditional occupations such as horse-dealing, street performances with trained bears and goats, and breeding a specific Central Asian species of greyhound (*sag-i tozi*). Women's occupations were begging and fortune-telling. The Luli, engaged in similar occupations, refrained from intermarriage with the Jugi.

Of the Jogi of Afghanistan, two groups, the Balkhiqi and Tashqurghani, have long been settled in the area. Two other groups, the Kulabi and the Bukhara'i (or Farari, "refugees"; also Naqshbandi) are relatively recent arrivals from Central Asia. The Bukhara'i apparently fled to Afghanistan during the early sovietization of Central Asia. They are engaged in the same occupations as the other groups.

Two other groups of Central Asia are also regarded as Gypsies, or sometimes more cautiously as gypsy-like: the Qavol and the Mazang. The former, who also call themselves Shekhmumadi, are found mainly in the Khatlon (formerly Kulab) region of Tajikistan and form the Central Asian branch of the Afghanistani SHEIKH-MOHAMMADI. The Mazang, found both in Uzbekistan and Tajikistan, seem to be a non-Gypsy peripatetic group akin to those known in Afghanistan under the umbrella name of JAT. (see also JATS II, KHAMSE)

H

HA A people in Tanzania who inhabit the stretch between Lake Victoria and Lake Tanganyika. The Ha territory includes highlands and valleys covered with woods, bushes, and grasslands. The Ha number more than 500,000, making them one of the largest ethnic groups in Tanzania. The Ha language belongs to the Bantu group of the Niger-Kordofan language family.

The Ha are mainly involved in cattle-grazing, fishing, and, at times, hunting. They live in beehive-shaped, grass-covered huts, which are in most cases scattered around the countryside.

During their history the Ha have been influenced by the TUTSI, and even politically dominated by them for a certain period. Ha worship is based on magic and family ancestor cults. The Ha are famous for their dances, as well as their music, which is played on drums and gourds.

HACHE WINIK see LACANDON.

HADDAD see DANOA.

HADENDOWA A Bedawiye-speaking subgroup of the BEJA.

HADIVA An ethnic group living in Ethiopia.

HADIYA A people numbering 650,000 (1980s) who live in the southern Shoa Province of Ethiopia. They are speakers of an eastern Cushitic language. The Hadiya are Sunni Muslims and there are also some Christian (Protestant and others) groups among them. They are agriculturalists (ensete, grains) and cattle-raisers. Historically they represent the legacy of the medieval Islamic kingdom of Hadiya.

The Hadiya consist of five subgroups (MARAKO, SASAGO, LEMO, SORO, BADAWACCO), but the ethnonym also sometimes includes culturally related groups (ALABA, TAMBARO, KABENA). In their political and social structure they combine a segmentary clan-structure with some traces of age- and generation-grading. (see also ETHIOPIANS, OROMO)

HADJERAY A generic term for many ethnic groups inhabiting the Gurea region of south-central Chad. In 1964 these groups numbered about 87,000.

The Hadjeray lack a centralized political organization or even a common origin. They migrated to their current home in the fifteenth century to escape slave raiders and converted to Islam during the period of colonial rule by the the FRENCH.

The DIONKOR and the YALNA are usually associated with the Hadjeray.

HAFT LANG A clan of the BAKHTIARI.

HAIDA A Native North American group numbering about 4,000 living today on the Queen Charlotte Islands, British Columbia, Canada, and the South Alaskan Peninsula, U.S.A. The Haida were the most numerous tribe of the West Coast Indians but a smallpox epidemic in the 1830s and 1860s nearly wiped them out. In the following years the Haida were largely assimilated into the predominantly European society and abandoned their traditional lifestyle, particularly the raising of magnificent totem poles, for which they were famous.

For years the Haida have been carrying on a struggle against the deforestation of the Queen Charlotte Islands, a territory dotted with hundreds of ancient Haida villages and totem poles. In 1986 the Canadian government declared a portion of the Queen Charlotte Islands to be a conservation area, and in addition the United Nations declared some of the ancient Haida villages to be protected international heritage sites.

Today the Haida in Canada manage their own affairs, working directly with the federal government, not through the Department of Indian Affairs.

Haida

HAISLA A Native North American group numbering about 2,500, living today in British Columbia, Canada, in two bands, Kitimat and Bella Bella.

A West Coast Indian group, they were traditionally fishers. The Aluminium Company of Canada (Alcan) built the largest aluminium smelter in the world beside the Kitimat Indian village.

HAITIANS The estimated 7 million inhabitants of Haiti, located in the western part of Hispaniola Island, which it shares with the Dominican Republic. Over 1 million Haitians live in the capital, Port-au-Prince.

Haitian society is divided into two cultures, Franco-Haitian and Afro-Haitian. The former dates back to the days of colonization. Many French customs were assimilated into Haitian culture, including language, education, religion (Catholicism), etiquette, and cooking. Afro-Haitian culture characterizes the descendants of the slaves shipped in from Africa; it includes its own religion (Voodoo), language (French-based Creole), music, dance, and cooking. These two cultures, when combined, form a composite Haitian culture; when separated, they divide Haiti into two social classes far removed from each other. In fact, Haitian society has always been divided into two groups: the small elite and the impoverished masses. The elite is made up of big business owners, including Haitian mulattoes, ARABS, some Europeans, CANADIANS, and DOMINICANS. The poorer classes are mainly black.

Although Roman Catholicism is the official religion, Voodoo is the most practiced. It is based on the worship of family spirits (*loua*) which protect family members and bring them good fortune. A special ritual is held once or twice a year to thank the spirits with offerings, such as foods. Haiti is known for its art, particularly primitive painting and wood carving, much of which depicts Voodoo rituals. The holidays most celebrated are Good Friday, Day of the Dead, and Christmas, all significant because they are mystical. Haitians are fascinated by the dead and the unknown.

The economy is largely based on agriculture; however, because of serious ecological problems such as deforestation and soil erosion, productivity has declined drastically. This has caused many Haitian farmers to leave their lands for the urban slums, or even to attempt the daring voyage to the United States in poorly made sailboats.

In 1804 Haiti earned the distinction of being the first black nation to acquire independence and abolish slavery, a great feat in view of the might of the army of the FRENCH. From independence to the ousting of the first democratically elected president, Jean B. Aristide, the military has been able to impose its will through a series of coups. Except for the oppressive thirty years of the Duvalier regime, the resulting government instability has created an atmosphere of distrust for and discontent with the military and the chief executive officer. Since the early 1950s there has been neither an improvement in infrastructure nor the institution of a system to maintain living conditions and enforce zoning regulations. Today Haiti is the poorest nation of the western hemisphere.

HAJONG A Hindu ethnic group of Bangladesh, who speak Assamese and Bengali. They have much in common with the KACHARI. An agricultural group, they have remarkable skills in weaving and embroidery.

HALANG An ethnic group, numbering about 10,000, speaking a Mon-Khmer dialect. Halang villages are found in central Vietnam and south Laos. They adhere to traditional religions and once practiced human sacrifice by crushing a victim under the supporting pillar when inaugurating communal buildings. They engage primarily in slash and burn cultivation of rice and maize.

HALBA A people, numbering 480,000 (1981), living in the districts of South Raipur and Bastar in Madhya

Pradesh and Maharashtra, India. They speak Marathi (Halbi), an Indo-Aryan language.

The Halba in Bastar occupy a high position. They are the highest local caste with the exception of the Brahmans, perhaps because they are landholders.

HALE PAIKA   (Divaru, Billava) An ethnic group, numbering a few thousand, found in the state of Karnataka in southeast India. Most engage in agriculture; others are hunters and foresters.

HALIPAN   A subgroup of the IFUGAO.

HAMALAISET   see FINNS.

HAMBAL   A southern subgroup of the NEGRITOS of the Philippines.

HAMMAR   (Amar, Kokke) An ethnic group numbering 30,000 (1980s) who live east of the Omo River in southern Gemu Gofa Province, Ethiopia. They speak Banna, a member of the Omotic language group, and adhere to traditional beliefs. The Hammar are predominantly cattle-raisers. Their social organization includes elements of an age-class system. Related groups are the BANNA, BESHADA, and KARO.

HAN I   A Native North American group of the Athapaskan-speaking people, numbering about 1,000. They live in Yukon Territory, Canada and in Alaska, U.S.A, and still maintain their traditional form of living, based on the hunting of moose and caribou.

HAN II   The single largest ethnic group in China, where they numbered some 937 million in 1982, ac-

Han

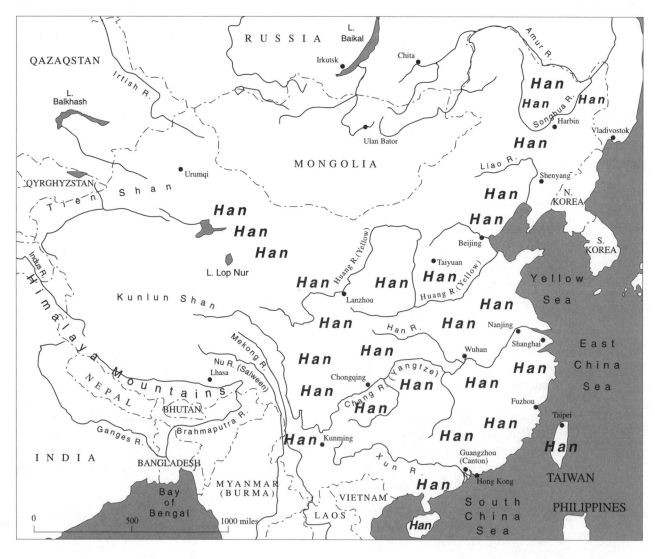

counting for over 90 percent of the population. The descendants of a neolithic culture established in the Yellow and Yangtze River basins in the third millenium B.C.E., they are by far the most influential group in modern China, dominating the country politically, culturally, and economically. (see also CHINESE)

HANDEA see SEDANG.

HANI (Houni, Woni) The approximately 1.1 million Hani are concentrated on the high southeastern plateau of the Yunnan Province of China. They are believed to be descended from tribes belonging to the larger YI ethnic group who first migrated from Tibet. In southern Yunnan, they share many characteristics with the DAI, while in the north they are similar to the TIBETANS.

The Hani language belongs to the Tibeto-Burmese group. They had no script until the Chinese government provided them with one based on the Latin alphabet in 1957.

Their religious beliefs include polytheism and ancestor worship. The cultivation of rice on terraced mountain slopes is their main economic activity.

HANTE see KHANT.

HANUNOO (s.d. Mangyan; Bulalakao) A Malayo-Polynesian ethnic group numbering several thousand, they live in the forest and grass covered lands of southern Mindoro, an island in the Philippines. They are mostly rural, with some living in the municipalities of Mansalay and Bulalacao. The Hanunoo are primarily a group of pagan mountain peoples who cultivate rice through slash and burn agriculture.

They speak the Mangyan language; 60 percent are literate in an ancient Indic-derived script which was once widespread but is now found only on the islands of Mindoro and Palawan. This literary language helps them preserve the cultural integrity of their culture as it existed before the Spanish conquest.

HANYA A pastoral people living in southern Angola.

HAPAO A subgroup of the IFUGAO.

HARAGE (Harari, Adare; Hara-ge, "people of the city") An ethnic group, numbering 30,000 (1984), who live in the walled city of Harar in eastern Ethiopia. Their language, Ge-Sinan, the "language of the city," belongs to the southern Semitic (Ethio-Semitic) grouping. The Harage are Sunni Muslims.

The city of Harar, a center of trade and of Islamic devotion ("the city of the saints") became, during the late Middle Ages the capital of the Islamic lowland empire of Zeyla. Forming an independent emirate in the late sixteeth century, the Harage were dependent for supplies on Oromo peasants (Kottu) who lived around the city. After a short Egyptian colonial interlude (1875–1884), Memelik of Shoa annexed the emirate in 1886. Since then, the Harage have specialized as traders. They are noted for their specific form of social organization based on neighborhoods (*afocha*).

HARARI see HARAGE.

HARASIIS (Harsuusi) A pre-Arab people living in the Jiddat plateau in the central desert of Oman. (see also OMANIS)

HARATIN A clan of the AIT ATTA living in Morocco. Because of their darker skins, they suffered from the rasicm of other AIT ATTA. Since Morocco's independence, however, many Haratin moved to the cities, where they have prospered.

HARE A Native North American nation of the Athapaskan-speaking group, numbering 1,400, living on two reserves in the Northwest Territories, Canada. They maintain their traditional way of life based on the hunting of large mammals.

HASALAR An ethnic group, numbering about 15,000, found in the state of Karnataka in southeast India. Traditionally, they were enslaved by neighboring groups, and they are still employed in menial professions and manual labor.

HASSAUNA (Shuwa) A small group of seminomadic Arab clans who migrated to Chad from the north between the fourteenth and nineteenth centuries. In 1954 they numbered around 20,000. The ASSALE, DAGANA, OULED MEHAREB, DULED MANSOUR, and BENI WAIL are all Hassauna clans. (see also CHADIANS)

HATA RUA see PALU'E.

HAUSA The largest ethnic group in Nigeria, where they live mainly in the northern states of Sokoto, Kano, Bauchi, and Kaduna. They also live in southern Niger and in small concentrations as traders throughout West and Equatorial Africa. In Nigeria they number, together with the FULANI, around 30.5 million; in Niger they number 3.3 million. Their main occupation is trade. The Hausa have been Muslims since the fourteenth century and formed several Muslim states in West Africa. They are a patrilineal and patrilocal society.

During the sixteenth century the FULANI settled in the Hausa states, where they served as religious counsellors to the Hausa kings. More orthodox than the Hausa kings, the FULANI demanded Islamic reforms towards the end of the eighteenth century and rebelled when their demands were not met. Led by Uthman dan Fodio, the FULANI declared a *jihad* (Muslim holy war), in which they were joined by Hausa subjects, who hated the despotic Hausa kings, and by non-Muslim nomadic FULANI. By 1810 the FULANI dominated the Hausa and the *jihad* movement spread eastwards to northern Cameroon and southward to the Yoruba states. The *jihad* resulted in heightened Islamic awareness in northern Nigeria and served as a unifying factor between the Hausa and FULANI. In the modern history of Nigeria they are referred to as one people, HAUSA-FULANI.

The Hausa are subdivided into nine main groups: DAURAWA, GOBIR, KANAWA, KATSENAWA, KEBBAWA, ZAMFARA, ZAZZAGAWA, AYOKAWA, and MAGUZAWA. (see HAUSA-FULANI)

HAUSA-FULANI Two peoples living in Northern Nigeria, they integrated during the nineteenth century into one people. They number about 30.5 million and constitute almost 30 percent of Nigeria's total population. During the colonial period the BRITISH did not try to change the political-religious system of the Hausa-Fulani. Nigeria was divided into three regions of which the Hausa-Fulani–dominated north was the largest. No missionary activities were allowed in the territory and Islam remained strong; however, as the missions were the only way of receiving Western education, the Hausa-Fulani lagged behind the two other major ethnic groups of Nigeria, the YORUBA and the IBO.

After independence in 1960, the Hausa-Fulani remained politically strong but, fearing competition with southerners, particularly the IBO who migrated north in search of jobs, they took discriminatory measures against them, culminating in a massacre of 30,000 southerners in 1966. Two million IBO fled back to their homeland and in 1967 declared their independence from Nigeria as the Republic of Biafra. The ensuing conflict lasted two-and-a-half years and left millions dead.

After the war Nigeria was divided into smaller units that cut across ethnic lines, an act that significantly reduced the ethnic tensions in that country. As a result the Hausa-Fulani of Nigeria now live in four states instead of one region. (see also FULANI, NIGERIANS, NIGERIENS)

HAVASUPAI (Supai) A Native North American group numbering about 500 and living on the Havasupai Federal Indian Reservation in Coconino County, Arizona, U.S.A. They are agriculturalists who grow corn and produce woven baskets for sale.

HAVU An ethnic group living in the Kivu region of east-central Zaire.

HAW (Ho) A Sino-Tibetan community of farmers and merchants living in the region where the borders of China, Thailand, and Laos converge. Although they number only about 1,000, their progressive methods of hillside agriculture and animal breeding have won them the esteem of other peoples in the region.

HAWAIIANS Descendants of the indigenous Polynesian population of the islands of Hawaii, located in the central Pacific Ocean. In the modern American state of Hawaii, some 190,000 people are of Hawaiian origin; they constitute about 20 percent of the population of the islands. Due to a high rate of intermarriage and assimilation, however, fewer than 10,000 can claim to be pure Hawaiians. The traditional Hawaiian language belongs to the Polynesian family of languages. Although few Hawaiian speakers remain, some words and phrases have entered the everyday speech of all islanders; the official language of the islands is English, but most islanders use Pidgin, an admixture of English and Hawaiian, for everyday affairs. In recent years attempts have been made to revive the Hawaiian language, with limited success. Most Hawaiians are Protestant or Roman Catholic.

Traditional Hawaiian occupations are centered on fishing and agriculture: about 25 percent of Hawaiians are still involved in agriculture on the extensive sugar and pineapple plantations on the islands. Most Hawaiians, however, are involved in the service- and tourist industries.

The first Polynesian settlers of Hawaii are believed to have arrived on the islands from the Marquesas islands in the middle of the first millenium C.E. Over the centuries, several dynasties emerged, competing for control of individual islands and the whole archipelago. The first European to visit the islands was Captain James Cook in 1778; his men introduced venereal disease, which devastated the Hawaiian population, starting a long process of population decline due to war and disease.

Soon after, Chief Kamehameha took advantage of the rapid death toll among his opponents and succeeded in defeating the chiefs of the other islands, thereby uniting the islands into a single kingdom by 1795. That year is considered to mark the foundation of a unified Hawaiian nation. The islands became an invaluable stopover point for whalers and traders. Many Europeans came to settle on the islands, suppressing traditional religions and exerting increasing influence on the kingdom's political and social life.

Hawaii subsequently became an important forward station for the U.S. navy and airforce; it was the attack on the U.S. naval installation at Pearl Harbor by the JAPANESE that precipitated U.S. entry into World War II. Hawaii became a state of the United States in 1959. In the early 1970s native Hawaiian groups began citing the precedent of Native North American peoples to achieve greater rights. This has even sparked a nascent independence movement among some islanders.

Hawaiian customs and traditions are common among all the islands' inhabitants: these include *aloha* shirts (flowery printed shirts), *leis* (flowery greeting wreaths), *luau* barbecues, the traditional *hula* dance, and Hawaiian music.

HAWAZMA   A subgroup of the BAGGARA.

HAWIYA   A clan of the SOMALI.

HAY   see ARMENIANS.

HAYA   (Wahaya, Ziba, Waziba) The Haya are among the largest Tanzanian ethnic groups, numbering 412,000 in 1967.

They inhabit territory in northwest Tanzania, between the Kagera River and Lake Victoria. They belong linguistically to (and are dominant in) the Interlacustrine cluster of the Bantu language group of the Niger-Kordofan family. The Haya consist of two main ethnic elements: the IRU, who were originally Bantu, and the HIMA, who are descendants of the previous Nilotic population of the territory and were absorbed by the Bantu. The IRU are mainly cultivators while the HIMA are shepherds.

The Haya economy includes coffee and indigenous crops. Their basic diet also includes beans, maize, sweet potatoes, sorghum, groundnuts, and fish products. Most families are cattle owners. Hunting and gathering wild foodstuffs do not play an important role in their subsistence. Many Haya have been food traders since pre-colonial times.

Politically, the Haya were divided into eight "early states" (BUGABO, IBANDIRO, KAIANJA, KIAMTUARA, KARAGWE, KIZIBA, MARYKU, and MISSENENYI). The Karagwe kingdom was a dominant force in this area in the eighteenth century. All these states were governed by a despotic king (*mukama*), who ruled through appointed chiefs and officials as well as the royal army, which was structured on age groups. Landsharing was in the hands of peasant communes, which consisted of about 130 patrilineal, exogamic clans. The Haya live in stable, compact village units in which the houses are set apart from one another. Their traditional dwellings are of a beehive shape.

The Haya are mostly Roman Catholics. They greatly value education and modern professions.

HAZARA   A people who inhabit the eastern part of Afghanistan's central massif (the Ghur), known today as Hazarajat. Their estimated number ranges between 870,000 and 1.1 million. The Hazara speak a dialect of Dari (the Persian spoken in Afghanistan) which has a strong admixture of Mongol and Turkic.

The Hazara are divided into several tribe-like local groups, the most important of which is the Day-Kundi, living in villages dominated by the castles of their former powerful chiefs. The ethnogenesis of the Hazara remains unclear. Up to the time of the emir Abd al-Rahman (1879–1901) they were practically independent. Most are sedentary peasants. Excellent soldiers, they have provided large numbers of recruits for the army. Nowadays many can be found among the manual workers in Kabul and other cities. They were actively involved in the guerrilla war against the Soviets after the 1979 Soviet invasion.

Hazara

They are Shi'ite Muslims. The Shaikh-Ali tribal group of the Hazara in the Bamian area, north-central Hazarajat, belong to the Isma'ili sect, and are accused by the surrounding Sunni population of practicing pagan ceremonies and of sexual promiscuity. The latter accusation may have been triggered by the fact that Hazara women wear long dresses without the long under-trousers customary in Afghanistan, as in most other Muslim societies.

Those Hazara dwelling in the northern part of Hazarajat may be defined as semi-nomads, pasturing their flocks in distant areas in summer. The name of the people, which means "thousand" in Persian, clearly reflects the Mongol military tribal organization in thousand-strong units of cavalry. However, the theory that they are MONGOLS and TURKS who settled there from the thirteenth century onwards and gradually abandoned their language is now regarded as dubious. Most probably they are the result of the mixture of MONGOLS and TURKS with the local pre-Mongol IRANIANS who evidently spoke not Persian but another Iranian language. The transfer to Persian and the emergence of the present Hazara dialect have been traced back to not earlier than the late fifteenth to sixteenth century.

There are also small groups calling themselves Hazara among the Dari-speaking Isma'ilis of the Afghanistani part of the Pamirs and among the TAIMANI (see AIMAQ). Their connection with the Hazara is uncertain. The so-called Berberi Hazara in the Iranian province of Khorasan, south of Mashhad, are nineteenth-century emigrants from Hazarajat. The Hazara are not to be confused with the HAZARA DEH-I ZAINAT AIMAQ of Afghanistan, nor with the multi-ethnic population of the Hazara district in west Pakistan. The BARBARIS of eastern Iran are related to the Hazara. (see also AFGHANS, BARBARIS)

HAZARA DEH-I ZAINAT   see AIMAQ.

HBAU   A subgroup of the JARAI.

HDRUNG   A subgroup of the JARAI.

HE DRONG   A subgroup of the JARAI.

HEHE   An aggregate of small ethnic groups with similar language and culture occupying the Iriga and Mufindi districts of highland grasslands in Tanzania. According to the 1967 census, they numbered 360,000. The Hehe speak a Bantu dialect of the Niger-Kordofan family of languages. Their religion includes the cult of ancestors, as well as elements of Christianity and Islam.

Originally, they consisted of fifteen tribal chiefdoms which in the mid-nineteenth century were organized into a unified state and then expanded into other areas. Nowadays they are divided into dispersed patrilineal clans. The Hehe have a reputation of being good warriors. They stood up to German colonial troops in 1898 and were defeated only after bloody fighting. Even now the Hehe supply a large proportion of recruits to the Tanzanian army.

The Hehe are basically cereal farmers, with maize as their main crop. They are also cattle grazers, and often hire themselves out as farm employees to supplement their income. (see also TANZANIANS)

HEILTSUK   A Native North American group, numbering about 1,500, living on the northwest coast of British Columbia, Canada. Their main source of livelihood is fishing, as it was in the past.

HELONG   An ethnic group numbering several thousand originating on the Indonesian island of Timor but now found primarily on the adjacent island of Semau. Once thought to have inhabited all of Timor, they were forced by the ATONI to the area surrounding the coastal town of Kupang.

Immigration further diminished their numbers on Timor, where they are now found in only one small village, and most fled to Semau. They are primarily Christians and engage in slash and burn cultivation of rice and corn.

HEMBA   A cluster of ethnic groups living along the Lualaba River in Zaire. Their society is matrilineal and they are related to the LUBA.

HERA   A subgroup of the ZEZURU.

HERERO   An ethnic group living in the Banguela, Mocamedes, and Huila districts of Angola, where they number about 20,000, and in Namaraland, central Namibia. Although traditionally a pastoral people, in recent years they have turned increasingly to agriculture.

The Herero are divided into several patrilinial clans which are, in turn, divided into villages. Each village is headed by a priest-chief named Makuru after the leading Herero divinity.

The CHIMBA of southern Angola are a subgroup of the Herero. (see also ANGOLANS, NAMIBIANS)

Herero

HETA   A South American Indian group living in the forests of the State of Paraná, south Brazil. Although this is normally considered a Guaraní area, the language of the Heta connects them to the Tupi language family. They number fewer than 100 and since 1955 they have been periodically interviewed by scholars from the University of Paraná.

HEWE   A subgroup of the TUMBUKA.

HIDATSA   A Native North American group, numbering 2,000 persons, most of whom live today on the Fort Berthold Federal Reservation in North Dakota. Unlike their nomadic plains neighbors, they lived in fixed village settlements of earth lodges along the Missouri River, growing corn and squash and hunting buffalo seasonally.

Culturally they were related to the MANDAN and ARIKARA tribes. In the 1830s a smallpox epidemic devastated their population, and a few years later they were moved by the U.S. army to their present location.

HIGAONAN   See BUKIDNON.

HIGGI   A subgroup of the TIV.

HILL KHARIA   A people, numbering over 100,000 (1961), living in the Dhalbhum area of Bi-

har, India. They worship a pantheon of gods, including the sun. They are agriculturalists; hunting, collecting forest produce, and day-laboring are secondary occupations.

HILL MARIA   see ABUJHMARIA.

HILL PANDARAM   (Pandaram) A group of nomadic and semi-nomadic hunters and gatherers numbering about 2,000 living in the forested hills of the Indian state of Kerala. They speak either a Malayalam or Tamil dialect which is virtually unintelligible to other speakers of those two languages.

The Hill Pandaram are nominally Hindus but identify their divinities with mountain peaks rather than with statues and images. Similarly, they have few rites and rituals and no communal places of worship. In recent years, some Hill Pandaram have become settled farmers.

HIMA   One of the eight "early states" of the HAYA. (see also GANDA, HAYA, NKOLE, NYORO, TORO, UGANDANS)

HLENGWE   A Tonga-speaking group living in the southeastern districts of Zimbabwe and in southern Mozambique.

HMONG   see MIAO.

HO   An ethnic group numbering 585,000 (1981), living in Bihar and Orissa, India. They speak Munda, a dialect belonging to the Austro-Asiatic family of languages, and are related to the ASUR.

They have always been fiercely independent, even during Muslim rule. In 1900 they were subdued by the BRITISH after a vigorous struggle that had continued for years.

The Ho belong to the Austro-Asiatic group of the Austric family. They worship the supreme god Singabonga, ancestral spirits, and other local and clan gods. Their main occupations are hunting, fishing, and cultivation of rice. (see also HAW)

HOEN   see NHA HUEN.

HOLLI   A subgroup of the YORUBA living along the border of Nigeria and Benin.

HOLO-HOLO   A subgroup of the NYAMWEZI.

HOLONTALO   see GORONTALO.

HOMR   A subgroup of the BAGGARA.

HONDURANS   The people of Honduras in Central America, numbering about 4.2 million, are mostly Roman Catholic, Spanish-speaking *mestizos*, a mixture of European and Indian stocks. Around 6 percent of the population are indigenous Indians, who are mainly concentrated in the west of the country, near Guatemala. Some Indian groups, such as the MOSQUITO, PAYA, XICAQUE, and ZAMBO, speak their own languages rather than Spanish.

Descendants of JAMAICANS (c.2 percent of the population) brought to work in the local banana plantations live in the northern coastal area on the Caribbean Sea, where there are also whites of ENGLISH stock, mainly Protestants, descendants of the settlers who developed the banana economy. The development of the plantation economy on the tropical coastal plains has caused a substantial migration from traditional settlement areas in the temperate mountainous regions.

Christopher Columbus arrived in Honduras in 1502, but no permanent Spanish settlement was established until 1522. Early struggles between indigenous Indians and SPANIARDS abated somewhat with the appointment of the first territorial governor in 1526, but major war between the colonists and the indigenes later broke out, lasting from 1537 through 1539. Honduras, never an independent colony, was part of Guatemala after 1570, at which time discovery of silver brought many new people, including the BRITISH, who threatened Spanish dominion over the country.

The Central American colonies separated from Europe in 1821 and, in 1823, Honduras, Guatemala, and Belize combined to form one country, called the United Provinces of Central America, from which Honduras withdrew in 1838. Early in the twentieth century, the unstable Honduran government was increasingly controlled by Nicaragua, until the United States sent Marines to protect U.S. economic interests, particularly banana production. A succession of military dictatorships was followed by the reestablishment of civilian government in 1982. Of the two major Honduran political parties, the Liberals are actually conservative, while the right-wing National Party is closely tied to the military.

HOOPACHUPA   A Native North American group numbering 2,500, many of whom live on the Hoopa Extension and Hoopa Valley Federal Indian Reservations in Humboldt County, in north California, U.S.A. These are the largest reservations in the state of California.

Some Hoopachupa villages are still located on their ancient sites. They were traditionally hunters of deer and cultivators of maize.

HOPI   A large Native North American Pueblo Indian people numbering about 10,000, many of whom live in Arizona, U.S.A. on the Pueblo Navajo Federal Reservation. There is friction between the Hopi and NAVAJO groups arising from the Navajo invasion of Hopi lands in the past.

Their culture is similar to that of the ZUNI. They are one of the few aboriginal groups to maintain their culture down to the present; their villages are ancient, some extending back 1,000 years. They are renowned for their elaborate basket-weaving and miniature sculpturing.

Hopi

The Hopi own and operate a cultural center, a museum, and a motel-restaurant complex. (see also PUEBLO INDIANS)

HOTTENTOT   see SAN, SOUTH AFRICANS.

HOUEDA   (Pedah) An ethnic group of about 15,000 living along the coastal lagoons of Lake Aheme, Benin. They are closely related to the AIZO. Their main occupation is fishing.

The Houeda kingdom of Ouida, founded in the sixteenth century, fell in the eighteenth century.

HOUSATONIC   see STOCKBRIDGE.

HOVA   see MERINA, MALAGASY.

HPON   A Tibeto-Burmese group of fewer than 1,000 living along the Irrawaddy River in northern Myanmar (Burma). They are shifting agriculturalists but are also employed in fishing and the timber industry. The Hpon are rapidly being assimilated by the surrounding SHAN people.

HRE   (in Vietnamese: Da Vach) A Mon-Khmer group, numbering about 30,000, living in the mountains of central Vietnam.

HROY   (Bahnar Cham, Cam) A Malayo-Polynesian group, numbering about 10,000, living in southern Vietnam. Their language is similar to Cham, and they are sometimes considered a subgroup of the BAHNAR.

HRUSSO   see AKA.

HRVATI   see CROATS.

HTEU LA   A subgroup of the AKHA.

HUAMBIZA   A subgroup of the JIVARO.

HUANCAVILVA   A Native South American group living in Ecuador.

HUARPE ALLENTICAC   A Native South American group living in Argentina.

HUARPE MILLCAYAC   A Native South American group living in Argentina.

HUARPE PUNTANOS   A Native South American group living in Argentina.

HUASTEC   An indigenous Mexican people, numbering slightly over 100,000. More than 50,000 speakers of Huastecan, a Maya-Totonac language, inhabit a mountainous, sparsely forested area in the Mexican state of San Luis Potosí, known as Potosí in Huastec. Another 50,000 Huastec live in the state of Veracruz. A third Huastec group, some 2,000 in all, inhabit the states of Hidalgo and Tamaulipas.

Although the Huastec language belongs to the Maya-Totonac group, the Huastec are located far from the present areas of Maya habitation. At an earlier period, speakers of these languages occupied the entire Gulf Coast, but as time passed, most migrated elsewhere.

As with many other indigenous MEXICANS, Huastec practice of Catholicism is combined with some pre-Hispanic beliefs. They worship a god called Mam, associated with fertility, lightning, rain, and storms; they also venerate the sun and moon, the former identified with a male divinity and the latter with a female. On the other hand, their Catholic festivals also celebrate the patron saint of each village, Holy Week, and All Souls' Day.

The climate in much of the Huastec territory is tropical and humid, with rains in the summer. Agriculture is the basis of their economy, but handicrafts are also produced. Beans, corn, fruit, squash, and sweet potatoes, grown for their own consumption, are complemented with market production of sugarcane and sesame. Cultivation in Veracruz and San Luis Potosí, traditionally emphasizing coffee, has recently been expanded to include peanuts and rice.

HUAVE   A Native American people living in southwest Mexico. (see also MEXICANS)

HUETARES-PACACUAS   A Native South American group living in Costa Rica.

HUI   (Huihui) At an estimated 7.5 million, the Hui are China's second largest minority. Concentrated mainly in the Ningxia Hui Autonomous Region, they are also perhaps the most scattered ethnic group in the country, intermingled with Han CHINESE and other minorities.

Speaking only Chinese, the Hui have so well assimilated into Chinese society that they are almost indistinguishable, except in dietary and religious aspects, from the HAN. Also called Chinese Muslims, they have a strong sense of community, with the mosque serving as the focus of communal life and a center for festivals and religious ceremonies. Descended from Chinese converts to Islam, and ARABS and IRANIANS who settled in northwest China over 1,000 years ago, the Hui emerged as a distinct nationality during the Ming dynasty (1368–1644).

The Hui have produced many famous scientists and literary and political figures, including Zheng He, a well-known Ming navigator who led China's large royal fleet across the Atlantic Ocean seven times and visited over thirty countries in Asia and Africa.

Outside China, Hui can also be found in southeast Asia and Russia. A number of Hui from the Chinese Kansu and Shensu provinces fled to the territory of the Russian empire between 1864 and 1881 after they

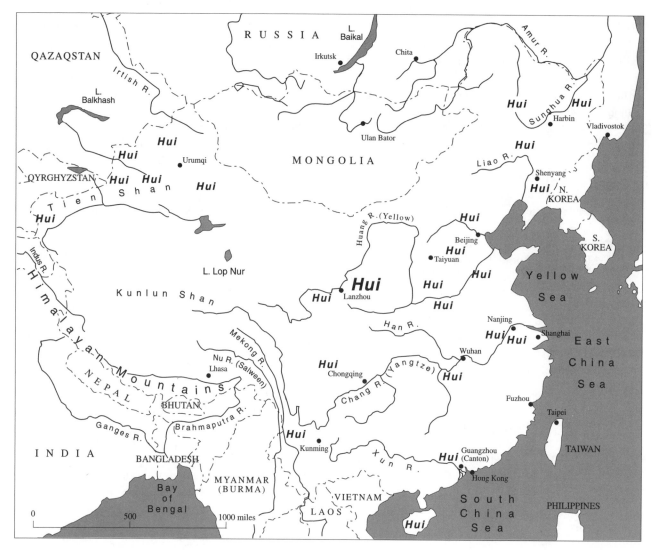

Hui

were defeated in a revolt against the Chinese emperor. They were called Dungan by the Russians. According to the 1989 Soviet census they numbered 70,000 (within the borders of the former Soviet Union). They speak the Kansu dialect of Chinese and use it also in writing, first with the Arabic, then, from the early 1930s, the Roman, and, since the late 1930s, with the Cyrillic alphabet. They are accomplished farmers.

HUICHOL An indigenous people of the Sierra Madre of northwest Mexico. They were still nomadic at the time of the Spanish Conquest. Their contact with Spanish missionaries and soldiers was limited due to the remoteness and inaccessibility of their habitat.

They are one of the few Mexican indigenous peoples who have retained their original religion. Their beliefs and way of life have changed very little over the cen-

turies. They are noted today for their "god's-eye" weaving, popular with tourists. (see also MEXICANS)

HUIHUI see HUI.

HUILICHE A subgroup of the ARAUCANIANS living between the Tolten River and the Reloncavi Gulf in Argentina.

HUMAHUACANS see PUNANS.

HUNDE An ethnic group living in in the Kivu region of central-eastern Zaire.

HUNGARIANS (s.d. Magjarok) Of the c.15 million Hungarians, 10.5 million live in Hungary, where they form a majority of 95 percent. More than 3 million live in adjacent areas in neighboring Croatia, Slovakia, and the Ukraine, including 400,000 in Vojvodina (Serbia) and 2.5 million in Transylvania (Romania). About 2 million Hungarians live in the United States, Western Europe, Scandinavia, and Australia.

Hungarian is the major non–Indo-European language spoken in Europe (the others are Finnish, Estonian, and Basque). Together with Khant and Mansi, it forms the Ugric subgroup of the Finno-Ugric group of Uralic languages. It is, however, quite removed from the other two and they are not mutually intelligible. Hungarian has been a literary language, written in the Roman alphabet, since the Middle Ages.

Despite widespread assimilation of neighboring Slavs and, to a lesser degree, ROMANIANS, the Hungarians form an almost homogeneous society linguistically and religiously (most are Roman Catholics). The only slightly distinguishable group are the Hungarians of Transylvania, many of whom are descendants of the Szekely, a people who settled in the area of what is modern Hungary before the Hungarians and who were later encouraged to colonize Transylvania.

The Hungarians probably originated in the basins of the upper Kama and Volga Rivers, and for unknown reasons migrated at an unestablished date to the steppes, where they adopted the culture of the steppe nomads. Although mainly of Finni-Ugric stock, they might have included a Turkic element which supplied their leadership. In the ninth century they were a federation of ten tribes which roamed the steppes west of the Don River. Pushed west by the Pecheneg, they were led by their khan, Arpad, across the Carpathian Mountains. Here they established themselves in the plains of modern Hungary at the end of the ninth century and destroyed Greater Moravia in the following decade. Until defeated at Lechfeld by the emperor Otto I in 955, they were the terror of Germany, their raids reaching as far as France and Italy.

Arpad's great-grandson, Geza, converted to Roman Catholicism in 975, and his son, Saint Istvan (Stephen) was declared king of Hungary by the pope; tradition claims that he was crowned on Christmas Day, 1000. Hungary thus became part of Western Christendom and its defender in southeast Europe. Istvan's successors extended their borders to the Carpathians, annexing Slovakia and Transylvania. The kingdom of Croatia in the south was united with the Hungarian crown in 1102, although it retained its autonomy. In 1241 the MONGOLS devastated the country, reducing the population by almost half, but since the MONGOLS did not remain in occupation, Hungary survived as an independent kingdom and retained its status as a great power.

In 1301 the Arpad line became extinct, and from that time, with two exceptions, the country was ruled by foreign dynasties, the Angevins, Luxembourgs, and Jagiellonians, all of whom were also rulers of other countries and thus involved Hungary in a web of internal and external struggles. In the mid-fourteenth century Hungary became involved in Balkan affairs, fighting the Ottomans; in 1396 a Hungarian-led crusade was defeated by the Ottomans at Nicopolis. In 1526 Süleyman the Magnificent defeated the Hungarian army in Mohacs and occupied the Hungarian capital, Buda. In 1566 four decades of struggle between the Ottomans and the Habsburgs came to an end with the Habsburgs ruling the western fringe of Hungary and Croatia, as well as Slovakia, for which they had to pay tribute to the sultan; the bulk of Hungary (and Croatia) came under direct Ottoman rule, while an autonomous principality was established in Transylvania. Although under the suzerainty of the sultan, Transylvania played an active part in European politics and especially in the wars of reformation.

Following the second Ottoman failure to conquer Vienna (1683), the Habsburgs conquered most of the previous kingdom of Hungary, including Transylvania, and the territories were ceded to them by the Ottomans in the Peace of Karlowitz (1699). Hungary became part of the extended Habsburg Empire, centrally ruled from Vienna, and underwent a series of administrative reforms and germanization at forced pace.

Partly in response to these policies and partly under the influence of ideas emanating from revolutionary France and Germany, a reform movement developed which, combined with a cultural revival, turned into a nationalist movement by the mid-nineteenth century. In 1848, Hungarian nationalists declared the independence of a restored Hungarian kingdom in its broadest scope. They were immediately crushed by the RUSSIANS in 1849. Following the Habsburg defeat in the Austro-Prussian war of 1866, a compromise was reached, which created a Great Hungarian kingdom in a dual Austro-Hungarian monarchy.

Throughout the nineteenth century the Hungarian nationalist movement had been at odds with the CROATS, SLOVAKS, and ROMANIANS under its control, practicing a policy of repression which sought to enforce the assimilation of minorities into Hungarian culture. After World War I and the collapse of the dual monarchy, Hungary was forced to cede large territories to Romania, Yugoslavia, and Czechoslovakia, and even to Austria, where great numbers of Hungarians lived. Thus, out of 10 million Hungarians, 1.7 million found themselves in Romania, 1 million in Czechoslovakia, over 500,000 in Yugoslavia, and 25,000 in Austria. This created strong irredentist pressures on Hungary's foreign policy. In World War II Hungary joined the Axis powers and was rewarded by Hitler and Mussolini with half of Transylvania and parts of Czechoslovakia and Yugoslavia. After the war Hungary was pushed back to its pre-war borders, except for an additional strip it lost to Czechoslovakia. A hard-line Communist regime was imposed by the Soviet troops which occupied Hungary.

In 1956 Hungary's Stalinist regime was toppled and a new democratic government under Imre Nagy announced its withdrawal from the Warsaw Pact and declared Hungary's neutrality. This prompted the Soviets to crush the new government by military force and reimpose a Communist regime under Janos Kadar. However, Kadar's administration proved mild, enabling private-sector activities and bringing economic development to the country. By the late 1980s, Hungary was among the most prosperous and free countries in Eastern Europe and in 1989–1990 led the other eastern bloc countries in overturning the Communist regime through the electoral process.

The Hungarian minorities in the neighboring countries underwent different experiences in the post-World War II period. Many Hungarians were expelled from Czechoslovakia and those who were left remained passive. Its large Hungarian minority was the reason for making Vojvodina an autonomous province within Serbia. In Transylavania, however, the large Hungarian minority was repressed especially harshly during the regime of Ceaucescu.This strained Romanian-Hungarian relations throughout the post-Stalinist period. The rise of Serb nationalism and the existence of a number of outstanding problems between Hungary and Slovakia makes the future of the Hungarian minorities in these two new states uncertain. (see also SLOVAKS)

HUNGWE   A subgroup of the SHONA.

HUNKPAPA   see SIOUX.

HUNZUKUT   (Burusho, Burushaski) An ethnic group, numbering under 50,000, which inhabits the rocky mountain regions of Hunza and Nagir in Pakistan. They are Muslims of the Ismaili school. Their language, Burushaski, is of obscure origin and attempts to link it with any other known language have failed. It may represent a proto-Aryan language once spoken throughout much of northern India and Pakistan. Although there is no literature in Burushaski, a rich oral tradition exists, dating back hundreds of years.

The Hunzukut are primarily farmers and herders. They grow a variety of fruits, vegetables, grains, and tubers and raise cattle, yak (from whose milk yoghurt is made), small animals, and fowl. They are known for their astonishing longevity.

HURONNE WENDAT   see WYANDOT.

HURUTSE   (Bahurutse) A subgroup of the SOTHO.

HUTU   A people, numbering an estimated 5 million, living in Rwanda and Burundi, east central Africa. They are divided almost equally between the two countries. Their language belongs to the central-Bantu group, with some Cushitic influences derived from the TUTSI. Most Hutu are Christians, belonging to various independent African churches or churches of European origin.

From their arrival in the area at the beginning of the millennium the Hutu have been mainly agriculturalists, although keeping cattle was common as well, and this economic structure still holds today. While a majority in their area, they yielded without a struggle to the fifteenth-century invasion by the TUTSI, which led to complete Tutsi domination over the Hutu, both political and economic.

In 1972 an uprising of the Hutu of Burundi against the TUTSI has resulted in massacres on both sides and a mass exodus of many refugees to neighboring countries, with the Hutu remaining under Tutsi supremacy. (see also BURUNDIANS, RWANDANS, TUTSI)

HWADUBA   A subgroup of the TSWANA.

H'WING   A subgroup of the RHADE.

I

IATMUL An ethnic group, numbering approximately 12,000, living in the Sepik River region in northern Papua New Guinea. They speak an indigenous local language. Their economy is based upon hunting, gathering, and fishing, as well as the importing of various types of fish. Their "men's house," among the most beautiful architectural displays in New Guinea, serves as the meeting place for religious ceremonies and assemblies.

IBALOI (Benguet Igorots, Benguetanos) An ethnic group, numbering 100,000, living in the upper Agno River region of Kabaya in the southern Benguet Province of northern Luzon, an island of the Philippines.

The Ibaloi have intermarried extensively with the KANKANAI. Gold abounds in their region and has compounded wealth gained through wet-rice agriculture in river settlements and root crops in the mountain settlements. Settlements are small, containing about twenty households who live in houses raised on stilts.

The Ibaloi consider themselves a community of the living and the dead. Ancestral cultural heroes are deified, the greatest spirit being named Kabigat.

IBAN (Sea Dayak) An ethnic group living on the Indonesian island of Kalimantan (Borneo). (see also DAYAK)

IBANDIRO One of the eight "early states" of the HAYA.

IBIBIO A people living mainly in the Calabar state of eastern Nigeria. They number about 6.3 million and adhere to either Christianity or traditional religions. Their main occupation is agriculture and they excel in wood carving. Having no tradition of migration, they have probably inhabited their present location for a long time. In the nineteenth century missions began to build schools in their region. Britain later engaged in several military expeditions to bring the Ibibio under their control. It took several years, however, before administrative control could be established.

In 1928 the Ibibio formed an ethnic organization, called the Ibibio Union, to unite all Ibibio to fight the injustices of British colonialism. The union encouraged the Ibibio to gain a Western education and established a teachers' training college. It also promoted peaceful coexistence between the Ibibio and other ethnic groups. When Nigerian party politics began to develop during the 1950s, most Ibibio leaders supported an Ibo-dominated party, but many later abandoned it, feeling that it held out little hope for non-IBO. These later joined minority parties, hoping to create a separate state for the minority groups of the Eastern Region. The Ibibio Union was disolved along with all other ethnic organizations following a 1966 military coup. In recent years the Ibibio have begun to reorganize. One new organization which attempts to unite all the Ibibio is often regarded as the legitimate successor of the Ibibio Union.

The Ibibio are subdivided into smaller groups: ANANG, EFIK, OGONI, EJAGHAM, BOKI, YAKO, EKURI, AKUNAKUNA, MBEMBE, ODODOP, and ORRI. (see also NIGERIANS)

IBILAO see ILONGOT.

IBO (Igbo) Located in the southeastern part of Nigeria, in the states of Anambra and Imo, the Ibo are the third largest ethnic group in this country. They number around 18 million people and constitute about 17 percent of the population.

The traditional religion of the Ibo is polytheistic but contains the concept of a supreme god that controls the world from afar, with a large number of lesser gods. Towards the end of the nineteenth century, following the British conquest of the area, missionaries arrived in

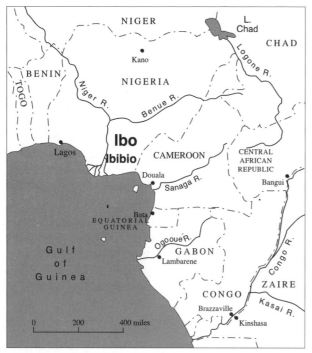

Ibibio and Ibo

the region and most Ibo converted to Christianity, encouraged by the Western education offered by the missions.

Before British colonization the Ibo did not consider themselves as one people. They lived in small isolated villages that served as separate political units. The BRITISH misinterpreted this social structure as anarchy. Since they could find no chiefs with any sway over a significant area they decided to rule the Ibo directly with the help of local chiefs who were not traditional leaders of the Ibo communities.

The sense of common identity among the Ibo developed only in the colonial period. Modernization and urbanization caused them to leave their isolated villages and meet other Ibo and non-Ibo. Another factor leading to the development of a shared sense of common identity was the declaration by British anthropologists that the Ibo are in fact a single ethnic group.

Towards the end of the nineteenth century the BRITISH conquered all of modern Nigeria and organized it into a single colony consisting of three regions: the north, with the HAUSA-FULANI as the predominant group; the mainly Yoruba-occupied southwest; and the Ibo territory in the southeast.

During the colonial period the Ibo underwent major social and economic changes. Many seized the new opportunities offered by capitalism and education, left their villages and moved to urban centers in Nigeria and in other countries, where they learned new professions and were integrated into the capitalist economy. Their rapid modernization provoked bitterness among the less-developed HAUSA-FULANI and YORUBA.

After World War II the BRITISH allowed the development of party politics. However, the political struggle soon became ethnic. After Nigeria's independence the HAUSA-FULANI who dominated Nigerian politics enacted a discriminatory policy towards the Ibo. Ethnic tensions intensified throughout the 1960s and culminated in the massacre in 1966 of some 30,000 Ibo in the north of the country by the HAUSA-FULANI. Two million Ibo spread across Nigeria fled to their homeland where in May 1967 they declared the Republic of Biafra. The ensuing civil war lasted two-and-a-half years, during which tens of thousands of soldiers on both sides were killed and some one million Ibo died of starvation. The war ended in January 1970 and Biafra was reincorporated into Nigeria.

In the aftermath of the war, the Nigerian government attempted to dilute ethnic identities in Nigeria by dividing the existing regions into twenty-one smaller units that cut ethnic lines. The Ibo are now divided between two states.

There are many different Ibo subgroups, varying slightly in terms of dialect and culture. Some, like the ARO, flourished during the pre-colonial period by dealing in slaves and palm oil. Their strong economic position diminished, however, as a result of British colonialism. Other Ibo subgroups are the ABADJA, ABAM, AHAM, ALENSAW, AWHAFIA, AWHAWZARA, AWTANZO, EDDA, EKKPAHIA, ETCHE, EZIAMA, EZZA, IHE, IJI, IKA, IKWERRI, IKWO, ISHIELU, ISU-OCHI, NDOKKI, NGBO, NGWA, NKALU, NRI, OKOBA, ONISHTA-AWKA, ORATTA, ORU, UBANI, and UTUTU. (see also HAUSA-FULANI, NIGERIANS)

ICELANDERS The 250,000 inhabitants of Iceland speak a language developed from archaic Norwegian; in the Middle Ages, this vernacular was used to articulate a rich mythological literature.

Iceland was first discovered in the eighth century by Celtic monks; from 872 it was colonized by Norse Viking rebels against the first attempts of Norway's monarchs to impose order, who brought their Celtic slaves with them. In due time Norway sent an elite class to Iceland, which established an original civilization dominating political life until the fourteenth century. While agriculture was hardly possible, pastures and fish fields abounded. There were no towns, only farms. The Icelanders' early history seems to have been peaceful and democratic. By the year 1000 they were christianized, and slavery disappeared. However, the situation deteriorated in the thirteenth century. Unending vendettas brought the republic down, and subjected the island to Norwegian sovereignty.

By 1380 Icelanders passed under nominal Danish sovereignty. Volcanic eruptions, deterioration of the climate, the plague, and the introduction of serfdom contributed to the islanders' ruin. In the sixteenth century Danish overlords imposed Protestantism. Epidemics and volcanic eruptions further decimated Icelanders in the eighteenth century. The nineteenth century witnessed gradual recovery, but many Icelanders escaped through emigration to Canada.

In 1904 Iceland became autonomous and parliamentarism was introduced. A new treaty in 1918 left only a personal union with Denmark. Total independence followed in 1944 as a result of World War II. In the Cold War, Iceland's importance as a prop for Western (North Atlantic Treaty Organization) bases often clashed with a popular tendency towards neutralism. The Icelanders were able to develop an extensive social security system, but in spite of recent prosperity, their economic basis, dependence on fishery, remains narrow and vulnerable. Extension of maritime zones has led to recent conflict with the BRITISH.

ICHKERI   see CHECHEN.

IDAHAN   (Sabah Murut) see MURUT.

IDOMA   An ethnic group living in central-south Nigeria.

IDU   A subgroup of the MISHMI.

IFE   A subgroup of the YORUBA living in Nigeria.

IFUGAO   (Ifugaw, Ipugao, Yfugao) A mountain people of northern Luzon, an island of the Philippines. Numbering c.150,000, they live on the slopes of Mount Data in western Bontok along the waters of the upper Abra, Chico, and Magat Rivers. Subgroups include the BANAUE, BUNHRAN, MAYAYAO, HALIPAN, HAPAO, and KIANGANG.

The Ifugao language is a Malayo-Polynesian language of the Northern Philippine grouping. They have been living in the same geographical area for several hundred years where they have maintained their traditional culture despite the pressures of modernization. They live in small hamlets along terraced hills. Sub-

sistence is mainly through wet-rice agriculture and slash and burn cultivation of tubers. Animals and farming implements are used to plow the land; a man's status is determined by his rice fields. In addition to agriculture, hunting and gathering are also important. The *ginga*, a water clam found in rice fields, is a main source of food. Coffee has recently become a main export.

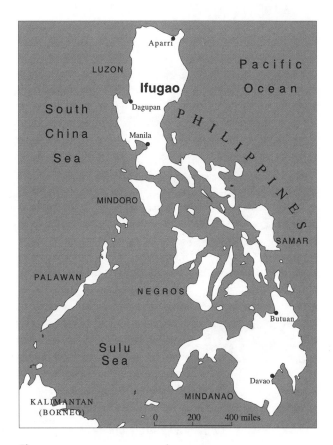

Ifugao

They are known for their sophistication in wet-rice terracing and intricate ritual and legal organization, despite the lack of an intervillage political system.

There are no formal political institutions and the society functions through the organization of mutual kinship obligations. The Ifugao have a pantheon of gods, and believe that the universe consists of five regions: earth, skyworld, underworld, downstream region, and upstream region. The spirits speak through tribal priests who call upon the deities during rituals and sacrifices.

IGALA   An ethnic group living in central-south Nigeria.

above: An Ifugao man in northern Luzon, the Philippines
below: Ifugao women

IGBO   see IBO.

IGEMBE   A subgroup of the MERU.

IGOJI   A subgroup of the MERU.

IGOROT   see BONTOK.

IHE   A subgroup of the IBO.

IJAW   An ethnic group, numbering about 2 million, living in Nigeria, where they constitute some 2 percent of the population. Most of them inhabit the Rivers State but some are also found in the Bendel State.

In the eighteenth century they served as middlemen in trade, particularly the slave trade, with European settlers along the coast. The discovery of petroleum in their region and the subsequent emergence of large cities altered the traditional Ijaw mode of living, although some still remain in villages and are dependent on fishing. (see also NIGERIANS)

IJEBU   A subgroup of the YORUBA living in the Ogun State of Nigeria. Although they originally served as middlemen to European traders, they were later one of the most active groups opposing British colonialism.

IJESHA   A subgroup of the YORUBA living in Nigeria.

IJI   A subgroup of the IBO.

IKA   A subgroup of the IBO.

IKWERRI   A subgroup of the IBO.

IKWO   A subgroup of the IBO.

ILA   (Shukulumbwe) An ethnic group numbering 35,000 living in south-central Zambia near the Kafue River. Their language, Ila, is related to Tonga. Some are Christians while others adhere to traditional African religions.

Much of their religion and culture is similar to that of the neighboring PLATEAU TONGA. They follow a matrilineal descent system but their residence pattern is patrilocal. They raise cattle and engage in trade. The Ila have a reputation as brave warriors. Harry Nkumbula, founder of the Northern Rhodesian African National Congress, was an Ila. (see also ZAMBIANS)

ILANON   An ethnic group, numbering an estimated 100,000, living concentrated around Polloc Harbor on the western side of Mindanao, an island in the Philippines. They are the best known people of the area, due to the fact that they were once feared as pirates throughout southeast Asia, having boats rowed by slaves and armed with brass cannons. The name "Ilanon" used to be the general term for any Mindanao Muslim.

The Ilanon language, which ties the Ilanon people into one group, is very closely related to Magindanao. The introduction of Malayan commerce (1000–1200 C.E.), helped create concentrated population centers and initiated their history of raiding and pirating. Although they are thought to have originated from the area around Lake Lanoa, that area was originally inhabited by the MARANAO and was only used as a base for the Ilanon during Spanish intrusion.

IL-E ARAB   A subgroup of the KHAMSE.

ILLINOIS   A Native North American group, numbering no more than a few hundred, living in Oklahoma.

ILONGOT   (Ibilao) An ethnic group numbering several thousand, living in southern Nueva Vizcaya Province on the Philippine island of Luzon. Their language consists of three distinctive dialects, Egongut, Italon, and Abaka.

Ilongot settlements contain up to seventy people living in four to nine houses. They are renowned traders who hold land in common and practice dry rice slash and burn cultivation. Headhunting is still practiced.

The Ilongot remained isolated until the 1950s, living in a society without any form of political system, but since that time, Protestant missionaries have been active among them.

ILSEVEN   A clan of the SHAHSEVEN.

ILTHURIA   A subgroup of the RENDILLE.

ILUMAN   An OTAVALO group.

IMENTI   A subgroup of the MERU.

IMRAGUEN   An ethnic group, numbering around 1,500, living in Mauritania, in the region stretching from Cape Timiris to Nouadhibou. They are nominally

Muslims, but have retained their traditional laws and customs.

IMUSHAR   A subgroup of the TUAREG.

INANLU   see EINALLU, KHAMSE.

INDIANS   The population of India, the world's most populous state after China, estimated at 871 million (1991). The country's 2.2 percent annual population growth rate, while slightly below the average for the developing world as a whole, currently represents an addition of over 19 million to that total each year. Despite increasing urbanization, the population remains overwhelmingly rural, with some two-thirds of workers engaged in agriculture. Probably the single most difficult perennial problem facing the state is the inability to generate economic growth sufficient to keep pace with the needs of its expanding population. Attempts at birth control have met with mixed results.

Bounded to the north by the Himalayan mountain chain, India can be more properly described as a subcontinent than a country. It has represented a cul-de-sac for the invasionary forces that have entered it from the northwest since time immemorial and its complex ethnic mix is primarily a result of successive groups of invaders remaining to intermingle with the indigenous population. While great kingdoms have flourished in different parts of the subcontinent over millennia (the civilization that built the cities of Moenjodaro and Harappa flourished in the Indus valley, in what is now Pakistan, some 4,500 years ago), India has been a single governmental entity for a relatively short time dating from the consolidation of British colonial rule in the first half of the nineteenth century.

Since it gained independence from Britain in 1947, India has been a sovereign democratic republic, currently divided into twenty-two states and nine union territories. National government is centered in the capital, Delhi.

Human settlement is pervasive and, with an average of over 264 persons per square kilometer, the country is densely populated, although not uniformly so: the Indo-Gangetic plain in the north is the area of greatest population concentration, while the northwestern desert and north and northeastern mountain regions are relatively sparsely inhabited.

With a per capita annual income of just $350 in 1989, the country is very poor, while the very high proportion of young people places a great burden on the resources of adult wage earners and state services.

Domestic overcrowding is endemic, with an average of 2.8 people per room, and an estimated 100 million Indians are shelterless. Despite the fact that the country possesses a sophisticated administrative structure, a well-equipped bureaucracy, and a large supply of educated manpower, only 36 percent of the population is literate.

India is one of the world's top twenty industrialized nations. While the capital goods and heavy industry sector is primarily government-owned and run, the consumer goods industries are largely in private hands. Given the enormous domestic market, exports account for a relatively small proportion of production.

India's main food crops are rice and wheat; its most important cash crops include sugarcane, cotton, tea, coffee, rubber, and tobacco. Agricultural output grew rapidly with the introduction of new farming techniques and the use of chemical fertilizers during the 1960s and 1970s, and India is nearly self-sufficient in food. How long these levels of production can be sustained is a matter for some concern. A combination of factors including increased population pressure on cultivable land, deforestation and resultant soil erosion, a receding water table, and diminishing returns from the use of artificial soil nutrients make farming an increasingly precarious business, with the lot of the smallholders who represent the majority of Indian farmers especially hard. Many have migrated to the cities in search of a livelihood, thereby exacerbating the problems of metropolises whose infrastructures are already inadequate to the needs of their residents.

Although India is a secular state, religion plays an integral part in the nation's life. Some 82.5 percent of the population is Hindu, and Indian culture and social mores are overwhelmingly a product of Hinduism, whose influence has been strong even among groups of a different religious affiliation. Islam, practiced by 11.5 percent of Indians, is the second largest religion in the country; it is the legacy of nearly 600 years of Muslim control over north India, which began in 1192 with Muhammad of Ghazni's capture of Ajmer (in modern-day Rajasthan) and ended with the defeat of the last Moghul emperor by the BRITISH at the Battle of Plassey in 1757. During this period Islam became well-established, with many Hindus, especially those from the lowest castes, converting to the religion of their conquerors. Persian became the language of government and was colloquialized as Hindustani, from which arose Urdu (a more strongly Persianized form using Persian script) and Hindi (rooted in Sanskrit, the Indo-

Aryan language of the 1500 B.C.E. Aryan invaders). In the modern era, these two languages are increasingly identified with particular religious communities, with Urdu the language of Islam and Hindi largely, although not exclusively, that of Hinduism.

India is also home to over 20 million Christians, 16 million Sikhs, 6 million Buddhists, and some 3.5 million Jains; the religions of the latter two groups are offshoots of Hinduism dating from the middle of the first millennium B.C.E., while Sikhism, founded in north India in the fifteenth century, also originated as a Hindu reform movement. Long-established, albeit numerically insignificant, communities of JEWS and PARSIS are currently in decline due to emigration or assimilation. Among India's 50 million tribal peoples are communities pursuing totemic and indigenous traditional religious practices.

The introduction of Hinduism to India has been ascribed to the Aryan tribes who arrived in the northern part of the subcontinent around 1500 B.C.E., but the religion is more probably a fusion of their religious practices with those of the Indus valley civilization and the Dravidian inhabitants of south India. Today, it is Hinduism rather than language or ethnicity that links the still predominantly Dravidian south with the Aryan north.

Perhaps the most distinctive feature of Hinduism as far as the outsider is concerned is its caste system. In fact, this system subsumes a twofold classification of social strata. One of these is textual, based on the scriptures, known as the Varna model, and divides society into four distinct, hierarchically ordered groups: Brahmans, the sacerdotal elite, the priests, the teachers, and religious guides; Kshatriyas, warriors and rulers, of whom the Rajputs of north India represent an important and powerful subgroup; Vaishyas, traditionally merchants and traders, and therefore an economically significant and often prosperous group; and Shudras, textually enjoined to serve the other three castes and widely represented as farmers in the Indian countryside. The other form of stratification is that of the Jati, or caste, model, the on-the-ground hierarchical arrangement whereby each Varna is divided into an immense number of subgroups bound by ties of conduct, kinship, and profession. Within this latter system, some subcastes of the lower Varnas may in fact enjoy higher social status than groups occupying a position within the higher Varnas. Traditionally, the individual's caste status rigidly determines the options available to him as to choice of marriage partner, friends, occupation, dwelling place, and a plethora of other variables. The systems' earliest origins are almost certainly pre-Aryan, although the Aryans appear to have developed caste differentiation to assert and consecrate their belief in their superiority to the pre-Aryan Indian people.

Although the influence of the caste system is now weaker than it used to be, with casteism (discrimination on the basis of caste) officially illegal in India and government initiatives to improve the conditions of those from the lower castes (initiatives which have been attacked on the grounds of both tokenism and favoritism), socio-economic standing is still significantly correlated with caste origin. Moreover, even among non-Hindu minorities, status and profession are often determined on quasi-caste lines, especially where the minority is living in a local environment which is predominantly Hindu. The inflexibility and conservatism engendered by the caste system have frequently acted as an inertial force militating against change in India.

The manifest diversity of languages and religions within the country has been dealt with since independence from Britain by a marked tendency to make state boundaries coextensive with linguistic or traditional regions. The search for and creation of a strong sense of national identity unifying the disparate groups within the republic is in great part a legacy of the role played in the struggle for independence from British rule by two men, Mahatma Gandhi and Jawaharlal Nehru. Both Hindus, they nonetheless stressed the importance of a non-sectarian approach to Indian affairs and affirmed the right of all Indians, regardless of creed or circumstance, to be regarded as equal members of society.

Gandhi emphasized the need to pursue an economic policy commensurate with the needs of India's rural masses and was instrumental in highlighting and moving to ameliorate the appalling deprivation and oppression faced by India's tens of millions of Untouchables, the lowest, casteless, class in Indian society for whom the most menial and degrading tasks are traditionally reserved and whom he renamed Harijans ("Children of God").

As the first prime minister of independent India, Nehru departed from Gandhi's economic blueprint by pursuing the goal of industrialization, but remained committed to preserving the democratic and secular values of the state. Both men were strongly opposed to the partition of India into a largely Hindu India and an overwhelmingly Muslim Pakistan, arguing that this was not an adequate solution to the problem of sectarian tensions and might even serve to exacerbate them.

The outbreak of communal clashes that cost over a million lives at the time of partition (1947–1948) seemed to support this contention.

A government of India is faced with administering a nation where until recently, linguistic rather than religious or ethnic affiliation has been the prime determinant of group identification. More than 700 main languages and dialects have been identified, while fifteen regional languages are recognized officially by the Indian government. Broadly speaking, the inhabitants of the northern part of the country speak languages of Indo-Aryan origin descended at least in part from Sanskrit and related to European languages. Prominent among these northern languages are Hindi, Urdu, Punjabi, Bengali, Marathi, Gujarati, Oriya, and Kashmiri; one of these, Hindi, is the official language of the state. The peoples of the south, in contrast, speak one of the Dravidian languages: Tamil, Telugu, Malayalam, and Kannada.

There are recurring charges from the south of "linguistic colonialism" on the part of the north, and there is considerable resentment of the fact that Hindi is a compulsory language in all schools, a status accorded to no southern tongue. Although it has no official status, it is in fact English, the legacy of British rule, that is most commonly used as a lingua franca between educated northerners and southerners.

The Austro-Asiatic language family is represented by tribal languages found in east and central India, northern Bengal, and Assam, while the predominantly tribal areas of the northeast are home to speakers of Sino-Tibetan languages. There are tribes in Bihar which speak a language of as yet unidentified origin.

Since the early 1980s Indian governments have been faced with unprecedented levels of civil unrest caused by religious conflict and separatist aspirations. In 1984 then-prime minister Indira Gandhi was assassinated by Sikh militants agitating for the creation of an independent Sikh homeland in what is now the Punjab; their activities have made that area, one of the most affluent and agriculturally developed in the country, the site of widespread and persistent acts of terrorist violence which have cost thousands of lives and led to significant levels of Hindu emigration from the state to surrounding areas and metropolises. Meanwhile, Kashmiri Muslims, who represent some 75 percent of the population of that state, have backed their demands for independence or union with Pakistan with attacks against state and federal law enforcement authorities. The northeastern state of Assam has also witnessed rebellion against central government rule. The reemergence of Hindu-Muslim rivalries, betokened by increased support for Hindu-nationalist political organizations and inter-communal clashes leaving several hundreds dead, has led many to surmise that the fragile national consensus has broken down.

In response to labor shortages around the world, the English exported Indian laborers to virtually all their farflung colonies. Since decolonization, Indians have become a significant minority, if not the majority, in many new states. Countries with substantial Indian communities include: the Gulf States of the Middle East (where they still maintain the status of migrant laborers), East Africa (whereas in Uganda Idi Amin Dada expelled all Asians in 1972; Indians still form an important middle class in Kenya and Tanzania), South Africa (where Indians are recognized as a distinct racial group with their own parliament), Mauritius (where they constitute the majority of the population), Guyana (the same), Fiji (where they have come into ethnic conflict with the native FIJI ISLANDERS), Europe, and America.

INDONESIANS   A people inhabiting Indonesia, a vast archipelago of 13,677 islands stretching for over 3,000 miles between mainland Southeast Asia and the island of New Guinea, the western half of which, Irian Jaya, is a province of Indonesia. There are about 200 million Indonesians, almost 90 percent of whom are Muslims, making it the most populous Muslim country in the world. The official language is Bahasa Indonesia, a variant of Malay with marked Portuguese and Dutch influence. Most Indonesians, however, prefer their native languages, of which there are over 200, and Indonesian is used only as a lingua franca, particularly in urban areas. Most local languages (excluding those spoken in the northern half of the island of Halmahera and throughout Irian Jaya) are members of the Malayo-Polynesian branch of the Austronesian family of languages, although most are mutually unintelligible. A Chinese minority of about 2.5 percent lives in urban areas and has preserved its own language and culture, further adding to the country's ethnic complexity. Two-thirds of the country's population live on the island of Java (Djawa) and the smaller adjoining islands of Bali and Madura. This is one of the most densely populated regions in the world and overpopulation is currently threatening the delicate sociological and ecological balance.

The indigenous cultures of Indonesia are often a conglomerate of diverse cultural elements, many of foreign origin. Certain regions of Indonesia, such as Java, were important trading centers in the ancient world; others, like the Moluccas, were coveted by foreign powers for their spices. Hinduism from India and Buddhism from India and China arrived in Java some two thousand years ago. Islam was introduced by Arab traders in the fifteenth century and Christianity was introduced by the DUTCH and PORTUGUESE in the seventeenth century. Many of the farflung islands and remote regions of the larger islands such as Borneo (Kalimantan) were only reached in the mid-nineteenth century. Their peoples often still live much as they did when discovered and have only minimal allegiance to the Indonesian state. The importance of regionalism and ethnic loyalty is further evidenced by the very name of the country, Indonesia, which was only invented to describe the islands as a geographic unit in 1857.

Despite limited arable land, nearly 70 percent of the population is engaged in agriculture. Rice is the staple crop in most regions, though rubber, sugar, and coffee are economically important as cash crops. There are also considerable oil and natural gas reserves, and deposits of nickel, tin, and bauxite. Literacy is increasing rapidly and many Indonesians are now finding employment in services.

Although different ethnic groups enjoyed considerable autonomy, early Indonesian history is dominated by the presence of several empires and sultanates such as Srivijaya, Majapahit, Ternate, and Tidore. The PORTUGUESE and the DUTCH fought over control of the islands from the sixteenth to the nineteenth centuries, with the DUTCH eventually gaining ascendancy and the PORTUGUESE left only with the eastern half of the island of Timor. Dutch colonial rule was marked by corruption and harsh exploitation of the native population. In 1860, however, the publication of *Max Havelaar,* by Dutch author Multatuli (Edward Douwes Dekker), with its scathing condemnation of conditions under colonialism, led the DUTCH to reconsider their position and improve conditions on the major islands.

Local nationalist sentiment increased between the world wars and many Indonesians viewed the Japanese occupation (1942–1945) and the nominal self-rule they then enjoyed as the first step toward independence. Nationalists led by Sukarno declared a republic; they continued to fight the DUTCH after ousting the JAPANESE. Independence was finally granted in 1949. To counter the vast ethnic and geographic diversity of the country, Sukarno introduced a state ideology which called for the unity of Indonesia and the suppression of secessionist attempts.

Since independence, Indonesia has expanded to include western Irian, formerly western New Guinea (1963) and the former Portuguese colony of East Timor (1975). The EAST TIMORESE long resisted Indonesian rule. The Central Moluccas also attempted to establish an independent state but the revolt was quelled upon independence; some 40,000 refugees have fled to the Netherlands, where they continue to agitate for independence.

Although one of the most important nations in Asia by virtue of its size and vast natural resources, Indonesia faces many problems. These include overpopulation, dwindling possibilities for agricultural development (centuries of slash and burn agriculture have all but destroyed the soil), regionalism and ethnic nationalism, and severe violations of human rights. At the same time, competent planning, careful utilization of vast natural resources, and mutual understanding among the various peoples can turn Indonesia into a regional economic and cultural force. (see also ATONI)

INGALIK   A Native North American group of the Athapaskan-speaking peoples, numbering about 500 and living in Alaska, U.S.A. They earn their livelihood today, as in the past, by hunting moose and caribou in season.

INGILOI   A small ethnic group in Azerbaijan. There are no estimates of their numbers, since they were not registered as a separate group in Soviet demographic statistics. They may number from several hundred to a few thousand.

The Ingiloi are a bilingual community using the Azerbaijani language outside the home and the Ingiloi east-Georgian dialect among themselves. Some Ingiloi have lost Georgian and are now Azerbaijani monolinguals.

Those living in the Kachi district of Azerbaijan are Eastern Orthodox Christians; others, living in the villages of Alibeglo, Mosul, and Ititala, have been Shi'ite Muslims since the seventeenth century. (see also GEORGIANS)

INGUSH   (s.d. Ghalghai) A people of the Central Caucasus, inhabiting the area between the middle course of the Terek River and the main Caucasian Ridge in the western part of the Chechen-Ingush Republic, and the eastern region of the North-Ossetian Republic of Russia. The total number in the USSR according to the 1989 Soviet census was 238,000, of whom c.164,000 lived in the Chechen-Ingush Republic.

The Ingush language belongs to the Nakh (or Veinakh) branch of the Ibero-Caucasian family. In the 1920s the alphabet was based on the Roman script; in 1938 it adopted the Russian Cyrillic script. They possess a rich folklore; their written literature dates back to the 1930s. Eastern Orthodox Christianity was brought to the Ingush from Georgia in the seventh and eighth centuries; Sunni Islam of the Hanafi school began to spread among them only in the eighteenth century, but at least until 1860 about one-quarter still professed Christianity.

Historically the Ingush are divided into clan-like communities: Ghalghai (which name became the common s.d.), Dgharkhol, Kistin (Veppi), Korin, and Metskhal. A part of the Kistin now lives in East Georgia, on the upper course of the Alazani River (Pankis-Kanyon). They are bilingual, with Georgian as the literary language.

The Ingush are traditionally mountain-dwellers, living in three-storey stone houses. In the old *auls* (villages) located on the steep slopes and in canyons, medieval stone towers for dwellings and defense have been preserved.

During the sixteenth, seventeenth, and nineteenth centuries a considerable number of Ingush resettled in the plains. One of the first settlements in the middle basin of the Terek River was the village of Angush (Ingush): hence the Russian name for the people. The territory of Ingush was annexed by the Russian Empire in 1810.

In the 1860s the Ingush began to be pushed back into the mountains by Russian Terek Cossacks. The large wave of Muslim emigration from the North Caucasus to the Ottoman Empire during the mid-nineteenth century took with it also a number of Ingush, who now dwell in Turkey and in other Near and Middle Eastern states which came into existence after the fall of that empire; they are known there, together with the descendants of other Muslim North Caucasian emigrants of that period, as Circassians (see CHERKESS).

Clashes between the Ingush and the Cossacks continued until the 1917 Bolshevik revolution. During the ensuing civil war the Ingush joined forces with the Bolsheviks, as the Cossack stand was outspokenly anti-Soviet. In 1924 the Ingush Autonomous *Oblast* (Region) was established, and united in 1936 with the Chechen Autonomous *Oblast* into the Chechen-Ingush Autonomous Soviet Republic. In 1944 the republic was liquidated and the Ingush as well as the CHECHEN were deported to Kazakhstan and Siberia; in 1957 they were "rehabilitated" and

returned to their ethnic territory. After the dismemberment of the USSR, ethnic tension between the OSSET and the Ingush erupted in armed conflict in the early 1990s.

The traditional economy in the mountains is based on cattle-breeding and terrace agriculture; in the low-lying plains, agriculture. Today the Ingush also work in urban industries. (see also CHERKESS)

INKASSA   see SAHWI.

INTONAMAN   A South American Indian ethnic group of lowland Bolivia. They engage in agriculture, growing maize, sweet manioc, sweet potatoes, peppers, pineapples, beans, and cotton. Hunting and fishing help supplement their diet.

INUIT   (Eskimo) A large Native North American people. "Inuit" is the Canadian designation of the group known as the Eskimo in Alaska and Greenland. The word Eskimo, meaning "eaters of raw flesh," is considered a term of derision by the Inuit who prefer their own self-designation (Inuit means "people").

The more than 150,000 Inuit are scattered along the shores of Alaska (U.S.A.), the Beaufort Sea, the Yukon and Northwest Territories (Canada), Siberia (Russia), and Greenland. Many Inuit communities are still engaged in their traditional modes of earning a livelihood: fishing, hunting, trapping, and whaling. A large number of Inuit communities have in recent decades suffered severely from the rise in public concern over trapping and especially the taking of seal skins from baby seals. Even though the Inuit were never engaged in the hunting of baby seals, the negative publicity in the international media had a spill-over effect which was serious enough to cut severely into their income.

For many years Inuit land claims were ignored by territorial and federal governments. In the former Soviet Union, all the Inuit communities near and on the Bering Strait were transferred inland to avoid contact with Native communities in Alaska. Only in the last few years have Inuit from both sides of the Bering Sea begun to meet. In Alaska the federal government recognized the Inuit title to their traditional land, and a proportion of the Alaska Native Land Settlement was reserved for them. Today in Alaska the sixteen Inuit villages are united in the Bering Strait Native Corporation. In Canada, the Inuit fought for legal title of their traditional land for more than thirty years. In 1992 Canada's federal government established an au-

Inuit

tonomous Inuit Territory which is the largest autonomous region in the world.

Catholic missionaries began their attempts to convert the Inuit in the beginning of this century. Several Protestant denominations also engaged in missionary work among the Inuit. The result was that many Inuit communities are now split along religious lines. Even today most of the Inuit communities are isolated from the larger society to the south and from one another. There are two reasons for this: one is the distance which separates the various Inuit communities; the second is the weather which, especially in the long winter months, is extremely severe. Most Inuit communities are heavily dependent upon air traffic for supplies and contact with the outside. Isolation has also served to enhance the presence and use of sophisticated equipment, especially in the area of telecommunications and medical diagnosis. (see also CANADIANS, GREENLANDERS)

IOWA A Native North American group numbering about 700, many of whom are living on the Federal Indian Reservation in Kensan and on the Iowa Federal Trust Area in Oklahoma, U.S.A., which they share with the SHAWNEE.

Like the HIDATSA and the MANDAN, they were traditionally earth lodge dwellers who lived as agriculturalists and seasonal buffalo hunters.

IPUGAO see IFUGAO.

IPURINA A group of South American Indians living in the extreme western portion of the Amazon basin in Brazil. They subsist primarily from fishing and hunting turtles and manatees from bark- or dugout canoes. They also grow maize, sweet manioc, beans, sweet potatoes, peanuts, and peppers. The villagers live in enormous, circular, communal dwellings.

IRANIANS The term used as a recent self-appelation by the Persian people of Iran. It is also applied as a metaethnic term to include all the peoples and ethnic groups forming the nation state of Iran: AFSHARS, AIRUMS, and ARABS in the southwest; AZERBAIJANI in the northwest; BAKHTIAR, BALUCH, BARBARI, GILAK, KHAMSE, KUHGULI, KURDS, LAQS II, LURS, MAMASANI, MAZANDERANI,

An Inuit man

above: An Inuit mother and child
below: An elderly Inuit woman with a child

PADAR, PERSIANS, QAJARS, QASHQAI, SHAHSEVEN, and TALYSH in northwest Iran; and TATS II and TURKMEN in northeast Iran.

The recent history of the peoples of Iran centers around the history of the PERSIANS, the backbone of the Iranian state. The peoples of Iran are overwhelmingly Muslim and speak a variety of languages. While Iranian languages are spoken by the bulk of Iranian peoples, Turkic languages are spoken in the north in regions bordering with Azerbaijan and Turkemenistan. Arabic is spoken in the extreme southwest, near Iraq.

IRAQIS (s.d. Iraqiyyun). Seventy-seven percent of the 19 million Iraqis are ARABS; they form the predominant nationality and speak a distinct Arabic dialect. Only some 4 million (20 percent of all Iraqis) are Sunnis, inhabiting the upper Euphrates region from the Syrian border to west of Baghdad and the Tigris region between Mosul and Samarra, who have for centuries been the politically dominant and more prosperous group. The 10 million (Twelver) Shi'ites, Iraq's most numerous group, are much poorer. Originally a rural population living in the south and center, many have migrated to Baghdad in search of better opportunities. Iraq contains the Shi'ite holy places of Karbala and Najaf. Fundamentalist Iran may have some influence on Iraqi Shi'ites.

Between an-Nasiriya and the confluence of the rivers Tigris and Euphrates in south Iraq live the Marsh Arabs or Madan, fishermen and cattlebreeders who for thousands of years have used reeds for building houses on artificial reedmat islands. They may descend from the Sumerians. In the western desert live a few thousand BEDUIN.

The KURDS, numbering 3.5 – 4 million, or 20 – 23 percent of the population, constitute Iraq's single largest ethnic minority. Since KURDS are nearly all Sunni, they bring the Sunni total to 42 percent. KURDS have demanded autonomy and engaged in multiple rebellions against central government. The 35,000 Yazidis in Jabal Sinjar are ethnically Kurdish. Other ethnic minorities are the TURKMEN, ASSYRIANS, PERSIANS, ARMENIANS, and Lur. Of more recent vintage are PALESTINIANS, refugees of the 1948 war.

Christians represent a tiny minority (3.5 percent) of the population. The largest denominations are the Nestorian (Chaldean and Assyrian) churches. A group of c.23,000 Mandeans (Sabeans), shipwrights and silversmiths, live near rivers so as to fulfill their religious duties, which emphasize ablutions.

Like elsewhere in the Middle East, population in Iraq tends to be compressed into a small part of the territory. Only one-third of the land is arable. Baghdad lies in the midst of Iraq's densest and most urbanized concentration. A metropolis of 4.6 million, it houses more than a quarter of all Iraqis. Intensive irrigated cultivation is concentrated between ar-Ramadi and an-Nasiriya and along the Shatt al-Arab, but high natural growth has turned Iraq in recent years into a food importer. Population has dropped here as a result of both Gulf wars.

More than a common nationality, Iraqis share the experience of living under the same state power. In its contemporary guise the state is a fairly modern creation, and has been only moderately successful in instilling a sense of collective national destiny among its diverse ethnic and religious components. State ideology combines pan-Arabism with glorification of the Mesopotamian past. However, the emphasis on a specific Iraqi identity is fairly recent and artificial.

The presumed ancestors of modern-day Iraqis created some of the world's oldest cultures: Sumer, Babylonia, and Assyria, which developed in the alluvial bed formed by the Tigris (Dijla) and Euphrates (Furat), the eastern leg of the Fertile Crescent. This is still the economic and cultural center of modern Iraq. In this "cradle of civilization," agriculture, domestication of animals, the wheel, cuneiform script, and urban life were all first invented. Babylonia and Assyria were succeeded by the Persian, then the Greek and Roman, empires. Conquered by the ARABS in 633, the area was subject to much ethnic admixture over the following centuries. Mesopotamia once more became a world power under the Abbasid dynasty which founded Baghdad, until the MONGOLS devastated their capital in 1258 and again in 1393. The genocide they committed has left an enduring mark on Iraq. In 1533 the TURKS took Baghdad and Iraq became a backward border province of the Ottoman Empire. In World War I Britain conquered the region.

Iraq as a modern state came only into being as a British mandate after World War I, but it has continued to suffer from internal disjunction. Created from three former Ottoman provinces, only its southern part (largely coextensive with ancient Mesopotamia) is Arab, while its northern mountainous part (Mosul Province) is Kurdish. Geopolitical juggling has created the preconditions of a longstanding feud of Iraqi Arabs with their Kurdish neighbours. The BRITISH imposed a Hashemite monarchy on Iraq and stimulated its integration into the world economy. In 1932 Iraq was the first mandate to graduate to independence. However,

British influence remained preponderant in the 1930s and throughout World War I.

In the 1950s Iraq began to develop into an oil economy. State revenues rose but were unequally distributed. Anti-Western, nationalist, and socialist impulses led in 1958 to a republican revolution, followed by nationalizations that broke up the landowner class. This ushered in a long period of instability, until the Ba'ath party consolidated its hold in 1968 by building a one-party state and taking full control over the army. Ever since, power has been the preserve of one clan stemming from the town of Tikrit.

At its outset, the secular Ba'ath regime still faced well-organized opposition parties: the Communists, strongest among the Shi'ites, and the KURDS in the north. After the Communists had been eradicated many Shi'ites turned to Islamic fundamentalism. The KURDS were decimated in repeated campaigns meant to eliminate any dream of autonomy. In 1979 Saddam Hussein al-Tikriti took power; by terrorizing and exterminating his opponents he transformed the Ba'ath party into an instrument enhancing his personal power. Iraq's succession of coups and countercoups progressively narrowed participation in the power elite, until it finally led to the current highly centralized and long-lasting dictatorship resting on a combination of brutally coercing the masses, pampering its hundreds of thousands of armed clients, and in general distributing the economic benefits that have come with the post-1973 oil boom (the Iraq Petroleum Company was nationalized in 1972).

Iraq's economy is now 90 percent based on oil exports; the petroleum bonanza has benefited mainly Iraq's traditional Sunni urban ruling class. It enabled the creation of a large services sector as well as a huge army of close to one million soldiers. Rapid industrialization led to massive importation of foreign laborers, particularly from Egypt. Saddam Hussein's regime has needed external successes for domestic purposes, and Iraq was well endowed to fulfill his ambitions to become leader of the Arab world. Favorably located, with a large population, a rich agricultural base supplemented by enormous oil wealth, Iraq's geopolitical position is at once superb and vulnerable. In fact Mesopotamia has historically been one of the Middle East's perennial power bases. Yet Saddam Hussein's adventurist foreign policies have squandered the country's resources and led the Iraqis from debacle to debacle. In the war against fundamentalist Iran, started in 1980, Iraq lost hundreds of thousands of soldiers, had its industrial infrastructure ruined, and incurred a stag-

gering war debt of $80 billion before agreeing to an inconclusive ceasefire in 1988. Within Iraq, the war served only to increase Shi'ite-Sunni antagonism.

The invasion and annexation in 1990 of Kuwait, Iraq's rich neighbor, although initially doubtless a popular move, led to the second Gulf War and unequivocal defeat for Iraq. The international embargo and bombings have caused widespread hunger and destruction. Still, Saddam Hussein was allowed to suppress ensuing Kurdish and Shi'ite rebellions, and has maintained his (somewhat shaken) hold on power.

IRAQW (Mbulu, Wambuly) A people, numbering 198,000 (1967), concentrated in the district of Mbulu in the Aushausha region of north-central Tanzania. Their language is considered to belong to the Rift cluster of the Cushitic group of the Afro-Asiatic family.

The indigenous social structure of the Iraqw is based on tribal democracy. The main political institution is a public meeting attended by all adult male heads of households. During the colonial period, a system of appointed chiefs was imposed. The household is the unit of production and consumption. Both men and women participate in agricultural work. Most families grow a wide range of staples. Crops include maize, sweet potatoes, beans, pumpkins, wheat, sorghum, millet, and other vegetables. The raising of cattle is another important branch of the traditional agriculture of the Iraqw. The use of natural resources is mainly based on regular land redistribution between the households.

The religious concepts of the Iraqw are connected with the spiritualization of natural features such as the sky, as well as on some abstract ideas and ritual worship of their land.

IRAYA An ethnic group, numbering c.10,000, living in the northern mountainous interior of the island of Mindoro, in the Philippines. They speak the Mangyan language, which belongs to the Malayo-Polynesian family of languages. (see also PAGAN GADDANG)

IREBU An ethnic group related to the MBOCHI, living in Congo.

IRISH (s.d. Gwyddel) The Irish living in Eire number 3.7 million; 600,000 Catholics in Northern Ireland are also ethnically Irish. Another 700,000 live in Britain. Four million people of Irish descent live in the United States.

Ninety-five percent of Eire is Catholic; a residual and dwindling Protestant minority lives mainly in districts adjacent to Northern Ireland (the old Ulster province). Gaelic, the Celtic language, has survived as a spoken language in poor outlying regions: 500,000 still speak it, mainly in the counties of Galway, Donegal, Kerry, and Connemara, and the isolated Aran islands. Elsewhere, English has become the dominant tongue. Gaelic is taught in schools and is considered a touchstone of national sentiment. Whole stretches of Ireland are depopulated and devoid of towns as a result of famine and war. Since the 1970s the population has slowly grown.

Gaels, the Iron Age Celtic forebears of the Irish, may have entered the island in the sixth century B.C.E. from Spain or southern France. After subduing the indigenous Picts, they built a hierarchical culture, religiously unified but divided by internal strife. In the fourth century C.E., the Celts adopted Christianity; the amalgamation of the Picts and the Celts gave rise to the Irish. The sixth to eighth centuries were the Golden Age of Irish civilization, which produced a very original and imaginative literature, architecture, manuscripts, and sculpture. The Irish were at the time much more advanced than continental Europeans. They sent their monks to rechristianize the European continent.

Viking invasions in the ninth century broke Irish power. Scandinavians settled Dublin and established towns and commerce, until driven out by the Irish monarchy. After conquest by the ENGLISH in 1171, Anglo-Norman landlords introduced feudalism, and from their castles and fortified towns reduced the Irish to serfdom. After a while, English nobles were assimilated and Irish culture revived. In the sixteenth century, however, the Tudors completed the English conquest of Ireland. A cruel campaign under Elizabeth I finally subdued the Irish.

The Reformation duplicated the ethnic English-Celtic contradiction with a Protestant-Catholic one. Most Irish remained Catholic, but English and Scottish colonization in the seventeenth century eventually turned Ulster into a predominantly British-Protestant region.

A Catholic Irish revolt in 1641 triggered the English civil war. The Irish were pacified by Oliver Cromwell and the original Catholic population dispossessed. Land grants were offered to any Englishman prepared to keep the rebels in check, while entrepreneurs drove out indigenous farmers and replaced them with colonists. Most of the Irish were reduced to poverty and survived as landless laborers for the ENGLISH. Ireland became a British colony, sending wool to England, prohibited from weaving themselves, victims of programmed underdevelopment. That policy was also harmful to the Anglo-Irish Protestant establishment, which aspired to greater autonomy, and in the late eighteenth century obtained legislative independence. In 1800 Ireland was annexed to Britain, a step which resulted in the formation of revolutionary Irish movements throughout the nineteenth century.

The failed potato harvests in 1845 to 1847 led to catastrophe: famine killed 1.5 million Irish, and millions more escaped to Britain and the United States, starting a process of depopulation. Since 1850 over 3 million Irish have left Ireland.

Misery stimulated nationalism, federalist agitation and rural guerilla warfare by secret societies. British land liberalization and tenant security against eviction only provoked secessionist tendencies among Protestant ultras. Presbyterians and Tories conspired to torpedo Irish autonomy, but land reforms undertaken to preempt the independence movement ended the supremacy of the landed aristocracy.

However, nationalist agitation was not to be contained. The early twentieth century was the era of Gaelic cultural renaissance. The Sinn Fein, established in 1905, boycotted colonial institutions. By World War I, England conceded Home Rule (although Protestants obtained promise of separate treatment for Ulster); but it was too late: in 1916, the Bloody Easter revolt broke out in Dublin, followed by a full scale war of independence. Britain recognized the Irish Free State as an autonomous dominion within the British Empire, but imposed partition and negotiated a separate status for Northern Ireland.

After a period of reconstruction in the 1920s, an economic crisis brought radical Eamon de Valera to power. In 1949 Eire (Southern Ireland) became a completely independent republic. The Irish remained, however, an overwhelmingly agricultural and poverty-stricken society of large families. From the 1950s a new, less ideologically-marked, generation came to power. Economic debates have since primed national ones. In the 1960s industrialization was successfully undertaken, as well as cautious rapprochement with Northern Ireland, although (at least officially) Eire maintains its claim over the whole of the island. Until entering the European Community in 1972, which put an end to isolationism, the southern Irish remained poorer than their northern brethren. The spillover effect of the civil war in Northern Ireland and global recession maintain them in a state of structural underdevelopment. The Irish live in a state where the Catholic church continues to wield old-style power over the private life of the citizen.

IRON see OSSET.

IROQUOIS CONFEDERACY (Six Nations) A Native North American group, numbering about 40,000, in Ontario and Quebec, Canada, and about 18,000 in New York, Wisconsin, and Oklahoma, U.S.A.

This group of nations (the MOHAWK, ONEIDA, ONONDAGA, CAYUGA, SENECA, and TUSCARORA) was the strongest in the eastern United States, having conquered the ERIE and the HURONS. They were the staunchest allies of the BRITISH in the wars first with the FRENCH and then with the rebel American colonies, and later with the United States. On account of their strong support of the British cause, many Iroquois moved to Canada.

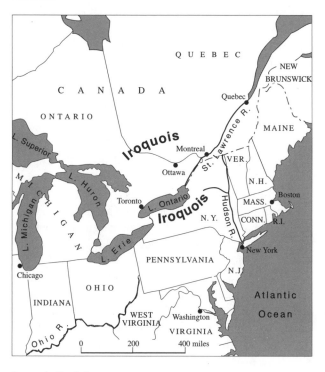

Iroquois Confederacy

The Six Nations Reserve near Brantford, Ontario, is the largest Indian reserve in Canada. Features of the Iroquois government influenced the founders of the American republic.

IRU see NKOLE, TORO, NYORO, UGANDANS.

IRULAR A group, numbering 125,000 (1981), living in the states of Kerala (where they are the second largest tribe), Karnataka, Mysore, and Tamil Nadu, India. They speak Tamil, a language belonging to the Dravidian family.

The Irular are Hindus. Their name is derived from the darkness of their complexion. Formerly a nomadic matrilineal group, they are now settling and changing over to the patrilineal pattern.

A number of the Irular are shifting cultivators, others food-gatherers, and some own government lands. They collect bamboo, firewood, and forest produce for sale in markets. They do not use leather.

ISALA An ethnic group living in Ghana.

ISAM (Pagu) An ethnic group closely related to the TOBELORESE, living on the Indonesian island of Halmahera.

ISHAAQ A clan of the SOMALI.

ISHAQZAI A subgroup of the PASHTUN.

ISHIELU A subgroup of the IBO.

ISHKASHIMI (s.d. Shkoshmi) An ethnic group inhabiting a small area in north Afghanistani Badakhshan and two villages (one only partially) in the Mountain Badakhshan Autonomous *Oblast* of Tajikistan. Their estimated number is 2,000, three-quarters of whom live in Afghanistani Badakhshan.

The Ishkashimi language belongs to the Pamiri division of the South-Eastern subgroup of Iranian languages. It has two dialects, Ishkashimi proper in the Mountain Badakhshan Autonomous *Oblast* and Sanglichi in Afghanistani Badakshan. Some scholars regard the latter as a distinct language, and its speakers are sometimes regarded as a separate ethnic group or as the SANGLICHI ethnic subgroup of the Ishkashimi ethnic group. The language is unwritten, with Tajik used as the literary language in Mountain Badakhshan and Dari in Afghanistani Badakhshan.

The Ishkashimi of Afghanistani Badakshshan (the SANGLICHI) belong to the Isma'ili sect of Islam, as, to the best of present knowledge, do the Ishkashimi of Mountain Badakhshan. Some sources, claiming that the majority of the latter are Sunni Muslims of the Hanafi school, are unsubstantiated. The date of their islamization is unknown, but cannot be earlier than the eleventh century.

The Ishkashimi live in small villages of between ten and fifty extended families, each family forming in its aggregate a clan-like unit known as the *kunda*. Villages are built mainly in the valley or on the slopes and at the feet of mountains. Dress, in Mountain Badakhshan, is now semi-European, but is still traditional in

Afghanistani Badakhshan. Their diet is predominantly vegetarian, including dairy products, with meat being reserved for festive occasions.

Their traditional occupation is grain and legume farming on small terraced plots, with some sheep-, goat-, and cattle-raising. (see also AFGHANS)

ISNEG see APAYAO, MANDAYA.

ISRAELIS The bulk (82 percent) of the population of Israel are JEWS. The rest are mainly ARABS, forming a part of the PALESTINIANS. Israeli Jews constitute not only the largest component of the population, they also are predominant in the political and economic structure of the country, running its government, forming its military power, and steering its economy. The JEWS live mainly in the urbanized central coastal plain, while most of the ARABS reside on the northern periphery (the Galilee), along the Samarian foothills and in the Negev. Many of the ARABS in Israel still live in villages and small towns while the majority of JEWS are highly urbanized, largely concentrated in the three metropolitan regions of Tel Aviv, Jerusalem, and Haifa.

While Palestine was never without a Jewish population, its numbers were small until the nineteenth century, but began to increase initially as a result of religious-oriented immigration from eastern Europe and the Muslim lands. The immigrants were for the most part Orthodox Jews and most lived in the four "holy cities," Jerusalem, Hebron, Tiberias, and Safed. Those who arrived from the 1880s onwards were mostly from eastern Europe, and created the basic modern institutions of the Jewish population.

The Israeli JEWS belong to three major communities: Ashkenazim, of Central and East European origin; Sefardim, of Iberian descent (*Sefarad,* or Spain); and Mizrahiyim, or eastern JEWS, who originate from Muslim lands or Asia. The last two are often grouped together in common usage as Sefardim. Ashkenazim and Sefardim diverge in ritual and liturgical details, usually minor, but there is no doctrinal difference. Israeli JEWS speak a modernized form of Hebrew, the ancient Semitic language in which the Old Testament is written, which was revived as a spoken language in its Sefardi pronunciation in Israel. Since Israel throughout this century has been a land of immigration, many other languages are still in use among Israeli JEWS, including Russian, Ladino (Judeo-Spanish), Yiddish (Judeo-German), Arabic, French, English, German, Spanish, and Romanian.

The ARABS of Israel comprise about a sixth of the population. They are mainly Muslims, with a minority of various Christian denominations. A tiny percentage of the Israeli population are DRUZE, a religious group allied to the DRUZE in neighboring Syria and Lebanon, who to a large extent form an ethnic group of their own. All these three religious communities use Arabic as their main language.

The country was under Ottoman rule until World War I, after which the League of Nations awarded a mandate to Great Britain, which had promised to create a Jewish National Home without prejudicing the rights of the Arab inhabitants. The Jewish enterprise developed against a background of growing local Arab hostility and resistance, especially as Jewish nationalism evoked the emergence of a Palestinian Arab nationalism.

Palestine already had a large Arab population when modern Jewish nationalism, or Zionism, began and the ARABS have continued to regard the establishment of the Jewish state as an invasion of their patrimony and as an alien intrusion in the Arab Middle East. Arab anti-Jewish outbreaks, first occurring in 1920, grew in momentum in the 1920s and 1930s. When the United Nations decided on partition, the ARABS of the country rose in armed opposition and after the state was proclaimed were joined by the armies of six Arab states. In the ensuing battle (the War of Independence), Israel's army emerged victorious. Palestine was divided into Israel, areas annexed by the kingdom of Jordan, and the Gaza Strip, ruled by Egypt. As a result of the 1967 Six Day War, in which Israel decisively defeated an alliance of Egypt, Syria, and Jordan, the whole of historic Palestine fell into Jewish hands. The future of the areas taken over, with their large Arab population and burgeoning Palestinian nationalism, became a crucial issue. The problem polarized Israeli society between those who were determined that these areas would remain under Israeli control and those who were prepared to grant the Palestinians autonomy or even statehood.

While the war of 1973 (the Yom Kippur War) paved the way for a peace agreement with Egypt in 1978, the Palestinian question was exacerbated and put into even sharper focus by the outbreak in 1988 of an intensified Arab campaign of civil uprising (the *intifada*). Following the 1991 Gulf War, U.S. pressure brought Israel, its Arab neighbors, and PALESTINIANS into talks on the possibility of a peace settlement.

The Jewish settlement developed an Ashkenazi-dominated ethos. After the establishment of the State this was gradually challenged by newcomers from

above left: An Israeli woman
bottom left: An elderly Israeli man from Yemen

above right: An Israeli yeshiva student
bottom right: A kibbutznik in Israel

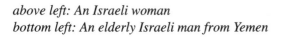

269

Muslim lands, who at first had a difficult time finding their niche but nonetheless moved up the socio-economic ladder and, with the immigration from North Africa in the 1950s, became numerically a majority. More recently the influx of immigrants from the former Soviet bloc has resulted in an approximate numerical parity between the immigrants of European origin and those coming from Muslim lands.

The relationship between religion and state is among the most controversial issues in Israeli politics. Religious Jews have established a number of political parties which, although representing only a sixth of the voters, have occupied key positions in almost all governments as they held the balance between the right and the left blocs of parties. They have obtained many concessions, some of which effect the way of life of even the secular Jewish community (such as the exclusive application of religious law in matters of personal status, including marriage and divorce).

Israel is today a predominantly urban society, with only 5 percent employed in agriculture. Two-thirds of the population is concentrated in the lowlands. To sustain their military strength, the absorption of immigrants, and high standard of living, Israelis remain heavily dependent on foreign subsidies from Jewish communities and other sources, particulary U.S. foreign aid.

ISSA   A people living in Djibouti, where they represent the largest ethnic group, at an estimated 200,000. They are considered to be closely related to the SOMALI both by language and by religion. They speak the Somali language and are Sunni Muslims of the Shafi'i school.

Traditionally, the Issa were a nomadic people wandering with their cattle in the Somali plains and desert. They see themselves as part of "Greater Somalia," a feeling which, supported for years by the Somali people, served as the base for a long and bloody dispute with the AFAR of Djibouti.

Under French colonial rule, the Issa constantly demanded independence or voiced their aspiration to reunite with their Somalian brothers in Somalia. Although the FRENCH gave their opponents, the AFAR, central political positions, the Issa preserved their dominance in Djibouti. Since independence in 1979 the Issa have taken hold of most key positions in both the political and the economic spheres. (see also AFAR, DJIBOUTIANS, SOMALI)

ISU-OCHI   A subgroup of the IBO.

ITALIANS   (s.d. Italiani) The 57 million, overwhelmingly Catholic, inhabitants of Italy speak a language directly descended from Latin, and largely influenced by the Tuscan vernacular popularized from the thirteenth century. In spite of the early creation of a national language, most Italians until recently continued to express themselves in their regional dialects.

Numerous invasions have created a very mixed and regionally diversified Italian population. North Italians, who are the most strongly modernized, are largely of Celtic origin. In Val d'Aosta lives a mixed Italian-French population. Venetians have maintained maritime folklore and glass-blowing crafts. The origin of the Etruscans, probable ancestors of the Tuscans, who ruled most of the Italian peninsula until the sixth century B.C.E., is unknown. The Tuscans are famous for their artistic traditions. Here like elsewhere in Italy, numerous historical and religious festivals are kept, such as the competition between Sienese neighborhoods in the yearly Palio. Umbrian popular culture is less exuberant and more religious. South Italians are Mediterraneans affected by successive Greek, Gothic, and Norman dominations, and are on average much poorer than northerners. By and large the south is ethnically more homogeneous than the north, but there are marked contrasts in popular culture, which is most "theatrical" in Naples. Banditry remains ingrained in isolated villages of the Calabrian Sila. SICILIANS are quite distinct from southern Italians proper, and are treated separately.

Italy formed the core of the Roman Empire which united the Mediterranean world two thousand years ago: this was the Italians' first collective experience. Overstretched and weakened Rome could not resist barbaric invasions in the first centuries C.E. Italy was divided among a number of successor monarchies of Germanic origin (viz. the Longobards in the sixth century). South and east Italy remained for some time outposts of the Byzantine Empire, but eventually were also swept away.

In the Middle Ages, Italian ports and artisan and merchant cities were among Europe's most advanced, and made Italy Europe's most prosperous (and coveted) region. From the eleventh century, the merchant republics of Venice and Genoa vied with each other to establish their dominion over the eastern Mediterranean. Florence, Siena, Milan, and a host of other towns, thrived on manufacture and banking, while Rome exploited its status as a sacred city for temporal gain. The very advance of the North Italians enabled them to defeat the German emperor's attempts at centralizing power. Since then, the North Italians have re-

above: Two Italian women
below: Italian school children

mained the richest and most urbanized part of the Italian population. Pisa, Amalfi, Genoa, Venice, and later Siena, Florence, and Milan were ruled by bourgeois bankers and entrepreneurs under whose patronage artists and intellectuals developed a wholly new culture: that of the Renaissance, which celebrated individualism and the heritage of the classical period.

However, the particularistic city-states also laid the base for the political fragmentation of the Italians that was to endure until the nineteenth century. After they had succeeded in defeating the ambitions of the German Hohenstaufen emperor to create a unitary state, in the sixteenth century Italy's competing and warring merchant republics succumbed to the more tightly disciplined armies of French and Spanish invaders, attracted by the prospect of rich booty. Ottoman expansion cut off traditional trade routes; the age of discoveries shifted commerce away from the Mediterranean to the Atlantic, sealing Italy's decline.

Thereafter, Italian unity and self-determination was only finally achieved in the 1860s, under the kingdom of Sardinia, by a combination of astute diplomacy and popular action, particularly Giuseppe Garibaldi's Expedition of the Thousand, which defeated the French Bourbon and papal forces. Plebiscites ratified the unification and established a monarchy.

However, after half a century of political crises capped by the miseries caused by World War I, the chasm between rich and poor in Italy very nearly brought about a socialist revolution. Upon its failure, Benito Mussolini installed a Fascist dictatorship. Restoring order and providing a modicum of economic progress bought the regime broad support, but the political capital was spent on grandiose foreign adventures which dragged the Italians into World War II on the German side. After the war, a none-too-stable democratic republic replaced Fascism.

Since 1945, fast economic and social modernization — frequently punctuated by fierce class struggles — has transformed Italian society. In spite of superficial westernizing fashions, family bonds remain very strong. Italians are a very urbanized people; even their villages often take an urban character. Contrast between regions remains the central fact of Italian life. Since World War II, the north has become heavily industrialized, while the south has remained relatively isolated, underdeveloped, and poor.

Population growth has led to massive emigration. Between 1860 and World War I, over two million migrated to the Americas and North Africa. After World War II four million moved to Switzerland, France (600,000), Germany (450,000), Belgium (200,000), and other, mainly European, destinations.

Domestic migration waves have been even more massive — population moves from countryside to city, from mountain to coast, from island to continent and from south to north. With the influx of millions of southerners, the industrial and prosperous north not only imported a pool of cheap labor, but also a host of social problems. Current regionalist anti-southerner movements such as the Lombard League may represent the Italian version of the anti-foreigner Right in Germany, France, and Britain — although today Italy itself has become an immigration country for 500,000 North Africans and Ethiopians. (see also AMHARA, ETHIOPIANS, SARDINIANS, SICILIANS, SOUTH JABARTI, TYROLEANS)

ITELMEN   The 2,500 or so Itelmen live in the Kamchatka peninsula in the Koryak Autonomous Province of the Russian Federation. Originally widespread throughout Kamtchatka, the Kurile islands, and Cape Lopatka, their numbers have been greatly reduced since the eighteenth century through both epidemics and russification.

The Itelman language is close to Chukchi and Koryak. It has no alphabet and Russian is used as the literary language.

Originally fishermen, hunters, and gatherers, the Itelmen live now mostly in mixed villages with RUSSIANS. Their religion has remained shamanist-traditional, like that of the CHUKCHI and KORYAK.

ITESO   An ethnic group, numbering an estimated 100,000, living in the Busia district of western Kenya. Their language belongs to the Karamajong-Teso-Ithunga branch of the Eastern Nilotic family.

Most of the Kenyan Iteso migrated during the nineteenth century from Uganda to Kenya in search of new lands suited to agriculture. Their economic base is agriculture, although some practice animal husbandry. Some have adopted Christianity, but the majority still retain their traditional African religion. The basic socio-political unit among the Iteso was and still is the clan, which in the past was a unifying factor in an otherwise segmented society.

ITNEG   see TINGGIAN.

ITSEKIRI   A Yoruba-speaking ethnic group living in Nigeria, on the western side of the Niger Delta in the Bendel State. Their area is currently a center of Nigeria's petroleum industry.

ITSHA   A subgroup of the EGBA. (see also YORUBA)

ITTU   A division of the eastern OROMO.

IULLEMEDEN   (Aullemende) A subgroup of the TUAREG.

IVOIREANS   Estimated to number nearly 10 million, the people of the Côte d'Ivoire are composed of over sixty ethnic groups. The AKAN, subdivided into the BAULE and the AGNI, the KRU, who are subdivided into several groups, and the small ethnic groups of the lagoon area, live in the southern part of the country. The MANDE (MALINKE, BAMBARA, and DIULA) and the SENUFO live in the north. The DAN, GURO, and GAGON live in the southwest, while the LOBI, subdivided into a number of groups, live in the northeast. The BAULE are the largest ethnic group in the Côte d'Ivoire, but constitute only 20 percent of the population.

Sixty-five percent of Ivoireans practice traditional religions, 23 percent are Muslims, and 12 percent are Christians. Most of the Muslims live in the north and are MALINKE. The official language of the Côte d'Ivoire is French. The most widely spoken local language is Akan.

The Côte d'Ivoire gained independence from the FRENCH in August 1960. During the decolonization period, which started after the end of World War II, the BAULE were the most active ethnic group in politics. A Baule chief named Félix Houphouet-Boigny founded in 1946 the PDCI (Parti Democratique de la Côte d'Ivoire). It was affiliated to the inter-territorial party of French West Africa, headed also by Houphouet-Boigny, the RDA (Rassamblement Democratique Africaine). Although he himself was a member of the BAULE, Houphouet-Boigny soon turned the PDCI into a party which represented all the ethnic groups in the country.

During the 1950s the PDCI became the only force in the Côte d'Ivoire, and Houphouet-Boigny was the uncontested leader. His speeches emphasized the ethnic diversity of the country and the importance of unity.

After independence, which was gained peacefully, Houphouet-Boigny became president, with the PDCI as the only party. No serious ethnic problems have emerged during his rule. However, the BAULE play a dominant part in politics.

Since the beginning of the 1990s there has been popular pressure for democratization. The government has only partly responded, and full democratization has not yet occurred.

IXIL   A subgroup of the MAYA.

IZHMI   (Izva Tas) A subgroup of the KOMI. They are often considered a distinct group because of their strong admixture of NENTSY.

IZHOR   (s.d. Karjalainen) The descendants of a group of Carelians who settled on the Izhora river in Russia in the eleventh and twelfth centuries. They number fewer than 1,000. Living among RUSSIANS and for centuries under Russian rule, they have been assimilated by the latter, which accounts for their decreasing numbers (21,700 in 1897; 16,100 in 1926).

The Izhor language belongs to the Finno-Ugric group of the Uralic language family. At the beginning of Soviet rule an attempt was made to transform it into a literary language, but it was soon abandoned and Russian serves as the Izhor literary language.

Living among RUSSIANS, the Izhors were assimilated into their culture, customs, and also into the Russian Orthodox Church.

J

JA'ALIYIN   An Arab group living in northern Sudan. (see also SUDANESE)

JABA   A subgroup of the FULANI.

JABARTI   An ethnic group, numbering several hundred thousand, who live among the AMHARA in the northern and central Ethiopian highlands. They are Amharic-speaking Sunni Muslims whose islamization may date from the early days of the Muslim sultanates in eastern Shoa (Ifat), between the ninth and thirteenth centuries. They were generally excluded from landownership and became traders.

In the Islamic-Arabic world, the term "Jabarti" was sometimes used for all Muslims originating from the Horn of Africa.

JABBARA   A subgroup of the KHAMSE.

JABELAWI   (Watawit, Dongolawi, Arab al-Aswad [Black Arabs]) The c.50,000 arabized population among the BERTA of Western Ethiopia along the border with Sudan. Originally the Jabelawi were a Nilotic peasant population (sometimes called *hamej*, Arabic for "rabble, savage") related to the eastern Sudanese empire of Funj. After the Egyptian invasion of the Sudan (1840), refugee ARABS from the northern Sudan (Dongolawi) established themselves through intermarriage as a new ruling stratum, and as slave-traders.

When the area was integrated into the Ethiopian empire during the last decade of the nineteenth century, this arabized stratum assumed administrative functions in the new state.

JADID   One of several tribes grouped together as NURESTANIS.

JADRAN   A subgroup of the PASHTUN.

JAGOI   An ethnic group living on the Indonesian island of Kalimantan (Borneo). (see also DAYAK)

JAHAI   A subgroup of the SEMANG.

JAH HUT   A subgroup of the SENOI.

JAJI   A subgroup of the PASHTUN.

JAKI   A subgroup of the KUHGILU.

JAKUN   (Aboriginal Malay) An assortment of small, forest-dwelling groups living in the southern extremity

Jakun

of the Malay Peninsula. They number about 15,000, divided into several subgroups, including the Jakun proper, BEDUANDA, BELANDA, BEREMBUN, KENABOI, MANTRA, SEMALAI, TEMUAN, TEMOQ, and UDAI.

The Jakun engage in some form of agriculture, indicating their abandonment of a nomadic lifestyle. They are dependent on the MALAYS, with whom they trade, and have come to be exploited by them. At the same time, they are losing their distinct identity and are being rapidly absorbed by the Malay majority. Their language is an archaic version of Malay.

JALAIR   A tribe of the UZBEKS.

JALALI   (Wotapuri) An ethnic group living dispersed in the northern part of Afghanistan. No data about their number are available, although a rough estimate puts them at about 2,000.

Their language, Inku, belongs to the Indian group of the Indo-European family of languages. Although it is also the mother tongue of several other dispersed ethnic groups of Afghanistan (cf. PIKRAJ, SHADIBAZ, and VANGAVALANS), the Jalali possess a distinct ethnic self-identity. Inku is unwritten. Practically all adult Jalali are equibilinguals, speaking Dari (the Persian spoken in Afganistan) as well as their mother tongue.

The Jalali are peripatetics, i.e., non-pastoral nomads. The men are mainly occupied in circus-style bazaar and street performances with monkeys and bears, and as street musicians. The main occupation for women is begging, and sometimes peddling, especially fruit. (see also AFGHANS, JATS II, VANGAVALANS)

JALATEC   A subgroup of the MAYA.

JALUO   see LUO.

JAMAICANS   Nearly 2.5 million Jamaicans occupy the Caribbean island of Jamaica. They have created a cultural as well as commercial crossroads: within the mixed population, largely composed of mulatto and black descendants of African slaves, are also minority communities of BRITISH, Continental Europeans, CHINESE, East INDIANS, and Middle Eastern ARABS. While English is the official language, and Spanish and French widely understood, what is most generally spoken is a creolized English, with African components. The world-wide popularity of Jamaican reggae music has made the unique Jamaican accent familiar elsewhere on the globe and has also focused attention on other Jamaican art forms, including its African-based folk music.

While Anglicanism was once the established religion, many Protestants belong to Baptist, Pentecostal, and other denominations. Spiritualist religious movements, based in Christianity and strongly embellished with belief in possession by spirits, are numerous: these include the Pocomanian and Cumina sects and the now well-known Rastafarians. There are also substantial Hindu, Jewish, and Muslim communities among Jamaica's diverse peoples.

Jamaica's relatively young population, with almost 40 percent under 15 years of age, is densest in the coastal lowlands and is nearly half urban, the result of considerable rural-to-urban migration in the 1960s and 1970s: urban unemployment and government-sponsored emigration programs have created substantial Jamaican expatriate communities in the United States, Canada, and the United Kingdom. A few Jamaicans are still engaged in subsistence farming, partly due to government agrarian reform programs, but of the vast majority of the remainder, those who are employed work in tourism (the main source of foreign exchange), mining, and the manufacture of molasses and its principal product, rum. The agricultural sector of the economy is small and labor-intensive.

Jamaica, whose historically indigenous (later exterminated) Arawak people were encountered by Columbus in 1494, was disappointing to the SPANIARDS because it lacked gold, and was therefore largely neglected, falling to the BRITISH in 1655. It became a base for British pirates preying on Spanish shipping, and of the slave trade.

The latter, introduced by the Spanish, enabled the development of one of the most flourishing sugar plantation economies in the Caribbean, but also imported enough Africans to organize a continuing guerrilla movement to harrass the BRITISH during the seventeenth and eighteenth centuries. The plantation economy collapsed with the abolition of slavery in the 1830s and in 1866 Jamaica was designated a crown colony. Initiating moves toward self-determination in the 1930s, Jamaica became internally autonomous in 1959 and an independent Commonwealth member in 1962. (see also HONDURANS)

JAMSHIDI   see AIMAQ.

JANJERO   (Yem) An ethnic group, numbering 120,000 (1980s), who live between the Omo and the Little Gibbi Rivers in northwestern Kefa Province, Ethiopia. They adhere to traditional beliefs, Ethiopian Orthodox Christianity, and Sunni Islam.

The history of the small kingdom of Janjero dates back to the Middle Ages. The kingdom was incorporated into the Ethiopian Empire in 1894. The Janjero are mainly agriculturalists, growing barley, sorghum, coffee, cotton, and ensete. Their society was highly stratified, with a royal clan, nine privileged clans, and lower classes of artisans and hunters. Their self-definition relates to clans which claim descent from YEMENIS.

JAPANESE

JAPANESE Racially, culturally, and ethnically, the Japanese (inhabitants of the Japanese archipelago, situated off the eastern edge of the Asian continent) are one of the most homogeneous peoples in the world. Of Mongoloid origin, the estimated 124 million Japanese account for about 97 percent of Japan's total population. Large Japanese communities also exist in the United States (especially Hawaii), Brazil, Canada, Peru, and Argentina. Within Japan, there are substantial Korean, Chinese, and Indochinese immigrant communities. The one remaining distinct indigenous ethnic group in Japan is the AINU, a people living on the northern island of Hokkaido, who have Nordic-like features including abundant facial and body hair. They currently number no more than 20,000.

The Japanese are known to have originated from a mixture of peoples who came to the Japanese islands at various times and from various places on the Asian continent and formed a group of tribes in the mid-first millennium B.C.E. Some time after 250 B.C.E., an influx of rice-growing people created the Yayoi culture which first flourished in western Japan before penetrating to the northeast. The Yayoi dominated the islands for five centuries; the first state, Yamato, founded in the fourth century, represented the Japanese transition from ancient tribes into a nationality.

Throughout their early history (third-tenth centuries), the Japanese developed a culture strongly influenced by the CHINESE and the KOREANS. Their first contact with Europeans (the PORTUGUESE and the DUTCH in particular) occurred during the sixteenth century, but was followed by 200 years of isolationism during the Tokugawa period. Contacts with the West were renewed following the arrival of Commodore Matthew C. Perry from the United States in 1853, and friendship treaties with the United States, Russia, Britain, and the Netherlands soon followed. Strong internal resistance to opening Japan to foreign contacts was finally overcome after the ascension of Emperor Meiji in 1868; the Meiji Restoration, as it is known, signaled the end of Japanese feudalism and isolationism and marked the entry of Japan into the modern era.

Japan's victories in the Sino-Japanese (1894–1895) and Russo-Japanese (1904–1905) Wars marked its emergence as a regional superpower; it was one of the Big Five powers at the post-World War I Versailles peace conference. Meanwhile, it rapidly transformed from an agricultural to an industrial nation. Japan's participation in World War II was ended by the destruction of Hiroshima and Nagasaki by U.S. atomic bombs in 1945; this ushered in the Atomic Era, precipitated the unconditional surrender of the Japanese to the Allied powers, and led to the institution of a parliamentary system of government based on the sovereignty of the people. The new constitution promulgated in 1946 also prohibited any political role for the emperor other than as titular head of state.

Japan's remarkable economic expansion in the postwar period (initially triggered by massive U.S. aid and the economic boom consequent upon Japan's role as a major supplier during the Korean War) has made it second only to the United States among non-Communist nations in total value of GNP. Japanese export penetration into foreign markets, coupled with Japanese consumer loyalty to home-produced goods, has enabled the country to continue to register substantial trade surpluses.

Japanese, the official language of Japan, is now accepted to be one of the branches of the Ural-Altaic family, the major language stock of Asia. Spoken Japanese bears some resemblance to Korean, and the writing system is derived from Chinese. Since earliest times, the Japanese have used characters borrowed from China in their written form, but later added phonetic signs and simplified some characters.

Most Japanese adhere to Buddhism, which was introduced through China in the sixth century. In addition, Shinto, the ancient Japanese and former state religion, is adhered to by most Japanese Buddhists, and Confucianism, also introduced through China, is influential. Christianity was introduced into Japan by the Jesuit saint, Francis Xavier, in 1549 and now claims some 1.7 million Japanese adherents.

An outstanding characteristic of the Japanese is their tendency to identify themselves through their affiliation to a group — be it the family, village, company, or nation — rather than in their capacity as individuals. As a result of successful industrialization since the nineteenth century, Japan has come to resemble a Western society. However, the Japanese still maintain much of their unique culture: the emperor is widely revered, the vast majority of homes contain a shrine to family ancestors, and a large number of traditional forms (such as particular modes of dress on ceremonial occasions, the tea ceremony, highly refined flower arrangements, calligraphy, and sumo wrestling) continue to prevail.

Japanese are among the world's most urbanized people, with some 77 percent of the population living in conurbations located in the archipelago's limited flat areas. Four out of five Japanese live on the Honshu island group. Life expectancy, per capita income, and birth- and death-rates conform to the highest Western standards rather than those prevalent in Asia as a whole.

Despite extensive industrialization, which has imposed severe pressures on the environment, agriculture is still vital to the Japanese. Most of Japan's needs for rice, vegetables, fruits, and eggs are provided by Japanese farmers. Fishing is another traditional occupation, and Japan is currently one of the world's foremost fishing nations.

JARAI (Anu Chu) One of the most important of the hill peoples of south-central Vietnam, numbering about 150,000. The term "Anu Chu" recently adopted as a self-designation by these hill peoples to define themselves as a single ethnic unit is a Jarai expression meaning "Sons of the Mountains."

Traditionally the Jarai are slash and burn cultivators of rice who lived in the vicinity of Pleiku. They attached prominence to several Jarai sorcerers, and a legend about the most powerful of these, the king of fire, has been used by some nationalist KHMER and MONTAGNARD to justify the unification of the hill peoples with Cambodia.

Jarai were influential in the Python God religious movement of the 1930s and the Python God himself was said to have been born of the union of a Jarai woman with a python. They were also active in FULRO, the United Front for the Protection of Oppressed Races, which sought to attain autonomy for the hill peoples of South Vietnam. Many Jarai supported the Viet Cong in the hope of achieving autonomy, but forced labor and the expropriation of food and property led the Jarai to believe that they were caught between two powers with little interest in their wellbeing.

The A-RAP, CHU TY, COR, HBAU, HDRUNG, HE DRONG, MDHUR, PLEI KLY, SESAN, and TOBUAN are Jarai subgroups distinguished by either cultural or geographical differences.

JARAWA I An ethnic group living in Nigeria.

JARAWA II A tiny ethnic group living in the western part of the Andaman Islands. They are hostile to modern civilization, and only a very small group began to respond to friendly overtures in 1974. Their main occupations include food collecting, hunting, and fishing.

JARE A subgroup of the TIV.

JARSO A subgroup of the OROMO. (see also SOMALI)

JATAPU An ethnic group, numbering 105,000 (1981), living in Andhra Pradesh and Orissa, in India. Their dialect belongs to the Dravidian family of languages.

The Jatapu are predominantly agriculturalists and work as forest and agricultural laborers, and collect and sell minor forest produce.

JATS I (Jats of the Indian subcontinent; also Jatt, Zutt) A people, numbering some 30 million, living in India and Pakistan, mainly in the regions of Uttar Pradesh, Rajasthan, Punjab, and Sind. Their language belongs to the Indian branch of the Indo-European family of languages.

In Pakistan the Jats are Sunni Muslims of the Hanafi school, in the central part of Punjab they are Sikhs, and in other parts of India they are either Sunni Muslims of the Hanafi school or Hindus. The written language of the Muslim Jats is Urdu, that of the Hindu Jats, Hindi, and that of the Sikh Jats, Punjabi. They are sedentary agriculturalists.

Among Muslim Jats, clan subdivisions still exist; among the Hindu Jats, fraternal polyandry existed until the mid-twentieth century and levirate marriage is still practiced. Killing of female newborns was usual until the end of the nineteenth century.

The founder of the shortlived eighteenth century Sikh independent state in Punjab, Ranjit Singh, was of Jat origin.

The islamization of the Jats of the Indian subcontinent was a steady process which was finalized only in the late seventeenth century.

JATS II The Jats of Afghanistan, where the name serves as a general appellation for a number of peripatetic ethnic groups: GHORBATIS, JALALI, PIKRAJ, SHADIBAZ, and VANGAVALANS. The Baluch and Afghanistani subgroups of the so-called Central Asian GYPSIES, the JUGI, are also regarded in Afghanistan as belonging to the Jats. The KUTANANS and SHEIKH-MO-

HAMMADIS also fall into the category, although they are not always included in it. (see also GYPSIES, KUTANANS, PAKISTANIS, SHEIKH-MOHAMMADIS)

JAUNSARI   A people, numbering about 75,000, living in the hills of the northern Indian state of Uttar Pradesh.

JAVANESE   (s.d. Wong Djawa, Tijang Djawi) An Indonesian people numbering about 53 million, occupying most of the central and eastern regions of the Indonesian island of Java (Djawa). There are also significant Javanese communities throughout Indonesia, indicative of their important role in the history of the Indonesian archipelago. The Javanese language is among the most widely spoken of Malayo-Polynesian languages and is written in a modified version of the Pallava alphabet of southern India. The language is considered particularly complex due to the large number of forms of speech, reflecting rank and status; the informal, *ngoko*, speech is greatly different from the deferential, *krama*, style. There are currently nine such styles, although rapid modernization and the emergence of Indonesia as an urbanized society (the capital, Jakarta, with a population approaching 8 million, is located on Java) has led to some decline in the use of stylized speech, which may all but disappear in the next century.

Most Javanese are Muslim, but there are also small Catholic and Protestant communities. Traditional Hindu and Buddhist beliefs are also strong, although generally integrated into Islamic beliefs. Pre-Islamic deities play special roles in the nominally Muslim life of Javanese peasants, who constitute the vast majority of the population. Ethnographers sometimes class the Javanese into two religious groups based on the degree of adherence to Islam and the retention of pre-Islamic customs.

Their traditional economy is based on the cultivation of irrigated rice. In recent years, however, serious problems of population density have resulted in considerable parts of the population shifting to manioc as a supplementary or even staple crop. The cultivation of vegetables and soy beans and fishing are used to supplement the diet. In the rural areas there are some small cottage industries revolving around local crafts such as batik and silver-smithing, while in urban areas such as Jakarta Javanese are employed in industry and services. The growing number of Javanese seeking employment in Jakarta has posed serious social problems for Indonesia.

Whereas the CHINESE and even the Romans (Ptolemy mentioned the island in the second century C.E.) knew of the existence of Java and carried on some form of trade with it from earliest times, it was Indian Brahmans who made the greatest impact on the local people. They apparently settled there at the behest of local rulers and their culture eventually merged with the local one to form a new, Javanese culture. Reports exist of an eighth-century Indo-Javanese kingdom called Mataram which abandoned Brahmanism in favor of Buddhism in the late ninth and early tenth centuries. This kingdom eventually came into conflict with the Sri Vijaya empire of Sumatra, while a vassal state in the east became the center of Javanese power. One Brahman king, Erlangga, stands out for his cultivation of the arts and the vernacular law code he enacted. Under him and his successors, Java became an important center of the spice trade and its influence spread as far as the Moluccas. Erlangga's dynasty was eventually supplanted by that of the Singhasari in the central highlands, which defeated the fleet of Kublai Khan. The last important Javanese dynasty was the Madjapahit, whose influence was felt throughout Indonesia. It was in this period that the great national poem, the *Nagakritagama*, was completed. Most important Javanese architecture also dates from this period. By the early sixteenth century, the native dynasties had declined considerably and Java fell to the Muslims.

The Muslim era led to the rise of several smaller, bellicose states and a decline in indigenous culture. The PORTUGUESE and later the DUTCH utilized the weakened state of affairs on the island to exert their own influence.

Only the western part of the island was commercially viable; the eastern and central regions had, as a result of the anarchy of warring states, reverted to agricultural societies, although the Muslim kingdom, Mataram, established a short-lived empire. Only in the latter half of the nineteenth century did efficient Dutch administration and investment result in some rise in the local standard of living. Because of its location and sizable population, Java played an important role in the postwar Indonesian independence movement. Indonesia's first president, Sukarno, was part Javanese, and the Javanese have continued to dominate the civil service of the country.

JAWI   One of four tribes comprising the MAMASAN.

JAZIRIYYUN   see ALGERIANS.

JEBELAWIN An ethnic group living in Ethiopia. They speak an Arabic dialect.

JEH A Mon-Khmer group, numbering about 20,000, living in southern Laos and central Vietnam. They cultivate upland rice, hunt small game, and trade salt, cloth, buffalo, and metals among themselves, possession of these items being considered prestigious.

JEKRI A subgroup of the YORUBA living in Nigeria.

JEN G'WE A subgroup of the AKHA.

JEWS A people associated with its own religion, Judaism, and as such broadly defined in terms of both ethnicity and religion. Jews are dispersed in many countries around the world; they are often considered, by themselves or by others, more as a religious denomination than as an ethnic group. They now number around 13 million; 5.5 million live in the United States of America, 4 million in Israel, and around 1.5 million in countries of the former Soviet Union. The rest are dispersed around the world with communites of over 200,000 in France, Britain, Argentina, and Canada.

In Israel, Jews are a majority of the population and also dominate politically and economically; Israel is defined as a Jewish state. In other countries Jews form only small minorities. In recent decades hundreds of thousands of Jews have settled in Israel. The largest waves of such immigration occured in the early 1950s, mainly from Central and Eastern Europe and from the Middle East, and in the early 1990s from the countries of the former Soviet Union. Only relatively small numbers of Jews have come to the Jewish state from Western Europe and the Americas.

In 1939 there were around 17 million Jews within Europe, concentrated mostly in Eastern Europe. During World War II this number was reduced to around 11 million due to the deliberate destruction of European Jews by the German Nazis and their European collaborators. The Holocaust, as this destruction is known, left Jewish communities in Europe shattered; many disappeared. The post-war years witnessed a large migration of European Jews to North and South America as well as to Australia and South Africa, alongside a large stream of Jewish immigrants moving to the newly formed Jewish state of Israel.

The Jewish religion is the oldest of the major monotheistic faiths. Its historical tradition firmly connects the concepts of peoplehood and faith. Its Orthodox version touches upon many aspects of life, rendering Jewish minority communities in many countries a distinct culture. The language of religious ritual is Hebrew, which is also the language currently spoken by ISRAELIS. It is a Semitic language, akin to Arabic.

The Jewish people derives from a group of Semitic tribes known as the Israelites, who settled in the land of Canaan (later known as the Land of Israel and also as Palestine) in the twelfth to thirteenth centuries B.C.E. They were united into a kingdom during the rules of Saul, David, and Solomon (eleventh to tenth centuries B.C.E.); in David's time, Jerusalem became the capital city and during the reign of Solomon a temple was built there as the focus of the cult. After Solomon's death, the realm split into the northern kingdom of Israel and the southern kingdom of Judah. The former came to an end in 722 B.C.E. when it was conquered by the Assyrians and most of its inhabitants exiled. In 586 B.C.E. the Babylonians conquered the kingdom of Judah, destroyed the Temple and exiled the elite to Babylonia. These exiles retained their identity and after some fifty years, when they were permitted to return to Jerusalem, a large contingent went back and rebuilt the Temple. However, a considerable number chose to remain in Babylonia. About this time, Jews were also living in Egypt, and these two communities constituted the beginning of the Diaspora (Jews living outside their own land).

In the early centuries of the Second Temple, the Jews in Judah lived under Persian and then Greco-Syrian rule until achieving a century of independence under the Hasmoneans (Maccabees) from 164 B.C.E. From 63 B.C.E. the country was ruled by the Romans. The Diaspora extended considerably and by the first century C.E. reached as far as Yemen, Armenia, and the western Mediterranean. After the Jews in their own land (Judea, the Roman form of Judah) rose in revolt against the Romans in 66–70 C.E. the last vestiges of their independence was eliminated and, with the destruction of the Temple, their religion became synagogue-oriented. After the revolt and following a further uprising in 132–135, many of the survivors were deported. Jews continued to live in the Land of Israel; however, from the sixth century their numbers in the country were comparatively small.

The Jews now spread to many parts of the world: along the North African littoral, in the wake of the Roman armies into Central and Northern Europe, and throughout western Asia as far as India. Three major groupings could be distinguished: Ashkenazi Jews of Central, and later Eastern, European origin; Sephardi Jews, the Jews of Spain and Portugal and their descendants; and Eastern Jews who lived in Muslim lands and Asia. Under both Christian and Muslim rule, the Jews were subject to severe persecutions and discrimination. Confined to ghettos, they developed their own culture, with little contact with the non-Jewish world. However, there were exceptional periods, such as the so-called "Golden Age" in Spain (around the eleventh century). This was under Muslim rule, which generally was less harsh than that of the Christians, although the Jews in Muslim lands were regarded as second-class citizens, subject to constant discrimination and periods of persecution.

The Jews were frequently on the move, migrating from one country to another, partly as a result of exterior pressures and expulsions, partly from economic motives. They were expelled from England (1290), France (1394), and Spain (1492). Many of the Jewish refugees from Spain found their way to Jewish communities around the Mediterranean Sea, in which they soon became the dominant element. Continuing expulsions from Western and Central Europe propelled the Jews eastward and large numbers settled in Poland and Lithuania, which from the fifteenth to sixteenth centuries constituted the leading religio-cultural center of the Jews and by the late nineteenth century accounted for 85 percent of the Jewish people.

The eighteenth-century Enlightenment and the American and French Revolutions heralded the emancipation of the Jews, who began to receive equal civil rights. With the abolition of the obligation to live in ghettos, they now entered general society. Emancipation was a gradual process: in Western and Central Europe it was complete by the mid-nineteenth century but did not reach Eastern Europe until the Russian Revolution and some of the Muslim lands until the twentieth century, if at all. Under the new circumstances, patterns of Jewish identity changed. Instead of a virtually monolithic religious orthodoxy, various patterns of non-Orthodox Judaism emerged (Reform, Conservative) while a considerable number of Jews now considered themselves secular.

Violent persecutions of Jews in czarist Russia toward the end of the nineteenth century led to a massive emigration. The major goal of the emigrants was the United States, where a community had been developing since the mid-seventeenth century. However, many settled in Western and Central European countries while others founded new communities in Latin America, Canada, South Africa, and Australia. The late nineteenth century also saw the emergence of political Zionism. Jews had always longed and prayed for the return to Zion, to go back to their original land (which, as Palestine, had been under Muslim rule since the seventh century with the exception of the Crusader period), but had never been permitted to enter in numbers. Now they began to organize and to settle in Palestine with the hope of rebuilding it as their homeland.

The number of Jews in Palestine had grown to about two-thirds of a million when in 1947 a United Nations resolution called for the partition of Palestine; in 1948 the State of Israel was proclaimed. The signal was now given for a massive immigration of Jews from many parts of the world, notably Holocaust survivors from Europe and Jews from Muslim lands. Some Jewish communities moved en masse, including the ancient communities of Iraq and Yemen. The political and cultural hegemony of the Jewish world now passed to Israel (the Jewish state) and the United States (the country with the largest number of Jews). From the 1970s a large emigration was permitted from the Soviet Union (whose Jews had been cut off from the rest of the Jewish world since 1917); the majority of the three-quarters of a million Jews who left went to Israel.

Hebrew, although it remained the "holy tongue," began to drop out of everyday use in late bibical times, being supplanted in Palestine by the cognate Aramaic language and in the rest of the Hellenistic world by Greek. In the Diaspora the Jews became familiar with the languages of their environment, which they often wrote in Hebrew script. The medieval German spoken by Ashkenazi Jews developed into Yiddish, until recently the most widely spoken of Jewish languages. The Jewish refugees from Spain spoke Castilian, which among their descendants became known as Ladino or Judeo-Spanish. Other Jewish languages included Judeo-Arabic and Judeo-Persian. Hebrew remained the language of prayer and literature until the nineteenth century, when it was revived as a spoken tongue and is now the everyday language of Israel. In the Diaspora Jews now communicate in the language of their country of residence and, apart from Hebrew, the use of Jewish languages is dying out. (see also ISRAELIS)

JICAQUE A South American Indian group living along the Mosquito Coast of Nicaragua and Honduras. Once cannibalistic hunter-gatherers, they now also grow bitter manioc and raise maize and cochineal-producing cactus as cash crops. They use dugout canoes to carry their trading products.

JICARILLA see APACHE.

JIE An Eastern Nilotic people living in Uganda between the DODOTH people in the north and the KARAMOJONG in the south. They regard both these groups as their enemies, while considering the TURKANA as closely related and the LABWOR as friends.

Like the KARAMOJONG, the Jie are cattle-herders. Cattle are a sign of wealth and provide the focal point of economic and social structure. Agriculture is of far less importance, although they grow a variety of vegetables and grains. In common with other Eastern Nilotic pastoralists, the kinship system of the Jie is that of a patrilineal clan-structure.

The Jie share basically the same religious beliefs as the other peoples of the Karamojong cluster, but they have in addition a cycle of rituals connected with rainmaking and fertility. All the initiated men take part in the rainmaking ritual in March when the rainy season is expected to begin. There is another central ritual of their transhumant cycle of cattle-herding, held when they reach the eastern pastures. This marks the turn of the year and is connected with a ritual of thanksgiving to their high god, Akuj. (see also KARAMOJONG)

JIMMA A subgroup of the OROMO.

JINGHPAW see KACHIN.

JIRAJIRA A South American Indian group of hunter-gatherers who inhabit the foothills of the Cordillera de los Andes in northwestern Venezuela. (see also VENEZUELANS)

JIVARO (s.d. Shuar) A South American Indian people living in the extensive jungles of the Oriental region of Ecuador and northern Peru. They are one of the most numerous South American Indian peoples living in the rainforests east of the Andes. The Jivaro are bounded to the west by the Andes, to the east by the Tigre River, and to the south by the Maranon River, which is one of the main branches of the Amazon. Spread through remote rainforest zones along riverbanks, the various Jivaro subgroups share physical, linguistic, and cultural characteristics which differ from those of the non-Jivaro peoples who surround them. Tribes belonging to the Jivaro ethnic group include the ARAPICO, CHILAPA, UPARA, PAUTA, SANTIAGO, GUALAQUIZA, CUSULIMA , HUAMBIZA, COPATAZA, ACHUARA, ANTIPA, and AGUARUNA. The AGUARUNA are the only Jivaro whose territory is completely within Peru. There are at least

Jivaro

15,000 Jivaro in all, including at least 5,000 members of "pure" tribes who have no contact with the world outside their rainforest. The Jivaro all speak Jivaro languages.

During the conquest and in colonial times the SPANIARDS tried to dominate the Jivaro, first through violent attacks and later through missionary activities. Jivaro fierceness as warriors and their notoriety as head shrinkers kept the outside world at bay for centuries. Today, some Jivaro tribes have developed friendly but cautious business relationships with visiting outsiders. Jivaro agriculturalists raise manioc, maize, cotton, and a variety of garden produce; skilled Jivaro hunters catch game animals for food and trade. Some Jivaro work as day laborers on the forest margins.

The Jivaro engage in inter-tribal battles as well as in conflicts with outsiders. Victory in a Jivaro war is obtained only with the capture of an enemy's head, which becomes a trophy (*tsantsa*) and source of prestige, and is shrunk in conjunction with a "head feast." The Jivaro also make animal *tsantsas*, especially from the heads of jaguars; they believe this animal possesses human characteristics. (see also ECUADORIANS)

JOGI, JUGI see GYPSIES, JATS II.

JOLA see DIOLA.

JOLOANOS see TAUSUG.

JOLO MOROS   see TAUSUG.

JOLONG   A subgroup of the BAHNAR.

JOMPRE   An ethnic group living in Nigeria.

JONAM   A small group, speaking a Western Nilotic language, living around Pakwach, between the Alur and the Albert Nile Rivers in Uganda.

JO-PADHOLA   see PADHOLA.

JORDANIANS   (s.d. Urduniyyun) The Jordanians are ARABS, number approximately 3.5 million, and inhabit the Hashemite Kingdom of Jordan; they are about equally divided into the original population, living east of the Jordan river, and PALESTINIANS who have settled there as refugees and migrants since 1948. By the early 1990s about 250,000 PALESTINIANS were still living in refugee camps, but most of them now live in Amman, Zarqa, and Irbid, Jordan's main cities.

Most Jordanians are Sunni Muslims. An estimated 5 to 13 percent are Christians (about one-tenth of the PALESTINIANS are Christian), who live mainly in the cities. Of these, two-thirds are Greek Orthodox, followed by Greek Catholics and Roman Catholics. The Circassians (see CHERKESS), about 2 percent of the population, live in Amman and villages around it established in 1880–1905 (the time at which they migrated from the Caucasus) and now form a well-integrated minority.

BEDUIN, who once constituted the majority of the population, number today only 100,000; they still form the core of the army. They are divided into ten tribal groupings with limited wandering grounds (some have become semi-sedentarized) and mainly live in the south (Wadi Mujib).

Roughly 20 percent of the population are agriculturalists (the Jordan River valley has become a fertile zone, irrigated by the East Ghor canal), but Jordanians are now 60 percent urban. PALESTINIANS in particular have substantially contributed to industrialization and the development of services such as banking, tourism, and trade. Jordanians have a somewhat diffuse identity because of Jordan's artificial origin, shifting geographical shape, its Palestinian minority (which has its eyes set west of the Jordan river), and neighbors with designs on its territory. Jordan boasts a strong army and its East Bank political elite has grown a specifically Jordanian identity.

Since the area of what is now Jordan never developed into an autonomous power center, it developed no specific regional identity until its establishment after World War I by Britain. In 1923 Transjordan was carved from the British mandate over Palestine, and created to compensate the emir (from 1946 king), Abdallah, for Hashemite efforts to aid the BRITISH during that war (the Hashemites had ruled over Hijaz in the Arabian peninsula until expelled by the Saudis).

Following the 1948 war with Israel, Transjordan had to cope with the influx of Palestinian refugees. In 1950 Jordan annexed the West Bank, the area west of the Jordan river which had been earmarked for a Palestinian state, thus increasing its population by one-third. The monarchy (from 1953 under Hussein), initially only supported by the BEDUIN and a few well-to-do merchant families, has weathered many crises and seems gradually to be gaining broader legitimacy, hand in hand with the crystallization of a separate Jordanian identity. Following the loss of the West Bank to Israel in 1967, Palestinian guerrillas posed the most serious threat to the monarchy.

In the ensuing "Black September" of 1970, thousands of PALESTINIANS in Jordan were killed; many more left for Lebanon. Still, the growth of Jordan's economy during the 1970s also benefiting the PALESTINIANS while satisfying various East Bank constituencies.

After the outbreak of the *intifada* (see PALESTINIANS), Jordan in 1988 formally disengaged from the West Bank and initiated cautious democratization. Elections in 1989 led to massive gains for Islamic fundamentalists. The 1991 Gulf War crisis imposed a severe burden on Jordan's economy: its trade was disrupted by the anti-Iraq embargo, financial support by Saudi Arabia and the Gulf states was cut, and hundreds of thousands of its migrant workers, mostly PALESTINIANS, were compelled to return home. Postwar recovery and the start of common Jordanian-Palestinian peace talks with Israel appear to have given Jordan new hope.

JSOKO   An ethnic group related to the EDO, living in southwestern Nigeria.

JUANG   A Munda-speaking group, numbering about 25,000, living in the northwest hills of India's Orissa State, as well as in Bihar. They practice communal ownership of their agricultural land which they cultivate using slash and burn methods. They also grow rice near local riverbeds.

The Juang are best known for their intricate dances mimicking birds and animals.

JUBU   A subgroup of the TIV.

JUKUN   An ethnic group living along the Benue valley in northern Nigeria and in smaller numbers in Cameroon.

A precolonial Jukun kingdom was destroyed in the Fulani *jihad* (Muslim holy war) of the nineteenth century. The British colonial power admired the political organization of the Jukun and enabled them to dominate the more numerous but less developed TIV, who shared their territory. Tiv resentment has led to sporadic violent incidents between the two groups since Nigeria's independence in 1960. In 1991 one such clash, which followed a contested municipal election, developed into an ethnic war during which villages were burned and thousands of people from both groups fled the region. Since then, attempts have been made to reconcile the two groups with the help of traditional northern rulers. (see also TIV)

JULA   see DYULA.

K

KABA A subgroup of the SARA.

KABAENAS see MARONENE.

KABARDIANS (s.d. Adyghe, Keberdei) A people located in the Central Caucasus Mountains in the basin of the Malka, Baksan and Terek Rivers, mainly in the Kabardino-Balkan Republic in Russia. According to the 1989 Soviet census they numbered 363,000.

Kabardians

The Kabardian (or Kabardino-Cherkess) language, in scholarly literature also known as High Adyghe, belongs to the Abkhazo-Adyghean branch of the Ibero-Caucasian family.

Literary Kabardino-Cherkess, based on the Baksan dialect of the Great Kabarda used the Roman alphabet between 1925 and 1938, when Cyrillic was introduced.

Since the sixteenth and seventeenth centuries the Kabardian have been Sunni Muslims of the Hanafi school; those living in the environs of Mozdok are Russian Orthodox Christians.

They are descendants of the ADYGHEANS who settled in the thirteenth and fourteenth centuries on the left bank of the Terek River (Great Kabarda) and later on the right bank (Little Kabarda).

Their traditional economy is based on agriculture, horse-breeding, and now also on various branches of urban industry. (see also ABAZIANS, ADYGHEANS, BALKAR, CHERKESS)

KABENA (Qabenna) An ethnic group, numbering 20,000 (1980s), who live in the southern Shoa Province in Ethiopia, north of the GURAGE. They speak an eastern Cushitic language and are Sunni Muslims. The Kabena are agriculturalists and cattle-raisers. Culturally and linguistically they are related to the HADIYA.

KABENDE An ethnic group related to the USHI, living in Zambia.

KA BEO see LAQUA.

KABILIA BERBERS see SANHADJA.

KABIRPATHI A subgroup of the PANIKA.

KABRE (Kabye, Cabrais; s.d. Lan-Mbe) An ethnic group living in the La Kara and Central Regions of northern Togo. They number around 275,000 and mostly practice traditional religions.

During the periods of colonial rule by the GERMANS (until World War I) and the FRENCH, the Kabre joined the colonial armies and police forces in large numbers, but their region remained underdeveloped. After independence, the Kabre joined Togo's army which they have dominated since the military coup of 1963. With the rise to power of a Kabre, Etienne Eyadema, following the coup, there were efforts to modernize the northern regions of Togo, especially the Kabre area.

The LOGBA are a Kabre subgroup.

KABUI A subgroup of the ZELIANGRONG.

KABYE   see KABRE.

KABYLE   (s.d. Tamourt) A Berber people numbering over 1 million living in Kabylia (al-Qabail), a mountain range east of Algiers. They retain a language, oral literature, and lifestyle of their own.

The name Qbayl (Arabic: "tribes") was used only from the eighteenth century, and originally referred to all the BERBERS of North Africa.

The inaccessible Kabyle mountains often served as a refuge and formed a basis for resistance, first against Romans, Vandals, and Byzantines, and later against the ARABS.

In the nineteenth century, three autonomous Kabyle principalities were recognized by the Ottoman Empire. In 1857 invasion by the FRENCH led to the pacification of the Kabyle, and also to the destruction of their political tribal structures. Resistance unified the three Kabyle groups: the SANHADJA, west of Dais (Dellys); the ZUWAWA, east of Bijaiah (Bougie); and the QUTAMA, in the Bijaiah-Annaba region.

Kabylia is traditionally little urbanized. In view of the poverty of the soil, which demanded extensive terrace agriculture, there is rural overpopulation, forcing the people into non-agricultural occupations or emigration to Algiers, Tunisia, and France, where today 75 percent of all Kabyle men live; many still living in Kabylia are dependent on their remittances.

The Kabyle live in large villages once administered by a council of arms-bearing men. Theirs is a polygamous society, from which smiths and butchers are excluded. Common law supersedes religious law, although the council has lost its functions, and common law was prohibited after Algerian independence. An independent-minded population, the Kabyle fought bloody battles during the war of independence. Early in the 1960s their guerrillas were defeated by the Algerian army.

The Algerian state has not recognized the Kabyle language and suppresses their customs. The Kabyle, for their part, have largely refrained from participating in Algerian public life. In the 1980s a Berber movement in favor of minority rights started in Tizi Wazu (Tizi-Ouzou). Currently the Kabyle are the backbone of the Berber-based Front des Forces Socialistes (FFS), which protests their accelerated arabization.

KACHA   A subgroup of the NAGA living in the eastern hill region of Nagaland, India, on the border with northwestern Myanmar (Burma).

KACHA NAGA   A subgroup of the ZELIANGRONG.

KACHARI   A people numbering about 1 million, living mainly in the state of Assam in eastern India. They are now located primarily in the foothills between the Brahmaputra River and the border with Bhutan, but until the Ahom invasion of 1228 Kachari kings were established in upper Assam. In 1790 the Kachari kings, by then located in Khaspur, Cachar District, formally embraced Hinduism and were recognized as belonging to the Kshatriya, or warrior, caste. The people have remained a dstinct ethnic group. Their language (variously known as Bodo, Kachari, and Mech) is of the Tibeto-Burman group, while the Kachari themselves have distinctively Mongolian-type features.

The Kachari are divided into clans named after natural phenomena (the heavens, earth and rivers, and flora and fauna) and practice a tribal religion incorporating an extensive pantheon of local village and household deities, with village elders officiating at religious ceremonies. Burial of the dead is the usual practice, although cremation is also permissible; there is a belief in life after death.

Descent and succession of property is through the male line. Although tribal institutions such as the community house for unmarried males link the Kachari to the NAGA and other hill groups of Assam, the growing influence of Hinduism in the region has meant that the Kachari are becoming assimilated into the caste society of the ASSAMESE in the plains. Marriage is arranged by parents and requires payment of a bride price. (see also MECH)

KACHEM   see GATAMI.

KACHIN   (Jinghpaw, Dashan, Khang, Singhpo) The term "Kachin" is derived from a Jinghpaw word that means "red earth," denoting the main territory of the Kachin people, located in Myanmar (formerly Burma) in Southeast Asia. Kachin can also be found in parts of northwest Thailand, the Yunnan region of China, and also in small numbers within India. In Myanmar (Burma) the Kachin are found mainly in the Kachin State, as well as in parts of the northern Shan State. There are also some closely related ethnic groups (such as the SINGHPO in the Hukawng Valley) which have branched off from the Kachin over the years. The JINGHPAW are the largest Kachin subgroup, followed by the MARU DANGBAU, ATSI, LASHI, and ACHANG. It is estimated that there are roughly 1 million Kachin today,

Kachin

but since part of the people live within China, and due to the lack of census-taking in Myanmar, accurate data are impossible to obtain. The Kachin language and its various dialects belong to the Tibeto-Burman family, with Jinghpaw creating its own branch. The languages of the MARU DANGBAU are more closely related to Burmese and classifed in the Lolo-Burmese branch.

The Kachin live mainly in single-family, stacked dwellings of bamboo, wood, and thatched roofs adjacent to the fields. Marriages are traditionally arranged, with a bride price usually paid by the groom's father. One lineage will provide wives for another, and that lineage will give wives to yet another, until the various groups are connected, creating a situation in which each family line is both *mayu* (wife-givers) and *dama* (wife-takers). Marriages among those of the same bloodline are traditionally restricted.

They are an agricultural society that practices slash and burn cultivation. The main crop is rice, and less frequently crops of maize, buckwheat, sesame, to-

bacco, and opium are grown. At one time, the Kachin collected trade-route revenues from the CHINESE who passed through their territory as traders.

They have been mainly Christians since the onset of missionary work in the late nineteenth century. Catholicism and Protestantism are the two main branches, and there are some dispersed Buddhist groups, especially in the city of Mandalay. However, most Kachin still believe in the local *nats* (gods), who preside over the earth and sky and are accompanied by many spirits who interact with the living. There is at least one *dumsa*, or priest, in each village, who is trained in the practice of sacrificial rites. There are also many female mediums and magicians who practice spiritual healing. Priests help guide the deceased to the afterlife after their bodies have been preserved for nearly a week.

Although there are traces of a Kachin presence in China dating back to the fourteenth century, a documented history of the people begins only in the eighteenth century. The Kachin have been very closely tied to the culture of the SHAN, who live in many of the same areas in Myanmar.

Although the Kachin were originally a northern people, they began making their way into the heart of the country and further southward along the Chinese trade routes. While the BRITISH were trying to take over Burma in the late nineteenth century, the Kachin were also attempting to control more of the area. Eventually the BRITISH won control of Burma, which led to many Kachin attacks on the British frontier administration. The 1942 invasion of Burma by the JAPANESE suppressed the Kachin even more heavily, and it was not until Burma's independence in 1948 that the Kachin were finally able to begin acquiring power. In 1962, a Kachin was to become president, but a military coup ended the democratic process. Since then, there have been many Kachin attempts to undermine the ruling regime. Many have subsequently left the country to find refuge in China, Thailand, and the bordering areas of India. (see also BURMANS)

KADAR An ethnic group, numbering 2,300 (1981), living in the Palghat and Trichur Districts of Kerala, India. They speak a dialect belonging to the Dravidian family of languages and are Hindu.

The Kadar are expert elephant-tamers. Their name indicates that they belong to the "*kadu*," or forest, and they were previously food-gatherers. They now engage in the cultivation of cash crops such as pepper, coffee, and rice.

KADARA   An ethnic group living in Nigeria.

KADAZAN   see DUSUN.

KADI   (Kwadi) A small ethnic group living in the Mossamedes Desert, nineteen miles from Porto Alexandre, Angola.

KADOMBUKU   An ethnic group living in the mountainous central region of the Indonesian island of Sulawesi (Celebes). (see also TORADJA)

KADU   An ethnic group speaking a Tibeto-Burman language and numbering about 40,000, living in northern Myanmar (Burma). They are rapidly assimilating into Burmese society; many speak Burmese and they are all Buddhists. Traditionally rice cultivators, many have sought employment among the BURMANS, particularly as elephant drivers.

KADUP   An ethnic group living on the Indonesian island of Kalimantan (Borneo). (see also DAYAK)

KAFFICHO   (Kafa, Kefa) A people, numbering about 500,000 (1980s), who live in the central part of Kefa Province, Ethiopia. They adhere to traditonal beliefs, Ethiopian Orthodox Christianity, or Sunni Islam.

The oral history of the empire of Kafa dates back to the late fourteenth century. The Kafficho formed a stratified society, with a royal clan (the Minjo) at the top, followed by various degrees of noble and less noble clans (sometimes claiming descent from the TIGRAY and AMHARA). Artisans and hunters were lower classes. The Kafa polity, including the rituals linked to its kingship, became a model for many neighboring states.

The Kafficho were engaged in cattle-raising and cultivated a variety of cereals, cotton, and coffee. A special export was the anal secretion of civet cats. During the nineteenth century the Kafficho participated actively in the slave trade with the AMHARA of Shoa Province. Kafa lost its independence in 1897.

KAFIRS OF AFGHANISTAN   see NURESTANIS, VAIGULI.

KAGOMA   A subgroup of the FULANI.

KAGORO   A subgroup of the FULANI.

K'AH   A subgroup of the RHADE.

KAHAYAN   An ethnic group living on the Indonesian island of Kalimantan (Borneo). (see also DAYAK)

KAIANJA   One of the eight "early states" of the HAYA.

KAIDAQAN   see KAITAG.

KAILI   An ethnic group living in the mountainous central region of the Indonesian island of Sulawesi (Celebes). (see also TORADJA)

KAINGANG   A South American Indian group living in southern Brazil, dispersed throughout the States of São Paulo, Paraná, Santa Catarina, and Rio Grande do Sul. They live in more than a dozen villages with an unequal population distribution, protected by official sponsoring. Rio Grande do Sul also provides for shelters at six points in the north of the state. The Kaingang number a few thousand. They speak a Guarani language, and have preserved their social and religious traditions. (see also ARGENTINES)

Kaingang

KAINGUA   see MBUA.

KAINULAISET   see FINNS.

KAITAG   (Khaidaq, Qaidakh, Khaitaq, etc.; s.d. Kaidaqan) An ethnic group living in the mountains of Daghestan, between the shore of the Caspian Sea and the basin of the Kazikumukh Koisu River. According to the Soviet 1926 census, the only one in which the

Kaitag were listed as a separate ethnic group, they numbered 14,430. Today they might number 25,000–30,000. One of the first Daghestani ethnic groups to become islamicized, the Kaitag have been Sunni Muslims of the Shafi'i school probably since the eighth century. The Kaitag language, recently regarded as a dialect of the Dargin language, belongs to the Daghestani branch of the Ibero-Caucasian family. It is unwritten, and Dargin is used as the literary language.

The Kaitag are first mentioned in Arab sources of the tenth century. In the fifteenth to eighteenth centuries the Kaitag *usmiyat* (principality) was one of the most important feudal principalities of Daghestan. In 1802 it became a Russian protectorate, and in 1844 it was abolished. The lowlands inhabited by the Kaitag came under direct Russian rule in 1920; only in 1962 did the mountain areas they inhabit also come into Russian hands. The Kaitag are now undergoing an intensive process of ethnic integration into the DARGIN. Today they use as self-designation the term "Dargin" alongside their own ethnic term.

Their traditional economy includes cattle-breeding, agriculture, horticulture, and home industry.

KAIWA A South American Indian group living in the southern part of the State of Mato Grosso, central-west Brazil, near the border with Paraguay. Their language connects them to the Guarani language family. They number a few thousand individuals and are settled in clusters of villages. (see also GUARANI)

KAJE A subgroup of the TIV.

KAKA An ethnic group living in Cameroon.

KAKADU An aboriginal group living in the Northern Territory, Australia. (see also AUSTRALIAN ABORIGINES)

KAKAR A subgroup of the PASHTUN.

KAKH see FEREIDANS.

KAKWA An ethnic group living in southern Sudan and northeastern Uganda.

KALAE An ethnic group living in the mountainous central region of the Indonesian island of Sulawesi (Celebes). (see also TORADJA)

KALAGAN see TAGAKAOLO.

KALAMIAN A Malayo-Polynesian people who originally occupied Coron Island and coastal settlements on Busuanga Island and other smaller islands in the Philippines. Linguistically they are related to the TAGBANUWA.

KALANADY An ethnic group living in the southern Indian state of Tamil Nadu. They are Hindus and practice mainly agriculture,

KALANGA An ethnic group living in Zimbabwe. They speak a distinctive Shona dialect which some scholars consider a separate language. (see also SHONA, ZIMBABWEANS)

KALASHANS An ethnic group living in the Chitral Region of Pakistan. Their estimated number (mid-1960s) was 3,000. The Kalasha language belongs to the Dardic branch of the Indo-Iranian family. It possesses two dialects, and is unwritten. Urdu, the official language of the state, is used as the literary language.

No details as to Kalashan religious beliefs are available. They are described as mainly pagans, which, in the context of the religious reality of Chitral, may mean that the majority are non-Muslims with a minority belonging to the Isma'ili sect of Islam. They are divided into several clans.

Their main occupations are agriculture and cattle-raising. They claim that they once inhabited a larger territory in Chitral, much of which was taken over by the KHO several centuries ago.

KALENJIN A people of western Kenya, living east of Lake Victoria, who form part of the Southern Nilotic-speaking people of East Africa. They include ethnic groups such as the KIPSIGIS, NANDI, SABAOT, TUGEN, ELGEYO, MARAKWET, and POKOT, together estimated at about 2 million people.

These Highland (Southern) Nilotic-speaking people arrived in western Kenya before the other Nilotic groups and intermarried with Southern Cushitic-speaking people, to produce a new people, the Kalenjin. The process took about 1,000 years. The Kalenjin today are mostly Christians but a high percentage (including the Christians) observe traditional rites and beliefs. Their dual base can be seen also in the Kalenjin culture; the ritual practice of circumcision as a rite of passage and prohibitions against eating fish are two Cushitic cultural characteristics in-

Kalenjin

corporated into the Kalenjin culture. The removal of the lower incisors in adolescence and intensive cattle husbandry are part of the Nilotic contribution to Kalenjin culture.

Although their history can be traced back at least a thousand years, the name Kalenjin is new. Meaning "I tell you," the term gained currency from a radio program during British colonial rule over Kenya; the Highland Nilotic-speaking radio announcer opened the program with this word, trying to attract attention, and eventually the term was adopted by the BRITISH for all the Highland Nilotic-speaking people of western Kenya for political-administrative reasons. Since then it has become an agreed term for these people. Most Kalenjin are still engaged both in agriculture and animal husbandry. Until 1978 they were a remote group, but as Kenya's second president, Daniel arap Moi, is a Kalenjin (from the TUGEN) they have gained positions of power. (see also KENYANS, KIKUYU, OKIEK)

KALERI   An ethnic group living in Nigeria.

KALINGA   An ethnic group, numbering about 150,000, living in what is today the Kalinga Province of northern Luzon, an island of the Philippines. "Kalinga" means "enemy" in the language of their lowland Christian neighbors. They populate the mountainous area of the Central Cordillera along the low river valleys of the middle Chico River. They speak a dialect similar to other languages in northern Luzon. There are marked differences between the Northern Kalinga and the Southern Kalinga. Female shamans are used against evil spirits among the Northern Kalinga, while funereal rites and ancestral spirits are crucial to the Southern Kalinga. Ceremonies generally deal with the harvest and the well-being of the village.

Both subgroups rely on wet-rice agriculture, supplementing this with slash and burn crops such as dry rice, beans, tubers, maize, tobacco, and coffee. Fields are all privately owned.

KALISPELL   A Native North American group, numbering about 400, many of whom live on the Federal Indian Reservation in Oreille County, Washington, U.S.A.

KALLAR   An ethnic group found in the southern Indian state of Tamil Nadu. Traditionally hunters, they are now engaged in agriculture. They have preserved many indigenous beliefs and Kallar men are commonly circumcised.

KALMYK   (s.d. Khalmg) Of the c.174,000 Kalmyk living in Russia, 146,000 inhabit the Kalmyk Autonomous Republic, west and south of the lower Volga River. Expatriate communities are also found in Europe (mainly Germany) and the United States.

The Kalmyk language belongs to the western (Oirat) branch of the Mongol group of Altaic languages. Kalmyk was written in the old Oirat (Mongol) script until 1925; after that date the Cyrillic alphabet was introduced.

The Kalmyk were the westernmost of the four Oirat (western Mongol) groups that roamed the lower Volga steppes from the turn of the seventeenth century. Having rejected Islam in favor of Mahayana Buddhism, they proved Russia's natural allies against the Muslim TATARS, BASHKIR, and QAZAQ. However, by the end of the eighteenth century, Russian attempts to bring them under centralized control caused the majority of Kalmyk, who lived east of the Volga, to flee to their ancient homeland. They were warmly welcomed by the newly-established Chinese authorities in Xinkiang (Sinkiang) in western China. Today the name Kalmyk refers only to the descendants of those who then lived west of the Volga and remained under Russian control.

Originally nomads, the Kalmyk began to settle in permanent villages in the second half of the nineteenth century, thus adding agriculture and domestic crafts to their traditional economy of cattle-, sheep-, and horse-raising.

Kalmyk

In 1935 an Kalmyk Autonomous Republic was established within the framework of the Russian Federation. In 1943 it was abolished and the Kalmyk were deported from their homes, mainly to Siberia. In 1957 they were allowed to return and their republic was reinstated. However, the deportation had a disastrous effect on their national culture: unlike some other deported nationalities, the Kalmyk were dispersed among Russian villages, a family or two in each. The result is that nowadays almost all Kalmyk below the age of fifty have lost their national language and the means of daily discourse is Russian.

The religion of the overwhelming majority of the Kalmyk is still Mahayana Buddhism, which makes them the only native Buddhist group in Europe. A minority has been converted to Russian Orthodox Christianity.

KALO I   A clan of the PARIA.

KALO II   (Ca Lo) A Mon-Khmer group, numbering about 20,000, living in the central highlands of Vietnam. They are related to the BRU and have had considerable contact with other groups, notably coastal VIETNAMESE.

KALULI   An ethnic group of a few thousand living in the mountainous area of central Papua New Guinea. They speak an indigenous regional language. They are gardeners whose staple crop is sago. They believe in an imperceptible shadow world which parallels the physical world and which is subject to many of the same laws. Their main ceremonial rites emphasize singing and dancing.

KALYO-KENGYU   A subgroup of the NAGA living in the eastern hill region of Nagaland, India, on the border with northwestern Myanmar (Burma).

KAMAN   A subgroup of the MISHMI.

KAMANGE   A subgroup of the TUMBUKA.

K'AMANT   see QEMANT.

KAMAR   A people, numbering 23,000 (1981), living in Madhya Pradesh and Maharashtra, India. They speak Marathi, a language belonging to the Indo-Aryan family, and are related to the GOND.

The Kamar are a Hindu group who also worship ancestral spirits. A taboo against touching a horse prevents them from horse-riding. Their main source of livelihood is agriculture; subsidiary occupations are hunting, fishing, basket-making, collection of edible forest produce, and occasional menial labor.

KAMBA   An ethnic group living in Congo. They are related to the KONGO and speak their language.

KAMBARI   A subgroup of the FULANI.

KAMBATA   A people, numbering 500,000 (1980s), who live west of the Bilate River in the southern Shoa Province, Ethiopia. They speak an eastern Cushitic language and are Ethiopian Christians, Sunni Muslims, or adherents of traditional beliefs.

The Kambata are sedentary agriculturalists (grains, ensete) and cattle-raisers. Their country is very densely populated. Before incorporation into the Ethiopian Empire, Kambata was a kingdom which shared many characteristics with the kingdom of Welamo to its immediate south. Kambata was dominated by a royal lineage. Other noble lineages claimed a northern pedigree (AMHARA, TIGRAY), related to the political expansion of the Ethiopian Empire during the Middle Ages. (see also ETHIOPIANS)

KAMBE   A subgroup of the MIJIKENDA.

KAMIAS   see GOND.

KAMMARA   An ethnic group, numbering 38,000, (1981), living in Andhra Pradesh, Karnataka, Kerala, and Tamil Nadu, India. They speak Telugu and Oriya, languages belonging to the Dravidian family.

The Kammara of Andhra Pradesh are blacksmiths. They manufacture agricultural implements and receive payment in cash or in kind. Some Kammara have abandoned their traditional profession and taken to agriculture.

KAMPUCHEAN   see KHMER.

KAMUKU   An ethnic group living in Nigeria.

KANAK   A Melanesian-speaking people, numbering c.75,000 (less than half the total New Caledonian population), who inhabit the large island of New Caledonia, in the Loyality Group located east of Australia. The majority are Christians, mainly Roman Catholics. There is a sizable number of Kanak in Noumea, the capital, but the majority are rural inhabitants engaged in agriculture, either of commercial or traditional subsistence crops.

Since the beginning of occupation by the FRENCH in 1853 the Kanak have constantly rebelled, the main cause being land appropriation. Their struggle against the FRENCH took to the political arena in 1969, with a demand to allow them to determine their own affairs. The French settlers' opposition to Kanak involvement in the governing of the territory has since increased the tension.

In recent years efforts based on rural development projects have been made to draw the Kanak further into the market economy. (see also NEW CALEDONIAN ISLANDERS)

KANAWA   A subgroup of the HAUSA.

KANAY   see KENOY.

KANET   see KHASA.

KANGWANE   A SWAZI clan.

KANIAWALI   A subgroup of the MAIYANS.

KANIKKAR   An ethnic group, numbering over 10,000, living in the Trivandrum and Quilon districts of Kerala, India. They speak Malayalam and Tamil, both belonging to the Dravidian family of languages, and are a Hindu group.

KANJOBAL   A subgroup of the MAYA.

KANKANAI   (Igorot) An ethnic group, numbering about 150,000, living in northwestern Benguet Province and in the adjacent mountains of Luzon, an island in the Philippines. They speak a distinctive dialect of the Malayo-Polynesian language of northern Luzon. They exploit the mineral-rich region they live in and subsist on wet-rice terraced agriculture.

KANOWAR   see KINNAUR.

KANSAS   (Kaw) A Native North American group numbering about 750, many of whom live in the Federal Trust Area in Oklahoma, U.S.A. Traditionally they were buffalo hunters of the plains who moved to the Indian Territory in 1873.

KANTWEU   An ethnic group living in the mountainous central region of the Indonesian island of Sulawesi (Celebes). (see also TORADJA)

KANURI   An ethnic group living mainly in the Lake Chad region of the Borno State, Nigeria where they number around 5.3 million, or 5 percent of all NIGERIANS. They also live in the eastern part of Niger where they number around 370,000. They speak Kanuri and have been Muslims since at least the eleventh century. They are mostly farmers who live in small agricultural villages. Their traditional political system was headed by a chief who was assisted by a council of elders.

During the eleventh century they established the kingdom of Bornu, which was a major power in West Africa until the fourteenth century. During the nineteenth century they successfully resisted the *jihad* (Muslim holy war) by the FULANI and managed to maintain their independence as well as their cultural and linguistic distinction. In the early twentieth century their region became part of the British colony of Nigeria. As a minority group in Nigeria, they play only a minor role in Nigeria's politics.

The MANDARA of Nigeria and Cameroon, and the BEDE, BOLEWA, KAREKARE, KOYAM, MANGA, MOBER, NGIZIM, and TERA of Nigeria are all subgroups of the Kanuri. (see also NIGERIANS, NIGERIENS)

KAONDE   (Kunde) An ethnic group, numbering about 150,000, living in the Solwezi and Kasempa Districts of northwestern Zambia. Some Kaonde live in Zaire, in neighboring areas across the border. They speak Kaonde; some are Christians while others prac-

A young Kanuri woman in Niger

Kaonde

tice their traditional African religion, which, like their culture, is similar to that of the BEMBA. The Kaonde follow a system of matrilineal descent and are organized in a unified political unit. They separated from the LUNDA in the sixteenth or seventeenth century. They often raided the ILA in order to acquire slaves. (see also KUNDA, ZAMBIANS)

KAPARIYA   A nomadic people living in the northern Indian state of Uttar Pradesh. They engage primarily in trading livestock.

KAPAUKU   (s.d. Me) An ethnic group of approximately 90,000 living in the mountainous area of western Irian Jaya, the Indonesian part of the island of New Guinea. They speak an indigenous regional language.

Their subsistence is based mostly on the cultivation of sweet potatoes, and to a lesser extent upon the raising of pigs. They believe in an omnipotent god, Ugatame, who created the world and predetermined all that has transpired since the beginning of time.

KAPINGAMARGANI ISLANDERS   A Polynesian-speaking people numbering a few hundred, inhabiting two isolated atolls, Kapingamargani and Nukuoro, in the southwest corner of Pohnpei State of the Federated States of Micronesia. The population is mostly confined to the tiny islet of Touhou.

KAPUCHA   see BEZHTIN.

KARACHAI   see QARACHAI.

KARADJERI   An aboriginal group numbering several dozen living in northern Western Australia. (see also AUSTRALIAN ABORIGINES)

KARAGAS   see TOFA.

KARAGWE   One of the eight "early states" of the HAYA.

KARAJA   A South American Indian group living in many communities around Bananal Island, between the States of Goiás and Pará, central-north Brazil. Their language is unclassified. They rove around the beach in small bands, moving up and down the river during the dry season.

KARAKALPAK   see QARAQALPAQ.

KARA-KIRGIZ, QARA QYRGHYZ   see QYRGHYZ.

KARAKORA   A subgroup of the SENUFO.

KARAMA   see LEBANESE.

KARAMOJONG   An ethnic group, numbering 100,000, living in the plain which carries their name, a semi-arid savanna in northern Uganda. They speak a Eastern Nilotic language.

They are mainly cattle-herders, with sorghum and other grains (maize and different kinds of millet) produced for consumption. Cattle are the focal point of their life.

The Karamojong live in permanent settlements, where crops are grown. Only the young men are sent with the herds on a seasonal migration cycle, mainly from eastern to western pastures, depending on rainfall seasons.

The settlement pattern is that of a group of huts inhabited by an extended family. Usually a group of families live in each hamlet. Several such settlements make one neighborhood region. The elders of each neighborhood region decide in local matters. The settlement pattern is dependent on the availability and amount of water.

Their kinship system is that of a patrilineal clan-structure. Their age-set system consists of older and younger sets. Chiefs, while they are elected, must be sons of chiefs. Cattle raiding is very common, as are incursions into the areas of other groups. As late as the 1980s the Karamojong raided the TESO.

Several peoples split from the Karamojong to develop as ethnic groups of their own, including the DODOTH, JIE, and TURKANA, usually referred to as the "Karamojong cluster." Altogether there are seven ethnic groups in the southern Sudan and Uganda which are closely related linguistically and share a belief in a high god named Akuj. The Karamojong regard the other groups as branches. This splintering of groups is mainly caused by life in a semi-arid territory, which demands a low population density and high group mobility. The groups belonging to the Karamojong cluster are those who proved the most resistant to external changes. They are the least christianized and islamized of all UGANDANS. Their conservatism is due to the fact that the BRITISH sought to preserve the traditional Karamojong way of life while they introduced new influences to the rest of Uganda. The peoples of the Karamojong cluster are the only ones in Uganda that have no ancestor cult. (see also DODOTH, JIE, KUMAN, TESO, UGANDANS)

KARANGA   An important Shona-speaking ethnic group living in southern Zimbabwe, between the towns of Gweru, Bikita, Chirezazi, and West Nicholson. Their Karanga dialect is used by one-third of all Shona-speakers. The early Karanga lived near a gold field, and mining and trading gold with ARABS were their primary occupations. They also raised cattle, possession of which is still an important status symbol in their society. Their vast wealth enabled them to establish a powerful dynasty which built the enormous structure known as Great Zimbabwe.

The DUMA of the Masvingo and Chipinge regions, the Sena living along the southern bend of the Zambezi River in Mozambique, the GOVERA, MARI, and NYUBA are all Karanga subgroups. (see also SHONA, ZIMBABWEANS)

KARATA   (Qarata; s.d. Kirtle) An ethnic group in the Caucasus Mountains of northwest Daghestan, Russia. They are estimated as numbering c.6,000.

The Karata language belongs to the Avar-Andi-Dido group of the Ibero-Caucasian family. It is unwritten, and Andi is used as the literary language. The Karata have been Sunni Muslims of the Shafi'i school proba-

bly since the end of the eleventh century. They are now undergoing an intensive process of consolidation with the AVAR. Among themselves they usually identify themselves by the name of their village. The AVAR refer to themselves as Karata. Other non-Avar groups considered the Karata as AVAR.

The traditional Karata one-floor whitewashed stone house has an external gallery and a cattle-shed under the house. Their traditional economy is based on sheep- and cattle-breeding, horticulture, and home industry.

KARAVAZHI   A Hindu group of agricultural laborers found in the state of Kerala in southern India.

KARAYU   A division of the OROMO living in the Awash Valley, Ethiopia.

KARBI   An ethnic group living in Assam, India. Their language belongs to the Tibeto-Burman family, and they are related to the MIKIR. The Karbi are Hindus.

Karanga

They are divided into three groups according to area of habitation: the CHINTHONG, RONGHANG, and AMRI.

A typical Karbi house is built on a bamboo platform using timber posts. Thatch is used for the roof. Cattle are generally kept under the bamboo platform. Their primary occupation is agriculture; in the hilly regions they practice shifting cultivation, growing paddy and mixed crops, while settled cultivation is practiced in plains districts. The handloom industry is another Karbi occupation.

KARBO   An ethnic group living in Chad.

KARELIANS   see IZHOR, FINNS.

KAREN   A people numbering 3–4 million, living mainly in the hills and lowlands along the Irrawaddy River in central Myanmar (Burma) in a region designated as the Karen and Kayah States, as well as in neighboring Thailand. Because of the civil war in Myanmar about 30,000 have fled to Thailand as refugees and there is also an important Karen community in California. Other large groups include the KAYEN-NI (Red Karen), SGAW (s.d. Pwakenyah), PWO (s.d. Phlong), and PA-O. They speak a Tibeto-Burman language and adhere to a variety of religions including traditional beliefs, Buddhism, and Christianity.

Karen

They engage primarily in agriculture, growing rice, maize, legumes, tubers, tobacco, cotton, and betel nuts. They also raise water buffalo, pigs, and chickens, and are skilled in handling elephants. The women weave, incorporating intricate patterns into their clothing and accessories. In recent years, the Karen in Thailand have developed a small but profitable tourist industry.

Little is known about the origins of the Karen, but it is surmised that they originated in Central Asia and only recently migrated to their present homeland. Most neighboring peoples such as the BURMANS, MON, and SHAN, oppressed the Karen, using them as slaves. In response, a sense of national identity united the disparate tribes into a cohesive ethnic unit with aspirations to independence. Many converted to Christianity; education in mission schools and a shared sense of purpose with the British colonial authorities in Rangoon resulted in many Karen assuming prominent positions in the local colonial administration. Karen nationalists had hoped to forge a federation out of the various ethnic groups in colonial Burma. They believed that their support of the BRITISH during occupation by the JAPANESE in World War II would be rewarded by considerable autonomy or even independence. The BRITISH, however, denied them statehood and they were incorporated into Burma in 1948. The new Burmese government granted the Karens limited autonomy in the form of two Burmese states, Kayah, inhabited by the KAYEN-NI subgroup, and Kawthoolei (later the Karen State) inhabited by the SGAW and PWO subgroups.

Since then, Karen living in the low-lying regions have undergone a rapid process of acculturation into the predominate Burmese culture. Hill Karen, however, have never abandoned their dreams of independence and have carried out an ongoing guerrilla war against the central government under the direction of the Karen National Union (KNU). The KNU is now a coalition of both hill Karen and more educated Christian Karen from the Irrawaddy delta region who, it is sometimes claimed, reject the idea of statehood, preferring a federated Myanmar. The KNU has recently joined forces against the government with the banned National League for Democracy.

Karen in Thailand are undergoing a rapid process of assimilation and are often included in a generic hill tribe category, Yang. (see also BURMANS, THAI)

KARIERA   A group of AUSTRALIAN ABORIGINES living along the Indian Ocean coast of northern Western Australia.

A young Karen woman in western Thailand

KARJALAINEN see IZHOR.

KARJALAISET see FINNS.

KARLANI A subgroup of the PASHTUN.

KARNATI see NAT.

KARO I A subgroup of the BATAK.

KARO II An ethnic group closely related to the HAMMAR.

KAROK A Native North American nation, numbering about 2,500, living in Del Norte County, California, U.S.A.

KARTVELI see GEORGIANS.

KARWAL An ethnic group located in Bihar and Uttar Pradesh, India. The Karwal are nomads who move about for hundreds of miles. They have a rigid system of gang control. The head (*mukhya*) of the gang is invariably a middle-aged, energetic, and assertive woman. Neither her husband nor her sons have any control over the gang.

Leadership descends not to sons and daughters but to the eldest daughter-in-law. She controls the movements of the gang, plans the next camps, punishes infractions, and settles all social and gang disputes. From every camp center, the Karwal move out in individual family units between sunrise and sunset, within a radius of five to six miles, to collect alms, a tenth of which is given to the leader. The members of the nomadic gang are not necessarily members of the same clan. They can join, leave, or rejoin the gang at will.

The Karwal are treated by the Bihar state government as a criminal group, closely watched and escorted from the limits of one police station to another.

KASENA An ethnic group living in northern Ghana and Burkina Faso. Together with other neighboring groups, they are classified as GRUSI.

KASHGHARLYQ A subgroup of the UIGHUR.

KASHKAI see QASHQAI.

KASHMIRI A people numbering more than 8 million, who inhabit the immense province of Kashmir, straddling the Indian border with Pakistan at the northern extreme of the Indian subcontinent. Most speak Kashmiri, the southernmost member of the Dardic family of languages. Geography has played an important role in the development of modern Kashmiri; proximity to enormous Indo-Aryan speaking populations had a significant effect on the language, which has borrowed extensively from both Sanskrit and, more recently, Hindi-Urdu in terms of vocabulary and grammar. Attempts to transcribe the language with either the Arabic (via Persian) or Sanskrit alphabets have met with little success due to phonetic complexities in the language. As a result, the emergence of an indigenous Kashmiri literature has been limited. The few existing works in Kashmiri, most notably by the fourteenth-century poet Lalla Devi, are unusually rich.

Religious strife has been endemic to the Kashmiri people since the early twentieth century. More than three quarters of the population are Muslims (both Sunnis and Shi'ites), about 20 percent are Hindus, and there are small Sikh and Jain communities. Nonetheless, until the independence of both India and Pakistan, the territory was dominated by a Hindu ruling family. The effect of the decision to partition British India into two states, one predominantly Hindu, the other Muslim, was particularly severe in Kashmir where both the ruling clan and a sizable minority were Hindu and wished to be incorporated by India. The majority, however, were Muslims who voted in a referendum to join Pakistan. To further exacerbate the situation, there were Muslims who supported Gandhi's ideology of a united India and a vocal group of nationalists who demanded the formation of an independent Kashmiri state based on cultural and linguistic rather than religious lines.

Since India and Pakistan's independence, three wars (1948, 1965, and 1971) and countless border skirmishes were fought over Kashmir and the threat of a fourth still lingers. Among the Kashmiri on both sides of the international boundary there have been repeated, often belligerent, calls for reunification of the territory.

The Kashmiri economy is generally based on the diverse geographic and climactic conditions of the country which range from the rich soil of the Vale of Kashmir to the towering peaks of the Himalalyas. Rice, corn, barley, and fruits are the main crops and sheep, goats, and yak are raised in the higher elevations. Local flocks produce a rich wool (cashmere) popular in the West. Although industrial development is limited, there are ex-

A Kashmiri

tensive timber forests and rivers to provide hydro-electric power. Tourism, once a mainstay of the economy of the Vale of Kashmir, has declined because of the endemic religious violence in the region.

KASHUBIANS   see POLES.

KASIMBAR   An ethnic group living on the Indonesian island of Kalimantan (Borneo). (see also DAYAK)

KASSENG   A Mon-Khmer group, numbering about 4,000, living in southern Laos. They engage in slash and burn agriculture and weave cloth to trade with neighboring peoples. They are particularly well-known for their handcrafted black lacquered shields.

KATAKOTI   An ethnic group found along the coast of the state of Kerala in southern India. Their principal occupation is fishing.

KATALO   An ethnic group living in Nigeria.

KATANG   (Katteng) A Mon-Khmer people, numbering about 13,000, living in southern Laos. They cultivate rice, both in irrigated fields and using slash and burn techniques. Katang villages consist of several longhouses built on piles and organized in geometric patterns for protection.

KATANGNANG   see LEPANTO.

KATARQAL'AI   (Wotapuri) An ethnic group living in two villages, Katarqal'a and Wotapur (hence the two names), in the Pech river area in Afghanistan. No data about their number are available, although a rough estimate puts them at several hundred.

The Katarqal'ai language belongs to the central subgroup of the Indo-Iranian group of the Indo-European family of languages. It is unwritten, Pashtun being used as the written language. The Katarqal'ai language may well have died out in the village of Wotapur, with Pashtun now being the language spoken there too. The Katarqala'i are Sunni Muslims of the Hanafi school. They are sedentary agriculturalists.

KATAYYAB   see LEBANESE.

KATHI   An ethnic group of agriculturalists found scattered throughout northern India and Pakistan. They are believed to be one of the most ancient peoples in the region, their presence having been recorded by the armies of Alexander the Great.

KATHODI   A group of Hindu farmers and merchants found in central India, mainly in the states of Maharashtra and Gujarat. They number approximately 200,000.

KATI   One of several tribes grouped together as NURESTANIS.

KATINGAN   An ethnic group living on the Indonesian island of Kalimantan (Borneo). (see also DAYAK)

KATSENAWA   A subgroup of the HAUSA.

KATTENG   see KATANG.

KATTITTURDUR   see KHINALUG.

KATU   (s.d. Monui + village name) A Mon-Khmer group, numbering 25,000, living in the central highlands of Vietnam. They practice slash and burn agriculture with hunting and gathering to supplement their diet.

The Katu have had only minimal contact with other peoples and have preserved many of their customs and religious traditions. There is a strict separation of the sexes, communal buildings being forbidden to women. Their religion centers on the dead, holding that each individual possesses two souls, one good and one bad, but that only the good soul survives after death.

KAUMA   A subgroup of the MIJIKENDA.

KAVANGO   An ethnic group, numbering about 120,000, living in northern Namibia. Their main occupations are fishing and agriculture. (see also NAMIBIANS)

KAVIRONDO NILOTES   see PADHOLA.

KAW I   see AKHA.

KAW II   see KANSAS.

KAWAHLA   An Arab group living in northern sudan. (see also ARABS, SUDANESE)

KAWAR   A group, numbering 591,000 (1981), living in Madhya Pradesh, Maharashtra, and Orissa, India.

They speak Chhattisgarhi and Hindi, languages belonging to the Indo-Aryan family. The Kawar are primarily farmers. (see also MAJHWAR)

KAYABI A South American Indian group living in a few villages in the State of Mato Grosso, central-west Brazil. They number several hundred persons, and their language connects them to the Tupi language family.

KAYAPO (Cayapo) A South American Indian group living in the Xingu Valley in the State of Pará, north Brazil. Formed by six different subgroups scattered in the valley, yet linguistically unified, they number around 2,000. They have lately fought the Brazilian government in an international court in an attempt to protect their land. (see also BRAZIIANS)

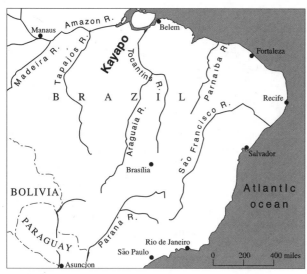

Kayapo

KAYEN-NI (Red Karen) A subgroup of the KAREN.

KAYONG (Ca Rong) A Mon-Khmer group living in southern Vietnam.

KAZAK, KAZAKH see QAZAQ.

K'DRAO A subgroup of the RHADE.

KEBBAWA A subgroup of the HAUSA.

KEBERDEI see KABARDIANS.

KEDAYAN (Kerayan) An ethnic group living along the northern coast of the island of Kalimantan (Borneo) in the Malaysian province of Sarawak, and in Brunei.

Thought to represent an indigenous population, they have been thoroughly acculturated by the MALAYS and virtually nothing remains of their traditional culture. They cultivate rice.

KEHAL A nomadic Muslim group inhabiting the banks of the Indus River in northern Pakistan. They are fishers.

KEI (Kei Islanders, Ewab Islanders) Name for the almost 50,000 inhabitants of the Kei Islands, part of the Flores-Banda chain of islands in Indonesia. They speak a Malayo-Polynesian language. There are Muslim, Catholic, and Protestant communities (the latter two encouraged by the Dutch colonial authorities to counter the influence of the BUGINESE) coexisting with traditional beliefs in the spirits of the dead and nature spirits. They are primarily slash and burn agriculturalists, with fishing playing an important role in supplementing the diet. The Kei also manufacture boats and grow coconut for the production and export of copra.

KEKCHI A group of MAYA, of indeterminate population, living in highland and lowland areas of Central Guatemala. They practice slash and burn agriculture, and their planting, accomplished with digging sticks, accompanies fertility rituals. The Kekchi prepare food outside and sleep in hammocks in their windowless thatched-roof pole-houses.

The Kekchi language belongs to the Mayan family of languages. Nominally Roman Catholic, the Kekchi religion remains traditionally syncretic, combining Catholic and indigenous elements. Contact with the non-Mayan world has increased in recent years, as evidenced by commercial cloth supplanting traditional weaving. (see also MAYA)

KELABATIC (Sarawak Murut) An ethnic group living in central Borneo, Indonesia. (see also MURUT)

KEL ADRAR (Ifoghas) A subgroup of the TUAREG.

KEL AHAGGAR (Kel Hoggar, Kel Howwar, Ahaggar) An ethnic group, numbering around 13,000, living in the central Saharan massifs of Ahaggar and Ajjer in southern Algeria. They speak the Berber language and are Muslims.

The Kel-Ahaggar belong, together with the AZJAR and the TASSILI, to the northern branch of the TUAREG.

They are divided into three subgroups: the KEL GHELA, TEGEHE MELLET, and TAIOQ.

In the past, each group was headed by a noble family after which it was named. They used to be seminomadic pastoralists. However, since the colonization of Algeria by the FRENCH in the nineteenth century, the Kel Ahaggar underwent a series of economic and social transformations. Many abandoned their nomadic way of life in favor of agriculture and trade. By the 1960s about half the Kel Ahaggar were sedentary.

Since Algerian independence, the Kel Ahaggar have undergone other rapid changes. The noble families lost their power over other clans, whose members joined the civil and military administration of the country. In addition, the Kel Ahaggar have been going through a process of arabization. (see also TUAREG)

KEL AIR   A subgroup of the TUAREG.

KEL AJJER   A subgroup of the TUAREG.

KELE   (Bakele; s.d. Bongom) An ethnic group living in Gabon, mainly in the Lambarene and other regions stretching from the Atlantic to Gabon's eastern border. Those Kele living in the far eastern part of the country are gradually being assimilated by the KOTA. Protestant missionaries tried to convert the Kele in the nineteenth century but their dispersion and seminomadic way of life hindered these efforts.

In the precolonial era the Kele were mostly elephant hunters and were active in the slave trade. Although they had no centralized political authority, some Kele chiefs entered into a treaty with the FRENCH in the early nineteenth century, according to which they recognized French sovereignty in their regions. Since these chiefs had no control over the majority of the Kele, the FRENCH found it difficult to impose their rule. Many Kele migrated to other parts of the country during the colonial period in search of jobs; at the time of Gabon's independence they were the most widely dispersed people in the country. (see also FANG)

KEL GHELA   A subgroup of the KEL AHAGGAR.

KEL HOGGAR   A subgroup of the KEL AHAGGAR.

KEL HOWWAR   A subgroup of the KEL AHAGGAR.

KEMANT   see QEMANT.

KEME TUN DJANG   see REDJANG.

KENABOI   A subgroup of the JAKUN.

KENGA   An ethnic group living in Chad.

KENOY   (Queney, Kanay, Kenne, Kenei) A Malayo-Polynesian people living deep in the mountainous interior of southern Palawan, an island in the western Philippines.

KENSIU   A subgroup of the SEMANG.

KENVI   A people, numbering a few thousand, living in Uganda on Lake Kyoga and the adjacent river systems, which are overgrown with papyrus and almost impassable. They live on the river in floating huts made of papyrus, which are only approachable by boat. The Kenvi are linguistically and culturally closely related to the SOGA people. Their language belongs to the group of Eastern Lacustrine Bantu languages.

Their main economic activity is fishing. Some of their catch is bartered for other foods with neighboring groups.

They are organized in exo- and polygamous patrilineal clans. Politically they are not unified. A limited authority is vested in headmen who are elected for life.

The Kenvi worship the high god Gasani, who has power over sky and water. A place of worship administered by a priest is dedicated to him. The Kenvi also recognize several water spirits.

KENYANS   The population of Kenya in East Africa, numbering 25 million. They are divided into Bantu, Nilotic, and Cushitic peoples. The latter arrived in central Kenya in antiquity from Ethiopia as pastoralists in search of grazing grounds. In Kenya they consist of small ethnic groups. The Nilotic and the Bantu arrived in Kenya around the turn of the first millennium C.E.; the Nilotic from the Nile valley mingled with Bantu groups settled mostly northeast of Lake Victoria. The Bantu arrived from southeast Nigeria as part of the spread of these peoples over central and southern Africa. The main Nilotic peoples in Kenya are the LUO and the KALENJIN; the main Bantu peoples are the KIKUYU, LUHYA, and KISII.

The KIKUYU make up some 20 percent of the Kenyans. They live in Central Province and are mostly Christians. The LUO, 14 percent of the population, live around Lake Victoria and are partly Christians and

The peoples of Kenya

partly adherents to traditional religions. The LUHYA, who live in Western Kenya, represent 13 percent of the population and are mostly Christians. The KALENJIN and the KISII, also inhabitants of Western Kenya, constitute 10 and 6 percent respectively of the population; only some are Christians. All these peoples are further subdivided into smaller groups.

Swahili and English are the official languages, although Kikuyu and Luo are widely understoood. Most Kenyans profess both Christianity and traditional African beliefs. Muslims are found mainly along the coastline but also around Nairobi and in the north. Agriculture is the occupation of the majority of the Kenyans, 90 percent of whom live in villages.

Kenya was declared a BRITISH protectorate in 1895. During the colonial era the British encouraged European settlement in Kenya, mostly on lands in the highlands which previously belonged to the KIKUYU. During the 1920s Kenyans, mainly from among the KIKUYU, began to organize. During World War II the economic situation of the Kenyan farmers deteriorated while the European settlers prospered. This situation led in 1944 to the creation of the Kenya African Union. It was a coalition of several peoples, but its main support came from the KIKUYU, one of whom, Jomo Kenyatta, who was to become Kenya's first president, was the head of this organization.

During the late 1940s and early 1950s a Kikuyu guerrilla organization known as the Mau Mau launched a militant campaign against European settlers. This developed into a civil war between the Mau Mau and British-supporting Kenyans, which led to the death of about 13,000 Kenyans and a few dozen Europeans. As a result the Kenya African Congress was banned and Kenyatta was jailed. In 1960 the BRITISH opened the political arena to Africans and two main parties competed for power: Kenya African National Union (KANU), headed unofficialy by Kenyatta, who was still in prison, and supported by the KIKUYU, LUO, and TEIDA peoples, and the Kenya African Democratic Union (KADU), which was supported by the smaller peoples of Kenya. KANU won the elections and Kenyatta led Kenya to independence in December 1963. He ruled the country until his death in 1978, kept close ties with the BRITISH, and invited the European settlers to stay in independent Kenya.

After his death he was peacefully replaced by Daniel arap Moi of the KALENJIN. Moi continued Kenyatta's policy but allocated more funds to the region of his own people. He declared Kenya a one-party state in 1982.

At the beginning of the 1990s protests and demonstrations of large scale erupted in Kenya demanding a multi-party democracy. Moi and his party won the multi-party elections of 1992, but his power was considerably reduced. The KIKUYU have been dominant in the government and civil service of the country since independence and remain the most powerful and influential people even after Moi's coming to power.

KENYI An ethnic group living in Uganda, on the islands of Lake Victoria. They are primarily fishers.

KERA An ethnic group living in Chad, east and south of Lake Tikun. They number around 25,000 and are similar to the TOUBOURI in all respects except language.

KERAKI An ethnic group numbering a few thousand living in southwestern Papua New Guinea. They speak indigenous languages and are slash and burn cultivators, with yams serving as their main crop. Their beliefs include both magic and myth, and they perform ritual ceremonies.

KERALITE see MALAYALI.

KERAYAN see KEDAYAN.

KERINTJI An ethnic group numbering about 100,000 and inhabiting the Kerintji Basin in western Sumatera (Sumatra), Indonesia. They are Muslims and their language, Kerintji, while sometimes considered a Minangkabau dialect, also has many similarities with Redjang and uses a similar script. Their territory is exceptionally fertile and they have well-developed methods of rice cultivation. Tea as a cash crop was introduced by the DUTCH during the colonial period. (see also MUKO-MUKO)

KERKETE see CHERKESS.

KERNOW see CORNISH.

KERU A subgroup of the YORUBA living in Nigeria.

KET The 1,000 Ket live in the Yenisey basin in western Siberia in Russia. They were originally more numerous and inhabited the entire Yenisey basin, but by the nineteenth century only their northernmost tribe survived assimilation by the RUSSIANS, EVENKI, and KHAKASS.

The Ket language is not related to any known language. No alphabet has been created for it, and Russian serves as the literary language.

Originally hunters and gathers, the Ket were shamanist-animist by religion.

KETU   A subgroup of the EGBA. (see also YORUBA)

KEWA   An ethnic group, numbering approximately 60,000, living in the mountainous area of central Papua New Guinea. They speak an indigenous language. Their subsistence is based on pig-raising and gardening. Although most are Christians, they maintain many of their traditional spiritual beliefs. They specialize in the production of various musical instruments such as flutes and drums.

KEYO   see ELGEYO.

KGALAGADI   An ethnic group living in or near the Kgalagadi desert in Botswana. They speak dialects of Sekgalagadi, a Sotho-Tswana language related to the Setswana of the TSWANA. They practice either Christianity or traditional religions.

In the nineteenth century the Kgalagadi played an important role as hunters in trans-Kgalagadi trade but they gradually lost their autonomy to the TSWANA. During colonial rule by the BRITISH they had to enter the migrant labor market in order to pay the colonial taxes. In the 1950s the Kgalagadi began to organize themselves through independent churches and later through party politics. (see also SOTHO)

KGATLA   (Bakgatla) see SOTHO, TSWANA.

KHA-AS   see KHAKASS.

KHAIDAQ, KHAITAQ   see KAITAG.

KHAIRWAR   An ethnic group, numbering 17,000 (1981), living in Madhya Pradesh and Maharashtra, India. They speak Rajasthani, a language belonging to the Indo-Aryan family. They are a Hindu group.

KHAKASS   (s.d. Kha'as; until 1923 they were called by the Russians Minusinsk or Abakan Tatars) A Turkic-speaking ethnic group who numbered c.81,000 in the 1989 Soviet census, most of whom live in the Khakass Autonomous Province of Russia, where they form about 10 percent of the population. The Khakass include several tribes of mixed origins. Their modern

Khakass

language, created in the former Soviet Union on the basis of tribal dialects, is currently written in Cyrillic script.

The Khakass lands were conquered by the RUSSIANS in the seventeenth century and have since been heavily colonized. Originally nomads raising cattle and reindeer, they were compelled under Russian rule to become first semi-nomadic and then settled farmers who assimilated most Russian cultural norms and adopted Orthodox Christianity. Today, only language and some enduring shamanist beliefs and ceremonies differentiate them from the RUSSIANS.

KHA KO   see AKHA.

KHA LAMET   see LAMET.

KHALKHA MONGOLS   see MONGOLS.

KHALMG   see KALMYK.

KHAMPA   A group living in Himachal Pradesh, India. No census has been possible as they are constantly on the move between Tibet and India (the word "khampa" means "nomad"). While they resemble TI-

BETANS, the Khampa do not consider themselves either TIBETANS or INDIANS.

The Khampa mostly live in tents and travel between Tibet and India, trading between the two countries. They carry their possessions on pony-back. They are neither agriculturalists nor herders.

KHAMPTI (Khamti, s.d. Tai) A group, numbering about 2,500 (1984 census), living in the Tengapani basin, Lohit district, in the east part of the state of Arunachal Pradesh, India.

They speak Thai and Kamit, belonging to the Siamese-Chinese group of languages.

A Mongolian people, the Khampti are Buddhist. They settled in their present abode during the eighteenth century. They are thought to be migrants from the Bor-Khampti area, the mountainous region between the eastern extremity of Assam and the valley of the Irrawady.

They are settled agriculturists. Their staple is rice, supplemented by vegetables, meat, and fish.

KHAMSE (lit. "five") A confederation of five tribal units inhabiting the Fars province in Iran. Three are tribes of Turkic origin: the AIANLU, BAHARLU, and NAFAR; one is an Iranian tribe named BASHIRI. The fifth unit, now known as IL-E ARAB (lit. "the tribe of ARABS") is made up of a number of clans of ARABS, mainly the JABBARA and SHAIBANI. All Khamse are Shi'ite Muslims.

The confederation first came to the fore in the early 1860s to counterweigh the QASHQAI. At first all were nomads. Nowadays the AIANLU and the BAHARLU are sedentary agriculturalists, while the others still pasture their flocks in the winter in the eastern part of the Zagros mountains, and in summer on the plains near the Persian Gulf.

Within the Khamse confederation the NAFAR are now in a close alliance with the BASHIRI. The latter, in their turn, are joined on their migration route by GYPSIES, whose relationship with the BASHIRI is that of clients serving their protectors. Khamse rugs are highly valued by connoisseurs.

KHANDEYAR A subgroup of the NENTSY.

KHANG see KACHIN.

KHANT (s.d. Hante) There are over 20,000 Khant living in the Khanty-Mansi autonomous province as well as in the southern Ob region in the

Yamalo-Nenets autonomous province and the northern part of Omsk province in Siberia, in the Russian Federation.

The Khant language is related to Hungarian and together with the Mansi language forms the Ugrian division of the Finno-Ugric group of the Uralic linguistic family. In 1930 it adopted a Roman alphabet, which was changed to a Cyrillic one in 1939.

The Khant were originally forest hunters and gatherers, but are now settled agriculturalists. Their religion is a mixture of traditional and Russian Orthodox Christian beliefs, with a strong emphasis on ancestor-worship.

KHA P'AI P'U NOI see P'U NOI.

KHARIA An ethnic group, numbering 304,000 (1981), living in Madhya Pradesh, Bihar, Maharashtra, and Orissa, India. They speak Munda, of the Austro-Asiatic family of languages, and Bengali, of the Indo-Aryan family. They are related to the MUNDA and the SAVAR.

The principal deity of the Kharia is a hero called Banda. They also worship their plows and axes, and make offerings to the sun.

The Kharia earn their living as laborers, cultivators, and collectors of forest produce. (see also SAVAR)

KHARWAR A Dravidian-speaking people, numbering about 200,000, found throughout northern India. They are Hindus and engage primarily in agriculture. They constitute one of the northernmost branches of the Dravidian-speaking peoples.

KHASA (Kanet) An ethnic group living in Himachal Pradesh, India. Previously nomadic shepherds, they are now settled.

KHASONKE An ethnic group living in the Kayes, Bafoulabe, and Kita regions of western Mali.

KHAS PACOH see PACOH.

KHATTAK A subgroup of the PASHTUN.

KHATU-KAI A subgroup of the ADYGHEANS.

KHEZAMA A subgroup of the CHAKHESANG.

KHINALUG (s.d. Kattitturdur) An ethnic group people living in the *aul* (village) of Khinalug, which they themselves call Kettsh. The *aul* is c.7,000 feet above sea level in the Shakhdagh mountain region of northern Azerbaijan. A few Khinalug families also live in the Kuba and Khuchmas region of Azerbaijan. Their estimated number is 1,000. They have been Sunni Muslims of the Shafi'i school since the sixteenth century. The Khinalug language belongs to the Lezghi group of the Ibero-Caucasian family. The language is unwritten, and Azerbaijani is used as the literary language.

The Khinalug are undergoing an intensive process of consolidation with the AZERBAIJANI. They have preserved some traditional components in women's dress, as well as two-storey stone houses and their economy (sheep-breeding).

KHMER (Cambodian, Kampuchean) The dominant ethnic group of Cambodia, where they constitute 90 percent of the population of over 7 million. Significant Khmer communities can also be found in both ancient communities and recent refugee camps in Thailand and Vietnam, bringing the total number of Khmer-speakers in Southeast Asia to c.8 million.

The Khmer probably migrated to their present location from the north in the early centuries C.E. They were the dominant ethnic group of the Chenla kingdom, which gained ascendancy over neighboring states during the sixth century. From the ninth to thirteenth centuries a Khmer kingdom known as Kambujadesa (the name Cambodia stems from the Hindi variant of the name, Kambuja) dominated southern Vietnam and significant portions of Laos and Thailand. Culturally, Kambujadesa was influenced by India, from which it adopted a writing system as well as Hinduism and Buddhism. Today the Khmer are predominantly Buddhist, although relics of traditional ancestor and spirit worship are also important. One of the most significant feats of the Kambuja state was the construction of the Angkor Wat complex of temples and public buildings, which can still be seen today. Also developed was a complex irrigation system which utilized waters from the Mekong River and Tonle Sap Lake to irrigate the flat interior savannah. Upon the kingdom's downfall in 1432, the Khmer underwent a series of invasions by their neighbors, the THAIS and VIETNAMESE, which culminated in the Khmer seeking the protection of the FRENCH in 1864.

Independence from France was granted in 1953, and the Khmer under King Norodom Sihanouk pursued a neutral stance to avoid entering the Vietnamese conflict. In 1965, a South Vietnamese air raid on Viet Cong bases in eastern Cambodia forced Cambodia into the war and provided impetus for its own Communist Khmer Rouge insurgency. The government collapsed in 1975 and the Khmer Rouge entered the capital, Phnom Penh.

The grim Khmer Rouge regime (1975–1979) nearly destroyed Cambodia. A radical variation of communism was pursued, cities were depopulated, and the entire population was forced into the countryside as slave labor. Between one and three million people died of deprivation or were executed for crimes ranging from failing to produce rice efficiently, to having an education, or even wearing spectacles. Border skirmishes with the VIETNAMESE led to a full scale war and the conquest of the country in 1979. A pro-Vietnamese regime was established in Phnom Penh, but the country remains ravaged by warring factions.

Despite Khmer Rouge excesses, certain elements of Khmer culture survive. Ninety percent of the Khmer still live in small villages and grow rice in irrigated paddies. They still use the red and white checkered cloth, practically a national symbol, for everything from a headdress to a means of carrying young children. The influence of Buddhism is felt everywhere. (see also THAI)

KHMU (s.d. Kumhmhu) A Mon-Khmer group, numbering 105,000 living in Laos. Having migrated to the country prior to the LAO, the Khmu are generally treated as second-class citizens. The LAO, however, have considerable respect for the Khmu as sorcerers indispensable in a number of religious rituals including royal purification ceremonies.

Many Khmu have assimilated into the LAO by adopting Buddhism and the Lao language. A minority has become Christian, while others retain their belief in powerful spirits of the home and village. Some such malevolent spirits are believed to possess people and these victims are generally ostracized and exiled from the village.

An interesting phenomenon among the Khmu is a native messianic movement which believes in the return of their ancient hero, Cuang.

KHO I (Koo) A generic term for several small agricultural hill groups, numbering several thousand people, found in northern India.

KHO II (Khowar, Chitrali, Chitrari) An ethnic group constituting the majority in the Chitral region of Pakistan. Their estimated number (mid–1960s) was 90,000. A small group of Kho, calling themselves CHITRALI, live in the Mountain Badakhshan Autonomous *Oblast* of Tajikistan. Their language, known as Khowar and also as Chitrali, Chitrari and Arnia, belongs to the central subgroup of the Dardic branch of the Indo-Iranian family. Only two publications in Khowar are known: the first, using the Roman alphabet, is dated 1902, and the second, published in 1958, utilizes the Arabic alphabet. Urdu is used as the literary language.

The Kho belong to the Isma'ili sect of Islam. The date of their islamization is unknown. They are divided into three clearcut social strata: nobles (*adamzada*), middle class (*arbabazada*), and the poor (*faqir-miskin*). Each stratum is divided into several clans, some of non-Kho origin.

Their main occupations are agriculture and cattle-raising. They originally lived in the northern part of Chitral, and their expansion over the region is said to have taken place several centuries ago. The Kho possess a rich folklore of poetry, music, and narration.

KHOIKHOI   Descendants of the aboriginal population of coastal South Africa and the Orange River. They numbered about 100,000 when the DUTCH arrived in the Cape region. The DUTCH called them Hottentot. The advance of the DUTCH and other Europeans in South Africa eventually cost the Khoikhoi their land through defeat in wars and as a result of decimation by smallpox. Later, they intermarried with Bantu slaves brought by the Europeans and with others to form the Cape Colored group. Some of them stayed as servants and workers in the areas developed by the European settlers, while others left the Cape region and settled in the Orange River basin. The Khoikhoi influenced the Bantu peoples, XHOSA, and ZULU, as is evidenced by the clicks characteristic of the Khoi language. They are currently associated with the SAN and are known together as the KHOISAN.

KHOISAN   A term used to refer to the KHOIKHOI and the SAN, the earliest known inhabitants of South Africa.

KHOJA   A subgroup of the TURKMEN.

KHOND   One of the Scheduled Tribes of India, numbering almost 1.5 million and living in the hilly region of Orissa State in eastern India. They speak the Kui language belonging to the Dravidian family, which they transcribe using the Oriya script.

Their religion is based on the relationship between two gods, the male figure, Buri, and the female figure, Tari, who are in conflict. Religious loyalties are divided between devotees of each god, although all accept the existence of lesser gods who regulate human affairs. In the past, the cult of Tari demanded extensive human sacrifices, which have since been replaced by animal sacrifices. Christian missionaries have had some success among the Khond in recent years.

The Khond grow rice, corn, and some legumes; they also raise animals and hunt. Their most important economic pursuit, however, is the harvesting of the abundant teak forests in their vicinity. The wood is sold to Hindu traders along the Orissa coast.

KHOWAR   see KHO.

KHOZZAM   see DJOHEINA.

KHUA   A Mon-Khmer group, numbering about 1,000, living on the mountain slopes in the Quang Binh province of northern Vietnam.

KHUANI   see KHVARASHI.

KHUFI   An ethnic group inhabiting the Khuf valley at the upper reaches of the Panj River in the Pamir region of the Mountain Badakhshani Autonomous *Oblast* (Region) in Tajikistan. Their estimated number (in the early 1980s) was 2,000.

The language of the group is now regarded as a dialect of the Rushani language. It is unwritten, with Tajik used as the literary language. Since the 1930s they have been regarded officially as part of the TAJIK. They are followers of the Isma'ili sect of Islam; the date of their islamization is unknown, but cannot be earlier than the eleventh century.

The Khuf valley is a deep cleft at a high altitude between steep mountain slopes. Its inaccessibility made it an ethnic reserve. The Khufi are one of the Pamir groups best known to anthropologists. They live in dispersed houses. The one-storey, one-room house is inhabited by an extended family of three generations.

Men's dress is now semi-European but women's is still traditional, and includes two long artificial plaits of sheep wool. Their diet is predominantly vegetarian, with a wide variety of dishes made of flour. Meat is reserved for festive occasions.

Their traditional occupation is grain and legume farming on small terraced plots, with some sheep-, goat-, and cattle-breeding, a cow being regarded as equal to ten sheep.

KHUGHNUNI   see SHUGHNI.

A Khoikhoi hunter in South Africa

KHUMI   see PANKHO.

KHVARASHI   (s.d. Khuani, Khvarshal) An ethnic group living in the Caucasus mountains of northwest Daghestan, Russia, estimated as numbering 800. The Khvarashi language, consisting of two dialects, belongs to the Dido subgroup of the Avar-Andi-Dido group of the Ibero-Caucasian family. It is unwritten, and Avar is used as the literary language. The Khvarashi have been Sunni Muslims of the Shafi'i school since the eleventh century.

The Khvarishi are now undergoing an intensive process of consolidation into the AVAR. However, they retain their traditional women's headdress made of one piece of cloth instead of the two that is the norm among neighboring ethnic groups. Their two- to three-storey houses, however, are typical for the region. Their traditional economy is based on distant sheep-breeding.

KIAMTUARA   One of the eight "early states" of the HAYA.

KIANGAN   A subgroup of the IFUGAO.

KICHAI   A Native North American group, numbering about 200, living with the WICHITA on the Federal Trust Area in Oklahoma, U.S.A.

KICKAPOO   A Native North American group originally living in Wisconsin, but moved by the United States government several times until they were settled together with the CHOCTAW on the Kickapoo Tribe of Oklahoma Federal Trust Area.

Some Kickapoo left for Mexico in the 1850s, returning to the United States at the beginning of this century and settling in Texas and Oklahoma. Some also live on the Kickapoo Federal Reservation Area in Kansas. (see also MEXICANS)

KIGA   A people, numbering more than 100,000, living in the Kigezi Highlands in southwest Uganda, near Lake Edward along the borders with Rwanda and Zaire. Their language belongs to the Western Lacustrine Bantu-language group and is related to that of the NYORO. Culturally they are closely related to their northern neighbors, the Bantu agriculturalists in the Ankole region of Uganda and in Rwanda.

Living in small hamlets, the Kiga are mainly agriculturalists, growing vegetables, millet, and maize and breeding sheep, goats, and some cattle. While the latter are of some importance in their social system, the Kiga do not have a ethnically defined cattle-herding aristocracy as do their neighbors in the Ankole region. They are organized in a segmentary lineage-system consisting of polygynous households and a kinship organization in patrilineal exogamous clans. They constitute an independent peasant population, without an institutionalized political rule, and are not unified. Fights between the different clans were frequent.

In the early twentieth century the Kiga were involved in a war with the TUTSI of Rwanda, who tried to subjugate them. They were also frequently the target of attacks by groups of PYGMIES. The Kiga cult of female Nyabingi spirits, communicated with by priests, was mobilized against the TUTSI and later against the BRITISH.

Besides the Nyabingi cult, the Kiga worship the spirits of their ancestors and a remote god, as well as many spirits, to whom evil influence is ascribed. Kiga religious specialists are not organized hierarchically.

KIKUYU   (Gikuyu, Akikuyu) The largest people in Kenya, numbering some 4 million in 1979, the Kikuyu are concentrated in the center of the country. They speak Kikuyu and are Christians, due to their contact with Christian missionaries in the late eighteenth century.

They have no written records, and all that is known of their early history is told in legends and transmitted by tradition. The Kikuyu people are an amalgam of different groups, a product of a long process of intermingling. Originally nomads living by hunting, gathering, and herding of cattle, sheep, and goats, they have gradually evolved into sedentary agriculturists. They developed a free market system of economy long before their contact with Europeans. As time passed, due to increase in population and herds, the Kikuyu separated into three main ethnic groups, each developing along slightly different lines in language and in culture: the Kikuyu proper, the MERU, and the KAMBA.

Traditionally, each individual was a member of a family unit (*mbari* or *nyambu*) first and foremost; then a member of the clan (*moherega*). Uniting the entire group of family units and clans was the *mariika*, the system of age-grades, which transcended territorial or kinship groupings. Of importance was initiation through circumcision and clitoridectomy into adulthood and therefore full status in Kikuyu society. In their traditional culture can be detected, in microcosm, two features of life characteristic of contemporary

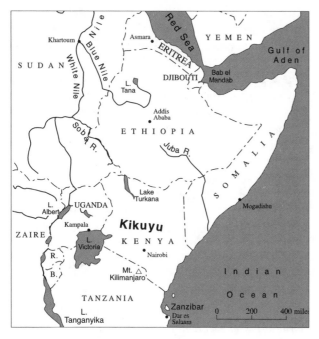

Kikuyu

Kenya: a basically egalitarian, democratic political system, and a productive expanding free market system of economy.

The Kikuyu are the most dominant and influential factor in Kenya's recent history. In the 1890s and early 1900s, the BRITISH, as rulers of Kenya, began to encourage European settlement in the highlands where the Kikuyu were living. This was the beginning of a long struggle accompanied by changes in the cultural, social, and political structures of the Kikuyu.

The Kikuyu led the struggle for Kenya's independence, with Jomo Kenyatta as their leader. Kenyatta is regarded as the "father" of the state, the *mzee* (honored elder), and was the first president of Kenya from 1963 until his death in 1978.

The most important stage in the Kikuyu struggle for independence was the Mau Mau rebellion which began in late 1952 and lasted until 1956. The cause of the rebellion was widespread unemployment and landlessness. It led to major social changes, particularly concerning land rights of Africans, which had been both ignored and denied them until then, and representation in government. These changes triggered the first exodus of Europeans out of Kenya, mainly to South Africa.

When Kenya gained its independence the Kikuyu occupied many of the highest government and military posts and were heavily represented in the business elite as long as Kenyatta, a Kikuyu himself, was the head of state. But after Kenyatta's death in 1978, the new president, Daniel arap Moi, favored his own KALENJIN people. The influence of the Kikuyu in the country was consequently reduced, and they moved to the opposition. (see also KENYANS)

KIL (Chil, Mnong Kil) A Mon-Khmer group in southern Vietnam, numbering over 10,000. Although they engage in slash and burn cultivation of rice, they own little land and often rent their fields from neighboring peoples. Hunting and gathering are also common. The Kil are often considered a subdivision of the MNONG.

KILENGE An ethnic group of approximately 5,000, living on the Pacific island of Bougainville within the state of Papua New Guinea, east of the mainland. They speak an indigenous local language.

The Kilenge are slash and burn cultivators whose main crops are sweet potatoes and taro. Although most are Catholics, many still believe in traditional spirits. Their ceremonies center around the life-cycle.

KILINGA An ethnic group, related to the BARIBA, living in Benin. The DOMPAGO are a subgroup of the Kilinga. (see also BENINIANS)

KIM see KRIM.

KIMBUNDU An ethnic group living south of the Dande River in Angola. They speak Kimbundu and are both Christians and adherents of traditional religions. Traditionally they were agriculturalists who grew cassava as a subsistence crop, but since the nineteenth century they have begun growing coffee for export.

The PORTUGUESE had a particularly strong influence upon their region. One group of Kimbundu, the Ambaca-speaking AMBAQUISTAS, were instrumental in the subjugation of Angola by the PORTUGUESE, but this created tension between them and other Kimbundu groups.

The Kimbundu produced the first Angolan literature.

KIMBY A subgroup of the NYAMWEZI.

KINNAUR (Kanowar) A Himalayan ethnic group living in the Khasa area of Himachal Pradesh, India. They differ ethnically and culturally from the KHASA. They are Buddhists who also worship various Hindu gods; their spiritual leaders are called lamas, and they practice polyandry.

The Kinnaur are a poverty-stricken tribe. They cultivate bathua, potatoes, koda, pulses, and wild fruits, which form their staple diet.

KINTAK A subgroup of the SEMANG.

KIOWA A large Native North American group numbering about 5,000, many of whom live today in the Kiowa Tribe Federal Trust Area with the COMANCHE and the CADDO. Traditionally they roamed the southern plains together with the COMANCHE, but were forced to move to the Indian Territory, Oklahoma, in the 1870s.

KIPSIGIS The largest people of the KALENJIN group, numbering 1 million, or c.4 percent of the population in Kenya. They occupy the highland region around Kericho town.

Traditionally Kipsigis family life is focused around the homestead. The homesteads are not grouped into villages but into a hierarchy of economic and political units. Christianity is practiced as well as traditional religious customs. Circumcision and clitoridectomy are the events of greatest significance in the extensive initiation ceremony which marks the transition from childhood to adulthood.

In the colonial period, the Kipsigis were active in the resistance against the BRITISH. Nowadays, as part of the KALENJIN, they enjoy a favored status because Kenya's president, Daniel arap Moi, is a member of this grouping.

Their main crops are pyrethrum, tea, and maize. Although they have a long tradition of cultivation, it is their other economic tradition, cattle-husbandry, which remains their passion. They have a history of herding, raiding and being raided in return in competition with the MASAAI, the KISII and the LUO.

KIPTANI A subgroup of the MARAKWET.

KIR A group of several thousand Hindu farmers found in western Madhya Pradesh, India. They are known for their devout religious practices, and some serve as priests for neighboring peoples.

KIRANT An ethnic group, numbering 500,000, living in Nepal, consisting of two main divisions, the LIMBOO and the RAI. Possessing their own religion and scripture, they are one of Nepal's ancient ethnic groups, and once ruled the country.

The LIMBOO speak a Limboo dialect, and adhere to Shiva Hinduism and Buddhism. Their main occupation

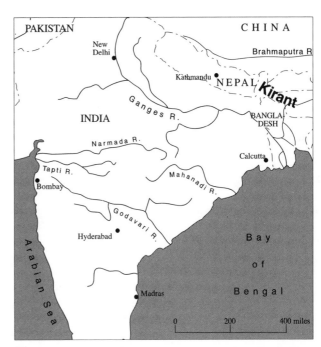

Kirant

is agriculture, growing rice in low-lying areas and potatoes, maize, wheat, and barley at higher altitudes. While over 90 percent of the LIMBOO are dependent on agriculture, some young LIMBOO seek employment in Malaya and India, and some join the Nepal State Army.

The RAI have pronounced Mongoloid features. They have a reputation of being absolutely fearless and have made a name for themselves in the Gurkha army. Their main occupation is agriculture, but some young men seek employment in India, Malaya, and Singapore.

KIRDI A generic term for a number of ethnic groups living in Chad and northern Cameroon. As practitioners of traditional religions, they fled the nineteenth-century *jihad* (Islamic holy war) of the FULANI and settled in their remote mountainous home, which remained underdeveloped during the period of colonial rule by the FRENCH. Many have since become Muslims, but have retained many pre-Islamic practices.

Important Sara-speaking groups include the MOUNDANG, with 100,000 people in the Mayo-Kebbi region of Chad and smaller numbers in Cameroon, the 80,000 TOUBOURI, who live mostly in Chad's Fianga region, and the MASSA, who live mainly in the Bongor sub-region of the Mayo-Kebbi region. Some 18,000 MUSGUM are closely related to these groups but speak Voloum instead of Sara. Other Kirdi groups include the MATAKAM, MOFU, GIZIGA, FALI, KAPSIKI, and DABA.

Although they constitute the majority population of northern Cameroon, the Kirdi never became an important political factor in the country. (see also CAMEROONIANS, SARA)

KIRGIZ   see QAZAQ, QYRGHYZ.

KIRGIZ-KAISAK   see QAZAQ.

KIRIBATI   see GILBERTESE.

KIRIRI   see CARIRI.

KIRTLE   see KARATA.

KISA   A group in Western Kenya, estimated as numbering 25,000; part of the LUHYA people. They speak Baluhya, a Western Bantu language. Most Kisa are Christians. A sense of Kisa identity still persists, despite acculturation into the broader LUHYA identity.

Most Kisa are agriculturalists; their main crops are maize, sukuma, and cassava.

KISAN   (Nagbansi, Nagesar, Nagesia) A people numbering 257,000 (1981), living in the states of Bihar, Orissa, and West Bengal, India. They speak Santali and Bhumij, of the Austro-Asiatic family, and Kurukh, of the Dravidian grouping. They are Hindus.

The Kisan raise dry, rain-fed crops. They live in hilly or dense jungle areas, which can be reached only by foot or pony.

Their houses are strong and substantial, containing rooms for sleeping and indoor work, and a kitchen with attached cattle-sheds and pigsties. They also rear poultry and goats.

Polygamy is practiced by the Kisan, although it is confined to those who can afford it. Conjugal relations cannot cross caste boundaries. (see also NAGESIA)

KISAN KORWA   see KORWA.

KISII   A people, numbering 1.5 million, living east of Lake Victoria, around Kisii town in Western Kenya. Their language, Kisii, is a Western Bantu one. They constitute the seventh largest ethnic group in Kenya.

Originally from Uganda, the Kisii people practice both agriculture and animal husbandry. Much of their income now comes from selling handicrafts, in the form of wooden and soapstone works, to tourists.

Most Kisii have converted to Christianity within the past century. Nevertheless, certain traditional rites still persist: boys continue to be initiated into manhood by group circumcision, and girls by clitoridectomy. The Kisii continue to live in scattered homesteads surrounded by agricultural land. (see also KENYANS)

KISSI   An ethnic group living in northwestern Liberia, in Upper Lofa County, where, together with the GOLA, they number around 200,000. They also live in southwestern Guinea, in the Guekedou and Kissidougou Regions, and in Sierra Leone in the eastern Province. They speak the Mel language and mostly practice traditional religions.

Before the arrival of the BRITISH, FRENCH, and AMERICO-LIBERIANS, the Kissi developed a centralized political system. In the late nineteenth and early twentieth century, the Kissi territory was divided between the French colony of Guinea, the British colony of Sierra Leone, and Liberia.

The Kissi in Liberia are one of the ethnic groups in conflict with the KRAHN ethnic group in an ongoing civil war. In Sierra Leone the Kissi have been largely influenced by the MENDE and many speak the Mende language. (see also LIBERIANS)

KISSII   An ethnic group of southern Tanzania living in the Rift Valley. According to the 1967 census they numbered 2,200. Their main economic activity lies in cultivating the land and in raising cattle. Their language belongs to the Bantu group of the Niger-Kordofan language family. They have been assimilated by the NYAKYUSA.

KISTIN   see INGUSH.

KITIMAT   A subgroup of the HAISLA.

KIVU   An ethnic group living in eastern Zaire.

KIWAI   An ethnic group of approximately 15,000, living in southern Papua New Guinea. They speak an indigenous regional language. They grow fruits and vegetables, hunt, and gather. They believe in a wide array of spirits, and many of them practice sorcery.

KIZIBA   One of the eight "early states" of the HAYA.

KLENG   A subgroup of the NGEH.

KLO   see KROBO.

KMRANG   A subgroup of the SEMANG.

KNOP NEUSE   see TSONGA.

KOBA   An ethnic group living in Botswana.

KOBCHI   A subgroup of the TIV.

KOCH   One of the BORO peoples living in Assam. (see also DIMASA-KACHARI)

KODOY   A subgroup of the MABA.

KOHATUR   see KOTA.

KOHISTANI   (Dard) A people numbering about 50,000 and living in Pakistan, between the northern reaches of the Indus River and the Afghanistan border. They speak several distinct Dardic dialects all influenced by the Burushaski language and grouped together by linguists as Kohistani. They have been devout Muslims since the eleventh century. The Kohistani are semi-nomadic, the men taking their flocks of sheep and goats to graze in higher elevations in the warmer summer months. Corn and millet cultivation in the more fertile valleys is generally the domain of the women.

The civil war in Afghanistan has resulted in some PASHTUN fleeing as refugees to the Kohistani lands, where they are slowly being integrated. Their effect on the local culture has yet to be determined. (see also MAIYANS)

KOHO   A generic term for several Mon-Khmer groups living in the mountainous region of southern Vietnam. The most important Koho group is the Sre (Cau Sre), numbering about 30,000. Other groups include the MA B'SRE, MA BLAO, and MA DODONG.

KOIARAI   An ethnic group of a few thousand living outside of Port Moresby on the southeastern coast of Papua New Guinea. They speak an indigenous local language.

KOKI   A people living in the southwest of the Buganda region in Uganda, bordering on the Ankole region. Their language is related to that of the TORO. They were politically organized in a kingdom of their own before they became incorporated into the kingdom of Buganda, ruled by the GANDA.

Like their neighbors, the Koki worship their ancestors, for whom they build shrines near their houses.

KOKKE   A subgroup of the HAMMAR.

KOL   An ethnic group numbering some 650,000, living in Bihar, Madhya Pradesh, Maharashtra, Orissa, and Rajasthan, India. They are Hindus.

The Kol, an ancient people of central India, are second only to the MUNDA as the largest Scheduled Tribe in India.

KOLAM   An ethnic group numbering 140,000 (1981), living in the states of Andhra Pradesh, Madhya Pradesh, and Maharashtra, in India. They speak Kolami, a member of the Dravidian family of languages.

Living near the GOND, the Kolam have adopted their lifestyle. They have a simple economic system. Many of them are forest laborers. They practice shifting cultivation and until recently possessed neither plows nor cattle. Even today many subsist by hoe cultivation on hill slopes.

KOLARIAN   A Munda people living in eastern India. (see also BHUMIJ, KORKU)

KOLCHA   An ethnic group, numbering about 100,000, living in the western Indian state of Gujarat. They speak Gujarati and are Hindus. Their economy is based on the provision of services to neighboring peoples.

Koli

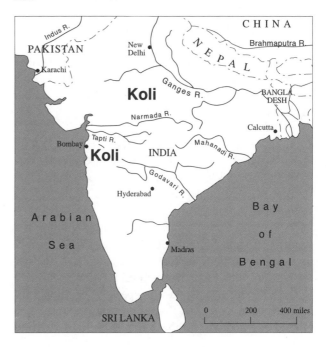

KOLHATI see NAT.

KOLI A Marathi-speaking people of unknown origins, numbering some 2 million. There are two subgroups: the Hill Koli, who live among other ethnic groups in the Madhya Pradesh State of India, and are involved in a number of service occupations (the term "coolie" is believed to derive from Koli); and the Sea Koli, who live mostly around the city of Bombay, where they are employed as fishermen.

KOLOLO (Makololo) An ethnic group living in southwest Zambia. They were involved in the slave trade. Their culture and social and political organization are similar to that of the LOZI, whom they subdued in 1836 after being forced to flee South Africa due to Zulu invasions in the early nineteenth century. In 1864 the LOZI defeated the Kololo and reestablished their kingdom.

KOMA I An ethnic group related to the LUYANA living in Zambia.

KOMA II (Ganza, Gunza) An ethnic group numbering 5,000, who live in the border triangle of the Blue Nile and Upper Nile Provinces of Sudan and Western Wallagga Province of Ethiopia. They speak a Nilotic language and adhere to traditional beliefs, but some are Sunni Muslims and Christians (Catholics, Sudanese Interior Mission). The Koma are sedentary agriculturalists and hunters.

During the late nineteenth century the Koma were strongly affected by the JABELAWI, Arab slave traders. They left their homes in the highland river valleys and took refuge in the Sudanese lowlands of the Nile. Between 1982 and 1991 the Koma territory on both sides of the Ethiopian border with Sudan was a retreat area for the Oromo Liberation Front (OLF). (see also ETHIOPIANS)

KOMI (s.d. Komi Nort, Komi Voityr) The 345,000 Komi and the 152,000 Komi Permyak regard themselves as one people with one language, despite their official division into two by the Soviet authorities.

They inhabit the Komi Autonomous Republic, the Komi Permyak Autonomous Province, and adjacent areas in the north of the Russian Federation. In the latter area are found the Zyuda Komi Permyak, who live in the Kirov province and who speak a transitional dialect between Komi and Komi Permyak; and the Yarza Komi Permyak, who although officially listed as Komi

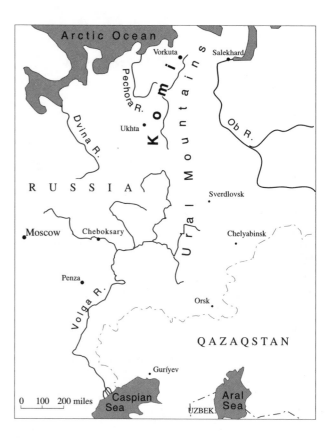

Komi

Permyak, speak (officially) a dialect of Komi. The IZHMI (s.d. Izva Tas: people of Izhma) form a distinct ethnic group among the Komi, having a strong NENTSY admixture. They live between the Izhma and Pechora Rivers in the Komi Autonomous Republic, the Yamalo-Nenets autonomous region, and the Tyumeni region.

The Komi and Komi Permyak languages belong to the Finno-Ugric group of the Uralic linguistic family. They are very close to and mutually intelligible with the language of the UDMURT. They were given the status of separate literary languages by the Soviet authorities and written in the cyrillic alphabet (although Komi was written in a mixed Roman-Cyrillic alphabet between 1918 and 1938).

Originally settled hunters and gatherers, the Komi and Komi Permyak became agriculturalists under the RUSSIANS. Many of them nowadays work also in the mining industry. Nominally Russian Orthodox Christians, both the Komi and the Komi Permyak have retained many of their traditional beliefs and rituals.

KOMI NORT, KOMI PERMYAK, KOMI VOITYR see KOMI.

KOMMA VOMNI A subgroup of the TIV.

KOMONO A subgroup of the SENUFO.

KONAMBEMBE An ethnic group related to the SANGA, living in northern Congo.

KONANGI One of the TENDA ethnic groups living in western Africa.

KONDA DORA An ethnic group, numbering 17,000 (1981), living in the states of Andhra Pradesh and Orissa, in India. Their language belongs to the Dravidian family.

The Konda Dora practice slash and burn cultivation on hill slopes. Their scanty crops are supplemented by minor forest produce.

KONDA KAPU An ethnic group, numbering some 35,000, inhabiting Andhra Pradesh, Karnataka, Kerala, and Tamil Nadu, India. They speak Telugu, a Dravidian language. They are primarily agriculturalists and agricultural laborers.

KONDA REDDI An ethnic group, numbering about 100,000, living in Andhra Pradesh, Kerala, and Tamil Nadu, in India. They speak Telugu, a language of the Dravidian group.

A Hindu grouping, the Konda Reddi adhere mainly to Shaivism (the worship of Shiva) but also revere a variety of other deities. They are basically agriculturists, and practice *podu* cultivation.

KONDOMA see SHORS.

KONGA A small Tamil-speaking group found in the southern Indian state of Kerala. They are primarily laborers.

KONGO (Bakongo) A people living in western Zaire, where they number around 10 million; in southern Congo, where they number around 850,000; and in northern Angola, where they number around 600,000. Two subgroups living in Angola are the SOSSO and the SORONGO (Solongo). Their language, Kikongo, is one of Zaire's four national languages.

The first contact of the Kongo with Europeans was as early as the fifteenth century. The PORTUGUESE traded with them and tried to convert them to Catholicism, but their conversion was only superficial. Protestant missionaries who arrived in their region in the nineteenth century found only vague signs of Christianity. At first the Kongo joined the missions and became Protestants but later an independent church was formed by Simon Kimbangu, regarded by the Kongo as a prophet. This is still the largest and most important independent church in Africa and most Kongo are members.

The Kongo formed a great kingdom that reached its zenith in the fifteenth and sixteenth centuries. During the seventeenth century the kingdom disintegrated but Kongo linguistic and cultural dominance continued to be felt. Towards the end of the nineteenth century the kingdom was conquered and divided by the PORTUGUESE, the FRENCH, and Leopold II of Belgium (in the early twentieth century the part that was the king's private territory was taken by the Belgian parliment and became Belgian territory). Most Kongo lived in the Belgian Congo (today Zaire).

During the period of colonial rule by the BELGIANS the Kongo seized educational opportunities and, thanks to their proximity to major cities including Leopoldville (Kinshasa), were well represented in the colonial civil service. They were, however, among the first groups to demand greater liberties and eventually independence. Their anti-colonial struggle was ethnic in character and included ideas of rebuilding the Kongo kingdom. In 1950 they formed the Association des Kongo to protect their culture from foreign influences in Leopoldville. Later this organization became a political party called the Alliance des Kongo.

Kongo

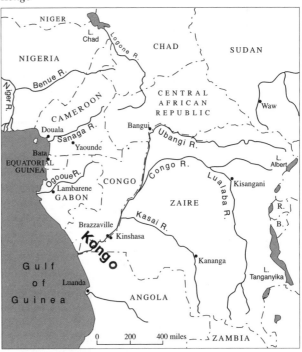

After independence the Kongo party leader, Joseph Kasavubu, became president of Zaire and supported a Federation in which the Kongo would have considerable autonomy. He was deposed, however, by Joseph Mobutu (Mobutu Sese Seko) in 1965, before his program could be enacted.

Following the Katanga crisis of 1960–1963, Zaire was divided into twenty-one provinces. The Kongo occupy the Congo Central province. They still dominate the government and civil service and are everywhere present in Zaire's capital.

The Kongo of Angola were also active in the decolonization struggle against the PORTUGUESE. In 1961 a revolt of Kongo farmers that was brutally crushed by the PORTUGUESE triggered the war of liberation that continued until independence in 1975. (see also ANGOLANS, CONGOLESE, YAKA, ZAIREANS)

KONIANKE   A subgroup of the MALINKE living in Guinea.

KONJO   A small ethnic group living to the west of the TORO in the Ruwenzori area in western Uganda. They speak Lukonjo, a language of the Western Lacustrine Bantu-language group.

Their main economic activity is hoe agriculture, producing cassava, yams, and coffee as cash crops. They keep no cattle, but raise sheep, goats, and pigs. On Lake Albert they also practice fishing. The Konjo are ironsmiths, potters, and weavers. They were cattle-herders until their herds were raided and driven away by the GANDA and NYORO. Culturally, they are related to the neighboring AMBO and SONGORO. Their kinship relations are patrilineal and they practice circumcision.

The land of the Konjo was once part of the Toro kingdom. For centuries they were the target of raids by the NYORO, the TORO, and the NKOLE.

Their religion places great emphasis on ancestor-spirits, for whom shrines of grass and twig are made. The Konjo also have religious specialists such as healers (medicine-men). The main spirit is Nyabingi.

KONKO   A subgroup of the BAHNAR.

KONKOMBA   (s.d. Kpunkpamba) An ethnic group living in northern Togo and northeastern Ghana. They speak a Gurma dialect.

The Konkomba had no centralized political organization. After World War I they found themselves divided between the territories mandated to the BRITISH and the FRENCH in Togo. In the late 1950s they voted against the union of British Togo with Ghana. Their neighbors the NANUMBA, however, voted for the union and won. The resulting Konkomba resentment led the Togo Konkomba to cross the border in 1981 to join the Ghana Konkomba in an interethnic war against the NANUMBA. Hundreds of NANUMBA were killed.

KONO   An ethnic group living in the Kono District of Sierra Leone and in small numbers in southeast Guinea and Liberia. Many Kono speak the Mende language. They practice either traditional religions or Christianity; their main occupation is agriculture.

According to their tradition the Kono immigrated to Sierra Leone, together with the VAI, in search of salt. After a long journey, part of the group, the Kono, stayed behind while the rest continued the search. Until colonization by the BRITISH in the late nineteenth century, the Kono were often attacked by the MENDE. (see also VAI)

KONOG   A subgroup of the NYAMWEZI.

KONSO   An ethnic group, numbering 100,000, who live north of the Sagan River in southwest Gemu Gofa Province, Ethiopia. They speak an eastern Cushitic language, and are mostly Sunni Muslims, with some following Ethiopian Orthodox Christianity or traditional beliefs. They are sedentary agriculturalists and weavers. In the regional division of labor, they had a special exchange-relationship with the Borona-OROMO. The social structure of the Konso is marked by age- and generation-grading. (see also ETHIOPIANS, OROMO)

KONTA   An ethnic group, numbering 45,000 (1980s), who live in eastern Kefa Province, Ethiopia. Their language belongs to the Omotic grouping, and they are either Ethiopian Orthodox Christians, Sunni Muslims, or adherents to traditional beliefs.

The Konta are grain- and ensete-farmers, and include the KOYSHA, KUCHA, and KULLO (Dawaro) ethnic groups. The small polities of the Konta were bordered on the west by the empire of Kafa, and on the east by the kingdom of Walayta. During the late eighteenth century, the Konta became dependent on the KAFICHO.

KONY   A subgroup of the SABAOT.

KONYA   A subgroup of the MALINKE living in Guinea.

KONYAK An ethnic group of 84,000 (1981), connected to the BONDO of Orissa, living in the Mon district of Nagaland, India. Since they are close to the Myanmar (Burma) border, they have economic and matrimonial ties with the people of that country, too. Many Konyak also live in the western part of Myanmar.

The Konyak are one of the largest ethnic groups in Nagaland, but not among the most prosperous. They also use opium, first planted in their area by the BRITISH in order to better control them. They practice slash and burn cultivation and the men are expert wood carvers, who make long drums in the shape of a canoe.

Leaders among the Konyak are called *Angs*; the position is hereditary and all-powerful. (see also NAGA)

KOO see KHO.

KOOTENAI see KOOTENAY.

KOOTENAY (Kootenai) A Native North American group, numbering about 600, living in British Columbia, Canada; a few hundred more live on the Federal Reservations in Idaho and Montana (with the FLATHEAD). Traditionally they lived on the west side of the Rocky Mountains, crossing seasonally to hunt buffalo.

KORA A group, numbering 137,000 (1981), living in the states of Bihar, Orissa, Maharashtra, and West Bengal, in India. The Kora speak Mundari, a language of the Dravidian family. They are closely related to the VODDE of Andhra Pradesh.

The Kora are Hindus and follow Hindu social customs. Their social status is very low. Village administration is left in the hands of a village head known as *majhi*, and his assistance, or *kotai*. Both offices are hereditary.

KORAGA An ethnic group, numbering 17,000 (1981), living in the states of Karnataka, Kerala, and Tamil Nadu, India. Their dialect belongs to the Dravidian family of languages.

The Koraga are regarded as a backward group in southern India, and in some areas they are treated more as a depressed caste than as a tribal group. They are traditionally non-vegetarians, and rice is also a staple of their diet. Agriculture is an important occupation for a very large number of Koraga, although they are also employed as scavengers and sweepers in towns.

KORANKO An ethnic group living in the Koinadugu District of Sierra Leone and in the northern part of the Kissidougou Region, Guinea. They are a branch of the MALINKE and mostly adhere to traditional religions. (see also SIERRA LEONEANS)

KOREANS An ethnically homogeneous Mongoloid people numbering about 60 million, who inhabit the Korean Peninsula, now divided between North and South Korea. There are also concentrated Korean communities in China, Japan, the United States, and the former Soviet Union.

It is generally believed that the Korean people's ancestors were migrants from the north who moved to the peninsula 4,000 years ago. Their name is derived from the Koryo, a dynasty that ruled the peninsula from 913 to 1392. Since at least the seventh century, when the peninsula was politically unified, Koreans have shared a common history, language, and culture. The Korean Peninsula is one of the few places in the world where no other sizable ethnic minority exists.

Although racially similar to the CHINESE AND JAPANESE, Koreans have a distinctive language with six major dialectic divisions, believed to have developed from a Tungustic prototype thousands of years ago. The most significant external influence on the language was Chinese, from which many words were borrowed. A system of transcribing Korean using Chinese characters was used until 1446, when the native and phonetic Korean alphabet, known as Hungul, was introduced. Hungul is claimed to have been the first phonetic alphabet in East Asia, but Chinese still remained the official writing system in Korea for some time. A mixed Chinese-Korean writing system, introduced in 1894, is still in use in South Korea.

The ancient religious beliefs of the Koreans included animism and shamanism. Buddhism reached Korea between the fourth and sixth centuries, and Confucianism, which had a decisive influence on the peninsula, was Korea's state religion from the fourteenth to the early nineteenth centuries. Christianity, introduced in the nineteenth century, failed to win mass appeal.

Although contacts with the CHINESE and JAPANESE have had a marked influence on Korean culture, and despite Japanese colonization in the early twentieth century, Koreans have maintained a separate and distinctive national identity. Following the Korean War (1950–1953), however, the peninsula was divided into two countries, one supported by the United States, and the other by the Soviet Union and China. Thirty-two percent of Koreans live in North Korea, which has a Marxist ideology and an economy based on the doctrine of self-sufficiency; the 68 percent residing in

318

above: A Korean couple
below: Koreans at a picnic

South Korea have a capitalist system and an export-oriented economy. Korean is the official language of both countries, and the people share the same cultural heritage although, being more exposed to the outside world, South Korea is more westernized.

The estimated 4.8 million Koreans living in China are relatively new immigrants who settled in the Jilin and Heilongjiang Provinces of China after the Japanese annexation of Korea in the mid-nineteenth century. Many Koreans living in China continue to use the Korean language.

The estimated 600,000 Koreans in Japan constitute that country's largest ethnic minority. They began settling there in the 1920s, when Korea was a colony of Japan. Most first-generation Koreans were brought over as forced laborers and military draftees to compensate for the manpower shortage resulting from the wartime economy. Some poor peasants also migrated to Japan in search of work. Although most of the present-day Korean population were born in Japan, have never been to Korea, and do not speak Korean, they are legally aliens. They are usually subject to discrimination in housing, employment, marriage, education, and social welfare.

KOREKORE An important Shona-speaking people living in Zimbabwe, numbering about 1.7 million (one-sixth of Zimbabwe's population). They live in the country's far north. The SHANGWE (Bashangwe), living along the Bumi River southeast of Lake Kariba, are a Korekore subgroup. (see also ZIMBABWEANS)

KORKU An ethnic group, numbering 183,000 (1981), living in the states of Madhya Pradesh and Maharashtra, in India. They speak Munda, a member of the Austro-Asiatic family of languages. They are an offshoot of the MUNDA or Kolarian ethnic group, akin to the KORWA.

The primary occupation of the Korku is cultivation, but they also collect forest produce and work as day laborers.

KORO I An ethnic group living in the mountainous central region of the Indonesian island of Sulawesi (Celebes). (see also TORADJA)

KORO II A subgroup of the TIV.

KORWA A people, numbering 40,000 (1981), living in the states of Madhya Pradesh, Bihar, and West Bengal, in India. Their language resembles those of the MUNDA and SANTAL, members of the Austro-Asiatic family.

The Korwa are Hindus. Their principal subdivisions are the Diharia or Kisan Korwa, those who live in villages and cultivate, and the Paharia Korwa of the hills, who are also called Benwaria because of their practice of *bewar*, or shifting cultivation. (see also KORKU)

KORYAK Almost all the 9,000 Koryak live in the Koryak Autonomous Province in northeast Siberia, Russia. They are closely related ethnically, culturally, and linguistically to the CHUKCHI and the ITELMEN. They are divided into nine tribes.

The Koryak literary language was established in 1932 and a Roman alphabet was adopted. In 1937 the alphabet was changed to Cyrillic.

The Koryak were traditionally divided between the CHAVCHYVAV, the settled, mainly fishermen on the coast, and the NYMYLYN, the nomadic reindeer-breeders inland. In the 1920s half the Koryak were nomads. Although most of them have been settled ever since, some of them remain semi-nomads. They practice their traditional religion.

KOSHI An ethnic group living in Angola.

KOSIAN see BALANTAK.

KOSRAE ISLANDERS (Kosraeans) A Micronesian-speaking people of about 6,500 who inhabit eight islands located in the eastern part of the Caroline Islands chain. The Kosrae (formerly Kusaie) island group was administered by Germany at the beginning of the twentieth century, under a Japanese mandate from 1920, and under U.S. sovereignty from 1945. At present the Kosrae island group is a member of the Federated States of Micronesia, associated with the United States.

The Kosraean society at the village level is dependent on subsistence cultivation and fishing. Postmarital residence is usually patrilocal. The population is divided between Roman Catholics and Protestants.

KOSSI (Bakossi) An ethnic group living in the greater part of the anglophone Meme region of Cameroon. Their relationship with their francophone neighbors, especially BAMILEKE who came as immigrants to the region, have been particularly tense and culminated in 1967 in a massacre of over 230 BAMILEKE by Kossi in the town of Tombel.

KOTA I (Bakota) An ethnic group living mostly in northeastern Gabon, where, with related groups, they number about 144,000. A few thousand Kota also live in the adjacent regions of Congo. In the precolonial period they faced a number of invasions from the POUNOU, KELE, and FANG, and gradually intermingled with these groups.

KOTA II (Kohatur, s.d. Kov) An ethnic group numbering a few thousand living in the Nilgiri Hills of the southern Indian state of Tamil Nadu. They speak a Dravidian language closely related to Toda, and most also speak Tamil or Malayalam. They are virtually all Hindus although they maintain their own names for important Hindu deities.

The Kota are agriculturalists who produce vegetables and legumes. The surplus is traded with neighboring peoples for grains. Tea is an important cash crop. Traditionally, they also provided their neighhbors with crafts and ornaments and were competent musicians who traded their skill for food, services which are no longer required.

The Kota have taken to modernization with great zeal. Educational standards are high and they are disproportionately represented on the local level in white-collar professions, including medicine and government.

KOTAWARINGAN An ethnic group living on the Indonesian island of Kalimantan (Borneo). (see also DAYAK)

KOTIA An ethnic group, numbering 51,000 (1981), located in the states of Andhra Pradesh and Orissa, India. They speak Oriya, a member of the Indo-Aryan family of languages.

The Kotia are farmers and day laborers. They collect minor forest produce for sale in weekly markets. Most have given up shifting slash and burn cultivation in favor of settled agriculture.

KOTOKO An ethnic group, numbering some 15,000, living along the lower course of the Logone River and the Chari River and Delta in Chad and on the other side of the border in Cameroon. Mostly Muslims, they speak a number of related dialects and do not have a common language.

The Kotoko did not have one kingdom but lived in separated and independent walled cities that owed nominal allegiance to the Bornu empire. During the periods of colonial rule by the GERMANS in Cameroon and the FRENCH in Chad, some of these political entities were split in two. After World War I all the Ko-

toko territory came under French rule but remained in two different colonies: French Cameroon and Chad.

KOTOKOLI (Temba) An ethnic group, numbering about 120,000, living in the Sokodo area of Togo. They speak the Tem language and are mostly Muslims.

KOTTUU A subgroup of the OROMO.

KOUKA An ethnic group, numbering about 30,000 living primarily in the Batha Region and among the BULALA along the eastern coast of Lake Chad. They are mostly Muslims.

KOUPUI An agricultural group found in northern India.

KOYA (s.d. Dorla Satam) An ethnic group, numbering 475,000 (1981), located in Andhra Pradesh, Karnataka, Maharashtra, and Orissa, in India. Most of the Koya in Andhra Pradesh speak Telugu, but some speak Koya. The Koya also speak Gondi, a dialect of the Dravidian family spoken by the GOND.

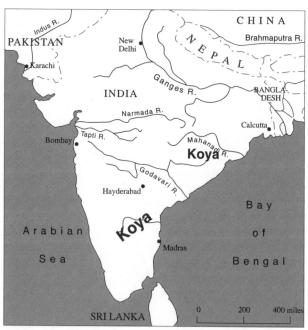

Koya

The Koya are Hindus, and they also worship *Bhudevi* (the earth mother), who is responsible for their agriculture.

Mexican villagers at a local store

A Ladakhi woman prepares butter tea, which is served frequently to welcome guests.

The Lhamo Healers of Ladakh

When, during a 1981 expedition to the Himalayas, the German doctor Walter A. Frank became severely ill, he was healed by a local female shaman in the remote Indian town of Sabu, in the northern region of Ladakh. Here is his account of this remarkable healing process:

"In the winter of 1981, my research expedition led me to Ladakh, a unique but inaccessible mountain region between the northwest Himalayas, Karakorum, and Tibet. Unfortunately, I had contracted a cold in Delhi, which soon developed into viral bronchitis and sinusitis. Soon, a three-and-a-half day cycle evolved: one day of relative wellbeing, one day of exhaustion, and a third day of fever. None of the medications, such as sulfonamide from my expedition pharmacy, had any impact whatsoever; nor did antibiotics. I hoped that the mountain air of Ladakh would help."

"After three weeks we found a pilot to fly us to Leh, the capital of Ladakh. Even there, however, my condition failed to improve. One morning, I drove to Sabu, a village about seven five miles east of Leh, to visit Sonam Zangmo. She was a *lhamo*, a "wise woman," reputed to have access to the heal-

Ladakh — also the land of Buddhist prayer flags, which are believed to carry blessings

ing powers of *lha*s (spirits). With my last strength I carried myself to her hut. After a friendly reception, I was invited to a cup of Tibetan butter tea. Then, however, she informed me that she was not feeling well and had no time to perform the healing. On request, I described to her my miserable condition. Suddenly, she started to tremble and to roll her eyes, murmuring, "The god is coming! The god is coming!" and fell into a trance. Her two daughters rushed to dress her in her ceremonial costume; the *lhamo* then lapsed into a singsong, squeaky voice and knelt before the house altar."

"I had received some information about the ritual process from a colleague who had previously been in Ladakh. While the *lhamo* was still busy with her prepara-

tions, my symptoms suddenly disappeared completely. My respiratory tract felt free and clear as never before. Thereafter, she began to suck at my solar plexus. As it was described to me later, following each suck she spat pitch-black mucus into a plate and then rinsed her mouth with clean water, spitting it out before continuing to suck the black illness from my body. To the astonishment of my very skeptical companions, my health was instantly restored. I felt as if my five weeks of severe illness had never been. I feared a relapse, but it did not occur, and I was able to continue immediately with my research."

"For me this miraculous healing was a key experience, one that induced me to

the world. On an expedition to the Himalayas, German doctor, Walter A. Frank, was healed by a shaman like the one pictured

urn my scientific interest even more to he phenomena of shamans and shamanstic healing. Right after my return to Leh, visited the teacher of Sonam Zango, the *hamo* from Tikse. He lived in an impressive farmstead just outside a village, bove which towered the majestic Cloister Mountain. Again I was lucky; atients were already waiting and I was ble to observe from close the ritual neeling in front of the altar and a sacrice of rice: all the participants received ice in their hands, which they dispersed s an offering to the gods and spirits."

"The healing again took place by sucking n the solar plexus, this time with a copper ube about seven inches long and half an nch in diameter. During the whole process an exuberent mood prevailed. The doctor joked with his patients, scolding them for their unhealthy lifestyle, particularly if they happened to be heavy smokers. Payment usually consisted of a few coins, however, some patients did not pay at all."

"At last, my turn came. First the *lhamo* sucked my neck and then again at my solar plexus. At the end he produced a piece of bone from my hip, which he presented to me. He repeated this treatment twice and extracted a small stone and a piece of goatskin from other parts of my body."

"I know on the base of scientific research that producing such objects is possible. But whether those from Tikse were genuine remains doubtful, because all three items were small enough to have fitted into the copper tubes. Shamans undoubtedly cheat from time to time in order to impress their clients with their skills. Nonetheless, this does not alter the success of the process, as proven through my spontaneous healing."

"Shamanistic healing does not fit easily into our scientifically oriented conception of the world. Generally, such phenomena are explained as charlatanism or, more generously, miracles. However, recent studies in physics have put into question our prevailing concepts about causality in the natural sciences and compel us to reevaluate basic assumptions about the world in which we live. Here the various disciplines (both traditional and modern) can learn from each other."

The commemoration of deceased ancestors, often celebrated with sacrifices, is an important element in all festivities and religious ceremonies of the Malagasy.

The Cult of the Dead in Madagascar

In Madagascar a natural death, whether from a severe illness or old age, results in the spirit returning home to the land of its ancestors and to God. Sudden, unexplained deaths are usually blamed on spells cast by a hostile *mpamosavy* (harmful magician). Although suicides bring shame on the deceased's family, even they are buried with all honors. In Madagascar a distinctive ceremonial system has developed around death and burial. Its striking monuments can be admired throughout the island.

After passing away (preferably in the presence of family) a coin is placed on the forehead of the deceased; it will serve as

the soul's fare money in its passage to the next world. Since the burial or reburial is a prolonged process, the corpse is protected from decay with phenoline injections. It is then placed in a zinc coffin, and carried to the highland home of its ancestors. There, family burial-chambers, built from stone and equipped with individual burial niches, are found. Should the family be unable to afford to transfer the corpse, it is buried temporarily in a local cemetery. Only after at least two years have elapsed, is it brought to its ancestral home, usually in a simple coffin made of wood and transported on the roof of a taxi.

Families unable to afford an expensive interment bury their loved ones on the morning immediately following death. The corpse is wrapped in a mat or piece of cloth and occassionally placed in a coffin made of wooden planks. It is then lowered into a shallow pit and covered with soil and stone slabs. The deceased

is buried with personal belonging (clothes, ornaments, etc.) and pierce plates are placed on top of the grave.

Designs of graves vary considerably The BEZANOZANO, Christian fishermen living along the coast, affix a wooden cross to their graves, as well as the traditional fishnets and boat paddles. The SAKALAVA, on the other hand, erec graves marked by wooden figures, characterized by frank eroticism as well a by their depiction of scenes from every day life in Madagascar.

In the eastern parts of the island the dead are buried in the forest. Coffins are placed on the ground, on a platform with a roof, or in a wooden hut to protect them from the elements. Among the ANTANOSY who live in southeastern Madagascar, the forest graveyard is levelled. At marked spots, upright stones, arranged in a circle and adorned with wooden pillars and the horns of sacrificial cattle, are erected for

A woodcarver preparing a death pillar for a member of the Maroseranana royal family.

the deceased, This is a practice commonly found in Indonesia and Southeast Asian, and an indication of the origins of the MALAGASY in that region.

The VAZIMBA of the Manombolo River valley bury their dead in mountain caves. Every year the remains of the deceased are exhumed, washed in the sand of the Manombolo River, and reburied.

In previous centuries only members of royal families had the right to be buried in stone graves. Today the practice is customary among all wealthy families. In recent decades, particularly in the south, an entirely new custom has evolved from this practice. Professional gravebuilders now erect huge grave buildings, sometimes of concrete. During the actual burial an additional small house, complete with windows and mirrors, is built for the individual grave, and sometimes a sarcophagus is fashioned. At the head and foot of the sarcophagus, "male" and "female" stones are inserted.

In the south the favorite cattle of the deceased is often slaughtered to mark the building of a grave or a burial. Their horns are then attached to the grave so that the animals' souls can unite with those of their owner.

After the kings of the Mahafaly State lost power in the early twentieth century, many simple peasants started to keep large herds of cattle as a status symbol. They also adopted burial customs hitherto restricted to royalty.

During the construction of a grave, the coffin is stored in a nearby hut. A fire is kept burning day and night and a guard keeps vigil over the site. Often the widow of the deceased remains with the corpse until interment, as was the custom with departed kings.

In the highlands it is customary to rebury the dead during the cool season. Once it has been returned to its ancestral home, the corpse is carried through the village and fields along a circuitous route, escorted in a procession and accompanied by musicians playing drums, flutes, and trumpets. The soul must be confused so that it will never find its way back to the village. At the same time, any dead who, until now, were temporarily buried near the family grave are reinterred. Yet even for those already buried, interment is not final. Every year, they are carried out, washed, wrapped in new shrouds of coarse, painted silk, and carried back to their niches.

A wooden display on a grave contains depictions of the everyday life of the Malagasy.

Secret Societies: the Lodges of the Powerful

Secret societies are not unique to Melanesia. There, however, and especially in New Britain and the surrounding islands of Papua New Guinea, they play a particularly prominent role in the social life of the community.

The existence of these societies is not what is secret. Rather, it is the knowledge of cult rituals, objects (including a variety of masks and flutes), and meeting places that is kept secret, and revealed only to a trusted circle of initiated members.

In patriarchal societies such as Melanesia, women are, of course, excluded from secret societies on principle. Even among adult males, power and material wealth are preconditions for acceptance. Nor are these associations limited to a single village; members can be found throughout a much wider region.

The best known Melanesian secret society is the Dukduk of the TOLAI, who inhabit the Gazelle Peninsula of New Britain. Members are divided into two ranks, each with distinctive masked costumes. The higher rank, Tubuan, can only be acquired by inheritance or through a substantial payment of shell-money. This rank is characterized as "mothers" to the second rank, the Dukduk, their "children."

The rank of Tubuan demands considerable personal expenditure. Members had to arrange numerous celebrations or risk humiliation at the hands of associates.

A prospective new member of the Dukduk requires the patronage of a Tubuan-rank member (his "godparent"), to sponsor and present his application. This godparent is usually the father or uncle of the novice, and is responsible for him until the termination of the initiation ceremony. If an application is accompanied by a sufficiently large payment, it is routinely accepted.

Soon after, members assemble for the initiation ceremony, which takes place at a secret cult site. Usually, the location and function of the site is common knowledge among the entire community, but only cult members have access to it. Outsiders may face severe punishment even for just trying to approach it. At the initiation ceremony, all those present are

Masks are an essential element of the secret societies of Melanesia. Cult objects such as flutes are entrusted only to a select circle of initiates.

arranged in a circle, with the novices in the middle. The master of ceremonies suddenly appears, wearing his Tubuan mask, and commences striking the novices with a stick; he is soon joined in this pursuit by other members. When the beating is over, godparents pay shell-money to all the other members present. The master of ceremonies then

lifts his secret mask and instructs the novices in the secret dances and rites of the society.

On the next day the novices receive their Dukduk masks and, rendered wholly unrecognizable by their disguise, dance through the village demanding payments from each hut. When this ceremony is completed, all the Dukduk

Two Dukduks (left) and a Tubuan. An early twentieth century photograph from the Gazelle Penisula of New Britain, then a German colony. Today, it is a part of the state of Papua New Guinea.

Dukduk secret associations still exist, as shown in this contemporary photo of Tubuan masks.

masks are "killed" — burnt. The Tubuan masks remain untouched. All phases of the ceremony are accompanied by lavish celebrations, making them an expensive affair.

Secret societies once demanded tribute, in the form of food or shell-money, from all the inhabitants of their area, an action that sometimes seemed akin to extortion. The society decided how much each individual or family should pay, and payments developed into a form of retributive law-enforcement. Offences against social mores and even crimes were dealt with through escalated payment demands. Since all the powerful men of the community were members of secret societies, there was no practical means of opposing ther demands.

These societies benefited their members in the form of respect and material advantages. Secret societies tended to serve the interests of their members rather than the social or religious interests of the community at large. Yet, although they functioned as exclusive clubs that enriched themselves at the expense of the public, they would sometimes arrange impressive festivities to demonstrate their generosity. Secret societies exploited the public's fear of the power wielded by members and the violent methods sometimes employed to achieve their ends.

Known less for their secret associations than for their cargo cults are many of the inhabitants of Vanuatu. They believe that a return to their traditional lifestyle will lead to a Golden Age, wherein they will acquire the great riches of the white man.

In a community with few organized political and legal organizations, secret societies were often the only institutions to maintain order. This somewhat mitigates the rather negative image of these societies that might result from an examination of their often brutal and arbitrary methods.

Because they acted in secret and were not answerable to any external authority, secret societies were vehemently opposed by church and state. Nevertheless, some traditional secret societies still survive. Although they have lost their political significance, they have retained their status as an assembly of notables.

The Yurt: The House of the Nomads

The traditional dwelling for many Turkic- and Mongolian- speaking nomadic peoples (qazaqs, qyrghyz, mongols) living in the Eurasian steppe is the yurt, a structure consisting of a cylindrical trunk and conical (among the mongols) or lightly arched (among the Turkic peoples) roof. Its fundamental building element is a wooden framework, including a door, grill, roof poles, and a circular aperture opening to allow the escape of smoke. Among the eastern mongols, two posts support this last opening. Sometimes a wooden floor is added to the structure. The framework is traditionally made from willow wood, (in modern times, the use of trucks for the transportation of materials has enabled nomads to use heavy larch wood as well), and is covered with felt mats. The most distinctive element of the yurt is the grill.

One wall of the structure consists of about forty long, flat strips, arranged one on top of the other in the shape of a grill. At the crossing-points they are drilled and bound together with short strips of leather. The grills are movable and easily dismantled. When set up, they reach a height of up to five feet. A wall has fifteen "heads," as the upper crosspoints of the poles are called; between five and six

Qazaqs in a yurt; the structure is also used by Mongols.

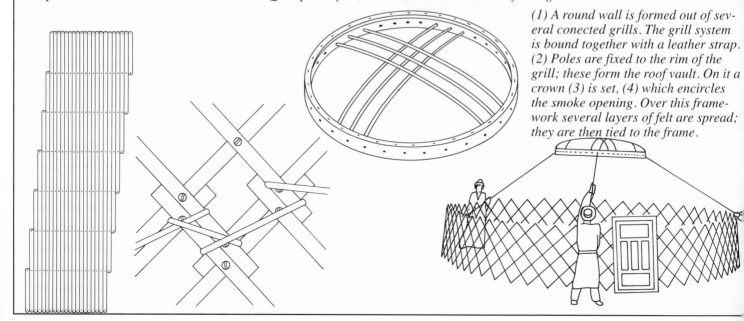

(1) A round wall is formed out of several conected grills. The grill system is bound together with a leather strap. (2) Poles are fixed to the rim of the grill; these form the roof vault. On it a crown (3) is set, (4) which encircles the smoke opening. Over this framework several layers of felt are spread; they are then tied to the frame.

walls bound together form the trunk of the yurt. To the south (among the mongols) or east (among the Turkic peoples), an opening is left for a door, consisting of side posts, lintel, and a relatively high threshold. The threshold is considered holy and may not be tread on. The door opening, originally closed with a piece of rollable felt, is now generally protected by one or two painted or carved door-wings.

The structure's framework is held together by a wide belt of wood at the height of the upper third of the grill. This belt is of decisive importance, since it bears the whole weight of the roof which, under the lower ends of the roof-poles, presses outward against the heads of the grills. The lower ends of the roof poles are fixed with a loop to the heads of the grills; the top ends are fitted into pre-prepared holes drilled into the smoke-opening. This last item is made of of two connected pieces of bent wood; its total diameter is about four feet. Over the wooden frame huge felt mats, not penetrable by light or water, are secured by horse-, camel-, or yak-hair ropes. It is customary among some Turkic peoples to place decorative raffia or reed mats between the grill and the felt.Finally, the smoke opening is covered with one or two felt pieces. During the daytime and in the warm season, these are thrown back, so that light can penetrate and smoke may escape. The occupants of the yurt are able to assess the time of day by reference to the angle of the sunrays penetrating the yurt through the smoke hole. Inside the yurt the space is divided into different functional areas. In the middle stands the stove, behind it, as seen from the entrance, is the seat of honor, on which the master of the house or important guests are seated. Two chests, either painted or decorated with metal fittings, are found against the back wall; these contain clothing and other valuable items. Using the seat of honor as a base point, the left side of the yurt looking from the seat of honor toward the door, is the domain of the lady of the house. There are found shelves for household utensils and food, a wooden bed, and a small cupboard. The right side belongs to the men; stored there are arms, saddles, a large bridle, and a big leather sack containing sour, fermented milk.

The yurt is an eminently practical and well-designed dwelling given the geographic, climactic, and economic conditions of the region. It is easily folded and transported, weighing just under 900 pounds when folded. It can be carried by just a single camel, an essential precondition for the nomadic lifestyle. Humidity causes the wool in the felt covering of the yurt to swell, making it entirely waterproof; moreover, the natural fat content of the wool enables it to repel water. Although not anchored to the ground, the yurt is little affected by the raging storms of the steppes because of its spherical shape. Despite its great strength, the light wooden frame is elastic enough to withstand even the heaviest storms.

Detail from a decorative wooden door of a Yurt. Felt doors also provide adequate protection from the elements.

A Kwakiutl cemetery. The colored woodcarvings represent family coats of arms.

The Totem-pole and the Potlach of the Northwest American Coast

The long, narrow, coastal strip along the Pacific Ocean, between southeastern Alaska and northern California, as well as the outlying islands, is home to the Northwest Coast Indians. The region is distinguished by its humid, mild climate and rich sea, river, and land fauna and flora. On the coast and in the rivers, fish, seals, beavers, and otters are plentiful; in the hinterland, which is blanketed with majestic cedars and coniferous trees, roam

The hosts of a potlach present blankets, masks, and chests to guests (circa 1900).

bears, elks, red deer, mountain goats, and sheep. In the past, the women of the region collected berries, roots, and nuts. A particularly hierarchical society evolved based on these abundant natural resources. Its material civilization centered on objects that were not only functional but also fulfilled certain esthetic demands. Spacious houses, large boats hewn from a single tree trunk, and monumental totem poles were built from cedar wood, as were boxes of all sizes. Some

The loincloth of a dancer in Chilkatsti, British Columbia, Canada. The eyes, ears, beak, claws, and tail suggest that it represents an eagle.

vessels, such as the ceremonial "fat-bowl," were carved from a single block of wood. Most of these objects were painted as well. The Northwest Coast Indians developed a distinctive style of artwork, which incorporated mostly animal motifs. Skilled craftsmen took advantage of the many natural raw materials to execute their creations. From the inner layers of the cedar bark, dresses and mats were woven; from the roots of spruce trees, women wove baskets; from horn, spoons were carved.

The *potlach*, an elaborate ceremony in which lavish gifts were given to guests, is among the most outstanding of these peoples' celebrations. The ceremony took place in honor of its major sponsor, usually an individual of rank. Common gifts included everyday items such as boxes and blankets, but each had to be unique and to meet the highest standards in terms of quality and workmanship.

Preparations for a *potlach* might last up to a year and occupy great numbers of artists. For bestowing presents on his guests so abundantly, the host could rightfully expected to receive a gift in return for his generosity. This principle of mutual commitment formed a basis of all *potlach* celebrations. The recipients of gifts were expected to surpass their former

hosts at their own *potlach*. It is no wonder that accumulation and distribution of gifts in the *potlach* often developed into a ruinously expensive competition. At the same time, it contributed greatly to artistic creativity with its never-ending demand for *objets d'art*.

Totem poles, still the most conspicuous symbol of the Northwest Coast Indians, were meant to demonstrate the impressive social status of their owners. Totem poles (actually "coats of arms poles"; the animals are symbols of the pole owner's prominence) are characterized by schematized representations of animals, depicting episodes from the family history. During the erection of the pole, often done during a *potlach*, the legendary exploits of ancestors were retold by a storyteller. This ceremony often took place during a *potlach*. Several distinct types of totem poles can be distinguished: to commemorate marriages; to venerate the dead; and to mark entry into a new home.

In the nineteenth century the encounter with white traders and access to iron tools enabled the Northwest Coast Indian culture to flourish. With the increase in material affluence came an upsurge in all the arts. The arts of carving and basketweaving developed even despite a Canadian government ban on *potlach* celebrations between 1884 and 1951. There is still an active and productive community of artists preserving the traditions of the Northwest Coast Indians. This new generationis currently experimenting with new forms. Growing public interest and the eagerness of contemporary art collectors to acquire their work have inspired many young Indians to continue their indigenous artistic tradition.

The upper part of a totem pole, representing various mythical creatures. Totem poles may reach a height of up to 45 feet.

Big Men: Great Men of Call

In many tribal societies in Papua New Guinea, a man's social role is rigidly fixed according to his social group, be it clan, age-group, or men's association. On the political level, however, there is no established leadership occupying honorable positions and legitimizing its authority by virtue of descent. Instead, the institution of the "Big Man" has evolved; this represents one of the few ways of rising through the social hierarchy. Given the patriarchial organization of Papuan society, it is not surprising that only men are eligible for Big Man status.

Early reports on the customs and social mores of the PAPUA NEW GUINEA ISLANDERS describe the Big Man as a chief. To outsiders he may, indeed, appear to act like one. The Big Man demands respect, possesses material wealth, and is the main speaker on official occasions. There are, however, many differences between the status of the Big Man and that of chiefs which preclude all but the most superficial comparisons. First of all, it is prestige rather than descent that validates the position of the Big Man. A potential Big Man must, therefore, demonstrate ability as a gardener and pig-farmer. No wealth accrued through these abilities may be hoarded, since only through the distribution of goods to individuals or the community does a man procure the respect needed to justify his elevation to the position of Big Man. Even such gift-giving requires tact: each gift obligates the recipient to reciprocate, so the aspiring Big Man must be certain that he is not placing anyone in the embarrassing situation of being unable to give an appropriate gift in return.

In the past Big Men were required to distinguish themselves in warfare, too. A trophy, usually the head of an adversary, was required to account for a victory.

Ritual cannibalism was also practiced — by eating an enemy, the victor "absorbed" his might. Such martial successes, however, endangered the life of the Big Man, because his own head became all the more attractive to his adversaries.

Although the hunting of wild animals was of only marginal importance to the food supply, it was a prestigious task and important in supplying the feathers and teeth used in ceremonial decorations. These decorations often represented the bond with ancestors that was integral to Papuan beliefs, and were sometimes attributed with special powers.

Perhaps the most important qualifications for the position of Big Man were a profound knowledge of the group's mythology and estimable oratorial skills. In a society where the ancestor cult occupies such a prominent position, myths are the "science of the ancestors," that provide the community with quasi-historical roots. Acknowledgment and respect is assured to those who possess and can transmit a detailed account of their people's history. Rhetorical skills are, even

In Papua New Guinea the breeding of pigs is often connected with prestige. A Big Man is also a successful pig farmer, which he proves during extended "pig celebrations."

occasionally tested in debates, in which the candidates compete for the favor of the tribe. Another prerequisite is artistic talent; proficiency in carving and painting the cultic and decorative motifs characteristic of Papua is an essential requirement of the Big Man.

Several Big Men may serve simultaneously within a single village. Since it is also possible for a Big Man to lose his coveted status, it is not surprising that competitors are constantly challenging his position. Every failure or violation of pre-sanctioned rules and customs is instantly punished with a loss of prestige and power.

The authority of the Big Man is based not on despotic power but upon the good will of the entire community and can, therefore, be easily withdrawn. The Big Man cannot enforce unpopular decisions, no matter how necessary, nor can he rely on the support of other influential men in the community, because they are also his competitors. This kind of meritocracy is a remarkably effective means of popular control.

Papuan societies are sufficiently small enough so that all important issues may be dealt with publicly. To some extent the institution of the Big Man has democratic elements: any man can achieve a leadership position if he can excel in important areas.

Big Men had to prove themselves as warriors, like this member of the Mendi from the southern highlands of Papua New Guinea.

The South Sea Islands: Reputation and Tourism

As early as the seventeenth century, explorers sought out the fabled southern continent, believed to exist in the South Pacific Ocean as a counterbalance to the great land masses of the Northern Hemisphere. It was called "Cytheria," reflecting a Greek description of Venus, the goddess of sensuality. And it was, in fact, in Polynesia, that European explorers and researchers such as Samuel Wallis, Louis-Antoine de Bougainville, and Captain James Cook found a world that corresponded almost completely to the European concept of paradise. The land boasted a pleasant climate, rich and diverse flora and fauna, and an abundance of culinary delicacies. Most of all, they perceived it as the home of a handsome people, who seemed to enjoy a life free of worries and hard labor.

This combination of factors has long made Polynesia a choice destination for tourists. Since many of the Pacific islands can easily be reached by airplane, South Sea tourism has developed rapidly. The first tourist center was Hawaii, America's fiftieth state, just a five hour flight from the American West Coast. The tourism industry, developed there during the last forty years, drastically changed the face of the island. Small villages were evacuated to make place for exclusive beach-hotels; Honolulu became an American-style city. Since these hotels are operated by foreign companies, HAWAIIANS have been reduced to menial positions as hostesses and servants. The rich cultural tradition has degenerated into tourist-oriented entertainment. Five million tourists a year have brought traffic, water shortages, mountains of rubbish, and prostitution to these once tranquil islands.

In response to the spread of western culture throughout Polynesia, indigenous movements have emerged, seeking to preserve local traditions and culture against the onslaught of commercial demands and to adapt fundamental elements of the traditional way of life to contemporary circumstances. This is a difficult process, often rendered near-impossible. In many

A cruise ship anchored in Huahine Bay, French Polynesia.

Tourists attending a dance show in the Hotel Taharaa, Tahiti.

instances tourists visiting the islands outnumber the indigenous population. Nevertheless, the deep-rooted Polynesian tradition of hospitality means that tourists continue to be welcomed warmly.

Naturally, tourism is most developed on islands such as Fiji, Tahiti, and the Cook Islands, with large airports served by international airlines. All these islands have a fully developed tourism infrastructure: western-standard hotels, holiday apartments, well-kept beaches, and organized excursions. A second group of islands, including Tonga, Western Samoa, and Tuvalu, have at their disposal large air-

ports but are only served by regional airlines. On these islands organized excursions are restricted to major cultural and population centers. The more remote regions are, of course, open to tourists but western conveniencies are often lacking. A third group of islands is only served by boats, and on these tourism is not yet fully established. While visitors are welcome, they are left largely to their own resources.

While Hawaii is a case in point of the negative effect uncontrolled tourism can have on indigenous populations, many Pacific Ocean states remain enthusiastic

South Sea repose and technological advances combine in this scene from Samoa.

A view from the Club Bali Hai, in front of Cook's Bay, Tahiti. In holiday villages such as this, the conventional South Sea dream vacation is offered to tourists.

about the prospects offered by foreign tourism. Exports such as tropical woods and agricultural products have limited potential as foreign income earners, so tourism currently offers the only viable source of foreign exchange. Many Polynesian countries are, therefore, keen to attract foreign investment in their tourism industry. More and more, development projects are avoiding large hotel complexes in favor of smaller, dispersed facilities with individual apartments. Guests must be ready to make do without luxuries such as swimming pools or entertainment centers.

Fortunately, it seems that the expectations of tourists in Polynesia is also undergoinhg change. They are proving increasingly ready to adapt themselves to the country rather than to demand the amenities they are accustomed to at home. Patience and ample time are necessary prerequisites for a meaningful tourist experience in the region. Hurried sightseeing is incompatible with an appreciation of Polynesia's rich traditional culture.

A Nepali man in Kathmandu

There are several divisions of Koya such as Raja Koya, Gutha Koya, Adlai Koya, Dallobe Koya, Bomme Koya, and others. Their primary occupation is slash and burn cultivation. Some collect herbs and roots, using them as medicines and selling them to the plains people. They also work as forest laborers. (see also DORLA, PORJA)

KOYRA   see AMARROO.

KOYSHA   A subgroup of the KONTA living in Ethiopia.

KOYUKON   A Native North American group of the Athapaskan-speaking peoples, numbering about 500 and living in Alaska, U.S.A. Their livelihood today is supplied, as in the past, by hunting moose and caribou in season.

KPA   A subgroup of the RHADE.

KPALLA   see KREICH.

KPELLE   (Guerze) The largest people in Liberia, numbering around 530,000, some 21 percent of LIBERIANS. They live mainly in Bong County but smaller groups are also found in Gibi Territory and Bomi and Lofa Counties.

The Kpelle probably began to migrate to their present location from neighboring Guinea in the sixteenth century. Their language is Kpelle. Many, particularly those along the coast, converted to Christianity in the nineteenth century following the arrival of the AMERICO-LIBERIANS. The remainder of the Kpelle practice traditional religions.

Following the arrival of the AMERICO-LIBERIANS in the nineteenth century they became increasingly westernized. One of the first changes they adopted was the introduction of money.

The Kpelle were not involved as a group in the 1980 coup against the AMERICO-LIBERIANS, and they are not participants in the ongoing war between the KRAHN and its Gio (DAN), MANO, and KISSI rivals. Like all the ethnic groups of Liberia, however, their social structure was severely disturbed by the war.

KPONG   A subgroup of the ADANGBE.

KPUNKPAMBA   see KONKOMBA.

KRAHN   (Wee) An ethnic group, numbering around 125,000, living in the Nimba, Grand Geden,

and Sinoe Counties of Liberia. In 1980, Samuel Doe, a member of the Krahn group, staged a military coup that took control of Liberia from the AMERICO-LIBERIANS who had ruled the country for almost 150 years.

Doe stayed in power for ten years, until a civil war erupted in 1990 between the Krahn and the Gio (DAN), MANO, and KISSI. Doe was killed, but the civil war still continues. (see also DAN, LIBERIANS)

KRANCHI   A subgroup of the GUAN.

KREEN-AKAKORE   A South American Indian group living in the Xingu Valley in the State of Goiás, central-west Brazil. Except to other Indians, they are unknown to outsiders.

KREICH   (s.d. Kpalla) An ethnic group living among the BANDA in the Upper Kotto region in the Central African Republic.

KREM   A subgroup of the BAHNAR.

KRIM   (s.d. Kim) An ethnic group living in the Pujehum and Bonthe Districts of Sierra Leone. They are closely related to the BULOM and speak a variant of their language. Most are Christians or practice traditional religions, with a minority professing Islam. They have been largely absorbed by the MENDE.

KRIVICHI   see BYELORUSSIANS.

KROBO   (Klo) A subgroup of the ADANGBE.

KRU   A people located along the southeastern coast of Liberia and in smaller numbers in the Côte d'Ivoire. Their language is Kru. Kru who live in the cities are usually Methodist Christians whereas most rural Kru practice traditional religions.

Kru-speaking peoples have occupied their present sites since at least the sixteenth century. By the nineteenth century they were organized in small independent political units called *dake*.

The Kru emerged as one distinct people only after their encounter with Europeans in the beginning of the nineteenth century, when they started working on European ships. There is an assumption that their name comes from the English word "crew."

In 1822 AMERICO-LIBERIANS settled and became rulers of Liberia. The settler community that arrived on the Kru coast in the 1830s was the poorest and weakest of the Americo-Liberian settlements and harsh commercial competition developed between them and the Kru. Throughout the nineteenth century relations between the Kru and the AMERICO-LIBERIANS grew more and more hostile. As a result the Liberian government took measures against the Kru to weaken them economically.

With the outbreak of World War I, commerce on the Liberian coast became scarce and the Kru found themselves in an economic crisis. This, together with a deep hostility and feelings of frustration led to a Kru revolt against the AMERICO-LIBERIANS in 1915. With the military help of the United States the government defeated the Kru a year later.

Kru migration to Monrovia, the Liberian capital, began before the revolt and continued afterwards. There they concentrated in one part of the city that was consequently called Krutown. After the revolt the Liberian government wished to control the Kru in order to avoid similar problems in the future. In 1916 the Municipal Corporation of Krutown was created for the Kru migrants in Monrovia. This organization was used by the government as a means of communication and control over the rural Kru.

Although the main purpose in the creation of the Kru corporation was to gain control over them, the Kru used this organization in order to obtain political power in Monrovia and through it to become more involved in Liberian politics.

In 1980 the Americo-Liberian elite was removed from power after 150 years by a military coup led by a member of the KRAHN, Samuel Doe. As a result, the Kru corporation lost its government's support and was clearly weakened. Ten years later a civil war errupted in Liberia between Doe's ethnic groups and its Gio (DAN), MANO, and KISSI rivals. This war is still going on. The Kru are not clearly associated with any of the opposing forces but their social fabric in both the rural and urban areas has been severely disturbed by these devastating events. (see also ADYUKRU, IVOIREANS, LIBERIANS)

KRUNG   A small group of Malayo-Polynesian speakers in southern Vietnam.

KRYZ   An ethnic group living in north Azerbaijan, in the Shakhdagh mountain region, estimated as munbering 6,000. The Kryz have been Sunni Muslims of the Shafi'i school since the sixteenth century.

The Kryz language belongs to the Daghestani branch of the Ibero-Caucasian family. It is unwritten, and Azerbaijani is used as the literary language. The Kryz are undergoing an intensive process of acculturation into the AZERBAIJANI.

In mountain villages the traditional type of stone house is found, with two storeys in the front and one in the rear. Villages are located on steep slopes and consist of several blocks inhabited by closely-related groups.

The Kryz traditional economy is based on sheep-breeding, terrace agriculture, horticulture (in the plains regions), and carpet-weaving.

KSHATRIYA   see THAKURI.

K'TUL   A subgroup of the RHADE.

KUAP   An ethnic group living on the Indonesian island of Kalimantan (Borneo). (see also DAYAK)

KUBA   An ethnic group living in Zaire, between the Sankuru and Lulua Rivers. Their precolonial kingdom reached its peak in the eighteenth century but disintegrated following a civil war in the nineteenth century.

KUBACHIANS   see QUBACHIANS.

KUBU   (s.d. Orang Darat) An originally derogatory term used to describe small groups of nomadic hunters and gatherers numbering fewer than 20,000 and living in the swampy eastern coastal regions of Sumatera (Sumatra), an island in the Indonesian archipelago. They are of Veddoid stock and generally adopt the language of those larger groups with whom they are in closest contact and with whom they sometimes trade. Some few Kubu have settled in villages belonging to these other groups, but they maintain their own neighborhoods, where they live in relative squalor. Settled Kubu are often Muslims; nomadic Kubu profess shamanistic beliefs.

Kubu groups include the AKIT, DUWABLAS, LUBU, MAMAK (Mamma), ORANG DARAT, ORANG KEPOR, ORANG LOM, ORANG MAPOR, ORANG RAWAS, ORANG UTAN, RAWAS, SAKAI, TALANG, TAPUNG, and ULU.

KUBUTAR   see NAT.

KUCHBANDHIA   A small group of Hindu hunters and subsistence farmers found in northwest India.

KUCHO   A subgroup of the KONTA living in Ethiopia.

KUDAWA A subgroup of the FULANI.

KUHGILU An ethnic group, part of the LUR people of Iran, living in the mountains between Behbehan and Zedun and from Tell-Khosrow to the area inhabited by the MAMASAN in south-central Iran. The last population figure available (1945) was about 75,000; they may now number 150,000. They are Shi'ite Muslims who have retained certain vestiges of an ancient hearth-fire cult and the veneration of tombs of local saints.

Kuhgilu

The Kuhgilu consist of three tribes: the Jaki (one of whose clans, the Boir-Ahmadi, has become preeminent); the Aqa-Jari (said to be of Mongol descent and retaining Turkish names); and the Bavi. Each tribe is divided into clans and subdivided into families of 30-100 tents. Although mainly nomadic pastoralists, they also engage in seasonal agriculture. Vendetta and clan conflicts characterize tribal life.

The Kuhgilu had tense relations with the central government until they were subdued by Reza Shah Pahlavi (1925–1941), who started a policy of enforced sedentarization, which had limited success. (see also LUR)

KUI (Soai) A Mon-Khmer group living along the border of Cambodia and Thailand. There are over 100,000 Kui, but intermarriage and assimilation into the surrounding KHMER is rampant and the Kui have generally adopted Buddhism and agricultural techniques from the KHMER. Apart from rice cultivation, the

Kui are skilled ironworkers and have a reputation among neighboring peoples as elephant hunters.

KUKI A generic term for several groups found in the state of Assam, northeast India. They number about 150,000. They speak a Tibeto-Burman language, and have preserved many of their traditional beliefs. In the past, the Kuki were feared as headhunters. (see also PURUM)

KUKNA A large Scheduled Tribe in the western Indian state of Gujarat. They number about 500,000 and speak a Gujarati dialect. They profess Hinduism. Most are employed in agriculture.

KUKURUKU An ethnic group, related to the EDO, living in southwestern Nigeria.

KULABI see GYPSIES.

KULAMAN (Manobo) An ethnic group, numbering several thousand, living along the Davao Gulf coast of Mindanao, an island in the Philippines. They speak a language belonging to the Manobo family. They are Muslims. Warriors have special status in their society.

KULANGO An ethnic group numbering about 50,000 living in northeastern Cote d'Ivoire. They are related to the LOBI and most adhere to traditional religions.

Merchants from the DYULA who settled among them since the fifteenth century have not managed to convert them to Islam. The Kulango were dominated by the BRONG from the seventeenth century until colonization of their area by the FRENCH in the late nineteenth century.

KULAWY An ethnic group living in the mountainous central region of the Indonesian island of Sulawesi (Celebes). (see also TORADJA)

KULFA An ethnic group living in Chad.

KULLO (Dawaro) A subgroup of the KONTA living in Ethiopia.

KULU An ethnic group living in Nigeria.

KUMAI BRAHMAN see BRAHMANS.

KUMAN A small ethnic group living north of Lake Kyoga in Uganda, between the LANGO and TESO peoples (to whom they are related). Their language is largely influenced by that of the LANGO and NYORO. Today they are regarded as Western Nilotes. They are thought to be a group that split off from the KARAMOJONG at the turn of the twentieth century and, while slowly moving westward, assimilated linguistically into Western Nilotic groups.

They are cattle-herders, but agriculture, which is the women's domain, also plays an important role in their economy. The main crops are millet and sorghum, as well as several kinds of vegetables. Agriculture is not only for subsistence, but has been market-oriented since the early twentieth century, when cotton was introduced as a cash crop. (see also LANGO, UGANDANS)

KUMHMHU   see KHMU.

KUMYK   see QUMUQ.

KUNAMA   An ethnic group, numbering 100,000 (1980), who live between the Gash and Sertit Rivers in southwest Eritrea. Their language belongs to the Nilotic group, and they are divided among Sunni Muslims, Christians (both Protestants and Catholics), and adherents of traditional beliefs. They are sedentary terrace agriculturalists, using the plow. Their exogamic clan system still bears traces of the older system of matrilineal descent. (see also ERITREANS, ETHIOPIANS)

KUNDA   A Nyanja-speaking group, numbering 65,000, living in southeast Zambia. They profess either Christianity or traditional religions.

The Kunda arrived in Zambia as part of the BEMBA migration, and were conquered by the NGONI in the nineteenth century. Their culture therefore contains elements similiar to those of both these peoples.

KUNDU VADIYAN   An agricultural people found in the southern Indian state of Kerala.

KUNTA   A nomadic group living in Mali.

KURAMA   A tribe of the UZBEKS.

KURDS   Spread out over five countries, the Kurds live in a contiguous zone spanning southeast Anatolia in Turkey, skirting northeast Syria, and reaching over north Iraq into west Iran. This area, known as Kurdistan, overlapped with that of the ARABS, ARMENIANS, TURKS, and others.

Kurdish identity, in many instances, is a matter of choice. Kurdish numbers are subject to controversy;

total Kurdish population may lie anywhere between 5 and 30 million; reasonable estimates are in the 20 million range. The estimates for Turkey range from 3.5 to 12 million. As Kurds have been denied official existence in Turkey, where they were called Mountain Turks, counts are especially vague here. Two to six million live in Iran, which also absorbed an unspecified number of Kurdish refugees from Iraq. Iraqi Kurds number between 3.5 and 4.5 million. Between 300,000 and one million live in Syria, mainly in the northern mountains; there is also a Kurdish quarter in Damascus.

About one-third of the Kurds dwell outside Kurdistan in the Middle East diaspora, dependent on their relationships with host societies. Urban Kurdish communities have sprung up in Baghdad, Basra, Aleppo, Damascus, and Beirut. Until recent deportations, 40,000 Kurds lived in Armenia and 21,000 in Georgia. The 150,000 Kurds in Azerbaijan and 50,000 in Turkmenistan are descendants of frontier guards sent in the sixteenth century by the PERSIANS, and of tribes that migrated in 1750–1800. Smaller groups in Qazaqstan and Qirgyzstan, who were deported from the Caucasus in 1937–1938, are now being ordered to leave. There are 380,000 Kurdish migrant laborers in Europe, most from Turkey.

The Kurdish language is akin to Iranian. It is not a unified language but consists of a number of mutually unintelligible dialects: Kirmanji is spoken in the area

Kurds

above left: A Kurdish woman
above right: A Kurdish child
below: A group of Kurdish men

of the former Ottoman Empire, north of Mosul and into the Commonwealth of Independent States. Sorani is spoken in former Persian territories: Iran and the eastern part of Iraq south of the Greater Zab (the Sulaymaniya region). The Iranian dialects Kirmanshahi, Leki, and Gurani are spoken between Kermanshah and Sanadaj; Zaza in eastern Anatolia between Diyarbakir, Sivas, and Erzurum.

Although Kurds have neither language nor religion in common, they share a common culture and history, which is expressed in Kurdish folklore and songs exalting heroism and self-sacrifice. However, classical literature was written in Arabic (and Persian) until the late nineteenth century.

Most Kurds are Sunni Muslims. In Iraq (Khanaqin province) and Iran (Kermanshah) some tribes are Twelver Shi'ites. There is widespread participation in religious brotherhoods such as the Naqshabandi and Qadiriya dervish orders. Part of the Zaza are Alawites. In southeast Kurdistan, a small portion belongs to the Ahl al-Haqq, a little-known Shi'ite syncretistic sect.

Yazidis (Dasnayis, Asdais) are ethnically Kurdish. They practice a religion of obscure origin incorporating Zoroastrian and Manichaean as well as Nestorian and Shi'ite elements. They believe the world was created by God but is sustained by a hierarchy of subordinate beings. Incorrectly known as devil worshippers, they propitiate the evil Peacock King. They are mainly farmers in Jabal Sinjar, west of Mosul (Iraq), its continuation in east Syria around Lake Khatun, and northwest Syria in Aintab, north of Aleppo. Smaller groups live in Turkey's Diyarbakir district, Iran, and Georgia. Yazidis have often been persecuted; this has rendered them secretive and endogamous. They may number 100,000 altogether. The LAK are another group of Kurds, living in the Luristan province in the central-west part of Iran. The Lak language is regarded as a dialect of Kurdish. They are Shi'ite Muslims and pastoral nomads. The LAK were settled in their present habitat by Persian rulers in the early seventeenth century.

The Kurds' troublesome relations with their neighbors reflect a longstanding tension between urbanized and government-controlled plainsmen and intractable hill-dwellers. Kurds used to be nomadic tribesmen moving uplands in summer; in winter they would come down with their flocks, terrorizing the lowlanders, Kurdish or other. Kurdish peasants in the plains stood in a near-serflike relation to the village landlord. Local sheikhs who led religious brotherhoods also elicited strong loyalty and sometimes formed dynasties. Today peasants are partly detribalized, but old traditions are slow to die. The isolation which has preserved Kurdish traditional identity also precludes the modernization which might overcome their fragmentation.

Many Kurds live outside the rural framework nowadays. Pressure on the land has driven many men to seek work in industry. One million Turkish Kurds moved westward in Turkey during the years 1950 to 1980.

Kurdish history is one of periodic revolts that failed to achieve political independence. In spite of their numbers they never attained their objective of independence.

Kurds believe they stem from the ancient Medes. Scholars disagree whether their origin is Indo-European or Caucasian. Iranized tribes settled "Kurdistan" in the seventh century B.C.E. Kurds found themselves successively under Seleucid, Parthian, Sassanid, Armenian, Byzantine, Arab, Mongol, and Turkic rule. The Kurd Salah-ed-Din (Saladin), who took on the Crusaders in the twelfth century, has become a prototype of the Muslim hero. In the Middle Ages Kurdish nomad tribes profited from the destruction of the Armenian peasantry by MONGOLS and TURKMEN to take over their lands for grazing, and gradually moved deeper into the Anatolian plateau. In the sixteenth century, the Ottoman Empire organized Kurdish tribal confederations, led by nobles (sayyids), and gave them frontier marches in fief, on condition they policed the border with Shi'ite Persia. The latter experimented with the same system but were less effective than the TURKS in using Kurdish self-rule for defensive purposes.

In the nineteenth century the Ottoman Empire attempted to install direct control over the Kurds. The PERSIANS tried likewise with their Kurds. This caused a series of unsuccessful revolts. A first quasi-national revolt broke out in 1880. However, many nobles remained loyal to the sultan, and Kurds were also employed to keep other minorities in order. The pattern of divide-and-rule was to become a recurrent theme in Kurdish history. During World War I Kurds played a role in the massacre of the ARMENIANS, but in 1916 the Young Turkish leadership began to persecute and deport them as well. The peace conference of Sevres prescribed in 1920 both an Armenian state and, south of it, a Kurdish autonomous area, with the prospect of a state that was to be joined by the British-occupied Mosul province. However, tribalism was still strong. Fearing Christian rule, Kurdish troops helped Ataturk drive out GEORGIANS and surviving ARMENIANS.

After Turkey had secured its independence, Kurds lost their protected status. In 1924 the Kurdish language and all Kurdish associations were banned, arousing a series of tribal revolts that were brutally crushed: tens of thousands were killed, hundreds of thousands fled to Syria, whole regions were depopulated. Unrest persisted till 1938. Attempts were made at forcible assimilation by displacement of 1 million Kurds and Turkish settlement of their areas. After World War II a relative liberalization set in, allowing Kurds to participate in political life as "TURKS." Deportation and migration meanwhile engendered vast urban Kurdish concentrations who could not be kept isolated indefinitely from the idea of liberation. In the 1960s and 1970s illegal secessionist Kurdish parties were established, some resorting to terrorist means of struggle. The city of Diyarbakir became the Kurdish nationalist center.

As Kurdish militantism grew, so did repression. In 1979 the Kurdish provinces were placed under martial law. Turkey was particularly suspicious of across-the-border Kurdish contacts, fearing a spillover of Kurdish revolts in Iran and Iraq, and tried to seal off its border with these two states. By the late 1980s, in reaction to PKK (the far-left Kurdish national movement) attacks, a policy of resettlement was resumed. In 1988 Turkey felt obliged to accept Kurdish refugees from Iraq. In 1991 spoken Kurdish became a legally tolerated language. However, anti-guerrilla oppression continued.

Reza Shah Pahlavi, who came to power in Iran in 1921, wanted to integrate his ethnically heterogeneous nation. He dealt with Kurdish separatism just as ruthlessly as he did with Iran's TURKS and ARABS. The deportation of recalcitrant tribes was, however, insufficient to suppress the Kurds. In the aftermath of World War II the Kurds set up their ephemeral autonomous Republic of Mahabad under Soviet auspices. In 1946, after the Soviets left, Tehran reconquered Mahabad, and the Kurdish national movement went underground. Only in 1975, after the Iraq-Iran agreement robbed Iraqi Kurds of Iranian support, was a new revolt against Tehran initiated. The 1979 Islamic revolution allowed the Kurds to take over limited power in Kurdistan. Khomeini offered the Kurds autonomy of a kind that denied them real self-determination. While the Shi'ite Kurds around Kermanshah rallied around him, most Sunni Kurds rejected the proposal. Their towns were retaken and Kurdistan was kept under military control, leaving the Kurdish movement in disarray.

Many of the Kurds of Iraq live in the oil-rich Mosul province, awarded in 1925 to Iraq with the proviso of Kurdish autonomy. Iraq formally accepted this when it acceded to independence in 1932, yet did not keep its promises, thus provoking a series of Kurdish uprisings. By 1943 the autocratic and charismatic Mullah Mustafa Barzani had become the predominant Kurdish leader. Defeated in 1946, he fled to Iran to fight with the Mahabad republic. After the 1958 coup the Kurds were granted equal rights, and Barzani returned from exile in the Soviet Union. In 1961 he mobilized an open revolt. Intermittent war continued until 1970.

In 1970 Barzani controlled two-thirds of Kurdish Iraq, and the Iraqi government concluded a ceasefire on the promise of wide-ranging autonomy and recognition of the Kurdish language. However, implementation met with so many obstacles that in 1974 Barzani's disgruntled warriors (*peshmergas*) started a new and rather successful guerrilla campaign with the support of Iran. In 1975 Saddam Hussein and the Shah signed the Algiers agreement in which Iraq ceded claims on the Shatt al-Arab in exchange for Iran's ceasing aid to Kurds, and Kurdish resistance crumbled. Iraq resettled a quarter of a million Kurds in southern Iraq and established a *cordon sanitaire* toward the Iranian border.

During the 1980 Iraq-Iran war the Kurds resumed rebellion. In 1987, when Iranian victory seemed imminent, the Iraqi Kurdistan Front held a vast territory, blocking two of Iraq's seven armies. But Iran was exhausted; in 1988 a ceasefire was signed. Iraq now restored control by a policy of systematic dekurdization, with mass killings, destruction of Kurdish villages, and deportations. Many Kurds fled to Turkey and Iran.

After the 1991 Gulf War a spontaneous Kurdish rebellion broke out. Unrestrained by the West, Iraq's counteroffensive forced 1 million Kurds to flee to Iran. Hundreds of thousands to whom Turkey refused entry were installed in fragile UN-protected "secure havens." Later, the Kurds were able to establish their own self-management in some of their areas of settlement under the protection of UN forces. (see also IRAQIS, LEBANESE, MESKH, SYRIANS, TURKS)

KURFEY (Soudie) A small Hausa-speaking group living in Niger, north of Tahoua.

KURI A subgroup of the YEDINA, living on the western shores of Lake Chad.

KURICHCHIAN An ethnic group, numbering 30,000 (1981), located in the states of Kerala (where they are the earliest known inhabitants) and Tamil Nadu, India. They speak Malayalam, a language belonging to the Dravidian family.

The Kurichchian are Hindus and their chief deity is the god of the hunt (Muttuppan, or Shiva). Some worship Vishnu.

They do not accept food cooked by any other but a Kurichchian. Before they enter their homes on return from a journey they take a purificatory bath. They refrain from eating when they visit neighboring villages. Those who break dietary laws are outcast.

On their small patches of land they raise pepper and a variety of cash crops.

KURTATCHI   An ethnic group of approximately 5,000 living on the Pacific island of Bougainville in Papua New Guinea, east of the mainland. Although the younger generation speak additional languages, all Kurtatchi speak Tunputz, an indigenous local language. In the rural sector, most are employed as slash and burn gardeners, while in the cities, most work in the modern economic sector. Although most are practicing Methodists, many still believe in traditional ancestral spirits.

KURTEY   An ethnic group numbering around 25,000, living in Niger, on the banks and islands of the Niger River, off the town of Tillaberi and in Niamey, the capital of Niger. They stem from the intermarriage of FULANI with the SONGHAI and DJERMA peoples. Every year large numbers of Kurtey go to Ghana to engage in seasonal labor.

KURUMAN   An ethnic group, numbering 36,000 (1981), living in the states of Kerala, Karnataka, and Tamil Nadu, India. They speak Kannada, a member of the Dravidian family of languages.

The Kuruman are Hindus. They worship Shakti and Shiva, and also practice ancestor worship. They were once suspected of practicing black magic, and were harassed and even killed for that reason. Until a few years ago they were food gatherers.

KURUMBA I   An ethnic group numbering about 20,000, living in southern India, mainly in the Nilgiri District of the Tamil Nadu state. They speak a Dravidian language and are mostly Hindus, although their particular rites and rituals are often connected with sorcery.

Among neighboring peoples the Kurumba have a reputation as powerful magicians who can turn themselves into any animal. In the past, these peoples feared Kurumba spells and occasionally massacred Kurumba villages in retaliation for a local mishap blamed on the powers of the Kurumba.

Traditionally the Kurumba were hunters and gatherers who also cultivated small plots of fruits and vegetables. They are in the process of adopting a more sedentary lifestyle, with many finding employment as itinerant workers in local plantations.

KURUMBA II   (Tellem) An ethnic group living in the Liptako, Djilogodjy, and Yatenga areas of Burkina Faso. In precolonial times they formed a kingdom called Laroun.

KURYK MARI   see MARI.

KUSAE   see KUSASI.

KUSAIE   see KOSRAE ISLANDERS.

KUSASI   (Kusae) A MOLE-DAGBANI group living in the Upper Region of Ghana and in small numbers in Burkina Faso and Togo. Their language is Kusal.

KUSU   An ethnic group living along the Lomani River in the western part of Kivu Region, Zaire.

KUTANANS   An ethnic group living in the vicinity of the town of Khost in the central-east part of Afghanistan, near the border with Pakistan. They are one of the lesser-known ethnic groups of Afghanistan, and there are no exact data on their number, language, and religion. They may number some few thousand. For contacts outside their group they use Pashto, the main language of their area of habitation. It may be assumed that, at least outwardly, they are Sunni Muslims of the Hanafi school. They are peripatetics (non-pastoral nomads). Unlike most other peripatetic ethnic groups of Afghanistan (cf. GHORBATIS, JALALI, PIKRAJ, SHADIBAZ, VANGAVALANS) except for the SHEIKH-MOHAMMADIS they are not dispersed but live in one area. Their main occupations are itinerant peddling and juggling, and therefore they are sometimes regarded as part of the so-called Jat population of Afghanistan. Male Kutanans also engage in unskilled itinerant day-labor. (see also AFGHANS, JATS II)

KUTCHIN   A Native North American group of the Athapaskan-speaking peoples, numbering about 2,500, making them one of the largest groups in the Yukon

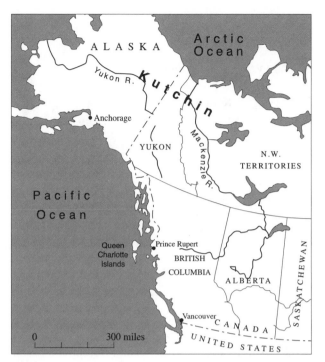

Kutchin

Territory, Canada. They are also found in Alaska and in the North-West Territories, Canada, on both banks of the Mackenzie River. Their area is rich in natural resources.

KUTSO-WLACH see VLACHS.

KUTURMI A subgroup of the FULANI.

KUWAITIS Of the more than 2 million people living in Kuwait before the Iraqi invasion of 1990 (1.8 million in Greater Kuwait City alone), only 42 percent were indigenous Arabic-speaking Kuwaitis: 49 percent were non-Kuwaiti ARABS (including IRAQIS and PALESTINIANS). The remainder were IRANIANS, INDIANS, PAKISTANIS, and ARMENIANS, nearly all recent arrivals attracted by Kuwait's oil economy. Most were Muslims: 73 percent Sunnite, and 18 percent Shi'ites (of the indigenous Kuwaitis, c.30 percent are Shi'ite; there were many Shi'ites among Iraqi and Iranian guest workers). The Iraqi occupation and Gulf War have brought about substantial changes in the composition of the population, and the situation is still in flux.

Kuwait was originally a small trading port in an otherwise desert area situated at the top of the Persian Gulf, at the nexus of an ancient overland caravan track and the sealane linking the Indus Valley and Mesopotamia. It was converted to Islam in the eighth century. In 1514 the PORTUGUESE established a trading and staple station which, in 1756, fell into the hands of a dynasty originating from the Hijaz, the al-Sabahs, who are still in power. The BRITISH established a presence in 1793, and their influence grew throughout the nineteenth century. In 1853 Kuwait, squeezed by the Ottoman Empire, was forced to promise allegiance to Istanbul; it was attached to the vilayet Basrah, thus providing a basis for later Iraqi claims. Seeking protection for their territory, in 1899 the Sabahs negotiated a treaty with Britain, granting in return free navigation and supervision of Kuwaiti foreign affairs.

Before World War II, pastoralism supported a few thousand. Fishing and boat-building constituted Kuwait's main sources of income; dhow-builders formed a Shi'ite guild. Pearling, Kuwait's traditional earner, suffered from competition with artificial Japanese pearls. Then, in 1938, oil was struck. Commercial exports led in the decade of World War II to rapid development. The population grew twelvefold, mainly through the influx of foreign workers: non-Kuwaitis formed 80 percent of the labor force.

In 1961 Kuwait became fully independent, and in the 1970s and 1980s it underwent rapid modernization and became one of the richest countries of the world. By 1980, it had nationalized its petroleum wealth. Indigenous Kuwaitis ("First Class Citizens") developed into a new class, an elite of merchant families who enjoyed free social services. In fact, the autocratic al-Sabah family tried to compensate for the lack of political participation by providing a wide array of free amenities. By contrast, most guest laborers did not share in the wealth. Denied political and economic rights, often living miserably and without the possibility of bringing over their families, the non-citizen Second Class majority depended on a First Class sponsor for their residence permits, inducing a new form of dependence. That position was particularly galling to the PALESTINIANS: preponderant in the press and mid-level management, they played a major role in the country's economic and cultural life, but were also a potential source of opposition. Troublesome noncitizen minorities were threatened with expulsion.

Kuwait holds enormous oil reserves, good for one century. Yet since the mid-1970s, as its technocrats realized how dependent it is on a single, depletable resource, Kuwait has started to reduce output. Attempts to diversify industry are, however, hampered by its small domestic market. By the 1980s Kuwaitis were living mainly on the interest on their gigantic foreign investments. The invasion by Iraq in 1990 ushered in seven months of occupation and systematic spoilation which has ruined Kuwait. Hundreds of thousands of guest laborers and

400,000 Kuwaitis (more than half the indigenous population) fled the country. Since the liberation of their land in the Gulf War of 1991, they have been returning only slowly.

KUYU   An ethnic group related to the MBOCHI living in Congo.

KUZNETSY   see SHORS.

KVANES   see FINNS.

KWADI   see KADI.

KWAHU   see KWAWU.

KWAKIUTL   A Native North American people numbering about 4,000, living on Vancouver Island, British Columbia, Canada. The Kwakiutl were considered the most artistic of the West Coast Indians, and their skill in sculpting totem poles and creating colorful masks was widely renowned.

They continued to practice the *potlach*, a traditional gift-giving ceremony used to distinguish social rank. Although the ceremony was outlawed between 1888 and 1951 to encourage assimilation, many Kwakiutl went to jail rather than give up the practice.

Today many Kwakiutl earn their livelihood through the operation of commercial fishing vessels. In recent years many Kwakiutal bands have taken education under their own control.

KWALA   (Likoula) An ethnic group living in Congo.

KWANDANG   A subgroup of the GORONTALO.

KWANDI   An ethnic group related to the LUYANA living in Zambia.

KWANGWA   (Makawangwa) A Luyana-speaking group, numbering about 75,000, living in southwest Zambia. They are related to the LOZI.

KWANYAMA   An ethnic group living in southern Angola. A centralized Kwanyama kingdom existed in the Mossamedes hinterland from 1870 to 1915, when their last leader was defeated by the PORTUGUESE.

They were hunters and cattle-breeders, and traded in iron, salt, copper, ivory, and slaves.

KWATAWA   A subgroup of the FULANI.

KWAWU   (Kwahu or Quahoe) An Akan-speaking ethnic group living in Ghana, between the Afram River to the north and the Accra-Kumasi railroad to the south.

KWEGU   (Gwagu, Manjo) An ethnic group, numbering about 1,000, who are related to the stigmatized strata of hunters (Manjo) among the Omotic-speaking people in southern Gemu Gofa Province, Ethiopia.

KWENA   (Bakwena) A subgroup of the southern SOTHO.

KWENI   see GURO.

KWERI   (Bakweri) A non-centralized ethnic group living in Cameroon in villages on the slopes of Mount Cameroon and along the coast.

Their main towns, Buea, Victoria (now Limbe), and Tiko, are the administrative and commercial centers of anglophone Cameroon. The region was developed after the discovery of petroleum oil in the late 1970s but the Kweri did not share the fruits of this development.

KWESE   An ethnic group living between the Kwilu and Kasai Rivers in the Kwango and Kasai Regions of Zaire.

KWOMA   An ethnic group of a few thousand living in the Sepik River region in northern Papua New Guinea. They speak an indigenous regional language. Their main crop is yams, with coffee as their main cash crop. They believe in two creators of the world and their chief ceremonies include dances.

KYOKOSHI   An Akan-speaking ethnic group living in Ghana. They are related to the AGNI-BAULE.

KYON-TSU   see LOTHA.

KYPRIANI   see CYPRIOTS.

L

LABEAU   A subgroup of the LAKI.

LABHU   see BAI.

LABWOR   A small ethnic group of northwest Uganda. Living between the cattle-herding KARAMO-JONG and the agriculturalist ACHOLI, the Labwor are mainly active as traders between their neighbors. As traders, they are bilingual, although they originally belonged to the Eastern Nilotic language group. They are also ironsmiths.

LACANDON   (s.d. Hach Winik) The last survivors of the ancient MAYA, still living a traditional life. Numbering fewer than 1,000, they inhabit the rain forests of Chiapas in Southern Mexico and also neighboring Belize. The name "Lacandon" (*acantun*) in the Mayan language means erectors of stone idols, but it is also a pejorative term originally applied to them by other Mayan groups. Their own self-designation, Hach Winik, means "True Men" or "Original People."

Most of the written records of their ancient civilization were destroyed by the SPANIARDS, whose zealous efforts to eradicate paganism prevented the Lacandon from preserving the astronomy, mathematics, or the extraordinary calendrical system of their ancestors.

Although there is a tendency to speak of the Lacandon as one group, they are actually divided into two, the Northern and the Southern Lacandon. There are differences between their customs and dress, as well as their languages. Over the past years the differences have been intensified by the southern group's receptivity to the teachings of Protestant missionaries.

Religion has also divided the northern group, families who live on the shore of Lake Metazabok having been converted to Seventh Day Adventism. It is only around Lake Naja, a few miles away, that a small group of Lacandon still worship their own gods.

The Lacandon are not incorporated into the political system of Mexico. At Naja, deep in the heart of the rain forest, they manage their own affairs. The men still wear long hair and the traditional tunic. Their diet consists mainly of corn, chili, and squash. (see also MAYA)

LADAKHI   A Tibeto-Burman speaking people living around the town of Ladakh in northern India. They are closely related to the TIBETANS.

LADINO   see GUATEMALANS.

LAGE   An ethnic group living in the mountainous central region of the Indonesian island of Sulawesi (Celebes). (see also TORADJA)

LA-GIA   see LAYA.

LAGURU   A Bantu-speaking ethnic group living in Tanzania.

LAHU   The approximately 300,000 Lahu inhabit the rugged hills in the southwestern part of China's Yunnan Province. Some have migrated to Burma and Thailand.

An ancient legend explains that the Lahu descend from hunters who, while chasing a red deer that fled into the southern forest, discovered rich grasslands, spurring a southerly migration. By the eighteenth century they had settled in their present home where, under the influence of the Han CHINESE and DAI, they adopted sedentary farming.

Their language is related to the Yi language of the Tibeto-Burmese group, with an animal vocabulary essentially the same as in Yi. As a result of close contact with the Han CHINESE and DAI, many can speak both these languages. In some areas, a writing system created by Western missionaries was once in use, but since the late

A Ladakhi shepherd crossing a Himalayan stream with his flock

1950s the Chinese government has helped them create their own alphabet. Most Lahu have preserved their ancient beliefs although some have become Christians.

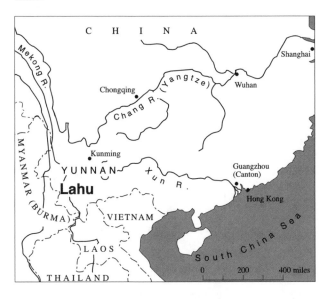

Lahu

Lahu homes are made of bamboo. Like those of the DAI, their homes consist of two storeys, with the ground floor reserved for animals.

LAHULI   An ethnic group numbering 1,900 (1981), located in Lahaul-Spiti, Himachal Pradesh, India. They speak Tibetan, a member of the Tibeto-Burman family of languages. They are Buddhist and polyandrous.

LAIWONU   An ethnic group living in the mountainous central region of the Indonesian island of Sulawesi (Celebes). (see also TORADJA)

LAK I   An ethnic group of approximately 5,000 living on the island of New Britain, off the northern coast of Papua New Guinea. They speak an indigenous regional language. They cultivate pigs and grow vegetables. They believe in a single mythical god as well as in sorcery. Their most celebrated ceremony involves honoring the spirits of the dead.

LAK II, LAKK   see KURDS.

LAKALAI   An ethnic group of approximately 10,000 living on the Pacific island of New Britain in the state of Papua New Guinea, east of the mainland. They speak an indigenous regional language. Their

subsistence is based upon the cultivation of various vegetables, as well as on the maintenence of cash crops such as coconuts. Most of their beliefs in traditional spirits have been replaced by Christianity. Their most important ceremony is one which honors the deceased.

LAKHER   (s.d. Mara) An ethnic group , numbering about 15,000, living in the state of Mizoram, eastern India. They speak a Tibeto-Burman language.

LAKI I   see ZAY.

LAKI II   (s.d. To Laki) A generic term for several ethnic groups numbering over 100,000 people and living in the southeastern peninsula of the island of Sulawesi (Celebes), Indonesia, including the ASERAWANUA, LABEAU, MEKONGGA, MOWEWE, TAMBOKI, and WIWIRANO. They are closely related to the MORI, from whom they apparently seceded, and are predominantly Muslim, although rites connected with ancestor worship have survived. They engage in the cultivation of rice and sago and in deer hunting.

In the past the Laki were feared as cannibals who often ate the brains of their victims, The name Laki, literally "big men," is thought to refer to their reputation as headhunters.

LAKOTA   see SIOUX.

LALA   A Chibemba-speaking group numbering about 140,000 living in central Zambia, west of the Luangwa River. They practice both Christianity and traditional African religions. As part of the BEMBA people, they share with them a similar culture and social and political organization. The Lala follow a matrilineal descent system and are known for their artistry. In the early twentieth century the Lala came under the influence of the Protestant millennarian movements that overwhelmed Zambia.

The Lala produced iron until the arrival of the Europeans, when they became farmers. They were originally part of the LUBA kingdom who migrated southward from southeastern Zaire.

LALAEO   An ethnic group living in the mountainous central region of the Indonesian island of Sulawesi (Celebes). (see also TORADJA)

LALI   (Lari) An ethnic group related to the KONGO, living in Congo.

LALUNG (s.d. Tiwa) A people numbering 163,000 (1987), living in Assam and Meghalaya, India. They speak Boro, a language of the Tibeto-Burman family.

Believed to be migrants from Tibet, the Lalung are Hindus. There are two subdivisions, the hill and the plains Lalung, which differ greatly in food, housing, agricultural, and other practices. The hill Lalung practice slash and burn cultivation while the plains Lalung cultivate paddy with settled plow cultivation. Their staple is rice.

The Lalung had a proud tradition of a well-run dormitory (called *samadi*). This institution used to be the nucleus for training youth in the arts, crafts, and musical lore of the Lalung. However, among the plains Lalung this institution is fast disappearing, while the hill Lalung still maintain it. (see also DIMASA-KACHARI)

LAMAHOLOT A subgroup of the SOLORESE.

LAMBA I An ethnic group numbering about 25,000 living in Zambia's copper belt. Their language, Ulu-lamba, is related to Chibemba. They practice both Christianity and traditional religions. They have a matrilineal descent system, and their culture is similar to that of the BEMBA. They have always resented copper-mining in their region because it resulted in the loss of much land.

LAMBA II An ethnic group living in the Kande region of northern Togo. They are related to the KABRE.

LAMBYA An ethnic group living in northeast Zambia. Their language, Lambya, is related to Tambo.

LAMDANI A subgroup of the GARO.

LAMET (Kha Lamet) An ethnic group numbering about 6,000 living in the hills of northern Laos. Their language, a member of the Mon-Khmer family, is closely related to that of the KHMU. Like most hill tribes, the Lamet practice traditional religions.

They practice a rice-based shifting slash and burn agriculture. The Lamet have developed few crafts and are dependent on trade with their neighbors for tools and ornaments.

LAMPONG see ABUNG.

LAMPU An ethnic group living in the mountainous central region of the Indonesian island of Sulawesi (Celebes). (see also TORADJA)

LAMUSA An ethnic group living in the mountainous central region of the Indonesian island of Sulawesi (Celebes). (see also TORADJA)

LAMUT see EVEN.

LANATAI see YUAN.

LAND DAYAK An ethnic group living on the Indonesian island of Kalimantan (Borneo). (see also DAYAK)

LANDUMA An ethnic group living in Guinea, West Africa, between the Rio Nunez and the Fatala River, and in Guinea-Bissau in the area around the southern town of Catio. They speak a Baga dialect. In Guinea most Landuma are assimilating into the larger Susu-speaking population living along the coast.

LANGBA A subgroup of the BANDA.

LANGO A people living in Uganda, in the area north of Lake Kyoga and south of the ACHOLI. They originally spoke an Eastern Nilotic language which was replaced by a Western Nilotic tongue as a result of their absorption of TESO groups.

Their economy is a mixed one of cattle-herding and shifting agriculture; after three years they abandon their fields and migrate to a new location. Since the plague of the 1890s, when they lost most of their herds, the Lango have concentrated on agriculture. They grow different kinds of millet and vegetables and keep domestic animals. Cattle still represent the most important kind of property, and are passed from father to son, but only with the consent of the lineage. The bride price was paid in cattle. The Lango also lived on hunting, including big game such as elephants.

They do not practice circumcision, but have initiation rites and separate living quarters for unmarried young men and women. Age-sets used to exist on the village level but as far back as the 1930s they became obsolete. The Lango have a kinship system of patrilineal exogamous clans, which displayed a tendency to subdivision. The basic unit is the village, varying in size from 10 to 150 huts. It is an economic unit and cooperation within a village in cattle-herding and horticulture is normal. The majority of villagers belong to the same lineage. There is no central authority and the village organization is largely egalitarian. Village elders have mediatory functions but no powers. The Lango have no formalized legal system and the arbitrator has no means to enforce his decision. Some headmen also exercise influence in neighboring villages and there was therefore a tendency towards leadership on a district level. This function was confined to military activities and was much weaker than among the ACHOLI. The office of war leader was not hereditary and depended on an individual's skill and success. Small-scale quarrels among the Lango were frequent, and they were involved in the wars between the GANDA and the NYORO.

The ACHOLI were traditionally the main enemies of the Lango, who were widely feared as warriors. Sometimes groups of Lango were employed as mercenaries, especially by King Kabelega of Bunyoro during encounters with his rivals and the BRITISH. The KUMAN seem to have been one of the major targets of Lango raids and a considerable number of KUMAN have been absorbed into the Lango.

Like their ACHOLI neighbors, the Lango used to live in large villages fortified against raiding enemies. Since the Ugandan state suppressed raiding, the settlement pattern has become one of more scattered homestead clusters. Attempts by the GANDA to conquer the Lango area after the subjection of the TESO were unsuccessful, and the Lango came under British colonial rule only in 1911. Milton Obote, prime minister of independent Uganda in the late 1960s, was himself a Lango.

The Lango had a special organization (*etogo*) for interlineage ceremonies, membership in which was inherited patrilineally. The *etogo* also played a role in burial rituals and rainmaking-ceremonies. Initiation into the *etogo* took place at the same time as initiation into the age-sets.

The Lango worship Jok, the creator, who is omnipresent, although in different manifestations. Jok is also held responsible for sickness and is, like the spirits worshiped by other Nilotic peoples, sometimes connected with specific places.

The ancestor spirits can intervene in everyday life, especially when they are perceived as being angry. Contact with the ancestors is established through rituals at the ancestor shrines without the aid of a religious specialist. However, other spheres require the services of a religious specialist, or *ajoka*, who interprets Jok's will. Both men and women can become *ajoka*, but religious and political authority are strictly separated. (see also UGANDANS)

LAN-MBE   see KABRE.

LANOH   A subgroup of the SEMANG.

LANTA I   (Balanta, Balante) The largest ethnic group, in Guinea-Bissau, numbering around 300,000 people or 32 percent of the population. They live to the north and south of the Geba River. They speak Balanta and mostly adhere to traditional religions. Their main occupation is rice cultivation.

At the end of the nineteenth and the beginning of the twentieth century the PORTUGUESE launched several campaigns against the Lanta until they succeeded in conquering their territory. During the colonial period the PORTUGUESE brought most of the local administration from the Cape Verde Islands. The Lanta served as forced laborers in projects such as railway building, while the CAPE VERDEANS served as foremen. This and the educational advantages enjoyed by the CAPE VERDEANS caused the Lanta deep feelings of frustration and resentment toward the PORTUGUESE and their Cape Verdean appointees.

The Lanta played an important role in the struggle for decolonization but often refused to fight the PORTUGUESE outside their own region because of their resentment towards other ethnic groups. Independence in 1974 did not end Lanta hostility toward the CAPE VERDEANS since the latter still dominated the new country. By 1980 very few Lanta had been promoted in the single ruling party, the government, or the army, and consequently, supported a military coup staged by the Principal Commander (a post equivalent to prime minister) and army commander of Guinea-Bissau, a member of the PAPEL, a traditional ally of the Lanta. After the coup most CAPE VERDEANS were removed from higher posts and these were filled by members of the Lanta, PAPEL, MANJACO, and other ethnic groups.

LANTA II   A subgroup of the DIOLA.

LAO   (Laotian, Laotian Tai, s.d. Phou Lao) A people numbering some 2 million, or 50 percent of the population of Laos. Although they are practically indistinguishable from their TAI neighbors in Thailand and Vietnam, they are considered a distinct ethnic group based on national as well as linguistic and minor religious differences. They are primarily Buddhists although traditional beliefs in spirits are still strong. The traditional religion is the religion of the living, it is said, while Buddhism is reserved for the dead. The Lao enjoy religious celebrations and village-sponsored ceremonies are quite common.

The original Lao state of Lan Xang lasted from the fourteenth to the eighteenth centuries. As colonial rulers, the FRENCH preserved the ancient dynasties ruling different regions of the country, with preference given to the dynasty ruling Luang Prabang. Upon independence, which was granted gradually in the 1950s, the ruling family of Luang Prabang was established as monarchs for the entire country, although certain sections were set aside for Communist insurgents known as the Pathet Lao, led by the king's half-brother. The Pathet Lao grew increasingly powerful and allowed the construction of the Ho Chi Minh Trail on its territory, connecting North and South Vietnam and Cambodia. A Pathet Lao regime was established throughout the country in 1975 and the monarchy was abolished.

Laos is one of the world's poorest countries. The population is 85 percent rural and much of the traditional village culture has survived. (see also KHMU)

LAOTIAN, LAOTIAN TAI   see LAO.

LAPPS   (s.d. Saami) The Lapps are natives of Lapland, a contiguous zone in the northern reaches of the Scandinavian peninsula, but due to long-lasting colonization by other peoples, they do not form a majority anywhere. Total numbers are variously given as 35,000-60,000: 20,000-40,000 in Norway, 10,000-

Lapps

15,000 in Sweden, 3,000-4,000 in Finland, and 2,000 in the Russian Kola peninsula.

The Saami language belongs to the western branch of the Finno-Ugric family. Saami is divided into a number of mutually almost unintelligible dialects. Most Lapps today are bilingual, and many are assimilating into their surroundings, passing within few generations from a near-prehistoric lifestyle to modernity. Written Saami developed in the seventeenth and eighteenth centuries in the framework of attempts at christianization. Before their conversion, Lapps, like many other circumpolar populations, were shamanists. Incantatory poems (*joik*) are until today characteristic of Lapp oral culture. In the 1830s many converted to Laestadianism, a Protestant fundamentalist movement. The use of the Saami language is declining. Lapp material culture is not rich.

The Lapps' origin is uncertain. Anthropologically a separate type, they possibly descend from a pre-Finnish population which later adopted a Finno-Ugric language. Until the middle ages, Lapps lived throughout Finland. During the sixteenth and seventeenth centuries, they retreated north and west into Sweden and Norway ahead of Finnish settlement. Swedish traders were instrumental in extending northern Sweden's scope and power of taxation.

Lapps, who used to combine herding with a sedentary life in winter villages, were forced, probably in the eighteenth century, to devote themselves entirely to reindeer pastoralism. Herding of reindeer plays a central role in the Lapp economy and culture to this day.

They were differentiated into three ecological groups. Mountain Lapps winter in forests and follow their herds upmountain in summer. They live off reindeer meat, use skis and a specific kind of tent (*kota*). The Forest Lapps are semi-nomadic fishermen along lakes. The Arctic Lapps are impoverished and completely sedentarized.

As long as national borders were not fixed, herders migrated from one territory to another. Indeed, even after the Swedish-Norwegian border was fixed in 1751, Lapps' rights to seasonal migration along traditional tracks were guaranteed. In practice, however, their rights were eroded, particularly by the expansion of agriculture in northern Sweden. This led to conflicts between the settled and nomadic population, and attempts to police Lapp-settled areas: in Sweden in the nineteenth century, grazing areas (*lappby*) were legally defined, and their members made collectively responsible for damages by reindeer to agricultural propriety.

above left: A Lapp man
above right: A Lapp woman
below: A Lapp couple

Lapps opting for the sedentary life lost their grazing privileges.

In the nineteenth century, many Lapps in Norway were forced to cede their lands to NORWEGIANS who settled their areas. During the twentieth century, as agriculture in northern Scandinavia declined, so did conflicts with the Lapps. But the emerging iron, timber, and meat production industries have led to the implantation of large non-Lapp populations in previously Saami territory, and affect the mosses and lichens which constitute reindeers' natural food. State policies have recently been geared to improve Lapp living standards, but to the detriment of their traditional lifestyles. Larger herds and fewer herders mean that herding is becoming a part-time occupation. Some Lapps have obtained financial compensation from the state for the loss of their herding rights, but many today have to supplement their incomes by the sale of handicrafts to tourists.

The radioactive fallout of the 1986 Chernobyl nuclear reactor disaster has further affected herding. Less than 10 percent of Lapps are engaged in pastoralism: the rest are hunters, fishermen, peasants, or have migrated to cities, where most Lapps live today. In Finland, combined herding-agriculture is permitted, and reindeer-herding is not a Lapp monopoly. In Russia the Saami were employed in *sovkhozes*. Reindeer-herding is more important for the Russian economy than for any other, and is not restricted to Lapps.

After an extended period of assimilation, the Lapp position has recently improved. Saami ethnic consciousness is on the rise and Saami parliaments are planned in Norway and Sweden. (see also FINNS)

LAQ I   An ethnic group living in a desert area in southern Iran, halfway between Kerman and Bandar Abbas. Little information or population data are available about them. Their language belongs to the Turkic family of languages, but nothing further is known about it. Judging by their environment, they are most likely Shi'ite Muslims and pastoral nomads. They may be connected with the AFSHAR, in whose immediate vicinity they live. However, they are not included in any listing of Afshar clans and tribes.

The Turkic language-speaking Laq of Iran are not to be confused with the LAQ of the Caucasus.

LAQ II   (Liak, Liakk, Qazi-Qumuq, Kazakumukh) A people living the mountains of central Daghestan and since 1944 also in the northwestern region of Daghes-

tan on the flat country (Novo-Laq region). In 1989 they numbered 120,000.

The Laq language, which has five dialects, belongs to the Daghestani branch of the Ibero-Caucasian family. Based on its Qumuq dialect, Laq is one of the first Daghestani languages to be written down (the first composition written in Laq dates back to 1734). Until 1928 it was written in the Arabic script, then in the Roman, and, since 1938, the Russian Cyrillic script.

The Laq have been Sunni Muslims since the thirteenth or fourteenth century.

The feudal state of Qaziqumuq Shamkhalate existed on Laq ethnic territory from the fourteenth century. As the Qaziqumuq Khanate, it was incorporated by the RUSSIANS into their empire in 1820.

Laq villages are usually located on steep slopes; livestock are housed on the lower floor of the stone house, traditional in Daghestan, while the family live on the upper floor. Laq men wear the clothing typical of the area, while women wear wide trousers and long dresses.

Their traditional economy includes agriculture, cattle-breeding, home industry, metal work (tableware, weapons), production of leather goods, and pottery.

LAQAY   A tribe of the UZBEKS.

LAQUA   (s.d. Ka Beo) A group of 200 speaking a Tai language and living in northern Vietnam. They are considered to be indigenous inhabitants of the region.

LARA   An ethnic group living on the Indonesian island of Kalimantan (Borneo). (see also DAYAK)

LARI   see LALI.

LASHI   A subgroup of the KACHIN.

LAT   A Mon-Khmer group numbering about 2,000, living in southern Vietnam. They are often classed with the NOP, LAYA, and other groups.

LATA   A subgroup of the NGUNI.

LATGALLIANS   (Latgolisi) see LATVIANS.

LATI   (s.d. A-khu) A group of 500 speaking a Tai language, living in northern Vietnam, where they are considered indigenous inhabitants.

LATUKA   A people living in the Equatoria Province of Sudan. (see also TOPOSA)

LATVIANS (Letts; s.d. Latviesi) There are about 1.7 million Latvians concentrated mainly in Latvia and in adjoining areas of neighbouring Estonia, Lithuania, and Russia. Sizable communities of Latvians in Western Europe and America date back mainly to the two World Wars and their aftermath.

Latvian is one of the two surving Baltic languages, which form a separate branch among the Indo-European languages. It is divided into three dialects; the central, spoken by the majority; eastern Augszemnicks; and northwestern Tamnieks. It has been written in the Roman alphabet since the sixteenth century.

Although ethnically and linguistically akin to the LITHUANIANS, the Latvians are closer in culture and religion to the ESTONIANS. This is due to the fact that whereas the Lithuanians were exposed to Polish influence and embraced Catholicism, the overwhelming majority of Latvians were exposed to the rule and influence of the GERMANS and joined the Lutheran church. However, they share with the LITHUANIANS the *dainas* tradition of folk songs.

In 1935, the last year for which population data are available, 68 percent of the Latvians were Lutheran. Almost all of the Catholics (26 percent in 1935) were Latgallians (s.d. Latgolisi), a distinct cultural and religious group living mainly in the eastern part of Latvia bordering on Russia, Belarus (Byelorussia), and Lithuania. This part of Latvia was under Polish-Lithuanian rule and its culture and religion were influenced accordingly. Latgali is a transitional dialect between Latvian and Lithuanian, and is mutually intelligible (though with some difficulty) by both. It has also been, and still is, used as a literary language, although the Latgallians use mainly standard literary Latvian.

The Latvians take their name from the Latgallians (Latgali), who originally lived in the northeast of present Latvia and absorbed the Selonians (Seli), the Semigallians (Zemgali), and the Couronians (Kursi). Whether these were Latvian tribes or separate Baltic peoples is the subject of debate. The Latgallians also assimilated the Finnic Livs (or Livonians), who inhabited the northwestern part of present Latvia.

In the first century C.E. Tacitus testified to contacts between the Roman world and the Baltic tribes, based on the amber trade. In the ninth century the Vikings crossed Latvia on their way to Russia. In the tenth and eleventh centuries both the SWEDES and the RUSSIANS tried to conquer and baptize the Latvians, but this was only achieved by the GERMANS in the first half of the thirteenth century; they divided Latvia among the Teutonic Order, the bishopric of Riga, and the free city of Riga.

The three centuries of German rule created profound change in the country. The country was westernized and both its nobility and its urban classes germanized. Riga's joining the Hanseatic League brought prosperity to the country, offset by the suffering inflicted on the population by constant wars with, and among, the neighboring kingdoms of Sweden, Poland, Lithuania, and Muscovite Russia.

Following the reformation, Poland and Sweden vied for the Baltic states, finally dividing Latvia in 1629. Vidrem (all territory north of Dvina) was annexed to Sweden, Latgale (the southeast) to Poland, and Courland became an autonomous duchy under the suzerainty of Poland. Following the Northern War, in 1721 Vidrem was annexed by Russia, to be followed by Latgale at the first Partition of Poland (1771) and Courland at the third (1795).

During the reign of Alexander I (1806–1825) the serfs were granted personal freedom, but only under Alexander II (1855–1881) were they given the right to own land. This, together with industrialization and urbanization, created a socio-economic change among the Latvians, which together with the spread of education and the revival of Latvian language and literature created the infrastructure for Latvian nationalism. Nationalism, however, finally rose as a reaction to the policy of forced russification pursued under Alexander III and Nicholas II.

The demand for a separate Latvian state was first made following 1905. In the wake of the 1917 revolutions Latvia proclaimed its independence, although it had to defend it (with foreign aid) against Soviet attempts at annexation. Following the Ribbentrop-Molotov agreement, Latvia was forced to grant bases to the Soviet Union and was then annexed to it in August 1940 as one of the Union republics.

During the first year of Soviet rule about 35,000 Latvians were arrested and deported to the Gulag, followed by almost 105,000 after the reconquest of Latvia from the GERMANS in World War II. About 65,000 Latvians fled to the West. The Soviet authorities initiated a policy of industrialization and russification which resulted in the 1980s in the de facto transformation of Latvia into a bi-national state in which the Latvians accounted for no more than 60 percent of the population, while the RUSSIANS comprised almost 40 percent. Riga became an overwhelmingly Russian city.

In the late 1980s Latvian nationalists organized a struggle for separation from the Soviet Union and reinstatement of complete independence. After the dissolution of the Soviet Union in 1991, Latvia became an independent state. It had still to solve the great problems related to the large Russian population within its borders.

LATVIESI   see LATVIANS.

LAWA   An ethnic group numbering about 10,000, living in northern Thailand. They speak a Mon-Khmer language and are Buddhists, although traditional beliefs retain great importance. They cultivate wet rice and were formerly known as miners of iron ore, although the practice has generally fallen into disuse.

LAWANGAN   An ethnic group living on the Indonesian island of Kalimantan (Borneo). (see also DAYAK)

LAYA   (La-Gia) A Mon-Khmer group numbering about 2,000, living in southern Vietnam. They are often classed with the LAT, NOP, and other groups.

LAZ   An ethnic group originating in the Caucasus who migrated to Turkey in 1878. (see also TURKS)

LAZI   see CHAN.

LEBANESE   (s.d. Lubnaniyyun) The Lebanese form a loose, mostly Arabic-speaking, conglomerate of religious and ethnic communities with a history of coexistence as well as of strife in a tiny mountainous country bordering the East Mediterranean. Lebanon's population is estimated at 3.5 million: Lebanese proper account for approximately 83 percent; the other 17 percent are PALESTINIANS, ARMENIANS, KURDS, and SYRIANS. The capital, Beirut, has a population of some 1.5 million.

Religion plays a dominant role in Lebanese life. In the mid-1980s, Christians, once the majority, constituted some 40 percent of the population (Maronites 25, Greek Orthodox 7, Greek Catholic 4, Armenian 4; smaller groups include Syrian Catholics and Syrian Orthodox, Chaldeans, Nestorians, Roman Catholics, and Protestants) and Muslims 60 percent (Shi'ites 32, Sunni 21, Druze 7; smaller groups are the 60,000 Alawites and a few thousand Isma'ilis).

Since the late nineteenth century, a large expatriate population has developed. More than half of all Lebanese reside abroad (total estimated at 2.6 million in 1970): 500,000 in the U.S.A., 250,000 in Brazil, 150,000 in Argentina, others in Africa and the Gulf. Due to the civil war untold numbers of Lebanese, PALESTINIANS, and SYRIANS have opted for exodus.

The Christian Maronites, numbering 900,000, are Arabic-speakers fluent in French as a second language. Maronite liturgy uses Syriac, a variant of the ancient Aramaic tongue. Founded officially by Saint Maron in the early fifth century, the Maronite Church was originally a monothelete church (preaching the unity of will in Jesus, a doctrinal compromise for monophysite quarrels, rejected by Byzantine Orthodoxy). Hailing from north Syria, it fled from persecution to the northern Mount Liban around the Qadisha Gorge. In 1099 Maronites accepted Orthodox dogma, but in 1216, under the influence of the Crusaders with whom they collaborated, went over to Catholic doctrines. The church is in communion with Rome since 1736. In the eighteenth century, the Maronites developed a feudal structure, partly under DRUZE overlordship. From the nineteenth century, the Maronite church was instrumental in the crystallization of a separate Lebanese identity. Its clergy, one of the pillars of Maronite power, owns a large part of Lebanon.

Maronite strongholds are the mountainous regions of Matn, Shuf, and Kisruan, but many migrated to East Beirut in the twentieth century. There is also a Maronite diaspora in America and in Black Africa, as well as a few in Syria, Israel, and Cyprus. Maronites claim descent from the Phoenicians and consider themselves Lebanese par excellence. Major clans are the Franji, Edde, Khoury, Chamoun, as well as the Gemayel, which controls the Phalange (*Katayyab*; since 1979 "Lebanese Forces"), militia of the Gemayel clan. Maronites advocate de facto partition of Lebanon into autonomous confessional cantons, although they have recently been forced into a modicum of cooperation with the Syrians.

The Greek Orthodox Christians (250,000) keep to the Chalcedonian dogma of Christ's double nature and to Byzantine rite (in Arabic), and are attached to the Patriarchate of Antioch. The oldest Christian group, they live dispersed. Most are city-dwellers; they control a large part of Beirut's wealth. Greek Catholics or Melkites (150,000) also follow the Byzantine rite, but in the eighteenth century attached themselves to Rome (Uniate).

The Sunni Muslims (750,000), once part of the "establishment," were eclipsed by the Christians. They are now the most urbanized community, entrenched in Beirut, Tripoli, and Sidon, and in the northern Akkar, southern Biq'a, and Shuf. More than any other group, they resented Lebanon's separation from Syria in 1920: the Sunni popular basis is still rather pan-Arab. Leading families are the Karam and Sulh.

above: Extracting pine nuts in the mountains of Lebanon
below: Lebanese in a Beirut market

The Shi'ite Muslims (Mutawalis; 1.1 million), the poorest, most oppressed, and largest group, live mainly in the south (Jabal Amil), Beirut's slums, the Biq'a, and the Hermel (in the northeast). They believe that the line of successors to Ali died out in the thirteenth century with the disappearance of the last imam, who will reappear to redeem the world: messianism and devotion to cult figures mark their religious practice. In the 1970s, Israeli bombing against Palestinian refugees living in their midst succeeded in alienating south Lebanese Shi'ites from the latter, but also politicized them. Many fled to West Beirut where they started the Movement for the Dispossessed, from which the al-Amal militia sprang. The Iranian revolution inspired pride: they came to reject traditional Sunni dominance. Amal supports secularization and democratization of the Lebanon, whereas the more radical Hizbullah propounds an Islamic state.

The DRUZE of Lebanon number 200,000 or more. They are concentrated in the Shuf mountains. Major clans are the Junblatis and Yazbaqis.

Of all ARABS, none have been more thoroughly influenced by the West than the Lebanese, and none are more divided. Commercial links with the West were maintained throughout centuries; in particular, ties with France go back to Maronite protection by the Crusaders. The Lebanese remained a village-oriented nation, in spite of the fact that nearly two-thirds were town-dwellers. Lebanese prosperity was largely based on incomes from services: trade, banking, investments, and insurance, shipping, airlines, oil terminals, education and medical services, and tourism, and remittances from Lebanese living abroad. Beirut was the cultural and leisure capital of the Arab world, and Lebanon seemed the epitome of successful modernization without revolution.

However, this open and pluralistic culture was plagued by a combination of social changes and regional conflicts that culminated in continuous civil war, leading to the collapse of the Lebanese economy. By the 1980s, manufacturing had declined by 75 percent, and narcotics had become a major export, providing the money for arms imports by the warring militias. Beirut's population declined by half.

Lebanon's many ethno-religious communities reflect a history of geographical isolation and foreign intervention at one and the same time. Phoenicians (Canaanites), the presumed forerunners of the modern Lebanese, developed the natural ports of Tyre, Sidon, and Byblos until Greek conquests supplanted Phoenician trade preeminence. The region then came under Seleucid, Roman, and then Byzantine control. The Muslim conquest changed its religious balance and language, but Christianity remained predominant in Mount Lebanon. Its fragmented coast and mountainous interior became a refuge for those fighting central authorities and/or dominant orthodoxies.

The late nineteenth century was an era of Maronite predominance and cultural revival spurred on by Western missionary efforts. Only the Maronites welcomed the French mandate after World War I. In 1920 the FRENCH added the predominantly Muslim regions to create "Greater Lebanon." The Syrians were outraged at this amputation. In its new borders, Lebanon had become much more religiously heterogeneous.

When Lebanon became independent in 1943, the leaders of its religious communities were forced to work out some formula for living together. The last census, of 1932, showing a slight Christian majority, became the basis for a carefully arranged power-sharing arrangement, whereby confessional identity determines allocation of parliament seats and of military and bureaucratic offices. Lebanese political culture came to be based on communal sectarianism.

Stability in the 1950s and 1960s made for prosperity, but also for a growing gap between rich and poor. A first civil war was fought in 1958 over Lebanon's adherence to conflicting political forces in the Arab world. In 1975 civil war broke out again, in the form of a power struggle between Maronite clans and Muslim Leftist-radicals supported by PALESTINIANS. Effective central government broke down, to be restored only in 1989.

In that year Lebanon's leaders agreed to the Syrian-backed Taif agreement, which called for a new equilibrium in Christian-Muslim relations, dissolution of all militias, and extension of state control over the whole territory. Controlled by a government of national unity, itself controlled by Syria, Greater Beirut has become a Syria-dependent city state which is gradually extending its hold. Reconstruction has begun, but Lebanon's overriding question of identity still hangs over this heterogenous state.

LEBONI   An ethnic group living in the mountainous central region of the Indonesian island of Sulawesi (Celebes). (see also TORADJA)

LEBU   An ethnic group living in Senegal. Their original homeland is in the Cape Verde peninsula. They speak Wolof.

LELA An ethnic group living in the Tenado region of Burkina Faso, west of Koudougou between the Black and Red Volta Rivers.

LELE A small ethnic group living in the Kissidougou region of Guinea along the Sierra Leone border. They have been almost completely absorbed into the surrounding groups, especially the MALINKE and the KISSI.

LEMBA A Shona-speaking group living in the Mberengwa area of Zimbabwe. They are traders and metal workers who converted to Islam before the eighteenth century. (see also VENDA)

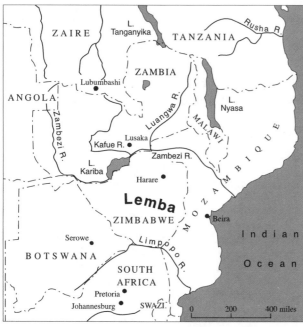

Lemba

LEMBAK (Sindang) An ethnic group numbering about 40,000, living among the REDJANG in south-central Sumatera (Sumatra), an island in Indonesia. They are Malay-speaking Muslims. Although both the REDJANG and the MALAYS consider the Lembak to be a subgroup of theirs, the Lembak see themselves as a distinct group, citing their precolonial state, Sindang Merdeka, which served as a buffer between the REDJANG and the sultanate of Palembang.

The highland Lembak have better preserved their traditions and culture than the lowland Lembak, who have incorporated considerable Malay cultural elements.

LEMBETU see REMBETU.

LEMBO An ethnic group living in the mountainous central region of the Indonesian island of Sulawesi (Celebes). (see also TORADJA)

LEMO A subgroup of the HADIYA.

LEMOUNTA A subgroup of the MAURE.

LENDU A people living in Uganda, to which they were brought by SUDANESE soldiers. Originally they lived on the high plateau of the southern part of Lake Albert, and there were later several settlements as far south as the town of Entebbe. They are therefore of mixed origin. Their language is not a Bantu, but a Sudanese one, although they are to a considerable extent assimilated into the ALUR.

The Lendu are agriculturalists. Their households are polygynous and their kinship system is one of patrilineal clans. Their highest authority are the chiefs. The Lendu are not politically unified.

Their religious specialists are the *jiko* (rainmakers) and *begiga* (healers); ancestor worship plays a prominent role in their religious system. (see also ALUR)

LENGI (Balenge) An ethnic group living in Equatorial Guinea. (see also EQUATORIAL GUINEANS)

LENJE A Tonga-speaking group numbering 125,000 living east of the Lukanga Swamp in southern Zambia. They trade in copper and ivory but are not organized into chiefdoms. In 1890 some Lenje signed treaties with Cecil Rhodes in return for protection against the NGUNI and CHIKUNDA.

LENTOUNA A subgroup of the SANHADJA.

LEPANTO (Sagada, Igorot; s.d. Katangnang) An ethnic group living in some thirty villages in the western part of Bontok subprovince and Ilocos Sur Province in northern Luzon, an island in the Philippines.

The Lepanto number 75,000 and are currently divided into six major bilateral descent groups. They speak a language similar to the Northern Kankanai languages and practice wet-rice terracing in the same way as their neighbors, the BONTOK. Settlements are compact, containing up to 700 persons. Houses may be of two or three storeys; households comprise a unit known as *obon*, and are not always kinship based. No marked differences in wealth exist. Funerary rites play an important part in their culture.

LEPCHA   An ethnic group numbering 50,000 (1981), located in Sikkim, West Bengal, and Tripura, India. They speak Himalayan languages belonging to the Tibeto-Burman family. The Lepcha are of Mongoloid stock, living in the Himalayas on the southern and eastern slopes of Mount Kanchen Junga.

The Lepcha religion is known as *Mun*. Its priests wear Buddhist robes and follow monks' duties. They are expected to protect the people from epidemics by communion with the supernatural and by periodical sacrifices.

When Tibet's suzerainty over Sikkim began in the early seventeenth century, the Lepcha were overshadowed by the BHUTIA of Sikkim, the latter being more industrious and accustomed to plow cultivation. In subsequent centuries the Lepcha joined the BHUTIA in their struggle against the more prosperous NEPALESE, but both NEPALESE and BHUTIA treated the Lepcha as slaves.

Some of the Lepcha are agriculturists, others day-laborers, carpenters, and goverment workers. (see also SIKKIMESE)

LESU   An ethnic group of approximately 1,000 living on the east coast of New Ireland, a Pacific island in the state of Papua New Guinea, east of the mainland. They speak an indigenous local language. They are slash and burn cultivators and fishermen. Their religious beliefs are a mixture of Christianity and traditional religion. Life-cycle events are celebrated in ceremonies involving singing and dancing.

LETO   An ethnic group living in Chad.

LETTS   see LATVIANS.

LEUFUCHE   A subgroup of the TEHUELCHE.

LEYA   (Baleya) A Tonga-speaking group numbering about 20,000 living along the Zambezi River in southern Zambia.

LEZGI   (Lezghi) A people living in southeast Daghestan and in northern Azerbaijan. In 1989 they numbered 470,000.

The ethnic term *Lezgi*, in various phonetic forms, has been known since antiquity and from Arab and Persian medieval sources. In these and in Russian sources, the term was erroneously used for all southern Daghestani mountain people.

The Lezgi language, with three dialects, belongs to the Daghestani branch of the Ibero-Caucasian family.

Lezgi

Literary Lezgi is based on its Gune (Kurin) dialect. It became a written language using the Arabic script in the second half of the nineteenth century. In 1928 it was reduced to the Roman and in 1938 to the Cyrillic script. The illiterate folk poet Suleiman Stalskii (1869–1937), was highly lauded by Soviet literary critics and historians as the founder of Soviet Lezgi literature.

The Lezgi are Sunni Muslims whose final islamization took place no earlier than the mid-fifteenth century. Some of the Lezgi living in Azerbaijan became Shi'ites, evidently in the sixteenth or seventeen centuries. The first Lezgi Khanate (principality) was founded in 1775 in the Kurin area. In 1812 it submitted to Russia and by 1864 all Lezgi territories were part of the Russian Empire.

Lezgi stone houses in the mountain regions consist of two or more storeys with recesses in the walls and an inner court. Traditional clothing for men is typical for all Daghestan; women wear wide trousers, long dresses, and headscarves.

Their traditional economy is based on distant sheep-breeding in the mountains, and cattle-breeding, agriculture, horticulture, metalwork (weapons, jewellery), and carpet-weaving in the foothills.

LHOTE   A subgroup of the NAGA living in the eastern hill region of Nagaland, India, on the border with northwestern Myanmar (Burma).

LI   The Li are the aboriginal inhabitants of Hainan Island, off the southern coast of China, where they constitute the largest minority group (numbering approximately 818,000), followed by the MIAO.

They are said to be descended from the ancient Yue tribes of China who settled on the island over 3,000 years ago. Since their language, belonging to the Tai family, had no written form, they used Chinese ideographs. In 1957, the government helped them create their own Roman alphabet.

Principal religious beliefs include the worship of ancestors, local earth gods, and other spirits.

Most Li settled in the upland river valleys, where their principal occupations are slash-and-burn agriculture, buffalo- and cattle-raising, and hunting.

Li culture is an intermediate stage between that of the THAIS and INDONESIANS. At weddings they refrain from using wagons or horses. The groom visits his prospective in-laws on a day selected as lucky, carrying a piece of red cloth with which he wraps the girl and carries her away. Soon after, he returns with her to her parents' home and lives there until his wife becomes pregnant. Only then can they establish their own home.

LIAK, LIAKK   see LAQ II.

LIANGMEI   A NAGA group. (see also ZELIANGRONG)

LIBERIANS
The population of Liberia in West Africa, which was founded in 1847 by freed black slaves from the southern United States of America. They number 2.7 million. The Liberians consist of a number of ethnic groups, including the AMERICO-LIBERIANS, the descendants of the original settlers, who now constitute fewer than 2 percent of the population. Other groups are the KPELLE, DAN (Gio), MANO, LOMA, GHANDI, and MENDE in the north of the country, the KRU, BASSA, GREBO, KRAHN, and DEI in the southeast, the GOLA, KISSI, and VAI in the southwest. More than 20 percent of the Liberians live around the capital, Monrovia.

The official language is English but the most widely spoken languages are Mande and Kru-Bassa. Liberia is officially a Christian state, although complete freedom of religion is guaranteed. Christianity and Islam are the two main religions but many Liberians adhere to traditional religions.

From the foundation of Liberia up to 1980 the AMERICO-LIBERIANS formed the ruling elite and local ethnic groups were usually hostile toward them. In 1915 the KRU revolted against the Americo-Liberians, but the revolt was crushed with the help of the United States. In 1980 a military coup carried out by Samuel Doe, who belonged to the KRAHN ethnic group, put an end to America-Liberian hegemony. He was in power for ten years. In 1990 a civil war broke out between his ethnic group and the DAN, MANO, and KISSI groups, during which he was killed. Despite efforts to end the war, it continues, disrupting the life of all Liberians.

LIBIYYUN   see LIBYANS.

LIBYANS
(s.d. Libiyyun) The 4.7 million inhabitants of Libya, except for a few Berber-speaking pockets, are ARABS. Nearly all are Sunni Muslims. The population is concentrated in a shallow zone along the coast. Only the areas around the capital, Tripoli, permit some modest agriculture. About 300,000 Libyans, mainly in the eastern region of Cyrenaica, are pastoralists. In the desert there are a large number of oases. Until petroleum was discovered, Libya was a very poor country.

After a confused history of successive conquests and colonizations by Phoenicians, GREEKS, Romans, Byzantines, and ARABS, the eleventh century invasions by nomad ARABS (the Bani Hilal) first created the core of the Libyan nation. An object of Spanish-Ottoman rivalry, Libya became a Turkish province in the sixteenth century. The Karamanli dynasty unified Tripoli, Cyrenaica, and Fezzan in the eighteenth century, and became hereditary rulers under Ottoman suzerainty until the Ottoman empire restored direct rule in 1835. In the same year, the religious leader Muhammad ben Ali al-Sanussi started a national-religious movement (Al-Sanussiya) based on autonomous oases. In 1890 his successors beat the Ottoman TURKS but were unable to ward off Italian ambitions. In 1912 Italy conquered Libya and proceeded to destroy its tribal society. Colonization by ITALIANS, mainly SICILIANS and Umbrians, in the 1930s led to the displacement of the local population. During World War II the refugee King Idris supported the BRITISH against Italy, and after the war was restored to power.

Starting in the 1960s, massive oil revenues enabled Libyans to become independent from foreign aid and turned the country into a wealthy state. However, the oil boom profited a narrow elite whose conspicuous consumption patterns did little to endear it to other Libyans. A nationalist opposition of military, students, and civil servants began to agitate against the monarchy, and demanded the evacuation of foreign military bases.

Modern Libyan history begins with the radical and anti-royalist revolution carried out in 1969 by Muammar Qadhafi and his "Free Officers." While the regime, initially, was dominated by the military, power shifted into civilian hands. However, Qadhafi's own role was only enhanced. Oil was nationalized in 1973; massive oil-derived revenues made possible a series of social-political experiments which have thoroughly changed the Libyans' archaic social life.

Libya's economic policy is now "Islamic socialist." Officially the salaried class has been abolished in favor of producers' associations where no private gains may be realized, laborers own and manage expropriated factories, monetary exchanges are restricted, consumption is limited, and private trade is abolished. In practice, Libyans needed foreign labor. By the end of the 1970s, one third of their work force consisted of non-Libyan guest laborers, some of them later replaced by Libyans.

A one-party state was established. In the 1970s Qadhafi launched his "people's revolution," a cultural revolution to purge "ill elements." Direct democracy was institutionalized by directly-chosen revolutionary committees, established to ideologically activate the masses. Theoretically anarchist, Qadhafi's dictatorship of the revolutionary committees in practice transformed Libya into a police state, harshly suppressing any opposition — the most dangerous being radical Islamic fundamentalists. But in spite of internal crises, Qadhafi has always won thanks to his symbolic function as victor over the monarchy and his charismatic power of mobilization.

In principle, Libya's leader has established a reputation for intransigence, adventurism, and unpredictability. Libyans have initiated a number of failed fusion attempts with other Arab countries and have repeatedly confronted the West. Declining oil incomes in the 1980s provoked unpopular austerity measures. Disaffection by the army showed in coup attempts. After keeping a very low profile in the Gulf crisis, the Libyan leadership in 1990 risked a very circumspect domestic liberalization program, restraining the Revolutionary Committee's power and timidly allowing a private sector to reappear.

LIETUVIAI   see LITHUANIANS.

LIKOULA   see KWALA.

LIKUBA   An ethnic group related to the MBOCHI living in Congo.

LILLOOET   A Native North American group numbering about 2,500, living in British Columbia, Canada. Many earn their living today working in the lumber industry. In the last few years they have taken a more vociferous stand to support their land claims against the provincial and federal governments. They have also spearheaded protests against logging in the Stein Valley in British Columbia. Some of the largest folk festivals in support of the environment have been held annually on the Lillooet Reserve. (see also COLVILLE)

LILVI   see LIVS.

LIMA   A Chibemba-speaking group numbering 36,000 living in central Zambia along the western region of the southern copper belt. They are Christians and also practice traditional religions. Their culture and social organization are similar to those of the BEMBA.

LIMBA I   An ethnic group numbering about 325,000 living in the northern province of Sierra Leone. They mostly adhere to traditional religions, but seem to be more attracted to Christianity than to Islam. Their main occupation is palm-wine production.

LIMBA II   An ethnic group related to the LAMBA living in Zambia.

LIMBOO   A subgroup of the KIRANT.

LIMBOTO   A subgroup of the GORONTALO.

LIMBU   see GURKHA.

LIMMU ENARYA   A subgroup of the OROMO.

LINDA   A subgroup of the BANDA.

LINDU   An ethnic group living in the mountainous central region of the Indonesian island of Sulawesi (Celebes). (see also TORADJA)

LINGA   An ethnic group related to the MBOCHI living in Congo.

LIONESE   (s.d. Lio) An ethnic group living in the mountainous region of central Flores, an island in Indonesia. They speak Endenese. Portuguese contact in the seventeenth century led many Lionese to adopt Catholicism and to establish a small Christian coastal state, Paga. Now, virtually all Lionese are Catholic.

LIPAN A subgroup of the APACHE.

LISI An ethnic group living in Chad. (see also CHADIANS).

LISU A group numbering approximately 500,000 mainly inhabiting the mountain villages of the Yunnan Province of southwest China. Some also live in Myanmar (Burma) and Thailand. Historical documents dating from the Ming dynasty refer to the Lisu as a branch of the YI people.

Their language is a member of the Yi group of the Tibeto-Burmese family of languages. An incomplete writing system was replaced in 1957, with the help of

Lisu

the Chinese government, by a new one based on the Roman alphabet.

Having retained their ancient beliefs, the Lisu worship their ancestors and gods of the earth, sky, wind, lightning, and forests. A priestly caste once existed, and priests are still regarded as the keepers of Lisu customs. Their specialized knowledge of Lisu traditions and folklore is essential in preserving Lisu identity.

Like other local groups, the Lisu hunt and cultivate dry hill rice, corn, and buckwheat. Their houses are built of wood or bamboo, with a fireplace in the main room serving as the social center. Opposite the door an altar to ancestral spirits serves as the household's center of ritual.

LITHUANIANS (s.d. Lietuviai) The approximately 3.1 million Lithuanians form about 80 percent of the population of Lithuania, which until 1991 was part of the Soviet Union. Several hundred thousand live in North America, Europe, Australia, or scattered throughout various former Soviet republics.

The Lithuanian language is related to Lettish (Latvian) with which it constitutes the Baltic group within the Indo-European family of languages. It is believed that the ancestors of the Lithuanians settled in the basins of the Neman and Dvina Rivers at the beginning of the second millennium B.C.E. Living as separate tribes, they worshiped forest divinities and venerated ancient oaks, a practice still observed among rural Lithuanians. Conversion in the mid-thirteenth century to Roman Catholic Christianity, still the predominant religion in the country today, helped to unite the Lithuanian tribes, which formed a unified state with Vilna as its capital in the first half of the fourteenth century. The Lithuanian principality later expanded its rule over Russian provinces and by the end of the fourteenth century had become the strongest power in eastern Europe. In 1569 the Lithuanians formed a union with the POLES, following which the Lithuanian aristocracy and urban population became in due time entirely polonized.

With the rise of Russia in the eighteenth century and following the division of Poland, the Lithuanians found themselves under the RUSSIANS. In the nineteenth century, especially after the Polish revolts of 1831 and 1863, the Russian authorities followed a policy of russification. Thus, in 1863 Russian was proclaimed the sole official language and the Cyrillic alphabet was imposed on the Lithuanian language. Many RUSSIANS were settled among the Lithuanians. The Lithuanian national revival, a backlash to russification, led to a nationalist movement which succeeded in proclaiming an independent state after World War I. Vilna was occupied in 1920 by Poland, and Kaunas (Kovno) was proclaimed the capital of Lithuania. Following the Ribbentrop-Molotov agreement, Lithuania was occupied in 1940 by the Soviets and incorporated into the Soviet Union as one of its fifteen republics. Between 1941 and 1945 it was occupied by the GERMANS. Following World War II about 100,000 Lithuanians took refuge in Germany from the Soviets, while 200,000 others were exiled to the eastern parts of the Soviet Union. At the same time about a quarter of a million RUSSIANS were settled in the Lithuanian Soviet Socialist Republic. The Lithuanian diaspora in western countries has served since 1940 as a cultural and political center, keeping alive aspirations for independence.

In the late 1980s the nationalist movement gained in strength. In 1989 Lithuania proclaimed independence, which caused a prolonged, mainly non-violent, con-

The Lisu

frontation with Moscow. Following the disintegration of the USSR in 1991, Lithuania reclaimed its independence and was accepted as a member of the United Nations. (see also LATVIANS)

LITHUANIAN TATAR   see CRIMEAN TATAR.

LIVS   (Livonians; s.d. Lilvi, Raandalii) The fewer than 5,000 Livs, who live in the westernmost part of Latvia, are the remnants of a much larger people assimilated by the LATVIANS and ESTONIANS. The ancient territory of Livonia, which covered the southern half of present-day Estonia and the northern half of Latvia, was named after them.

The Livonian language belongs to the Finnic branch of the Finno-Ugric group of languages. It has been written since the nineteenth century, although Latvian is generally used by the Livs as their literary language. (see also LATVIANS)

LOBEDU   (Lovedu) A subgroup of the SOTHO.

LOBI   An ethnic group living in the Gaoua and Diebougou regions of Burkina Faso and in the Côte d'Ivoire, where they originally inhabited the area between the Black and White Volta Rivers. They are now scattered across that country.

The Lobi never had a centralized political organization. While their territory was colonized by the FRENCH in 1901, they were little affected by colonization. In the Cote d'Ivoire they are considered among the country's poorest ethnic groups. The TUSIA (Tusyan) who live east of Banfora and the DOROSIE (Dorobe) who live around Lakosso (both in Burkina Faso) are subgroups of the Lobi. (see also BURKINABES, IVOIREANS, MOLE-DAG-BANI)

LOHRA   An ethnic group numbering 193,000 (1981), living in Bihar and West Bengal, India. They speak Ho, a dialect of the Austroasiatic family of languages.

They are mainly blacksmiths, living scattered in villages of other peoples and ethnic groups. They make the tools required by neighboring farmers, such as sickles, ax heads, arrows, and plowshares, receiving food in return.

LOI   An ethnic group related to the MBOCHI living in Congo.

LOIKOP   see SAMBURU.

LOINANG   see SALUAN.

LOLO   An ethnic group numbering about 120,000 living in Sierra Leone. (see also SIERRA LEONEANS)

LOLODA   An ethnic group closely related to the TO-BELORESE, living on the Indonesian island of Halmahera.

LOLOKA   see PALUO.

LOMA   (Toma) A Mande-speaking group living in Upper Lofa County, Liberia. They number around 125,000, or 5 percent of the country's population. Loma living in the Macenta administrative region of Guinea are called Toma. In the latter country, they are gradually assimilating into the larger MALINKE population. (see also LIBERIANS)

LOMWE   see LIBERIANS, MAKUA-LOMWE.

LONGKEA   An ethnic group living in the mountainous central region of the Indonesian island of Sulawesi (Celebes). (see also TORADJA)

LOPAWA   A subgroup of the FULANI.

LORRAINES   see ALSATIANS.

LOSSO   An ethnic group related to the KABRE living in northern Togo. They mostly adhere to traditional religions.

LOTHA   (Kyon-tsu, Miklai, Tiontz, Tson-tsu) An ethnic group numbering 58,000 (1981) located in the Wokha district of Nagaland, India. They are related to the RENGMA and the AO, and their customs and dress are very similar.

Unlike the majority of NAGA, the Lotha own land in common, although they do allow some private land holdings as well.

LOUCHEUX   A Native North American group of the Athapaskan-speaking peoples numbering about 2,500, making them one of the largest tribes in the Yukon region in Canada.

LOVALE   An ethnic group numbering about 100,000 living in northwest Zambia. They speak Lovale and profess both Christianity and traditional religions. Lovale initiation ceremonies for girls and boys include masked dancers representing various spirits. They are primarily fishermen and hunters, but also grow cassava. (see also GANGUELA, LUNDA)

LOVE   see BRAO.

LOVEN   A Mon-Khmer group numbering about 20,000 living in southern Laos. They are becoming increasingly Buddhist, although remnants of traditional religions and ancestor-worship linger, particularly in rites related to death.

The Loven have been particularly influenced by the surrounding LAO and the FRENCH. They are primarily agriculturalists, and have adopted several new crops such as potatoes and coffee.

LOZI   (Barotse, Rozi, Barozi) A people numbering 235,000 living in southwest Zambia. They speak Lozi and are predominantly Christians, although some still adhere to their traditional religion, which, focused on the cult of a high god, developed into a cult of the king. Lozi agriculture, centered in the Kafue River flood plain, was the most complex and intensive system in pre-colonial Africa. They also engaged in fishing, cattle-raising, and trade.

The Lozi descent system was bilateral, but only the royal clan and lineage was of any significance. A centralized Lozi empire developed when their king defeated neighboring peoples inhabiting areas near the Kafue River. The king ensured loyalty by distributing land grants to his officers.

The development of a royal bureaucracy is unique to the Lozi. It consisted of three types of officials; members of the court who performed religious rituals and supervised the tribute received from subject peoples, territorial governors who served as judges, and officers responsible for tributary peoples and recruitment for the army.

In the mid-eighteenth century the Lozi conquered the SUBIYA, LOVALE, ILA, TOTELA, TOKA, MBUNDA, and KWANGWA. In the mid-nineteenth century, the Lozi were temporarily conquered by the KOLOLO but the monarchy was restored in 1864.

In the twentieth century many Lozi attended schools opened by the Europeans and became clerks in the colonial administration. The majority, however, continued to work in the copper belt. Toward the end of the colonial period, the Lozi fought to maintain a separate status for their people. They petitioned the BRITISH in 1961 for an independent state, but this was refused. In 1969, the Zambian government recognized the tradi-

tional rights of the Lozi within the country. (see also ZAMBIANS)

LUANO   An ethnic group numbering about 10,000 living in south-central Zambia, east of Lusaka. They speak Chibemba.

LUBA   (Baluba) A people of around 9 million (together with the MONGO) living in the Kasai and Shaba (Katanga) Regions of Zaire. Their language, Tshiluba, is one of Zaire's four national languages. They profess either Christianity or traditional religions. The Luba are subdivided into three groups: LUBA-KASAI, LUBA-SHABA, and SONGYE.

From the fourteenth to eighteenth centuries the Luba controlled a large empire in the southeastern part of present-day Zaire. During the eighteenth and nineteenth centuries their kingdom disintegrated into small rival princedoms following the outbreak of a civil war and invasions by the CHOKWE, YEKE, and LUNDA. Under colonial rule by the BELGIANS many Luba moved to cities and to mission centers to take advantage of educational opportunities. The Luba were very active in colonial administration and commercial life.

Many Luba who lived in Kasai migrated to the mineral-rich and relatively developed Katanga region. These newcomers were highly resented by the local LUNDA group in Katanga. In 1960, when Belgium abandoned its colony, the LUNDA led the secession of Katanga. At first, the local Luba saw the conflict as one of poor locals against rich foreigners and supported the LUNDA, but the conflict soon became ethnic and the local Luba joined the Kasai Luba and their organization, Balubakat, which opposed the secession. After the Katanga crisis ended in 1963, with Katanga remaining part of Zaire, some Luba became involved in politics and acquired high positions in the administration of the country while many others were critical of the regime of Mobutu Sese Seko and remained highly independent of the central government. The Lunda-Luba conflict in Katanga is manifested today by the flight of Luba from Katanga to Kasai following severe attacks upon them by the LUNDA. (see also ZAIREANS)

LUBA-KASAI   A subgroup of the LUBA.

LUBA-SHABA   A subgroup of the LUBA.

LUBICON   A Native North American group of CREE who until 1985 did not have an "official" existence. It was the protest of the CREE living in the Lubicon Valley against the incursion of the pipeline into their traditional hunting lands that brought them together as a recognized group. Only recently has the government provided a reserve for them and recognized them as having Native status in Canada.

LUBNANIYYUN   see LEBANESE.

LUBU   see KUBU.

LUCHAZI   An ethnic group numbering about 50,000 living in northwestern Zambia. They are part of the Lunda-Lovale language group and are related to the CHOKWE and LOVALE.

LUENA   see GANGUELA.

LUGBARA   A people living in the densely populated area of northwestern Uganda (West Nile District), and in Zaire. They speak a Central Sudanic language. The two subgroups of the Lugbara, the High and the Low, regarded as historically distinct, are also linguistically different. High Lugbara, spoken in the west, is closely related to Kiliko, a language spoken in Zaire, whereas Low Lugbara is intelligible to speakers of Madi.

The Lugbara are predominantly agriculturalists, growing a variety of vegetables, fruits, and grains: sorghum, bananas, cassava, and maize, with tobacco as a cash crop. They also keep animals: cattle, goats, sheep, and fowl. They live in scattered settlements. They have very few specialists, mainly smiths (men) and potters (women). Since the 1920s there has been a growing number of migrant wage-laborers working in southern Uganda.

The kinship system of the Lugbara is based on patrilineal exogamous clans. They have no chiefs. The elders have only the function of arbitrators.but do not possess the means to enforce their decisions.

The Lugbara were in contact with Europeans since the early nineteenth century. Since 1914 their region has been part of Uganda.

The majority of the Lugbara are Christians, although a minority profess Islam. Traditionally the Lugbara believed in one creator god, worshiped ancestor spirits, and practiced witchcraft. (see also UGANDANS)

LUHYA   The Luhya people of western Kenya are estimated as numbering 2 million and are the third largest group in the country. They live in three western districts of Kenya: Bungoma, Busia, and Kakamega. They speak the Baluhya language, a Western Bantu tongue, and most of them have been Christians for the last century. The Luhya are a conglomerate of 15–20 different groups of people who emigrated to the Buluhya region between the sixteenth and eighteenth centuries. All these groups, whether Nilotic - or Cushitic - speaking people by origin, were bantuized, retaining neither their original language nor their other traditional characteristics.

The Luhya are in fact regarded as a separate entity solely by virtue of being distinct from their neighbours in Western Kenya, the Luo- and Nilotic-speaking peoples. However, while there are variations in the dialects, rituals, economic pursuits, and culture of the various Luhya groups, there are also features common to them all: a language and certain cultural elements.

There are fifteen groups that are generally agreed as belonging to the Luhya people. Those groups are: the Abaisukha, Abaidakho, BUKUSU, Abakabrasi, Abawanga, Abanyala, Nyole, Maragoli, Samia, Shisa, Trichi (Tiriki), Marama, Marachi, Tsotso, and Khekhe.

Most Luhya people engage in agriculture, and some keep cattle and other domestic animals. The main crop is maize, both as a staple and a cash crop. Other cash crops are sugar cane, cotton, cassava, and tobacco.

Various traditional rituals are still observed by most Luhya. The most important is male circumcision, which is practiced by all Luhya groups, but with variations between the different groups.

LUISENO   A Native North American group also known as the Mission Indians, living on several Federal Reservations such as La Jolla, La Posta, and Los Coyotes, California. They earn their livelihood today by means of farming.

LULI   see GYPSIES.

LULUA   A people living in the Western Kasai Region of Zaire, between the Lulua and Kasai Rivers. They are related to the LUBA.

During colonial rule by the BELGIANS the Lulua did not try to seek educational and employment opportunities. They began to organize politically only after World War II and in 1959 they called for autonomy rather than independence. There have been tensions between them and the LUBA.

LUMBU   An ethnic group related to the ILA living in Zambia.

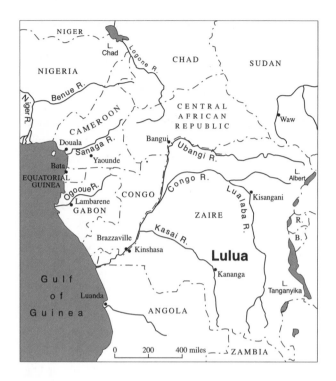

Lulua

Lunda

LUMMI A Native North American group numbering about 3,000, many of whom live on the Lummi Federal Reservation in Washington State, U.S.A. Today, as in the past, they earn their livelihood through fishing.

LUNDA An people living in the Lunda and Moxico Provinces of eastern Angola (where they number about 400,000), in the northwest region and Luapula Province of Zambia (where they number about 150,000), and in southwestern Zaire. They speak Lunda and are Christians or retain traditional beliefs in a supreme deity called Lesa and nature spirits. Other religious beliefs and rituals were influenced by the BEMBA and the Christian Watchtower Movement. Although traditionally agriculturalists, the Lunda also participated in the slave trade with the PORTUGUESE.

The Lunda follow a patrilineal descent system with political authority formerly centralized in a Lunda kingdom which emerged in southwestern Zaire in the tenth and eleventh centuries. The Lunda king was served by district governors and a bureaucracy peopled by members of the royal family, commoners, and even people of other ethnic origins who had been absorbed by the Lunda.

While most scholars believe that the Lunda did not expand into Zambia and Angola until the seventeenth century, there is evidence in oral tradition that they may have begun their migration and absorption of new peoples as early as the sixteenth century, but it only gained momentum in the early eighteenth century along the Zaire-Zambia watershed. Leaders of these newly adopted chiefdoms were given important positions in the Lunda government, which prepared them to secede and establish their chiefdoms (cf. the NDEMBU, who settled along the Zambezi River headwaters, and the LOVALE, who settled in Luapula Province).

In the eighteenth century the Lunda began moving east in search of salt and seized the salt pans at Kecila, eventually controlling the area east of the Lufira river.

In Angola, groups such as the OVIMBUNDU, the GANGUELA, and the MBUNDU were particularly influenced by Lunda migrants. Lunda influence in the region was brought to a halt by rapid expansion and colonization of Lunda regions by the CHOKWE in eastern Angola. Interaction between the Lunda and CHOKWE in eastern Angola led to the Lunda adopting many aspects of Chokwe life; today, Lunda in eastern Angola are sometimes referred to as Lunda-Chokwe. (see also LUBA, ZAIREANS, ZAMBIANS)

LUNDA-CHOKWE see ANGOLANS.

LUNDU An ethnic group living on the Indonesian island of Kalimantan (Borneo). (see also DAYAK)

LUNDWE An ethnic group related to the ILA living in the Namwala District of Zambia.

LUNGU An ethnic group living along the southern part of Lake Tanganyika in northeastern Zambia and in Tanzania, north of the border. Most Lungu speak Mambwe but some who live further south speak Chibemba. They are Christians or practice traditional religions. Lungu living in the south follow a matrilineal descent system, but those living in the north follow a patrilineal system.

The Lungu produce iron and raise cattle; those living along Lake Tanganyika are also fishermen and farmers. The BRITISH protected them from various African and Arab raiders. (see also MAMBWE)

LUO (Jaluo) A people of western Kenya, living in Nyazna Province, on the shores of Lake Victoria. They are estimated to number about 2.3 million and are the second largest people in Kenya. The main town in the Luo territory is Kisumu, which is also the most important Kenyan town on Lake Victoria. Their language belongs to the Western Nilotic family. There are also some Luo-speaking subgroups in Sudan, notably the THURI and ACHOLIARE: the latter live near the town of Opari on the Uganda border. Most Luo are Christians, members of local African churches, or churches of western origin.

The Luo-speaking people originated in the area of the confluence of the Nile and the Bahr el-Ghazal Rivers and were the first to arrive in Kenya, in the sixteenth century. Their traditional economy was based on animal husbandry, but during the eighteenth and nineteenth centuries this was gradually replaced by agriculture, using techniques of cultivation and irrigation that were advanced for the times. Fishing and trading also developed, and became as important as agriculture. Nevertheless, traditional attitudes toward cattle have hardly changed: a rich Luo is one who possesses a large herd, and a man who has no cattle is considered poor, no matter how full his granary.

Luo social structure was complex, consisting of at least forty groups, each associated with a territory and each possessing autonomous political leadership and a separate, clearly-defined lineage system. Today, however, the framework exists more in principle. In practice, their culture has undergone many changes, reflecting their predominent role in the modernization of

Kenya. They are known for the high percentage of intellectuals and professionals, both men and women. (see also KENYANS, NUER, SHILLUK, TANZANIANS, UGANDANS)

LUPACA A subgroup of the AYMARA.

LUR I A people who live in the Luristan province of southwest Iran, and to its south. Small groups also live in the southeast of Iranian Azerbaijan, in Gilan, near Qazvin in the northwest of Iran, and dispersed in some urban settlements around the country. They are estimated to number between 500,000 and 2 million.

The Lur speak a number of cognate dialects which belong to the southwest group of Iranian languages. Most Lur are Shi'ite Muslims, and some are followers of the Ahl-e Haqq sect. The Lur of Luristan are divided into two main tribal groups: the POSHTE KUH ("overhill"), cattle-raising nomads, roaming northwest Luristan; and the PUSH-E KUH ("foothill"), who are predominantly sedentary agriculturalists, as are the Lur in the northern area of Luristan and those of a small Lur enclave near Qazvin. Lur-related nomadic ethnic groups to the south of Luristan are the MAMASAN and KUHGILU.

Lur groups are composed of clans, some evidently of Kurdish or Turkic origin. Most families are large and traditionally patriarchal. Nomadic Lur live in wool tents and wear felt jackets and felt hats of a special form, which afford protection against both heat and cold. They possess a rich folklore including epic and lyric poems and fairytales. They are closely connected

Lur

with the BAKHTIAR, and sometimes both groupings are regarded as two branches of one ethnos.

LUR II   see IRAQIS.

LUSATIANS   see SORBS.

LUSHAI   see MIZO.

LUSITANIANS   see PORTUGUESE.

LUSO-INDIANS   see ANGLO-INDIANS.

LUTZU   (Nutzu, s.d. Anu, Nusu, Nu) A Tibeto-Burman people living in Yunnan in southwest China. They inhabit the Salween valley in a stretch of territory extending from Tibet to the Myanmar (Burma) border. The approximately 25,000 Lutzu are often classified as northern or Black Lutzu, who have adopted many Tibetan conventions, and southern Lutzu, who have better preserved their traditional mode of life.

They are shifting agriculturalists. Over the past several years, they have also begun trading opium for alcohol, a staple of the Lutzu diet, with the CHINESE. They practice a form of Lamaist Buddhism which has retained many elements of their traditional beliefs.

LUXEMBOURGERS   The 370,000 Luxembourgers form a population of mixed Celtic, Germanic, and French origin. They have a collective identity, supported by a separate German dialect (Letzeburgish) which is their everyday language. Medieval Luxembourg supplied the Holy Roman Empire with several emperors before being absorbed by ambitious Burgundians and Habsburgs; thereafter, the Luxembourgers shared the fortunes of the BELGIANS until the Grand Duchy was created in 1815. After the Belgian revolution, the statelet was again split between Belgian and rump-Luxembourg, maintaining a personal union with Dutch kings.

Later in the nineteenth century, power passed to another branch of the Nassau dynasty (and soon evolved from absolutism to democracy), and Luxembourg became fully independent. Luxembourgers enjoy a high standard of living thanks to their heavy industry; long a fiscal paradise, one quarter of their population is foreign.

LUYANA   An ethnic group living along the upper part of the Zambezi river in Zambia. They speak Luyana and are related to the LUNDA. The LYUWA, NDUNDULU, and SIMAA are Luyana subgroups.

LYUDINIKAD   see VEPS.

LYUWA   A subgroup of the LUYANA.

M

MA A people numbering about 30,000, speaking a Mon-Khmer language, and living along the banks of the Donnai River in southern Vietnam. Traditional Ma territory consists of both fertile valleys and mountainous regions covered with dense tropical forests. Various subgroups of Ma have therefore emerged: the MA TO, MA RO, and MA SOP, classified according to geographical location and corollary agricultural methods.

The Ma share a common history and were probably united as a single political unit at one time. The disintegration of this unit led to internecine tribal warfare which was only suppressed by the FRENCH in 1937.

MAALE An ethnic group, numbering 30,000, (1980s), who live south of the upper bend of the Woito River in central Gemu-Gofa Province, Ethiopia. Their language belongs to the Omotic grouping, and they adhere to traditional beliefs. Maale was a small kingdom before being incorporated into the Ethiopian empire. The Maale are agriculturalists and cattle-raisers.

MAANYAN An ethnic group living on the Indonesian island of Kalimantan (Borneo). (see also DAYAK)

MAAQUIL A subgroup of the MAURE.

MABA I A subgroup of the SAWAI.

MABA II A group of primarily agricultural and stockbreeding clans numbering about 180,000 living in the Ouadai and Biltine regions of Chad. Smaller numbers are found in the neighboring Central African Republic. The Maba language is called Duramabang.

Between the seventeenth and nineteenth centuries, the Maba were the core group of the Ouadai kingdom that encompassed much of eastern Chad. Today several Maba subgroups have emerged. One such group, the DJEM, can also be found in neighboring Cameroon. In Chad live the KODOY (north of Abache in the Ouadai

region), ABISSA, DEBBA, DEKKER, MADABA, and MALANGA subgroups. (see also CHADIANS, SAWAI)

MABAN An ethnic group living on the border of Sudan and Ethiopia.

MA BLAO A subgroup of the KOHO.

MA B'SRE A subgroup of the KOHO.

MACASSARESE (s.d. Makassar) The dominant population of the southernmost part of the island of Sulawesi (Celebes), Indonesia.

They number over 2 million. They are closely related to the neighboring BUGINESE who live slightly to the north and share most cultural elements except history and language. Because of rich agricultural land and advanced irrigation of rice, their territory is able to sustain a relatively large population.

Macassarese

A local Macassarese kingdom, named Goa after the ruling family, exerted considerable influence in the precolonial period and all but dominated the lucrative spice trade with the Molucca Islands. Islam, introduced in the seventeenth century, played a considerable role in the development of an indigenous culture, but pre-Islamic elements were also important as is evidenced by the emergence of a local script, generally thought to have been adopted from the MALAYS. Although Islamic beliefs and rituals are now central to the Macassarese, they have also preserved certain elements of their traditional religion, particularly with regard to veneration of the dead.

Since colonization by the DUTCH, the role of the royal family has altered considerably. No longer absolute monarchs, they continue to play an important role in administering their territory as part of post-independence Indonesia. Similarly, a rigid class system based on personal wealth as demonstrated by bride-price has survived, although there is considerable mobility among the lower classes. The upper classes are held to be of divine (possibly foreign) descent.

MACEDONIANS   A southern Slavic people living in Macedonia, until 1991 a republic of Yugoslavia. Some two-thirds of the 2 million inhabitants of Macedonia are Slavic Macedonians who adhere to Eastern Orthodox Christianity; in the Middle Ages they were deeply involved in the heretic Bogomil religious movement that swept the Balkan region. The other major ethnic group in Macedonia is the ALBANIANS, who profess Islam.

The Slavic Macedonian language, formalized after World War II by the Yugoslav authorities, is part of the Bulgarian group of southern Slavic languages.

Macedonia was a part of the Ottoman Empire until 1912, but became part of Serbia in 1913 as a result of the Balkan War. Bulgaria claimed that the Macedonians were BULGARIANS, while Serbia maintained that the Macedonians had been forcibly bulgarized. The SERBS tried to assimilate the Macedonians immediately upon taking control of Macedonia.

After World War II the Communist regime in Yugoslavia under Tito established Macedonia as one of the constituent republics of Yugoslavia and made great efforts to develop Macedonian nationalism as a bulwark against Bulgarian irredentism among the Macedonians.

Following the disintegration of Yugoslavia and the subsequent war between Croatia and Bosnia-Herzegovina in 1991, Macedonia declared its independence.

However, the new state had problems gaining international recognition, with the GREEKS officially objecting to the use of the name Macedonia (on the grounds that it is also the name of a region in northern Greece that is intimately associated with ancient Greek history, having been the birthplace of Alexander the Great) and the BULGARIANS repeating their longstanding claim to the region.

MACHA   A division of the OROMO living in western Shoa, southern Gojjam, and the Wallaga, Illubabor, and Kefa Provinces of Ethiopia.

MACHOSHEI   A subgroup of the ADYGHEANS.

MACUXI   see MAKUXI.

MADA   A subgroup of the TIV.

MADABA   A subgroup of the MABA.

MADI   A people dwelling in the lowlands of the Nile Valley in Uganda and Sudan. They speak a Central Sudanic language.

They are mainly agriculturalists, practicing some cattle-raising. During the 1920s cassava was introduced into the area as a food crop. It was accepted by the LUGBARA and Madi very quickly and developed into the main food staple. Besides cassava the Madi also grow millet, sorghum, and maize, as well as tobacco as a cash crop. (see also UGANDANS)

MA DODONG   A subgroup of the KOHO.

MADURESE   (s.d. Wong Medura, Tijang Medura) A people, numbering over 5 million, inhabiting the island of Madura lying off the eastern coast of the Indonesian island of Java. The Madurese are closely related to the JAVANESE; they speak a similar language and share much the same cultural, ethnic, and religious history. The Javanese script is traditionally utilized for both an indigenous literature and for stories influenced by Javanese traditions. The Madurese are virtually all nominal Muslims, but many of the Hindu and Buddhist elements conspicuous to Javanese culture are absent among the Madurese.

Because the island of Madura is less fertile than Java, cattle and fishing are much more prominent. Bulls are particularly valued and bull racing is a popular sport. The most developed crafts are those associated with bull racing.

The Madurese emerged as a unified ethnic entity only as a result of Javanese pressure. Prior to this, local legends concentrated more on the origins of villages and local groups than on the Madurese as a group. A short-lived independent kingdom emerged during the decline of the Javanese Madjapahit empire; and it flourished with the arrival of Islam in the sixteenth century. With the ascension of the second Javanese empire of Mataram, Madurese independence was lost, but nationalist sentiment was particularly strong and led to a number of revolts, the most important being the Trunodjojo Revolt of the late seventeenth century. With the imposition of colonial administration by the DUTCH in the second half of the nineteenth century, the status of the Madurese nobility declined sharply. Today they are little more than low-ranking civil servants.

MAE ENGA   An ethnic group of approximately 20,000 living in the mountainous region of central Papua New Guinea. They speak an indigenous local language and are gardeners who employ slash and burn cultivation. Although influenced by Christianity, they retain traditional religious beliefs, and the practice of magic is quite common.

MAFULU   An ethnic group of approximately 15,000 living in southeastern Papua New Guinea. They speak an indigenous regional language. They are slash and burn cultivators; their main crops are yams and they breed pigs. Their religion is based upon a mixture of traditional magic and sorcery and Christian beliefs. Their most important ceremony is the tribal feast.

MAGAHAT   A Proto-Malay non-Christian people who live in the mountainous areas of southeastern Negros, an island in the Philippines. Most are shifting cultivators who live in the municipalities of Tanjay, Santa Catalina, Bayawan, and Sinton. Their language is a mixture of Sugbuhanon and Kiligaynon, two lowland Christian Filipino languages.

MAGAR   A people numbering 500,000 (1991) living in eastern Terai and midwestern areas in Nepal. Their language belongs to the Tibeto-Burman family. Most Magar are craftsmen, although some own land and practice agriculture. Some also work as miners, blacksmiths, basket weavers. They also trade in salt which they bring from Tibet. (see also GURKHA)

MAGH   A Buddhist ethnic group living in the Chittagong hill tracts and Cox's Bazaar areas of Bangladesh, said to be descendants of the Arakanese who ruled the region from the tenth to the sixteenth centuries. The Magh of the Patuakhali district are said to have sailed up the Bay of Bengal from Rangoon and settled in the region from 1789.

Important tasks in Magh society, such as breadwinning and farming, are mostly entrusted to women, but clan and family structure is based on the dominance of the male.

The primary occupation of the Magh is slash and burn cultivation. Their staples are rice and liquor.

MAGHARULAE   see AVAR.

MAGHRIBIYYUN   see MOROCCANS.

MAGINDANAO   A Muslim people numbering about 600,000, living on the west coast of Mindanao, an island in the Philippines, around the town of Cotabato. Their language belongs to the Malayo-Polynesian family. They are wet-rice cultivators who plant their crops in flood waters from the local river systems.

MAGJAROK   see HUNGARIANS.

MAGUZAWA   A subgroup of the HAUSA.

MAGWE   see BETE.

MAHA   A subgroup of the NUBIANS.

MAHAFALY   A tribal division of the MALAGASY.

MAHI   A subgroup of the FON.

MAHICAN   (Mohican) A small Native North American group, many of whom live on the Golden Hill State Reservation in Connecticut and the Stockbridge-Munsee Federal Reservation in Wisconsin. Originally inhabitants of New York State, they were pushed west by European settlers. James Fenimore Cooper immortalized them in his classic work *The Last of the Mohicans*.

MAHLI   An ethnic group numbering 103,000 (1981), located in Bihar, Orissa, and West Bengal, India. They speak Santali, a member of the Austroasiatic family of languages, and their customs are close to those of the MUNDA and ORAON.

The Mahli worship the sun as a supreme deity. Theirs is a highly forest-based economy. They are professional basket makers skilled in working with bamboo. Their level of literacy is low.

MAHON   A Mandé-speaking ethnic group living in the Côte d'Ivoire.

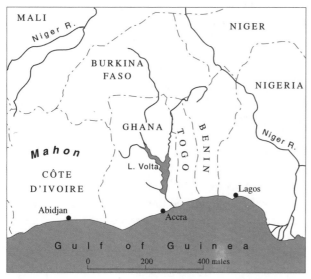

Mahon

MAHONGWE   (Hungwe) An ethnic group living in the southern part of the Mekambo region, Gabon. They are linguistically related to the KOTA.

MAI   see T'IN.

MAILU   (s.d. Magi) An ethnic group of approximately 5,000 living on the southeastern coast of Papua New Guinea as well as on small nearby islands. They speak an indigenous local language. Their subsistence is based mostly upon fishing and pottery making. An elaborate annual pig feast honoring their mythological hero serves as their most important ceremony.

MAINGTHA   see ACHANG.

MAISIN   An ethnic group of a few thousand living in northeastern Papua New Guinea. They speak two indigenous regional dialects. While they practice slash and burn cultivation, they are also hunters and gatherers. Their religion is a mixture of Christianity and traditional beliefs.

MAIYANS   An ethnic group living in the mountainous area along the upper flow of the Indus River in the Swat region of North Pakistan and also in some adjacent areas. An estimation of the early 1980s puts them at about 100,000. The Maiyan language belongs to the Dardic group of Indo-Iranian languages of the Indo-European family. It consists of several dialects, speakers of one of which, Kaniawali, constitute an enclave amid the SHINANS and can be regarded as a subgroup of the Maiyans. The language is unwritten, and Urdu is used as the official language of writing and education, with Pashto, the language of the PASHTUN, used for oral communication with non-Maiyans.

The Maiyans are Sunni Muslims of the Hanafi school and are sedentary agriculturists. Since their main area of habitation forms a part of the so-called Swat Kohistan ("mountainland"), the term Kohistani (or Kuhistani) is also applied to them and to their language, alongside the term Maiyan, which they themselves use as self-designation. However, in the ethnogeographic context of Swat, the term Kohistani lacks precision, since it is sometimes used to cover all the ethnic groups of the Swat Kohistan, including the GARWI and TORWALI.

MAJANGIR   (Masongo, Ojang, Tama) An ethnic group numbering 15,000 (1980) who live at the head of the Akoba, Gilo, and Aluoro Rivers in the Illubabor Province of western Ethiopia. They speak a Nilotic language and adhere to traditional beliefs. During the nineteeenth century, the Majangir were a dependency of the empire of Kafa, and they are culturally influenced by the contacts with their Omotic-speaking neighbors.

The Majangir are settled agriculturalists who cultivate root crops (yams, taro), and who practice shifting cultivation. They live in a tsetse fly infected zone (below 5,000 feet); however, since the early 1950s their region has been affected by the expansion of coffee as a large-scale cash crop. The Majangir have a clan-system, but their social organization functions mainly on the level of cooperatives (coffee-sharing groups). The only hereditary positions used to be those of shamanic priests. (see also ETHIOPIANS)

MAJHWAR   (Manjhi) An ethnic group numbering 6,500 (1981), living in the Raigarh and Surguja districts of the state of Madhya Pradesh, India. They are considered a mixed tribe originating from the GOND, MUNDA, and KAWAR.

MAKA   An ethnic group related to the FANG living in Cameroon.

MAKAH   A Native North American group numbering about 1,200, many of whom live on the Makah Federal Reservation, Washington State, U.S.A. They are related to the NOOTKA. After World War II they purchased a facility from the U.S. government and established a new reserve there.

MAKASSAR   See MACASSARESE.

MAKAWANGWA   See KWANGWA.

MAKIANESE   Inhabitants of the island of Makian, off the southwest coast of Halmahera, an island of Indonesia. They cultivate bananas, corn, and coconuts and engage in fishing.

MAKOLOLO   See KOLOLO, LOZI.

MAKONDE   An ethnic group numbering over 1 million living in the Newala, Mtawara, and Linda districts of southeastern Tanzania (in which country they are the second largest ethnic group), and in the Makonde Plateau of northern Mozambique. The Makonde language belongs to the Bantu group of the Niger-Kordofan family of languages. Most of the Makonde profess traditional African religions, though some have converted to Islam.

The Makonde have no tradition of a unified political system. Their political units encompass a few villages; each village has a hereditary headman and a council of

Makonde

elders. The traditional Makonde family structure is matrilineal.

Geographically and ecologically the Makonde are more isolated and, as result, relatively less developed than some other main ethnic groups of Tanzania. The Makonde people are considered to be one of the the the least influenced by the colonial and post-colonial development and have the reputation of being conservative. The economy of Makonde rests mainly on slash-and-burn agriculture, the major crops being maize, sorghum, and cassava. The Makonde have developed special agricultural techniques in dealing with the lack of water on the Newala Plateau. They also enage in fishing and hunting and have a reputation as great warriors, a skill they learned defending themselves against Arab slave raiders. They refused to adopt Arab culture and were therefore subject to intense missionary activity, but the Makonde were the last group to be defeated by the PORTUGUESE.

Tanzanian independence had a marked influence on the Makonde, who formed their own political party, the União Makonde de Moçambique, which in turn joined the Mozambique African National Union. The Makonde were later victims of the infamous Muede Massacre during the Portuguese repression of FRELIMO (Liberation Front of Mozambique) fighters for Mozambique's independence.

Since independence the Makonde have made the difficult transition from a subsistence economy to one in which a sizabale proportion of the population is engaged in migratory labour, production of cash crops and in other aspects of market econmy. The Makonde are famous for their imaginative woodcarvings, which are sold internationally. They are farmers who live in small family units combined into villages. (see also MOZAMBICANS, TANZANIANS)

MAKSHA   The western subgroup of the MORDVIN.

MAKU I   An ethnic group related to the M'BOCHI living in Congo.

MAKU II   A South American Indian group living in the jungles of the State of Amazon, north Brazil. Numbering a few hundred, they were the original inhabitants of the area, but have since been dominated mostly by the BANIWA and the TUKANA, who hunted them down and turned them into slaves. (see also TUKANA)

MAKUA-LOMWE   An ethnic unit comprising two groups, the Makua and the Lomwe, living along the lower Zambezi River, in the Nyasa and Cabo Delgado Provinces and on parts of the northeastern coasts of Mozambique. Makua groups are also found in Tanzania in the districts of Masasi, Kilosa, and Tanduru. In Malawi, Lomwe are found in the Incholo and Chradzulu Districts and near the towns of Zombe, Mlanje, and Blantyre. The Lomwe are the second largest ethnic group in Malawi. In Mozambique Makua-Lomwe number about 1 million and in Tanzania, 40,000.

Most speak Lomwe, but those along the coast speak Swahili. They are predominantly Christians or adherents of traditional religions, but the Makua have adopted Arab customs. In earlier times they had a single, centralized chieftainship but this had disintegrated by the twentieth century into several chieftainships which met only to decide on foreign affairs. They are primarily agriculturalists. Their culture is similar to that of the YAO and they have elaborate initiation ceremonies.

In 1582, the Makua-Lomwe defeated the PORTUGUESE along the Mozambique coast. There is still considerable animosity between them and the MAKONDE, who raided them for slaves. This animosity was used by the PORTUGUESE during Mozambique's War of Independence to deprive the FRELIMO (Liberation Front of Mozambique) army of members: the Makua-Lomwe were warned that FRELIMO was dominated by the MAKONDE. Although four chiefs claiming to represent the Makua-Lomwe used this as a pretext to demand a federal goverment after independence, most Makua-Lomwe ignored the Portuguese and allied themselves with FRELIMO, denouncing these chiefs as renegades. (see also MOZAMBICANS)

MAKUXI (Macuxi) A South American Indian group, numbering several thousand, living in villages around the northern part of the State of Amazon, northern Brazil, and across the border with Guyana. They are closely related to another Carib-speaking group called TAULIPANG.

MALA ADIYAR An ethnic group found in southern Kerala, India. They generally work as plantation laborers.

MALA ARAYAN An ethnic group numbering about 25,000, living in central Kerala, India. Their economy is based on slash and burn agriculture and gathering.

MALAGASY Collective name for some twenty groups comprising the predominant population of the island of Madagascar off the southeast coast of Africa (other less significant groups include ARABS, Africans, CHINESE, and INDIANS). The 12 million Malagasy are a hybrid group of mixed African-Indonesian descent. Their language belongs to the Malayo-Polynesian family, and their traditional religion, based on ancestor worship, shares many features with indigenous Malay religions. Today, about 40 percent are Christian.

The most important Malagasy groups include the ANTEIFASY, ANTEIMORO, ANTANKARANA, ANTANDROY, ANTANOSY, BARA, BETSILEO, BETANIMENA, BETSIMISARAKA, BEZANOZANO (Tankay), MAHAFALY, MERINA (Hova), SAKALAVA, SIHANAKA, TANALA, and TSIMIHETY. The BETSILEO have best preserved traditional Indonesian characteristics, while the BETSIMISARAKA are most noticeably African, but cultural and linguistic differences between the various groups are minimal. Africanization and geographic diversity are most recognizable in economic pursuits. While almost 80 percent of the Malagasy are rural agriculturalists, those along the west coast continue the African traditions of herding cattle and fishing. Those along the east coast and in the central plateau are dependent upon rice, a crop apparently brought over by the original migrants from southeast Asia. In some areas, particularly the central plateau, rice is grown in a sophisticated system of irrigated terraces. Today, vanilla is also an important cash crop; Madagascar produces two-thirds of the world's supply.

It is generally believed that the Malagasy first migrated from Indonesia some 2,000 years ago. Some may have reached the African coast where a hybrid Indonesian-African culture is thought to have flourished until it was obliterated during the Bantu expansion in the seventh and eighth centuries C.E. Over the centuries, African and Arab immigrants intermingled with the Malagasy, but their contribution to the racial and ethnic makeup of the present population is still subject to debate.

A well-developed hereditary class system of nobles, commoners, and slaves led to the emergence of numerous mini-states. From the sixteenth to eighteenth centuries, the MERINA began a series of conquests from which a unified kingdom emerged. Towards the end of the eighteenth century, Merina dominance waned. Madagascar became a protectorate of the FRENCH in 1885 and a colony in 1896.

Although Madagascar became an independent republic in 1960, dissatisfaction with continued French involvement in internal affairs led to a coup in 1972. The new Marxist government adopted many xenophobic policies including the expulsion of foreigners, but this also led to a revival of Malagasy culture after years of French domination. In recent years, the government has rejected dogmatic Marxism in favor of economic and political liberalization.

Ethnic politics still figure prominently in Malagasy politics. The MERINA who, with 26 percent of the population, constitute the largest group, form the bulk of the middle class and still dominate the political arena.

MALAITA An ethnic group of approximately 70,000 living on a mountainous island belonging to the Solomon Islands chain in the southwest Pacific Ocean. They speak an indigenous local language. Their subsistence is based upon slash and burn cultivation with their main crop being taro. Although Christianity has taken hold among most of the islanders, many still believe in ancestral spirits.

MALAKKARAN An ethnic group living in northern Kerala, India. They have only recently abandoned their traditional economic activities based on hunting, gathering, and small scale agriculture in favor of agricultural work on plantations.

MALAKKURAVAN A ethnic group numbering only a few hundred, found in central Kerala, India. They engage in hunting, gathering, and small-scale agriculture.

MALANGA A subgroup of the MABA.

MALASAR A ethnic group numbering a few thousand found in central Kerala and Tamil Nadu in southern India. They are generally employed as plantation workers.

MALA VEDAN A Hindu ethnic group found in the states of Kerala and Tamil Nadu, India. Once hunters and gatherers, they are generally engaged as plantation laborers.

MALAWIANS The 9 million inhabitants of Malawi are divided into six distinct ethno-linguistic groups: the CHEWA of the south; the NYANJA of the eastern littoral of Lake Malawi (Nyasa) and in the area of the basin of the Shire River; the YAO, who live along the upper Shire River near Blantyre, Chiradzulu and Zomba districts; the LOMWE, of the Incholo and Chiradzulu districts; the NGONI of the central and southern regions; and the TUMBUKA of the extreme north. In addition, by mid-1991 there were an estimated 1 million refugees from Mozambique in the country.

These groups possess not only different languages (the official languages are English and Chichewa) but also adhere to different religions. The YAO are Muslim, as are some of the CHEWA, while the NYANJA adhere to Christianity and traditional religions. The population distribution is uneven; only 12 percent of Malawians live in the northern regions while the rest inhabit the southern and central regions. Around 13 percent of the population is urbanized, and the two main cities are Lilongwe, the capital, and Blantyre, the commercial center in the south.

Agriculture is the mainstay of Malawi's economy; the country is the second largest producer of tobacco in Africa, and tea and sugar are also produced for export. Staple food crops are maize, millet, sorghum, groundnuts, rice, cassava, and pulses. The industrial sector is undeveloped and the government has placed a high priority on its improvement, encouraging private enterprise and foreign investment. These efforts have been marginally successful as a result of the limited local market and limited possibilities for export. Tourism is also an important industry in Malawi. Some minerals, such as asbestos, bauxite, coal, limestone, uranium, graphite, and vermiculite have been discovered but only a few, including limestone, have been exploited.

Malawi, which was a protectorate of the BRITISH, became independent in 1963 under the leadership of Dr. Hastings Kamuzu Banda's Malawi Congress Party. Banda's regime is known as one of the most conservative governments in Africa, and this is partly because at the time of independence it was heavily dependent on Rhodesia and the Portuguese territories for access to the sea; these territories were also its principal trading partners. As a result, Banda not only has maintained diplomatic relations with South Africa and the former colonial regimes of Portuguese Africa, but has also rejected requests for africanization of the civil service. In addition, Banda has mobilized support from his own ethnic group, the CHEWA. In 1966 Malawi became a one-party state with Banda as its president; in 1971 he became life president. He has consistently suppressed all opposition and as a result most of the opposition parties have had to operate outside the country, at one time or another claiming responsibility for raids and sabotage against government installations.

Since the early 1990s, two internal opposition movements, the Alliance for Democracy (AFORD) and the United Democratic Front (UDF), have led demands for a national referendum on the option of a multi-party system. Both groups are particularly strong in the north, where the TONGA and TUMBUKA peoples live. These peoples have educational advantages over others further south, including the majority CHEWA and other smaller ethnic groups, due to the north's superior mission schools. Dr. Banda has long campaigned against northern teachers, civil servants, and students in the southern and central regions. The slow pace of africanization of the civil service, army, and police force has been attributed to attempts to prevent domination by northerners.

In June 1993 the Malawians voted in a referendum for a multi-party system.

MALAYALAR   An ethnic group found in northern Kerala, India. They are generally engaged in agriculture.

MALAYALI   (Keralite, Travancorean) Name for the almost 30 million inhabitants of the Kerala State along the southern coast of India. They speak Malayalam, a Dravidian language closely related to Tamil. Half are Hindus, and the other half are almost equally divided between Muslims and Christians.

As an important trading center from ancient times, the area has also been influenced by cultures as diverse as those of ancient Rome and China. Each group of ar-

rivals left a distinct impression on the indigenous population.

Popular legend posits a local king, Agastya, with developing the region and inventing various sciences and technologies; some scholars now claim that Agastya is a corruption of the Latin Augustus. It is known that there was a sizeable colony of Roman merchants and soldiers here and Kerala once boasted the only Roman temple in southern Asia.

The Malayali are also among the most educated people in India, and the state maintains the highest literacy rate in the country. At the same time, unemployment is also high, due in part to the large numbers of university graduates who are unable to find work in what is one of India's most densely populated regions. While many Malayali have emigrated, others have found solace in Marxism and other similar political philosophies.

MALAYAN   One of the hill peoples of Kerala, India. They are gatherers but also find employment as laborers.

MALAYS   (s.d. Melayu) A people inhabiting Malaysia, Singapore, and the coastal regions of Indonesia and the southern Philippines (where they are sometimes refered to as Coastal Malays). Most Malays live in Malaysia. They speak a Malayo-Polynesian language closely related to Indonesian and are virtually all Muslims. Two Malay scripts are currently in use: Rumi (Roman) using the Latin alphabet, and Jawi (Javanese), based on the Javanese variant of an Indian alphabet. (see also BRUNEIANS, NIASANS, SEMANG, THAI)

MALAYSIANS   The 16 million population of Malaysia is 60 percent Malay. Malaysia consists of the southern Malay Peninsula and the states of Sarawak and Sabah on the northern coast of the island of Borneo (Kalimantan). There are also sizable communities of CHINESE and INDIANS originally brought by the BRITISH in the nineteenth century to work in the tin mines and rubber plantations, as well as smaller groups of aboriginals forming a negligible percentage of the Malaysian population.

Sixty-five percent of the total population of Malaysia live in rural areas and are engaged primarily in the cultivation of wet rice. Fishing is also important and there are extensive rubber plantations, a legacy from the British colonial period. In recent decades Malaysia has experienced something of an economic boom; it now boasts the fastest growing economy in Southeast Asia.

Malayali

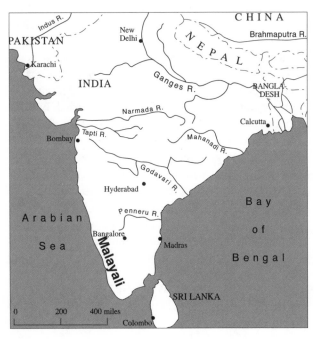

above: A Malayali rope maker in southern India
below: Malayali boatmen in southern India

Much of the wealth comes from extensive tin mines which produce 35 percent of the world's output. Local crafts such as brass, silver, and ironsmithery are also important as is the manufacture of batik cloth.

Until the colonial period, there was no distinct Malaysian identity. Rather, eleven independent sultanates ruled the territory. By the early twentieth century, Great Britain had concluded a series of deals with the local sultans giving it control over the area which controlled the strategic Straits of Malacca. In 1948, the eleven Malay states were united into the Federation of Malaya; independence was granted in 1957. In 1963, plans were made to unite the country with the island of Singapore off its southern coast and three British colonies in northern Borneo (Kalimantan), North Borneo (Sabah) Brunei, and Sarawak. Brunei withdrew shortly before the emergence of the new state of Malaysia, and Singapore withdrew from the federation in 1965. Today Malaysia is a constitutional monarchy with a king elected from among the nine hereditary sultans of mainland Malaysia for a five-year term. British interests are still important, as are increasing American interests. Islam plays an important role in affairs of state, and Islamic scholars are often consulted over points of law.

In the 1950s and 1960s Malaysia experienced a violent communist insurgency which threatened to sweep the country into civil war. The rebels were backed by Peking, leading many MALAYS to question the loyalties of the ethnic CHINESE minority, about 30 percent of the population, and several racially-motivated riots erupted. In the 1960s Malaysia went to war with the Philippines, over possession of the province of Sabah on Borneo. Local government officials, in turn, were suspected of aiding Muslim Moro secessionists in the southern Philippines.

MALDIVIANS (s.d. Divehi) Inhabitants of the Republic of the Maldives, an archipelago of 1,300 small islands and atolls (only 200 of which are inhabited) situated in the Indian Ocean south of the Indian subcontinent. They are also found on the island of Minicoy, politically part of India. The Maldivian population stands at about 220,000; about 10,000 Divehi live on Minicoy. They are Muslim and speak an Indo-Aryan language related to Sinhalese but with many Tamil, Persian, and Arabic loan words. A singular Divehi script, developed 300 years ago, combines Indian and Arabic elements.

Maldivians are generally fishermen and traders who excel in boat building and have exploited their position

in the center of the Indian Ocean trade routes. Recently, tourist ventures have been encouraged on several uninhabited islands and there is some agriculture, particularly the cultivation of millet and taro and the gathering of coconuts.

The Maldives were first settled by Tamil traders in about 1000 B.C.E. Their descendants, known as Giravaru, are today virtually indistinguishable from other Maldivians but nevertheless constitute a separate group. From the tenth century SINHALESE from Sri Lanka (Ceylon) began migrating to the islands and became the dominant ethnic group. Traditionally Buddhist, the islanders were converted en masse to Islam by ARABS in the twelfth century and Islam has since emerged as the dominant culture. An attempt at colonization by the PORTUGUESE in the fifteenth century was short-lived and incidental. Colonization by the BRITISH beginning in the late nineteenth century similarly failed to leave a mark on the islanders. Independence was achieved in 1965 and the traditional sultanate was abolished in 1968.

Despite their importance in international trade, the Maldivians have been little influenced by the outside world and modernization has only recently been initiated. The low-lying islands have slowly begun sinking into the ocean, leaving the people's future in question.

MALECITE (Maliseet) A Native North American group living in southern Quebec and New Brunswick, Canada. They number some 3,500 in New Brunswick. There are also several hundred Malecite in Maine, U.S.A.

MALEKU A Native American group living in Costa Rica.

MALETE A subgroup of the TSWANA.

MALI An ethnic group, numbering 2,500 (1981), living in Andhra Pradesh, India. They speak Oriya, a member of the Indo-Aryan family of languages. The Mali are mostly cultivators, especially skilful at growing vegetables, but their traditional occupation is garland-making.

MALIANS (Maliens) The people of Mali in West Africa, numbering 8.2 million. The main ethnic group is the MANDE, which consists of the BAMBARA, MALINKE, and DIOULA, linguistically and culturally related, who live in the southeast; the FULANI, who live in the Mopti region in the center of the country; the SENUFO; in the extreme south; the SONINKE in the west; the SONGHAI; in the center, the TUAREG; in the north; and the DOGON; who live in the Bandiagra plateau; east of Mopti. The official language of Mali is French; the most widely spoken is Bamana, which is the language of the BAMBARA but is also spoken by other ethnic groups. Eighty percent of the Malians are Muslim, 18 percent practice traditional religions, and only 1.2 percent are Christians.

The Malians gained their independence from the FRENCH in 1960 after a short-lived federation with the SENEGALESE, called the Mali Federation. Containing only two states with major cultural and historical differences made the federation highly unstable and caused it to collapse.

After independence the leader of Mali, Mobido Keita, abolished all opposition parties. In 1968 he was overthrown in a military coup by Mousa Traore. Since independence, the main ethnic conflicts in Mali are with the TUAREG, a nomadic people of Berber origin and the black African majority. Incidents between government forces and the TUAREG are quite frequent.

In 1991, following popular pressures for political reforms, Traore's regime was overthrown and a process of democratization has started.

MALIENS see MALIANS.

MALIKI see AIMAQ-I DIGAR.

MALILI MORI see MORI.

MALINKE (Maninka, Mandinka) A people belonging to the MANDE grouping who are found throughout West Africa. In Guinea, the Malinké, counted with other Mandé peoples, number 2.4 million; in the southern and northwestern Côte d'Ivoire they and other MANDE number 1.5 million; in Senegal, 480,000; in western Mali, about 400,000; and in the Gambia, 286,000. Smaller numbers are found in Sierra Leone, Liberia, and Guinea-Bissau. They speak Mandé and are either Muslims or adherents to traditional religions. In most of the countries in which they live their main occupations are trade and agriculture.

Until the eleventh century the Malinké lacked a centralized political structure and thus became easy targets for raids of the SONINKE of the Ghana Empire. During the eleventh century the region of the Malinké in Mali became integrated into the commercial network between North and West Africa. Consequently, small Malinké princedoms were established. In the thirteenth century one of these princedoms, under the leadership of its king, Soundiata, conquered the neighboring princedoms. In the following decades it expanded to the desert and became the Mali empire. The empire's revenue was derived from taxes imposed on the gold and ivory trade in its territory. In the fifteenth century the Mali empire declined and collapsed.

The KONIANKE, KONYA, MIKIFORE, OINCA, TENE, and TOUBACAYE of Guinea are all subgroups of the Malinké. (see also IVOIREANS, GAMBIANS, GUINEA-BISSAU, THE PEOPLE OF, GUINEANS, MALIANS, SIERRA LEONEANS)

MALISEET see MALECITE.

MALKARLY see BALKAR.

MALO An ethnic group numbering 60,000 (1980s), who live between the Omo and the Ergine Rivers in central Gemu Gofa Province, Ethiopia. Their language belongs to the Omotic grouping and they adhere to traditional beliefs. The Malo are grain (durra, teff) and ensete-farmers.

MALORUSSY see UKRAINIANS.

MAL PAHARIYA An ethnic group living in the states of West Bengal and Bihar, India, numbering 96,000 (1981). They speak Bengali, a member of the Indo-Aryan language family, and are Hindus.

The common form of agriculture is shifting cultivation, and they also have a hunting season which runs from May to August.

MALTESE The 350,000 Maltese living on the tiny, densely-populated archipelago of Malta between Sicily and Libya, speak a Semitic language derived from either Phoenician or Arabic. They are predominantly Roman Catholics.

Malta's central position in the Mediterranean made it a meeting point where Italian, Arab, and British influences mingled. Traditionally, most inhabitants were mariners, others worked in quarries or as filigree artisans. Malta's elite spoke Italian, and bought provisions in Sicily for the whole population. The present-day economy includes tourism, trade, port facilities, and some industry.

Malta was colonized by, successively, Phoenicians, GREEKS, Carthaginians, and Romans. In 870 ARABS from Tunis occupied the island, and converted its Christian population. The following centuries saw an influx of ARABS and BERBERS. Malta became a pirate base and slave market. The Sicilian Normans conquered it in 1090, but by the thirteenth century there were still more Muslims and JEWS than Christians. When Muslims were expelled, most opted for conversion to Christianity, but kept customs like seclusion and the veiling of women. Ruled by the houses of Anjou, then Aragon, Malta's importance grew as Ottoman maritime expansion threatened Spain.

After the fall of Rhodes, stronghold of the Order of the Knights of Saint John of Jerusalem, in 1522, Malta became a prime strategic outpost. In 1530 Charles V gave Malta to the order, henceforth known as the Knights of Malta. Repeated Turkish attacks necessitated the construction of fortifications which helped the Maltese withstand a siege in 1565. However, the Maltese population hated the Knights; their power was broken as a result of the French Revolution. In the nineteenth century, Britain turned Malta into a major naval base. Maltese trade became more significant after the opening of the Suez Canal. Population growth led to economic problems and to emigration to North Africa, the United States, and Britain and its colonies.

After World War II the Maltese obtained autonomy and in 1964, full independence. In 1974 Malta became a parliamentary democratic republic. The last foreign troops left in 1979. In spite of close links with the Arab world, Malta seeks integration in the European Community. (see also ARABS)

MALTIN   see MALTESE.

MAMA   A subgroup of the TIV.

MAMAK   (Mamma) A subgroup of the KUBU.

MAMANUA   A northern subgroup of the NEGRITOS of the Philippines.

MAMASAN   An ethnic subgroup of the LUR, living between Ardakan and Kazerun in south-central Iran. The latest figures available (1945) estimated them as numbering 35,000; by the early 1990s they might have increased to 70,000.

The Mamasan are divided into four tribes: RUSTAMI (the most numerous), BAQISH, JAWI, and DUSHMAN-ZIARI. They were only subdued by Iran's central government after World War I. Reza Shah Pahlavi (1925–1941) initiated a policy of enforced sedentarization, and they are now mainly sedentary agriculturalists. (see also LUR)

Mamasan

MAMBILA   An ethnic group living in Nigeria.

MAMBWE   An ethnic group numbering about 63,000 living in northeast Zambia. They speak Mambwe and are divided among Christians and followers of their traditional religion. Although they are mostly farmers, some Mambwe raise cattle. Cotton is an important crop, and they were among the first Zambians to weave cloth.

Originally part of the LUNGU, the Mambwe separated from them in the nineteenth century. They were influenced by Christianity in the 1880s. In 1890 two Mambwe chiefs signed treaties with Britain hoping for protection from the BEMBA. They later regretted their submission to the Europeans, and many joined the millennarian Watch Tower movement in 1917. (see also ZAMBIANS)

MAMEAN MAYA   A subgroup of the MAYA.

MAMELUCO   A Native South American group living in Brazil.

MAMVU   An ethnic group living in Zaire between the town of Isiro and the border with Sudan and Uganda.

MAN   see YAO.

MANAGO   A subgroup of the EGBA. (see also YORUBA)

MANALA   A subgroup of the NDEBELE.

MANAM   An ethnic group of approximately 7,000 living on an island off the northern coast of Papua New Guinea. Many speak more than one indigenous language. Their economy is based upon slash and burn cultivation, and their main crops are sweet potatoes and bananas. Their religion is a mixture of Catholicism and the traditional belief in spirits.

MANAO   An Arawak-speaking group of South American Indians who inhabit the triangle between the Amazon and the Rio Negro Rivers in Brazil. Once famous river traders who brought gold from the far west to the mouth of the Amazon in large dugout canoes, thus giving rise to the El Dorado legend, they are now almost completely extinct.

MANCHU   For centuries, the Manchu (now estimated as numbering 4 million) lived mainly in former Manchuria and adjacent areas; they are now settled in the Liaoning, Jilin, and Heilongjiang Provinces of northeastern China.

The Manchu are descendants of a people called the Tungus who inhabited northeastern Manchuria in prehistoric times. The Manchu conquered China in 1644 and founded that country's last imperial dynasty, the Qing dynasty. In the approximately 250 years of Manchu rule. the Chinese empire reached its geographical zenith, but the dynasty began to decline in the latter half of the nineteenth century and was overthrown in 1912.

The Manchu have their own language, Manchu-Tungus, which belongs to the Altaic family. Its traditional

Manchu

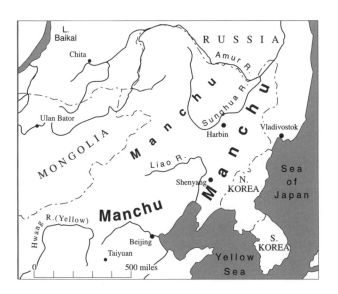

script, first created in the seventeenth century, borrowed from the Mongolian Uighur script, but later added dots and circles to mark phonetic differences. Since the founding of the Qing dynasty, many Manchu migrated to other parts of China; similarly, a sizeable Han population migrated to Manchuria. Despite the Qing authority's attempts to preserve Han-Manchu distinctions, the Manchu, like the HUI, have become almost completely sinicized. The Manchu language is used today by a dwindling number of elderly people in remote areas; most Manchu speak only Chinese.

The Manchu were once shamanists who used shamans to exorcise malevolent spirits and perform religious ceremonies. Most Manchu engage in agriculture; scattered urban Manchu are usually workers and intellectuals.

MANDA   see HIDATSA.

MANDADAN CHETTI   An agricultural ethnic group living in the state of Tamil Nadu, India.

MANDAEANS   (Sabeans) see IRAQIS.

MANDAI   see GARO.

MANDAILING   A subgroup of the BATAK living in the interior highlands of the Indonesian island of Sumatera (Sumatra).

MANDAK   An ethnic group of approximately 5,000 living in central New Ireland, a Pacific island in the state of Papua New Guinea, east of the main island. Comprising five dialects, their language is an indigenous regional one. Their economy is based on slash and burn cultivation, hunting, fishing, and pig- and chicken- raising. While most are Christian, many still believe in magic and spirits. Their ceremonies revolve around the dead.

MANDAN   A Native North American group numbering 1,000, many of whom live on the Fort Berthold Federal Reservation, North Dakota, U.S.A.

In the past they lived along the Missouri River in earth lodges. Most of the tribe was wiped out by the smallpox epidemic of the 1830s. However, George Catlin recorded their culture in a series of paintings. Catlin's painting of Mandan Chief Four Bears is among the most famous paintings of Indian chieftains.

MANDAYA   (Isneg, Apayao) The largest ethnic group to be found in the eastern Davao province of southeastern Mindanao, an island in the Philippines. They number about 40,000, two-thirds of whom are Christians, with a small percentage of self-declared Muslims. The Mandaya practice upland slash and burn agriculture, mainly of rice and tubers.

After the turn of the twentieth century, the autonomous rule of the headman (*bagani*) shifted to an elected government. Traditional beliefs have lingered side by side with Christianity, and female shamans (*ballyan*) are still credited with the power to heal or to cause suffering. The Mandaya are known to have been headhunters.

MANDE (Manding) A term denoting a number of West African peoples, mainly the MALINKE, BAMBARA, and DYULA, who speak dialects of the same language and share a similar culture. The Mande heartland is in the upper Niger River along the Mali-Guinea border. This region was the center of the ancient Mali empire which was founded in the thirteenth century. (see also IVOIREANS, GUINEANS, MALIANS, SENEGALESE, SIERRA LEONEANS)

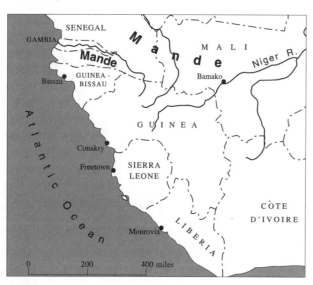

Mande

MANDERA A subgroup of the KANURI.

MANDING see MANDE.

MANDINKA see MALINKE.

MANDJIA A subgroup of the BAYA. (see also CENTRAL AFRICAN REPUBLIC, THE PEOPLE OF THE).

MANDYAKO see MANJACO.

MANGA A subgroup of the KANURI.

MANGAL A subgroup of the PASHTUN.

MANGBETU An ethnic group living in Zaire between the Ituri and Vele Rivers near the towns of Poko, Isiro, and Rungu. In the precolonial era they created a number of states and have assimilated other ethnic groups.

MANGGARAI An ethnic group numbering over 500,000 living in the western half of the island of Flores in Indonesia.

They are divided equally among Catholics (in the eastern part of their area), Muslims (in the western part), and adherents of their traditional religion (in the center). They are slash and burn cultivators of rice and corn. Vestiges of a traditional caste system persist; although slavery has been abolished, descendants of slaves, constituting the lowest of the former castes, are still disdained by both land-owning nobles and commoners.

MANGHIT A tribe of the UZBEKS.

MANGWATO A subgroup of the TSWANA.

MANGYAN see HANUNOO.

MANHICA A subgroup of the SHONA.

MANIGRI A subgroup of the EGBA. (see also YORUBA)

MANINKA see MALINKE.

MANIPURI A group numbering over 30,000 (1961), living in Bangladesh. They speak Manipuri and the Moi dialect. Said to have come to this region from Assam, the Manipuri are Vaishnava Hindus.

MANJACO (Mandyako) An ethnic group numbering c.137,000 living in Guinea-Bissau mainly in the area south of the Cacheu River and north of the Mansoa River. They mostly adhere to traditional religions but a small number are Muslims. They are related to the BRAME and PAPEL.

In the late nineteenth century the Manjaco tried to resist settlement by the PORTUGUESE in their region. After independence the Manjaco did not play an important role in Guinea-Bissau's politics until the 1980 coup which was led by a member of the PAPEL ethnic group. Following the coup, members of the Manjaco were promoted to important positions in the administration and government. (see also GUINEA-BISSAU, THE PEOPLE OF)

MANJHI   see MAJHWAR.

MANJO   see KWEGU.

MANNAN   An agricultural ethnic group, numbering about 5,000, living in central Kerala, India.

MANNEWAR   A small ethnic group living in the state of Maharashtra, India. They are Hindus and speak Telegu.

MANO   (Ma) An ethnic group living in Nimba County, Liberia. They number about 175,000 people, or 7 percent of the LIBERIANS. Smaller numbers live in Guinea in the Nzerekore administrative region. The Mano of Liberia are fighting together with the Gio (DAN) and KISSI against the KRAHN in the ongoing civil war in Liberia and a large number of them have fled to the Cote d'Ivoire and Guinea. (see also LIBERIANS)

MANOBO   see KULAMAN.

MANSI   (Vogul) The 8,000 Mansi live mainly in the Khanty-Mansi Autonomous Province along the Ob River basin in western Siberia, Russia. Some also live among RUSSIANS in the Yekaterinburg Province of Russia, at the eastern foothills of the Ural Mountains.

The Mansi speak Vogul, which together with Khanty belongs to the Finno-Ugric family of languages. Many Mansi speak Russian as well. In the early seventeenth century they were converted to Russian Orthodox Christianity but retained their ancestors' shamanistic beliefs.

They are related to the KHANT people, along with whom they are known as Ugrians or Voguls. Their chief occupations are hunting, fishing, reindeer-herding, and farming. Some Mansi are industrial workers.

MANTRA   A subgroup of the JAKUN.

MANUS   An ethnic group of approximately 25,000 living on a group of islands a few hundred miles north of Papua New Guinea. They speak many different dialects of an indigenous regional language. They are slash and burn agriculturalists and fishermen. Although

formally Christian, most center their religious beliefs upon ancestral spirits.

MANUSH   see GYPSIES.

MANX   The 65,000 inhabitants of the Isle of Man, a British Crown dependency with political and legal autonomy located in the Irish Sea. They are primarily (over 60 percent) of indigenous origin, although there are many ENGLISH, IRISH, and SCOTS living on the island. The Manx speak English, although there has been an attempt in recent years to revive Manx Gaelic, which was threatened with extinction with the death of the last native speaker in 1973. The island's economy is dependent upon agriculture, fishing, and tourism. While the islanders' principal religion is Protestantism, belief in Celtic supernatural beings persists.

MANYEMA   A Bantu ethnic group inhabiting an area stretching from the northwestern corner of Tanzania to the main tributaries of the Congo River. Their main area of settlement is in Zaire. They live in fortified villages and practice only agriculture and fishing

Mansi

in a subsistence economy, but no stockraising. Initiates are circumcised. Politically they are organized in chiefdoms.

MANYIKA   (Manyike) One of the important Shona-speaking peoples in eastern Zimbabwe, numbering about 1.2 million people or one-ninth of the population. A smaller number also live in western Mozambique. Their language, Chimanya, is a Shona dialect. (see also SHONA, ZIMBABWEANS)

MANYUKEI   An ethnic group living on the Indonesian island of Kalimantan (Borneo). (see also DAYAK)

MAO   (Anfillo) An ethnic group numbering 30,000 (1984), who live in the southern highlands of western Wallagga Province, Ethiopia. Some are Ethiopian Orthodox Christians, others Sunni Muslims. Linguistically they are related to the KAFFICHO. The Mao of Anfillo represent the legacy of a christianized ruling stratum, linked to the late medieval expansion of the Ethiopian empire. They live among the OROMO of Leqa-Sayo.

MAORI   A Polynesian-speaking people numbering 306,000 (1990), who were the indigenous inhabitants of New Zealand.

Prior to colonization, during the eighteenth century, intertribal warfare was a constant part of Maori life as a means of gaining land and slaves. The Maori social organization rested upon genealogical links carefully preserved in oral tradition. Membership of a tribe was

Maori

determined by descent through both the male and the female lines. For most of the nineteenth century this framework was affected by contact with the European population. The consequences for the Maori people were varied. They had no defense against such diseases as influenza, measles, and whooping cough. Their adoption of new technologies and Christianity was selective. Although their lifestyle was disrupted, it was not necessarily undermined, especially in the case of those tribes located away from the coast. Above all their life was dominated by the progressive loss of land to the European settlers.

The Treaty of Waitangi, signed in 1840 by the BRITISH and by most major Maori chiefs, had acknowledged Maori ownership of land, but had not served to prevent the unscrupulous practices of British settlers anxious to obtain land. The last decades of the nineteenth century brought about cultural upheaval among the Maori due to confiscation and individualization of land ownership and replacement of the traditional communal form of ownership.

In 1865, the Native Land Act set up the native land court to establish titles to land and supervise land purchase. The Native Land Development Act of 1929 was a significant milestone for the Maori, making funds available for the development of Maori lands. The alienation of tribal lands slowed down in the 1970s and the 1980s. In the 150 years since organized British settlement, Maori land had been reduced to less than 3 percent of the total. Government reorganization of Maori affairs (The Runanga Iwi Act of 1990) recognized the importance of tribal social organization and evolved new policies which promoted tribal self management and tribal development.

Today, individual titles to land are fragmented, and multiple ownership has considerably lessened the value of the land to the Maori owner. The unit farms are too small to be economicallly viable in modern times and the population pressure on land has led to underemployment in Maori areas. Urbanization was the major demographic process of the Maori population throughout the third quarter of the twentieth century, and brought about high rates of unemployment among the Maori, much higher than for the rest of the labor force in New Zealand. In general, urbanization did not improve the Maoris' social conditions, although they are slowly integrating into New Zealand society. (see also NEW ZEALANDERS)

MAPPILA   (Moplah) A Malayalam-speaking people numbering about 6 million living in the Malappuram

District (the Malabar Coast) of the southern Indian state of Kerala. They have been Muslims since the eighth century although many have come to reject the doctrines of Orthodox Islam in favor of political ideologies such as socialism. Despite efforts by Christian missionaries to introduce Catholicism and later Protestantism, the economic mismanagement by the PORTUGUESE and later by the BRITISH nurtured animosity to the church and hostility toward Western European traditions and customs.

Unemployment is particularly severe among the Mappila. Despite their high level of education, the state economy is primarily agricultural, while the entire region suffers from overpopulation. Some primitive industries do exist, but they are based on the now dwindling natural resources of the state and often present an ecological threat to the region; whole forest areas have been cut down to produce charcoal. Currently, Mappila constitute a significant segment of the migrant workers in the Persian Gulf states.

MAPUCHE A subgroup of the ARAUCANIANS living between the Tolten and Itata Rivers in Argentina.

MARA A subgroup of the TIV.

MARAKAPAN A Native South American group living in Venezuela.

MARAKKALA see SRI LANKANS.

MARAKO A subgroup of the HADIYA.

MARAKWET A Kalenjin-speaking group living to the north of the ELGEYO people in the Elgeyo-Marakwet District in Kenya, and numbering over one million. Like the ELGEYO, they are cliff-dwellers.

The Marakwet are a cluster of six groups: the ENDO, Markweta, BOROT, ALMO, and KIPTANI live along the Kerio valley; the sixth group, the CHERANGANY, live in the hills to the west. Within these natural borders, the Marakwet were relatively safe. However, they frequently fought among themselves. Their most common external enemies were the TUGEN from across the valley and the POKOT from the north, but they rarely fought as a territorial unit against outsiders. Offensive warfare was generally waged over livestock, either seizing that of groups or reclaiming their own stolen animals.

Goats constitute the main stock, sheep are numerous and important, but cattle are few and their possession is of social importance. Both men and women may own stock. The Marakwet also practice mixed farming with irrigation.

They hold traditional religious beliefs. The most important ritual operations are circumcision and clitoridectomy, which mark the entry into adulthood. (see also KALENJIN)

MARALINGA An Australian Aboriginal group living in South Australia. (see also AUSTRALIAN ABORIGINES)

MARANAO (Ranao: lit. "residing near a lake") An ethnic group numbering 900,000, located in the Philippine island of Mindanao, around Lake Lanao, the largest lake in the chain. The Maranao are Sunni Muslims, with a minor Shi'ite influence; while they were the last major group in the Philippines to become Muslims, more Maranao make the pilgrimage to Mecca each year, than any other group.

They live in small villages near rivers or another source of water, in groups of five to fifty multi-family houses raised on stilts and usually centered on a mosque and/or a "great house" where the community leader lives. The Maranao are an agricultural society, growing mainly rice, and also trade in food and crafts at markets. They are known to have joined the ILANON in the past as raiders and pirateers, and to have resisted the influence of the SPANIARDS. Marriages are arranged with a bride-price to be paid (usually land, animals, and previously even slaves); polygyny is accepted, but can usually be afforded only by the wealthy. They also retain their belief in local spirits and hold elaborate, long-lasting funerary rites. (see also ILANON)

MARBA An ethnic group closely related to the MASSA and the MUSEY, living in the Tandjile Region of Chad.

MARDUDJARA An Australian Aboriginal group numbering about 1,000 living in Jigalong and other small clusters in the Gibson Desert of central Western Australia. They subsist on hunting and gathering. (see also AUSTRALIAN ABORIGINES)

MARGAL see MEGREL.

MARGI An ethnic group living in Nigeria.

MARI I A subgroup of the KARANGA of Africa.

Mari

MARI II Most of the c.650,000 Mari live in the Mari Autonomous Republic in Russia, with minorities in the neighboring republics and provinces along the Volga River. They are divided into two distinct groups: the Kuryk (forest) Mari, inhabiting the western bank of the Volga River, and the Olyk (meadow) Mari, on its eastern bank. The Upo (eastern) Mari are a subdivision of the Olyk Mari. They live mainly in Bashqortstan, Tatarstan, and the Sverdlovsky Province.

This division between the Olyk and Kuryk Mari dates back to the twelfth century and is linguistic rather than cultural-ethnic, the dialects (in fact separate languages) not being mutually intelligible. The Mari languages form a distinct subgroup within the Finnic group of the Finno-Ugric languages. Both were made into literary languages in the nineteenth century by the Russian Orthodox Mission in Kazan, and Cyrillic alphabets were adopted for them.

During the centuries of Russian rule the Mari stubbornly and quite successfully resisted all efforts at christianization and russification, which sets them apart from all other non-Muslim peoples conquered by Russia. Accordingly, the Mari preserved their ancient religion with only minor influences of either Christian-

ity (mainly among the Kuryk Mari) or Islam (mainly among the Upo Mari). Mari nationalism, which began to develop in the second half of the nineteenth century, was connected to their religious distinction. In the 1870s it manifested itself in the Kugu Sort (Great Candle) movement which was particularly strong among the Olyk and Upo Mari.

MARIA see ABUJHMARIA.

MARIANA ISLANDERS A Micronesian-speaking people numbering about 43,000 who inhabit sixteen islands in the Pacific Ocean west of Hawaii. English is widely spoken, but the indigenous Chamorro and Carolinian languages are spoken in the family. Only six of the islands have been regularly inhabited: Saipan, Rota, Almagan, Tinian, Agrihan, and Anatahan (evacuated in 1990 owing to a volcanic eruption). The people are Christians, although traditional beliefs and taboos are still practiced.

As a result of external influences, starting with the first contact with the Spanish in 1521, there is great cultural and social diversity among the present inhabitants. The indigenous inhabitants are the Chamorro-speaking majority, and there is an important minority group of Carolinian background; however, their colonial history has also given rise to a mixture of many immigrant groups, including SPANIARDS, GERMANS, and JAPANESE. The traditional Chamorro society was based on matrilineal clans, which have now disappeared, due to Spanish, German, Japanese, and American policies which encouraged a patrilineal system. The solidarity of lineages has been destroyed, and today the majority of households consist of a nuclear family unit.

The economy of the northern Mariana Islands is dominated by tourism; agriculture is based on small holdings and the important crops are coconuts, breadfruit, tomatoes, and melons.

In the twentieth century the islands have been administered successively by Germany, Japan, and the United States from 1947, as part of the United Nations Trust Territory of the Pacific Islands. In 1975, the islanders voted for a separated status as a U.S. Commonwealth Territory.

MARICHE A Native South American group living in Venezuela.

MARINDANIM An ethnic group of approximately 5,000 living on the southern coast of Irian Jaya, the Indonesian part of the island of New Guinea. They speak an indigenous local language. Their subsistence is based upon their main crop of sago. Although most are Christian, they nonetheless use traditional sorcery in various ceremonies.

MARING An ethnic group of approximately 10,000 living in the mountains of central Papua New Guinea. They speak an indigenous regional language. They are hunters, gatherers, fishermen, pig-raisers, and slash and burn cultivators. They are ardent believers in the power of their ancestral spirits.

MARINGGAI A subgroup of the ABUNG.

MA RO A subgroup of the MA, living in southern Vietnam.

MARONENE (Kabaenas) A small group inhabiting the southeastern tip of the island of Sulawesi (Celebes), Indonesia, and the outlying island of Kabaena. They are predominantly Muslims who speak a language related to those of the Philippines. Sago is the staple crop although rice is also cultivated, and hunting is important.

MARONITE CLANS (Franji, Edde, Kohuru, Chamoun, Gemayel) see LEBANESE.

MARONITES see LEBANESE, SYRIANS.

MARSHALL ISLANDERS (Marshallese) A Micronesian-speaking people who inhabit a chain of 33 islands known as the Marshall Islands, located in the center of the Pacific Ocean. The population of 45,000 (1988) is spread over the eastern chain of the islands, known as Ratak, and the western chain known as Ralik. About 20,000 live in the capital, Majuro. In 1920 Japan was given a League of Nations mandate over the Marshall Islands, and began large-scale colonization, which was interrupted during World War II. Administered by the United States since 1947, the Marshallese voted in 1991 to form their own republic to be freely associated with the USA. The economy is based on copra, fisheries, and tourism. The traditional society of the Marshallese consists of a complex system of matrilineal clans, socially stratified.

MARSH ARABS see IRAQIS.

MARTINIQUE, THE PEOPLE OF Inhabitants of the French overseas departement of Martinique, situated among the Lesser Antilles in the Caribbean Sea. The island has a predominantly Roman Catholic population of 365,000, most of whom are descendants of black African slaves. The economy is based on agriculture, with sugarcane and bananas as leading crops. French is the official language, but a Creole dialect is widely spoken. There exists a strong movement for independence from rule by the FRENCH.

MARU DANGBAU A subgroup of the KACHIN.

MARYA A subgroup of the TIGRE.

MARYKU MISSENENYI One of the eight "early states" of the HAYA.

MASA A group living in southern Chad. They practice their traditional religion.

MASAAI A people estimated at 200,000, or about 1 percent of the population, living in southern Kenya between the towns of Narok and Namanga, and in northern Tanzania. They speak Maa, which is an Eastern Nilotic language. Most Masaai retain their traditional religion although some have adopted some form of Christianity.

The Masaai are pastoral nomads who live today much as they always have in the open plains of southeast Kenya and Tanzania. Their life and culture traditionally revolve around their cattle, which are the only wealth they recognize, and they move to wherever conditions are best for their herds.

Before the BRITISH occupied Kenya in the beginning of the twentieth century, the Masaai wandered freely after grazing land. The creation of borders and the territorial limits put upon them have forced a change in their lifestyle, although not as drastic as with other nomadic people.

The Masaai live in settlements called *bomas*, circles of huts made from twigs and surrounded by barricades to fence in their cattle. Their cultural life is full of celebrations, starting with birth. The Masaai version of age-sets consists of childhood, junior warrior (*moran*), senior warrior, junior elder, and senior elder. Each generation of men constitutes an age-set which passes through each age-grade in succession. After circumcision boys become men and junior warriors.

The Masaai political system is decentralized; meetings of elders and public discussions are held to decide on more general matters. What ruled, and continues to rule, are the lives of their cattle. Their religion is cen-

A Masaai family in northern Tanzania

tered around mystical beliefs concerning the Masaai, their cattle, and God. The cows are sacred, and therefore their land and all other elements concerning cattle are sacred. Cattle provide all the needs of the Masaai: milk, blood, and meat as their diet, and hides and skins for clothing. (see also ARUSHA, TANZANIA)

MASALIT An ethnic group numbering around 67,000 living in the Ouadai region of Chad especially along the Sudanese border. Their language is related to Duramabang, spoken by the MABA. Although mostly Muslims, they have retained many pre-Islamic practices. (see also CHADIANS)

MASANGO see MAJANGIR.

MASCOI A South American Indian group inhabiting the Gran Chaco region of central South America. They subsist primarily by hunting, fishing, and the gathering of wild products, most notably algarroba pods. They also grow maize, sweet manioc, beans, and pumpkins (all cultivated by the menfolk only), and herd livestock.

MASHACALI (Maxakali) A South American Indian group living in government-sponsored reserves in the State of Minas Gerais, southeastern Brazil. Like the FULNIO group, they have preserved their own traditions and language (which belongs to the Ge family).

MASHASHA A Nkoya-speaking group numbering 9,000 living in southwest Zambia.

MASHI A group of Luyana-speakers numbering 9,000 living in the extreme southwestern corner of Zambia.

MASHONA see SHONA.

MASMUDA A people living in Morocco who form, together with the SANHADJA, the main stock of the BERBERS of that country. They are now dispersed over the area from Rabat to Azru and Khanifra, although their original homeland was in the western part of the High Atlas mountains. They speak a dialect of the Berber language, and were converted to Islam in the seventh century. The Masmuda are sedentary agriculturalists and cattle-raisers.

In the eleventh century they became subject to the Almoravids, an Islamic reform movement which destroyed the kingdom of Ghana, conquered Morocco

and much of western Algeria, and reunified Muslim Spain against the *Reconquista*. In the early twelfth century they rebelled against the Almoravids under the leadership of Ibn Tumart, bringing about the foundation of the Almohad dynasty. During the first half of the thirteenth century, the power of this dynasty began to decline, and the Masmuda of the Atlas region took the opportunity to regain their independence.

When the FRENCH occupied the region in the late nineteenth century, the Masmuda were divided into three groups, each ruled by a local family. Today, the name "Masmuda" is still preserved in the north of Morocco, but seems to have disappeared in the south, where the former Masmuda people are now known as the Shuluh. (see also SANHADJA)

MA SOP A subgroup of the MA, living in southern Vietnam.

MASOUFA A subgroup of the MAURE. (see also SANHADJA)

MASSA A subgroup of the KIRDI.

MASSANGO (Sangou) An ethnic group living in Gabon, in the forested mountainous area of the south-central interior between the Ogoulou and Offoue Rivers. They are linguistically related to the ESHIRA. In the early twentieth century they resisted French colonization but were suppressed after only two years of fighting.

MATACO see MATACO-MATAGUAYO.

MATACO-MATAGUAYO The indigenous inhabitants of Argentina. At the time of the Spanish Conquest, they occupied the west and central parts of the Chaco area.

They consist of the MATAGHUAYO, VEJOZ, GUISNAY, MIBALA, MAKA, MATARA, TONOCOTE, MATACO, CHOROTE, and CHULUPI. At present, just eighteen Mataco-Mataguayo communities remain in Chaco, thirty in Formosa, and forty-four in Salta, including nine communities of CHOROTE and CHULUPI.

MATAGAM A subgroup of the KIRDI.

MATAGHUAYO see MATACO-MATAGUAYO.

MATARA A tribe of the MATACO-MATAGUAYO.

Mataco-Mataguayo

MATENGO   A people numbering some 180,000 living on the eastern side of Lake Tanganyika in Tanzania. Their language belongs to the Niger-Kordofan family of languages.

The Matengo live in compact villages along the shores of the lake and subsist primarily from fishing.

MATHA   An agricultural group living in northern Kerala, India.

MA TO   A subgroup of the MA, living in southern Vietnam.

MAUE   (Mawe) A South American Indian group living south of the Amazon River, in the State of Amazon, northern Brazil. They live in a dozen villages on river locations, and have been strongly influenced by missionary activities. Some of them are known as SA-TARE. They number a few thousand.

MAULIK   see DHIMAL.

MAURES   (Moors) An Arab-Berber people living in Mauritania, numbering around 1.3 million, and constituting about two-thirds of the population. They speak the Hassaniya dialect of Arabic and are predominantly Muslims. The term Maure or Moor was often used in European languages to describe North Africans in general or even Muslim people in other parts of the world.

The FRENCH conquered the Maure territory in the early twentieth century and ruled them indirectly with the help of appointed chiefs until the eve of World War

II. Since Mauritania was of little economic value to the FRENCH, barely any investment was made in its development.

Maure society is traditionally divided into classes which include the aristocracy, the Islamic clerics, and the tribute-paying third class. This social division still exists in modern Mauritania, and blacks, historically of the third class, are still treated as slaves.

Slavery was last abolished only in 1980, in response to the pressures of a local liberation movement aided by anti-slavery movements from abroad. It is still common, however, in various parts of the country. The anti-slavery struggle has brought attention to the injustices and inequalities tolerated by traditional Maure society despite their being contrary to Islamic law.

Maure sub-groups include the AZARZIR, DUAISH, LEMOUNTA, MAAQUIL, MASSOUFA, REGEIBAT, TOLBAS, and ZENAGA. (see also MAURITANIANS)

MAURITANIANS   The people of the Islamic republic of Mauritania which forms a geographic link between the Maghreb and sub-Saharan West Africa. They number c.2 million. Two-thirds of the population are the MAURES, people of Arab-Berber origin, while the rest are black Africans divided into several ethnic groups of which the principal are the FULANI (20 percent) and the WOLOF (12 percent). The black minority are mainly sedentary cultivators and are concentrated in a relatively narrow zone in the south of the country. Islam is the official religion of Mauritania and almost all Mauritanians are Muslim.

The Mauritanians became independent from colonial rule by the French in November 1960. Since then, Mauritanian political life has been dominated by the MAURES and the black minority has suffered a great number of injustices and inequalities. Until 1980 slavery was legal in Mauritania, and only following the pressure of human rights movements was it abolished. However, it still exists in various parts of the country and the main sufferers are the black Mauritanians.

Following a dispute with Senegal in 1989, light-skinned Mauritanians living in Senegal were attacked while SENEGALESE and black Mauritanians were also attacked in Mauritania. About 48,000 black Mauritanians took refuge in Senegal. The conflict between the two countries has not yet been resolved.

MAURITIANS   The national designation of the inhabitants of the island republic of Mauritius located in the Indian Ocean about 500 miles east of Madagascar. Mauritius has no indigenous population; its approximately 1 million inhabitants are descended from a variety of ethnic groups who were brought over during the colonial period to work on the extensive sugar plantations. Bhojpuri-speaking INDIANS comprise the largest ethnic population with about 68 percent of the total. African Creole-speakers constitute another 27 percent and the remainder are descended from FRENCH and BRITISH who come as colonialists and from CHINESE who came as immigrants. About half the population practices Hinduism, 30 percent are Christians, 15 percent are Muslims, and the remainder Buddhists, Taoists, and Confucianists.

The island's first settlers were ARABS who arrived as traders in the tenth century but left shortly after. The DUTCH discovered Mauritius in 1598 and introduced sugar cane, which accounts for almost 90 percent of the country's exports and 70 percent of the labor force. The FRENCH gained control in 1715 and brought African slaves to work the extensive sugar plantations. The Creole language developed from a fusion of French and African elements. In 1810 the BRITISH captured Mauritius and began importing INDIANS as laborers. Independence was granted in 1968.

Inter-ethnic tensions, coupled with the decline in world sugar prices, have resulted in several violent clashes between the island's peoples. A state of emergency was declared in 1968–1970 and again in 1971–1978 after Africans and Muslims clashed over attempts to declare Creole the national language. The Hindu Indian majority still dominates local politics, but ethnic political parties have some leverage in determining national affairs.

MAUTONG   (Mouton) An ethnic group living on the Indonesian island of Kalimantan (Borneo). (see also DAYAK)

MAVILAN   An ethnic group living in northern Kerala, India. Originally engaged in hunting and gathering, they are now moving to agriculture and services.

MAWE   see MAUE.

MAWRI   A subgroup of the TURKMEN.

MAXACALI   see MASHACALI.

MAY   A Mon-Khmer group, numbering about 1,000, living on the mountainsides in the Quang Binh Province of northern Vietnam. Traditionally nomadic, the May have become increasingly sedentary in recent years.

MAYA   The Maya, indigenous MEXICANS who were settled villagers as early as 1500 B.C.E., have become renowned in recent years for their pre-Colombian achievements in art, architecture, astronomy, and mathematics. The southern Maya reached the zenith of their classic phase in about 700 C.E., at which point hundreds of ceremonial centers and as many as fifty large towns flourished. The northern Maya of the present Mexican states of Yucatán and Quintana Roo began their ascent in c.800 C.E., but soon fell under the ideological, political, and artistic influence of the Toltec Empire; their centers had been abandoned by the time of the Spanish conquest in 1519.

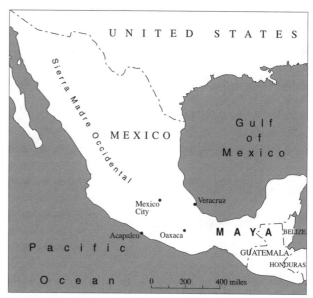

Maya

The Maya are both numerous and widely dispersed: unreliable censuses and periods of intense violence in Guatemala and El Salvador have resulted in greatly varying population estimates, but they number more than 5 million and are characterized both geographically and by altitude. They currently inhabit Mexico and four Central American countries, and are divided into highland and lowland Maya. Most numerous in Guatemala and southern Mexico, they are also dispersed over parts of Belize, El Salvador, and Western Honduras.

Linguistic and geographic groupings provide a regional classification system. The Yucatec Maya inhabit the Yucatán, north Belize, and northeast Guatemala; the LACANDON, small in number, extend from the Mexican-Guatemalan border into Belize; while the QUICHE are concentrated in the western highlands of Guatemala. The QUICH-CAKCHIQUEL people, most numerous of the Maya, number more than a million, and include several subgroups of which the KEKCHI, numbering at least 250,000, are probably the largest.

Other groups include the MAMEAN MAYA of the western Guatemalan highlands, numbering almost 400,000. Among the Mexican Maya are the CHAMULA, TZOTZIL and TZELTAL, and ZINACANTECAN peoples of the state of Chiapas, and the CHONTAL of the state of Oaxaca. Smaller Guatemalan groups include the AGUATEC, CHORTI, IXIL, JALALTEC, KANJOBAL, POCONCHI, POCOMAN, TZUTUHIL, and USPANTEC.

Central American veneration of its ancient Maya past has unfortunately not been paralleled by an equal reverence for its Maya present. On the contrary: brutally subjugated during the conquest and colonial period, the Maya have also suffered greatly since independence. Over the last two decades of the twentieth century, this has been especially true in Guatemala, which has the largest Maya population of any central American country, and where more than 100,000 village-dwelling Maya have died violently. (see also CHAMULA, CHONTAL, GUATEMALANS KEKCHI, HUASTEC, LACANDONES, MEXICANS, QUICHE, TZETLTAL, YI, YUCATEC, ZINACANTECOS)

MAYANGA   see SUNDI.

MAYAYAO   A subgroup of the IFUGAO.

MAYO   An ethnic group, numbering some 30,000, living in northwest Mexico along the Mayo River Valley of southern Sonora and the Puerte River Valley of northern Sinaloa, not far from the Mexican-U.S. border. Their location in low-lying and fertile lands left them vulnerable to Spanish attacks. They were converted to Christianity by Jesuit priests, and are today among the most deeply religious of all Indian peoples of Mexico. The religion they practice is, however, syncretic. It is difficult to separate the pagan aspects of their observance from Catholic ritual; in this regard, their Easter celebrations are especially noteworthy.

The Mayo revolted twice against what they saw as outside domination. In the first revolt, in the late 1880s, they allied themselves with the neighboring YAQUI but lost. The second occurred around 1917, during the Mexican Revolution: again they lost, not just the struggle, but their lands and self-determination as an Indian tribe as well. As a result of these setbacks

and later economic deprivation, they have sought solace in religion, to the extent that they are often regarded by other groups as fanatics. The Mayo average about two years of schooling, resulting in their performing the lowest, most poorly paid work in the region. (see also MEXICANS)

MAYORUNA   A South American Indian people living in the extreme western regions of the Amazon basin in Brazil. They subsist primarily from hunting and gathering. They also engage in limited agriculture, cultivating maize and sweet manioc.

MAYOTTE, THE PEOPLE OF   The inhabitants of Mayotte, the southernmost island in the Comoros chain lying in the Mozambique Channel between Madagascar and the African mainland. The estimated population is 77,000. They are of mixed Arab, Malagasy, and African origin. Comorian, the common language, is a variant of Swahili heavily influenced by Arabic and written in Arabic characters. The people of Mayotte engage mainly in agriculture, growing vanilla, coffee, and rice. Islam is the predominant religion.

In both 1974 and 1976 the people of Mayotte voted overwhelmingly to retain their links with France rather than to join the independent Comoro Islands.

MAZAHUAS   An Otomi-Mixteca subgroup of the Mexican Olmecs that constitutes one of the largest indigenous groups of people in that country, living in the states of Mexico and Michoacan, and in the Federal District. They number approximately 200,000. They were one of the five tribes that founded the important ancient centers of Culhuacan, Otompan, and Tula prior to conquest by the SPANIARDS.

The Mazahua economy is now based on subsistence agriculture, involving the cultivation of corn, beans, and squash. They also engage in domestic crafts. Their social structure is patriarchal.

The Mazahua have retained few pre-Hispanic traditions, although their Catholicism is infused with traditional elements. (see also NAHUA)

MAZANDARANI   A people living in a fertile and densely populated area near the Caspian coastal lowlands and nearby mountains. Their estimated number is 1.5–1.8 million. The Mazandarani language belongs to the western subgroup of the Iranian group of languages. They are Shi'ite Muslims.

The Mazandarani are mainly sedentary agriculturalists, specializing in cultivating tea; some are urban craftsmen and traders. For a long period they were ruled by virtually independent or semi-independent dynasties, the most outstanding of which was the Bavandids (665–1349), and were more or less brought under central Iranian authority only by Shah Abbas I the Safavid in 1596.

MAZANG   see GYPSIES.

MAZATECOS   A part of the Otomi-Mixteca subgroup of Olmecs, numbering some 125,000; 90 percent of them inhabit the Mexican state of Oaxaca, the remainder, the neighboring states of Puebla and Veracruz. Some 40 percent speak no Spanish.

The Mazateco engage in subsistence agriculture, growing corn, beans, squash, and a variety of tropical fruits, both for home consumption and for sale in itinerant open markets or in small stores (the owners of which enjoy considerable prestige among the Mazateco). They also cultivate coffee, sugarcane, tobacco, rice, and cocoa as cash crops; Mazateco in the Ayautia and Jalapa de Diaz areas also collect tubers from which hormones are synthesized for the European pharmaceutical market.

Mazateco families are patriarchal, their residence patrilocal. The Mazateco have perpetuated a strong tradition of collective work that has served to fortify community spirit. In many villages councils of elders continue to function as the principal administrative and moral authority.

While all Mazateco are nominally Catholic, their festivities and ceremonies contain many indigenous elements. Thus, celebrations for a child's birth are scheduled according to the Aztec calendar, from which the name of the child's totem animal is derived. This name, and that of the saint on whose day the child is born, is given to the infant.

MAZOVIANS   see POLES.

MBAI   (Mbaye) A subgroup of the SARA.

MBAKA   (Ngbaka) An ethnic group living in the Lobaye Region of the Central African Republic. Jean-Bedel Bokassa, the despotic ruler of this country from 1965 till 1979, was a member of the Mbaka group. (see also CENTRAL AFRICAN REPUBLIC, THE PEOPLE OF THE)

MBALA   An ethnic group living in southwestern Zaire between the Kwango and Kasai Rivers. Their language is related to that of the KONGO.

MBALIS   An ethnic group living in Angola.

MBAMBA   see OBAMBA.

MBANJA   (Mbanza) An ethnic group living in the Equator Region of Zaire, mainly between the Zaire and Ubangui Rivers. They speak the language of the BANDA. (see also ZAIREANS)

MBANZA   see MBANJA.

MBEMBE   A subgroup of the IBIBIO.

MBERE   A people living on the southeastern slopes of Mount Kenya, near the EMBU people. The Mbere are part of the Central Bantu-speaking people of East Africa and are estimated as numbering about 100,000. Mbere land being poor and rainfall sparse, they have always concentrated on animal husbandry and bee-keeping, together with agriculture. Cultivation in the rainy areas of Mbere land consists of cash crops such as cotton and tobacco, as well as maize and vegetables for daily use.

Although most Mbere people are today Christians, aspects of the traditional religion are still strong. Other traditional elements include round houses with conical thatched roofs, as well as dancing ceremonies and rhythmic drumming.

MBIMU   An ethnic group related to the SANGA living in northern Congo.

MBIRE   A subgroup of the ZEZURU.

MBO   An ethnic group related to the BASSA-BAKOKO, living in Cameroon.

M'BOCHI   An ethnic group living along both banks of the Alima River in Congo. They number about 200,000, or 11 percent of the population, and are mostly Christians.

In the early twentieth century the M'bochi were influenced by the education provided by the FRENCH in Catholic missions and became one of the most westernized ethnic groups in Equatorial Africa. During the French colonial period the M'bochi supplied the African cadres for the colonial administration and were active in the private business sector. During the period between the two World Wars the M'bochi gradually lost their dominance in the administration to members of other ethnic groups, mainly the VILI and the LALI. After World

War II, when party politics began to develop in the French colonies, most M'bochi supported the Congo branch of the French Socialist party. (see also CONGOLESE)

MBO DLAMINI   A subgroup of the NGUNI.

MBOKO   An ethnic group related to the M'bochi living in Congo.

MBOUM   see MBUM.

MBUA   (Kaingua) A South American Indian group dispersed among the States of São Paulo, Paraná, Santa Catarina, and Rio Grande do Sul, all in southern Brazil. They live in shelters called *toldos* (tents), maintained mainly by the Rio Grande do Sul authorities. Their language belongs to the Guaraní language family. (see also GUARANI)

MBULU   see IRAQW.

MBUM   (Mboum) An ethnic group living in northern Cameroon and the western Central African Republic. They are related to the BAYA. (see also CAMEROONIANS, CENTRAL AFRICAN REPUBLIC, THE PEOPLE OF THE)

MBUNDA   An ethnic group numbering 67,000 living in northwest Zambia. Their language, Mbunda, belongs to the Wiko language group. They are Christians still adhering to traditional beliefs. The Mbunda are an agricultural people and are known for their expertise in handling the bow and arrow and ax. While originally from Angola, Mbunda are now found only in Zambia near LOZI centers.

MBUNDU   An ethnic group numbering 1.3 million living in northeast Angola, in the Luanda, Malanje, and North and South Kwaza Districts. They speak Kimbundu and are Christians who retain elements of their traditional religion. In the sixteenth century, the Mbundu were mainly farmers, craftsmen, and traders organized into small but centralized chiefdoms. The establishment of colonial rule by the PORTUGUESE had a profound effect on the Mbundu and many are now *assimilados* — Africans who have adopted Portuguese values and customs.

Most Mbundu belonged to the Soviet- and Cuban-backed Popular Movement for the Liberation of Angola (MPLA). The founder of this movement, Agostinho Neto, and many other prominent ANGOLANS, are Mbundu.

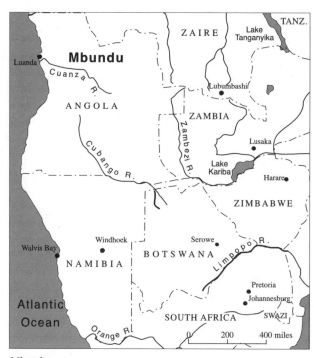

Mbundu

MDHUR   A subgroup of the JARAI.

M'DUR   A subgroup of the RHADE.

MECH   An ethnic group numbering 27,000 (1981), living in the Darjeeling, Cooch Behar, and Jalpaiguri regions of West Bengal, India. They are related to the KACHARI, and speak an Assamese dialect belonging to the Tibeto-Chinese family of languages.

The Mech worship the *sij* plant as a symbol of their supreme deity, Bathow, as well as other deities. They practice shifting cultivation and also pursue spinning, weaving, and fishing. The Mech are adapting to changing conditions, and are also employed as policemen, teachers, and forest laborers.

ME'EN   An ethnic group living in Ethiopia. They speak a Nilotic language. (see also SURMA)

MEGREL   (s.d. Margal) A large ethnic group in Georgia who now consider themselves GEORGIANS, located mainly in the Kolkhida lowland, extending along the Black Sea shore and the foothills of the Caucasus mountain range. They number an estimated 400,000. The Megrel have been Eastern Orthodox Christians since the sixth century.

The Megrel language belongs to the Kartvelian branch of the Ibero-Caucasian family of languages. In the 1920s and 1930s attempts were made to reduce it to writing, and Georgian is now used as the literary language.

The chief occupations of the Megrel are agriculture, horticulture, and viticulture. (see also CHAN, GEORGIANS)

MEJBRAT An ethnic group of approximately 15,000 living in the western peninsula of Irian Jaya, the Indonesian part of the island of New Guinea. They speak an indigenous local language which is a composite of seven dialects. They are hunters, gatherers, and cultivators of various food crops, most prominent among which is taro. Their beliefs include mythical and magical elements.

MEKAN An ethnic group living in Ethiopia. They speak a Nilotic language. (See also SURMA)

MEKEO An ethnic group of approximately 20,000, living on the southeastern coast of Papua New Guinea. Their language consists of three indigenous dialects. They are hunters, gatherers, and slash and burn farmers. They believe in a mixture of Catholic doctrine and traditional myth. Their ceremonies feature sorcery and magic.

MEKONGGA A subgroup of the LAKI.

MELAKUDI A Dravidian-speaking group of herders and farmers found in the southern Indian states of Kerala and Karnataka. They number about 10,000.

MELANAU (s.d. A-Liko [with place-name]) A generic term for several groups, speaking dialects of the same language (although not all dialects are mutually intelligible) and sharing many cultural patterns, living in the Malaysian province of Sarawak and in the neighboring sultanate of Brunei on the island of Borneo. They number about 100,000, most of whom are Muslims. There are also smaller Christian and traditional communities.

Swampy conditions have precluded much agriculture in their region except for small garden plots and sago-growing. Most Melanau engage in hunting and gathering while fishing is important along the coast.

MELATUNG An ethnic group living on the Indonesian island of Kalimantan (Borneo). (see also DAYAK)

MELAYU see MALAYS.

MELPA An ethnic group of approximately 50,000 living in the mountainous area of central Papua New Guinea. They speak an indigenous regional language. Their economy is based upon the cultivation of vegetables, especially sweet potatoes. Although members of Christian churches, they still maintain their belief in ghosts and cults.

MENAM A Mon-Khmer group numbering 5,000 living in southern Laos and central Vietnam. They cultivate upland rice and trade cinnamon and medicinal herbs with neighboring peoples. They are often identified with the DUANE, JEH, NOAR, and SAYAN.

MENDE An ethnic group living mainly in the Southern and Eastern Provinces of Sierra Leone where they number about 1.3 million, or 30 percent of Sierra Leone's population. Smaller numbers are also found in Upper Lofa County, Liberia. They speak Mande and are gradually converting to Islam and Christianity. Their main occupation is agriculture. The Mende have been absorbing other ethnic groups since precolonial times and they dominate their region culturally.

In the late nineteenth century the BRITISH turned the Mende region into a protectorate. At first the Mendef tried to resist the BRITISH, who responded by appointing loyal Mende as chiefs, thereby altering the precolonial Mende political system. During the colonial period the BRITISH invested heavily in the infrastructure of the Mende territory in the south of Sierra Leone. The Mende took greater advantage of educational opportunities than did than other ethnic groups in Sierra Leone. After independence, they struggled with the TEMNE for power in government, which they maintained until 1973. (see also LIBERIANS, SIERRA LEONEANS)

MENDI An ethnic group of approximately 30,000 living in the mountainous region of central Papua New Guinea. Like other neighboring groups, they speak an indigenous local language. Their economy is based upon the raising of pigs and the growing of sweet potatoes. Although several Christian missions are active among them, they retain traditional beliefs in ancestral spirits.

MENDRIQ A subgroup of the SEMANG.

MENOMINI (Menominee) A Native North American group numbering about 3,500, many of whom live on the Stockbridge-Munsee Federal Reservation in

Wisconsin. Traditionally they were harvesters of wild rice and hunters of small game.

MENSA   A subgroup of the TIGRE.

MENTAWEIANS   Inhabitants of the Pagai Archipelago and the islands of Sipora and Siberut, in Indonesia. They number about 20,000 and speak an obscure language, generally believed to belong to the Western Indonesian language family. Since the 1950s they have adopted Christianity and only a handful of elders still adhere to their traditional belief in spirits.

The Mentaweians are of Mongoloid stock with Veddoid and possibly even Caucasian strains. They lack some of the cultural components common to most Indonesian peoples such as pottery-making and the use of betel. Only recently has the government introduced rice cultivation; taro and occasionally sago remain the staple crops.

MERILLE   see DASSANETCH.

MERINA   The largest tribal division of the MALAGASY. They constitute about one-quarter of the island of Madagascar's population.

MERU   A people living in the Meru district in central Kenya, where they constitute the sixth largest group, numbering an estimated 800,000. They speak a Central Bantu language with several dialects. Most Meru are Christians, of all denominations, although some still follow traditional African religions, while male circumcision and initiation ceremonies remain a basic part of life.

The Meru are actually a conglomerate of several subgroups closely related by linguistic and cultural similarities. Only in the twentieth century have they emerged as a recognized social and political unit. The Meru, as a unit, encompass the IGEMBE, IGOJI, IMENTI, MIUTINI, TIGANIA, MUTHAMBI, MWIMBI, and the CHUKA. The last group named is least related to the Meru and does not possess the strongly-held tradition of migrating from the coast characteristic of the others.

All the Meru subgroups, except the CHUKA, believe in common ancestors who dwelled in a place called Mbwa. This common origin, however, did not prevent the various subgroups from fighting among themselves, and fragmentation was at a peak by the beginning of the nineteenth century. The advent of colonialism re-established the sense of unity and common

identity among the various Meru groups. One of the major cultural similarities between the groups is a prohibition against eating fish, probably adopted from the Maa-speaking nomads with whom they had contact over the centuries.

Today most Meru practice a mixed economy of cultivation and annimal husbandry. The main cash crops are coffee, potatoes, and miraa, a narcotic plant in use among the SOMALI people.

MESCALERO   A subgroup of the APACHE.

MESHALIT   A subgroup of the TIGRE.

MESKH   (Meskhi Turks) A Turkish-speaking heterogenous ethnic group consisting of QARAPAPAKH and turkified GEORGIANS, ARMENIANS, CHEMSHINS, and KURDS, all professing Sunni Islam of the Hanafi school. They lived in southwest Georgia, near the Turkish border, until 1944, when the Soviet authorities deported them to Uzbekistan. Their estimated number is 200,000.

In exile they developed a common ethnic consciousness and began to define themselves as Meskh or Meskhi Turks. In the 1960s and 1970s they became known for their struggle to be allowed to emigrate to Turkey or return to Georgia. In 1989 anti-Meskh disturbances broke out in the Ferghana valley of Uzbekistan, and many Meskh fled to other areas of the USSR. The Georgian authorities were hesitant about allowing the mass return of Meskh unless they took on Georgian identity. In 1990 their umbrella association, *Vatan* (Homeland), was established.

MESME   An ethnic group living in Chad.

MESMEDJE   A Nilotic ethnic group living in Chad.

MESSIRIYYAH   A subgroup of the BAGGARA.

META   An ethnic group related to the BAMILEKE living in Cameroon.

METIS   An ethnic group numbering about 100,000 living in western Canada, primarily in Manitoba. Most speak French and profess Catholicism. They are descended from FRENCH and SCOTS who settled along the Red River as traders and hunters and intermarried with the native Indian population. After some generations a distinctive culture emerged which incorporated European and Native Indian elements, and the Metis came to regard themselves as an ethnic group detached from both the Europeans and the Indians.

The incorporation of the Northwest Territories (now Manitoba, Saskatchewan and Alberta) by Canada was opposed by the Metis who believed that this threatened their own existence. Tensions culminated in the capture of Winnipeg in 1869 and the establishment of a provisional Metis government there, headed by Louis Riel. This short-lived attempt at creating an independent Metis homeland was suppressed by the Canadian government the following year and the Metis leaders fled to the United States. A second such attempt in 1885 ended with the capture and execution of Riel.

The Metis have since integrated into Canadian society, although like the indigenous Indian peoples they suffer poverty and many live on reservations. They are classified by the Canadian government together with the Indians and INUIT as an indigenous people and in recent attempts to rewrite the Canadian constitution there has been some effort by the federal government to redress the claims of the Metis. (see also CANADIANS)

MEXICANS The approximately 90 million Mexicans are a particularly heterogeneous population. Some two-thirds of the people, the *mestizos*, are of mixed Spanish and indigenous ancestry and have produced a culture combining aspects of their diverse backgrounds. The varied indigenous groups scattered throughout the country are another significant factor. They constitute 9 percent of the population, but are generally somewhat isolated from mainstream Mexico's industrial civilization. Most have preserved their native languages, using them either exclusively or with Spanish as a second language. Missionary efforts to introduce a more Orthodox version of Catholicism have been largely unsuccessful. Some have retained their native religions; others have integrated traditional beliefs and rituals into Catholicism.

The following thirteen Mexican states are inhabited primarily by indigenous groups: Oaxaca, Chiapas, Quintana Roo, Campeche, Guerrero, Hidalgo, Nayarit, Puebla, San Luis Potosí, Veracruz, Yucatán, Michoacán, and the State of Mexico. These indigenous peoples are divided into fifty-six distinct ethnic groups, grouped into several linguistic families. Indigenous groups include the MAYO, SERI, YAQUI, TARAHUMARA, and KICKAPOO in the north, the HUICHOL, OTOMI, PUREPECHA, and NAHUA in the areas surrounding the Central Valley of Mexico, the TOTONAC in the east, the MIXTEC, ZAPOTEC, and HUAVE in the southwest, the MAYA in Yu-

catán, and the CHIAPAS in the far south. There are also many small tribes such as the CHONTAL who are of Mayan origin but are today counted as a distinct group.

Mexico's indigenous peoples lead a precarious existence: their houses are inadequately protected against heat and cold and, living in poverty, they are particularly susceptible to disease and infection. Some still subsist by traditional means such as fishing, hunting, and agriculture. This is sometimes supplemented with income from traditional crafts such as carving (particularly beautiful are their musical instruments), rope-making, and weaving. Others seek menial employment in the cities, while still others migrate, both legally and illegally, to the United States, where they seek employment as agricultural workers.

Soon after the establishment of the colony of New Spain, Mexican society was divided by a class system. Class distinctions gradually became more graded over time. The highest class was composed of full-blooded descendants of original Spanish colonists. These were followed by the *mestizos*, Indians, blacks, and *zambos* (descendants of mixed Indian and black blood). While racial discrimination is officially denied today, it lingers as an historical fact, basically unaltered from colonial times.

Catholicism is the predominant religion in Mexico although church and state have been officially separated for over a century. Some Mexicans have converted to Protestantism and there are small Jewish and Muslim communities, particularly in Mexico City.

Indigenous Mexicans have been settled cultivators for at least 3,500 years. The Olmec, originally of the Gulf Coast, while yet little-known, are considered to have given rise to the first great Mesoamerican civilization in about 1100 B.C.E. Much better-known, but still not completely understood, were the MAYA, whose towns and ceremonial centers (c.250–750 C.E.) spanned southern Mexico and four Central American countries. They were extraordinarily advanced for their time and place in mathematics, astronomy, arts, architecture, and medicine, and possessed a written language. The MAYA resisted the SPANIARDS until disease accomplished what force of arms and religious conversion could not.

The ZAPOTEC and MIXTEC peoples also constructed major proto-urban sites at Mitla and Monte Alban in Oaxaca in the first millennium C.E., slightly predating the Teotihuacanos. The second millennium opened with the rise of the Toltecs to power over central Mexico. The Mexica, coming from the north along with other migratory tribes of the Chichimeca, founded a new empire along the shores of Lake Texcoco and established their capital, Tenochtitlan, on a man-made island on the lake itself, some two centuries before the coming of the Spanish *conquistadores*.

Inevitably, Spain came into conflict with the *criollos*, SPANIARDS born in Mexico, eventually precipitating a struggle for independence (1810–1821). Loss of territory to the United States in the late 1840s and occupation by the FRENCH during the brief reign of Maximilian in the 1860s were the result of the weakness of the early post-independence period. Stability was, however, restored during the administrations of Benito Juarez and Porfirio Diaz, although the latter established a dictatorship overthrown by what is now referred to as the Revolution, which began in 1910.

Since that time the Mexicans have established the most politically stable government in Latin America. While attempts to establish a correspondingly stable rural economy based on *ejidos* (agricultural cooperatives) have not met with much success, and with uneven industrialization, based largely on import substitution, the strong Mexican extended family, the central focus of Mexican cultural values, seems to have been able to weather all economic blows. Oil, nationalized in the late 1930s, is a powerful symbol of national self-determination and a non-negotiable item in attempts to establish a North American common market.

Some 25 per cent of all Mexicans live, at an altitude of 8,000 feet, in the capital, Mexico City. The official population in 1990 was 15.5 million, but many observers consider this to be grossly underestimated by as much as a third. The population has burst beyond the municipal boundaries into the adjacent State of Mexico. During the pre-1980 economic boom, many impoverished rural peasants moved to the city where, they believed, life would be better for themselves and their children. Hospitals and schools were plentiful and government subsidies made buying food cheaper than producing it in rural areas.

Since Mexico's economic crisis, many of these migrants have been unable to find regular work and consequently suitable housing. As a result, they move in with relatives, one room sometimes sheltering as many as ten people. Others construct makeshift housing of cardboard or corrugated, galvanized metal. Such settlements now form satellite towns around the capital. Mexico City is now the world's most unhealthy environment.

MIAMI A Native North American group numbering about 500 living in Oklahoma. Originally they inhab-

ited northern Illinois and Wisconsin. After the war of 1812 they were removed to Kansas and from there to the Indian Territory.

MIAN BALANTAK see BALANTAK.

MIAN BANGGAI see BANGGAI.

MIANGO An ethnic group living in Nigeria.

MIAN SEA-SEA see BANGGAI.

MIAO (Meo, Hmong, Hmung) An estimated five million Miao live mainly in southern China (Hunan, Guizhou, Sichuan, and Yunnan Provinces). Some Miao also live in Vietnam, Laos, Thailand, and Burma.

The Miao are one of the most ancient peoples in Southeast Asia. Their ancestors settled in southern China as early as the second millennium B.C.E. They speak a language of the Miao-Yao group and are closely related to the YAO. There are an estimated seventy to eighty groups of Miao distinguished by differences of dialect, dress, and customs. Some Miao claim to be descendants of the CHINESE.

The Miao have a long history of resistance to the CHINESE imperial authorities. The most violent encounter took place in the eighteenth century when local troops called on the imperial armies to quell a Miao uprising.

Their shamanist religion involves the worship of spirits, demons, and ancestral ghosts. Shamans are used to exorcise malevolent spirits. Miao youths are allowed to

Miao

A Miao girl

select their mates using traditional forms of courtship, including antiphonal singing or tossing a ball between groups of boys and girls from different villages.

The Miao economy is based on slash and burn agriculture on the mountain slopes and on raising draft animals such as cows or buffalo. The Miao are well-known for their songs and dances and for their fine jewelry and embroidery. Their houses are usually constructed on piles, with their animals kept at night in the hollow beneath the piles. (see also TUJIA)

MICMAC   Native North American group numbering about 16,000, living in New Brunswick, Nova Scotia, and Prince Edward Island, Canada. They are the only native group on Prince Edward Island and in Nova Scotia. They maintain their traditional practice of hunting moose and caribou and fishing. Recently they won the right to fish Atlantic salmon commercially.

MIBALA   A subgroup of the MATACO-MATAGUAYO.

MICHIA   see BAI.

MICHIK   see CHECHEN.

MIDOB   A subgroup of the NUBIANS.

MIDOGO   An ethnic group living in Chad.

Mijikenda

MIHUANE   A subgroup of the CHARRUA.

MIJIKENDA   A people in eastern Kenya, living north of the Galana River down to the Tanzanian border. ARABS traditionally lived on the Indian Ocean coast, with the Mijikenda dwelling on a very narrow inland plain. They belong to the Eastern Bantu-speaking people. Today part are Christians and part Muslims, due to their close connections with the Muslims on the coast.

The Mijikenda are divided into nine subgroups, each speaking its own dialect and numbering between 40,000 and 60,000 people. Predominantly Muslim subgroups are the CHONYI and the KAMBE. Predominantly Christian subgroups are the RABAI and the RIBE, who were the first native African groups to come into contact with the Protestant Christian missionaries who settled along the Kenya coast in the nineteenth century. The GIRIAMA, KAUMA, and GIBANA are equally divided between Christians and Muslims. The DIGO and the DURUMA are those Mijikenda groups that have best preserved their traditional religion.

Most Mijikenda are farmers, their main crops being coconut palms and cashews, grown mainly for export. Their social system is based on clans and subclans. Additionally, the RABAI, GIRIAMA, and particularly the DIGO were renowned as traders in the eighteenth century. Commerce originated in the seventeenth century among the GIRIAMA, who traded with the Swahili SHIRAZI along the coast. They specialized in acquiring ivory from Sanye hunters in exchange for domestic animals and other goods.

GIRIAMA have preserved their traditional houses made of grass thatch and their women have retained their costume. This includes a well padded rump covered by a long, colorful dress. The amount of padding indicates the woman's status and beauty.

MIJU   see MISHMI.

MIKIFORE   A subgroup of the MALINKE living in Guinea.

MIKIR   (s.d. Arleng) A people numbering between 250,000-300,000 located in the northeastern Indian state of Assam. Most live in the Mikir Hills region of that state. They speak a language belonging to the Tibeto-Burman family. The Mikir religion, an indigenous but highly hinduized faith, is of only marginal importance and has no communal places of worship. There are, however, community agricultural and other festivals, accompanied by feasting and animal sacrifice.

The Mikir engage primarily in agriculture. Rice and cotton are the most important crops although a wide variety of tubers and vegetables are also grown. Some small animals are domesticated, and hunting and fishing supplement the diet. There are few crafts, mostly of an ornamental nature, and almost no trade with neighboring peoples.

Little is known about the Mikir people's remote history. Since anthropological surveys were first conducted they have been subsistence agriculturalists. Nonetheless, some impressive but abandoned stone structures dot the Mikir Hills, hinting at the existence of an ancient Mikir civilization. (see also KARBI)

MIKLAI   see LOTHA.

MILANG   A subgroup of the ADI.

MIMAT   A subgroup of the ADI.

MIMIKA   An ethnic group of approximately 10,000 living in southwestern Irian Jaya, the Indonesian western half of the island of New Guinea. They speak an indigenous local language. They are farmers and slash and burn gardeners. Traditional religious beliefs have come under the influence of Christianity.

MINA   A name given to parts of the GA and ANE ethnic groups who migrated to Benin and Togo from El Mina in Ghana in the middle of the seventeenth century. They live along the coast from Lome, Togo's capital, to Ouidah in Benin. Despite their relatively small number they are particularly involved in Togo's commercial, intellectual, and political life.

MINAHASANS   A confederation of ethnic groups, living on the Indonesian island of Sulawesi (Celebes), formed against the neighboring Bolaang Mongondow people. Together they number about 50,000 people speaking dialects of the same language. Minahasan groups include the Christian groups of BANTIK, BELANG, BENTENAN, TOMBALU, TONDANO, TONSAWANG, TONSEA, TONTEMBOAN, and TOULOUR, and the Muslim group of PONOSOKAN. They cultivate rice, corn, and sago and raise goats, pigs, and chickens. Tobacco, cloves, and coffee are grown as cash crops.

MINANGKABAU   A people speaking a Malayo-Polynesian language originally inhabiting the high-lands of west-central Sumatera (Sumatra), an island of Indonesia. Minangkabau speakers number c.6 million, over half of whom are ethnically Minangkabau. Twentieth-century trends such as emigration and urbanization have resulted in Minangkabau communities being scattered across Sumatera and the outlying islands and as far abroad as the Malaysian peninsula. Minangkabau living in their ancestral homeland sometimes refer to themselves as Urang Padang after their historic capital; those living in other areas call themselves Urang Awak (our people). The scattered communities have resulted in distinct dialectal variations, and a unified form of the Minangkabau language is currently being developed. They are Muslims, but vestiges of indigenous beliefs have survived, particularly in their devotion to magic rituals.

A Minangkabau state apparently controlled much of western Sumatera and the outlying islands in the precolonial period. Its economy was based on the pepper trade leading to increased contacts with neighboring Islamic states in Sumatra such as Atjeh and with Java. The conflict between traditional and Islamic beliefs culminated in a civil war in the first half of the nineteenth century, enabling the DUTCH to exert their colonial influence by supporting the traditional rulers. Since then, Islam has become an important factor in the society. Early Dutch influence had a moderating effect and led to importance being placed on such things as secular education. Traditionally cultivators of rice,

Mina

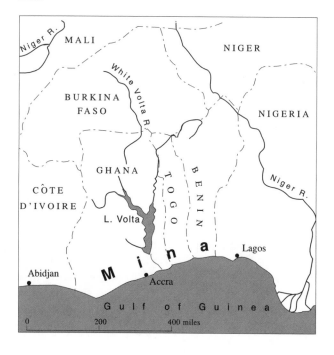

the Minangkabau are now among the most educated and urbanized of INDONESIANS. There is a significant community in the capital, Jakarta, and Minangkabau played important roles in the struggle for independence and in the postcolonial administration. (see also MUKO-MUKO)

MINDASSA   An ethnic group related to the KOTA living in Gabon.

MINDOUMOU   (Ndoumou) A Mbete-speaking group living along the Mipassa River in southeastern Gabon in the area of Franceville.

MINIANKA   An ethnic group living in the Côte d'Ivoire, in southwest Burkina Faso, and in southeast Mali among the SENUFO, with whom they are closely associated. They mostly practice their traditional religion.

MINTIL   A subgroup of the SEMANG.

MINUSINSK   see KHAKASS.

MINYAMIN   An ethnic group of a few thousand living in the mountainous area in the Sepik River region in central Papua New Guinea. They speak Minyamin, an indigenous language. Their economy is based upon hunting and pig-raising. Except among the elderly, traditional beliefs in sorcery have been replaced by Christianity. Among their most celebrated ceremonies is the initiation of boys.

MINYONG   A subgroup of the ADI.

MIRI   (Mishing) A people numbering 420,000 (1987), living in the states of Arunachal Pradesh and Assam (where they are the second largest group of Scheduled Tribes), in northeastern India. Their language belongs to the Tibeto-Burman family. They are Hindus.

The plains Miri now inhabiting the riverine areas of the Upper Assam Valley are blood relations of the tribal people living in the Abor hills of Arunachal Pradesh.

Miri houses are constructed on raised platforms five feet above the ground. A typical house is some 120 feet in length and contains 30–40 persons living in a hall without compartments. The roof is thatched and the walls are made of bamboo. The *morung* (bachelors' dormitory) is an important feature of the village.

Their main occupation is agriculture, mainly of the subsistence type. Agricultural lands are suitable mainly for paddy cultivation. Traditionally the Miri loved hunting and fishing, but today group hunting is almost extinct and community fishing has lost much of its original character. However, individual as well as group fishing is done with much merriment.

MIRRIAM   A subgroup of the TIV.

MISHING   see MIRI.

MISHMAST   A subgroup of the AIMAQ-I DIGAR.

MISHMI   A people numbering 8,500 (1981), living in the Lohit district of the state of Arunachal Pradesh, northeast India. Their language belongs to the Tibeto-Burman family.

Miri

The Mishmi are divided into three subgroups, IDU, TARAON, and KAMAN, who are called by the plains people of Assam Chulikatta, Digaru, and Miju, respectively.

They practise slash and burn agriculture. Their houses are divided into a number of rooms for every married person. Unmarried youth, both male and female, live in separate rooms in the house.

MISRIYYUN   see EGYPTIANS.

MISSION INDIANS   see LUISENO.

MIUTINI   A subgroup of the MERU.

MIWOK   A Native North American Indian group numbering about 500 living in California.

MIXTEC   An indigeneous Indian people in Mexico, numbering 300,000, and living mainly in the state of Oaxaca. They call themselves the "People of the Rain." They inhabited parts of what are now northern Oaxaca and southern Puebla during the sixth and seventh centuries C.E. They conquered the ZAPOTEC and

Mixtec

lived in the same region until the arrival of the SPANIARDS, adapting many ZAPOTEC elements into their own culture.

The Mixtec religion is a mixture of the old Mixtecan-Zapotecan and Catholic, the maize and sun god having been replaced by the Guadalupe Virgin, the Virgin of Jaquila, and the Lord of Esquipulas. Their festivals represent the Spanish conquest in dances that mimic Spanish characteristics, using costumes made of feathers.

The finest of the Mixtec settlements, many of which were built over earlier Zapotec sites, was Mitla, which included five main groups of ceremonial and elite residential buildings. Mixtec goldware marked the zenith of metalworking in ancient Mexico. Today's inhabitants of Oaxaca continue some traditional crafts, making small articles of gold to special order and hats for tourists. Pottery-making, another ancient craft, is still

an important cottage industry. Techniques of rural agriculture continue to prevail, crops consisting of maize, beans, and squash. Shifting cultivation is practiced, and when the land is exhausted the family moves elsewhere, leaving it to lie fallow for four to five years. (see also MEXICANS)

MIZO   ("people of the high land"; Lushai, Zomi) A general term applied to the peoples who speak the Duhlian dialect and live in the states of Mizoram and Manipur in northeast India, on the border with Myanmar (Burma). The term has come to be accepted by these people in place of the name "Lushai," which was given to them by the BRITISH. The Mizo represent most of the population of the state of Mizoram and number over 600,000 in all the northeast states of India. The Mizo language belongs to the Sino-Tibetan branch of the Tibeto-Burman family of languages. They had no script of their own, and have adopted, through the help of Christian missionaries, a phonetically-based Roman script.

Most of the Mizo are engaged in slash and burn agriculture and wet-rice cultivation. The biggest cash crop is ginger. Each village has a smithery which produces weapons and tools.

Christianity is the dominant religion of the Mizo. Nearly 85 percent of the population of the state of Mizoram is Christian, with the majority being Protestants. The Mizo believe that their ancestors lived in China and first migrated to the Kabaw Valley in what is today Myanmar during the tenth century C.E. Forced by the SHAN to move to the Chin Hills, the Mizo came under British rule in the middle of the nineteenth century. British administration continued until Indian independence in 1947. In the 1960s the Mizo became active politically; only in the 1980s, however, did they come to see themselves as part of the Indian constitutional framework.

MIZRAHIYIM   see ISRAELIS.

MNAMI   An ethnic group living in Guinea on the Atlantic coast.

MNONG   A Mon-Khmer group numbering about 40,000 living in the mountainous jungles of central Vietnam. They are divided into many subgroups including the BIET, BUNUR, CIL, GAR, NONG, PNONG, PREH, ROHONG, RLAM, and ROLOM, each of which has a distinct dialect sometimes classified as a language. The Mnong worship a wide variety of spirits. They are primarily slash and burn agriculturalists but also grow fruits, vegeta-

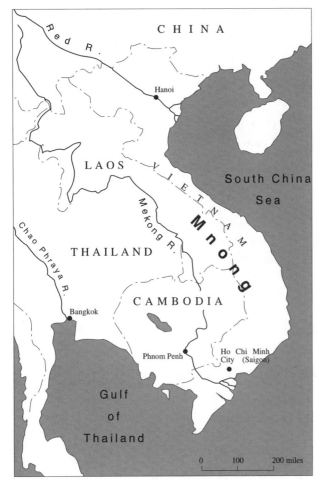

Mnong

bles, and cotton in small gardens near their longhouses. They also engage in trade with neighboring CHINESE and VIETNAMESE. Salt, and, especially, jars are considered valuable and their possession is a status symbol.

Before World War I the Mnong were hostile to the colonial authorities of the FRENCH and led a Montagnard insurrection in the central highlands. They were also prominent in the messianic Python God religious movement which promised to rid the highlands of the FRENCH and the VIETNAMESE.

MNONG KIL   see KIL.

MO   A small ethnic group living in northern Ghana and Burkina Faso. Together with other neighboring groups, it is classified as GRUSI.

MOBA   The name for several ethnic groups living in the northern Dapaong, Kara and Sansanne-Mango areas of Togo and in the capital, Lome. They number around 96,000 and speak a Gurma dialect. (see also TOGOLESE)

MOBER   A subgroup of the KANURI.

MOCHA   (Seka) An ethnic group numbering 60,000 (1980s) who live at the headwaters of the Baro River of the Illubabor Province, Ethiopia. They adhere to traditional beliefs. The Mocha are sedentary agriculturalists, cultivating cereals and ensete. They are related to the KAFFICHO, and live to the west of the Nilotic MAJANGIR.

MOCOVI   A subgroup of the GUAYCURU, living in Argentina.

MODOC   A Native North American group numbering about 500 living in Oklahoma and Oregon. This group is remembered for the fierce resistance it showed to white settlers in California in the aftermath of the American civil war. The Modoc resisted almost to the last warrior.

MODOLE   An ethnic group closely related to the TOBELORESE, living on the Indonesian island of Halmahera.

MOFU   A subgroup of the KIRDI.

MOHAPI   An ethnic group living in the mountainous central region of the Indonesian island of Sulawesi (Celebes). (see also TORADJA)

MOHAVE   (Mojave) A Native North American people, numbering about 3,500, most of whom live on the Colorado River Federal Reservation in Arizona, on the California border, and the Fort Mojave Federal Reservation in California.

MOHAWK   The largest ethnic group of the Native North American IROQUOIS CONFEDERACY, numbering more than 20,000, living today in Quebec and Ontario, Canada, and New York, U.S.A. In recent years, the Mohawk were involved in a violent conflict with the Canadian authorities over land use and aboriginal rights. The bands which spearheaded this uprising were those in Oka and Caughnawaga, Quebec. (see also IROQUOIS CONFEDERACY)

MOHICAN   see MAHICAN.

MOHMAUD   A subgroup of the PASHTUN.

A Mober woman, of the Kanuri people, in front of her home in southern Niger

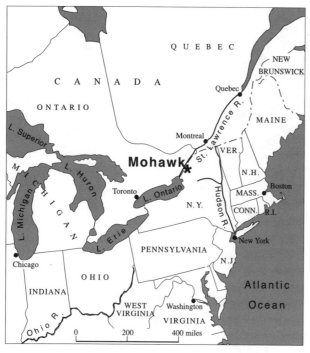

Mohawk

MOI see MONTAGNARDS.

MOJAVE see MOHAVE.

MOJO A South American Indian people living in lowland Bolivia. They subsist primarily from agriculture, their staple crops being maize and sweet manioc. Hunting and fishing help supplement their diet. There are marked class distinctions among the villagers, with succession to the office of local headman determined patrilineally.

MOKEN (Selung, Sea Nomads) A group of nomadic boat people living along the coasts throughout most of southeast Asia. Their population is rapidly decreasing and may now number only a few thousand. Their original Austronesian language has been lost and most now speak a dialect of Malay.

The nuclear family lives together on a boat, and several boats may sometimes group together in bad weather. They have a variety of traditional religious beliefs colored by Christianity, Islam, and Buddhism. They engage primarily in fishing and in trade, selling sea products such as pearls, tortoise shells, and shark fins to coastal merchants.

MOLDOVANS Most of the 4.5 million inhabitants of Moldova, a state of the former Soviet Union situated between northeast Romania and southwestern Ukraine, are Romanian-speaking, the rest being UKRANIANS (750,000), RUSSIANS (700,000), and GAGAUZ (300,000).

The Romanian-speaking Moldovans were an integral part of Romania between 1918 and 1940. In the latter year the Bessarabian province of Romania was annexed by the Soviet Union and was established as the Moldovan Soviet Socialist Republic. The Soviets tried with little success to develop a distinct Moldovan nationality and language, for which a Cyrillic alphabet was adopted.

In 1991 Romanian-speaking Moldovans seceded from the Soviet Union and established an independent Moldova. The RUSSIANS and UKRANIANS (most of whom lived east of the Dniestr River) and the GAGAUZ objected, fearing that the Romanian-speaking Moldovans would seek to merge with Romania, an idea to which the Romanian state is known to be sympathetic. As a result, fighting broke out between Moldova's ethnic groups, threatening the territorial integrity of the region. (see also ROMANIANS)

MOLE see MOSSI.

MOLE-DAGBANI A generic term for several culturally and linguistically related groups: the DAGABA, DAGOMBA, FRAFRA, GRUSI, KUSASI, LOBI, MOSSI, NANKANSI, TALENSI, and WALA. (see also GHANAIANS)

MON (Peguan, Talaing) A people numbering almost 1.5 million, 90 percent of whom live in eastern Myanmar (Burma) and the remainder in Thailand. They speak a Mon-Khmer dialect and are Theravada Buddhists. Rice cultivation and fishing are the primary economic activities.

The Mon had an independent state until the mid-eighteenth century, when they were conquered by the BURMANS. There is still considerable hostility toward the BURMANS and a Mon insurgency movement has threatened the Myanmar (Burmese) military regime in the area. Some insurgents have an openly secessionist platform; others are attempting to create a federation out of the various ethnic groups that comprise Myanmar.

MONEGASQUES The people of Monaco, numbering about 30,000, inhabit the smallest country in the world after the Vatican City. Located in the French Riviera, near the Italian border, Monegasques have integrated both French and Italian cultural elements.

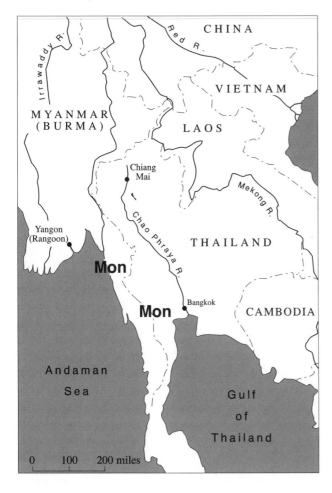

Mon

French is the official language and the population is predominantly Roman Catholic.

Most Monegasques are employed in services, the tourism industry, and in the world-famous casino in Monte Carlo.

MONGHSA see ACHANG.

MONGO An ethnic group living in Zaire, along most of the Congo Basin. Together with the LUBA-KA-SAI, they number around 5 million. The Mongo language is the lingua franca for most of northwestern Zaire.

In precolonial times the Mongo did not have kingdoms and the village was their basic political unit. For that reason their common identity was cultural rather than political. During the colonial period under the BELGIANS the Mongo region was divided by the BELGIANS into five provinces in order to weaken them. However. the Mongo did manage to organize them-

selves, and during the 1950s they created the Union Mongo.

The NGOMBE living along the Zaire River are a subgroup of the Mongo.

MONGOLS The Mongols constitute over 90 percent of the population of Mongolia (Outer Mongolia). They are divided into several tribes, the largest being the Khalkha Mongols. An additional 3.4 million Mongols live in China's Inner Mongolian Autonomous Region and the Xinjiang Uighur Autonomous Region. There are also some Mongols in eastern Russia.

Among the earliest inhabitants of the territory now known as Mongolia was a Mongolian people, the Huns, who created a nomadic empire and warred with the CHINESE for centuries before dissolving in the fifth century. The Mongols became a major factor in world history in the early thirteenth century; under the leadership of Genghis Khan, the Mongol tribes were united and reached their zenith of power. Their empire was the largest the world has ever known, extending south to China, southwest to Turkestan, Iran, and Iraq, and northwest to Russia. After Genghis Khan's death, the empire was divided among his sons, one of whom, Kublai Khan, later conquered China and founded the Yuan dynasty (1279–1368). The once powerful Mongol states had largely disappeared by the end of the fourteenth century, and the Mongols returned to their homeland in East and Central Asia. They were later subdued by the MANCHU who conquered China and founded the Qing dynasty (1644–1911), the last impe-

Mongols

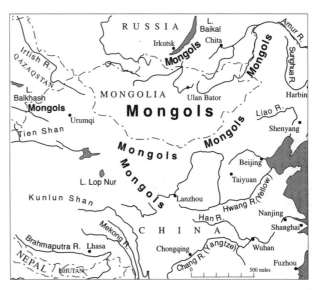

rial dynasty in China's history. After the 1911 Chinese Revolution, Outer Mongolia declared its independence, and in 1924, the Mongolian People's Republic was declared with Soviet support.

The Mongol language, a sub-family of the Altaic languages, is composed of nine major dialects, one of which, Khalkha, serves as the official language of Outer Mongolia. In the early thirteenth century, the Mongols adopted a script from the Turkic UIGHURS which they retained until 1941, when the Mongolian government announced the adoption of a new phonetic alphabet derived from a modified Cyrillic script.

Traditionally, most Mongols practiced Tibetan Mahayana Buddhism, and that religion had a strong influence on Mongolian society. As a result of an anti-religious movement launched by the current government in the 1930s, about two-thirds of the people profess no religion or are avowed atheists.

The traditional economic occupation of Mongol society was nomadic animal husbandry. Even today, pastoral activities still dominate the economy, although farming has played an increasingly significant role.

A distinctive feature of the Mongol dwelling is the *yurt* or *yer*, a cone-shaped, latticed structure used by herdsmen moving from pasture to pasture. The traditional society was based on blood relationship through the common male ancestor who gave his name to the clan. Marriage between members of the same clan was forbidden. Favorite Mongol sports include wrestling, archery, and horse-racing.

The Mongols in China are practically identical to the Mongols of Mongolia, but speak different dialects of the Altaic Mongolian language. Most Mongols can understand one another, although the written language, based on the Uighur script, has far fewer variants than the spoken language. Mongols in China have long been influenced by Han Chinese culture. Some now have Chinese names, speak Chinese, and wear Chinese clothing.

During the Yuan Mongol dynasty, contacts with other countries were expanded and encouraged. The authorities also welcomed foreign religions such as Christianity and Islam, and encouraged Tibetan Buddhism. Numerous foreigners were employed by the state bureaucracy, among them Marco Polo, who returned to Europe to write the famous account of his travels in China. The Mongol Empire finally collapsed as a result of infighting among Mongol princes and extensive peasant uprisings.

Mahayana Buddhism was reintroduced from Tibet in the seventeenth century by Mongol princes attempting to unite their people. For centuries the religion was influential and widespread among the Mongolians.

While some Mongolians have taken up farming, most maintain their nomadic traditions, living in round, felt-covered tents, and roving with their herds of horses, sheep, cattle, and goats according to season. (see also AFGHANS, BURYAT, BYELORUSSIANS, DAURS, DONGXIANG, EVEN, KACHARIANS, KOREANS, NIASANS, TU, UZBEKS, YAKUT)

MONOM (Bonom) A Mon-Khmer group living near the town of Kontum in southern Vietnam.

MONPA An ethnic group numbering 22,000 (1981), living in the Kameng district of the state of Arunachal Pradesh, northeastern India. They are Buddhists and speak Tibetan, a member of the Tibeto-Burman family of languages.

Monpa life centers around the great Buddhist monastery of Tawang. They are a mild and industrious people living in a well-wooded and low-lying region where they practice terrace cultivation and keep bees. Monpa houses are two-storeyed and constructed of stone or wood. The Monpa also manufacture carpets, mats, and saddle bags.

MONTAGNAIS A Native North American group numbering about 10,000, living along the north shore of the Gulf of Saint Lawrence in Quebec, Canada. Originally they were woodland hunters living in wigwams. Today they earn their livelihood by hunting, fishing, trapping, and by working in the forest industry.

MONTAGNARDS (Moi, s.d. Anu Chu) A generic term for the inhabitants of the densely forested mountain chain running on a north-south axis through most of Vietnam. Although they constitute less than 15 percent of Vietnam's population, they are the dominant ethnic category in much of the country's land mass. They represent a cultural mosaic, speaking dozens of languages belonging to the Mon-Khmer, Malayo-Polynesian, and other families, and worshiping in a variety of ways. The RHADE is one of the most prominent and advanced groups among the Montagnards.

Recent times have seen the emergence of a well educated Montagnard class with national aspirations of its own. In the early colonial period under the FRENCH they were simply referred to as savages or the Vietnamese equivalent, Moi. Montagnard is a more recent French appellation, which came into vogue only in the 1930s;

they themselves prefer the JARAI term "Anu Chu," meaning "Sons of the Mountains."

Many Montagnard groups are descended from the original inhabitants of Vietnam and have come to resent what they consider foreign incursions in their land. However, even the most important Montagnard peoples lacked any significant unifying factor broader than the village where they engaged primarily in agriculture. In the colonial period, their territory was recognized for its abundant mineral wealth which the FRENCH and VIETNAMESE began to exploit. The Montagnards attempted to resist outside penetration in their land, but at the same time, many took advantage of missionary activities such as education, and a new elite class emerged. Some groups saw the FRENCH and later the communists as their saviors from domination by the VIETNAMESE.

Among the most important nativist movements was the Python God religious movement of the 1930s and the FULRO (United Front for the Protection of Oppressed Races) movement of the 1950s and 1960s. The former appealed to the religious sentiments of the hill peoples by promising the imminent arrival of a messianic figure who would restore their dominance in their ancestral lands. The latter struggled to achieve autonomy or independence and was able to elicit some minor concessions from the South Vietnamese government. In North Vietnam, the government promised autonomy, but with unification of Vietnam in the 1970s this promise was abandoned and the former South Vietnamese policy of settling ethnic VIETNAMESE in Montagnard regions was again adopted.

It is estimated that some 200,000 Montagnards died during the Vietnamese War. Countless others fled their homes and have recently begun to return to the hills. In the aftermath of the war, many of the national aspirations of the Montagnards disappeared. (see also VIETNAMESE)

MONTENEGRINS   (s.d. Crno Gortsi) A Slav people numbering some 500,000 and living in Montenegro, for several decades a part of Yugoslavia; they are closely related to the SERBS. SERBS and ALBANIANS constitute the rest of the population of Montenegro.

The Montenegrins are Eastern Orthodox Christians who speak a southern Slavic language which is a dialect of Serbo-Croat. They use the Cyrillic script, as do the SERBS.

Living in their inaccessible mountain region bordering the Adriatic Sea, the Montenegrins have preserved social and cultural customs, traditions, and institutions long abandoned by other southern Slavs. Kinship systems based on clans are still deeply entrenched in their social and economic life.

The Ottoman Empire had great difficulty in controlling the Montenegrins, who resisted subjugation for years. After World War II the Montenegrins joined Yugoslavia; they remained loyal to the SERBS when the country disintegrated in 1991. (see also SERBS)

MONTUVIO   A Native South American group living in Ecuador.

MONUI   see KATU.

MOORS   see MAURE, PORTUGUESE, SPANIARDS, SRI LANKANS.

MOPLAH   see MAPPILA.

MORDOVIANS   see MORDVINS.

MORDVINS   (Mordovians) The Mordvin people, numbering about 1.4 million, live mainly in the middle

Mordvin

Volga region in Russia. One-third live in the Mordovian Autonomous Republic, where they constitute only one-third of the population, RUSSIANS forming the majority. The remaining Mordvins live in the neighboring regions.

Agriculture is their main occupation, especially apiculture. Mordvin handicrafts are embroidery, woodcarving, and metal ornaments.

The Mordvins are divided into the Erzya in the east and the Maksha in the west. The dialects spoken by the two are not mutually intelligible, and they form, in fact, two separate languages, constituting the Mordvin branch of the Finnish group of languages. Both are now literary languages, using the Cyrillic alphabet.

The first written reference to Mordvin tribes dates to the sixth century. Between the thirteenth and fifteenth centuries they were within the sphere of the "Golden Horde," the Mongol-Tatar state that ruled Russia. After the fall of the Tatar Kazan Khanate in 1552, the Mordvins came under Russian rule and their lands were parceled out among Russian landlords. In the sixteenth and seventeenth centuries the Mordvins were forcibly converted from paganism to Russian Orthodox Christianity, a process which caused mass migration of Mordvins eastward to Siberia.

With the implementation of the Peasant Reform of 1861 in Russia, many Mordvins were left with very small parcels of land, and more than 100,000 were resettled in the Urals and Siberia.

MORI   (s.d. To Mori) An ethnic group numbering about 15,000 living in central Sulawesi (Celebes), an island of Indonesia. They are predominantly Muslims and speak an Austronesian language, thought to have ties with the languages of the Philippines. They cultivate rice, taro, corn, and tobacco, with coffee as a cash crop. The Mori are commonly divided into three subgroups, the Upper Mori, Lower Mori, and Malili Mori, but distinctions appear to be geographical rather than cultural.

Prior to their conquest by the DUTCH in the early twentieth century, the Mori were dominated by the BUNGKU and TERNATANS. Ties with the BUGINESE are also evidenced by the existence of a powerful Buginese aristocracy. (see also LAKI)

MORISCOS   see ANDALUSIANS, SPANIARDS.

MOROCCANS   (s.d. Maghribiyyun) The 26 million inhabitants of Morocco, in North Africa, are nearly all Sunni (Malikite) Muslims. Moroccan Islam evinces some specific traits, centered in particular around the cult of saints' tombs (maraboutism). The Moroccan Arabic dialect and three Berber dialects are the main languages. Although identified with the Islamic and Arab world, Moroccans historically have undergone less Arab influences than ALGERIANS or TUNISIANS. There is a sharp division between the Mediterranean-Atlantic coast (where two-third of Moroccans dwell) and the desert hinterland, sparsely populated by semi-nomads and sedentary oasis dwellers. Between the two, the range of mountains from Tangiers to Agadir has constituted a historical refuge for archaic populations, in particular Berber villages characterized by *ksur* (ancient fortified granaries). The Shleuh are BERBERS in the High Atlas Mountains. Demographic pressures have induced migration to the Atlantic coast and to Western Europe. The Berber region has a tradition of particularism, and resisted both Moroccan sultans and the FRENCH.

Agriculture and husbandry are preponderant, but water scarcity is a major obstacle to development. Rural Morocco has remained a traditional society. Religious brotherhoods are still powerful. At least half the population is illiterate. Remittances of Moroccan workers abroad and income from tourism have become increasingly vital to the balance of payments.

BERBERS doubtless were Morocco's original population. However, the coast was colonized first by Phoenicia, then by Romans, who ruled first through local Berber dynasties, then directly. In the seventh century North Africa was conquered and converted to Islam by ARABS: Berber tribes, previously divided in many minute realms, integrated into Arab armies.

In the ninth and tenth centuries Morocco fell prey to struggles between competing Arab dynasties, and was wrecked by the Hilali invasions. In the eleventh century, the Almoravids, a Berber tribe controlling trans-Sahara caravan routes, conquered Morocco, combining religious passion with ethnic and economic motives. Once in power, they built Marrakesh, and went on to conquer Spain. After a while, religious zeal decreased and centrifugal tendencies reappeared: their place was taken by another Berber dynasty, the Almohads.

In the fifteenth century, Spanish expansionism cost Morocco a number of harbors. In the sixteenth century, the Sa'dians, another reformer dynasty, liberated the country in a holy war, and resisted Turkish advances in Algeria. Moroccan identity has since been anchored in the historical fact that they were never subdued by the TURKS. The Alawite dynasty, which is still ruling today, came to power in the seventeenth century, and knew its

above: A Moroccan coppersmith
below: Moroccan women in festive dress

heyday under Mullah Isma'il (1672–1727), after whose reign a decline set in. In 1856 the isolated kingdom was forcibly opened to European trade, and became an object of interest to the SPANIARDS, FRENCH, BRITISH, and GERMANS. After temporarily delaying European penetration by playing off imperial rivals, early-twentieth century Moroccan kings were weakened by tribal revolts, while Moroccan economy was dislocated by European products. French claims were recognized in the 1906 Algeciras Treaty. From 1912 on, France imposed a direct protectorate. Spain obtained zones in the Rif mountains as well as Spanish Morocco. It took the FRENCH the better part of the 1920s to pacify the tribes and strengthen the *makhzen* (central administration): at first French authority was indirect and rested on the absolute monarchy. After Morocco was opened to European immigration and colonization, an anti-European revolt broke out in the Rif under Abdelkrim After its suppression, colonization was facilitated by direct rule. From the 1930s, nationalist (partly pan-Arab) resistance originated with Morocco's urban elites, not from its mountain tribes any more. World War II put a stop to French colonization and renewed hopes for independence. France granted Morocco independence in 1956.

MORU   see AZANDE.

MOSHI   see MOSSI.

MOSHWESHWE   (Lesotho Sotho) A subgroup of the SOTHO.

MOSQUITO   (Miskito) A South American people Indian inhabiting the Mosquito Coast of Nicaragua and Honduras. They continue their traditional practices of hunting, gathering, and fishing, but these have now been superseded by the cultivation of bitter manioc and cash crops, such as cochineal-bearing cactus. Village shamans continue to be responsible for curing illnesses, prophesying, and placating the nature spirits believed to control human destiny. (see also HONDURANS, NICARAGUANS)

MOSSI   (Mole, Moshi) A people living in the Northern and Upper Regions of Burkina Faso and in smaller numbers in northern Ghana and Togo. The arrival of Muslims in Mossi territory had little effect on them and although some chiefs converted to Islam most Mossi clung to their traditional religion. The Catholic and Protestant missionaries who arrived after colonial occupation by the FRENCH did not convert many Mossi because of the refusal of the chiefs to cooperate. The Mossi were and still are mainly an agricultural people.

During the precolonial period the Mossi established four kingdoms: Ouagadougou (the strongest of the four), Yatenga, Tenkondogo, and Fada-N'Gourma. These kingdoms reached their apogee in the fourteenth or fifteenth century.

Towards the end of the nineteenth century the FRENCH attempted to reach the region of the Mossi. They sent expeditions to persuade them to sign a treaty ceding rights over their region. When this method failed the FRENCH decided to conquer the Mossi region.

In 1919 the FRENCH established the colony of Upper Volta. In 1932 over half this colony, which included the Mossi territory, was annexed to the Cote d'Ivoire and the rest was divided between Niger and Mali. During the colonial period the FRENCH tried to change the political organization of the Mossi. When a ruler died they appointed a Mossi of their own choice who would be easy to control. Economic development of the Mossi region was limited and the Mossi were used as labor for agriculture in more developed colonies such as the Cote d'Ivoire. A large number of Mossi were drafted into the French army.

When party politics began in the French colonies after World War II, the Mossi formed the UDIHV (Union de la Defence des Interets de la Haute Volta), which stressed the need to abolish forced labor, especially among the Mossi. They also wished to be separated from the Cote d'Ivoire, where their political power was limited. In 1947 the French National Assembly agreed to that request and Upper Volta was reconstituted as a separate territory. The separation gave the Mossi a large political party in Upper Volta, which dominated all the political institutions created by the colonial adminstration. During the 1950s a group of young Mossi who resented the power of the chiefs created another Mossi party, the MDV (Voltaic Democratic Movement).

Since independence in 1960 a large number of Mossi migrate every year to earn a living in relatively wealthy neighboring countries such as Ghana and Togo.

The NYONYOSE and YATENGA are subgroups of the Mossi. (see also also BURKINABES, MOLE-DAGBANI)

MOTU   An ethnic group of approximately 30,000, living near Port Moresby on the southeastern coast of Papua New Guinea. They speak an indigenous language. They subsist by growing various crops as well as by overseas trade. The Motu were the first group in New Guinea to come into contact with missionaries and their traditional beliefs have been replaced by Christianity.

MOUBI   An ethnic group living east of Abou Telfan in the Oum Hadjer District, Chad. They are mostly Muslims but have retained pre-Islamic practices. Since Chad's independence in 1960 they have rebelled against the central government several times.

MOUNDANG   A subgroup of the KIRDI.

MOUNTAIN ARAPESH   An ethnic group of approximately 5,000 living in the mountain ranges of the northern part of Papua New Guinea. They speak an indigenous local language. Their economy is based upon the growing of taro and yams. Believers in spirits, their main rituals are centered around the life-cycle.

MOUNTAIN JEWS   see TAT I.

MOUNTAIN TURKS   see KURDS.

MOUSGOUM   An ethnic group classed among the KIRDI groups, living in Chad.

MOVIMA   A South American Indian group inhabiting lowland Bolivia and speaking their own language. They depend on agriculture, cultivating maize and sweet manioc as their staples, supplementing these crops by hunting and fishing.

MOWEWE   A subgroup of the LAKI.

MOZAMBICANS   The 16 million inhabitants of Mozambique are divided into eight distinct ethnic groups: the MAKUA-LOMWE of the provinces of Zambezia, Nampula, Niassa and Cabo Delgade; the YAO, of Niassa; the MAKONDE, who are found on either side of the Tanzanian border; the CHEWA, of the Tete district; the NYANJA, who also reside in Tete; the TONGA, of the southern regions; the CHOPI, of the province of Inhambane; and the SHONA, who live north of the TONGA near the border with Zimbabwe.

The MAKUA-LOMWE and the YAO adhere to Islam while the other groups comprise both Christians and adherents to traditional religions. The CHEWA are divided among Christians, adherents of traditional religions, and Muslims. Portuguese is the official language of Mozambique but each group also speaks its own language.

Agriculture is Mozambique's main economic activity; 80 to 90 percent of the work force engage in tea, cotton, sugar, and sisal farming. Livestock is of secondary importance because of the prevalence of the tsetse fly in two-thirds of the country. The industrial sector focuses on the processing of primary products and accounts for only 10 percent of the GNP. Manufacturing is an underdeveloped element of the economy; Mozambique is dependent on manufactured goods from South Africa.

Mozambique became an independent state in 1975 following a long civil war led by the Liberation Front of Mozambique (FRELIMO). In 1977 FRELIMO declared itself a Marxist-Leninist vanguard party and embarked on a series of policies to establish a socialist state. One source of conflict was the violent actions of RENAMO (National Resistance of Mozambique). Supported by South Africa, it sought to challenge the regime, as peaceful political dissent was forbidden. RENAMO was not supported by any one ethnic group and has been accused of not adhering to any specific ideology other than the destabilization of the FRELIMO regime. The signing of the Nkomati Accord with South Africa in 1984 precipitated a series of peace talks which continued throughout the decade; in 1991 a timetable was set for discussions on the cessation of hostilities and the possibility of elections.

MPONDO   A subgroup of the NGUNI.

MPONDOMISI   A subgroup of the NGUNI.

MPONGWE   An ethnic group living on the Como River Estuary in Gabon, where the modern capital of Libreville is located. They speak Myene and are mostly Christians.

During the precolonial period the Mpongwe served as middlemen between European traders on the coast and the peoples of the hinterland such as the KELE and SEKE. In the mid-nineteenth century they unsuccessfully tried to resist French colonization of their region, while many acquired skills in local missions enabling them to work for European trading firms and the colonial administration.

During the 1920s and 1930s educated Mpongwe organized to defend their land rights against both the FRENCH and the FANG and to gain access to quality education. At independence 1,200 out of the estimated 1,800 Mpongwe lived in Libreville and relative to their small number played important roles in the Gabonese civil service, education and business. (see also ADYUMBA, FANG)

MRASS TATARS   see SHORS.

MUALANG   An ethnic group living on the Indonesian island of Kalimantan (Borneo). (see also DAYAK)

MUBUKUSHU   An ethnic group related to the LUYANA, living in Zambia and Angola.

MUCKLESHOOT   A Native North American group numbering about 3,500, one-third of whom live on the Muckleshoot Federal Reservation, King County, Washington, U.S.A.

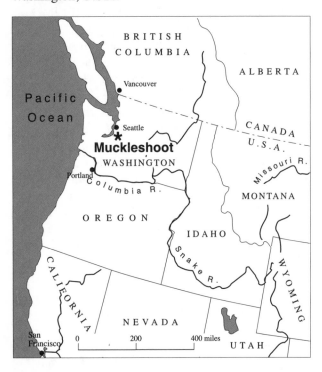

Muckleshoot

MUDEJAR   see SPANIARDS.

MUEMBA   see BEMBA.

MUGAT   see GYPSIES.

MUHER   A subgroup of the GURAGE.

MUIDU   A Native American group numbering 500, many of whom live on the Berry Creek Rancheria, Butte County, California, U.S.A. Today they earn their livelihood through farming.

MUKHA DHORA   An ethnic group, numbering 18,000 (1981), living in the state of Andhra Pradesh,

India. They speak Telugu, a member of the Dravidian family of languages.

An agricultural people, most Mukha Dhora work as day-laborers for the forest department. They adhere to their own traditional religion.

MUKO-MUKO   A people numbering about 20,000 living in southern Sumatera (Sumatra), an island in Indonesia. They are a composite group, comprised of MINANGKABAU, KERINTJI, PEKAL, and MALAYS. They made occasional bids for independence and had considerable influence over other coastal groups in southwest Sumatera.

MUKULU   (Bena Mukulu) An ethnic group numbering about 44,000 living in Zambia, northwest of Lake Bangweulu near the Chimpili Hills. While some still practice their traditional religions, many converted to Christianity, particularly under the influence of the Catholic Order of the White Fathers who worked extensively among them.

They follow a matrilineal system of inheritance and engage in trade and ironwork. They have intermarried extensively with the BEMBA and have a similar culture and social organization.

MUMUYE   A subgroup of the TIV.

MUNA   (To Muna) An ethnic group, numbering over 20,000, living on the island of Muna off the coast of southern Sulawesi (Celebes), an island of Indonesia.

They are closely related to the neighboring BUTONESE whose sultanate, Butung, ruled them until occupation by the DUTCH in the early twentieth century. Like other inhabitants of southern Sulawesi and the outlying islands, their language shows some affinities with those of the Philippines. The Muna, however, consider themselves to be a aggregate of the BUGINESE and TORADJA. They are Muslim.

Remnants of a well-entrenched class system, originating in the group's close affiliation with the Sultanate of Butung, are still quite strong, with each class having certain privileges and cultural norms such as costumes and music. There is limited mobility between the classes.

MUNDA   A group, numbering 1.5 million (1981), living in the states of Bihar, Madhya Pradesh, Orissa, and West Bengal, India. They speak Munda and Kolarian, members of the Austroasiatic family of languages.

The Munda worship Singa-bonga, the sun god, and a number of other minor deities, including a goddess of rivers and springs. They have a history of conflict with the BRITISH rulers of India, notably their revolts of 1894 and 1895. (see also BHUMJI, KHARIA, KORKU, MAJHWAR, NAGESIA)

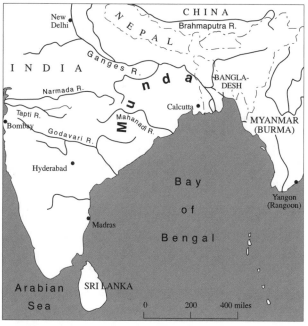

Munda

MUNDO   see SULOD.

MUNDUGUMOR   (s.d. Biwati) An ethnic group, numbering several thousand, living near a tributary of the Sepik River in northern Papua New Guinea. Their language, Biwat, is an indigenous local one. They are gardeners and pig-raisers. Although most are Catholics, they also retain their traditional beliefs in universal forces. Among their ceremonies is the initiation of young men.

MUNDURUKU   ·(Mundurucu) A South American Indian group living east of the Tapajos River and around it, in the States of Amazonas and Pará, northern Brazil. They number a few thousand. In the past they were known for their aggression and were strongly feared by their neighbors. Today they make a living by collecting latex from wild rubber trees and bartering it for consumer goods. Although some groups still use their native language (thought to belong to the Tupi family) exclusively, others have become acculturated to their more modern surroundings.

MUNJANI   see MUNJI.

MUNJI   (Munjani) An ethnic group inhabiting the Munjan and Tagabe valleys on the northern slope of the Pamir mountains. Their estimated number is 1,500 to 2,000. The Munji language belongs to the Pamir subgroup of the southeast Iranian language family. An offshoot of the Munji language, called Yidgha, is spoken in the Kutkuh valley of Chitral. It was brought there by migrants from the Munjan valley, according to its speakers, several generations (apparently between 150 and 200 years) ago. The Munji belong to the Isma'ili sect of Islam. They are mountain agriculturists.

MUONG   (s.d. Mwal, Mwon, Ngue) The most northerly of the Mon-Khmer groups. They number about 300,000 and live in the mountains and along the southwest Red River Delta of Vietnam. The Muong are believed to have been closely related to the VIETNAMESE and to have emigrated to the country at the same time.

Muong

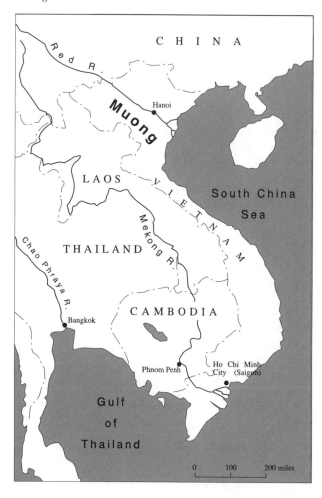

Unlike the VIETNAMESE, however, they rejected the cultural influence of the CHINESE during the HAN occupation of northern Vietnam, which led to their divergence from the bulk of the Vietnamese population.

Today they live in isolated villages and cultivate rice using both slash and burn methods and irrigation. They also hunt and fish; some Muong are craftsmen. They have a well developed clan system much like that of neighboring TAI groups. The Muong religious pantheon includes various spirits representing natural phenomena and local heroes who have been deified.

MURA A South American Indian group of the western Amazon basin in Brazil. Their main activities are fishing and hunting turtles and manatees. They also engage in limited cultivation of maize, sweet manioc, and beans.

MURIA An ethnic group living in the Bastar district of the state of Madhya Pradesh, India. They are related to the GOND and have been influenced by ABUJHMARIA customs.

The Muria are a settled tribe practicing agriculture. They are noted for their *ghotul*, a dormitory for the unmarried of both sexes, which is supported by the entire village.

MURIK An ethnic group, numbering a few thousand, living in the flatlands of the northern coast of Papua New Guinea. Comprising many dialects, their language is an indigenous regional one. Their economy is based upon fishing, trading, and gardening. They practice their own form of Christianity, which acknowledges the power of the spirits. Their most common ceremonies are the life-cycle rituals.

MURNGIN see YOLNGU.

MURSI An ethnic group numbering several thousand, who live in the lower Omo valley in southern Gemu Gofa Province of Ethiopia. They are linguistically related to the Sudanese DIDINGA, and adhere to traditional beliefs. The Mursi are agriculturalists and nomadic cattle-raisers.

MURUNG An ethnic group numbering 16,000 (1980), living in the Chittagong hill tracts of India and Bangladesh.

The Murung have had little contact with the outside world and are perhaps the most primitive group in the Chittagong region. Their small settlements of ten to fifteen families are separated by many rivulets and streams. Family units are self-sufficient and practice slash and burn agriculture. (see also DAYAK)

MURUT A collective term for two ethnic groups living in central Borneo, an island of northern Malaysia. The Idahan (Sabah Murut) number about 40,000; the Kelabat (Sarawak Murut) number about 5,000. They speak two distantly related languages belonging to the Austronesian family, and have preserved their traditional religion. Both groups cultivate rice. However, the Idahan employ slash and burn agricultural techniques, while the Kelabit have irrigated fields. Similarly, the Idahan graze pigs, while the Kelabit raise cattle.

MUSAHAR An ethnic group found in the states of Uttar Pradesh and West Bengal, India. They engage in agriculture and in gathering.

MUSEY An ethnic group living in Chad, in the region of Gounougaya in the Chari River Valley.

MUSULMAN see SRI LANKANS.

MUTAWALIS see LEBANESE.

MUTHAMBI A subgroup of the MERU.

MUWAHHIDUN see DRUZE LEBANESE.

MUYU An ethnic group of approximately 15,000 living in the mountainous area of eastern Irian Jaya, the Indonesian western half of the island of New Guinea. They speak an indigenous local language. As slash and burn cultivators, their most important crops are bananas and sweet potatoes, while the most commonly raised animal is the pig. They are Roman Catholics who believe in supernatural beings as well.

MVAE An ethnic group related to the FANG, living in Gabon.

MWAL see MUONG.

MWENJI A group of Luyana-speakers numbering about 13,000 living along the Luanginga River in western Zambia.

MWIMBI A subgroup of the MERU.

MWON see MUONG.

Mzabite merchants in southern Algeria

MYANMARESE   see BURMANS.

MYASA BEDA   An ethnic group living in central Karnataka State, India. They practice traditional religions; their economy is based on agriculture and gathering.

MZABITES   A Berber people living deep in the Sahara desert, in the Mzab oases of southern Algeria. They number some 80,000 and are distributed over four villages, Ghardaia, Beni Isguen, Melika, and Beni Noura. They subsist from cultivation irrigated by subterranean wells.

The Mzabites are puritanical Ibadi Muslims descending from a group which fled Basra in Iraq and established a community in Oran in 760. Successive religious persecutions in the eleventh century brought them first to the Ouargla oasis and thence to the Mzab. Their isolation has allowed them to preserve their customs, including isolation of the womenfolk. Young men tend to migrate to northern Algerian cities and return when they have made enough money to marry and establish themselves. The strict codes of conduct of the Mzabites are enforced by their leaders, a council of pious elderly scholars. *Hamrias* are halfcaste descendants of black slaves who work among the Mzabites, and also serve as musicians at their lavish weddings.

N

NADZE A Khoisan-speaking ethnic group living in Tanzania.

NAFAR A subgroup of the KHAMSE.

NAGA A generic term for a group of Sino-Tibetan speaking tribes inhabiting hilly Nagaland in eastern Indian along the border with Myanmar (Burma). They number almost one million, divided into numerous groups and subgroups including the ANGAMI, AO, CHANG, KACHA, KALYO-KENGYU, KONYAK, LHOTE, NAKED RENGMA, RENGMA, SANGTAM, SEMA (Zeme), TANGKHUL, TUKOMI, and YACHUMI, each of which speaks one or more diverse, mutually unintelligible dialects. To resolve the linguistic difficulties of the region a pidgin language, Nagamese, or Bodo, has emerged. Traditional religious beliefs are similarly numerous, although most share many common elements including the belief in a variety of deities and spirits and rituals connected with the annual and life cycle. Each group has a unique oral literature and most emphasize music and dance in religious rituals. Christian missionaries, mainly American, have had considerable success among the Naga peoples.

The Naga peoples engage mainly in the terrace cultivation of various grains, legumes, and vegetables. Livestock and dogs are raised for food, and some groups also hunt and fish. Each tribe also specializes in certain crafts such as blacksmithing, pottery making, weaving, and salt manufacturing the products of which they trade with other Naga peoples.

Little is known about the origins of the Naga. It is surmised that they originated in one of the great river basins of China, but they are believed to have begun migrating to their present homeland between two and three thousand years ago: the reasons for this migration have been lost in time. The BRITISH first reached Nagaland in the early nineteenth century and met with harsh resistance. Anti-British guerrilla warfare was

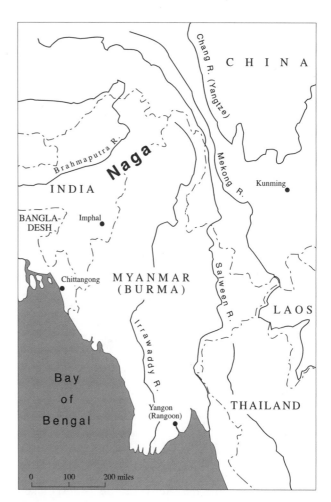

Naga

met with severe retribution and the frequent razing of villages until the region was subdued. Although the colonial authorities later treated the Naga favorably, it was American missionary and educational activity which promoted a sense of united Naga identity and the establishment of the Naga National Council, which promoted the establishment of an independent Naga state.

Soon after India's independence, Naga political aspirations erupted into a full scale civil war and the unilateral declaration, in 1956, of an independent Naga state. By 1963 India gave in to many of the Naga claims by creating the state of Nagaland in a federal India. A shortlived peace lasted until 1972, when Nagaland's chief minister was assassinated. American missionaries were finally called in to negotiate a truce between the Nagas and the federal government of India, concluded in Shillong in 1975. Although there is still some secessionist activity and a handful of guerrilla camps in neighboring Myanmar (Burma), since 1979 Nagaland has been relatively peaceful.

NAGAIBAK (s.d. Noghaibak) Descendants of NOGHAI who converted to Russian Orthodox Christianity in the eighteenth century, although many of them reverted to Islam in the nineteenth century. They number some 15,000.

The Soviet authorities tried to develop the Nagaibak into a distinct nationality, and their language, a dialect of Tatar, was provided with a Cyrillic script in 1923. Some publications, including a periodical begun in 1934, have since appeared in it, but after World War II, the Nagaibak were grouped together with the TATARS, and nothing more was published in their language. (see also BASHKIRS)

NAGBANSI see KISAN.

NAGESAR see KISAN.

NAGESIA (s.d. Kisan) An ethnic group, numbering 22,000, living in the states of Madhya Pradesh, Maharashtra, and West Bengal, India. Their language belongs to the Dravidian family of languages and they are related to the MUNDA.

The tribe is divided into three groups, the Telha, Dhuria, and Senduria. The Telha are so called because at wedding ceremonies they mark the bride's forehead with *tel* (oil), while the Dhuria use *dhul* (dust) taken from the sole of the bridegroom's foot, and the Senduria, like most Hindu castes, apply vermilion. (see also KISAN)

NAGOT (Nago) A subgroup of the YORUBA living in Nigeria.

NAHAL An ethnic group of about 15,000, found in the states of Madhya Pradesh and Maharashtra, India. They are related to the BHIL and KORKU peoples.

NAHANE A Native North American Athapaskan-speaking group numbering about 2,000, living in the Yukon Territory, Canada. At present they are in the final stages of negotiating their land claims against the federal government of Canada. This will secure for them not only traditional fishing rights but also ownership of a large territory rich in natural resources.

NAHUA Together with the OTOMI and MAZAHUA, the largest indigenous group in Mexico. As the native group living closest to the capital, Mexico City, they have been the most influenced by urbanization. Scattered throughout the country, they do not form a political unit, nation, or tribe. Some 880,000 Indians still speak the Aztec language, Nahuatl, the only element which unites them. Nahuatl coexists with Spanish, the elaborate vocabulary once used by priests and politicians augmented by a number of words representing modern concepts.

The ancestors of the Nahua were the Aztecs, or Mexica, who directly or indirectly dominated a large part of what is now Mexico during the pre-Colombian epoch. The Spanish destroyed the Aztec capital of Tenochtitlan, the ruins of which were uncovered during construction in Mexico City.

Their economy is based on corn. The Nahua closest to the capital have assimilated into Mexican society. The less fortunate work, along with their children, as street vendors, while the luckier ones trade in the public market. Urban Nahua are poorly nourished.

Nahua

In spite of christianization, the Nahua still practice rituals derived from pre-Christian times, closely connected with crop-blessing ceremonies and the cycle of the seasons. Elders who are expert "rain petitioners" or who "prevent hail" can still be found in some villages. Bread, fruit, and other delicacies are sometimes left in caves as offerings to both the ancient gods and the saints. Most festivities are in honor of the Catholic saints, but the symbolic and exquisite dances and customs for which the Nahua are still renowned continue pre-Hispanic traditions designed to please both pagan gods and Catholic saints, and thus to guarantee abundant crops and healthy livestock. (see also SALVADOREANS, MEXICANS)

NAKED RENGMA A NAGA group living in the hills of Nagaland on the border between eastern India and Myanmar (Burma).

NAKOTA see SIOUX.

NALOU A tiny ethnic group living along the lower Nunez River and on the Tristão Islands, Guinea.

NAMA An ethnic group numbering about 60,000 living in Namibia. They speak the same language as the DAMARA and are descendants of hunter-gatherers (collectively referred to as KHOISAN) who have since become stock farmers.

NAMADI An ethnic group of hunters numbering around 800 people living in the el-Djouf desert of Mauritania. They speak their own dialect, called Ikoku by the MAURES.

NAMA SONTA see NAYAKA.

NAMAU An ethnic group of approximately 5,000 living in the marshlands of southern Papua New Guinea. They speak Purari, an indigenous language which is unrelated to any of the languages spoken by neighboring peoples. They are hunters and gatherers, as well as cultivators of various crops such as sweet potatoes and taro. Their religion is centered around the belief in *imunu*, the omnipotent and boundless force.

NAMBIKUARA (Nambicuara) A South American Indian group living in the State of Mato Grosso, west Brazil, close to the border with Bolivia. Survivors of a once powerful group, they now number only a few hundred. This group suffered from the intrusion of whites searching for rubber, and were decimated by both intertribal warfare and epidemic diseases. They occupy a relatively large area. Their speech is apparently unrelated to any other language group.

NAMCHI An ethnic group related to the BAYA living in Cameroon.

NAMIBIANS The people of Namibia in Southern Africa, numbering 1.8 million. They are composed of several ethnic groups: the OVAMBO who live mainly in the north and are subdivided into eight groups, the KAVANGO, who also live in the north, the HERERO, who live north of the central plateau, the DAMARA in the west, the CAPRIVIANS and the SAN in the extreme northeast, and a small number of TSWANA. There are also significant communities of AFRIKANERS, BRITISH, and GERMANS.

Until World War I Namibia, which was then called South-West Africa, was under German colonial rule. In 1920 it became a mandate of the Union of South Africa. Following World War II the United Nations contested South Africa's continued control of the territory and opposed its integration into South Africa in the late 1960s. After a lengthy guerrilla war Namibia became independent in 1990. SWAPO (the South-West African People's Organization), a political force that emerged from the Namibian liberation movement, won the multi-party elections and formed the new state's government.

NANAI see NANI.

NANDEVA A South American Indian group dispersed throughout the states of Mato Grosso, São Paulo, and Paraná, in southern Brazil. They number several hundred, and speak a Guarani language. (see also GUARANI)

NANDI (Chemwal) The second largest Kalenjin-speaking group, numbering some 500,000, or c.2 percent of Kenya's population. They occupy the highland region around Kapsabet, the Nandi's foremost town and administrative center, in the Rift Valley Province, and are similar in most respects to the KIPSIGIS. Once called Chemwal, the Nandi have had their present identity from pre-colonial times.

Today they are agriculturalists and keep cattle, which retain great ritual and material value. The possession of some livestock is almost a social necessity. Nandi social life begins at the homestead level. Their homesteads are dispersed, but organized in a hierarchy of political-residential units, regulated by councils of elders.

They have a record as one of the most militant people in the region, having fought against both neighboring ethnic groups and the BRITISH, whom they resisted from 1895 to 1905. Some Nandi practice Christianity while others preserve their traditional religion. Circumcision and clitoridectomy are important symbols of the passage into adulthood. (see also KALEJIN)

NANGODI   An ethnic group living in Ghana.

NANI   A self designation used by four groups which, although divided by the Soviets into separate nationalities, consider themselves a single people. They inhabit the eastern edge of the Russian Federation. The NANAI, numbering about 12,000, live along the lower Amur River: about 80 percent live in Russia and the remainder in China. Some 2,500 OROCHI live south of the Amur River in the Khabarovsk Province. There are fewer than 200 OROK, living on the northern half of the island of Sakhalin. An estimated 300 lived in southern Sakhalin under Japanese rule, but following the annexation of southern Sakhalin by Russia after World War II, the entire community was executed as traitors and collaborators with the JAPANESE. The ULCHI, numbering under 2,000, live along the lower Amur River.

The four Nani languages (in fact, mutually intelligible dialects) belong to the Manchu group of the Tungus-Manchu languages. Of the four, only Nanai was established as a literary language and given a Cyrillic alphabet. However, only few publications have appeared in Nanai, and Russian serves as a literary language.

Originally the Nani were fishermen and hunters, who had a common culture with the NIVKHI. Since Russian conquest and colonization in the nineteenth century they have been rapidly assimilated by the RUSSIANS. Although they still adhere to traditional religions, Russian Orthodox Christian and Chinese influences are particularly strong.

NANKANSI   (s.d. Gurense) A MOLE-DAGBANI ethnic group living in the Upper East Region of Ghana. Their language is called Gurensi. They have intermingled with the FRAFRA.

NANUMBA   (Nanum, Nanune) A MOLE-DAGBANI group living in the Northern Region of Ghana, between the Daka and Oti Rivers. (see also KONKOMBA)

NANZWE   A Shona-speaking group living in the Hwange district of Zimbabwe. They suffered incessant attacks by the NDEBELE, LOZI, and KOLOLO in the early nineteenth cenmtury.

NAO   An ethnic group, numbering 13,000 (1980s), who live south of the KAFFICHO people in central Kefa Province, Ethiopia. They adhere to traditional beliefs. The Nao formed a small kingdom which, during the second half of the nineteenth century, became incorporated into the Kafa kingdom.

NAPORE AND NYANGEA   These two groups, which regard themselves as one people, inhabit the Nyangea and Rom Mountains in northeastern Uganda. They live close to the cattle-herding DODOTH and speak an Eastern Nilotic language.

They are agriculturalists but, like the LABWOR, as a small population living near larger agriculturalist and pastoralist peoples, they have become mainly traders, especially in grain and tobacco.

NAPU   An ethnic group living in the mountainous central region of the Indonesian island of Sulawesi (Celebes). (see also TORADJA)

NAQSHBANDI   see GYPSIES.

NARA   see BARIA.

NARRAGANSETT   A Native North American group, numbering a few hundred, living on Long Island, New York. They are one of the few surviving peoples native to Long Island.

NARYM SELKUP   see SELKUP.

NASIOI   (Kietas) An ethnic group of approximately 15,000, living on the Pacific island of Bougainville in the state of Papua New Guinea, east of the main island. They speak a several Austronesian dialects, although most young people now speak Pidgin English. They are slash and burn cultivators whose main crop is sweet potatoes and chief cash crops are cocoa and copra. While some have been converted by Christian missionaries most still adhere to traditional beliefs in ancestral spirits.

NASKAPI   A Native North American group numbering about 500, living in Quebec. They are closely related, culturally and linguistically, to the MONTAGNAIS.

NAT (Navidigar, Kubutar, Badi, Karnati, Garudi, Kolhati, Sapera) A nomadic ethnic group of performers, numbering about 10,000, found throughout northern, western, and central India. They contain both Hindu and Muslim adherents.

NATIORA An ethnic group living in Burkina Faso.

NATUKHAI A subgroup of the ADYGHEANS. (see also CHERKESS)

NAURU ISLANDERS (Nauruans) A Micronesian-speaking people of mixed Micronesian, Melanesian, and Polynesian descent. They number about 10,000 and inhabit Nauru, a small island in the southwest Pacific Ocean. Formerly a joint trust territory of Australia, New Zealand, and the United Kingdom, Nauru won independence in 1968. The island contains some of the richest and most highly developed phosphate deposits in the Pacific Ocean, but these are expected to be exhausted in the near future, and the current decline in production is the islanders' most significant economic problem.

NAVAJO (Navaho) The largest Native North American people, numbering 175,000, living in Arizona, New Mexico, Utah, and Colorado, U.S.A. They also

Navajo

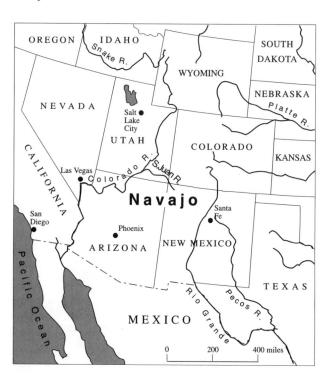

have the largest single reservation of any Native people in North America, encompassing more than 15 million acres of land.

An Athapaskan-speaking group, they originated in Canada and migrated to the American southwest only in the thirteenth century. From their contact with the SPANIARDS they learned to raise sheep and to work with silver and precious stones. In the nineteenth century they had several violent confrontations with United States armed forces, but in the end they received a very large area of land from the U.S. government.

During World War II several thousand Navajo joined the U.S. armed forces, where they were often used as radio operators, speaking their native tongue, which was impossible for the JAPANESE to understand.

Today the capital of the Navajo is in Window Rock, Arizona. They are involved in a wide variety of economic ventures including farming, mining, and the production and sale of woven carpets and costume jewelry. (see also ATHAPASKAN)

NAVIDIGAR see NAT.

NAXI (Nasi, Nakhi) A people, numbering approximately 245,000, living mainly in the Yunnan Province of southwest China. Their language, belonging to the Tibeto-Burman group, has two dialects. A hieroglyphic writing system, invented over one thousand years ago, failed to win widespread use and was replaced, with the help of the Chinese government, with a Roman alphabet in 1957. Increasing contact with the CHINESE has resulted in Chinese becoming a common form of communication among the Naxi.

Like the TIBETANS, with whom they coexist in the north, many Naxi have embraced Tibetan Mahayana Buddhism. Shamanist worship of wind, fire, mountains, water, and other natural phenomena and objects is also common.

Although they share many Han Chinese customs and festivals, the Naxi have maintained a distinctive culture, including their timber-framed dwellings and their dress. They engage primarily in the cultivation of rice and corn.

NAYADI A group of Untouchables found in Kerala, India. They are hunters and gatherers.

NAYAKA (s.d. Nama Sonta) An ethnic group numbering only a few thousand, living along the border of the Kerala and Tamil Nadu states of southern India.

They speak a Dravidian language which has incorporated considerable elements from neighboring languages. Most Nayaka practice traditional religions which have integrated Hindu beliefs and deities; the majority of their religious rites focus on death and burial.

The Nayaka live in the forests, where they gather honey, and occasionally cultivate small plots of land. It is common for Nayaka to find part-time employment among neighboring peoples.

NAYAMWEZI   A Bantu-speaking ethnic group living in Tanzania.

NBAKA   An ethnic group living in northern Zaire.

NCAMU   A subgroup of the NGUNI.

NDAONESE   (s.d. Ndau Ndau) Inhabitants of the small islands of Ndau and Nuse in the Timor Archipelago, Indonesia. They number about 4,000 and speak a Savunese dialect; many also speak Rotinese. Rotinese culture has traditionally dominated Ndau, and many Ndaonese have settled on the island of Roti.

Because of the small size of their islands (only five square miles are habitable) and poor conditions for cultivation, the Ndaonese engage in gold- and silversmithing and in trade. Agriculture is limited to small household gardens.

NDAU   A Shona-speaking group living south of the Zambezi and Save Rivers in Mozambique. (see also SHONA)

NDEBELE   (Matabele) A people related to the Ntungwa NGUNI. They live in the central Transvaal, South Africa, where they number 800,000 and in southwest Zimbabwe and the adjacent areas of northeast Botswana, where together they number almost 2 million. A non-urbanized people, they are divided into two groups: the Northern Ndebele, that speaks the Sotho language and is practically assimilated into the SOTHO people, among whom it lives; and the Southern Ndebele, which is itself divided between the MANALA and the NDZUNDA.

Both Ndebele groups are predominantly Christian; about two-thirds of the Northern Ndebele and over four-fifths of the Southern Ndebele have specific church affiliations. Among both groups, approximately half the Christians belong to African Independent Churches; the largest minority is Roman Catholic.

Ndebele

In 1981 a self-governing state, Kwandebele, was established in the central Transvaal for the Southern Ndebele. It is the poorest of the Bantustans established by the South African government, with its major products being manufactured goods and sugar cane.

While the Northern Ndebele have adopted many SOTHO customs, the Southern Transvaal Ndebele practice general NGUNI customs. The Southern Ndebele are also known for their elaborate beadwork, neckrings, and colorful murals (generally incorporating geometric designs) on the external walls of their homes.

The Zimbabwe Ndebele, numbering c.1.7 million, live in southwest Zimbabwe around Bulawayo. They speak Sindebele and some are Christians while others practice their traditional religion which is similar to that of the Nguni.

The Ndebele originated in Natal, where they had a highly centralized kingdom. Ethnic identity was based on allegiance to the king who was the centre of religious and economic life as well as commander of the army.

In 1821 the Ndebele fled to eastern Transvaal until attacks by the PEDI, KORA, and AFRIKANERS forced some to move to their present location in the Mutapo Hills near Bulawayo. Capable of rapid and efficient military mobilization, they attacked and conquered many peoples as they moved. After a prolonged conflict the Zimbabwe Ndebele were defeated by the BRITISH in 1893; they rebelled in 1896.

A Ndebele chief in South Africa

In Zimbabwe's struggle for independence, the Zimbabwe Ndebele supported Joshua Nkomo's Zimbabwe African Peoples' Union (ZAPU). (see also NGUNI, PEDI, SOUTH AFRICANS, ZIMBABWEANS)

NDEMBU   A Lunda-speaking group numbering 50,000 living in northwest Zambia. A nomadic group who travel in search of fertile land and better hunting prospects, the Ndembu worship their ancestors and practice divination. They were originally part of the Lunda empire. When the BRITISH occupied the area, they established a Ndembu administration and bureaucracy. (see also LUNDA)

NDOGO   see AZANDE.

NDOKKI   A subgroup of the IBO.

NDORAWA   A subgroup of the TIV.

NDOROBO   (Dorobo) An ethnic group living in the Rift Valley province of Kenya. They share the Maa language with the MASAAI and are estimated at about 25,000. They are hunters and gatherers but some have also begun to raise cattle.

The Ndorobo follow traditional African religions; only a few have adopted Christianity. In the Masaai language their name means "poor folk," i.e., people with no cattle. Over the years many smaller ethnic groups whose way of life has disintegrated have been absorbed into the Ndorobo.

NDOUMOU   see MINDOUMOU.

NDRE   A subgroup of the BANDA.

NDUKA   A subgroup of the SARA.

NDUNDULU   A subgroup of the LUYANA.

NDWANDWE   A subgroup of the NGUM.

NDZUNDA   A subgroup of the NDEBELE.

NEDERLANDERS   see DUTCH.

NEGIDAL   (s.d. El'kan Beyenin, Eleke Beye; "local person") The Negidal, numbering about 500, live in two villages, one on the Amur and the other on the Amgun River, some 100 miles apart, in Khabarovsk, on the southeastern border of Russia with China.

Their language belongs to the Tungus division of the Tungus-Manchu group. It has no alphabet, Russian being used as their literary language.

In the eighteenth and nineteenth centuries many Negidal were assimilated by the NANI. Since the nineteenth century they have been assimilated by the RUSSIANS.

Their culture and religion are similar to those of the EVENKI, but also contain many NIVKHI, NANI, and UDEGEY elements.

NEGRITOS   (Agta, Zambales Negritos, Aeta, Hambal, Sambal, Ati, Mamanua) Ethnic groups of forest dwellers of unknown population living in the Philippines. Once predominant in the area, they were small, dispersed bands of hunters and gatherers who lived in the lowland and coastal areas until being forced into the mountainous forests they inhabit today. Intermarriage with MALAYS who migrated to the islands throughout history has obscured cultural and ethnic distinctions which might otherwise have been more pronounced.

The original non-Austronesian language which probably existed has disappeared and most Negritos speak the languages of their non-Negritos neighbors. They practice slash and burn agriculture as well as hunting and gathering, and have good trade relations with neighboring highland and lowland peoples.

The several thousand Zambales Negritos of the mountains of southern Zambales Province (northwest of Manila) are considered to be of the purest stock. They live in a highly patriarchal society with scattered settlements of no more than three or four bamboo-thatched houses which are moved every year or so. They are largely vegetarians, practicing limited slash and burn agriculture and trading forest products such as beeswax, tobacco, and tree sap with their neighbors. Women do most agricultural work while men hunt and trade. They have no formal political system, as they believe that the world is ruled by a spiritual domain. They are a highly ritualistic society.

The islands of the southern Philippines are inhabited by scattered Negrito-like peoples numbering 20,000 to 30,000. They live in the interior mountainous regions of the islands of Negros, Panay, and Mindanao. In Negros and Panay they are known as ATI and in Mindanao as MAMANUA. They are semi-nomadic and practice an inefficient form of slash and burn agriculture, sweet potatoes being the staple crop. Hunting and gathering are also important. Their society is highly patriarchal; the local shaman is looked on as a priest who communicates with a "supreme being" responsible for the community's general welfare. (see also SEMANG)

NENTSY (Nenets, Samoyed) The Nentsy live in the far north of Russia, between the Kola and Taymyr Peninsulas, on the Kara and Laptev Seas, and in the Kulgaev and Novaya Zemlya Islands. They are mainly concentrated in the Yamalo-Nenets, Taymyr, and Nenets Autonomous *Oblasts* (Regions). They numbered 30,000 in 1979.

Nentsy

The Nentsy are divided into two main groups: Khandeyar (forest dwellers) and tundra dwellers. Their language, belonging to the Samoyed division of the Uralic languages, is divided into two group of dialects, which reflect the ecological division. A literary language based on a tundra dialect was established in 1932 using the Cyrillic alphabet. However, very little has been published in it and Russian is used as the literary language.

Their traditional, nomadic, tribal way of life and their religion are preserved in part, and they subsist on fishing, reindeer-herding, and fur-trapping.

NEPALI (Nepalese) A term referring to the inhabitants of the kingdom of Nepal, rather than to a distinct ethnic group. Located at the mountainous crossroads of the primarily Buddhist Tibeto-Burman culture in the north and the Hindu Indian culture in the south, in an area of great geographic diversity, Nepali cultural and ritual life is one of vast diversity.

Despite ethnic diversity within the national borders, the people of Nepal share an identity derived from a unique political heritage. Nepal is the only Hindu monarchy in the world; the king is commonly held to be an incarnation of the Hindu god Vishnu. The official language is Nepali, an Indo-Aryan language, although most people speak one of appproximately two dozen ethnic languages.

Having successfully resisted British colonization in the early nineteenth century, the Nepali remained relatively closed to international influence until the 1950s, with the opening of borders to trade and travel.

The vast majority of Nepal's inhabitants live in villages and small towns in the arable hills flanking the Himalayan range. The local economy in a Nepali village is invariably based on small-scale, family-based, subsistence farming. Rice, the main staple crop, is grown in irrigated terraces carved into the rolling hillside. Steeper tracts of land are also terraced by hand and intercropped with corn, soybeans, and squash. Land that is too steep or rocky for cultivation is used to graze goats and cattle. Small gardens provide vegetables.

Despite legislation in 1963 abolishing the Hindu caste system, caste hierarchy remains a dominant factor in the socio-economic life of the Nepali. Many occupations, such as haircutting, butchering, and goldsmithing continue to be carried out by traditional lineage groups. The NEWARI (who are not a caste but a distinct Nepali ethnic group) continue to dominate in crafts based on a technique of metal casting originally developed by them. (see also GURKHA, SIKKIMESE)

NESTORIANS see ASSYRIANS, IRAQIS, KURDS, LEBANESE, SYRIANS.

NETHERLANDS ANTILLEANS Inhabitants of five islands in two groups at the extreme southern and northern ends of the Lesser Antilles. Bonaire and Curaçao (Aruba was a member until 1986, prior to which this three-island group was often called the "ABCs") are just off the north coast of Venezuela; Saba, Sint Eustatius, and Sint Maarten are just east of Puerto Rico.

The population (usually called by their respective island names) is estimated at 183,000; of these, 85 percent live on Curaçao, mostly in Willemstad, the capital. Dutch is the official language, but English is common in the northern group and Spanish in the southern;

above: Hindu Nepali in the Kathmandu Valley
below: Tibetan Nepali women carrying produce to market

the lingua franca, however, especially in the south, is Papiamento, a mixture of Spanish, Portuguese, and Dutch. The islands are racially mixed, with African elements predominating in the northern group and Native American elements strong in the southern; whites are a small minority on all islands except Saba. About 80 percent of the population are Roman Catholics, with Protestant and Jewish minorities (the oldest continuously functioning Jewish community in the western hemisphere is here, and Curaçao is the site of the first synagogue in the Americas).

The SPANIARDS landed on Curaçao in 1499, and had also claimed Aruba and Bonaire, then inhabited by peaceful Arawak, by 1527. The DUTCH, who had set up colonies among the less peaceful CARIB inhabitants (subsequently exterminated) of the Windward Islands, did not arrive in Curaçao until 1643; their hold over the "ABCs" was not fully consolidated until 1845, when the Netherlands Antilles came into formal existence. Curaçao, a Caribbean center of the slave trade, suffered a severe economic downturn when in 1863 Holland decreed emanicipation in its colonies. Netherlands Antilleans did not recover until the discovery of oil in Venezuela in the early 1900s turned Aruba and Curaçao into important refining and transhipment centers. Refining Venezuelan oil was the major base of the islanders' economy until very recently. The people of these islands, who became an integral part of the Netherlands in 1954, have been assuming increasing autonomy in domestic decisions since the occurrence of severe, partly racial, internal disturbances in the 1970s and 1980s.

NEUA   A Tai-speaking group considered to be the original TAI population of Laos. They are Buddhists and cultivate rice. Contact with the VIETNAMESE has influenced their dialect.

NEWAR   A people, numbering some 450,000 (1981), living in Nepal. Its largest concentration is in the Kathmandu Valley. There are two groups, the Hindu and the Buddhist Newar. They speak Nepal Bhasa, also called Newari Bhasa, and use the Devanagari script.

The Newar are the aborigines of Nepal. They possess more Mongoloid than Indo-Aryan features. Most are traders by profession, though some are also employed in government service and some engage in agriculture. They are also good masons, carpenters, plasterers, painters, dyers, sculptors, goldsmiths, blacksmiths, and woodcarvers.

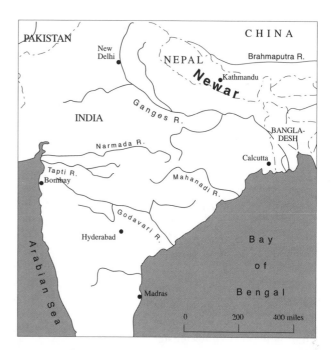

Newar

The Newar of the Kathmandu Valley live in brick houses of two, three, or even five storeys, with tiled roofs and artistically carved wooden windows. In comparison with other NEPALI, their standard of living is high. Their staple food is rice. Although the joint family system still exists among them, it is disintegrating rapidly in the face of modernization.

NEW CALEDONIAN ISLANDERS   The inhabitants, numbering 170,000, of the large island of New Caledonia and several smaller islands of the Loyalty Group in the Pacific Ocean, east of Australia. They are divided among several ethnic groups, with the KANAK (an indigenous people of Melanesian origin) constituting about 45 percent; Europeans, mainly FRENCH, one-third, Polynesians 11.5 percent; and others, mostly Asians, one-tenth. Almost all are Roman Catholics. The major urban center is the capital, Noumea, situated on the main island. French is the official language and mother tongue of the French settlers, and there are some thirty Melanesian languages spoken by the KANAK.

New Caledonia became a French possession in 1853 and a French Overseas Territory in 1946. Since then the KANAK have made numerous attempts to achieve independence, resisted by FRENCH settlers who remain loyal to the French republic.

New Caledonia has been strongly influenced by the presence of large scale mining enterprises of nickel, cobalt, and chromium, discovered on the islands in the nineteenth century. New Caledonia has the largest known nickel deposits in the world, accounting for about 30 percent of the world's known reserves. After mining, tourism is the most important sector of the economy. The New Caledonian economy benefits from its status as a French overseas territory in association with the European Economic Community.

NEW ZEALANDERS   The 3.4 million inhabitants of the two main islands of New Zealand (North Island and South Island) and several smaller islands, the largest of which is Stewart Island. Population distribution is uneven, determined by the country's physical features and resultant agriculture. The highest concentrations of population are on the western and southern coasts of North Island, and to a lesser extent on the eastern coast of South Island; this population lives mainly in urban concentrations — over 70 percent in cities with populations greater than 25,000.

Most New Zealanders are of European origin predominantly the descendants of BRITISH, who immigrated to the islands from the end of the eighteenth century. They speak English and are mostly Christians. About 306,000 are MAORI of Polynesian origin, and there is a sprinkling of Pacific Islanders, mainly Polynesians, who are concentrated in Auckland. The MAORI are native to New Zealand, and their culture has developed in isolation as a variant of Polynesian culture.

New Zealand underwent various waves of settlement before officially becoming part of the British Empire in the 1840s. The ever-increasing demand of European settlers for land was a major factor in promoting conflict between the MAORI and the Europeans during the nineteenth century. The 1840 Treaty of Waintangi between the BRITISH and most major MAORI chiefs acknowledged, without really protecting, Maori land rights.

New Zealand played an increasingly important role in the South Pacific Islands after joining the South Pacific Commission as a founder member in 1947. It administered the United Nations Trust Territory of Western Samoa until the latter's independence in 1962 and assisted the Cook Islands in achieving self-government. New Zealand has a say in the affairs of Niue and Tokelau, and provides economic and administrative support to the tiny British territory of Pitcairn Island.

Traditionally the economy relied on a narrow range of primary export products, including dairy products, meat, and wool. In 1990–1991 agriculture accounted for more than 60 percent of total exports. Manufacturing employs about 20 percent of New Zealanders, one-fifth of whom work in processing primary products. (see also MAORI)

NEYO   A small ethnic group numbering around 5,000, living in twenty villages around the town of Sassandra, Côte d'Ivoire. They belong to the KRU ethnic grouping, and their language is related to those of the BETE and the GODIE.

NEZ PERCE   (Sahaptini) A Native North American people numbering 2,400, many of whom live on the Nez Perce Federal Reservation in Clearwater County, Idaho, U.S.A.

The group is remembered for its ill-fated attempt to escape commitment to a reservation, during which it was pursued for over one thousand miles by the United States Cavalry and caught just south of the Canadian border in 1877. Chief Joseph, the leader of the attempt, became a well-known symbol of Native American resistance to forced relocation.

NGACHANG   see ACHANG.

NGADADJARA   see PIDJANJARA.

NGADJU   An ethnic group living on the Indonesian island of Kalimantan (Borneo). (see also DAYAK)

NGALA   An ethnic group living in northwestern Zaire, between the Zaire and Ubangi Rivers. Their language, Lingala, is one of Zaire's four national languages.

NGAMA   An ethnic group living in Chad.

N'GAM-GAM   (Ngam) An ethnic group living in northern Togo.

NGANASAN   (s.d. Nya) The fewer than 1,000 Nganasan live mainly in the Taymyr Autonomous Province in northwest Siberia, Russia. Their language belongs to the Samoyedic group of the Uralic languages. It is close to and mutually intelligible with Nentsy. It has no an alphabet, and Nentsy and Russian serve as literary languages. They adhere to their traditional shamanist religion. Ethnically the Nganasan are of mixed NENTSY-EVENKI-DOLGAN origin.

NGANGULU   An ethnic group living in Congo.

N'GAO   A subgroup of the BANDA.

NGBA   An ethnic group living in Cameroon.

NGBAKA   A subgroup of the BANDA.

NGBANDI   An ethnic group living in northwestern Zaire, between the Zaire and Ubangi Rivers. Zaire's president Mobutu Sese Seko is a member of the Ngbandi ethnic group. (see also ZAIREANS)

NGBO   A subgroup of the IBO.

NGEH   (Nghe) A Mon-Khmer group numbering 3,000, living in Laos and Vietnam. The KLENG are a subgroup of the Ngeh.

NGHE   see NGEH.

NGIAW   see SHAN.

NGIO   see SHAN.

NGIRIL   An ethnic group related to the MBOCHI living in Congo.

NGIZIM   A subgroup of the KANURI.

NGOLOGA   An ethnic group living in Botswana.

NGOMBE   A subgroup of the MONGO living along the Zaire River.

NGONDE   An ethnic group living in southern Tanzania. (see also NYAKYUSA)

NGONI   A people living in southeast Zambia, where they number 180,000, in southern Mozambique (100,00), and in central Malawi (720,000). Most Ngoni speak Nyanja, but some in central Malawi speak Chewa. Some are Christians and some practice traditional religions.

The Ngoni were characacterized by strong, centralized chiefdoms and much of their ritual was aimed at strengthening the monarchy. The age-set was used in an attempt to unite the villages. The Ngoni used ZULU military techniques and thus attained a reputation as fierce warriors.

Today, however, they are no longer warriors, but have become farmers and raise cattle. They have also abandoned the patrilineal descent system in favor of the matrilineal system of the CHEWA and NSENGA.

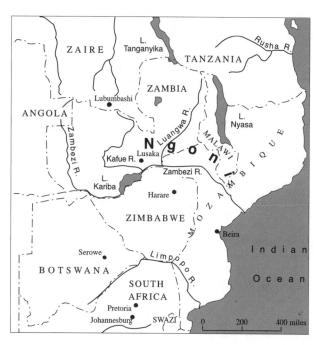

Ngoni

The Ngoni originated in South Africa where they lived along the coastal areas of Natal, the Cape, and southeastern Transvaal. With the nineteenth-century upheavals in southeast Africa (the *mfekane*), the Ngoni fled north, absorbing other ethnic elements as they travelled.

One of the Ngoni groups which fled South Africa at this time, led by chief Soshangana, founded the Gaza dynasty in southern Mozambique. At the height of their power, in 1850, they dominated the territory between the Zambezi and the Incomati Rivers. They were known for their harassment of the PORTUGUESE and fought a series of battles against these colonial rulers from 1832 until 1895 when they were finally conquered. They were then used by the PORTUGUESE as mercenaries because of their reputation as fierce warriors. The Soshangana Ngoni also conquered the TONGA and CHOPI. Intermarriage with these defeated peoples diluted their distinctive ethnic character.

The Ngoni came to Zambia and Malawi in a mass migration from South Africa led by Chief Zwangendaba. By the time of his death in 1848, he had reached the area of what is now the Malawi-Tanzanian border. However, the conflict over his successor led to the migration of several groups: one northward, one west, and another east toward Lake Malawi (Nyasa). Some had moved into lands occupied by the BEMBA in 1850, but were defeated by them in 1870 and moved to Malawi to join the Ngoni already living there. Other Ngoni established permanent settlements in Zambia. In 1860 they reached the territory of the NSENGA and made repeated attempts to take over the prosperous CHEWA kingdom until they succceeded in 1880. As a consequence of intermarriage with the CHEWA, the Ngoni adopted most of their culture and social customs, including language. The Ngoni of Zambia were conquered by the BRITISH in 1898, and a Ngoni chief was appointed administrative head of the region.

The Ngoni chiefdoms of central and southern Malawi were established as a result of the movements of other Ngoni groups seeking to establish new chiefdoms. There they intermarried with the local CHEWA, and their ethnic character was further diluted. The area of the central Ngoni chiefs came under British rule in 1896. In 1897 the Ngoni revolted against the BRITISH, forcing many to flee to Malawi. These groups of Ngoni are known as the Mchingi Ngoni. Having also settled in a CHEWA society, they live in predominantly CHEWA villages governed by CHEWA headmen. There are only a few distinctly Ngoni villages. As in the other areas conquered by the Ngoni, intermarriage has caused them to lose their unique character and their culture is mainly that of the CHEWA. (see also MALAWIANS, NGUNI PEOPLES)

NGOROS   An ethnic group living in Cameroon.

NGOVA   An ethnic group living in Zimbabwe.

NGOWE   An ethnic group living in Gabon, on the coast around Cape Saint Catherine and the Iguela Lagoon. They number only a few thousand. Though they are probably a branch of the ESHIRA, they speak the same language as their northern neighbors, the NKOMI. In the precolonial period they served as middlemen between European traders on the coast and the peoples in the hinterland.

NGUE   see MUONG.

NGUMBO   An ethnic group related to the USHI living in Zambia.

NGUNG BO   A Mon-Khmer group numbering about 3,000, living in some twenty villages in southern Laos. They are primarily slash and burn agriculturalists but also breed buffalo and produce baskets to trade with neighboring VIETNAMESE. Their villages consist of several longhouses arranged in a circle with a palisade to protect them from marauders.

NGUNGWE   see NYANJA.

NGUNI PEOPLES   A cultural-linguistic grouping of southeastern Bantu-speakers who migrated into the southern African subcontinent between 500 and 1000 C.E. Today they are found in Malawi, Zambia, Zimbabwe, Swaziland, southern Mozambique, northern Botswana, and South Africa, and number around 20 million.

The largest and most important Nguni peoples today are the SWAZI, ZULU, XHOSA, NGONI, and NDEBELE (Matabele). There are also a large number of smaller groups of Nguni, most of whom were organized as independent states or chiefdoms prior to the late nineteenth century. The Nguni are generally ordered under two genealogical parent groups, the NTUNGWA and the TEKELA. The former include the XHOSA, ZULU, and the NDEBELE of the Transvaal. Among the Tekela Nguni, in addition to the SWAZI, the NDEBELE of Zimbabwe and the NGONI, other groups are the THONGA (Tonga), MTHWETHWE, EMBO, PHONDO, NGWANE, NDWANDWE, BEHELEZIZI, MFENGU, TSHANGE, ZOTSHO, BEHELE, RAULE, RELEDWANE, FINGO, HLUBI, TOLO, RADEBE, ZIZI, and MADUNA. Other Nguni groups are the CELE, TULI, QWABE, MBODLAMINI, XOLO, MPONDOMISI, BOMVANA, BOMVU, LATA, BELISI, and NCAMU.

Historically Nguni polities experienced a large number of fissions due to the political structure of Nguni chiefdoms. The principal line of cleavage has been between followers of the chief's eldest son (known as the right-hand son) and those of the senior son (known as the paramount son), legal heir of the Great Wife, a later-married wife, also known as the "mother of the country."

The Nguni today are largely Christians, although this self-definition does not necessarily preclude the practice of traditional religious rituals or negate traditional religious-moral codes. Within the traditional cosmology, ancestors play an active role, primarily in a protective capacity and as representatives of group values.

In pre-colonial times the Nguni were primarily pastoralists for whom cattle had ritual as well as status importance, not unlike among the peoples of East Africa. In addition to each man's identification with a favorite ox, cattle were lavishly tended and trained to respond to distinctive whistles; the horns of oxen were esthetically bent and shaped, displayed at dances, and were the subject of poems. Cattle also played an important role in numerous rituals. Marriage was recognized only if the *lobola*, a bride price conferring rights to the reproductive and productive potential of the bride (and usually set at a given number of cattle), had been paid by the groom to the bride's father. That the *lobola* symbolically associated cattle with women's reproductive functions (and was not purely a material exchange) is reflected in the elaborate taboos surrounding women in their relations with cattle. In addition to herding (which was a male occupation), other economic activities included the cultivation of millet, corn sorghum, maize, calabashes, pumpkins, and beans, traditionally female occupations. Hunting was also an important economic activity among the Nguni in early times, both for food and for ivory (the primary export article).

Until the late eighteenth century, Nguni chiefdoms remained small. Among the northern Nguni, particularly the HLUBI, NGWANE, and NDWANDWE, as with the ZULU and the THEMBU, early state formation seems to have been connected with participation in trade with the PORTUGUESE at Delagoa Bay. The goods exchanged were primarily ivory and, to a lesser extent, cattle, for brass, iron, copper, glass beads, and, where possible, firearms. With the exception of the NGONI, the Nguni states and chiefdoms generally did not participate in the slave trade.

Historically all Nguni practiced male circumcision at the age of puberty. Usually contemporaries of each locality were circumcised together, and it was considered appropriate that they be led by the son of a chief. Circumcision was dropped by the northern Nguni, particularly the ZULU, SWAZI, and MPONDO, but maintained by the southern Nguni, in particular the XHOSA and THEMBU.

In their early history in the southern African subcontinent, there was a great deal of mixing and intermarriage between the incoming Nguni and the local KHOIKHOI and SAN peoples. Evidence of this derives from the high percentage of Khoisan-associated clicks in many of the Nguni languages, particularly in Zulu and Xhosa (in which click-words make up six and seven percent of their respective vocabularies). Further evidence of cultural admixture derives from the San-related practice of amputating the end joint of the little finger, which has been adopted by some Nguni groups, specifially the THEMBU, BOMVU, TULI, NCAMU, BELESI, and LATA. Other Nguni groups, like the MPONDO, XHOSA, and ZULU, amputate one joint of the finger in the case of a sick child. Yet, unlike both the KHOIKHOI and the SAN, most of the Nguni groups have fish taboos, with the notable exception of the THONGA of Delagoa Bay and the TULI. (see also NSENGA, SOUTH AFRICANS, SOUTHERN SOTHO, SWAZI, ZULU)

NGUOI KINH   see VIETNAMESE.

NGUON MUONG   An ethnic group living in southern Vietnam. (see also SACH)

NGWA   A subgroup of the IBO.

NGWAKETSE   (Bangwaketse) One of the largest TSWANA subgroups living in Botswana. They grew wealthy in the nineteenth century mainly by trading in ostrich feathers. Towards the end of that century they accepted British protection against AFRIKANER expansionism but later joined other Tswana groups in trying to limit British authority. Due to ecological crises in that period and taxes imposed by the colonial administration, the Ngwaketse were forced into migrant labor. They remained dependent economically on this type of work after Botswana's independence in 1966. (see also SOTHO)

NGWANE   A subgroup of the NGUNI.

NHA HUEN   (Hoen) A Mon-Khmer group numbering about 3,000, living in southern Laos. Traditionally, cultivators of rice, they have also begun growing coffee. Their native religion is gradually giving way to Buddhism. Domestic animals, including elephants, are important to the Nha Huen.

NHANECA HUMBE   An ethnic group numbering about 250,000, living in the Huile and Cunene Provinces of Angola. Most practice traditional religions, and they engage in agriculture, animal husbandry, hunting, and fishing. Cattle is important to their economy and serves as a status symbol.

The Nhaneca Humbe are divided into four chieftainships, two of which consider themselves to be independent. They believe that their ruler is sacred, and have resisted the influence of the PORTUGUESE.

NHANG   (Giai, Nung) An ethnic group numbering about 12,000 living in northern Vietnam. They are most similar to the Black TAI except in their use of a unique cotton gin.

NIANTIC   A Native North American Indian group, numbering a few hundred, living in Connecticut, U.S.A.

NIASANS   (s.d. Ono Niha) Inhabitants of the island of Nias located off the western coast of Sumatera (Sumatra), Indonesia. They number about 600,000 and are comprised of several racial and cultural strata, including Veddoid, Malay, and even Mongoloid elements. Their language, which is divided into northern and southern dialects, is believed to be a member of the Malayo-Polynesian family. The indigenous religion is still strong, although both Christianity and Islam have made considerable inroads and 95 percent of the population now identify themselves formally as Christians.

The native religion extolled head-hunting and human sacrifice. It had a complex cosmology apparently influenced by Hinduism and this belief was utilized in many daily events; the patterns of villages and houses were fashioned to represent this cosmology and are particularly ornate. Crafts such as goldsmithing and carpentry are of particular importance and a unique monetary system evolved in which dried pig meat was used as a recognized currency. Rituals connected with head-hunting and human sacrifice have since been replaced by animal sacrifices, elaborate dances, and mock battles.

The Niasans possess a rigid class system with the landowners forming an aristocracy and commoners and slaves being kept perpetually indebted. Slaves, generally taken in battle, are sometimes mistreated. Evidence of the secondary status of slaves is seen by their exclusion from the ceremonies involved in rites of passage.

Contemporary Niasan society is based on agriculture and the raising of pigs. There is also some fishing and a nascent tourist industry. Traditionally, the Niasans were acclaimed for their elaborate architecture.

NICARAGUANS   The nearly 4 million inhabitants of Nicaragua, the largest of the Central American republics. About 70 percent of the people are *mestizo* (of mixed European and Indian ancestry). MOSQUITO Indians and blacks constitute an additional 15 percent, the remainder being European. The population is predominantly Roman Catholic.

Most of the population is concentrated around Lakes Nicaragua and Managua, adjacent to a string of active volcanoes lining the west coast. Nicaraguans are constantly exposed to the danger of earthquakes, one of which devastated Managua, the capital city, in the 1970s is sometimes accredited with the unrest which precipitated the later overthrow of the government by the Sandinistas.

Nicaragua was discovered by Columbus in 1502 on his last voyage to the New World, but permanent settlements were not founded by the SPANIARDS until 1524. With the end of the War of Independence in 1821, Nicaragua was annexed to the Mexican empire under Emperor Augustin Iturbide. In 1823, when the empire collapsed, Nicaragua formed a political union with Costa Rica, Honduras, and El Salvador, which lasted only until 1838, when Nicaragua gained political independence. In the early twentieth century, however, Nicaragua became effectively an economic dependency of the United States, which supported the Somosa family dictatorship until Sandinista forces took power in the late 1970s after sustained civil war. Initially favorable to the new regime, which achieved world renown for its remarkable literacy campaign and efforts at land reform, the United States turned against the Sandinistas, supporting Somocista and counter-Sandinista forces (called "Contras") throughout the 1980s. The Sandinistas were ousted in free elections at the end of that decade.

Due in part to restrictions imposed by the United States, Nicaragua's former principal trading partner, the economy failed to flourish during the Sandinista period. The most important source of income for Nicaraguans has been agriculture: 60 percent of the people raise crops, especially in the western part of the country, where the soil is suitable for mechanized farming. Important crops include cocoa, coffee, cotton, fruit, sesame, sugar cane, and tobacco. Much of the land, however, is not arable. Forestry and mineral resources have also remained underdeveloped. Some forest products, including balsa, cedar, mahogany, pine, rosewood, and rubber, are exported; mining industries have produced small amounts of copper, gold, and silver.

NICOBARESE   An ethnic group, numbering 22,000 (1981), living in the Nicobar Islands, India. Their language, Nicobarese, belongs to the Austroasiatic family of languages. They are located in almost all the inhabited islands of the Nicobar group except Great Nicobar, traditionally the domain of the SHOM-PEN.

The Nicobarese are the more progressive section of the population on the Andaman and Nicobar islands: they are acquiring modern technology and education at a very fast pace. The coconut is the mainstay of their economy, supplemented by other types of nuts and plantations of bananas and other fruits. They also engage in fishing, shell collecting, and poultry- and pig-farming.

Although they have their own tribal language, they understand other languages such as Portuguese, English, German, Malay, Chinese, Burmese, and Hindi.

NIENDE   A subgroup of the SOMBA.

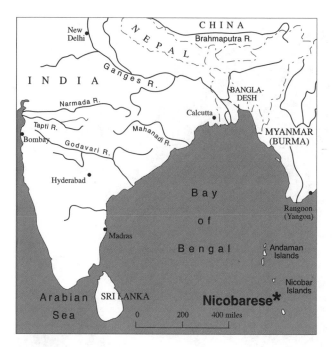

Nicobarese

NIGERIANS   A people living in Nigeria, West Africa. In 1990 their estimated number was 108 million. Well over 250 ethnic groups make up the Nigerian people, some numbering fewer than 10,000. The main ten groups which together account for nearly 80 percent of the population are the HAUSA-FULANI (two groups) of the north, the YORUBA in the southwest, IBO in the southeast, KANURI in the northeast, TIV in the central east, EDO in the southwest, NUPE in the central west, IBIBIO in the southeast, and IJAW in the Bendel state. Each of these ethnic groups is subdivided into a number of linguistically and culturally related groups. The remainder of the population is divided between a large number of smaller ethnic groups.

Much of the population is concentrated in the southern part of the country as well as in the area around Kano in the north. The Middle Belt between these two areas is sparsely populated. The official language of Nigeria is English. The most widely spoken languages are Hausa, Yoruba, and Ibo. About 52 percent of the Nigerians are Muslims, 42 percent are Christians, and 6 percent follow traditional religions.

The Nigerians became independent from British colonial rule in October 1960. During the colonial period the BRITISH divided Nigeria into three regions. The north, in which the HAUSA-FULANI were the main ethnic group, was the largest and dominant region. The BRITISH did not allow missionaries to act among the HAUSA-FULANI, and so Islam remained strong in the region. However, as the missions were the only way of receiving western education the HAUSA-FULANI lagged behind the two other major ethnic groups of Nigeria, the YORUBA in the west and the IBO in the east.

During decolonization the political parties in Nigeria were formed along ethnic lines and the political struggle soon became ethnic. After independence the HAUSA-FULANI dominated Nigerian politics, but they feared competition with the southern people, especially the IBO, who arrived in the north in large numbers to seek jobs. As a result discriminatory measures were applied. These ethnic tensions intensified during the 1960s and in 1966 some 30,000 IBO were massacred in the north by the HAUSA-FULANI. Following the massacre 2 million IBO, who had been dispersed all over Nigeria, fled to their original homeland in the southeast. In May 1967 the IBO declared independence from Nigeria and their region became the Republic of Biafra.

This act resulted in a war that lasted two and one-half years, during which thousands of soldiers on both sides were killed and about a million IBO died of starvation in Biafra. The war ended in 1970 with Biafra becoming part of Nigeria again.

After the war there were attempts to weaken the ethnic tensions in Nigeria by dividing the existing regions into smaller units that would cut across ethnic lines.

In 1968 Nigeria adopted a federal structure comprising twelve states; in 1976 seven more states were added, and another two were added in 1987. Although Nigeria's ethnic problems were not completely solved, the new federal structure contributed greatly to the lessening of ethnic conflicts. At the beginning of the 1990s the Nigerian government started a hesitant democratization process, allowing the creation of a two-party system. In order to ease ethnic tensions before the elections, nine more states were added in 1991, making a total of thirty states. The president denied allegations that the real purpose of this move was to postpone the elections.

NIGERIENS   The people of Niger, West Africa, numbering 7.8 million. The ethnic groups which make up the Nigeriens are the HAUSA and the FULANI in the south, the DJERMA and the SONGHAI in the southwest, the KANURI in the southeast and the TUAREG in the north. The TUAREG, a nomadic people of Berber origin, have been the main source of ethnic problems in Niger. Most of the northeastern region of the country is uninhabited. Eighty-five percent of the Nigeriens are Muslims, less than 1 percent are Christians, and the rest practice traditional religions. The official language of

above: Bororo Fulani women in Niger
below: a dugout piroque on the marshy banks of the Niger River

Niger is French, but the most widely spoken language is Hausa.

The people of Niger gained independence from the FRENCH in August 1960. In the decolonization period two main parties competed for power: the Parti Progressiste Nigerien led by Hamani Diori eventually gained control of the new state and banned all opposition parties. Diori was overthown in a military coup in 1974.

Since independence there have been a series of ethnic incidents in the Tuareg region in the north of the country. In 1984 a large number of TUAREG were expelled from Niger. In 1990 ethnic unrest resurfaced following the return to Niger of many TUAREG who had migrated to Libya and Algeria in the early 1980s to escape the drought. These incidents were caused by TUAREG dissatisfaction with the fact that the leader who came to power in 1987, Ali Saibou, did not fulfill his promise to rehabilitate the TUAREG who returned to Niger.

NIKIM An ethnic group living in Nigeria.

NINGALAM see GLANGALI.

NINGERUM An ethnic group of approximately 5,000, living in the mountainous region of western Papua New Guinea. They speak an indigenous language. Their subsistence is based upon the cultivation of mixed gardens, with bananas and sago as main crops. Their religious beliefs revolve around the worshipping of ancestral ghosts.

NINGO A subgroup of the ADANGBE.

NIPMUC A Native North American group numbering a few hundred, living in Massachusetts, U.S.A.

NISHANG see DALFA.

NISHGA (Nishka) A Native North American group numbering 5,000, many of whom live in four villages along the Nass River in British Columbia, Canada. They are related to the TSIMSHIAN and the GITKSAN.

The Nishga were, and remain, in the forefront of aboriginal land claims activism in Canada. They refused to recognize the reserve system and attempted to exert their control over the Nass Valley by sending a delegation to London, England, to appeal directly to the British monarch.

In 1973 they won a major judicial victory when the Supreme Court of Canada agreed that they had a legiti-mate title to their native lands. This forced a change of policy on the part of the Canadian government. At present they are in the final stages of negotiating a settlement of their land claims.

NISI see DAFLA.

NI-SO-MEH see AO.

NISQUALLY A Native North American group numbering 2,000, many of whom live on the Nisqually Federal Reservation, Thurston County, Washington, U.S.A. On account of the reservation's proximity to the city of Tacoma, many Nisqually are employed in the town.

NISSAN An ethnic group of several thousand, living in the Bismarck Archipelago of Papua New Guinea, east of the main island. They speak two dialects of an indigenous local language. Their subsistence is based on the cultivation of sweet potatoes and yams. They are practicing Catholics who also believe in traditional supernatural entities. Their most celebrated ceremonies are pig feasts.

NIUE ISLANDERS (Niueans) A Polynesian-speaking people numbering about 3,000 (1989). They inhabit a single island of 100 sq.m. located 700 miles west of Rarotonga. Niue Island is a self-governing state is in free association with New Zealand, where an estimated 1,200 Niueans live. The islanders are mainly Protestants. Niue Island possesses a limited amount of natural resources, and copra, tropical fruits, and high-quality honey constitute its most important products.

NIVKHI (from *Nivkh*, "man") The 6,000 Nivkhi live on the lower Amur River near its estuary and on the northern part of Sakhalin Island in Russia. The Nivkhi who lived in the southern part of the island were executed upon its annexation by the Soviet Union in 1945, as collaborators with the JAPANESE.

Their language is not related to any other known language. In 1931, it was given a Cyrillic alphabet, but little has been published. Russian serves as the literary language for the Nivkhi. The Nivkhi share a culture with their neighbors the NANI. Since Russian occupation and colonization of their region in the nineteenth century they have been assimilated into the RUSSIANS.

The Nivkhi religion is shamanist-animist with some Russian Orthodox influences. Like the AINU, they reserve a special place in their religion for worship of the bear.

NJAI A subgroup of the TIV.

NJEMP An ethnic group numbering c.9,000 living near Lake Barinao in the Rift Valley of Kenya. Their language, Maa (also spoken by the MASAAI), belongs to the Plains Nilotic family. Most Njemp have retained their traditional beliefs and rites, but a minority has converted to Christianity, mainly after receiving church schooling and medical services.

The Njemp are sedentary agriculturalists, although they keep cattle, considered their most important source of income and pride. Those living on the shores of Lake Baringo are engaged in fishing. While differing by occupation from the SAMBURU and MASAAI, the Njemp resemble these two groupings both culturally and socially, especially with regard to circumcision, the warrior system (*moran*), dress, and dance.

NKALU A subgroup of the IBO.

NKOLE (Nyamkole) A people living in the region of Ankole in southwestern Uganda. The name Nkole refers to the population of Ankole, consisting of two stratified groups: the IRU, who speak a Bantu dialect related to the language of the NYORO, which belongs to the group of Western Lacustrine Bantu languages, and the HIMA, who, although probably originally Nilotic-speakers, were linguistically absorbed by the IRU ma-

Nkole

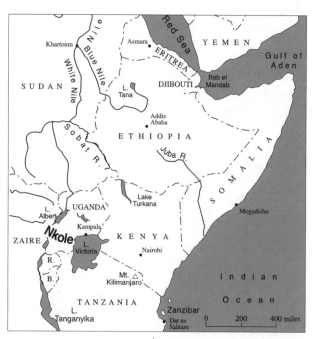

jority. The IRU are agriculturalists, living in loose settlements near their plantations. The HIMA are cattle-herders, breeding the longhorn cattle common among Nilotic people.

In the past, the Nkole worshiped a remote god, Lugaba, and various lesser gods and spirits. Most important were the spirits of ancestors, especially those of the ruling dynasty. The spirits had their own priests, although Lugaba had none. The clans had their own gods as well and their priests were members of the clan. Today the Nkole are largely Protestant Christians. (see also UGANDANS)

NKOMI A Myene-speaking ethnic group living in Gabon, around Lake Nkomi and in the Port Gentil Region. They are either Christians or follow traditional religions.

In the late nineteenth century the FRENCH signed treaties with some Nkomi chiefs allowing them to take over their region. During the French colonial period other ethnic groups such as the ESHIRA and the FANG settled in the Nkomi region around Lake Nkomi and hundreds of Nkomi migrated to Port Gentil.

NKOYA An ethnic group numbering under 50,000, living in southeastern Zambia. They speak Nkoya. The WANDYA are a subgroup of the Nkoya.

NKUM An ethnic group living in Nigeria.

NOANG A Malayo-Polynesian-speaking group numbering over 10,000, living in southern Vietnam. The Noang have preserved various elements of their traditional religion, particularly the use of sorcerors called *ibojou*.

NOAR A Mon-Khmer group living in Vietnam and Laos. They are often identified with the DUANE, JEH, MENAM, and SAYAN.

NOCTE An ethnic group, numbering 20,000 (1981), living in Arunachal Pradesh, India. They speak Naga, a member of the Tibeto-Burman family of languages.

The Nocte belong to the Mongoloid group. They are heavily tattooed on their faces and bodies. Their houses are built on stilts so that the ground floor can be used for keeping domestic animals. Their chiefs' houses are the largest in Arunachal Pradesh, and are constructed with massive blocks and wooden pillars. They have a system of male and female dormitories which play a crucial role in courtship.

NOE (Wanoe, Nhohwe) A subgroup of the ZEZURU.

NOGAI see NAGAIBAK.

NOGENG A subgroup of the TSWANA.

NOGHAI A people living primarily in several neighboring areas in the Caucasian region of Russia. According to the Soviet 1989 census they numbered 75,000. Their language belongs to the northwest Qypchaq group of Turkic languages. They consist of three groups, each speaking its own dialect: the Aq (lit. "white") Noghai dwelling in the Stavropol area and in the Qarachai-Cherkess Autonomous *Oblast* (Region); the Achiqulaq Noghai dwelling in the Chechen-Ingush Republic; and the Qara (lit. "black") Noghai dwelling in Daghestan. Their dialects are closely related. Literary Noghai, combining the Aq and Qara Noghai dialects, was established only in the late 1920s. In 1928 it was provided with a Roman alphabet, which was replaced in 1938 with a Cyrillic alphabet. Since the fourteenth century the Noghai have been Sunni Muslims of the Hanafi school. In 1888 many Noghai migrated to the Ottoman Empire, where they were assimilated by the TURKS.

The modern Noghai are a remnant of the once numerous Noghai Horde, a strong nomadic political entity which was formed in the fifteenth and sixteenth centuries but later disintegrated into a nomadic group that roamed with its herds in the steppes between the Ural and Dnieper Rivers. The Noghai first adopted a sedentary way of life in the Kuban River basin in the eighteenth century; in all other places, they became sedentary only in 1920. As nomads, they lived in large *yurts* (tents) which could be dismantled. As dwellers in permanent settlements, they adopted the Caucasian type of house.

Their economy is based on cattle-breeding and agriculture.

NOGHAIBAK see BASHKIRS, NAGAIBAK.

NOKHCHIY see CHECHEN.

NOLE A subgroup of the OROMO.

NONG A subgroup of the MNONG.

NOOTKA (Aht) A Native North American group numbering 6,000, living on Vancouver Island, British Columbia, Canada. As part of the West Coast Indian culture, they have traditionally been considered great whalers. Some members of the group own their own fishing vessels, while others are employed in the forest industry. (see also MAKAH)

NOP (To Lop) A Mon-Khmer group numbering a few thousand, living in southern Vietnam. They are often classed with the LAT and LAYA.

NORTHERN IRISH The 1.5 million inhabitants of Northern Ireland consist of two ethno-religious groups who are engaged in a prolonged civil war: some 1 million (60 percent) are Protestants of English and Scottish descent. They often refer to themselves as Ulstermen and consider themselves BRITISH. The remainder are Catholics and form part of the IRISH people living across the border in Ireland.

Protestant ascendancy in Northern Ireland dates back to the seventeenth century, when masses of Scottish Presbyterians, who were facing persecution by Anglicans, were transplanted to Ireland. Eventually these Presbyterian smallholders, who looked down upon Celtic culture, became the majority in the northern counties of Ulster (later Northern Ireland). Throughout the nineteenth century Protestants, feeling surrounded by hostile Catholics, struggled in vain to ward off Home Rule for Ireland. However, although they were unable to prevent the advent of the Irish Free State after World War I, their resistance won them separate status. Protestants believed that peaceful coexistence of the two religious communities was inconceivable and that Catholics posed a threat; they insisted on the need for separate jurisdiction.

In 1920 the British partitioned Ireland, cutting out a territory with a Protestant majority in Ulster which was to remain part of the United Kingdom. To ensure economic viability, some Catholic districts were added. The Northern Irish were granted a local parliament, the Stormont, with administration shared between the "motherland" and Ulster. Britain tolerated the Protestants' systematic economic and social discrimination of Catholics, who refused assimilation and boycotted Northern Irish political institutions. The close proximity of the Protestant and Catholic communities made the latter easy targets for discrimination.

Unlike the Republic of Ireland, Ulster underwent an industrial revolution. After the 1940s, however, industry declined, leading to high unemployment and adding fuel to the communal fire. Catholic resentment of fifty years of deprivation, lack of equal opportunities in housing and jobs, gerrymandering of voting districts, and other practices to protect Protestant privileges, exploded in the late 1960s, when a younger and more assertive generation came of age. When, in 1969, demands for equal rights were refused by the Stormont, armed rioting broke out in Belfast. The attack of a Catholic quarter by Protestant squads led Britain to send in troops, adjourn the Stormont, and establish direct rule. Attempts to restore order were met in the 1970s by Catholic urban guerrilla action and growing Protestant counterviolence. The Provos (the Provisional wing of the Irish Republican Army [IRA]) took up the defense of Catholic quarters and initiated terrorist attacks against Protestant strongholds. While Protestant radicals now fight a rearguard battle to maintain their prerogatives, IRA aims have expanded to include unification of both Irelands.

Britain failed to improve community relations or achieve a solution founded on powersharing and devolution of authority. Reforms deemed insufficient by Catholics were considered too threatening by Protestants and both camps regard British authorities as biased towards the other side.

While industry and urbanization are concentrated east of the Bann river, in the Protestant heartland, the poorer, rural, and heavily Catholic counties west of the Bann are particularly underdeveloped. Violence, as well as crime and alcoholism, is largely confined to laborers' ghettoes, where unemployment runs high. The Northern Irish conflict is largely over collective identity and borders: marches, parades, barricades, and bonfires are means of affirming or transgressing boundaries. Both communities live completely segregated lives, but each is a close-knit group that maintains strong social control over its members, often nurturing its prejudices and grievances. (see also BRITISH, IRISH)

NORWEGIANS The 4.5 million Norwegians live in a sparsely-populated country the size of Germany, in Northern Europe. The largest concentrations of population are found in southern Norway. The Norwegian language belongs to the Scandinavian branch of Germanic languages. As a result of long Danish domination, it exists today in two forms: the former official Danish-Norwegian Ryksmal, and folk Norwegian or Landsmal. The two are currently fusing to form neo-Norwegian, or Nynorsk. Until the recent boom in the oil industry, Norse lifestyles were largely dominated by agriculture and life at sea (fishing and the merchant marine).

In the eighth century petty kings commanding oligarchies of peasants-landowners colonized the moun-

tainous regions of coastal Scandinavia. The first unified monarchy was established in the ninth century. However, limited arable land resulted in overpopulation, the peasantry was displaced by an emerging aristocracy, and the new aristocrats were dissatisfied with the monarchy. These factors, combined with technical advances in shipping, caused many Norwegians to embark on Viking expeditions of conquest and dicovery. England and Scotland were terrorized by Viking raiders; in northern France and Sicily they established Norman rule. In expeditions to the east, the Faroe Islands, Iceland, and Greenland were settled.

In 1030 the Norwegians officially adopted Christianity. Soon after they became implicated in a series of inter-Scandinavian conflicts, in which independence was asserted and a strong hereditary monarchy was established. In 1397 the Union of Kalmar united Norway with Sweden and Denmark, creating what appeared to be a major power in Northern Europe, but the ensuing period was catastrophic. Plague decimated the population, while the combined onslaught of the Danish monarchy and German merchants virtually eradicated the local aristocracy. Large numbers of DANES settled the country, establishing their own aristocracy there.

Growing European demands for shipping timber permitted some economic growth in the sixteenth century, while throughout the following centuries, urban entrepreneurs profited from fishing and whaling. In order to export their wood and fish, Norwegians started building their own merchant marine — it was to grow into the world's third largest. Denmark's implication in the Napoleonic wars finally opened the way to dissolve the Union of Kalmar in 1809; despite a clamour for independence, however, the Norwegians were forced into a union with Sweden.

Throughout the nineteenth century economic expansion continued to fuel the Norwegians' longing for total independence, while the emergence of a national literature emancipated the Norwegian language from Danish influence. From the middle of the nineteenth century tensions mounted as the independence movement became more vocal. The Kingdom of Norway was proclaimed in 1905, but by then some 700,000 Norwegians migrated to North America. Despite its declaration of neutrality, Norway was occupied by Nazi Germany in 1940; following World War II a vast reconstruction program was begun and social-democratic governments developed an extensive social security system. From the 1970s, exploitation of North Sea oil further enriched the Norwegians. At the same time progressive redistribution policies remained in force.

above left: A Norwegian street scene
above right: A Norwegian fisherman
below: Norwegians in traditional dress

Only in the 1980s did inflation and unemployment erode the Norwegian welfare state, enabling the conservatives to take over the reins of government.

NRI   A subgroup of the IBO.

NSENGA   A Nyanja-speaking group numbering 200,000 living in southeast Zambia. In the eighteenth and nineteenth centuries they traded ivory with the Europeans and grew cotton. The Nsenga were originally part of the CHEWA group. In the 1870s they were conquered by the NGUNI, who intermarried with them and adopted their language.

NTHALI   A subgroup of the TUMBUKA.

NTUM   A subgroup of the FANG.

NTUNGWA   One of the two major divsions of the NGUNI, the other being the TEKELA. Major Ntungwa groups include the XHOSA, ZULU, and NDEBELE.

NU   see LUTZU.

NUBIANS   A people of northeastern Sudan; with a population of approximately 2.7 million, they constitute the largest ethnic group in the northern part of the country. The Nubians of the Halfa District and Dungulah speak Nubian, although most Nubians speak Arabic.

The Nubians, traditionally living in the Nile River valley linking Sudan with Egypt, have always been a settled people, living in towns and villages and cultivating irrigable land. The poverty of their region, however, encouraged them to migrate and they can now be found in all parts of Sudan and Egypt.

The Nubians include many subgroups such as the MAHA and, further south, the DONGOLAWIN (Dangla). The GERKID and the MIDOB of the Darfur area speak Nubian languages. (see also EGYPTIANS, SUDANESE)

NUER   A people of southern Sudan, numbering an estimated 1.4 million. Their language, Nuer, belongs to the Eastern Sudanic family of languages. Cattle are their basic economic unit and they play a major role in Nuer rites and beliefs, even among that segment of the population that has adopted Christianity.

Together with the LUO, NYAMANG, and SHILLUK, they form the regional opposition to the leadership of John Garang in the southern Sudan's war against the Khartoum government.

Nubians

Another group of Nuer are found in the lowlands of Gambela, on the Ethiopian border with Sudan. They are a mixed population of Sunni Muslims, Christians, and adherents of traditional African religions. During the late 1980s the Nuer came into conflict with the DINKA living in their region and with SUDANESE refugees. They are currently contesting the resettlement in their region of AMHARA and TIGRAY refugees. (see also ETHIOPIANS, SHILLUK, SUDANESE)

Nuer

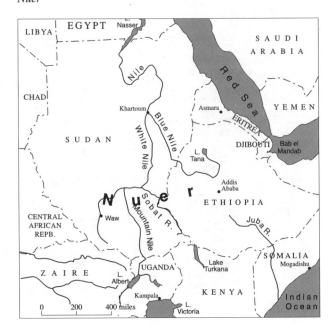

A Nubian boatman on the Nile River

NUNG see NHANG.

NUNUMA A small ethnic group living in northern Ghana and Burkina Faso. Together with other neighboring groups, the Nunuma are considered part of the GRUSI.

NUPE An ethnic group living mainly in the Niger State, Nigeria. They number about 1.2 million, 1.2 percent of Nigeria's total population. Mostly Muslims, they are divided into a large number of subgroups who speak related Nupe languages. Their precolonial state reached its zenith between the sixteenth and eighteenth centuries but fell to the BRITISH in the late nineteenth century.

Many Nupe are craftsmen organized into societies and guilds. Agriculture is another important occupation of the Nupe. (see also NIGERIANS)

NU-QUAY A subgroup of the AKHA.

NURESTANIS (Jadid) The general designation of a number of ethnic groups inhabiting the Nurestan region of Afghanistan. These groups are the KATI, VAIGALI (Vai or Vaialans), TREGAMI (Gambiri), ASHKUN, VAMAI, and PRASUN (Paruni). The KATI are called by their neighbors *Siyah-posh* ("black-clad") and the other groups are called *Safid-posh* ("white-clad"), referring to their traditional goat pelts and leggings.

The TREGAMI are sometimes regarded as a subgroup of the VAIGALI, and the VAMAI may be considered a subgroup of the ASHKUN. The speakers of the Bashgali dialect of Kati, a small part of whom inhabit an adjacent area in Pakistan, are sometimes regarded as a distinct subgroup of the KATI. In 1981 the overall number of Nurestanis was estimated at about 120,000, with the KATI (c.100,000) representing the majority

The Nurestani languages form a subgroup of their own in the Indo-Iranian branch of the Indo-European family of languages; they are sometimes regarded as a subgroup of the Dardic branch of the Indo-Iranian group. All Nurestani languages, save Kati, are unwritten; however, the use of Kati as a written language is very recent and its real extent in this capacity is still uncertain. In 1981 the main dialect of Kati was proclaimed "the Nurestani language" and made a national language of Afghanistan. Regular radio broadcasts and attempts to produce newspapers and elementary school textbooks were launched. All other Nurestani groups,

and de facto the KATI, continue to use Pashto as their literary language.

The Nurestanis have been Sunni Muslims of the Hanafi school since 1895–1896. Until then, they had resisted the Muslim conquest and rejected Islam. Their religion was a mixture of polytheism and animism, and exhibited some Hindu influences, especially the cult of Shiva. The pantheon differed from one place to another but it seems to have been headed by Imra, the creator, from whom stemmed other gods of varying degrees of importance. The Nurestanis also believed in a great number of demons and evil spirits whom they had to placate constantly. Some vestiges of pre-Islamic beliefs are retained to this day.

Nurestani houses are built of wood (Nurestan being one of the few wooded areas in Afghanistan) and are usually three storeys high. The upper floor serves as the living quarters and its flat roof is used as a threshing floor. The ground floor is used for sheltering livestock, and the middle floor for storage. The Nurestanis engage in the cultivation of cereals and legumes on small terraced and irrigated plots. They also raise goats and cattle in common pastures shared by the village. The diet is predominantly vegetarian and dairy.

The village consists of several quarters, each headed by an elected leader. Internal conflicts are judged by a gathering of the most respected members of the community. A sharp division is made between the Nurestanis and the *bari*, descendants of former slaves, who provide them with services such as carpentry and masonry.

Until the twentieth century the Nurestani were known as Kafirs ("infidels"). They were vitually independent until the Kabul agreement of 1893, in which Britain abandoned any claim to their territory, then called Kafiristan. In 1895 Abd al-Rahman, the king of Afghanistan (1880–1901), staged a campaign against the Kafirs. By 1896 the conquest of the area and its forced islamization were complete and the name of their province was changed to Nurestan ("land of light"). The name Jadid ("new") refers to the Nurestanis as new converts to Islam. (see also AFGHANS)

NURZAI A subgroup of the PASHTUN.

NUSU see LUTZU.

NYA see NGANASAN.

NYAKWAI A people living in northeastern Uganda, in the area of the KARAMOJONG cluster of peoples. They speak an Eastern Nilotic language and are pastoralists with a culture similar to that of the KARAMOJONG.

NYAKYUSA A people living in southern Tanzania, in the Rift Valley at the head of Lake Nyasa (Malawi). In 1967 they numbered 307,000. Their language belongs to the Southern Highland cluster of the Bantu group of the Niger-Kordofan language family. Today, the name "Nyakyusa" is used by a number of other groups of similar origins, speech, and culture, who consider themselves ethnic subgroups of the Nyakyusa people. Some other neighboring ethnic groups (such as the KISSII and NGONDE) were, and still are, being assimilated by the Nyakyusa.

Nyakyusa

Historically, Nakyusaland is divided into approximately 100 "princedoms," each headed by a chief. The basic social unit of the Nyakyusa was a unique system of "age-villages," each ideally occupied by men of approximately the same age with their wives and children. Boys usually left home at about the age of ten. Upon reaching adulthood and marrying, young people established their own settlement which later became politically, economically, and ritually autonomous. Nyakyusa villages are compact, composed of well-built houses, situated close together. (see also KISSII, TANZANIANS)

NYAMANG An ethnic group inhabiting part of southwestern Sudan. They speak Nuer, the language of

the NUER people. Some Nyamang are Christians, while others follow traditional African religions.

In recent years the Nyamang have opposed John Garang's war against the Arab-dominated central government of Sudan in Khartoum. (see also NUER, SHILLUK)

NYAMKOLE see NKOLE.

NYAMWEZI (in Swahili, "people of the moon," i.e., of the west) One of the largest peoples of west-central Tanzania, numbering 406,000 in 1967. Of heterogeneous origin, they belong linguistically to the Western Tanzanian Bantu Niger-Kordofan family of languages. Although they are akin to the SUKUMA in language and traditions, they have quite recently developed a unique and separate ethnic consciousness.

Historically the Nyamwezi were divided into a number of small states. At the end of the nineteenth century the Unyanyembe, the strongest among them, dominated the caravan trade, until then under Arab control. At that time the Nyamwezi town of Tabora was the most important trading center of the region. As the most prominent political force, the Nyamwezi assimilated a number of neighboring peoples such as the KIMBY, KONOG, SHUMBWA, TONGWE, BENDE, and HOLO-HOLO, who later became their ethnic subgroups.

Traditionally, Nyamwezi states were ruled by sacred kings (*ntemi*). The traditional Nyamwezi village is a dispersed rather than a compact settlement. They are primarily cultivators although they also raise cattle. In modern times their traditional agriculture has declined mainly due to land erosion and an inadequate water supply.

NYANG An ethnic group living in Cameroon.

NYANGATOM (Bume) An ethnic group numbering 6,000 (1980s), living in the lower Omo Valley, north of Lake Turkana (Ethiopian-Kenya-Sudanese borderlands). They are related to the Toposa-speaking cattle-raising groups (TOPOSA, TURKANA, KARAMOJONG) in Kenya, the Sudan, and Uganda. The Nyangatom adhere to traditional beliefs. Their social organization is marked by age-grading. In the 1980s the Nyangatom were affected by recurring droughts, the presence of a Sudanese guerrilla organization, and systematic cattle-raids.

NYANGEA see NAPORE.

NYANJA (Ngungwe) An ethnic group numbering 1.2 million, living on the east littoral of Lake Nyasa

(Malawi) and in the Shire River basin, Malawi. There are also Nyanja in the Tete District of Mozambique. They speak Nyanja, and are either Christians or followers of traditional African religions. They are agriculturalists, and have a matrilineal descent system. The Nyanja were ruled by a chief who divided their territory among headmen.

The Nyanja came in contact with Anglican missionaries in the late nineteenth century, and as a result many speak English rather than Portuguese. They are descendants of the Maravi Empire, which rose prior to the sixteenth century.

The resettlement policies of the PORTUGUESE caused many Nyanja to flee to Tanzania. Other Nyanja contributed significant numbers to the war against the PORTUGUESE. (see also MALAWIANS, MOZAMBICANS)

Nyanja

NYANTRUKU   A subgroup of the YORUBA living in Nigeria.

NYANYEKE-HUMBE   see ANGOLANS.

NYIHA   An ethnic group related to the NKOYA living in Zambia.

NYINBA   (Barthapalya,) An ethnic group, numbering a few thousand, living along the Tibetan border with Nepal. They speak a Tibetan dialect and are Tibetan Mahayana Buddhists. They cultivate grains and vegetables and herd cattle. Because of the poor agricultural conditions in their region, which ranges in elevation from 7,500 to 11,000 ft., they are also dependent on the gathering of salt which they trade with the NEPALI for food.

NYMYLYN   A subgroup of the KORYAK. They were traditionally reindeer herders.

NYOKA   An ethnic group related to the NYIHA living in Zambia.

NYONYOSE   A subgroup of the MOSSI.

NYORO   (Banyoro) A people living in western Uganda, on the high plateau east of Lake Albert. Their language is one of the Western Lacustrine Bantu languages. Most Nyoro are agriculturalists, but the ruling elite are cattle-herders. The latter were originally Nilotic-speakers, but became linguistically assimilated into the sedentary majority.

The Nyoro played an important role in a system of inter-ethnic trade and exchange. As ironworkers they produced hoes which were bartered for cattle and other goods with their northern neighbors. They established a trading network over considerable distances and bartering with the TESO, KUMAN, LANGO, ACHOLI, and ALUR.

There are over one hundred Nyoro clans. Politically they constitute a stratified society with an aristocracy

Nyoro

of HIMA descent. Their ancient kingdom of Bunyoro formed the core of the kingdom of Kitara, which in the fifteenth century controlled most of present-day Uganda. It was ruled by the Bachwezi dynasty, which emerged from the HIMA aristocracy. At some time in the sixteenth century, a new HIMA dynasty, the Bito, took power in Kitara, but lost control over most of its empire. The kingdom continued to disintegrate and was reduced to the core area of Bunyoro when in 1870 Kabalega came to power. After reforming the military into a standing army, he changed Bunyoro from a political entity largely controlled by the Hima aristocracy into a highly centralized kingdom. He cut the aristocracy's power and based his own rule on the army, which was recruited mainly from the majority IRU as well as from other ethnic groups, especially the LANGO and the ACHOLI.

Kabalega's attempts to expand his kingdom were thwarted by the GANDA and the BRITISH, who exiled him to the Seychelles in 1899. The Bunyoro kingdom retained a special status within Uganda, but lost some of its territories to the Buganda kingdom, which were returned shortly before independence. The kingdom was finally abolished by the constitutional reform of 1967.

The traditional Nyoro religion is characterized by ancestor worship with specialized priests, or *muchwezi*, a term used to describe both priests and ancestor spirits. The king's ancestors are of special importance and their graves play an important role. The Nyoro also have rainmakers and healers. (see also KIGA, SOGA, TORO)

NYUBA   A subgroup of the KARANGA.

NYULI   (Banyuli) One of several smaller Bantu groups settled in southeast Uganda, between Mount Elgon and Busoga. Their language, Lunyuli, is related to Lugishu and belongs to the group of Eastern Lacustrine Bantu family of languages.

According to their own tradition, they came from the Lake Victoria region to Busoga. About half migrated further north to the Bukedi District. They are culturally related to the SOGA, their neighbors to the south.

NZABI   see BANDJABI.

N'ZAKARA   An ethnic group, numbering around 82,000, living in the Central African Republic. They are a residual group of the SABANGA, who had a powerful kingdom in the nineteenth century.

NZEMA   (Nzima) An Akan-speaking group living in the Western Region of Ghana between the Tano and Ankobra Rivers. The first president of Ghana, Kwame Nkrumah, was a member of the Nzema group. (see also AKAN)

O

OBAMBA (Ambamba or Mbamba) A Mbete-speaking group living in the northern part of the Franceville Region and in the Okondja Region, Gabon.

OBORRA A subgroup of the OROMO.

OCHOLLO A subgroup of the GAMO.

ODODOP A subgroup of the IBIBIO.

OESTERREICHER see AUSTRIANS.

OGADEN A clan of the SOMALI.

OGHUZ A subgroup of the TURKMEN.

OGLALA A subgroup of the SIOUX.

OGONI A subgroup of the IBIBIO.

OGUZ see GAGAUZ.

OINKE A subgroup of the MALINKE living in Guinea.

OJANG see MAJANGIR.

OJIBWA see CHIPPEWA.

OKAK An ethnic group related to the FANG, living in Gabon.

OKANAGAN A Native North American group, numbering 2,300, living in British Columbia, Canada. Traditionally they were a hunting people but today they are agriculturalists raising cattle and growing a variety of crops.

OKANDE An ethnic group living in Gabon on both sides of the middle Ogooue River.

Okanagan

OKEBO An ethnic group living in Zaire. (see also ALUR)

OKIEK A group of Kalenjin-speaking hunters and gatherers who live in forest regions, adjacent to areas inhabited by the KALENJIN, in Kenya. Their name derives from the Kalenjin word meaning "hunter."

OKINAWANS (s.d Okinawajin, Ryukyujin; Ryukyu Islanders) Inhabitants of the Ryukyu Islands, stretching approximately 700 miles between Japan and Taiwan. They number over one million and are culturally similar to the JAPANESE. They have, however, preserved a distinct dialect and had a long history as an independent kingdom before their occupation by the JAPANESE under the emperor Meiji in 1872. Most islanders live on the large island of Okinawa.

Traditionally the Okinawans engaged in agriculture and fishing but these are rapidly being supplanted by tourism and providing services to American soldiers stationed on some eighty-eight bases there. Considerable contact with these soldiers has resulted in a significant percentage of the population being of mixed American and Okinawan origin. Such people enjoy practically no rights and are often subject to discriminatory policies.

The AMERICANS captured Okinawa from the JAPANESE in 1945 in a campaign in which over 110,000 Okinawans were killed by both American troops and the retreating Japanese armies who challenged the loyalty of the local population. The islands were returned to Japan in 1972: 20 percent of Okinawa's territory was to remain under American rule as military bases. Under the AMERICANS, the Okinawans enjoyed limited autonomy, including a chief executive in power from 1968–1972, but this was curtailed by the JAPANESE. A further problem facing the Okinawans today is the high rate of unemployment stemming from both the loss of arable land and the rapid influx of Japanese consumer goods, precluding the establishment of local industry.

Attempts by the JAPANESE to create local industry such as oil and aluminum processing were made more to avoid the restrictive ecological guidelines on the Japanese mainland, and have caused considerable environmental damage. All these factors have led to the emergence of several independence-minded groups that play an increasing role in local politics.

OKOBA   A subgroup of the IBO.

OKO-JUWOI   An ethnic group living in the Andaman Islands in the Indian Ocean. They subsist on fishing, gathering, and small-scale cultivation.

OLMEC   see MEXICANS.

OLOH KAHAYAN   An ethnic group living on the Indonesian island of Kalimantan (Borneo). (see also DAYAK)

OLYK MARI   see MARI.

OMAGUA   A Tupi-speaking Native American agricultural ethnic group of the upper Amazon River in Brazil. They are now almost extinct.

OMAHA   A Native North American group, numbering 2,000, many of whom live on the Omaha Federal Reservation in Thurston County, Nebraska, U.S.A. Traditionally hunters of buffalo and cultivators of maize, today many raise cattle and cultivate grain.

Omaha

OMAITO   An ethnic group numbering about 25,000, found in the Indian state of Orissa. They are primarily Hindus and engage in agriculture.

OMANIS   (s.d. Umaniyin) An Arab people numbering c.1.5 million, living in Oman (until 1971: Muscat and Oman). Arabic-speaking Omanis, forming three-quarters of the population (the rest are INDIAN, PAKISTANI, IRANIAN, and SOMALI), are divided between some 200 tribes.

Small unassimilated pre-Arab peoples live in mountain areas. A few thousand in Dhofar (Zufar) still speak an ancient South Arabic language, as do HARASIIS (Harsuusi) in the central desert Jiddat plateau. Another group speaks Komzari (an Iranian dialect). Among the fishermen and traders on the coasts, there are ARABS with a strong African element, who presumably descend from slaves.

86 percent of the population is Muslim. While most are Sunnis, the sedentary peasants and artisans living in the well-watered and fertile valleys of the mountainous interior are Ibadi Shi'ites.

Historically, the restive interior contrasts with the well-controlled seat of central authority, the predominantly Sunni seaports along the coast. Oman's climactic conditions allow agriculture mainly in Batinah, along the east coast, and in the interior, south of Hajjar, the country's most populated region. The southern part of Oman does not permit permanent settlement. Dhofar is populated by semi-nomadic pastoralists; one-fifth of the Omanis are nomads.

In the fourteenth and fifteenth centuries, Omani merchants traded caravan goods overseas from the port of Suhar. From 1508 to 1688, Muscat (Masqat) was in the hands of the PORTUGUESE, who used it on their way to Goa. In the eighteenth century Ibn Sa'id consolidated Arab power in Zanzibar and on the East African coast. The slave trade brought Oman prosperity, and an alliance of traders and rulers was able to transform Muscat into a major Indian Ocean power and the leading port of the Persian Gulf. During the zenith of Oman's power (1800–1860) many Omanis migrated to Zanzibar, and for a time, the island was the center of Oman's commercial empire. In 1856, however, it lost Zanzibar and the slave islands off the East African coast, while Britain's proscription of the traffic in slaves and arms led to prolonged economic depression.

In the 1930s Oman's rulers tried to prevent social unrest by imposing medieval isolation on the state. In 1970, when a Dhofar secessionist movement, supported by South Yemen, threatened the country's integrity, the sultan cautiously opened up his country to outside influence.

The rebels were defeated in 1973; that same year Oman experienced a boom in oil production. Reserves, however, are meager and alternative sources of future income are uncertain.

OMASUYO   A subgroup of the AYMARA.

OMEGUA   A Native South American group living in Venezuela.

OMETO   (Domete) A people numbering 275,000 (1980s) who live in the eastern part of the Kefa Province, Ethiopia. They speak Welamo and are either Ethiopian Orthodox Christians, Sunni Muslims, or adherents of traditional beliefs.

ONA   A Native South American group living in Tierra del Fuego, southern Argentina. Of the 10,000 original inhabitants of Tierra del Fuego, there remain today only a few persons of mixed blood. (see also ARGENTINIANS)

ONDA'E   A subgroup of the TORADJA.

ONDO   A subgroup of the YORUBA living in Nigeria.

ONEIDA   A Native North American group, the smallest member of the IROQUOIS CONFEDERACY in the United States. They live in New York and in Wisconsin. In Canada, however, where they are found only in the province of Ontario, they number more than 5,000.

ONGE   An ethnic group numbering 10,000 (1981), located in the Andaman Islands, India. Living in Little Andaman, with some in Rutland Island, they are the most widespread of the Andaman aborigines. Their language is unclassified.

The Onge are organized into clans with well-defined hunting boundaries for each group. There is no permanent Onge habitation or village in any part of Little Andaman. Until recently they were hunters and gatherers, but they now they live in quarters built for them by the administration in Little Andaman Island and work in plantations established in their region by the government. (see also SENTINELESE)

ONISHTA-AWKA   A subgroup of the IBO.

ONONDAGA   A Native North American group, part of the IROQUOIS CONFEDERACY. About 800 live in New York, and another 900 in Ontario, Canada.

ONO NIHA   see NIASANS.

ONTONG JAVA   Inhabitants of the island of Ontong Java (Lord Howe's Island) in the Solomon Islands, in the southwest Pacific Ocean. Most of their traditional beliefs have been transformed by Anglican missionaries.

ORAKZAI   A subgroup of the PASHTUN.

ORANG AMBON   see AMBONESE.

ORANG ASLI   see SEMANG.

ORANG BABIAN   see BAWEAN ISLANDERS.

ORANG DARAT   see KUBU.

ORANG GLAI   see RAGLAI.

ORANG KEPOR   A subgroup of the KUBU.

ORANG LOM   see KUBU.

ORANG MALUKA SELATAN   see AMBONESE.

ORANG MAPOR   see KUBU.

ORANG MELAYU   see DAYAK.

ORANG RAWAS   see KUBU.

ORANG TIMOR ASLI   see ATONI.

ORANG UTAN   see KUBU.

ORAON   (Dhangara, s.d. Kurukh, Kurunkh) An ethnic group, numbering 1.9 million (1981), living in the states of Bihar, Madhya Pradesh, Maharashtra, Orissa, and West Bengal, in India, and in Bangladesh. They speak Kurukh and Sadri, languages belonging to the Dravidian family.

According to tradition, the Oraon originally hailed from Gujarat but were expelled from their land. The Oraon of Orissa have no villages exclusively their own, although they form the dominant part of the population in many villages. In Orissa, before building a new house or founding a new settlement, the Oraon employ magical-religious procedures to select the site.

Oraon

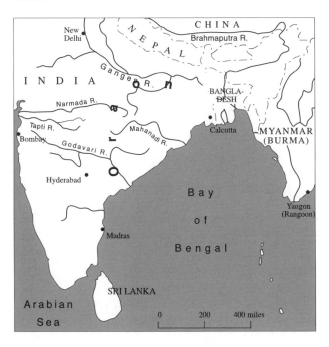

Villages have a bachelors' house (*dhumkuria*) where unmarried males are obliged to sleep.

In Bangladesh, the Oraon live in the Rangpur, Dinajpur, Bogra, and Rajshahi districts. They are said to have migrated to Bangladesh from the hilly areas of Orissa. They worship the sun and other deities as well as the principal Hindu deities and those of the SANTAL.

ORATTA   A subgroup of the IBO.

ORIYA   The c.27 million inhabitants of the state of Orissa, India. Their language, also called Oriya, belongs to the Indo-Aryan branch of the Indo-European family of languages.

Orissa has had a long history, and its culture has been influenced not only by neighboring cultures, but also by its former Hindu, Muslim, and British rulers. It has an exalted place in ancient Indian history; in 261 B.C.E. the emperor Asoka fought a bloody battle to conquer Kalinga, as it was then known, and became disenchanted with war at the sight of the aftermath of the battle. He became a Buddhist and helped spread Buddhism throughout India and South Asia.

Orissa's economy includes the cultivation of rice, betel leaves, coconuts, coffee, cocoa, spices, and fruit; raising dometic animals, the manufacture of cotton textiles, and local industrial arts are also important.

ORKNEY ISLANDERS   (Orcadians) Some 20,000 people inhabit the Orkneys, a group of islands northeast of Scotland. Their local dialect of English is derived from early forms of lowland Scottish English mixed with Norn, a Norwegian dialect which died out as a separate language in the seventeenth century. The people, of Norse and Scots origin, are now primarily Protestant. They have benefited from the prosperity brought by commercial agriculture and the North Sea oil industry. Fishing and tourism are also significant sources of revenue.

ORMURI   (Baraki, Bargista) An ethnic group living in the Logar Valley south of Kabul, Afghanistan, and in the Kaniguram area of Pakistan. They are estimated as numbering c.100 in Afghanistan and c.1000 in Pakistan.

The Ormuri language belongs to the eastern group of Iranian languages and consists of two dialects, one spoken in Logar and the other in Kaniguram (regarded as more archaic). The Ormuris are Sunni Muslims of the Hanafi religious school. They are rapidly being assimilated linguistically into the TAJIK in Afghanistan and the PASHTUN in both Afghanistan and Pakistan.

The Ormuri of Logar are mainly agriculturalists and those of Kaniguram are artisans and tradesmen. (see also AFGHANS)

OROCHI   One of the four NANI groups.

OROK   One of the four NANI groups.

OROKAIVA   An ethnic group of approximately 30,000, living in the lowlands of northeastern Papua New Guinea. They speak an indigenous regional language. They are slash and burn cultivators, with their main crop being taro. They have been heavily influenced by the Anglican church. Their major indigenous rituals are associated with the taro cult.

OROKOLO   An ethnic group of approximately 10,000, living near Orokolo Bay on the southern coast of Papua New Guinea. They speak an indigenous regional language. They are gardeners, hunters, and fishermen. They believe in spirits of the dead and of nature. Many of their ceremonies are characterized by decorative masks.

OROMO   (Galla) Numerically the largest people in Ethiopia. For political reasons, the numbers of the 1984 census (12.4 million) were probably too low. Oromo-speakers (Afaan Oromo, Orominya) now make up 40–50 percent of the total population of the ETHIOPIANS and live in most provinces of the country. They are the majority population in the provinces of Shoa (including Addis Ababa), Wallo, Wallagga, Kefa, Illubabor, Harage, Bale, Arsi, and Sidamo. They also live in southern Tigray, southern Gojjam, and part of Gemu Gofa. The degree of urbanization among the Oromo is relatively high. An Oromo-speaking population of about 240,000 lives in northern Kenya, and a small minority lives in Somalia. Between 1978 and 1991, Somalia also hosted about 250,000 to 300,000 Oromo refugees. In the 1980s both these trends contributed to the growth of a Oromo nationalism. Most Oromo are Sunni Muslims (55–60 percent), followed by Ethiopian Orthodox Christians (30–35 percent), and members of the Ethiopian Protestant Mekane Yesus or Roman Catholic Churches (several hundred thousand). The influence of Islam has grown constantly since the eighteenth century, but there are also traces of an older legacy of islamization between the thirteenth and fifteenth centuries. A small minority of Oromo still adhere to traditional beliefs (Oromee).

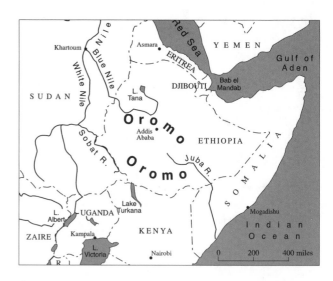

Oromo

The Oromo are mainly agriculturalists and cattle-raisers, living in the most fertile part of Ethiopia, the general altitude being 5,000 to 8,000 feet. Major cash-crops such as coffee and the narcotic *qat* are grown, as well as all major grains (teff, wheat, barley), which made their lands of special interest to settlers from the north (AMHARA, TIGRAY). Agriculture is sometimes intensified by terracing, irrigation, rain-pools and elaborate systems of wells. Some subgroups in the Sidamo province are specialized cattle-raisers. This, together with nomadic pastoralism, gave Oromo culture a specific pattern, but it was more a secondary development. The historical mode of livelihood among the Oromo was a combination of highland farming and lowland cattle-breeding.

Most of the southern Oromo area became incorporated into the Ethiopian Empire between 1868 and 1899. The more northerly Oromo participated since the eighteenth century in imperial Ethiopian politics, eventually dominating the imperial court during the first half of the nineteenth century.

The inclusion of the Oromo into the Ethiopian empire gave them a disadvantaged and discriminated status. The ethnonym "Galla," used since the sixteenth century in written sources (Ethiopian, Arabic, Portuguese), became associated by Oromo nationalists with such discrimination. During the 1970s, the term "Oromo" (connected since the 1840s in European writings with the specific religious beliefs among the Galla) became used for national mobilization and public self-identification.

Between 1974 and 1991 several Oromo organizations participated in guerrilla activities against

Mengistu Haile Mariam's regime. Major organizations today are the Oromo Liberation Front (OLF), the Oromo People's Democratic Organization (OPDO), the Islamic Front for the Liberation of Oromia (IFLO), the Oromo-Abbo Liberation Front (OALF), and the United Oromo People's Leadership (UOPL).

During the sixteenth and seventeenth centuries the Oromo became a major challenge for the Ethiopian Empire. While their original settlements seem to have been in the highlands of the Bale region, they had begun to settle in regions deserted after wars. By that process, remaining populations were often assimilated.

Historically the Oromo were divided into an eastern (*baretuma*) and a western (*borana*) half. Each half included segmentary clusters organized in federations. The Oromo polities included hierarchized status groups, based on a division of labor between cattle-raisers, agriculturalists, and stigmatized castes. The ruling strata of these federations dominated a political structure based on an age- and generation-grading system known as *gadaa*. Access to temporal political office was organized according to age and by elections. Comparable *gadaa* existed among other peoples speaking eastern Cushitic languages (HADIYA, SIDAMO, KONSO, DARASA, ARBORE).

During the eighteenth and nineteenth centuries, local states evolved among several subgroups of the Oromo. The decline of the *gadaa* polities, state-building, incorporation into the Ethiopian empire, and religious conversions, contributed to the processes of acculturation into the AMHARA or SOMALI, but many distinctive cultural features were retained.

Three major divisions exist among the Oromo: northern, western-central, and eastern. The northern groups include the RAYYA (Azebo) in southern Tigray, and the WALLO (Yajju) in Wallo and northern Shoa. Among the Wallo the degree of assimilation into the dominant AMHARA population is particularly high. The northern Oromo are mainly Muslims, but many converted during the nineteenth century to Ethiopian Orthodox Christianity.

The western and central groups include the large federations (clan-cluster) of the MACHA (in western Shoa, southern Gojjam, Wallaga, Illubabor, Kefa), the TULAMA (in Shoa), the KARAYU (in the Awash Valley), and the ARSI (in Arussi, Bale, and northern Sidamo).

Ethiopian Orthodox Christianity is strong among the TULAMA and eastern MACHA, Islam among the southwestern MACHA. Among the TULAMA, the Muslim Worji became an urbanized trading community.

Protestant minorities are particularly strong among the MACHA.

The eastern Oromo include the federations of the ITTU, ANIA, the AFRAN QALLUU (OBORRA, ALA, NOLE, JARSO), and Oromo-speakers among the GURGURA and BABILLE, all in northern Hararge. The eastern Oromo are sometimes also called "Baretuma" (the former ruling stratum) or "Kottuu" (peasants). They are predominantly Muslims. Mixed Oromo-Somali populations (GURGURA, JARSO) live in the vicinity of the towns of Harar and Diredawa.

The southern groups include the GUJJI (northern Sidamo), BORANA (southern Sidamo and northern Kenya), GABRA (camel-herders and former vassals of the BORANA, east of Lake Turkana in northern Kenya), and the TANA-ORMA (along the Tana River in northern Kenya).

The GABRA live in a very dry desert area. The GUJJI (1984: 480,000) and the BORANA (1984: 238,000) are specialized cattle-breeders, with strong remants of the *gadaa* system. Traces of the old religion (Oromee) are strong among them, but Islam is increasing. Culturally mixed groups in southern Sidamo are the GARRI, GURRA, GERRI, GERRI-MERO (agriculturalists in the Juba valley), and SAKUYE (Ajuran). (see also AMHARA, ETHIOPIANS, SOMALI)

OROSHORI (Roshorvi) An ethnic group living in a small area of the upper reaches of the Burtang River in the Mountain Badakhshan Autonomous *Oblast* (Region) of Tajikistan, mainly in the village of Roshorv and in some adjacent smaller villages. The last estimation of their number, dating from the late 1970s, puts them at about 2,000.

The Oroshori language belongs to the Pamir branch of the southeast subgroup of Iranian languages. It is unwritten, and the Tajik language is used for culture and communications with other ethnic groups of the region. The Oroshori have belonged to the Isma'ili sect of Islam since the eleventh century. They are mainly agriculturalists. Not listed separately in Soviet demographic statistics, until recently they were regarded as part of the TAJIK people.

ORRI A subgroup of the IBIBIO.

ORU A subgroup of the IBO.

ORUNGU An ethnic group living in Gabon. They once inhabited the Ogooue River delta but moved northward and inland in the nineteenth century. They speak Myene and are mostly adherents of traditional religions.

During the eighteenth and nineteenth centuries they developed a centralized kingdom that became involved in the slave trade. At first they migrated to a region called Sangatanga ("shallow waters") to avoid British anti-slavery patrols, following the abolition of slavery in the early nineteenth century, but they eventually succumbed to pressure by the BRITISH and abandoned the slave trade. In the late nineteenth century their chiefs signed treaties with the FRENCH, allowing them to colonize the area.

The Orungu did not accept the missions and were thus denied a western education. For that reason they did not play an important role in the French colonial administration. During the colonial period most abandoned their original homeland and only a small minority remained there after Gabon's independence in 1960.

OSAGE   (Wazhazhe) A large Native North American group numbering 7,500, many of whom live on the Federal Trust Area in Oklahoma. They are related to the OMAHA.

Earthen hut dwellers and cultivators of maize, they were removed to the Indian Territory in 1870. Oil was discovered on their land during the earlier part of the century, making the group one of the wealthiest Native North American peoples.

OSSET   (Oset s.d. Iron, Digor) A people inhabiting the North Ossetian republic of Russia and the South Ossetian Autonomous *Oblast* of Georgia. The internationally-accepted designation of the people as Osset stems from "Os", their appellation in Georgian. According to the Soviet 1989 census they numbered nearly 600,000.

The Osset language belongs to the northeast subgroup of Iranian languages and consists of two main dialects: Iron, spoken by most of the Osset, and Digor, spoken in some valleys in the western part of the North Ossetian republic. The Digor dialect is regarded as more archaic. Since the twelfth century, Iron-speakers have been Eastern Orthodox Christians. Speakers of Digor, comprising about one-quarter of the Osset, were converted from Christianity to Sunni Islam of the Hanafi school in the seventeenth and eighteenth centuries.

The substantial differences in dialect, and especially the adherence to different religions, shaped different Iron and Digor awarenesses, with each group regard-

Osset

ing itself as a separate entity. This phenomenon has not yet been completely overcome. Osset in Georgia (s.d. occasionally Tuallag), regard themselves as a subgroup or, more recently, an integral part of the Iron, belonging to the same religion and speaking virtually the same dialect, although it combines lexical borrowings from Georgian. An unknown number of Digor had left the Caucasus in the period 1859–1864 with the great exodus of North Caucasian Muslims to the Ottoman empire; although some of their descendants retain Digor as their mother tongue, most were assimilated by the CHERKESS and, to a lesser extent, by the TURKS.

The Osset are directly descended from the once-numerous and powerful Allan tribes that roamed with their herds in the steppes near the Black and Azov Seas and the northern Caucasus as early as the first century C.E. Osset territories were gradually incorporated into the Russian empire in the 1820s. In 1921 the northern Ossetian territories were proclaimed the Ossetian *Okrug* (district) of the Mountain Autonomous Soviet Socialist Republic within the framework of the Russian Soviet Socialist Federated Republic. In 1924 they were given the status of autonomous *oblast* and in 1936 that of an autonomous republic. The southern Ossetian territory was given the status of an Autonomous *Oblast* in 1922. With the collapse of the Soviet Union the latent tensions between Osset and GEORGIANS in the South-Ossetian Autonomous *Oblast*, sharpened by the demands of the South Ossetian national movement to secede from Georgia and unite with the North Ossetian Republic, led to severe armed clashes. Latent tensions between Osset and INGUSH in North Ossetia also led to conflict in that republic.

The complicated history of the Osset literary language deserves special mention. The Allan, ancestors of the Osset, used the Greek alphabet (as evidenced by an inscription dated c.941). Attempts at reducing Osset to writing in the Cyrillic alphabet of Church Slavonic and in the Georgian script were undertaken in the eighteenth century. By the mid-nineteenth century literary Osset was established on the basis of the Iron dialect. From 1844 to 1923 the Russian Cyrillic alphabet was employed; in 1923 this was replaced by the Roman alphabet. At the same time a separate literary language for the Muslim Osset based on the Digor dialect and Roman alphabet was also introduced, preceded by a number of attempts at using the Arabic script. In 1938 Iron-based literary Osset reverted once more to the Russian Cyrillic alphabet in North Ossetia, and to the Georgian alphabet in South Ossetia. In that year the Digor-based (Muslim) literary Osset was abolished. Finally, in 1954 the North Ossetian Cyrillic-based script replaced the Georgian-based writing system in South Ossetia. Only since then has unified literary Osset taken its final form.

The first collections of Osset folklore were published by Russian scholars in the period 1860–1880. Written literature in Osset dates back to the second half of the nineteenth century. (see also QARACHAI)

OSTYAK   (Khanty) An ethnic group living in western Siberia. Together with the MANSI they form the VOGUL people.

OSUDOKUA   A subgroup of the ADANGBE.

OT   see PUNAN.

OTAVALO   A Native South American group living in the Andean uplands of Imbabura Province, northern Ecuador. The city of Otavalo, the commercial and political center of the region, has a mostly white and *mestizo* population; the Otavalo Indians live among the hills and valleys of the outlying areas. The population is estimated at several thousand, divided among a number of distinct tribes, each of which is bounded by geographic feature such as rivers or ravines.

Each tribe has its own traditions. The PUNYARO are basket makers and hat knitters; the SAN JUAN are cotton fabric weavers; the PEGUCHE and the ILUMAN are cashmir fabric weavers; the CARABUELA are poncho weavers; the QUICHICHE are bedspread weavers; the PUCARA knit fans and mats from a large, thick, native herb; and the CALPANQUI make pottery. Some Otavalo who live near the city have become textile factory workers; others have be-

come day laborers, domestics, and construction workers. Most Otavalo are farmers, raising barley, corn, quinoa, and other crops. Their crafts are sold around the world.

Most Otavalo are highly literate: in addition to the Quechua language, which they adopted after Spanish missionaries used it as the common language to convert all Andean Indians, they are fluent in Spanish.

OT BALUI   An ethnic group living on the Indonesian island of Kalimantan (Borneo). (see also DAYAK)

OT DANUM   An ethnic group living on the Indonesian island of Kalimantan (Borneo). (see also DAYAK)

OT MARUWEI   An ethnic group living on the Indonesian island of Kalimantan (Borneo). (see also DAYAK)

OTO   A Native North American, group numbering 1,500, most of whom live on the Otoe-Missouria Federal Trust Area in Noble County, Oklahoma. They are earthen-hut dwellers and cultivate maize. They were removed to the Indian Territory in 1870.

OTOMAC   A Native South American group living in eastern Venezuela, in the lower basin of the Orinoco River. They are primarily agriculturalists, their staple crop being maize. They fertilize their fields using the flood waters of the Orinoco River.

OTOMI   An generic term for several culturally similar indigenous groups inhabiting Mexico's central plateau.

Otomi

The linguistic label "Otomi" is applied to at least four closely-related languages spoken by these farming people. Their economy ranges from complete subsistence agriculture and animal husbandry to cash cropping, their settlement patterns from dispersed to highly concentrated, housing from brush shelter to concrete-block homes, and dress from the most traditional to the most contemporary.

The Otomi kinship system is based on godparenthood, and the reciprocal privileges and obligations this entails. The religious ceremonies of the most rural Otomi, while fundamentally Catholic, contain pre-Christian elements. (see also MEXICANS, NAHUA)

OT SIAU   An ethnic group living on the Indonesian island of Kalimantan (Borneo). (see also DAYAK)

OTTAWA   A Native North American group of about 4,000, 2,500 of whom live in Ontario, Canada, 450 in Oklahoma, and the rest in Michigan and Kansas.

They belong to the group of woodland Indians who became allies of the BRITISH against the FRENCH in North America. Siding with the BRITISH against the AMERICANS in the war of 1812, they were removed first to the Ohio Valley and then to the Indian Territory.

OT USU   An ethnic group living on the Indonesian island of Kalimantan (Borneo). (see also DAYAK)

Ottawa

OUASSOULOUNKE   (Wasulunka) An ethnic group living in the southeastern part of upper Guinea.

OULAD DELIM   A Berber people living in the southwest region of Western Sahara. In 1974 they numbered approximately 5,500. They are descendants of the founders of the Almoravid, an Islamic reform movement of the eleventh century, and arrived in the Western Sahara in the thirteenth and fourteenth centuries.

During the sixteenth century, the Oulad Delim were described by travelers to their region as a people who possessed "neither dominion nor tribute". However, during the eighteenth century they began to gain power over other groups by force. Until the arrival of the SPANIARDS in the end of the nineteenth century, they were involved in many tribal conflicts and wars. At first the Oulad Delim resisted the SPANIARDS, but a *modus vivendi* was gradually established between them, which included trade agreements.

During the colonial period the Oulad Delim were forced to stop raiding other groups and thus lost the base of their economy. As a result, many joined the Spanish army and police force. In 1975, when Spain did not fulfill its promise to grant self-determination to the people of Western Sahara and allowed Morocco to enter the territory, most of the Oulad Delim, including those in the army, gave their support to the Polisario Front.

Now, most of the Oulad Delim are sedentary.

OULED HEMAT   see DJOHEINA.

OULED MANSOUR   A subgroup of the HASSAUNA.

OULED MEHAREB   A subgroup of the HASSAUNA.

OULED RACHID   see DJOHEINA.

OUTACHI   A subgroup of the EWE.

OVAMBO   An ethnic group living along the border of Namibia and Angola. There are 120,000 Ovambo in Angola. They are a semi-pastoral group of cattle herders that has resisted European influences.

Because of the arid and open nature of their territory, the Ovambo role in Angola's war of independence was initially marginal. However, in 1968 when the PORTUGUESE demanded that they relocate, they refused. In Namibia, they founded the Ovamboland Peoples' Organization in 1959, forerunner of the South-West

African Peoples' Organization (SWAPO), which demanded that Angolan Ovambo be reunited with their kinsmen in Namibia. (see also ANGOLANS)

OVIMBUNDU   A people, numbering 1.1 million, living in the central highlands of Angola. They speak Umbundu and are mostly Christian. Originally an agricultural people, they began serving as middlemen in the slave trade in the seventeenth century; by the nineteenth century trade this had become their primary occupation. They also engage in fishing, hunting, and blacksmithing.

Ovambo and Ovimbundu

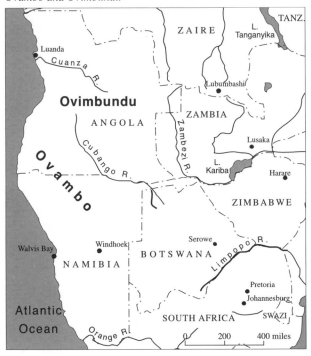

In the nineteenth century Protestant missionaries from North America began working among the Ovimbundu, who enthusiastically adopted the new religion and even created their own Protestant villages with Ovimbundu-operated schools, churches, and clinics. Their Council of Evangelical Churches of Central Angola has 400,000 members and is the largest Protestant community in that country.

The Ovimbundu were the main supporters of the National Union of Angolan Workers (UNITA), and its leader, Jonas Savimbi, is a member of the group. There is traditional animosity between the Ovimbundu and the MBUNDU. (see also ANGOLANS)

OWE   An ethnic group living in Nigeria.

OY   A Mon-Khmer group, numbering about 5,000, living in southern Laos. They have a developed religious system based on various taboos called *kalam*, but Buddhism is also prevalent, while Catholic missionaries have succeeded in converting several villages.

The twentieth century has seen the slow demise of the Oy people. There were an estimated 20,000 at the turn of the century, but TAI slave raids and a smallpox epidemic greatly reduced the population.

OYDA   (Ayda) An ethnic group numbering 20,000, living north of the upper bend of the Woito River in central Gemu Gofa Province, Ethiopia. They belong linguistically to the Omotic language group, and adhere to traditional beliefs. The Oyda are grain- and ensete-farmers.

OYO   A subgroup of the YORUBA living in Nigeria.

P

PACCIOCA   A chiefdom of the DIAGUITA.

PACOH   (Khas Pacoh) A Mon-Khmer group living west of the Vietnamese city of Hue.

PACSA   A subgroup of the AYMARA.

PADA   An ethnic group living in the mountainous central region of the Indonesian island of Sulawesi (Celebes). (see also TORADJA)

PADAM   A subgroup of the ADI.

PADAR   A subgroup of the AZERBAIJANI people living in the eastern part of Azerbaijan. No exact population figures are available; they may number several tens of thousands. They are Shi'ite Muslims. Historically seminomads, they are now mainly sedentary agriculturalists. They are currently being assimilated by the AZERBAIJANI.

PADHOLA   (Jo-Padhola, Kavirondo Nilotes) A Nilotic group living in areas settled mainly by Bantu peoples south of Mount Elgon and along the shores of Lake Victoria in Uganda and Tanzania. They live in villages and do not intermarry with the Bantu. Their language, Dhupadhola, belongs to the Western Nilotic family, and is closely related to that of the ACHOLI.

Living in a fertile region, their main economic activity is the cultivation of millet, maize and vegetables. They also keep cattle, sheep, and goats.

The Padhola originated in the northwest and are related to the LUO of Kenya. Their formation as a people took place only after they settled in their present region, which seems to have been uninhabited at the time of their arrival. However, the Padhola were later forced to share their territory with other small Nilotic and Bantu groups which, yielding to pressure else-where, moved into this area (the TESO) or who were remnants of greater entities (the SAMIA).

The Padhola are divided into exogamous clans, half of which originate in different Western Nilotic groups. The rest were incorporated from neighboring groups such as the TESO, GWERE, and SOGA. The Padhola settle in villages and have age-sets introduced into Padhola society by TESO groups. They have no centralized authority, although in some cases they acknowledge the authority of Bantu chiefs.

Their traditional religion is marked by an ancestor cult. Each clan had one or several shrines for ancestor worship. There existed one cult centered around a shrine common to all Padhola. Their religion was largely influenced by other groups which they absorbed, most notably the GWERE. They have religious specialists in the form of healers, while their highest god, Nyasi, is only appealed to in time of difficulty.

PADKOLO   An ethnic group living in Cameroon.

PAGAN   One of three Native American groups which compose the BLACKFOOT nation.

PAHARIA KORWA   (Benwaria) A subgroup of the KORWA.

PAHOUIN   see FANG.

PAI   see T'IN.

PAI-I   see SHAN.

PAIUTE   A Native North American group numbering 7,500, many of whom live on reservations such as the Duck Valley Federal Indian Reservation and colonies such as the Las Vegas Colony, in Nevada.

The Ghost Dance religion, which gave expression to the futile hopes of the Plains Indians for the disappearance of the white man from their land, originated with the Paiute. Traditionally small game hunters and gatherers of wild fruits and roots, today they engage predominantly in agriculture.

PAIWAN-RUKAI An ethnic group, numbering approximately 80,000, living in mountainous central Taiwan. In addition to being slash and burn agriculturalists, they are also hunters and fishermen. They produce artwork of stone and wood and bronze dagger-handles. They have preserved their traditional religion.

PAJINARA (Pajis) A subgroup of the SOLORESE.

PAKAMBIA An ethnic group living in the mountainous central region of the Indonesian island of Sulawesi (Celebes). (see also TORADJA)

PAKAWA An ethnic group living in the mountainous central region of the Indonesian island of Sulawesi (Celebes). (see also TORADJA)

PAKISTANIS The 110 million inhabitants of Pakistan. Two thirds of all Pakistanis are PUNJABIS living in the Punjab plain, and 11 percent are SINDHI living in the region of the lower Indus River and delta. The Pathan (see PASHTUN), a warlike, semi-nomadic people living in the north and northwest of the country, constitute 9 percent of the population. The BALUCH, living in the western regions, comprise just under 7 percent. The remainder are non-Islamic RAJPUTS and JATS, of Indo-Aryan origin, inhabiting the eastern and central regions.

Ninety-five percent of the Pakistanis are Muslims, mostly members of the Sunni sect; there are smaller numbers of Shi'ites and Isma'ilis. The c.3 million Ahmadis are no longer considered Muslims. Christians and Hindus together represent approximately 3 percent of the population; the remainder includes PARSIS, who practice Zoroastrianism.

The Urdu language emerged in the sixteenth and seventeenth centuries, during the Mogul period. Half of all Pakistanis speak this mixture of local dialects, which is now the official language of the state. The other major languages are, according to region, Punjabi, Baluchi, Pushtu, Gujarati, and Sindhi.

Pakistan is primarily an agricultural country with wheat, rice, and corn as staple crops and cotton as a cash crop. One-quarter of the land is farmed and nearly half the labor force works in agriculture. Industry, which is on the rise, employs just over one fifth of the labor force. Although women are restricted as to the jobs in which they can be employed, Benazir Bhuto was the first woman to serve as head of government in an Islamic country.

Islam arrived in the area of present day Pakistan in the eighth century with the conquering armies of the Umayyad Caliphate. The Muslims ruled the area of northern India (of which Pakistan was a part) until the BRITISH established colonies in the nineteenth century. In the long struggle for independence from British rule, Muslim groups founded the All-India Muslim League in 1906, and by the 1930s there were calls for the establishment of an independent Muslim state detached from Hindu-dominated India. In August 1947, Pakistan, split by the large expanse of India into East and West, gained independence. In 1971, civil war broke out in East Pakistan, and with the help of India the independent state of Bangladesh was created there. Modern Pakistan ("land of the pure") is now comprised of what was West Pakistan.

PAKPAK (Dairi) A subgroup of the BATAK living in the interior highlands of the Indonesian island of Sumatera (Sumatra).

PAKULI An ethnic group living in the mountainous central region of the Indonesian island of Sulawesi (Celebes). (see also TORADJA).

PALAQUA see BAJAU LAUT.

PALAU ISLANDERS (Palauan, Belauan) A Malaysian-speaking people, numbering 15,000, inhabiting eight principal and 252 small islands located in the Western Carolines, about 720 miles south of Guam. They speak Palauan, a derivative of the Malayo-Polynesian linguistic family. They are predominantly Christians, mainly Roman Catholics. The largest concentration of Palauans is found in the administrative and commercial center of Palau on the island of Koror.

Matrilineal families and clans characterize Palauan society. Early in the twentieth century they were administered by Germany, from 1920 they were under a Japanese mandate, and from 1945 under U.S. trusteeship.

PALAUNG (s.d. Ta-ang) An ethnic group living in the Shan states of Myanmar (Burma). No precise population figures exist but they are estimated to number about 250,000. They speak a Mon-Khmer language ap-

above left: A Pakistani woman
above right: A Pakistani man
below: A Pakistani man with his camel

parently related to that spoken by the WA, and practice Buddhism alongside traditional beliefs. The Palaung are traditionally slash and burn cultivators of rice, grains, and vegetables, with tea as a commercial crop. They are vegetarians, and therefore do not raise animals or hunt.

The most recent anthropological survey of the Palaung was conducted in 1931. Current information is scarce.

PALAWAN   A Malayo-Polynesian people living in southern Palawan, an island in the Philippines. Numbering approximately 90,000, they live in interior regions south of Apurauan on the west coast and south of Aboabo on the east coast. Roughly 15 percent are Muslims while the remainder practice traditional religions. They cultivate rice.

Palawan

PALAWO   A Nilotic-speaking ethnic group living in northwestern Uganda. (see also UGANDANS)

PALENDE   An ethnic group living in the mountainous central region of the Indonesian island of Sulawesi (Celebes). (see also TORADJA)

PALENQUE   A Native South American group living in Venezuela.

PALESTINIANS   (s.d. Filastiniyyun) The Palestinians are an Arab people living partly in historic Palestine (Israel, the West Bank, and the Gaza Strip) and partly dispersed in neighboring countries, particularly in Jordan. Without a state of their own, they have striven since 1948 to obtain self-determination and statehood.

The vagaries of history and war have divided the Palestinian people into three segments: Israeli Arabs, Palestinians of the Israeli-occupied territories (the West Bank and the Gaza Strip), and the Palestinian diaspora. Of the c.5 million Palestinians, 750,000 live in Israel, less than one million in the West Bank (including 150,000 East Jerusalem Palestinians who refuse Israeli citizenship), 650,000 in the Gaza Strip, 1.5 million in Jordan, 350,000 – 400,000 in Lebanon, 250,000 in Syria, and a similar number in Saudi Arabia. An estimated 200,000 can be found in Kuwait. Smaller Palestinian diaspora communities exist in Egypt, Iraq, and other Arab countries, as well as in Europe and America.

The great majority of Palestinians are Sunni Muslims, but there are significant Christian and Druze minorities. They speak a Palestinian dialect of Arabic and consider themselves part of the Arab nation.

In the wake of the Arab conquest of Palestine in 637, a process of arabization and islamization took place among the Christian Byzantine population of the country. However, substantial Christian communities continued to exist. The Crusades brought additional Christian, non-Arab elements, but under subsequent Mameluke and Ottoman rule islamization progressed.

Palestine's economy decayed. By the beginning of the nineteenth century, the country contained c.275,000 ARABS, most of whom lived in villages in the hills. Under the impact of mid-nineteenth century Ottoman reforms and Jewish- and Christian-initiated economic development, the Palestinian Arab population rose to c.600,000 by 1914. ARABS living in towns — many of them Christian traders — were more open to foreign influences. The Palestinian economy became increasingly export-oriented, and many impoverished peasants joined the ranks of the urban poor. Improving economic conditions attracted immigration from neighboring Arab countries in the first half of the twentieth century. Simultaneously, many Palestinians, particularly Christian groups, emigrated overseas.

Palestinian collective identity has been crystallized by the struggle for self-determination against the

above: A Palestinian man drinking coffee
below: A Palestinian woman in the market

BRITISH and the JEWS. The confrontation with competing Jewish nationalism in the first half of the twentieth century was an important factor in the formation of a distinct Palestinian identity. Calls for the cessation of Jewish immigration and land acquisition go back to the early twentieth century. Palestinian resistance became more forceful under the British mandate (1920–1948) and a Palestinian national movement emerged in the 1920s. Resistance against Britain's Balfour Declaration, calling for the establishment of a Jewish homeland in Palestine, and the imposition of the mandate led to violent riots. The 1936–1939 Arab revolt, which began as a popular revolt against Britain, developed into a civil war against the local Jewish population. By the time it was suppressed, it had also witnessed internecine Palestinian fighting.

The United Nation's partition of Palestine (1947) into an Arab and a Jewish state (Israel), and the ensuing war between Israel and her neighbors resulted in the exodus of c.750,000 Palestinians from Israeli territory. Few were permitted to return. This single most traumatic episode in Palestinian history dashed Palestinian hopes for independence and resulted in the formation of a Palestinian diaspora in neighboring Arab countries. 200,000 Palestinians from the southern Mediterranean coast found refuge in the Egyptian-held Gaza Strip; another 200,000 fled from the Galilee to Lebanon and Syria; from the center of Palestine, c.350,000 fled to the projected Arab state of Palestine (where 400,000 were already living). In 1950 this area, known as the West Bank, was annexed by the Hashemite Kingdom of Jordan and many refugees eventually crossed the Jordan River to settle on the East Bank (Jordan proper) — its capital, Amman, became the city with the largest Palestinian population in the world. By the end of the war, only 150,000 remained in Israel. The June 1967 (Six Day) War saw Israel occupy both the West Bank and the Gaza Strip, and many new refugees fled from the West Bank to Jordan.

While Palestinian refugees in Syria are kept under strict control, in Lebanon many have succeeded in escaping the squalor of their refugee camps and have found their way into business and liberal professions. They have also tipped the delicate balance between the Christian and Muslim population, and have played an important role in that country's civil war. Others migrated to the Gulf states, where they were indispensable to the regional oil boom. In many Gulf states, however, notably Kuwait, they came into conflict with the ambitions of the indigenous ARABS and are often

mistreated and even expelled. The Palestinians of the West Bank and Gaza Strip that remained under Israeli occupation found themselves increasingly bound to the Israeli economy — many work in Israel as migrant laborers. They now constitute the core of the Palestinian people, and are the most vocal group in the ongoing struggle for independence, the *intifada*.

Although Palestinians who remained in Israel after 1948 were formally granted equal rights (they are eligible to vote like other Israeli citizens), the military administration imposed on them remained in force until 1966. Many of their lands were expropriated by the Israeli government and they suffered social and economic discrimination. However, after the military administration was lifted, they were soon absorbed in the lower strata of the Israeli economy and have improved their standard of living. Education has increased awareness of their deprived position. This, together with contacts with Palestinians in the West Bank and Gaza, has led to a process of "Palestinization" of Israeli Arab consciousness, and to a more forceful assertion of their claim to equal rights. Israeli Arabs constitute a fast-growing group, numbering c.750,000, most of whom are Sunni Muslims. There are c.140,000 Christians (divided into a multitude of denominations, the most important being the Greek Orthodox) and c.43,000–70,000 DRUZE. The latter form a separate religiously-defined group which has throughout the years enjoyed more cordial relations with the Jewish authorities, and has better integrated into Israeli life. Nomadic Beduin in the Negev and Galilee are undergoing sedentarization. Approximately 2,500 Circassians (see CHERKESS) live in two villages in the Galilee. They are Sunni Muslims who fled from the Caucasus in the 1860s.

In the early 1960s, as a new generation of Palestinian militants sprang up from among the refugee camps, Palestinians began creating their own liberation organizations. The first Palestinian commando group, the Fatah (1959), began guerrilla activities against Israel in the mid–1960s, and contributed to the destabilization of the Arab-Israeli armistice. The Palestine Liberation Organization (PLO) was established in 1964 as an instrument of Palestinian nationalism.

After being driven out of Jordan in "Black September," 1970, Palestinian organizations rebuilt their infrastructure in southern Lebanon. When Syria's intervention in 1976, and Israel's in 1978 and 1982, destroyed this infrastructure, the PLO was forced to move its headquarters to Tunis. The political program of the PLO has shifted from "liberating the whole of

Palestine" to the acceptance of a Palestinian state co-existing with Israel. The emphasis on armed struggle has given way to attempts at using diplomatic means to achieve this end. The major opposition to the PLO has come from fundamentalist Islamic organizations, mainly the Hamas, that oppose any partition of historic Palestine. The *intifada* uprising in the West Bank and the Gaza Strip against Israeli occupation, began in 1987.

In 1992 a joint Jordanian/Palestinian delegation, with representatives from the West Bank and Gaza, joined the peace negotiations between Israel and the Arab states of Jordan, Lebanon, and Syria. (see also ISRAELIS, JORDANIANS)

PALICUR (Palikur) A South American Indian group numbering several hundred, living in the northern part of the State of Amazonas in northern Brazil. A few hundred reportedly live in French Guiana. They are highly acculturated and mostly bilingual.

PALIKUR see PALICUR.

PALLIYAN A group of about 6,000 agriculturalists found in southern Kerala and southern Tamil Nadu, India.

PALU An ethnic group living in the mountainous central region of the Indonesian island of Sulawesi (Celebes). (see also TORADJA)

Palliyan

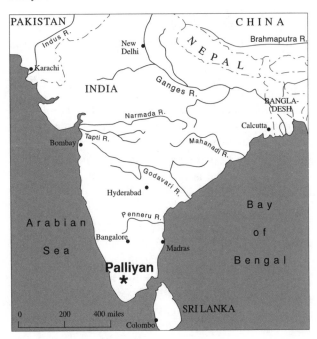

PALU'E (s.d. Hata Rua) The approximately 20,000 inhabitants of the island of Palu'e in the Lesser Sunda Islands chain of Indonesia. Some are also found along the coast of Flores.

They speak a language called Sare Lu'a belonging to the Austronesian family and are mostly Catholics, although traditional religious beliefs are evident. They cultivate yams, cassava, taro, corn, and mung beans.

PALUO (Loloka)A people inhabiting the northern part of the Bunyoro region of the NYORO people, south of the Victoria Nile River in Uganda. They number several thousand and speak a Western Nilotic language. They are stock-raisers, but also agriculturalists, practicing shifting cultivation. The ACHOLI call them Loloka.

PAMATSI (Pomaks) see BULGARIANS.

PAMINGGIR A subgroup of the ABUNG.

PAMIR ETHNIC GROUPS see BAJUWI, BARTANGI, ISHKASHIMI, KHUFI, MUNJI, OROSHORI, RUSHANI, SARIQOLI, SHUGHNI, WAKHI, YAZGULOMI, ZEBAKI.

PAMUE see FANG.

PANAMANIANS The 2.5 million inhabitants of Panama. They are largely *mestizo*, of mixed European and Indian ancestry, but also include small groups of blacks, whites, and Indians. Most are Roman Catholic, and speak Spanish.

The Panama Canal Zone and its surrounding area, including the capital, Panama City, and the major city of Colon, constitute the most densely populated part of Panama. Earlier, this Zone was the basis of much of the Panamanian economy, which consisted of providing goods and services to the "Zonians" (a name given to U.S. citizens and military living in the Canal Zone).

In fact, the Panamanians have failed to exploit their natural resources, which include minerals and rich fishing grounds along the coast. Small and relatively primitive farms cultivate only a small portion of the available land.

The first European expedition arrived in Panama in 1501. Panama rapidly became the point of embarkation for expeditions to Peru. The Panamanians enjoyed relative autonomy until Spain entered a period of political and economic decline in the mid-1700s; in 1751, the area became part of the territory of New Granada, now Colombia.

Upon achieving independence in 1821, Colombia, Ecuador, and Venezuela formed the Republic of Gran Colombia; when it dissolved after nine years, Panama remained part of Colombia. In 1903 the Colombian government refused to allow the United States to build a canal across Panama and the Panamanians, with considerable North American assistance, revolted, declared independence, and promptly leased the Canal Zone to the United States "in perpetuity." The U.S. proceeded to exert total sovereignty over the Canal Zone, administering it essentially as a colony. Although this arrangement was a source of political embarrassment to the Panamanians, they were economically dependent upon the AMERICANS living there, and public opposition to U.S. sovereignty did not erupt until after World War II. In 1979 the United States formally returned the Canal Zone to Panama. This symbolic victory over U.S. domination, however, did not resolve Panama's continuing problems: Panamanians have since had to contend with political instability.

PANANA, PANI   see PAWNEE.

PANANJOI   An ethnic group living on the Indonesian island of Kalimantan (Borneo). (see also DAYAK)

PANGAN   see SEMANG.

PANGGEE   A subgroup of the ADI.

PANGU   A subgroup of the TIV.

PANGWALA   An ethnic group numbering 11,000 (1981), living in the state of Himachal Pradesh, India. They speak Western Pahari, a member of the Indo-Aryan family of languages. They are Hindus.

The Pangwala are the indigenous inhabitants of the Pangi region of the Chamba District, Himachal Pradesh. Their main occupation is generally farming but a few rear sheep and goats as well.

PANGWE   see FANG.

PANIKA   An ethnic group numbering 53,000 (1981), living in the hill tracts of Maikal, Madhya Pradesh, in India. They are Hindus of Dravidian origin.

PANJAWANG   An ethnic group living on the Indonesian island of Kalimantan (Borneo). (see also DAYAK)

The Panika live in mixed villages with the GOND, BAIGA, PARDHAN, AGARIA, and other tribes. Exclusively Panika villages are seldom found. They are generally divided into two subgroups: the Kabirpanthi and the Sakta (Sattaha). The former, a larger group, consider themselves purer, more advanced, and higher in the social hierarchy than the Sakta. They engage in settled cultivation.

The Sakta are poor. They live in the hilly tracts and, like other hill peoples, engage in slash and burn cultivation, clearing of forests, and collecting forest produce. Some weave cloth in return for grains and forest produce.

PANKHO AND BANJOGI   A Buddhist ethnic group living in Bangladesh. They were ousted from their original home, thought to have been in Myanmar (Burma), along the southern slope of the Chin Hills and on the plateau of Zao, by KHUMI in the seventeenth century.

The Pankho and Banjogi are slash and burn agriculturalists.

PANNIYAN   An ethnic group, numbering 57,000 (1981), living in the Palghat, Calicut, and Cannanore Districts of the state of Kerala, India. They speak Malayalam, a member of the Dravidian family of languages, and are Hindus, worshiping the Kadu Bhagawati and Kali. There is a legend that shipwrecked Africans might have occupied this particular part of the country, and in fact the Panniyan do have a close physical resemblance to African peoples.

The Panniyan have no clans or social gradations. They are reputed to be competent hunters, capable of trapping tigers with only a spear and a net. Good agricultural laborers, they live in shacks near farms and plantations.

PA-O   A subgroup of the KAREN.

PAPAGO   A Native North American group numbering 25,000, many of whom live on a few federal reservations such as the Ak Chin Federal Indian Reservation in Arizona, U.S.A., which is widely known for its success in raising and marketing cotton. They are one of the best examples of self-management and self-reliance among Native American peoples.

PAPEL   (Pepel) An ethnic group numbering around 66,000, living in Guinea-Bissau. They are closely related to the BRAME and MANJACO. The Papel became im-

Papago

portant in Guinea-Bissau's politics only after a military coup staged by a member of this group in 1980. Following the coup, most CAPE VERDEANS in high positions were dismissed while members of the Papel, BALANTA, MANJACO, and several other groups were promoted. (see also GUINEA-BISSAU, THE PEOPLE OF)

PAPUA NEW GUINEA ISLANDERS (Papuans)

The Melanesian population, numbering 3.7 million, of Papua New Guinea (PNG) an area which includes the eastern part of the island of New Guinea (the western part of which, Irian Jaya, is part of Indonesia) and some smaller islands, including the Bismarck Archipelago (mainly New Britain, New Ireland, and the Manus Islands) and the northern part of the Solomon Islands (mainly Bougainville and Buka).

Population distribution is extremely uneven. Nearly half the total population lives in a restricted belt, mainly at high altitude. The swampy lowlands of some of the coastal areas are very sparsely settled.

The country's population is very diverse, and scholars of different disciplines are making only moderate progress in deciphering the complicated native social structure. It is agreed, however, that there was much migration and mixing among the ancestors of the present population, which created a great number of linguistic groups and cultural patterns. The differences between neighboring communities, exemplified by the

variety of languages, have been influenced by the mountainous topography and isolation. Each ethnic group, especially in isolated valleys, formed a distinct culture.

The indigenous languages fall into two groups: Austronesian and Papuan. The Austronesian languages, numbering around 200 and often referred to as Melanesian, are mostly located in coastal, near-coastal and insular regions, and are spoken by about 15 percent of the population. The Papuan languages, numbering about 500, are found mostly in the mainland, and the southern half of Bougainville. Most languages are spoken by only small groups. Pidgin English has spread throughout the country and is replacing the vernacular languages to a great extent.

Only one percent of the population is non-Melanesian. There are some tiny groups of Micronesian (in the Manus Islands) and Polynesian origin (Takau and Nukumanu Islands), which have mixed with the Melanesian population.

During the last third of the twentieth century, the PNG Islanders have undergone social and economic changes. Rural-urban migration has increased rapidly and shanty towns are already a feature of all major urban centers. Nevertheless, most of the population still lives in villages. Those of the coastal areas are generally small (up to 300 people) and those in the highlands are often large, with up to 2,000 inhabitants. In some areas people live in hamlets with two or three dozen inhabitants. The present village economy still contains some typical features of subsistence or semi-subsistence agriculture, where the common crops are cassava, taro, yam, cocoa, and sweet potatoes; pig husbandry is also of great significance. The simple digging-stick is still in use, and handmade tools from readily available local materials are common. Land is usually vested in wide kinship groups, although individuals may control its use. Some groups adhere to matrilineal inheritance of land, while others exercise patrilineal inheritance. The exchange of valuables, in trade, ceremonial offerings, and as gifts, is an integral part of life. Kinship relations are the basis of every aspect of traditional life. Men and grown boys have one house and women, girls, and small children another. Polygamy is present in many of the groups. There is no imposed order from a chief or a council, and public opinion, shame, reciprocal obligations, and religious beliefs encourage conformity to society's norms. The belief in magic, spells, and sorcery is widespread, even among the significant proportion that has adopted Christianity (nominally more than 90 percent). These

Papua New Guinea Islanders participating in a traditional festival

beliefs and practices, which differ in detail from area to area, are based largely on a form of ancestor and spirit worship.

The island of New Guinea was visited by European navigators from the early sixteenth century, but exploration and colonial settlement did not begin until the mid-nineteenth century. In 1884 Papua, the southern part of eastern New Guinea, and adjoining islands, was proclaimed a British protectorate, and the northern part of eastern New Guinea came under German administration. Australia formally administered Papua from 1906. From 1945 Papua and the former German New Guinea, administered since World War I by Britain (except for a brief period of Japanese occupations during World War II), became the Territory of Papua New Guinea. As the Australian administration was extended into the interior, the country's largest population concentration was discovered, and by the 1950s all groups were brought under administrative control. PNG attained independence in 1975. Although it inherited from the Australian authorities a highly centralized administration, the heterogenous and fragmented nature of the country and its society resulted in the introduction of decentralization. By 1978 all twenty provinces had been granted provincial government status.

More than two thirds of the working population are engaged in subsistence and semi-subsistence agriculture. The rest are engaged mainly in commercial agriculture in which the principal export cash crops are coffee, cocoa, coconuts, palm oil, rubber, and tea. Since independence, copper, gold, and silver have taken over as principal export commodities. More recently substantial deposits of chromite, cobalt, nickel, and quartz have been discovered, all of which attract labor to the mining areas. Tourism is another expanding sector.

PARACHI   An ethnic group of Afghanistan living in small enclaves in three valleys on the southern slopes of the Hindu Kush, north of Kabul. They are estimated as numbering about 5,000.

The Parachi language belongs to the eastern group of Iranian languages. They have been Sunni Muslims of the Hanafi school since the end of the sixteenth century. They were first mentioned at the very beginning of the sixteenth century as an ethnic group in the Kabul region engaged in trade and agriculture.

Their number began to decrease rapidly in the nineteenth century, due to political and administrative developments which brought an end to the isolation of the area. Presently undergoing an intensive process of assimilation into the surrounding PASHTUN and TAJIK, they may be regarded as an ethnic group on the verge of disappearance. (see also AFGHANS)

PARAGUAYANS   A people inhabiting Paraguay, an inland country of South America, bounded by Bolivia, Brazil, and Argentina. Numbering c.4 million, most live in the area east of the Rio Paraguay. West of this river is the sparsely-populated but much disputed Gran Chaco which cost Paraguay more than 75 percent of its population during a disastrous nineteenth-century war. Overwhelmingly Roman Catholic, at least 50 percent of the population speaks both Spanish (the official language) and Guarani.

The GUARANI are the indigenous people of Paraguay. During the sixteenth century, their territory spread to the Andean foothills, the Brazilian frontier, and the Amazon basin. The SPANIARDS arrived at the Rio Paraguay in 1524. The capital city of Asunción was founded in 1537 on the Day of the Assumption of the Virgin. Later, members of the Jesuit and Franciscan orders founded agricultural colonies. They became both protectors and teachers of the indigenous peoples, instructing them to develop their skills, achieve relative autonomy, and avoid exploitation. This angered the European colonists, anxious to increase their labor supply through the enslavement of the Indians, and resulted in the expulsion of the Jesuits from the New World. Paraguayans initiated a rebellion against Spain in 1810: the last Spanish governor left in 1811.

Paraguayans are 95 percent *mestizo*. Of the fewer than 50,000 unassimilated Indians, the majority lives in the Chaco region and a minority in southern Paraguay. Among the *mestizo* population, 44 percent live in towns. As the least advanced country in Latin America, Paraguay also has the lowest annual rate of population increase, partly because many have left Paraguay and moved to neighboring countries; nearly 25 percent of Paraguayans live abroad. Over the years, the Paraguayan government has encouraged immigration, especially of skilled workers. Of these, North AMERICANS constitute the largest western and JAPANESE the largest nonwestern groups. Paraguay has attracted few Europeans, with the notable exception of Mennonites and members of the associated Hutterite sect from Germany.

The influence of the SPANIARDS on Paraguayans was felt less than almost anywhere else in Hispanic America. In Asunción, Spanish is the predominant language, but outside the capital Guarani is spoken and is taught in schools. However, although the spoken language is indigenous, the preferred music is predominantly European, setting the Paraguayans apart from people in other Latin American countries, whose preferred musical forms are more dependent on indigenous and folkloric tradition. This unique feature of Paraguay apparently stems from the Jesuit discovery that the GUARANI possessed extraordinary musical ability; they began teaching these people European music, which they performed exquisitely. They did not, however, compose original musical works in the same idiom — performance by the indigenous peoples was rewarded, but not creativity.

Although religious freedom is guaranteed by law, the government is officially Catholic. The president must be Roman Catholic and the church is governmentally subsidized and has the right to be represented in the Council of State. Governmental recognition and support notwithstanding, during the dictatorship of Alfredo Stroessner (1954–1989) the church was, ironically, the most outspoken critic in Paraguay and the major agitator for human rights and change.

Paraguay's economy is predominantly agricultural. The country is substantially self-sufficient in this sector, and agricultural products constitute about 90 percent of exports (predominantly cotton, soya, and wheat). Paraguayans also raise cattle; their volume of meat exports, however, has been reduced by noncompetitive pricing policies and import restrictions in potential markets. Other major products include oil, oilseeds, timber, and tobacco.

Paraguayan industry is limited, employing less than an eighth of the work force in the processing of raw materials and basic goods. Trade deficits have been serious, with substantial drains of international reserves in the mid-1980s.

PARAHURI A subgroup of the YANOMAMI.

PARAKANA A South American Indian group living in the State of Pará, north Brazil, close to the ASURINI. They speak a Tupi language.

PARBATIYA UPADHYAYA see BRAHMANS.

PARDHAN An ethnic group numbering 133,000 (1981), living in the states of Andhra Pradesh, Madhya Pradesh, and Maharashtra, India. They speak Telugu, Marathi (their mother tongue), and Gondi, languages belonging to the Dravidian and Indo-Aryan families.

The Pardhan are musicians and hereditary bards of the GOND, and also act as their advisers, companions, and genealogists. They play the trumpet at weddings and funerals. The songs and stories which they preserve by oral transmission are the most important repositories of Gond tradition, and as such they play a vital role in Gond culture. The GOND pay them in cash and in kind for their services. The Pardhan also engage in day-labor and agriculture. (see also PANIKA)

PARDHI A nomadic group of farmers and hunters located throughout northern, western, and central India. They number about 60,000.

PARESSI (Paresi) A South American Indian group living in a dozen or more small villages in the state of Mato Grosso, central-west Brazil, close to the Bolivian border. Their speech ties them to the Arawak language family, and although they trade with outsiders, they have maintained their native culture and language.

PARHAIYA An ethnic group, numbering 28,000 (1981), living in Bihar and West Bengal, India. They speak Munda, a member of the Austroasiatic family of languages, and are one of the Scheduled Tribes.

The Parhaiya have lived for centuries on the hills and in the forests of Palamau. Their houses are tiny, constructed from bamboo and thatch grass, and accommodate only nuclear families. Adult sons and daughters erect their own huts. They grow vegetables for their own consumption, but being semi-nomadic, also engage in hunting and foraging. Unlike other nomadic groups, they have no clan divisions.

Due to rigorous enforcement of forest laws, the Parhaiya were forced to abandon their mountain habitat and live in the foothills. This has disrupted their ancient pattern of life: having no land, they eke out a precarious living by menial labor.

PARIA I An ethnic group living in several districts of Uzbekistan and Tajikistan, in the Hisar Valley, and along the upper stream of the Surkhan-Daria River. In the mid-1970s they were estimated as numbering 1,000. Their language belongs to the central group of Indian languages of the Indo-European family, and is the only Indian language known to be spoken in Central Asia. It is unwritten, Uzbek and Tajik being used in writing and education. All Paria speak both Paria and Tajik, while some speak Uzbek as well. They are Sunni Muslims of the Hanafi school who engage in sedentary agriculture. Cotton is the most important crop.

The Paria are divided into six clan-like subdivisions, the largest of which, the KALO, is also regarded as the most prestigious. A seventh subdivision, Shuia, disappeared in the 1930s.

They live in small groups of three to twenty families dispersed among the TAJIK and UZBEK, who refer to them as "Afghon" (i.e., Afghanis). In fact, they probably originated in the Punjab of India, migrating to Central Asia through Afghanistan in several waves in the nineteenth century. The ethnonym Paria should not be confused with the South Indian caste term "pariah."

PARIA II A Native South American group living in Venezuela.

PARIGI An ethnic group living in the mountainous central region of the Indonesian island of Sulawesi (Celebes). (see also TORADJA)

PARJA see DHURWA.

PARSIS (Zoroastrians) An ethno-religious grouping numbering more than 100,000, living in India, particularly in the city of Bombay. They are adherents of the Zoroastrian religion who, by dint of their long isolation and particular language, have developed into a separate ethnic group. Together with Zoroastrians in Iran, they number an estimated 150,000. Indian Parsis differ linguistically from Iranian Zoroastrians.

The Zoroastrian religion is based on the ancient dualistic Persian religion of Mazdaism which, under the influence of Zarathustra and his holy book, the *Avesta*, received a more ethical monotheistic slant. Fire temples, purification rituals, and elaborate initiation rites for adolescents are characteristic. The dead are left to be devoured by birds of prey in "towers of silence." Zoroastrianism developed under the Achaemenids and became Persia's state religion under the Sasanids (fourth century C.E.). In the seventh century, while most Persians accepted Islam, minorities resisted. Minute remnants of these pockets survive in Yazd, Kerman, Shiraz, and in Tehran (Teheran) and are recognized as a legitimate monotheistic faith in the Islamic Republic of Iran.

However, most Parsi believers fled to the Iranian trading stations along the western coast of India in the ninth and tenth centuries. With the opening of Indian-European maritime channels, many Zoroastrians, who came to be known in India as Parsis, engaged in trade. Since the nineteenth century they have become prosperous merchants and industrialists, well known for

their welfare and mutual aid programs. Hinduism adopted the Parsis as a special caste. By participating in the Indian struggle for independence (including in the Congress Party), the Parsis carved out a niche of their own in modern India. The question facing them now is whether to assimilate into India's modernizing and increasingly secular society. (see also INDIANS, PAKISTANIS)

PARSIVAN, PARSIBAN see FARSIVAN.

PARUNI One of several tribes grouped together as NURESTANI.

PASHAI An ethnic group of peasant mountain-dwellers inhabiting the southern fringes of Nurestan in northeastern Afghanistan, and the Kohistan region, northwest of Kabul. Estimates of their number vary from 60,000 to 100,000. Their language belongs to the Dardic group, an intermediate linguistic subgroup between the Indian and the Iranian languages, and is divided into several widely divergent dialects regarded by some scholars as separate languages. Although it is unwritten, it was proclaimed one of the officially recognized languages of Afghanistan.

The Pashai are Sunni Muslims of the Hanafi school. According to Marco Polo they were still pagans in the late thirteenth century and it appears that they only adopted Islam in the end of the sixteenth century. (see also AFGHANS)

PASHTUN (Pushtun, Pukhtun, Pathan, Afghan) A people living in Afghanistan and Pakistan numbering an estimated 13 million. In Afghanistan they inhabit an

Pashtun

above: Pashtun men in Ladakh, India
below: Pedi women in South Africa

area extending from north of Jalalabad to Qandahar and westward to Sabzawar, as well as several enclaves in the west and the north; in Pakistan, from Dir and Swat southward, and in some enclaves in the Punjab and in Baluchistan. Pashtun colonies exist also in Xinjiang (China), some Persian Gulf states, and in eastern Iran (c.50,000). The 1989 Soviet census listed some 9,000 Pashtun, but this includes all AFGHANS who lived in the Soviet Union at that time.

The Pashto language belongs to the eastern subgroup of the Iranian branch of the Indo-European family. It consists of some twenty dialects which are usually divided into two main groups, the eastern (northeastern, or "hard") and western (southeastern or "soft"). Pashto is written in an adapted form of the Arabic alphabet. It has a rich literary tradition of poetry and prose, the latter mainly religious and historical. The earliest literary works whose dating is not disputed were written in the seventeenth century. The authenticity of works reputedly composed between the eighth and fourteenth centuries is doubtful. In 1936 Pashto was proclaimed the official language of Afghanistan, a role it has shared with Dari (the Afghanistani version of Persian) since 1964. Modern unified literary Pashto is still developing. Since the late 1940s it has tended to comprise more and more components of the eastern dialect group, which is utilized by most Pashto-speakers.

The overwhelming majority of Pashtun are Sunni Muslims of the Hanafi school. The TURI and some clans of the ORAKZAI are Shi'ite Muslims. The Pashtun are divided into sedentary agriculturalists, pastoral nomads, and semi-nomads. Depending on region, irrigation may be utilized. The foremost crops are wheat and barley; livestock raised includes cattle, sheep, goats, camels, donkeys, and horses. While on the move, nomads live in tents of black goat-hair. Houses are mostly flat-roofed adobe dwellings. Both men and women adhere to traditional forms of dress, sometimes including European additions such as trousers. Men wear a turban which indicates their tribal affiliation, women wear a head-covering. They possess an elaborate code of conduct known as *Pashtunvali*, based on concepts of honor, valor, and hospitality.

The Pashtun are divided into many tribes (in Afghanistan alone, according to an estimate made in the early 1980s, there were thirty-six tribes). Many belong to the DURRANI (Abdali), GHILZAI, or KARLANI confederations. Tribes may also contain Pashtun clients (*hamsaya*) who are regarded as full members. Each tribe is usually headed by a hereditary *khan* of restricted power. All matters of importance are settled by a council (*jirga*) of the chiefs of clans. All tribal subdivisions, down to the level of the village or the camp, have such councils. On the village or camp level, the *jirga* played an important role in the customary periodic redistribution of land, which has been dying out in recent decades.

Main Pashtun tribes in Afghanistan of the DURRANI confederation are: POPOLZAI, ALIKOZAI, BARAKZAI, ALIZAI (all sedentary), NURZAI (nomadic), ISHAQZAI (Sakzai; semi-nomadic); of the GHILZAI confederation: TOKI (sedentary), TARAKI (semi-nomadic); the POVINDA, originally part of the SULAIMAN branch of the GHILZAI, is now a large nomadic tribe in its own right, which until the 1961 tensions between Pakistan and Afghanistan, crossed the international border yearly. The KARLANI confederation includes the MANGAL, JADRAN, and JAJI (semi-nomads), and the VARDAK (sedentary). Other groups include the semi-nomadic and non-confederated MOHMAUD, SAFI, and KAKAR. Pakistani tribes include the AFRIDI, YUSUFZAI, VAZIR, KHATTAK, BANGASH, TURI, and ORAKZAI. Some tribes live in both countries.

The legendary genealogy of the Pashtun, as recorded in the seventeenth century, traces their ancestry back to Afghana, the grandson of the biblical king Saul (Talut, Sarul). They are first mentioned as Avagana in an early sixth-century Indian source. They remained of marginal importance in the political history of the area up to the thirteenth-century Mongol conquest. The first ruler to establish Pashtun as an independent state was Ahmad Shah Durrani (1747–1773), who established the Sadoqzay dynasty. His fragile empire was kept intact during the rule of his son, Timur Shah (1773–1793), but disintegrated during the struggles among Timur's sons and grandsons, which led to Britain's first intervention in the area. Throughout the nineteenth century the BRITISH tried to gain control of Afghanistan. The 1893 Durand delineation of the border between Afghanistan and India left the Pashtun divided between the two states, a situation still in force today. With the 1947 partition of India and Pakistan, the idea of unifying the Pashtun into one state (Afghanistan) was raised, but never fulfilled. Politically, the Pashtun of Pakistan were and remain marginal to that country's development.

Following World War II, and especially after Britain's withdrawal from India in 1947, Afghanistan was increasingly drawn into the sphere of Soviet influence, manifested in the growing Soviet involvement in development projects as well as in the rise of Marxist forces. Muhammad Zahir Shah (1933–1973) was destined to be the last king of Afghanistan. Following a decade of internal reform and a neutralist foreign policy, he was deposed by his cousin Muhammad Daoud Khan, who established a republic and proclaimed himself its president.

In March 1978 an alliance of the Marxist parties Khalq ("The People") and Parcham ("The Flag") carried out a coup and established the People's Democratic Republic of Afghanistan. An internal struggle between the two components of the new regime, coupled with growing armed resistance in the countryside, led to the Soviet military intervention of December 1979, which in turn ignited the thirteen-year war in Afghanistan. The Pashtun were one of the leading forces in resisting the USSR and the Moscow-backed government which fell in 1992. (see also AFGHANS)

PASSAMAQUODDY   A Native North American group numbering about 1,100, who live in Quebec, Canada. Originally they were woodland hunters and today they supplement their income by means of fishing and by working in the forest industry. They are closely related to the ABNAKI.

PASSI   A subgroup of the ADI.

PATAI   An ethnic group living on the Indonesian island of Kalimantan (Borneo). (see also DAYAK)

PATANI   A subgroup of the SAWAI.

PATASHO-HA-HA-HAI   (Pataxo) A South American Indian group living in the State of Bahía, northeastern Brazil. Only two dozen living members are left of this group, in a government-sponsored village.

PATHAN   SEE BAKARWAL, PAKISTANIS, PASHTUN.

PATHIYAN   An ethnic group living in northern Kerala.

PAUMARY   A South American Indian people inhabiting the drainage basin of the Juruá and Purus Rivers of the western Amazon in Brazil. Their primary pursuits are fishing and the hunting of turtles and manatees from bark or dugout canoes. They also grow sweet manioc, maize, and a range of secondary crops. They live in huge communal houses.

PAUTA   A subgroup of the JIVARO.

PAWI   (Poi) A Paleo-Mongoloid people numbering about 30,000, found in the state of Mizoram in north-eastern India. They engage in slash and burn agriculture.

PAWNEE   (Pani, Panana) A Native North American group numbering 2,000, many of whom live on the Pawnee Tribe Federal Trust Area, Pawnee County, Oklahoma, U.S.A.

In the past they lived along the Missouri River in earth lodges. They were traditional cultivators of maize, squash, and other vegetables, and seasonal buffalo hunters. In the mid-1850s they were removed to Kansas and in 1876 to the Indian Territory in Oklahoma, U.S.A.

PA-Y   A Tai-speaking group numbering about 600 living along the Vietnamese border with China. They are believed to have emigrated from China to their present location in recent times.

PAYA   A South American Indian group of the Mosquito Coast of Nicaragua. They now cultivate bitter manioc and plantains, crops which supplement the products of their traditional pursuits of hunting, fishing, and gathering. They are also traders in forest products. (see also HONDURANS)

PAYAPI   An ethnic group living in the mountainous central region of the Indonesian island of Sulawesi (Celebes). (see also TORADJA)

PEANA   An ethnic group living in the mountainous central region of the Indonesian island of Sulawesi (Celebes). (see also TORADJA)

PEAR   (Bahr, Pohr, Samre, Phnong) A Mon-Khmer group numbering about 10,000, living in northeast Cambodia above the Tonle Sap Lake. They are often grouped together with the SAOCH along the southern coast and called Samre; Cambodians also refer to them as PHNONG, a generic term for all groups living in the uplands.

Most Pear engage in slash and burn agriculture. Rice is the staple crop but sweet potatoes, bananas, peppers, and tobacco are also grown. Hunting and gathering are also pursued to supplement their diet, as is fishing in nearby streams. They have preserved their traditional religious belief in spirits.

PEBATO   An ethnic group living in the mountainous central region of the Indonesian island of Sulawesi (Celebes). (see also TORADJA)

PECHENEG   see HUNGARIANS.

PEDAH   see HOUEDA.

PEDI   (Bapedi, Northern Sotho) A people belonging to the SOTHO peoples of Southern Africa. They number about 3 million, and those not urbanized today live in the area of the Northern Transvaal province of South Africa, where they are also known as the Northern SOTHO. The original Pedi had the *noko* (porcupine) as their totem, although today other totemic groups such

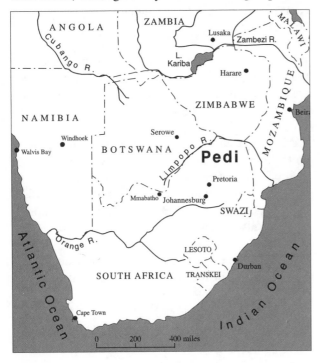

Pedi

as the *tau* (lion) and the *kewna* (crocodile) are also included.

The Pedi speak a northern Sotho language. Over half the Pedi are Christians, the remainder adhering to traditional beliefs. Of the Christian Pedi, some 60 percent belong to African Independent Churches, another 17 percent are Lutherans, and 16 percent are Roman Catholics.

Under South Africa's Grand Apartheid scheme, the Pedi were granted a Tribal Homeland called Lebowa, situated in the northern Transvaal. Lebowa became a self-governing state in 1972. Its major products are platinum, chrome, citrus fruits, and sisal.

The Pedi Empire originated early in the nineteenth century, but they were routed by the NDEBELE in the 1820s. Pedi influence again grew in the 1860s. Between 1861 and 1879, their expanding empire was attacked by the ZULU and the SWAZI, both of whom regarded the Pedi as their subjects at varying times. The Pedi were also seen as a threat to the interests of both the AFRIKANERS and the BRITISH. A massive British offensive against them destroyed the empire in 1879.

Culturally, the Pedi belong to the SOTHO peoples and share their customs. They are renown for the mural art which adorns the internal walls of homes (as opposed to the NDEBELE, whose murals are on the external walls and enclosures). The Pedi art style is distinctive in form, color, and design. Since these murals are women's work, beautiful wall decorations are considered an indication of a woman's housekeeping talents. (see also SOTHO, SOUTH AFRICANS)

PEGUAN   see MON.

PEGUCHE   An OTAVALO tribe.

PEHUENCHE   A subgroup of the TEHUELCHE.

PEKAL   A group numbering about 15,000, living in western Sumatera (Sumatra), Indonesia. They are a composite of MINANGKABAU, KERINTJI, and REDJANG populations and each of these groups consider the Pekal to be their subgroup. They speak a Minangkabau dialect with considerable Redjang influence. (see also MUKO-MUKO)

PEKI   An ethnic group related to the EWE living in Togo.

PENDE   A cluster of ethnic groups living in Zaire, between the Kwilu and Kasai Rivers.

PENOBSCOT   A Native North American group numbering 1,500, many of whom live on the Penobscot State Reservation near Augusta, Maine, U.S.A. They are one of the few East Coast Native American groups to survive to the present day.

In the aftermath of the British-Indian War, many of the Penobscot migrated north to Canada, where they were absorbed by other Algonkian-speaking peoples. Traditionally woodland hunters, many Penobscot find employment today in the lumber industry.

PEPEL   see PAPEL.

PERSIANS   (s.d. Irani) A people inhabiting the Islamic Republic of Iran, mainly in the center and east of

Persians

the country. They number c.20 million and constitute about 45 percent of the population. A relatively large number of Persians, apparently 2–3 millions, live outside Iran, mainly in Europe and North America.

Iranian groups began to settle in what is present-day Iran toward the end of the second and beginning of the first millennia B.C.E. Persians were the ruling ethnic element already in the Achaemenid Iranian empire (559–330 B.C.E.). They actively assimilated other groups in the Iranian highland, particularly those whose languages belonged to the Iranian group, thereby becoming the dominant ethnic element there.

The Persian language, Farsi, belongs to the southwestern subgroup of the Iranian group of the Indo-European family of languages. Persians are Shi'ite Muslims.

About half the Persians are sedentary agriculturalists chiefly dependent on primitive artificial irrigation. They practice handicrafts such as handweaving, rug-weaving, and pottery-making. The typical Persian rural dwelling is constructed of clay with a framework of wooden columns, a flat roof, and no windows. Light comes in through the door or an opening in the roof.

Urban Persians are divided into more or less clearcut social strata. The lowest of these are former villagers who flocked to the towns between the late 1950s and the late 1970s. They are unskilled manual laborers, dwelling in shantytowns on the outskirts of the larger cities, in slums, or on the streets. They are, however, well represented among skilled urban factory workers and form the majority of the so-called Bazari, i.e., bazaar craftsmen and/or shopkeepers among the lower

and upper middle class and the country's religious and administrative groups. The traditional urban house is constructed of burnt bricks over a high foundation and contains a terrace.

Since the 1930s, and especially after World War II, urban building has followed the European pattern. Reza Shah Pahlavi (1925–1941) enforced European-style dress including a modified French military *képi* known as *kolah-e Pahlavi* (the Pahlavi head dress). This style and variations of it gradually became more entrenched among all strata of the population except for religious functionaries and for women, whose dress retained more traditional aspects. This tendency was reversed by the 1979 Islamic revolution, with men reverting to traditional dress and women wearing the traditional *chador* (long black robe and headcovering).

Persian written literature is among the oldest and richest in the world. Inscriptions in ancient Persian date back to the sixth century B.C.E. The writings of Firdawsi (941–c.1012), Omar Khayyam (1048–c.1132), Rumi (1207–1273), and Hafiz (1325–1390), have become world-famous. (see also FARSIVAN, TANZANIANS, TURKS)

PERUVIANS　　The people of Peru, the third largest South American republic, number today over 21 million. Pre-Columbian civilizations developed in Peru as far back as the end of the third millennium B.C.E. The Chavin, Nazca, and Tiahuanaco cultures preceded the establishment of the Inca Empire that controlled Peru and also parts of Ecuador, Bolivia, northern Argentina, and Chile in the fifteenth century.

The country was conquered by the SPANIARDS in 1531. This brought about the destruction of the Inca Empire, the foundation of Lima (1535), near the Pacific coast, in order to facilitate naval communications and transport with Panama and Spain, and the establishment of the viceroyalty of Peru. Spanish colonization lasted until the end of 1824, when the Peruvians, with the aid of Simon Bolívar, finally routed the Spanish armies and became fully independent.

Social stratification was established at the beginning of the colonial period on ethnic grounds, with the Spanish conquerors and colonists forming the upper classes. Today, white Europeans constitute approximately one-tenth of the total population. The *mestizos* (mixed white-Indian) account for one-third to one-half, and the rest (c.35 percent of the population, are a large group of Quechua-speaking Indians (estimated at more than 3 million) and a sizable group of Aymara-speaking Indians. There are also two small minorities of

above: Two Peruvian women
below: A Peruvian market

Africans and Asians (mainly CHINESE, but also JAPANESE), totaling c.1 percent of the population.

White Peruvians are mostly urban dwellers, but 50 percent of the people live in the Andes Mountains (Sierra), where most of the Indian population is concentrated. The Montaña or Selva (eastern slopes of the Andes extending into the Amazonian tropical forest) covers most of Peru but only 8 percent of the population lives there, including Amazonic indigenous groups.

The formation of a clear Peruvian national identity was conditioned by the ethnic composition of the population and by the country's historical development. Indian antagonism toward Spain and the white creole elite brought about the 1780 revolt in Alto Peru (later Bolivia) against oppressive taxes and the forced labor imposed on them by the SPANIARDS. The revolt lasted for three years before it was finally suppressed, and it became a historical landmark for popular Latin American revolutionary movements.

After independence, Peru was dominated by the army and fought, together with Bolivia, two wars against Chile (1836–1839 and 1879–1883), losing both. The first war reasserted Peruvian national identity. The Chilean invasion of Peru during the Pacific War (Lima was occupied by the CHILEANS from January 1881 until the beginning of 1884) brought about fierce Peruvian resistance in the Sierra, which consolidated Peruvian nationalism and patriotic feelings.

The ethnic and socio-economic divisions within Peru have led to frequent historical and political discussions on the problems of Peruvian national identity. Some praise the historical role of Spain in Peru and hold that the nation's future will depend upon Peruvians of European descent, those able to lead the modernization of their society and economy. Others look for solutions based on a fusion of the European and Indian components of the nation. The left-wing Alianza Popular Revolucionaria Americana (APRA) was in favor of regenerating the indigenous Indian society through land reform. The guerrilla movement *Sendero Luminoso* (Shining Path) violently rejects Western liberal democracy and culture as well as the capitalist organization of the economy and attempts to impose an agrarian collectivist model of Marxist-Maoist revolutionary principles.

After a twelve-year populist-military dictatorship that tried to impose land and economic reforms without much success, Peru returned to democracy in 1980. Since then, right and left wing policies have been unsuccessful in the effort to stabilize Peru's economy and social development. Both rural and urban guerrilla warfare complicate the situation by introducing further divisive elements. In 1990 a Peruvian of Japanese descent, Alberto Fujimori, was elected to the presidency. His government has applied strong neo-liberal economic adjustment policies and perpetrated a self- coup d'etat in 1992. This was done in order to fight guerrillas more effectively and to apply effective policies without parliamentary blockage.

PETAPA   An ethnic group living on the Indonesian island of Kalimantan (Borneo). (see also DAYAK)

PEUL   see FULANI.

PHALABORWA   A subgroup of the SOTHO.

PHALANGES   see LEBANESE.

PHILIPPINES, THE PEOPLE OF THE   The 66 million inhabitants of the Philippines, a tropical archipelago of some 7,100 islands stretching 1,100 miles from north to south, can be referred to collectively as "Filipinos." This term is often used to designate only those who profess Christianity. They represent a wide range of peoples and ethnic groups. Most of the population is of Malay origin, and is divided into a number of groupings, based on language, religion, and island locality. Among these are the BONTOK, COTABATO MANOBO, IFUGAO, ILONGOT, KALINGA, KENOY, LEPANTO, MAGAHAT, NEGRITOS, SUBANUN, TADYAWAN, and YAKAN. The largest non-Malay group is the CHINESE, who number approximately 1 million.

Habitation is concentrated on the eleven largest islands, which account for 95 percent of the population. The islands' one major urban concentration is metropolitan Manila with a population of 8 million. It is a conglomeration of four cities (Manila [the country's de facto capital], Quezon [the nominal capital], Caloocan, and Pasay) and thirteen surrounding municipalities located on the island of Luzon.

The vast majority of Filipinos are Christians, making the country the only predominantly Christian nation in Asia. Catholicism was first introduced by the SPANIARDS in the sixteenth century, and is professed by over 80 percent of Filipinos, while Protestantism, which entered the Philippines with the American occupation, counts less than 10 percent of the population as its adherents. Islam is the religion of about 5 percent of the people, including the MARANAO and MAGINDANAO, who live on the southern island of Mindanao, while the archipelago is also home to a number of small groups which continue to practice their traditional religions. Tensions between Christians and Muslims in the southern islands and Muslim demands for autonomy have led to the creation of government agencies and institutions (under the auspices of the Ministry of Muslim Affairs), which seek to cater to the special educational, legal, and religious needs of the Muslim minority.

The official languages of the Philippines are Filipino (Pilipino) and English. Both are widely spoken and comprehended. Filipino is based upon Tagalog, the language of the region around Manila in central Luzon. Spanish was classed as an official language until 1973 but is only spoken by a small minority. There also exists a plethora of indigenous languages and dialects, essentially of Malay-Indonesian origin, which exhibit considerable grammatical and phonetic similarity to one another and are all classified as Austronesian. In addition to Tagalog, these include: Visayan, the largest major language group, spoken in the central islands around the Visayan Sea, including the islands of Panay and Tagbilaran; Cebuano, spoken by the inhabitants of the island of Cebu; Samaran, the language of the island of Samar; and Ilocano, the dominant language of northern Luzon.

The Philippines is primarily a rural, agrarian country, with about two thirds of people living in villages and nearly half involved in agriculture, forestry, and fishing. There is a great disparity between the great majority of Filipinos, who are poor, and a tiny minority of wealthy people.

Rice and corn, the principal subsistence crops, cover roughly half the available arable land: smallholdings and tenant farming are the norm. Commercial agriculture, by contrast, is dominated by large plantations producing coconuts for copra (of which the Philippines is the world's largest producer), sugarcane, tobacco, bananas, pineapples, and coffee. People also engage in subsistence fishing throughout the Philippines.

The ancestors of the Malay peoples of the Philippines most probably migrated from Southeast Asia. The Filipinos were mostly hunters, fishers, and shifting cultivators at the time when they first came into contact with the ARABS, who came as traders and introduced Islam to the region in the fourteenth century. Ferdinand Magellan, a Portuguese-born explorer working for Spain, was the first European to discover the islands, which were then conquered and controlled by the SPANIARDS by 1571. Sporadic Filipino agitations for independence were boosted by the successful rebel-

lions of the Spanish colonies in the Americas in the 1820s. Filipino opposition to colonial rule by Spain culminated in the unsuccessful revolt of 1896–1898, at the end of which the SPANIARDS sold the Philippines to the AMERICANS; Filipino demands for independence continued.

American rule of the islands lasted nearly fifty years. During that period, the Philippines were used as a supplier of raw materials to and buyer of goods from the United States. During World War II, the islands were the major theater of military operations in the Pacific and were occupied by the JAPANESE between 1942 and 1945, when they were recaptured by the AMERICANS.

The islands became a fully independent republic in 1946. However, the United States has maintained a significant naval and military presence in the region, however. The new state faced a difficult period of reconstruction after the damage the region incurred during the war. The government of the Philippines also faced insurrection by the Hukbalahaps, communist guerrillas whose revolutionary demands included calls for land reform. President Marcos quelled renewed Hukbalahap activity in 1969, but was then faced by Muslim rebel groups, including the Moro National Liberation Front (MNLF), whose strongholds were in the southern islands; their armed opposition to his regime was used to justify the imposition of martial law in September 1972.

Corruption and human rights abuses lost Marcos the support of the Roman Catholic church and led to popular discontent. The rigging of elections in 1986 precipitated an uprising against him, resulting in his flight to Hawaii. Corazon Aquino became president. She quickly instituted land reforms designed to transfer ownership of land into the hands of the tenant farmers who work it. However, communist insurgency, widespread poverty, a weak economy, and the power of the military to influence internal affairs continue to pose problems for the people of the Philippines.

PHINOI   see FINNS.

PHIRING   A subgroup of the TSWANA.

PHNONG   A generic term for groups living in the Cambodian uplands. (see also PEAR)

PHOU LAO   see LAO.

PHUTING   (Bapthuting) A subgroup of the SOTHO.

PIANOCOTO-TIRIYO (Pianokoto) A South American Indian group living near the Trombetas River in the State of Pará, northern Brazil, and in neighboring Suriname. They number over 1,000 and are formed of several closely related dialect groups.

PIDJANJARA (Ngadadjara) An Australian aboriginal group numbering a few thousand found in the Gibson Desert in Western Australia. They speak Pidjanjara. (see also AUSTRALIAN ABORIGINES)

PIH see BIH.

PIKINCHE A subgroup of the TEHUELCHE.

PIKRAJ An ethnic group living dispersed in the north and northeast of Afghanistan. They are estimated as numbering 2,000 (1980s).

Their language, Inku, belongs to the Indian group of the Indo-European family of languaages. Although it is also the mother tongue of several other dispersed ethnic groups of Afghanistan (JALALI, SHADIBAZ, VANGAVALANS), the Pikraj retain their distinct ethnic self-identity. The language is unwritten. Practically all adult Pikraj are bilingual, speaking Dari (the Afghanistani form of Persian) as well as Inku.

The Pikraj are Sunni Muslims of the Hanafi school. They are peripatetics (non-pastoral nomads). The men mainly trade in animals or engage in begging. Women generally engage in peddling. (see also AFGHANS, JALALI, JATS II, VANGAVALANS)

PILAGA A semi-nomadic South American Indian subgroup of the GUAYCURU, living in the Gran Chaco region of Argentina and Paraguay. They practice limited agriculture (growing maize, sweet manioc, beans, and pumpkins), but are primarily dependent on gathering wild products, hunting, and fishing. (see also GUAYCURU)

PILA-PILA (s.d. Yowa) An ethnic group numbering about 20,000 living mainly in the Djougou region of Benin, south of the town of Natitingou in the Atakora Province.

PIMA A Native North American group numbering 13,000, many of whom live on the Gila River Indian Federal Community and on the Salt River Reservation in Maricopa County, Arizona, U.S.A. Traditionally they were hunters of small game and gatherers of roots and wild plants, but today they are farmers growing cotton, corn, and other crops which can grow in Arizona.

One of the most famous Pima in this century was Ira Hayes, a U.S. Marine who participated in raising the American flag at the famous battle of Iwo Jima in World War II.

PINTUBI A group of AUSTRALIAN ABORIGINES living in the Gibson Desert in central Australia. They depend on government subsidies for their livelihood.

PIPIKORO An ethnic group living in the mountainous central region of the Indonesian island of Sulawesi (Celebes). (see also TORADJA)

PITCAIRN ISLANDERS The population of Pitcairn Island, a small, isolated, and remote island in the South Pacific, a British possession with strong ties to New Zealand. They are of Anglo-Tahitian stock, descendants of the Bounty mutineers who landed on the island in 1790 with six Tahitian men and twelve Tahitian women. In 1937 the population reached its peak of 233, and since then has declined, due to migration, to fewer than sixty today. All Islanders are members of the Seventh Day Adventist Church.

Two-thirds of Pitcairn's revenue is derived from the sale of postage stamps.

PIT RIVER TRIBE see ACHUMAWI, ATSUGEWI.

PLA An ethnic group related to the EWE living in Togo.

PLATEAU TONGA A Tonga-speaking group living in southern Zambia on the Batoka Plateau, north of Lake Kariba. Unlike the Valley TONGA they raise cattle in addition to farming, and have a system of age mates which helps unite their village units. The Plateau Tonga also made weapons and sold them to other African peoples.

In 1937 a group of Tonga chiefs, farmers, and teachers formed the Northern Rhodesian African National Congress to protest land alienation and discrimination against African food production for market. This was mainly a local group and it did not muster sufficient support to withstand government condemnation. The congress was not a significant political force until its revival in 1951. (see also TONGA)

PLEI KLY A subgroup of the JARAI.

PNONG A subgroup of the MNONG.

PO   A subgroup of the TSWANA.

POCOMAN   A subgroup of the MAYA.

POCONCHI   A subgroup of the MAYA.

POHNPEI ISLANDERS   (Pohnpeians, Ponapeans) A Micronesian-speaking people of about 31,000, who inhabit ten islands located at the center of the Caroline Islands in the Pacific Ocean. Early in the twentieth century they were administered by Germany; from 1920 they were under a Japanese mandate; and from 1945, under U.S. sovereignty. At present the island group is a member of the Federated States of Micronesia, associated with the United States.

The population is predominantly Roman Catholic. Their most common residential social unit is a matrilocal extended family, part of a matriclan. They possess the most complex sociopolitical organization in Central Micronesia, much affected by years of colonial occupation. Originally they practiced subsistence agriculture. Under the JAPANESE their agriculture underwent intensive development.

POI   see PAWI.

POK   (Bok) A subgroup of the SABAOT.

POKOMO   The estimated 68,000 Pokomo of eastern Kenya live on the banks of the Tana River from the coast up toward the towns of Hola and Garissa. Their language belongs to the Coastal Bantu grouping. Some

Pohnpei Islanders

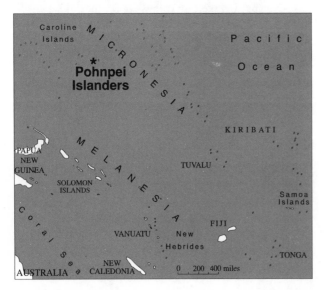

Pokomo retain their traditional religion but the majority today are Muslims.

The Pokomo economy is based on agriculture, with the Tana River as the major source of water. Their main crops are sugar cane, rice, and maize. Agriculture is also the basis of their culture and social structure, as well as wealth: a bride's price is set in products such as bags of rice, sugar, maize, etc. The Pokomo always manage to produce a surplus which is traded with neighbors.

POKOT   A Kalenjin-speaking ethnic group living in western Kenya.

POLES   (s.d. Polace; sing. Polak) The inhabitants of Poland, numbering 38 million, or 98 percent of the population. Another c.1.5 million Poles live in the neighboring Czech Republic, Slovakia, the Ukraine, Belarus, and Lithuania. Over 10 million Poles or their descendants live in the United States and Canada, and many others have migrated to France, Germany, Britain, Italy, and Australia.

The Polish language belongs to the Western branch of the Slavic group of Indo-European languages. It has been a literary language since the creation of the Polish state, and numerous texts, dating from the fourteenth century, have been preserved in it. It is written in the Roman alphabet.

The Polish nation was formed by the union of about twenty tribes: the Polish heartland still exhibits traces of the old divisions. Five major areas are distinguished by dialect, culture and folklore: Wielkopolska (Greater Poland) in the basin of the middle Warta up to the middle Odra (Oder) Rivers; Slask (Silesia) in the basin of the upper and middle Odra; Mazowrze (Mazovia) in the basin of the middle Wista River; Pomorze (Pomerania) along the Baltic coast from the Odra to the Wista; and Malopolska (Lesser Poland) in the basin of the upper Wista.

The Gorale (mountain dwellers) living in the Carpathians form a markedly distinguished group within Malopolska. The Karzuby (Kasubians) of the north, although forming part of Mazowrze, speak a distinct dialect considered by many to be a separate language. The eastern part of modern Poland, in the basin of the Neman and the Narew Rivers, was not part of the original Polish homeland; it was inhabited by East Slavic tribes who were colonized and assimilated by Poles from Mazowrze. However, some East Slavic traits remain which distinguish them from other Poles. Another area colonized by Poles from Mazowrze was the frontier of Prussia. Unlike the rest of the Polish people, these "Prussian Mazovians" are Lutherans.

Over the centuries, large parts of Slask, Mazowrze, and Wielkopolska came under rule by the GERMANS. With their annexation in 1945 and the expulsion of the German population, these areas became a target for Polish migration.

Slavic tribes seem to have inhabited the area of today's Poland since the early centuries C.E. In the ninth and tenth centuries tribal states were formed, the strongest of which was that of the Wislanie that ruled over most of Lesser Poland. A second state evolved in Slask (Silesia). However, the tribe which established Poland as a state was that of the Polanje under the Piast dynasty. The name "Pole" is derived from their name (lit. "forest clearing dwellers").

Mieszko I (963–992) conquered Pomerania, Silesia, and Lesser Poland. In 966 he converted to Roman Catholicism: Poles date the foundation of their country from that year. His son, Boleslaw I (992–1025), expanded the Polish domain westward and eastward into the basins of the Bug and Sam Rivers. He was the first crowned king of the Poles. Boleslaw III (1102–1138) divided Poland among his sons: the country, although officially one kingdom, remained divided for the following two centuries until it was reunited by the last Piasts, who forged an alliance with Hungary and Lithuania. Under the Jagiellonian kings (1385–1572) the United Kingdom of Poland-Lithuania reached its zenith as one of the major powers in Europe, extending over a huge territory from the Baltic to the Black Seas, and from the Odra River to about fifty miles west of Moscow.

As a major power, the kingdom was involved in the affairs of far removed areas and frequently had to fight the Ottomans, the Muscovites, the SWEDES, and other regional powers to the southeast, north, and west. Internally, the country evolved into a parliamentary monarchy of the aristocracy with the Sejm (Diet) being convened regularly after 1493. In 1569, lacking an heir to the last Jagellonian ruler, the Sejm formed the Union of Lublin, Poland, Lithuania, Prussia, and Livonia, a *rzeczpospolita*, (unified and indivisible commonwealth). This commonwealth, however, could only survive while it had a powerful monarch, such as the Vasa kings (1587–1668), or Jan III Sobieski (1674–1696). Under weak or corrupt rule it became a battlefield for its neighbors, whose strength was increasing. Following the rule of Peter the Great in Russia, and especially after the Northern War, Poland became a de facto Russian protectorate, and was finally partitioned among Russia, Prussia, and Austria in 1772, 1793, and 1795.

After the Napoleonic wars, in which a Duchy of Warsaw was created, Poland was redistributed among its neighbors. A kingdom of Poland was carved out by the Congress of Vienna and united with the Russian empire, while Krakow (Cracow) was made a free city. The Polish nobility and gentry had waged a struggle for the reinstatement of Polish independence from the first partition. Many now joined the French revolutionaries and Napoleon. In 1830 the Poles revolted but were crushed in 1831 by the RUSSIANS and Prussians. In 1846 an insurrection in Krakow resulted in the city's annexation to Austria. A second revolt in Poland in 1863 again took more than a year to be crushed by Prussia and Russia. This time the Russian authorities took steps to prevent the Polish nobility from revolting again.

After 1864 all three divisions of Poland underwent rapid industrialization and urbanization, which caused in their turn great social changes and the emergence of modern nationalism. During World War I both coalitions courted the Poles. After the war a Polish republic (the Second Commonwealth) was created by reuniting the areas which had belonged to Austria, Germany, and Russia. The new Polish state had to fight for survival, annexing large territories in the east. As a result more than a third of Poland's inhabitants belonged to minority groups, almost all of whom (the notable exception were the 3 million JEWS) continued to remain loyal to their previous nationalities. Internally unstable and externally a target for irrendentism, Poland became a dictatorship. Having defied Hitler's territorial demands, Poland was invaded by Germany in 1939, sparking off World War II and leading to Poland's being partitioned between Germany and the Soviet Union.

After the war Poland's borders underwent a drastic change. The eastern territories inhabited mainly by UKRAINIANS, BYELORUSSIANS, and LITHUANIANS were annexed to the Soviet Union. In compensation the Poles received all the German territories east of the Odra-Nysa Rivers line as well as the southern part of East Prussia. Some 4 million GERMANS escaped before the Soviet army's arrival in the country; after the war another 3.3 million GERMANS were expelled.

By 1947 Poland, like the rest of Eastern Europe, was ruled by a communist regime; unlike in other communist states, however, the Catholic church maintained a powerful political position and gave significant support to the anti-communist opposition. During its forty-two year existence the communist regime underwent several major crises, all involving food riots and strikes by well-organized industrial workers. In August 1980 there was a widespread strike in the shipyards and coal mines. This time, however, circumstances had changed. A Polish cardinal had been elected pope, lending moral and political strength to the Polish opposition. Under the church's wing a free trade movement was formed, called *Solidarnosc* (Solidarity). Following the collapse of Communist regimes in East Europe Solidarity came to power and its leader, Lech Walesa, was elected president. Since then the Poles have been struggling to build a democratic regime with a viable market economy.

POLESHCHUK see BYELORUSSIANS, UKRAINIANS.

POMAKS (Pamatsi) see BULGARIANS, TURKS.

POMO A Native North American group numbering 800, many of whom live on the Dry Creek Rancheria, Sonoma County, California, U.S.A. Originally from the San Francisco area, today they live in northern California. Since they have no reservation they live scattered over a wide area.

PONAPEANS see POHNPEI ISLANDERS.

PONCA A Native North American group numbering 3,200, many of whom live on the Ponca Tribe Federal Trust Area in Kay and Noble Counties, Oklahoma U.S.A. Some also live in Nebraska.

They are earth lodge dwellers and cultivators of maize and squash. Most of the tribe moved to the Indian Territory of Oklahoma in the 1870s, the remainder joining the Omaha Reservation in Nebraska. At the end of the nineteenth century, a separate section of the reservation was established in Nebraska for the Ponca, and many Ponca chose to move there from Oklahoma.

PONOSOKAN A subgroup of the MINAHASAN.

PONTIC An ethnic group originating in the Black Sea region, but now found primarily in Athens, Greece, and in North America. Their language is of unknown origins and is unrelated to any known language. The Pontic community has dwindled rapidly in recent years due to assimilation and acculturation into the dominant GREEKS.

POPOLZAI A subgroup of the PASHTUN.

PORAJA An ethnic group numbering about 350,000, living in the states of Madhya Pradesh and Orissa in central India. Their primary occupation is the cultivation of rice.

PORJA An ethnic group numbering 16,000 (1981), living in Andhra Pradesh, India. They speak Oriya, a member of the Indo-Aryan family of languages. The Porja are agriculturists and day laborers. The women sell firewood.

PORTUGUESE The 10 million Portuguese are a predominantly Catholic people speaking a Romance language closely akin to Galician. Counting former colonies Brazil, Mozambique, and Angola, Portuguese is spoken worldwide by over 160 million people.

The Portuguese are believed to descend from the Lusitan tribe who, in the third century B.C.E., entered into a compact with Rome. During the first millennium C.E., however, Portugal as such did not exist. The country was overrun first by the Suevi and West Goths, Germanic invaders from the north, then conquered in 711 by Muslim Moors. A long process of *Reconquista* against the North African rulers ensued: the Portuguese nation was shaped in this crucible. The process of reconquest was completed by the mid-thirteenth century, rounding off the territorial basis of Europe's oldest nation-state. The influence of the ARABS has remained stronger in the south, but the overall Arab imprint is less strong on the Portuguese than on the SPANIARDS.

The next episode in the crystallization of the Portuguese nation was the era of exploration and the establishment of the first worldwide seaborne empire in the fifteenth and sixteenth centuries. Portuguese mariners opened the Atlantic and established colonies from the African coast to insular Southeast Asia, China, and Brazil. Behind the establishment of this immense empire lay not only economic interests but the aspiration to spread Christianity.

Portugal's period of glory was brief and was followed by a long era of decline. The last Portuguese king mysteriously disappeared in 1578. The SPANIARDS occupied the country, and during the next decades the Portuguese lost most of their overseas empire to the DUTCH and ENGLISH. In 1640 they regained their independence. Emphasis was placed on the colonization of Brazil and the exploitation of sugar, cotton, and tobacco from plantations cultivated by imported African slaves.

Attempts at creating an industrial base in the eighteenth century failed. Portugal was practically a British colony, trading local wines for English textiles. By the nineteenth century, the Portuguese had become isolated from European currents and lost Brazil. Civil wars between the peasants and the bourgeoisie shook the country. After the establishment of a radical anti-clerical republic early in the twentieth century, a confused period of coups and countercoups exhausted the country's resources. This deepened the economic crisis and undermined the legitimacy of politicians, so that in 1926 a fascist military coup led by Oliveira Salazar was hailed as providing a measure of stability. Although the regime managed to provide some material progress, the army and secret police dominated the country and imposed isolationism on the people. Salazar became all-powerful from 1933.

Portugal has been a perpetual reservoir of cheap manpower: from the sixteenth century the dearth of arable land stimulated emigration. Between 1820 and 1935, 1.5 million Portuguese immigrants colonized Brazil. Post-World War II emigration was directed towards France and other European countries. By the middle of the twentieth century the Portuguese were among Europe's poorest and least developed peoples. However, the migrants' experiences, along with growing mobility and urbanization, began to change outlooks, and destabilized the regime. 1968 was the end of the Salazar era. His technocratic successors failed to modernize the economy and liberalize the political structure. Unpopular colonial wars in Africa were the catalyst of the April 1974 Revolution of Carnations, which liquidated Portugal's colonial heritage. A parliamentary democracy was institutionalized. In the 1980s, mass tourism, the beginnings of industrialization, and integration into Europe have brought about the rapid modernization of Portuguese society.

POSHTE KUH see LUR.

POSO An ethnic group living in the mountainous central region of the Indonesian island of Sulawesi (Celebes). (see also TORADJA)

POSO-TOJO An ethnic group living in the mountainous central region of the Indonesian island of Sulawesi (Celebes). (see also TORADJA)

POTAWATOMI A Native North American group numbering 3,200, many of whom live in the Citizen Band of the Potawatomi Tribe Federal Trust Area in Potawatomi County, Oklahoma, on the Potawatomi Federal Reservation in Jackson County, Kansas, and on the Hannahville Federal Reservation in Michigan, U.S.A.

Traditionally they were hunters and gatherers but some also cultivated maize and wild rice. Their traditional dwellings were wigwams (tents covered by birch bark). They were also known for their birch bark canoes. They were allies of the FRENCH in their war against the BRITISH and allies of the BRITISH against the AMERICANS in the Revolutionary War. As a result the Potawatomi were scattered over a large geographic area.

POTIGUARA A South American Indian group living in villages along the northern coastline of Brazil, at the border of the States of Paraíba and Rio Grande do Norte. Numbering over 1,000, they have retained their traditional lifestyle.

POTOSON HUASTEC see HUASTEC.

POUNOU (Bapounou) An ethnic group living in southwestern Gabon, in the upper N'Gounie and Nyanga River systems. They speak a language which is related to that of their ESHIRA neighbors.

According to their tradition they migrated to their present location from the south before the nineteenth century. During the nineteenth century they participated in the slave trade and exported rubber.

POVINDA A subgroup of the PASHTUN.

PRAI see T'IN.

PRAMPRAM A subgroup of the ADANGBE.

PRASUN (Paruni) One of several clans grouped together as NURESTANI.

PREH A subgroup of the MNONG.

PRINCIPE ISLANDERS see SAO TOME AND PRINCIPE, THE PEOPLE OF.

PRU A small Mon-Khmer group living in southern Vietnam.

PUBIAN A subgroup of the ABUNG.

PUCARA An OTAVALO clan.

PUEBLO INDIANS A Native North American people of about 40,000. The term "pueblo" (Spanish for "people") refers both to the grouping and to its dwelling pattern: a multi-level housing complex made of mud and stone, with a beam roof covered with mud.

Pueblo groups include the HOPI, the ZUNI, and other smaller groups. They are modern descendants of the Anasazi, an ancient civilization that flourished between the thirteenth and the sixteenth centuries. The most ancient Pueblo village is Acoma, which has a continuous history of about 1,000 years. They were efficient agriculturalists who developed a system of irrigation. The Pueblo villages were built on high ground for defense purposes.

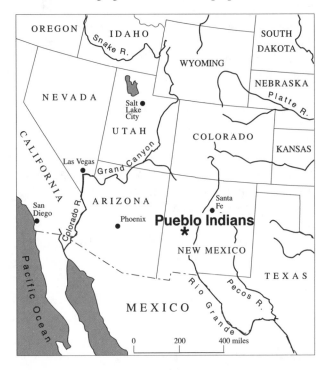

Pueblo Indians

Today the Pueblo Indians live in a combination of ancient and modern dwellings and earn their livelihood from agriculture and pottery, for which they are world famous. Friction continues to exist today between the Pueblo Indians and the NAVAJO, who consider the former invaders of their territory.

PUELCHE   A South American Indian nomadic group living on the Argentinian pampas. They were dependent on hunting the rhea and guanaco (which they pursued with the help of domesticated dogs) for their subsistence. They also gathered wild produce such as algarroba pods. They are now almost extinct. (see also TEHUELCHE)

PUERTO RICANS   Puerto Ricans, some of whom call themselves "Borinquenos" after their

Taino/Arawak ancestors, number over 3.3 million on the Caribbean island itself, with large expatriate populations in such major cities of the Continental U.S.A. as New York, Boston, Chicago, and Los Angeles, and in many smaller cities. Economic pressures have forced many families to lead a dual existence, oscillating between the island and mainland. Of the permanent inhabitants of this mountainous island, most are concentrated in the coastal lowlands, with almost half in the San Juan metropolitan area. Roman Catholicism is the predominant faith among Puerto Ricans, who were ruled by the SPANIARDS for several hundred years. In spite of heavy North American influence since 1898, when the island was occupied by the U.S. in the Spanish-American War, Puerto Ricans have retained much of their own mixed Spanish, African, and American Indian culture: attemps by the U.S.A. to impose English as the official language failed early in the present century, and Spanish was subsequently restored.

To some extent, it is the mountain peasant, or *jibaro*, depicted with a guitar in one hand and a field machete in the other, who has symbolized the island's culture to its own people. The mountain music is less well-known than the renown coastal *salsa*, but it is the combination of the two, together with a unique pattern of dances and celebrations partly shared with Cuba, that give Puerto Rican culture its character.

Puerto Rico's economy is more industrialized than that of any other Caribbean island, dependent to a considerable extent upon labor-intensive manufacturing complemented by trade enterprises and financial services. While agriculture, dominant until the 1940s, has declined considerably, plantation sugar cane and distilled rum are still important products.

The island, designated by the U.S.A. as the "Commonwealth of Puerto Rico" in 1952, has the status of a "Free Associated State." The United Nations has directed the U.S.A. to divest itself of the island under decolonization statutes, but neither the Puerto Rican indedpendence movement strongest in the 1960s and 1970s, nor the statehood movement, have been able to marshall sufficient force and adherents to resolve the island's anomalous political status.

PUKHTUN   see PASHTUN.

PULARE   A chiefdom of the DIAGUITA.

PULI   A subgroup of the AKHA.

PULIYAN   An ethnic group numbering 61,000 (1981), living in the states of Tamil Nadu and Kerala, India. They speak Tamil, a member of the Dravidian family of languages. They are nomads who subsist by hunting and fishing.

PUNA   A Native South American group living in Ecuador.

PUNAN   (Bukitan Ot) A generic term for several nomadic, forest-dwelling groups living in the interior of the Indonesian island of Kalimantan (Borneo). They number about 3,000. Their language is related to that of the Kenyah, but is divided into numerous, often mutually unintelligible dialects. This is due in part to the extensive use of loan words adopted from the sedentary populations with whom they come into contact. Although they possess no writing system, they can relay messages through sticks set in the ground. They employ terraced irrigation systems to cultivate corn, beans, and pumpkins; in recent times they have adopted potato-cultivation and cattle-raising. Their religious beliefs are similar to those of the KENYAH but recent contact with Christian missionaries has had some influence.

The sedentary population among whom the Punan live regard them as little more than animals, and often claim them as slaves. (see also DAYAK)

PUNAN KARAHL   An ethnic group living on the Indonesian island of Kalimantan (Borneo). (see also DAYAK)

PUNJABIS   The inhabitants of the Punjab region of India and Pakistan. They speak Punjabi, an Indo-European language. The name Punjab denotes the area lying between the Indus River and the five rivers (Jhelum, Chenab, Ravi, Beas, and Satluj) originating in the Himalayas. In 1981 the combined population of Indian and Pakistani Punjab was 64 million.

The Punjab region has unique historic significance as the traditional route through which invaders and migrants have come to India. It is also the region of the prehistoric civilizations of Harappa and Mohenjodaro. Alexander the Great is recorded to have come as far as the Ravi River during his incursions.

Punjab has seen massive agricultural development; it is often referred to as the wheat bowl of India. It also has many agro-processing and agro-service industries. Its culture has been molded by events during the partition of India in 1947, which separated Hindus and

Sikhs from Muslims, and made Sikhs a majority in the Indian Punjabi countryside. Recently, the Sikhs in Indian Punjab have been agitating for an independent state within the region. (see also PAKISTANIS)

P'U NOI   (Kha P'ai P'u Noi) A Mon-Khmer group numbering about 10,000 living in southern Laos. They originated in the north of that country but migrated southward as a result of pressure from the CHINESE, BURMANS, and VIETNAMESE. They engage in slash and burn cultivation of rice and are nominally Buddhists, although they also worship a variety of local spirits.

PUNYARO   An OTAVALO people.

PUREPECHA   An indigenous Mexican people numbering almost 100,000, inhabiting the mountain, gorge, and lake areas of northern Michoacan, a state in Mexico. Their language, Purepecha, is a member of the Maya-Totonac family.

Nominally Roman Catholic, the Purepecha attribute special powers to Jesus and the Virgin Mary, and the devil is in many ways seen as more important than the saints. Their festivals, the most important of which honor the patron saints of each village, are punctuated with masked dances: the best known is *Los Viejitos* (the "dance of the old men"). The Purepecha believe that the dead who have left work unfinished, promises unredeemed, or vows to saints unsatisfied, wander the earth until relatives complete their obligations.

Sometimes known by the derogatory name Tarasco, the Purepecha have subsisted through agriculture, forestry, animal husbandry, and, in such lake areas as Pátzcuaro, by fishing. The men, many of whom are now emporary migrants to towns in search of work, dress in less traditional fashion than the women. They are famed for their work in copper, pottery, weaving, and lacquered wood. (see also MEXICANS)

PURUHA   A South American Indian group living in Ecuador.

PURUM   (Burum) A KUKI people, living in the Manipur Hills of India and Myanmar (Burma). Numbering several hundred, they live in four villages. The language they speak belongs to the Tibeto-Burman language family.

The people primarily subsist on slash and burn agriculture accompanied by animal domestication. The Purum practice a traditional religion which has been influenced by Hinduism.

A Punjabi Sikh man

PUSH-E KUH   see LUR.

PUSHTUN   see PASHTUN.

PUTIAN   see SULOD.

PU'U MBANA   An ethnic group living in the mountainous central region of the Indonesian island of Sulawesi (Celebes). (see also TORADJA)

PU'U MBOTO   An ethnic group living in the mountainous central region of the Indonesian island of Sulawesi (Celebes). (see also TORADJA)

PUYALLUP   A Native North American group numbering 8,000, some of whom live on the Puyallup Federal Reservation in Pierce County, Washington, U.S.A. Originally part of the West Coast Indian culture, today they maintain a small reservation on the outskirts of Tacoma, Washington, U.S.A. Many work in local industry.

PUYI   see BUYI.

PUYUMA   An indigenous ethnic group numbering approximately 20,000, living in Taiwan. Originally agriculturalists but also hunters and fishermen, they adhere to traditional religious beliefs.

PWO   (Phlong) A subgroup of the KAREN.

PYGMIES   An ethnic group living mostly in southern and northeastern Gabon, in the forest area of southern Cameroon, in Congo, in the Congo River

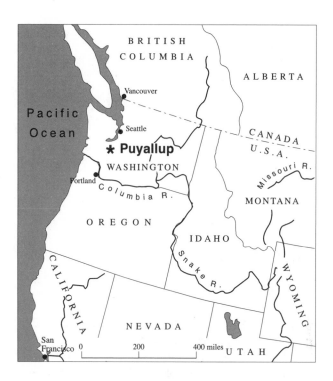

Puyallup

basin of Zaire, in Equatorial Guinea, and in small numbers in Rwanda, Burundi, and Uganda. The Pygmies have generally rejected a modern economy and lifestyle. They still live from hunting and gathering and raise food crops and livestock. They are known for their small size. They generally adopt the language and customs of their neighbors. (see also AMBO, BAYELE, CENTRAL AFRICAN REPUBLIC, THE PEOPLE OF THE)

Q

QABENNA   see KABENA.

QACHALYQ   see CHECHEN.

QAITAGH   see KAITAG.

QAJAR   An ethnic subgroup of the AZERBAIJANI. In Iranian Azerbaijan they still form a more or less compact group, living as an enclave among the MAZANDARANI, to the southeast of the Caspian coast, where they number an estimated 100,000. In Azerbaijan, where historically they had a strong presence in the Qarabagh (Ganja) area, they have abandoned their specific identity in favor of that of the general Azerbaijani one. The Qajar dynasty, which ruled Iran from 1779 to 1925, originated from this subgroup.

QARACHAI   (s.d. Qarachaily, Karachi) A people, numbering 156,000 (1989), living on the northern slopes of the main Caucasian Ridge, in the upper basin of the Kuban River and its tributaries. The Qarachai lan-

Qarachai

guage belongs to the Qypchaq group of the Turkic family. A unified Qarachai-Balkar literary language, based on Qarachai, was created in the mid-1920s for both the Qarachai and the BALKAR, whose spoken language is regarded as a Qarachai dialect. In 1925 it was reduced to the Roman and in 1938 to the Cyrillic alphabets.

Since the seventeenth to early eighteenth centuries the Qarachai have been Sunni Muslims of the Hanafi school, although up to the twentieth century some traditional beliefs have been preserved (e.g., the worship of sacred stones).

According to accepted opinion, they descend from Qypchaq tribes, who incorporated the aboriginal population of the Central Caucasus, among them part of the Allan, the ancestors of the OSSET. The Qarachai material culture and folklore show considerable similarity with those of the OSSET.

In 1922 the Cherkess-Qarachai Autonomous *Oblast* was proclaimed, divided in 1926 into two separate administrative units. In 1944, charged with collaborating with the Nazi GERMANS during World War II, the Qarachai were deported to Central Asia. They returned in 1957, and a Qarachai-Circassian Autonomous *Oblast* was reinstalled. They were formally "rehabilitated" only in November 1989. In November 1990 a Qarachai republic was proclaimed, an act which remained, however, merely formal. Demands that the Russian authorities recognize Qarachai statehood continued to be a major feature of Qarachai ethnic self-awareness in the early 1990s.

QARAPAPAKH   (lit. "black hats") Historically, a Turkish ethnic group which from the 1930s has gradually assimilated into the TURKS, AZERBAIJANI, and MESKH.

QARAQALPAQ   A people living mostly in Qaraqalpaqstan in Uzbekistan, near the Aral Sea and along the Amu-Darya River. In 1989 census they numbered 423,000. They speak a language which belongs to the Qypchaq-Noghai group of Turkic languages. Its literary form, based on its northeastern dialect, developed only in the mid-1920s. It was reduced to the Roman alphabet in 1928 and to the Cyrillic one in 1938. The Qaraqalpaq are Sunni Muslims of the Hanafi school. Ethnically and linguistically they are close to the QAZAQ. Traditionally, they have been divided into several tribes, each usually consisting of several clans. They are first mentioned within the realm of Central Asia only in the late seventeenth century.

Traditionally they were nomad cattle-breeders and to a lesser extent fishermen and sedentary agriculturalists. Until the 1960s the Qaraqalpaq remained mostly rural, with only 10 percent of the population occupied in industry. Between 1960 and 1990 the situation changed: Qaraqalpaqstan became the most urbanized region of Uzbekistan, with 50 percent of the population concentrated in cities.

The capital city, Nukus, grew fivefold in thirty years and other cities tripled in size. The main reason for this mass exodus from the countryside was an ecological disaster in the area of the Aral Sea, which caused pollution of both water and land, and led to a high child mortality rate.

The area inhabited by the Qaraqalpaq became part of the Russian empire in 1873. In 1925 the Soviets proclaimed the establishment of the Qaraqalpaq Autonomous *Oblast* within the framework of the Qazaq Autonomous Soviet Socialist Republic which, in turn, was a part of the Russian Soviet Socialist Federative Republic. An autonomous republic since 1932, it was included in the Uzbek Soviet Socialist Republic in 1936. The Qaraqalpaq now constitute only 31 percent of the total population of their autonomous republic.

In the rise of Qaraqalpaq ethnic self-awareness in the late 1980s and early 1990s, three tendencies stand out: the demand for the return of lands seen as taken by UZBEKS; the demand for secession from Uzbekistan and reintegration into Russia with the status given to other former autonomous republics; and finally, the demand for the status of a fully independent republic within the framework of the Commonwealth of Independent States.

QARATA   see KARATA.

QARBULAQ   A tribal community of the CHECHEN.

QARLUQ   A tribe of the UZBEKS.

QASHQAI   A people dwelling in the Fars province of Iran. Their estimated number is 650,000. The Qashqai language is unwritten and belongs to the Oguz group of Turkic languages. They are Shi'ite Muslims.

The Qashqai as an ethnic unity are a relatively recent phenomenon. As an ethnic name, Qashqai is first mentioned only in the eighteenth century. Evidently, the Qashqai as a people emerged at that time as the result of the consolidation of several Turkic-speaking tribes, joined by smaller tribes of non-Turkic origin.

About two-thirds of the Qashqai are nomads who live mainly from cattle-, camel-, and horse-breeding and partly from agriculture. Qashqai winter pastures are located mainly to the south of Shiraz, the capital of the Fars province, on the southern mountain slopes, close to the shores of the Persian Gulf. Summer pastures are in high mountain regions. Most nomad Qashqai also have plots of agricultural land near their pastures. Sedentary Qashqai work mainly at agriculture, and Qashqai women are carpet-weavers.

Until 1930 the union of Qashqai tribes was headed by *ilkhans*, whose power is hereditary. In 1930 the Qashqai, with all the other nomadic peoples of Iran, were forcibly brought under the control of the central government, the *ilkhan*, Sanlat ad-Dawla, was imprisoned and subsequently died in prison, while his sons were forced out of the country. During World War II the rule of the *ilkhan* was restored and one of Sanlat ad-Dawla's sons, Nasir, took over the post. In 1963, however, the Qashqai were once more brought under the control of the central government and the *ilkhan* was forced to leave Iran.

Qashqai

Since the 1960s an evergrowing number of Qashqai have been migrating to towns, mainly Shiraz. Most urbanized Qashqai are engaged in services.

QATARIS The approximately 80,000 indigenous Arabic-speaking Muslim Qataris today constitute only one fifth of the 420,000 inhabitants of Qatar, a state on the Persian Gulf. Another 25 percent are other ARABS: PALESTINIANS, EGYPTIANS, LEBANESE, SYRIANS, and YEMENIS; 16 percent are IRANIANS, and 34 percent South Asians. By religion, 92 percent of the Qataris are Muslims, most of them Sunni.

Qatar is a barren desert and its modest aquifers support only limited agriculture. It was sparsely populated and poor, with its people lived mostly from fishing and pearling, until oil was found in the late 1940s. The oil economy now earns 90 percent of the tiny state's revenues and supports a high per capita income. It also attracts thousands of migrant laborers, who, in spite of their low incomes, were much better integrated here than in other Gulf states. Nearly all live in the capital, Doha (Ad-Dawhah). Only a few thousand Beduin live in the desert.

In 1860 the currently reigning ath-Thani family took control in the shadow of growing Ottoman and, later, Saudi power in the Gulf region. In 1916 Qatar became a protectorate of the BRITISH. Save for Britain, it is unlikely that the Qataris would have escaped absorption into Saudi Arabia, the fate of most other neighboring ARABS.

In 1971 Qatar became independent from Britain. In 1972 a bloodless coup brought Khalifah bin Hamad ath-Thani to power, who allowed a very limited broadening of political participation, and installed a comprehensive social security system for Qatari nationals. Oil was nationalized in 1976. In 1981 Qatar became a member of the Gulf Cooperation Council. The regime maintains a strict Wahhabite Muslim lifestyle.

QAVOL see GYPSIES.

QAZAQ (Kazakh) A people living in Qazaqstan and adjacent areas of Russia and Uzbekistan. A sizable number of Qazaq is also found in the Xinjiang Uighur Autonomous Region of China and in Mongolia. A small number of Qazaq live in northern Afghanistan.

In 1989 there were 8.1 million Qazaq in the Soviet Union, of whom some 6.7 million lived in the Kazakh Republic and the remainder in the Russian and Uzbek republics. Within their own republic (16.7 million residents) the Qazaq make up 40 percent of the total population, with RUSSIANS as the second largest group at 38 percent of the population (6.2 million). The number of Qazaq in China is approximately 1 million. The number in Mongolia is unknown, but estimated to run to tens of thousands. There are some 3,000 Qazaq in Afghanistan (mid-1980s), all of whom fled Soviet rule in the 1920s.

The Qazaq language belongs to the northwestern Qypchaq-Noghai group of Turkic languages. In the Soviet Union the Arabic script was used until 1929, followed by the Roman, and, since 1938, Cyrillic. In China the Qazaq developed a writing system based on the Roman alphabet in the 1950s. They possess a rich oral folklore, and their written literature dates back to the second half of the nineteenth century.

In Russian pre- and early Soviet ethnography the Qazaq were designated as Kirgiz to distinguish them from the QYRGHYZ, or as Kirgiz-Kaisak. In their turn, the QYRGHYZ, to be distinguished from the Qazaq, were named Kara-Kirgiz by the RUSSIANS. With the stabilization of Soviet Russian ethnography their name was spelled "Kazakh" in Russian and not "Kazak" as could have been expected, since the latter form had already existed in Russian as the designation of Slavic (Russian and historically also Ukrainian) Cossacks.

The Qazaq are Sunni Muslims of the Hanafi school. Their islamization was a steady process which was completed only in the eighteenth century. Some remnants of shamanism and ancestor worship remain.

Qazak

Historically, the area of contemporary Qazaqstan, as part of the great European chain of steppes and deserts, served as a corridor for the many migrations and invasions of nomadic peoples on their way from east to west. This continuous procession created powerful ethnic interaction among the indigenous tribes and the tides of newcomers. By the end of the first millennium C.E. numerous Turkic tribes, among them Qypchaq, dominated the area. During the thirteenth and fourteenth centuries many MONGOLS were gradually integrated into the local nomadic groups. Toward the beginning of the sixteenth century these tribes became consolidated into the Qazaq people, and for a short time a state, the Qazaq Khanate, emerged, which later broke into three federations: the Great, the Middle, and the Lesser Hordes (*Zhuzes*, lit. "parts"). During the eighteenth and nineteenth centuries these Qazaq federations gradually became part of the Russian Empire.

With the breakdown of this empire in 1917, a short-lived Qazaq autonomy headed by the Alash Orda national modernist party existed until 1919. The Russian Bolsheviks crushed it and established the Kirghiz Autonomous Soviet Socialist Republic (ASSR), in 1920 renamed in 1925 the Qazaq ASSR within the framework of the Russian Federation. In 1936 it was given the status of a Soviet Socialist Republic (SSR). In 1991 Qazaqstan became an independent state within the framework of the Commonwealth of Independent States.

Traditionally, the Qazaq were, and in China and Mongolia still are, pastoral nomads. This traditional framework was destroyed by the massive influx of RUSSIANS, who came as settlers beginning in the nineteenth century, and was greatly accelerated under the Soviets, especially in the 1950s and early 1960s, who implemented industrialization, urbanization, and forced sedentarization. The major demographic catastrophe for the Qazaq occurred at the beginning of the 1930s when, due to forced settlement and collectivization, close to 1.5 million died of hunger. The very landscape of the Qazaq steppes was reshaped through extensive agricultural and industrial construction.

The process of change alongside forcible sedentarization produced a new occupational structure for the Qazaq, creating workers and farmers and a relatively broad stratum of intelligentsia. At the same time it brought both de-ethnicization of the Qazaq people (by the late 1980s 40 percent of its youth could not speak Qazaq) and ecological disasters near the Aral Sea and in Samipalatinsk, where for many years the Soviet military carried out underground nuclear tests. The move-

ment against Russian domination in the party-political apparatus and for the strengthening of the status of the Qazaq language served as a rallying focus for national assertiveness from the late 1980s, which reached its climax in the above-mentioned formal 1991 proclamation of an independent Qazaqstan. (see also AFGHANS, QARAQALPAK, UZBEKS)

QEMANT (K'amant, Kemant) An ethnic group numbering 170,000 (1984), who live to the north and west of the town of Gondar, Ethiopia. They speak a central Cushitic language as well as Amharic and are a subgroup of the AGAW. Many now adhere to a form of Ethiopian Orthodox Christianity. They are plow-using agriculturalists.

Socially, the Qemant like other Cushitic groups, stress patrilineal descent, but in regard to land tenure they follow the cultural tradition of the AMHARA.

QIPCHAQ A subgroup of the UZBEKS.

QIZILBASH (Turkic "redhead") An ethnic group living in three major cities of Afghanistan (its capital Kabul, Herat, and Qanlahur), and also in the vicinity of Beshul, a town southwest of Kabul. Their estimated number (1970s) ranged from 30,000 to 40,000.

The Qizilbash speak Dari, the Afghanistani version of Persian. They are Shi'ite Muslims. Overwhelmingly urban, they are engaged mainly in trade and in administrative work, and are well represented in the free professions. They are descended from Turkic-speaking soldiers from Iran garrisoned in Afghanistan by the Iranian king Nadir Shah (1739–1747).

Historically, the term *qizilbash* was used from the thirteenth century to refer to the Shi'ites of Asia Minor and Kurdistan, and from the late fifteenth century as a cognomen for tribes (predominantly Turkic) who became followers of the Safavid Sufi sheikhs and, with the establishment of the Safavid Shi'ite state in Iran (1501), formed the core and elite of the Safavid army. (see also AFGHANS)

QUAHOE see KWAWU.

QUAPAW (Capaha) A Native North American group numbering 1,500, many of whom live on the Quapaw Tribe Federal Trust Area, Ottawa County, Oklahoma, U.S.A. Originally they lived in thatched huts along the Mississippi River, near the Arkansas River. They moved to the Indian Territory of Oklahoma and settled there with the OSAGE. Today they work in local industry.

QUBACHI (s.d. Urbugh) An ethnic group of the single *aul* (village) of Qubachi in the Caucasian Mountains of Daghestan, Russia, between the Caspian Sea coast and the Qaziqumukh Koksu River. The most recent population data available are that of the Soviet 1926 census, when they numbered 2,322. They have been Sunni Muslims of the Shafi'i school since the nineteenth century.

The Qubachi language is unwritten, and Dargwa is used as the literary language. Over the last decades Qubachi has been regarded as a dialect of the Dargwa language belonging to the Dargwa-Lak group of the Ibero-Caucasian family of languages. Soviet ethnography has regarded the Qubachi as a subgroup of the DARGIN which uses its mother tongue. Until 1820, when they were included in the Russian empire, the Qubachi had formed one of the Dargin "free communities."

The Qubachi are known throughout the Caucasus as highly skilled metalworkers (weapons, jewelery, and coining). Hence in medieval ethnographic nomenclature they were named Iranian Zirijhgaran, or hauberk makers.

QUEBECOIS (French Canadians) French-speaking inhabitants of the Canadian province of Quebec, numbering about 6.8 million. Unlike other Canadian provinces, Quebec is predominantly French-speaking and Roman Catholic. Its inhabitants, although now mostly urbanized, are descendants of the FRENCH, who came as settlers to Canada and who have tenaciously preserved their French heritage despite the lures of English-speaking society in both the rest of Canada and the neighboring United States.

The first French settlement in Canada was established in present-day Nova Scotia in 1604. In 1608 the town of Quebec was established along the banks of the Saint Lawrence River; Montreal was established on an island to the southwest of Quebec City in 1642. In 1663 the area was incorporated as the French territory of New France.

The early settlers were a hardy lot, generally originating in Normandy and Brittany in France: Quebecois French, sometimes known as Joual, has preserved some of the archaic forms and dialectal distinctions of European French from this period and location. Over the following century, thousands of French settlers flocked to Quebec as farmers and trappers. There, their rural French culture gradually diverged from that of France, forming a distinctly French Canadain tradition.

Expansion by the BRITISH from their Atlantic colonies led to the collapse of French Atlantic settlements and the concentration of most of the FRENCH along the Saint Lawrence River.

In the early 1700s the French settlers of Acadia (present-day New Brunswick) were conquered by the ENGLISH and many were exiled to the Gulf of Mexico. Among their descendants are the Cajuns of Louisiana. A French-speaking community which survived in northern New Brunswick is still known as ACADIANS.

The BRITISH captured Quebec City in 1759 and the rest of New France in 1763. The French defeat was particularly traumatic for the local population whose present motto, *Je me souviens* ("I remember"), refers to the indignity of defeat by the ENGLISH. Although the preservation of French language, religion, and culture were assured by an act of British Parliament in 1774, the FRENCH felt increasingly swamped by the burgeoning English population and feared that their distinctive cultural identity would soon disappear. This was exacerbated by the union of English Upper Canada (now Ontario) with Lower Canada (now Quebec) into the single territory of Canada. With the formation of the Dominion of Canada as a federation of British North American territories in 1869, the union was finally dissolved to assure the FRENCH in the province of Quebec, now known as Quebecois, some degree of autonomy in what had become an overwhelmingly English-speaking country.

Although the Quebecois played an important role in the emergence of Canada and provided the country with several of its most significant leaders, there was the constant fear of English cultural dominance and the loss of their own heritage through a slow process of assimilation. At the same time, they resented the English conquest of the eighteenth century and sought to assert themselves as a society distinct from the rest of Canada. Tensions erupted during both world wars over national conscription, with the FRENCH refusing to be forced into a war they considered to be solely for the defense of Britain. By the late 1960s the traditional devout agrarian Quebecois society had been transformed by rapid urbanization and a new intellectual elite emerged which demanded independence to preserve their French-speaking society in an overwhelmingly English-speaking continent. Sparked by De Gaulle's declaration in Montreal, "Long Live Free Quebec," the Front de la Liberation de Quebec (FLQ), a separatist organization, committed several terrorist attacks, prompting Canadian prime minister Pierre Trudeau, himself a Quebecois, to proclaim a state of emergency in the province. This crushed the FLQ but separatist sentiment remained high, culminating in the formation and eventual election of the Parti Quebecois, a separatist party, to power in the province in the 1970s. French was declared the province's sole official language; education in French was made compulsory, and special units of language police were formed to assure that only French signs were displayed in public places. A referendum on "sovereignty-association" was voted down by a slim margin, prompting the Canadian government to make further concessions to Quebec to preserve the country.

In the 1980s, the Canadian government proposed to rewrite the constitution, assuring Quebec's status as a distinct society and providing for a set number of representatives in any future Canadian parliament. In a nation-wide referendum in 1992, the new constitution was rejected; English-speaking CANADIANS were alarmed at the power promised Quebec, while the Quebecois spurned the offer as being insufficient. As a result, Quebecois separatism again threatens to divide Canada.

QUECHUA Over 10 million Native South Americans of the Andean Highlands speak the ancient Inca language, Quechua. They are spread out across present-day Ecuador, Peru, Argentina, Chile, and Bolivia. The two largest concentrations of Quechua-speaking peoples are in Peru and Bolivia, where they comprise about 40 percent of the population. Quechua was recognized as an official language of Peru (alongside Spanish) in 1975. Apart from language, the Quechua and AYMARA are virtually indistinguishable. (see also AYMARA)

QUENEY see KENOY.

QUERANDI A Native South American group, originally nomadic horsemen of the Argentinian pampas. Never numerous, they are now almost completely extinct.

QUICHE The most numerous of Guatemala's highland Mayan groups, numbering more than a million. They are the largest linguistic group in Guatemala and practice both Catholic and indigenous rituals, sometimes in the same church.

They live in scattered small villages, surrounded by fields and pastures. A major Quiche center is the re-

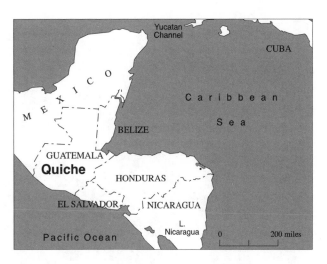

Quiche

gion surrounding the market town of Chichicastenango, south of their pre-Hispanic capital of Atilan where all the inhabitants were massacred by the SPANIARDS in the early 1500s because they had no gold. (see also MAYA)

QUICHE-CAKCHIQUEL A subgroup of the MAYA.

QUICHICHE An OTAVALO subgroup.

QUILLACA A subgroup of the AYMARA.

QUINAULY A Native North American group numbering 2,300, many of whom live on two Quinauly Tribe Federal Reservations in Washington State, U.S.A. Traditionally they were part of the West Coast Indian culture that lived near the Pacific.

In the last decade, they achieved a degree of autonomy, receiving federal funds directly, not through the Bureau of Indian Affairs. They own and operate a salmon hatchery and a lumber company. They have more than 400 square miles of reservation land and a beach stretching for thirty miles along the Pacific Ocean, making the Quinauly the group that owns the largest area of beach.

QUIRIQUIRE A Native South American group living in Venezuela.

QUITU A Native South American group living in Ecuador.

QUMUQ A people living in the flat lowland region of northern Daghestan and in the Chechen-Ingush and

above: Quechuan children in the Andean countryside
below: Quechua llama-herders on an Inca road in the Andes Mountains

A young Quiche girl

North Ossetian autonomous republics of Russia. In 1989 they numbered 282,000. Their language belongs to the Qypchak (northwest) group of the Turkic family and includes three territorial dialects, Buinak, Qaitagh and Khasaviurt. Formerly, the Arabic script was in use; in 1927 a Qumuq alphabet was created on the basis of the Roman alphabet; in 1938 it was changed to Cyrillic. Their literary language is based on the Khasaviurt dialect. The Qumuq have been Sunni Muslims of the Shafi'i school since the fourteenth century.

The formation of the Qumuk people was a long and steady process which began in the seventh century and was finalized in the thirteenth. Ethnically they can be defined as the result of the mixture of various Turkic ethnic groups who arrived in the region in several waves with the original northeast Caucasians. Since the sixteenth century the Qumuq were the dominant ethnic group of north Daghestan and formed a kind of feudal state, headed by a hereditary ruler, or *shamkhal*, whose seat from 1640 was in the *aul* (village) of Tarku. Their territory was finally incorporated into the Russian Empire only after the RUSSIANS crushed the great Daghestani revolt of 1834–1859.

Their traditional economy is based on distant cattle-breeding, bee-keeping, wine, and house handicrafts. They possess a rich folklore, their written literature dating back to the early nineteenth century.

QUNGRAT   A subgroup of the UZBEKS.

QUTAMA   A subgroup of the KABYLE.

QWABE   A subgroup of the NGUNI.

QWANNAW   see ANDI.

QYPCHAQ   A subgroup of the BALKAR.

QYRGHYZ   A people living mainly in Qyrghyzstan and its neighbors, Uzbekistan, Tajikistan, and Qazaqstan, and in the Xinjiang Uighur Autonomous Region and the Heilongjiang Province of China. Their estimated number in China is about 114,000. The 1989 Soviet census showed the number of Qyrghyz in the territory of the former USSR as 2.5 million. Several thousand Qyrghyz who had lived in the Pamir area of Afghanistan fled to Pakistan following the Soviet 1979 invasion and subsequently were resettled in a mountainous area in the east of Turkey.

The Qyrghyz language belongs to the northwest Qypchaq-Noghai group of Turkic languages. In Qyrghyzstan and other former Soviet states the language contains a substantial admixture of Russian and international (via Russian) lexical borrowings; in China its vocabulary has been embellished with Chinese words.

In the the former Soviet Union it was written in the Arabic alphabet until 1928, when it was reduced to the Roman alphabet and in 1940 to the Cyrillic. Since the eclipse of the Soviet Union there has been a growing tendency to return to the Roman script. In China a Roman alphabet was adopted in the late 1950s; in some areas the Uighur script is also used.

The Qyrghyz have been Sunni Muslims of the Hanafi school since the sixteenth to eighteenth centuries, but preserve many pre-Islamic beliefs.

In tzarist and early Soviet Russian ethnography the Qyrghyz were named Qara-Qyrghyz (pronounced, and transcribed in Russian as Kara-Kirgiz) to distinguish them from the Qazaq, named at that time Kirgiz or Kirgiz-Kaisak.

The first historical evidence of a Qyrghyz people dates back to the eighth century when they lived in the area of the Yenisey or the Irtysh Rivers in Siberia. They are first mentioned in the area of central Asia in the tenth century. After a number of migrations (at times forced) to and from the area of their present abode, they became its permanent inhabitants in the eighteenth century.

Qyrghyz

Traditionally, Qyrghyz tribes were built around three greater divisions which were composed of "wings" (right and left) and "branches". The memory of this tribal affiliation is still preserved. The Qyrghyz possess a very rich oral literature. Their *Manas* is probably the longest of world epics. Its two basic versions, written down only in the twentieth century, have 200,000 and 379,000 lines. It is a major repository of Qyrghyz collective memory, depicting the history, way of life, and values of their ancestors.

For centuries the Qyrghyz were nomads, moving with their herds in a yearly nomadic cycle from the plains to the mountains and back to find summer and winter grazing pastures. In the second half of the nineteenth century the Qyrghyz lands were conquered by the Russian Empire. Russian settlers expropriated much of the grazing land of the Qyrghyz, leading to many conflicts. In 1916 the Qyrghyz participated in the abortive revolt of Central Asian Muslims against the tzarist Russian regime. Many lost their lands and many fled to China; nearly one-third of the people perished. In 1924 the Qara-Qyrghyz Autonomous *Oblast* (region), renamed in 1926 the Qyrghyz Autonomous Soviet Socialist Republic, was established within the framework of the Russian Soviet Federative Socialist Republic. In 1936 it was given the status of a Soviet Socialist Republic within the framework of the Soviet Union. Many Qyrghyz died during the forced sedenterization campaign and famine of the 1930s.

At the end of the 1980s there emerged a Qyrghyz movement of national awakening. In 1989 a law was passed making Qyrghyz the state language of the republic. In 1991 an independent Qyrghyzstan was proclaimed within the framework of the Commonwealth of Independent States. (see also AFGHANS)

QYRYM TATARLYI, QYRYMLY TATAR see CRIMEAN TATARS.

R

RAANDALI see LIVS.

RABAI A subgroup of the MIJIKENDA.

RABARI (Raika) An ethnic group numbering approximately 6,000, found in the Pakistani province of Sindh and the Indian state of Gujarat. They are predominantly Hindus and engage in herding.

RABHA An ethnic group numbering 11,000 (1981) living in Assam, Meghalaya, and West Bengal, in India, and in Bangladesh and Nepal. They speak Boro, a language belonging to the Tibeto-Burman family. Of Mongolian stock, they include five to seven sub-tribes. They are Hindus.

Their livelihood is derived mainly from agriculture. They cultivate paddy along with pulses, mustard seeds, and jute; their staple is rice, together with dried and powdered fish, pork, and rice-beer. The women are experts in spinning and weaving, and also have excellent knowledge of dyeing yarn by indigenous processes. (see also DIMASA-KACHARI)

RADIMICHI see BYELORUSSIANS.

RAGLAI (Orang Glai) A Malayo-Polynesian-speaking group numbering about 40,000, living in southern Vietnam. The Raglai are sometimes divided by geographical location into Northern and Southern Raglai, the latter heavily influenced by the NOANG and the CHAM. They have preserved their ancient religious beliefs and consider the village of Choah to be sacred.

RAHANWEN A clan of the SOMALI.

RAI I A subgroup of the KIRANT.

RAI II A small Malayo-Polynesian-speaking group inhabiting the area surrounding Ho Chi Minh City (Saigon) in southern Vietnam.

RAIKA see RABARI.

RAJBANSI A Bengali-speaking Hindu group living in Bangladesh. No current population figures are available.

RAJI An ethnic group, numbering about 2,000, found in the Himalayan foothills of Uttar Pradesh, India. They are Hindus and engage in slash and burn agriculture.

RAJPUTS A people living in northwest India, in the Ganges Plains, Madhya Pradesh, and the Himalayas. After India's independence in 1947 the twenty-three Rajput states of Rajputana were united into the single state of Rajasthan. Traditionally, the Rajputs were of the fighting, landowning, and ruling castes. While still known as fighters today, they are predominantly landowners.

There are over 100 known Rajput clans which are divided hierarchically. They are highly cultured people, who are skilled in Sanskrit literature, Hindi music, and drama presented in many vernacular tongues. They are also well known as great builders of palaces and temples. Most practice Hinduism, but there are more than one million Muslim Rajputs. Most Hindu Rajputs are Shaivites, but some are followers of the Swaminarayan sect of Ramanjua or Vallabhacharya. (see also BHILALA, BUKSA, GURKHA, INDIANS, PAKISTANIS)

RAMPI An ethnic group living in the mountainous central region of the Indonesian island of Sulawesi (Celebes). (see also TORADJA)

RANAO see MARANAO.

RANGA A subgroup of the SARA.

RANKULCHE A subgroup of the TEHUELCHE.

RAPA NUI   A people, numbering about 3,000, native to Easter Island, a small isolated volanic island in the southern Pacific Ocean. They have lived on the island continuously for over 1,500 years, a span of time that encompassed a remarkable cultural flowering followed by disintegration and population collapse; all of this occurred in isolation from the outside world.

Contact with passing European ships began in 1722, and subsequent interactions with missionaries and colonists have affected the Rapa Nui, but their culture survived domination by Chile, and is now experiencing a renaissance.

Local legends claim that the Rapa Nui arrived in several boatloads of sea voyagers under the leadership of Hotu Matua. The origin of these initial settlers has been the subject of much dispute. Thor Heyerdahl popularized the notion that they came from South America. Most scholars today reject this hypothesis; the evidence suggests that the Rapa Nui are of Polynesian origin. The famous stone heads, known as *moai*, that are scattered throughout the island, were clan totems.

Easter Island became a Chilean territory in the nineteenth century, and the CHILEANS relocated the Rapa Nui to the town of Hanga Roa on the western edge of the island. They were confined to Hanga Roa and the rest of the island was converted to grazing land for Chilean sheep ranchers. The native language, Rapanui, was suppressed, and children had to speak Spanish in school. Today only one-fourth of the younger Rapa Nui can speak Rapanui.

Regular airline services and the popular appeal of the stone statues have spawned a massive increase in tourism in recent years. This has transformed Easter Island both physically and culturally; the Rapa Nui have increasingly become involved in economic enterprises rather than the traditional subsistence farming and fishing. They are enjoying a cultural resurgence.

RASHA'AIDA   An ethnic group living in Eritrea. (see also ERITREANS)

RATAGNON   A Malayo-Polynesian group, numbering a few thousand, living in the extreme southwest of the island of Mindoro in the Philippines. They speak the Mangyan language, which is also spoken by their neighbors, the HANUNOO.

RATO   An ethnic group living in the mountainous central region of the Indonesian island of Sulawesi (Celebes). (see also TORADJA)

RA'U   An ethnic group living in the mountainous central region of the Indonesian island of Sulawesi (Celebes). (see also TORADJA)

RAWAS   A subgroup of the KUBU.

RAYYA   (Azebo) A division of the northern OROMO, living in southern Tigray, Ethiopia.

REDDI   (Kapu, Suryavanisa) An ethnic group inhabiting an area of the Eastern Ghats extending from the Mackund and Goperu Rivers south to the delta plain between the Godavari and Kistna Rivers. They are hill people who live in three types of settlements: hill, riverside, and those of the Andhra Plains. The dominant language is Telugu. They are slash and burn agriculturalists whose diet consists mainly of garden vegetables and the meat of domesticated animals.

REDJANG   (s.d. Keme Tun Djang) The collective term for members of four semi-autonomous clans, with a total population of about 250,000, living along the coast and in the highlands of south-central Sumatera (Sumatra), an island in Indonesia. They consider themselves the indigenous inhabitants of the region. Their language, Redjang, is closely related to Malay but possesses a traditional script, which recent efforts have been made to preserve. Rice cultivation is of particular importance to the Redjang and each family maintains a

Redjang

small rice field near their home, notwithstanding their primary economic occupation. En masse conversion to Islam in the mid-nineteenth century has virtually eradicated remnants of their indigenous religion.

The Redjang believe themselves to be descendants of a common ancestor, Djang, who lived in Lebong and whose four sons were the founders of the four Redjang clans. These formed a federation but by the thirteenth century social conditions had so deteriorated that four Javanese princes were selected to govern them. Since Indonesia's independence the Redjang have attempted to revive their traditions and language, which had fallen into some disuse.

REE   see ARIKARA.

REER BARE   A clan of the SOMALI.

REGEIBAT   A subgroup of the MAURE.

REGUIBAT   A subgroup of the TUAREG.

REMBETU   (Lembetu) An ethnic group living in Zimbabwe.

RENDILLE   An ethnic group, estimated as numbering c.14,000, living in the Northeast District of Kenya. Their language, Rendille, is part of the Eastern Cushitic family.

The Rendille are camel nomads roaming the region of northern Kenya between Lake Turkana to the west and Mount Marsabit to the east, between the Merille River and the Ndoto Mountains to the south, and the Chabi Desert to the north. Extensive intermarriage with neighboring groups of SAMBURU has created the small subgroups of ARIAAL and ILTHURIA. The life and livelihood of the people are intricately bound up with the camel, their beast of burden, source of food, and symbol of social values.

They also keep sheep and goats, and a minority herd cattle. The clan is the basic social unit. Traditionally, an entire clan, of which there are ten, lived together as one settlement.

RENGAO   A subgroup of the BAHNAR.

RENGMA   (Anzang) An ethnic group numbering 15,000 (1981 census) in the Phek District of Nagaland and in the State of Assam, northeastern India. They are related to the MIKIR.

The Rengma practice both terrace and slash and burn agriculture in their territory, known as the Rengma Region. Clan endogamy is forbidden among them. They adhere to both traditional religions and Christianity. (see also LOTHA, NAGA, SEMA)

RENNEL ISLANDERS   An ethnic group of a few thousand living in the central part of the Solomon Islands, in the southwest Pacific Ocean, northeast of Australia. They speak an indigenous regional language. They are slash and burn cultivators, fishermen, hunters, and gatherers. Today most are Christians. Their most celebrated ceremonies are centered around the harvest.

RESHEVAT   see DASSANETCH.

REUNION, THE PEOPLE OF   The inhabitants of the island of Réunion, located in the Indian Ocean about 400 miles east of Madagascar. They number over 600,000, of whom about 30 percent are of French origin, the remainder being of mixed Arab, African, and Malagasy decent. The population is predominantly Roman Catholic although there is also a significant Muslim community. Sugar is the single most important cash crop, but coffee, tropical fruits, and geraniums are also grown, the latter providing oil for the manufacture of perfumes. Many islanders provide services to the extensive French naval presence on the island.

RHADE   One of the most prominent ethnic groups of south-central Vietnam. Numbering about 120,000, they are also among the most advanced among the MONTAGNARDS (hill people) of the country. Their language is often used as a lingua franca by other hill peoples. The Rhadé religion is based on a pantheon of deities arranged according to a distinct hierarchy and involves numerous rituals. They are slash and burn cultivators of rice.

The Rhadé took advantage of the educational opportunities offered in the French colonial period, and a stratum of native administrators, medical personnel, and tradesmen emerged. This accounts for the predominance of Rhadé in the various Montagnard national movements that evolved in southern Vietnam, most notably in FULRO, the United Front for the Protection of Oppressed Races, which sought to attain autonomy for the hill peoples and whose leader, Y Bham, was himself a Rhadé.

Negotiations with the FRENCH and, later, South Vietnamese enabled the Rhadé to enjoy some degree of prominence in the federal South Vietnamese government and they supported the AMERICANS during the Vietnam War. As a result, they found themselves among the victims of the Viet Cong insurgents and many were forced to flee their ancestral homes. The unification of North and South Vietnam crushed Rhade aspirations for greater autonomy and they are currently trying simply to preserve their cultural identity.

The A'DHAM, BLO, EPAN, H'WING, K'AH, K'DRAO, K'TUL, KPA, and M'DUR are Rhade subgroups. (see also MONTAGNARDS)

RHETO-ROMANS   A residual population speaking Romanche, an old Gallo-Roman language, divided among many dialects. They live in eastern Switzerland (Graubunden, Grisons, and Grigioni cantons). Hardly reaching 50,000 (1 percent of the SWISS) and dwindling in numbers, this group is one of Switzerland's oldest. They are also found in a few villages in the Austrian Tyrol; 17,000 Ladin speakers in Italian South Tyrol speak a related tongue. (see also SWISS)

Rheto-Romans

RIBE   A subgroup of the MIJIKENDA.

RICARA   see ARIKARA.

RIEN   A Mon-Khmer group living in southern Vietnam. They are similar to their neighbors, the SRE and MA.

RIGEZAT   see DJOHEINA.

RIKHUNI   see RUSHANI.

RIZAYGAT   A subgroup of the BAGGARA.

RLAM   A subgroup of the MNONG.

ROH   A subgroup of the BAHNAR.

ROHONG   A subgroup of the MNONG.

ROLOM   A subgroup of the MNONG.

ROLONG   A subgroup of the SOTHO, TSWANA.

ROMA   see GYPSIES.

ROMANIANS   (s.d. Romanii) Known also as Rumanians. The difference between the O and U has political and cultural significance, the O form signifying a connection to Rome and the U to Byyzantine; the Romanians themselves prefer the former. Of the 27 million Romanians, about 21 million live in Romania and neighboring Hungary, Serbia, and Bulgaria; 3 million live in Moldova and adjacent areas in the Ukraine and are known as MOLDOVANS. The Romanians are divided by dialect, history, and culture into three groups: the Wallachs, the MOLDOVANS, and the Romanians of Transylvania. All are Eastern Orthodox Christians by religion. Their language, Romanian, belongs to the eastern branch of the Romance (Latin) group of Indo-European languages. It is divided into regional dialects. The modern literary language is based on the Wallachian dialect of Bucharest. Originally written in Cyrillic, its alphabet was changed to Roman in the mid-nineteenth century. In the Soviet Union a Moldovan language was created based on the Bessarabian dialect with a strong admixture of Russian words.

The ancient inhabitants of modern Romania were the Dacians, wbo were conquered by the Romans under Emperor Trajan in the first years of the second century C.E. Roman rule was followed by massive colonization, and it is now a maxim in Romanian historiography that the Romanians are the descendants of this fusion. This is, however, difficult to prove as settled life came to a halt for more than a millennium after Roman withdrawal from Dacia in 270, and the land was conquered by consecutive waves of nomads. According to Romanian scholars, the Latinized population found shelter in the Carpathian Mountains and Transylvania, and their counterparts south of the Danube River found shelter in the Pindus Mountains, where they are known as VLACHS. Some Western scholars hold that the Romanians are descendants of VLACHS who crossed the Danube northward in the early thirteenth century, while others try to connect their origin to Romance-speaking crusaders.

In the last decade of the thirteenth century and over the following fifty years, the two principalities of Wallachia (known in Romanian as Muntenia, or Tara Romaneasca [Romanian land] and Moldavia [Moldova]) were founded southwest and northwest of the Carpathians by Romanian *voivodes* (princes) from Transylvania. These grew in strength and territory, alternately fighting off and submitting to strong neighbors: Wallachia to Hungary and Moldavia to Poland. In 1417 Wallachia accepted Ottoman suzerainty and almost a century later, in 1513, Moldavia followed suit. This lasted, not without occasional conflict, until 1878. The Ottomans moved the capital of Wallachia to Bucharest and that of Moldavia to Iasi (Jasi). The treaty of Kucuk Kaynarca (1774) between Russia and the Ottomans and subsequent treaties made both principalities a de facto Russian protectorate. After the Crimean War, the Peace of Paris (1856) placed the principalities, still under formal Ottoman suzerainty, under the collective guarantee of the European powers, but the two were not allowed to unite. In response, both principalities elected the same prince in 1859 and with the assent of the powers, including the Ottomans, they merged into a single Romania.

The Congress of Berlin, following the Russo-Ottoman War of 1877–1878, granted the Romanians independence and in 1881 they formed a kingdom. In 1913 Romania took part in the second Balkan War and gained southern Dubroja from Bulgaria. In World War I Romania joined the entente powers and gained Transylvania and Bukovina from Austria-Hungary, and Bessarabia from the RUSSIANS. This fulfilled Romanian nationalist demands, but the incorporation of HUNGARIANS, GERMANS, UKRAINIANS, and RUSSIANS now gave rise to animosity and irredentism. During World War II, Romania stayed neutral at first, which cost it dearly. In June 1940 the Soviet Union recaptured Bessarabia. In August Hitler and Mussolini forced Romania to transfer the northern half of Transylvania to Hungary and in September the GERMANS forced Romania to return southern Dobruja to the BULGARIANS. Following that, and after an internal coup in Bucharest, Romania joined the Axis powers. It took part in the invasion of the Soviet Union in 1941 and was rewarded with Bessarabia and further territories east of the Dniester River as far as the Ukrainian city of Odessa.

In 1944 Romania was occupied by Soviet forces. By 1948 sovietization was complete and a Communist regime was in power in Bucharest. Under the peace treaty Romania gave up southern Dubroja to Bulgaria, and Bessarabia and Bukovina to the Soviet Union, but was returned Transylvania. In 1965 Nicolae Ceausescu came to power, which he retained until 1990. He enforced a large, oppressive, apparatus of terror and brought the Romanians to the verge of starvation. In 1990 a popular uprising and coup toppled Ceausescu, and he and his wife were executed. (see also MOLDOVANS)

ROMENII   see VLACHS.

RON   A subgroup of the TIV.

RONGA   see TONGA.

RONGMEI   A NAGA group. (see also ZELIANGRONG)

ROSHANI   see RUSHANI.

ROSHORVI   see OROSHORI.

ROSSELL ISLANDERS   (s.d. Yelatpi) An ethnic group of approximately 5,000, living on the small mountainous Rossell Island, east of the island of New Guinea and about 500 miles southwest of Port Moresby, the capital of Papua New Guinea. Their language, Yelatnye, is an indigenous local language. They are slash and burn cultivators, whose main crops are sweet potatoes and taro. Their religious beliefs combine Christianity and traditional beliefs in spirits.

ROTINESE   (s.d. Atahori Rote) Inhabitants of the island of Roti which, lying south of the island of Timor, is the southernmost island of the Indonesian archipelago. Some 100,000 Rotinese live on Roti, along with CHINESE and NDAONESE who came as immigrants. Rotinese have also migrated to nearby Timor, where they number about 50,000, and as far as Flores and the Sumba Islands. They speak an Austronesian language with several distinct spoken dialects: one was reserved solely for ritual and poetic use. Christianity was first introduced into the island in the early seventeenth century and is now the dominant religion, particularly as a result of extensive missionary work in the early twentieth century. Missionaries promoted education and literacy, and today, despite their small numbers, the Rotinese are active in both regional and national government and services.

The staple Rotinese crop is the lontar palm, the juice of which is tapped and converted into a number of food products. Rice and other grains are also cultivated, as are fruit trees. Fishing is important seasonally and horses and livestock are raised. The importance of hunting and gathering is rapidly diminishing. Crafts include weaving, basket-making, and the manufacture of distinctive broad-rimmed sunhats.

ROTUMANS A Polynesian-speaking people numbering about 10,000, native to Rotuma Island, north of the Fiji archipelago. They are mostly Christians. There are just over 2,500 Rotumans on the island itself. Its small size and scarce employment opportunities have encouraged its inhabitants to migrate to other parts of Fiji, mainly to the capital, Suva, on the main island of Viti Levu, and to engage in urban occupations.

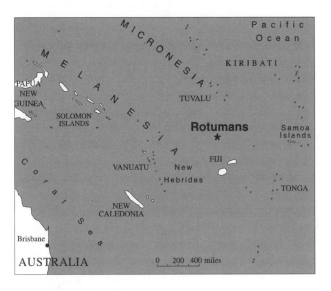

Rotumans

The Rotuma Island economy is based on agricultural production, which includes the major staple crops common to the area, such as taro, yams, and cassava. Administered by the BRITISH from their local colonial headquarters in Fiji, the island became a province of Fiji on independence in 1970. In 1988 the Rotumans, announcing that they did not recognize Fiji's newly declared status as a republic and attempted to declare independence from the FIJIANS, so as to remain within the British Commonwealth. In a constitutional settlement in 1990 Rotumans were granted special status within Fiji.

ROZI see LOZI.

ROZVI see RUZWI.

RUBUKA A subgroup of the TIV.

RUC A Mon-Khmer group, numbering a few hundred, who live in the Quang Binh province in northern Vietnam.

RUMANIANS see ROMANIANS.

RUMELI see TURKS.

RUS see RUSSIANS.

RUSHANI (s.d. Rikhuni; Roshani) An ethnic group inhabiting an area along the Panj River in the Mountain Badakhshan Autonomous *Oblast* (Region) of Tajikistan and in Afghanistani Badakhshan. Their estimated number (in the early 1980s) was 15,000.

The Rushani language belongs to the Pamiri division of the Iranian languages. It is unwritten, with Tajik used as the literary language in Mountain Badakhshan and Dari in Afghanistani Badakhshan. Although recognized as a specific ethnic group, the Rushani were officially regarded in the Soviet Union as part of the TAJIK. They are followers of the Isma'ili sect of Islam; the date of their islamization is unknown, but cannot be earlier than the eleventh century.

Until the late nineteenth century the Rushani ethnic territory was ruled by the *kha* (from the Persian *shah,* "king") of Shughnan through his Rushani vassal. As the *khas* were predominantly Sunni Muslims who regarded their Isma'ili subjects as infidels, the selling of Rushani into slavery in neighboring Sunni regions was widely practiced. Their territory was divided into two parts between the Russian empire and Afghanistan by the 1893 British-Russian agreement on the Pamir frontier.

The Rushani live in villages of ten to fifty extended families, built mainly in the valley or on the mountain slopes. In Mountain Badakhshan, men's dress is now semi-European with traditional elements; in Afghanistani Badakhshan it remains traditional. In both areas women's dress is still traditional. Their diet is predominantly vegetarian, with the addition of dairy products, meat being reserved for festive occasions.

Their traditional occupation is grain and legume farming on small terraced plots, with some sheep-, goat-, and cattle-breeding. (see also AFGHANS)

RUSSIANS (s.d. Russkiye) Most of the 150 million Russians live in Russia, where they form a majority (about 88 percent) of the population, and in adjacent northeast Ukraine and northern Qazaqstan (where they are 20 percent and 41 percent of the population respectively). Large numbers of Russians live in all the other republics of the former Soviet Union. Relatively small emigre communities may be found in Western Europe, the United States, Canada, and Australia. Russian Orthodox Christianity is the predominant religion of the Russians.

Russian is one of the East Slavic languages. It is very homogeneous despite the fact that its speakers spread from the Baltic Sea to the Pacific Ocean, the only differences between the numerous dialects being in pronunciation. The dialects are divided into northern and southern groups. The modern literary language was created at the end of the eighteenth century and has been the vehicle of a great and world-renown literature, especially during the nineteenth century.

The Russian people are descended from East Slavic tribes who lived on the northeast fringes of the Kievan Rus state and who, expanding eastward and northward, mixed with speakers of Finno-Ugric languages. The original homeland of the Russians (although they regarded all the territory of Kievan Rus as their patrimony) was in the Oka and Upper Volga basins, with easy access to the Baltic, White, Caspian, and Black Seas. Since then the Russians have been increasing in numbers by assimilating many of the ethnic groups around them.

The ethnonym "Russian" comes from Rus, the name by which the Eastern Slavs, following their Finnic neighbors, called the Scandinavian Vikings. It was the Vikings who organized the Russians and established the Kievan state in the late ninth century. These Rus, under the leadership of descendants of Prince Rurik of Jutland, soon became slavicized as their names testify. Vladimir (972–1015) gave Kievan Rus its territorial extension, the watersheds of all the rivers leading to the Baltic, Black, and Caspian Seas, its first code of law, and its dynastic seniority system. But most important, in 989 he converted his people to Orthodox Christianity, thus linking the Eastern Slavs culturally to the rich Byzantine civilization but isolating them from the

Russians

Catholic West and from the neighboring Western Slavs.

His son Jaroslav (1019–1054) started the "Golden Century" when Kievan culture reached its zenith, which afterwards influenced all its successor states and peoples. Soon after his death, however, the Kievan state was divided into a growing number of principalities, and the center moved from Kiev to Vladimir. This change reflected the moving of the demographic, economic-commercial, and cultural center of Kievan Rus to the northeast where the forefathers of the Russians were beginning to emerge as a separate people.

After the Mongol invasion of 1238–1240 the princes ruling in the central Russian lands were subjugated to the *khans* of the Golden Horde for about 240 years, while those in the west were gradually absorbed by Lithuania and Poland. It was through loyalty to the *khans* that the princes of Moscow (originally a small peripheral principality of Vladimir) managed to annex much territory. The process of "regathering the Russian lands" became part of the official ideology in the mid-fifteenth century under Ivan III, the first Muscovite ruler to declare himself "czar" (caesar) as a demonstration of independence from and claim of overlordship over the TATARS. He was also first to claim to be the head of the Christian world as heir to the Byzantine Empire.

Under Ivan IV, the Russians conquered Kazan (1552) and Astrakhan (1556) and began the expansionary process that brought them to the far eastern areas of Okhotsk within a century. In the middle of the seventeenth century under Alexis Romanov the eastern Ukraine was annexed. Peter the Great conquered the Baltic provinces and turned the Russians towards rapid westernization, but at a terrible cost in lives. Catherine the Great completed the "regathering of the Russian lands," in the eighteenth century by acquiring Lithuania and parts of Poland. In another direction she annexed the northern coast of the Black Sea and the Crimea and started expansion into the Caucasus. In the nineteenth century the czars rounded off their empire by conquering the Caucasus (in a lengthy and very costly war), Central Asia, and the Russian Far East.

The Russians spread through large parts of their expanding empire through colonization and assimilation, mainly of Finno-Ugric, Turkish non-Muslim, and various Siberian groups. This assimilation was frequently facilitated by these groups' conversion to Russian Orthodox Christianity. The participation of BYELORUSSIANS and UKRAINIANS in the colonization of newly conquered lands facilitated in many cases both their own russification and the assimilation of the native population.

In the second half of the nineteenth century, however, with the spread of nationalism, the Russian empire found itself sharing the predicament of other multi-national empires and used the same remedy: forced assimilation. This was also connected with the regime's attempt to divert grievances arising from social, economic, demographic, and educational changes which found no adjustment in the political structure, by encouraging Russian chauvinism.

World War I and the 1917 Revolution brought down the czarist regime and, following a bitter civil war, the Soviet Union was established on the principles of Marxism and recognition of the rights of all ethnic groups. Nevertheless, the Russians soon proved to be the dominant people of the Soviet Union as they had been in czarist Russia. The Russian Soviet Federated Socialist Republic (RSFSR) was the strongest and largest in population and area and was, in fact, the core of the Soviet Union. If in the first years of the new regime there were attempts to put down the centrality of the Russians, during Stalin's long rule it gradually became a principle, and the Soviet Union was proclaimed "a happy family of peoples, led and guided by the elder brother: the Russian people."

Accordingly, a policy of assimilation was carried out using different means, not all subtle. These included wholesale registration of ethnic groups as Russians; failure to provide small ethnic groups with alphabets, thus assimilating them by making Russian their literary language; and migration, both forced and encouraged. The subtlest and most widespread method was the creation of a "Russian-speaking population" through making Russian the only language of education. At the same time, the various officially-recognized national languages were subjected to creeping russification of their alphabet, vocabulary, and even grammar.

Following the dissolution of the Soviet Union the RSFSR separated from the other fourteen republics. It was officially renamed the Russian Federation, but has come to be known as "Russia" around the world. This, however, did not seem to resolve the problems resulting from the country's remaining under the dominance of the Russians. In addition, 25 million Russians found themselves living outside Russia, including 11 million in the Ukraine alone. (see also BYELORUSSIANS, UKRAINIANS)

RUSTAMI   One of four groups comprising the MA-MASAN.

RUTUL   (s.d. varies from village to village) An ethnic group living in southern Daghestan (within Russia) and in Azerbaijan. According to the 1989 Soviet census they numbered 21,000. The general appellation "Rutul" derives from their main place of habitation, the village of Rutul in Daghestan.

The Rutul language belongs to the Lezgi group of the Ibero-Caucasian family of languages. Consisting of four closely-related dialects and several subdialects, it is unwritten, Lezgian in Daghestan and Azerbaijani in Azerbaijan being used as the literary language.

The Rutul are Sunni Muslims of the Shafi'i school. The exact period of their islamization is unknown. On the basis of the general history of the region, this probably took place no earlier than the fifteeenth to sixteenth centuries. Their ethnic territory was included in the Russian Empire in 1839.

The Rutul in Azerbaijan are undergoing a process of assimilation into the surrounding population.

Their traditional economy is based on sheep-breeding, agriculture, and horticulture, and on carpet-making, pottery, and metal work.

RUZWI   (Rosvi, Barozwi, Varozvi) A Shona-speaking group dispersed throughout Zimbabwe. (see also SHONA, ZIMBABWEANS)

RWANDANS   The approximately 7 million inhabitants of Rwanda, an independent state in east-central Africa. The official languages are Kinyarwanda and French, but some peoples, mainly along the Ugandan and Tanzanian borders, speak Swahili. About 75 percent of the population are Christians, mostly Catholics. One-fifth adhere to traditional beliefs in spirits and a supreme deity called Imama, and there is a small Muslim minority.

Rwanda is a fertile country, with good soil and sufficient rain for intensive agriculture and animal husbandry. There are no mineral sources, however, and foreign currency is earned only from coffee, introduced by the BELGIANS in 1932. One of the major problems facing Rwanda today is overpopulation (it is Africa's most densely-populated country) and the resulting demand for land, which has led to the poor economic situation and a low average standard of living. Most Rwandans today keep cattle as an economic investment, but in the past the ownership of these animals was not only an important status symbol but also an essential element in the traditional socio-political system.

Rwanda's two major ethnic groups are the HUTU, an indigenous peasant group and the largest grouping (85 percent of the population) and the TUTSI, originally invaders from the north who have dominated the HUTU since the fifteenth century with their strong, centralized state and competent military establishment. A third group, the TWA, are forest-dwelling pygmies. With the establishment of the Tutsi state, a strict class system evolved in which the HUTU were subservient to the TUTSI. There was, however, considerable intermarriage between the two groups, and the TUTSI came to adopt the language of the HUTU, Kinyarwanda.

Colonized by the GERMANS in the late nineteenth century, the region, along with neighboring Burundi, was conquered by the BELGIANS in World War I. Initially Belgium favored the TUTSI, but Catholic missionaries eventually persuaded the colonial authorities to transfer their support to the majority HUTU shortly after World War II. The Tutsi king was deposed, and in 1962 Rwanda became an independent state. Characteristic of the independence movement was marked opposition by all parties to unite the country with neighboring Burundi as a single political entity.

In 1963, Tutsi refugees who had fled to Uganda attempted to invade Rwanda and reestablish their hegemony. The HUTU responded by massacring 12,000 TUTSI. By 1964 as many as 150,000 TUTSI fled Rwanda; they are still living as refugees along the border. The remaining TUTSI still form a sizable proportion of the educated elite, however, and Hutu resentment is still characteristic of relations between the two groups. Following the 1970s there have been continuing bloody clashes between the two groups and many more TUTSI have fled the country.

A small group, known as the TUSSI, mostly refugees from Rwanda, live on the border with southwest Uganda, although some have lived in that area since the days of British rule. They speak a Southern Lacustrine Bantu language called Lunyarwanda. In 1990 they started an invasion of Rwanda under the leadership of military officers who had defected from Uganda, where the bulk of the Rwandan Patriotic Front fighters were born.

RYUKYU ISLANDERS, RYUKYUJIN   see OKINAWANS.

S

SAAMI   see LAPPS.

SAB   A subgroup of the SOMALI. They are primarily sedentary agriculturalists.

SABA   An ethnic group living in Chad.

SABAOT   A recently-contrived collective name for four groups of Kalenjin-speaking people, the KONY, SAPEI (Sabei), POK (Bok), and BUNGOMEK (Bonam), which are included under that name in the Kenya population census. They number over 50,000 and live in the region of Mount Elgon on the Kenya-Uganda border. Like other KALENJIN, they practice highland agriculture, although originally they were largely pastoralists and hunter-gatherers.

Typical agricultural products are maize, millets, beans, and potatoes. Although cattle husbandry is now less important in their economy, its social and ritual importance remains. Their social structure, beliefs, and traditional dress and ornamentations generally resemble those of the NANDI. (see also also KALENJIN)

SABDARAT   A subgroup of the TIGRE.

SABE   An ethnic group living in Benin.

SAC   (Sauk) A Native North American group numbering 2,300, many of whom live today on the Sauk and Fox Federal Reservation, Tama County, Iowa, and the Sac and Fox Tribe Federal Trust Area, Oklahoma, U.S.A.

Originally they were hunters in Michigan but in the aftermath of battles with American forces, they were removed to the Indian Territory of Oklahoma, where many work in the local economy. The American athlete and hero of the 1912 Olympic Games, Jim Thorpe, was a member of the Sáuk.

SACH   A Mon-Khmer group living in northern Vietnam. Intermarriage, particularly with the NGUON MUONG, is common.

SA'DAN TORADJA   An ethnic group living in the mountainous central region of the Indonesian island of Sulawesi (Celebes). (see also TORADJA)

SAFI   A subgroup of the PASHTUN.

SAFID-POSH   One of several groups collectively known as NURESTANIS.

SAGADA   see LEPANTO.

SAHA   see YAKUT.

SAHAPTINI   see NEZ PERCE.

SAHO   A federation of ethnic groups numbering 150,000 (1980), who live in the lowlands of south-central Eritrea, bordering northeast Tigray, and in neighboring Ethiopia. They are Sunni Muslims, with some Ethiopian Orthodox Christians. The Saho are nomadic pastoralists, grazing between the coastal plain and the Tigray highlands.

SAHWI   (Sefwi, Encassar, Inkassa) An Akan-speaking group living between the Tano and Ankobra Rivers in Ghana. During the latter part of the seventeenth century they were dominated by the DENKYIRA and over the next two hundred years by the ASHANTI.

SAINT KITTS AND NEVIS, THE PEOPLE OF Part of the Leeward Islands in the Caribbean Sea, these islands have a population of about 40,000, of whom over 90 percent are of black African origin. The country was first colonized by the BRITISH in 1623 and became independent in 1983. English is the main language and the people are predominantly Christians, with three-quarters of the population professing Protestantism. The sugar industry generates over 50 per cent of total revenues, but tourism is also a significant income earner. Nevis recently seceded from the federation.

SAINT LUCIANS   The island of Saint Lucia in the Caribbean Sea has a population of some 153,000. It was ceded by France to Great Britain in 1814 and achieved full independence (after a twelve-year period of self-government) in 1979. Nearly 90 percent of the population is descended from black Africans brought as slave laborers for the sugar, tobacco, ginger, and cotton plantations established in the seventeenth and eighteenth centuries. The Saint Lucians speak both English and a French *patois*, and the majority is Roman Catholic. The small community of East Indians is divided between Hindus and Muslims.

The island's manufacturing sector is the largest and most diversified in the Windward Islands, while its single largest industrial investment is a petroleum storage and transshipment terminal. Agriculture and tourism are the main foreign exchange earners.

SAINT VINCENT AND THE GRENADINES, THE PEOPLE OF   Located in the Windward Islands in the Caribbean Sea, the island of Saint Vincent controls about half of the Grenadines, a chain of more than 100 small islands scattered between Saint Vincent and Grenada to the southwest. Some three-quarters of the inhabitants of the country are descendants of Africans brought to work as slaves during occupations by the BRITISH and the FRENCH. Perhaps 20 per cent of the population is of mixed origin, with a small minority of European descent and a community of around 1,000 Black CARIBS, descendants of the intermingling of Native Americans and runaway African slaves from other islands that predates European colonization.

The people speak English as well as a French *patois*. The majority is Protestant, but there is also a significant Roman Catholic community. The country became independent in 1979 and has an economy dominated by agriculture, the processing of agricultural products, and tourism.

SAISIAT   An ethnic group numbering approximately 5,000, living in northwestern Taiwan.

SAKAI   A subgroup of the KUBU.

SAKALAVA   A tribal division of the MALAGASY.

SAKATA   An ethnic group numbering about 93,000, living in the Lake Mai-Ndombe subregion of Zaire. They were never organized in a central political framework.

SAKHA   see DOLGAN.

SAKTA   (Sattaha) A subgroup of the PANIKA.

SAKUYE   (Ajuran) A subgroup of the OROMO.

SAKZAI   A subgroup of the PASHTUN.

SALA   (Zala) A Tonga-speaking group numbering about 14,000, inhabiting the region west of Lusaka, Zambia. Their native language, Sala, has become extinct due to domination by the ILA and TONGA. (see also GOFA)

SALAIR-OZON   A part of the BURYAT.

SALAJAR   A group numbering about 100,000 living on the island of Salajar and on smaller neighboring islands off the coast of southern Sulawesi (Celebes), an island of Indonesia. Inhabitants of northern Salajar speak a Macassarese dialect; inhabitants of the south speak a Butonese dialect.

They are Muslims, although traditional beliefs are of considerable importance. Once traders and pirates, they have recently adopted agriculture.

SALAMAT ARABS   see DJOHEINA.

SALAR   (Salyr) An ethnic group numbering approximately 85,000, who live mainly in the Qinghai and Gansu Provinces of China. Their ancestors are believed to have originated in Central Asia and to have migrated to their present regions during the Yuan (Mongolian) dynasty (1279-1368).

The Salar language belongs to the Qurluq group of Turkic languages. Lengthy contacts with Han CHINESE and TIBETANS have resulted in the introduction of many loan words from those languages (most young Salar speak Chinese). Salar is sometimes regarded as a dialect of the Uighur language and as such defined as the language of the Sary UIGHUR (lit. Yellow Uighur). It is unwritten, Chinese being used as the literary language.

The Salar are Sunni Muslims of the Hanafi school. The main occupation is agriculture, followed by

Salar

forestry, logging, and salt-making. Their culture generally resembles that of the HUI.

SALIVA   A South American Indian group of the Orinoco River delta in western Brazil. Very little is known of them, but it is supposed that their primary pursuits are those prevalent among other peoples of the region: fishing, collecting shellfish, hunting large river animals such as crocodiles and manatees, and growing maize irrigated by river flooding. (see also VENEZUELANS)

SALUAN   (Loinang) An ethnic group numbering about 85,000 living in central Sulawesi (Celebes), Indonesia. They speak an Austronesian language. Both Christianity and Islam have won adherents among them since the early twentieth century. They cultivate rice, corn, sago, and millet, and raise chickens, goats, and dogs for consumption.

SALVADOREANS   (s.d. Salvadorenos) The 5.25 million inhabitants of El Salvador, a small Central American country. It is one of the world's most densely-populate states. They are 94 percent *mestizo* (racially mixed), 5 percent Native Indian, and 1 percent white. The people speak Spanish and are 96 percent Roman Catholic. El Salvador's geographic situation between two volcanic mountain ranges parallel to the Pacific has meant that San Salvador, the capital city, undergoes frequent earthquakes.

Agriculture represents nearly a quarter of the gross national product and employs two-fifths of the labor force, who produce cash crops of coffee, cotton, and sugar cane. Nearly a third of the land area is devoted to pasturage. A limited fishing industry exports small quantities of lobster and shrimp.

In 1524 Spanish *conquistadores* encountered culturally-advanced Indians of Nahua descent and the Pipil kingdom of Cuzcatlan. The Indians were completely subjugated by 1539, by which time what is now El Salvador (divided into San Salvador and Sonsonate) became a subordinate territory of Guatemala. In 1811 San Salvador issued the first Central American declaration of independence. In 1821 El Salvador was incorporated into the Mexican empire until its fall in 1823, and in 1840 it was the last state to withdraw from the Federation of Central America. The country first experienced prolonged political turmoil, then a succession of military dictatorships.

The Salvadoreans have suffered from profound economic inequality: until the emergence of the land reform movement in the 1980s, almost all the wealth was controlled by a few powerful families. The result has been extreme underdevelopment, associated unemployment (30-40 percent), educational deprivation (two-thirds of the population is illiterate), heavy dependence upon American aid, and political instability. Demands for social justice have fueled guerrilla opposition to the government in a civil war, which began in the 1970s, and more than a decade of violence on both sides further oppressed the poverty-stricken people. In 1979 the government was ousted. A new constitution was adopted in 1983 and a civilian president freely elected in 1984.

SALYR   see SALAR.

SAMA, SAMA LAUT, SAMA MANDELAUT   see BAJAU LAUT.

SAMAALE   A clan of the SOMALI. They are primarily camel-raisers.

SA-MAI-NA   see AO.

SAMANTHULU   see KHOND.

SAMARAHAN   An ethnic group living on the Indonesian island of Kalimantan (Borneo). (see also DAYAK)

SAMBAL   A southern subgroup of the NEGRITOS of the Philippines.

SAMBIA   An ethnic group of a few thousand living in the mountainous region of central Papua New Guinea.

They speak an indigenous language. Their subsistence is based on hunting, pig herding, and gardening. They practice traditional religions.

SAMBURU   (s.d. Loikop) An ethnic group numbering an estimated 100,000 living in the Samburu district of central Kenya, to the south and southeast of Lake Turkana, around the district town of Maralal. They are the northernmost of the Maa-speaking peoples. Most Samburu have retained their traditional African religion, which is well-suited to their pastoral way of life, with cattle at the center of religious rites, wealth, and social status.

A minority of the Samburu engage in cultivating land and tourism as alternative sources of income, but the major economic occupation was and is cattle-herding. The almost total dependence on a pastoral economy is reflected in the Samburu diet (milk and meat), in their traditional dress (skins and hides), and in their songs and dances, which are mainly connected with their cattle.

As a pastoral society, the Samburu depend on the warriors (*moran*) of the group. These are unmarried men who defend their territory and their cattle, particularly along the border with the TURKANA. Clans are the second major social and economic institution. They are dispersed within the Samburu territory, each member having obligations to the clan, especially in times of danger or celebrations. The Samburu have no centralized political institutions and traditionally authority is held by the elders.

SAMIA   A small ethnic group living in southeast Uganda. They share the area with other small Bantu-groups as well as the Western Nilotic PADHOLA. The Samia speak an Eastern Lacustrine Bantu language. Living on the border with Kenya, the Samia are culturally related to the LUHYA of Kenya. (see also PADHOLA)

SAMO   An ethnic group living in the northern Dafina area of Burkina Faso, along the Sourou River. Many of them are Muslims. (see also BURKINABES)

SAMOANS   A Polynesian-speaking people inhabiting American Samoa and Western Samoa, in the southern Pacific Ocean. In America Samoa there is a population of 35,000, living on five main islands and two smaller islands. Its main island is Tutuila, where the administrative center, Pago-Pago, is situated. In Western Samoa there is a population of 165,000, on two main islands: Upolu, with the capital, Apia, and Savai'i, and about twenty small islands.

American Samoa has been administered by the United States since 1899 and became an incorporated territory of the U.S.A. in 1920. Western Samoa was administered by Germany from 1899, and by New Zealand from 1919. It became an independent state in 1962.

The basis of the social and economic life is the *aiga* (clan), ruled by a *matai*, a headman, who may be either a chief or an orator. An intricate hierarchy of graded titles has developed comprising titular and orator chiefs.

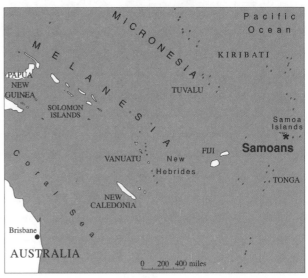

Samoans

Native or communal land accounts for more than 90 percent of all lands in American Samoa. The major agricultural crops are coconuts, tropical fruits, especially bananas, taro, yams, and breadfruit. Local fisheries are at subsistence level, but tuna products constituted most of the island's exports in 1989.

SAMORR   see TUGEN.

SAMOYEDS   see NENTSY.

SAMRE   see PEAR, SAOCH.

SAN   (Khoisan, Bushmen) The original inhabitants of East, Central, and Southern Africa. Having been variously exterminated, decimated by diseases, or assimilated into other populations, today only around 50,000 remain, located primarily in the Kalahari

Samburu women of central Kenya performing a traditional dance

514

above: A Samoan dancer
below: Samoans in a country restaurant

Desert in Namibia (c.20,000) and parts of Botswana (around 30,000).

The origins of the San in the Kalahari are not entirely clear. Scholarly opinion is divided between those who identify them as descendants of local San, traditionally found in this area; and those who see this population as remnants of Khoikhoi (Hottentot) and San refugee populations from all parts of the Southern Africa.

San social organization today, as before, is based on the band, consisting of several interrelated families. These highly mobile bands, which rarely encompass more than fifty people, are the largest social unit. Bands have specific, rather ill-defined, areas in which they move, and they are autonomous. Bands do not interact for economic, ritual, or social activities, have no chief or leader, and are highly egalitarian.

The San are a hunting-gathering people, and much of their diet consists of wild plants, which are the property of the band but, once collected, belong to the collector and her family. Small hunted animals are the property of the hunter and his family, while the meat of large animals (which are hunted by a party) is distributed to everyone in the band according to definite rules based on each man's role in the particular hunt. (see also NAMIBIANS, NGUNI, SOUTH AFRICANS, SOUTHERN SOTHO)

SANAVIRON   see COMECHINGEN.

SANDA TEMNE   see TEMNE.

SANDWE   (Wasaanday) A Khoisan-speaking ethnic group living in western Tanzania near the Nponde River. They number about 50,000. The Sandwe were anthropologically and culturally influenced by both the Cushitic and Bantu peoples. They both raise cattle, sheep, and other domestic animals, and engage in tropical agriculture. They supplement their diet by hunting, fishing, and gathering.

The Sandwe largely adhere to their traditional religion, although some have been converted to Protestant Christianity.

SANGA   An ethnic group numbering about 92,000 living in northern Congo. They constitute 5 percent of Congo's total population. (see also CONGOLESE)

SANGIR   (Sangil, Sangirezen, Talaoerezen) An ethnic group numbering 250,000, living on the Philippine islands of Sangihe (Sangir) and Talaud, as well as on the southern coast of Mindanao. They speak their own language, Sangir, which belongs to the Austronesian family. Although they originally grew sweet potatoes, maize, bananas, and rice by the slash and burn method, the DUTCH helped create a market for (and dependency on) such export crops as coconuts and nutmeg. Fishing and boat building are also part of the Sangir economy.

The Sangihe island group consists of the Soa "from the coast," who are the upper class, and the Tau Ruku, "inland grass people," who are of lower status and have been enslaved by the Soa in the past. The people of the Talaud islands also belong to this latter category. The DUTCH introduced a new social structure including a *radja* (head chief) who is assisted by the village chiefs.

The Sangir were formerly Muslims, Islam apparently having been brought over from the sultanates in the east, but Christianity became predominant with the coming of the DUTCH in the 1890s. However, neither Christianity nor Islam have been able to overcome the strong traditional beliefs of Sangir-speaking peoples, which include spirit possession and ritual ceremonies that once involved human sacrifice.

SANGLICHI   An ethnic group living in Afghanistan. They are often considered a subgroup of the ISHKASHIMI. (see also AFGHANS, ISHKASHIMI)

SANGO   An ethnic group living in the Ubangui Valley of the Central African Republic. During the period of colonial rule by the FRENCH, the Sango language became the lingua franca for the entire colony of Ubangui-Shari (now the Central African Republic), and since independence in 1966 it, along with French, is that country's official language. (see also CENTRAL AFRICAN REPUBLIC, THE PEOPLE OF THE)

SANGOU   see MASSANGO.

SANGTAM   A subgroup of the CHAKHESANG. (see also NAGA)

SANHADJA   (Zanaga) One of the two major Berber peoples, widely dispersed in the Maghrib. They are split into two main branches, the sedentary Kabyle and the nomadic Sanhadja, whose traditional home has been the western Sahara from Senegal to the southern parts of the Anti-Atlas mountains. They speak the Berber language. They are Muslims but have retained pre-Islamic practices.

The Sanhadja migrated to the western stretches of the Sahara Desert in about 1,000 B.C.E. Their use of horses and iron gave them an advantage over the previous inhabitants of the region. They were gradually, although superficially, converted to Islam from about the mid-eighth century. In the eleventh century, they nurtured the Almoravid Islamic reform movement, which destroyed the kingdom of Ghana, conquered Morocco and much of western Algeria, and reunited Muslim Spain against the challenge of Christian Spain. They reached their zenith in the tenth to twelfth centuries, but the Sanhadja-based Almoravid state collapsed in the thirteenth century under the attack of the MASMUDA of the High Atlas.

The Sanhadja of the Middle Atlas resisted French penetration in 1913–1914 out of fear of submitting to the ruling Arab dynasty, which they had previously resisted in the seventeenth century. They are divided into a large number of subgroups, the main ones being the LENTOUNA, MASSOUFA, and GADALA. (see also KABYLE, MASMUDA)

SAN JUAN An OTAVALO group.

SANPOIL A Native North American group numbering a few hundred, living in Washington State, U.S.A.

SANTA CRUZ ISLANDERS An ethnic group of approximately 6,000 living on the three Santa Cruz islands in the Solomon chain, in the southwest Pacific Ocean. They speak three related indigenous languages. Their economy is based on slash and burn cultivation. They adhere to a combination of Christian and traditional beliefs.

SANTAL A people numbering over 4.2 million (1981), living in Bihar, Orissa, West Bengal, and Tripura, in India and Bangladesh. They speak Munda, a member of the Austroasiatic family of languages.

Based on physical characteristics, they are regarded as being of Dravidian stock. The Santal worship many gods. Like the MUNDA, their supreme god is Singabonga, the sun god. In addition to tribal gods and goddesses, the Santal have also adopted the Hindu deities Siva and Durga.

The Santal social structure is very similar to the Hindu Varnasrama structure, on which the system of castes is based. They are divided into seven clans. They live in elementary as well as extended patterns of family units, and have their own traditional administra-

Santal

tive units. The office of headman (*manzhi*) is hereditary. The *manzhi* collects rent for a small commission, holds rent-free land, gives consent for any marriage negotiations, and settles village disputes through the village council.

His assistant (*jog manzhi*), also a hereditary office, regulates social behavior. The village priest is the ritual specialist; his assistant propitiates the spirits.

Young men are initiated before they are admitted into village society and receive burn marks on their left arms as a token of initiation.

In addition to producing crops of millet, maize, sesame, paddy, and pulses, the Santal retain their ancient practices of hunting (including snaring birds and small game), fishing, and food gathering activities.

The rules of Santal inheritance are akin to those of the Hindus. All sons live with the father during his life time and after his death set up different homes. The eldest receives a bullock and a rupee more than the others. Women have no rights of ownership in property whether moveable or immoveable.

The Santal believe in life after death. The dead are anointed with oil and are provided with new clothes, food, weapons, pots, and pans. They are then cremated. (see also ORAON)

SANTEE A subgroup of the SIOUX.

SANTIAGO   A subgroup of the JIVARO.

SAOCH   A Mon-Khmer group numbering about 3,000, living on the southern slopes of the Elephant Mountains of the Cambodian coast. They are closely related to the CHONG.

The Saoch are generally hunters and fishers, but many also find employment as farmhands for the KHMER. Their religious beliefs include the adoration of a sacred stone located in the nearby woods and a nebulous form of ancestor worship. (see also CHONG, PEAR)

SAO TOME AND PRINCIPE, THE PEOPLE OF
The population of the smallest independent country in Africa, situated on two islands in the Gulf of Guinea. The islands had no indigenous population prior to colonization by the PORTUGUESE toward the end of the fifteenth century, and its inhabitants, now numbering 120,000, are divided into two groups. The larger is the Forros, descendants of Portuguese colonists and their African slaves brought to work the islands' plantations; the second is the Angolares, descended from shipwrecked slaves from Angola who formed small fishing communities on the southern coast of São Tome. The local variant of Portuguese, the official language, has been heavily influenced by various African languages. Roman Catholicism, the predominant religion, has similarly been influenced by traditional African beliefs.

The islands became independent from the PORTUGUESE in 1975. Since the mid-1980s, the government of São Tome and Principe has inclined toward democratization and capitalism and in 1991 multi-party elections were held.

Most of the islands' inhabitants find employment in the extensive cocoa and coffee plantations.

SAPEI   (Sabei) A subgroup of the SABAOT.

SAPERA   see NAT.

SAPUAN   A Buddhist Mon-Khmer group, numbering about 1,000, living in southern Laos. Most Sapuan have been assimilated into the predominant LAO, largely through intermarriage.

SARA   A large ethnic group living in southern Chad along the Chari and Logone River valleys. They number around 1.5 million and constitute about 30 percent of Chad's population. The Sara mostly adhere to traditional religions, although many have recently con-

verted to Islam, and Protestant and Catholic missions have also had some success. They are divided into a large number of clans, some of which, notably the MOUNDANG, TOUBOURI, and MASSA are also considered part of the KIRDI. The GOULAYE clan of the Moyen-Charo region has been particularly influenced by local missionary activities. Other Sara clans are the KABA, who live along the border with the Central African Republic, the MBAI (Mbaye) of the Doba and Moissala region, and the DIJIOKO, DINDE, NDUKA, and RANGA. All Sara groups engage primarily in agriculture and fishing.

Since the Sara failed to organize themselves into large political units in the precolonial period, larger neighboring kingdoms such as Bornu, Baguirmi, and Ouadai often raided them for slaves. Their reputation as menial laborers was continued by the colonial administration of the FRENCH, who recruited them for forced labor. By the 1930s, their traditional lifestyle was upset by severe colonial taxation policies, and the Sara were forced to take up the cultivation of cotton to pay taxes.

Soon after World War II, with the introduction of party politics in French Africa, the Sara organized their own political party, which, because of the group's numerical advantage, became an important political force in the independence movement. Its leader, François (later Ngarta) Tombalbaye, became Chad's first president in 1960 and the Sara became the dominant ethnic group in the new state's armed forces and civil administration. Neighboring groups, particularly from the Muslim north, still regarded the Sara as subject people or slaves and remained openly hostile to Sara hegemony. Tombalbaye was deposed in a 1975 coup with considerable backing from the LIBYANS. (see also CENTRAL AFRICAN REPUBLIC, THE PEOPLE OF THE, CHADIANS)

SARADOL   A subgroup of the BURYAT.

SARAKOLE   see SONINKE.

SARAMBAU   An ethnic group living on the Indonesian island of Kalimantan (Borneo). (see also DAYAK)

SARCEE   A Native North American Athapaskan-speaking group numbering 1,000, many of whom live on the Sarcee reserve in Alberta, Canada. They are the only Athapaskan-speaking Plains Indian group in Canada. (see also ATHAPASKAN)

SARDARJI   see INDIANS.

SARDINIANS   The 1.5 million inhabitants of the Mediterranean island of Sardinia are a component of the ITALIANS. They speak an archaic Latin dialect; in some villages Catalan is still spoken, a remnant of Spanish rule of the island. They live in a poor pastoral island, where the inland remains partitioned among gangs, which historically provided a minimum of security, where the state was too weak to do so. Costumes, songs, and original customs, such as bride-stealing, remain in force.

The island was successively occupied by the Carthaginians, Romans, Vandals, and Byzantines, and thus became the a lair of Saracen pirates. After a period of semi-independence following 1164, it fell to Spain in 1355, passed later to Austria, and in the eighteenth century finally became the seat of a kingdom which in 1861 united Italy. The island was recognized as an autonomous region in 1948. Recently, tourism has been developing as an income earner and may counteract the perennial emigration.

SARIQOLI   (Sarykoli) An ethnic group living in most of the villages in the Tajik district of the Xinjiang Uighur Autonomous Region of China. Their estimated number is about 23,000. The area they inhabit has been named the Tajik District since they, together with the WAKHI of Xinjiang, are regarded by the CHINESE as one ethnic group and defined in their aggregate as TAJIK.

The Sariqoli speak the Sariqoli dialect of the Shughni language, which, in turn, is divided into three subdialects, Tashqurghani, Vachani, and Byryugsoli. These dialects are unwritten, and Uighur is used as the literary language. Many Sariqoli speak both Sariqoli and Uighur. They belong to the Ismai'il sect of Islam.

The Sariqoli are generally semi-nomadic mountain farmers and herders, growing wheat, barley, and peas in spring before leaving their villages in the early summer to graze their herds in mountain pastures. They return to their villages in time for the autumn harvest. (see also WAKHI)

SARUYAN   An ethnic group living on the Indonesian island of Kalimantan (Borneo). (see also DAYAK)

SARYKOLI   see SARIQOLI.

SARY UIGHUR   A subgroup of the UIGHUR.

SASAGO   A subgroup of the HADIYA.

Sasak

SASAK   The predominant ethnic group on the Indonesian island of Lombok, east of Java. They number approximately 1 million and are divisible into two culturally distinct groups, the WAKTU LIMA and the WAKTU TELU. Both groups speak the same Malayo-Polynesian language related to the languages of the JAVANESE and BALINESE. The language has three major dialects used by members of different castes. An indigenous script called Kawi is rapidly being replaced by a new Roman alphabet. The Sasak are nominally Muslims, with the WAKTU LIMA being more orthodox in their observance of religious tenets.

Rice is the most important crop, and water buffalo are occasionally herded for their meat. Chickens are also raised but usually only for cock fighting.

Since the colonial period, there has been increasing antagonism between the WAKTU LIMA and the WAKTU TELU.

SATAR   An ethnic group living in the forests of Morang and Jhapa, Nepal. Although their origin is obscure, they are believed to have migrated from Santal Parganas and Chhota Nagpur, in the state of Bihar, India.

Like Hindus, the Satar believe in one creator. They also believe in other gods and goddesses. Their guardian deities are called Marang Baru and Marang Thakur, and their village deity is called Aoto Bouga. They have no caste system.

The Satar's main occupation is agriculture, but their farming implements and methods of cultivation are extremely simple. Some Satar keep cattle and goats. They are also skilled in weaving cloth and making brooms and mattresses from the leaves of trees.

SATARE A subgroup of the MAUE.

SAU see DAYAK.

SAUDI ARABS The 12 million indigenous Saudi Arabs, 99 percent of whom are Sunni Muslims, constitute an estimated 82 percent of the population of Saudi Arabia. Because of the dearth of water, less than 1 percent of the country is permanently inhabited. Population is concentrated in the Nejd around Riyadh, the Hijaz, and in the eastern provinces. While the Nejd is a land of oases, the southern Hijaz (Asir) is the best watered region. Rain-fed agriculture is possible only here. Oil is mostly exploited in the Eastern Province.

The Hijaz is the heartland of Islam, and boasts the holy cities of Mecca and Medina, the destination of nearly 2 million *hajj* pilgrims anually, nearly half of them from abroad. There are Shiite c.300,000 Iranian-speakers in the Eastern Province, especially in the al-Qatif and Hufuf (Hasa) oases.

Saudi Arabs are organized in tribes and, although weakening, tribalism remains strong. The requirements of the oil industry have led to a mass import of labor: an estimated 15 percent of the population now consists of foreign workers, 1.5 million of these are ARABS, mainly EGYPTIANS, PALESTINIANS, and YEMENIS. There are also large numbers of INDIANS, PAKISTANIS, and short-term contractees from Korea, the Philippines, Thailand, and Sri Lanka.

The Beduin once formed a substantial element of the indigenous ARABS, but official policy since King Abdul Aziz Ibn Sa'ud, the founder of the Saudi state, has been to sedentarize them. In the era of oil production, pastoralism has decreased from 25 to 4 percent of the labor force, and many Beduin have been absorbed into the oil industry. Major tribes include: in the Nejd region, the Anazah, Mutair, Otaibah, Shei, Dawassir, Ruwallah, Shammar, and Rashid; in Hassa, the Maara and Ajman; in Hijaz, Banı Atiyah and Bani Wahhab. The Harb in the Hijaz descend from Beduin and black female slaves: slavery in Saudi Arabia was officially abolished in 1962. The Sulaba (or Sulayb) are a gypsy-like people following Beduin tribes and serving as their musicians and entertainers.

The rural population, essentially oasis-dwellers, has declined considerably. By the mid-1980s agriculture and fishing accounted for only 4 percent of the labor force. In the 1970s and 1980s Saudi Arabia built huge airports, harbors, roads, and water projects, but non-petrochemical heavy and hi-tech industry are still lacking.

The Saudi Arabian polity is based on strict adherence to a puritanical form of Sunni Islam, which includes a ban on alcohol, the prohibition of usury, the imposition of the veil, and the observance of Islamic penal law. Males wear traditional dress. The country is ruled as a royal patrimony, and an absolute monarchy has suppressed all attempts at widening political participation. Instead of democracy, Saudi Arabs have a king who is approachable to all his subjects. Political stability is further sustained by lavish subsidies to tribes and to the hundreds of princes belonging to the ruling house. Huge incomes from oil exports have transformed Saudi society. New classes are developing, which until recently did not exist at all: an urban bourgeoisie, white collar workers, and laborers. However, tribalism remains the overriding structure.

It is with the sudden emergence of Islam around the holy places, Mecca and Medina, in the early seventh century that Arabia, the area of modern-day Saudi Arabia, became globally important. ARABS spread their religion and language, and in time mingled with the populations they conquered. When, in the late seventh century, political power passed from Arabia to Damascus and thence to Baghdad and Cairo, Arabia became once more an isolated and fragmented tribal frontier. From 1517 on, it fell under Ottoman protection, at least nominally.

The modern history of Saudi Arabia began in the eighteenth century with the emergence of the Saudi tribal dynasty in Nejd. It allied itself with the puritanical Wahhabi reform movement, which demanded strict obedience to the tenets of the Koran. The Saudi dynasty conquered neighboring tribes and imposed a righteous lifestyle on them. By 1800 they had overrun most of the Arabian peninsula. In the nineteenth century the Saudis established their capital in Riyadh. In 1925 they defeated the Hashemite rulers of the Hijaz (including the holy city, Mecca) and established the kingdom of Hijaz and Nejd. In 1932 the kingdom was renamed Saudi Arabia.

In 1938 oil was discovered and production started. Until 1981 Saudi exports met ever rising oil demands. But proven reserves grew even faster: the Arabian peninsula contains 45 percent of the world's proven oil reserves, and the Saudis control the single largest part of it. The past decades have seen the creation of a huge petrochemical infrastructure. Development was especially rapid from the 1960s until the early 1980s, but the Saudi economy suffered from a chronic lack of skilled labor (women have been largely excluded from social and economic life).

Foreign laborers were therefore hired. However, Saudi policy has been to limit to the utmost the impact of foreigners on the mores and political expectations of the population. Expatriates live in segregated communities and their movements are strictly controlled. Iraq's occupation of Kuwait in 1990 and the ensuing Gulf War brought about the enforced departure of foreign workers, including 800,000 YEMENIS.

SAUK   see SAC.

SAUNDIKA   see SUNDI.

SAURIA PAHARIA   A people numbering over 2 million (1981), living in Bihar and West Bengal, India. Their language belongs to the Dravidian family of languages.

SAUSU   An ethnic group living in the mountainous central region of the Indonesian island of Sulawesi (Celebes). (see also TORADJA)

SAVAR   A group numbering 40,000 (1981), living in the states of Bihar, Orissa, and West Bengal, India. They are related to the KHARIA. They live on hills and in jungles, where they hunt with bows and bamboo- or metal-tipped arrows, but this is a subsidiary occupation. They also forage in the jungle for edible roots and yams and till small portions of land. The Savar do not, however, practice shifting cultivation. Some work for daily wages. The Savar family is patrilineal and nuclear. Their houses are windowless and have only one room. (see also KHARIA)

SAVARA   A group numbering 82,000 (1981), living in the state of Andhra Pradesh, India. Their language belongs to the Dravidian family of languages.

The Savara live in a world of spirits and deities. They are agriculturists, supplementing their diet by hunting and food-gathering. Forestry and agricultural labor are their other modes of occupation.

SAVUNESE   (s.d. Dou Hawu) Inhabitants of the Savu islands in Indonesia. There are also Savunese communities, mostly Christian, in the nearby islands of Timor and Sumba. They number approximately 50,000 and speak a language closely related to Ndaonese. The Savunese pantheon consists of a number of deities presided over by a god known by nine names. There are six principal religious ceremonies: birth; naming; baptism and haircutting; marriage; house building; and complex funeral rites. Boys are circumcised between the ages of six and fifteen; both boys and girls undergo tooth-filing between the ages of fifteen and seventeen. Neither ceremony is accompanied by any specialized ritual. Other religious ceremonies include ritual warfare held annually. Marriages are strictly monogamous.

Products of the lontar palm are essential to the Savunese. Other important crops include sorghum, corn, millet, and peanuts. Horses are raised for export, and tie-dyeing is a well developed craft.

SAWAI   Generic term for six small ethnic groups inhabiting southern Halmahera, an island in eastern Indonesia. The total population is estimated to be about 10,000. They have preserved their traditional religious beliefs.

Sawai groups include the BULI, GANE, GEBE, MABA, PATANI, Sawai proper, and WEDA.

SAYAN   A Mon-Khmer group living in Vietnam and Laos. They are often identified with the DUANE, JEH, MENAM, and NOAR.

SCANDINAVIANS   see DANES, FINNS, LAPPS, NORWEGIANS, SWEDES.

SCHWEIZER   see SWISS.

SCOTS   Most of the 5.2 million Scots living in Scotland in the north of the British Isles currently speak an English dialect. Only in the Western Highlands and in the islands do c.75,000 continue to speak Gaelic (Celtic), the original language of the Scots before they were united with the ENGLISH to their south.

Historically, the Scots were characterized by extended family structures or clans, recognizable by their kilt patterns. The Lowlands are the Scots' economic and population center: the main cities are Edinburgh and Glasgow, where many ENGLISH also live. The hilly Highlands are less open to non-Scottish influences, and have retained their Gaelic color, manifest in songs, bagpipe dances, and various traditional celebrations.

Scotland's original inhabitants were the Caledonians, or Picts, subjugated in antiquity by Celtic Scoti from Ireland. Living to the north of Hadrian's wall in Roman times, they remained unconquered and their civilization unaffected. Christianity was introduced by the IRISH, whose monks brought with them a specific Celtic rite. In 700–800 the Pict and Scot realms were united in West Scotland, while the ENGLISH (Angles and Saxons) conquered East Scotland. The current Scottish people descends from a mingling of these diverse groups.

In 1174 Scotland became a fief under English kings, who introduced feudalism into the Lowlands. English became the dominant language. In the Highlands, clan leaders resisted this process, tribal structures lived on, and the Gaelic language was preserved, especially in the northwest. English efforts to pacify the Scots provoked ceaseless border wars between the two peoples, lasting until the seventeenth century. In the late Middle Ages, ruinous private wars and incessant civil wars obstructed economic growth; towns were depopulated, and the peasantry oppressed. The Scots remained much poorer and more backward than their English neighbors.

Scottish orientation was always balanced between the ENGLISH and the FRENCH. An anti-French reaction in the 1550s facilitated conversion to Calvinist Protestantism, although Highlanders long remained faithful to Catholicism. Complicated inter-Protestant disputes kept the ENGLISH involved in Scottish affairs. Elizabeth I supported the Anglican-oriented Episcopalian aristocracy against the more democratic Calvinist Presbyterians. Since 1603, when a Scottish king ascended the English throne as James I and brought about a personal union, of the two realms Scottish history became inextricably bound up with that of the ENGLISH. The Scots' revolt against the imposition of Anglicanism by Charles I in 1638 triggered the Puritan Revolution in England. Conversely, restoration in England in 1660 led, in Scotland, to the suppression of the Presbyterians by the Episcopalians. The Presbyterian church was restored after the Glorious Revolution of 1688.

In 1707 the union between Scotland and England became official, and the United Kingdom was established. The Scottish parliament was abolished, but Scots retained their separate church and law. Abolition of custom duties opened the way for Scottish economic growth. However, it did not profit the lower gentry; hence in 1748 they supported Bonnie Prince Charlie to assume the crown. The defeated Scottish nobles were dragged down in his fall.

In the eighteenth century, Scots became trailblazers of the Enlightenment and technological innovators. In the nineteenth century, the industrial revolution engulfed Lowland Scotland. Cheap labor combined with a poor domestic market to propel the Scots to produce cotton, iron, steel, and ships for export. They also became active in the expansion of the British Empire, but the working class experienced extreme misery. By the early twentieth century they created a strong labor movement.

In comparison with the modernized Lowlands, the Highlands remained impoverished. Landlords drove tenants off their land; mid-nineteenth century crop failures initiated a still-continuing process of depopulation and emigration. In the post-World War I years, Scottish industry, obsolescent by then, collapsed: it did not recover in the post-World War II era. From the 1970s onward, economic crises, high unemployment, and disappointment with British governments led to a strengthening of Scottish nationalism. The Scottish National Party, striving for independence, won 30 percent of the vote in 1974. Nationalists hope to finance an independent state from North Sea oil fields. British government plans to grant extensive autonomy to the Scots failed to mobilize enough support. Scottish nationalism dwindled during the 1980s. It remains strongest in the border zone with England. (see also BRITISH)

SEA DAYAK   An ethnic group living on the Indonesian island of Kalimantan (Borneo). (see also DAYAK)

SEA NOMADS   see MOKEN.

SEBA   An ethnic group related to the LAMBA, living in Zambia.

SEBEI   An ethnic group inhabiting the northern and northwestern slopes of Mount Elgon and the surrounding plains in eastern Uganda. They live mainly on the mountain itself, the plains having become largely depopulated when they were raided in the nineteenth century by the KARAMOJONG, POKOT, NANDI, and MASAAI.

The Sebei language belongs to the Southern Nilotic group of languages. They were originally cattle-herders who also raised sheep and goats. They practice shifting hoe agriculture and grow millet and sorghum for subsistence and coffee as a cash crop.

In contrast to their neighbors, age-sets play no significant role in Sebei social life. Both men and women (at ages thirteen and sixteen respectively) are initiated by circumcision. The Sebei consist of different groups, which are interrelated but formally independent from each other. Today they are largely christianized. (see also SUK, UGANDANS)

SECHELT A Native North American group numbering 850, most of whom live on the Sechelt Reserve, British Columbia, Canada.

SEDANG (s.d. Ha Ndea) A Mon-Khmer group numbering about 80,000 living in southern Vietnam. They cultivate rice and raise vegetables and tubers. They have a stratified social structure with the wife of the village chief representing the spirit of the rice crop and playing an important role in agricultural religious rituals.

Another aspect of their religion is the belief that gods and men were once equal. Until the 1930s human sacrifice and ritual cannibalism were practiced. This was suppressed by the French colonial authorities, and resulted in a fierce war between the Sedang and the FRENCH. Only animal sacrifices are currently practiced.

Sedang

The COR, DANJO, DUONG, KMRANG, and TO-DRAH are subgroups of the Sedang.

SEDUMAK An ethnic group living on the Indonesian island of Kalimantan (Borneo). (see also DAYAK)

SEFARDIM see ISRAELIS, JEWS.

SEFWI see SAHWI.

SEID A subgroup of the TURKMEN.

SEK A Mon-Khmer group living along the Mekong River in northern Thailand and Laos. They practice Buddhism and have been considerably influenced by the LAO.

SEKA see MOCHA.

SEKANI A Native North American group numbering 900, most of whom live on reserves in British Columbia, Canada.

In the 1960s several villages of Sekani north of Prince George were relocated when their lands were flooded to provide hydro-electric power. Many of them still practice their traditional way of life which is based on hunting and trapping. Others are employed in the lumber industry in and around the city of Prince George. (see also CARRIER)

SEKE An ethnic group living in Gabon on the northern coast at Cocobeach and in neighboring Equatorial Guinea. They adhere mostly to traditional religions.

During the eighteenth and nineteenth centuries, the Seke were involved in the slave trade. Their chiefs signed treaties with the FRENCH in the late nineteenth century allowing them to colonize the region.

SEKOYA A small group of South American Indians inhabiting the West Amazonia region of Ecuador. Their name is derived from the Sekoya River, along which some Sekoya live. They speak a language belonging to the Western Tukano family.

Sekoya living near the Aguarico River have intermarried with the SIONA, and are referred to as the Siona-Sekoya.

SELAKAN An ethnic group living on the Indonesian island of Kalimantan (Borneo). (see also DAYAK)

SELEKA A subgroup of the TSWANA.

SELEPET An ethnic group of approximately 7,000 living in northeastern Papua New Guinea. They speak an indigenous regional language. They are slash and burn cultivators whose main crop is sweet potatoes while their chief cash crop is coffee.

SELIMA A subgroup of the BAGGARA.

SELKUP Fewer than 3,000 Selkup live mainly in the Yamalo-Nenets Autonomous Province and the Tomsk Province in the Russian Federation.

The Selkup language belongs to the Samoyedic group of the Uralic linguistic family but is far removed from the other Samoye tongues. It is divided into three major dialects. The Soviet authorities did not provide for an alphabet for Selkup, and Russian serves as the literary language.

The Selkup are divided into two groups, the Taz-speaking Turukhan Selkup who live in the *tunda*, and the Narym Selkup, who live in the *taiga* forests and speak the Tym and Ket dialects.

Traditionally hunters, fishermen and gatherers, the Selkup, especially the Narym Selkup, have been steadily assimilated by the RUSSIANS. They practice traditional religions.

SELONIANS (Seli) see LATVIANS.

SELUNG see MOKEN.

SEMA (Zeme) A group numbering 95,000 (1981), living in the states of Manipur, Nagaland, Assam, and Arunachal Pradesh, in northeast India. Their language belongs to the Tibeto-Burman family and they are related to the RENGMA, who are NAGA.

In the past, the Sema were migratory. They would set up new villages by declaring the first person to have migrated to that place, as the leader and by calling him the father of that village. (see also NAGA)

SEMAI A subgroup of the SENOI.

SEMALAI A subgroup of the JAKUN.

SEMANG (Negritos, Pangan, Orang Asli) A generic term for the indigenous inhabitants of the forests of the Malay Peninsula, numbering about 2,000. They are divided into several tribes: the BATEK (including the BATEK DE, BATEK NONG, BATEK TE, and MINTIl), JAHAI, KENSIU, KINTAK, LANOH, and MENDRIQ.

They speak languages belonging to the Asli (native) language family, which have incorporated many Malay words. Religious beliefs differ from group to group, but all share a belief in supernatural beings living both above and beyond the earth. Traditionally hunters and gatherers, they are gradually adopting agriculture.

The Semang have apparently lived in the Malay Peninsula for as long as 10,000 years. The MALAYS generally despise the Semang; they used them as slaves until the practice was banned by the BRITISH in the late nineteenth century.

In the 1950s the British government in Malaya attempted to bolster ties with the Semang in order to prevent them from collaborating with Communist insurgents.

SEMELAI A subgroup of the SENOI.

SEMIAHMOO The smallest Native North American group. Numbering fifty, they live in British Columbia, Canada. They are part of the Salishan linguistic group.

SEMIGALLIANS (Zemgali) see LATVIANS.

SEMINOLE (Alachua, Apachicila, Apalachee, Ays) A Native North American people numbering 6,000, many of whom live on two federal reservations, Big Cypress and Brighton, and one State Trust Area in Oklahoma, U.S.A.

Originally the largest group of indigenous peoples in Florida, they fought a guerrilla-style war with the Americans, which reduced their numbers significantly. In the aftermath of their war, around 1840, they were removed to the Indian Territory of Oklahoma. A peace treaty was signed only in the 1930s making the Semi-

Semang

nole the native group which was at war with the United States for the longest period of time.

Today the Seminole in Florida use their privileges to sell commodities without taxes to the public.

SEMOQ BERI   A subgroup of the SENOI.

SENA   A subgroup of the KARANGA.

SENDURIA   A subgroup of the NAGESIA.

SENECA   A Native North American group, one of the smallest of the IROQUOIS CONFEDERACY, living in Oklahoma, U.S.A., and Ontario, Canada.

SENEGALESE   (in French: Senegalais) The people of Senegal, numbering about 7 million, are unevenly distributed throughout the country, reflecting variations in land fertility and the concentration of government and business activity around the capital, Dakar. More than 70 percent of the Senegalese labor force is employed in the agricultural sector.

The Senegalese people is composed of a number of ethnic groups, the largest of which, the WOLOF, live mainly in the northwest. SERER live in the central-west, FULANI and TOUCOULEUR in the north, and DIOLA and MANDE in the south. About 95 percent of the Senegalese are Muslims, with Christians found mainly among the DIOLA and SERER. In recent years, the latter have become increasingly islamicized. French is the official language, but the lingua franca is Wolof.

Senegal became independent in 1960. Leopold Sedar Senghor, a member of the SERER and first president of the country, ensured that his party would represent all ethnic groups by merging it with all other parties and creating a single-party state. His 1974 democratization process was continued by his successor Abdou Diouf after Senghor's resignation in 1980. In 1982 the Senegambian (Senegal-Gambia) confederation was established after the Senegalese army saved Gambia's president from a military coup. The confederation was created as a result of the close ethnic relations between the two countries, separated only by colonial borders: Gambia was a British colony but the same ethnic groups live in it. Despite cultural and linguistical connections, the confederation was dissolved in 1990 as a result of severe disagreements between the two countries. Until 1980 ethnic factors almost did not affect Senegalese political life. Since the early 1980s, however, the emergence of a separatist movement among the DIOLA in the southern province of the Casamance

region, separated from the rest of the country by the Gambia and subject to some neglect, has periodically presented the government with considerable security problems. (see also MALIANS)

SENGA   A Tumbuka-speaking group numbering 45,000 living along Zambia's eastern border. Some are Christians while others practice traditional religions. Their culture and social organization resemble that of the TUMBUKA but unlike most peoples of Zambia their descent system is patrilineal. The Senga raise and trade cotton and tobacco.

SENGELE   An ethnic group living in the Bandundu Region of Zaire west of Lake Mai-Ndombe. Their language is related to Mongo.

Sengseng

SENGSENG   (s.d. Arawe) An ethnic group of approximately 1,000 living in southwest New Britain in Papua New Guinea, to the east of the main island. They speak an indigenous regional language. Their main crops are taro and various green vegetables. Their religious beliefs include the worship of ancestral ghosts. Music and dance are their major artforms.

SENNAH   An ethnic group living on the Indonesian island of Kalimantan (Borneo). (see also DAYAK)

SENOI   (Sakai [derogatory]) A generic term for a group of indigenous inhabitants of peninsular Malaysia numbering about 25,000. They speak Asli (native) languages and have generally preserved their traditional religious beliefs.

They are often divided into SEMAI (the largest tribe), CHE WONG, JAH HUT, SEMELAI, SEMOQ BERI, and TEMIAR. Unlike the hunter-gather SEMANG, they are primarily slash and burn cultivators of rice and manioc.

Most older Senoi still remember oppression and slaving raids by the MALAYS. In recent years the government has attempted to convert the Senoi to Islam and educate them in Malay norms.

SENTAH   see DAYAK.

SENTINELESE   The least known aborigines of the Andaman Islands, India. They live in North Sentinel Island. Their affinity with the ONGE has been noted but their language, which has not been classified, differs from that of the ONGE. They continue to lead their traditional life of hunting, fishing, and food gathering.

SENUFO   (Senoufo) An ethnic group living in north-central Côte d'Ivoire where they number around 1.3 million, in southeastern Mali where there are about 1.2 million, and in Burkina Faso where they number around 630,000. In the Côte d'Ivoire and Burkina Faso, most Senufo are Muslims while in Mali they generally adhere to traditional religions.

In the nineteenth century, the Senufo had an Islamic kingdom called Sikasso in the area of the city of Korhogo in modern Côte d'Ivoire which conquered rival

Senufo

kingdoms to the south. Another kingdom called Kenedougou co-existed in present day Mali. Prior to French colonization, the Senufo suffered from the attacks and domination of the leader of the MALINKE, Samori, who established an empire in that region.

The KARAKORA, KOMONO, and TURKA of Burkina Faso are subgroups of the Senufo. (see also BURKINABES, IVOREANS, MALIANS)

SERBS   (s.d. Srbi) There are about 8.8 million Serbs, most of whom live in the former Yugoslavia; 6.2 million in Serbia (66 percent of the population), including Vojvodina and Kosovo, 500,000 (including MONTENEGRINS) in Montenegro (79 percent), 1.5 million in Bosnia-Herzegovina (30 percent), and 600,000 in Croatia.

The Serbian language belongs to the southern branch of the Slavic group of Indo-European languages. It is so close, dialectical differences nothwithstanding, to Croatian that the two are considered a single language, Serbo-Croat, which is spoken in Serbia, Croatia, Bosnia-Herzegovina, and Montenegro (Crna Gora). Yet, it is written in two alphabets: the Eastern Orthodox Serbs use the Cyrillic and the Catholic Croats the Roman.

The Serbs are very close to the CROATS and BOSNIAN MUSLIMS anthropologically and linguistically. The main difference lies in religion. The Serbs are Eastern Orthodox Christians while the CROATS are Roman Catholics. Being separated by religion and history (Ottoman-Muslim rule) from the West, the Serbs were slower than the CROATS (but faster than the BOSNIAN MUSLIMS) to become modernized and westernized.

The MONTENEGRINS form a distinct group within the Serbs. Living in an inaccessible mountain home bordering the Adriatic Sea, they have preserved into the second half of the twentieth century social and cultural institutions, customs, and traditons abandoned long ago by other Serbs.

Slavic tribes settled the present day Serbia and Montenegro in the sixth and seventh centuries C.E. By the ninth century they formed separate tribal states ruled by chiefs (*zupans*). The Zupan Mutimir converted in 879 to Eastern Orthodox Christianity, but until the mid-twelfth century the Serbs were under the overlordship of the Byzantines and/or Bulgars. The Neumanja dynasty established Serbia as an independent kingdom and founded, under Saint Sava, the Serbian Orthodox church. Serbian power reached its zenith under Stefan Dusan (1331–1355) who conquered Macedonia, Albania, Epirus, Aetolia, and Thessaly and crowned himself tzar of the Serbs and GREEKS. The last Serbian king, Lazar, was captured and beheaded by the Ottomans at the battle of Kosovo (1389) and the Serbs came under Ottoman rule. Some Serbs fled into Hungary to continue to fight the Ottomans from there but were subdued during the Ottoman conquest of Hungary in 1527.

The only Serbs who never submitted to Ottoman rule were the MONTENEGRINS, who as vassals of Venice kept fighting the Ottomans. Between 1516 and 1855 the MONTENEGRINS were ruled by elected *vladikas* (bishops), although after 1697 the election was limited to the Petrovic Njegos family.

Ottoman defeats in the wars against Austria and Russia during the late seventeenth into the eighteenth centuries, the advancement of the Austrian border into Serbian lands, and encouragement by Russian and Austrian agents, helped to ignite a Serbian rebellion in 1804. By 1806, the rebels succeeded in occupying most of Serbia, including Belgrade, but following the conclusion of the Russo-Ottoman War of 1806–1812, the Serbs were defeated and in 1813 the Ottomans reentered Belgrade. A second rebellion in 1815 was more successful and by 1830 the Ottomans officially declared Serbia an autonomous principality under their suzerainty. Following the Balkan crisis of 1875–1878 Serbia gained independence and enlarged its territory, although territorial continuity with Montenegro was prevented by the Austrian occupation and administration of Bosnia-Herzegovina and the district of Novi Pazar. In 1882 Serbia was proclaimed a kingdom.

Between autonomy and World War I, Serbian internal politics were characterized by the ongoing feud between the houses of Karageorge and Obrenovi, which influenced Serbia's foreign orientation to either Russian or Austria. Its foreign policy was based on the idea of a general uprising of the Christians against the Ottomans and the creation of a large South Slav state under Serbian leadership. According to the accusations of other southern Slavs, it was under the guise of a South Slav union that the Serbs had been continuously and singlemindedly trying to create a Greater Serbia at the expense of neighboring peoples and to dominate the other southern Slavs. Thus, for example, when Bulgaria united in 1885, Serbia, perceiving a threat to its supremacy among the southern Slavs, was quick to try and undo the union by use of force; it was the only party to make such an attempt.

After the Crimean War Serbia's autonomy was guaranteed by the Great Powers. In the 1860s and 1870s Serbia entered into a series of treaties with Greece, Romania, Montenegro, and the Bulgarian revolutionary committee, thus creating a precedent for the Balkan League of 1912.

In the twenty-two years preceding World War I, a competition developed between the dynasties of Montenegro and Serbia over overall leadership of the Serbs. Under Nikolai (1860–1918), the MONTENEGRINS managed to double their territory and have its independence recognized at the Congress of Berlin (1878); in 1910 it was proclaimed a kingdom. The timing of the outbreak of the First Balkan War (1912) was greatly influenced by the Serbian-Montenegrin competition. Both Serbia and Montenegro gained large territories in the Balkan Wars, and had now, in addition, a joint border.

In World War I Serbia and Montenegro fought on the side of the Entente Powers and were occupied by Austro-Hungarian forces. In November 1918, after their withdrawal, representatives of the Slavs of the regions of Dalmatia, Croatia, Slavonia, Slovenia and Bosnia-Herzegovina proclaimed the union of their territories with Serbia and Montenegro in one state of Serbs, Croats, and Slovenes. The Serbs of Vojvodina joined Serbia, and the Grand National Assembly of Montenegro, under Serbian bayonets, voted unanimously to depose Nikolai and join Serbia too.

The Serbs were, from the start, the dominant element in the new South Slav state. Croat and Slovene disappointment at Serb dominance in the new kingdom, which in 1929 changed its name to Yugoslavia, led to a separatist movements developing, mainly among the CROATS. In World War II Yugoslavia was partitioned among Germany, Italy, Hungary, and Bulgaria. An independent Greater Croatia led by Croat fascists was created by the GERMANS, while the Serbs remained under direct German occupation.

Liberated by its own Communist-led partisans under Josip Broz Tito, Yugoslavia was reinstated under a Communist regime and proclaimed a federation, with Serbia, Montenegro, Macedonia, Bosnia-Herzegovina, Crotia, and Slovenia as its constituent republics. Nevertheless, communist Yugoslavia continued to be dominated by the Serbs, despite the fact that Tito himself was a Croat. Following the death of Tito, the rise of nationalism among the different groups in Yugoslavia and a mounting economic crisis caused relations among the republics and peoples of Yugoslavia to become increasingly strained. Relations became polarized between Slovenia and Croatia, which were pursuing an open market economy and political democratization, and Serbia, which was promoting Serbian nationalism and clinging to an orthodox Communist economy.

In 1991 Slovenia and Croatia seceded from Yugoslavia and proclaimed their independence. The Serbs living in Croatia, assisted by the predominantly Serbian Yugoslav army and air force, rebelled, starting a civil war which spread to Bosnia-Herzegovina. In this war the Serbs, more than the CROATS and BOSNIAN MUSLIMS, were accused of pursuing a policy of ethnic cleansing, of war crimes, and of rape and slaughter on a massive scale, aimed mainly against the BOSNIAN MUSLIMS. (see also CROATS, SLOVENES)

SERER   A people living in the Sine-Salum and Bawol Regions of Senegal. They are the second largest group in that country, after the WOLOF, numbering about 1 million people and constituting about 16 percent of the population.

Their original language is Serer but many now speak the language of their neighbors, the WOLOF. At the beginning of the colonial period some Serer converted to Catholicism. After Senegal's independence the Serer who migrated to the cities adopted the Wolof culture, language, and religion, thus becoming Muslims. However, a strong Catholic minority still exists among the Serer.

The Serer are sedentary agriculturalists, originally from the Senegal valley. In the eleventh century the region was influenced by the expansion of Islam from North Africa and the Serer moved southward because of their refusal to convert to Islam.

In the twelfth or thirteenth century the Serer formed the small but powerful kingdom of Sin and by the end of the fifteenth century, the kingdom of Salum. Both kingdoms were absorbed into the Jolof kingdom of the WOLOF.

Until the colonization of the region by the FRENCH at the end of the nineteenth century, Serer society was divided into classes and castes. There were three classes: nobles, freemen, and slaves. The castes were established according to the economic activity of the family. In the colonial period these divisions became less and less important. Until World War II political activity in Senegal was limited to the residents of four communities: Dakar, Rufisque, Goree, and Saint Louis. After the war, when the political arena was opened to all SENEGALESE, the Serer became involved in politics through the activity of Leopold Sedar Senghor, who led his country to independence and was its president until 1980, when he voluntarily retired from office.

Despite Senghor's being a Serer, the dominant ethnic group in Senegal's political and administrative systems was the WOLOF.

Since Senegal's independence the Serer have undergone a rapid process of islamization and "wolofization." They have started to move to the cities and adopt the Wolof culture. Those who stay in the rural areas adopt the Wolof lifestyle and agriculture techniques, with groundnuts as their main crop. Many have joined Wolof Islamic brotherhoods. (see also SENEGALESE)

SERI   Numbering 300–400, the Seri are native to the Mexican state of Sonora, living both on the mainland coast of the Sea of Cortes and on adjacent Tiburon Island. These remaining Seri, descendents of distinct earlier groups, now constitute a single community made up of mobile hunting and gathering bands. Their homeland, in spite of its proximity to the United States border, was largely bypassed for centuries and their life, customs, religion, and economy remained largely traditional. Recently, however, tourism has come to Sonora's Kino Bay and the Seri have increasingly sought employment in commercial fishing and migrant farm labor, some supplementing their income with craft sales. (see also MEXICANS)

SESAN   A subgroup of the JARAI.

SESE   An ethnic group living on the Sese Islands in Lake Victoria. (see also GANDA)

SETY   see ESTONIANS.

SEYCHELLOIS   The approximately 70,000 inhabitants of the Republic of Seychelles, an Indian Ocean archipelago about 1,000 miles off the east coast of Africa. Although the chain consists of over 100 islands, about 90 percent of the population lives on the principal island of Mahe. They are of mixed African, Asian, and French descent. French Creole is both the offical and common language, but English and French are used by the government. The population is predominantly Christian. Until recently, the people were dependent on agriculture; with the opening of an international airport on Mahe, tourism has become increasingly important.

The Seychelles became independent from Great Britain in 1976.

SGAW   (s.d. Pwakenyah) A subgroup of the KAREN.

SHADIBAZ An ethnic group living dispersed in central-east Afghanistan. In the 1980s they were estimated as numbering 1,500. Their language, Inku, belongs to the Indian group of the Indo-European family of languages.

Although it is also the mother tongue of several other dispersed ethnic groups of Afghanistan (JALALI, PIKRAJ, VANGAVALANS), the Shadibaz have a distinct ethnic self-identity. Practically all adult Shadibaz speak Dari (the Persian spoken in Afghanistan) as well as Inku.

The Shadibaz are Sunni Muslims of the Hanafi school. They are peripatetics, i.e., non-pastoral nomads. Their main occupation is leading monkeys or bears in circus-like bazaars and street performances, and peddling cloth, clothing, and perfume. Women peddle bangles. (see also AFGHANS, JATS II)

SHADU ANDH A subgroup of the ANDH.

SHAHSEVEN (lit. shah-lovers) A subgroup of the AZERBAIJANI, living mainly in dozens of enclaves spread throughout northwest Iran from eastern Iranian Azerbaijan (around Ardabil) southeast to the steppes between Zanjan and Teheran. Some are found in southern Azerbaijan. Their estimated number in Iranian Azerbaijan is between 200,000 and 300,000; in Azerbaijan they may number tens of thousands. They are Shi'ite Muslims.

In Iranian Azerbaijan half the Shahseven are sedentary stockraisers and agriculturists; most others are seasonal semi-nomads, with about 5,000 purely nomadic families. Sedentary and semi-nomadic Shahseven live in villages, which form enclaves in the territories shared by them with the AZERBAIJANI. Nomadic Shahseven live in sturdy, well-isolated tents resembling the traditional *yurt*. They exchange milk from their herds for grain. Shahseven women are not veiled and choose their partners themselves; older women may attain positions of authority.

In Azerbaijan, although historically nomadic, Shahseven are now sedentary agriculturalists, rapidly losing their self-identity in favor of the general Azerbaijani ethnic identity.

The Shahseven first came to the fore as a group of Turkic tribes faithful to the Iranian shah Abbas I the Safavid (1587–1629). He organized them into a tribal confederation with privileged status, including rights over lands. In the nineteenth century, the inclusion of the northern part of Azerbaijan into the Empire, RUSSIA deprived the Shahseven of their winter pastures in the Mughan steppe. By the end of that century, a gradual sedentarization process began, speeded up between the 1920s and 1960 by Reza Shah (1925–1941) and Muhammad Reza Shah (1941–1979). After the 1979 Iranian revolution, the name Shahseven was officially changed to Ilseven ("people-lovers"). However, the new appellation has remained merely formal act and the Shahseven are still commonly known by their traditional name. (see also AZERBAIJANI)

SHAI A subgroup of the ADANGBE.

SHAIBANI A subgroup of the KHAMSE.

SHAKE An ethnic group living in Gabon along the upper Ogooue River above Booue and along the road from Booue to Lalara. They belong to the Bakota linguistic group and are closely related to the DAMBONO and the SHAMAI.

SHAMAI An ethnic group living north of Okondja in the Haut-Ogooue Province of Gabon. They are closely related to the SHAKE.

SHAMBAA (Sambaa) A Bantu-speaking ethnic group living in the western Usambara Mountains of Tanzania. The name probably means "the people of the banana trees region." The Shambaa language belongs to the Bantu group of the Niger-Kordofan family of languages. The Shambaa are the largest among a group of culturally related peoples, including the MBUGU, ZIGULA, and ZARAMO.

They are primarily farmers, but also raise livestock. They traditionally practiced an advanced form of shifting agriculture but now face the problem of land shortage as well as soil erosion. Bananas were formely their staple, but nowadays have been largely superseded by maize and cassava. Among other crops coffee, vegetables, and, more recently, tea are very important.

The Shambaa live in villages whose population derives from closely-related families or descent from the same lineage. Their agricultural system is based on individual land ownership. Each family farms its own plots scattered in the valleys and on the hillsides surrounding the settlement. Nevertheless, until recently, the community was considered to be the official owner of all the land.

Most of the Shambaa settlements are situated on ridges or spurs. The number of houses varies from five to more than one hundred.

Peoples of Papua New Guinea

Llama and Alpaca Breeders of the Andean Highlands

The Puna region extends from central Peru, through Bolivia, and up to northern Chile. *Puna* means "highland" in Quechua. The region has an average altitude of 11,500 feet, and it is divided into two climatic zones: the Puna Baja (lower Puna) and the Puna Alta (higher Puna); the latter, at a height of over 12,000 feet, experiences some 300 days of frost per year. This makes the cultivation of crops difficult.

The Puna is the habitat of the QUECHUA. Given the harsh conditions, the QUECHUA make their living herding llamas and alpacas, subspecies of the wild guanaco and members of the camelid family, which were first domesticated in prehistoric times. Now, the QUECHUA also raise sheep, but these animals are less suited to the harsh climate of the high Andes than the camelids.

Llamas reach a shoulder height of between three and four feet; alpacas are substantially smaller and grow only up to three feet at most, although their silky hair grows to a length of six inches, while the llama's hair is much shorter and coarser. Llamas serve mainly as a source of meat, while alpacas are bred primarily for their fine wool. Llama skins are processed into blankets and leatherware. In addition, the llama is valued as a patient pack-animal, ideally suited to the demands imposed upon it during the long trading trips engaged in by the QUECHUA. In the treeless Puna, llama dung is also a useful source of fuel.

Llamas and alpacas occupy a position of great importance in the life of the QUECHUA. The social status of peasants depends more on the number of herd animals they possess than upon the extent of the fields in their possession. In the Quechua language, *waxchay* or *wakcha* mean poverty, both in terms of animals and of human relations. An individual with no llamas or alpacas is, therefore, by definition, poor.

The prominent position of the llama and alpaca in Quechua culture is also expressed in the indigenous religion.

The Quechua protect themselves against the cold of the Andes with blankets and caps

Among the many gods worshiped by the QUECHUA, the most important are depicted as having a close relationship with these animals. Thus, Pachamamna, the mother of the earth, is also considered the patroness of the camelids. Sacrifices to her testify to the Quechua's gratitude for her gift of such serviceable beasts.

The mountain peaks worshiped as gods are also considered great llama and alpaca owners. Sacrificies are made to them so that they enable the animals to multiply freely. Preferred sacrifices are llamas and alpacas. The pulsating heart is ripped from the chest cavity, and the blood, fat, and legs of the sacrificial beast are presented as an offering to the gods.

Camelids also play a major role in the mythological traditions of the mountain people. According to these traditions, the animals have only been given by the gods to humans on loan; if the beasts are mistreated, the gods may demand their return.

The QUECHUA believe that the camelids originated in the interior of the earth, reaching man in the outer world through springs and lakes. According to Quechua beliefs, a reduction in the number of llamas and alpacas signifies the imminent end of the world. In order to avert such a catastrophe, the QUECHUA of the high Andes have a yearly ceremony to ensure the perpetuation and multiplication of their herds. During these festivities, which last several days, a number of rites are performed. Young animals have their earlobes marked, and they are ritually married.

Given the immense importance of their herds to the QUECHUA, belief in the continued existence of mankind is based solely on the welfare of the llamas and alpacas in their custody. This welfare must be ritually secured again and again, and is a reflection of their very real dependency on these animals. Were llamas and alpacas to disappear from the highlands of the Puna, the Quechua believe that their culture, too, would cease to exist.

llama breeder decorating his herd for a ritual celebration.

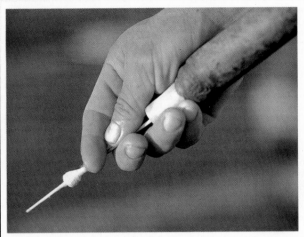

Cotton fiber is wrapped around an arrow's tip for greater stability in flight.

Curare is applied to arrows using a small stick. The arrows are made of palm leaf ribs.

Death by Blowpipe: Curare as an Arrow Poison

Many Indians in the area of the Amazon and Orinoco Rivers use a blowp

Soon after the discovery of America, news of a deadly arrow poison, curare, used by the Indians of South America, reached Europe. Curare is a plant-derived alkaloid. Injury from a curare-tipped arrow results in quick death due to paralysis of the muscles of the respiratory system.

The poison, produced in the Orinoco and Amazon Rivers regions, is used by numerous Indian groups, including the MAKU and Huitoto of Colombia, and the YANOMAMI, TUKANA, Akuweya, and Piaroa of Venezuela. Although each group has its

own name for the poison, curare is its most common designation.

The historian, Peter Martyr, described how several old women had died from inhaling the fumes of the poison they had been brewing. He seems to have been influenced by rumors. Curare's paralyzing effect occurs only if the poison is injected directly into the bloodstream. Missionaries supplied some information about curare, but the first detailed description of its effect was made by Alexander Humbolt, who visited South America during 1799–1804.

Curare is extracted from various wil plants and from the roots and bark o some Strychnos (family: *Loganiaceae* and Chondodendron (family: *Manisper maceae*) species. The number of ingred ents is considerable: twenty or mor plants may be used to prepare the poiso. According to Humbolt's description, th teeth of venomous snakes and ants an beetles were also added to the concoctio. Chemical analysis substantiates the pres ence of the alkaloid responsible for th poison's effect. An animal killed b curare is fit for consumption since th

...effective and noiseless weapon.

A Yanomami boy becomes accustomed to handling a bow and arrow from an early age.

...poison is harmless as long as it is not injected directly into the bloodstream. Another amazing aspect of curare is its remarkable durability: analyses of old museum samples show that it maintains its effective even after one hundred years! Until now, over seventy different types of curare have been identified, each particular to various peoples and regions.

Many attempts have been made to find an antidote for the poison: in colonial times, sugar, salt, and papaya were all tried, but their efficiency is dubious. The traveller, La Condamine, who visited the Amazon region in the late eighteenth century, reports feeding sugar to a hen poisoned with curare. Although the hen recovered briefly, the prospective antidote was incapable of saving its life.

In hunting, palm wood arrows, six to eight inches long, are brushed with curare and carefully stored in a bamboo quiver. The arrows are shot with a blowpipe, sometimes as long as six feet, made of either two connected bamboo tubes or two bamboo halves glued together with tar. A skilled hunter can blow arrows with such force that they hit targets more than ninety feet away. Birds, small mammals, and monkeys are the main victims of curare's deadly poison. Even with rifles becoming increasingly popular, the blowpipe and poisoned arrows are still the preferred means of hunting game in many instances. While a rifle shot will scare away other animals, the blowpipe is noiseless.

Native South Americans now use curare exclusively in hunting. In the past, however, it was often applied to spears and used in inter-tribal warfare. The use of curare was widespread throughout the entire Amazon and Orinoco Rivers regions and the poison was often used to pay for goods and in trade. In the eighteenth and nineteenth centuries curare produced by the TUKANA and the MACUXI of the Rio Grande region of Brazil was traded as far away as Manaus and the Atlantic coast.

Other poisonous extracts are also found among Native South Americans. The Choco and Noanama of the Pacific coast of Colombia use the secretion of a frog; the GOAJIRO of La Goajiro Penisula between Columbia and Venezuela use the poisonous gland of a tree snake. No other poison, however, has been found to be as potent as curare. Its manufacture illustrates the considerable pharmaceutical skills of the lowland Native South Americans.

The art of body painting: a young man in Kau uses a wooden stick to mark lines on the background color, which has been applied with the hands.

Changing Pictures in Southern Sudan

In the three villages of Kau, Nyaro, and Fungor, in the southeastern Nuba Mountains of southern Kordofan (Sudan), there exists an art form which, in its refinement, abstraction, and strength of expression, is unique in Africa. Fantastic shapes and designs are painted onto the human skin; they combine with the lines of the body and face to create a magnificent human work of art. These moving pictures are not limited to particularly gifted artists, but are produced by all, supposing that they have the essential prerequisite of an unblemished body. Individuals paint their own faces, arms, legs, chest, and bellies with the help of a mirror; a friend will paint the back.

These body paintings are not tattooed onto the skin and are, therefore, of limited durability. The artists first wash themselves and rub their skin with peanut-oil. They then apply the colors and designs using their hands, wooden sticks or stamps. When a painting must be removed, it is covered with clay and wet- ted. This absorbs the colors and the layer of oil, so that after rinsing the skin is again visible.

Before blue was available as a commer cially-produced color in Arab countries only natural colors were used: black derived from coal dust, white from pul verized shells or limestone, and red and yellow from various shades of ochre found in a certain cave. The symbolic sig nificance of each of these four traditiona colors is difficult to determine. Black i preferred before the bloody knife battle common among the peoples of souther Sudan because it makes the body appea igger. They also believe that dark colors offer protection from the evil eye. The choice of other colors depends on both family traditions and personal taste. This, and the imaginative vision of the artist who uses his own body as his canvas, is the essence of this creative form. Yet, although it is a form of personal expression, it can also be compared to to a fashion statement in other societies and countries.

The art of body painting is best understood when seen in the context of the social order of the three villages in which it is practiced, lying between the granite blocks of Kordofan and the steppes leading down to the alluvial Nile River basin. Tradition determines who are allowed to express themselves with body paintings. The art is limited to young men between the ages of seventeen and thirty, when they are believed to reach manhood. Body painting can, therefore, be seen as a sign of membership in an exclusive group, much in the same way as a uniform or badge. Men of this age are sent to guard the farthest herds, engage in the most violent knife battles, and are the main rivals for the attentions of marriageable young women.

The young men of Kau, Nyaro, and Fungor and their tattooed female counter-

young man has adorned himself with an attractive leopard design.

An artistic haircut is an integral part of the makeup. Decorative white feathers are also very popular.

parts are the hope of the community. Their paintings indicate a sacred, albeit finite state. On the one hand, the body painting is an indication of the juvenile strength, vigor, and beauty of their naked bodies, but it also serves to estrange them from the social mainstream. These men are excluded from everyday relationships and from the agricultural work of the community. The body painting is also a sort of festive dress, worn and reapplied for thirteen years until it is left to wear off under the clothes donned once the young man reaches adulthood.

The artistic repertoire in southern Sudan is not exhausted by body paintings: hair-cuts, dances, songs, music, and rites of passage into adulthood are also prevalent among them.

In recent years, new, modern styles have also been introduced in southern Sudan as a result of contact with the outside world. Together with traditional body painting, they have been adopted by the young men of Kau, Nyaro, and Fungor as further means of self-expression: sunglasses and silk cloth wrapped around the loins are increasingly popular. The new draperies notwithstanding, the art of body painting has lost neither its bizzare beauty nor its artistic distinction.

Sigiriya frescoes of the fifth century c.e., on Lion Rock, Sri Lanka, show women emerging from the clouds.

Illnesses and Demons: Healing Rituals in Sri Lanka

In many places in Sri Lanka, sculptures of the Buddha, such as this one in Aukana, are found

Among the Buddhist SINHALESE, inhabiting the southern and eastern parts of the island of Sri Lanka, contact with demonic and divine powers is an ever-present phenomenon. In traditional mythological works such as the *Mahavamsa* (the Great Chronicle), Sri Lanka is described as the land of the *yakku* (devils), demonic, ignorant creatures whom the Buddha had terrified into submission, expelled from the island, or liberated from the bondage of their fears and deprivations so as to placate their hostile intentions.

In the bas-reliefs and friezes commonly found in Sri Lankan assembly halls, these demons are represented as dwarfs who crave earthly wealth, and attack humans to achieve it. But *yakku* are not just the remote and fearsome inhabitants of a bizarre underworld: they are, according to Sinhalese beliefs, also present in the world inhabited by animals, humans, and gods. They are, therefore, summoned dur-

Fifth-century Sigiriya frescoes showing women emerging from the clouds.

ing magical religious ceremonies, only to be assuaged and driven out.

Since *yakku* are believed to be capable of damaging the delicate balance of nature, they are held responsible for any disturbances of the body and soul. Fortunately, their personification and representation in pictures and statuettes enable humans to interact with them. During magical rites, and particularly during healing rituals, they are treated as if they have specific bodily needs which must be sated, and they are housed and fed. The invocation of their powers is an important precondition for the healing of the patient, who must be freed from fears and disturbances and brought back into harmony with nature.

Y Traditional Sri Lankan religion plays an important role in ceremonies held to perform such exorcisms. *Yakku* are invoked through dances or by the creation of clay figurines, known as *bali*. Sacrifices and prayers seek to make them favourably inclined to the sufferers. *Yakku* are invoked in the name of the Buddha, the *Dharma* (the body of religious teachings), and the *Sangha* (the community of spiritual aspirants). They are requested to receive the sacrifices of humans, not to bring them any further suffering, and not to disrupt the equilibrium by causing further illnesses.

Some of the best-known and ubiquitous *yakku* are the *sanni yakku*, found in eighteen different manifestations. They are

considered to be the cause of all diseases and the embodiment of the various bodily and mental afflictions of mankind. They are invoked through the *Tovil*, or "Devil Dance," and are only exorcized in a nightlong struggle. The *sanni yakku* are treated as a community and are always honored as a group with sacrifices and food-offerings.

Different illnesses are attributed to specific groups of demons. The most dangerous among the demons are the *Maru Sanni*, who cause frenzies and twitches, the *Amuku Sanni*, who cause vomiting and diarrhea, the *Bihiri Sanni*, responsible for fainting, the *Kora Sanni*, who cause lameness, the *Naga Sanni*, who cause bad dreams and poisons the body, and the *Kalu Sanni*, the black death, particularly threatening to women and children.

In the figure of the *Mahakola*, all the *sanni yakku* are jointly represented, although they can be differentiated by color and other characteristics. They are invoked through verses (known as *mantras*) and are then chased away using mystic symbols (*yantras*).

Technical knowledge for the production of effective magical artifacts such as masks, has been passed down by families over the centuries. The information is copied down on palm leaf manuscripts and passed down from generation to generation. Certain of these arts are traditionally the realm of specific clans and familes. Groups of fishermen from small agricultural settlements along the southern and western coasts of Sri Lanka are particularly noted for their skill in both carving and animating special *Sanniya* masks. These are carved from kaduru wood and elaborately decorated. Their hideous features are believed to represent the *yakku*.

Sanniya mask dances take place secretly in the middle of the night. They are an exclusive affair, in which only the patient, relatives, and neighbors are permitted to participate. During the dance, the abrupt and twisted movements of the Devil Dancer personifies the character of the malevolent ghost.

Even with the advent of modern medicine, these rituals remain a vibrant component of Sri Lanka's rich religious culture and are often performed during periods of political and economic turmoil so prevalent among the ethnic groups of Sri Lanka.

A Devil Dancer appears in the mask of Kalu Sanni to the accompaniment of drum-beats.

Susani Embroidery in Central Asia

The Tajik word *susani*, meaning "needlework," is used to describe the large embroidered blankets and scarfs produced by the TAJIKS and UZBEKS of Central Asia. The manufacture of *susani* is restricted to the agricultural areas of contemporary Uzbekistan and northern Tajikistan.

Once, *susani* were of great importance to both the urban and rural populations of Central Asia. In weddings they often formed part of the bride's dowry. At the wedding ceremony the bridal couple's room and part of the surrounding courtyard were decorated with *susani* and embroidered blankets were spread on the bridal bed. Tradition dictated how many and what kind of embroidered fabrics the family of the bride was to contribute as a dowry. In Murata, a small village lying northeast of the town of Bukhara, two large and two small wall-hangings, two bridal bedsheets, and two prayer rugs, each produced by the women of the family, formed an integral part of the dowry.

Traditonally, a girl's mother began preparing *susani* for her daugther's dowry shortly after the child's birth. Originally, *susani* were made from home-spun cotton cloth interwoven with silk threads colored with dyes made from local plants. Later, imported Russian cloth and dyes were used. Young girls would first begin to learn embroidery from their mothers between the ages of four and six. The child would continue to embroider for her dowry until her wedding day, although sometimes the mother would ask relatives and neighbors to help get the bridal *susani* finished in time.

Some women specialized in making preparatory sketches of *susani* designs and in choosing the appropriate dyes. This skill would be passed down to their daughters, ensuring the embroideries' continuity of design and composition. In this way, *susani* often preserved pre-Islamic motifs. Plant motifs can be traced to a belief in the significance of trees, a concept which has also survived in the oral traditions and legends of the region. Some legends tell of trees that sprouted from the graves of the departed heroes. In other tales, the fruit of certain trees (espe-

A blanket for a bridal bed, from the second half of the nineteenth century: silk o *cloth. (from the Museum of Textiles, Krefeld).*

cially apples) brought blessings upon children or had miraculous medicinal powers. Others describe water accumulating at the foot of such trees in the form of a spring, a pond, or a stream. When the hero drinks or bathes in this "water of life," he is healed, rejuvenated, or even resurrected. On *susani*, these waters are alluded to by small almond-shaped designs, often of a dazzling yellow color, that blossom from the trees. Designs of animals, usually birds, are only infrequently depicted on *susani*. The

Islamic prohibition against depictions o living things has had a marked impact o traditional motifs. At the same time bird believed to mediate between this world an the world beyond, play an important role i local traditions. To the trained eye, an entir realm of traditional mythological and rel gious concepts can be found on *susani*.

The conquest of Turkestan by the RUS SIANS in the mid-nineteenth century wit nessed a decline of the magical belief embedded in the region's traditional cu

...sani embroideries were once produced exclusively by hand. Today even the most complicated designs are machine-made.

ture. The scientific values of the post-Enlightenment era undermined both the old conceptions of nature and, as a result, the symbolic world of Central Asian decorative artwork. *Susani* were no longer believed to possess mystical powers, and modern motifs were introduced. Graphic examples are the designs that became popular in the early twentieth century, representing contemporary objects.

Rapid cultural developments in the late nineteenth and early twentieth centuries, interrupted the continuity of traditional *susani* embroidery. Among the changing social conditions in Central Asia to have the greatest impact were the introduction of compulsory education for girls and the introduction of women into the work force. However, the continued need for such needlework has resulted in the emergence of a commercial form of the traditional embroidery, now sold worldwide.

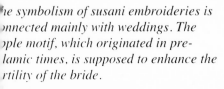

...he symbolism of susani embroideries is ...nnected mainly with weddings. The ...ple motif, which originated in pre-...lamic times, is supposed to enhance the ...rtility of the bride.

The choice of colors and design was left to susani specialists. Colors were derived from natural materials such as the skin of apßples (yellow) or indigo (blue).

A Tswana celebration of the marriage of a chief's son in Bophuthatswana, a bantustan "homeland" established by the South African government.

When a Cousin Becomes a Wife

Among the TSWANA, who inhabit the area between the Kalahari Desert and the eastern coastal mountain ranges of southern Africa, cousin marriage, taboo in the West, is a long-established tradition. Certain cousin marriages are preferred to others: first cousins are considered a particularly good match. For men, the daughter of a paternal aunt or a maternal uncle are the most preferred marriage partners. If this, however, is impossible, the daughter of a paternal uncle or a maternal aunt are also desirable. In the absence of a suitable cousin for marriage, one should at least endeavor to marry a relative.

To understand the reasons underlying these marriage preferences, it is necessary to study the social structure of the TSWANA. Originally a part of the SOTHO (they share many of their customs and traditions), the TSWANA emerged as a distinct ethnic group in recent times. Among the traditions developed to preserve this distinct identity is a rejection of intermarriage with other ethnic groups, although the practice was apparently quite common in the past.

The TSWANA now classify themselves into groups of relatives, who trace their origin to a common ancestor of the male line (forming patriclans). Another social structure is that of three hierarchical strata: the nobility, commoners, and newcomers (members of other peoples who have been absorbed by the TSWANA in the course of time). According to Tswana law, the bridegroom is required to pay a steep bride-price, in cattle, to the family of the bride. This is paid so as to secure for the bridegroom's relatives rights over the offspring of the union.

A comparison of the weddings of the nobility with those of the commoners brings several important differences to light. In the mid-twentieth century only about a quarter of men of common status married a relative, usually the daughter of a maternal uncle (a cross-cousin). For the nobility, however, the figures were much higher. For them, marriage within the kinship group is important because it ensures that cattle, the commonly accepted measurement of wealth, are not lost to them. In this way, the status of the nobility, based on the retention of wealth, remains unchallenged.

For commoners, however, it is more important to seek a reliable and permanent marriage partner. As such, marriage with the daughter of a maternal uncle belonging to a different kinship group has proved to be a popular strategy in that it links different groups of relatives in a

four-legged spectator looks on quietly at the happy bustle. On the occasion of a marriage, crocodiles, a popular Tswana totem animal, are less in demand than cattle, paid as a bride-price.

Tswana Cousin Marriages

The parallel cousin marriage (above): The marriage partners (male = ▲; female = ●) come from brothers or sisters of the same sex. The cross cousin marriage (below): The marriage partners come from a brother-sister relationship. Altogether, there are four possible cousin marriage variations. Married couples are represented with double lines, brothers and sisters, with single horizontal lines. The vertical lines show a person's descent.

indirect exchange system. While group A will always take women as their partners from group B, it will always provide marriageable women to group C.

Since Tswana society is organized on patrilineal lines, rights of inheritance and communal position are passed down through the male line. While maternal relatives are, therefore, no competition in terms of the acquisition, through inheritance, of power and influence they do have an interest in the profits earned by their in-laws. Marriage with a maternal uncle's daughter thus helps to establish a deep-rooted system of mutual assistance and cooperation between various groups of relatives. It is different if a man marries a paternal uncle's daughter.

On the one hand these marriages bring a degree of uncertainty to the relationship of the marriage partners, since patrilineal relatives become in-laws, with all the ambiguity such a relationship entails. On

the other hand, such a marriage also creates room for redefinition: a father's brother can eventually be redefined as a mother's brother. This may be in the interests of both sides since one side loses a potential competitor for power and status, while the other secures for itself the influence of the first party in its new role as an in-law.

To a Westerner, the marriage customs of the TSWANA may seem strange. In the West, marriages are usually based on a loving relationship between two people. Among the TSWANA, the principal underlying factor behind cousin marriages is the fulfilment of socio-economic obligations for present and future generations. The romantic inclinations of the marriage partners are of little consequence. More important is the fact that cousin marriages offer both the nobility and the commoners a means of securing material prosperity and social cohesion.

The Shapono: An Entire Village Under One Roof

The mountains near the sources of the Orinoco River, the Rio Blanco, and Rio Negro, on the border of Venezuela and Brazil, are home to the YANOMAMI. The area is covered with thick tropical rainforest, and has a grassy savannah to the north. For most of the year the YANOMAMI live in villages of between forty and two hundred inhabitants. Two or three times a year they leave their village settlements for a few weeks to visit neighboring communities. At that time, they live in the forest under temporary windbreaks.

The YANOMAMI describe themselves as "house dwellers" (*yano* means "house" in their language). While the YANOMAMI of Brazil construct large communal houses, those of Venezuela build the *shapono*, a circular structure resting on poles.

The *shapono* is divided into sections of between 45 and 60 feet, each of which houses a single family. In this way, all the inhabitants of a village are united under one roof. Tied to the supporting poles are hammocks made from bark, linen, or woven cotton. Generally, the roof reaches to the ground, thereby constituting the border between the village and the forest. In times of war, however, the village is protected by an additional pallisade. Three entrances connect the village compound with the outside world. The *shapono* is usually constructed near a brook. This not only provides the YANOMAMI with drinking water; it also serves for washing and bathing and as a playground for the children.

Each family has its own hearth. Older children and secondary wives or husbands (the YANOMAMI practice polygamy and polyandry) have a separate hearth near that of the family. Children who have been weaned (i.e. those older than four) occupy hammocks above those of their parents. Between three and seven family groups related by marriage live in one *shapono* and each group is represented by an older and experienced member in the assembly of elders. This assembly decides by consensus on all matters of concern to the entire community, including whether to relocate the village, to develop new agricultural

The bow and arrow remains the main weapon of the Yanomami.

plots, to visit other communities, or how to best deal with hostile groups. Although women have no formal say, they have much influence in the final decision.

The *shapono* is the social center of the YANOMAMI community. In it the bulk of the daily routine takes place. Here the YANOMAMI spend their afternoons in a leisurely fashion, chatting, repairing tools and weapons, producing ornaments from feathers and fiber, and dozing. The *shapono* is also the site of festivities, ceremonies, and the reception of guests. From it shamans call upon the spirits to heal illnesses, to divert natural catastrophies, and to protect the group from hostile neighbors.

At the same time, most economic activities of the YANOMAMI take place outside the *shapono*. In the morning women work the surrounding cultivated

inomami women return from a foraging expedition and sort out their finds.

Yanomami man looks skeptically aside. The Yanomami have come to expect from "civilization" nothing better than the xtermination of their habitat.

In the Orinoco River region, the shapono remains the traditional home of the Yanomami. The population of a whole village lives under one circular roof.

plots; two or three times a week they leave the village in larger groups to forage for wild fruit, crabs, and small fish. Upon their return in the early afternoon, they then prepare food in the *shapono*. Shortly before sunset mothers leave the *shapono* again to bring firewood and water for the night. The men also tend the cultivated plots, growing bananas, manioc, and other crops. They also hunt, either alone or in groups of two or three, tapirs, wild pigs, antelopes, birds, and anteaters. During celebrations, when guests from other villages are invited, the men join together in larger hunting groups and go out on extended excursions, often lasting several days.

Currently, the YANOMAMI are subject to growing external pressures and influences. Most notably, the penetration of goldminers into their Brazilian settlements threatens their traditional way of life. International protests, however, might save the YANOMAMI from extinction.

above: Young Thai Buddhist monks
below: A floating market in Thailand

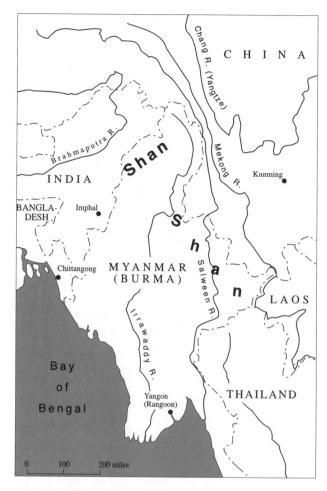

Shan

The traditional cults of the Shambaa included magical elements. Parts of the banana tree are often used as an important element in rituals.

SHAN (Tai, Dai, Pai-I, Ngiaw, Ngio) The term "Shan," of Burmese origin, is used by Westerners to describe the large cluster of peoples found throughout western Myanmar (Burma), Thailand, and parts of southern China. Shan peoples usually refer to themselves as "Tai," followed by another word which indicates the person's specific origin (Tai Khe, Tai Lu, Tai Wu, etc.). "Dai" and "Pai-I" are used by the southern CHINESE to label the Shan people, and "Ngio" and Ngiaw" are used by those of northern Thailand.

The largest percentage of Shan peoples can be found in the Shan State, located in eastern Myanmar. The total number of Shan is estimated to be between 2 and 4 million. Their official language is Tai (which is similar to Lao and Thia), but there are many differences be-

tween the written languages of the various Shan peoples. The Shan are Theravada Buddhists.

They are mainly an agricultural society, utilizing both irrigated flatland farming and a hill-terraced slash and burn method. The main food crop is rice. Although there seems to be increasing use of machine-oriented farming, especially in Thailand, the Shan traditionally rely on water buffalo and bullocks to work the land.

The Shan are thought to have migrated from China to Burma around the end of the first millennium C.E. Shan princes ruled many small states throughout northern Burma and had close ties with the KACHIN. When the BRITISH assumed control of Burma at the end of the nineteenth century, many Shan princes became their political puppets.

At this point, the Shan of Thailand were cut off from those in Burma. When Burma gained independence in 1948, the Shan states were combined into one large state. In the second half of the twentieth century, the Shan have begun to try to separate themselves from the Burmese government in order to create an autonomous Shan state. (see also BURMANS)

SHANGAAN A Tonga-speaking subgroup living along the Limpopo River. Originally a Tonga military organization named after a Nguni chieftain, they resisted incursions by the PORTUGUESE throughout the nineteenth century. (see also TSONGA)

SHANGAWA A subgroup of the FULANI.

SHANGWE (Bashangwe) A subgroup of the KOREKORE.

SHANKALLA (Shangalla) A derogatory term for people in Ethiopia speaking Omotic or Nilotic languages.

SHANKILA A name often used for the 40,000 (1980s) southern Gumuz-speakers, living in Ethiopia in the Blue Nile River valley (southern Gojjam Province, northern Wallagga). "Shankila" is a typical Ethiopian term used to denote a population which can be enslaved. Since 1984, the Gumuz territory in southern Gojjam Province has been affected by resettlement programs for the TIGRAY and AMHARA.

SHAPSUG A subgroup of the ADYGHEANS. (see also CHERKESS)

SHATKASI   see CHERKESS.

SHAVANTE   see XAVANTE.

SHAWNEE   (Abaentee Shawnee) A Native North American group numbering 1,500, many of whom live on the Sac and Fox Tribe Federal Trust Area in Oklahoma, U.S.A.

Originally they lived in Tennesee where they were hunters of small game. Their most famous leader was Tecumseh, who attempted to unite the Native North American groups of the Ohio Valley to fight against the AMERICANS. He was killed in the war of 1812, the alliance collapsed, and the Shawnee were relocated, first in Kansas and then in Oklahoma, where two

Shawnee

Shawnee subgroups arrived at different times but were united again into one group.

SHE   The She, numbering approximately 370,000, are a minority nationality located mainly in China's Fujian, Zhejiang, Jiangxi, and Guangdong Provinces. Their language, a member of the Sino-Tibetan group, is similar to the Kejia dialect of Han Chinese and is linguistically related to Yao. Since the She have no writing system of their own, Chinese is the commonly used written form.

The She belong to the aboriginal population of south China, and regard Chaozhou in the Guangdong Province as their place of origin.

Characteristic of She villages are the ancestral halls, with members of a clan generally belonging to the same ancestral hall. Each family retains an ancestral cane with a carved dragon's head as a symbol of totem worship. They also worship their ancestors and believe in ghosts and spirits.

Highly sinicized by the Han CHINESE, many She speak Chinese among themselves, but their ethnic characteristics are preserved in their folk songs, dress, and handicrafts.

The She chiefly engage in cultivating rice and sweet potatoes, in forestry, and in tea-planting.

SHEIKH-MOHAMMADIS   An ethnic group living in the central-east part of Afghanistan, to the east of Kabul, the capital. No population data are available, but a rough estimate puts them at about 2,000.

The Sheikh-Mohammadis speak Dari (the Afghanistani form of Persian) and Pashto. Among themselves they use Adurgari, a language about which little is known, which they learn to speak at the age of six or seven. It apparently belongs to the so-called Kohistani, i.e., eastern, subgroup of the Dardic branch of the Indo-Iranian group of languages.

Sunni Muslims of the Hanafi school, they are peripatetics (non-pastoral nomads). They differ from other such ethnic groups in Afghanistan in that they are more or less concentrated in one area. Their main occupation is peddling, and, therefore, they are sometimes regarded as part of the Jat population. (see also AFGHAN, JATS II)

SHEKMUMADI   see GYPSIES.

SHEKO   An ethnic group numbering 25,000 (1980s) who live east of Gurafarda in the western Kefa Province of Ethiopia. They speak a language called Gimira and adhere to traditional beliefs. The Sheko are extensive root-crop cultivators. Socially, they are stratified into master clans and dependent clans. Artisans and hunters were stigmatized.

SHERBRO   see BULOM.

SHERDUKPEN   A Mongoloid group of fishers, farmers and craftsmen found in Arunachal Pradesh, in northeast India. They number about 2,000.

SHERENTE   see XERENTE.

SHERPA A tribe living in northeast areas of Nepal (Namche Bazar, Solu Khumbu, and Helambu). They speak Sherpa, and also understand Tibetan. It is surmised that they came from Tibet and settled in the northern part of Nepal. "Sherpa" in Tibetan means "easterners."

The Sherpa are Buddhists. Although they eat meat, they do not slaughter animals themselves. In every village there is at least one monastery where religious ceremonies are conducted in a serene atmosphere. The head of a monastery is called a lama.

Agriculture, trade, yak farming, and sheep rearing are the main occupations of the Sherpa. They grow wheat, maize, and potatoes. Rice is also grown on the banks of rivers. Some Sherpa trade with India and Tibet. Some prepare *ghee* (clarified butter), *durukho* (a kind of dried cheese) and Nepali paper. They also weave woolen blankets and carpets, and make wooden utensils and baskets. Sherpa act as porters for mountaineering expeditions.

SHETLANDERS The 23,000 inhabitants of the Shetlands, a cluster of islands northeast of the Scottish mainland, speak a local dialect of English derived from earlier forms of Scottish English combined with many words of Norn, the Norwegian dialect once spoken on the islands. They are primarily of Scottish or Norse origin. Fishing or farming smallholdings constitute the main economic activities, and the islanders are also famous for their fine woolen sweaters and shawls. Protestantism is the dominant religion, although older folk beliefs concerning fairies, seal people, ghosts, and witchcraft persisted until very recently.

SHI An ethnic group living in the highlands of the Kivu Region between Lake Tanganyika and Lake Kivu, Zaire.

SHIKH A subgroup of the TURKMEN.

SHILA A Chibemba-speaking group numbering about 30,000 living in the Luapula River valley in Zambia. Some are Christians, while others adhere to traditional religions, with many rituals revolving around fishing, their chief occupation. Their culture resembles that of the BEMBA.

SHILLUK A people living in southwestern part of Sudan. They speak a Southern Nilotic language, indicating that they formed part of the southern Nilotes who arrived in this area about 1,000 years ago. Their

territory lies north of that of the NUER and west of the northern DINKA, on the west bank of the Nile River near its confluence with the Sobat River.

Most of the Shilluk are settled agriculturalists. They live in villages based on extended families or small lineage groups. The Shilluk are Christians but some follow their traditional religion, sometimes mixed with Christianity to form a local independent Shilluk Church.

Together with the NUER, the LUO, and the NYAMANG, they form the opposition to John Garang, who in recent years has been waging war in southern Sudan against the central government in Khartoum, controlled by the Muslim ARABS of northern Sudan. (see also NUER, SUDANESE)

Shinans

SHINANS An ethnic group living mainly in the region of Gilgit in northwest Pakistan and in some adjacent areas. An estimate of the early 1980s puts them at about 100,000. The Shina language belongs to the eastern subgroup of the Dardic group of Indo-Iranian languages. It consists of several greatly differing dialects and is unwritten, Urdu being used as the official language of writing and education.

The Shinans were converted from Buddhism to Sunni Islam in the twelfth century. They have been predominantly Shi'ite Muslims since the end of the sixteenth century.

Their early history is relatively obscure. From the early twelfth century to 1822 the Shinans of Gilgit were ruled by the Turkic Tara-Khan dynasty, then by various short-lived ruling groups of outsiders. The British-controlled Maharajah of Jammu and Kashmir ruled from 1846 to 1889; from 1899 to 1947 the BRITISH ruled directly.

SHINASHA   see GONGA.

SHINNECOCK   A Native North American group numbering a few hundred, most of whom live in Long Island, New York, U.S.A.

Many Shinnecock intermarried with African-Americans and members of other Native groups. Some are part of the local economy and others work on the reserve's shellfish farm.

SHIRAZI   (Zanzibarians) The inhabitants of the Zanzibar and Pemba islands of which are now a part of Tanzania. The language of the Shirazi is Swahili. There are some 30,000 Shirazi, "proper" but the name is also used as a self-definition by the vast majority of Zanzibarians of African origin.

The Shirazi are the product of intermarriages between the indigenous African population of the islands, invaders from the mainland, and Asian immigrants. A large number of the Asians were Persians (see IRANIANS) who settled in Zanzibar and Pemba around the tenth century. These Persian immigrants gradually disappeared as a separate ethnic entity, but their cultural influence on the native population was considerable in that it provided a focal point for the consolidation of the local communities into new ethnic groups. Today the Shirazi are subdivided into the HADIMU, the TRUMBATU, and the PEMBA. The members of these groups still retain their Shirazi identity as distinct from that of more recent, mainly involuntary, immigrants from the continent.

The Shirazi were first organized into village communities. Such a unit included either a single settlement or a small number of neighboring ones. The traditional economy of the Shirazi is based on agriculture and fishing. Since the Middle Ages they have maintained close contact with the ARABS and their maritime commerce (including the slave-trade), for which Zanzibar was an important location.

The Shirazi were among the first African peoples to be converted to Islam. The establishment of the Omani Sultanate's power over the islands and, later on, the establishment of the Sultanate of Zanzibar with the ARABS as the ruling aristocracy, made the Shirazi an integral part of the local Arabic-Swahili civilization.

By the end of the nineteenth century the Sultanate had become a protectorate of the BRITISH. During the late colonial period the Shirazi played an important role in the national liberation movement. In post-colonial days they supported the Afro-Shirazi Party, the leading force of the local revolutionary movement during the 1960s and 1970s.

SHIRIANA   Nomadic inhabitants of the savanna of southern Venezuela, this Native South American group depends on hunting, gathering, and fishing. Agriculture is completely unknown to them.

SHKOSHMI   see ISHKASHIMI.

SHLEUH   A group of nomadic BERBERS living in the Atlas mountains of Morocco. (see also BERBERS, MOROCCANS)

SHOLIGA   A group numbering about 30,000 living along the border of the Indian states of Karnataka and Tamil Nadu. They are gatherers who also engage in part-time work as laborers.

SHOM-PEN   A small group (about 200 persons in 1981) living in the Great Nicobar Islands, India. They speak Nicobarese, a language of the Austroasiatic family, and another unclassified language.

Effective communication has not been established with the Shom-Pen because of their reserved nature. Nomadic by habit, they depend on horticulture, and agriculture is still foreign to them. Efforts are being made to make closer contact with them. (see also NICOBARESE)

SHONA   (Mashona) A people inhabiting most of Zimbabwe as well as the Manica and Sofala provinces of Mozambique. In Zimbabwe, the 7.5 million Shona represent 75 percent of the population; in Mozambique they number 765,000.

The Shona are divided into seven major groups: KALANGA, KARANGA, KOREKORE, MANYIKE, NDAU, RUZWI, and ZEZURU. Each group is further divided into various subgroups.

Ancient centralized Shona kingdoms developed into vast empires in earliest times but began to disintegrate in the eighteenth century. They were finally destroyed in the 1830s by the NGONI, but the Shona reorganized into independent chiefdoms.

The Shona are primarily agriculturalists and practice animal husbandry. They speak Shona and practice both Christianity and their traditional religion, worshipping a hierarchy of spirits headed by Mwari, the supreme god. They also practice healing and divination. In Zimbabwe many have converted to Christianity; 17 percent belong to mission churches and 8 percent to independent churches brought to Zimbabwe by Shona who had worked in South African mines. These churches developed a unique character in the 1930s, and their numbers grew rapidly.

They were the first Bantu-speaking group to arrive in Zimbabwe. Their first kingdom, established by the KARANGA at the site of the Zimbabwe ruins, declined suddenly in the fifteenth century, but another empire was established in the northern Dande region by the Munhumutapa dynasty. This state soon disintegrated too as tributary territories seceded and became important kingdoms such as Changamire, Torwa and Mutasa. In the seventeenth century the Changamire state, known as Rozvi, ruled most of the country but its decline was hastened by invasions by the NGONI in the eighteenth century. In 1897, the Shona attempted a failed revolt against the BRITISH.

The Shona have always been the main supporters of the Zimbabwe African National Union (ZANU) led by Robert Mugabe, himself a Shona. As Zimbabwe's predominant ethnic group, ZANU became the ruling party. During the 1985 election there was considerable conflict between the Shona and the NDEBELE, who feared ethnic discrimination. To resolve the issue, ZANU and the predominantly Ndebele party, the Zimbabwe African Peoples' Union (ZAPU) decided to merge.

The Shona of Mozambique originate from the Munhumutapa empire. They are mainly hunters and fishermen and are part of the KARANGA. Some Shona subgroups in Mozambique include the CHIRUMBA, HUNGWE, MANHICA, NDAU, TEMBO, and TSWA. (see also MOZAMBICANS, TSONGA, VENDA, ZIMBABWEANS)

SHORS   (s.d. Shor-Kizhi, Abat-Kizhi, Chysh-Kizhi ["Taiga people"]; previous Russian designations: Kuznetsy, Kondoma, Mrass Tatars) A group of Taiga peoples of mixed origin who speak Turkic dialects. Their original habitat in the Kuznetskii Ala Tai Mountains of southern Siberia was conquered by the RUSSIANS in the early seventeenth century and colonized steadily since. Under Russian rule the Shors abandoned shamanism for Russian Orthodox Christianity.

A Shor National Region, formed by the Soviet authorities in 1929, was disbanded in 1939. Thus denied education and publications in their language (which was standardized and provided with a Cyrillic alphabet in 1929), they assimilated into the predominantly Russian population. Their number has remained static at around 16,000.

Originally trappers, hunters, gatherers, and primitive farmers, the Shors were also exceptionally skilled miners and blacksmiths. Under Russian rule they became mainly peasants and miners. Today, many live and work in the coal-mining centers of the Kuznetskii basin.

SHOSHONE   (Agaiduka) A Native North American Plains Indian group numbering 1,500, many of whom live in Nevada on the South Fork and Odgers Ranch Federal Reservations and in the Winnemucca Federal Colony. The American explorers Lewis and Clark were guided to the Rocky Mountains by Sacagawea, a female member of the Shoshone people.

SHQIPTIAR   see ALBANIANS.

SHUA   see BAI.

SHUAR   see JIVARO.

SHUCURU   see XUKURU.

SHUGHNI   (Shughnani; s.d. Khughnuni) An ethnic group inhabiting the Mountain Badakhshan Autonomous *Oblast* (Region) and the Badakhshan region of Afghanistan on both sides of the Panj River. Their estimated number was 50,000 (mid-1980s).

The Shughni language belongs to the Pamiri division of the southeastern subgroup of Iranian languages. It has four dialects: Shughni proper, Shakhdara, Barwazi, now rapidly disappearing, and Bajuwi, which is sometimes regarded as a language of its own. In the late 1920s–1930s Shughni was regarded as an official language of the Mountain Badakhshani Autonomous *Oblast*. Literary Shughni, based on Shughni proper, the main dialect, and written with the Roman alphabet, was used in publications and in the region's educational network. Attempts at creating a literature in it were also undertaken. In 1938 all publishing and educational activities were switched to Tajik. No attempts at using Shughni as a written language are known to have been undertaken in Afghanistani Badakhshan.

The Shughni have belonged to the Isma'ili sect of Islam since the eleventh century. They live in villages of ten to fifty extended families. Aggregates of closely-related families form a clan-like unit known as a *guru*. Villages are built mainly in valleys or on mountain slopes. The only town in the Shughni ethnic territory is Khorugh (Khorog) which is the administrative center of the Mountain Badakhshan *Oblast*. In Tajikstan a considerable number of Shughni live outside the Shughni territory, many in Dushanbe, the capital.

In Mountain Badakhshan men's dress is now semi-European; urbanized Shughni, have mostly abandoned traditional styles. In Afghanistani Badakhshan it is still traditional, as it is in both areas for women. Their diet is predominantly vegetarian, with the addition of sour dairy products, meat being reserved for festive occasions. However, urbanized Shughni tend to switch to the general Tajik or urban Tajik-Russian diet. The main occupation of non-urbanized Shughni is grain and legume farming on small terraced plots, with some sheep,-goat,-and cattle-breeding.

The first mention of the Shughni ethnic territory, as Shiqnan, dates back to the late ninth century. For many centuries the Shughni formed the core of independent or semi-independent Badakhshan feudal state-like structures, each headed by a *kha* (Persian *shah*, "king"). The *khas* were predominantly Sunni Muslims who regarded their Isma'ili subjects as infidels: this served as a legal pretext for the widespread practice of selling Shughni into slavery to neighboring Sunni regions. In 1895 the British-Russian 1895 agreement on the Pamir frontier brought about the division of the Shughni ethnic territory into two parts; that to the right of the Panj River became part of the emirate of Bukhara, which at the time had been a protectorate of the RUSSIANS for nearly three decades; that to the left became part of Afghanistani Badakhshan. In 1925 the Soviets established the Mountain Badakhshan Autonomous *Oblast* as part of Soviet Tajikistan. While recognized as a specific ethnic group, the Shughni have, in the Soviet Union, been officially regarded as part of a broader Tajik ethnos since the 1930s.

Since the 1940s Shughni representation in the ruling and intellectual elite of Tajikistan has been disproportionately high. The revival of Shughni as a written language was discussed in Tajikistan in the late 1980s and resulted in the Tajikistan 1989 Language Law, which promised to pay special attention to the Pamiri languages. Attempts at its revival include the proposal of creating a new Cyrillic-based Shughni alphabet. In the early 1990s the Shughni of the Mountain Badakhshan Autonomous *Oblast* were in the forefront of those who demanded the raise in status of the district to that of a republic. (see also also AFGHANS, BAJUWI)

SHUI The approximately 290,000 Shui live mainly in China's Guizhou Province, where neighboring

groups include Han CHINESE, MIAO, BUYI, DONG, and YAO. Believed to be descended from one of China's ancient

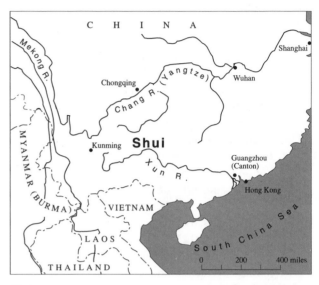

Shui

Yue tribes, their name first appears in documents dating from the Ming dynasty (1368–1644).

The Shui language belongs to the Zhuang-Dong group of the Sino-Tibetan family. It was written in an ancient hieroglyphic script consisting of only about 100 words, most related to religious activities. Chinese is now the commonly used language in daily life.

The Shui mainly practice their traditional religion. Western influence penetrated Shui-populated areas in the late nineteenth century and resulted in large-scale opium planting that damaged traditional agriculture.

The Shui have their own calendar in which the ninth lunar month marks the beginning of the new year.

SHUKULUMBWE see ILA.

SHULUH see MASMUDA.

SHUMASHTIANS An ethnic group inhabiting the Shumashti village on the right bank of the Kuna River in Afghanistan, in the proximity of the PASHAI. No population data are available, but a rough estimate puts them as numbering no more than 2,000.

The Shumashtian language belongs to the central subgroup of Indo-Iranian languages. It is unwritten, Pashto being used as the literary language.

The Shumashtians are Sunni Muslims of the Hanafi school. They are sedentary agriculturalists.

SHUMBWA A subgroup of the NYAMWEZI.

SHUSWAP A Native North American group numbering 7,000, many of whom live on several reserves in British Columbia, Canada.

The Alkali Lake subgroup of the Shuswap was the first in British Columbia to ban the use of alcohol on the reserve. Other reserves have attempted to emulate it, but with little success.

SHUWA see HASSAUNA.

SHWAN see SVAN.

SIAMESE see THAI.

SIANE An ethnic group of approximately 20,000 living in the mountainous region of central Papua New Guinea. They speak an indigenous language. They are slash and burn cultivators, with their main crop being yams and taro. They practice a traditional religion which focuses primarily on ancestral spirits. Their ceremonies, which take the form of pig feasts, are celebrated mostly on the occasions of birth and initiation.

SIANG An ethnic group living on the Indonesian island of Kalimantan (Borneo). (see also DAYAK)

SIBO (Xibo) An ethnic group numbering approximately 84,000 who live mainly in the Xinjiang Uighur Autonomous Region and the northeast Liaoning Province of China. In origin and culture, they are related to the MANCHU; they speak a Manchurian dialect and employ the Manchurian script.

Over 200 years ago, part of the Sibo, together with some other minority ethnic groups in China, were sent to defend the northwestern frontiers in Xinjiang. Since then, two groups of Sibo have developed distinct characteristics. The Sibo who remained in the northeast share many similarities with the neighboring HAN and MANCHU in language, dress, food, and dwelling. Those in the northwest have preserved their original ethnic characteristics, although many of them speak the languages of the UIGHUR and the QAZAQS.

Most Sibo practice their traditional religion, although some are Lamaist Buddhists. Their primary occupations are agriculture, raising livestock, and fishing. The Sibo family unit usually consists of three generations.

SIBUNGO An ethnic group living on the Indonesian island of Kalimantan (Borneo). (see also DAYAK)

SICILIANS The 5 million inhabitants of the island of Sicily, Italy, are a subgroup of the ITALIANS. Due to their central location in the Mediterranean Sea, the Sicilians have been subjected to a great number of influences. The resulting ethnic mix combines predominantly Mediterranean with (particularly in West Sicily) North African elements. Sicilian culture and customs show the impact of the ARABS; popular culture (including puppetry) is Norman-influenced. Premodern social and economic relations have maintained their grip on Sicilians. The Sicilian Mafia, once an organized crime syndicate may originally have constituted a crude form of righting injustices inherent in the feudal system.

In spite of land reform, modest industrialization, and the development of tourism, unemployment remains high. Sicilians form a pool of cheap labor and are a traditional source of migrants, formerly to the United States, of late to North Italy.

Sicily's history was shaped by the GREEKS, Carthaginians, Byzantines, and ARABS. These were followed in the Middle Ages by the Normans and the GERMANS. The FRENCH, who succeeded the GERMANS, were soon followed by the SPANIARDS. Sicilians then entered a long period of decay, made worse by epidemics and banditry.

Centuries of exploitation and mismanagement by the various foreign rulers created the foundation for today's underdevelopment. Famine brought revolts in the seventeenth century. Mid-nineteenth century particularist agrarian revolts led the way for eventual unification with Italy in 1860. Since 1948 the Sicilians have enjoyed limited self-rule.

SIDAMO A people numbering 1.3 million (1980s) who live northeast of Lake Abaya in northern Sidamo Province of Ethiopia. They speak an eastern Cushitic language and adhere to traditional beliefs; some are Sunni Muslims or Christians (Ethiopian Orthodox and diverse minorities). The Sidamo are agriculturalists (grains, ensete), and cattle-raisers.

Although they are one of the larger population groups in Ethiopia, they are also strongly segmented. Their social and political structure is based on patrilineal primogeniture, age- and generation-grading, and councils of elders. The term "Sidamo" is sometimes used among Oromo-speakers to denote those with relations to Ethiopian Christianity. (see also ETHIOPIANS, OROMO)

SIDIN An ethnic group living on the Indonesian island of Kalimantan (Borneo). (see also DAYAK)

SIDONDO An ethnic group living in the mountainous central region of the Indonesian island of Sulawesi (Celebes). (see also TORADJA)

SIERRA LEONEANS The people of Sierra Leone in West Africa, numbering an estimated 4.2 million. The two main ethnic groups which make up the Sierra Leonean people are the TEMNE who live in the northwest of the country and constitute 45 percent of the population and the MENDE who live in the south and constitute 30 percent of the population. Both groups are subdivided into a number of linguistically and culturally related subgroups. Other groups are the Mande-speaking peoples in the north (KORANKO, YALUNKA, SOUSOU, and MALINKE), the FULANI, the LOLO and the SIERRA LEONE CREOLES.

Most of the Sierra Leoneans practice traditional religions, although there are significant Muslim and Christian communities. The official language of the country is English. The two local lingua francas are Mende and Krio, the Creole language.

Sierra Leone became independent from British colonial rule in 1961. Since then the country's political life has been highly unstable and characterized by an incessant ethnic struggle for power between the TEMNE and the MENDE.

At the beginning of the 1990s popular demands for political reforms and democratization were raised. Sierra Leone became involved in the civil war in Liberia which began in 1990, and during which around 125,000 LIBERIANS took refuge in Sierra Leone.

SIERRA LEONE CREOLES Descendants of liberated slaves, who were settled by the BRITISH in Freetown, Sierra Leone towards the end of the eighteenth century. Having been exposed to Western culture, the Creoles are English-speaking Christians. They number about 40,000 or 1 percent of Sierra Leone's population.

Toward the end of the nineteenth century, the Creoles faced rejection by the British, which sparked a crisis of cultural self-confidence: many questioned their acceptance of European values as African standards. During decolonization after World War II the Creoles played an active role in the Sierra Leone nationalist movement.

SIGI An ethnic group living in the mountainous central region of the Indonesian island of Sulawesi (Celebes). (see also TORADJA)

SIGU An ethnic group living on the Indonesian island of Kalimantan (Borneo). (see also DAYAK)

SIHANAKA A tribal division of the MALAGASY.

SIKHS see INDIANS, PUNJABIS.

SIKKA (s.d. Ata Sikka) An ethnic group numbering about 200,000, living in the central region of the Indonesian island of Flores. They speak Sara Sikka, an Austronesian language with three discernible dialects. The population is primarily Catholic although vestiges of their traditional religion persist. As gods were once paired as male and female counterparts, current Catholic doctrine among the Sikka places inordinate emphasis on the Virgin Mary as a female counterpart to Jesus. Non-Christians are often referred to as Ata Krowe.

The Sikka are primarily slash and burn cultivators of rice, corn, and cassava. Coconuts are raised as a cash crop and fishing is becoming increasingly important. Slash and burn techniques have caused considerable damage to the environment; poor soil conditions are making agricultural development difficult.

A Catholic Sikka sultanate existed since the early seventeenth century, and was granted considerable autonomy by the DUTCH, who were the colonial power. As a result, the Sikka were incorporated into the Republic of Indonesia only in the mid-1950s.

The ATA TANA AI numbering fewer than 10,000, are a subgroup of the Sikka. They have preserved their traditional religion and place greater emphasis on the role of women in the internal government of the village. They engage in similar forms of agriculture, but hunting and gathering are also important.

SIKKIMESE A Himalayan people numbering 350,000, living in the Himalayan state of Sikkim in northern India, bordering on Tibet, Nepal, and Bhutan. The Sikkimese consist of various Asian peoples who have no linguistic or ethnic connections with one another. The largest groups include INDIANS, NEPALIS (55 percent), LEPCHA, (25 percent), and BHUTANESE. The official language is English, although not many actually speak it. Sikkimese and Gurkhali are the primary languages. Sikkim's capital, Gangtok, has about 50,000 inhabitants.

Agriculture is the main economic activity despite the harsh climate and adverse topography. Staple crops are rice, corn, cardamom, citrus fruits, and apples; potatoes are a major cash crop. Domestic livestock are used for work and the abundant bamboo forests in the region supply another source of income.

above: A Sikkimese couple
below: A Sikkimese ritual dance

The state religion is Tibetan Buddhism, to which 30 percent of the population adhere; 60 percent of the population is Hindu. There is continual conflict between the Tibetan BHUTANESE, and the LEPCHA over land rights.

SIKSIKA   A Native North American group of Plains Indians, one of the three which make up the BLACKFOOT. An Algonkian-speaking people, they were dependent upon the buffalo for their livelihood. During the seventeenth and eighteenth centuries, they were at war with the CREE, ASSINIBOIN, SHOSHONE, and SIOUX.

The Siksika were and remain divided by the border between the United States and Canada. On the American side they settled on reservations in Montana in 1855; in Canada they settle on reserves east of Calgary in Alberta, in 1877. In 1912 they sold half the reserve in Canada and had, as a result, one of the highest standards of living among Plains Indians in Canada. The Blackfoot in Canada today number about 4,000. There is a much smaller number on the Blackfeet Federal Reservation in Montana, where they have established and operate the Northern Plains Indian Museum. (see also BLACKFOOT)

SILTI   A subgroup of the GURAGE.

SIMAA   A subgroup of the LUYANA.

SIMALUNGUN   (Timur) A subgroup of the BATAK living in the interior highlands of the Indonesian island of Sumatera (Sumatra).

SIMONG   A subgroup of the ADI.

SIMPOKE   An ethnic group living on the Indonesian island of Kalimantan (Borneo). (see also DAYAK)

SINDANG   see LEMBAK.

SINDI   (Sindhi) A people of the Sind region in southern Pakistan in India, mainly in the states of Rajasthan and Gujarat. They number about 15 million, most within Pakistan. Their main concentration is in the lower Indus River valley. The important urban centers of the Sindi population are the Pakistani cities of Karachi and Hyderabad.

The Sindi in Pakistan are Sunni Muslims, while in India they are Hindus. Their language, Sindi, belongs to the Indo-European family and has been heavily influenced by Arabic. It uses a Persian-Arab script similar to the one used by Urdu, the national language of Pakistan. (see also PAKISTANIS)

SINGAPOREANS   The inhabitants of the small island republic of Singapore in the Strait of Malacca off the coast of mainland Malaysia. Founded by Sir Thomas Raffles in 1819 as a port midway between India and China, Singapore was originally uninhabited and its present population consists primarily of descendants of nineteenth-century immigrants and laborers. More than three-quarters of the total population of 2.8 million are CHINESE, 15 percent are MALAYS, and the remainder are Tamil-speaking INDIANS and Europeans. Most of the island is occupied by the city of Singapore and the population is over 90 percent urban. Chinese, Malay, Tamil, and English are all official languages, and religions include Buddhism, Hinduism, Taoism, Islam, and Christianity.

Singapore joined with the British colonies of Malaya, Sarawak, and Sabah to form the Federation of Malaysia in 1963. Ethnic tension between predominantly Chinese Singapore with its western-oriented, urban, and mercantile culture, and the Malay-dominated remainder of Malaysia resulted in the amicable secession of Singapore from the Federation in 1965. As an independent nation with one of the world's largest ports, Singaporeans have fared well. Ethnic tensions between the various communities are minimal although there has been some trouble, particularly with Malay Muslim fundamentalists. Under Lee Kuan Yew, Singaporeans developed a "clean cut" society with strict penalties for any infringement on what became defined as the national character. Behavior such as smoking and chewing gum in public is penalized by stiff fines and tourists have been turned away for having long hair. At the same time, Singaporeans live in the wealthiest country in Southeast Asia with the highest standards of education, health, and welfare.

SINGGIE   An ethnic group living on the Indonesian island of Kalimantan (Borneo). (see also DAYAK)

SINGHALESE   see SINHALESE.

SINGHPO   (Ching-Po) A Mongoloid agricultural group found in northern Arunachal Pradesh, northeast India.

SINGO   A subgroup of the VENDA.

SINHALA   see SINHALESE.

SINHALESE (Singhalese, Sinhala) A people numbering an estimated 13 million living mainly in the central drylands and the southern and western wetlands of Sri Lanka (formerly Ceylon). They make up nearly 73 percent of the population of Sri Lanka, most of the rest of the population being TAMILS, who live mainly in the northeast of the island. The Sinhalese had previously lived in northeast Sri Lanka but during the thirteenth century, for reasons unknown, migrated to the southern and western parts of the island.

Sinhala, an Indo-European language of the Indo-Aryan group, has undergone many changes since it first arrived in Sri Lanka from northern India at the turn of the sixth century B.C.E. It still retains traces of southern Indian languages. The predominant religion is Theravada Buddhism, whose roots in Sri Lanka go back as far as the third century B.C.E. The Sinhalese have also been influenced by Christianity, Hinduism, and Islam.

Sinhalese culture exists within a family-tied caste system. There tends to be a hierarchy of castes and families try to use marriage as a way to improve their social status. Usually small problems and conflicts within communities are solved internally, with either local officials or those from higher castes presiding. Marriages are usually arranged. It is usual for the bride to live with the family of the groom, who is expected to be of an equal or higher caste.

The Sinhalese can be divided into the Kandyan Sinhalese of the central highlands, whose central city is Kandy, and the low country Sinhalese, who reside in the southern city of Colombo (the capital of Sri Lanka) and the surrounding southwest wetlands. Agriculture remains the main source of livelihood for many Sinhalese. Most of the farmlands are still worked with the help of water buffalo, and the crops range from rice, manioc, coconut, breadfruit, and other vegetables used for subsistence, to cash-crops of chilies, spices, herbs, eggs, marijuana, and some Ayurvedic medicinal plants. Small animals are also raised. The introduction of the plantations created some low-paid jobs in the production of coffee, tea, tobacco, and coconut for consumption in Europe, and increased the development of a cash-dependent society.

After over 300 years under European rule, including 130 years of rule by the BRITISH, Sri Lanka (Ceylon) achieved autonomy in 1932, and in 1948, gained independence. Nearly a decade of peaceful co-existence between the different ethnic cultures ensued, until the 1956 elections, when a Sinhalese politician gained an overwhelming victory and declared Sinhala the only national language. The northern TAMILS initiated increasing civil disturbances; the Sinhalese have been hardpressed since then to retain their predominance among the SRI LANKANS. The Sinhalese-based political parties are the UNP (United National Party), in power since 1977, and the SLFP (Sri Lanka Freedom Party). (see also SRI LANKANS)

SIO An ethnic group of several thousand, living on the northern coast of Papua New Guinea. They speak an indigenous language.

Their subsistence is based on shifting cultivation, hunting, and fishing. Their religious beliefs are centered around ancestral spirits. The most important ceremony, the rites of initiation, take place during the rainy season.

SIONA (Siona-Sekoya) see SEKOYA.

SIONGO An ethnic group living on the Indonesian island of Kalimantan (Borneo). (see also DAYAK)

SIOUX (s.d. Dakota, Lakota, Nakota) A Native North American group, numbering 8,500, living in Saskatchewan and Alberta, Canada. 75,000 live in North and South Dakota and Montana, U.S.A.

Sioux

The Sioux were traditionally and remain today one of the largest of the Native North American peoples. They refer to themselves as Dakota, Lakota, and Nakota, depending on their dialect. Traditionally they were buffalo-hunters, living in large buffalo-hide teepees. There were a number of Sioux tribes, such as the Hunkpapa, Oglala, Santee, Teton, Yankton, and Yanktonaie.

The Sioux were at war with the United States from the 1850s to the 1890s. The war began with the migration of white settlers westward. The first Sioux group to engage the whites in combat was the SANTEE in Minnesota, the most easterly of the Sioux. The fiercest series of battles occurred in the 1870s, and included the most famous, the battle of the Little Big Horn.

After this battle, in 1876, even though they were victorious, both the lack of buffalo herds and the arrival of cavalry reinforcements caused many Sioux to follow Chief Sitting Bull to Canada, where their descendants live today. The Ghost Dance Religion adopted by the Sioux, in the 1890s disappeared shortly after the massacre at Wounded Knee.

Today the Sioux are in the forefront of Native activism and were founders of the American Indian Movement, widely known at the time as Red Power. In 1973 they occupied the offices of the Bureau of Indian Affairs in Washington, D.C. and then seized and fortified the site of the Massacre at Wounded Knee, which led to a violent confrontation with the U.S. army.

The Sioux to this day are fierce defenders of their rights and identity. Many of them live in appalling conditions. Their reservations, while large, are underdeveloped and under-funded, and many are now partly flooded by dams such as Fort Randall, Big Bend, and Gavins Point on the Missouri River in South Dakota.

SIRIONO   A group of South American Indians, numbering a few hundred, living in Bolivia along the Blanco and Grande Rivers in the eastern part of the country. They speak Guarani.

Those living in the forests in small bands are hunters and gatherers. Others work in agricultural and pastoral estates. They adhere to traditional religions.

SISALA   A small ethnic group living in northern Ghana and Burkina Faso. Together with other neighboring groups, it is classified as GRUSI.

SIWAI   An ethnic group of approximately 15,000 living on the Pacific island of Bougainville in Papua New Guinea, east of the mainland. They speak an indigenous regional language. Their main crop is taro and their chief cash crop is cocoa. Christianity has almost completely replaced traditional beliefs in spirits. Their most important ceremonies are associated with the life-cycle.

SIX NATIONS   see IROQUOIS CONFEDERACY.

SIYAH-POSH   One of several tribes grouped together as NURESTANIS.

SKOKOMISH   A Native North American Indian group numbering 1,200, many of whom live on the Skokomish Reservation in Mason County, Washington, U.S.A.

Skokomish

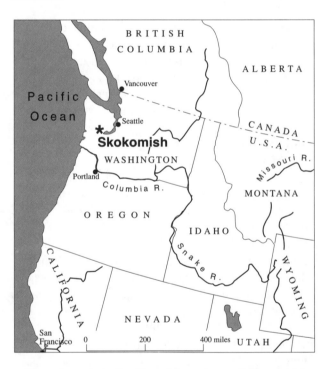

They earn their livelihood by salmon fishing and by working in the forest industry. Some are also employed in the general economy of Tacoma, Washington.

SLAVE   A large Athapaskan-speaking Native North American group numbering 5,500, many of whom live in the Yukon and Northwest Territories, Canada. They have been relatively successful in maintaining their language and culture.

Many continue to practice their traditional occupations of hunting moose and caribou and of trapping. The Slave are in the final stages of negotiating their land claims with the federal goverment of Canada.

SLOVAKS Of the 6.1 million Slovaks, 5 million live in Slovakia and the adjacent areas of the Czech Republic, Austria, Hungary, the Ukraine, and Poland. Expatriate communities exist in the United States and Canada, Western Europe, and the Commonwealth of Independent States.

The Slovak language belongs to the Western Slavic languages. It is closely related to and mutually intelligible with Czech. Until the mid-nineteenth century Czech was the literary language of the Slovaks. Since the 1840s, however, a Slovak literary language has been developed which utilizes the Roman alphabet.

In culture and religion, as well as in language and origin, the Slovaks are closely related to the CZECHS. The main difference in religion is the existence of a sizeable Protestant minority in Catholic Slovakia, while the Czechs are almost entirely Catholics. In culture, the main difference between the two stems from the strong influence of the HUNGARIANS on the Slovaks - the result of a distinct historical destiny.

Slavic tribes settled the area of modern Slovakia in the sixth-seventh century C.E. However, unlike the Czechs, the Slovaks never managed to establish their own state. After being ruled by the AVAR in the seventh century and by Greater Moravia in the tenth century (when they adopted Christianity), the Slovaks became part of Hungary and thus shared all the vicissitudes of the HUNGARIANS. The nobility and burghers were or became Hungarian and so did the many peasants who, due to overpopulation moved into the Hungarian plain. In 1526 the Slovaks came under the Habsburgs.

Slovak nationalism emerged at the beginning of the nineteenth century, first as part of Czech nationalism and later separately. The factor which marked separate Slovak conciousness was the development in the 1840s of the Slovak literary language, based on a dialect of central Slovakia. After suppressing the Hungarian revolution in 1849 the ruling AUSTRIANS facilitated the growth of Slovak nationalism by putting the Slovak-settled region under a de facto separate regime which favored the Slovaks over the HUNGARIANS. However, after the establishment of the dual monarchy of Austria-Hungary in 1867, the Slovak region reverted to the control of Budapest, which pursued a policy of forced assimilation. This only helped drive Slovak nationalists to demand independence and to cooperate with other Slavs, mainly the CZECHS.

In 1918, following World War I, the Slovaks joined the CZECHS in establishing Czechoslovakia. However, the CZECHS, being stronger numerically and more developed economically and socially, took the leadership of the new state. This growing resentment among the Slovaks, which found its expression in a strong autonomist movement. After the Munich agreement of 1938, Slovakia proclaimed its autonomy and was forced by Nazi Germany and Italy to surrender territories inhabited mainly by HUNGARIANS to Hungary. Following the occupation of Bohemia and Moravia by the GERMANS, Slovakia was granted independence under German protection.

After World War II Czechoslovakia was reconstituted under a Communist regime and many of the HUNGARIANS living in the Slovak part of the country were expelled. Despite efforts by the communist regime to industrialize Slovakia, the Slovaks remained generally less developed than the CZECHS and their standard of living, lower. In 1969 Czechoslovakia was made into a federation and a Slovak Socialist Republic was established alongside a Czech one. After the collapse of the communist regime in 1990, Slovakia experienced a strong growth of nationalist demands to separate from the Czech republic. In 1992 the two component republics of Czechoslovakia reached an agreement on separation, and in 1993, Slovakia became an independent, sovereign state.

SLOVENES The 1.75 million Slovenes live mainly in Slovenia, where they form an overwhelming majority (91 percent of the population), and in adjacent areas of neighboring Italy, Austria, and Croatia. Expatriate communities exist in other republics of the former Yugoslavia, Germany, and North America.

Slovene belongs to the southern branch of Slavic languages. It is close to, but clearly distinct from, Serbo-Croatian. It has been a literary language, although not in much use, since the Middle Ages. The modern literary language was formed in the nineteenth century and uses the Roman alphabet.

Ethnically and religiously close to the CROATS (both are overwhelmingly Roman Catholic), the Slovenes are distinguished culturally, having been influenced by German culture while the Croats were influenced by Hungary and Italy. The Slovenes, together with the CZECHS, are the most westernized of the Slavic peoples. In former Yugoslavia the Slovenes were the most urbanized and industrialized people. They had the highest rates of literacy and participation in higher education and enjoyed the highest standard of living. Slovenia was first among Yugoslavia's republics in terms of economic prosperity.

Slavic tribes, the ancestors of the Slovenes, settled in the territory of present-day Slovenia and further north in the sixth century C.E. They were subjugated by the BAVARIANS in the mid-eighth century and formed part of the Carolingian empire, being divided among the *marks* of Carinthia, Carniola, and Styria. The ascent of the HUNGARIANS at the beginnning of the tenth century and German colonization of present-day Austria separated them from the CZECHS.

German colonization assimilated most of the Slovenes north of the Drava River. From the thirteenth century onward Slovenia formed part of the Habsburg lands of contemporary Austria and shared their historical destiny. The fact that the Slovenes withstood acculturation is due exclusively to an intensive educational work by native Catholic priests who used Slovene as a literary language.

The origins of Slovene nationalism date back to the Napoleonic era when territories inhabited by Slovenes formed part of the Illyrian provinces of the French empire (1809–1814). The French encouraged the use of Slovene as an official language as part of their policy favoring Slovenes over GERMANS. In 1848 Slovene nationalists demanded for the first time an autonomous province within the Austrian empire.

In the second half of the nineteenth century Slovene nationalism was replaced by the idea of a union of all the southern Slavs within the Habsburg Empire. Following World War I, the Slovenes joined the CROATS and SERBS in establishing the Kingdom of the Serbs, Croats, and Slovenes, which in 1929 changed its name to Yugoslavia. Serb domination in Yugoslavia aroused some resentment among the Slovenes, but it never reached the intensity and proportions of that of the CROATS.

In World War II, Slovenia was divided between Italy, Germany, and Hungary. After the war it again became part of Yugoslavia and a Slovene republic was established as one of the five federated republics of Yugoslavia. In the 1980s with the economic deterioration and the general rise of nationalism among the various peoples of Yugoslavia, the demand grew for Slovenia's separation from Yugoslavia. This demand was based on the feeling that Slovenia, the most prosperous among the five republics, contributed much more to Yugoslavia than it received in return. In 1991, following an electoral victory of the nationalists, Slovenia proclaimed its independence from Yugoslavia, which was achieved almost without bloodshed.

SO   A Mon-Khmer group numbering 10,000 living along the Mekong River in northern Thailand and Laos. They have been influenced by the surrounding LAO and TAI and speak their languages.

The So cultivate rice, fruits, and vegetables, but are poorer than most surrounding peoples and are therefore dependent on the Lao for a variety of services such as religion. There is considerable intermarriage between the So and the SEK.

SOA   A subgroup of the SANGIR.

SOAI   see KUI.

SOBO   An ethnic group related to the EDO living in southwestern Nigeria.

SODDO   A subgroup of the GURAGE.

SOEWAWA   A subgroup of the GORONTALO.

SOGA   A people living in a small but densely populated area in eastern Uganda, north of Lake Victoria. Their language, Lusoga, belongs to the Eastern Lacustrine Bantu languages, but many Soga also speak Luganda, the language of the GANDA of Uganda, to whom they are culturally related.

The Soga grow plantains, sweet potatoes, and millet. They used to engage only in subsistence agriculture, although their area is particularly fertile. Under the Uganda British Protectorate they began to grow cash crops such as coffee and cotton.

In the northern part of their territory cattle-herding is of some importance. Their region is very densely settled and was for many years the target of slave-raids.

The Soga are organized in an exogamous lineage-system, consisting of several small chiefdoms. The chiefs do not possess strong influence but are nominally the owners of the land. Political authority is executed in territorial, rather than kinship, units.

In the past their country was subordinated to three peoples: the north was under the influence of the NYORO, the center was dominated by the TESO, and the south by the GANDA.

Later they were, for a long period, ruled by the Ganda. During British colonial rule the Soga were granted special status along with the kingdoms of Buganda, Bunyoro, and Toro.

Their traditional religion centered around ancestor worship. The gods were remote and did not interfere in everyday life. Today they are largely Christianized and have a high literacy rate.

SOKORO   An ethnic group related to the KOTOKO living in Chad.

SOLI   A Tonga-speaking group numbering 40,000, living near Lusaka, Zambia.

SOLOMON ISLANDERS   A Melanesian-speaking people numbering about 300,000, inhabiting twenty-one large and numerous small islands in the Pacific Ocean, east of Papua New Guinea and north of Vanuatu. The principal islands are Guadalcanal, Malaita, Choiseul, Santa Isabel, San Cristobal, and New Georgia. The majority of the population is Christian, and the lingua franca is Pidgin English. The Solomon Islands were a British protectorate since the late nineteenth century. During World War II Japan occupied the main islands and the group became a theater of war. In 1978, the islands became an independent state within the British Commonwealth.

Most Solomon Islanders continue to follow traditional village life, in which every family produces its own food and builds its own house. About 90 percent of the population depends on subsistence agriculture, the main crops being coconuts, sweet potatoes, taro, yams, and cassava. Fishing is a traditional subsistence activity, which has increased commercially with the assistance of the JAPANESE. The government pursues a policy of rural development with the aim of increasing production and its commercialization. Agriculture accounts for half the local production. The principal commercial crop is copra, which was for many years the main export. The Islands depend heavily on overseas aid, mainly from Austrialia and Japan.

SOLONGO, SORONGO   A subgroup of the KONGO.

SOLORESE   (Lamaholot; s.d. Ata Kiwan) A people numbering approximately 300,000, inhabiting the Indonesian islands of Solor, Adonara, and Lembata, and the eastern part of the island of Flores. They speak a Malayo-Polynesian language. Most are Catholics, although there are also Muslim, Protestant, Hindu, and Buddhist communities, as well as adherents of traditional beliefs. Agriculture is the primary economic occupation, and fishing and whaling are common along the coasts. Hunting is also important and there is some trade.

The Solorese have long been in contact with inhabitants of other islands and with both the DUTCH and POR-TUGUESE as colonial powers. They were converted to Islam before the JAVANESE, and Catholicism was introduced in the mid-sixteenth century. Until 1859, when the PORTUGUESE ceded their rights to the island to the DUTCH, the Solorese were caught in ongoing colonial warfare which pitted family members and clans against one another. Remnants of this persist today; the Solorese are divided arbitrarily into Demonara (Demons), associated with the PORTUGUESE, and Pajinara (Pajis), associated with the DUTCH, who still occasionally fight among themselves.

Many young Solorese males have left their homes in search of employment, causing severe demographic problems, especially in terms of the extremely low ratio of men to women.

SOMALI   A people estimated to number between 4 and 5 million, occupying most of Somalia, the southern part of Djibouti, the Ethiopian part of the Ogaden Desert, and part of northeast Kenya. All Somali speak one common language, Somali, a member of the Semito-Cushitic language family, and are linguistically related to the OROMO and AFAR. Some Oromo-speakers, Somali-speaking Bantu, and Swahili-speakers (Bajun) live among the Somali; in urban areas there are also groups of ARABS, southern ETHIOPIANS (Adare) and INDIANS (Banian).

Most Somali occupy plains regions and are primarily nomadic herdsmen with the camel as the basic economic unit. It is believed that in the fourteenth century the Somali were converted to Islam by ARABS from

Somali

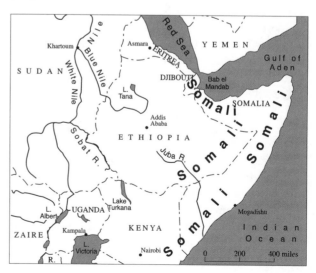

across the Red Sea. Today, all Somali are Sunni Muslims of the Shafi'i school.

Part of the Somali are townspeople and agriculturalists living in urban centers, especially along the coast and around Mogadishu, the capital. This town, which has existed since at least the tenth century, was in the Middle Ages divided into a seaside quarter (Shangama) for Asian traders and settlers (Persians [see IRANIANS], ARABS) and an inland quarter (Hammar-Wen) for their Somali counterparts.

The political, social, and economic basis of the Somali people is the *rer*, a large self-contained kinship group consisting of a number of families claiming common descent as an agnatic kinship line. The basic loyalty and kinship of a Somali is to his *rer*, and the clan has always played a decisive role in the history of the people.

The major Somali clan-clusters (HAWIYA, DAROOD, DIR, ISHAAQ, DIGIL, DAHANWEN), which claim a fictional Arab ancestor, are divided between the northern SAMAALE, traditionally mainly pastoral camel-raisers and the southern SAB, who are mainly sedentary agriculturalists. The former possess a stronger corporate character than the latter.

The independent Somali Democratic Republic was formed in 1958, out of the British colony of Somaliland in the north, and the Italian colony of Somalia in the south. The unification of Somalia with the Somali in Djibouti (former French Somaliland), southern Ethiopia, and northern Kenya, was long a strategic aim for the leading political strata of Somalia. This encouraged several wars with Ethiopia (1963, 1977–1978) and continuous guerrilla activities in south Ethiopia and north Kenya. Internal friction after the fall of former president Siad Barre (1969-1990) led to a de facto division of Somalia, and the self-proclamation of a northern republic of Somaliland (1991). Clan-based politics proved crucial for these developments, although this was officially discouraged in favor of nation-building during Siad Barre's reign.

Since the 1960s, the Somali living inside Ethiopia (1984: 1.6 million), have been known as Western Somali. They mainly live in the Haud (bordering northern Somalia) and the Ogaden (Hararge, southern Bale, south Sidamo) regions. They are Sunni Muslims. Most are nomadic pastoralists (camel- and cattle-breeders), but there are also traders, drivers, and mechanics.

The main Somali clans inside Ethiopia are the Issa, Gadabursi, Ishaaq, Ogaden (Darood), and Hawiya. In the Shaballe valley live the Reer Bare (acculturated Bantu agriculturalists). In the vicinity of the towns of Harar and Diredawa live mixed Oromo-Somali populations (Gurgura, Jarso). Culturally mixed groups in the southern Sidamo region are the Garri, Gurra, Gerri, Gerri-Mero (agriculturalists in the Juba valley), and Sakuye (Ajuran). Muslim Somali preachers played an important role in the Islamization of the southern Oromo region. Mutual adherence to an Islamic saint (the famous sanctuary of Sheikh Hussein in Bale) sometimes provided a focus for political alliances.

SOMBA   (Tamberna) An ethnic group living in the Atakora mountains of northwestern Benin and in smaller numbers in the adjoining parts of Togo. Their region has poor soil and they are among the poorest groups in Benin. The Benin Somba tried to resist colonization by the FRENCH. After Benin's independence in 1960, the Somba were disappointed by the new government's policies and avoided contact with it as far as possible.

Somba subgroups include the BIYOBE, DYE, NIENDE, SORUBA, and WOABA.

SOMRAI   An ethnic group living in Chad.

SONGHAI   (Songhay) A people living in Niger and Mali, along the south bank of the Niger River. In extreme southwestern Niger, around Niamey, the capital, they number, with the DJERMA, around 1.4 million. In eastern Mali, south of the town of Timbuktu they number around 480,000. They are also found in smaller numbers in northern Benin and other areas. They speak the Songhai language and have been Muslims since the thirteenth century. They are primarily sedentary subsistence farmers whose main crop is millet.

During the fourteenth and fifteenth centuries the Songhai developed one of the largest of the West African empires. It originated in a small chiefdom that was established in the seventh century in eastern Mali. The Songhai king converted to Islam at the beginning of the eleventh century but the new religion reached the masses only in the thirteenth century. By the end of the sixteenth century the Songhai empire collapsed following an Almoravid invasion from the north.

The FRENCH conquered the Songhai territory at the end of the nineteenth century. At the begining of the twentieth century the Songhai tried to resist French rule but the uprising was severely repressed. In the 1950s many Songhai supported the Union Soudanaise, the main political party of Mali, then called the French Sudan. They are relatively unimportant in Mali's contemporary politics.

SONGOROB An ethnic group living in western Uganda. They are related to the KONJO and the AMBO.

SONGYE A subgroup of the LUBA.

SONINKE (Sarakole) A people numbering around 640,000, living mainly in northwest Mali in the Kayes, Yelimane, Nioro, and Nara Regions. A Soninke diaspora is found throughout West and Central Africa. They speak Sarakole and are Muslims. They are mainly merchants, who have migrated from their homeland to most of the important marketplaces in West and Central Africa.

Between the eighth and the eleventh centuries the Soninke ruled the Empire of Ghana, an ancient empire that was established as early as the fourth century. In the eleventh century the empire reached its climax but it was weakened by Almoravid (an Islamic reform movement) invasions. During the precolonial period the Soninke accumulated wealth because of their proximity to the desert trade route from North Africa. They exchanged salt and cattle for cereals. They also traded in slaves and were the major suppliers of the Atlantic slave trade in the eighteenth century. After the abolition of the slave trade in the nineteenth century, the Soninke lost their economic power. During the French colonial period they began to migrate. Today they have one of the highest rates of labor migration in West Africa.

SONOWAL see BORO-KACHARI.

SOP A Mon-Khmer group living in southern Vietnam. They are generally considered a subgroup of the MA.

SORBS (also Wends, Lusatians) The fewer than 50,000 Sorbs live in the mountains of Lusatia in the east of Germany. They are remnants of the large Slavic population between the Elbe and Odra Rivers, which has been acculturated by the GERMANS since the Middle Ages.

The Sorb language belongs to the Western branch of the Slavic languages. It is not a literary language, although it has sporadically been written in the Roman alphabet. German is the Sorbs' literary language.

The Sorbs were peasants, enserfed by German landlords before the emancipation of the serfs. By religion they are Lutheran Christians.

SORK A people numbering less than 1,000 living in southern Laos. They speak a Mon-Khmer language

Sorbs

similar to that of the SAPUAN and have begun assimilating into that slightly larger group which, in turn, is increasingly influenced by the LAO. Although vestiges of traditional beliefs remain, the Sork are generally Buddhists.

SORO A subgroup of the HADIYA.

SORUBA A subgroup of the SOMBA.

SOSSO A subgroup of the KONGO.

SOTHO Southern Bantu peoples numbering as many as 8 million, living in southern Africa. Around 1.6 million live in Lesotho, where they are the predominant ethnic component; some 1 million live in Botswana; around 5 million, in South Africa (traditionally concentrated between the Limpopo and Orange Rivers and in parts of Natal); and the remainder, in southwestern Zimbabwe. Today they are divided into three main groups: the Northern Sotho (the PEDI), the SOUTHERN SOTHO (the Basotho) and the Western Sotho (the TSWANA).

The Sotho are primarily Christians. Their traditional cosmology includes a conception of a supreme being and a pantheon of lesser spirits more immediately involved in the lives of individuals. Ancestors continue to form part of the community, as do unborn children. The Sotho place greater emphasis on the impersonal causation of evil than do other southern African groups. This is reflected in more elaborate ritual purification techniques than those of, for example, the NGUNI.

There are two schools of thought on early Sotho history: one finds evidence for the claim that they moved into southern Africa in three distinct migrations from the northeast; the second supports the theory of migrations over relatively short distances from the southwestern Transvaal. Certain features of the rituals of the PEDI are suggestive of links with the lake chiefdoms north of Malawi, thus supporting the first school. Yet archeological evidence of the Buispoort and Uitkomst Late Iron Age cultures (respectively in the area of Magaliesberg and between Pretoria and Warmbaths) has been supportive of the second school; pointing to the unmistakable similarities between these material cultures from c.1000 C.E. and that of the present-day Sotho. The second school is also supported by certain oral traditions. Working with these traditions, historians have dated the period of fission of the original chiefdom and consequent dispersal from the Buispoort-Uitkomst areas as some time between 1440 and 1550. The earliest Sotho speakers were the KGALAGADI and the Hurutse (Bahurutse), the ancestors of the NGWAKETSE (Bangwaketse) and PEDI. Before the *Mfekane* (see NGUNI, ZULU) in the 1830s, only the PEDI seem to

Sotho

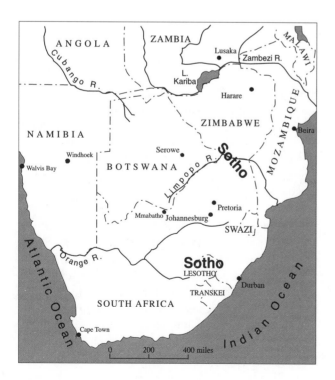

have successfully united a group of chiefdoms into a paramountcy. The organization of early chiefdoms centered on the village, which was an important administrative unit and economically self-sufficient. The settlements of the HURUTSE had a population of 10,000 to 20,000, their settlements great size distinguishing them from their neighbors, the NGUNI. Sotho society was organized in age-sets, with each age group assigned specific herding or household duties. Transition from one age-group to another was accompanied by specific initiations. The principal rituals of ancestor cults were performed at initiations. The age-set was also the basis of the Sotho military organization, and was directly linked to political authority. Sotho settlements were constructed in stone from at least 1800 onwards. The office of chief was hereditary and the chief was executive head and commander-in-chief, assisted by a cadre of advisors and councilors. Trade was controlled by the chiefs and the Sotho had no regular markets.

The Sotho are distinguished from the NGUNI primarily by their rules of marriage. For both groups lineage is an important factor in marriage. But while the NGUNI are strictly exogamous, the Sotho are endogamous and marriage between cousins is the preferred custom.

The Sotho are traditionally cultivators of grains and tobacco and herders of cattle, goats and sheep. As opposed to the NGUNI, the Sotho used sheep in rituals and associated them with chiefs. Animal sacrifices, however, were less common among the Sotho than among the NGUNI. In addition, the Sotho were skilled craftsmen, a feature which distinguished their economy from that of their neighbors. They were metalworkers, leatherworkers, wood- and ivory-carvers, and miners of salt and iron ore. Traditionally they were distinguished from other peoples by their particular dress: the name "Sotho" possibly derives from a Nguni jest about their clothing. The Sotho did not participate in the slave trade.

The Sotho are characterized by totemism, groups being mystically bound to specific natural objects or animals which, for that group, are both objects of particular honor and surrounded by ritual taboos. The particular taboo was often reflected in the chiefdom-clan name, e.g., Taung (lions), Tloung (elephants), Phuting (antelopes), Kwean (crocodiles), and Tlhaping (fish).

SOU A Mon-Khmer group numbering 1,000, living in Laos. They have been influenced by the culture of the LAO and speak the Lao dialect of Tai. Their small numbers are due to both a low birthrate and a high mortality rate during several epidemics in the past century.

SOUDIE SEE KURFEY.

SOUEI A Mon-Khmer group numbering about 10,000, living in southern Laos. They have been assimilated into the culture of the neighboring LAO.

SOUTH AFRICANS The total population of South Africa is around 36 million, including the population of the four independent tribal homeland republics of the Transkei, Bophutatswana, Venda, and Ciskei. The largest group is of southern Bantu-speaking peoples, who today number around 28 million. Within this group, the largest subgroup is the NGUNI, who number around 17 million in South Africa, and include the ZULU, XHOSA, SWAZI, and the southern Transvaal NDEBELE. The next largest subgroup is the Sotho-speakers, who number c.5 million and include the PEDI, the SOUTHERN SOTHO (Basotho), and the TSWANA. The TSONGA (Shangana) are the third largest group, numbering around 1.5 million. The VENDA, the fourth group of southern Bantu in South Africa, number around 550,000.

South Africa's white population numbers around 5 million, with around 3 million AFRIKANERS and the remaining 2 million mainly English-speakers, mostly descendants of BRITISH who colonized and immigrated to the area, but also including a minority of immigrants from Eastern and Western Europe. The South African population also includes around 3.5 million *coloureds*, people of mixed black, white, and Khoi (Hottentot) descent (around 80 percent of whom speak Afrikaans at home); and around 1 million Asians. The original inhabitants of the country, the KHOIKHOI and the SAN, hardly exist in South Africa today.

While the Bantu and European populations are scattered throughout the four provinces of South Africa, around 82 percent of the Asian population lives in Natal, and around 86 percent of the *coloureds* live in the Cape Province.

Around 77 percent of the entire population is Christian. The African Independent Churches constitute the largest Christian group in South Africa, followed by the Dutch Reformed Church groups. The latter are stronger in the rural areas among all population groups, but other churches predominate in towns. Among the Asian population, in urban areas 62 percent are Hindus and 20 percent are Muslims, while in the rural areas 70 percent are Hindus and 8 percent Mus-

lims. The Asian population has a Christian minority of 12 percent, the *coloured* population has a Muslim minority of 8 percent. There is also an English-speaking minority of JEWS, who account for 4 percent of the white population.

South Africa's history is one of alternating periods of conflict and cooperation between its various peoples. The KHOIKHOI (Hottentot) and the SAN (Bushmen), known jointly as the KHOISAN, were the earliest inhabitants of South Africa. At some time between 500 and 1000 C.E., Iron Age migrants of Negroid Bantu-speaking peoples crossed the present northern border of South Africa. From their ancestral homeland in the Nigeria-Cameroon area, these Bantu-speakers came to populate virtually all areas of central and southern Africa. Traditionally the Bantu-speaking NGUNI lived in the areas of the eastern Cape, Natal, and parts of the Transvaal; the SOTHO lived in the areas of the Transvaal, the Orange Free State, and the northern Cape; the VENDA in the area of the Soutpansberg, and the TSONGA in the coastal area from the Mozambique border to Saint Lucia Bay in Natal.

Prior to the late eighteenth century, most of these groups (with the notable exception of the SAN, who were organized in small family-based bands) were organized into a number of politically independent chiefdoms. Many of these were ethnically mixed, and modern scholarship has argued for the irrelevance of ethnicity in early South African history.

White settlement in South Africa began in 1652 with the establishment of a refreshment station at the Cape under the Dutch East India Company. These early Company settlers were the forefathers of the present day AFRIKANERS. In 1820, in an attempt to alleviate the chronic labor shortages, the BRITISH, who then ruled the Cape Colony, settled a group of ENGLISH in the area of Algoa Bay (present day Port Elizabeth). These early settlers form part of the ancestry of present-day white European English-speaking South Africans.

Slave-labor was resorted to at an early date. In addition to locally-captured slaves, others were imported into the Cape Colony from the East Indies and India, beginning almost from the inception of white settlement in the mid-seventeenth century. These were later supplemented with African slaves. The present day *colored* population of South Africa emerged in consequence of settler-slave/Khoi/Bantu mixing and intermarriage from an early time. South Africa's present-day Asian population is descended from indentured laborers, INDIANS and CHINESE, brought into South Africa from the second half of the nineteenth century.

above: A racially-mixed school in South Africa
below: Afrikaners in traditional dress

Since the mid-sixteenth century, people in South Africa were plagued with political-military conflict and epidemic disease. The first military disputes between the DUTCH and the KHOIKHOI began in 1659 and sporadic conflict between the two continued until 1802. In 1779 the first armed confrontation began in what has been called the Hundred Years' War between the XHOSA and the white colonists.

In 1815, the *Mfekane* erupted. This was a series of dramatic political-military upheavals originating in the northeast sector of South Africa, which destroyed many of the existing African polities in the area and scattered peoples over half the African continent. Modern scholars are divided in their interpretations of these events. One school posits the view of a revolution in military tactics among the ZULU under King Shaka, who then went on a genocidal rampage against all neighboring polities, each of which followed with like rampages outwards from the Zulu epicenter. A more recent school locates the origin and momentum of the *Mfekane* in accelerated slave-raiding expeditions by the PORTUGUESE from the northeast and white settlers from the south; expeditions which created havoc and prompted the emergence (and location) of the particular ethnic groups found in modern South Africa.

These dramatic events were enacted against the background of waves of epidemic human and bovine diseases. In 1713 a smallpox epidemic devastated the Khoisan population; and from the 1850s to the early 1900s plagues of locusts and cyclical cattle epidemics afflicted Bantu and European agriculture alike.

South Africa's unitary political system was constructed in 1910, following the loss of independence of Khoikhoi and Bantu chiefdoms and states by the end of the nineteenth century, and the defeat of the independent Afrikaner Republics in the Anglo-Boer War of 1899–1902. Racial segregation and discrimination became progressively more rigid under successive white administrations, culminating in the formal institution of apartheid in 1948 under the Afrikaner Nasionale Party. In 1961 South Africa withdrew from the British Commonwealth and declared itself a republic.

Under the scheme of apartheid, which aimed at the creation of ten independent tribal homelands for South Africa's Bantu peoples, four such independent republics were established between 1976 and 1981: the Transkei and Ciskei (which divide the XHOSA between them), Bophuthatswana (for the TSWANA), and Venda (VENDA).

In addition, there are six self-governing states (which declined independence): Lebowa (for the PEDI),

Gazankulu (Shangaan-TSONGA), Qwaqwa (SOUTHERN SOTHO), KwaZulu (ZULU), KwaNdebele (NDEBELE of the Transvaal), and KaNgwane (SWAZI). All of South Africa's Bantu peoples were considered de jure citizens of one or another of these homelands. However, the Restoration of South African Citizenship Act of 1988 has requalified some of these peoples for South African citizenship. The future political settlement in South Africa will no doubt affect the fate of these homelands as quasi-separate territories.

Since the late 1980s violent clashes between the Inkatha party and the African National Congress have dominated Bantu politics in Natal and in the industrial Witwatersrand region in Transvaal. There are two interpretations of these clashes. One sees them as an expression of ethnic conflict between the Zulu Inkatha and the Xhosa-dominated African National Congress. The second sees this violence as an outcome of conflicting political visions for the future South Africa: Inkatha is fighting for a South Africa in which traditional authorities and ethnicity form the basis of national politics; the African National Congress fighting for a supra-ethnic and unitary South African nationhood.

SOUTHERN SOTHO   (Basotho) A part of the Sotho peoples of southern Africa. The Southern Sotho today number around 3.5 million. Around 1.6 million live in Lesotho, where they constitute almost the entire population; and around 1.9 million live in South Africa in the Transkei, the Orange Free State, and the self-governing tribal homeland of Qwaqwa.

The Southern Sotho are primarily Christians. In Lesotho, around 80 percent are Christians, Protestantism predominating in the densely-populated lowlands, and Catholicism in the mountain areas. In South Africa, around 88 percent have specific church affiliations. Of the entire Southern Sotho population in South Africa, around 22 percent belong to African Independent Churches, around 16 percent are Roman Catholics, and around 12 percent are Methodists.

The Southern Sotho share the cultural and political customs of other SOTHO. They were welded into a people by King Moshoeshoe I in the nineteenth century. He had become leader of the Kwena and Fokeng early in the century, absorbing peoples from other SOTHO and NGUNI groups who had become refugees during the *Mfekane* upheavals in the 1830s. The Fokeng, in particular, had lived in small, scattered communities intermingled with San groups, which accounts for the Khoisan-associated click-words in the Basotho language. The language of the Southern Sotho is in fact the only Sotho language to contain such click words. The written form of Southern Sotho was created by French missionaries.

SOUTH MOLUCCANS   see AMBONESE.

SOUTH TYROLEANS (s.d. Tyroler) The 285,000 South Tyroleans are a Germanic minority living in Italy, in Alto Adige (South Tyrol). Before World War I the region was purely German and this group formed a whole with the other Tyroleans living in the Austro-Hungarian empire. After World War I, however, Austria was forced to cede the area to Italy. Under fascism, South Tyrol was forcibly colonized by Italian industrial laborers sent purposely to Bolzano (Bozen) in order to dilute its German character. The Tyroleans, overwhelmingly agricultural, remained poor.

After 1939, as a result of an agreement between Fascist Italy and Nazi Germany, many South Tyroleans were forced out to Germany. Although a large majority wanted the region to be returned to Austria, it remained in Italy's hands after World War II. The Italian authorities granted cultural autonomy but kept economic and social development under their control. Pro-Austrian irredentism died out after Austria's neutralization in 1955. However, tensions with Austria continued and South Tyrolean dissatisfaction and acts of sabotage pressured Rome to improve its autonomy package: in 1972 it prescribed proportional representation in all functions and budgets. The South Tyroleans, who profited from the tourist boom, now became richer than their Italian neighbors and reciprocated by accepting Italian citizenship. Meanwhile, local ethnic ITALIANS suffering from unemployment, threatened to turn to fascism.

SPANIARDS   (Spanish s.d. Espagnoles;) The 39 million Spaniards, today overwhelmingly Catholic, have an extremely heterogeneous background. The contemporary Spanish people is made up of ANDALUSIANS, CASTILIANS, CATALANS, GALICIANS, and others, including even the highly particularized BASQUES.

Castilian, the Romana language spoken in the politically dominant kingdom of Castile, became the official Spanish, and by 1500 became a vehicle of hispanization of the new territories in southern Spain and in the Americas. Spanish is today spoken worldwide by c.280-300 million people, most in the Americas. Only a minority among them stems from the 4 to 5 million Spaniards who emigrated from the sixteenth century onwards. In Spain itself, Catalan, Galician, and Basque remain regional languages.

In antiquity, the prehistoric ancestors of the Spaniards underwent Phoenician, Greek, and Celtic influences before the Romans conquered the Iberian Peninsula in the last centuries B.C.E. The next invaders were the Germanic Visigoths and Vandals, not particularly numerous and hardly mingling with the indigenous population, but creating the first specifically Spanish civilization. The Muslim-Moorish conquest in the eighth century, lasting until the fifteenth, left deep and permanent marks (on Spanish culture and language). Asturias, Navarre, and part of the Pyrenees in northern Spain were the only regions left untouched. From here started the *Reconquista*, a long crusade during which Castilian supremacy affirmed itself. Zones abandoned by Muslims were repopulated by Christian settlers. Those who stayed, the industrious *mudejars* (conquered Muslims) and Jewish merchants and financiers, were originally left in peace. However, under the impact of a series of hardships in the later Middle Ages, religious tolerance declined severely. The Inquisition created a sharp split between Christians and others. Under the unifying ideology of staunch Catholicism, the monarchs of Castile and Aragon attained control over the whole Iberian peninsula: Spain's final unification in 1492 coincided with the forced baptism or expulsion of all remaining JEWS and Muslims (*moriscos*). The JEWS took their Spanish heritage (including language) with them throughout the Balkans, North Africa, and the Levant. Those who stayed and converted remained suspect and persecuted. The expulsion of the JEWS was an economic blow for trade; that of the Muslims for agriculture.

In the sixteenth century, the Spaniards under the Habsburg dynasty became the dominant European and world power, controlling Sicily, southern Italy, and the Netherlands. The discovery of the Americas, the urge to extend the Catholic faith, and lust for precious metals soon resulted in an overextended empire encompassing the greater part of Latin America and the Philippines. Within a century, this superpower was economically ruined and politically marginalized. Epidemics in the seventeenth century hastened the decline. Spain first lost its European dominions and then, in the nineteenth century, its American empire. This was an unstable era for Spain, plagued by a series of military coups and by the struggle between absolutists and liberals. Political tranquility returned when a constitutional monarchy was installed in 1874, but a corrupt oligarchy soon deprived parliamentarism of any legitimacy.

above: A Spanish farmer on his donkey
below: Spanish women engaged in lacework

The twentieth century witnessed the establishment of modern industry in Catalonia; the rest of the country remained primarily agriculurated. The misery of agrarian laborers in the south led to violent revolts, nourished a strong anarchist movement, and strengthened regionalist and labor movements. The Second Republic (1931–1936), dominated by the Left, initiated agrarian, federal, and anticlerical reforms, but revolutionary rhetoric frightened the propertied classes and alienated conservative peasants. The traumatic Civil War (1936–1939) part Catholic crusade, part reassertion of centralism against regionalists, and part ideological class struggle, was won by the fascist Phalanges led by Francisco Franco, whose reign survived into the 1970s. His dictatorship, based on army and church, epitomized the supremacy of CASTILIANS over the more outward-looking and economically more advanced CATALANS and BASQUES.

After the mid-1950s, Catholic technocrats (Opus Dei) undertook a program of modernizing Spain's economy: opening Spain to foreign investment and importing technologies finally brought the industrial revolution to hitherto rural Castile. Gradually, the old contradiction between the underdeveloped center and the advanced periphery lost its edge. A rural exodus inflated the urban population and reduced the number of peasants, rendering the question of agrarian reform less significant. In the cities a modern entrepreneur class emerged. The mass export of cheap manpower (mainly to France, Germany, and Switzerland) masked unemployment. Tourism, work abroad, the media, and European influences introduced modern and democratic values. Eventually even the church rallied the anti-authoritarian opposition. Franco's death in 1975 made possible a peaceful transition to a liberal, federal democracy. In the 1980s regional decentralization was begun, and Spain moved to become a growing industrial power. (see also CANARY ISLANDERS)

SPOKANE   A Native North American group, numbering 2,200, many of whom live on the Spokane Federal Reservation at the junction of the Spokane River and Lake Franklin Roosevelt in Washington, U.S.A.

Traditionally they were hunters and gatherers living in underground dwellings. Many now work in the local economy.

SQUAMISH   A Native North American West Coast Indian group, numbering 1,800, most of whom live in Vancouver, British Columbia, Canada, and on the Port

Madison Federal Indian Reservation on Puget Sound, near Seattle, Washington.

Many own and operate small fishing vessels while others work in the forest industry.

SRBI   see SERBS.

SRE   (Cau Sre) A KOHO group, numbering about 30,000, living in southern Vietnam. They are similar to their neighbors the MA and the RIEN.

SRI LANKANS   The inhabitants of Sri Lanka (Ceylon), an island located on the southeastern tip of the Indian subcontinent. The southern part of the island is a plateau broken by a range of mountains; the northern part is a coastal plain. The population numbers 18 million, about half of whom live in the southwest part of Sri Lanka.

Sri Lanka has been populated by peoples migrating from India across the Palk Strait. The largest group is the SINHALESE (73 percent of the population). The largest minority is the TAMIL (18 percent), followed by the Muslim Sri Lankans (Moors: 7 percent), VEDDA, BURGHERS, and Eurasians. English was the official language until 1956, when it was replaced in that capacity by Sinhala. This was strongly opposed by the Tamil minority, and led to inter-ethnic tension. In 1978 Tamil became a national language, but it was made an official language only in 1987. Most Sri Lankans speak either Sinhala or Tamil. The former, related to Pali, belongs to the Indo-Aryan subgroup of the Indo-European family of languages; Tamil is a 2,000–year-old Dravidian language.

Sri Lanka is a secular state; approximately 70 percent of the population are Buddhist, 15 percent Hindus, 8 percent Muslims, and 7 percent are Christians. Most SINHALESE are Therevada Buddhists, while the TAMILS are largely Hindus. A majority of the Eurasians are Roman Catholics.

Agriculture is the mainstay of Sri Lankan society. It employs nearly half the labor force and accounts for one quarter of the nation's economy. About three quarters of those working in agriculture grow export crops such as tea, rubber, and coconut products. Rice is the largest staple crop, with sugar, pepper, cardamom, tobacco, coffee, and cocoa also widely grown.

The SINHALESE were the first settlers in Sri Lanka, arriving in the sixth century B.C.E. from northern India. Buddhism first entered the island in the second century B.C.E. The Sinhalese civilization was destroyed by civil war and the establishment of an invading Tamil king-

A Sri Lankan man

dom in the north of the island. The first Europeans arrived in the early sixteenth century. The PORTUGUESE, having introduced Christianity and opened the island to the west, were defeated by the DUTCH, who built up trade and established a colonial administration. The BRITISH, coming after the DUTCH in the early nineteenth century, established a highly centralized colonial state which introduced education among other welfare benefits. Today more than 80 percent of the population is literate.

In 1948 Ceylon, as it became known, gained independence; in 1972 it was renamed Sri Lanka. The centralized nature of the political system has created strife between the Buddhist SINHALESE and the Hindu TAMIL. The TAMIL have been fighting for an independent state in northern Sri Lanka since 1983. Their battle escalated in the late 1980s when India attempted to negotiate a settlement but found itself on the offensive against Tamil rebels. By the early 1990s the situation was worsening.

The Muslims of Sri Lanka, known as Moors, Marakkala, Musalman, Sonar, or Sonakar, consist of three groups: SRI LANKANS (c.1 million), MALAYS (60,000), and INDIANS (40,000). The majority speak Tamil, while others speak Sinhala; most are Sunni Muslims.

Muslim ARABS first arrived in Sri Lanka in the eighth century and eventually dominated Colombo, the capital. Others (the Malay and Indian Muslims) arrived through the colonialist developments of the PORTUGUESE and the BRITISH. Their society tends to be strongly bound by religion and a well-controlled family lineage. They are competent as traders and have dominated the Sri Lankan jewelry trade as well as other lucrative branches of commerce.

STIENG (Bulip) A Mon-Khmer group, numbering about 35,000, living in the southern Vietnamese highlands along the Vietnamese-Cambodian border. They believe in spirits and are particularly cautious of sorcerers. They live in longhouses and are primarily agricultural.

The Stieng participated in the anti-French revolt of 1864 and again rebelled against the colonial authorities in the 1930s. Many also participated in the communist insurgency in Vietnam, hoping to gain autonomy under a socialist regime, but others were forced to flee to the Cambodian border as refugees. In 1967 the inhabitants of the Stieng refugee camp of Dak Son were massacred by Communist insurgents from Vietnam.

Stieng

STILLAGUAMISH A Native North American group, numbering 650, living in Washington State, U.S.A.

STOCKBRIDGE (Housatonic) A Native North American group, most of whom live on the Stockbridge-Munsee Federal Reservation in Wisconsin, U.S.A. They number about 1,000.

SUBANUN An ethnic group, numbering roughly 60,000, who live on the inlands of the Zamboanga Peninsula of the island of Mindanao, in the Philippines. They speak Subanda and are mix-field farmers who mainly grow rice, maize, and other crops. They usually own very little land and have been exploited in the past by Muslim groups. Their name is the term used by both the Christians and Muslims of Mindanao for "pagan." Under the influence of neighboring Christian groups, they abandoned slash and burn farming practices for a more permanent field agriculture.

The Subanun usually live on their farms in shack-like houses arranged in small clusters. Marriage often takes place before puberty, after the families have negotiated the bride-price, and divorce is rare. Younger women usually file and blacken their teeth. The Subanun are known to be a non-violent society; those with skills in litigation are called upon to settle disputes.

They adhere to their traditional religion. Although it does not play a large part in their lives, ceremonies are held for spiritual reasons during death, sickness, and harvest, and even seances are occasionally practiced.

SUBIYA (Subia) An ethnic group living between the Chope and Zambezi Rivers in Zambia and in the Caprivi Strip of Namibia. In Zambia they number 23,000. Some speak the language of the TONGA, but most speak Lozi as a result of extensive contact with the LOZI.

SUBU An ethnic group living in Cameroon.

SUDANESE The population of Sudan, numbering 25 million, is divided ethnically and culturally between north and south. The Arab language and culture and Islam are dominant in the north, while the south is inhabited by Nilotic peoples and is divided between Christians and adherents of traditional religions.

The ARABS of the north, who are the largest people in Sudan and make up over half the population, are divided into several groups including the JA'ALIYIN, GUHANA, and KAWAHLA, but all of these groups share the same culture and all are Muslims.

The main ethnic groups living in the south of the country are the DINKA, who form 12 percent of the population, the NUER (6 percent), SHILLUK, and AZANDE (5 percent of the population), who absorbed other smaller ethnic groups over the years. They are Christians who also retain practices associated with their traditional religions. The NUER, speakers of a Nilotic language, live in the lowland of Gambela on the Ethiopian border. They are semi-nomadic cattle-raisers. During the late 1980s the Ethiopian NUER were strongly affected by Dinka-Nuer frictions, by the influx of SUDANESE as refugees, and by resettlement schemes for AMHARA and TIGRAY within Ethiopia.

There are also non-Arab ethnic groups who live in the north but underwent a process of arabization and islamization, one of which is the BEJA (5 percent of the population). Another group is the KAKWA, who also inhabit two enclaves in northwestern Uganda. They were a segmentary society speaking an Eastern Nilotic language, whose nationalist awareness grew when one of their members, Idi Amin, became dictator of Uganda during the 1970s. The MABAN, a group of Nilotic-speakers, mainly live in the northeast of the Upper Nile province of Sudan, as well as in the western Wallagga and Ilubabor Provinces, Ethiopia. They are sedentary agriculturalists. Their home area has also been affected by the civil wars in both Sudan and Ethiopia.

The religious difference, combined with the ethnic separateness and the extreme remoteness of the south from the center of the state in the Arab Muslim north, are all expressed in the economic backwardness and political separatism characterizing the south of Sudan in the last decades of the twentieth century.

Since the late nineteenth century Sudan was nominally an Anglo-Egyptian territory, but the British character of the regime became evident when in 1924 all EGYPTIANS were evacuated from Sudan. The BRITISH ruled the Sudanese indirectly through sheiks and chiefs. As a result, tribalism, which had been greatly weakened in the late nineteenth century, was revived and encouraged.

Sudan became independent in 1956. Since then Sudanese political life has been very unstable. Civilian parlimentary governments were often replaced by military regimes. The governments under all these regimes faced two major problems: Sudan's economic dependence on one cash crop, cotton; and the ongoing rebellion in the south. The war between the south and the north had started even before independence, as a result of the political frustrations of the southern population. The Sudanese, mainly those living in the south, have suffered greatly in recent years from the civil war and natural disasters. It is estimated that hundreds of thousands have died of starvation since 1986. (see also TOPOSA)

SUGALI A people, numbering over 1 million (1981), living in the state of Andhra Pradesh, India. They speak their own language, which is similar to Gujarati.

Many Sugali are roving traders; others settled in suitable pasture lands to raise the cattle that serve as pack-animals. In the Kurnool and Anantapur Districts, these people live as a pastoral group, rearing the cattle of the plains people for remuneration. Some have resorted to agriculture and many are laborers.

SUISSES see SWISS.

SUKU An ethnic group living in Angola. (see also YAKA)

SUKUMA (Usukuma) The largest ethnic group of Tanzania, constituting about 13 percent of the total population of the country. They number some 3 million. The heart of their historical territory is south of Lake Victoria, and also covers a small part of southeast Uganda. The ethnic denomination "Sukuma" (which

Sugali

means "people of the north") includes a great number of ethnic subgroups, of common as well as of heterogeneous origin, who have only recently acquired their common ethnic consciousness. The Sukuma language belongs to the West Tanzanian cluster of the Bantu Niger-Kordofan family of languages. They are predominantly Muslims, but their cultural traditions include several mystical elements of other indigenous cults.

Most Sukuma practice a mixed form of agriculture. For some, life centers around the growing of cereal crops and tobacco in changing locations, with a high concentration of labor during the planting and harvesting seasons. The Sukuma region is also the major source of cotton, a prominent Tanzanian export. Cattle are an important part of Sukuma agriculture and are rarely integrated with crop farming. Some cattle farms possess over 2,000 head of cattle. Sukumaland, with its urban centers of industrial and commercial activity, as well as gold and diamond mining, has become a major wealth-producing area of Tanzania.

The traditional village organization of the Sukuma was highly developed. Settlements were ruled by chiefs in conjunction with councils of elders and there were several dozen chiefdoms. The distribution of land and assignment of labor were in the hands of village age-group organizations. Sukuma settlements are dispersed, but each has a fixed natural boundary. The houses are of the cone-on-cylinder type or are in the "long-house" shape. The roof space is used for storage. (see also TANZANIANS)

SULABA (Sulayb) see SAUDI ARABS.

SULAIMAN A subgroup of the PASHTUN.

SULH see LEBANESE.

SULOD (Mundo, Putian) A proto-Malay mountain group, numbering about 25,000, who inhabit the banks of the Panay River between Mounts Siya and Baloy in central Panay, an island in the Philippines. The lowlanders refer to them as *bukidnon*, or mountain-dwellers. They speak dialects similar to lowland Kiniraya.

The Sulod live in small semi-permanent, autonomous settlements, situated primarily, on high ridges along riverbeds, and generally consisting of five to seven scattered bamboo houses raised on stilts. They practice slash and burn agriculture, growing rice, maize, and sweet potatoes. With no work animals or large farming implements, they move every two years or so.

Religion is an important part of Sulod life. No important decision is undertaken without consulting the community's spirits and deities.

SULUK, SULUS see TAUSUG.

SUMAU see GARIA.

SUMBANESE Inhabitants of the eastern half of the Indonesian island of Sumba, numbering approximately 100,000. Traditionally divided into as many as fifty oft-warring mini-states, they share a common language, culture, and religious beliefs. An oral tradition, *li ndai*, recounts the belief in a common ancestor. The traditional religion focuses on the cult of the dead. In recent years, practices such as headhunting, human sacrifice, and ritual cannibalism have been abandoned.

Rice and corn are cultivated using slash and burn methods, and horses and cattle are raised. These animals are often traded for ornamental goods.

SUMBAWANESE (s.d. Tau Semawa) The predominant ethnic group living of the western half of the island of Sumbawa, Indonesia. They number about 500,000, and are virtually all Muslims. Rice cultivation in the primary economic activity.

Descendants of the aristocracy of the former Sultanate of Sumbawa have been incorporated into the civil service of modern Indonesia.

SUMBURU   An ethnic group living in northeast Kenya. They have intermarried extensively with the RENDILLE.

SUMO   A South American Indian group of the Mosquito Coast of Nicaragua. They used to depend primarily on hunting and fishing, but now cultivate plantains and bitter manioc and raise cash crops for trade. Most modern Sumo villages have a practicing shaman to cure illness and placate the numerous malevolent nature spirits in which this people believe.

SUNDANESE   (Orang Prijangan) A people numbering 19 million living in the western half of the Indonesian island of Java. Most speak Sundanese, although a minority, living in northwestern Java, also uses a Javanese dialect called Banten-Javanese. Sundanese is closely related to Malay. It is sometimes believed to have had an indigenous script which was replaced by both the Javanese and Arabic script in ancient times and of which no examples remain. Modern Sundanese literature only emerged in the 1920s.

The Sundanese are Muslims, but the peasantry still adheres to a local rice goddess and various natural spirits. Hindu and Buddhist influence is less marked than among the JAVANESE. Unlike the JAVANESE, the Sundanese strictly adhere to the Muslim prohibition against the consumption of alcohol.

Much of what is known about Sundanese history is conjectured from legends. There were apparently several kingdoms, and one leader, Siliwangi, stands out because of the abundant myths describing his exploits.

The colonial administration of the DUTCH was particularly unpopular among the Sundanese for their imposition of coffee cultivation (the Sundanese traditionally grow irrigated and slash and burn varieties of rice). Opposition to Dutch rule climaxed in the late nineteenth century in a peasant uprising led by Muslim clerics in Banten.

SUNDI I   (Mayanga) An ethnic group, related to the KONGO, living in Congo.

SUNDI II   (Saundika) An ethnic group, numbering about 80,000, living in central India. They are Hindus

Sundanese

who engage primarily in brewing alcoholic beverages, which they sell to neighboring groups.

SUNWAR   An ethnic group, numbering 200,000, living in Janakpur and Sagarmatha, Nepal. They are Hindus.

The Sunwar live in one-storey houses built of stone and mud. Their main occupation is agriculture: they grow rice, wheat, and barley in the river valleys, and maize and millet on the hill slopes. They also serve with the armed forces in India and Nepal. (see also GURKHA)

SUOMALAISET   see FINNS.

SUPAI   see HAVASUPAI.

SURI   An ethnic group, numbering 10,000, who live north and south of the Akkobo River in southwestern Kefa Province of Ethiopia. They speak a Nilotic language, and share the characteristics of speakers of Surma. They adhere to traditional beliefs. (see also ETHIOPIANS)

SURINAMESE   A people inhabiting Suriname (formerly Dutch Guiana) on the northeastern coast of South America. The population numbers 450,000, over one third of whom are East Indians (Hindustanis), another third Creoles (Africans and people of mixed African-European heritage), just under a sixth JAVANESE, a tenth are descendants of escaped African slaves, and the remainder South American Indians,

CHINESE, LEBANESE, JEWS, NETHERLANDS ANTILLEANS, North Americans, and PORTUGUESE. The major contact among the various ethnic groups, 80 percent of which live in and around Paramaribo, the capital city, is economic, government policy being the maintenance of traditional cultural values.

While the official language is Dutch, Creole languages, Sarnami (derived from Hindi and Urdu), and Javanese are widely spoken by the people.

Two-thirds of the Surinamese are Christians, divided evenly between Protestants and Catholics, with the remainder Confucian, Hindu, Jewish, or Muslim, and, in interior areas, devotees of South American Indian or African religions.

Only one half of one percent of the land is arable; of this, half is planted with rice. Suriname's small fishing industry exports shrimp to North America: the United States and the Netherlands are Suriname's major traditional partners.

Although what is now Suriname was sighted by Columbus in 1498, the Native South American Indians repelled successive colonization attempts by waves of SPANIARDS, DUTCH, BRITISH, and FRENCH until British planters and their slaves from Barbados established the first European settlement in 1651. Suriname, extensively settled by Dutch sugar-, coffee-, cotton-, and co-coa-planters driven out of Brazil, passed into Dutch hands in 1610 and remained primarily a plantation economy. Slaves were in the majority during the early part of this period: of the white minority, a third were JEWS and the remainder FRENCH, GERMANS, and BRITISH. After emancipation, CHINESE were brought in as contract laborers, followed by East Indians and JAVANESE between 1873 and 1939. Mining, first of bauxite and aluminium, supplanted planting in importance early in the twentieth century.

The Surinamese, who achieved internal autonomy in 1954, were soon beset by interethnic strife between East Indians and Creoles. European, American, and Dutch aid was suspended in 1983, three years after military seizure of power, in the wake of the execution of civilians. In 1986 military forces confronting the Surinamese Liberation Army raided Bush Negro villages in the interior, killing many people and driving thousands into exile in French Guiana: the increasingly unpopular military government was defeated in elections a year later.

SURMA An ethnic group numbering 60,000, who live south of the Maji River and the lower Omo River valleys in southern Kefa Province of Ethiopia.

They speak Surma, a Nilotic language, and adhere to traditional beliefs. They are related to the Surma-speaking MEKAN and ME'EN ethnic groups living in the region.

The Surma practice intensive cultivation of grain, nomadic cattle-raising, and occasional hunting. (see also ETHIOPIANS)

SURRIYYUN see SYRIANS.

SURUI A South American Indian group living in the State of Mato Grosso, central-west Brazil. They number a few hundreds and speak the language of the neighboring GAVIAO. (see also GAVIAO)

SUSU (Soussou) An ethnic group living on the coast of Guinea, where they number around 815,000 and constitute 16 percent of the population, and in smaller numbers in Sierra Leone, in the Kambia, Port Loko, and Koinadugu Districts. The Susu languge is now the lingua franca of most of the peoples living in Lower Guinea. The Susu are mostly Muslims and their main occupations are agriculture and trade. Their culture has influenced that of other ethnic groups, especially in Guinea. The Susu who migrated to Sierra Leone have intermingled with the FULANI and other ethnic groups. (see also SIERRA LEONEANS)

SUYA A South American Indian group living in one village in the Upper Xingu area, between the States of Mato Grosso and Pará, central-north Brazil. Their language belongs to the Ge language family. In the past

Suya

they were known for their numerical size, but having lost a high number of their people as the result of a strong "pacification" policy, they number fewer than 100. Wooden lip disks mark the married men. (see also TRUMAI)

SVAN (s.d. Shwan) An ethnic group living in Georgia, on the southern slopes of the main Caucasian range, in the upper basin of the Tskhenis-Tskali and Inguri Rivers. No population data are available, but a rough estimate puts them as numbering 60,000-80,000.

The Svan language, Lushnunin, belongs to the Ibero-Caucasian family. It consists of four dialects (Upper and Lower Bal, Lashkh, and Lentekh). Attempts at using it as a written language, undertaken in the 1920s and early 1930s were soon abandoned. Georgian is now used as the language of education and writing.

The Svan have been Eastern Orthodox Christians since the sixth century. They are mainly a rural population, chiefly occupied in livestock-raising. Until the 1930s, they were regarded as a separate ethnic group in the Soviet Union. Since then they have been considered and, consider themselves part of the GEORGIANS. (see also GEORGIANS)

SVIZZERI see SWISS.

SVOBODNIKI see CANADIANS.

SWAKA A Chibemba-speaking group living in eastern Zambia, where they constitute 1 percent of that country's population. They are an offshoot of the LALA.

SWAZI (KaNgwane) A people that is part of the NGUNI in southern Africa, numbering around 2.3 million. Around 850,000 live in the kingdom of Swaziland, some 1.3 million in South Africa, and the remainder in southern Mozambique. The Swazi have two states of their own: the kingdom of Swaziland, and the self-governing state of KaNgwane in the eastern Transvaal in South Africa. Swaziland, which became independent in 1968, is a land-locked country, bounded in the north, west, and south by South Africa, and in the east by Mozambique.

The Swazi are predominantly a Christian people. In South Africa, around 80 percent have specific church affiliations. More than half the Swazi Christians in South Africa belong to African Independent Churches, and the largest minority are Roman Catholics. In Swaziland, around 70 percent of the Swazi population are Christians; the remainder follow traditional African religions where communication with ancestors is important. In Swaziland the Swazi king is ritual head of state; as head of the most senior lineage of the most senior clan, he consults with the ancestors of the nation. The Swazi practice general Nguni customs; however, Swazi society is formally hierachical to a greater extent than that of other NGUNI peoples.

The Swazi people trace their ancestry to a small group of the Embo-Nguni, led by the dominant clan of the DAMINI, who lived in the area of Delagoa Bay in the sixteenth century. The DAMINI are still dominant in Swaziland. When the proto-Swazi split from the Embo nucleus in the eighteenth century and moved into the area of present-day Swaziland, they were led by King Ngwane III, who gave this people one of their names: the KaNgwane. The Swazi emerged as a coherent and homogeneous nation in the nineteenth century under Kings Sobhuza I and Mswati II; their name derives from the latter king. His death in 1868 ended both the era of Swazi territorial expansion and the process of assimilation of various local NGUNI and SOTHO groups into the Swazi people.

Swazi political history has been dominated by two issues, both focusing on the usurpation of the land. The first was the late nineteenth-century struggle to prevent the incorporation of large parts of the historical Swazi kingdom into the Afrikaner (Boer) republic of South Africa, the second to maintain the separate status of the remaining parts of Swaziland. Failing in their bid for the first, the Swazi achieved a preliminary victory for the second through the 1881 Convention of Pretoria, agreed between the BRITISH and the Boers, which delineated the present boundary between South Africa and Swaziland. The Swaziland Convention of 1894, however, made Swaziland a Protectorate of the Transvaal and it was only in 1902, after the Anglo-Boer War, that Swaziland became a British colony. Swaziland's separate status nevertheless remained tenuous until the late 1940s when a newly installed British Colonial Office was willing to guarantee that Swaziland would not be incorporated into the Union of South Africa.

The second issue was concerned with the loss of land within the boundaries of present-day Swaziland. In his struggle to regain for the Swazi the more than two-thirds of the present country which had been given to white farmers and the British crown, King Sobhuza II (1921–1982) appealed repeatedly to the British government. In the 1940s Britain ceded a large part of Crown lands to the Swazi and allocated funds for the repurchase of other Swazi lands from South African and Euroopean interests. By the early 1980s two-thirds of the land of Swaziland was in Swazi hands, realienation having been made criminal by the Land Speculation Control Act of 1972.

In April 1973 the constitution was changed from a Westminster-type system to a traditional one in which the king has unlimited power. The king functions as executive, legislative, and judicial head, and succession is governed by Swazi law and custom. In 1986 King Mswati III was crowned.

The present Swazi political system is characterized by tensions between modernists and traditionalists which erupted during the 1970s in labor actions and violence. These were suppressed in autocratic fashion, sometimes violently. Both traditionalists and modernists are also to be found within the traditional aristocracy. (see also NGUNI, SOUTH AFRICANS)

SWEDES The 8.5 million inhabitants of Sweden, one of Europe's largest countries, are Europe's most homogeneous people. They are overwhelmingly Swedish, with weak Finnish, Lapp, and German influences. The Swedish language belongs to the Scandinavian branch of Germanic languages. The Norrland dialect is considered the most archaic. Formally, most Swedes are Lutheran Protestants, though some pre-Christian practices survive in folklore.

Swedish communities are also found in Finland. Already in the first millennium, Swedish migrants settled on the Aland Islands which control the Gulf of Bothnia, and from there reached the Finnish west coast (Osterbotten); subsequently Swedish sailors, peasants, and fur traders colonized Finland's south. From the thirteenth to the eighteenth century Sweden ruled supreme over the FINNS. A substantial Swedish population of approximately 450,000 still lives along the Finnish coast. Its number is in decline due to emigration and intermarriage. Swedish is an official language in Finland.

The Swedes participated in Viking expeditions; in the ninth century, Viking traders (*vareges*) established merchant colonies in Letland, then sailed down Russian rivers to trade furs and slaves with the Byzantines and ARABS, creating settlements in the process. However, they soon assimilated into the Slavs.

The Swedes resisted exchanging their Germanic deities in favor of Christianity until the thirteenth century, when a medieval Christian civilization evolved. However, the 1397 Union of Kalmar, superficially uniting Sweden with Norway and Denmark under Danish hegemony, provoked revolts of peasants and miners. Cooperation with Denmark became impossible after the 1523 "Stockholm bloodbath" massacre of the Swedish leadership. The Swedes regained their independence (save for the southernmost province, Scania) and soon embarked on a program of expansion. Under the Vasa dynasty, Sweden became a Lutheran monarchy; free peasants were its mainstay. From 1611 to 1721, the Golden Age of Sweden became a great power, leading wars against Poland and Denmark, and dominating the Baltic region. In the late seventeenth century the power of metallurgy and armaments manufacturers increased, Sweden's economy grew and Scania was incorporated back into Sweden. However, this extensive territory, gained within a brief period of time, was lost just as quickly. A disastrous Nordic War against Poland, Russia, and Denmark ended Sweden's great power status. Defeat in the Napoleonic Wars led to the loss of Finland in 1808 (Sweden was compensated by the addition of Norway, a union that lasted until 1905) and marked the last occasion in which Sweden participated in an armed conflict.

The nineteenth century was the heyday of Swedish liberalism; a constitutional monarchy was established. Swedes saw neutralism as a guarantor of their prosperity. But agricultural expansion and, after 1870, industrialization could not keep up with population pressure: one million Swedes migrated to North America.

From the 1930s social-democrats built a welfare state based on agricultural cooperatives, high salaries, social contracts, and extensive social security. This has led to the highest living standard in the world, paid for by the world's highest taxes, and, lately, unbalanced budgets. The 1970s–1980s crisis has affected the "Swedish model": industrial decline, coupled with the growth of public consumption (which finances educational expenses and social employment policies), deficits, growing inflation, and an unfavorable balance of trade have resulted in a conservative backlash. In 1990 the Swedes took their first steps away from the welfare state and towards a freer market. (see also FINNS)

SWINOMISG A Native North American group, numbering 800, living on the Federal Swinomisg Indian Tribal Community near Burlington, Washington, U.S.A.

SWISS (s.d. Schweizer, Suisses, Svizzeri) The 6.7 million Swiss are divided among German- (70 percent), French- (20 percent), and Italian-speakers (c.4 percent). Rheto-Romanche speakers (1 percent) are restricted to the Graubunden (Grisons-Grigioni) canton. The Swiss are about evenly divided between Catholics and Protestants. They constitute a very dense and highly urbanized population.

The current Swiss population may be traced back to the Helveti and Rhaeti, of the fifth century B.C.E. Celtic tribes. Burgunds and Alemans pushed the original population to remote valleys, where they partially adopted a Germanic language. Aleman tribes settled in Mittelland and in the Prealps; Latin dialects retrenched themselves deeper in the Alps. Other Germanic-speaking elements came under French and Italian influence: Christian Burgund auxiliaries, settled in the Rhone-Saone zone and adopted the Roman language. Thus the language frontier became more or less fixed.

When transalpine traffic began to increase again after the Crusades, German emperors in search of power over Italy attempted to subdue the Alpine forester and pastoralist communities who controlled the vital passes. To defend their liberties, a revolt against the Habsburg overlords broke out. The alliance of three cantons, Uri, Schwyz (which gave its name to the confederation), and Nidwald (Unterwald) in 1291 became the core of the future confederation. The Swiss defeated the Austrians, and soon other cantons joined: Luzern (Lucerne), Zurich, Glarus (Glaris), Zug (Zoug), and Bern (Berne). The confederation became a center of particularism, expanding by adherence (Appenzell, Valais-Wallis, Geneva, Sion, Sankt Gallen-St-Gall, Neuchatel-Neuenburg, Basle, Shaffhausen-Schaffhouse, Soleure-Solothurn, Fribourg-Freiburg cantons) and conquest (Thurgau-Thurgovie, Vaud).

Located at the crossroads of northern and southern Europe, the Swiss reacted favorably to the Protestant Reformation, which added religious contrast to their ethnic/linguistic contrasts. Jean Calvin even established a Protestant theocracy in sixteenth-century Geneva. Swiss unity survived the wars of religion; the 1648 Peace of Westphalia at the end of the Thirty Years' War formalized its independence and armed neutrality.

From the sixteenth century on, overpopulation stimulated emigration: mercenary soldiers became the main export. Their remittances were responsible for economic growth and prosperity throughout the seventeenth and eighteenth centuries, along with banking, and industrialization. This was the aristocratic-oligarchic era: cantons were ruled by paternalist patrician elites. Geneva became one of the intellectual capitals of the Enlightenment. Meanwhile social tensions caused by oppression of the peasants exploded in re-

volts. Revolutionary currents influenced by the French Revolution led to a brief French occupation and democracy, until Napoleon restored the Confederation. By the mid-nineteenth century, power passed to the liberal bourgeoisie, and Switzerland turned into a liberal democracy.

Thanks to a second industrial revolution based on hydro-electricity, tunnels, watchmaking, and tourism, the later nineteenth century was an era of prosperity and stability for the Swiss; this has continued throughout the twentieth century. Since 1864, when the Red Cross established its headquarters in Switzerland, the country has become famous as a location for international organizations, and a refuge for the politically and religiously proscribed, as well as for capital fleeing the taxman. Switzerland remained neutral in both world wars and ever since. Lately its isolationism has become an obstacle to its integration in Europe.

The Swiss example represents an unusual achievement on three levels: first, they are made up entirely of heterogeneous and unconnected linguistic and religious minorities, yet judicious powersharing has permitted coexistence without major disruptions in one state. In spite of a certain rivalry between its multiplicity of subcommunities, federal government is carefully shared by representatives of various religions, tongues, and cantons. Direct participatory democracy, referenda, and other instruments maintain the citizens' influence on the polity. Secondly, thanks to a tradition of studious neutrality, they have managed to stay out of all international conflicts over the past five hundred years (with one exception); still, the Swiss feel besieged and threatened. All adult males serve in the citizen reserves' army. Lastly, devoid of natural resources, the Swiss economy sustains one of the world's highest living standards, based on advanced industry and services. The Swiss nowadays share their land with numerous foreign workers (some 1 million foreigners forming a quarter of Switzerland's labor force): mainly ITALIANS and SPANIARDS who, even if born in Switzerland, cannot become citizens.

SYRIANS (s.d. Suriyyun) Eighty-eight percent of the 12 million Syrians are ARABS speaking a distinct Syrian-Arabic dialect. The country's 700,000 to 1 million (6–8 percent) KURDS are mostly refugees from Turkey living mainly in the northeast (the Jazirah) and in Damascus; smaller, unrelated Kurdish groups, the Kurd Dagh, dwell in the hills northwest of Aleppo, and are largely arabized. Discrimination in the 1960s led many KURDS to migrate to Damascus or Lebanon. Another substantial minority is the 300,000 ARMENIANS, mainly craftsmen in Aleppo and Damascus. Smaller minorities include 110,000 mainly Sunni Turkmen nomads in the Jazirah and 50,000 Circassians (see CHERKESS) originally settled mainly in the southwest. Syria also harbors 210,000-250,000 PALESTINIANS, refugees from the 1948 war with Israel.

Including the Kurds, 70 percent of the Syrians are Sunni Muslims, and 12 percent (1 million) are Alawite Muslims, once the poorest farmers, found mostly in northwestern Syria (Jabal al-Nusayriyah), where they form two-thirds of the population. A split from Isma'ili Islam, Alawites consider Ali, the fourth caliph, as incarnation of God. Their rituals include pre-Christian pagan and Sabean elements and are conducted near shrines and sacred groves, but their doctrines are kept esoteric. After long having been persecuted by Syria's orthodox Sunni rulers, they were employed by the FRENCH in the army and given partial autonomy. The secularism of the Ba'ath (Arab Renaissance) party attracted many Alawites, and they have dominated Syria politically ever since Salah Jadid took power (1966). The 150,000 Isma'ilis, concentrated in the Hama region, are Shi'ite Muslims.

Approximately 15 percent of the population are Christians, who live mostly in cities in western Syria. The largest Christian denominations are the Greek Orthodox, with Arabic as their liturgical language, and the Syrian Orthodox (Jacobite) Church, which is monophysite and uses Syriac; Greek Catholics (Melkites), Syrian Catholics, Maronites, Roman Catholics, and Protestants form smaller churches. A small community of Nestorian ASSYRIANS settled in East Syria in the 1930s. The 300,000 DRUZE (3.5 percent) live mainly in the Jabal al-Druze region.

Many Syrians probably descend from pre-Arab civilizations which occupied the western portion of the Fertile Crescent, such as Ugarit, Mari, the Aramaeans (who spoke a North Semitic language related to Hebrew), and others. In 636 Christian Byzantine Syria, weakened by Byzantine-Sasanid wars, fell prey to the ARABS and shortly afterwards became the center of the first, Umayyad dynasty. Arabic supplanted Aramaic

and most Syrians embraced Islam. From 1516 to 1918 it was part of the Ottoman Empire. At the beginning of the twentieth century, nationalism in Syria, organized in secret associations, was pan-Arab as well as Greater Syrian. Syria as a modern state was created by the FRENCH, who ruled the country under a League of Nations mandate (1920–1946) and delineated its current borders. The FRENCH, first detaching Syria from Lebanon, then gave autonomy status to Druze and Alawite areas and ceded the Iskenderun (Alexandretta) region to Turkey in 1939. Iskenderun is still claimed by the Syrians.

After independence in 1946, parliamentarism failed, and coup followed coup. Syria's recent political history is one of the progressive narrowing of the social base of its regime, which correspondingly increases the need for harsher repression. The upshot of this prolonged crisis was a strengthening of an anti-liberal, state socialist, military-based regime. Political stability was only imposed after 1970 by the authoritarian military regime of Hafiz Assad who concentrated power in his hands and has meanwhile grown into one of the Middle East's longest surviving rulers.

In 1976 Syria first opposed Maronite hegemony in Lebanon, then invaded it in an attempt to forestall the victory of a leftist-Palestinian block. The Syrian economy suffered from the military occupation of Lebanon, and an arms race which absorbed a large portion of the budget. Discontent in the late 1970s fed support for the Muslim Brothhood among the Sunni middle class in Aleppo, Homs, and Hama. Assad responded to the challenge with unprecedented brutality, razing parts of Hama in 1982 and massacring thousands.

For years, Syria dug itself into the role of spoiler of the Israeli-Arab peace process, striving to impel Israel to return to Syria the Golan, lost in the Six Day War in 1967. The collapse of Soviet military aid and the 1991 Gulf crisis combined to give Syrians the opportunity to mend fences with the West, to consolidate their hold over Lebanon, and to join the Arab-Israeli peace process.

SZEKELY   see HUNGARIANS.

T

TAAISHA   A subgroup of the BAGGARA living in the Darfur Province of Sudan.

TA-ANG   See PALAUNG.

TABAHOI   A subgroup of the DAYAK living on the Indonesian island of Kalimantan (Borneo).

TABASARANS   An ethnic group living in southeastern Daghestan, Russia. They number some 99,000.

The Tabasaran language belongs to the Daghestani branch of the Ibero-Caucasian family. The literary language is based on its southern dialect; from 1932 the alphabet was Roman-based; in 1938 the Cyrillic alphabet was adopted.

The Tabasarans have been Sunni Muslims of the Shafi'i school since the fourteenth and fifteenth centuries. Prior to annexation by the RUSSIANS in 1820, the Tabasarani ethnic territory, which had existed since the fifteenth century, was divided into two separate principalities.

Their villages are located on steep slopes and consist of several sets of living quarters, usually inhabited by

Tabasarans

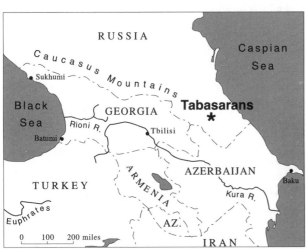

families belonging to the same *tukhum* (loose nexus of families claiming common origin).

The Tabasarans adhere to the traditional dress common in Daghestan. Their economy is based on agriculture, horticulture, sheep-breeding, and carpet-making.

TABUYAN   A subgroup of the DAYAK living on the Indonesian island of Kalimantan (Borneo).

TABWA   A Chibemba-speaking group numbering about 50,000, living on both sides of the Zambia-Zaire border. Some are Christians, while others adhere to traditional religions; their culture, religion, and social organization resemble those of the BEMBA. They first settled in Zambia, between Lake Mweru and Lake Tanganyika, in the late eighteenth century.

TADMAKKA   A confederation of Berber groups living in the central Sahara Desert in North Africa. This tribal confederation was established during the sixteenth century in the region of Ad-Fafrikanerrar (in what is now west-central Algeria) with the fall of the Songhai Empire. They are Muslims and speak the Berber language.

In the mid-seventeenth century the Tadmakka left Adrar and settled south of the Niger River bend. In the beginning of the eighteenth century they were the dominant power around the town of Timbuktu (in present day Mali). During the 1750s, however, the Tadmakka were weakened by internal quarrels.

TADVI BHIL see DHANKA.

TADYAWAN   A Malayo-Polynesian group, numbering a few thousand, who live in the mountainous northern interior of Mindoro, an island in the Philippines. They speak the Mangyan language, as do their neighbors the HANUNOO.

Tadyawan, Tagakaolo, and Tagbunawa

TAGAKAOLO (Kalagan) An ethnic group, numbering several thousand, who live between the western coast of the Gulf of Davao and the interior uplands of Mindanao, an island in the Philippines. Their language belongs to the Central Philippines group of languages. They are slash and burn agriculturalists, who have made corn their staple crop. Their hamlets generally contain eight to ten households. Some have converted to Islam, while most still maintain traditional beliefs.

TAGBANUWA An ethnic group, numbering 25,000, living in eastern Palawan, an island of the Philippines. Their language belongs to the Malayo-Polynesian family. They use an ancient syllabic script of Indian origin.

The Tagbanuwa live in small, compact villages of up to 500 persons. They are slash and burn cultivators of dry rice, hunters and gatherers. The nuclear family is of utmost importance.

TAGISH A Native North American group, numbering 700, living in the Yukon Territory, Canada. They are related to the TLINGIT.

TAGOUANA An ethnic group related to the LOBI living in the Cote d'Ivoire.

TAHIRI One of five groups constituting the AIMAQ-I DIGAR.

TAHITIANS The indigenous inhabitants of the island of Tahiti, part of the French department of French Polynesia, in the southeastern Pacific Ocean. An influx of Polynesian peoples from neighboring islands has made it impossible to distinguish between native Tahitians and these new imigrants. The estimated Polynesian population of Tahiti is about 12,000. They speak Tahitian (an eastern Polynesian language) and are Christians. Tahitians apparently arrived from the Marquesas Islands in the latter half of the first millenium C.E.

The most important cultural influence upon the islanders was the arrival of Europeans in 1767. By 1812 Ponare II, the island's leading chief, had adopted Christianity, and used missionaries to crush opposition to his reign. Both he and his successors encouraged American and European whalers and sealers to use the island as a stopover and trading point. In 1842 Queen Pomare allowed the french to annex the island, thereby ending the rule of the native dynasty.

In 1880 Tahiti became a French colony. In 1945 Tahitians were declared citizens of France. During the era of decolonization they chose to remain French nationals, although recently an independence movement has emerged.

Most Tahitians engage in agriculture, but others can be found in services and in the tourism industry. (see also PITCAIRN ISLANDERS)

TAHLTAN A Native North American group, numbering 1,100, living in northern British Columbia, Canada. They are hunters and salmon fishers. Traditionally they were a trading group, moving between the coast and the inland areas of British Columbia.

TAI see KHAMPTI.

TAI KHE, TAI LU, TAI WU Subgroups of the SHAN.

TAIMANI One of the four AIMAQ clans.

TAIMURI (Timuri) One of five groups constituting the AIMAQ-I DIGAR.

TAINOS see CUBANS, DOMINICANS, PUERTO RICANS.

TAI OF VIETNAM (Black Tai, s.d. Tai Dam; White Tai, s.d. Tai Khao; Red Tai, s.d. Tai Deng; Tho) There are several Tai groups in North Vietnam and Laos. The Black, White, and Red Tai number an estimated total of 385,000, while the Tho number some 600,000, making them the largest non-Vietnamese ethnic group in northern Vietnam and Laos. The Black and White Tai are named for the color of their women's clothing; the Red Tai acquired their name from the Red River, along whose banks they live. *Tho* is a Vietnamese word for soil — it is used to refer to several Tai groups in northern Vietnam.

All Tai groups engage in rice cultivation, but opium is also grown and traded with the neighboring CHINESE and VIETNAMESE. The groups are divided into major families, some of which have specific taboos attached to them. One group is forbidden to eat certain plants or the meat of various birds; another is forbidden to use wood in home construction. Red Tai religion focuses on the belief that the heavens consist of a parallel world to this.

In the fifteenth and sixteenth centuries Vietnamese rulers overran the Tai regions and sent administrators to govern the area. These intermarried with the local population and their descendants, known as Tho-ti, are empowered to perform certain religious rituals and form an elite class among the Tai groups. They have adopted Buddhism from the VIETNAMESE.

On the withdrawal of the FRENCH from Vietnam, the Tai peoples of the north opposed the communist regime of Tonkin, later North Vietnam, and supported the FRENCH. France in turn organized an autonomous Tai Federation in 1948, many of whose leaders aspired for eventual independence from Vietnam. Viet Minh forces, however, were in desperate need of the strategic advantages afforded by the highlands and assaulted the Black Tai village of Diem Bien Phu. The ensuing French defeat led many Tai to shift allegiances to the Viet Minh in the hope of maintaining their semi-autonomous status under their auspices. This and inter-ethnic conflicts within the Tai Federation eventually led to its demise.

The Tai of northern Vietnam are part of a huge population of Tai-speakers in southwestern China, Laos, Thailand, and Myanmar (Burma). (see also DAI, LAO, THAI, SHAN, YISAN)

TAIOQ A subgroup of the KEL AHAGGAR.

TAI-ORA An ethnic group of approximately 15,000 living in the mountainous region of northern Papua New Guinea. They speak an indigenous regional language. They are slash and burn cultivators, as well as hunters, gatherers, and pig-raisers. Some have retained their traditional beliefs in supernatural entities; others have adopted Christianity.

TAITA An ethnic group, numbering an estimated 180,000, living around the Taita hills in the Taru Desert of southeastern Kenya. They speak Jagalla, a language belonging to the Coastal Bantu grouping. Some of the Taita are Muslims, although the majority is Christian. The Taita area was on the route from the coast to Mount Kilimanjaro and Lake Victoria; the many trading caravans and missionaries who used this route made their mark on Taita culture.

The Taita have always been agriculturalists. In the past they were the only group with an innovative irrigation system, enabling them to grow maize, cassava, millet, and sugar cane. Agriculture has influenced Taita social structure and a set of values, rites, ceremonies, and rituals has been created around it. Labor is almost equally divided between men and women. In addition, a cooperative system of land working, harvesting, and distributing has evolved. Taita produce is sold in the markets of the towns of Voi and Mombasa.

TAIWANESE A people, numbering about 20 million, who inhabit the island of Taiwan in the South China Sea. Only about 350,000 of the islanders are indigenous Taiwanese of Malayo-Polynesian origin. The vast majority are Han CHINESE and are relatively recent immigrants to the island. The Mandarin dialect of Chinese is the official language but most islanders speak the Hakka dialect. In other aspects they are similar to the CHINESE and consider themselves part of the CHINESE.

Taiwan is currently governed by Chinese mainlanders who opposed communism and fled to the island, where they formed the government of Nationalist China, which they claim to represent all of China — a claim not recognized by the mainland CHINESE. Officially there is a state of war between mainland China and Taiwan. At the same time, the Taiwanese economy has boomed; Taiwan now boasts one of the highest annual economic growth rates in the world. Many young Taiwanese have begun advocating a form of independence that would put an end to the current totalitarian government and establish Taiwan as an entity distinct from the Chinese mainland, thus ending the longstanding state of war between the two countries and bringing about foreign recognition of the island.

TAJIKS A people, numbering an estimated 8 million, living in Tajikistan, Uzbekistan, and Afghanistan. Of that number, 3.6 million live in Afghanistan, a considerable number of them being descendants of refugees from Soviet rule in Tajikistan in the 1920s and 1930s.

The Tajiks speak a number of Central Asian and Afghanistani dialects of Persian. The former have, since the 1920s, been called the Tajik language, and the latter, since the 1960s, have been known as Dari.

Tajiks

The literary form of Tajik, based on the Samarkand-Bukharan group of dialects, has been used since the 1920s as one of Tajikistan's three official languages (the other two are Russian and Uzbek); in 1989 it was proclaimed the state language. Until 1929 it used the Arabic alphabet; from then until 1938 the Roman alphabet was used, at which time it was replaced by the Cyrillic. The literary form of Dari, based primarily on the Kabul dialect, was in 1964 proclaimed one of Afghanistan's two official language, the other being Pashto. Dari utilizes the Arabic alphabet.

The Tajiks are Sunni Muslims of the Hanafi school. The majority live in rural areas; indeed, the percentage of urban population has been shrinking recently in Tajikistan. The Tajiks of the Central Asian flatlands are engaged mainly in cotton production, the cultivation of fruits and vegetables being an auxiliary, although not insignificant, branch of loca agriculture. In the mountains of Tajikistan and Afghanistan they engage mainly in both irrigated and unirrigated cultivation of cereals

(wheat, barley, and some local varieties of maize), and also in short-range herding of sheep, goats, and cattle. Little use is made of horses or donkeys, whether for riding or as beasts of burden.

The characteristic Tajik flatland village consists of several dozen flat-roofed adobe houses. Villages in mountainous areas contain fewer houses, of either adobe or of stone, with up to three storeys (the ground floor is reserved for livestock during the winter, the middle floor for dwelling, and the upper for storage).

Urban middle-class Tajiks, both men and women, have adopted a mainly European style of dress; those of lower status, like those in rural areas of Central Asia, wear a combination of traditional and semi-European clothing. Tajiks of Afghanistan adhere to the traditional style of dress.

In 1924 the Tajik Autonomous Soviet Socialist Republic was created within the framework of the Uzbek Soviet Socialist Republic. The latter included the cities of Bukhara and Samarkand, which contained large populations identified as Tajiks, as well as a flatland area with a considerable Tajik population. In effect, large numbers of Tajiks, whose main center was the town of Khujand, remained excluded from Tajik autonomy. In 1929, after heavy political bargaining, Tajikistan, now including the Khujand region, was elevated to the status of a Soviet Socialist Republic. During the decades of Soviet rule, a massive effort was made to rewrite Tajik ethnic and political history according to new ideological standards. Their emergence as a separate people was dated from the ninth-tenth centuries. The Central Asian Khorasian state of the Samanid dynasty (864–999) was thus seen as the first Tajik state. In the same way Tajik cultural history was created by retroactively adopting political and cultural heroes of the region.

Soviet rule introduced drastic educational, political, and economic changes, established new occupations, and paved the way for the emergence of a versatile, modern, indigenous intelligentsia. On the other hand, it brutally exterminated the pre-Soviet economic, political, and cultural elites, created sharp antagonism between Tajiks and UZBEKS, and aggravated the tension between the northern (flatland) Tajiks and those of the mountainous south. The latter claim that the former exercise political and cultural domination.

In the late 1980s new political-cultural trends came to the fore. One of these, associated with groups of the intelligentsia, emphasized the need to revise Tajik history during the Soviet period, focusing on the plight of Tajiks in neighboring Uzbekistan, who were losing their ethnic identity and being reclassified as UZBEKS. The movement advocated changes in the Tajik language, bringing it closer to Iranian Farsi and Afghan Dari. The other trend, supported mostly by southerners, favored a return to traditional aspects of Tajik identity, including Islamic values and the virtues of rural society, as opposed to the vices of modern secular life. A third trend, supported by the former political elite, centers upon a somewhat revised view of Tajik identity as it emerged in the former Soviet Union.

The proclamation of independence in September 1991 did not eradicate the deep cleavages between these groups. The breakup of the Soviet Union accelerated the eruption of civil war which has resulted (up to 1993) in the loss of 50,000–80,000 lives. The Afghan Tajiks actively participated in resisting the 1979 Soviet invasion and were one of the main forces which led to the fall of that government in 1992. (see also AFGHANS, FARSIVANS, SARIQOLI, UZBEKS, WAKHI)

TAKOGAN   see BILAAN.

TALAING   see MON.

TALAMANCA   A Native American group living in Costa Rica. (see also COSTA RICANS)

TALANG   A subgroup of the KUBU living on the Indonesian island of Sumatera (Sumatra).

TALAOEREZEN   see SANGIR.

TALENSI   (Talene) An ethnic group of the MOLE-DAGBANI, living in the upper East Region of Ghana. Their language is Talene. (see also MOLE-DAGBANI)

TALLION   see BELLA COOLA.

TALYSH   (Talesh; s.d. Talush) An ethnic group living in the Talysh Mountains in northern Iran and Azerbaijan. They were first mentioned in the thirteenth century. Their estimated number in Iran (late 1970s) was 283,000; the Soviet census of 1989 put them as numbering 22,000. However, their real number in Azerbaijan is probably higher. In the 1930s all Talysh were registered as AZERBAIJANI, and various steps were taken to ensure their assimilation into this group.

The Talysh language belongs to the Northwest subgroup of the Iranian group of the Indo-European fam-

Talysh

ily. Attempts made in the Soviet Union in the 1930s to reduce it to a written language using the Roman alphabet were abandoned. At the end of the 1980s modest attempts were made to revive Talysh as a written language using the Cyrillic alphabet, but it is now practically unwritten. Persian in Iran and Azerbaijani in Azerbaijan serve as the languages of education and literature. There are some differences between the Talysh spoken in Iran and that spoken in Azerbaijan.

The Talysh are Shi'ite Muslims. In Iran they are predominantly agriculturalists, with tea and tobacco serving as cash crops, and cattle-breeders; in Azerbaijan they cultivate citrus and rice and breed cattle.

TAMA   see MAJANGIR.

TAMAN   A subgroup of the DAYAK living on the Indonesian island of Kalimantan (Borneo).

TAMANG   An ethnic group, numbering 550,000 (1985), living in the districts of Nuwakot, Phedigram, and Makwanpur in northern Nepal.

Tamang houses are constructed of unbaked brick. They are primarily agriculturalists, growing maize (their staple food), rice, and potatoes. They also engage in animal husbandry. The sale of potatoes forms the bulk of their income. They are Buddhists. (see also GURKHA, NYINBA)

TAMBARO   (Timbaro) An ethnic group, numbering 50,000 (1980s), who live east of the Gibbi River in the

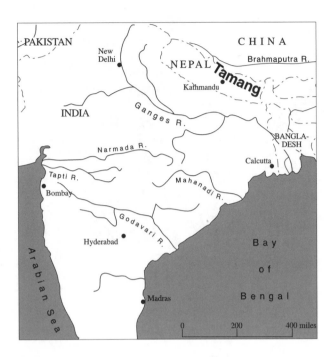

Tamang

southern Shoa Province, Ethiopia. They speak an Eastern Cushitic language and are Sunni Muslims. The Tambaro are agriculturalists and cattle-raisers. Culturally and linguistically they are related to the HADIYA.

TAMBERNA   see SOMBA.

TAMBO   A Mambwe-speaking group, numbering 15,000, living in northeastern Zambia. They were originally part of the BISA but separated from them in an easterly migration. They raise cattle.

TAMBOKI   A subgroup of the LAKI.

TAMILS   A people living in southern India and in northern Sri Lanka (Ceylon). All speak either Tamil or a dialect of Tamil, a language belonging to the Dravidian family.

The Tamil of India (Tamilar, Tamilian) live in what is traditionally referred to as Tamil Nadu (home), which now encompasses the Indian state by the same name, and in Pondicherry, located in the southeasternmost part of the Indian subcontinent. Close to 90 percent of the 60 million Tamil live in Tamil Nadu. The population originally centered around the area of Madras, now the capital of Tamil Nadu. From there they began to migrate into other areas of what is today India in the first century C.E. Even when conquered by

Telugu-speakers in the sixteenth century, they resisted assimilation into northern Indian culture. From 1801 until the eve of Indian independence the BRITISH ruled most of southern India; the FRENCH governed Pondicherry and Karikal.

While many Indian Tamil settlements are large, housing up to 10,000 persons, they retain the characteristics of smaller villages. Approximately 35 percent of the population lives in what can be termed an urban setting. Established quarters separate the higher castes from their lower counterparts. Houses are built of mud and thatch or of brick and tile. The infrastructure of most towns is underdeveloped, however; electricity is found only infrequently. Living on subsistence agriculture, most farmers grow wet rice and dry field crops such as rice, millet, sorghum, coconuts, bananas, mango, and tamarind. Large irrigation systems have been used for many centuries where there are reservoirs for growing rice. Domesticated animals are used to work the land. They are rarely used for food, as many Tamil are vegetarians. Coastal settlements rely heavily on fishing and often trade inland for various crops. While men and women divide the labor, many women are excluded from professional positions.

Extended nuclear families generally live together, but it is not unusual for a couple to live alone. Education is strongly emphasized, and literacy is as high as 60 percent. The caste system is slowly being replaced by an economic class system. The Tamil have a strong

Tamils

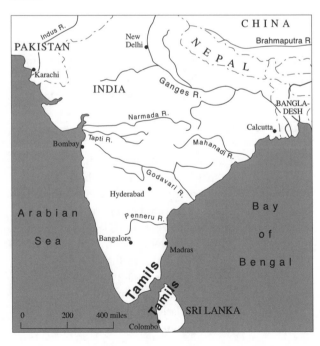

above: Tamils at a public gathering
below: Tamil farmers

sense of pride and often actively distinguish themselves from northern Indians. Hindi, the official language of India, is not compulsory in school; many students prefer pursuing English.

Hinduism is practiced by 90 percent of Indian Tamils; 5 percent are Christians and an equal number are Muslims. Ceremonies are held for deities representing various aspects of daily life such as health, fertility, and protection. Pongal, a Tamil communal rice celebration, is held annually with a special ceremony-honoring oxen. Tamil temples are characterized by soaring towers. Faith-healing, rather than conventional medicine, is common. The belief in reincarnation is uncommon except in instances of a child's death: the child is thought to be reborn into the same family. Many Tamils bury their dead rather than cremate them.

The 3.2 million Tamil of Sri Lanka (Tamilarkal, Tamilian) live in the northern and eastern regions of the island. They represent about 10 percent of Sri Lanka's population. Some 70 percent are refugees of the 20-year guerrilla war for independence from the island's majority SINHALESE. They speak a Tamil dialect and, while constituting a distinct culture, are related to the Tamil and Malayalam-speaking peoples of southern India. Their traditional homeland is known as Tamil Eelam, which today encompasses the densely populated Jaffna Peninsula of the north. They are mostly Hindus, although there are some Roman Catholics and Protestants. Music and dance are not encouraged. Medicinal practices are much like those of the Indian Tamil. They do not believe in an afterlife, and cremation is widely practiced.

It is not known when the Tamils first appeared in Sri Lanka, but by the thirteenth century a Tamil Hindu kingdom arose in the area surrounding the Jaffna Peninsula. In 1619 the PORTUGUESE conquered Sri Lanka, only to lose it to the DUTCH in 1658. The island became one of the Netherlands' most profitable colonies, with extensive plantations for tea and other commodity crops. In 1796 the BRITISH captured the island and introduced Christian missionaries and English-language schools. These greatly benefited the Tamil minority, who entered professions such as law and medicine. After independence (1947) conflict erupted between the majority SINHALESE and the Tamils. Since 1974 the Tamils have been fighting for an autonomous state in the north and east. Both sides have suffered severe casualties.

The Tamil population of Sri Lanka is primarily rural. There is virtually no industrial development, and subsistence agriculture is practiced. Rice is grown in surplus only in the eastern coastal region. The Jaffna Peninsula is an important source of garden crops. Remittances from Tamils living abroad comprise one of the most important elements of the economy. The society is male-dominated and highly patriarchal. Marriages are arranged and women are forced to remain in traditional roles within the family and the society. The dowry is an essential part of the marriage ceremony and often becomes the focus of honor for the bride's family. Extended nuclear families live together in a male-dominated environment.

Many Tamil youths fighting with the guerrillas have made Tamil politicians completely ineffective in what is a battle between generations and economic classes as much as it is against the Sri Lankan government.

The civil war in Sri Lanka has its roots in the strong centralized government which the BRITISH left in the wake of colonialism. Tamils, as a minority, found that their representatives had little power in the independent government. This radicalized the youth, who were already disenchanted with the traditional Tamil culture. The Liberation Tigers of Tamil Eelam is the dominant rebel group; they nearly crippled the central government when, in 1987, the Colombo government invited the Indian army to help suppress the insurgents. As a result, violence has spread and, in 1991, Sri Lankan Tamils assassinated the former Prime Minister of India, Rajiv Gandhi. (see also MALDIVIANS, SINHALESE, SRI LANKANS, VEDDANS)

TAMOAN   A subgroup of the DAYAK living on the Indonesian island of Kalimantan (Borneo).

TAMOURT   see KABYLE.

TAMPOLENSE   One of the GRUSI groups living in Ghana and Burkina Faso.

TANAINA   A small Native North American group of Athapaskan-speakers, numbering about 1,500, living in Alaska, U.S.A.

TANALA   A tribal division of the MALAGASY.

TANANA   A Native North American group, numbring 8,500, living in Alaska, U.S.A. While some have retained their traditional occupations of hunting and fishing, others work in the oil, natural gas, and forest industries.

TANANDOA   A subgroup of the TORADJA.

TANA-ORMA   A subgroup of the OROMO, living along the Tana River in northern Kenya.

TANDA see TENDE

TANGHUL One of the NAGA groups living in the mountainous eastern Indian state of Nagaland.

TANGSA An ethnic group, numbering c.10,000 (1981), divided into a number of subgroups and clans, living in Arunachal Pradesh, India, on the Indo-Burmese border. They speak Tolo-Maso and Naga, languages belonging to the Tibeto-Burman family.

Tangsa houses are built on stilts. Their staple food is rice, and they practice shifting cultivation; settled agriculture was introduced after 1950. Communal hunting and fishing form an important part of Tangsa life. They are also keen traders.

TANGU An ethnic group of a few thousand, living near the northern coast of Papua New Guinea. They speak an indigenous language. Their economy is based on slash and burn cultivation, fishing, hunting, and gathering. They believe in numerous ghosts and spirits. Frequent Tangu ceremonies are accompanied by singing and dancing.

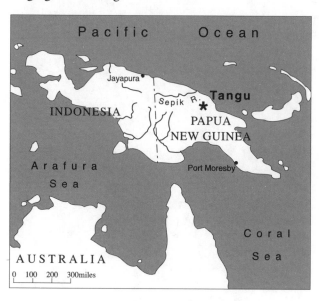

Tangu

TANIMBARESE The name given to the approximately 200,000 inhabitants of the Tanimbar Islands group in the Southeast Moluccan Archipelago of Indonesia. About half are Catholics, and the remainder are evenly divided between Protestants and Muslims. They speak several languages, often mutually unintelligible, but all classified as Austronesian. They engage in agriculture and fishing; weaving is an important craft among the women.

TANKAY A tribal division of the MALAGASY.

TANLU see BALKAR.

TANZANIANS The inhabitants of the United Republic of Tanzania number 26 million. Their country was formed in 1964 as a result of the union of mainland Tanganyika (a German colony from 1891 to 1919, which became a British mandate in 1920 and later a trustee territory; it achieved independence in 1961) and the former sultanate of Zanzibar (a British colony, 1860–1963), which includes the Indian Ocean islands of Zanzibar and Pemba.

The term, Tanzanian, reflects a political reality more than ethnic unity. The Tanzanians' national identity, backed by relative stability in ethnic relations, is mostly due to the unitary, one-party state. The important element of an overall ethnic identity is language: English and Swahili. The latter is the mother tongue of the indigenous populations of Zanzibar and Pemba and of many of the mainland's coastal peoples. Swahili has, since the Middle Ages, become the lingua franca in some areas of East Africa and the language of Afro-Asian sea-trade. It is based on several Bantu languages with a substantial amount of Arabic, Portuguese, English, and Hindi.

The population of modern Tanzania includes more than 120 ethnic language and culture groups belonging to five language families. The contemporary ethno-linguistic map of the country was formed by inter- and extra-continental migration and language assimilation and by mutual cultural and religious influences. Bantu peoples constitute about 95 percent of the Tanzanian population. Their language groups belong to the Niger-Kordofan family, which is represented in Tanzania by seven clusters: Inter-Lacustrine, Western Tanzanian, Southern Highlands, Southern Tanzanian, Central Tanzanian, Coastal and Hinterlands, and Highland Bantu. The fifteen largest Bantu ethnic groups, which include approximately half the population of the country, are: SUKUMA, MAKONDE, CHAGA, HAYA, NAYAMWEZI, HA, GOGO, HEHE, NYAKYUSA, SHAMBAA, LAGURU, BENA, TURU, ZARAMO, and YAO.

The Bantu first invaded Tanzania as early as the middle of the first millennium C.E.; they are considered the latest African settlers of Tanzania. They introduced a well-developed culture of land cultivation and iron production, while expelling or assimilating

A banana market in Arusha, Tanzania

most of the previous population. Those who remained are represented by peoples speaking various languages, among whom are the "tribes" of the Cushitic group, belonging to the Afro-Asiatic family of languages. Although their original anthropological characteristics are now quite mixed, they remain similar to the ETHIOPIANS.

Another non-Bantu branch of the African population in Tanzania is the Nilotic (including so-called Para-Nilotic) group, belonging to the Nile-Saharan (or Shari-Nile) language family. Their cluster (subgroup) structure reflects the wave-like character of the Nilotic infiltration of the Tanzanian mainland. The first to arrive were, most probably, the Nilotes of the Highland subgroup. Later came tribes of the Plains branch (mainly MASAAI); the last were the River-Lake Nilotic peoples (mainly LUO). The oldest part of the native population of Tanzania belongs to members of the Khoisan language family.

The non-African population is represented in Tanzania by Europeans, INDIANS (the most veteran non-Africans in the country), descendants of PERSIANS, and ARABS (especially in Zanzibar, where they were the former ruling aristocracy of the local sultanate). Tanzanians are also religiously heterogeneous; approximately half adhere to different traditional African religions. Others are Christians (from a quarter to a third of the population) and Muslims. Many Tanzanians belong to various syncretic cults, Afro-Christian, and Afro-Islamic sects and churches. A small Parsi community professes Zoroastrianism.

Due to the above, the future of Tanzania as a homogenous nation remains doubtful. The populist regime of the "socialist orientation" based on *ujamaa*, the ideology of Julius Nyerere, pushed ethnic tension below the surface, but could not eliminate them. In fact, the new ethnic awareness led to the assimilation of smaller ethnic units into larger ones, as well as the breakup of some large language and culture groups. The contemporary government's efforts toward implementing a representative, multi-party democracy could increase these tendencies even further.

TAPANTA   A subgroup of the ABAZIANS.

TAPIRAPE   A South American Indian group living near Bananal Island, between the States of Mato Grosso and Goiás, central-west Brazil. Once a strong group, whose language belongs to the Tupi language family, there are today only a handful of survivors.

TAPUNG   A subgroup of the KUBU living on the Indonesian island of Sumatera (Sumatra).

TARAHUMARA   The largest group of indigenous Indians of northern Mexico, inhabiting a considerable part of Chihuahua State. They are a mobile herding people, whose seasonal migrations lead them from the top to the bottom of Copper Canyon, a depth of more than 2,000 meters. The Chihuahua al Pacifico railroad, completed in 1960 after more than seventy-five years of construction, still offers the only transportation from the city of Chihuahua through the Tarahumara region, among the very few heavily-wooded areas of Mexico north of Chiapas, to the Pacific Ocean. Prior to its completion the Tarahumara were relatively isolated from the rest of Mexico.

The Tarahumara, who travel primarily on foot, are among the world's most noted runners. Their footraces are exciting events. (see also MEXICANS)

TARANCHI   A subgroup of the UIGHUR.

TARASCO   see PUREPECHA.

TARGUI   see TUAREG.

TARIBA   see USINO.

TASADAY   see COTABATO MANOBO.

TASHQURGHANI   see GYPSIES.

TASSILI   One of several groups constituting the northern branch of the TUAREG people. (see also KEL AHAGGAR)

TAT I   (Transcaucasian Tat) An ethnic group living mainly in Azerbaijan and in some villages near the Azerbaijani border in the Republic of Daghestan. No population data on their number are available, but a rough estimate puts them at several tens of thousands. The 1989 Soviet census figure of 31,000 is misleading since this refers to the Mountain JEWS of the Caucasus, who speak several distinctively Jewish dialects of Tat I, known in their aggregate as Judeo-Tat. The Tat I language belongs to the Northwestern subgroup of Iranian languages of the Indo-Iranian family. Transcaucasian Tat speak several dialects of this language which are all unwritten, Azerbaijani being used for writing and education. Practically all Transcaucasian Tat are Tat-Azerbaijani equibilinguals.

While most Transcaucasian Tat are Shi'ite Muslims, some are Sunni Muslims of the Hanafi school. They live in a number of enclaves, each of several settlements, concentrated mostly in northeastern Azerbaijan. They are sedentary agriculturalists, cultivating wheat, barley, maize, peas, sunflowers, rye, millet, grapes, and tobacco. Their livestock consists of cattle, buffalo, sheep, donkeys, horses, and in some places, camels. Carpet-making is an exclusive occupation of women. Their material culture is identical to that of the AZERBAIJANI.

A peculiar feature of the Tat is the near-absence of original verbal and musical folklore; both are recited, sung, or written in Azerbaijani. The assimilation of the Tat into the AZERBAIJANI, observed by researchers for about a century, still continues. Since the 1930s they have been registered and officially regarded as AZERBAIJANI; their ethnic self-identification has become increasingly blurred; however, some symptoms of its reawakening have been noted since the late 1980s.

TAT II (Northwest Iranian Tat) An ethnic group living in northwestern Iran, in a range of settlements stretching from the Aras River (Araxes) to the north of the town of Save. No population data are available, but a rough estimate puts them at several tens of thousands. The Tat II language belongs to the Northwestern subgroup of Iranian languages of the Indo-Iranian family. It consists of five groups of unwritten dialects, Persian being used for writing and education. Practically all adult male Tat have a good command of neighboring dialects of Azerbaijani. They are Shi'ite Muslims.

The Tat II are engaged mainly in irrigated agriculture, particularly grain farming. Cotton, sugar beets, and grapes are also grown, and cattle are raised. In larger settlements, part of the population engages in peddling, shopkeeping, and cattle trading. Each family of agriculturalists has its own plot and a number of families form a *boneh*, or structural unit, cooperating in tillage and irrigation. Each such unit is headed by a hereditary *sarboneh*, whose main responsibility is the equitable distribution of irrigation water to the members' plots. All *sarbonehs* of a settlement cluster form the decision-making elite.

The Tat II group of Iran should not be be confused with the Tat I of Azerbaijan. It should also be noted that the term "Tat" has, in the Turkic world, not only ethnic but social meanings.

TATARS A people living mainly in Russia; they are also found in the all the former republics of the Soviet Union, Poland, Afganistan, Turkey, and the Xinjiang Province of China. Since World War II there have been small Tatar minorities in Germany and elsewhere in Western Europe, the United States, and Canada. The total number of Tatars is about 6.7 million, of which 6.6 million live within the boundaries of the former USSR.

The main Tatar territory is the Republic of Tatarstan, an autonomous republic of Russia, located on the Volga River. There they number about 1.8 million, or half of that republic's total population. There are 1.2 million Tatars in the Republic of Bashqortstan, 1 million in the Central Asian republics, and half a million in the Cheliabinsk and Orenburg *Oblasts* (Regions) of the Russian Republic. More than fifty percent of the Tatar diaspora live in urban areas. The Tatars speak a Turkic language; contemporary literary Tatar is based on the Qazan dialect. Until 1928 it used the Arab alphabet; from 1928 to 1938, the Roman alphabet; and since 1939, the Cyrillic alphabet. Of late there has been a growing inclination to restore the Roman alphabet. The Tatars of Lithuania, Belarus, and Poland apparently abandoned Tatar for local languages in the

Tatars

sixteenth century. The Tatars of Afghanistan, numbering about 10,000, now speak Dari (the Afghanistani version of Persian). In the later nineteenth century small but influental groups of Tatar intellectuals, motivate by pan-Turanianism, emigrated to Turkey and adopted Turkish.

The overwhelming majority of Tatars are Sunni Muslims of the Hanafi school. The only exception are the Kriashens (from the Russian, *kreshchenye,* the baptized), a subethnic group of Tatars numbering about 250,000 and found in the mid-Volga area alongside the bulk of the Tatar population (the Qazanlyg). Other Tatar subgroups include the Siberian Tatars (150,000), composed, in turn, of the Baraba, Tobolluq, Tom, and Tomenli. Included among the Siberian Tatars are descendants of Muslim Turkic-speaking merchants of Central Asias who settled in Siberia between the mid-seventeenth and the early nineteenth centuries and were known as the Siberian Bukharans.

Some Tatars living in Bashqortstan form a specific subethnic group known as Teptiars. They are now mainly distinguished by their spoken language, which combines traits both of Tatar and Bashkir.

In Tatarstan and Bashqortstan the Tatars are mainly rural agriculturalists; in other areas they are predominantly urban.

The Tatars emerged as a distinct people in the thirteenth century. They are a fusion of pre-Mongol Turkic groups, Bulgars, immigrant TURKS, MONGOLS, and Finno-Ugric groups. The name was first applied by

Taulipang

RUSSIANS to designate the Golden Horde Mongols and Turks in the thirteenth and fourteenth centuries and was later attached to the Turkic population of the Kazan principality.

From the second half of the nineteenth century through the early twentieth century the Tatars embarked on modernization, disseminating a modernist, pan-Turanian ideology among other Turkic and Muslim peoples of the Russian Empire. In 1920 the Tatar Autonomous Soviet Socialist Republic was proclaimed. In the early 1990s, with the collapse of the USSR, calls were heard for the establishment of an independent Tatarstan and attempts were made to create an educational and cultural network for the Tatar diaspora within the Commonwealth of Independent States. (see also AFGHANS, BASHKIR, CHUVASH, CRIMEAN TARTARS, TURKS)

TATOG   (Dadog) see BARABAIG.

TAUADE   An ethnic group of approximately 10,000, living in eastern Papua New Guinea. They speak an indigenous regional language. They are slash and burn cultivators, whose staple crop is the sweet potato. They have very complex religious beliefs, prominent among which are the relationship between wild and the domesticated animals and the cult of ancestral spirits. In their varied ceremonies vegetables are distributed and pigs sacrificed.

TAULIPANG   A South American Indian group, living in the northern part of the State of Amazonas, northern Brazil. Closely related to the MAKUXI, their language belongs to the Carib family. They number over 1,000.

TAUNG   (Bataung) An historical chiefdom of the SOTHO.

TAU-OI   A Mon-Khmer group, numbering 11,000, living in Laos and central Vietnam. They cultivate rice and engage in fishing.

TAUP   A subgroup of the DAYAK living on the Indonesian island of Kalimantan (Borneo).

TAU RUKU   see SANGIR.

TAU SEMAWA   see SUMBAWANESE.

TAUSUG   (Suluk, Taw Suluk, Sulus, Joloanos, Jolo Moros) An ethnic group, numbering over 400,000, living on the island of Jolo in the Sulu Archipelago of the

Philippines. Although Jolo is their settlement center, Tausug ("men of the current") can also be found in heavy concentrations on adjacent islands in Sulu, in northern Borneo, and recently on Mindanao. They are Sunni Muslims. The Tausug language is closely related to Visayan of northeastern Mindanao, and the Malay-Arabic script is still used for religious purposes. It is thought to have been introduced on Jolo at the time of the Sung dynasty of China (960–1279), due to increased trade with the CHINESE. Although this trade decreased substantially when the SPANIARDS achieved naval superiority after 1840, many Chinese influences are still found among the Tausug.

The Tausug tend to inhabit volcanic islands like Jolo, which provide good conditions for intensive upland rice cultivation. Agriculture, fishing, and animal husbandry are the main occupations, with rice the predominant crop. Natural resources such as bamboo are used for a variety of tools. The Tausug live in small thatched huts, in clusters of between twenty and one hundred houses. Such clusters are found in most areas, although there are higher concentrations on the coast.

Traditionally, the Tausug were ruled by a sultan, with power distributed among a close-knit staff of political and religious advisors. Jolo was never fully controlled by outside forces until the AMERICANS took control of the Philippines in 1899. Tausug internal structures have remained more or less intact, with emphasis on heritage and tribal rivalries. Laws are based primarily on the Koran.

TAVARA An ethnic group living mainly in Mozambique, although a substantial minority is also found between the Zambezi and northern Mukumbura Rivers in Zimbabwe. They speak the Chitavara subdialect of the Korekore dialect of Shona.

TAVASTES see FINNS.

TAVETA An ethnic group, numbering about 10,000, living in southeastern Kenya near the town of Voi, on the Kenya-Tanzania border. They are mostly Christians. Their language belongs to the northeastern Coastal Bantu group, linguistically relating them to the TAITA, their neighbors in southeastern Kenya.

The Taveta engage in agriculture as well as fishing on Lakes Jipe and Chala.

TAWAELIA A subgroup of the TORADJA living on the Indonesian island of Sulawesi (Celebes).

TAWANA (Batawana) An historical chiefdom of the SOTHO.

TAWI A subgroup of the TORADJA living on the Indonesian island of Sulawesi (Celebes).

TAW SULUK see TAUSUG.

TCHAMBA An ethnic group related to the KOTOKOLI living in Togo.

TEDA (Tedagada) A clan of the TOUBOU, numbering about 20,000.

TEDURAY see TIRURAY.

TEGEHE MELLET A subgroup of the KEL AHAGGAR.

TEGURAY see TIRURAY.

TEHUELCHE A major South American Indian group living in Argentina in parts of Neuquen, North Rio Negro, and the Chubut Mountains. They are composed of various subgroups, including the PUELCHE, PIKINCHE, WILLICHE, FURILOCHE, PEHUENCHE, CHAZICHE, RANKULCHE, and LEUFUCHE.

After three centuries of acculturation by the ARAUCANIANS, the Tehuelche suffered virtual extinction, with the exception of a few very scattered and depleted groups. The northern Tehuelche, the original inhabitants of the pampas, are now extinct. Of the southern Tehuelche, whose habitat extended from the Andes Mountains to the Atlantic coast, and from the Chubut River to the Straits of Magellan, only dispersed groups remain in the province of Santa Cruz in southernmost Argentina, and near Cardiel Lake, Three Lakes (on the way to Lago Argentino and Rio Gallegos), Camazu Aike, and in Chubut, on the Chalia reserve. Their language is nearly extinct. (see also ARGENTINES)

TEIDA An ethnic group living in Kenya. (see also KENYANS)

TEKE (Bateke) A people living in Congo, where they number c.370,000. Smaller numbers can also be found in Zaire on both sides of the Zaire River, between Kinshasa and the confluence of the Kasai and the Congo (Zaire) Rivers.

They were one of the first groups in the region to have contacts with Europeans. They did not have a

Tehuelche

centralized political organization. The BAKOUKOUYA of Congo are a subgroup of the Teke. (see also CONGOLESE)

TEKELA   see NGUNI.

TEKKE   A tribe of the TURKMEN.

TELEFOLMIN   An ethnic group of approximately 5,000, living in the Sepik River region of western Papua New Guinea. They speak an indigenous Papuan language. They are slash and burn cultivators, hunters, and gatherers.

While most are Baptist Christians, some, especially the older members, adhere to traditional beliefs. Their most celebrated ceremonies center around male initiation.

TELEUT   A subgroup of the ALTAI.

TELHA   A subgroup of the NAGESIA.

TELLEM   see KURUMBA.

TELUGU   Speakers of the Telugu language, which belongs to the Dravidian family of languages and is related to Tamil. While living in a number of states in southern and central India, most inhabit the state of Andhra Pradesh. Telugu communities also exist in the United States, Fiji, Malaysia, Mauritius, Singapore, and South Africa. The total number of Telugu-speakers is estimated at around 70 million.

Nearly 90 percent of the Telugu are practicing Hindus; the remainder is roughly 6 percent Muslim and 4 percent Christian. The heirarchic caste system is a very important part of Telugu society.

Agriculture is the main means of both subsistence and cash income, with rice as the main crop, followed by tobacco, sugarcane, and cotton. There is also some raising of livestock such as fowl, goats, pigs, and sheep.

Within the lower castes much of the fieldwork is done by women, but this is not permitted in the higher castes. Labor separation occurs within the caste system, with manual labor reserved for the lower castes. Those of higher castes often own the land being worked. Traditional crafts such as pottery, goldsmithing, carpentry, and weaving are usually passed down patrilinealy through the caste system.

As early as the third century B.C.E. Buddhism had a great influence on the Telugu region. The following centuries saw many dynastic changes until Muslims established the Bahmani kingdom in the seventh century. Eventually the DUTCH, BRITISH, and FRENCH came to the region for its textiles and spices. British colonial rule was imposed on the region in the eighteenth century. After many years of Congress Party domination, the Telugu Desam party assumed power in Andhra Pradesh.

TEM   An ethnic group living in Ghana.

TEMBA   see KOTOKOLI.

TEMBE   A South American Indian group living in the State of Pará, northern Brazil. They number only a few hundred and are well assimilated into the local peoples.

TEMBO   A subgroup of the SHONA.

TEMIAR   A subgroup of the SENOI.

TEMIRGOI   A subgroup of the ADYGHEANS.

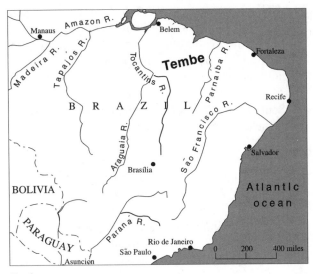

Tembe

TEMNE   A people living in Sierra Leone, numbering approximately 1.2 million, c.30 percent of the population. They are divided into two major groups, the Sanda Temne in the north and the Yoni Temne in the south, both Temne-speaking. Most Temne are Muslims; of late many have begun to adopt Christianity. They are mainly agriculturalists and some raise cattle. In recent decades some have taken to trade.

The Temne migrated southward to their present location from the Futa-Jallon region in present day Guinea in the late fourteenth or early fifteenth century under pressure by the SUSU. In the sixteenth century European traders arrived on the coast of Sierra Leone, and the slave trade became an important element of Temne society. Its abolition by the BRITISH in the nineteenth century weakened the Temne economically, although some moved to other branches of trade and continued to accumulate wealth. The BRITISH tried to persuade Temne chiefs, sometimes by force, to sign treaties ensuring British rule over Temne territory, thus consolidating their rule over the region and enabling them to collect taxes. However, although the Temne lost their independence they managed to preserve their social structure and heritage through secret societies, whose role it was to hand down traditional customs and laws from one generation to another.

After Sierra Leone's independence in 1961 most Temne supported the All People's Congress party of Siaka Stevens, himself a Temne. Stevens gained power in 1968 and ruled the country till 1985. During his reign the Temne dominated the Sierra Leone's government and administration. (see also SIERRA LEONEANS)

TEMOQ   A subgroup of the JAKUN.

TEMUAN   A subgroup of the JAKUN.

TENDE   (Tanda) A cluster of ethnic groups, numbering around 30,000, living mainly in northern Guinea but also found in Senegal and Guinea-Bissau. These groups include the BASSARI and KONAGI.

TENGGERESE   (s.d. Wong Tengger) A small ethnic group living on the slopes of the Tengger Mountains in eastern Java, Indonesia. They speak an archaic form of Javanese and worship ancestral and nature spirits, leading anthropologists to conjecture that they are descended from JAVANESE, who fled to their remote mountain homeland following the collapse of the Javanese empire of Madjapahit. They engage primarily in slash and burn agriculture, but their limited territory has resulted in increasing numbers finding employment in the capital Jakarta and other Javanese cities in recent years. There, as they rapidly become acculturated to the dominant culture, Tenggerese survival as a distinct ethnic group has become questionable.

TENGIMA   see ANGAMI.

TENGUEREDIFF   A subgroup of the TUAREG.

TEOTIHUACANOS   A Native American group living in Mexico. (see also MEXICANS)

TEPETH   An ethnic group living in Uganda, in the three mountainous regions (Moroto, Kadam, and Nepak) of the territory of the KARAMOJONG. They are considered the original inhabitants of these areas. Their language is unclassified, but differs from those of the surrounding peoples.

The Tepeth were hunter-gatherers, but today are largely agriculturalists. Although their areas of settlement are separated physically, there is contact between them, and the Tepeth regard themselves as related in terms of kinship. They are considered by the KARAMOJONG as experts in magic.

TEPTIAR   see CRIMEAN TATARS.

TERA   A subgroup of the KANURI living in Nigeria.

TERENA   A South American Indian group living in the State of Mato Grosso, central Brazil, close to the border with Paraguay. Dispersed in many villages, they are sedentary agriculturalists. They have assimilated the mores and customs of the local peoples.

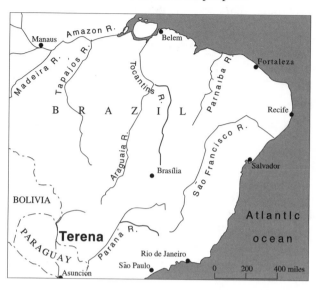

Terena

TERNATANS   The inhabitants of the island of Ternate, situated off the coast of Halmahera, an island in Indonesia, and their descendants, scattered throughout the Indonesian archipelago. They number about 50,000, fewer than a quarter of whom still live on Ternate. Islam was introduced in the fifteenth century, and the ensuing Ternatan sultanate was unusually influential in the history of the region. Its role as an important center of the spice trade enabled it to control much of Halmahera and even parts of the island of Sulawesi (Celebes). For some 300 years it was at war with the rival neighboring sultanate of Tidore, but the supremacy of Ternate can be seen in its adoption by the DUTCH as the center of their colonial administration prior to the establishment of Dutch Batavia (present-day Jakarta).

The Ternatan language is one of the North Halmaheran languages; it may be related to the languages spoken by the AUSTRALIAN ABORIGINES and the inhabitants of western New Guinea (Irian Jaya).

Today the Ternatans engage in the cultivation of sago, bananas, and cassava. (see also ALFUR)

TERRABA   (Terbi) A Native American group living in Costa Rica. (see also COSTA RICANS)

TESO   (Bakedi) A people living in central Uganda, north of Lake Kyoga. A minority also lives in Kenya and in southeastern Uganda. They speak a language of the Eastern Nilotic branch of the Nilo-Saharan language family. Linguistically they are related to the KARAMOJONG. They are the second largest ethnic group in Uganda and the largest branch of Eastern Nilotic speakers.

At some time in the past the Teso switched from cattle-herding to agriculture, adapting to a higher, moister environment and adopting the ox-drawn plow introduced during the early colonial years. They therefore have more in common with their southern Bantu neighbors than with the KARAMOJONG, to whom they are closely related linguistically. They grow millet, maize, sesame, beans, and other grains and vegetables, and still keep animals, especially sheep and goats. They are the most modernized of the Eastern Nilotic peoples, due to early and intensive contact with Europeans, and were among the first to enagage in commercial agriculture, producing mainly cotton as a cash crop.

Teso society was egalitarian with an exogamous clan structure and the age-sets common among the KARAMOJONG. The age-sets, which were connected in times of war, became obsolete after Teso lands were conquered by the GANDA and later taken over by the BRITISH. The GANDA, who call the Teso "Bakedi," introduced a system of chiefs which was not indigenous to the Teso. The BRITISH adopted this system but supported Teso attempts to fill these offices with their own people.

Teso tradition claims that they used to live in what is now the area occupied by the KARAMOJONG. Over a period of 250 years they moved into their present locale, adapting to the new, more fertile, environment with its more reliable rainfall. In 1830, when the KARAMOJONG destroyed the Iworopom people, the Teso granted refuge to a considerable number and absorbed them. This was accompanied by an adaptation of Iworopom culture, which contributed to the development of a clearly distinguishable Teso culture. On the other hand, friction with the KARAMOJONG led some Teso to migrate southward, where they live today among small groups of Bantu peoples such as the GWERE and the SAMIA. Today most Teso are Christians. (see also LANGO, PADHOLA, SOGA, UGANDANS)

TETELA   An ethnic group living in Zaire, between the town of Lusamba and the Upper Zaire River. They are closely related to the KUSU. Some Tetela converted to Islam in the late nineteenth century. Zaire's first president, Patrice Lumumba, was a member of this group; he failed to unite them with the KUSU.

TETON   A tribe of the SIOUX.

TETUM   Inhabitants of the south-central part of Timor, an island in Indonesia. They number about 350,000 and speak dialects of the same Austronesian language. Catholicism, with elements of indigenous beliefs, is the predominant religion.

Slash and burn agriculture is the primary occupation, although crops vary according to location and topographic conditions. Buffalo and pigs are also raised. The Tetum have suffered considerably in the ongoing civil war between Indonesia and EAST TIMORESE secessionist insurgents.

TEUSO   An ethnic group living in northeastern Uganda, along the Kenyan border, on the western side of the eastern Rift Valley.

They were hunter-gatherers, but became agriculturalists. The Teuso are people of small stature and, due to their lack of resemblance to their neighbors, they are, like the TEPETH, regarded as remnants of the region's original population.

TEVE   A subgroup of the SHONA living south of the Zambezi and Save Rivers in Mozambique.

THADU   A people, numbering almost 200,000 living in the northeastern Indian state of Manipur and in neighboring Myanmar (Burma). They speak a Kuki dialect and have generally preserved their traditional belief in a supreme god, Pathen, and innumerous minor deities. They engage in slash and burn agriculture, animal husbandry, hunting, and fishing, with women performing most agricultural work.

Although their precise location of origin is unknown, it is generally believed that the Thadu are recent arrivals to their present area, having been forced there by neighboring peoples. A series of defeats in wars with their neighbors and the BRITISH culminated in the disastrous Kuki rebellion in the early twentieth century.

THAI   (Siamese) The predominant people in Thailand, inhabiting the central and southern regions of that country. They number almost 46 million and constitute about 80 percent of the total population. They speak a monosyllabic tonal language with apparent affinities with Chinese, but there are also similarities with Indonesian languages and Kadai, sometimes leading linguists to group these languages together in a Proto-Austric family. The Thai script, based on an Indian script, attests to the richness of the language. There are forty-four consonants and thirty vowels, as well as nine characters to indicate tone. Most of the Thai are

Theravada Buddhists, and almost all men spend some time as priests and monks. Other important ethnic groups in Thailand include the CHINESE (18 percent), MALAYS (3 percent), and KHMER, KAREN, and other mountain ethnic groups. In recent years there has been a movement among Thai-speaking Muslims, who constitute about 4 percent of the population and are concentrated in the south, to demand autonomy and even independence.

The Thai people originated in the Chinese province of Yunnan. They began migrating to their present home in 1050, establishing a kingdom centered at Sukothai in the mid-thirteenth century. As the population gradually moved south, the capital was reestablished in several locations, the last being Bangkok in the late eighteenth century. From early in its history, Thailand was open to western influence. It was, however, the only country in the region not subject to colonial rule, allowing the indigenous culture to flourish. Although the king relinquished absolute power in favor of democracy in 1932, in 1976 a military coup gained virtual control of the country and curtailed political rights. This has resulted in several violent protests in the early 1990s, led by students demanding a more democratic form of government.

The people of Thailand have faced several armed threats in recent years. Chief among these was a penetration from Cambodia of VIETNAMESE in search of rebels, the war against opium growers and drug lords in the infamous Golden Triangle, Muslim insurgents in the south and north, and ethnic Meo insurgents along the Laotian border. Despite these problems, the country has adopted a decidedly pro-Western attitude which has resulted in considerable aid being granted to encourage development.

THAKALI   An ethnic group, numbering 4,000 (1961), living in the Thak region of Mustang-Manang, Nepal. Their language belongs to the Tibetan group.

The Thakali, of Mongoloid stock, are Buddhist. They are traders by profession, and their group is among the most financially successful in Nepal.

THAP   A Mon-Khmer group living in southern Laos. They grow rice and maize using slash and burn methods, and collect betel leaf which they sell to the VIETNAMESE.

THARAKA   An ethnic group of central Kenya, numbering an estimated 100,000, living on the southeastern slopes of Mount Kenya, in the Meru district. They speak Tharaka, one of the Central Bantu languages of

East Africa. Their economy combines agriculture and animal husbandry. A traditional form of wealth respected among the Tharaka people was cowrie shells. A married woman wore a long triangular leather apron embroidered with cowrie shells. The longer the apron and the more shells it had, the richer the family was. Today most traditional Tharaka features have vanished, as have their traditional religion and rites. Today most are Christians and only a few traditional songs, dances, and other rituals are preserved among Tharaka elders.

THARU   A people, numbering 500,000 (1985), living in the Terai region of Nepal. They speak a mixture of Prakrit, Bhojpuri, and Magadhi. They are Hindus.

Their main occupation is agriculture and husbandry, and rice is their staple. They live in rectangular mud huts, one side of which serves as a kitchen, the other as a bedroom. (see also BUKSA)

THE   A Mon-Khmer group living in southern Laos. Often considered a subgroup of the OY, they number under 2,000. The population was reduced dramatically by an epidemic in 1944.

THENGAL KACHARI   see BORO-KACHARI.

THO   see TAI.

THONGA   see NGUNI, TONGA, TSONGA.

THOTI   A people, numbering under 2,000 (1981), living in the states of Andhra Pradesh, Karnataka, and Maharashtra, India. Their language, Gondi, also spoken by the GOND, belongs to the Dravidian family of languages. Most Thoti are day-laborers; some are agriculturalists.

THURI   A subgroup of the LUO.

TIBETANS   The Tibetans of China, numbering 3.9 million, live mainly in Tibet, southwestern China, on "the roof of the world," the highest plateau and one of the most sparsely populated regions on earth. China calls Tibet the Xizang Autonomous Region. Tibetans also live in the Qinghai, Sichuan, and Yunnan Provinces, with smaller groups of Tibetans living in India, Nepal, and Bhutan.

All Tibetans share the same language, a member of the Sino-Tibetan family. It is highly stylized, with both an honorific and an ordinary word for most terms of reference. The honorific expression is used when

Tibetans

speaking to equals or superiors; the ordinary term is used when speaking to inferiors or referring to oneself. The written language, created in the seventh century, is based on an Indian script.

The Tibetans' formal religion is a form of Mahayana Buddhism which retains elements of Bon, the traditional pre-Buddhist religion of the Tibetans. It is divided into four schools, which adhere to the same scriptural canon but differ slightly in their religious and spiritual practices. Monks (lamas) head the great monasteries, holding political power and owning land. The Dalai Lama, believed to be the reincarnation of Avalokiteshvara, patron saint of all Tibetans, is their temporal and spiritual leader. Lamas maintained a form of theocratic rule in Tibet for centuries until, in 1959, the present (fourteenth) Dalai Lama and 80,000 of his followers fled to India after the CHINESE sent troops to occupy Tibet. There, he established the Tibetan government-in-exile which, although not formally recognized on the international stage, enjoys the allegiance of the vast majority of Tibetans both within and outside Tibet. It calls for withdrawal of the Chinese occupiers of Tibet and the establishment of an internationally recognized demilitarized zone and ecological preserve within the region.

Chinese attempts to destroy the traditional Tibetan culture and religion through the destruction of Buddhist monasteries, the resettlement of ethnic CHINESE in the region, the frequent implementation of compulsory

above left: A Tibetan woman
above right: A Tibetan man
below: A Tibetan monastery in Potala

abortions for pregnant Tibetan women, and the torture and execution of Tibetans who voice their opposition to the occupation, have failed to silence Tibetan protests, despite the fact that as many as 1 million Tibetans have died as a result of the policies of the Chinese authorities in the region.

Some 80 percent of Tibetans are sedentary farmers, whose livestock includes yaks, sheep, goats, and horses. Dwellings usually consist of one- or two-storey buildings with brick or stone walls and flat clay roofs. Nomadic herdsmen live in yak-hair tents.

Most marriages are monogamous, but under certain circumstances polyandry (several brothers sharing the same wife) and polygamy are practiced. Tibetan women, whether married or single, are particularly independent, and are commonly found taking full responsibility for household affairs, trade, and agriculture. Kinship on the mother's side is almost as important as that on the father's side.

The Tibetans' typical diet consists of barley flour, yak meat, mutton, cheese, and tea mixed with butter and salt. (see also CHINESE, DAUR, HANI)

TICOIS   see COSTA RICANS.

TICUNA   (Tukuna) A South American Indian group living partly in the State of Amazonas in northern Brazil, and in Peru and Colombia. The Ticuna are an unusually large group, numbering several thousand; their language has not been definitely identified. Together with the BANIWA, they are the most important group in the region. They hunted and enslaved the MAKU, who were the original inhabitants of the area.

TIDONG   A generic term for those members of indigenous groups in the Malaysian province of Sabah on the island of Borneo, who have adopted Islam in recent years. They number about 10,000.

TIDORESE   The inhabitants of the island of Tidore, off the coast of the Indonesian island of Halmahera, and their descendants, scattered throughout Indonesia. They number about 50,000, half of whom still dwell on Tidore. They speak a language affiliated with the North Halmaheran family and with possible ties to the languages of New Guinea and those of the AUSTRALIAN ABORIGINES. The Tidorese were converted to Islam in 1430 and established a powerful sultanate which rivaled that of the neighboring island of Ternate. This sultanate played an important role in the precolonial spice trade, but declined with the arrival of the DUTCH.

Today the Tidorese are best known for their expertise in fishing. (see also ALFUR)

TIDULAY   see TIRURAY.

TIGANIA   A subgroup of the MERU.

TIGON   A subgroup of the TIV.

TIGRAWAI   see TIGRAY.

TIGRAY   (Tigrean, Tigrawai) A people, numbering 4.2 million, living in south-central Eritrea and in the Tigray Province in northern Ethiopia. They reside in all major urban centers in both countries. The Tigray are speakers of a southern Semitic (Ethio-Semitic) language (Tigrinya). They are mainly plow-using, grain-producing (teff, millet, barley), highland agriculturalists.

The Tigray adhere to Ethiopian Orthodox Christianity (with some Roman Catholics in Eritrea), and are one of the core populations of the historical Ethiopian Empire. Linguistically, the Tigray language (Tigrinya) is more related to the classical written Ethiopian church-language, Ge'ez, than to Amharic. Political competition between Tigrinya- and Amharic-speaking nobilities were a recurrent trend in the history of the Ethiopian Empire. The traditional social institutions of the Tigray were once similar to those of the AMHARA, although descent-groups (*enda*) had a stronger corporate character than among the AMHARA. Communal and village life is strongly influenced by the rituals of the Ethiopian Orthodox Church. Land was once held in the unalienable collective ownership of the peasants.

Tigray and Tigre

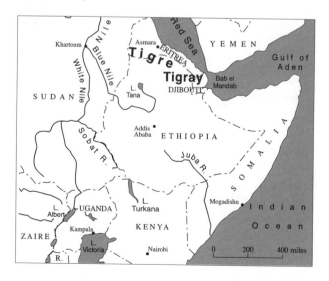

Rights in tribute and surplus labor were temporally distributed inside the hierarchical power structures, which linked the Tigray territory and nobility with the overall structures of the empire.

During the second half of the nineteenth century Tigray dominated the Ethiopian Empire, but their power was weakened by Italian colonialism in Eritrea. Axum, the classical religious and political center identified with Tigrean culture, is now in Eritrean territory. Under kings Menelik II and Haile Selassie, the Tigray became junior partners in the domination and administration of Ethiopia. However, many Tigray attempted to resist cultural assimilation by the AMHARA. Under the military regime of Mengistu Haile Mariam (1974–1991), Tigray intellectuals, in opposition both to the regime and to the old Tigray nobility, formed the Tigray People's Liberation Front (TPLF) which took power in Addis Ababa in 1991. Former TPFL leader Meles Zenawa became the new Ethiopian president.

The highlands of Tigray, to the north of the old Ethiopian Empire, were less fertile and more prone to drought than the southern parts of the empire, those settled by the AMHARA. The Tigray compensated for that shortcoming by controlling trade between the Sudan and the Red Sea coast (Massawa), and the development of internal migration strategies in times of need. Thus, they developed a specific kind of internal social cohesion different from that of groups like the AMHARA or the OROMO. The organized flight of about 240,000 Tigray to the eastern Sudan after the drought of 1984, can be seen as a modern adaptation of a traditional pattern dealing with natural and man-made disasters. The recent success of the TPLF is internally linked to the successful management of a regional crisis situation, based on older strategic patterns. (see also ERITREANS, ETHIOPIANS)

TIGRE   A people, numbering 600,000 (1984), living in the lowlands of Keren and the coastal plains of northern Eritrea. They speak Tigre, a southern Semitic (Ethio-Semitic) language, as well as Bedawiye and Arabic. They are Sunni Muslims or Ethiopian Orthodox Christians. A major shift from the latter to the former religion took place during the first half of the nineteenth century, which also loosened Tigre links with the ETHIOPIANS.

The Tigre are semi-nomadic pastoralists and sedentary agriculturalists who use the plow. Historically, "Tigre" was used to denote a vassal to a ruling stratum claiming descent from the BENI AMER or SAHO.

The Tigre include ten major tribal units: AD SAWRA, AD SHEIKH, AS MU'ALLIM, AFLENDA, BET ASGEDE, BET JUK,

MARYA, MENSA, MESHALIT, and SABDARAT. (see also ER-ITREANS, ETHIOPIANS)

TIJANG   see JAVANESE.

TIKAR   A generic term for all major ethnic groups living in the Bamenda highlands of Cameroon. One sub-group is the BALI, once possessed of a hierarchical political structure headed by a king. They were the major allies of the GERMANS during the latter's colonization of the area.

TIKOPIA   An ethnic group, numbering a few thousand, living on Tikopia Island in the Solomon Islands, in the southwest Pacific Ocean. They speak an indigenous language. Their economy is based upon fishing and gardening. Nearly all practice Christianity, which has replaced their traditional beliefs in spirits.

TIMBARO   see TAMBARO.

TIMBIRA   Ge-speaking South American Indians of the central Brazilian state of Goiás. They grow sweet and bitter manioc and maize. Hunting, fishing, and gathering help supplement their diet.

TIMORESE   see ATONI.

TIMOTE   A South American Indian group living in Venezuela. (see also VENEZUELANS)

TIMURI   A subgroup of the AIMAQ-I DIGAR.

T'IN   (s.d. Mai, Prai, P'ai) An ethnic group, numbering c.40,000, living in northern Thailand and Laos. They speak a Mon-Khmer dialect. Traditional religious beliefs in the worship of a variety of spirits are still important. They are slash and burn cultivators of rice.

TINDIANS   (from the village of Tindi, s.d. according to village: Anghidy, Aknada, etc.) An ethnic group living in the mountains of northwestern Daghestan. They are estimated as numbering 5,000. They have been Sunni Muslims of the Shafi'i school apparently since the sixteenth century. Their language belongs to the Andi subgroup of the Avar-Andi-Dido group of the Ibero-Caucasian family. It is unwritten, and Avar is used as the literary language.

During the twentieth century, the Tindians have undergone an intensive process of ethnic consolidation into the Avar. They now tend to identify themselves as

above: A Tigre woman
below: Tigre women carrying water jars

Avar in non-Daghestani and non-Avar contexts, retaining their self designation as Tindians (according to village) among other Daghestani and Avar groups.

Their traditional economy is based on agriculture, horticulture, and cattle-breeding.

TINGGIAN (Itneg) An ethnic group, numbering about 30,000, who live either on the valley floors of the Abra River in northwestern Luzon, the large northern island of the Philippines, or in the surrounding mountains. Their language is part of the Iloko-Cagayan branch of Northern Philippines languages.

The Tinggian are pagan wet-rice cultivators who have intermarried with many other ethnic groups and have been influenced by Christian settlers. Those Tinggian who have settled on mountains practice the slash and burn cultivation of dry rice and root crops.

TINITIANESE see BATAK.

TINOMBO A subgroup of the DAYAK living on the Indonesian island of Kalimantan (Borneo).

TIPRA An ethnic group living in the Chittagong Hills of eastern Bangladesh. No current population figures are available. They are Hindus and speak a dialect of Hallami. They practice slash and burn agriculture.

TIRAHI (Tiru) An ethnic group living in several villages in Afghanistan, southeast of the town of Jalalabad. No population data are available, but a rough estimate puts them at numbering several thousand.

The Tirahi language belongs to the central subgroup of the Dardic languages of the Indo-Iranian family. It is unwritten, Pashto being used as the literary language. Many Tirahi are Tirahi-Pashto equibilinguals, and the change-over to Pashto is well under way. They are Sunni Muslims of the Hanafi school.

The Tirahi are sedentary agriculturalists. As their name implies, they came to their present habitation from the Tirah area now inhabited by the AFRIDI and ORAKZAI tribes of AFGHANI. (see also AFGHANS, PASHTUN)

TIRURAY (Teduray, Teguray, Tidulay) An ethnic group, estimated as numbering 40,000, inhabiting the province of Cotabato, on the southwestern side of Mindanao, a southern island in the Philippines. They can be divided into three subgroups, those of the river, the coast, and the mountains. The latter group has been much less, if at all, affected by Christian missionaries.

All speak Tiruray, with some also speaking a special language used in ceremonies.

Increasing deforestation has forced many to move their small houses to the mountains. Although hunting and fishing are part of their economy, they exist mainly off the products of slash and burn agriculture (rice, sweet potatoes, sugar cane, and maize). They also engage in basketry and woodworking. Polygyny is a common practice, with women usually regarded as little more than property.

The Tiruray believe in the existence of a supreme being, and also hold that dreams are the experiences of the soul outside the body.

TIV A people living in the Benue State of northern Nigeria, south of the Benue River. Together with other related groups they number around 10 million. They are mostly Muslims. Despite their large numbers, the Tiv failed to create a centralized political framework and were often the victims of attempts by their neighbors to subjugate them. The FULANI tried to conquer the Tiv in the nineteenth century, but during the colonial period, the smaller JUKUN, who shared the Tiv's territory, were promoted by the BRITISH to dominate them. The Tiv began to assert themselves only after Nigeria's independence in 1960 by rejecting the mainstream Northern Peoples' Congress party in favor of the United Middle Belt Congress Party. Enmity between the Tiv and the JUKUN escalated into a series of clashes, the most severe of which took place in October 1991. Villages were razed, and thousands of refugees from both groups fled for their lives. Recently, attempts have been made to reconcile the two peoples with the help of traditional northern rulers.

Because of the lack of political cohesion and the relatively large number of Tiv, many subgroups have emerged. These are the AFUNU, ANGAS, ANKWAI, BANKAL, BASA, BASSA-KOMO, BIROM, BOKOKO, BURA, BURMAWA, CHAMBA, EGGAN, GADE, GLAVUDA, GUDE, GWANDARA, GWARI, HIGGI, JARE, JUBU, KAJE, KOBCHI, KOMMA VOMNI, KORO, MADA, MAMA, MARA, MIRRIAM, MUMUYE, NDORAWA, NJAI, PANGU, RON, RUBUKA, TIGON, and YERGAN. (see also JUKUN, NIGERIANS)

TIWANAKU see AYMARA.

TIWI An Australian aboriginal group living on Melville and Bathurst Islands off the northern coast of the Northern Territory, Australia. Originally semi-nomadic hunters, fishers, and gatherers, they are now employed in public services and reside in fixed settlements provided by the government. (see also AUS-TRALIAN ABORIGINES)

TLAPANECOS   An indigenous Mexican people, numbering some 35,000, living in southeastern Guerrero State, Mexico, from the mountains of the Sierra Madra Occidental to the Pacific coast. Their language, Tlapaneco, is a member of the southern Hokan family.

Their religion is a combination of officially accepted Catholicism and an ancient belief in deities related to water and fertility. The Catholic afterlife is complemented by the Tlapaneco belief that the souls of the departed wander the paths the people knew in life, evading the devil to ensure that in the afterlife the soul will work only in fertile cornfields. Catholic festivals are celebrated side-by-side with others honoring Akuniy, the god of water. As a legacy of colonial times, masked dancers at Catholic festivals re-enact pre-sixteenth century struggles beteen Christians and Muslims.

Municipal government is a combination of official and indigenous political authority and religious authority. Tlapanecos generally marry within their own village, often moving in with the bride's parents while the son-in-law works temporarily for them to pay off the bride price. The birth of the first child makes the marriage permanent.

TLHAKO   A subgroup of the TSWANA.

TLHALERWA   A subgroup of the TSWANA.

TLHAPING   (Batlhaping) see SOTHO, TSWANA.

TLINGIT   (Auk) A Native North American group, numbering 10,000, making them the largest Native American group living in Alaska, U.S.A. For more than one hundred years they were at war with the Russian Empire and were successful in preventing the RUSSIANS from establishing a foothold in Alaska.

They continue to live in large villages and are famous for their artistry and totem poles. Many of them are salmon- and halibut-fishermen, and many Tlingit women work seasonally in the salmon canneries. (see also TAGISH)

TLOKWA   A subgroup of the TSWANA.

TLOUNG   (Batloung) An historical chiefdom of the SOTHO.

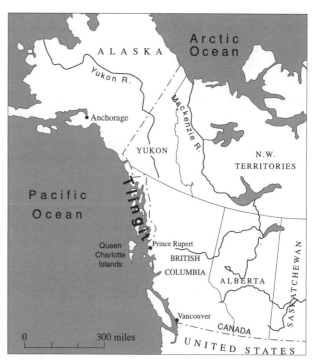

Tlingit

TOALA   (To Ale) The indigenous Veddoid inhabitants of the Indonesian island of Sulawesi (Celebes). Although they number only about 100, virtually all in the village of Samudae, they have had a marked impact on the other inhabitants of Sulawesi. While the influence of the BUGINESE has caused them to abandon their cave-dwelling, hunter-gatherer lifestyle in favor of agriculture, it has not entirely succeeded in introducing Islam to the Toala.

TOBA I   see BATAK.

TOBA II   A semi-nomadic South American Indian people of the Gran Chaco region of Paraguay. They are horsemen, and depend on herding and hunting for their livelihood. They also engage in limited cultivation of maize, sweet manioc, beans, and pumpkins. (see also GUAYCURU)

TOBAGOANS   see TRINIDADIANS AND TOBAGOANS.

TOBELORESE   An ethnic group living in the northern peninsula of the Indonesian island of Halmahera. Their language belongs to the North Halmaheran family of languages and is closely related to those of neighboring groups such as the GALALARESE, the nomadic TOGUTIL, and the ISAM (Pagu), LOLODA, and MODOLE. Once feared as brutal pirates, the introduction of

Christianity has had a moderating effect on the To-belorese, and they currently engage in agriculture. To-belorese communities are also found on the neighboring islands of Batjan, Morotai, and Obi.

TOBUAN   A subgroup of the JARAI.

TODA   (Tutavar, s.d. O·l) An ethnic group of obscure origins, numbering about 1,000, living in the Nilgiri Mountains of the southern Indian state of Tamil Nadu. They speak a Dravidian language related to Tamil and Malayalam. Although most Toda have preserved their traditional religion, Hinduism has had considerable influence. Some Toda have adopted Anglican Christianity and are excluded from traditional Toda society. Most have intermarried with other local peoples, mainly the TAMILS. As a result, Tamil is increasingly their first, and often their only, language.

The most important element of Toda religious beliefs centers around the production of buffalo milk. Agriculture is slowly gaining ground among them, and some have entered the professions.

TODJO   A subgroup of the TORADJA living on the Indonesian island of Sulawesi (Celebes).

TO-DRAH   A subgroup of the SEDANG.

TOFA   (former Russian designation, Karagas; s.d. Tubalar) A group of mixed origins, numbering fewer than 1,000, living in the Irkutsk Region, in the eastern part of the Russian Federation. They speak a Turkic dialect and are closely related to the TUVINIANS. The Tofa language was never given literary status in the USSR, and no alphabet was provided. They are primarily shamanists.

Originally from the Sayan Mountains, where they were nomadic hunters, trappers, and reindeer breeders, they were forcibly settled during Soviet collectivization and are now agriculturalists.

TOFINU   A subgroup of the GUN, itself a subgroup of the FON.

TOGBO   A subgroup of the BANDA.

TOGOLESE   The people of Togo, West Africa, numbering 3.5 million. They are composed of a large number of ethnic groups. In the southern part of the country the dominant group is the EWE, who are subdivided into a number of groups and constitute 44 percent of the population. The northern part of Togo is more ethnically diverse. The largest group in the north is the KABRE, which constitute 23 percent of the population. Other groups in the north are the MOBA, KOTOKOLI, and the GURMA. In central Togo live the AKPOSSO, AKEBOU, AGNAGAN, ADELE, AHLON BASSILA, and BUEM.

Fifty percent of the Togolese practice traditional religions, 35 percent are Christians, and 15 percent are Muslims. The official language of Togo is French, while the most widely spoken languages are Ewe and Kabre. In 1974 these languages replaced French as the languages of education.

The territory of Togo was ruled by the GERMANS until World War I. After the defeat of Germany it was divided between France and Britain as a mandate. The larger eastern part was entrusted to the FRENCH, while the western, smaller, part became a British mandate, which joined Ghana when that state became independent in 1957.

The Togolese of French Togoland gained their independence in April 1960. During decolonization two main parties emerged. The Commite de l'unite togolaise (CUT), led by Sylvanus Olympio, began its political course by campaigning for the unification of the EWE in both parts of Togo with the EWE of Ghana. Toward independence, however, this goal was abandoned and the CUT demanded independence for French Togo. The FRENCH tried to encourage an opposition party, but it was Olympio's party that led Togoland to independence. In 1963, Olympio was overthrown in a military coup by Etienne (Gnassingbe) Eyadema, whose support came mainly from his own ethnic group, the KABRE. The northern ethnic groups generally supported the coup because their region remained underdeveloped by the CUT government. When Eyadema gained power, the army was predominantly northern, but in order to avoid ethnic discontent in the south, he kept some southerners in top military and government posts.

In the beginning of the 1990s violent protests erupted in the capital demand of political reform. Eyadema, who feared the situation might develop into an ethnic conflict between the EWE and the KABRE, promised a new constitution and a multi-party system. The democratization process started in 1991 but was halted by an outbreak of serious violence.

TOGUTIL   A nomadic group living on the Indonesian island of Halmahera. (see also TOBELORESE)

TOKA   A Tonga-speaking group, numbering 22,000, living in the southernmost region of Zambia, north of Victoria Falls. The Toka are mainly cattle raisers, but they also cultivate grain and engaged in trade. A small-pox epidemic in 1892 severely reduced their numbers. In the 1890s they migrated southward in search of employment. In 1900 the British South Africa Company gave Europeans land grants in Toka territory.

TOKELAU ISLANDERS (Tokelauans) A Polynesian-speaking group, numbering c.4,000, nearly half of whom inhabit three small islands, the only territory of New Zealand, 250 miles north of Western Samoa. They are Christians, mainly Protestants, who face problems of overcrowding. Remittances from New Zealand Tokelauans are an important source of income on the islands. Agriculture is of a basic subsistence nature.

TOKI A subgroup of the PASHTUN.

TOLAI An ethnic group of approximately 100,000, living on the Gazelle Peninsula in New Britain, an island to the east of mainland Papua New Guinea. They speak Kunaua, an indigenous regional language. Their economy is based on slash and burn cultivation, with sweet potatoes and taro as their main crops. They believe in traditional spirits and sorcery, although many claim to be Christians.

TO LAKI see LAKI.

TOLBAS A subgroup of the MAURE.

TOLE A subgroup of the TORADJA living on the Indonesian island of Sulawesi (Celebes).

TOLI-TOLI A subgroup of the DAYAK living on the Indonesian island of Kalimantan (Borneo).

TOLO A subgroup of the BAHNAR.

TO LOP see NOP.

TOLTEC see MEXICANS.

TOMA see LOMA.

TOMBALU One of the Minahasan groups living on the Indonesian island of Sulawesi (Celebes).

TOMINI An ethnic group, numbering about 50,000, living in the northern peninsula of the Indonesian island of Sulawesi (Celebes). Inland groups have better preserved their traditional way of life than coastal

groups, who have been influenced by various foreign groups, particularly the BUGINESE. They are Muslims, but there are reports of vestiges of ancestor worship still surviving. The Tomini are primarily agriculturalists, growing corn and sago. Rice, only introduced in the beginning of the twentieth century, is increasingly popular.

Tomini subgroups include the BALAESAN, BOANO, DAMPELASA, DONDO, KASIMBAR, MAUTONG (Mouton), PETAPA, TINOMBO, TOLI-TOLI, and UMALASA.

TONDANO One of the Minahasan groups living on the Indonesian island of Sulawesi (Celebes).

TONGA (Thonga, Tsonga, Batoka, Bathonga) A people, numbering 750,000, living in southern Zambia along the western part of the Zambezi River border with Zimbabwe. They also live in Zimbabwe, between Victoria Falls and Kariba, and in the southernmost region of Mozambique. In Zambia they are divided into two groups, the GUEMBE, or Valley Tonga, and the Plateau Tonga. They speak Tonga and adhere to either traditional African religions or Christianity.

The Tonga had no centralized political organization. They lived in small, loosely connected villages that shared common "rain shrines," built near the graves of prominent men and venerated to bring the infrequent and much-needed rain. Plateau communities were more unstable than valley communities and local rain shrines were short-lived. The Tonga also practiced an-

Tonga

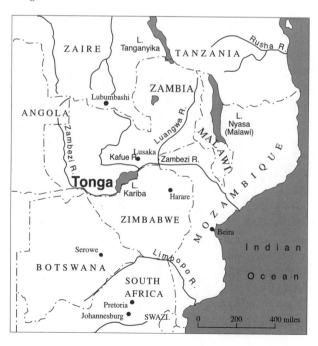

cestor worship and performed initiation ceremonies for boys and girls, which included circumcision. Most Tonga were cultivators and fishermen. During the nineteenth century the Tonga of Zambia and Zimbabwe gained a reputation as boatmen for transporting warriors across the river during the wars of the NDEBELE in 1840. More recently, they have been active in Zambian politics and were the main source of support for the Zambian African National Congress. The Tonga of Mozambique arrived in their region only in the nineteenth century. Until FRELIMO (the Liberation Front of Mozambique) took control of Mozambique, 40 percent travelled to South Africa and Zimbabwe to work in the mines. As a result they learned English instead of Portuguese and brought the African Independent Churches to Mozambique. Edward Mondlane, the leader of FRELIMO, was of Tonga origin. The RONGA are a Tonga subgroup. (see also MOZAMBICANS, TSONGA, ZAMBIANS, ZIMBABWEANS)

TONGA ISLANDERS (Tongans) A Polynesian-speaking people, numbering c.90,000, inhabiting three main island groups located in the central South Pacific Ocean, east of Fiji. Most are Christians, the leading denomination being the Wesleyan Church. Over one-half of the population resides on the largest island, Tongatapu, where the capital, Nuku'alofa, is situated.

Tonga is a kingdom that became independent from Britain in 1970. Fishing and agriculture are the traditional and principal economic activities and 90 percent of the population farm their own plots. The gov-

Tonga Islanders

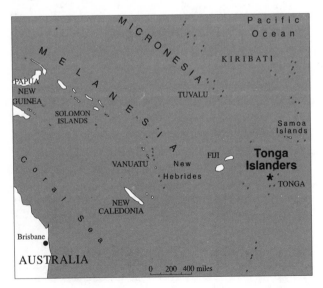

ernment is the main employer. Tourism is on the increase.

TONGWE A subgroup of the NYAMWEZI.

TONKAWA A Native North American group, numbering a few hundred, living in the Tonkawa Tribe Federal Trust Area, Oklahoma, U.S.A.

TONOCOTE A subgroup of the MATACO-MATAGUAYO.

TONSAWANG One of the Minahasan groups living on the Indonesian island of Sulawesi (Celebes).

TONSEA One of the Minahasan groups living on the Indonesian island of Sulawesi (Celebes).

TONTEMBOAN One of the Minahasan groups living on the Indonesian island of Sulawesi (Celebes).

TOPOSA A people living in the eastern part of the Equatoria Province, the Sudan. They number around 28,000, most of whom are nomadic and semi-nomadic. Together with the LATUKA, they migrate from the southwest to the northeast and alternate their loyalties to either the Muslim Arab northern SUDANESE or the African southern SUDANESE. Both groups form an armed militia of nomads, raiding cattle and smuggling goods across Sudan.

Some Toposa are nominally Christians but most of them still profess pre-Christian African religious beliefs. Toposa society is based on the principle of age-grades which constitute the basic units of the armed militia.

TOR An ethnic group of several thousand, living in the mountainous region of northern Irian Jaya, the Indonesian western half of the island of New Guinea. They speak several indigenous regional languages. Their staple crop is sago, and their only cash crop is dammar (resin). Their religious beliefs center around various spirits and ghosts. Male and female initiation rites are the focus of their ceremonies.

TORADJA The generic term for the numerous ethnic groups inhabiting the mountaineous central region of the Indonesian island of Sulawesi (Celebes). They number about 500,000 and are predominately Christian. About 10 percent still adhere to traditional beliefs.

Western Toradja groups include the BADA, BANASU, BANAWA, BAKU, BESOA, DOLAGO, DONGGALA, GANTI, GIMPU, KAILI, KANTEWU, KORO, KULAWY, LEBONI, LINDU, MOHAPI,

NAPU, PAKAWA, PAKULI, PALU, PARIGI, PEANA, PIPIKORO, RAMPI, RATO, SAUSU, SIDONDO, SIGI, TAWAELIA, TOLE, TORO, and WINATU; Eastern Toradja groups include the BANTJEA, BAU, BUYU, KADOMBUKU, KALAE, LAGE, LAIWONU, LALAEO, LAMPU, LAMUSA, LEMBO, LONGKEA, ONDA'E, PADA, PAKAMBIA, PALENDE, PAYAPI, PEBATO, POSO, POSO-TOJO, PU'U MBOTO, PU'U MBANA, RA'U, TANANDOA, TAWI, TODJO, and WOTU. The Southern Toradja are also called the Sa'dan Toradja and are more homogeneous. The Western Toradja are particularly diverse in terms of language and culture, while the Eastern Toradja share many cultural norms. In recent years, Islam and especially Christianity have become more widespread, although most Toradja still adhere to traditional beliefs.

Anthropologists in the early twentieth century took a special interest in the Toradja because of their diversity and their rich culture, which included head hunting, intricate rites connected with death and burial, and ornately carved stone statues. Today most Toradja engage in the the subsistence cultivation of rice. Coffee and cloves are cultivated as cash crops.

TORO I   A subgroup of the TORADJA living on the Indonesian island of Sulawesi (Celebes).

TORO II   A people living in Uganda on the border with Zaire, south of the NYORO, east of the Ruwenzori Mountains, and north of the NKOLE. In 1967 they numbered 255,000 and constituted over 3 percent of the UGANDANS. They speak a Western Lacustrine Bantu language. They are agriculturalists, growing sweet potatoes as a staple, and coffee and cotton as cash crops.

The Toro form a stratified society consisting of a Nilotic HIMA aristocracy and IRU agriculturalists, who are the greater part of the population. The HIMA imposed their rule in the fifteenth or sixteenth century. The Toro were often the target of raids from neighboring NYORO, with whom the Toro have many cultural traits in common and into whom they were incorporated in various periods. The Toro area was inhabited by a diversity of people of different origins.

During the gradual erosion of the power of the NYORO, the Toro became independent (1830), but were reconquered in 1873. In order to smash the power of the NYORO, the BRITISH declared the Toro lands an independent kingdom in 1891. The kingdom lasted as such until 1967. It was not until independence that a distinct common Toro identity seems to have emerged.

Like their neighbors, the Toro worship the spirits of their ancestors, especially those of their kings. (see also AMBO)

TOROM   An ethnic group living in Chad.

TORWALI   An ethnic group living in the mountains of Swat in northern Pakistan, along the Swat and Panjkora Rivers. No statistical data are available, but they are estimated as numbering several thousand. The Torwali language belongs to the Dardic group of the Indo-Iranian branch of the Indo-European family of languages. It is unwritten, and Urdu is used as the official language of writing and education. The main language of oral communication with non-Torwali is Pashto.

The Torwali are Sunni Muslims of the Hanafi school and are sedentary agriculturalists.

TOSKS   A subgroup of the ALBANIANS.

TOTELA   An ethnic group living in southwestern Zambia. Their language, Totela, is related to the language of the TONGA.

TOTO   A Mongoloid group, found mainly in West Bengal, India. They speak a Tibeto-Burma language and engage in slash and burn agriculture, hunting, and fishing.

TOTONAC   An indigenous Mexican people, numbering 200,000, inhabiting northern Puebla and southeast Veracruz States in Mexico. Their language, of the Maya Totonac group, is comprised of several dialects, all mutually unintelligible. Totonac Catholicism is syn-

Totonac

cretic: in addition to Catholic saints, the sun, earth, fire, mountains, and wind are venerated, and Saint John is seen as another representation of their ancient god of lightning and rain.

The Mountain Totonac believe that people share their lives with animal "doubles." The rich stock of traditional Totonac stories deals with celestial bodies and the universe, creation, nature, and the spirit world. Best-known of the Totonac ceremonies is the "dance" of the *voladores*. The five dance participants climb a pole, sometimes as high as ninety feet, to a tiny platform (*tecomate*). One plays a flute and dances on the platform while the others, ropes tied to their ankles, jump into space and slowly descend in widening circles as the ropes unwind from the pole, landing on their feet at the last moment. (see also MEXICANS)

TOUBOU (Toubouri) A people, consisting mostly of semi-nomadic Muslim pastoral clans, living in northern Chad. In 1975 they numbered around 250,000. The two major Toubou clans are the DAZA (Dazagada), numbering 135,000, who speak the Dazaga language related to the language of the KANURI, and the TEDA (Tedagada), numbering about 20,000.

The Toubou resisted French colonization; the FRENCH, in turn, refrained from intefering with them in return for the safety of communication routes through Toubou territory.

After Chad's independence in 1960 the Toubou rebelled against the government and demanded continued non-interference with their traditional way of life. Order was restored only in the mid-1970s after a compromise was achieved.The BULGEDA are a subgroup of the Toubou. (see CHADIANS, KIRDI, SARA)

TOUCOULEUR, TOKOLOR   see TUKULOR.

T'OU LAO   A group related to the TAI and numbering about 600, living along the Vietnamese border with China.

TOULOUR   One of the Minahasan groups living on the Indonesian island of Sulawesi (Celebes).

TOUNDJOUR   An ethnic group living in Chad.

TRAVELLERS   see GYPSIES.

TREGAMI   (Gambiri) A subgroup of the NURESTANIS.

TRING   A Mon-Khmer group living in southern Vietnam.

TRINIDADIANS AND TOBAGOANS   The inhabitants of the islands of Trinidad and Tobago, the southernmost of the Windward Islands of the Lesser Antilles, which were united as a single nation in 1962. The combined population of the two islands is 1.3 million. The people are a mixture of Africans, CHINESE, East Indians, and SPANIARDS: people of African descent constitute 40 percent of the population, and East Indians another 40 percent. The population is about equally divided among Roman Catholics, Protestants, and Hindus, with Muslims and Rastafarians as small but significant minorities. The main language is English and, as a result of substantial immigration from rural areas, the population is largely urban.

The economy is dominated by petroleum and natural gas production and processing, which employ a sixth of the labor force. Although the Trinidadian and Tobagoan GNP is among the highest in the Caribbean, falling petroleum prices have resulted in a declining GNP, high inflation, and increasing unemployment. Agriculture accounts for about a tenth of the GNP and pastoralism is prevalent (the sight of water buffalo cultivating rice paddies is reminiscent of Southeast Asia). Tourism, mostly from the United States, Canada, and Europe, is enthusiastically encouraged.

Trinidadians and Tobagoans are famous for their music, especially Calypso (which combines political, sexual, and social meaning), and their extraordinary Carnival, a celebration preceding Lent. The best Calypso of the preceding season is chosen as the "Road March" of that year's Carnival.

When the islands were visited by Columbus in 1498, Trinidad was inhabited by the ARAWAK and Tobago by the CARIB: these peoples were subsequently worked to death by the SPANIARDS.

The islands were neglected Spanish possessions until 1797, when they surrendered to a British naval expedition. Slaves were imported to cultivate tobacco and, later, cocoa.

Tobago was acquired by the BRITISH in 1802 and adminstratively combined with Trinidad in 1889; prior to this time, after the abolition of slavery, Britain was already subsidizing the immigration of plantation labor from India. The inhabitants were granted self-government in 1925, entered the Federation of the West Indies in 1958, gained independence in 1962, and became members of the British Commonwealth, as a parliamentary republic, in 1976. Recent legislation has granted considerable autonomy to Tobago.

TROBRIAND ISLANDERS An ethnic group of approximately 25,000, living on an island north of the southeastern edge of the mainland of Papua New Guinea. Various indigenous dialects are spoken. Their economy is based mainly on the cultivation of yams. Their religious life revolves around a belief in spirits and magic. Their main ceremonies are performed in honor of pregnant women.

TRUKHMEN see TURKMEN.

TRUMAI A South American Indian group, living in the Upper Xingu area, between the states of Mato Grosso and Pará, central-north Brazil. They number fewer than two dozen, with no village or clear linguistic affiliation. They live with the SUYA, another South American Indian group, or by themselves.

TRUNG-CHA A subgroup of the TAI, numbering a few hundred.

TSAKHUR (the name of their largest village; s.d. also Yikhi) An ethnic group living in the southern mountains of Daghestan, in the eastern Caucasus Mountains of Russia, and in northern Azerbaijan. In 1989 they numbered some 20,000.

The Tsakhur have been Sunni Muslims of the Shafi'i school since the fourteenth-fifteenth centuries. Their language belongs to the Lezgin group of the Ibero-Caucasian family. It is unwritten; attempts in the 1930s to reduce it to a written language based on the Roman alphabet were abandoned by the end of that decade. The Tsakhur of Daghestan use Russian and those of Azerbaijan use Azerbaijan as their literary language. The latter have been heavily influenced by the AZERBAIJANI.

From the fifteenth century the Tsakhur ethnic territory constituted a sultanate based in the village of Tsakhur. In the seventeenth century the center was moved to the village of Elisu in modern Azerbaijan. The sultanate was incorporated into the Russian Empire in 1803; in 1852, during an uprising, the Tsakhur of Daghestan were resettled by the RUSSIANS. They were permitted to return to their homes in 1860.

Their traditional stone houses have two rooms, one of which is used only in summer and the other, dug at a depth of up to six feet into the ground, in winter. Their economy is based on distant sheep-breeding, carpetmaking, metal work, and jewelry.

TSAMA (Kuile) An ethnic group, numbering 12,000 (1980s), living in the lowlands of the Woito River in southern Gemu Gofa Province, Ethiopia. They speak an Eastern Cushitic language and adhere to traditional beliefs. The Tsama are sedentary agriculturalists and cattle-raisers. (see also ETHIOPIANS)

TSANGUI (Batsangui) A M'bete-speaking group living in southeastern Gabon and Congo. They are closely related to the BANDJABI.

TSHANGANE see TSONGA.

TSHANGE A subgroup of the NGUNI.

TSHOKWE see CHOKWE.

TSILKOTIN see CHILCOTIN.

TSIMIHETY A tribal division of the MALAGASY.

TSIMSHIAN A Native North American group living on the northwestern coast of British Columbia, Canada. The Tsimshian are composed of three separate tribes, the NISHGA, GITKSAN, and Coastal Tsimshian. Most of the latter live in bands near Prince Rupert and along the Skeena River.

They work in the local forest industry and in the salmon canneries of Prince Rupert. They have maintained their language, clan system, and *potlach* ceremony, in which gifts are exchanged.

TSONGA (Shangaan Tsonga, Thonga, Tonga, Gwamba, Knop Neuse) A group of Southern Bantu-speakers occupying the eastern coastal area between the Kosi Bay in southern Mozambique. They are also found in northern Natal, South Africa. They number 6 million; some 4.5 million live in Mozambique, and 1.5 million live in South Africa. They are a distinct group, not connected with the TONGA of Inhambane and Mazabuka, or those in the Zambezi River valley or Malawi.

The Tsonga in South Africa were granted a Tribal Homeland in the northeast Transvaal called Gazankulu, which became a self-governing republic in 1973. Its major products are gold and manufactured goods.

Around 50 percent of the Tsonga in South Africa are Christian, with around half belonging to African Independent Churches; the largest minority is Roman Catholic.

A Tsonga woman with child in Natal, South Africa

Oral traditions of the Tsonga place them for centuries along the coastal areas of Mozambique and Natal, from where they moved (or were pushed) westward. Several of their lineages claim links with the SHONA, while one lineage claims links to the PEDI. The Tsonga were conquered by Shoshangane of the ZULU in 1820–1821, and were influenced by the Zulu language and customs. In consequence, many Tsonga call themselves Tshangane or Shangaan after Shoshangane. The

Tsonga

ZULU and Tsonga nevertheless retained their distinctive identities, and their languages are mutually unintelligible. Prior to the Zulu conquest, the Tsonga lived in small independent chiefdoms of between 6,000 to 8,000 people.

The earliest Tsonga are said to have lacked mastery over fire and to have eaten raw meat. Cattle were scarce in the tsetse-infested lowlands, and they kept fowl, which were used in rituals (as with the Bantu-speakers of Central Africa). Goats were the common domestic animal and sorghum was the primary cultivated crop. The Tsonga are renown as master fishermen. They also participated in the slave trade, selling women prisoners-of-war. Tsonga inheritance laws stipulate that a man's heir is his younger full brother and only after the death of all full brothers does a son become his father's heir. In this inheritance system the Tsonga resemble many peoples of Central Africa. (see also SOUTH AFRICANS, TONGA)

TSOU An ethnic group, numbering approximately 8,000, originally located in mountainous central Tai-

wan. The Tsou were encouraged to move southward and adopt the cultivation of rice by the TAIWANESE. The group, which also engages in hunting and fishing, believes that the infringement of strict segregation of the sexes can lead to divine retribution.

TSWA A subgroup of the SHONA.

TSWANA (Batswana, Western Sotho) A people belonging to the SOTHO of southern Africa. They number about 4 million, of whom c.1 million live in Botswana (where they constitute 90 percent of the population). Around 3 million live in South Africa, where those not urbanized are located in the western Transvaal and the northern Cape provinces and within the segmented homeland of Bophuthatswana, which achieved independence in 1977.

Botswana became an independent republic in 1966. While the Tswana form the overwhelming majority of its population, there are also small minorities of KOBA, HERERO, KGALAGADI, SAN, and NGOLOGA. The official languages are English and SeTswana.

The Tswana may be divided into two main groups: the Western Tswana, including the TLHAPING, ROLONG HURUTSHE, NOGENG, and the Western KWENA; and the Eastern Tswana, including the Eastern KWENA, TLHALERWA, PHIRING, TAUNG, KGATLA, BIDIDI, TLOKWA, MALETE, TLHAKO, SELEKA, PO, and the HWADUBA.

Tswana

In South Africa around 90 percent of the Tswana are Christians, with around 30 percent of all South African Tswana belonging to African Independent Churches; around 12 percent are Methodists, and around 11 percent, Lutherans. In Botswana around 30 percent of the Tswana are Christians; the remainder adhere to traditional religions.

The Tswana are part of the SOTHO and share their general customs. They were, however, traditionally more highly stratified than both other SOTHO groups and the NGUNI. The southern Africa system of clientage was highly developed among the Tswana, with Tswana clients receiving dogs as well as cattle in return for meat and pelts. Historically, the Tswana have had close relations with the SAN, many of whom were Tswana clients. Intermarriage, however, has been strongly disapproved of since the late nineteenth century. The Tswana were also distinguished from other peoples by their elaborate legal and court systems, as well as by the brutality of their court sentences and other official deployments of coercive violence.

The Tswana regard pollution as an inevitable result of contact with those in "natural" but not "normal" states: for example, the dead, the incarcerated, and women during their menses. In addition to this, around 90 percent of urban Tswana in South Africa have been found to accept the possibility of a sorcery-related etiologies for certain illnesses. The disease most commonly attributed to sorcery in urban areas is *kokwana-phogwana,* a type of gastroenteritis, which is the major cause of infant deaths (around 25 percent). In SeTswana, the general term for health is *boitekanelo,* meaning "to be equal," indicating that good health depends on a balance between man, the environment, and mystical forces.

During the seventeenth and eighteenth centuries the Tswana were subdivided into numerous, politically independent groups. In the nineteenth century, there was friction between some of these groups and the Boer (AFRIKANERS), who settled Transvaal. By the end of that century all of the Tswana territory was divided between the Cape Colony in the south, the BRITISH in the north, and the Boer republics in the east. In 1910 the Cape Colony and Transvaal were incorporated into the Union of South Africa. The Tswana chiefs lost most of their powers and the people were forced to pay taxes. During that period missions began to work among the Tswana and many converted to Christianity. The Tswana also became dependent on migrant labor, especially as miners, for their livelihood.

In Botswana, the BRITISH ruled the Tswana indirectly through rural committees. When Botswana gained its independence in 1966, the government recommended major changes in the administration of rural committees in order to weaken the position of the traditional chiefs. Botswana became a multi-party democracy after independence.

The Tswana living in South Africa bitterly opposed the apartheid legislation of 1948. In 1959 the "Bantu Self-Government Act" of the South African government recognized eight ethnic units, of which the Tswana were one.

In 1970 the government established Bophuthatswana as a nominally independent Tswana homeland and encouraged a political party that would support its bantustan policy. Many Tswana organized a second party that opposed this alleged independence and continued to fight against apartheid. Eventually, the South African government was forced to abandon the Homelands project. (see also NAMIBIANS, SOTHO, SOUTH AFRICANS)

TU   A minority people, numbering no more than 160,000, found mainly in the Qinghai and Gansu Provinces of northwestern China. They call themselves MONGOLS, believing that they are descended from Mongolian soldiers stationed in the region during the Yuan dynasty (1279–1368), who intermarried with the local population.

Their language is related to Mongolian, with which it shares a basic vocabulary. Religious terms have been borrowed from Tibetan, and daily words and new terms from Chinese. With no writing system of their own, the Tu use the Chinese script.

Most Tu are Mahayana Buddhists; enormous temples once rose over Tu-populated areas. In earlier times, they engaged in livestock-breeding, but they have since adopted agriculture.

TUAREG (s.d. Imushar) A Berber people, numbering c.1 million, living in the southern Sahara Desert, dispersed in southern Algeria (490,000), Libya, northern Mali (354,000, or 6 percent of the population), northern Niger (700,000, or 10 percent of the population), and Chad. Main Tuareg subgroups are the KEL AHAGGAR in the Hoggar Mountains (center Tamanrasset), the KEL AJJER in Tassili N'Ajjer (centered around Djanet), both in Algeria; the KEL AIR in Niger, the KEL ADRAR (Ifoghas) in Algeria and Mali, the IULLEMEDEN, and the TENGUEREDIFF. The Tuareg are Muslims but have kept many pre-Islamic customs.

above: A Tuareg man serving tea in Niger
below: Tuareg horsemen entering a market in Niger

They are of North African origin, but were chased southward by Hilal invaders in the eleventh century. Mobile tent-dwelling pastoralists and warriors, they subsisted from camel-breeding and as guides and guardians of desert caravans. Raids against sedentary settlements and caravans were central to their ethos and hierarchy, and increased their herds of cattle. Because of their swift camels and superior weapons, the Tuareg generally had the better of their enemies.

Tuareg society consists of matrilineal clans and is hierarchically organized into ruling and vassal tribes. Each tribe is led by an elected chieftain. Authority is linked to the symbolism of war drums. Within each tribe there are three castes: the white-skinned nobles (*iharragen*); free vassals (*imrad*), who would pay protection money and were eligible for conscription, — they were often descendants of mixed Tuareg-Arab marriages; and the *iklan*, domestic slaves taken from among the SUDANESE. Outside the formal hierarchy stand the *maalmines*, a professional caste of smiths, tanners, and amulet-makers. Agriculture is the obligation of the HARATIN, black African serfs who are periodically plundered for rice, millet, and dates.

Called the "Blue People" because of the indigo headdresses of their nobles, Tuareg men are known for their

Tuareg

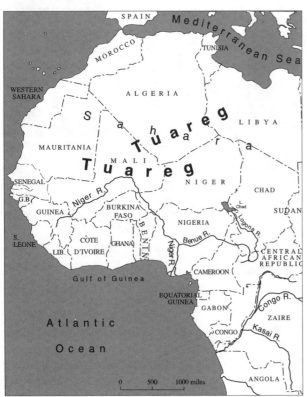

veils. In contrast to other BERBERS, women play a significant public role in Tuareg society (which is monogamous). Freed from domestic chores by the servants, they may be poets or musicians; among the AZJA, women are literate in *tifinar*, the traditional Berber script, and own cattle of their own.

The REGEIBAT are long-distance nomads in the Sahara related to the Tuareg.

Tuareg are the Berber people who have longest resisted modernization. They have been romanticized for their independent behavior, but paid a heavy price for maintaining their lifestyle. In resisting subjugation by the state, the larger part of Tuareg aristocracy was eventually killed. In the post-colonial period, independent black African republics tried to limit Tuareg mobility. A rebellion of the Tuareg in Mali was crushed in 1962.

In Algeria, the government was successful in its attempts to denomadize local Tuareg. In the wake of Algeria's oil and gas boom and the 1968–1974 drought in the southern Sahel, most Algerian Tuareg opted for urban life. The catastrophic droughts of 1982–1985 also drove thousands of Tuareg from Mali and Niger into Algeria and Libya. Muammar Qadhafi, Libya's ruler, proposed the idea of a Tuareg republic and gave them military training.

In 1987 Niger and Mali invited the Tuareg to return, but once they were home, the governments failed to honor prior promises and kept the Tuareg in detention camps and deprived them of aid. In Niger, where Tuareg occupy the mining district of Aïr, an army massacre at Tchin Tarabadene became the signal for a general Tuareg revolt in 1990; it was brutally suppressed. When the revolt spread to the towns of Gao and Timbuktu in the Niger River valley, thousands were killed and hundreds of thousands fled to Algeria and Mauritania. In 1991 Algeria drew up the Accord of Tamanrasset between Mali and four unified Tuareg groups, which installed an autonomous government in the Adrar Region. It failed, however, to put an end to the Tuareg rebellion. A revolution in Mali in 1992 necessitated a new agreement in 1992, reaffirming Tuareg autonomy in the north, but the pact did not end hostilities. Tuareg revolt also continues in Niger. (see also KEL AHAGARR, MALIANS, NIGERIENS)

TUBA   see ALTAI, TUVINIANS.

TUBALAR   see TOFA

TUDAG   see COTABATO MANOBO.

TUGEN (Tuken) The third largest Kalenjin-speaking group in Kenya, numbering over 270,000, or about 1.1 percent of all KENYANS. They occupy the lowland region to the east of the Kerio River and a range of hills above the Kerio River valley, with Kabarnet as the administrative center.

Tugen in the north are more agricultural than pastoral, with pastoralism generally limited to flocks of sheep and goats. In the south the Tugen (Samorr) are more pastoral then agricultural, herding cattle as well as goats. Economic practices detrimental to the environment and rain run-off have contributed to considerable soil erosion in the area, already noted in the 1930s as one of Kenya's most economically-devastated regions.

Daniel arap Moi, president of Kenya, is a Tugen. He was often accused by the opposition of promoting the interests of his own and other KALENJIN groups. Indeed, since his assuming office, the Tugen have been favored over other ethnic groups.

Tugen culture is similar to that of the NANDI, although varying in details. However, despite the practice of stock-raiding and historical references to ambushing caravans, the Tugen were never as militant as the NANDI.

While some Tugen are Christians, most practice their traditional religions. Circumcision and clitoridectomy are important elements of Tugen life. (see also KALENJIN)

TUHUN NGAAVI see DUSUN.

TUJIA A minority group of approximately 2.8 million, inhabiting mainly the Hunan, Hubei, and Sichuan Provinces of southwestern China, whose origins are traced to peoples of the Tibeto-Burmese linguistic group. Highly sinicized by the HAN CHINESE for centuries, they have no written language of their own, and most speak and write Chinese. Some are also fluent in the Miao language.

The Tujia and the MIAO are similar, and intermarriages between the two groups are common. Their religious beliefs, consisting of spirit and ancestor worship, are also influenced by the HAN CHINESE.

The Tujia economy is based on forestry and the cultivation of rice and sweet potatoes. Of their original culture, they have retained folk songs, dances, and silver ornaments.

TUKEN see TUGEN.

TUKOMI A subgroup of the NAGA living in mountainous state of Nagaland, India.

TUKULOR (Toucouleur, Tokolor) A people whose home territory is in Futa Toro, a Senegalese region in the middle valley of the Senegal River and extending from Dagana to Bakel. They also live in Mauritania and in Guinea. The Tukulor emerged as a people after nomadic FULANI reached Futa Toro from the north and intermarried with the local population.

The Tukulor speak Fulani and converted to Islam as early as the eleventh century. They are mainly agriculturalists and traders.

Traditional Tukulor society was divided into three broad social ranks: freemen, skilled craftsmen, and bondsmen. The Islamic clerics, as freemen, had spiritual authority and held political office.

As clerics and traders the Tukulor spread Islam throughout the Sudan. In the eleventh century they established the Tekrur kingdom, which was conquered by the FRENCH in the late nineteenth century. During the French colonial period the center of activity was shifted from the Tukulor region to the areas inhabited by the WOLOF, surrounding Dakar. Those Tukulor who have migrated to the Wolof regions since the nineteenth century have tended to gradually take on a Wolof cultural identity. (see also SENEGALESE)

TUKUNA see TICUNA.

TULA An ethnic group living in Nigeria.

TULALIP A Native North American group, numbering 2,000, living on the Tulalip Federal Reservation, North Puget Sound, Washington U.S.A.

Their occupations center around the Pacific Ocean, where they have successfully established a salmon hatchery and a commercial smoking-house for salmon-curing.

TULAMA A subgroup of the OROMO.

TULI A subgroup of the NGUNI.

TUMANAO see BILAAN.

TUMBUKA (Batumbuka) An ethnic group, numbering about 80,000, living in Malawi, near the eastern Zambian border. They speak Tumbuka and are mostly Christian, although some still practice traditional religions. The Tumbuka lived in decentralized chiefdoms and still follow a matrilineal descent system. Subjugation by the NGONI in 1855 resulted in an overall deterioration of their ethnic identity. The situation was somewhat ameliorated, however, with the establishment of colonial rule. In 1909 the Tumbuka came under the influence of the preaching of Kamwana of the Christian Watchtower movement.

The FONGWE, HEWE, KAMANGA, and NTHALI are Tumbuka subgroups. (see also MALAWIANS)

TUMUZU   A Native American group living in Venezuela. (see also VENEZUELANS)

TUNISIANS   The people of Tunisia number 8 million. Most Tunisians are ARABS, although there are small groups of BERBERS. Nearly all are Sunni Muslims. Since the departure of the FRENCH and ITALIANS and the emigration of the JEWS, Tunisians form a nearly homogeneous population. The east coast, where three quarters of the population is concentrated and which has always been open to foreign influences, is urbanized and intensively cultivated; today it is also the center of tourism. The interior remains rural and pastoral, a land of steppes, large landed property, and extensive grain-farming estates, where past decades have seen a process of both sedentarization and rural exodus; beyond lies Saharan Tunisia, sparsely settled except for a number of palm oases.

Tunisia lacks the natural resources of some of its neighbors, but enjoys high educational levels. However, its successful educational efforts have saturated the labor market, resulting in a brain drain to other Maghreb states (in particular Libya), the Gulf, sub-Saharan Africa and (until the mid–1970s) Europe. The Tunisians were once regarded as one of the Arab world's most secularized peoples. Polygamy is prohibited and an active family planning policy is promoted. Tunisia has adopted a Western-style development strategy. However, in recent years Tunisians have reasserted their Arab and Islamic identity. Of late, Islamic fundamentalism and active anti-Westernism have emerged.

BERBERS may have been the original Tunisians, but the first great civilization (Punic) was imported by Phoenicians in the ninth and eighth centuries B.C.E. Punic was still spoken in the Tunisian countryside in the fifth century C.E. Two centuries later, Arab invaders overran the Tunisian Berber tribes, leading to gradual but complete islamization and arabization. In the eleventh century, the Fatimid rulers of Egypt launched the BANI HILAL against the BERBERS, resulting in the laying waste of large parts of the North African Maghreb. Cities declined and many Tunisians reverted to nomadism. In the sixteenth century Tunisia became entangled in Spanish-Ottoman rivalry, and from 1564 it was an Ottoman province ruled by Mamelukes. In the seventeenth century Tunisia became semi-autonomous.

In the nineteenth century Tunisians increasingly came under European influence: France and Italy vied in their designs on them, resulting, in 1881, in the establishment of a French protectorate.

French administration left little power to indigenous ARABS. Tunisian nationalist agitation broadened after World War I into a campaign for a constitution, but was preempted by the gradual introduction of reforms. Habib Bourguiba, who was subsequently to mould modern Tunisia, established the Neo-Destour party in the 1930s. Since the FRENCH were not responsive to local demands, riots broke out in 1938. Bourguiba was exiled but returned in the 1950s to fan the fires of national revolt. In 1954 a guerrilla movement forced France to grant the Tunisians autonomy; full independence followed in 1956.

As the only active pre-independence political party, the Neo-Destour assumed power. At first a trade union tendency toward a state-controlled economy carried the day. However, in the 1970s the country was threatened with an agriculture crisis and a liberal economy was restored. Despite talk of political liberalization, however, the Neo-Destour party maintained control. Discontent erupted in 1978, when workers' and students' strikes demanding the abolition of the one-party system threatened the regime. A controlled experiment in democratization and multi-party politics was begun and Bourguiba lost power.

Throughout the 1980s the intellectual elite seemed unable to stop the emergence of the fundamentalist Islamic movement, which boycotted the 1990 elections. However, the Gulf crisis in 1991 split the fundamentalists, and the government introduced harsh repressive measures against them; the An-Nahda Islamic Movement was disarmed without provoking massive protests. Economic growth has since permitted some relaxation of social tensions. (see also ARABS)

TUPI-GUARANI   see COLOMBIANS, GUARANI.

TUPINAMBA   The collective name for a group of Tupian-speaking South American Indian peoples of the lowlands of southeastern Brazil (variously known as the Potiguara, Caete, or Tupinikin). They now depend primarily upon extensive agriculture, with the men clearing the fields and the women tilling them. Their staples are maize and bitter and sweet manioc, but they also grow beans, sweet potatoes, peppers, pineapples, and cotton. Tupinamba chieftains have extensive authority over a number of communities. They were once a ferocious and cannibalistic warrior people.

TUPINIKIN   See TUPINAMBA.

TURCOMANS   See IRAQIS, SYRIANS, TURKS.

TURI   A subgroup of the PASHTUN.

TURKA   A subgroup of the SENUFO, living in Burkina Faso.

TURKANA   A pastoralist Nilotic people, numbering an estimated 300,000, living west of Lake Turkana around the town of Lodwar in northwest Kenya. Their language belongs to the Eastern Nilotic family. The Turkana follow their own traditional African religion and only a very small number have converted to Christianity.

The Turkana are nomad pastoralists with mixed cattle-, camel-, sheep-, and goat-herds; animals are the basic source of wealth and social status. They have no centralized political institutions and the importance of age-sets and clans is nominal. The only obligation and loyalty of a Turkana is to his family and homestead. The Turkana raid neighboring peoples, stealing their cattle and engaging in warfare with them. Kenya's central government is unable to control the Turkana and their region is considered problematic. Recently, the central government has tried to exercise more control over the Turkana by providing more schools, clinics and other services, to enhance the ongoing process of sedentarization. (see also KARAMOJONG)

TURKMEN   A people living mainly in Turkmenistan and also in Uzbekistan, Tajikistan, and the Stavropol Province of Russia and the adjacent north Caucasian regions. Groups of Turkmen also live in Afghanistan, Iran, Iraq, Syria, and Turkey. The general estimation of their number today is about 3.8 million. According to the Soviet 1989 census there were c.2.8 million Turkmen in the former Soviet Union. There are about 400,000 in both Iran and Afghanistan, 170,000 in Iraq, 88,000 in Syria (all estimates of the 1980s), and apparently the same number in Turkey, although no population data are available there.

The Turkmen language belongs to the Oghuz group of Turkic languages, but contains some elements of the Qypchaq group of Turkic languages. It consists of several dialects and has been a written language since the eighteenth century. Its classical form was heavily influenced by the Chaqhatai (classical Central Asian) literary language. The Soviet literary Turkmen language is based on its Yomud and Tekke dialects. It utilized the Arabic alphabet until 1928, when this was replaced by the Roman script, which was in turn replaced by Cyrillic in the 1940s. In 1980 it was proclaimed one of the official languages of Afghanistan, but publications utilizing the Arabic script are limited.

The Turkmen are overwhelmingly Sunni Muslims of the Hanafi school. Somes sources list several groups of Turkmen of Iraq, Syria and Turkey as Shi'ite Muslims.

For centuries the Turkmen have been predominantly nomads whose livestock consisted mainly of sheep, horses, and camels. Some were semi-nomads and smaller groups were sedentary agriculturalists engaged in the irrigated cultivation of cereals (wheat, barley, millet, and sorghum). An essential part of the economy of both nomads and semi-nomads was the periodic raiding of Shi'ite areas in Iran to take captives of both sexes and of working age. These were sometimes kept as slaves, but more often sold in the slave markets of Merv (now Mary), Bukhara, and Samarkand.

The Soviets invested much effort in sedentarizing the Turkmen and were to a great extent successful. Today the Turkmen of Turkmenistan are sedentary agriculturalists, combining agriculture with seasonal long-distance herding. The main crop is now cotton, traditional cereals taking second place alongside irrigated horticulture. About one-third are urbanized, engaged mainly in gas and oil production, local urban industry and services. Turkmen carpets are still mainly handwoven by women, but imitations are also produced in urban carpet factories. In other areas of the Commonwealth of Independent States (CIS) and in Syria and Turkey, the Turkmen are sedentary agriculturalists, in Iran and Afghanistan mainly nomads, and in Iraq, sedentary semi-nomads.

In Turkmenistan men now dress in European or semi-European style. However, most Turkmen still wear the specific high lambskin hat, and traditional dress is still worn in Iran and Afghanistan. Women tend to adhere to the more traditional forms of dress.

Tribal structure is still strong in Turkmenistan, Iran, and Afghanistan, but has apparently weakened in Iraq, Syria, and Turkey. The Turkmen consist of about thirty tribes, the major being the TEKKE, ERSARY, YOMUD, and Goklen. Of the smaller tribes, four (SEID, KHOJA, SHIKH, and ATA) are venerated as possessing saintly ancestry. Another group, the c.20,000 North Caucasian Turkmen, usually called Trukhmen, were

above: Turkmen elders in Turkmenistan
below: A Tuvaluan family

split off from the main body of Turkmen in the eighteenth century and have long been sedentary agriculturalists. Their dialect has been strongly influenced by that of the NOGHAI. The c.4,000 MAWRI of north Afghanistan (originating, according to their name, from the Merv area of Turkmenistan) identify themselves as Turkmen, but are not recognized as such by other Afghanistani Turkmen.

Historically, the Turkmen are direct descendents of the Oghuz, who entered Central Asia from the east in about the tenth century. They were gradually converted to Islam and absorbed some pre-Oghuz, mostly Iranian, inhabitants of the area of present day Turkmenistan. Although formally dominated at various times by Iran and the Central Asian principalities of Khiva and Bukhara, they remained virtually independent for centuries until they were subdued by the Russian empire in the 1870s and 1880s. In 1924 the Soviet authorities promoted the creation of the Turkmen Soviet Socialist Republic.

Since 1989 the Turkmen of the former Soviet Union have experienced a process of political and national awakening, and the awareness of Turkmen roots has become strongly stressed. In 1991 Turkmenistan proclaimed its sovereignty, but with the collapse of the Soviet Union it remained within the framework of the CIS. (see also AFGHANS)

TURKS   Most of the estimated 56 million Turks live in Turkey. Their language, Turkish, belongs to the large group of Turkic tongues. Besides native Turks from Anatolia proper, there are Rumeli (European) Turks, most of whom left their countries of birth as Serbia, Greece, Albania, Bulgaria, and Romania gained independence in the nineteenth century. These returnees from the shrinking Ottoman Empire numbered 4.5 million, and were given land throughout Anatolia. Their descendants today number close to 12 million.

After World War I, 400,000 Rumeli from Greece were exchanged; along with Turkish returnees came 150,000 Pomaks, islamicized Bulgars. These are now turkified and dwell in west Anatolia. However, not all Rumeli returned. Six million ethnic Turks living in the Balkans, Bulgaria, Hungary, Cyprus, and northern Greece represent the remnant of centuries of Turkish presence in these areas. The largest concentration is in Moldova, where they identify themselves as GAGAUZ. A large number of Anatolian Turks live in Europe as migrant laborers, mostly in Germany. In the northern part of Cyprus there are 160,000 Turks who speak Turkish as their mother tongue. In 1974 Turkish troops occu-

pied and partitioned Cyprus, and a Turkish republic was set up.

Turkic-speaking Turcomans or TURKMEN in central and East Anatolia, Qypchaq-speaking TATARS (who immigrated in the nineteenth century from Russia), and YORUK are classified as Turks. The YORUK are nomads living in the south-central interior, where they continue their ancestral pastoral life, alternating seasonally between valleys and mountains. They are non-orthodox Sunni Muslims, and are known for their rug knotting.

Turkey has only one large non-Turkish minority: the KURDS, variously estimated at between 3.5 and 12 million (as much as 20 percent of the population), who are officially known as Mountain Turks. Other small ethnic groups include the CHERKESS (2.1 percent of the population, in the Adana region). The LAZ left the Caucasus after Russia seized their country in 1878, and are often fishermen and mariners; like the Hemsin GEORGIANS, who are undergoing a process of assimilation, and the ABKHAZIANS, they live along the southeast coast of the Black Sea, numbering together possibly 100,000. There are also ARMENIANS and GREEKS, who are mainly businessmen in Istanbul, as are the JEWS. These groups are a mere shadow of their former selves, when they had a substantial share in the Ottoman Empire's trade and manufacture. In the Urfa area in South Turkey live 600,000 ARABS.

The overwhelming majority of Turks are Sunni Muslims, with a minority adhering to Shi'ah Islam. In the Tunceli province of Eastern Anatolia, many poor peasants belong to the Shi'ite sect of the Alawites. Sufi *tariqat* (brotherhoods) played a large role in Turkish life, sometimes combining Islamic mysticism with pre-Islamic practices, including the Mevlevis (dancing dervishes) and the less elitist Alevi Bektasi, instrumental in converting Anatolian Christians to Islam. Turkish culture was always marked by latent tension between city-centered Sunni orthodoxy and a nomadic-rural popular culture which retained shamanistic elements.

The Turkish invasions in the Middle Ages initially led to large-scale abandonment of land by peasants. The dominance of nomad pastoralism in large parts of the Anatolian plains left only small pockets permanently cultivated. Demographic pressure in the first half of the twentieth century led, however, to the transformation of central Anatolian shepherds' habitations into permanent settlements. Crucial to repopulation were the *muhacir*, or Rumeli returnees. Although long-distance nomadism has greatly diminished, millions of peasants still practice some kind of short-term summer

above: Turkish men in a coffeeshop
below: Turkish women doing housework

pastoralism near their villages, living in tents or temporary dwellings. Modernized city dwellers contrast strongly with the conservative rurals. Roads bring contact with modernity everywhere and facilitate ubiquitous migration to towns, where more than half the population now dwells. Cities were also the locus of Turkish high culture. Traditional architecture has been preserved in typical mosques with slender minarets, *medreses*, wooden houses with latticework, etc. This is only the most visible aspect of the Turkish artistic heritage. Rugs, ceramics, and music and other arts betray central Asian influences, overlaid with Persian, Arab, and Byzantine motifs.

Extended patriarchal families are still the rule, and women have remained subordinate in spite of efforts at modernization. Social life is segregated according to gender. Mosques thrive and the officially disbanded Sufi brotherhoods have clandestinely revived and provide a focus of anti-secular identity.

Until a thousand years ago, the territory of what is today Turkey was settled by populations unrelated to the Turks: Hittites and Urartu (claimed for ancestors by the Armenians), Phrygians and Lydians, Romans and Parthians. It was also home to some of the earliest Christian communities, and subsequently became the heart of the Byzantine Empire. However, between the eleventh and the fifteenth centuries, it was conquered and settled by a nomadic people driven from its ancestral homes in central Asia: the Turks.

From the tenth century, Turkish soldiers and slaves adopted Islam. Before long they took over the authority of their Arabic and Persian masters and founded realms of their own based on Sunni Islam, Arab-Iranian culture, and the Arabic alphabet. Seljuq Turks pushed through Iran and Iraq into North Syria. In the eleventh century, they conquered and settled the larger part of Byzantine Anatolia. The invaders succeeded in thoroughly islamicizing and turkifying the larger part of Anatolia, in the process submerging Armenian and Greek culture. Only the Aegean area remained predominantly Greek until the 1920s. However, the thirteenth century saw the weakening of the Seljuqs, who had established their capital in Konya. A new, dynamic tribe appeared on the scene: the Ottoman Turks, or Osmanlis, who completed the conquest of Anatolia and from there established the Ottoman Empire, which at its peak encompassed the Balkans, Arabia, and North Africa.

The Ottoman Turks conquered Constantinople in 1453 and named it Istanbul, thereby finishing off the moribund Byzantine Empire. Subsequently, all of Arabia, North Africa, and the Balkans were brought under Turkish rule. The Ottoman Empire reached its apogee under Suleiman the Magnificent (1520–1566) who laid siege to Vienna. The empire rested on an impressive administration and a formidable army. From the seventeenth century on, the empire gradually shrank under the impact of attacks by Christian states and the rising nationalism of minorities within the empire, as well as corruption.

Efforts at centralization and modernization of the empire came too late. The last sultans stifled efforts at parliamentarism and restored absolutism in 1877. From the army, the only thoroughly modernized institution of the empire, came in 1908 the Young Turkish revolution. Originally Ottomanist in intent, it soon lapsed into vain attempts at imposing turkification on the empire's mixed nationalities. As a result of the failure of Ottomanism, a narrow Turkish nationalism retrenched itself in the Anatolian heartland. It attempted to turkify the motherland by suppressing non-Turkish minorities. The massacres of the ARMENIANS continue to cloud relations between the two peoples. Turkey chose the losing side in World War I. The Arab peoples shook off the yoke. Just as the victors intended to carve up the empire, Mustafa Kemal succeeded in galvanizing the Turkish masses: the invading armies were thrown out. The Turkish war of independence in 1922–1923 resulted in the establishment of a republic, and led to the uprooting of millennial Greek communities and wholesale population transfers between Greece and Turkey.

The significance of Mustafa Kemal Ataturk ("Father of the Turks") in restoring pride to his people and in forcing upon them drastic modernization cannot be overstated. He abolished the sultanate and the khalifate, instituted a one-party republic, and endeavored to thoroughly secularize social life, granting equal rights to women, prohibiting the veil, and imposing Western clothes (the visored cap is still the favored headgear of Turkish men), introducing the Latin alphabet and family names, purifying Turkish of Arab and Persian accretions, and starting industrialization. The republic's capital was shifted from cosmopolitan Istanbul (Constantinople) to inward-looking Ankara.

After World War II, Turkey became a democracy with competing political parties — although the army, standardbearer of Kemalism, has repeatedly taken power. Mechanization of agriculture led to a mass migration to the slums around the big cities and to Western Europe.

The military coup of 1980 was widely applauded because it addressed the generalized sense of insecurity. Socially, the generals tended to steer Turkey into a disciplined hierarchical society. A restricted democracy was restored in 1982.

Turkey's role in the region is bound up with national questions, in at least three directions. First, continued suppression of the restive Kurds at home has failed to prevent the reopening of the Kurdish file internationally. The 1990 Iraqi crisis also reawakened feelings towards the province of Mosul. Secondly, the fragmentation of the former Soviet Union has created a power vacuum that invites Turkey to involve itself with its Turkic relatives in Azerbaijan, Turkmenistan, and other new republics rife with ethnic conflict. Lastly, the explosion of Yugoslavia carries with it the risk of dragging the Turks down into civil strife. (see also CYPRIOTS, MESKH)

TURKS AND CAICOS ISLANDERS The inhabitants of a Caribbean British dependency, situated south of the Bahamas and north of Hispanola. They number just over 11,000, and are one-third black and two-thirds racially mixed. Predominantly Protestant, their language is English.

The Turks and Caicos Islanders were under Bahamian authority until 1874, when their territory was annexed to the Jamaican colony. Independence efforts were initiated in the 1980s, but have thus far achieved neither resolution nor firm results.

TURPANLYQ A subgroup of the UIGHUR.

TURU An ethnic group living in Tanzania. (see also TANZANIANS)

TURUKHAN SELKUP see SELKUP.

TUSCARORA A Native North American group, numbering 1,200, living in New York, U.S.A., and Ontario, Canada. They are part of the IROQUOIS CONFEDERACY.

TUSIA (Tusyan) A subgroup of the LOBI.

TUTAVAR see TODA.

TUTCHONE A Native North American subgroup of the Athapaskans, numbering 500, living in the Yukon Territory, Canada. Many continue to hunt and trap in the traditional way.

TUTSI A people numbering an estimated 1.5 million, divided almost equally between the African states of Rwanda and Burundi. A Cushitic-speaking people, they probably originated from the area of the OROMO in Ethiopia and their penetration into the region was a slow and peaceful process. They first subjugated the indigenous inhabitants of eastern Rwanda around the end of the fourteenth century, then gradually extended their dominion towards the west, abandoning their own language for the Bantu language of the HUTU. The Tutsi were cattle herding pastoralists who managed to dominate a numerically larger agriculturalist HUTU. The extent of Tutsi domination of HUTU varied from region to region but was usually both political and social. They formed the ruling class of the Rwanda and Burundi kingdoms and their cattle-centered culture became the dominant one. Physically the Tutsi are very different from the HUTU and TWA, the two other main groups in the area.

In Burundi, the Tutsi retained their dominance of the HUTU, despite the 1972–1973 massacres and the flight of Tutsi refugees caused by a revolt by the HUTU. In Rwanda, however, the Tutsi lost their political supremacy when the HUTU began a peasant revolt. Nevertheless, they retained their place among the intellectual elite. (see also BURUNDIANS, HUTU, KIGA, RWANDANS)

TUVALUANS A Polynesian ethnic group, numbering about 10,000, who inhabit nine small atolls, formerly known as the Ellice Islands, in the western Pacific Ocean. There are more than 1,500 Tuvaluans in the Pacific islands of Nauru, Vanuatu, and Fiji. About 98 percent of the population are Christian Protestants, and their language (Tuvaluan) belongs to the Polynesian family.

The capital and main island is Funafuti. On the coral atolls the quality of the soil is poor and expansion of agriculture is limited. Although many Tuvaluans earn wages from local and external sources, and from selling copra, the main export product, the cultivation of gardens on the atolls, together with fishing, are still fundamental to their way of life.

The Ellice Islands were declared a British protectorate in 1892 and linked adminstratively with the Gilbert Islands. In a 1974 referendum over 90 percent of the voters favored a separate status for the atoll group and, in 1978, Tuvalu became independent as a special member of the British Commonwealth.

TUVINIANS (s.d. Tuba, Tuwa, Tyva-Kizhi) A Turkic group of mixed origins living in the Tuvinian Au-

Tuvinians

tonomous Republic in southern Siberia, Russia. According to the 1989 Soviet census they numbered 207,000. Over 20,000 Tuvinians live in Mongolia. Originally shamanist, they converted to Mahayana Buddhism in the eighteenth century. Their language, Tuvinian, belongs to the Turkic family and contains many Mongol loan words. It is currently written with a Cyrillic script.

The area of the contemporary Tuvinian Autonomous Republic was conquered in 1757–1758 by the MANCHU, then rulers of China. It was opened to Russian commerce and settlement under the Peking Treaty of 1860. In 1914, turmoil in China following the 1911 Revolution enabled the RUSSIANS to establish a protectorate in the area, and in 1921 to establish the "independent" Tannu-Tuva People's Republic. In 1944, Tannu Tuva was incorporated into the Federated Russian Soviet Socialist Republic, first as an autonomous province, and then as an autonomous republic in 1961.

Though they were forcibly sedentarized by the Soviet authorities, traditional hunting and gathering are still important to the Tuvinians. They have only recently begun finding employment in agriculture, mining, and industry.

TUWA   see TUVINIANS.

TWA   A group of PYGMIES who live in both Rwanda and Burundi in Central Africa. Their exact number is not known, but various estimates recorded at the beginning of the twentieth century placed them at 3,000–4,000 in each of the two states; they have always represented under 1 percent of the total population. Small groups also live in Uganda.

The Twa are considered the original inhabitants of Rwanda and Burundi, probably coming from the rainforest area of present Zaire. In the past they occupied the western Mfumbiro region and the swampy country in the north, where they were mainly hunters. Some Twa in other parts of Rwanda and Burundi were metal workers and potters.

Originally the Twa spoke a unique Pygmy language, related to that of South Africa and also to the click language of the rainforest people of Zaire. Their religion was based on a belief in a supreme power. (see also BURUNDIANS, PYGMIES, RWANDANS)

TXUKAHAMAI   A South American Indian group living in a government-controlled village in the Upper Xingu Valley, near the Xingu River, in the State of Goiás, central-west Brazil. Their language links them to the language family of the KAYAPO. They presently number a few hundred.

TYITSO   A subgroup of the AKHA.

TYROLEANS   see SOUTH TYROLEANS

TYVA-KIZHI   see TUVINIANS.

TZELTAL AND TZOTZIL MAYA   Two groups living in the central area of the southeastern Mexican state of Chiapas. While not identical, they have many elements of culture and language in common.

They are an agricultural people cultivating beans, chile, corn, manioc, squash, and peanuts with traditional hoes and digging sticks. Most families live in thatched wattle-and-daub or log houses in tiny dispersed communities, characterized by distinctive costumes. Roman Catholic observance is combined with indigenous religion. (see also MAYA)

TZUTUHIL   A subgroup of the MAYA.

U

UBA A subgroup of the GOFA.

UBANI A subgroup of the IBO.

UBINE A subgroup of the AYMARA.

UBYKH An ethnic group living since 1864 in Turkey. Until then they were located on the Black Sea coast, north of the modern town of Sochi between the ADYGHEANS, the SHAPSUG, and the ABAZIANS. Some few descendants of the Ubykh in the Caucasus live among the ADYGHEANS. No population data are available: a rough estimate puts them at several hundred.

The Ubykh language belongs to the Abkhazo-Adyghean branch of the Ibero-Caucasian family of languages. It was never written. In the first quarter of the twentieth century it was still spoken by the Ubykh of Turkey, before they began to speak Turkish exclusively. Ubykh in the Caucasus had apparently been linguistically assimilated into the larger Adyghean group by the beginning of the twentieth century.

The Ubykh have been Sunni Muslims of the Hanafi school since the sixteenth century. They retain their ethnic identity despite the loss of their language.

UDAI A subgroup of the JAKUN.

UDEGEY (s.d. Udee, Udekhe) The 2,000 Udegey live in the Sikhate Alin Mountains south, of the Amur River in the Pacific area of the Russian Federation. Their language belongs to the Manchu branch of the Tungus-Manchu group of the Altaic linguistic family. In its group, Udegey is the closest to the Tungusic languages. No alphabet was adopted, and Russian serves as the literary language of the Udegey.

The Udegey, like their neighbors the NANI, NIKHVI, EVENKI, EVEN, and NEGIDAL, were originally hunters and horse- and cattle-raisers. Since their conquest by the RUSSIANS they have become agriculturalists as well.

Their original religion was shamanism, with strong Chinese influences.

UDI An ethnic group living in two villages (Nidz, Vartashen) in northern Azerbaijan and in one village (Zinobiani) in the eastern part of Georgia. The estimated total number of Udi is 7,000. Their language belongs to the Daghestani branch of the Ibero-Caucasian family. It consists of two dialects: Vartashen (including Zinobiani) and Nidz. It is unwritten, with Georgian being used as the literary language in Georgia, and Armenian and Azerbaijani in Azerbaijan. Names and surnames follow the language of the country of residence.

The Udi of Vartashen and Zinobiani are Eastern Orthodox Christians, while those living in Nidz are Monophysite Christians.

According to sources dating from the fifth to the tenth centuries, the Udi were a numerically large people located on a wide territory in Eastern Transcaucasus from the Caucasian ridge to the Aras (Araxes) River. The Udi Christian ceremonies preserve traces of moon worship; the moon was the main deity of the ALBANIANS.

Their traditional economy is based on agriculture and horticulture. Stone (in Georgia, wooden) houses are characteristic; they contain a chimney corner used for drying and storing fruits. They adhere to the traditional Azerbaijani dress and are highly influenced by the culture of the AZERBAIJANI, ARMENIANS, and GEORGIANS.

UDMURT The c.750,000 Udmurt live mainly in the Udmurt Autonomous Republic, with some minorities in the neighboring Tatar, Mari, and Bashkir Republics and the Kirov and Perm Provinces of Russia.

The Udmurt language belongs to the Finno-Ugric group of Uralic languages. It is closely related to, and mutually intelligible with Komi and Komi Permyak. In 1910 the Cyrillic alphabet was adopted, but only in 1920 was the literary language standardized.

Udmurt

Like the KOMI, the Udmurt were hunters and gatherers who became agriculturalists under Russian rule and influence. They retained their traditional religion, although in different areas they borrowed, due to contact with other peoples, either Russian Orthodox Christian or Muslim beliefs and practices.

The Besermen (from Busurman = Musulman = Muslim) are a distinct group, of Volga Turkic origin, which was assimilated into the Udmurt. Their dialect has a great number of Tatar (and to a markedly lesser degree Chuvash) words. Although their name indicates that their nominal religion is Islam, some sources state that they are Russian Orthodox Christians. In either case, the Besermen have retained a great deal of their traditional religious beliefs and rites.

UGANDANS   The population of Uganda, a country in Africa, is an estimated 16.7 million, although reliable figures are impossible to arrive at due to the civil war and bloodshed of the 1980s. Population density is highest at Mount Elgon, in the extreme southwest, and

on the northern shores of Lake Victoria. The lowest density is in the semi-arid areas inhabited by the KARAMOJONG in the central north, and east of Lake Albert.

Ugandans can be divided into several language groups. The largest, consisting of about two-thirds of the population, is the Bantu-speakers, which include the Luganda-speaking GANDA. Nilotic-speakers constitute about a quarter of Uganda's population, subdivided into Western, Eastern, and Southern Nilotic. Eastern Nilotic languages are spoken by the cattle-herding KARAMOJONG as well as by the agriculturalist TESO living in the the northeast. Western Nilotic-speakers occupy northwestern Uganda and are mainly represented by the large ethnic groups of the ACHOLI and the LANGO, as well as by smaller ones like the ALUR, KUMAN, and PALAWO. Southern Nilotic is spoken only by minority groups on the border with Kenya, such as the SUK and the SEBEI. In the far northwest the LUGBARA and MADI, as well as the LENDU, speak Central Sudanic languages.

Luganda, the language of the GANDA, became a lingua franca in southern Uganda not only by being the vernacular of the largest precolonial political entity but also because the Ganda were the earliest group exposed to missionary activity and subsequently to standardization and literacy. In the north no indigenous lingua franca developed, but for a long time Swahili fulfilled this function. The question of Uganda's national language is still not solved. While Luganda seems the obvious candidate, resistance is strong, especially in the north of the country. English is mainly used by the ruling and educated classes, but it cannot be regarded as a truly national language understood throughout the country.

Christianity has prevailed, especially in the Lake Victoria region, whereas in other areas traditional religions still command some following; 70 percent of the population are Christians, two-thirds of whom are Catholics, the rest belonging to Protestant and independent churches. Ten percent are Muslims, living mainly in the south, and 20 percent adhere to traditional religions. The largest Protestant church is the Church of Uganda, an offspring of the Anglican Church Missionary Society, which was active during the colonial era. The greatest resistance towards christianization and islamization comes from the KARAMOJONG. Nevertheless, those Ugandans who are christianized or islamized have frequently absorbed the imported faiths into their traditional religions to form a widely-spread syncretism which even led to the founding of indigenous churches such as the "Society of the One Almighty God" and the "African Orthodox Church," usually headed by a charismatic religious leader. Political affiliations tended to be organized along religious lines, particularly during the years leading to independence.

Traditional religions share some basic traits, such as the belief in a remote god who created the universe, with an accompanying pantheon of spirits, sometimes localized in rocks, rivers, and trees, or embodied in snakes. Very important, except among the KARAMOJONG, is the ancestor-cult, which holds that ancestors are guardians of the social order.

The Bantu peoples are socially differentiated between the HIMA and IRU, who are not themselves ethnic groups. Rather, HIMA is the name given to the cattle-herding aristocracy by the NYORO, GANDA, TORO, NKOLE, KAGWE, and BUSINJA, while IRU signifies peasant or slave. The HIMA arrived in the fifteenth or sixteenth century from the north and imposed their rule over the local Bantu population, whom they named IRU and with whom they intermarried to a varying extent. Originally the Hima were probably Nilotic-speakers, subsequently absorbed linguistically by the majority people on whom they imposed their rule. Their main economic activity was cattle-herding (longhorn), but at least in Ankole they also engaged in some agriculture (sorghum, yams, beans.) Age-sets play a prominent role in their social system. The highest authority is vested in the *kabaka*, who is the overlord of Ankole. At the same time he is regarded as the supreme chief of all HIMA, although the *kabaka* of Buganda is much more powerful and comes from the ranks of the Hima aristocracy. The traditional religion was characterized by ancestor worship, but the HIMA also had the concept of a supreme god and believed in witchcraft and in evil spirits, with possession cults and professional healers. Today they are Christians.

The IRU are the majority of the Bantu-speaking population in the stratified societies of Central and Western Uganda. They were the bulk of the population in societies of Bantu-speaking agriculturalists dominated by Hima cattle-breeders. The main kingdoms of Uganda (Buganda, Bunyoro, Toro, Ankole) were characterized by a stratified society, although in some, such as Buganda, the social division became largely blurred. Another similar group, the BUDDU, live further to the east, on the western shore of Lake Victoria. Their country used to be tbe southern province of Buganda. The IRU are specifically known under that name in the kingdom of Ankole, but they are also known as NKOLE throughout Uganda.

The country can be roughly divided into south and north. Traditionally the south is characterized by subsistence agriculture focused on the production of plantains, with some stock-raising, although this does not play a decisive role. In the north cattle-herding traditionally played a very important role, not only in the economy but even more in the traditional culture and society. It was the adaptation to new environments as well as the rinderpest plague that devastated the herds, which contributed to the shift toward agriculture, varying from a complementary production among the KARAMOJONG to an even more important part of the economic production among peoples like the TESO and the LUGBARA.

Fishing is important among almost all the peoples of Uganda. For some, such as the KENYI or the island dwellers on Lake Victoria, it is even a major part of their income. Cash crop production is centered mainly in the south, particularly in the southeast. The main cash crop is coffee (up to 99 percent of export revenues). Ugandans have experienced the structural problems of a monoculture economy. The civil war brought economic life to a standstill as far as cash crop production was concerned. Uganda had up to the late 1980s a negative economic growth, the gravest decline in the whole of Africa during that period. As a result, the country increasingly fell back on subsistence production.

It is estimated that the Bantu peoples arrived in their present settlement areas in southern Uganda at least 1,000 years ago. Present-day ethnic identities emerged with the formation of kingdoms. This openness to adaptation and change is a feature not unique to Bantu groups; it is also found among Nilotic- and Sudanic-speakers. From about 1500, groups of Western Nilotic-speakers (LUO) moved south, founding the Bito dynasty in Kitara and imposing themselves in most of the Bantu areas as a cattle-herding aristocracy, out of which several kingdoms emerged. Nevertheless, they were linguistically assimilated by the Bantu majority. In northern Uganda the LUO settled in areas in which today they are the sole inhabitants. The most important of the Luo-speakers are the ACHOLI, but Western Nilotic-speakers are to be found also in southeast Uganda, which is inhabited by a number of small ethnic groups of Bantu and Nilotic origin.

Further to the east the more arid areas were settled by the Eastern Nilotic-speakers who, more than the Western Nilotes, adhered to an economy relying almost exclusively on cattle-herding. The only exception are the TESO, who early showed an eagerness to adapt to the new circumstances and economic possibilites provided by colonial rule. The Eastern Nilotic-speakers split up into several groups known collectively as the KARAMOJONG. The LANGO, one of the largest ethnic groups in the north, are probably the result of a fusion between Eastern and Western Nilotic groups, as are the smaller KUMAN and the ethnic groups of the LABWOR. Until the eighteenth century much of what is today Uganda was controlled by the kingdom of Kitara Bunyoro, a stratified society of Hima cattle-herding aristocracy and Bantu agriculturalists. The decline of Kitara-Bunyoro coincided with the ascent of Buganda which developed out of its core area on the northern shore of Lake Victoria to become the most powerful kingdom in Uganda at the time of the arrival of the BRITISH.

The BRITISH established a protectorate over Buganda in 1894, after a short interlude of Imperial British East Africa Company rule during the years 1888–1893. The BRITISH were interested in the area of the Nile sources for strategic reasons. The kingdom subsequently became the base for colonial expansion, a process in which the GANDA themselves played a prominent role. They were not only instrumental in conquering territories, like that of the TESO, but also as agents of administrative penetration. For that reason Buganda always retained a special status within Uganda, and political developments in Uganda during the following decades centered to a certain extent around the GANDA and their kingdom. The conquest of Bunyoro (the region of the NYORO) proved difficult, and only after a prolonged war were the BRITISH able to impose their rule. The areas in the north were incorporated only later, and it took until 1914 for Uganda to assume the approximate borders it has today. Even then the KARAMOJONG were not yet brought under the administrative system taken over by the BRITISH from the GANDA. This system was changing the traditional pattern of society, most notably among the segmentary societies in the northern part of the country, by introducing chiefs.

Uganda was, in terms of administration, by no means uniform, due to the special role conceded not only to Buganda but also to the kingdoms of the NYORO, TORO, and SOGA. The British government succeeded in streamlining the system of colonial rule in 1900, when they divided Uganda into four provinces, one of which was Buganda. The BRITISH restricted the autocratic rule of the king by strengthening the role of a council of chiefs. In the following decades the colonial system was slowly democratized, giving Africans more say in the central administration. Political differences in colonial Uganda were largely formulated along religious affiliations, especially Catholic or Protestant, but the separatist tendencies of the GANDA always played a major role.

In 1962 Uganda became independent under Milton Obote. In 1967 the kingdoms were abolished and dismembered into districts. Obote, himself a LANGO, was deposed in a military coup led by Idi Amin in 1972. During Amin's dictatorship over 300,000 Ugandans were killed by his army, and the entire Asian population was expelled from the country. As well, the role of the south, the area of the main cash crop production, was strengthened. When Amin was deposed in 1979, Obote came back to power. His heavy dependence on support from the LANGO and the ACHOLI, especially in the army, resulted in internal strife which developed into civil war. Yoweri Museveni, a southerner, started a guerrilla war, which brought him to power in 1986.

UGOGO see GOGO.

UGRIANS see MANSI.

UIGHUR (Uygur, Uyghur) A people living in the Xinjiang Uighur Autonomous Region of China and also in Uzbekistan and Qazaqstan. Their estimated number is about 6.3 million, of whom 6 million (1980s estimate) live in China and the remainder in the Commonwealth of Independent States (CIS).

The Uighur language belongs to the Qarluq group of Turkic languages. It consists of three main dialect groups: the central (called also northwestern), southern (the Khotan dialect group), and eastern (Lobnor dialect group). Some scholars add as a fourth group the languages of the SALAR and the Sary Uighur, which are closely related. In China it is written in a reformed Arabic script; in the former Soviet Union it used the Arabic script until the 1930s, when this was replaced by the Roman alphabet. Publications in Uighur were stopped by the end of the 1930s, but renewed in 1947 in the Cyrillic script. Since the late 1940s some Soviet publications destined for the Uighur of China have been printed in the alphabet used there. Ancient Uighur, whose earliest texts date back to the eighth century and which differs considerably from the modern language, utilized an alphabet of its own.

The Uighur are Sunni Muslims of the Hanafi school. They are sedentary agriculturalists and urban dwellers, utilizing an irrigation system (based on wells connected by underground canals in China). In China the main

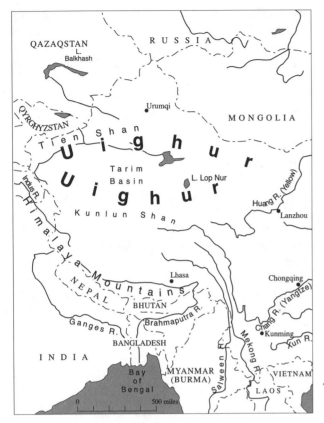

Uighur

crops are wheat, maize, and cotton, with some horticulture; urban dwellers are mainly engaged in crafts and trade. In Uzbekistan and Qazaqstan urban Uighur work in factories, crafts, services, and free professions.

The ethnonym "Uighur" has been traced back to the eighth century, although it fell into disuse in the fifteenth century. The closely cognate Turkic groups dwelling in Xinjiang called themselves by the name of their locality: KASHGHARLYQ (Kashghar), TURPANLYQ (Turpan), AQSULUQ (Aqsu), YAKANLYQ (Yakan). One such group, dwellers in the Ili valley, became known as Taranchi (lit. agriculturalist). They came to Central Asia in large groups in the early 1880s and were resettled by the czarist authorities, mainly in the Jetisu (Semirechie) area of present day Qazaqstan. Small groups of Kashgarlyq and Yakanlyq were the first to migrate to Central Asia. In the mid-nineteenth century they settled in the Ferghana valley (present-day Uzbekistan), where they were known under the general name of Kashgharlyq. "Uighur" was revived as a generic name for all these groups by an assembly in Tashkent in 1921. It steadily became accepted as the general denomination of all the above-mentioned cognate groups in China too, as evidenced by the name given to their region there.

The Uighur of Qazaqstan and Qyrghyzstan still firmly retain their ethnic identity, which was further strengthened by an influx of considerable numbers of Xinjiang Uighur fleeing China in the 1950s and 1960s during the accelerated ethnic sinization of Xinjiang by the central Chinese authorities. On the other hand, the Uighur living in Uzbekistan seem to be undergoing a process of steady assimilation into the UZBEKS.

UKRAINIANS (s.d. Ukraintsy) About 75 percent of the 60 million Ukrainians live in the Ukraine, where they form c.80 percent of the population, and in adjacent areas in neighboring Poland, Slovakia, Hungary, Romania, Moldova, Russia, and Belarus. Large numbers of Ukrainians live throughout Russia, Moldova, Qazaqstan, and Uzbekistan. Large expatriate communities live in Canada, the United States, France, Britain, and Germany.

The Ukrainian language belongs to the eastern subgroup of the Slavic languages and is mutually intelligible (though not necessarily with ease) with Russian and Byelorussian. It is divided into three groups of dialects, southern, northern, and southwestern, which correspond roughly to Ukrainian ethnographic-cultural divisions. An old Ukrainian literary language, formed in the fourteenth century, was replaced by Polish and Russian. The modern literary language was created in the nineteenth century and is based mainly on the Kiev dialect. It uses the Cyrillic alphabet. Parallel literary languages were created in the nineteenth century in Galicia (using Polish orthography) and in Carpathorus (using Hungarian orthography), but both gave way to the Kiev-based one.

Living in a large country with divergent ecological conditions and numerous neighbors, and having a complicated history, the Ukrainians are divided into three major ethnographic-ecological-cultural groups.

The Central-Eastern (or Southeastern) group live roughly south of the Kiev-Poltava line, i.e., in the steppe zone. The population of this area was strongly influenced by the neighboring TATARS and, in the southeast, by CHERKESS, and here the Ukrainian Zaporozhtsy, Black Sea, and Don Cossacks emerged. The Ukrainians of this group are mainly livestock-raisers and grain farmers.

The Northern group live north of the Sumi-Kiev-Zhitomir-Rivno line, i.e., the steppe forest zone. They were influenced mainly by the RUSSIANS and BYELORUSSIANS, and are mainly dairy and grain farmers, foresters, and flax-raisers.

The Western (or Southwestern) group live west of the Rivno-Kamenets line. They were strongly influenced by the POLES, HUNGARIANS, and to a lesser degree, the ROMANIANS and SLOVAKS. They are mainly foresters, semi-nomadic shepherds, and grain-, cattle-, and pig-farmers.

The first two groups are closer to each other than to the third in language, culture, and religion, belonging mainly to the Russian Orthodox Church. The third group is regarded by some as a transitional group between the eastern and western Slavs. They belong to the Ruthenian-Uniate Church, which was formed at the synod of Brzesc (Brest Litovsk) of 1596 when nine Orthodox bishops recognized the primacy of the pope but retained their separate church rites. They came under Soviet rule only following World War II.

The Poleshchuk form a distinct group among the Ukrainians. Living in the Pripet Marshes of Polesia they were heavily influenced by the neighboring BYELORUSSIANS and might be regarded as a transitional group between these two peoples, as is their dialect.

East Slavic tribes settled in the area of present day Ukraine in the sixth-seventh centuries C.E. From the ninth to thirteenth centuries they were part of Kievan Russia. It is in the centuries that followed invasions by the MONGOLS (1238) that the Ukrainians, like the neighboring eastern Slavic peoples, were formed. Unlike them, however, the ethnogenesis of the Ukrainians, their part in the inheritance of Kievan Russia, and their status vis-a-vis the RUSSIANS were all subject to heated dispute, which gave rise to a wide range of theories. One of the more extreme of these holds that the Ukrainians were the original people of Kievan Russia while the RUSSIANS were descendants of frontier settlers who intermingled with a variety of other peoples. The other theory holds that the Ukrainians were not part of Kievan Russia but lived west of it, and only settled their present areas following the destruction and depopulation of Kiev by the MONGOLS.

While Kiev was, indeed, destroyed and depopulated by the MONGOLS, other principalities west and north of it survived. These were gradually absorbed by Poland and Lithuania. After the dynastic union between the two (1386) the Ukraine became part of Poland. In that period the term *Ukraina* (lit. "borderland") originated; it was Poland's southeastern frontier against the CRIMEAN TATARS and the Ottomans.

The western and northern parts of the Ukraine were subjected to a strong Polish and Catholic influence. A Polish nobility enserfed the peasants, who largely retained their East Slavic speech and Slavonic service in the church (whether Russian Orthodox or Uniate). In the more turbulent borderlands beyond the Dnieper River, fugitives from the Polish border formed the Cossack bands which created the *Zaporizhska Sich* and, at the beginning of the sixteenth century, were strong enough to be mobilized by the Polish kings to protect them from Tatar raids.

In spite of this, inherent social, national, and religious contradictions existed between the Cossacks and the Polish state. They erupted in a series of rebellions, the most powerful and famous of which was led in 1648 by Bohdan Khmielnycki. In 1654 he appealed to the RUSSIANS for help and swore allegiance to the czar, an event celebrated in the Soviet Union as the "Union of the Ukraine and Russia." A Polish-Russian struggle followed. Although the two partitioned the Ukraine along the Dnieper River in 1667, Ottoman and Swedish involvement prolonged the struggle until 1709.

In 1775 Catherine the Great suppressed and disarmed the Zaprozhian Cossacks and brought the Ukraine under regular Russian administration. At the second partition of Poland (1793) a large part of the Ukraine was added to the Russian Empire. During the last two decades of the eighteenth and the first half of the nineteenth centuries, the Ukraine went through rapid socio-economic changes and the steppe belt was developed and colonized, making the Ukraine the center of gravity of the Russian empire's economy first as the main grain producer and exporter and then as an important mining and industrial center.

This rapid economic development was followed by great demographic, social, and socio-economic changes, which produced a revival of Ukrainian literature and the use of the Ukrainian language in education and scholarship during the middle of the nineteenth century. Among the leaders of this process was Taras Shevchenko (1819–1860) the national poet, and Mykola Kostomariv (1817–1885) and Panteleimon Kulysh (1819–1897), the founding fathers of Ukrainian historiography. In 1846 the short-lived "Secret Society of Saints Cyril and Methodius" was established in Kiev, an event which is commonly regarded as marking the birth of Ukrainian nationalism.

The Russian authorities regarded the Ukrainians (as well as the BYELORUSSIANS) as part of the Russian people. They even banned the name "Ukrainians," replacing it with the old term Malorussy (Lesser Russians). Alarmed at the growing use of the Ukrainian language in education and publication, they banned it in 1876

Ukrainians

and started a campaign of forced russification, which ended only after the revolution of 1905. During these years the center of Ukrainian nationalism, literature, and scholarship moved to Austro-Hungarian Lvov, and then to Lemberg.

Following the revolution of 1917, a national Ukrainian congress proclaimed in Kiev a "free sovereign" Ukrainian republic. In a countermove the Bolshevik regime formed a Ukrainian Soviet government in Kharkov. After the civil war most of the Ukraine remained under Soviet rule and was one of the founding republics of the Soviet Union. Western Ukraine came under POLISH rule. In World War II the Ukraine was conquered by the GERMANS, who enjoyed the cooperation of some Ukrainian nationalists. Following the war, the western Ukraine, Transcarpathia (Carpathorus), Bukovina, and southern Bessarabia were annexed to the Ukrainian Soviet Republic from Poland, Czechoslovakia, and Romania. In 1954 the Crimea was annexed to the Ukraine as part of the celebration of the tricentennial of the "unification of the Ukraine and Russia."

While the Ukraine underwent further industrial development and became a crucial part of the Soviet economy (its economic far surpassing its demographic weight), the Ukrainians suffered great losses (in the millions) in the civil war, the collectivization and famine that accompanied it, and then again in World War II and during the incorporation of western Ukraine into the Soviet Union.

In addition, during the entire Soviet period the Ukrainians were under strong, albeit generally subtle, pressure to russify, which further decimated their numbers (in one such case the Soviet authorities changed the nationality of the Kuban Cossacks in 1929 from Ukrainian to Russian, thus depriving the Ukrainians and adding to the RUSSIANS 2–3 million people).

Following the dissolution of the Soviet Union the Ukraine became a fully independent state. Although it joined the CIS, being the strongest member after Russia, it was an extreme advocate of keeping the CIS as loose an organization as possible. (see also BYELORUSSIANS)

ULBARAG   A subgroup of the GURAGE.

ULCHI   One of the four NANI groups.

ULLADAN   An ethnic group, numbering about 5,000, found in the state of Kerala, southern India. They are primarily nomadic hunters but also engage in farming and forestry.

ULSTERMEN   see NORTHERN IRISH.

ULU   A subgroup of the KUBU.

UMALASA   An ethnic group living on the Indonesian island of Kalimantan (Borneo). (see also DAYAK)

UMANIYIN   see OMANIS.

UMATILLA   A Native North American group, numbering 1,900, many of whom live on the Umatilla Federal Reservation, Umatilla County, Oregon, U.S.A.

Traditionally they were hunters of small game and fishers. Today many have become ranchers and workers in the local forest industry.

UNGA   A Chibemba-speaking group, numbering about 23,000, living near the Banguelu swamps in Zambia. They were originally part of the BEMBA. Fishing is their traditional source of livelihood.

UNITED ARAB EMIRATES ARABS   The United Arab Emirates (UAE, formerly the "Trucial States" or "Trucial Oman") are a conglomerate of seven Arab sheikhdoms along the southwestern coast of the Persian Gulf: Abu Dhabi, Dubai, Sharjah, Ajman, Umm al-Qaywayn, Ras al-Khaymah, and Fujayrah. Their combined population is 1.9 million. However, only a minority of some 30 percent are indigenous ARABS; other ARABS (including 37,000 PALESTINIANS) make up 56 percent, PAKISTANIS and INDIANS account for 9 percent, PERSIANS, 1.7 percent, and BALUCHS and Africans, 1 percent each. The official language is Arabic. Seventy-six percent are Sunni Muslims, 19 percent Shi'ites, and 4 percent Christians. Only intervention by the BRITISH brought these ARABS together and kept them from being swallowed by their more powerful neighbors.

Until the 1700s there were only fishing, pearling, and smuggling villages in the region, without known resources, yet strategically controlling the entrance to the Gulf. For this reason, the BRITISH signed a series of treaties giving them exclusive control over maritime relations but leaving the tribal sheikhs control over land. In 1892 the relationship was formalized in protectorate treaties. The sheikhs received subsidies in return, but were forced to (officially) suppress slave traffic.

After the 1950s oil exports created a boom, particularly in Abu Dhabi, causing explosive development and the highest per capita income in the world. Moderate amounts of oil were later found in Dubai, Sharjah, and Ras al-Khaimah.

As Britain prepared to leave in 1971, the emirates united in a confederation. They created an army with British support. Nevertheless each state maintains its own emir and princely families, and remains internally an absolute monarchy, with little mutual coordination. Abu Dhabi, five times bigger than the other emirates together and with the largest population and immense oil reserves, dominates politically. Competing against it is Dubai, until 1825 considered a dependency of Abu Dhabi. Its wealth was first based on smuggling gold, but Dubai and Sharjah are now developing as a shipping and commercial center. Throughout the emirates there are some agricultural oases; industrialization has been lagging due to water and labor shortages. Economic development transformed the sparse indigenous population into an upper class enjoying free education and medical services. As in other Gulf states, this situation has also made them extremely dependent on migrants, who constitute 80 percent of the labor force. The foreigners are concentrated in Abu Dhabi City and Dubai-Sharjah, there forming a powerless underclass whose political aspirations are feared. In Dubai alone there were 30,000, mostly Shi'ite, IRANIANS out of a total population of 210,000 (1983). The recession following the fall of oil prices in the 1980s led to attempts at repatriation.

UNYANYEMBE   A subgroup of the NYAMWEZI.

UPARA   A subgroup of the JIVARO.

UPO MARI   see MARI.

UPPER VOLTA, PEOPLE OF   see BURKINABES.

URANG AWAK   see MINANGKABAU.

URANG KANEKES   see BADUI.

URANG PADANG   see MINANGKABAU.

URANG PARAHIANG see BADUI.

URANG PRIJANGAN see SUNDANESE.

URANG TAWAJAN see BADUI.

URBUGH see QUBACHI.

URDU see PAKISTANIS.

URDUNIYYUN see JORDANIANS.

UREUENG BROLI A subgroup of the ATJEHNESE.

UREUENG TUNONG A subgroup of the ATJEHNESE.

URHOBO An ethnic group living in the Bendel State in west-central Nigeria. They are related to the EDO and speak their language. Although they engage primarily in agriculture, since independence some Urhobo villages have become centers of Nigeria's timber industry.

URIDAVAN A Kannada-speaking group of farmers living in the northern part of the state of Kerala, southern India.

URIRO A subgroup of the GURAGE.

URUBUS-KAAPOR A South American Indian group living between the States of Pará and Maranhao,

Urubus-Kaapor

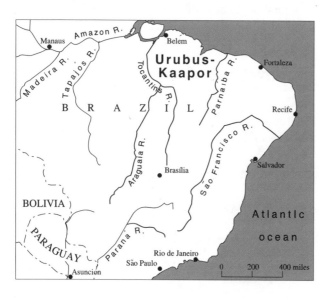

northeastern Brazil. They number around 1,000, dispersed in more than fifteen villages. Although an acculturation process has been under way for a long time, some parts of the group have not yet been affected by it.

URU-EU-WAU-WAU A South American Indian group living in the territory of Rondonia, north Brazil. This group, first contacted in 1984, has been dying of diseases (mostly tuberculosis) contracted through their contact with civilization. Their reservation has been undergoing extensive lumbering since 1988.

URUGUAYANS The over 3 million inhabitants of Uruguay, South America's smallest Spanish-speaking country, are mainly of European descent; *mestizos* account for about 5 percent, blacks slightly less, of the population. About half the Uruguayans (who are 80 percent urbanized) live in the region of Montevideo, the capital city; about 60 percent profess Roman Catholicism and over 30 percent no religion at all; the rest are Protestants or JEWS.

For nearly 200 years after the SPANIARDS first reached the Plata region, they established no fixed settlement in what is now Uruguay. The region was occupied chiefly by nomadic cattle herders (*gauchos*). There was no attempt to claim ownership of the land or even to establish ranch headquarters. The idea of landownership was slow to reach Uruguay, but once it did, the zone of *estancias* (ranches) moved northward from the Plata shore and the nomadic *gauchos* were pushed to more remote parts of the country. Landowners gradually replaced the *gauchos* with hired workers. As this type of occupation spread northward, Uruguay became a land of small scattered trading villages and widely spaced ranches. By the 1830s, the country was already grazed by millions of cattle, but the only products exported were hides, tallow, and salt beef.

In 1840 high grade merino sheep were introduced from Britain, and the grazing of wool sheep spread rapidly. In the 1870s two inventions reached Uruguay that initiated major changes in the pastoral economy. One was barbed wire, which made possible the fencing of pastures and control of animal breeding, the other was the refrigerator ship, which made possible the shipment of frozen meat across the tropics. It is estimated that by 1900 there were in Uruguay 18.5 million head of sheep and 7 million head of cattle.

This transformation was made possible by the initiative of European immigration during the nineteenth century. By 1852 more than a fifth of the Uruguayan population was foreign-born. Work was plentiful in the cattle industry and the *saladeros* (salted beef plants), due to the expansion of the British market for Uruguayan meat. The 1860 census revealed that the proportion of foreigners in Uruguay had grown to 35 percent, while in 48 percent of the total population lived in Montevideo. BRAZILIANS constituted the largest foreign colony, almost 20,000 people, or a fourth of the foreign total. SPANIARDS ran a close second with some 18,000. The ITALIANS and FRENCH created communities which stabilized in number at around 10,000 each. Almost half the population of Montevideo itself was foreign-born. By 1908 foreigners constituted 42 percent of the labor force in the industrial sector of Montevideo and 28.4 percent at the national level. Between the middle of the nineteenth century and 1903, the population of Uruguay grew almost thirteen times. By 1908 in Montevideo almost one-third of the inhabitants were foreigners. In the period 1881-1924, ITALIANS made up 41 percent of the total immigrants, SPANIARDS, 30 percent, and FRENCH, 6 percent. These immigrants made great contributions to the modernization of the country. The role of immigration in the rapid economic growth of Uruguay was crucial, specially in the secondary and tertiary sectors in the cities, as well as in the national urbanization process. Under the impact of immigration the old cultural patterns practically dissolved.

Uruguay's territory has served throughout much of its history as a buffer zone. The colonial empires of the SPANIARDS and PORTUGUESE disputed the area, invading Uruguay repeatedly in the attempt to occupy and retain a strategic position at the mouth of the Rio de la Plata. Uruguay (Banda Oriental, or East Bank) was an integral part of the viceroyship of Rio de la Plata, and gained independence through the intervention of the BRITISH and an agreement between Argentina and Brazil to recognize its sovereignty.

The Uruguayan republic soon became the most stable and democratic state in Latin America. During the early twentieth century, it made rapid economic and social progress. Exports of meat, wool, leather and grain continued to expand the nation's prosperity until the 1950s. Uruguay attained distinction in Latin America though the socio-political model implemented by Jose Batle y Ordoñez, who organized the urban and working-class population under the banner of the Colorado party. He and his successors created a welfare state that provided social benefits seldom equaled elsewhere in the developed world. The welfare state collapsed by 1965, however, as the largely pastoral economy proved unable to support a system in which most people worked in nonproductive activities. Instead, an authoritarian political regime took power with military intervention in 1973 to fight armed insurgency (the Tupamaros guerillas), and Uruguay became an oppressive state oriented by a neo-liberal economy policy that provoked a large wave of emigrants, including political exiles and refugees. Since 1984 re-democratization is gradually under way.

URUM (s.d. Urumchu) Turkish-speaking Christians of the Greek Orthodox denomination. During the 1922 population exchange between Greece and Turkey, many of the GREEKS repatriated to Turkey were in fact Urum (as many of the TURKS repatriated to Turkey were Greek-speaking Muslims). In the Caucasus, they are descended from two waves of Urum emigration from the Ottoman Empire in the eighteenth and nineteenth centuries. There they settled in Georgia, Abkhazia and the Kuban area, but have not been listed separately in Soviet statistics.

One group of Urum, the Greeks of Mariapol, spoke a Tatar dialect and were deported to Central Asia together with the CRIMEAN TATARS in 1944. In the early 1990s some Urum immigrated to Greece as repatriates.

USHI (Aushi) A Chibemba-speaking group numbering about 125,000 living in Zambia in the region northeast of the upper Luapula River and west of Lake Bangweulu. The Ushi believe in a god called Makumba. They trace their origins to the LUBA and were ruled by the LUNDA.

USINO (s.d. Tariba) An ethnic group numbering several hundreds living in the Ramu River region of northern Papua New Guinea. They speak various related indigenous languages. Their subsistence is based on slash and burn cultivation and pig raising. Although most are practicing Lutherans, many still possess traditional religious beliefs in spirits and ghosts. The most important ceremonies center around male initiation.

USPANTEC A subgroup of the MAYA.

USUKUMA see SUKUMA.

UTE A Native North American group numbering 6,000, living in Colorado, U.S.A., on several Federal Reservations, the Southern Ute and Ute Mountain Reservations and the Goshute Federal Reservation in Utah.

Traditionally they were hunters of small game and gatherers of wild plants. Today they are agriculturalists.

UTUTU   A subgroup of the IBO.

UYGHUR, UYGUR   see UIGHUR.

Uzbeks

UZBEKS   A people living mainly in Uzbekistan and in the adjacent areas of Turkmenistan, Qazaqstan, Qyrghyzstan, and Tajikistan. They are also found in Afghanistan and in the Xinjiang Uighur Autonomous Region of China. They are the second largest Turkic people in the world (following the TURKS of Turkey). Their estimated number is about 18.5 million, 16.6 million of whom live in the Uzbekistan and other countries of the Commonwealth of Independent States (CIS), 1.3 million in Afghanistan, and about 12,500 in Xinjiang. The Uzbeks of Afghanistan are descendants of those who fled Soviet rule in the 1920s and early 1930s.

The Uzbek language belongs to the Qarluq group of Turkic languages. It consists of two main dialect groupings, each containing a considerable number of dialects. By the mid-1930s, Soviet literary Uzbek was finally based mainly on the Tashkent and Ferghana dialects. In 1923 the traditional Arabic alphabet was replaced by a reformed vocalized version, which was replaced by the Roman and in 1940 by the Cyrillic alphabets. Together with Russian, Uzbek was one of the official languages of the Uzbeks, and together with Tajik and Russian one of the official languages of the Tajik SSR. In 1980 Uzbek was proclaimed one of the national languages of Afghanistan; it utilizes the traditional Arabic alphabet, but publications in the language are scarce. In Xinjiang it is practically an unwritten language, Uighur being used as the language of writing and education.

The Uzbeks are Sunni Muslims of the Hanafi school. Most are sedentary agriculturalists and some are urban dwellers. The main crop in the Uzbek-populated areas of Central Asia is cotton, cultivated in soil irrigated predominantly by the traditional system of regulated channeling of water. Additional crops are cereals and grapes; there is also some herding, mainly of sheep. Urban dwellers work in factories, at crafts and services, and since the end of the 1980s in legalized private trade. In Afghanistan main rural occupations are cereal-growing, horticulture, and herding, and main urban occupations are crafts and trade. The Uzbeks of Xinjiang are predominantly urban craftsmen and traders.

The typical Uzbek village consists of one-storey mud brick (often built over a wooden frame) flat-roofed houses, each with a front yard and surrounded by a high outer wall of mud or a mixture of stone and mud. The largest and finest building in the village is usually the mosque. Since the late 1920s most village mosques were closed or converted into local clubs, but in the late 1980s their reconversion was begun. In traditional parts of Central Asia Uzbek-populated towns, living compounds followed the same pattern as in villages, but may be larger and sometimes having a second floor. The streets are usually very narrow. Such a traditional town consists of a number of quarters, each with its own mosque, and each town would have a central mosque too. Towns would also have several *madrasa* (Islamic seminaries). The process of reopening the town mosques and *madrasas* has been underway since the end of the 1980s. Some mosques and *madrasas* are of great esthetic value. Since the end of the nineteenth century European-type buildings have been constructed in many towns and even in villages.

In Central Asia urban Uzbeks, both men and women, follow a European style of dress, with the traditional

above: Uzbeks in a tea house in Bukhara, Uzbekistan
below: Uzbeks in the market in Orgot, Uzbekistan

cap still being worn by many men. Rural Uzbeks follow a semi-European style, but in Afghanistan and Xinjiang the traditional form of dress is adhered to by both sexes.

The ethnogenesis of the Uzbeks has been a long and steady process which is not yet complete. Its main component is the ancient Central Asian Iranian ethnic groups which have been undergoing a centuries-long, almost latent, process of turkification. The process has been artificially hastened by the authorities since the 1920s, which has caused strong resentment among the intellectual strata of Tajiks. Its second component was the older Turkic settlers of Central Asia, whose first appearance in the present territory of the Uzbeks is traced back to the sixth century. The last component was the confederation of Turkic and turkified nomad MONGOLS, known under the general name of Uzbeks, who began expanding into Central Asia in the fifteenth century and finally conquered it in the sixteenth century. It was this Uzbek confederation to which all the rulers of the sixteenth to nineteenth century Central Asian principalities belonged (in the aftermath of the late 1860s to early 1870s Russian conquest of Central Asia one of them, the Khuqand (Kokand) principality

was abolished in 1876, and two others, the Bukharan and the Khivan, became, with very diminished territories, Russian protectorates). It was this name that was chosen as a unifying ethnic designation for the population of a republic established in 1924 on most of the Russian territories in Central Asia: the Uzbek Soviet Socialist Republic. In the longer run this engineering of a new ethnicity proved successful: the common Uzbek self-identification now strongly prevails over tribal identifications. Nevertheless, the latter still exist, albeit in a secondary and/or residual form. The following tribes deserve mentioning: the QARLUQ, QYPCHAQ, JALAIR, BARLAS, QUNGRAT, MANGHIT, LAQAY, and YUZ. Although not a tribe, the KURAMA group dwelling near Tashkent, also has a subethnic identity of its own (they are in all probability uzbekified QAZAQS). In Afghanistan the QARLUQ and QYPCHAQ regard themselves as distinct ethnic entities.

In September 1991 Uzbekistan proclaimed its sovereignty but remained within the framework of the CIS. In Afghanistan Uzbeks were very active in the resistance to the Soviet 1979 intervention and played a leading role in the downfall of the Moscow-backed Afghanistani government in 1992. (see also AFGHANS, TAJIKS)

V

VADDA, VADDO   see VEDDA.

VAD'D'ALAISET   see VOTES.

VAGALA   A small ethnic group living in northern Ghana and Burkina Faso. Together with other neighboring groups, it is classified as GRUSI.

VAGHRI   An ethnic group of farmers, shepherds, and hunters found in Gujarat, western India. They are Hindus and number several thousand.

VAI   An ethnic group living in Liberia, on Grand Cape Mount, where they number about 75,000, or 3 percent of the population, and on the coast of Sierra Leone where, together with the KONO, they number about 200,000. In Sierra Leone the Vai are either Muslims or Christians while in Liberia they are mostly Muslims. According to their tradition, they migrated to Sierra Leone with the KONO in search of salt. After a long journey, the KONO gave up while the Vai continued the search and eventually settled farther along the coast.

The Vai who live in Sierra Leone have been largely absorbed by the MENDE and most speak the Mende language. In Liberia, the Vai political and judicial structure was shaken by Americo-Liberian government intervention in the nineteenth and twentieth centuries. In reaction, many Vai converted to Islam, but some intermarried with the AMERICO-LIBERIANS and thus became involved in the political and economic life of the country.

The Vai are not directly involved in the ongoing civil war in Liberia between the DAN, MANO, and KISSI against the KRAHN, but like all ethnic groups there, they are deeply affected by it. (see also KONO, LIBERIANS)

VAIGALI   (Vai, Vaialans) One of several tribes grouped together as NURESTANIS.

VAKHAN   see WAKHI.

VAKHI   An ethnic group living in Afghanistan.

VALLEY TONGA   see TONGA.

VALMIKI   An ethnic group, numbering 43,000 (1981), living in Andhra Pradesh, India. They speak Oriya, of the Indo-Aryan family of languages. They are mostly agriculturalists and day-laborers. Some are merchants and moneylenders, and a few possess arable land.

VAMAI   One of several tribes grouped together as NURESTANIS.

VANGAVALANS   An ethnic group dispersed in the northern, eastern, southeastern, and central-eastern parts of Afghanistan. They are estimated as numbering 5,000.

The Vangavalans are Sunni Muslims of the Hanafi school. Their language, Inku, belongs to the Indian group of the Indo-European family of languages. Although they share Inku with several other dispersed ethnic groups of Afghanistan (JALALI, PIKRAJ, SHADIBAZ), they have their own distinctive self-identity. Practically all adult Vangavalans speak Dari (the Afghanistani form of Persian) and/or Pashto as well as their mother tongue.

They are peripatetics, i.e, non-pastoral nomads. Most men engage in trading animals, smuggling, and cloth-peddling; in central-east Afghanistan they are also jugglers, snake-charmers, haberdashers, and perfumists. The women's main occupation is peddling, mainly of bangles. (see also AFGHANS, JATS II)

VANUATU ISLANDERS   A people numbering about 136,000, or 95 percent of the population of some eighty islands in the Pacific Ocean (formerly the New Hebrides), north of Australia. The main island is Efate

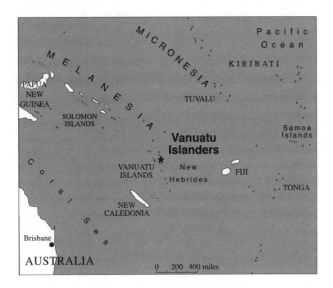

Vanuatu Islanders

and the largest is Espiritu Santo. While they are a Melanesian-speaking people, their lingua franca is the Bislama (Vanuatu Pidgin). They are Christians, mainly Presbyterian. The church hierarchy has replaced the graded society as a structural framework within which leaders exercise authority. The chief activity is traditional subsistence agriculture, and about 70 percent of the Islanders live in rural communities.

Until 1980 Vanuatu was jointly governed by an Anglo-French condominium established in 1906. The islanders achieved independence in 1980, and controversy over issues of land rights were settled by the new constitution, which ruled that the land belong to the indigenous owners and their descendants. In March 1988, Vanuatu signed an agreement with Papua New Guinea and the Solomon Islands to form the "Spearhead Group," which aimed to preserve Melanesian cultural traditions and to campaign for New Caledonian independence.

The principal exports are cocoa, copra, beef, and timber. In 1989 agriculture, forestry, and fishing contributed about 18.9 percent of Vanuatu's national product, about half their proportional contribution in the early 1980s.

VARDAK A subgroup of the PASHTUN.

VARMA (Bavarma) An ethnic group, related to the ESHIRA, living in Gabon.

VAROZVI see RUZWI.

VARSINAIS SUOMALAISET see FINNS.

VAZIR A subgroup of the PASHTUN.

VEDDA (Vadda, Veddah, Veddha, Vaddo; Dravidian for "hunter") An ethnic group inhabiting the island of Sri Lanka (Ceylon), mainly in the dry midlands between the TAMILS in the north and the SINHALESE in the south and west. They are divided into three main groups: the Anuradhapura Vedda, who live in the center-north of Sri Lanka, the Bintenne Vedda of the southeast portion of the island, and the Coastal Vedda who live along the coast between Tricomalee and Batticaloa. The Coastal Vedda live in close proximity to the TAMILS and therefore speak the Dravidian Tamil language, whereas the Anuradhapura and the Bintenne Vedda speak Sinhalese. Although the Vedda have been overwhelmingly absorbed into the neighboring cultures, both the TAMIL and the SINHALESE consider them a pagan, uncivilized group and, as such, a lower class. The Vedda themselves claim to be direct descendants of the original Sri Lankans.

Traditionally hunters and gatherers, the Vedda have moved toward shifting agriculture inland and fishing on the coast. Inland Vedda usually plant manioc, millet, beans, maize, and other vegetables for both subsistence and as a cash crop. The Coastal Vedda are net fisherman who also work small vegetable plots for subsistence. There has been an increasing need for most Vedda to hire themselves out as low-wage field hands.

The Vedda caste system is considerably weaker than that of the TAMILS and SINHALESE. Much of the administration of Vedda society is run or overseen by the SINHALESE or TAMIL.

In the past, Vedda worshiped local deities and spirits (both good and evil), but now tend to worship in either Buddhist temples or the Hindu shrines. The Coastal Vedda practice Hinduism, like their Tamils neighbors, and the Anuradhapura Vedda are Buddhists like the SINHALESE. The Bintenne Vedda, for the most part, still believe in local deities and worship the recently deceased. Most Vedda believe that people's souls can be possessed by evil spirits, thus creating the need for large ceremonial exorcisms.

VEH see VEN.

VEJOZ A tribe of the MATACO-MATAGUAYO.

VEN (Veh) A Mon-Khmer group living in southern Laos. They cultivate rice using slash and burn methods, and raise livestock.

VENDA One of the southern Bantu-speaking peoples, numbering c.550,000. They are found in the Soutpansberg area of the northern Transvaal of South Africa, and in southern Zimbabwe.

The Venda are an exceptional case among the black people of South Africa in that the majority (around 60 percent) adhere to traditional religious beliefs, the remainder being Christian. Of the latter, some 50 percent belong to African Independent Churches; another 18 percent are Lutherans; and 10 percent are Roman Catholics.

The Venda in South Africa accepted self-government under South Africa's homeland plan in 1971; Venda, the smallest of South Africa's Tribal Homelands, has been independent since September 1979. It is also the poorest in every respect. Its major products are tea, tropical fruit, and sisal.

There are two schools of interpretation of early Venda history, one emphasizing migration, the other local development. The Venda do not have a historical memory of themselves as a culturally or politically homogeneous people. Their language, which emerged as a distinct tongue in the early sixteenth century, is an amalgamation of the archaic forms of the languages spoken by the SHONA and SOTHO, peoples with whom the Venda also share a number of cultural elements. Considerations of personal safety when travelling among the SOTHO country are probably responsible for the Vendas' adoption, in the nineteenth century, of the Sotho custom of male circumcision. The Venda include an endogamous group called the LEMBA who have taboos against the consumption of pork, while their animal slaughtering traditions bear close resemblance to those practiced on the Swahili coast. The LEMBA, however, are not Muslims.

Since earliest times, the Venda have been divided into small-scale kinship groups (*mitupo*, sing. *mutopo*), sharing common views of origin, totemic oaths and taboos, burial customs, and political rituals. The *mutopo* does not necessarily constitute a corporate body. The politically-dominant *mutopo* among the Venda is the SINGO. After the late seventeenth century, the SINGO subjugated many communities in the Soutpansberg area. Non-Singo traditions refer to some of these groups as Venda, while most early ethnographers adopted the general Singo term for them: Ngona. The Singos' allies in this subjugation process were the Nadalamo and the Mphaphuli. In the eighteenth cen-

tury, the SINGO incorporated all remaining communities in the Soutpansberg area.

Traditionally, social and political stratification within the Venda is symbolically expressed in burial rites. Within this system there are three broad *mitupo* strata. The politically dominant stratum claims to have originated in the mountains, and is also buried there. The second stratum is the "pool people" and the third is the much despised "dry ones." Members of this last category are believed to wield malignant anti-social powers. (see also SOUTH AFRICANS, ZIMBABWEANS)

VENEZUELANS The 20 million inhabitants of Venezuela are 70 percent *mestizo* (descendants of both SPANIARDS and Indians), 20 percent Europeans, and 10 percent Indian and black. Indigenous peoples inhabit the Guyana Highlands and the forests west of Lake Maracaibo. In the Amazon region, diminishing numbers live in the states of Apure, Bolívar, Sucre, and Zulia. Less than thirty years ago it was predicted that indigenous tribes would suffer extinction by the year 2000, but liberalization of government policy toward indigenous Venezuelans since 1961 has altered this. Recently, for example, a special reserve was established for the YANOMAMI, who also inhabit northeastern Brazil.

Venezuelans of African descent inhabit mainly the coastal areas, with high concentrations in the vicinity of ports. European immigration to Venezuela has been heavy since the 1950s, as a result of which it is estimated that one in every six Venezuelans is foreign-born.

The Indian population consists of forty groups, speaking 170 languages and dialects. The most important and numerous tribes are the ACHAGUA, ARAWAK, CABERRE, CARACAS, CUMANANGOTO, GANDULE, GUAHIBLO, GUAJIRO, GUAYUPE, JIRAJIRA, MARAKAPAN, MARICHE, MOTILONES, OMEGUA, OTOMAC, PALENQUE, PARIA, QUIRIQUIRE, SALIVA, TEQUES, TIMOTE, TUMUZU, and ZORCA. Although some have converted to Catholicism, most have retained their traditional cultures and religions, altered only slightly by contact with outsiders. In spite of increased government protection, however, they are now being affected by development projects or tourism.

While the *mestizo* population continues to increase and its penetration of Venezuelan culture to spread, Venezuela has also been encouraging ITALIANS, PORTUGESE, SPANISH, and COLOMBIANS to immigrate to the country: at least a million foreigners currently reside in Venezuela. A strong economic incentive is Venezuela's rich supply of oil and well-developed oil refining industry, which have attracted many guest workers from the Caribbean region.

With the exception of relatively isolated Indian groups, almost all Venezuelans speak Spanish. The majority (94 percent) of the population is Roman Catholic. Relations between the church and state are friendly, and the presence of statutory religious freedom has enabled religious minorities, including Protestants and JEWS, to flourish there.

Venezuela was named "Little Venice" by Alonso de Ojeda, who sailed into the Gulf of Venezuela in 1499. The territory, Spanish control of which was fiercely resisted by Indians, was under the control of a German banking firm during much of the early 1500s. The indigenous people were decimated by smallpox in the late 1590s. From then until independence was declared in 1811, Venezuela fared much the same as the rest of Hispanic America.

What established Venezuela most securely as a keystone in the modern history of Latin America, however, were the exploits of the Venezuelan Simon Bolívar, who entered Caracás as "the Liberator" in 1813 to establish the shortlived Second Republic. Bolívar, driven out of the country by royalists in 1814, regrouped his forces in Haiti and re-entered Venezuela, proclaiming the Third Republic of Gran Colombia, a union of Venezuela and Colombia, which subsequently collapsed, and Venezuela was declared an independent state in 1829.

The constitution of 1961 established a strong presidential form of government under a system of legislation which, through protection of private enterprises and a system of social welfare, effectively guarantees a mixed economy. Suffrage is both universal and compulsory.

VEPS (s.d. Lyudinikad) The 12,500 Veps live in three non-contiguous territories in the Karelian Autonomous Republic, and in the Saint Petersburg and Vologda Provinces of Russia. Once inhabitants of a much larger territory, they were reduced in number and land during centuries of Russian settlement and cultural imposition.

The Veps language belongs to the Finno-Ugric group of Uralic languages. It has no alphabet, Russian serving as the literary language. The Veps have been assimilated by the surrounding RUSSIANS in culture and customs, and belong to the Russian Orthodox Church.

VIETNAMESE (Annamese, Cochinese, Tonkinese; s.d. Nguoi Kinh) The predominant people of Vietnam, where they number around 58 million, or 85 percent of the population. Significant Vietnamese refugee and immigrant communities are also found in France and the United States. Other important groups in Vietnam include ethnic CHINESE, although many have fled the country in recent years, and sixty-three distinct groups of hill peoples, or MONTAGNARDS. The term Nguoi Kinh has recently been adopted to indicate ethnic Vietnamese. They are mostly found along the country's coast and lowlands, particularly around the Red and Mekong River deltas in the north and south respectively.

The Vietnamese language is a monosyllabic tonal language of the Austronesian family. Originally written in Chinese characters, a Roman script called *quoc ngu*, employing diacritical marks to distinguish tones, was developed by Catholic missionaries in the late nineteenth century and rapidly gained acceptance.

The Vietnamese are descended from nomadic groups from central China who migrated to the Red River delta and intermingled with Indonesian immigrants in the pre-Christian era. They were subdued by the CHI-

Vietnamese

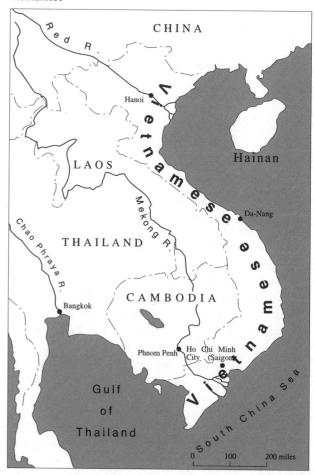

NESE in the second century B.C.E. and only reasserted their independence in the mid-tenth century. At the same time, they began migrating southward to the Mekong River delta, dominating or assimilating the local CHAM and KHMER. For 900 years, Vietnam was an independent empire modeled largely on the Chinese system. Cultural and religious activity centered on Chinese traditions and on Buddhism, Taoism, and Confucianism which coexisted alongside traditional beliefs in spirits and ancestor worship.

Vietnam reached its present territorial form only in 1780. Less than a century later, the FRENCH conquered the country and divided it into three sections, the colony of Annam in the south, and the protectorates of Cochin and Tonkin in the center and north. The FRENCH provided western education, a Roman alphabet to replace complicated Chinese ideographs (almost 90 percent of the Vietnamese are literate), and Catholicism. It was at this time that a native religion, Cao Dai, emerged, synthesizing Judeo-Christian traditions with Chinese religious values and Indian mysticism.

Led by Ho Chi Minh, Vietnamese students studying in France were attracted to the communist teachings of Karl Marx and Vladimir Ilych Lenin and sought to apply them in a future independent Vietnam. Following the Japanese occupation of the country (1940–1944) a short-lived communist regime was established in Tonkin in the north but this was quashed by returning French colonial troops. In 1954, France promised to grant independence under emperor Bai Dai, but this was rejected by the communists, now known as the Viet Minh, who were still influential in Tonkin. In the First Indochina War, French troops were severely beaten at Dien Bien Phu, and the partition of the country into North and South Vietnam was inevitable. The monarchy was deposed the following year.

The reunification of Vietnam was an important goal of the northern government and the two countries maintained a hostile relationship. By 1964 the two were at war, with the north being supported by China and the south by the United States. Until 1972 no side had the advantage. Finally public pressure in the United States, sparked by American losses in such violent encounters as the 1968 Tet offensive, forced President Richard Nixon to reduce American troops in Vietnam. By 1975, the North Vietnamese and their communist allies in the south, the Viet Cong, managed to break through South Vietnamese lines. By the end of April, the southern capital of Saigon (now Ho Chi Minh City) had fallen. Official reunification was proclaimed in 1976.

Scars of the Vietnamese War can still be felt among the Vietnamese. Two million civilians died in the conflict and many more were permanently injured. Moreover, Vietnam was soon involved in further conflicts with its former ally China and with neighboring Cambodia.

Many ethnic CHINESE, once a flourishing middle class, fled the country, as did Vietnamese seeking security on foreign shores. Known as "boat people," they captured world attention for a short time, but many still remain in incarceration camps in neighboring countries, unable to return home and with no country willing to accept them. In Vietnam, however, Buddhist resolve and recent political and economic liberalization are enabling the slow reconstruction of the country.

VILELA   An indigenous group dispersed throughout the regions of Tucumán and Santiago del Estero, Argentina.

VILI   An ethnic group living in southwestern Gabon and the adjacent coasts of Congo. Their language is related to that of the KONGO, and they adhere mainly to traditional religions.

In the nineteenth century the Vili served as middlemen between European traders on the coast and peoples in the hinterland. During the colonial period many became agents for European firms. (see also CONGOLESE)

VILLU VEDAN   A subgroup of the ERAVALLAN.

VIRGIN ISLANDERS   The inhabitants of over 100 islands in the Caribbean Sea constitute the Virgin Islands, with Britain administering the easterly islands and the United States the westerly ones. The population of some 130,000 is descended mainly from black Africans brought as slaves during the early years of Danish rule; nearly 60 percent are Protestants and some one third are Roman Catholics. English is the official and most widely spoken language. The economies of the two halves are interdependent, with agriculture, light industry, and tourism the primary economic activities.

VIRYAL   A subgroup of the CHUVASH.

VITOLANA   An ethnic group, numbering about 20,000, found in the state of Gujurat in northern India.

VLACHS   (Kutso-Vlachs; s.d. Romenii) The term Vlachs, Wallachs, or Vollochs is a Slavic form of the

A Vlach in northern Greece

German "Waelch," which designated Latin-speakers of the Balkan Peninsula (thus Wallach is one of the names for the ROMANIANS). For hundreds of years they have been assimilated by neighboring GREEKS and Slavs. The 400,000 or so Vlachs are concentrated mainly in the Pindos Mountains of Greece, but large groups can also be found in southern Macedonia, Bulgaria, Serbia, Albania, and northwestern and western Greece.

Together with Romanian, the Vlach language belongs to the eastern branch of the Romance group of Indo-European languages. It has been sporadically written in the Cyrillic and Greek alphabets but has not been used as a literary language. The Vlachs used to be mountain agriculturalists and semi-nomadic shepherds. They belong to the Eastern Orthodox Church. (see also BULGARIANS, ROMANIANS)

VLAMINGEN   see FLEMINGS.

VODDE   An ethnic group living in Andhra Pradesh, India. (see also KORA)

VODES   see VOTES.

VOGUL   see MANSI.

VOLGA-BULGARS   see CHUVASH.

VOLLOCH   see VLACHS.

VOTES   (Vodes, s.d. Vad'd'alaiset) Numbering fewer than one hundred, the Votes are the remnants of a once-numerous people who inhabited the area between the Narva and Neva Rivers. Since the eleventh century, they have been assimilated by the RUSSIANS, bringing the Votes to the brink of extinction.

The Vote language belongs to the Finnic branch of the Finno-Ugric languages and is mutually intelligible with Estonian. It has never been written, and Russian serves as the literary language.

VOUNGOU   (Bavoungou) An ethnic group, related to the ESHIRA, living in Gabon.

VUMA   An ethnic group living on seven islands in Lake Victoria, Uganda. They are related to the SOGA people but possess their own distinct cultural traits. Their language is a distant dialect of Luganda, the language of the GANDA. There are also differences between the dialects spoken on the islands.

The Vuma are agriculturalists, growing bananas and vegetables; they also keep animals, especially cattle, sheep, and goats. Fishing is important in their economy. Their pottery is famous and was once sold on the mainland.

Politically they are organized in chiefdoms, which were grouped together under one king, who lost his power under British rule.

The Vuma practice ancestor worship. The dead are buried near their houses. Bad events are ascribed to the rage of an ancestor, who must be appeased through sacrifice.

VUTE   An ethnic group, related to the BAYA, living in Cameroon.

W

WA (Hkawa, Kala, Va) A minority group inhabiting the southwest Yunnan Province of China. The Wa (numbering approximately 300,000) are a collection of subgroups believed to be among the oldest inhabitants of the southeastern Indochinese Peninsula. Other Wa communities can be found in Thailand and Burma.

Their language, comprising many dialects, belongs to the Mon branch of the Mon-Khmer language group. Although a Roman-based alphabet once existed in some areas, it failed to achieve popular usage. Instead, people generally sent objects as a means of communication: sugarcane, bananas, and salt represented good will; pepper meant anger; chicken feathers, urgency. In 1957 the Chinese government helped them create a new writing system.

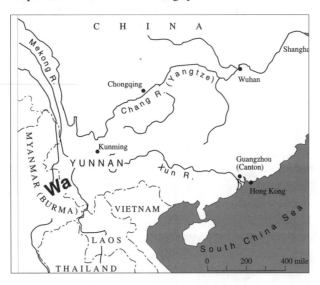

Wa

The Wa practice their traditional religion, in which the worship of skulls is prominent. As a protection from ghosts and spirits, frequent religious ceremonies are held. They are diligent farmers who use mountain slopes to plant corn, buckwheat, beans, and rice. Most Wa villages are built on the top of mountains.

Rich mineral deposits, particularly of silver and aluminum, are found in Wa-populated areas.

WAELCH see VLACHS.

WAGEVA see WOGEO.

WAHAYA see HAYA.

WAIMIRI-ATROARI A Native South American group living in the State of Amazonas, northern Brazil, near the border with Guyana.

WAJA A subgroup of the FULANI.

WAKHI (Vakhan, Wakhan; s.d. Khik) An ethnic group inhabiting the Mountain Badakhshan Autonomous *Oblast* (Region) of Tajikistan, the Wakhan District in Afghanistan, and the regions of Chitral, Gilgit, and Hunza in Pakistan. They also occupy the Tajik District of the Xinjiang Uighur Autonomous Region in China where, together with the SARIQOLI, they are known as TAJIK. Their estimated number is 20,000, of whom about 7,000 live in Tajikistan and Afghanistan each, about 3,000 in Pakistan, and the same number in China.

The Wakhi language belongs to the Pamiri division of the southeastern subgroup of Iranian languages. In Tajikistan it is spoken in three closely cognate dialects. Its dialectical differentiation in Afghanistan, Pakistan, and China has not yet been firmly established, although some specific linguistic traits of Wakhi in what is now Pakistan had been noted already in the 1930s. The Wakhi language is unwritten; Tajik in Tajikistan, Dari in Afghanistan, Uighur in China, and Urdu in Pakistan (and/or Kashmiri in the Hunza region) are used as literary languages. An attempt to establish literary Wakhi using a Roman alphabet was undertaken in Tajikistan in the 1930s but was abandoned in 1938.

In the late 1980s a project to reestablish Wakhi as a written language, this time using the Cyrillic alphabet was suggested.

The Wakhi belong to the Isma'ili sect of Islam. Although it is uncertain when they first adopted Islam, the date is surmised to be no earlier than the eleventh century.

Except in the relatively large settlement of Khandud, the administrative center of the Wakhan District of Afghanistan, the Wakhi live in small villages of ten to fifty extended families. Villages are built mainly in the valley or on mountain slopes. The typical Wakhi one-storey house consists of a single room.

In the Mountain Badakhshan Autonomous *Oblast*, Wakhi men have adopted semi-European dress. In other areas, men's dress is still traditional, and women in all areas have generally maintained their traditional attire. The Wakhi diet is predominantly vegetarian, with the addition of milk products: meat is reserved for festive occasions. The Wakhi consume large quantities of strong black tea with salt and milk. Among the Wakhi of Afghanistan addiction to opium is quite widespread. Their main occupation is grain and legume farming on small terraced plots, with some sheep-, goat-, yak-, and cattle-breeding.

While recognized by scholars as a distinct ethnic group, in the USSR the Wakhi have been officially regarded as part of the TAJIK people since the 1930s. (see also SARIQOLI)

WAKTU TELU, WAKTU LIMA Subgroups of the SASAK.

WALA (Wile) A MOLE-DAGBANI ethnic group living in the Wa State of Ghana and in the Diebougou region of Burkina Faso. Their language is called Wale or Wali. (see also MOLE-DAGBANI)

WALANI-WORIRO A subgroup of the GURAGE.

WALAYTA see WELAMO.

WALBIRI A group of AUSTRALIAN ABORIGINES, numbering about 2,000, found in the southern part of the Northern Territory in central Australia. Originally hunters and gatherers, they now find employment in cattle ranches.

WALLACHS see ROMANIANS, VLACHS.

WALLIS AND FUTUNA ISLANDERS A Polynesian-speaking people, numbering c.29,000, half of whom live on the Wallis and Futuna Islands, some 370 miles northeast of Fiji. The remainder have migrated to New Caledonia. The major concentration of population is on Uvea Island.

The islands form part of the French Overseas Territories and the islanders hold French citizenship. The entire population is Roman Catholic. Many still engage in subsistence farming, supplemented by copra production. Most monetary income is derived from government employment and remittances sent home by relatives employed abroad.

WALLO (Yajju) A division of the northern OROMO, living in the Wallo and northern Shoa Provinces, Ethiopia.

WALLOONS (s.d. Wallons) The Walloons share Belgium with the FLEMINGS. They live in Wallonia, the Belgian provinces south of the old Roman road from Boulogne to Cologne, the ancient frontier between the Romance and Germanic groups of Indo-European languages. Numbering 3.5 million, they constitute 33 percent of the BELGIAN population.

The Walloons are descended from Germanic (Frankish) invaders who were culturally absorbed into the romanized sphere in which they settled and eventually came to speak a French dialect. Culturally there is continuity between the FRENCH and the Walloons, Walloon culture consisting mainly of dialect literary productions (although there is also a rich folklore). While historically most Walloons came within France's cultural orbit, Liege was more influenced by Germany.

In Napoleon's time, Wallonia became one of the earliest industrialized regions on the European continent. Rich iron and coal deposits enriched the Walloons and enabled them to dominate Belgium after independence in the nineteenth century. Recently mining and industry have attracted POLES, UKRAINIANS, SLOVAKS, and other worker-immigrants. Today foreigners represent nearly 9 percent of the population in Wallonia.

The position of French as Belgium's dominant language was challenged early on and, by the late nineteenth century, Walloons were already on the defensive against the growing numbers of Flemish-speakers. A nationalist Walloon movement developed in reaction to the militancy of Flemish demands. Although mainly a post-World War II phenomenon, it had earlier precursors - cultural nationalism in the 1840s led to the proliferation of French-dialect studies and by 1890 the Walloons were organizing to defend the interests of French-speakers. At the same time, an enduring connection developed between the Walloons and the socialist movement.

The Walloons have consistently voted more radically than the pro-monarchist and conservative FLEMINGS. Debates pitted extreme Wallonists, who demanded abrogation of the Belgian state and attachment of Wallonia to France, against (more influential) moderates opting for a federal Belgium on a parity basis. Ethnic interests, however, were often dwarfed by national questions. By the 1960s and 1970s, however, the decline of mining and the steel industry, deindustrialization of the Walloon region, and high unemployment figures contrasted painfully with Flemish economic successes. In 1961 a mass strike by Walloon workers against budget cuts was broken by Flemish conservative trade unions.

This reawakened Walloon assertiveness and triggered the establishment of the Mouvement Populaire Wallon (Popular Walloon Movement) which clamored for federalism. Walloon nationalists in the Rassemblement wallon linked up with the Front Democratique Francophone, the party of French-speaking natives of Brussels who demanded *federalisme a trois*, which would include Brussels as a third, equal partner: Greater Brussels includes in fact one-tenth of all Belgians — 80 percent of them French-speakers. Federalism eventually brought constitutional recognition of Walloon cultural autonomy; in the 1980s Walloon political institutions were installed. The Brussels controversy remains unresolved. (see also also BELGIANS, FLEMINGS, SWEDES)

WALNE   A subgroup of the GURAGE.

WAMBULY   see IRAQW.

WAMIRA   An ethnic group of a few thousand, living in southeastern Papua New Guinea. They speak Wedau, an indigenous local language. Their economy is based upon slash and burn cultivation. Although most have become Christians, they retain traditional beliefs. Their ceremonies celebrate marriage and other stages of the life-cycle.

WANCHO   An ethnic group, numbering c.32,000 (1981), living in the state of Arunachal Pradesh, in mountainous northeastern India. They speak a Tibeto-Burman language. Most Wancho villages are situated on the slopes of the Patkoi range (above 3,000 feet).

WANDYA   A subgroup of the NKOYA.

WANTAOT   An ethnic group of approximately 10,000, living near the eastern coast of Papua New Guinea. They speak an indigenous Papuan language. Their subsistence is based upon the cultivation of various vegetables, especially yams and sweet potatoes. They believe in a complex mythological world.

WAPE   An ethnic group, numbering over 10,000, living in northwestern Papua New Guinea. They speak an indigenous Pauan language. Their economy is based on the cultivation of sago and the hunting of wild game. Their religion combines Christian tenets with a traditional belief in ancestral spirits.

WAPISHANA   A Native South American group living on both sides of the border between Brazil and Guyana. Only a few hundred out of a total of several thousand Wapishana live on the Brazilian side.

WARAZA   An ethnic group living in Ethiopia. They speak an Eastern Cushitic language.

WARLI   A Hindu people, numbering about 600,000, found in the states of Maharashtra and Gujarat in western India. Many work as laborers for the dominant groups in the region.

WAROPEN   An ethnic group of approximately 10,000, living on the northern coast of Irian Jaya, the Indonesian western half of the island of New Guinea. They speak a local language. Their economy is based on slash and burn cultivation and fishing. They prac-

Wamira, Wantaot, Wape, and Waropen

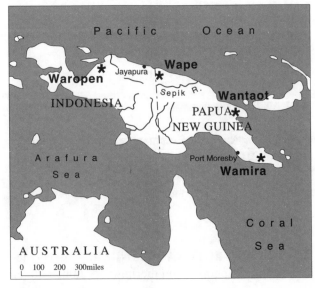

tice ancestor worship. Their most important ceremonies are initiation rites.

WARRAU   A Native South American people living in the Orinoco River delta in Venezuela. They depend primarily on fishing, collecting shellfish, and hunting such marine animals as manatees, crocodiles, and turtles. They also gather eggs and forest products. Agricultural activity is minimal.

WASA   (Warshas) An Akan-speaking ethnic group living in the Western Region of Ghana. In the seventeeth century they were under DENKYIRA control and they fought several wars with the ASHANTI during the following century. In the nineteenth century the Wasa allied themselves with the coastal peoples and joined the Fante Confederacy Movement to defend themselves against other ethnic groups.

WASHOE   A Native North American group, numbering 700, living on Carson Federal Colony, near Carson City, Nevada, U.S.A. They practice agriculture but most earn their livelihood by working in the local economy.

WASULUNKA   see OUASSOULOUNKE.

WATAWIT   see JABELAWI.

WAYTO   see WETO.

WAZIBA   see HAYA.

WE   see GUEMBE.

WEDA   A subgroup of the SAWAI.

WEE   see KRAHN.

WELAMO   (Walayta) A people of over 1 million, inhabiting the well-watered plateau north of Lake Abaya in eastern Kefa Province, Ethiopia. They adhere to traditional beliefs, Ethiopian Orthodox Christianity, or Sunni Islam. The Welamo are one of the major peoples in Ethiopia. Their kingdom, the largest such polity among the Welamo-speaking peoples (OMETO, GAMO, GOFA), was annexed to the Ethiopian Empire in 1894.

Most Welamo-speakers follow patrilineal descent systems and were traditionally organized in small polities (sometimes on the level of village societies), with a "sacred king." Dominant lineages in the large polities

often claimed a northern pedigree (AMHARA, TIGRAY), related to the political expansion of the Ethiopian Empire during the Middle Ages.

They are predominantly hoe-cultivators, growing tuberous plants (ensete) and cereal grains. Fields are often terraced.

WELSH   (s.d. Cymru) The 2.8 million Welsh, living mostly in Wales, are part of the BRITISH people. While English is their dominant language, over half a million continue to speak Welsh, an ancient Celtic tongue, more closely related to Breton than to Irish or Scottish Gaelic. Since industrialization in the nineteenth century there has been extensive immigration of and intermingling with the ENGLISH. The Anglo-Welsh now form the majority in South Wales.

Wales's inaccessible mountains were a refuge for Celts fleeing conquerors. North Wales, a region of shepherds, fishermen, and porters, has preserved its Celtic heritage more than the heavily industrialized south, but is subject to depopulation. Although most Welsh are Anglican Protestants, pre-Christian traditions, such as the annual Eisteddfodau singing and poetry championship, live on in the north.

Wales was conquered, but not romanized, in the first century C.E. In the fifth century it served simultaneously as safe haven for Celts fleeing Anglo-Saxon invasions and as bridgehead for Gaelic invaders who brought Christianity from Ireland. They maintained Wales's Celtic character, but from the seventh century their rule gradually weakened and Welsh power diminished. While ENGLISH settlers built castles and towns, the countryside remained Celtic. In the eighth century the many small Welsh kingdoms united to protect themselves against Vikings and Saxons - the Saxons built Offa's Dike as a barrier between themselves and the Welsh - but they soon fell prey to internal quarrels.

The eleventh-century Norman invasion of Britain ended in a standoff, with the Welsh resisting attacks against their own territory. In the following centuries, Welsh princes initially succeeded in keeping the ENGLISH at bay, but the latter conquered them after the sovereign prince of Wales refused to pay homage to the king of England. In 1284 Wales was annexed; the territory has since been reserved for the English crown prince. Welsh land was divided among royal officers; a last uprising failed in 1400-1415. In 1536 Henry VIII fully integrated Wales into England and prohibited Welsh language and customs. While the upper classes were overwhelmingly anglicized, the subsistence peasantry clung to its traditional ways.

Although the Welsh converted to Protestantism, they resisted the tithe to the Anglican church. In the mid-eighteenth century Welsh nationalism expressed itself in mass conversions to Calvinist Methodism.

In the nineteenth century, Welsh interest in their own history spawned a Celtic revival. Interest in Welsh heritage has been rekindled over the past decades, mainly in the revival of the Gaelic language, but this has led to tensions with the Anglo-Welsh and with a more recent influx of affluent ENGLISH settlers in rural Wales. The Welsh language is now officially taught in schools but other affirmations of a distinctive Welsh identity, such as devolution proposals to grant limited autonomy to the Welsh, have failed to mobilize significant support. (see also BRITISH)

WEMBA   see BEMBA.

WEND   see SORB.

WETO   (Wayto) An ethnic group, numbering several thousand, living on the shores of Lake Tana in the Gondar region of northern Ethiopia. They speak Amharic and are Sunni Muslims. They are fishermen and hippopotamus hunters.

WET'SUWET'EN   A Native North American group, numbering about 2,000, half of whom live in two villages (Moricetown and Hagwilget) in the Bulkley Valley, north-central British Columbia, Canada. They speak an Athapaskan dialect closely related to those spoken by the BABINE and BEAVER.

They converted to Catholicism only in 1890. In the last decade they have succeeded in gaining significant rights to their ancient land, a territory covering over 7,500 square miles. They work mainly in lumbering and salmon fishing, and maintain a well-functioning clan system. (see also ATHAPASKAN, BABINE, CARRIER)

WHITE MOUNTAIN APACHE   A subgroup of the APACHE.

WICHITA   A Native North American group, numbering 700, living on the Wichita Tribe Federal Trust Area in Caddo County, Oklahoma, U.S.A. They were among the first Plains peoples to move to the Oklahoma Territory.

WIDEKUM   An ethnic group related to the BAMILEKE living in Nigeria and Cameroon.

WIK   A group of AUSTRALIAN ABORIGINES living on the Cape York Peninsula in northern Queensland. They number several hundred. Originally hunters and gatherers, they now live in permanent settlements, where they are dependent on government subsidies.

WILE   see WALA.

WILLICHE   see TEHUELCHE.

WINAMWANGE   An ethnic group, related to the MAMBWE, living in Zambia.

WINATU   An ethnic group living in the mountainous central region of the Indonesian island of Sulawesi (Celebes). (see also TORADJA)

WINNEBAGO   A Native North American group, numbering 4,000, living on the Winnebago Federal Reservations in both Wisconsin and Nebraska. Today many Winnebago are farmers.

WINTUN   A Native North American group, numbering a few hundred, most of whom live on the Federal Rancheria in Colusa County, California, U.S.A.

WIWA   An ethnic group related to the MAMBWE living in Zambia.

Wichita and Winnebago

above: Wet'suwet'en women working hides in British Columbia, Canada
below: Wet'suwet'en salmon fishermen

WIWIRANO   A subgroup of the LAKI.

WOABA   A subgroup of the SOMBA.

WOBE   (Ouobe) An ethnic group, numbering about 53,000, living in the western Cote d'Ivoire around the town of Man. They belong to the KRU ethnic cluster and are closely related to the GUERE.

WOGEO   (s.d. Wageva) An ethnic group of a few thousand, living on an island off the northern coast of Papua New Guinea. They speak a local language consisting of various dialects. They are slash and burn cultivators and fishermen. They practice sorcery.

WOGO   An ethnic group numbering about 20,000, living in Mali, Nigeria, and Niger. They speak Songhai and are predominantly Muslim. Their main occupation is agriculture.

WOLOF   A people living in northwestern Senegal, the Gambia, and Mauritania. They are the dominant ethnic group of Senegal, where they number about 2.5 million, or 41 percent of the population. Their language, Wolof, is one of six official languages in that country and serves as the lingua franca. In the Gambia they number about 90,000, or 13 percent of the population. They are found mainly in Upper and Lower Salum districts and in the northern sections of Niani, Sami, Niumi, and Jokadu. Gambia's capital, Banjul, is a predominantly Wolof town. In Mauritania they number some 200,000, or c.10 percent of the population.

The vast majority of Wolof are Muslims; initial contacts with Muslim northerners and the slow process of islamization date from the eleventh century. Wolof Muslims are divided among several brotherhoods (*Murridiyya, Tijaniyya, Qadiriyya*). The leaders of these brotherhoods are known as *marabouts*.

The Wolof probably originated in Mauritania and migrated southward under pressure from the BERBERS of North Africa. Arriving in Senegal, they started a dual process of driving the SERER farther south and "assimilating" them. By the thirteenth century distinct Wolof states appeared, but they were conquered, like the rest of the Senegambia region, by the expanding Mali Empire. According to Mali oral traditions the Wolof were under Mali's rule for about a century. In the mid-fourteenth century the Wolof broke away from Mali and formed the Jolof empire, providing them with political, cultural, and linguistic unity. The empire included the Wolof states of Kajoor, Bawol, and Waalo; the SERER states of Siin and Salum; and western and central Fuuta Toro, home of the TUKULOR people.

Toward the end of the fifteenth century the Jolof Empire began to disintegrate. The revolt of Kajoor in the mid-sixteenth century marked its downfall. Some Wolof states with a similar social and political system continued to exist until conquest by the FRENCH in 1886.

The Wolof states were ruled by a governing class of semi-pagan aristocrats, called *garmi*. The rest of the population was divided into freeborns, members of castes, and slaves. From the eleventh century there were also Muslim leaders in the Wolof society but they remained subject to the *garmi*.

The final conquest of the Wolof states by the FRENCH caused a major crisis in the Wolof social and political structure. The aristocracy lost its control to Muslim leaders who set about reorganizing the disoriented society. The abolition of slavery in the end of the nineteenth century undermined the economic base of the traditional aristocracy, whereas the Muslim leadership was not affected by the abolition because of its involvement in the less demanding groundnut trade introduced by European traders (groundnuts are now Senegal's main export).

During the colonial period the FRENCH established first Saint Louis and then Dakar as Senegal's capital. These two cities and other major railroad towns were all in the Wolof area. As a result the Wolof underwent

Wolof

a rapid process of urbanization and their language became the lingua franca of the cities. Non-Wolof urban migrants often adopted the Wolof language and ethnicity within a generation or two.

After Senegal's independence the Wolof became the dominant ethnic group in that country. They are particularly powerful in the civil service and hold important leadership positions in Muslim organizations. Many Wolof migrated to the cities, while those who remained in rural areas continued to cultivate groundnuts.

The Wolof have been deeply involved in Senegalese politics even before independence and today hold a majority of the cabinet posts and seats in the National Assembly. (see also GAMBIANS, MAURITANIANS, SENEGALESE)

WONG DJAWA   see JAVANESE.

WONG MEDURA   see MADURESE.

WONG TENGGER   see TENGGERESE.

WORJI   A subgroup of the OROMO.

WOTAPURI   see JALALI. (see also KATARQALAI)

WOTU   An ethnic group, living in the mountainous central region of the Indonesian island of Sulawesi (Celebes). (see also TORADJA)

WOVAN   An ethnic group, numbering approximately 1,000, living in the Arame River valley of central Papua New Guinea. They speak an indigenous regional language. Their economy is based on slash and burn cultivation, pig-raising, and hunting. They believe in ancestral spirits and their main ceremonies involve male initiation rites.

WUNDA   An ethnic group living in Zimbabwe.

WYANDOT   A Native North American group, known in Canada as the Nation Huronne Wendat. They number 2,600 in Quebec and 700 in Oklahoma. They were a large group at the time of contact, but were nearly decimated by the warriors of the IROQUOIS CONFEDERACY, and their war with the BRITISH, and American policies. The American branch of the tribe was removed to the Indian Territory of Oklahoma.

X

XAVANTE   (Chavante, Shavante) A Native South American group numbering a few thousand, living in five villages in the State of Goiás, central-west Brazil. Their language connects them to the Akwe linguistic group. For many years, the Xavante resisted contact with outsiders. The most famous Xavante was Mario Juruna, who left his mission village to work as a laborer and years later was elected deputy to the National Congress of Brazil.

XERENTE   (Sherente) A Native South American group living south of the Xingu valley in the State of Goiás, central-west Brazil. With the XAVANTE, their language connects them to the AKWE. They number a few hundred.

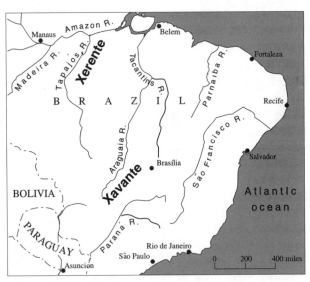

Xavante and Xerente

XETA   see HETA.

XHOSA   A people numbering 7 million, living in South Africa. They are part of the southern NGUNI. Non-urbanized Xhosa are concentrated primarily in the country's southeastern coastal areas. In 1834 Xhosa became the first South African black language for which a grammar was published. The Xhosa are primarily Christians: about four fifths have specific church allegiances. The Methodists are the largest Christian group (around 23 percent), followed by members of African Independent Churches (18 percent), and Anglicans (9 percent).

Two independent Xhosa homelands were established under South Africa's Grand Apartheid scheme: the Transkei, homeland of the Gcaleka Paramount (the Great House) Xhosa; and the Ciskei, homeland of the Ngqika Paramount (the Right-Hand House) Xhosa. The Transkei is a segmented state in the northeast Cape and Natal Provinces: it became an independent republic in 1976. The Ciskei, which became independent in 1981, is in the northeast Cape Province, located south of (but not contiguous with) the Transkei. Population figures for these states are extremely unreliable, given that citizenship in them has been very broadly defined to include non-resident Xhosas. Their major export products are tea, manufactured goods, wool, and pineapples.

Linguistic evidence and European accounts corroborate Xhosa oral traditions of a history of considerable, generally peaceful, interaction between the Xhosa and the indigenous SAN (Bushmen) and KHOIKHOI (Hottentot). There were, however, also periods of conflict between the peoples. Some seventeenth-century Khoikhoi chiefdoms became ethnically mixed with Xhosa elements and espoused distinctively Xhosa customs. Like the KHOIKHOI, the Xhosa were cattle-herders, cultivators, and hunters; the Xhosa and KHOIKHOI both trained their cattle as riding, pack, and racing animals.

In the eighteenth century the Xhosa nucleus split into two under the Gcaleka and Ngqika Houses. Also today included within the Xhosa people are chiefdoms originally stemming from the TEKELA line of NGUNI. In addi-

Xhosa pineapple farmers in South Africa

Xhosa

tion, the Xhosa also include a mumber of refugee chiefdoms of mixed (mostly SOTHO) or unknown origin.

Culturally, the Xhosa share the customs of the NGUNI. As with the NGUNI, the productive unit among the Xhosa was not the family but the homestead, a dynamic unit which expanded by acquiring indebted adherents from among the poor, who lacked cattle to start their own homesteads and gained access to cattle by serving the homestead head. This system was critical in the organization of a dominant class around the chief. Xhosa chiefs often redistributed cattle, not as an egalitarian measure but as a manipulation of the social structure; it was a means of enabling certain household heads to enhance their social status by expanding their circle of adherents. While the Xhosa are polygamous, only between 20 and 50 percent of Xhosa men were actually able to afford the *lobola* (bride-price, paid generally in cattle) for more than one wife.

The Xhosa were traditionally known for their great hospitality and their strict adherence to the rule of law. Disputes were settled in court, trade was regulated, and chiefs ruled by consent. The powers of witchcraft and sorcery were universally accepted, and torture was a recognized procedure against the accused in obtaining confessions. As a corollary to witchcraft and sorcery, prophecy, in the form of communication with ancestors through dreams and visions, was equally widely accepted. Belief in ancestor intervention in daily life and personal fortunes has been found to persist among Christian Xhosa in the urban environment in recent times. Whereas tribal and clan ancestral rituals have fallen into disuse in the cities, about 90 percent of urban Xhosa Christians see immediate ancestors and the spirits of senior kinsmen as active wielders of beneficial or malignant powers.

The African National Congress is said to be predominantly Xhosa. (see also NGUNI, SOUTH AFRICANS)

XICAQUE   A Native North American group living in Honduras.

XOKLENG   A Native Central American group living in the State of Rio Grande do Sul in southern Brazil. Today they number only a few hundred, having suffered heavy losses upon contact with non-Indian BRAZILIANS.

XOLO   A subgroup of the NGUNI.

XUKURU   (Shucuru) A Native South American group living in the State of Pernambuco, northeastern Brazil. Numbering a few thousand, they are well integrated into Brazilian society and speak their own language mixed with Portuguese.

Y

YACHE   An ethnic group living in Nigeria.

YACHUMI   A subgroup of the NAFA.

YAGHNOBI   An ethnic group living in Tajikistan. Until the early 1970s they lived mainly in the Yaghnob valley, and now live dispersed in compact groups, mostly in the Zafarabad District in Tajikistan and in the Varzob Valley near the republic's capital, Dushanbe. No population data are available, but a rough estimate puts them at about 4,000, of whom only 300 (1990) live in the Yaghnob valley itself.

The Yaghnobi language belongs to the Iranian group of the Indo-European family. It is the only surviving remnant of Sogdian, which was the main language of the most densely populated part of Central Asia prior to its islamization. Yaghnobi possesses two dialects. It is unwritten, and Tajik is the language of writing and education. Practically all Yaghnobi speak both Tajik and Yaghnobi. They also use a secret argot in which Tajik loan words abundant in Yaghnobi are replaced by specific coinings. They are Sunni Muslims of the Hanafi school and are sedentary agriculturalists.

The Yaghnob valley is situated c.7,500–9,000 feet above sea level and consists of a gap of c.900–9,000 feet between the steep slopes of two mountain ranges. It can be entered only by means of a difficult path along the Yaghnob River, and its near-impenetrability has made it a kind of ethnographic preserve. Villages form a sequence of one-storey stone flat-roofed houses built on or against the slopes. One of the roofs in the central part of the village was used as a gathering place. Each village had an uninhabited house, regarded as common property and used for hosting guests. In a number of villages there are ruins of fortresses built, apparently in the early Middle Ages, to defend the valley.

The main occupation of the Yaghnobi remains wheat and barley farming on small plots of slope or valley land. Peas were also cultivated. The second branch of the economy was cattle- and sheep-herding; oxen were used in tillage and donkeys for transport. Hunting, mainly of mountain goat and sheep, was practiced as an additional source of meat. Specifically feminine skills were weaving and producing earthenware without using a potter's wheel, a device unknown in the valley.

The first migrations of the Yaghnobi into the Varzob valley date back to the sixteenth century. In the 1950s the Soviet authorities encouraged the settling of larger groups of Yaghnobi in that area due to the need for additional manpower. In 1969 a decision was taken to transfer all the Yaghnobi still in the Yaghnob valley to a newly established Zafarabad district in the so-called Hunger Steppe in northern Tajikistan, to land earmarked for cotton, which badly lacked working hands. The transfer took place mainly in 1970–1971. Formally it was voluntary: in fact intimidation and force were used. Those who dared return were brutally extradited to the Zafarabad district for the second time in 1978. The adaptation of the Yaghnobi to their new surroundings was painful, and accompanied by high mortality. A second, tiny flow of returnees began by the end of the 1980s.

Since the 1930s the Yaghnobi have been officially regarded as part of a broader Tajik ethnic entity and accordingly registered as TAJIKS. The 1989 Tajikistani Language Law promised to take steps to ensure the continuing existence of the Yaghnobi language.

YAGULEMI   see YAZGULOMI.

YAHGAN   A migratory South American Indian group inhabiting the offshore islands of Tierra del Fuego. They practice no agriculture, but depend on collecting shellfish and mussels, fishing, and hunting seals, porpoises, and marine birds.

YAKA An ethnic group living in southwestern Zaire, between the Kwango and Wamba Rivers. During the period of colonial rule by the BELGIANS, the Yaka avoided contacts with the colonial authorities. After independence in 1960 there were a few ethnic incidents between the Yaka and the KONGO in the capital, Kinshasa. They tried occasionally to resist the central government's attempts to assume control over their lands.

The SUKU who live in southern Zaire between the Inzila and Kwilu Rivers are a Yaka subgroup.

YAKALYQ A subgroup of the UIGHUR.

YAKAN (Yakanese) The indigenous inhabitants, estimated as numbering 110,000, of Basilan, an island in the Philippines located just off the southwestern tip of the Zamboanga Peninsula. They are also found in smaller numbers on the islands of Sakol, Malanipa, and Tumalutab. Their language is similar to that of the BAJAU LAUT (Sea Samal) and although they maintain traditional beliefs, they are mainly considered Muslims.

The Yakan live by means of agriculture and some hunting, growing sweet potatoes, rice, and copra. Originally maintaining villages in the interior mountains, they are now more widely dispersed throughout the flatlands and coastlines.

YAKIMA A Native North American group, numbering 8,000, many of whom live on the Yakima Federal Reservation, Yakima County, Washington, U.S.A.

Traditionally hunters and diggers of roots, today many Yakima work in the forest industry.

YAKO A subgroup of the IBIBIO.

YAKOMBA An ethnic group living near the Kotto-Ubangui Rivers juncture in the Central African Republic.

YAKORO An ethnic group living in Nigeria.

YAKPA A subgroup of the BANDA.

YAKUT (s.d. Saha) The approximately 450,000 Yakut live in northeastern Siberia between the Arctic Ocean and the Stanovoi Range, most in the Yakut Autonomous Republic of Russia, where they make up about half of the population.

The Yakut language belongs to the Turkic family of languages. It is also used by the DOLGAN, the EVEN,

and the EVENKI. Isolated from other Turkic languages, its contact with the Evenki, Mongolian, and Russian languages led to the development of its particular system of phonetics. The first writing system for the Yakut language was created in 1922, based on the international phonetic alphabet. This was replaced in 1929 by the Roman, and in 1939 by the Cyrillic, alphabet.

The Yakut are believed to be of Mongol-Tungus origin, assimilated into pastoral Turkic tribes which penetrated into their area from the Baikal region and Central Asia in the thirteenth to fourteenth centuries. They are divided ecologically into northern (tundra) hunters, fishers, and reindeer-breeders, and southern (tayga), mainly cattle-herders, who form the majority of the people. In more recent times numbers of them have taken up farming, relegating hunting and fishing to a secondary role. Their original type of dwelling was the log *yurt* (hut). In the sixteenth to seventeenth centuries the Yakut, who originally lived in dispersed family groups, formed tribes and clans.

The RUSSIANS occupied the Yakut territory around 1630, subjected them to the heavy burden of a fur tax, and forced them to abandon their traditional religion and convert to Russian Orthodox Christianity. However, the Yakut have preserved many shamanist elements in their religious ritual.

Yakima

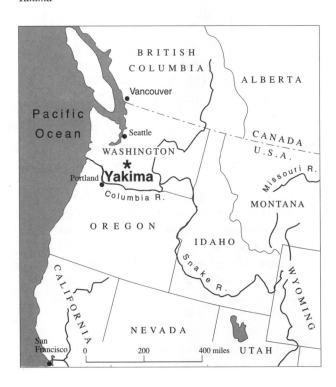

A Yakut woman

In the Soviet period further economic and social changes took place at an accelerated pace. The majority of Yakut are now industrial workers and miners. (see also DOLGAN, YUKAGIR)

Yakut

YALNA An ethnic group in central Chad, closely related to the HADJERAY.

YALUNKA (Djallonke) An ethnic group, closely related to the SUSU, living on the Guinea coast and in the Kamba, Port Loko, and Koinadugu Districts of Sierra Leone. They speak Susu and adhere to either their traditional religion or Islam. Their main occupation is agriculture. (see also SIERRA LEONEANS)

YAMANI see YEMENIS.

YAMBO see ANUAK.

YANADI A people, numbering over 300,000, found in central India. They are apparently of Australoid origin.

YANBASA An ethnic group related to the BAMILEKE, living in Cameroon.

YANGORU BOIKEN An ethnic group of approximately 15,000, living on the northern coast of Papua New Guinea. The various dialects which they speak are all part of an indigenous Papuan language. They are slash and burn cultivators, whose staple crops are taro and yams (edible roots). They believe in magical forces and ancestral spirits. Their most important ceremonies are associated with the life-cycle.

YANGUR An ethnic group living in Nigeria.

YANKTON, YANKTONAIE A subgroup of the SIOUX.

YANOMAMI (Yanomamo) A South American Indian group living in an extensive area of tropical rainforest straddling the border between Venezuela and Brazil. The remoteness of their homeland has preserved their isolation from the outside world until quite recently, and their traditional culture and lifestyle are more intact than those of many indigenous peoples. Their total number is about 25,000, but it is shrinking, due primarily to epidemics of contagious diseases introduced in recent years by outsiders, especially gold miners from other regions of Brazil.

The Yanomami consist of many subgroups who share a closely-related set of languages, one of whom is the PARAHURI, who live in more than ten villages along the Parima River near the Brazil-Venezuela border. Their culture includes constant low-level warfare between groups inhabiting different territories within their larger region, manifested in an endless pattern of grudges that triggers killings to avenge previous killings, or to avenge fatal diseases believed to have been induced by hostile shamans from other groups. Intergroup relations, however, are more complex and can include alliances and intermarriages. Specific groups may split apart, and others may recombine to form new communities over time.

The Yanomami are shifting cultivators, who combine slash and burn cultivation (manioc, plaintains, cotton, and a variety of other crops) with hunting and gathering in the rainforest. Extended families, which may include multiple wives and their children, live in thatched circular longhouses. Traditional Yanomami culture includes the extensive use of hallucinogenic drugs by adults.

The isolation of Yanomami lands has become increasingly compromised in recent decades, as missionaries, gold miners, loggers, peasant settlers, and even some tourists, have begun to enter the Yanomami domain. In 1991 Venezuela established the Orinoco-Casiquare Biosphere Reserve along its border with Brazil;

it is intended to keep miners and colonists out of the area. The Yanomami living in Brazilian territory have had more problems with encroachments by gold miners and colonists than those living in Venezuela. Depopulation from introduced disease has decimated some villages in the headwater regions of the Rio Negro, a major tributary of the Amazon River. In 1992, after years of pressure, the Brazilian government announced its intention to establish a protected reserve for the Yanomami. (see also VENEZUELANS)

YANZI An ethnic group living in Zaire.

YAO I (Ajava) An ethnic group living in the Niassa and Lago Districts of Mozambique. In Malawi they live in the Southern Province along the Shire River with other small groups of the west coast of Lake Nyasa (Malawi). They are also found in southern Tanzania. In Malawi they number over 1.1 million; in Mozambique there are 170,000 Yao.

Yao relations between kinship groups are defined by a sorority group in which a man cares for a group of women consisting of his sisters, daughters, and granddaughters. Domestic slavery was vital to the Yao social system and slaves were obtained through purchase, capture, or compensation. The abolition of slavery had an effect on Yao society. Many abandoned hunting and fishing for agriculture while others acted as middlemen for Arab traders. Contact with ARABS led the Yao to adopt Arab customs and dress, which they have since adapted to their traditional religion.

The Yao entered Tanzania in the 1850s and in 1912, when they were brought there as prisoners of war. Early migration to Malawi was peaceful at first, but by 1876 they had subjugated the faction-ridden NYNJA. Twenty years later the Yao themselves were subdued. This and the abolition of the slave trade caused their communities to break up. In Mozambique many Yao joined the army, controlled by the PORTUGUESE, as a result of Portuguese propaganda that emphasized their discord with the MAKONDE. (see also MALAWIANS, MOZAMBICANS, TANZANIANS)

YAO II (Man) A minority group, numbering approximately 1.8 million, who live mainly in China's Guangxi, Hunan, Guangdong, and Guizhou Provinces. Yao are also found in northern Vietnam, Laos, and Thailand, where they are known as Man.

Legends claim that the Yao are descended from the five-colored dog P'an Hu who saved a Chinese emperor the trouble and expense of a major military expedition by bringing him the severed head of a rival monarch.

Their language is closely related to that of their mountain neighbors, the MIAO (Hmong), both belonging to the Sino-Tibetan family. Knowledge and use of Chinese is common among the Yao. Centuries of association with the Han CHINESE has also left its mark on Yao religious beliefs and practices; they worship spirits, ghosts, and ancestors.

Living in mountainous regions, their main occupations are hoe-farming and logging. They grow millet, beans, and sweet potatoes.

The head of the Yao household is usually the eldest male; his authority over members of the household is absolute as long as they remain under his roof. Premarital sex is accepted; a woman moves in with her husband only after her first child is born. Traditional Yao dress varies according to area, but the elaborate dresses of the women are colorfully adorned   (see also MIAO)

YAP ISLANDERS   (Yapese) A Micronesian-speaking people, numbering about 12,000, who inhabit four islands located in the Western Caroline Islands, about 540 miles southwest of Guam. They are mainly Roman Catholics.

Early in the twentieth century the islands were administered by Germany. In 1920 they came under a Japanese mandate, and from 1945 under U.S. sovereignty. At present the island group is a member state of the Federated States of Micronesia, associated with the United States. The two important kin groups in Yapese society are based on patrilineal lineage and the matrilineal clan. Postmarital residence is usually patrilocal. The rank of a lineage is derived from the rank of the land it controls and on which it resides. The Yapese subsistence economy is based on fishing and agriculture (taro, yams, sweet potatoes).

YAQUI A Native North American group, numbering some 25,000, whose habitation spans the border between the United States (Arizona) and Mexico (Sonora). Currently, they are most concentrated in southern Sonora, where, with the MAYO, they are the only surviving speakers of Cahita, a Uto-Aztecan language. With the coming of the Spanish in the sixteenth and seventeenth centuries, the Yaqui were converted to the Catholic faith, some moving into mission communities.

The Yaqui retained their tribal territory, which Mexico attempted to seize in the mid-nineteenth century. This provoked a series of uprisings which led to the

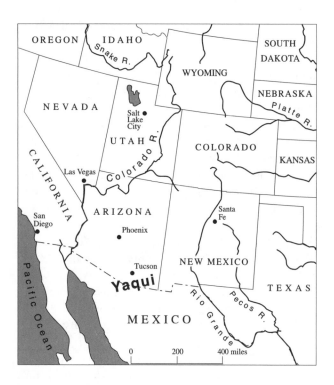

Yaqui

forced removal of many Yaqui in 1887 as near-slaves to other parts of Mexico. Demoralized, the remaining Yaqui declined in number. After newly-implemented policies of national land reform resulted in restoration of land to them in the 1930s, large irrigation projects on the Yaqui River forced conversion from subsistence agriculture to market production of cotton, wheat, and vegetable oils. As settled agriculturalists they have managed to farm fertile oases in one of the most arid areas on earth. (see also MEXICANS)

YARO A subgroup of the CHARRUA.

YARSE An ethnic group, living in Burkina Faso, which has intermixed with the MOSSI. Most are Muslims and their primary occupation is commerce.

YARURO A South American Indian people of the Orinoco River delta in Venezuela. They subsist primarily on harvesting and hunting marine animals ranging from shellfish to crocodiles. They also gather a range of forest products to supplement their diet.

YARZA KOMI PERMYAK see KOMI.

YATENGA see MOSSI.

YAZGULOMI (Yazgulami, Yagulemi, Yazghulami; s.d. Zgamig) An ethnic group living in the valley of the Yazgulom River in the eastern part of the Mountain Badakhshan Autonomous *Oblast* of Tajikistan. They are estimated as numbering 2,000. The Yazgulomi language belongs to the Pamiri division of the southeastern subgroup of Iranian languages. It has two closely cognate dialects: the "high," that of the villages situated along the higher stream of the Yazgulom River, and the "low," that of the villages along the lower stream of that river. It is unwritten, Tajik being used as the literary language. Practically all Yazgulomi speak both Tajik and Yazgulomi. They also use a kind of secret intonated argot in which Tajik loan words are replaced by Yazgulomi present participles.

Until the nineteenth century all Yazgulomi belonged to the Isma'ili sect of Islam. The time of their islamization is unknown, but cannot be earlier than the eleventh century. In the late nineteenth century some became Sunni Muslims of the Hanafi school. They are sedentary agriculturalists, and their main occupation is grain and legume farming on small plots of slope land. They also have small herds of cattle. The diet is predominantly vegetarian and dairy; meat is usually eaten on festive occasions.

Except for two larger villages, Andarbagh and Jamak, situated in the low-stream part of the valley, Yazgulomi villages comprise between ten and fifty extended families. The villages are built mainly in the valley or on the lower slopes of mountains. The one-storey house consisting generally of one room, is inhabited by the whole extended family. Closely related families form in their aggregate a clan-like unit or *gawm* (a borrowing from Arabic through Tajik; lit. tribe). Men's dress is now semi-European, although the traditional long robe is still worn; women's dress remains mainly traditional.

In 1954 all Yazgulomi inhabiting the villages in the upper part of the Yazgulom Valley were transferred to the Vakhs Valley in southwestern Tajikistan, one of the main areas of cotton production badly in need of manpower. Officially the transfer was voluntary; in fact it was made by administrative means. Their adaptation to their new environment was painful. According to unofficial data about one-third died, mainly of gastric diseases caused by drinking polluted irrigation ditch water. Reportedly all or almost all of those who survived and their Vakhs Valley-born descendants returned to the abandoned and ruined villages in the upper part of the Yazgulom valley by the end of the 1980s.

Though recognized as a specific ethnic group, the Yazgulomi have been regarded officially since the 1930s as a part of the TAJIK.

YAZIDIS (Dasnayis, Asdais) see ARMENIANS, IRAQIS, KURDS.

YEDINA An ethnic group of around 33,000, living in Chad, in the Bol District by Lake Chad and in the Massakory District. Their language is related to that of the KOTOKO. They adhere to their traditional religions and have only recently been exposed to Islam. Their main occupation is fishing.

The Yedina are divided into two major subgroups, the BUDUMA (numbering 23,000), who inhabit the islands and peninsulas of Lake Chad, and the Kuri who live along the western shores of the lake. There are also many small subgroups, among which the GURIA is the largest.

YEHUDIM YISRA'ELIYIM see ISRAELIS.

YEKE (Bayeke) An ethnic group living in the southern Shaba (Katanga) Region of Zaire, near the Zambian border. They speak Swahili.

In the nineteenth century the Yeke established a large kingdom which controlled the trade of slaves, copper, ivory, salt, and iron in the region. During the Katanga crisis of the early 1960s the Yeke joined the LUNDA in the creation of the Conakat party, that called for the secession of Katanga. (see also ZAIREANS)

YELATPI see ROSELL ISLANDERS.

YELE see BAYELE.

YELLOWKNIFE A Native North American group, numbering 900, living in the Northwest Territories, Canada. Many still practice their traditional ways of hunting.

YELLOW UIGHUR A subgroup of the SALAR, UIGHUR.

YEM see JANJERO.

YEMENIS (s.d. Yamani) The 11.7 million Yemenis are ARABS living in the southwestern corner of the Arabian peninsula in the recently united state of Yemen. The inhabitants of the Tihamah coastland are a mixture of Yemenis and Africans. The Arabic spoken in the south is a dialect with Hindi, Malay, and Swahili influences. A few thousand on the island of Suqutra (Socotra) still speak an ancient South Arabic language. Nearly all Yemenis are Muslims; the warlike Zaydi hillmen in the north follow a Shi'a sect and have traditionally dominated the merchant Shafi'i Sunnites, concentrated in the south and along the coast. A few thousand are Isma'ili Muslims.

Although Yemenis live in villages and hamlets, they have maintained their tribal affiliations. The primitive economy and repressive political system have kept them very poor, inducing mass migration to Britain, the U.S.A., and Ethiopia, as well as more temporary departures to work in the Gulf's oil industry. Perhaps 30 percent of the total working male population has emigrated. The south is worse off, with scarce water in the small part of its area that is suitable for agriculture. In Hadhramaut live both sedentary ARABS and nomadic Beduin tribes. Along the coast, fishing is the main resource.

The Yemenis may descend from famous pre-Islamic kingdoms that thrived on long-distance trade. They were islamicized by 650. In the nineteenth century the BRITISH occupied Aden and its hinterland in southern Yemen. After the collapse of the Ottoman Empire in 1918, northern Yemen became the independent kingdom of Yemen while southern Yemen was established as a British zone of influence in the Aden hinterland.

Northern Yemen was still a medieval kingdom when the last Zaydi ruler died in 1962. A bloody civil war broke out between republicans supported by Egypt, and royalists, aided by Saudi Arabia. This war reflected the tension between isolationism and openness to modernity. In 1970 a ceasefire established a republican regime; but many royalists kept key posts, and in fact Saudi, tribal, and Islamic influences remained predominant.

The South Arabian Federation, which Britain had installed in 1959 in southern Yemen, was forced to give way to radical republican nationalists who eliminated the power of both the BRITISH and the sultans. In 1967 southern Yemen became independent as the Democratic People's Republic of Yemen, governed by a Marxist-Leninist regime which leaned increasingly towards the Soviet Union.

In North Yemen after 1974 a succession of violent government changes exacerbated tension between modernizers (supported by the South) and Islamic traditionalists (allied with Yemen's northern tribes and the pro-Saudi faction). Domestic strife soon expanded into war between the two Yemens. The "forgotten civil

Yemeni women in a street in Tula, Yemen

war" continued for years. In the mid–1980s, however, a more moderate trend became manifest in both North and South Yemen, leading to a rapprochement between them. The thaw thus ushered in has, over the past years, led to liberalization of South Yemen's economic system, and to a expansion of political liberties in North Yemen. Finally reunited in 1991, Yemen is now experiencing the transition to a multiparty system with a free press. However, when it refused to abide by sanctions against Iraq, Saudi Arabia retaliated by suspending financial support and sent 800,000 Yemeni migrants back home, plunging the country into an acute financial crisis.

YENADI   A people, numbering 320,000 (1981), living in the state of Andhra Pradesh in central India. Their language, Telugu, belongs to the Dravidian family of languages.

The Yenadi live on edible jungle produce and small game. They also work as laborers.

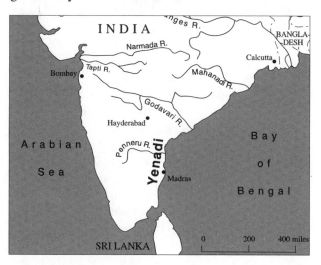

Yenadi

YERGAN   A subgroup of the TIV.

YERUKULA   A subgroup of the KORWA.

YFUGAO   see IFUGAO.

YI   (Lolo) Estimated as numbering 5.5 million, this people inhabits the mountains of southwest China, including the Liangshan Yi Autonomous Prefecture in the Sichuan Province, and the Yunnan, Guizhou, and Guangxi Provinces.

The Yi are believed to be descendants of the Tusan, six tribes which founded a kingdom called Nanchao in

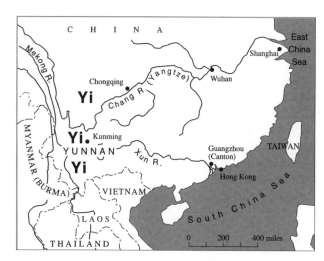

Yi

the seventh century; the kingdom lasted 600 years during which time they developed a hieroglyphic writing system during this period. Their language, belonging to the Tibeto-Burmese branch of the Sino-Tibetan family, is divided into six dialects, although all have the same historical origins and have borrowed an extensive vocabulary from Chinese.

Traditionally the Yi were divided into two castes. The Blackbone Yi were the ruling group possessing all property and slaves; far more numerous was the subjected group, consisting of poor Whitebone Yi and CHINESE who were slaves. This caste system was preserved among the Yi in the Liangshan area until the 1950s.

The Yi traditionally engaged in hoe agriculture, livestock-herding, and hunting. They believe that all objects contain good or bad spirits. Their unique solar calendar, invented 6,000 to 7,000 years ago, divided the year into five seasons or ten months of thirty-six days each, which made up a year of 360 days. The remaining five days were reserved for festivals. (see also LISU)

YIKHI   see TSAKHUR.

YIRA   An ethnic group living in the Kivu Region of central-eastern Zaire.

YIR YORONT   An Australian aboriginal group living on the Cape York Peninsula in northern Queensland. Originally hunters and gatherers, they are now employed primarily as laborers on cattle ranches and in services in nearby towns. (see also AUSTRALIAN ABORIGINES)

YOABU   An ethnic group living in Benin.

YOCAVIL   A chiefdom of the DIAGUITA.

YOKUT   A Native North American group, numbering 700, living in California. Traditionally they were hunters of small game and cultivators of maize and acorns; today they are mainly engaged in agriculture.

YOLNGU   (Murngin) An Australian aboriginal group numbering about 5,000, living on the northern edge of the Northern Territory, Australia. They are hunters and gatherers. (see also AUSTRALIAN ABORIGINES)

YOMBE   An ethnic group, numbering 10,000, living in the easternmost region of Zambia. They speak Tumbuka. Another group lives in the Congo.

YOMUD   A subgroup of the TURKMEN.

YONI TEMNE   see TEMNE.

YORUBA   A people found mainly in Nigeria, where they number around 21 million, or 20 percent of the population, and constitute the country's second largest ethnic group. The Yoruba live in southwestern Nigeria, including the area of Lagos, Ogun, Ondo, and Oyo States and the southern part of Kwara State. In the northwest they extend across Benin into central Togo. Their language, Yoruba, remained unwritten until the 1840s but has a rich oral literature and many dialects. Historically, Yoruba unity was linguistic and cultural rather than political.

The traditional Yoruba religion postulated a supreme deity, several hundred lesser gods, ancestral spirits, and different categories of spiritual beings. They believed that the supreme deity created the world in Ife, the center of all later Yoruba kingdoms, and sent Oduduwa, the father of all Yoruba kings, to that city to found his dynasty. Islam was introduced in the seventeenth century, probably by Muslims from the NUPE ethnic group who were brought to the Yoruba region as slaves. Christianity, mainly Protestantism, was first spread among the Yoruba in the 1840s by different missions, and competed with Islam. While Islam was better adapted to the polygamous Yoruba social structure, Christianity offered Western-type education in the mission schools. Today, the Yoruba are equally divided between Islam and Christianity.

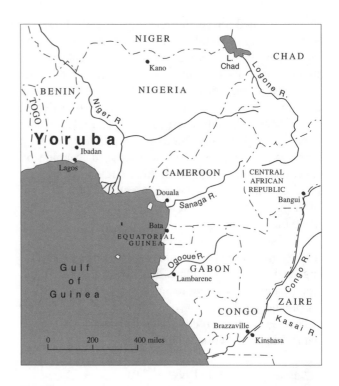

Yoruba

In the pre-colonial period, the Yoruba were divided into many independent political units, each ruled by a king who was considered to be a friend of the gods and to have spiritual powers which set him apart from his people.

Great power was also in the hands of commoner chiefs who formed a powerful council of state which could even select a new king. One of the earliest and most important kingdoms was Oyo, founded in 1100 and reaching its zenith in the sixteenth to eighteenth centuries; it survived until the nineteenth century.

Most Yoruba kingdoms declined during the nineteenth century as a result of penetration by the FULANI and Europeans from the north and south respectively. Towards the end of that century the BRITISH consolidated their rule over all of modern Nigeria and attempted to rule the Yoruba indirectly by using their kings as agents. This system of administration continued until the 1950s.

By the 1930s an elite class of literates and wealthy businessmen had developed among the Yoruba as a result of education and the growth of the cocoa industry. Members of this elite became increasingly involved in local politics.

Following constitutional changes in 1945, power shifted from the local level to the central government. In the decade after 1945 party politics began to develop and the anti-colonial struggle intensified.

Upon Nigeria's independence in 1960, the traditional British division of the country into three regions (the north, dominated by the HAUSA-FULANI; the southeast, dominated by the IBO; and the southwest, dominated by the Yoruba) resulted in ethnic and political instability, which climaxed in the bloody Biafra War of 1967, after a secessionist bid by the IBO. The Yoruba were divided over whether to demand independence for their region or to stay within the Nigerian federation.

To resolve the situation, the federal government divided the three regions into smaller units that cut across ethnic lines. As a result, the Yoruba now live in five states together with other ethnic groups instead of in one, almost homogeneous region.

The most important Yoruba subgroup is the EGBA. The IJEBU of the Ogun State were important for the role they played as middlemen in European trade and for their attempt to resist British colonialism. Other groups include the AHORI, AKOKO, BUNE, EKITI, EKO, IFE, IJESHA, JEKRI, KERU, NYANTRUKU, ONDO, and OYO of Nigeria, the DASSA and NAGOT (Nago) of Benin, and the HOLLI, who live along the border of both countries. (see also ADJA, BENINIANS, CUBANS, EGBA, NIGERIANS)

YORUK   see TURKS.

YOWA   see PILA-PILA.

YRRAYA   see GADDANG.

YUAN   (Lanatai) A Thai-speaking people numbering 6 million and inhabiting northern Thailand. Although assimilated into the dominant THAI, their historic connection to the Mekong Delta, their association with Indian Pali-Buddhism, and differences in dialect lead anthropologists to consider them a distinct ethnic group.

YUCATEC MAYA   An ethnic group inhabiting the Yucatan Peninsula. Largely Roman Catholic, they range from almost completely traditional, village-dwelling agriculturalists, cultivating beans, chilis, corn, squash, and yams, to fully acculturated town and city dwellers. Half speak the Yucatec language, and a fifth of these speak only Yucatec, which, also spoken in Belize and northern Guatemala, is believed to be the language closest to the classical Mayan tongue.

Many of the more acculturated Yucatec participate in one of the economic mainstays of the Yucatan, henequen-fiber harvesting and processing in which the fiber agave plant is used for making ropes. (see also MAYA)

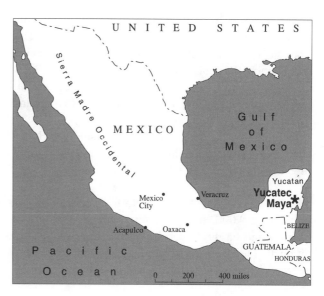

Yucatec Maya

YUCHI   A Native North American group, numbering 1,400, living in Oklahoma with the CREEK tribe. They originated in Georgia, U.S.A.

YUE   see GAOSHAN, LI, SHUI.

YUKAGIR   Numbering fewer than 4,000, the Yukagir are the remnants of a much larger population which

Yuma

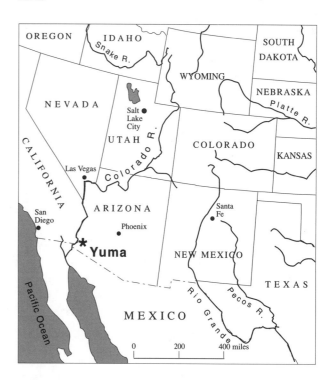

either perished in epidemics or was assimilated into the neighboring RUSSIANS, YAKUT, EVEN, and CHUKCHI. They now live in the Magadan Province and the Yakut Autonomous Republic in central Siberia,-Russia. They are divided into two groups distinctly different in culture and language. The Yukagir use both Russian and Yakut as literary language.

Traditionally they were hunters and fishermen. In recent decades they have moved into industry and mining. They practice their traditional religion.

YUMA (Yuman) A Native North American group, numbering 9,000, living scattered across the state of Arizona and on the Cocopah Federal Reservation. Traditionally they were agriculturalists and they continue to grow corn, beans, watermelon, and other desert crops.

YUMBRI A tiny group of nomadic hillspeople living in northern Thailand. They are gatherers who live in the dense forests of their region. The Yumbri are rapidly becoming extinct, victims of the hardship of jungle existence and the brutal hostility of neighboring peoples.

YUNAM see YUMA.

YUROK A Native North American group, numbering 1,200, living on several Federal Rancherias in California, U.S.A. They were a large group in the past and the only Algonkian-speakers native to California. They were traditionally hunters, fishers, and gatherers.

YURUMANGUI A Native South American group living in Colombia.

YUSUFZAI A subgroup of the PASHTUN.

YUZ A subgroup of the UZBEKS.

Z

ZABARMA   A subgroup of the FULANI.

ZAGHAWA   An Arab ethnic group living in north-eastern Sudan, in the deserts of northern Kordofan and Darfur Provinces. They are the sixth largest Arab sub-group in northern Sudan. They number an estimated 100,000, including related ethnic groups such as the BERTA.

The Zaghawa are Muslims, although they profess many pre-Islamic religious rites and beliefs. Their language is a local dialect of Arabic. They own cattle but also engage in agriculture.

ZAIREANS   The people of Zaire, the second largest country in Africa, situated in the center of the continent, number an estimated 36 million. They consist of numerous ethnic groups divided by external boundaries. The KONGO of the southwest are divided between Zaire, Congo, and Angola, the ZANDE in the northeast between Zaire and Sudan, the CHOKWE in the southwest between Zaire and Angola, the BEMBA in the southeast between Zaire and Zambia, and the ALUR in the northeast between Zaire and Uganda. Other groups include the LUBA of the Kasai Region and the Shaba (Katanga) Province in the south, KIVU in the east, NGBANDI, NBAKA, and MBANJA in the north, and LUNDA and YEKE in the Shaba Province.

These groups constitute over 80 percent of the Zairean people; the remainder are divided between a large number of smaller ethnic groups. About 80 percent of Zaireans live in the rural areas. The official language is French, but the most widely spoken languages are Lingala, Kikongo, and Swahili. Fifty percent of the Zaireans follow traditional religions; the rest are mostly Christian.

Prior to independence from Belgium, granted in June 1960, Zaire was known as Belgian Congo. The BELGIANS left their colony without preparing it for self-rule and grave ethnic conflicts erupted almost immediately after independence. The foremost of these was the attempt of the LUNDA and YEKE of the mineral-rich province of Katanga to secede. At first the LUBA of Katanga regarded the struggle as a conflict between the impoverished locals and the rich foreigners from among the Kasai LUBA and the CHOKWE, who arrived in Katanga during the colonial period. Soon, however, the struggle became an ethnic one and the local LUBA joined the Kasai LUBA and the CHOKWE in opposing secession. The Katanga crisis was resolved only in 1963. Since then Zaire has been ruled by Mobutu Sese Seko.

All groups in Katanga continued to feel disgruntled over the government's refusal to repay the money it appropriated from the region or to invest it in local development projects. In the 1970s two more crises shook the region, while the LUNDA-LUBA conflict simmered. In 1992 and 1993 many LUBA fled Katanga (renamed Shaba by Mobutu) after violent LUNDA attacks.

Since the early 1990s popular demands for democratization were heard, but Mobutu squashed all opposition harshly.

ZAMBALES NEGRITOS   A southern subgroup of the NEGRITOS of the Philippines.

ZAMBIANS   The 8 million inhabitants of Zambia are divided into seven major ethno-linguistic groups: the BEMBA of the northeast, also predominant in the Copper Belt; the TONGA of the extreme south; the CHEWA of the Eastern Province; the LUNDA of the north-west and the Luapula Province; the KAONDE of the Solwezi and Kasempe Districts of the northwest; the MAMBWE of the northwest; and the LOZI of the southwest. Each group is further divided into a total of seventy-three subgroups, based on their cultural and linguistic affinity to the major groups. Zambia is the third most urbanized country in sub-Saharan Africa; according to the 1980 census, 41 percent of the population lives in urban areas.

Zambia is the fifth largest producer of copper in the world, and this is its main source of income. Cobalt, lead, zinc, and coal are also produced. As a landlocked country, Zambia was formerly dependent on railroad lines through the white-dominated regimes of Angola, Mozambique, Rhodesia, Zimbabwe, and South Africa to the south. Zambian politics and foreign relations became obsessed with the liberation of the Portuguese colonies, Rhodesia, and South Africa, and provided supported to regional liberation movements. For rerouting its railroad as a sanction against Ian Smith's regime in Rhodesia, Zambia became the target of counterattacks by white minority governments, hindering Zambian economic development.

Agriculture has been given high priority by the Zambian government. In addition to large commercial farms there are a growing number of small-scale farmers scattered throughout the country; the most noteworthy are the TONGA and the ILA. The staple crops are maize, cassava, beans, sorghum, and tobacco, although wheat, cotton, and sugar are also grown.

Zambian independence from Britain was officially declared in 1964. The new government was led by Kenneth Kaunda and his United National Independence Party (UNIP), of Bemba origin. Other parties were supported by other ethnic groups: the African National Congress was dominated by the TONGA and the United Party was the voice of the LOZI. At independence the Kaunda government was faced with the Lozi wish to maintain the separate status granted to them by the colonial government. Kaunda recognized these rights in the Barotse Agreement of 1964.

In time Kaunda consolidated his power by outlawing all opposition: a one-party state was instituted in 1972. Although minority rule has all but disintegrated in most of southern Africa, the economic situation in Zambia failed to improve and political disquiet increased. Most parliamentarians are BEMBA but the diversity of other ethnic groups precluded political opposition movements based on ethnic divisions. Rather, opposition was led by trade-union leaders and politicians from different ethnic backgrounds. Discussions in 1990 over multiparty elections and constitutional amendments led to free elections in 1991, in which Kaunda was defeated by trade-union leader Frederick Chiluba.

ZAMFARA   A subgroup of the HAUSA.

ZAMUCO   A semi-nomadic Native South American group of the Gran Chaco region of Paraguay. Their main economic activities include hunting, fishing, and gathering forest products, but they also herd livestock and engage in limited cultivation of maize and sweet manioc.

ZAN   see CHAN, MEGREL.

ZANAGA   see SANHADJA.

ZANDE   see AZANDE.

ZAPARO   A Zaparoan-speaking Native South American group inhabiting the border area of Ecuador and the Loreto Province of northeastern Peru. They depend primarily upon the cultivation of sweet manioc, maize, beans, and peanuts. Agriculture is done by the women, while the men practice hunting and gathering. They have joined with other native peoples in the Shuar Federation, which strives to preserve indigenous cultures.

ZAPOROZHTSI COSSACKS   see UKRAINIANS.

ZAPOTEC   A native Mexican group, numbering c.300,000, living in Oaxaca, a predominantly native state in Mexico. They were among the first peoples to develop a more comprehensive form of writing in pre-Colombian Mexico; they were also famous for their calendrical science. Little is known about their origin, although it is generally assumed that they came from the northeast, attracted by the richness of this semitropical region. Having invaded Oaxaca, they established their sacred city at what is now called Monte

Zapotec

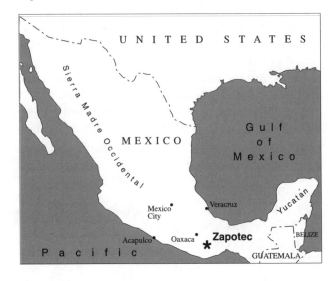

Alban. Some elements of classical Zapotec culture are still nurtured by their descendants.

While now dispersed throughout Mexico, the Zapotec still maintain a strong sense of identity: some use ancient techniques passed on orally and by example from parents to children in traditional ceramic and other craft industries. Dependence on a cash economy with scant rewards has caused others to seek work in Mexico City or the United States, many as seasonal migrants. (see also MEXICANS)

ZARAMAO   A Bantu-speaking ethnic group living in Tanzania.

ZARMA, ZERMA   see DJERMA.

ZAY   (Zeway, Laki) A small group living on the islands of Lake Zeqay in Ethiopia, south of the capital, Addis Ababa. Their language is related to that of the GURAGE, and they are Ethiopian Orthodox Christians. The Zay are fishermen. They represent small remnants of a population linked to the expansion of the Ethiopian Empire during the late Middle Ages.

ZAYDI   see YEMENITES.

ZAYYAN   (Zaian, Zayan) A BERBER group living in the center of Morocco. They are Muslims and speak a Berber language. During the colonial period the FRENCH permitted them to retain their own judicial system.

ZAZZAGAWA   A subgroup of the HAUSA.

ZEBAKI   An ethnic group inhabiting the Zebak subdistrict of the Badakhshan District in Afghanistan. No statistical figures about them are available, but their population is very roughly estimated at running into several hundred. Their vernacular, a dialect of Ishkashimi, has been extinct for some generations. They now speak a Dari (Afghanistani Persian) dialect.

The Zebaki have been followers of the Isma'ili sect of Islam since no earlier than the eleventh century. They live in small villages situated in valleys or on mountain slopes. Mountain agriculturalists, they also have a near-monopoly in the local salt trade. (see also AFGHANS)

ZELIANGRONG   An ethnic group, numbering 21,000 (1981), living in the states of Nagaland and Manipur in northeastern India. They speak a Sino-Ti-

betan language. They are a mixed group of the ZEMEI, LIANGMEI, and RONGMEI tribes of Nagaland. The ZEMEI and the LIANGMEI are known in Manipur as Kacha Naga and the RONGMEI as Kabui. They build their houses on piles above the ground and on hill-ridges. Their main source of livelihood is slash and burn agriculture, but terrace cultivation is also practiced by some in suitable sites. The women are noted for their weaving. The Zeliangrong have preserved their traditional religion.

ZELMAMO   see ZILMAMU.

ZEMEI   A NAGA group. (see also ZELIANGRONG)

ZEMMOUR   A Berber group living in the hinterland of the city of Rabat-Sale, Morocco, between the high and middle Atlas and the Atlantic shores. They are Muslims and speak a Berber language. As they become increasingly involved in trade, they have begun speaking Arabic outside their homes.

The Zemmour were semi-nomadic pastoralists, and their juridical and economic unit was the extended family. They left the pre-Sahara region by the sixteenth century but only settled in their present location in the nineteenth century, under the leadership of El-Rhazi. After El-Rhazi's death they refused to pay taxes or to acknowledge the sultans of Morocco. Attempts by the latter to enforce their authority over the Zemmour were barely perceptible; by the late nineteenth century anarchy was so prevalent in Zemmour territory that the sultan was afraid to traverse their lands. However, the lack of centralized rule also led to internal wars between Zemmour subgroups and weakened their power.

In the 1920s the FRENCH began occupying the Zemmour region and gained control over much of their lands. As a result, the Zemmour underwent a rapid economic and social transformation. Their pastoral way of life was replaced by settled agriculture and trade, and their juridical system was reformed. In the 1950s, due to their proximity to the cities of Rabat and Meknes and their affiliation with neighboring peoples, the Zemmour absorbed the nationalist ideas of the period, and participated in the Moroccan independence movement.

ZENAGA   A subgroup of the MAURE.

ZEWAY   see ZAY.

ZEYSE   An ethnic group, numbering 20,000, living on the southwestern side of Lake Chamo in eastern Gemu Gofa Province, Ethiopia. They are related linguistically to the AMARROO (the Omotic language group), and adhere to traditional beliefs. The Zeyse plant grains and ensete.

ZEZURU (Chizezuru) A Shona-speaking group living near Harare in central Zimbabwe. Some are Christians and some practice traditional African religions. They are divided into individual kingdoms which are united by a common language and culture. As they live close to the capital, they have been more affected by industrialization than have other groups. The Shona spoken by the Zezuru has been used as a basis for standardized Shona, or Chishona.

Subgroups of the Zezuru are the HERA, MBIRE, NOE (Wanoe, Nhowhe), and SHAWASHA. (see also SHONA, ZIMBABWEANS)

ZHUANG (Chuang) Estimated as numbering 13.4 million, the Zhuang are the largest ethnic minority in China. Most live in the Guangxi Zhuang Autonomous Region in southwest China, with smaller communities in the neighboring Yunnan and Guizhou Provinces.

Their language is related to the Tai language of Thailand. Their first written language, based on Chinese ideographs, appeared more than 700 years ago, but in 1955 the Chinese government helped them adopt the Roman alphabet, which is now the official script. Most Zhuang adhere to traditional religions, although Taoism is also widespread. The impact of Western missionaries has been limited to a few urban areas.

The chief occupation of the Zhuang has been farming, particularly rice cultivation. It is believed that they once lived farther north, migrating southward in re-

sponse to the encroaching HAN CHINESE. Han culture has had a marked impact on Zhuang dress and dwelling, but in some areas one can still find people living in traditional platform houses, built on pilings and similar to Dai and Burmese homes. People live on the top floor; the ground floor is reserved for animals.

The Zhuang's rich cultural history dates back over 3,000 years. Among their most famous cultural relics are cliff frescoes and bronze drums. Tattooing was once common, and chewing areca is still a popular tradition. Other social customs include premarital sexual freedom; after the wedding brides stay with their parents, moving in with their husbands only after a child is born. Until then, women may have relations with many other men.

ZIBA see HAYA.

ZIKRI see BALUCH.

ZILMAMU (Zulmamu, Zelmamo) A group of Suri-speakers, numbering 6,000 (1980s), living west of Maji in southern Kefa Province, Ethiopia.

ZIMBA A CHEWA subgroup living in the Tete District, north of the Zambezi River in Mozambique.

ZIMBABWEANS The 10 million inhabitants of Zimbabwe are divided into two major ethno-linguistic

Zhuang

Zimba

above: A Zhuang woman in southwestern China
below: A Zhuang farmer in southwestern China

groups, the SHONA and the NDEBELE. The majority of the population belongs to seven SHONA subgroups: the KOREKORE of the extreme northwestern region, near Lake Kariba; the MANYIKA of the eastern region, near the border with Mozambique; the KARANGA of the southern area, near the South African border; the ZEZURU of the region around Harare; the NDAU of the southeast; the KALANGA of the southeast; and the RUZWI, who are scattered throughout the country. The NDEBELE live in the southwest, mainly around Bulawayo. In Zimbabwe there are also small ethnic groups such as the VENDA of the southernmost region; the SOTHO of the southwest; and the TONGA, who live near Lake Kariba. Although English is the official langauge, the SHONA speak Shona and the NDEBELE speak Sindebele.

Zimbabwe's agricultural sector is highly developed, comprising 70 percent of the work force. The staple crop is maize; millet, sorghum, and barley are also grown. The main cash crops are tobacco, cotton, and sugar. Zimbabwe also has deposits of over forty different minerals; gold, asbestos, nickel, coal, copper, iron ore, and chromium are leading sources of income. In addition, Zimbabwe manufactures a variety of goods for export.

In 1923 Southern Rhodesia (as Zimbabwe was then called) became a white-dominated, self-governing colony with internal autonomy in all matters except foreign policy and legislation affecting the African population. In 1965 Ian Smith proclaimed his Unilateral Declaration of Independence and Rhodesia became independent of Britain under a white minority government. In response, African liberation movements, founded a few years earlier, launched a guerrilla war to end white rule. The Zimbabwe African Peoples Union (ZAPU), led by Joshua Nkomo, was supported by the NDEBELE, and the Zimbabwe African National Union (ZANU), led by Robert Mugabe, was supported by the SHONA. In 1980, after negotiations between ZANU, ZAPU, Britain, and the Smith regime, free elections were held: ZANU won the majority of seats in the new parliament. Mugabe aspired to establish a one-party state on the Marxist model after establishing a base of popular support throughout the country. Nkomo, who considered the election results to be invalid, rejected Mugabe's offer of the presidency and a merger between ZAPU and ZANU. In 1982 Nkomo and his colleagues were dismissed after arms were found on ZAPU property in Matabeleland. Despite some pro-Nkomo violence, the remaining ZAPU parliament members remained in the the government and Nkomo was not brought to trial.

This was, however, only the beginning of the ethnic conflict. In 1982 the military wing of ZAPU initiated acts of violence in the poverty-stricken Ndebele region. In 1983 and 1984 a ZANU army unit was accused of committing atrocities against NDEBELE civilians; despite objections from international organizations such as Amnesty International, the government denied the accusations. Mugabe's government then launched a military campaign against the dissidents in the Ndebele area. ZANU's representation in the government was increased, further alienating the two groups. In the midst of this deteriorating situation, talks between ZANU and ZAPU took place. In 1987 Mugabe withdrew from the talks, claiming that they had accomplished nothing. Only following a brutal massacre of NDEBELE in November of that year were the talks resumed. They culminated in a merger of the two parties and the formation of a single-party Marxist state. This agreement, signed in December 1987, was ratified in 1988.

ZINACANTECOS An ethnic group living in the Zinacantan district of the state of Chiapas, Mexico. They are Tzotzil-speaking descendants of the MAYA.

Zinacantecan religion mixes Catholicism with indigenous beliefs and rituals. The nominally Christian deity they worship is identified with the sun, and the Virgin Mary, with the moon: thus they have been able to preserve their belief that the sun is a male entity and the moon a female one. In their syncretic religious ceremonies, the Zinacantecos pray to their ancestral gods as much as to the Christian deity: although ceremonies are held in front of a cross, a shaman intercedes. Zinacantecan ceremonies, marked by the uniformity of their distinctive costumes, are extremely expensive, averaging one person's annual income.

Zinacantecan one-room houses, usually made of adobe with tile roofs, dot the precipitous Chiapas Highlands. The diet staple is maize, cultivated on smallscale farms and garden plots and consumed mainly in the form of tortillas. Beans and squash are also cultivated, the combination of the three foods constituting a whole protein and making up for the protein deficiency which would otherwise have been precipitated by absence of animals larger than chickens or small pigs suitable for domestication. Small game mammals are scarce in the densely-peopled Chiapas Highlands, but iguanas, considered a delicacy, are plentiful and widely consumed. (see also MAYA)

ZIRIJHGARAN see QUBACHI.

ZOMI see MIZO.

ZORCA A Native South American group living in Venezuela.

ZORO A Native South American group living in the State of Mato Grosso, central-west Brazil. Their region has been encroached upon by non-Indian settlers with the intention of initiating lumbering projects.

ZOROASTRIANS see PARSIS.

ZULMAMU see ZILMAMU.

ZULU A people, numbering 7 million, belonging to the northern NGUNI peoples of South Africa. Many Zulu are urbanized city dwellers: rural Zulu live in the southern Transvaal and Natal. The Zulu are predominately Christian: about three-quarters of them have specific church affiliations. One third are members of African Independent churches; 13 percent are Roman Catholics; and 7 percent are Methodists.

KwaZulu, the Zulu homeland in Natal, was granted nominal self-government in 1977, under Chief Mangosuthu Buthelezi of the Inkatha Freedom Party. The University of Zululand is situated in KwaDlangezwa.

Zulu

KwaZulu is the wealthiest of the Bantustan homelands. Its major products are manufactured goods and sugar cane. Population figures for KwaZulu are extremely unreliable, given that citizenship in them has been very broadly defined to include non-resident Zulus.

In addition to ruling Kwazulu, the Inkatha Freedom Party is also active within South Africa as a whole, particularly among Zulu migrant workers in the mining compounds of the Transvaal. The party claims an overall membership of 1.7 million and, although in 1976 it opened membership to all South African blacks, over 95 percent of its members are Zulu. The name "*Inkatha*" derives from a royal coil of woven grass, viewed historically as containing ingredients of mystical significance. It symbolized supreme power and represented the unity and spiritual essence of the Zulu people. The royal *inkatha* was passed from king to king until 1879 when it was destroyed in a British assault on the Zulu capital. In the twentieth century, the hereditary Buthelezi chieftaincy emerged as the focus of effective Zulu political power under a declining Zulu Paramountcy (presently headed by King Goodwill Mbangi Zwelethini).

Zulu history is currently undergoing academic reevaluation and revision. Traditional interpretations of early Zulu history are, nevertheless, as yet uncontested. At the turn of the nineteenth century the Zulu were an insignificant conquered clan. In 1817 Shaka of the Zulu clan assumed a pivotal role in the creation of a mighty Zulu empire. From here, however, interpretations diverge. According to traditional interpretations, Shaka revolutionized NGUNI warfare techniques and went on the rampage against all neighboring peoples. These, in turn, imitated Zulu tactical innovations and weaponry and themselves ravaged other peoples on the outskirts of the Zulu periphery. This was the *Mfekane* (the "crushing" or "hammering") which scattered peoples over half the African continent, some fleeing as far as the equator. Under Shaka's successor, Dingane, Zulu expansionism was finally curtailed: Dingane provoked and was defeated by AFRIKANERS in 1838–1839. The Zulu military system was finally destroyed by the BRITISH in 1879, after which Zululand was annexed by Britain in 1887, and incorporated into Natal in 1897. In 1906, a Zulu uprising under a minor Zulu chief, Bambata, in protest against the imposition of a poll tax, was the last chiefdom-based armed conflict prior to the establishment of the Union of South Africa.

Images of the Zulu and of Shaka have played an important role in the historical consciousness of both blacks and whites in South Africa. For blacks, the Zulu

A Zulu warrior in South Africa

have symbolized pre-colonial black power and grandeur, ruthlessly crushed by the forces of white imperialism. Shaka has been the symbol of this power, and his image has featured prominently in Inkatha, African National Congress, and Pan-Africanist Congress propaganda. For whites, Shaka and the rise of the Zulu empire have featured as proof of aboriginal black heathen barbarism and the inherently aggressive attitudes and policies of black groups toward one another.

The Zulu are exceptional among South Africa's black peoples in the twentieth century in that, in additional to specifically Zulu political organizations (such as Inkatha), a number of specifically Zulu labor organizations have been formed. One example of such organization was the *AmaWasha*, or Zulu Washermen's Guild, which operated in Natal and in the Witwatersrand region of the Transvaal in the late nineteenth and early twentieth centuries. Another example from the first half of the twentieth century was the Zululand Planters' Union.

Culturally, the Zulu share the customs of the NGUNI peoples. However, they differ from most NGUNI in that they have not practiced circumcision since the early nineteenth century. In urban areas, the religious-cultural modes of the modern day Zulu appear to follow the patterns of other urbanized black groups. Among urban Christian Zulu, the belief in the power of ancestors to influence human fortunes persists; in fact, 55 percent perform regular rituals to honor and placate ancestors (the highest percentage of all urban black Christian peoples). In some independent churches, the original group-founder, personal ancestors of the congregation, and King Shaka are all expected to appear during night services.

In addition to their elaborate "mime dances" performed in frequent galas for tourists, the contemporary Zulu are known for their intricate beadwork, symbolically coded in terms of design and color. (see also NGUNI, SOUTH AFRICANS)

ZUNI A Native North American group numbering 9,000, living on the Federal Zuñi Pueblo in New Mexico, U.S.A. One of the largest Pueblo groups, the Zuñi continue to practice agriculture and are famous for their silver and turquoise artistry. Many still live in their ancient villages. (see also HOPI, PUEBLO INDIANS)

Zuñi

ZURI see AIMAQ-I DIGAR.

ZUTT see JATS.

ZUWAWA A subgroup of the KABYLE.

ZYUDA KOMI PERMYAK see KOMI.

SELECT BIBLIOGRAPHY

General

Barth, Frederik, editor. *Ethnic Groups and Boundaries*. Boston: Little Brown and Co., 1969.

Comrie, Bernard. *The World's Major Languages*. New York: Oxford University Press, 1987.

Esman, Milton J, editor. *Ethnic Conflict in the Western World*. Ithaca, N.Y.: Cornell University Press, 1977.

Levinson, David, editor. *Encyclopedia of World Cultures*. 10 vols. Boston: G.K. Hall & Co., 1992–1993.

Murdock, George P. *Outline of World Cultures*. New Haven, Conn.: Human Relations Area Files, 1983.

Murdock, George P. *Ethnographic Atlas*. Pittsburgh: University of Pittsburgh Press, 1967.

Ruhlen, Merritt. *A Guide to the World's Languages*. Vol. 1, *Classification*. Stanford, Calif.: Stanford University Press, 1991.

Saches, Moshe Y, editor. *Worldmark Encyclopedia of Nations*. 7th edition. New York: Worldmark Press, 1988.

Snyder, Louis L. *Encyclopedia of Nationalism*. New York: Paragon House, 1990.

Weekes, Richard V. *Muslim Peoples, A World Ethnographic Survey.* 2 vols. London: Aldwych Press. 1984.

North America

Allen, James P. and Turner, Eugene J. *We the People: An Atlas of America's Ethnic Diversity*. New York: Macmillan, 1988.

Bumstead, John. M. *The Peoples of Canada,* Toronto: Oxford University Press, 1992.

Driver, Harold E. *Indians of North America*. Chicago: University of Chicago Press, 1969.

Jorgensen, Joseph G. *Western Indians*. San Francisco: W. H. Freeman and Co., 1980.

Leitch, Barbara A. *A Concise Dictionary of Indian Tribes of North America*. Algonac, Mich.: Reference Publications, 1979.

Markotic, Vladimir and Hromadiuk, Robert F. *Ethnic Directory of Canada*. Calgary: Western Publishers, 1983.

Marsh, James, H, editor. *The Canadian Encyclopedia*. 3 vols, Edmonton: Hurtig Publishers, 1985.

Miller, Charles W, editor. *A Comprehensive Bibliography for the Study of American Minorities*. New York: New York University Press, 1976.

Rachelis, Eugene, and Ewers, John C. *Indians of the Plains*. New York: American Heritage Pub. Co., 1960.

Robinson, Guy M, editor. *A Social Geography of Canada*. Toronto: Dundurn Press, 1991.

Ruby, Robert H, and John A. Brown. *Indians of the Pacific Northwest*. Norman: University of Oklahoma Press, 1988.

Sachs, Moshe Y, editor. *Worldmark Encyclopedia of the States*. New York: Worldmark Press, 1981.

Theodoratus. Robert, editor. *Immigrant Communities and Ethnic Minorities in the United States and Canada*. New York: AMS Press, 1989.

Thernstrom, Stephan, editor. *Harvard Encyclopedia of American Ethnic Groups*. Cambridge: Harvard University Press, Belknap Press. 1980.

Waldman, Carl. *Atlas of the North American Indian*. New York: Facts on File, 1985.

Yenne, Bill. *The Encyclopedia of the North American Indian Tribes*. London: Bison Books, *1986*.

Central America

Bell, Betty, editor. *Indian Mexico: Past and Present*. Los Angeles: University of California: Latin American Center, 1967.

Horowitz, Michael M. comp. *Peoples and Cultures of the Caribbean*. Garden City, N.Y.: Natural History Press, 1971.

Olien, Michael D. *Latin Americans: Contemporary Peoples and their Cultural Traditions*. New York: Holt, Rinehart and Winston, 1973.

Ryan, John. M, and others. *Area Handbook for Mexico*. Washington: The American University, 1970.

Spahni, Jean Christian. *The Indians of Central America*. Guatemala City: Piedra Santa, 1982.

Wauchope, Robert, and others. *Handbook of Middle American Indians*. 16 vols., Austin, Texas: University of Texas Press, 1964–1976.

Woodward, Ralph L. *Central America: A Nation Divided*. New York: Oxford University Press, 1985.

Wolfe, Eric. R. *Sons of the Shaking Earth*. Chicago: University of Chicago Press, 1959.

South America

Lyon, Patricia J, editor. *Native South Americans, Ethnology of the Least Known Continent*. Boston: Little, Brown and Co., 1974.

Steward, Julian H, editor. *Handbook of South American Indians*. 2 vols. Washington: Smithsonian Institute, Bureau of American Ethnology, 1946–1959.

Steward, Julian H, and Louis C. Faron. *Native Peoples of South America*. New York: McGraw-Hill, 1959.

Stoddard, Theodore L, editor. *Indians of Brazil in the Twentieth Century*. Washington: Institute for Cross-cultural Research Studies. No. 2, 1967.

Europe

Chadwick, H. Munro. *The Nationalities of Europe and the Growth of National Ideologies*. New York: Cooper Square Publishers, 1973.

Collins, Roger. *The Basques*. Oxford: Blackwell, 1987.

Comrie, Bernard. *The World's Major Languages*. New York: Oxford University Press, 1987.

Elton, Geoffrey R. *The English*. Oxford: Blackwell, 1992.

Gimbutas, Marija. *The Slavs*. London: Thames & Hudson, 1971.

Horak, Stephan M. *Eastern European National Minorities, 1919/1980: A Handbook*. Littleton, Colo.: Libraries Unlimited, 1985.

Jelavich, Charles, editor. *Language and Area Studies, East, Central and Southeastern Europe*. Chicago: University of Chicago Press, 1969.

Murdock, George P. *Ethnographic Atlas*. Pittsburgh, Penn., University of Pittsburgh Press, 1967.

Stephens, Meic. *Linguistic Minorities in Western Europe*. Llandysul Dufed, Wales: Gomer Press, 1976.

Theodoratus. Robert J. *Europe: A Selected Ethnographic Bibliography*. 1969.

Africa

Adamson, Joy. *The Peoples of Kenya*. New York: Harcourt, Brace and Jovanovich, 1967.

Bourdillon, M. F. C. *The Shona Peoples: An Ethnography of the Contemporary Shona, With Special Reference to Their Religion*. Gawelo: Mambo Press, 1976.

Bryan, M.A. *The Bantu Languages of Africa*. London: Oxford University Press, 1959.

Caldwell J, and others. *Population Growth and Socioeconomic Change in West Africa*. New York: Columbia University Press, 1975.

Christopher, A.J. *Southern Africa*. Folkston: Dawson, 1976.

Delange, Jacqueline. *The Art and Peoples of Black Africa*. New York: Dutton, 1974.

Douglas, Mary. *Peoples of the Lake Nyasa Region*. London: Oxford Universtiy Press, 1950.

Eades, J. S. *The Yoruba Today*. New York: Cambridge University Press, 1981.

Fedders, Andrew. *Peoples and Cultures of Kenya*. Nairobi: Transafrica, 1979.

Gibbs, James L, editor. *Peoples of Africa*. New York: Holt, Rinehart and Winston, 1978.

Greenburg, Joseph H. *The Languages of Africa*. Bloomington: Indiana University, 1966.

Lewis Ian M. *Islam in Tropical Africa*. London: Oxford University Press, 1966.

Lewis Ian M. *Peoples of the Horn of Africa: Somali, Afar and Saho*. London: International African Institute, 1969.

Morrison, Donald G, and others. *Black Africa. A Comparative Handbook*. New York: The Free Press, 1972.

Morrison, George G, and others. *Understanding Black Africa,* New York: Paragon House and Irving Publishers, 1989.

Murdock, George P. *Africa: Its People and Their Culture History*. New York: McGraw Hill, 1959.

Nelson, H.D. and others. *Area Handbook for Nigeria,* 4th ed. Washington D. C.; Government Printing Office, 1982.

Nurse, George T., and Weiner, Joseph S. *The Peoples of Southern Africa and Their Affinities*. Oxford: Clarendon Press, 1985.

Shack, William A. *The Central Ethiopians: Amhara, Tigrina, and Related Peoples*. London: International African Institute, 1974.

Skinner, Eliot, P., editor. *Peoples and Cultures of Africa*. Garden City, N.Y.: Doubleday, 1973.

Tringham J. Spencer. *The Influence of Islam upon Africa*. New York: Praeger, 1968.

Wellington, J H. *Southern Africa: A Geographical Study*. London: Oxford University Press, 1978.

North Asia (including the former Soviet Union)

Akiner, Shirim. *Islamic Peoples of the Soviet Union*. London, Kegan Paul International, 2nd ed. 1986.

Allworth, Edward, editor. *The Nationality Question in Soviet Central Asia*. New York: Praeger, 1973.

Allworth, Edward. *Nationalities of the Soviet East: Publications and Writing Systems*. New York: Columbia University Press, 1971.

Bennigsen, Alexandre, and Wimbush S. Enders. *Muslims of the Soviet Empire: A Guide*. London: Christopher Hurst & Co., 1986.

Bennigsen, Alexandre, and Lemercier-Quelquejay Chantal. *Islam in the Soviet Union*. New York: Praeger, 1967.

Geiger, Bernard, and others. *Peoples and Languages of the Caucasus*. The Hague: Monton & Co., 1959.

Goldhagen, Erich, editor. *Ethnic Minorities in the Soviet Union*. New York: Praeger, 1968.

Kolarz, Walter. *The Peoples of the Soviet Far East*. London: G. Philip, 1954.

Kozlov, Viktor. *The Peoples of the Soviet Union*. London: Hutchinson, 1988.

Krader, Lawrence. *Peoples of Central Asia*. Bloomington: Indiana University Press, 1966.

Lamont, Corliss. *The Peoples of the Soviet Union*. New York: Harcourt Brace, 1946.

Menges, Karl. *The Turkic Languages and Peoples*. Weisbaden: Otto Harrssowitz, 1968.

Ramet, Pedro, editor. *Religion and Nationalism in Soviet and East European Politics*. Durham, N.C.: Duke University Press, 1984.

Symmons-Symonolewica, Konstantin. *The Non-Slavic Peoples of the Soviet Union*. Meadville Pa.: Maplewood Press, 1972.

Wheeler, Geoffrey. *The Peoples of Soviet Central Asia*. London: Bodley Head. 1966.

Wixman, Ronald. *Language Aspects of Ethnic Patterns and Processes in the North Caucasus*. University of Chicago Department of Geography, Research Paper No. 191, 1980.

Wixman, Ronald. *The Peoples of the USSR: An Ethnographic Handbook.* Armonk, New York: M.E. Sharpe, 1984.

Wurm, Stephen A. *Turkic Peoples of the USSR*. Oxford Central Asian Research Center, 1954.

West Asia

Air Universtiy (U.S.0. Aerospace Studies Institute). *The Peoples of the Middle East*. Alabama: 1971.

Andrews, Peter A. *Ethnic Groups in the Republic of Turkey*. Wiesbaden: Reichert, 1989.

Arfa, Hasan. *The Kurds: An Historical and Political Study*. New York: Oxford University Press, 1966.

Bates, Daniel G. and Rassam, Amal. *Peoples and Cultures of the Middle East*. Englewood Cliffs, N.J.: Prentice Hall, 1983.

Dupries, Louis. *Afghanistan*. Princeton: Princeton University Press, 1980.

Edmonds, Cecil. *Kurds, Turks and Arabs: Politics, Travel and Research in North-Eastern Iraq*. London: Oxford University Press, 1957.

Esman M. and Rabinovich, I. *Ethnicity, Pluralism, and the State in the Middle East*. Ithaca: Cornell University Press, 1988.

Francisse, A.E. *The Problems of Minorities in the Nation-Building Process: The Kurds, The Copts, The Berbers*. New York: Vantage Press, 1971.

Gulick, John. *The Middle East: An Anthropological Perspective*. Pacific Palisades, Calif.: Goodyear Publishing, 1976.

Hourani, Albert H. *History of the Arab Peoples*. Cambridge, Mass.: Belknap Press, 1991.

Hourani, Albert H. *Minorities in the Arab World*. London: Oxford University Press, 1947.

Shiloh, Ailon, editor. *Peoples and Cultures of the Middle East*. New York: Random House, 1969.

Sweet, Louise E, editor. *Peoples and Cultures of the Middle East*. 2 vols. New York: The Natural History Press, 1970.

Tapper, Richard, editor. *The Conflict of Tribe and State in Iran and Afghanistan*. London: Croom Helm, 1983.

East Asia

Bannister, Judith. *China. A Country Study*. Washington, D.C.: Government Printing Office, 1981.

Bonavia, David. *The Chinese*. New York: Lippincott & Cromwell, 1980.

Collcutt, Martin, Jansen, Marius and Kumakura, Isao. *The Cultural Atlas of the World: Japan*. Alexandria, Va: Stonehenge Press, 1988.

Dryer, June Teufel. *China's Forty Millions: Minority Nationalities and National Integration in the People's Republic of China*. Cambridge, Mass.: Harvard University Press, 1976.

Grunfeld, A. Tom. *The Making of Modern Tibet*. Armonk, N.Y.: M.E. Sharpe, 1987.

Moser, Leo J. *The Chinese Mosaic: The People and Provinces of China*. Boulder, Colorado: Westview Press, 1984.

Southeast Asia

Center for Applied Linguistics. *The Peoples and Cultures of Cambodia, Laos and Vietnam*. Washington, 1981.

Cole, Fay-Cooper. *The Peoples of Malaysia*. Princeton N.J.: Van Nostrand, 1945.

Dobby, Ernest. *Southeast Asia*. London: University of London Press, 1973.

Fisher, Charles. *Southeast Asia: A Social, Economic, and Political Geography*. London. Methuen,1966.

Gibbons, Robert, and Ashford, Robert. *Himalayan Kingdoms: Nepal, Sikkim, and Bhutan*. New York: Hippocrene, 1983.

Heihus, Mary F. *Southeast Asia's Chinese Minorities*. New York: Hawthorn, 1974.

Krieger, Herbert W. *Peoples of the Philippines*. Washington: Smithsonian Institution, 1942.

Kunstadter, Peter, editor. *Southeast Asian Tribes, Minorities, and Nations*. Princeton, N.J.: Princeton University Press, 1967.

Lasker, Bruno. *Peoples of Southeast Asia*. New York: A. A. Knopf, 1944.

LeBar, Frank, editor. *Ethnic Groups of Insular Southeast Asia*. Vol. 1 *Indonesia, Andaman Islands, and Madagascar*. New Haven: Human Relation Area Files Press, 1972.

LeBar, Frank, editor. *Ethnic Groups of Insular Southeast Asia*. Vol. 2 *Philippines and Formosa*. New Haven: Human Relation Area Files Press, 1975.

LeBar, Frank,and others, editors. *Ethnic Groups of Mainland Southeast Asia*. New Haven: Human Relation Area Files Press, 1964.

Robequain, Charles. *Malaya, Indonesia, Borneo, and the Philippines*. London: Longmans, 1955.

Seidenfaden, Erik. *The Thai Peoples*. Bankok: Siam Society.

Sopher, David, E. *The Sea Nomads*. Singapore: National Museum, 1977.

Spencer, Joseph E. *Shifting Cultivation in Southeastern Asia*. Berkeley and Los Angeles: University of California Publications in Geography, 1966.

South Asia

Brass, Paul R. *Language, Religion, and Politics in North India*. London: Cambridge University Press, 1974.

Cassen, Robert H. *India: Population, Economy and Society*. New York: Holmes & Meir, 1978.

Gilbert, William H. *Peoples of India*. Washington: Smithsonian Institute 1944.

Maloney, Clarence. *Peoples of South Asia*. New York: Holt Rinehart & Winston, 1974.

Muthiah, S. and others, editors. A *Social and Economic Atlas of India*. New Delhi: Oxford University Press, 1987.

Robinson, Francis, editor. *The Cambridge Encyclopedia of India, Pakistan, Bangladesh, Sri Lanka, Nepal, Bhutan, and the Maldives*. Cambridge: Cambridge University Press, 1989.

Schermerhorn, Richard A. *Ethnic Plurality in India*. Tuscon, Ariz: University of Arizona Press, 1978.

Shackle, Christopher, editor. *South Asian Languages: A Handbook*. London: School of Oriental and African Studies, 1985.

Shapiro, Michael C., and Schifman Harold F. *Language and Society in South Asia*. Delhi: Motilal Banarsidass, 1981.

Sopher, David E, editor. *An Exploration of India: Geographical Perspectives on Society and Culture*. Ithaca: Cornell University Press, 1980.

Majundar, Dhirendra Nath. *Races and Cultures of India*. Bombay: Asia Publishing House, 1961.

Oceania

Berndt, Ronald M., and Berndt Catherine H. *The World of the First Australians: Aboriginal Traditional Life Past and Present*. Canberra: Australian Institute for Aboriginal Studies, 1985.

Brookfield, Harold C. with Hart Doreen. *Melanesia: A Geographical Interpretation of an Island World*. London: Methuen, 1971.

Brown, P. *Highland Peoples of New Guinea*. Cambridge: Cambridge University Press, 1978.

Chowning, Ann. *An Introduction to the Peoples and Cultures of Melanesia*. Menlo Park, Calif.: Cummings, 1977.

Dixon, R.M.W. *The Languages of Australia*. Cambridge: Cambridge University Press, 1980.

Elkin, A.P. *The Australian Aborigines*. Sydney: Angus and Robertson, 1979.

Foley, William A. *The Papuan Languages of New Guinea*. Cambridge: Cambridge University Press, 1986.

Howard, Alan, editor. *Polynesia*. Chandler Rub Co., 1971.

Howells, William. *The Pacific Islanders*. New York: Charles Scribner's Sons, 1973.

Isaacs, Jennifer. *Australian Dreaming: Forty Thousand Years of Aboriginal History*. Sydney: Ure Smith Press, 1992.

Jeans, D.N, editor. *Australia: A Geography: The Natural Environment*. Sydney: Sydney University Press, 1986.

McGregor, C. *The Australian People*. Sydney: Hodder & Stoughton, 1980.

May, R.J, and Nelson, H, editors. *Melanesia: Beyond Diversity*. 3 vols. Canberra; The Australian National University, Research School of Pacific Studies. 1982.

Nordyke, Eleanor C. *The Peopling of Hawaii*. Honolulu: University of Hawaii Press, 1989.

Oliver, Douglas. *Oceania: The Native Cultures of Australia and the Pacific Islands*. 2 vols. Honolulu: University of Hawaii Press, 1988.

Oliver, Douglas. *Native Cultures of the Pacific Islands*. Honolulu: University of Hawaii Press, 1989.

Smith, L.R. *The Aboriginal Population of Australia*. Canberra: Australian National University Press, 1980.

Tindale, Norman B. *Aboriginal Tribes of Australia: Their Terrain, Environmental Controls, Distribution, Limits, and Proper Names*. 2 vols. Berkeley: University of California Press, 1974.

Vayda, Andrew, editor. *Peoples and Cultures of the Pacific: An Anthropoligical Reader*. Garden City, N.Y.: Natural History Press, 1968.

Sherington, Geoffrey. *Australia's Immigrants*. London: Macmillan, 1978.

Ward, R.G. and Lea, D.A.M, editors. *An Atlas of Papua and New Guinea*. Department of Geography, University of Papua and New Guinea, and Collins/Longman, 1970.

Whiteman, Darrell L. *An Introduction to Melanesian Cultures*. Goroka, Papua New Guinea: Melanesian Institute, 1984.

INDEX

This index provides a key to all ethnic groups and subgroups mentioned in this encyclopedia, as well as to self-designations, alternative names, and alternative spellings. It also provides information as to where the reader might find additional information on many groups. Bold highlighting in the first column indicates that the group appears as a separate entry in the encyclopedia.

A

Cayapo → Kayapo
Cayuga → Iroquois Confederacy
Cele → Nguni
Central African Republic, The People of the
Cewa → Chewa
Chaba → Egba
Chachi → Cayapas
Chadians
Chaga → Tanzanians
Chaha → Gurage
Chahar Aimaq → Aimaq
Chahar (Char) Lang → Bakhtiari
Chakhesang
Chakhuma → Chakhesang
Chakma
Cham → Hroy
Chamalal
Chamarro → Mariana Islanders
Chamba → Tiv
Chambri
Chamorros
Chamula → Maya
Chana → Argentines
Chang → Naga
Chaobon
Chara
Charca → Aymara
Charkas → Cherkess
Charrua → Argentines
Chaubo
Chaudhri
Chavante → Xavante
Chavchu → Chukchi
Chavchyvav → Koryak
Chaziche → Tehuelche
Chechen → Cherkess
Chechi → Czechs
Chegmly → Balkar
Chehali
Chelkan → Altai
Chemwal → Nandi
Chenchu
Cheng
Chepang
Cherangany → Marakwet
Cherkas → Cherkess
Cherkess
Chero
Cherokee
Chewa → Malawians, Mozambicans, Nsenga, Zambians
Che Wong → Senoi
Cheyenne
Chhazang
Chiapas → Mexicans
Chibcha → Colombians, Guaymi
Chickahominy
Chickasaw
Chik Baraik
Chikunda
Chil → Kil
Chilapa → Jivaro
Chilcotin
Chileans → Araucanians
Chimba → Herero
Chimbu
Chin → Burmans
Chinese → Thai
Ching-Po → Singhpo
Chingathan
Chinook → Chehali
Chipewyan
Chippewa
Chiquito
Chiricahua → Apache

Chiriguanos
Chirima
Chirumba → Shona
Chishinga
Chitimacha
Chitrali → Kho
Chizezuru → Zezuru
Choctaw
Chodhara
Choiseul Islanders
Chokossi
Chokwe → Zaireans
Chong
Chono
Chontal → Maya, Mexicans
Chonyi → Mijikenda
Chopi → Mozambicans
Chorote → Mataco-Mataguayo
Chorotega → Costa Ricans
Chorti → Maya
Chrau
Chru → Churu
Chuchugasta → Diaguita
Chuka → Meru
Chukchansi
Chukchi
Chulikatta → Mishmi
Chulupi → Mataco-Mataguayo
Chumash
Chung-chia → Buyi
Churahi
Churu
Chutia
Chutiya → Deori
Chu Ty → Jarai
Chuukese → Chuuk Islanders
Chuuk Islanders
Chuvash
Chysh-Kizhi → Shors
Cibecue → Apache
Ciboneyes → Cubans
Cil → Mnong
Circassians → Cherkess
Cocama
Cochinese → Vietnamese
Cochinoc → Punans
Cocopah
Cofan
Collagua → Aymara
Collahuaya → Aymara
Colombians
Colville
Comanche
Comechingon and Sanaviron
Comorians
Comox → Colville
Congolese
Cook Islanders
Copataza → Jivaro
Copts → Egyptians
Cor I → Jarai, Sedang
Cor II → Semang
Cornish
Corsi → Corsicans
Corsicans
Cossacks (Zaporozhtsi) → Ukrainians
Cossacks → Qazaq
Costa Ricans
Cotabato Manobo
Cote d'Ivoire, The People of → Ivoireans
Couronians → Latvians
Cowichan
Cree → Lubicon
Creek
Crimean Tatars

Crno Gortsi → Serbs
Croats → Serbs, Slovenes
Crow
Cua
Cubans
Cumanangoto → Venezuelans
Cuna
Curaçao, The People of
Cusulima → Jivaro
Cuyo → Argentines
Cymru → Welsh
Cypriots
Czechs → Slovaks

D

Daba → Kirdi
Dafi
Dafla
Dagaba → Mole-Dagbani
Dagana → Hassauna
Dagari → Dagaba
Dagati → Dagaba
Dagbamba → Dagomba
Dagbon → Dagomba
Dagomba → Mole-Dagbani
Dahayat
Dai → Hani, Shan
Daju
Dakarkari → Fulani
Dakota → Sioux
Dakpa → Banda
Dalabon → Australian Aborigines
Damara → Namibians
Damara
Dambono
Dameli
Dami → Dime
Dampelasa → Dayak
Dan → Ivoireans
Danakil → Afar
Danes
Dangla → Nubians
Dangme → Adangbe
Dani
Danjo → Semang
Danoa
Danwar
Darasa → Ethiopians, Oromo
Dard → Kohistani
Darghin → Dargin
Dargin
Dargwa → Dargin, Qubachi
Daribi
Darood → Somali
Dashan → Kachin
Dassa → Yoruba
Dassanetch
Daur
Daurawa → Hausa
Da Vach → Hre
Dayak
Day-Kundi → Hazara
Daza → Toubou
Dazagada → Daza
Debba → Maba
Dei → Liberians
Dekker → Maba
Delaware
Demonara → Solorese
Dene → Athapaskan
Denkyira → Akan
Deori
Desa → Dayak
Deutsche → Germans

ACKNOWLEDGMENTS

The Publishers wish to express their appreciation to the following individuals and institutions for their help:

Illustrations:

Bertelsmann Lexikon Verlag GmbH, Gütersloh/München for the use of color illustrations from their book *Die Völker der Erde*. p. 20 Dr. Zvi Ron; p. 28 Gilad (Gili) Haskin; p. 40 Dr. Zvi Ron; p. 41 above and below right A.A.M. van der Heyden; below left Gilad (Gili) Haskin; p. 47 above right Duby Tal, Albatross, above left Yoel Shitrug, below Dr Zvi Ron; p. 50 above and below Ofer Bersham; p. 61 above Gavriela Zur, below Courtesy of the Australian Embassy, Tel Aviv; p. 64 Shaul Shmuel (Muli); p. 66 Gilad (Gili) Haskin; p. 74 above A.A.M. van der Heyden, below Mirjam Rabelink; p. 78 No'am Ron; p. 81 middle 2.v left W.D.Schurig/Okapia, Frankfurt/Main, below left Eberhard Grames/Bilderberg, Hamburg, middle left Jose Vincente Resino/Black Star, Hamburg, above left Christian Heeb/Look, Hamburg, below right Michael Friedel, above middle and right Mittermeier/WWF-Bildarchiv, Hamburg, above right Jeff Jacobson/Focus, Fritz Trupp, below middle Fritz Trupp; p. 82 Gert Chesi/Museum für Völkerkunde; p. 83 Gert Chesi/Museum für Völkerkunde; p. 84 Werner Gartung; p. 85 Fiedler/IFA Bilderteam; p. 86 Michael Friedel; p. 87 Michael Friedel; p. 88 Mareile Flitsch; p. 89 Museum für Völkerkunde; p. 90 Tobia Wendl München; p. 91 Tobia Wendl, München; p. 92 Walter Hermann, Berlin; p. 93 above left Walter Hermann, Berlin, above right H. Forsthoff/wings; p. 94 Peter Butzke/wings; p. 95 above left Jacques Perno/Explorer, above right Paul C. Pet, upper left H. Forsthoff/wings; p. 96 Gilad (Gili) Haskin; p. 108 Dr. Peter Demant; p. 113 Dr. Joseph Hadass; p. 116 Ofer Bersham; p. 118 Dr. Joseph Hadass; p. 123 Gilad (Gili) Haskin; p. 140 Gilad (Gili) Haskin; p. 146 Ofer Bersham; p. 148 Mirjam Rabelink; p. 160 Prof. Amiram Gonen; p. 164 Dr. Zvi Ron; p. 167 Yoel Shitrug; p. 178 Dr. Joseph Hadass; p. 183 Dr. Zvi Ron; p. 188 above Ofer Bersham, below Eyal Biger; p. 198 Dr. Zvi Ron; p. 204 Gilad (Gili) Haskin; p. 208 Duby Tal, Albatross; p. 223 Boaz Tsairi; p. 227 Dr. Peter Demant; p. 254 above Eyal Ron, below Gilad (Gili) Haskin; p. 262 Duby Tal, Albatross; p. 263 Duby Tal, Albatross; p. 269 above left S. Gafni, above right and below David Harris; p. 271 Duby Tal, Albatross; p. 292 Dr. Joseph Hadass; p. 296 Gilad (Gili) Haskin; p. 298 Gilad (Gili) Haskin; p. 302 Duby Tal, Albatross; p. 308 Courtesy of the South African Tourism Agency, SATOUR, Tel Aviv; p. 318 Tamar Beyth-Sharon; p. 321 A.A.M. van der Heyden; p. 322 Aberham/IFA-Bilderteam; p. 323 Walter A. Frank, Sinzig; p. 324 Bruce Coleman; p. 325 Lotte Schomeurs-Gernböck; p. 326 B & U; p. 327 left Linden-Museum für Völkerkunde, above right Brian Coates/Bruce Coleman, below right Hans Jürgen Burkhard/Bilderberg; p. 328 B & U; p. 329 B & U; p. 330 Jean-Loup Rousselot; p. 331 left Jean -Loup Rousselot, right Don Klumpp/The Image Bank; p. 332 Bruce Coleman; p. 333 A. Schaefer/wings; p. 334 Hans-Jürgen Burkhard/Bilderberg; p. 335 above Thomas Nebbia/Focus, below Bavaria; p. 336 Eyal Ron; p. 341 Gilad (Gili) Haskin; p. 348 No'am Ron; p. 353 Gilad (Gili) Haskin; p. 357 Dr. Zvi Ron p. 364 Gilad (Gili) Haskin; p. 379 Dr. Peter Demant p. 390 A.A.M. van der Heyden; p. 401 Gilad (Gili) Haskin; p. 407 Dr. Joseph Hadass p. 413 above Dr. Peter Demant, below A.A.M. van der Heyden; p. 419 Dr. Peter Demant; p. 427 Courtesy of the South African Embassy, Tel Aviv; p. 430 Prof. Amiram Gonen; p. 438 Dr. Joseph Hadass; p. 443 Gilad (Gili) Haskin; p. 445 Duby Tal, Albatross; p. 462 Gilad (Gili) Haskin; p. 464 Duby Tal, Albatross; p. 469 Billie Salmon; p. 473 above No'am Ron, below Courtesy of the South African Embassy, Tel Aviv p. 478 above Eyal Biger, below Dr. Zvi Ron; p. 488 Gilad (Gili) Haskin; p. 496 Ofer Bersham; p. 497 Gilad (Gili) Haskin; p. 513 Aibie Erez; p. 514 Eyal Biger; p. 529 Eran Sharon; p. 530–531 Maria Susana Cipolletti, Wasser Emmendingen; p. 322 below Bruce Coleman; p. 531 below Maria Susana Cipolletti; p. 532 Fritz Trupp; p. 533 Fritz Trupp; p. 534 Leni Riefenstahl-Archiv Starnberg; p. 535 Leni Riefenstahl-Archiv Starnberg; p. 536 above left E. Winkler, below B & U, p. 536–537 Wirtz-Liaison/Gamma, p. 537 below Lydia Icke-Schwalbe; p. 538 Erika Taube; p. 539 Charles Lenars/Explorer; p. 540 Andrej Reiser/Bilderberg; p. 541 Andrej Reiser/Bilderberg; p. 542 Fritz Trupp; p. 543 Fritz Trupp; p. 544 A.A.M. van der Heyden; p. 553 No'am Ron; p. 564 above Tal Kelem, below Courtesy of the South African Embassy, Tel Aviv; p. 567 Yoel Shitrug; p. 569 Gilad (Gili) Haskin; p. 585 Eyal Biger; p. 588 A.A.M. van der Heyden; p. 598 A. Bruno; p. 601 Dr. Zvi Ron; p. 610 Courtesy of the South African Embassy, Tel Aviv; p. 613 Dr. Joseph Hadass; p. 618 above Zur Shizef, below Ron Laufer; p. 620 Dr. Peter Demant; p. 635 Zur Shizef; p. 642 Dr Zvi Ron; p. 649 Boaz Tsairi; p. 653 Courtesy of the South African Embassy, Tel Aviv; p. 662 A.A.M. van der Heyden; p. 671 Gilad (Gili) Haskin; p. 674 Courtesy of the South African Embassy, Tel Aviv.

Typesetting and Pagination: Michael (Mitch) Abramson — The Jerusalem Publishing House; *Copyeditors:* Susanna Shabetai, Rohan Saxena; *Proofreading:* David Hamburger; *Secretary:* Shoshanna Lewis.

Films: Printone Ltd., Jerusalem.

Printing and Binding: Graphischer Großbetrieb Pößneck GmbH.

The Publishers have attempted to observe the legal requirements with respect to copyright. However, in view of the large number of illustrations included in this volume, the Publishers wish to apologize in advance for any involuntary omission or error and invite persons or bodies concerned to write to the Publishers.

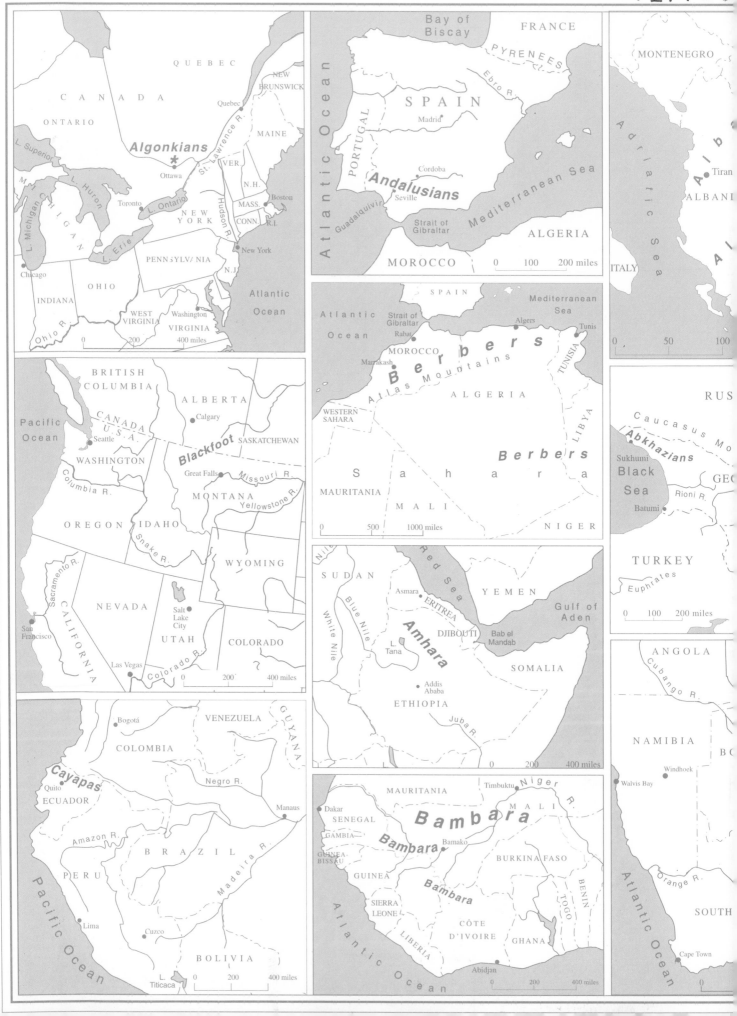

Map 1 (top left — Eastern North America):

QUEBEC

CANADA

ONTARIO

NEW BRUNSWICK

Quebec

MAINE

Algonkians

L. Superior

L. Michigan

L. Huron

Ottawa

St. Lawrence R.

VER.

N.H.

Toronto

L. Ontario

NEW YORK

Hudson R.

Boston

MASS.

CONN.

R.I.

L. Erie

Chicago

INDIANA

OHIO

PENNSYLVANIA

New York

N.J.

Ohio R.

WEST VIRGINIA

Washington

VIRGINIA

Atlantic Ocean

0 200 400 miles

Map 2 (left, second — Pacific Northwest):

BRITISH COLUMBIA

ALBERTA

Calgary

Pacific Ocean

CANADA

U.S.A.

Seattle

SASKATCHEWAN

Blackfoot

WASHINGTON

Columbia R.

Great Falls

Missouri R.

MONTANA

Yellowstone R.

OREGON

IDAHO

Snake R.

WYOMING

Sacramento R.

NEVADA

Salt Lake City

UTAH

COLORADO

San Francisco

CALIFORNIA

Las Vegas

Colorado R.

0 200 400 miles

Map 3 (bottom left — South America):

Bogotá

VENEZUELA

GUYANA

COLOMBIA

Cayapas

Quito

ECUADOR

Negro R.

Manaus

Amazon R.

Madeira R.

BRAZIL

PERU

Lima

Cuzco

Pacific Ocean

L. Titicaca

BOLIVIA

0 200 400 miles

Map 4 (top middle — Iberia):

Bay of Biscay

FRANCE

PYRENEES

Atlantic Ocean

SPAIN

Ebro R.

PORTUGAL

Madrid

Mediterranean Sea

Andalusians

Cordoba

Seville

Guadalquivir

Strait of Gibraltar

ALGERIA

MOROCCO

0 100 200 miles

Map 5 (middle — North Africa):

SPAIN

Mediterranean Sea

Atlantic Ocean

Strait of Gibraltar

Algiers

Tunis

Rabat

MOROCCO

Berbers

TUNISIA

Marrakash

Atlas Mountains

ALGERIA

LIBYA

WESTERN SAHARA

Berbers

MAURITANIA

Sahara

MALI

NIGER

0 500 1000 miles

Map 6 (middle — Horn of Africa):

SUDAN

Red Sea

YEMEN

White Nile

Blue Nile

Asmara

ERITREA

Gulf of Aden

Amhara

DJIBOUTI

Bab el Mandab

L. Tana

Addis Ababa

SOMALIA

ETHIOPIA

Juba R.

0 200 400 miles

Map 7 (bottom middle — West Africa):

MAURITANIA

Timbuktu

Niger R.

MALI

Bambara

Dakar

SENEGAL

Bambara

Bamako

GAMBIA

BURKINA FASO

GUINEA-BISSAU

GUINEA

Bambara

BENIN

TOGO

SIERRA LEONE

LIBERIA

CÔTE D'IVOIRE

GHANA

Atlantic Ocean

Abidjan

0 200 400 miles

Map 8 (top right — Adriatic):

MONTENEGRO

Adriatic Sea

Alb

Tiran

ALBANI

ITALY

Al

0 50 100

Map 9 (middle right — Caucasus/Black Sea):

RUS

Caucasus Mo

Abkhazians

Sukhumi

Black Sea

GEO

Rioni R.

Batumi

TURKEY

Euphrates

0 100 200 miles

Map 10 (bottom right — Southern Africa):

ANGOLA

Cubango R.

NAMIBIA

BO

Windhoek

Walvis Bay

Orange R.

Atlantic Ocean

SOUTH

Cape Town

0